THE BBI DICTIONARY OF ENGLISH WORD COMBINATIONS

Minyoung Song
HCI Master's Program.
School of Information
U of M
mysong @ umich. edu

The BBI Dictionary of English Word Combinations

Revised edition

Compiled by

Morton Benson

Evelyn Benson

Robert Ilson

John Benjamins Publishing Company

Amsterdam/Philadelphia

TM The paper used in this publication meets the minimum requirements of American National Standard for Information Sciences — Permanence of Paper for Printed Library Materials, ANSI Z39.48-1984.

Library of Congress Cataloging-in-Publication Data

Benson, Morton.
  The BBI dictionary of English word combinations / compiled by Morton Benson, Evelyn Benson, Robert Ilson. -- rev. ed.
    p.   cm.
  Rev. ed. of: The BBI combinatory dictionary of English. 1986.
    1. English language--Terms and phrases. I. Benson, Evelyn. II. Ilson, Robert. III. Benson, Morton. BBI combinatory dictionary of English. IV. Title.
PE1689.B46   1997
423'.1--dc21   97-34474
ISBN 90 272 2166 9 (Eur.) / 1-55619-520-6 (US) (Hb; alk. paper)   CIP
ISBN 90 272 2167 7 (Eur.) / 1-55619-521-4 (US) (Pb; alk. paper)

John Benjamins Publishing Co. • P.O.Box 75577 • 1070 AN Amsterdam • The Netherlands
John Benjamins North America • P.O.Box 27519 • Philadelphia PA 19118-0519 • USA

Contents

Preface to the
BBI Dictionary of English Word Combinations

Revised edition of the
BBI Combinatory Dictionary of English

In this revised edition we have expanded and updated the First Edition (1986) and the New Printing (1993) of the BBI, both of which were very favorably received. In selecting new material, we have made use of a variety of sources, such as: (1) critical appraisals from over 50 reviews in numerous journals; (2) additions to the bilingual versions of the BBI, specifically the Maruzen edition (Tokyo, 1993) and the *Longman Dictionary of English Collocations* (Hong Kong, 1995); (3) comments and suggestions of users of the BBI from around the globe, not all of whom can be mentioned here. We would, however, like to acknowledge the contributions of the following three scholars who have made a special effort to send in material: Mrs. Leatrice Lock Fung of Honolulu (Hawaii), Professor Mohamed H. Heliel of Alexandria University (Egypt), and Professor Zai Ming Li of Fuzhou University (People's Republic of China).

The Revised Edition includes items that were missed in the First Edition. Examples of collocations that were added are: *to access data, a blank cassette, a borderline case, a cellular phone, to come on strong, a computer virus, corporate downsizing, a credit note* (in British English), *cultural diversity, a digital clock, to downsize the workforce, to gather speed, a laptop computer, legally binding, to level an accusation at, to nominate a candidate, to over-shoot the runway, to program a VCR, to put a spin on something, to remove graffiti, to run a spell check, a security camera, to send a fax, to sound the all clear, twenty-twenty vision, to wave goodbye,* etc.

In addition, a special effort has been made to identify and incorporate collocations that have entered the English language in recent years since the interlinking of computers. Thus, collocations such as *to browse the web, to create a home page, to cruise the World Wide Web, to go online, to send*

E-Mail, to surf the Internet, to visit a web site, welcome to cyberspace! etc., have been included. We wish to express our sincere gratitude to Professor John F. Fritz, specialist in computers at the Allegheny University School of Nursing in Philadelphia, who assisted us in gathering these examples.

As in the First Edition, we have adhered to the principle of citing examples in clear, natural, normal English and have excluded collocations that are strictly technical. Once again, we will be grateful for comments and suggestions from users of this *Dictionary*.

M.B., E.B., R.I.

A Practical Guide to the BBI

Background

Learners of English as a foreign or second language, like learners of any language, have traditionally devoted themselves to mastering words — their pronunciation, forms, and meanings. However, if they wish to acquire active mastery of English, that is, if they wish to be able to express themselves fluently and accurately in speech and writing, they must learn to cope with the combination of words into phrases, sentences, and texts.

Students must learn how words combine or 'collocate' with each other. In any language, certain words regularly combine with certain other words or grammatical constructions. These recurrent, semi-fixed combinations, or *collocations,* can be divided into two groups: *grammatical collocations* and *lexical collocations.* Grammatical collocations consist of a dominant word — noun, adjective/participle, verb — and a preposition or a grammatical construction. Lexical collocations, on the other hand, do not have a dominant word; they have structures such as the following: verb + noun, adjective + noun, noun + verb, noun + noun, adverb + adjective, adverb + verb.

The BBI is a specialized dictionary designed to help learners of English find collocations quickly and easily. The BBI consistently pays attention to differences between American English and British English.

How to Find Grammatical Collocations in the BBI

Typical grammatical collocations in English are: (with prepositions) *admiration* (for), *acceptable* (to), *amazed* (at), (by) *accident, to adhere* (to), *eager* (for); (with grammatical constructions) *eager* (to do something), *eagerness* (to do something), *to want* (someone to do something), *to become* (someone or something). In such collocations the noun or the adjective or the verb is the dominant word. The **BBI** lists **grammatical collocations under the dominant word.**

Thus, in order to express in English the collocation *Feindseligkeit gegenüber,* the German speaker must find in the BBI the equivalent of the dominant word, that is, the noun *Feindseligkeit.* Learners of English may already know the dominant word; if not, the word can be found easily in any bilingual dictionary. The user of the BBI would then look up the entry for the noun *hostility* and find corresponding English collocations such as *hostility to* and *hostility towards,* both of which correspond to the German *Feindseligkeit gegenüber.*

The French speaker wishing to express in English the collocation *curieux de* (as in *curieux de quelque chose)* would look up the entry for the adjective *curious* and see that one says in English *curious about* (as in *curious about something).*

Spanish speakers seeking the translation of *los vimos entrar* would find at the entry for the verb *see* that one says in English either *we saw them enter* or *we saw them entering.*

How to Find Lexical Collocations in the BBI

Typical lexical collocations in English are: *to put up resistance, to override a veto, a formidable challenge, a dog barks, a herd of cattle, deeply absorbed, to argue heatedly.*

In order to find lexical collocations in the BBI, follow this step-by-step procedure: **if there is a noun in the collocation, look under the noun; if there are two nouns, look under the second; if there is no noun, look under the adjective; if there is no noun or adjective, look under the verb.**

Consequently, in order to find the English for *poner la mesa* a Spanish speaker would look up the entry for the noun *table* and find that in American English one usually says *to set the table* and that in British English one usually says *to lay the table.* Or, the same speaker would find for *prender fuego a* the corresponding English collocation *to set fire to* in the entry for the noun *fire.* The speaker of Italian who wishes to say in English *sfondare la porta* will find at the entry for *door* the collocations *to break down the door* and *to force the door.*

In order to render *eingefleischter Junggeselle* as *confirmed bachelor* and *der Hund bellt* as *the dog barks,* the German speaker would look up the entries for the nouns *bachelor* and *dog.*

French speakers would find that *un troupeau de moutons* is in English *a flock of sheep* by looking up the entry for the noun *sheep,* and that *un troupeau de bétail* is *a herd of cattle* by looking up the noun *cattle*.

Spanish speakers learn that they can express *bien caliente* in English as *piping hot* by consulting the entry for the adjective *hot*.

Speakers of Russian can find for *krepko spat'* the English equivalent *to sleep soundly* by looking under the entry for the verb *sleep*.

For more detail, see the Introduction to this Dictionary and *Using the BBI: A Workbook with Exercises.*

Abbreviations

adj.	adjective
adv.	adverb
AE	American English
Am.	American
anat.	anatomical
BE	British English
Br.	British
CA	creation and/or activation
CE	Common English
cf.	compare
colloq.	colloquial
comm.	commercial
derog.	derogatory
EN	eradication and/or nullification
esp.	especially
fig.	figurative
GB	Great Britain
imper.	imperative
inf.	infinitive
intr.	intransitive
ling.	linguistics
lit.	literary
math.	mathematics
med.	medicine, medical
mil.	military
misc.	miscellaneous
mus.	music
n.	noun

neg.	negative
obsol.	obsolete
occ.	occasionally
pol.	politics, political
pred.	predicative
prep.	preposition
refl.	reflexive
rel.	religion, religious
smb.	somebody
smt.	something
subj.	subjunctive
(T)	Trademark
tr.	transitive
usu.	usually
US	United States
v.	verb
*	incorrect English

The letters A to S denote the verb patterns, explained in the Introduction, Grammatical Collocations, section G8.

How Entries are Structured in the BBI

A Visual Guide

appointment *n.* ["agreement to meet"] 1. to have; keep; make, schedule an ~ with 2. to break; cancel; miss an ~ 3. by ~ (she sees patients by ~ only) 4. an ~ to + inf. (she had an ~ to see the dean) ["selection"] 5. to confirm; make an ~ 6. to block an ~ 7. ~ to (they announced her ~ to the commission) 8. an ~ as (an ~ as professor) ["position"] 9. to have, hold; receive an ~ 10. an interim; permanent; temporary ~ 11. a political ~ ["designation"] 12. by ~ to Her Majesty

— Definition (of noun in square brackets, other typeface and double quotation marks), referring to 1. – 4.

— Definition, referring to 5. – 8.
— Definition, referring to 9. – 11.
— Definition, referring to 12.

clock I *n.* 1. to regulate, set; wind a ~ 2. to advance a ~; or: to put, set, turn a ~ ahead/forward (by one hour) 3. to put, set, turn a ~ back (by ten minutes) 4. an alarm; digital; cuckoo; electric; grandfather; wall ~ 5. a time ~ 6. a biological ~ 7. a ~ is fast; right; slow 8. a ~ gains time; goes, runs; keeps time; loses time; runs down; stops; tells (the) time 9. a ~ strikes the hour 10. the dial; face; hands of a ~ 11. (misc.) to watch the ~ ("to wait impatiently for the end of the working day"); to work around the ~ ("to work without rest"); to work against the ~ ("to strive to meet a deadline"); the ~ ran out ("the allotted time expired"); to stop the ~ ("to suspend play in a game so that the clock stops running")

— 1. – 10. = Lexical collocations

— 11. = Idioms with paraphrases in double quotation marks

concerned *adj.* 1. deeply, gravely, greatly ~ 2. ~ about, for, over; with (~ about safety) 3. (esp. BE) ~ to + inf. (~ to know your decision) 4. ~ that + clause (we are ~ that they might have missed the train) 5. (misc.) as far as I'm ~
USAGE NOTE: The phrases *concerned about*, *concerned over* and less frequently, *concerned for*, mean "worried about" (concerned about your safety). The phrase *concerned with* means "interested in" (concerned with establishing the truth).

— 2. – 4. = Grammatical collocations

— USAGE NOTE providing additional information

Used only in American English

meat *n*. 1. to barbecue; broil (AE), grill; cook; cure; fry; roast; sear; stew ~ 2. to carve, cut; slice ~ 3. dark; red; white ~ 4. fatty; lean ~ 5. raw; tender; tough ~ 6. halal; kosher ~ 7. canned (AE), tinned (BE); fresh; frozen ~ 8. boned; chopped (AE), ground (AE), minced (BE); soup ~ 9. ~ goes bad, spoils 10. a slice of ~

Used only in British English

excited *adj*. 1. ~ about, at, over (to get ~ about smt.) 2. ~ to + inf. (she was ~ to learn the news) 3. ~ that + clause (we were ~ that they were coming) ——— Illustrative phrase

——— Compound verb

come out *v*. 1. (d; intr.) to ~ against ("to oppose") (to ~ against a proposal) 2. (d; intr.) to ~ for, in favor of ("to support") (to ~ for a bill) 3. (d; intr.) to ~ for ("to try out for") (are you ~ing out for the team?) 4. (d; intr.) to ~ with ("to make known; to publish") (to ~ with a new book; to ~ with the truth) 5. (L) it came out that he had cheated 6. (P; intr.) ("to end up, result") to ~ on top ("to be victorious") 7. (s) the pictures came out fine 8. (misc.) to ~ in spots ("to be covered with spots as a result of illness"); they came out from behind the bushes; she meant it as a compliment, but it came out as an insult

——— Definition (of verb in parentheses and double quotation marks)

Verb patterns

Introduction

General

In English, as in other languages, there are many fixed, identifiable, non-idiomatic phrases and constructions. Such groups of words are called *recurrent combinations, fixed combinations,* or *collocations.* Collocations fall into two major groups: *grammatical collocations* and *lexical collocations.*

Grammatical Collocations

Background

A grammatical collocation is a phrase consisting of a dominant word (noun, adjective, verb) and a preposition or grammatical structure such as an infinitive or clause. For example, Noam Chomsky in his *Aspects of the Theory of Syntax* (page 191) points out that *decide on a boat,* meaning 'choose (to buy) a boat' contains the collocation *decide on* (in his terminology: *close construction*), whereas *decide on a boat,* meaning 'make a decision while on a boat' is a *free combination* (in his terminology: *loose association*). Any native speaker of English feels that the components of *decide on* 'choose' and of other fixed phrases such as *account for, accuse (somebody) of, adapt to, agonize over, aim at,* etc. 'collocate' with each other. The native speaker will reject violations of collocability such as **decide at a boat, *account over a loss, *accuse somebody on a crime, *adapt towards new conditions*, etc.

Free combinations, on the other hand, consist of elements that are joined in accordance with the general rules of English syntax and freely allow substitution. For example, in English a verb may be followed by adverbials (of time, place, and manner). The resultant number of possible combinations is limitless: *they decided — after lunch, at three o'clock, during recess, immediately, in the library, on the boat, quickly, reluctantly, unhesitatingly, with a heavy heart,* etc.

Collocations should be included in dictionaries; free combinations, on the other hand, should generally not be included. (The inclusion of free combinations is sometimes essential to illustrate a sense of a polysemous entry in a general-purpose dictionary.)

We will now describe eight major types of grammatical collocations; all of these are included in this *Dictionary*. The types are designated by G1, G2, etc.

G1

G1 collocations consist of noun + preposition combinations. We do not normally include noun + *of* combinations. A very large number of English nouns can be used with *of*, especially to denote the concepts of 'direct object', 'subject', or 'possession'. Thus, we include the combination *blockade against,* but not *blockade of.* The phrase *the blockade of enemy ports* is a regular transformation of *to blockade enemy ports.* We include *apathy towards,* but not *apathy of.* A phrase such as *the apathy of the electorate* is predictable on the basis of the known functions of the preposition *of.*

We also do not include noun + *by* combinations. The phrase *the blockade of enemy ports by our navy* is a predictable and regular transformation of the sentence: *our navy blockaded the enemy ports.* In addition, as already indicated, we will not include free combinations, such as *apathy among (the members of our party), apathy in (France),* etc.

To save space, we usually do not include such derived prepositions as *concerning, regarding, in regard to, with regard to.* Note that the prepositions just listed are usually synonymous with *about.* Thus, an *argument about* is synonymous with an *argument concerning, an argument regarding,* etc.

G2

G2 collocations consist of nouns followed by *to* + infinitive. There are five syntactic patterns in which this construction is most frequently encountered; these patterns are the following:

1. It was a *pleasure* (*a problem, a struggle*) to do it.
2. They had the *foresight* (*instructions,* an *obligation, permission,* the *right*) to do it.
3. They felt a *compulsion* (an *impulse,* a *need*) to do it.
4. They made an *attempt* (an *effort,* a *promise,* a *vow*) to do it.
5. He was a *fool* (a *genius,* an *idiot*) to do it.

Some nouns can also be used with a verb form in *-ing: it's a pleasure to work* *there = it's a pleasure working there = working there is a pleasure (= to work there is a pleasure)*. Such nouns usually occur in the first syntactic pattern listed above. The use of the *-ing* form is shown in the entries.

We do not include nouns if they are followed by infinitives normally associated with the whole sentence rather than with the noun. Such infinitives express purpose; the phrase *in order* may be inserted between the noun and the infinitive with no change of meaning: *they sold their house (in order) to cut down on expenses, he mowed his lawn (in order) to impress his new neighbors, she closed the window (in order) to keep the flies out,* etc.

Nor do we include nouns that occur in phrases such as *a procedure to follow, a book to read, a place to eat, a way to do it,* etc. In such constructions, the infinitive can be replaced by a relative clause: *a procedure that is to be followed, a book that should be read, a place at which one can (should) eat, a way in which one may (should) do it.* The *BBI* does not include colloquial phrases often found in advertisements: *the dictionary to end all dictionaries, a computer to satisfy all needs,* etc.

Lastly, we usually do not include nouns preceded by a descriptive adjective: *an interesting book to read, a difficult person to understand, a clever thing to say,* etc.

Note that in addition to nouns, some adjectives (G6) and some verbs (Pattern E) are followed by *to* + infinitive.

G3

We include here nouns that can be followed by a *that* clause: *we reached an agreement that she would represent us in court; he took an oath that he would do his duty.* The *Dictionary* does not include nouns followed by relative clauses introduced by *that,* i.e., when *that* can be replaced by w*hich: we reached an agreement that would go into effect in a month; he took the same oath that his predecessor had taken.* Nor does it include nouns that can be followed by a clause only when they are objects of a preposition: *it was by chance that we met; it was with (considerable) pride that he presented his findings.*

Some nouns can be followed by a clause with the present subjunctive in formal English: *it was his desire that his estate be divided equally.* See the comments on the use of the subjunctive G8L. The use of the subjunctive is indicated in the entries for such nouns.

G3 nouns expressing emotion *(astonishment, surprise)* may take a 'putative' *should: she expressed surprise that he should be thinking of changing jobs.*

G4

G4 collocations consist of preposition + noun combinations. Examples are: *by accident, in advance, to somebody's advantage, on somebody's advice, under somebody's aegis, in agony, on (the) alert, at anchor,* etc.

G5

G5 collocations are adjective + preposition combinations that occur in the predicate or as set-off attributives (verbless clauses): *they were angry at everyone — angry at everyone, they stayed home — my friends, angry at everyone, stayed home.*

Some adjectives must be followed by a prepositional phrase: *they were fond of children.* One does not normally say: **they were fond.* In the sense 'craving' the adjective *hungry* is always followed by *for* in the predicate: *they were hungry for news.* The sentence *they were hungry* would have a different meaning. In a similar manner the adjective *deaf* in the sense 'unwilling to listen' is always followed by *to: they were deaf to our pleas for help.* Adjectives that are consistently used with a preposition in at least one sense are marked 'cannot stand alone' in the entries.

Derived prepositions such as *concerning, regarding, in regard to, with regard to,* are not included in the entries. Note that the prepositions just listed are usually synonymous with *about.*

In general, we do not include past participles (formed from transitive verbs) followed by the preposition *by*: this construction is regular and predictable. Thus, this *Dictionary* does not give such phrases as *abandoned by, absolved by,* etc.

We include adjective + *of* constructions when the subject of the construction is animate (usually human): *they are afraid (ashamed, confident, critical, demanding, envious,* etc.) *of him.* See G6 for a discussion of adjective + *of* constructions used with a 'dummy' *it* subject.

G6

G6 collocations consist of predicate adjectives and a following *to* + infinitive. Adjectives occur in two basic constructions with infinitives.

1.   *it was necessary to work*

In this construction, the *it* is a 'dummy' or 'empty' subject; it has no antecedent. Prepositional phrases with *for* can be inserted into this construction with many adjectives: *it was necessary for him to work.* If the verb is transitive, a direct object is, of course, added: *it was necessary to supervise them closely.* Some adjectives can be used with a prepositional phrase beginning with *of: it was stupid to go* — *it was stupid of them to go.* (Sometimes, both *of* and *for* are possible: *it was stupid of them to go; it was stupid for them to go.*)

Most adjectives that appear in adjective + *of* constructions (with the 'dummy' *it* subject) followed by *to* + infinitive can also be used in sentences without the infinitive. An example is: *it was stupid of them to go* — *it was stupid of them* (or: *that was stupid of them*). The possibility of dropping the *to* + infinitive is usually not indicated in the *Dictionary.*

2. *she (the girl) is ready to go; it (the machine) was designed to operate at high altitudes*

In this construction, the subject is 'real' and usually animate. Some adjectives, however, normally occur in this construction with an inanimate subject: *calculated, designed,* etc. (See the example provided above with *designed.*) Several adjectives can occur in this construction with either an animate or an inanimate subject; an example is *bound: she was bound to find out* — *it ('the accident') was bound to happen.* Other adjectives of this type are *destined, known, liable, likely,* etc.

Several adjectives can be used in both constructions: *it was supposed to rain* — *she was supposed to work today.* Some adjectives have the same meaning in both constructions: *it was difficult to convince him* — *he was difficult to convince.* Other adjectives of this type are *easy, hard, impossible,* and *tough.*

It should be noted that a large number of adjectives, when used with adverbs such as *too* and *enough,* can be followed by an infinitive: *he was too absorbed to notice; she was alert enough to see it.* These are not included in the *Dictionary.* The *Dictionary* does not include past participles that can be followed by a *to* + infinitive phrase of purpose: *the text was proofread (in order) to eliminate errors.* Nor does the *Dictionary* include past participles that are used in passive constructions: *she was appointed* (*chosen, designated, elected,* etc.) *to serve as our delegate.* Such constructions represent, in fact, the passive transformation of verb pattern H. (See below).

The *Dictionary* does, however, include many other past participles: *he was amazed* (*amused, annoyed, appalled, astonished,* etc.) *to see the results of our research.*

G6 collocations are normally illustrated in the *Dictionary* by examples. The examples will show in which construction (or constructions) each adjective is used. Note that many adjectives used with *it* and *of* can also be used with *he/she: it was stupid of him/her to go — he/she was stupid to go.*

Some G6 adjectives are normally not used without a following infinitive (or prepositional phrase), especially with an animate subject. We usually do not say **he is destined, *he is easy, *he is likely,* etc., but rather *he is destined to go far, he is easy to get along with, he is not likely to be late,* etc. G6 adjectives of this type are marked 'cannot stand alone' in the entries.

A few G6 adjectives (usually used with the 'dummy' *it*) can also be followed by a verb form in *-ing: it's nice to work here = it's nice working here.* The use of the *-ing* form is shown in the entries.

Note that in addition to adjectives, some nouns (G2) and some verbs (pattern E), are followed by *to* + infinitive.

G7

G7 adjectives (many of which are also in G6) can be followed by a *that* clause: *she was afraid that she would fail the examination; it was nice that he was able to come home for the holidays.* Several adjectives are followed by the present subjunctive in formal English: *it was imperative that I be there at three o'clock; it is necessary that he be replaced immediately.* See the comments on the use of the present subjunctive in G8L.

G8

G8 collocations consist of nineteen English verb patterns, designated by the capital letters A to S. A description of each verb pattern follows.

A. Pattern A verbs allow the *dative movement transformation,* that is, allow the shift of an indirect object (usu. animate) to a position before the direct object, with deletion of *to* when both objects are nouns and when the direct object is a noun: *he sent the book to his brother — he sent his brother the book* and *he sent the book to him — he sent him the book.* However, when both objects are pronouns, this transformation is common only in BE: *he sent it to him — he sent him it* (marginal in AE). BE also allows *he sent it him.*

B. Pattern B verbs are transitive; when they have an indirect object, they do *not* allow the *dative movement transformation,* i.e., the shift of the indirect object (usu. animate) to a position before the direct object with the deletion of *to.* Thus, we have *they described the book to her, they mentioned the book to her, they returned the book to her,* but not **they described her the book,* etc. Compare the A pattern verb *send,* which does allow the transformation: *they* *sent him the book.* Verbs denoting types of noise fit pattern B: *he screamed something to her.* Other such verbs are: *babble, bark, bellow, growl,* etc.

In a few rare cases, AE and BE usage differs. An example is the verb *recommend,* which in AE belongs to pattern B and in BE to pattern A. Such differences are indicated in the *Dictionary.*

C. In pattern C, transitive verbs used with the preposition *for* allow the *dative movement transformation,* i.e., allow the deletion of *for* and the shift of the indirect object (usu. animate) to a position before the direct object: *she bought a shirt for her husband — she bought her husband a shirt, she bought a shirt for him — she bought him a shirt.*

It must be emphasized that the *Dictionary* gives only those verbs that occur most frequently in the various meanings of *make — create.* For example, in regard to culinary operations, the *Dictionary* includes the verbs *bake, boil, brew, broil, chop, cook, fry, grill, grind, peel, scramble, slice,* and *toast* (as in: *bake me a cake, boil him an egg, brew her some tea, broil us a few steaks,* etc.). However, the *Dictionary* does not include less frequently used verbs that can be used in the same constructions. Examples are: *barbecue, braise, brown, devil, fricassee, oven bake, pan broil, pan fry, parboil, poach, sauté, scallop, shirr, steam, stew,* etc.

D, d. In this pattern, the verb forms a collocation with a specific preposition (+ object). Free combinations such as *to walk in the park* are excluded. In addition, combinations of the type verb + *by* or *with* are excluded when the latter denote 'means' or 'instrument': *they came by train, we cut bread with a knife,* etc.

Collocations consisting of a verb + *as* (+ object) are included in the *Dictionary: to act as, to interpret as, to serve as, to treat as,* etc.

Some D-pattern verbs are normally *not* used without a prepositional phrase. For example, one does not say: **we will adhere, *they based their conclusions, *our committee consists,* etc. Well formed sentences are: *we will adhere to the plan, they based their conclusions on the available facts, our committee consists of six members,* etc. When a verb (or a certain sense of a verb) is normally followed by a prepositional phrase, its pattern is designated by the small letter *d.*

The *Dictionary* does include *compound verbs* followed by prepositions: *break in on, catch up to,* etc. Note that *out of* is treated as a compound preposition.

Transitive D-pattern verbs used with *to* and B-pattern verbs produce identical constructions. We assign to B those verbs that are normally used with an animate indirect object, and to D — verbs normally occurring with inanimate indirect objects. Compare B: *we described the meeting to them* and D: *we invited them to the meeting.*

E. In this pattern, verbs are followed by *to* + infinitive. Examples of this construction are: *they began to speak, she continued to write, he decided to come, we offered to help,* etc. Verbs are not included if they are normally used in phrases of purpose, that is, if *in order* can be inserted with no change of meaning: *they were drilling (in order) to improve their pronunciation, he was running (in order) to catch a train, she stopped (in order) to chat,* etc.

F. This pattern includes the small number of verbs that are followed by an infinitive without *to: we must work.* These verbs, with the exception of *dare, help* (esp. AE), and *need,* are called *modals.* The verbal phrases *had better* and *would rather* also fit this pattern: *he had better (would rather) go.*

G. In this pattern, verbs are followed by a second verb in *-ing.* Typical examples of this construction are: *they enjoy watching television, he kept talking, we miss going to work every day, the house needs painting, she quit smoking, he regrets living so far from his family,* etc.

Note that some pattern G verbs are also in pattern E. Thus, we have approximately synonymous constructions: *he began reading — he began to read, she continued speaking — she continued to speak.*

Several verbs, however, that appear in both G and E have a different meaning in each construction. The sentence *he remembered to tell them* means that 'he intended to tell them and told them'; *he remembered telling them* means that 'he remembered the act of telling them'. In a similar manner, the construction *he forgot to tell them* means that 'he intended to tell them, but forgot to do so'; *he forgot (about) telling them* means that 'he forgot that he (had) told them'.

Note also the difference between the pattern G construction *she stopped chatting* 'she terminated her chat' and *she stopped to chat.* The latter construction contains an infinitive phrase of purpose similar to that in *she dropped in (in order) to chat, she telephoned her friend (in order) to chat,* etc.

H. In this pattern, transitive verbs are followed by an object and *to* + infinitive. Typical examples of this construction are: *she asked me to come; they challenged us to fight; we forced them to leave; he invited me to participate; she permitted the children to watch television.*

Many of the verbs in this pattern can take the infinitive *to be* after the direct object: *we advised them to be careful, she asked us to be punctual, the director authorized us to be in the laboratory,* etc. For verbs that are normally used only with *to be* after the direct object, see pattern M.

Most H-pattern verbs can be passivized: *I was asked to come, we were authorized to use the laboratory,* etc. Some, however, cannot be: *beseech, bring, cable, cause, commit, get, have, intend, like, prefer, telegraph, telephone, thank, trouble, want, wire, wish,* and *write.*

I. In this pattern, transitive verbs are followed by a direct object and an infinitive without *to.* Examples of this construction are: *she heard them leave, we let the children go to the park, they saw her drive up to the house, he watched them unload the car,* etc. Some of these verbs are also used in pattern J.

The use of I-pattern verbs in the passive occurs occasionally: *we felt the earth move — the earth was felt to move; they made us get up — we were made to get up.* Note the appearance of *to* + infinitive in the passive construction. In some instances, the *-ing* form seems more natural when the verb is passivized: *she was seen driving up to the house.* Most I-pattern verbs cannot be passivized: *we had them fix our roof, she helped us move the furniture, they let the children go home, I watched them unload the car,* etc.

J. In this pattern, verbs are followed by an object and a verb form in *-ing.* Typical examples of this construction are: *I caught them stealing apples, we found the children sleeping on the floor, he kept me waiting two hours,* etc. Note that some verbs in this list are also used in pattern I. Thus, we have approximately synonymous constructions: *she heard them leaving — she heard them leave, he felt his heart beating — he felt his heart beat, we watched them dancing — we watched them dance,* etc.

J-pattern verbs can usually be passivized: *they were caught stealing apples, the children were found sleeping on the floor, I was kept waiting two hours,* etc.

K. In this pattern, verbs can be followed by a possessive (pronoun or noun) and a gerund, i.e., a verbal noun. Typical examples of this construction are: *please excuse my waking you so early, this fact justifies Bob's coming late.* Some of these constructions are very close to those in pattern J, which consist of verb + direct object + present participle. Note the following constructions that are virtually synonymous: *I cannot imagine them stealing apples — I cannot imagine their stealing apples; they remembered Bill making that mistake — they remembered Bill's making that mistake,* etc.

The possessive construction is awkward when two objects are joined by a conjunction. Thus, the construction *I can't imagine Bill* (or *Bill's*) *and Mary's doing that* is far less likely to occur than the pattern J construction *I can't imagine Bill and Mary doing that.*

Native speakers of English often have individual preferences for one construction and may not find the other construction acceptable. Some speakers tend to avoid the possessive construction, which is considered to be bookish. Thus, instead of *we excused his coming late,* many will say *we excused him for coming late;* instead of *we anticipated his refusing,* they prefer *we anticipated his refusal,* etc. In this *Dictionary* we have attempted to include only the most frequently occurring verbs that can be followed by a possessive.

L. In this pattern, verbs can be followed by a noun clause beginning with the conjunction *that.* Examples are: *they admitted that they were wrong, she believed that her sister would come, he denied that he had taken the money, we hoped that the weather would be nice.* In colloquial English the *that* may be omitted: *they admitted they were wrong, she believed her sister would come,* etc.

Some verbs always take a noun or pronoun object before the *that* clause: *she assured me that she would arrive on time, they convinced us that we should invest our money at once, he informed his students that the examination had been canceled.* Such verbs are marked 'must have an object' in the entries. Other verbs can be used with or without a nominal object: *he bet that it would rain — he bet me that it would rain; we cabled that we would arrive on Tuesday — we cabled them that we would arrive on Tuesday; she promised that she would come — she promised her brother that she would come; we showed that we were good workers — we showed everyone that we were good workers,* etc. Such verbs are marked 'may have an object' in the entries. Most of the objects in the sentences just cited seem to be direct objects, i.e., cannot be preceded by *to.* Note however that the (especially AE) construction *he wrote me that he would come next month* has the CE variant *he wrote to me that he would come next month.* Certain verbs in pattern L (often belonging also to pattern B) may be followed by a prepositional phrase with *to: he swore that he would stop drinking — he swore to us that he would stop drinking.* Such verbs are marked 'to' in the entries.

Some verbs in pattern L allow the insertion of *the fact* with little or no change in meaning: *he acknowledged* (*admitted, confirmed, forgot, mentioned,* etc.) *that he was guilty* or *the fact that he was guilty.*

Verbs denoting types of noise fit pattern L: *growl, grumble, grunt, mumble,* etc.

Several verbs, in 'correct' or formal English, are followed by a verb in the present subjunctive in the *that* clause. Examples are: *he demanded that I be there tomorrow at ten o'clock, we moved that the resolution be accepted, the officer ordered that the soldier report to his unit immediately, she proposed that our class hold a reunion, they suggested that the firm appoint a new personnel manager.* In BE the modal *should* is normally used (also in AE as a variant): *they suggested that the firm should appoint a new personnel manager.* The verbs used with a following subjunctive in formal English are marked *subj.* in the entries. The variant with *should* is also shown in the entries.

Some L-pattern verbs can be followed by a clause either with the subjunctive or with the indicative; there is a difference in meaning. Compare: *I suggest that she be/should be there at two o'clock — the facts suggest that she is there.*

A few L-pattern verbs regularly have 'dummy' *it* as their subject: *it appears that they will not come.* Other verbs of this type are: *follow, seem, transpire, turn out,* etc.

M. In this pattern, transitive verbs can be followed by a direct object, the infinitive *to be,* and either an adjective, or a past participle, or a noun/pronoun. In most instances, the same verb can be followed by any of these three forms. Examples of this construction are: *we consider her to be very capable — we consider her to be well trained — we consider her to be a competent engineer; the court declared the law to be unconstitutional — the court declared the law to be superseded by more recent legislation — the court declared the law to be a violation of the Constitution; we found the roads to be excellent — we found the roads to be cleared of snow — we found the roads to be a serious problem for the state treasury.*

Note that this pattern includes verbs that normally take *to be* after the direct object. For verbs that combine freely with infinitives other than *to be,* see pattern H.

N. In this pattern, transitive verbs can be followed by a direct object and an adjective or a past participle or a noun/pronoun. Here are several examples of this construction with an adjective: *she dyed her hair red, we found them interesting, he made his meaning clear, the police set the prisoner free.* Verbs used with adjectives in this construction are marked 'used with an adjective' in the entries.

Examples with a past participle are: *the soldiers found the village destroyed, she had her tonsils removed, we heard the aria sung in Italian.* Verbs used with past participles are marked 'used with a past participle' in the entries. Examples with a noun/pronoun are: *we appointed (designated, elected, made, named) Bob secretary, her friends call her Becky, they ordained him priest.*

Verbs used with nouns/pronouns are marked 'used with a noun' in the entries. Many of these verbs are also used in pattern H (*appoint, designate, elect, name*). Approximately synonymous constructions of the following types can thus be formed: *we appointed (designated, etc.) him secretary;* or: *we appointed him to serve as secretary;* or: *we appointed him to be secretary.*

Some pattern N verbs are also used in pattern M. Note the following synonymous constructions: *we consider her (to be) a competent engineer; the court declared the law (to be) unconstitutional; we found the roads (to be) cleared of snow; we proved him (to be) guilty,* etc.

Finally, it should be noted that some N-pattern verbs are used only with certain adjectives or with a certain adjective. For example, with the verb *paint,* we can say *to paint the walls blue/green/white,* etc. With the verb *shoot,* we can only say *to shoot somebody dead.*

O. In this pattern, transitive verbs can take two objects, neither of which can normally be used in a prepositional phrase with *to* or *for.* Examples of sentences with such double objects are: *the teacher asked the pupil a question, we bet her ten pounds, the police fined him fifty dollars, God will forgive them their sins, she tipped the waiter five dollars,* etc. Note the superficial similarity of the constructions *we bet him ten pounds* and *we sent him ten pounds.* (See pattern A.) Only the second construction allows the transformation *we sent ten pounds to him.*

Pattern O is also very close structurally to pattern N (which has a noun/pronoun following the direct object: *they called him a fool*). The latter construction has one direct object (him), followed by a predicate (object) complement (*a fool*).

Some pattern O verbs can be used with either of their objects alone: *the teacher asked the pupil — the teacher asked a question.* Such verbs are marked 'can be used with one object' in the entries.

Verbs pertaining to gambling such as *bet, lay,* and *wager* are noteworthy in being able to take in effect three objects — a person, an amount, and a clause denoting the point of the bet: *we bet him ten pounds that it would rain. Bet* can be used with any of the three objects alone; *lay* seems to require the first and the second; *wager* can be used with either the second or the third alone.

O-pattern verbs can usually be passivized; in most instances, at least one object can become the subject of the passive construction. Examples are: *no questions were asked, ten pounds were bet, he was fined fifty dollars, they will be forgiven, the waiter was tipped five dollars.*

P. In this pattern, intransitive, reflexive, and transitive verbs must be followed by an adverbial. The adverbial may be an adverb, a prepositional phrase, a noun phrase, or a clause. For example, we cannot normally say in English **he carried himself.* An adverbial is required to form a complete sentence: *he carried himself well;* or: *he carried himself with dignity.* In a similar manner, without adverbials the following sentences are not complete: **Tuesday comes, *we fared, *the meeting will last, *my brother is living* (= 'dwelling'), **a strange man was lurking, *I nosed the car, *she put pressure* (cf.: *she exerted pressure,* which is acceptable), **the boys sneaked, *they tramped, *the trunk weighs,* etc. Acceptable sentences can be formed only if an appropriate adverbial is added: *Tuesday comes after Monday, we fared well, the meeting will last two hours, my brother is living in Utah, a strange man was lurking where we least expected him, I nosed the car (out) into the street, she put pressure on them, the boys sneaked into the auditorium, they tramped through the woods, the trunk weighs thirty pounds.*

Note that some polysemous verbs cited above may have senses that do not require an adverbial: *they are coming, is he still living? a shot-putter puts the shot,* etc.

Some adverbials of duration may resemble direct objects: *the meeting will last all day, this job took two hours,* etc. In fact, these verbs are intransitive; we can say, for example, *the meeting will last long.* We must also mention here sentences with verbs of measurement, such as *the trunk weighs thirty pounds.* We treat *thirty pounds* as an adverbial complement rather than as a direct object, thus distinguishing this sense of *weigh* (which we consider to be intransitive) from the sense used in the sentence *she weighed the trunk* (which we consider to be transitive) .

Some verbs are invariably followed by a particle: *hang around, well up,* etc. Such forms can be considered compound verbs (phrasal verbs) and should be given in dictionaries as separate entries. They are not included in this pattern.

In this *Dictionary* we have attempted to give only the most commonly used verbs and senses that have obligatory adverbials. We have not included all verbs that are followed by a *way*-phrase and an obligatory adverbial: *we elbowed (fought, jostled, made, pushed, worked,* etc.) *our way through the crowd, they bribed their way to success, the Tatar cavalry burned its way through Eastern Europe,* etc. The number of such verbs is very large.

Q. In this pattern, verbs can be followed by an interrogative word: *how, what, when, where, which, who, why*; to these we add *whether* (which often alternates in clauses with *if*). These interrogative forms are often called *wh*-words.

Note: verbs that can be followed only by *what* are not included. An example is the verb *want;* we can say *he wants what I want,* but not **he wants how I want.*

The verbs entered in the *Dictionary* can be followed by a *wh*-word and usually by either a *to* + infinitive construction *or* by a clause: *he asked how to do it, she could not decide whether or not to begin, she knew when to keep quiet — he asked how he should do it, she could not decide whether (if) she should begin, she knew when it was best to keep quiet.*

Although most pattern Q verbs do not take a noun/pronoun object before the *wh*-construction, several must have an object: *we told them what to do, they informed us where applications were being accepted,* etc. Such verbs are marked 'must have an object' in the entries. A few verbs can be used with or without an object: *she asked why we had come — she asked us why we had come.* Such verbs are marked 'may have an object' in the entries.

R. In this pattern, transitive verbs (often expressing emotion) are preceded by the dummy *it* and are followed by *to* + infinitive or by *that* + clause or by either. The construction (or constructions) in which each verb usually seems to occur is shown in the entries. Examples are: *it behooves/behoves you to study more; it puzzled me that they never answered the telephone; it surprised me to learn of her decision* and *it surprised me that our offer was rejected.*

S. In this pattern, a small number of intransitive verbs are followed by a predicate noun or by a predicate adjective: *she became an engineer; he was a teacher; he became smug; she was enthusiastic.* The verb *make,* used intransitively, belongs here: *he'll make a good teacher.*

A somewhat larger group of intransitive verbs can be followed only by a predicate adjective; these verbs are coded with the small letter *s.* Examples are: *she looks fine; the flowers smell nice; the food tastes good.*

Special Note on Transitivity

Verbs are always transitive in the following patterns: A, B, C, H, I, J, K, M, N, O, and R. In four other patterns verbs are consistently intransitive: E, F, G, and S. In the fifteen patterns just listed, verbs are not marked for transitivity. In patterns D, d, and P, verbs of both types occur and are marked as *tr.* or *intr.* In patterns L and Q, verbs can be followed by a clause, and consequently, can be considered to be transitive with a few exceptions such as *appear, emerge, feel, seem.* If another object must be used, the verb is marked 'must have an object'. If another object may be used, the verb is marked 'may have an object'.

Survey of Verb Patterns

In this survey the following special symbols are used: s = subject; v = verb; o = object (direct or indirect); c = complement; a = adverbial (when obligatory); v-ing = verb form in *-ing*.

Pattern Designation		Pattern
A	=	svo *to* o (or) svoo
B	=	svo *to* o
C	=	svo *for* o (or) svoo
D, d	=	sv prep. o (or) svo prep. o
E	=	sv *to* inf.
F	=	sv inf.
G	=	svv-ing
H	=	svo *to* inf.
I	=	svo inf.
J	=	svov-ing
K	=	sv possessive v-ing
L	=	sv(o) *that*-clause
M	=	svo *to be* c
N	=	svoc
O	=	svoo
P	=	sv(o)a
Q	=	sv(o) wh-word
R	=	s(*it*)vo *to* inf. (or) s(*it*)vo *that*-clause
S	=	svc (adjective or noun)
s	=	svc (adjective)

Note that collocational types G2 and G3 (for nouns) and G6 and G7 (for adjectives) are closely related grammatically to some of the verb patterns given above.

Lexical Collocations

Background

Lexical collocations, in contrast to grammatical collocations, normally do not contain prepositions, infinitives, or clauses. Typical lexical collocations consist of nouns, adjectives, verbs, and adverbs. An example of an adjective + noun collocation is *warmest regards,* as in *I send warmest regards.* Typical violations of lexical collocability are **I send hot regards and *I send hearty regards.*

Many lexical collocations in English consist of a verb and noun, such as *bring in an acquittal, file an affidavit, put on airs,* etc. The various types of lexical collocations included in the Combinatory *Dictionary* will be described below.

The Combinatory *Dictionary* does not include free lexical combinations. Free lexical combinations are those in which the two elements do not repeatedly co-occur; the elements are not bound specifically to each other; they occur with other lexical items freely. Thus, a construction such as *condemn murder* is a free combination. The verb *condemn* occurs with an unlimited number of nouns: *they condemned — the abduction, abortion, abuse of power, the acquittal,* etc. In a similar manner, *murder* combines freely with hundreds of verbs: *abhor, accept, acclaim, advocate,* etc.

On the other hand, *commit murder* is a collocation. The verb *commit is* limited in use to a small number of nouns, meaning 'crime', 'wrongdoing'; it collocates specifically with *murder.*

We will now describe seven major types of lexical collocations; all of these are included in the *Dictionary*. The types are designated by L1, L2, L3, etc. The *Dictionary* attempts to give only those lexical collocations that are in common use.

L1

L1 collocations consist of a verb (usually transitive) and a noun/pronoun (or prepositional phrase). Most L1 collocations consist of a verb denoting *creation* and/or *activation* and a noun/pronoun. We call such fixed lexical combinations *CA collocations.* Here are examples of collocations with verbs denoting creation: *come to an agreement, make an impression, compose music, set a record, reach a verdict, inflict a wound.* Here are examples of collocations that express the concept of activation: *set an alarm, fly a kite, launch a missile, punch a time clock, spin a top, wind a watch.*

In some instances, the same noun collocates with one verb (or verbs) to denote creation and with another verb (or verbs) to denote activation: *establish a principle* (= creation) — *apply a principle* (= activation); *draw up a will* (= creation) — *execute a will* (= activation).

In many instances the meanings *creation* and *activation* are united in one verb: *call an alert, display bravery, hatch a conspiracy, impose an embargo, produce friction, inflict an injustice, offer opposition, pose a question, lay a smoke screen, put out a tracer, commit treason, issue a warning.*

CA collocations are arbitrary and non-predictable. Non-native speakers cannot cope with them; they must have a guide. They have no way of knowing that one says in English *make an estimate* (but not **make an estimation), commit treason* (but not **commit treachery*). In English one says *commit fraud and perpetrate fraud.* However, only the collocation *commit suicide* is possible; one does not say **perpetrate suicide.*

Even the native speaker may need at times to refer to a list of CA collocations. Many may not know which verbs collocate with such nouns as the following: *acquittal, afterburners, authority, barrage, bench warrant, Caesarean section, cartwheel, circuit breaker, cloture, copyright, counsel, coup de grâce, coup d'état,* etc. A native speaker of AE, who says *to take up a collection,* will not know which verb collocates with the colloquial BE synonym of CE *collection,* namely *whip-round (have).* Speakers of BE prefer *to have a bath;* AE speakers invariably *take a bath.* CE speakers *make a decision;* BE speakers can also *take a decision.*

Many nouns collocate with verbs that refer to the actions of more than one participant. Such nouns will have different CA collocations according to which participant's role is being described. Thus, a copyright office *grants or registers* a copyright, but an author or publisher *holds or secures* one.

CA collocations for polysemous nouns are extremely important. For example, the entry for the noun line has the following collocations: *draw a line* (on paper); *form a line* (= 'line up'); *drop smb. a line* (= 'write smb. a letter'). The entry for *operation* has: *perform an operation* (in a hospital); *carry out (conduct) an operation* (on the battlefield).

As indicated above, the Combinatory *Dictionary* does not include free combinations. Thus, we exclude many combinations with verbs such as *build, cause, cook, grow, make, manufacture, prepare,* etc. even though, strictly speaking, they convey the meanings of 'creation' or 'activation'. Such verbs form an almost limitless number of combinations: *build bridges (houses, roads), cause damage (deafness, a death), cook meat (potatoes, vegetables),* etc.; such combinations seem to be predictable on the basis of the meaning of their component elements.

On the other hand, we have included in L1 many collocations even if they do not mean 'creation' or 'activation'. Examples are: *do the laundry, decline a noun, take one's seat, carry a story, confirm a suspicion, resist temptation, conjugate a verb,* etc.

L2

L2 collocations consist of a verb meaning essentially *eradication* and/or *nullification* and a noun. Such fixed lexical combinations are called *EN collocations.* Typical examples are the following: *reject an appeal, lift a blockade, break a code, reverse a decision, dispel fear, squander a fortune, demolish (raze, tear down) a house, repeal a law, revoke a license, annul a marriage, suspend martial law, scrub (cancel) a mission, withdraw an offer, countermand an order, renege on a promise, crush (put down) resistance, break up a set* (of china), *rescind a tax, ease tension, quench one's thirst, denounce (abrogate) a treaty, exterminate vermin, override a veto,* etc.

The Combinatory *Dictionary,* does not include predictable free EN combinations. For example, the verb *destroy* can be used with a very large number of nouns denoting physical objects; these have not been entered. Examples are: *to destroy — a barn, bridge, building, city, document, factory, harbor, house, laboratory, port, road, school, village,* etc.

L3

L3 collocations consist of an adjective and a noun. One well known pair of examples is *strong tea* (not **mighty tea*) and *weak tea* (not **feeble tea*). In many instances, more than one adjective (or more than one form of the same adjective) can collocate with the same noun: *warm, warmest* (not **hot*); *kind, kindest; best* (not **good*) *regards.* Other examples of L3 collocations are: *reckless abandon, a chronic alcoholic, a pitched battle, a formidable challenge, a crushing defeat, a rough estimate, an implacable foe, a sweeping generalization,* etc.

As already indicated, the *Dictionary* attempts to give only the most commonly used lexical collocations. Many L3 collocations can be considered to be clichés. The *Dictionary* does not normally give collocations that are used solely in technical language. However, the *Dictionary* does give some technical collocations that will be of interest to students and teachers of English for Special Purposes.

In English, nouns are often used as adjectives. Nouns used attributively may enter into L3 collocations: *house arrest, jet engine, land reform, aptitude test.* These collocations are given at the entry for the second noun. However, if in a 'fused' compound the second noun does not have the same basic meaning as it has when used alone, the compound is not included as an L3 collocation.

Examples of such *Multi-Word Lexical Units* (MLUS) are: *bowling alley, sitting duck, long shot, stuffed shirt,* etc. An MLU is listed as a separate headword if it enters into a collocation. For example, the colloquial MLU *double take* ('delayed reaction') is given as a headword since it is part of the collocation *to do a double take.*

In some instances, noun + noun collocations can be found more easily by the user of the *Dictionary* when they are listed at the entry for the first noun rather than at the entry for the second noun. For example, *cabinet reshuffle is* given at **cabinet,** *drug pusher* at **drug,** etc. Such collocations are listed in the entries under *misc.*

L4

L4 collocations consist of a noun and verb; the verb names an action character-istic of the person or thing designated by the noun: *adjectives modify, alarms go off (ring, sound), bees buzz (sting, swarm), blizzards rage, blood circulates (clots, congeals, flows, runs), bombs explode (go off),* etc. The *Dictionary* does not include predictable combinations such as *bakers bake, boxers box, cooks cook, dancers dance, fencers fence,* etc.

L5

L5 collocations indicate the *unit* that is associated with a noun. The structure of an L5 collocation is often *noun$_1$ of noun$_2$.* Such collocations may indicate:

a. the larger unit to which a single member belongs: *a colony (swarm) of bees, a herd of buffalo, a pack of dogs, a bouquet of flowers, a pride of lions, a school of whales,* etc.
b. the specific, concrete, small unit of something larger, more general: *a bit (piece, word) of advice, an article of clothing, an act of violence,* etc.

L6

L6 collocations consist of an adverb and an adjective. Examples are: *deeply absorbed, strictly accurate, closely (intimately) acquainted, hopelessly ad-dicted, sound asleep, keenly (very much) aware,* etc.

L7

L7 collocations consist of a verb and an adverb. Examples are: *affect deeply, amuse thoroughly, anchor firmly, apologize humbly, appreciate sincerely, argue heatedly,* etc.

Arrangement of Entries

General

The *Dictionary* provides entries primarily for nouns, adjectives, and verbs. A few entries for adverbs and prepositions are also given. We will now describe the arrangement of each type of entry. Note that the following five principles apply to all entries.

1. Collocational types are indicated by illustrative phrases or sentences rather than by type designations. Verb entries are also coded.

2. Lexical collocations precede grammatical collocations.

3. Words characteristic of one variety of English are marked AE (for American English) or BE (for British English). For details concerning variety labeling, see the Style Guide, Collocational Strings, 9.

4. This *Dictionary* does not normally include idioms, i.e., frozen expressions in which the meaning of the whole does not reflect the meanings of the component parts: *to kill two birds with one stone* 'to achieve two aims with one action'; *to be beside oneself* 'to be in a state of great emotional confusion'. Some phrases, especially those expressing a simile, are transitional between collocations and idioms, that is, the meanings of the component parts are reflected partially in the meaning of the whole. The *Dictionary* does include important phrases of this type. For example, under *misc.,* the entry for **bird** has *as free as a bird,* the entry for **feather** has *as light as a feather,* the entry for **sugar** has *as sweet as sugar,* etc.

5. The *Dictionary* does include important fixed phrases that do not fit into any of the types of grammatical and lexical collocations described above. Thus, the entry for **business** gives *to mix business with pleasure,* the entry for **eye** gives *to feast one's eyes on smt.,* etc. Such phrases are normally given under *misc.*

Order of Entries

Headwords, including compounds, are listed in strictly alphabetical order. Thus, the phrasal (compound) verb **go along** follows **goal**. Solid compounds precede those written as two words. For example, **makeup** *n.* precedes **make up** *v.* Homographs, i.e., words with the same spelling, are listed according to the alphabetical order of their part of speech. Their order is, consequently, adjective, adverb, noun, verb. For example, **abandon** I *n.* precedes **abandon** II *v.*

Noun Entries

Collocational types given in noun entries are customarily arranged in the following order: L1, L2, L3, L4, L5, G1, G2, G3, G4. Usually, each collocational type is given in a separate numbered item. However, in order to save space, two collocational types may be shown in the same item. For example, in the entry for **allusion,** we have *to make an allusion to.* This construction shows both L1 and G1.

Adjective Entries

Collocational types are arranged in the following order: L6, G5, G6, G7.

Verb Entries

L7 collocations are given first; they are followed by the verbal patterns of G8, namely A to S. Items showing G8 items are coded, that is, each collocation is marked by a letter designating the appropriate verbal pattern. G8 items are listed in the alphabetical order of their letter codes. When there are several D/d collocations, these are given in the alphabetical order of the collocating prepositions.

Style Guide

The Swung Dash

1. The swung dash (~) usually replaces the headword within the entry. The swung dash is repeated only when necessary.

2. In entries for compound (phrasal) verbs the swung dash represents both the verb and the particle only when they are used in the unseparated infinitive or imperative form and also in the simple present tense, unseparated, with no (third-person singular) ending. The entry for **get away** has an infinitive in the collocation *to ~ from;* the entry for **reach out** has an imperative in the illustrative phrase: *~ your hand to me.* The entry for **run short** has the illustrative phrase *they never ~ of money.* In all other instances, the swung dash represents only the verb; the particle is shown separately. The entry **take down** has the illustrative phrase *to ~ testimony down in shorthand.* (Here the verb and particle are separated in the infinitive form.) The entry **set apart** has the phrase *certain traits ~ them apart from the others.* (Here in the simple present tense the verb and particle are separated.) The entry **run around** has the phrase *he ~s around with a fast crowd.* (Here the verb in the simple present tense has the third-person singular ending.)

3. The headword is used rather than the swung dash when irregular grammatical forms occur. Usually, these are irregular past tense forms of verbs. Occasionally noun plurals must be shown. For example, in the entry for **prisoner of war** we have *to interrogate; repatriate prisoners of war;* in **goose** we have *geese cackle, honk.*

Collocational Strings

1. When a headword collocates with various other words, the *Dictionary* usually lists the resultant collocations in strings. The presentation of collocations in strings not only saves an enormous amount of space, but it also allows the concentration of a great deal of material, facilitating the use of the *Dictionary* by its readers.

2. When collocations are listed in a string, a comma separates synonyms or near synonyms. Members of the collocational string are listed in alphabetical order. The entry for **advice** gives *to give, offer ~.* This string represents the synonymous collocations *to give advice* and *to offer advice.*

3. A semicolon separates non-synonymous collocations that are presented in a string. The entry for **answerable** has ~ *for; to.* This string represents the non-synonymous collocations *answerable for* and *answerable to.*

4. Both synonymous and non-synonymous collocations may be listed in one string. The entry for **booth** has *an information; phone, telephone; polling, voting; projection* ~. This string represents the collocation *an information booth,* the synonymous collocations *a phone booth* and *a telephone booth,* the synonymous collocations *a polling booth* and *a voting booth,* and the collocation *a projection booth.* Note that synonymous members of a string are grouped together, even though this upsets the overall alphabetical order. Note also that the article is not repeated in the string.

5. When the same noun collocates with different verbs and with different prepositions, the resultant collocations must be shown in different strings. Thus, under **degree** ('academic title') we have *to award a* ~ *to; to confer a* ~ *on.* Note that these collocations are synonymous; the semicolon between them separates different collocational strings rather than non-synonymous members of the same string. Another example is found in the entry **damage** ('harm'), which gives *to cause, do* ~ *to; to inflict* ~ *on.* These two strings represent the three synonymous collocations *to cause damage to, to do damage to, to inflict damage on.*

6. Separate strings are required when differences in the use of articles or of number must be shown. Differences in the use of articles are indicated in **business** 5: *a mail-order* ~; *show* ~; *the travel*~. In **atrocity** 2 we see a string of adjectives for the singular: *a dreadful, grisly, gruesome, heinous, horrible, horrid, monstrous, revolting, vile* ~; in **atrocity** 3 we see the allocations normally used in the plural: *death-camp; wartime atrocities.*

7. As indicated above under *Lexical Collocations,* some nouns collocate with verbs that refer to the actions of more than one participant. Only verbs referring to the actions of the same participant may be listed in one string. Thus, the entry for **copyright** has one string for the actions of the copyright office *(to grant, register a* ~*)* and a different string for the actions of an author or publisher *(to hold; secure a* ~*).*

8. The examples given above show that normally each string has one swung dash. The sole exception occurs in strings that include a compound word, i.e., a word consisting of two (or more) roots spelled as one word. The last element of the compound is the same element with which the other members of the string

collocate. In such instances, the member of the string preceding the compound must be followed by the swung dash. Under **boat** we have an *assault~; flying ~; gunboat; lifeboat; mosquito ~.*

9. Stylistic and variety labels referring to one member of the string normally follow that member. Under **show** I we have *to catch* (colloq.), *see, take in a ~.* The entry **accountant** has *a certified public* (AE), *chartered* (BE) *~.* Note that the variety label CE is usually not used. Thus, the entry for **different** 2 has *-from, than* (AE), *to* (BE). This means that CE has *different from,* AE has *different than,* and BE has *different to.*

Definitions and Paraphrases

1. Definitions and paraphrases are enclosed in double quotation marks.

2. Definitions of nouns and adjectives in double quotation marks, other type-face, and square brackets refer to items that follow. Note the following example: **accent** *n.* ["pronunciation"] *to affect, assume, imitate, put on; cultivate an ~,* etc. When 'miscellaneous' items are not covered by any previously given definition, they are listed at the end of the entry and are preceded by *misc.* in double quotation marks, other typeface, and square brackets. For an example, see the entry for **account** I.

3. Definitions of senses of verbs and paraphrases of illustrative phrases are given in double quotation marks and parentheses. Such definitions and para-phrases refer to the preceding item. An example of a paraphrase is provided in the entry **aback**. The collocation given is *taken aback;* the illustrative phrase is *I was taken aback,* which is paraphrased as *I was startled.*

4. When verb definitions refer to the headword, they stand immediately after the coding. For example, **go** II 11 has the coding (d; intr.), followed by the definition (*"to pass"*), the collocation *to ~ by,* and the illustrative phrase *to ~ by smb.'s house.* If, however, the meaning of the verb is clear only in combination with the following preposition, the definition follows not the coding, but the collocation. Thus, **go** 12 has the coding (d; intr.), the collocation *to ~ by,* the definition (*"to follow"*), and the illustrative phrase *to ~ by the rules.*

Illustrative Phrases

1. Illustrative phrases follow the collocation that they refer to; they are given in parentheses. The entry **adherence** 2 has the collocation *~ to* followed by the illustrative phrase *strict ~ to a plan.*

2. When synonyms are indicated in an illustrative phrase, they are separated by a slash (/). The entry for **state I** 9 has the illustrative phrase: *affairs/matters of ~.*

3. Note that a collocation may be expanded so as to serve as an illustration. Under **river** 4 we have the L4 collocation *a ~ flows* expanded by the phrase *(into the sea),* enclosed in parentheses. Thus, **river** 4 has: *a ~ flows (into the sea).*

Usage Notes

Usage Notes in the *BBI* provide additional information about the appropriate use of headwords and their collocations. The views of purists concerning correct usage are sometimes given. Usage Notes may also include details about the differences between AE and BE; for additional information about these differences, see the *Lexicographic Description of English.* Note that the swung dash is not used in the Usage Notes.

Pronunciation

In general, the *BBI Dictionary* does not indicate pronunciation. In a few instances, however, phonemic transcription is provided in order to differentiate homographs. Thus, **bow** I is transcribed as /bau/ and **bow** III as /bou/; **use** I is transcribed as /ju:s/ and **use** II as /ju:z/. For details concerning the simplified transcription used in the *BBI,* see the *Lexicographic Description of English.*

It should be noted that in some English homographs the stress of adjectives and nouns on one hand, and that of verbs on the other, may be different. In such instances, the adjective or noun has the stress on the first syllable, and the verb has the stress on the second syllable. Entries given in the *BBI* for such homographs with stress differences include: *absent, abstract, address, ally, annex, compress, conduct, conflict, contract, contrast, convert, defect, discourse, escort, excerpt, extract, impact, implant, increase, intrigue, object, overhaul, permit, present, produce, progress, prospect, protest, rebel, rebound, recall* (in AE), *record, recount, refund, refuse, relay, remit* (in BE), *subject, suspect, transfer, transplant, transport, upset.*

A few nouns have variant stresses, i.e., either on the first or on the second syllable. Examples are: *address* ("place of residence"), *ally, intrigue, recall* (in AE), *remit* (in BE; this noun is not used in AE). Several verbs have variant stresses. Examples are: *ally* (in AE), *annex, transport* (in AE). In the meaning "to summarize", the verb *abstract* is stressed on the first syllable. Note that the noun *upset* is stressed on the first syllable, whereas both the adjective and the verb are stressed on the second syllable; the adjective is, in fact, a past participle form.

A

aback *adv.* taken ~ (I was taken ~) ("I was startled")

abacus *n.* to operate, use an ~

abandon I *n.* 1. reckless, wild ~ 2. in, with ~ (in reckless ~)

abandon II *v.* (D; tr.) to ~ to (they ~ed us to our fate)

abbreviate *v.* (D; tr.) to ~ to (*Esquire* can be ~d to *Esq.*)

ABC *n.* as easy, simple as ~

abdication *n.* ~ from

abduct *v.* (D; tr.) to ~ from (to ~ a child from its home)

aberration *n.* a mental; sexual; statistical; temporary ~

abet *v.* (formal) (D; tr.) to ~ in (to ~ smb. in doing smt.; to aid and ~ smb. in doing smt.)

abeyance *n.* in; into ~ (to hold in ~; to fall into ~)

abhor *v.* 1. (G) he ~s being idle 2. (K) she ~s his smoking

abhorrence *n.* 1. to show ~ 2. in, with ~ (of)

abhorrent *adj.* (formal) ~ to (his behavior was ~ to everyone)

abide *v.* (d; intr.) 1. to ~ by ("to agree to, obey") (we must ~ by her decision) 2. (obsol. and formal) (d; intr.) ("to stay") to ~ with

ability *n.* 1. to demonstrate, display, exhibit, show ~ 2. to appreciate, recognize ~ 3. creative; leadership ~ 4. exceptional, great, outstanding, remarkable ~ 5. genuine, innate, natural; latent ~ 6. an ounce of ~ (he doesn't have an ounce of ~) 7. ~ at, in (to display ~ in mathematics) 8. the ~ to + inf. (the ~ to reason) 9. of ~ (a person of great ~; to the best of one's ~)

ablaze *adj.* 1. ~ with (the city was ~ with lights) 2. to set ~

able *adj.* ~ to + inf. (she was not ~ to reach him)
USAGE NOTE: In passive constructions, *able* is replaced by the verb *can*—he cannot be reached.

ablutions *n.* (formal or humorous) to perform one's ~

aboard *adv.* 1. to climb, come; go ~ 2. all ~!

abode *n.* 1. (legal) of no fixed ~ 2. (formal or humorous) to take up one's ~; welcome to my humble ~

abortion *n.* 1. to do, perform an ~ on 2. to induce an ~ 3. to get, have an ~ 4. a criminal, illegal; induced; spontaneous; therapeutic ~ 5. legalized ~

abound *v.* (formal) (d; intr.) to ~ in, with (this country ~s in opportunities; that book ~s with misprints)

about I *adj.* (cannot stand alone) ["ready"] 1. ~ to + inf. (the performance is ~ to begin) ["willing"] (colloq.) (AE) 2. not ~ to + inf. (we are not ~ to

stop now; we are not ~ to be taken in by their campaign promises) ["misc."] 3. to set ~ doing smt.

about II *prep.* 1. be quick ~ it ("do it quickly") 2. how/what ~ us? what ~ your promise? how ~ (having) a drink?

about-face *n.* ["sudden change in attitude"] to do an ~

about-turn *n.* (BE) see **about-face**

above *adv.* way; well; up ~

abreast *adj.* (usu. does not stand alone) ~ of (to be, keep, stay ~ of the news; to keep smb. ~ of the latest developments)

abroad *adv.* 1. from ~ (he had to return from ~) 2. to go; live; study; travel; work ~

abscond *v.* (D; intr.) to ~ from; with (they ~ed from the country with the funds)

absence *n.* 1. an excused; unexcused ~ 2. a prolonged ~ 3. ~ from (an unexcused ~ from school) 4. during, in smb.'s ~ 5. in the ~ of smt. (in the ~ of concrete evidence, we had to drop the charges)

absent I *adj.* ~ from (she was ~ from school)

absent II *v.* (D; refl.) to ~ from (to ~ oneself from a meeting)

absentia *n.* in ~ (to be tried in ~)

absolution *n.* (rel.) 1. to give, grant, pronounce ~ from (to grant ~ from sin) 2. to seek ~

absolve *v.* (D; tr.) to ~ from, of (he was ~d from his promise)

absorb *v.* 1. (D; tr.) to ~ from (to ~ drainage from a wound) 2. (D; tr.) to ~ into (to ~ a small firm into a large cartel)

absorbed *adj.* 1. deeply, completely, thoroughly, totally ~ 2. ~ by, with; in (she was ~ by/with the problem; the children were ~ in their homework; ~ in thought)

absorbent *adj.* highly ~

abstain *v.* (D; intr.) to ~ from (to ~ from alcohol)

abstention *n.* ~ from

abstinence *n.* 1. to practice ~ 2. complete, total ~ 3. ~ from (~ from alcohol)

abstract I *n.* in the ~

abstract II *v.* (technical) (D; tr.) to ~ from (to ~ iron from ore)

absurd *adj.* 1. patently; totally, utterly ~ 2. ~ to + inf. (it was ~ to leave such a large tip) 3. ~ that + clause (it's ~ that we have to/should have to get up so early)

absurdity *n.* it was the height of ~ (to insist on a refund)

abundance *n.* 1. an ~ of (there was an ~ of water power) 2. in ~ (we had food in ~) 3. of ~ (a society of ~)

abundant *adj.* (formal) ~ in (~ in natural resources)

abuse *n.* ["insulting language"] 1. to heap, shower ~ on, upon; to hurl, shout ~ at; to shower smb. with ~ 2. to take ~ (she took a lot of ~ from him) 3. verbal ~ 4. a shower, stream, torrent of ~ 5. a term of ~ ["rough use"] 6. to take ~ (this car has taken a lot of ~) ["mistreatment"] 7. domestic; emotional; personal; physical; sexual ~ 8. child; elder; spousal ~ 9. human rights ~s ["improper use, misuse"] 10. alcohol, drug, substance ~

abusive *adj.* ~ to, toward (he became ~ to his guests)

abut *v.* (D; intr.) to ~ against, on, upon

abyss *n.* 1. a gaping, yawning ~ 2. on the brink, edge of an ~

academe *n.* (formal) the groves, halls of ~

academy *n.* 1. a military; naval; police; riding ~ 2. an ~ for (an ~ for boys) 3. at an ~

accede *v.* 1. (D; intr.) ("to agree") to ~ to (they ~d to our demands) 2. (D; intr.) ("to ascend") to ~ to the throne

accelerator *n.* 1. to depress, step on an ~ 2. to ease up, let up on an ~

accent *n.* ["pronunciation"] 1. to affect, assume, imitate, put on; cultivate an ~ 2. to speak with an ~ 3. to get rid of an ~ 4. a broad; heavy, noticeable, pronounced, strong, thick; slight ~ 5. a foreign; phony; regional ~ ["stress"] 6. to place, put the ~ on (to place the ~ on a syllable) 7. (ling.) an acute; grave; pitch; tonic ~ (see also **stress**)

accept *v.* 1. to ~ blindly; fully; readily; unreservedly, without reservations 2. to ~ gracefully, graciously; gratefully 3. to ~ grudgingly, reluctantly 4. (D; tr.) to ~ as (they ~ed us as their equals) 5. (D; tr.) to ~ for (she was ~ed for admission) 6. (formal) (BE) (L) I ~ that the proposal may be defeated

acceptable *adj.* 1. completely, fully; mutually; socially ~ 2. ~ to (the conditions are ~ to all concerned)

acceptance *n.* 1. to gain, win; meet with ~ 2. to seek ~ 3. blind ~ (blind ~ of dogma) 4. general, universal, widespread; public ~ (to meet with universal ~) 5. a degree of ~

accepted *adj.* 1. generally, widely ~ 2. ~ that + clause (it is widely ~ that exercise is beneficial)

access I *n.* 1. to gain, get; have ~ 2. to seek ~ 3. to deny, refuse; give, grant ~ 4. direct; easy, free, unlimited, unrestricted; immediate, instant, quick, ready; limited, restricted ~ 5. (computers) random ~ 6. ~ to (we gained/got ~ to the files; ~ to a building)

access II *v.* (D; tr.) to ~ from (to ~ information from a computer)

accessary (esp. BE) see **accessory** 1, 2

accessibility *n.* ~ to (the professor's ~ to all students)

accessible *adj.* 1. directly; easily, readily; immediately ~ 2. ~ to (the stacks are ~ to the public; the director is ~ to everyone) 3. wheelchair ~

accession *n.* 1. on one's ~ (on his ~ to the throne he inherited vast estates) 2. ~ to (her ~ to power) 3. a new ~ (as in a library)

accessory *n.* ["accomplice"] 1. an ~ to (an ~ to a crime) 2. (legal) an ~ before the fact; an ~ after the fact ["optional equipment"] 3. auto (AE); matching; skiing; smoking ~ries

accident *n.* ["unexpected, unpleasant event"] ["catastrophe"] 1. to cause an ~ 2. to have, meet with (they had an ~ during their trip) 3. to survive an ~ 4. to prevent ~s 5. an awful, bad, dreadful, frightful, horrible, nasty, serious, shocking, terrible, tragic; fatal; unavoidable; unfortunate ~ 6. a minor, slight; near ~ 7. an automobile (AE), road, traffic; hit-and-run; railroad (AE), railway (BE), train ~ 8. a boating; hunting ~ 9. an industrial; nuclear ~ 10. an ~ happens, occurs (a bad ~ happened there) 11. in an ~ (he was in a hunting ~) 12. (misc.) an ~ waiting to happen ["chance"] ["luck"] 13. pure, sheer ~ 14. an ~ that + clause (it was pure ~ that we met; it was no ~ that we met) 15. by ~ (we discovered it by ~; it was by pure ~ that we found the money)

acclaim I *n.* 1. to receive, win ~ 2. critical ~ 3. general, public ~ 4. international, universal, wide, worldwide; national ~ 5. ~ for (she won critical ~ for her performance)

acclaim II *v.* 1. (d; tr.) to ~ as (the new medication has been ~ed as a miracle drug) 2. (d; tr.) to ~ for (she was ~ed for her research) 3. (N; used with a noun) the mob ~ed him emperor

acclamation *n.* by ~ (to elect smb. by ~)

acclimate (AE) see **acclimatize**

acclimatize *v.* (D; intr., refl., tr.) to ~ to (we ~d quickly/~d ourselves quickly to the jungle; he became ~d to the new surroundings)

accolade *n.* 1. to bestow an ~ on 2. to receive, win an ~ (from) 3. the ultimate ~

accommodate *v.* (D; intr., refl., tr.) to ~ to (they ~d easily/~d themselves easily to the new conditions)

accommodation I *n.* ["agreement"] ["adjustment"] 1. to come to, make; reach, work out an ~ 2. to seek an ~ 3. an ~ between; on; to; with (to make an ~ to wartime conditions; to reach an ~ with neighboring countries)

accommodation II (BE) see **accommodations**

accommodations *n.* (AE) ["place to live"] 1. to secure; seek ~ 2. deluxe; first-class ~ 3. hotel; living ~ 4. tourist; travel ~

accompaniment *n.* 1. an ~ to (a piano ~ to a song) 2. to the ~ of (to the ~ of soft music)

accompany *v.* 1. (D; tr.) to ~ on (to ~ a singer on the piano) 2. (D; tr.) to ~ to (I will ~ her to the station)

accomplice *n.* 1. an unwitting ~ 2. an ~ in, to (an ~

in crime)

accomplished *adj.* ~ at, in

accomplishment *n.* 1. see **achievement** 1 for adjective + noun collocations 2. no mean ~ 3. an ~ to + inf. (it was a real ~ to defeat them) 4. of ~ (a man, woman of many ~s)

accord I *n.* 1. to come to, reach; sign an ~ 2. complete, full ~ 3. a peace ~ 4. an ~ with smb. about/on smt. (we reached an ~ with the neighboring country about our common border) 5. an ~ that + clause (they came to an ~ that profits would be shared equally) 6. in ~ (with) (we are in complete ~ with each other) 7. (formal) of one's own ~ (he participated of his own ~)

accord II *v.* (formal) 1. (A) we ~ed a hero's welcome to him; or: we ~ed him a hero's welcome 2. (d; intr.) to ~ with (our information does not ~ with his report)

accordance *n.* in ~ with (in ~ with your instructions)

account I *n.* ["description"] ["report"] 1. to give, render an ~ 2. an accurate, factual, true; blow-by-blow, detailed, full, graphic; clear; eyewitness; first-hand; running; verbatim ~ (she gave a detailed ~ of the incident) 3. a glowing; lively, vivid ~ 4. a biased, one-sided ~ 5. a brief ~ 6. newspaper, press ~s (according to press ~s) 7. by all ~s ["explanation"] 8. to call smb. to ~ ["consideration"] 9. to take ~ of smt; to take smt. into ~ ["arrangement with a bank"] 10. to open an ~ 11. to close, settle an ~ 12. to have, keep an ~ (I keep an ~ in that bank) 13. to overdraw an ~ 14. to audit; credit, debit an ~ 15. a bank; checking (AE), current (BE); deposit (BE), savings; money-market; individual retirement (AE) ~ 16. an active; blocked; inactive ~ 17. a joint; numbered ~ 18. an overdrawn ~ 19. in an ~ (the funds were in her ~) ["business arrangement"] ["record of a business arrangement"] 20. to open an ~ (with a store) 21. to close an ~ 22. to have an ~ (with) 23. to charge, debit; credit smb.'s ~ 24. to charge smt. to one's/smb.'s ~ 25. to pay smt. on ~ 26. a charge (AE), credit (BE); expense ~ ["dispute"] 27. to settle an ~ (I have an ~ to settle with him) ["sake"] 28. on smb.'s ~ (do not refuse on my ~) 29. on ~ of (he did it on ~ of me) ["showing"] ["performance"] 30. to give a good ~ of oneself ["misc."] 31. on no ~ ("under no circumstances"); of no ~ ("of no importance")

account II *v.* 1. (d; intr.) to ~ for ("to explain") (he could not ~ for the missing funds; how do you ~ for the accident?) 2. (d; intr.) to ~ for ("to cause the destruction of") (our battery ~ed for three enemy planes) 3. (d; intr.) to ~ (for) ("to explain") (she has to ~ to the supervisor for time spent in travel) 4. (BE) (N; used with an adjective, noun) ("to consider") we ~ed her guilty; she was ~ed a

prodigy

accountable *adj.* 1. strictly ~ 2. ~ for; to (we are ~ to our parents for our actions) 3. to hold smb. ~ for smt.

accountant *n.* a certified public (AE), chartered (BE) ~

accounting *n.* 1. to give, render an ~ 2. a strict ~ 3. cost ~

accounts *n.* ["books, ledgers"] 1. to keep ~ ["record of transactions"] 2. ~ payable; receivable ["differences"] 3. to settle, square ~ (with)

accredit *v.* (D; tr.) to ~ to (our envoy was ~ed to their new government)

accreditation *n.* 1. to receive (full) ~ 2. to deny ~

accrue *v.* 1. (D; intr.) to ~ from 2. (D; intr.) to ~ to (the interest ~d to our account)

accuracy *n.* 1. historical; pinpoint; reasonable; scientific; strict, total ~ 2. ~ in

accurate *adj.* 1. deadly; fairly, pretty, reasonably; historically; strictly ~ 2. ~ in 3. ~ to + inf. (it would be ~ to say that he is lazy)

accusation *n.* 1. to bring, make an ~ against (he brought an ~ of theft against Smith; more usu. is: he accused Smith of theft) 2. to level an ~ against, at 3. to deny, reject; refute an ~ 4. a damaging, grave; false, groundless, scurrilous, unfounded, unjust; sweeping; veiled ~ 5. an ~ against; of (an ~ of gross negligence) 6. an ~ that + clause (he denied the ~ that he had accepted bribes)

accuse *v.* (D; tr.) to ~ of (he was ~d of murder)

accused *adj.* 1. falsely ~ 2. to stand ~ (of)

accustom *v.* (d; refl., tr.) to ~ to (we had to ~ ourselves to the new working conditions; more usu. is: we had to get ~ed to the new working conditions)

accustomed *adj.* (cannot stand alone) ~ to (~ to hard work; ~ to walking long distances; he got ~ to the warm climate)

ace *n.* ["a serve that an opponent cannot touch"] (tennis) 1. to score an ~ ["expert combat pilot"] 2. an air, flying ~ ["misc."] 3. within an ~ of ("very close to"); an ~ in the hole ("a concealed advantage")

ache I *n.* a dull; steady ~ (he felt a dull ~ in his shoulder) (see **backache, earache, headache, stomachache, toothache**)

ache II *v.* 1. (d; intr.) 1. to ~ for (to ~ for company) 2. (E) he is ~ing to get even 3. (misc.) to ~ all over

achievement *n.* 1. a brilliant, crowning, dazzling, epic, glorious, great, lasting, magnificent, major, memorable, monumental, notable, outstanding, phenomenal, remarkable, signal, staggering, superb, wonderful ~ 2. an ~ in (outstanding ~s in science)

acid *n.* 1. corrosive, strong ~ 2. acetic; boric; carbolic; citric; hydrochloric; sulfuric ~ 3. ~ burns (a hole); corrodes 4. (misc.) (slang) to drop ~ (LSD)

acknowledge *v.* 1. to ~ frankly, openly; gratefully 2. (B) the author ~d her debt to her research assistants 3. (D; tr.) to ~ as (she ~d him as her heir) 4. (G) he ~d being ignorant of the facts 5. (K) he ~d my being the first to think of it 6. (L; to) she ~d (to us) that she was to blame 7. (rare) (M) they ~d us to be the winners of the contest 8. (formal and rare) (N; used with a past participle) he ~d himself defeated

acknowledgment *n.* 1. to make an ~ of 2. a frank, open; grateful; public ~ 3. in ~ of

acme *n.* to attain, reach the ~ of

acquaint *v.* 1. to ~ thoroughly 2. (D; refl., tr.) to ~ with (the lawyer ~ed herself with the facts of the case)

acquaintance *n.* ["familiarity"] 1. to have an ~ with (he has some ~ with statistics) 2. a slight, superficial ~ 3. on ~ (on closer ~ he proved to be a nice person) 4. an ~ with ["casual friendship"] 5. to make smb.'s ~ 6. to keep up; renew; strike up an ~ with 7. a casual, nodding, passing, slight ~ (to have a nodding ~ with smb.) ["friend"] 8. a casual; intimate; old ~

acquaintanceship *n.* 1. to strike up an ~ with 2. a casual; close, intimate ~ 3. an ~ with

acquainted *adj.* 1. casually; closely, intimately, thoroughly ~ 2. ~ with (he got/became ~ with the situation; are you ~ with him?)

acquiesce *v.* (D; intr.) to ~ in, to (they ~d in the decision)

acquiescence *n.* 1. complete, total ~ 2. ~ in, to (~ in a decision)

acquisition *n.* 1. to make an ~ 2. (BE) an ~ to (he is a valuable ~ to our firm) 3. (misc.) language ~

acquit *v.* 1. (D; tr.) ("to exonerate") to ~ of (the jury ~ted her of all charges) 2. (P; refl.) ("to behave") she ~ted herself well; he ~ted himself like a veteran

acquittal *n.* (legal) 1. to bring in an ~ (the jury brought in an ~) 2. to win an ~ (the lawyer won an ~ for her client)

acrimony *n.* bitter, sharp ~

acrobatics *n.* 1. to perform ~ 2. (fig.) mental ~

acronym *n.* 1. to form an ~ 2. an ~ for

across *adv.* ~ from

act I *n.* ["action"] 1. to commit; consummate; perform an ~ 2. a barbaric, barbarous; despicable, hostile; terroristic; unfriendly ~ 3. a criminal, illegal, illicit ~ 4. a desperate; foolish, irresponsible, rash; impulsive ~ 5. a courageous; heroic, noble; justified ~ (she performed an heroic ~) 6. a friendly, humane, kind; thoughtful ~ 7. an ~ against (that was an ~ against company policy) 8. an ~ of (an ~ of faith; he committed an ~ of folly) 9. in the ~ (caught in the ~) ["performance"] 10. a circus; nightclub; variety (BE), vaudeville (AE) ~ 11. (misc.) to put on an ~ ("to pretend"); to do a balancing ~ ("to maneuver skillfully") ["legislation"] 12. by ~ of (Congress) ["misc."] 13. to get into the ~ ("to participate"); to get one's ~ together ("to begin to work effectively"); to do a disappearing ~ ("to vanish from the scene"); it's a tough ~ to follow ("it is difficult to emulate or to equal")

act II *v.* 1. to ~ impulsively; irresponsibly, rashly; responsibly 2. (d; intr.) ("to perform") to ~ against (to ~ against one's own client) 3. (d; intr.) ("to serve") to ~ as (she ~ed as our interpreter) 4. (d; intr.) to ~ for ("to replace", and, esp. BE "to represent as one's lawyer") 5. (d; intr.) ("to behave") to ~ like (the soldier ~ed like a real hero) 6. (D; intr.) ("to take action") to ~ on, upon (to ~ on smb.'s advice; to ~ on a request) 7. (d; intr.) ("to take action") to ~ out of (they ~ed out of fear) 8. (d; intr.) ("to behave") to ~ towards (how did they ~ towards you?) 9. (P; intr.) ("to behave") the soldier ~ed bravely 10. (s) (esp. AE) ("to behave") to ~ guilty 11. (misc.) they ~ed as if they were pleased

action *n.* ["activity"] ["act"] 1. to initiate; take ~; to go, swing into ~ (we took immediate ~) 2. to put smt. into ~ (we put our plan into ~) 3. to prod, spur smb. into ~ 4. concerted, united; decisive, firm; direct; vigorous ~ 5. immediate, prompt, swift ~ (we must take immediate ~) 6. drastic; emergency ~ 7. disciplinary; remedial ~ 8. hasty, rash ~ 9. affirmative ~ ("giving preference to members of minority groups") 10. industrial (BE), (a) job (AE), (a) strike ~ ("a protest by workers") 11. congressional; political ~ 12. (a) reflex ~ ["combat; military or police activity"] 13. to go into ~ 14. to see ~ ("to participate in combat") 15. to break off ~ 16. to take evasive ~ ("to maneuver in order to escape enemy fire") 17. enemy ~; a delaying, holding; police; punitive; rearguard ~ 18. in ~ (killed in ~) 19. out of ~ (two tanks were put out of ~) ["lawsuit"] 20. to bring, institute, take ~ against smb. for smt. (he brought legal ~ against his neighbor) 21. to dismiss an ~ (the judge dismissed the ~) 22. a civil; class; divorce; legal; libel ~ ["initiative"] ["enterprise"] 23. a man, woman of ~ ["plot of a play, novel"] 24. the ~ drags; picks up; takes place (the ~ picks up in the third act) ["misc."] 25. (colloq.) a piece of the ~ ("participation in an activity"; "a share of the profits"); the time for ~ is now ("this is the moment to act")

active *adj.* 1. sexually ~ 2. ~ in

activity *n.* 1. to engage in, participate in, take part in an ~ (all students take part in extracurricular ~ties) 2. to stimulate ~ (to stimulate economic ~) 3. to resume one's ~ties 4. to break off, terminate an ~ 5. to curb; paralyze ~ (business ~ was paralyzed) 6. bustling, constant, feverish, furious, uninterrupted ~ 7. business, economic; cultural; political; scientific ~ 8. extracurricular; leisure, recreational; social ~ 9. intellectual ~ 10. indoor; outdoor; physical ~ 11. subversive; terrorist; undercover ~ 12. union ~ties 13. to buzz, hum with ~ 14. a burst, flurry, whirl of ~

actor, actress *n.* 1. to cast an ~ 2. a character; ham ~

actuality *n.* in ~

act up *v.* (D; intr.) ("to function badly") to ~ on (my leg has been ~ing up on me)

acuity *n.* mental; visual ~

acumen *n.* 1. to demonstrate, display ~ 2. business, financial; legal; political ~ 3. the ~ to + inf. (she had enough ~ to see through the scheme)

acupuncture *n.* to do, perform ~ (on)

ad *n.* a classified, small (BE); help-wanted; lonely-hearts; want ~ (see also **advertisement**)

adage *n.* a familiar; old ~

adamant *adj.* 1. ~ about; in 2. ~ that + clause; may have subj. when the subjects of the clauses are different (he was ~ that he was fit to go; she was ~ that he not/should not go)

adapt *v.* 1. (D; tr.) to ~ for; from (to ~ a novel for the stage; to ~ a film from a novel) 2. (D; intr., refl., tr.) to ~ to (we ~ed quickly to life in Paris; she had to ~ herself to local conditions) 3. (D; tr.) to ~ to + inf. (we ~ed our schedule to meet their requirements)

adaptation *n.* 1. to make an ~ 2. an ~ for (an ~ of a novel for television)

add *v.* 1. to ~ considerably, greatly 2. (D; intr., tr.) to ~ to (we ~ed this amount to the bill; these changes ~ed greatly to the confusion) 3. (L) she ~ed that she would not bring the children

addendum *n.* an ~ to

addict *n.* a confirmed; drug ~

addicted *adj.* 1. chronically, hopelessly ~ 2. ~ to (~ to drugs)

addiction *n.* 1. chronic, hopeless ~ 2. drug ~ 3. (an) ~ to (~ to drugs)

addictive *adj.* highly ~

adding machine *n.* to operate, use, work an ~

addition *n.* ["adding of numbers"] 1. to do ~ ["part added"] 2. to make an ~ 3. a welcome ~ 4. an ~ to (an ~ to the family; an ~ to a report) 5. in ~ (in ~, she brought some fresh fruit) 6. in ~ to (in ~ to his salary, he earns a lot from royalties)

add on *v.* (D; tr.) to ~ to (to ~ a garage to a house)

address I *n.* ["speech"] 1. to deliver, give an ~ 2. an eloquent, moving, stirring ~ 3. a commencement; inaugural; keynote ~ 4. an ~ about, concerning ["place of residence"] ["place for receiving mail"] 5. to change one's ~ 6. a business; E-mail; forwarding; home; mailing; permanent; return; temporary; (BE) term-time ~ 7. at an ~ (at what ~ does she live?)

address II *v.* 1. (B) she ~ed her remarks to us; I ~ed the letter to him 2. (d; tr.) to ~ as (you should ~ him as "sir") 3. (d; tr.) to ~ to (~ her mail to this post-

office box) 4. (d; refl.) ("to deal with") to ~ to (the candidates did not ~ themselves to the issues; the book ~es itself to the problem of poverty)

USAGE NOTE: While this reflexive form in the meaning of "to deal with" is used as shown in the examples, nowadays the transitive form is more typical — "the candidates did not address the issues" and "the book addresses the problem of poverty".

add up *v.* (d; intr.) to ~ to (it all ~s up to a hoax; the figures ~ to fifty)

adept *adj.* ~ at, in (~ at solving crossword puzzles)

adequate *adj.* 1. barely ~ 2. ~ for (the food was ~ for all of us) 3. ~ to (she was ~ to the task) 4. ~ to + inf. (it would be ~ to list just the basic objections)

adhere *v.* 1. to ~ closely, doggedly, strictly, stubbornly, tenaciously 2. (d; intr.) to ~ to (to ~ strictly to a plan)

adherence *n.* 1. close, strict ~ 2. ~ to (strict ~ to a plan)

adieu *n.* to bid smb. ~

adjacent *adj.* ~ to (~ to our building)

adjective *n.* 1. to compare an ~ 2. an attributive; demonstrative; descriptive; gradable; non-gradable; possessive; predicate, predicative ~ 3. ~s modify nouns

adjourn *v.* 1. (D; intr.) ("to stop") to ~ for (to ~ for lunch) 2. (d; intr.) ("to move") (to ~ to the living room for brandy)

adjudge *v.* (formal) (M and N; used with an adjective) the court ~d him (to be) guilty

adjunct *n.* an ~ to (an adverb is often an ~ to a verb)

adjure *v.* (formal) (H) to ~ smb. to tell the truth

adjust *v.* (D. intr., refl., tr.) to ~ to (he had to ~ to the new climate; we ~ed our watches to local time)

adjuster *n.* a claims, insurance ~

adjustment *n.* 1. to make an ~ 2. a price; rate ~ 3. an ~ in, of (an ~ in/of his salary; an ~ of the brakes) 4. an ~ to (an ~ to a new environment)

adjutant *n.* an ~ general

administer *v.* 1. (B) ("to give") to ~ an oath to smb.

administration *n.* ["management"] 1. business; public ~ ["government"] 2. a centralized; civil; colonial; decentralized; federal ~ ["body of administrators"] 3. a college, university; hospital; school ~

USAGE NOTE: Consider such phrases as the "Clinton Administration" and the "Thatcher Administration".

administrator *n.* a civil; health; hospital; nursing; school; university ~

admiral *n.* a rear; vice ~; a fleet ~ (US); an ~ of the fleet (GB)

admiration *n.* 1. to arouse, win; command ~ 2. to express; feel; show ~ 3. (a) blind; deep, great, sincere, strong, undying; grudging; mutual; secret; ungrudging; universal ~ 4. ~ for (he felt great

~ for them) 5. in, with ~ (to look at smb. with ~) 6. (misc.) (humorous) a mutual ~ society

admire *v.* 1. to ~ greatly, very much 2. (D; tr.) to ~ as (we ~d her as a devoted teacher) 3. (D; tr.) to ~ for (we ~ her for her tact) 4. (K) they all ~d his behaving in that manner

admirer *n.* 1. to attract ~s 2. an ardent, devoted, enthusiastic, fervent, great, sincere; secret ~

admission *n.* ["access"] 1. to apply for; gain; seek ~ 2. to deny, refuse; grant ~ 3. free, open; restricted, selective ~; rolling (esp. AE) ~s 4. ~ to (she applied for ~ to the university) ["confession"] 5. to make an ~ of (he made an ~ of guilt) 6. a damaging ~ 7. a grudging ~ 8. an ~ that + clause (his ~ that he had been at the scene of the crime led to his conviction) 9. by, on smb.'s own ~ ["entry fee"] 10. general ~

admit *v.* 1. to ~ freely, openly, readily 2. to ~ grudgingly 3. (B) ("to confess") the accused ~ted his guilt to the police 4. (D; tr.) ("to allow entry") to ~ into, to (the manager ~ted him to the theater; she was ~ted to the university) 5. (formal) (d; intr.) ("to tolerate") to ~ of (the situation ~s of no delay) 6. (formal) (d; intr.) ("to confess") to ~ to (he ~ted to his complicity in the crime; the boy ~ted to stealing the apples) 7. (G) ("to confess") the employee ~ted stealing the money 8. (L; to) ("to confess") the clerk ~ted (to the police) that he had taken the jewels

admittance *n.* 1. to gain ~ to 2. to deny ~ to (he was denied ~ to the concert)

admonish *v.* (formal) 1. (D; tr.) to ~ for (the teacher ~ed the child for coming late to school) 2. (H) to ~ smb. to do smt.

ado *n.* 1. to make much ~ about, over 2. without further, much ~

adopt *v.* (D; tr.) to ~ as (they ~ed the child as their heir)

adoption *n.* to give up, put up for ~ (to put a child up for ~)

adore *v.* 1. (D; tr.) to ~ for (we ~ them for their generosity) 2. (G) she ~s visiting museums 3. (misc.) I ~ it when you look at me like that

adorn *v.* (D; tr.) to ~ with (the table was ~ed with flowers)

adrenaline *n.* the ~ was flowing

adrift *adj.*, *adv.* 1. to cast, set ~ 2. to cut ~ (from)

adroit *adj.* ~ at, in (~ at staying out of trouble)

adroitness *n.* ~ at, in (~ at giving injections)

adultery *n.* to commit ~ (with)

adulthood *n.* to reach ~

adults *n.* consenting ~

advance I *n.* ["forward movement"] 1. (usu. mil.) to make; press an ~ 2. (usu. mil.) an ~ against, on, to, towards (our troops made an ~ against the enemy) 3. an ~ into (an ~ into enemy territory) ["progress"] 4. a scientific; technological ~ 5. an ~

in (~ in science) ["early payment"] 6. to receive an ~ 7. to pay an ~ 8. an ~ on (to receive an ~ on royalties) ["misc."] 9. she paid her rent in ~; in ~ of the main party

advance II *v.* 1. (A) we ~d a month's salary to him; or: we ~d him a month's salary 2. (D; intr.) to ~ against, on, to, towards (our troops ~d on the next town) 3. (D; tr.) to ~ to (he was ~d to the rank of corporal)

advanced *adj.* 1. technologically ~ 2. ~ in (~ in industrial development)

advancement *n.* 1. to further, speed smb.'s ~ 2. to block smb.'s ~ 3. personal; professional; social ~ 4. rapid; slow ~

advances *n.* ["effort to become friendly or to enter into negotiations"] 1. to make ~ to (he made ~ to her) 2. to rebuff, reject smb.'s ~ 3. improper ~ (to rebuff smb.'s improper ~)

advantage *n.* 1. to have an ~ of; over (our team had the ~ of experience; her connections gave her an ~ over the others) 2. to gain; press (home) an ~ 3. to take ~ of ("to exploit") 4. to outweigh an ~ 5. a big, great; clear, decided, definite; mutual; unfair ~ 6. an ~ to (his wealth was an obvious ~ to us) 7. an ~ to + inf. (it was an ~ to have that team as our opponent in the first round = it was an ~ having that team as our opponent in the first round) 8. the ~ that + clause; may be subj. (it was to his ~ that she not/should not participate; it was to our ~ that they did not participate) 9. to smb.'s ~ (see also 8) 10. at an ~ 11. (tennis) ~ in; ~ out 12. (misc.) (BE) you have the ~ of me ("you know more than I do"); their political connections were used to good ~

advantageous *adj.* 1. clearly ~ 2. ~ to (his decision was ~ to us) 3. ~ to + inf. (it would be ~ to wait)

adventure *n.* 1. to have, meet with an ~ 2. a bold; breathtaking, exciting, real, thrilling; romantic ~; high ~ 3. an ~ to + inf. (it was an ~ to visit that place = it was an ~ visiting that place) 4. (misc.) a sense of ~

adventurer *n.* a bold, dauntless, intrepid; unprincipled ~

adverb *n.* an interrogative; negative ~

adversary *n.* 1. to come up against an ~ 2. a formidable, powerful; political; worthy ~

adverse *adj.* (formal) ~ to (~ to our interests)

adversity *n.* 1. to face (up to); overcome ~ 2. (misc.) in (the face of) ~

advert I (BE) see **advertisement**

advert II *v.* (formal) (d; intr.) ("to refer") to ~ to

advertise *v.* 1. (D; tr.) to ~ as (the match was ~d as the event of the decade) 2. (D; intr.) to ~ for (to ~ for a maid) 3. (L) they ~d that a position was open

advertisement *n.* 1. to place, publish, run an ~ (to run an ~ for a used car) 2. a classified; full-page; magazine; newspaper ~ 3. an ~ for

advertising *n.* classified; outdoor; word-of-mouth ~

advice *n.* 1. to give, offer ~ 2. to act on, follow, heed, take ~ 3. to ask for, seek, solicit ~ 4. to disregard, ignore, refuse, turn a deaf ear to ~ 5. good, practical, right, sage, sensible, sound, useful, valuable ~ 6. friendly; parting; unsolicited ~ 7. professional; technical ~ 8. misleading; useless; wrong ~ 9. a bit, piece, word of ~ 10. ~ about, on 11. ~ to (my ~ to him was that...) 12. ~ to + inf. (we took his ~ to remain silent) 13. ~ that + clause; subj. (my ~ is that you see/should see a doctor) 14. against smb.'s ~ 15. on, upon smb.'s ~ (on ~ of counsel; I acted on her ~)

advisable *adj.* 1. ~ to + inf. (it was ~ to leave immediately) 2. ~ that + clause; subj. (it is ~ that she leave/should leave early)

advise *v.* 1. to ~ strongly 2. (D; tr.) to ~ about, on 3. (d; intr., tr.) to ~ against (to ~ smb. against a course of action) 4. (formal) (d; tr.) to ~ of (to ~ smb. of the facts) 5. (G) who ~d making that statement? 6. (H) she ~d us not to wait 7. (K) who ~d his making that statement? 8. (L; must have an object in AE) she ~d (us) that we should leave 9. (Q; must have an object) he ~d us what to do; they ~d us where to go

advised *adj.* ill; well ~ to + inf. (you would be well ~ to stop smoking)

advisement *n.* (often legal) to take smt. under ~

adviser, advisor *n.* 1. an academic; careers (BE) ~ spiritual ~ 2. an economic; financial; foreign-policy; legal; military; political ~ 3. a senior; technical ~ 4. an ~ on; to (an ~ on foreign policy; an ~ to the president)

advisory *adj.* 1. merely, only, strictly ~ 2. ~ to

advocate I *n.* 1. an aggressive, strong; ardent ~ 2. a client, patient; consumer ~ 3. (the) devil's ~ (to play the devil's ~)

advocate II *v.* 1. to ~ strongly 2. (G) he ~d bringing legal action 3. (K) she ~d our withdrawing from the contest 4. (formal) (L; subj.) they ~d that one candidate withdraw/should withdraw

aegis *n.* under smb.'s ~, under the ~ of

aerial *n.* (esp. BE) a television, TV ~ (AE has *antenna*)

aerobics *n.* to do, go in for, take up ~

aeroplane (BE) see **airplane**

aether (old-fashioned BE) see **ether**

afar *adv.* from ~

affair *n.* ["romantic liaison"] 1. to carry on, have an ~ (with) 2. a casual; clandestine, secret; extramarital, illicit; love; passionate, tempestuous, torrid ~ ["matter"] ["event"] ["situation"] ["scandal"] 3. to investigate an ~ 4. to cover up, hush up an/the (whole) ~; to wash one's hands of an/the (whole) ~ 5. a delicate; embarrassing; private ~ 6. a sinister, sordid, ugly; sorry ~ 7. an ~ of honor ["social event"] 8. a dull; exciting ~ 9. a formal; gala; informal ~ 10. a catered ~ ["misc."] 11. a long-drawn-out ~

affairs *n.* 1. to administer, conduct ~ (of state) 2. to arrange; manage, run; settle one's ~ 3. to put one's ~ in order 4. to straighten out one's ~ 5. to wind up one's ~ 6. civil; community; cultural ~ 7. domestic, home (BE), internal; external, foreign; international; national ~ 8. legal; military; political; public; veterans' (AE) ~ 9. current ~ 10. (misc.) to interfere, meddle in smb.'s ~; a state of ~

affect *v.* 1. to ~ adversely; deeply, profoundly, strongly 2. (formal) (esp. BE) (E) he ~ed not to hear

affection *n.* 1. to demonstrate, display, show; return ~ 2. to feel; have ~ 3. to gain, win smb.'s ~ (she won the children's ~) 4. deep, great, strong, warm ~ 5. little ~ 6. ~ for (to feel ~ for smb.) 7. with ~ 8. (misc.) a token of one's ~

affectionate *adj.* ~ to, towards, with (~ with children)

affections *n.* 1. to gain, win smb.'s ~ 2. to alienate smb.'s ~ 3. (misc.) the object of smb.'s ~

affidavit *n.* (legal) 1. to file, submit; sign an ~ (the lawyer filed an ~ on behalf of her client) 2. a sworn ~

affiliate *v.* (D; intr., refl., tr.) to ~ to, with (to ~ oneself with a movement; they are ~d with the national committee; to become ~d with)

affiliation *n.* 1. to form, have an ~ 2. business; party, political ~s 3. an ~ to, with

affinity *n.* 1. to demonstrate, show (an) ~ 2. to feel; have (an) ~ 3. (a) close; elective; natural; strong ~ 4. ~ between; for; to; with (he always felt a close ~ with the underdog)

affirm *v.* (L) the ministry ~ed that the visit had been postponed

affirmation *n.* ~ that + clause (I believed her affirmation that she would not go back on her word)

affirmative *n.* to answer, reply in the ~

affix *v.* (D; tr.) to ~ to (to ~ one's signature to a document)

afflicted *adj.* 1. grievously ~ 2. ~ with (~ with a disease)

affluence *n.* in ~ (to live in ~)

afford *v.* 1. to ill; well ~ 2. (formal) (A) it ~ed great pleasure to him; or: it ~ed him great pleasure 3. (E; preceded by the forms: can — cannot — can't — could — couldn't) we cannot ~ to buy a new house; we can ill ~ to lose this contract 4. (formal) (K; preceded by the forms: can — cannot — can't — could — couldn't) we couldn't ~ his signing up for another course

affront *n.* 1. (formal) to suffer an ~ 2. a personal; shocking ~ 3. an ~ to (it was an ~ to common decency)

afloat *adj.* 1. to keep smt. ~ 2. to set (a ship) ~ 3. to keep, stay ~

aflutter *adj.* (colloq.) 1. all ~ 2. ~ with (~ with excitement)

afoul *adv.* (AE) to run ~ of (to run ~ of the law) (also **foul I**)

afraid *adj.* 1. deathly, terribly ~ 2. ~ for (to be ~ for the future) 3. ~ of (the child was ~ of the dark) 4. ~ to + inf. (he was ~ to dive from the high board) 5. ~ that + clause (we were ~ that he would find out) 6. (misc.) is it true? I'm ~ so; is she coming? I'm ~ not

after I *adv.* 1. immediately; long; shortly, soon; well ~ 2. the day ~ 3. forever ~

after II *prep.* the police were ~ them

afterburners *n.* to activate, go to ~ (our interceptors had to go to ~)

aftereffects *n.* to feel the ~

aftermath *n.* 1. a grim ~ 2. an ~ of, to 3. in the ~ (in the ~ of that incident, he had to leave town)

afterglow *n.* to bask in the ~

afternoon *n.* in the ~; ~s (AE), every ~, on any ~; on the ~ of; on Wednesday ~, Wednesday ~ (AE)

aftershave *n.* to apply, put on; use ~

aftertaste *n.* 1. to leave an ~ 2. a bitter, unpleasant; nice, pleasant ~ (it left a pleasant ~)

afterthought *n.* as an ~ (the most important detail came out almost as an ~)

afterward (AE), **afterwards** see **after I**

agape *adj.* (formal) ["gaping"] ~ with (~ with astonishment)

age *n.* ["stage of life"] 1. to live to, reach an ~ 2. an advanced, (ripe) old, venerable ~ (she lived to a ripe old ~) 3. an early, tender, young; impressionable ~ (at an early ~; at a very young ~) 4. middle ~ 5. college; high-school (AE); preschool; school ~ 6. (a) retirement, retiring (BE) ~ 7. (a) legal ~; the ~ of consent 8. at an ~ (at a tender ~; at the ~ of six; she died at the age of eighty) 9. of an ~ (people of all ~s; of childbearing ~) 10. (misc.) to come of ~ ("to reach one's majority"); to act one's ~ ("to behave maturely"); to look, show one's ~ ("to not have a youthful appearance"); to feel one's ~ ("to feel old"); over ~ ("too old"); under ~ ("too young"); in old ~ ("of advanced years") ["era"] ["period"] 11. to usher in an ~ (to usher in the computer ~) 12. a golden; heroic ~ 13. the Dark; Middle ~s (during the Middle ~s) 14. the Bronze; Ice; Iron; Stone ~ 15. the atomic, nuclear; computer; space ~ 16. in an ~ (in the nuclear ~) 17. for ~s (and ~s) 18. through the ~s

agency *n.* 1. an adoption; health-care; home-health (AE); welfare ~ 2. a private; public; voluntary ~ 3. an advertising; detective; employment; escort; ticket; travel ~ 4. a government; intelligence; law-enforcement; regulatory; watchdog ~ 5. a news ~ 6. at, in an ~ (she works at a travel ~)

agenda *n.* 1. to draw up, make up, put together an ~

2. to place, put smt. on the ~ (to put an item on the ~) 3. a hidden ~ ("a secret plan") 4. an item on the ~ 5. (misc.) high on the ~

agent *n.* ["representative"] 1. an estate (BE), real-estate (AE); insurance ~ 2. a literary; press ~ 3. a purchasing; shipping ~ 4. a ticket; travel ~ 5. a free ~ 6. an ~ for (an ~ for a large firm) ["smb. engaged in intelligence activities"] 7. a double; enemy; espionage, secret, undercover; special ~ 8. (misc.) an ~ provocateur ["substance"] 9. an asphyxiating; chemical; toxic ~ 10. a cleaning; cleansing ~

aggrandizement *n.* personal; territorial ~

aggregate *n.* in the ~

aggression *n.* ["attack"] 1. to commit ~ (against) 2. to repel ~ 3. armed; brazen, flagrant, naked, outright, stark, unprovoked ~ ["aggressiveness"] 4. to display, manifest, show ~ 5. to control, stifle ~ 6. deep-seated, hidden, deep-rooted ~ 7. an act of ~ (to commit an act of ~)

aghast *adj.* 1. ~ at (~ at the very thought of going back to work) 2. ~ to + inf. (they were ~ to learn of the bank's failure)

agitate *v.* 1. to ~ strongly 2. (D; intr.) to ~ against; for (they were ~ing for reform)

agitation *n.* 1. political; student; subversive ~ 2. ~ against; for 3. (misc.) in a state of great ~ ("feeling high anxiety")

agitator *n.* a political ~

aglow *adj.* ~ with (~ with happiness)

ago *adv.* 1. ~ that + clause (it was five years ~ that we met) 2. (misc.) a week ~; a long time ~, long ~; a while ~; many years ~, years and years ~

agog *adj.* 1. ~ over; with (she was all ~ over her new granddaughter) 2. ~ to + inf. (they were all ~ to hear the news)

agonize *v.* (D; intr.) to ~ about, over (to ~ over a decision)

agony *n.* 1. to endure, experience, feel ~ 2. to prolong the ~ 3. acute, deep, great, indescribable, untold; mortal ~ 4. in ~ (in great ~)

agree *v.* 1. ("to concur") to ~ completely, entirely, fully, totally, wholeheartedly; readily 2. (D; intr.) ("to concur") to ~ about; on, to; upon; with (to ~ with smb. about smt.; to ~ on/to a compromise) 3. (d; intr.) (of food, climate) to ~ with ("to suit") (the food doesn't ~ with me) 4. (grammar) (D; intr.) ("to correspond") to ~ in; with (Latin adjectives ~ with nouns in gender) 5. (E) ("to consent") they ~d to help 6. (L) ("to concur") we ~d that everyone would receive an equal share 7. (misc.) I could not ~ more

USAGE NOTE: In BE, *agree* can be used as a transitive verb — *to agree a plan.*

agreeable *adj.* 1. mutually ~ 2. ~ to (they were all ~ to our proposal; is this ~ to you?)

agreement *n.* ["contract, settlement, treaty"] 1. to arrive at, come to, conclude, enter into, negotiate, reach an ~ 2. to draw up, make, work out an ~ 3. to seal, sign an ~ 4. to carry out, honor, live up to an ~ 5. to break, violate an ~ 6. to cancel, denounce, rescind an ~ 7. a binding; contractual; ironclad; legal; secret; tacit; tentative; verbal; written ~ (we reached a tentative ~) 8. a prenuptial ~ 9. an armistice, ceasefire, peace ~ 10. an arms control, nonproliferation ~ 11. a sales, trade ~ 12. a bilateral; international; multilateral ~ 13. an ~ about, on; between; with (an ~ was worked out between them on all points) 14. an ~ to + inf. (we reached an ~ with them to cooperate fully at all times) 15. an ~ that + clause (the negotiators came to an ~ that all troops would/should be withdrawn) ["concord, harmony"] 16. to express; reach ~ 17. basic, essential; bipartisan; complete, full, solid, total, unanimous; mutual; tacit ~ (they reached full ~ on all points) 18. ~ about, on, over 19. by ~ (by mutual ~) 20. in ~ (we were in full ~ with them on all points) ["grammatical concord"] 21. grammatical ~ 22. ~ in (~ in case, gender, and number)

aground adj., adv. to run ~ (the ship ran ~)

ahead adj., adv. 1. comfortably, considerably, far, way, well ~ 2. ~ by (our team was ~ by three points) 3. ~ of (~ of one's competitors; to finish ~ of schedule) 4. (misc.) dead, straight ~; full speed ~; Danger ~!

aid I n. 1. to extend, give, offer, provide, render ~ 2. to come to, go to smb.'s ~ 3. to cut, reduce ~ 4. cut off, withdraw ~ 5. to increase ~ 6. generous, unstinting ~ 7. audiovisual; teaching ~s 8. first ~ (first ~ to the injured) 9. a hearing ~ 10. economic, financial; emergency; federal (US); foreign; government; humanitarian; military; state (US) ~ 11. legal ~ (for the poor) 12. (an) ~ for; in; to (an ~ to memorization; economic ~ to developing countries) 13. with; without the ~ of (to walk with the ~ of crutches) 14. (misc.) to enlist smb.'s ~; (BE; colloq.) what's all this in ~ of ? ("what's all this for?")

aid II v. 1. (D; tr.) to ~ in (she ~ed him in his work) 2. (rare) (H) to ~ smb. to do smt. 3. (misc.) to ~ and abet

aide n. 1. a home health ~ (AE) (BE has *home help*) 2. a military; presidential; senior ~ 3. an ~ to

aids n. audiovisual; teaching ~

AIDS n. to contract, get; have ~

ailment n. 1. a chronic; common; minor, slight; serious ~ 2. a back; heart; kidney; skin; stomach ~

aim I n. ["purpose"] ["goal"] 1. to achieve one's ~ 2. a chief; immediate; long-range, longterm; shortterm ~ 3. an avowed; idealistic, lofty, worthy ~ 4. an ~ to + inf. (it was our ~ to complete the work before the end of the month) 5. with an ~ (the project was launched with the ~ of retraining the unemployed) ["aiming of a weapon"] 6. to take ~ at 7. careful; steady ~ (she took careful ~ at the

intruder)

aim II v. 1. (D; intr., tr.) to ~ at (he ~ed at me; I ~ed the revolver at the intruder) 2. (d; intr.) to ~ for (he ~ed for the heart; she was ~ing for a promotion) 3. (E) we ~ to please 4. (misc.) to ~ high (fig.)

air I n. ["atmosphere"] 1. to clear the ~ 2. to breathe (in), inhale; exhale ~ 3. to pollute the ~ 4. balmy, mild; bracing, brisk, crisp, refreshing; clean; compressed; country; dry; foul; fresh; frigid; humid; moist; polluted; sea; stale ~ 5. a breath of (fresh) ~; a blast of hot ~; a puff, whiff of ~ 6. in the ~ (the decisive battles were fought in the ~) ["transportation by aircraft"] 7. by ~ (to travel by ~) ["medium through which radio signals are transmitted"] 8. on the ~ (to go on the ~; our station is on the ~) 9. off the ~ (that station never goes off the ~) ["appearance"] 10. to assume an ~ (to assume an ~ of innocence) 11. a detached; knowing; nonchalant; superior, triumphant ~ ["tune"] 12. a martial ~ (the band struck up a martial ~) ["misc."] 13. in the ~ ("current, imminent"); to walk on ~ ("to be elated"); to give smb. the ~ ("to reject smb."); up in the ~ ("unsettled"); to disappear into thin ~

air II v. (B) he is ready to ~ his views to anyone

air conditioner n. 1. to run; turn on an ~ 2. to turn off an ~ 3. a central; room ~ 4. the ~ was on, was running

air conditioning n. central ~

aircraft n. 1. commercial; enemy; friendly; jet; military; private; unidentified ~ 2. (misc.) to shoot down enemy ~; lowflying ~ strafed enemy lines; to ground all ~

airing n. ["public discussion"] 1. to give smt. an ~ (they gave our proposal a good ~ at the conference) ["ventilation"] 2. to give smt. an ~ (we gave the blankets a good ~)

airlift v. (D; tr.) to ~ from; to (the refugees were ~ed to safety from the flooded areas)

airline n. a domestic; feeder; international, overseas; local ~

airmail n. by ~ (to send a letter by ~)

airplane (AE), **aeroplane** (BE) n. 1. to board, get on; take an ~ 2. to get off an ~ 3. to bring down, land; ditch; fly, pilot; navigate an ~ (a pilot flies an ~) 4. to bring down, shoot down; force down; hijack an ~ (our fire brought down an enemy ~) 5. a jet; propeller-driven ~ 6. an ~ banks; crashes; cruises; flies; gains altitude; lands, touches down; levels off; loses altitude; reaches an altitude; takes off; taxis along the runway (see also **plane**)

airport n. 1. an international; local; military ~ 2. at an ~

air raid n. to carry out, conduct an ~ against

airs n. ["affected manners"] 1. to give oneself, put on ~ 2. (misc.) (BE) ~ and graces

air show n. to have, hold, put on, stage an ~

air space *n.* to enter; respect; violate a country's ~

air superiority *n.* 1. to establish; gain ~ 2. complete, overwhelming, total ~

aisle *n.* 1. to clear the ~s 2. in the ~ (don't stand in the ~) 3. on the ~ (to sit on the ~) 4. (misc.) to roll in the ~s ("to laugh heartily")

ajar *adj.* to leave ~ (she left the door ~)

akin *adj.* (formal) (usu. does not stand alone) ~ to (a feeling ~ to love)

alarm *n.* ["warning device"] ["warning"] 1. to activate; give, raise, set off, sound; set; trigger, trip an ~ (she set the ~ to go off at five) 2. to deactivate, turn off an ~ 3. an air-raid; burglar; fire; silent; smoke ~ 4. a false ~ 5. an ~ goes off, rings, sounds ["apprehension, fear"] 6. to express; feel ~ 7. to cause; spread ~ (the incident caused great ~) 8. ~ at, over (to express ~ at the danger of war) 9. ~ that + clause (she expressed ~ that they would miss the train) 10. in ~

alarm clock *n.* 1. to set an ~ (she set the ~ to go off at five) 2. an ~ goes off, rings, sounds

alarmed *adj.* 1. unduly ~ 2. ~ at, by (we were ~ at the news of the earthquake)
USAGE NOTE: Currently *alarmed* is also used in the meaning "provided with an alarm" — *this room is alarmed.*

alarming *adj.* ~ to + inf. (it was ~ to think of the possible consequences)

album *n.* an autograph; photograph; stamp; wedding ~

alcohol *n.* 1. to distill, make ~ 2. to abstain from ~ 3. to reek of ~ 4. ethyl, grain; methyl, wood; pure, unadulterated; rubbing (AE; BE has *surgical spirit*) ~

alcoholic *n.* a chronic ~

alcoholism *n.* acute; chronic ~

alert I *adj.* 1. to keep, stay ~ 2. ~ to (~ to danger)

alert II *n.* 1. to call an ~ 2. to place, put (troops) on ~ 3. to call off, cancel an ~ 4. (a) full; high; preliminary; red ~ (the troops were on full ~) 5. on (the) ~ (for) (to be on the ~ for trouble) 6. (misc.) in a state of ~

alert III *v.* (D; tr.) to ~ to (we must ~ the public to the danger)

A levels *n.* ["advanced-level secondary-school examinations"] (GB) to do, sit, take one's ~

algebra *n.* to do ~

alias *n.* 1. to use an ~ 2. an ~ for 3. under an ~

alibi *n.* 1. to give; have; provide an ~ (for) 2. to check out, confirm smb.'s ~ 3. to disprove an ~ 4. an airtight, cast-iron, foolproof, unassailable ~ 5. his ~ held up

alien I *adj.* (formal) ~ to (such ideas are ~ to us)

alien II *n.* 1. to deport; intern an ~ 2. an enemy; illegal; resident ~

alienate *v.* (D; tr.) to ~ from (she was ~d from her family)

alienation *n.* ~ from (~ from one's old friends)

alight *v.* (formal) (D; intr.) to ~ from; on (to ~ from a vehicle; to ~ on a branch)

align *v.* (D; refl., tr.) to ~ with (the wheels must be ~ed with the frame; he ~ed himself with the left wing of the party)

alignment *n.* in; out of ~ (the wheels are out of ~)

alimony *n.* to award, grant; pay ~ (the judge awarded the ex-wife ~)

alive *adj.* 1. very much ~ 2. (cannot stand alone) ~ to (~ to the danger of becoming overconfident) 3. ~ with (the campus was ~ with students)

all I *n.* to give one's ~

all II *determiner, pronoun* ~ of (we saw ~ of them)
USAGE NOTE: The use of the preposition *of* is necessary when a personal pronoun follows. When a noun follows, *of* is omitted—the dean saw all (the) students ("the dean saw every student"). To express limited meaning, *of the* or *the* (very common in BE) can be inserted—the dean saw all students who had received poor grades = the dean saw all (of) the students who had received poor grades.

all clear *n.* 1. to give, sound the ~ 2. the ~ sounded

allegation *n.* ["assertion"] 1. to make; substantiate an ~ 2. to drop, retract, withdraw an ~ 3. to deny; reject; rebut, refute an ~ 4. a false; serious; slanderous; unproved, unsubstantiated, unsupported; vague ~ 5. an ~ about; against (~s of fraud were made against him) 6. an ~ that + clause (their ~ that she had taken the money proved to be false)

allege *v.* (L) it has been ~d that you stole the money

alleged *adj.* ~ to + inf. (she was ~ to have stolen the money)

allegiance *n.* 1. to give; owe; pledge, swear ~ 2. to switch one's ~ (from; to) 3. to disavow, forsake one's ~ to 4. true, unfailing, unswerving ~ 5. ~ to (~ to a cause)

allergic *adj.* ~ to (~ to dust)

allergy *n.* to acquire, develop; have an ~ to

alliance *n.* 1. to enter into, forge, form an ~ 2. to dissolve an ~ 3. a close; defense; military; political; unholy ~ 4. an ~ against; between; with (to form an ~ with one's neighbors against the common enemy) 5. an ~ to + inf. (an ~ to defend an area against any invader) 6. in ~ with

allied *adj.* ~ against; to, with (we were ~ with them against the aggressor)

allocate *v.* 1. (B; more rarely — A) the dean ~d the funds to several students 2. (D; tr.) to ~ for (our committee ~d money for the memorial)

allocation *n.* 1. to make an ~ 2. a budget ~ 3. an ~ for; to

allot *v.* 1. (A) the city has ~ted space to us; or: the city has ~ted us space 2. (D; tr.) to ~ for 3. (D; tr.) to ~ to (to ~ funds to the arts)

allow *v.* 1. (A; usu. without the preposition *to*) ("to permit") she did not ~ herself time for relaxation 2. (d; intr.) ("to provide") to ~ for (we ~ed for the difference in age; you must ~ for shrinkage) 3. (D; tr.) ("to give") to ~ for (they ~ed an hour for lunch) 4. (formal) (d; intr.) to ~ of ("to permit") (our financial situation ~s of no unnecessary expenditures) 5. (H) ("to permit") we ~ed the children to go to the park 6. (formal) (L) ("to admit") I must ~ that he is capable

allowance *n.* ["taking into account"] 1. to make (an) ~ for (to make ~/an ~ for inexperience; to make ~s for wear and tear) ["sum granted"] 2. to draw; give, grant an ~ 3. to live on an ~ 4. a cost-of-living; depletion; entertainment; housing; mileage; subsistence; trade-in; travel ~ 5. a daily; fixed; weekly ~ 6. an ~ for
USAGE NOTE: Parents may regularly give their children *pocket money*, which in AE is called *an allowance.*

all right *adj.* (colloq.) ~ to + inf. (it's ~ to take a break)

allude *v.* 1. to ~ vaguely 2. (d; intr.) to ~ to (the story ~d to a mystery in his past)

allusion *n.* 1. to make an ~ to (she made no ~ to the incident) 2. a vague ~

ally I *n.* a close, faithful, staunch ~

ally II *v.* (D; intr., refl.) to ~ against; to, with (we ~ied ourselves with our friends against the common enemy)

alms *n.* (formal) 1. to dispense, give ~ 2. ~ for (~ for the needy)

alone *adj.* 1. to leave, let smb./smt. ~ 2. ~ in (one's grief) 3. (misc.) to live ~; she's all ~ (in the world)

aloof *adj.* 1. to hold oneself, keep, remain, stand ~ 2. ~ from (he remained ~ from the others)

alphabet *n.* 1. the Arabic; Cyrillic; Greek; Hebrew; Latin, Roman; Phoenician; Sanskrit ~ 2. a phonetic; runic ~

altar *n.* 1. at the ~ 2. to lead smb. to the ~

alteration *n.* 1. to make an ~ 2. a major; minor, slight ~ 3. an ~ in

altercation *n.* (formal) 1. to have an ~ 2. an ~ about, over; between; with (to have an ~ with smb. about smt.)

alternate *v.* 1. (D; intr.) to ~ between (they ~ between supporting us and opposing us) 2. (D; intr.) to ~ in (we ~ in doing the household chores) 3. (d; intr., tr.) to ~ with (sunny weather ~d with rain; the coach ~d Jones with Wilson)

alternative *n.* 1. to propose an ~ 2. to fall back on an ~ 3. a viable ~ 4. an ~ to 5. no ~ but to + inf. (we have no ~ but to compromise)

altitude *n.* 1. to gain ~; to reach an ~ of 2. to lose ~ 3. a cruising ~ 4. at an ~ (at high ~s)

altogether *n.* ["nude state"] in the ~

amalgamate *v.* (D; intr., tr.) to ~ with (our firm will be ~d with a Japanese company)

amateur *n.* 1. a rank ~ 2. an ~ at, in

amaze *v.* (R) it ~d me (to learn) that he had been promoted

amazed *adj.* 1. ~ at, by (he was ~ at what he saw) 2. ~ to + inf. (she was ~ to see the results of the research) 3. ~ that + clause (we were ~ that he agreed so quickly)

amazement *n.* 1. complete, total, utter 2. ~ at (they expressed their ~ at our performance) 3. in, with ~ (they stared in ~) 4. to smb.'s ~ (to my utter ~, he arrived on time)

amazing *adj.* 1. ~ to + inf. (it was ~ to watch them perform) 2. ~ that + clause (it was ~ that she was able to solve the problem so quickly)

ambassador *n.* 1. to appoint an ~; to exchange ~s 2. to recall an ~ 3. an ~ extraordinary; an ~ plenipotentiary; an ambassador-at-large 4. a goodwill; roving ~ 5. an ~ to (our ~ to Rome)

ambiguity *n.* 1. to clear up, remove an ~; to avoid ~ 2. an ~ about, concerning

ambition *n.* 1. to achieve, attain, fulfill, realize one's ~ 2. to spur, stir smb.'s ~ 3. to limit, restrain one's ~ 4. boundless, unbridled; burning, consuming, devouring; driving ~ 5. frustrated; unrealized ~ 6. personal; political ~ 7. territorial ~s (of an aggressor) 8. an ~ to + inf. (he achieved his ~ to become mayor)

ambitious *adj.* (esp. BE) ~ to + inf. (she is ~ to succeed)

ambivalent *adj.* ~ about

amble *v.* (P; intr.) to ~ along the road

ambush *n.* 1. to lay, set an ~ for 2. to draw smb. into an ~ 3. to hide, lie, lurk, wait in ~ (for) 4. to run into, walk into an ~ 5. from ~ (to attack from ~)

amen *n.* 1. to say ~ 2. (informal) to say ~ to ("to endorse")

amenable *adj.* ~ to (~ to compromise)

amendment *n.* 1. to adopt; propose; ratify an ~ 2. a constitutional ~ 3. an ~ to (an ~ to the constitution)

amends *n.* to make ~ for (she wanted to make ~ for the damage that she had caused)

amenities *n.* ["comforts"] 1. to provide the ~ for ["greetings"] 2. to exchange ~ ["proper manners"] 3. to observe the ~

American *n.* 1. a Native ~ ("an American Indian of the US") 2. General ~ ("the English spoken in most of the US")

amiss *adj., adv.* (formal) 1. to take smt. ~ 2. to go ~ (a little courtesy would not go ~)

ammunition *n.* 1. to provide ~ for (also fig.) 2. to issue ~ 3. blank; dummy; live; tracer ~

amnesty *n.* 1. to declare, grant, offer (an) ~ (he was granted ~) 2. a full; general; partial; political ~ 3. an ~ for (the government declared a general ~ for political prisoners)

amok, amuck *adv.* to run ~

amount I *n.* 1. to calculate, figure out an ~ 2. an

ample, considerable, enormous, huge, large, tremendous; moderate; negligible, paltry, small ~ 3. the exact; full ~ 4. (misc.) an equivalent ~ in francs

amount II *v.* (d; intr.) to ~ to (it ~s to fraud; he'll never ~ to anything)

amuse *v.* 1. to ~ greatly, thoroughly, very much 2. (D; refl., tr.) to ~ by, with (she ~d the children with tricks; they ~d themselves by playing games) 3. (R) it ~d us to watch them play; it ~d me that they would never admit to being wrong

amused *adj.* 1. greatly, highly, thoroughly, vastly ~ 2. ~ at, by (she was ~ at/by that story) 3. ~ to + inf. (I was ~ to see him playing up to the boss) 4. to keep smb. ~ (he kept the children ~ by reading stories)

amusement *n.* 1. to provide ~ for 2. to find ~ in 3. in ~ (to look on in ~) 4. to smb.'s ~ (much to my ~, everyone believed her story)

amusing *adj.* 1. highly ~ 2. ~ to (it was ~ to everyone) 3. ~ to + inf. (it was ~ to watch the trained elephants perform)

anaemia (BE) see **anemia**

anaesthesia (BE) see **anesthesia**

anaesthetic (BE) see **anesthetic**

analogous *adj.* ~ to, with

analogy *n.* 1. to draw, make an ~ 2. a close; superficial ~ (there is a close ~ between these two phenomena) 3. an ~ between; to, with 4. by ~ (to reason by ~) 5. on the ~ of (to say *thunk* on the analogy of *sunk*)

analysis *n.* ["examination of component parts"] 1. to make an ~ 2. a careful, painstaking, thorough; critical; in-depth; objective; penetrating; subjective ~ 3. (ling.) discourse ~ 4. (chemistry) qualitative; quantitative ~ 5. (math.) vector ~ 6. on, upon ~ (upon further ~, we concluded that...) 7. in the last, final, ultimate ~ ["psychoanalysis"] 8. to undergo (an) ~

analyst *n.* financial; political; systems ~

anarchy *n.* 1. complete, total, utter ~ 2. ~ reigns

anathema *n.* 1. to declare, pronounce an ~ on 2. to lift an ~ from 3. ~ to (his theories were ~ to his colleagues)

anatomy *n.* comparative; descriptive; human ~

ancestor *n.* a common; remote ~

ancestry *n.* 1. to trace one's ~ (back to) 2. of (a certain) ~ (to be of French ~)

anchor I *n.* 1. to cast, drop ~ 2. to raise, weigh ~ 3. at ~ (to ride at ~)

anchor II *v.* to ~ firmly

anecdote *n.* 1. to relate, tell an ~ 2. an amusing, funny, witty; off-color; personal ~ 3. an ~ about

anemia, anaemia *n.* 1. to develop, have ~ 2. pernicious; sickle-cell ~

anesthesia, anaesthesia *n.* 1. to induce, produce ~ 2. to undergo ~ 3. general; local ~ 4. the ~ takes effect; wears off 5. under ~

anesthetic, anaesthetic *n.* 1. to administer, give an ~ 2. to have, take an ~ 3. a general; local ~ 4. the ~ takes effect; wears off 5. under an ~

angel *n.* (lit.) an avenging; fallen; guardian; ministering ~

anger I *n.* 1. to arouse, stir up ~ (the new taxes stirred up ~ against the government) 2. to express; feel; show ~ 3. to contain, restrain, suppress (one's) ~ 4. to repress, swallow one's ~ 5. to allay, appease, calm smb.'s ~ 6. to vent one's ~ (on) 7. blind, burning, deep, profound, seething, unbridled; mounting, rising ~ 8. righteous ~ 9. ~ subsides 10. a blaze, explosion, fit, outburst of ~ 11. ~ about, over; at smt. (he could hardly suppress his ~ about/over the matter; they expressed their deep ~ at being mistreated) 12. ~ at (esp. AE), towards, with smb. (their ~ at/towards/with me was ill-concealed) 13. in; with ~ (she struck back in ~; burning with ~)

anger II *v.* (R) it ~ed me (to learn) that they had not kept their promise

angle I *n.* ["space between two straight lines that meet"] 1. an acute; alternate; complementary; exterior; interior; obtuse; right; solid; supplementary ~ 2. a sharp ~ (at a sharp ~) 3. the side; vertex of an ~ ["deviation from a straight line"] 4. at an ~ (at an ~ of thirty degrees; at a rakish ~; at a right ~) ["viewpoint"] ["aspect"] 5. from an ~ (to examine a question from various ~s) ["motive; scheme"] (colloq.) (esp. AE) 6. to have an ~

angle II *v.* (d; intr.) to ~ for ("to try to obtain") (she was ~ing for an invitation)

angry *adj.* 1. to become, get ~ 2. ~ about, at, over smt. (they were ~ about the changes; we were ~ at being disturbed; they get ~ over every trifle) 3. ~ at (esp. AE), with smb. (he was ~ at his neighbor; she was ~ with me for being late) 4. ~ to + inf. (I was ~ to learn of his refusal to help) 5. ~ that + clause (we were ~ that our request had been rejected)

anguish *n.* (formal) 1. to cause ~ 2. acute; bitter; deep; mental ~ 3. ~ at, over 4. in ~ (in ~ over smb.'s death)

animadversion *n.* (formal) to make an ~ on, upon

animadvert *v.* (formal) (D; intr.) to ~ on, upon (to ~ on corruption)

animal *n.* 1. to domesticate an ~; to tame; train a wild ~ 2. to breed, raise ~s (in captivity) 3. to trap an ~ 4. to hunt wild ~s 5. to butcher, slaughter ~s (for food) 6. to skin an ~ 7. to stuff an ~ 8. to neuter an ~ 9. a carnivorous, flesh-eating, meat-eating; herbivorous, plant-eating ~ 10. a dangerous; predatory; wild ~ 11. a domestic; tame ~ 12. a draft; pack ~ 13. (misc.) like a caged ~; human beings are social ~s

animation *n.* computer; suspended ~

animosity *n.* 1. to arouse, stir up ~ 2. to feel, harbor ~ 3. bitter, burning, deep, seething ~ 4. personal ~

5. racial; religious ~ 6. ~ against, to, towards (she felt a burning ~ towards them) 7. ~ between

ankle *n.* 1. to sprain, turn, twist, wrench one's ~ 2. a well-turned ("shapely") ~ 3. (misc.) ~ deep in mud

annals *n.* to go down in the ~ (of history as)

annex I annexe *n.* an ~ to (an ~ to the main building; an ~ to a treaty)

annex II *v.* (D; tr.) to ~ to (they ~ed the conquered territory to their country)

annihilation *n.* nuclear ~

anniversary *n.* 1. to celebrate, commemorate, mark, reach an ~ 2. a wedding ~ 3. a diamond; golden; silver ~ 4. on an ~ (on their tenth wedding ~) 5. (misc.) (I wish you) a happy ~!

annotation *n.* 1. to make an ~ (to make ~s in/on/to a text) 2. copious ~s

announce *v.* 1. (B) they ~d the news to the reporters 2. (L; to) the president of the firm ~d (to the employees) that there would be a bonus

announcement *n.* 1. to issue, make an ~ 2. a birth; wedding ~ 3. a dramatic; formal, official; public ~ 4. a spot ~ 5. an ~ about, of 6. an ~ that + clause (they made a public ~ that an amnesty would be declared)

announcer *n.* a radio; sports ~

annoy *v.* 1. to ~ greatly, very much 2. (R) it ~ed me to be kept waiting so long; it ~ed us that they took so long to answer

annoyance *n.* 1. to express; feel; show ~ 2. great ~ 3. ~ at (esp. AE), with smb. 4. ~ at, over smt. 5. ~ that + clause (his ~ that he had been awakened so early was evident) 6. to smb.'s ~ (much to my ~, he was late)

annoyed *adj.* 1. greatly, very, very much ~ 2. ~ about, at smt. (we were ~ at losing the order) 3. ~ at (esp. AE), with smb. (he was ~ at/with the children) 4. ~ to + inf. (he was ~ to find his door unlocked) 5. ~ that + clause (she was ~ that the library was still closed)

annoying *adj.* 1. highly, most, terribly, very ~ 2. ~ to (it was ~ to everyone) 3. ~ to + inf. (it is ~ to read nothing but bad news) 4. ~ that + clause (it's ~ that there is no hot water)

annulment *n.* 1. to grant an ~ 2. to obtain an ~

anoint *v.* 1. (D; tr.) to ~ with (to ~ smb. with oil) 2. (N; used with a noun) they ~ed him king

anonymous *adj.* to remain ~

another *determiner, pronoun* one way or ~; one after ~; yet ~

USAGE NOTE: The preposition *of* is used before the plural — *he had another of his crazy ideas.*

answer I *n.* 1. to give, offer, provide an ~ 2. to come up with; have an ~ 3. to guess; know the ~ 4. to get, receive an ~ (from) 5. a clear, definite, straight, straightforward, unequivocal; definitive; direct ~ 6. a civil; diplomatic; wise ~ 7. a favorable; witty ~ 8. an immediate; ready; simple ~ 9. a glib; imperti-

nent; simplistic; stock ~ 10. an equivocal; evasive, vague ~ 11. a blunt, brusque, curt ~ 12. an affirmative, positive ~ 13. a negative ~ 14. a correct, right ~ 15. an incorrect, wrong ~ 16. (BE) a dusty ("unsatisfactory") ~ 17. a written ~ 18. an ~ to 19. in ~ to (in ~ to your question)

answer II *v.* 1. ("to respond") to ~ immediately 2. (d; intr.) ("to be responsible") to ~ to smb. for smt. (the directors had to ~ to the stockholders for the loss) 3. (d; intr.) ("to respond") to ~ to (to ~ to a name; the child ~s only to its nickname) 4. (d; intr.) ("to correspond") to ~ to (she ~s to the description) 5. (D; intr., tr.) (" to respond") to ~ with (she ~ed me with a nod) 6. (L; may have an object) ("to respond") they ~ed (us) that they would come 7. (misc.) can you ~ me this?

answerable *adj.* ~ for; to (we are ~ to our superiors for our actions)

answer back *v.* (D; intr.) to ~ to (children should not ~ to their parents)

ant *n.* 1. army; carpenter; fire; harvester; honey; leafcutter; worker ~s 2. white ~s ("termites") 3. a colony of ~s

antagonism *n.* 1. to arouse, stir up ~ 2. to feel (an) ~ 3. bitter, deep, deep-rooted, deep-seated, profound, strong ~ 4. ~ between; to, towards (to feel a strong ~ towards smb.)

antagonist *n.* a formidable ~

antagonistic *adj.* ~ to, towards (he is very ~ to us)

ante *n.* ["stakes"] (colloq.) to up the ~ (also fig.)

antelope *n.* a herd of ~

antenna *n.* a loop; outside; radio; television, TV ~ (BE also has *aerial*)

anterior *adj.* (formal) ~ to

anthem *n.* a national ~ (the band played/struck up the national ~)

anthropology *n.* cultural; physical; social ~

antibiotic *n.* 1. to prescribe an ~ 2. to take an ~ 3. a broad-spectrum ~ 4. a course of ~s

anticipate *v.* 1. to ~ eagerly 2. (G) we ~ spending two weeks here 3. (K) we ~d his winning first prize 4. (L) I ~d that they would be late 5. (Q) we could not ~ when they would arrive

anticipation *n.* 1. eager, keen ~ 2. in ~ of (an exhibit was scheduled in ~ of his visit) 3. with ~ (to look forward to smt. with eager ~)

anticlimax *n.* an ~ to (everything was an ~ to winning an Olympic gold medal)

anticlockwise (BE) see **counterclockwise**

antidote *n.* 1. to administer, give an ~ 2. to take an ~ 3. an ~ against, for, to (he took an ~ for the poison; an ~ to complacency)

antifreeze *n.* to add; drain ~

antipathy *n.* 1. to feel (an) ~ 2. (a) deep, strong; natural ~ 3. ~ against, to, towards (he felt strong/a strong ~ towards foreigners)

antique *n.* 1. to collect ~s 2. a genuine; priceless,

valuable; rare ~

antithesis *n.* 1. the direct, very ~ 2. an ~ between 3. an ~ of, to (the ~ to my theory)

antithetical *adj.* ~ to

antlers *n.* 1. to lock ~ 2. to shed ~ 3. a pair of ~

anxiety *n.* 1. to cause, create ~ 2. to feel ~ 3. to alleviate, ease, relieve one's ~ 4. acute; deep, grave, great, high; gnawing, unrelieved ~ 5. ~ about; for (~ for smb.'s safety) 6. ~ to + inf. (in his ~ not to offend them, he agreed to concessions) 7. in ~ (see 6)

anxious *adj.* 1. ~ about (~ about the world situation) 2. ~ for (we were ~ for their safety) 3. ~ to + inf. (she is ~ to help; we were ~ for them to meet you) 4. ~ that + clause; subj. (he was very ~ that we meet/should meet)

any I *adv.* (used with the comparative form of adjectives and adverbs and with *good*) ~ better (I wonder if they can work ~ better); ~ good (I don't think that this wine is ~ good); ~ easier (that doesn't make my job ~ easier); ~ more easily (the door will not shut ~ more easily now than before); ~ more difficult (do not make my job ~ more difficult than it is now); ~ less difficult (you haven't made my job ~ less difficult)

any II *determiner, pronoun* 1. ~ to + inf. (we don't have ~ books to sell; we don't have ~ to sell) 2. ~ of (I did not see ~ of them)

USAGE NOTE: The use of the preposition *of* is necessary when a pronoun follows. When a noun follows, the use of *of the* limits the meaning—did you see any students? did you see any of the students whom we had discussed earlier? (see the Usage Note for **something**)

anybody *pronoun* do you have ~ to talk to? (see the Usage Note for **something**)

anyone see **anybody**

anyplace (AE) see **anywhere**

anything *pronoun* 1. do you have ~ to say? 2. (misc.) ~ but ("not at all") (see the Usage Note for **something**)

anywhere *adv.* 1. do you have ~ to go? 2. ~ else; ~ near (see the Usage Note for **something**)

apart *adj., adv.* 1. to come, fall; tear ~ 2. to tell ~ 3. far; wide ~ 4. ~ from (~ from everything else) 5. (misc.) to come ~ at the seams

apartment *n.* (esp. AE) 1. to rent an ~ from 2. to rent (out) an ~ to 3. to furnish; redecorate; renovate an ~ 4. a basement; duplex; efficiency; furnished; garden; high-rise; luxury; penthouse; studio; unfurnished ~

apathetic *adj.* ~ about; to, towards (he is ~ about everything)

apathy *n.* 1. to feel; show ~ towards 2. to cast off, shed, throw off one's ~ 3. ~ towards

apes *n.* the anthropoid, great, higher ~

apex *n.* 1. to reach an ~ 2. at the ~

aplomb *n.* 1. the ~ to + inf. (she had the necessary ~ to order the meal in French) 2. with great ~

apologetic *adj.* 1. deeply ~ 2. to feel ~ 3. ~ about, for (she was deeply ~ for her blunder)

apologist *n.* an ~ for

apologize *v.* 1. to ~ humbly; profusely 2. (D; intr.) to ~ for; to (he ~d to us for being late) 3. (misc.) to ~ from the bottom of one's heart

apology *n.* 1. to make, offer, present; send an ~ 2. to demand an ~ 3. to accept an ~ 4. a full; heartfelt; sincere ~ 5. an official; public; written ~ 6. an abject, humble; belated ~ 7. an ~ for; to (Jim made an ~ to the teacher for his rude behavior)

apostasy *n.* (formal) (an) ~ from

apostate *n.* (formal) an ~ from (an ~ from the true faith)

apostle *n.* an ~ to

appall, appal *v.* (R) it ~ed me to see such sloppy work; it ~ed them that no preparations had been made

appalled *adj.* 1. ~ at, by (we were ~ at/by the news) 2. ~ to + inf. (I was ~ to see the results of their work) 3. ~ that + clause (everyone was ~ that the murderer had been released on parole)

appalling *adj.* 1. ~ to + inf. (it was ~ to see him in that condition) 2. ~ that + clause (it is ~ that so many people evade paying taxes)

apparel *n.* wearing ~

apparent *adj.* 1. clearly; increasingly ~ 2. ~ to 3. ~ that + clause (it was ~ to all that he was guilty)

apparition *n.* 1. a strange ~ 2. an ~ appears; disappears

appeal I *n.* ["request"] ["request for review"] 1. to issue; make an ~ 2. (legal) to file, lodge, make; lose; win an ~ 3. (legal) to take an ~ to a higher court 4. (also legal) to deny, dismiss, reject, throw out an ~ 5. (legal) (BE) an ~ lies against the decision ("there is an appeal pending") 6. a broad; desperate, urgent; eloquent, irresistible, moving, ringing, stirring; emotional; final, last; personal ~ 7. an ~ against, from; for; to (to file an ~ against a decision; to make an ~ to the public for donations; there is no ~ from a verdict of the higher court) ["attraction"] 8. to have ~ 9. esthetic; strong; universal, wide ~ 10. box-office; sales; sex; snob ~

appeal II *v.* 1. (D; intr.) ("to request a review") to ~ against (to ~ against a decision) 2. (D; intr.) ("to request") to ~ for; to (they ~ed to us for help) 3. (d; intr.) ("to request") to ~ to smb. to + inf. (he ~ed to them to support his campaign) 4. (d; intr.) to ~ to ("to resort to") (to ~ to common sense) 5. (d; intr.) to ~ to ("to please") (he doesn't ~ to her)

appear *v.* 1. (D; intr.) to ~ against; for (she ~ed against him in court; she ~ed for the defense) 2. (D; intr.) to ~ as (to ~ on stage as Hamlet) 3. (d; intr.) to ~ before (she had to ~ before the judge) 4. (D; intr.) to ~ in (to ~ in a leading role) 5. (D; intr.)

to ~ on (to ~ on stage) 6. (D; intr.) to ~ to (she ~ed to him in a dream; how does that ~ to you?) 7. (E) she ~s to be well 8. (L; to) it ~s (to me) that they will not come 9. (S) to ~ sad; (esp. BE) to ~ a fool 10. (misc.) to ~ before a committee; to ~ in print; to ~ on the scene; to ~ in person; to ~ live (in concert); to ~ at the door; the story ~ed in the newspaper

appearance *n.* ["appearing"] 1. to make, put in an ~ (the policeman made a timely ~) 2. a court; guest; personal; public; stage; TV ~ (the actor made a personal ~) 3. at smb.'s ~ (the crowd went wild at their first ~ on stage) ["outward impression"] 4. a disheveled; shabby; unkempt, untidy ~ 5. an immaculate, neat ~ 6. personal ~ (he was careless in his personal ~) 7. in ~ (neat in ~) 8. at first ~

appearances *n.* ["outward looks"] 1. to keep up ~ 2. outward ~ 3. by ~ (to judge by ~) 4. for the sake of ~, for appearances' sake 5. from, to all ~ (to all ~, the matter is closed) 6. (misc.) ~ can be deceiving (AE)/deceptive (BE)

append *v.* (D; tr.) to ~ to (to ~ a translation to a document)

appendage *n.* an ~ to

appendectomy, appendicectomy *n.* 1. to do, perform an ~ on 2. to have an ~

appendix *n.* 1. (anatomical) to have one's ~ out/removed 2. (anatomical) an inflamed; ruptured ~ 3. (anatomical) an ~ bursts, ruptures 4. an ~ to (an ~ to a textbook)

appertain *v.* (formal) (d; intr.) to ~ to

appetite *n.* 1. to have; work up an ~ 2. to whet smb.'s ~ 3. to satisfy smb.'s ~ 4. to lose one's ~ 5. to curb; spoil, take away smb.'s ~ 6. a good, healthy, hearty ~ 7. a huge, ravenous, voracious; insatiable ~ 8. a poor ~ 9. an ~ for

applaud *v.* 1. to ~ heartily, loudly 2. (D; tr.) to ~ for (we ~ed them for their courage)

applause *n.* 1. to draw, get, win ~ for 2. to burst into ~ 3. to hold the ~ 4. enthusiastic; heavy, lengthy, prolonged; loud, thunderous, wild ~ 5. light, weak ~ 6. the ~ dies down 7. a burst; ripple; round of ~ 8. to (the) ~ (she appeared on stage to the thunderous ~ of her admirers)

apple *n.* 1. to core; peel an ~ 2. cooking; eating ~s 3. a baked; green; sour ~ 3. (misc.) a rotten ~ ("an undesirable person"); the ~ of one's eye ("one's darling")

apple cart *n.* (colloq.) ["status quo"] to upset the ~

appliances *n.* ["devices"] domestic, household; electrical; kitchen; major; small ~

applicable *adj.* ~ to (~ to a case)

applicant *n.* an ~ for (an ~ for a position)

application *n.* ["request"] 1. to file; fill out, make, put in, send in, submit an ~ 2. to process; screen ~s 3. to reject, turn down an ~ 4. to withdraw an ~ 5. a fellowship; membership ~ 6. a formal; written ~ 7.

an ~ for; to (an ~ for admission to a university) 8. an ~ to + inf. (he filed an ~ to be admitted to the intensive course) 9. by, on ~ ["putting to use"] 10. ~ to (the ~ of theory to practice) ["placing"] 11. ~ to (the ~ of ice to the forehead)

application form *n.* 1. to fill in (esp. BE), to fill out (esp. AE), fill up (BE, obsol.) an ~ 2. to file, submit an ~

apply *v.* 1. (D; intr.) ("to request") to ~ for; to (we ~lied to the authorities for assistance; the captain ~lied to headquarters for a transfer; she ~lied for a fellowship) 2. (D; intr.) ("to seek admission to") to ~ to (she ~lied to three universities) 3. (D; intr.) ("to be relevant") to ~ to (the rule does not apply to this case) 4. (D; refl.) ("to concentrate one's efforts") to ~ to (she ~lied herself to her new duties with great energy) 5. (D; tr.) ("to put on") to ~ to (to ~ paint to a surface; to ~ ointment to a rash) 6. (D; tr.) ("to put to use") to ~ to (to ~ theory to practice) 7. (d; tr.) ("to channel") to ~ towards (to ~ money towards a purchase) 8. (E) ("to request") he ~lied (to them) to be transferred

appoint *v.* 1. (D; tr.) to ~ as (we ~ed him as treasurer) 2. (D; tr.) to ~ to (they ~ed her to the committee) 3. (H) they ~ed me to serve as secretary 4. (M and N; used with a noun) we ~ed her (to be) treasurer

appointment *n.* ["agreement to meet"] 1. to have; keep; make, schedule an ~ with 2. to break; cancel; miss an ~ 3. by ~ (she sees patients by ~ only) 4. an ~ to + inf. (she had an ~ to see the dean) ["selection"] 5. to confirm; make an ~ 6. to block an ~ 7. ~ to (they announced her ~ to the commission) 8. an ~ as (an ~ as professor) ["position"] 9. to have, hold; receive an ~ 10. an interim; permanent; temporary ~ 11. a political ~ ["designation"] 12. by ~ to Her Majesty

apportion *v.* (D; tr.) to ~ among, between (the funds were ~ed among the various departments)

apposition *n.* (grammar) in ~ to (the second noun is in ~ to the first)

appraisal *n.* 1. to give, make an ~ of 2. a down-to-earth; fair; objective; realistic ~

appraise *v.* (D; tr.) to ~ at (the house was ~d at seventy thousand dollars)

appreciate *v.* 1. to ~ deeply, greatly, keenly, sincerely, very much 2. (K) we ~ your helping us 3. (misc.) we ~ the fact that you have helped us; to ~ in value by ten percent

appreciation *n.* 1. to demonstrate, display, show one's ~ for 2. to express; feel ~ 3. deep, great, keen, sincere ~ 4. in ~ of (he did this in ~ of the help that he had received) 5. (misc.) to cultivate an ~ of art and music; as a token of my ~

appreciative *adj.* 1. deeply, greatly, keenly, sincerely ~ 2. ~ of (~ of help)

apprehension *n.* ["foreboding"] ["fear"] 1. to express; feel; show ~ 2. to allay smb.'s ~(s) 3. grave ~ 4. ~ about; for (we felt ~ for their safety) 5. (misc.) a feeling of ~; a state of ~

apprehensive *adj.* 1. ~ about; for (~ about recent developments; we were ~ for their safety) 2. ~ that + clause (we were ~ that they might forget)

apprentice I *n.* an ~ to (he was an ~ to a master craftsman)

apprentice II *v.* (B) at an early age, I was ~d to a carpenter

apprenticeship *n.* to fill; have; serve an ~

apprise *v.* (formal) (d; tr.) to ~ of (he was ~d of the decision by his lawyer)

apprised *adj.* to keep smb. ~ of (she will be kept ~ of the latest developments)

approach I *n.* 1. to make an ~ 2. to take an ~ (to take a judicious ~ to a problem) 3. a creative, innovative; fresh, new, novel; holistic ~ 4. a careful, cautious; conservative; judicious ~ 5. a direct, forthright; down-to-earth, no-nonsense, pragmatic, realistic ~ 6. an objective; rational; scholarly; scientific ~ 7. an easygoing; indirect ~ 8. a simplistic; unrealistic ~ 9. a hard-nosed, inflexible, uncompromising ~ 10. (applied linguistics) the audio-visual; oral-aural ~ 11. with the ~ (with the ~ of spring, we began to feel better) 12. an ~ from; to (I like her ~ to the problem; the ~es to a stadium; the pilot began her ~ to the runway)

approach II *v.* 1. (D; tr.) to ~ about (I was afraid to ~ them about this matter) 2. (D; tr.) to ~ for (she ~ed us for a loan) 3. (D; intr., tr.) to ~ from (to ~ from the other direction) 4. (d; tr.) to ~ with (to ~ smb. with a request)

appropriate I *adj.* 1. highly ~ 2. ~ for; to (~ for us; ~ to the occasion) 3. ~ to + inf. (it is not ~ to tip a bus driver) 4. ~ that + clause; may be subj. (it is ~ that he/should be present; it is ~ that we are meeting here)

appropriate II *v.* 1. (B) Congress ~d the funds to the states 2. (D; tr.) to ~ for (the committee ~d money for the memorial)

appropriation *n.* 1. to make an ~ for (our government made an ~ for the project) 2. defense; foreign-aid ~s

approval *n.* 1. to give one's ~ for 2. to nod; show; voice one's ~ 3. to gain, get, meet with, receive, win ~ 4. complete, full, unqualified, wholehearted ~ 5. universal, widespread ~ 6. official; public; tacit ~ 7. limited, qualified ~ 8. final ~ 9. ~ to + inf. (we received their ~ to continue the research) 10. on ~ (we bought it on ~) 11. (misc.) a roar of ~; to receive smb.'s seal, stamp of ~

approve *v.* 1. to ~ wholeheartedly 2. (D; intr.) to ~ of (we ~d of his decision)

approximate *v.* (BE) (D; intr.) ("to come near") to ~ to (to ~ to the truth)

approximation *n.* to give, make a rough ~

apropos *adv.* ~ of

apt *adj.* (cannot stand alone) ~ to + inf. (he is ~ to exaggerate)

aptitude *n.* 1. to demonstrate, display, show (an) ~ 2. (a) great, outstanding; inborn, innate, natural; special ~ 3. mechanical; scholastic ~ 4. an ~ for, in (an ~ for painting)

arbitrate *v.* (D; intr.) to ~ between (to ~ between opposing parties)

arbitration *n.* 1. to conduct ~ 2. to go to; resort to ~ (the union and management went to ~; the dispute went to ~) 3. binding; voluntary ~ 4. ~ between; of

arcade *n.* an amusement (BE); penny; video-game ~

arch *n.* a triumphal ~

architecture *n.* 1. classical; contemporary, modern ~ 2. Baroque; Byzantine; Colonial; Gothic; Greek; Modern; Renaissance; Roman; Romanesque ~

ardor, ardour *n.* 1. to demonstrate, display ~ 2. to cool, dampen one's ~ 3. fervent, intense; patriotic ~ 4. ~ for

area *n.* 1. to close off, rope off, seal off an ~ 2. a metropolitan, urban; rural ~ 3. a built-up; catchment; residential ~ 4. a no-smoking; service; storage ~ 5. a disaster; distressed ~ 6. an assembly, staging ~ 7. an impacted (AE) ("crowded with federal employees") ~ 8. (soccer) a penalty ~ 9. (meteorology) a high-pressure; low-pressure ~ 10. (misc.) a gray ("unclear") ~

arena *n.* 1. a sports ~ 2. the political ~ (to enter the political ~)

arguable *adj.* ~ that + clause (it is ~ that some unemployment is necessary)

argue *v.* 1. to ~ bitterly, heatedly, passionately, strenuously, vehemently 2. to ~ calmly, logically, plausibly, sensibly 3. (D; intr.) to ~ about, over; with (we ~d with them about the new law) 4. (d; intr.) to ~ against; for (to ~ against the amendment; to ~ for the new policy) 5. (d; tr.) to ~ out of (to ~ smb. out of doing smt.) 6. (L) she ~d logically that the new regulations would harm the poor 7. (misc.) to ~ from a position of strength

argument *n.* ["dispute"] 1. to get into, have; start an ~ 2. to lose; win an ~ 3. to break off, end, terminate an ~ 4. to clinch, settle an ~ 5. an angry, bitter, heated, loud, violent ~ 6. an animated, lively ~ 7. an ~ breaks out 8. an ~ about, over; between; with (I had a bitter ~ with him about politics) ["statement"] 9. to drive home, press (home) an ~ 10. to offer, present, put forward an ~ 11. to confute, rebut, refute; reject an ~ 12. an airtight, balanced, brilliant, cogent, compelling, conclusive, convincing, irrefutable, logical, persuasive, powerful, rational, solid, sound, telling, trenchant, unassailable, valid ~ 13. a circular; convoluted ~ 14. a groundless; tenuous, weak ~ 15. a specious, spurious ~ 16. an ~ about, over; against; between; for

(she presented a convincing ~ against the proposal) 17. an ~ that + clause (I cannot accept his ~
that war is inevitable) 18. (misc.) the point, thrust
of an ~; (legal) to hear ~s (against; for)

arise *v.* (D; intr.) to ~ from (to ~ from a deep
slumber)

arithmetic *n.* to do ~

arm I *n.* ["upper limb"] 1. to bend; cross; fold;
lower; raise; stretch; swing; wave one's ~s 2.
(misc.) to take smb. by the ~; to fling/put/throw
one's ~s around smb.; to carry smt. under one's ~;
to greet smb. with open/outstretched ~s; to hold
smb./smt. in one's ~s; to walk ~ in ~ with; with ~s
akimbo ["power"] 3. the long ~ of the law ["division"] 4. our naval air ~ ["attachment"] 5. a
pickup, tone ~ ["misc."] 6. to greet smb. with open
~s ("to give smb. an enthusiastic welcome"); to
keep smb. at ~'s length ("to keep smb. at bay"); to
twist smb.'s ~ ("to exert pressure on smb.")

arm II *v.* 1. (D; intr., refl., tr.) to ~ against (to ~
against a potential enemy) 2. (D; refl., tr.) to ~ with
(they ~ed the peasants with rifles)

armed *adj.* ~ to the teeth

armistice *n.* 1. to agree on, work out; declare; sign
an ~ 2. to violate an ~ 3. to suspend an ~ 4. an ~
between

armor, armour *n.* 1. heavy; light ~ 2. (misc.) to
pierce ~

arms *n.* ["weapons"] 1. to bear; take up ~ 2. to call
to ~ 3. (mil.) inspection; left shoulder; order; port;
present; right shoulder; trail ~! 4. to lay down
one's ~ 5. small ~ 6. under ~ ("armed") ["misc."]
7. up in ~ (about, over; against) ("stirred up")

arms race *n.* 1. to accelerate, step up the ~ 2. to curb
the ~ 3. the nuclear ~

army *n.* 1. to command, lead; drill, train; rally an ~
2. to mobilize, raise, recruit an ~ 3. to equip,
supply an ~ 4. to array, commit, deploy, field;
concentrate, mass an ~ 5. to inspect, muster, review an ~ 6. to encircle, envelop, surround;
outfight; outflank; outmaneuver; overrun; surprise an ~ 7. to crush, decimate, defeat, rout an ~;
to put an ~ to flight 8. to demobilize, disband an ~
9. a rebel; regular, standing; territorial; volunteer
~ 10. an advancing; conquering; defeated; occupying; retreating; victorious ~ 11. an ~ advances;
attacks; conducts war, engages in combat, fights;
pulls back, retreats, withdraws 12. (misc.) an ~ of
occupation; to join the ~

aroma *n.* 1. to have an ~ 2. a delicate, delightful,
fragrant, pleasant, pleasing; faint; tantalizing ~ 3.
an ~ emanates from 4. (misc.) a pleasant ~ wafted
in from the kitchen

around *adv.* 1. ~ here 2. to have been ~ ("to have
had considerable experience")

arouse *v.* (D; tr.) to ~ from (to ~ smb. from a deep
sleep)

aroused *adj.* easily; sexually ~

arraign *v.* (D; tr.) to ~ on (a certain charge)

arraignment *n.* 1. (legal) to hold an ~ for 2. a public
~

arrange *v.* 1. to ~ neatly; tastefully 2. (d; intr., tr.) to
~ for (to ~ for a series of lectures; we ~d for him to
give a concert) 3. (E) they ~d to leave early 4. (L) I
~d that they should be seated next to each other 5.
(Q) we ~d where we should meet; we ~d where to
meet

arrangement *n.* 1. to come to, make, work out an ~
(with) 2. to handle (the) ~s 3. a floral; seating;
working ~ 4. an ~ for; with 5. an ~ to + inf. (they
made an ~/~s to meet secretly) 6. by ~ (by special
~) 7. under an ~ (under a special ~)

array I *n.* ["order"] 1. in battle ~; drawn up in full ~
["display"] 2. a bewildering; dazzling, glittering;
imposing, impressive; vast ~

array II *v.* (D; tr.) to ~ against (~ed against the
enemy)

arrears *n.* in ~ (he is in ~ with his rent)

arrest I *n.* ["detention"] 1. to make an ~ 2. to resist
~ 3. a citizen's; false ~ 4. an ~ for (to make an ~ for
murder) 5. an ~ on a charge/charges of (to make an
~ on a charge of murder) 6. under ~ (to be under ~;
to place/put smb. under ~) 7. (misc.) house ~
["stoppage"] 8. a cardiac ~

arrest II *v.* 1. (D; tr.) to arrest ~ for (the police ~ed
her for murder) 2. (D; tr.) to arrest on a charge/
charges of (he was ~ed on charges of murder)

arrest warrant *n.* (AE) to issue an ~

arrival *n.* 1. an early; late ~ 2. an ~ at, in; from 3. on
smb.'s ~ (on our ~ in Chicago) 4. (misc.) to announce an ~ (as at an airport)

arrive *v.* 1. (D; intr.) to ~ at, in; from (they ~d from
Paris) 2. (s) they ~d safe and sound 3. (misc.) to ~
early; late; on time

arrogance *n.* 1. to demonstrate, display, exhibit ~
2. insufferable, overpowering, overwhelming ~ 3.
~ towards 4. the ~ to + inf. (he had the ~ to ask for
more money)

arrogant *adj.* 1. ~ towards 2. ~ to + inf. (it was ~ of
them to expect us to do all the work)

arrogate *v.* (formal) (B) to ~ a privilege to oneself

arrow *n.* 1. to shoot an ~ at 2. a poisoned; spent ~ 3.
(misc.) as straight as an ~

arson *n.* to commit ~

art *n.* 1. to practice an ~ (to practice the occult ~ of
the alchemist) 2. abstract; classical; contemporary; folk; impressionist; modern; primitive; pop;
surrealistic ~ 3. commercial ~ 4. an ~ in, to (there
is an ~ to making a good omelet) 5. a work of ~ 6.
(misc.) to exhibit, hang works of ~ (see also **arts**)

artefacts (BE) see **artifacts**

artery *n.* ["blood vessel"] 1. a blocked, occluded;
ruptured ~ 2. a coronary; main; pulmonary ~ 3.
(misc.) hardening of the ~ries ["channel"] 4. a

major; traffic ~

arthritis *n.* to develop ~

article I *n.* ["essay"] 1. to submit; write an ~ 2. to accept; publish; referee; reject an ~ 3. a journal; leading (BE, old-fashioned); magazine; newspaper; op-ed ~ 4. an ~ about, on (she wrote an ~ about her research) ["section"] 5. according to, under an ~ (according to ~ two of our constitution) ["object"] 6. household; secondhand; toilet ~s 7. (misc.) ~s of clothing; ~s of furniture ["grammatical affix"] 8. to take an ~ (certain nouns always take the definite ~) 9. the definite; indefinite ~

article II *v.* (BE) (d; tr.) ("to apprentice") to ~ to, with (to ~ smb. to a firm of solicitors)

articulate *v.* (d; intr.) to ~ with (these bones ~ with each other)

artifacts, artefacts *n.* ancient; cultural ~

artillery *n.* antiaircraft; coast; field; heavy; light; long-range; medium; self-propelled ~

artist *n.* 1. a gifted, great, talented; struggling ~ 2. a commercial; folk ~ 3. a pavement (BE), sidewalk (AE) ~ 4. a con, flimflam, rip-off, scam; escape; quick-change ~ 5. (misc.) an ~ in-residence

artistry *n.* brilliant ~

arts *n.* 1. (the) creative; fine; visual ~ 2. (the) decorative; graphic; plastic ~ 3. (the) applied; industrial ~ 4. the healing ~ 5. (the) liberal ~ 6. (the) martial ~ 7. the performing ~ 8. (misc.) ~ and crafts

ascend *v.* (D; intr.) to ~ to

ascendancy *n.* 1. to attain, gain ~ over 2. (a) clear-cut; overwhelming ~

ascendant *n.* in the ~ (which faction is in the ~?)

ascent *n.* 1. to make an ~ (to make the ~ of a mountain) 2. a gentle, gradual ~ 3. a steep ~

ascertain *v.* 1. (L) she ~ed that fraud had been committed 2. (Q) can you ~ who he is?

asceticism *n.* to practice ~

ascribe *v.* 1. (B) the painting was ~d to an unknown artist 2. (d; tr.) to ~ to (she ~d her success to hard work)

ash *n.* volcanic ~

ashamed *adj.* 1. deeply, thoroughly ~ 2. ~ about, of (she was ~ about what had happened; he was ~ of himself) 3. ~ to + inf. (she was ~ to admit her mistake) 4. ~ that + clause (he was ~ that his family was poor)

ashes *n.* 1. to rake; scatter, spread ~ 2. to reduce to ~ 3. (misc.) to rise from the ~; they sprinkled her ~ in the sea

ashore *adv.* 1. to put, set ~ 2. to come; go ~

aside *adv.* 1. to move; stand; step ~ 2. to brush; draw, take; leave; push, shove; put, set, sweep ~ 3. (AE) ~ from ("apart from")

asinine *adj.* ~ to + inf. (it was ~ to behave like that)

ask *v.* 1. (D; intr., tr.) ("to inquire") to ~ about, after (BE) (they ~ed me about my work; he ~ed about/

after her mother) 2. (d; intr., tr.) ("to request") to ~ for (she ~ed me politely for the book; the guest ~ed for the manager) 3. (D; tr.) ("to request") to ~ smt. of (I have a favor to ~ of you; he is ~ing a great deal of us) 4. (D; tr.) ("to invite") to ~ to (we ~ed them to the party) 5. (E) ("to request") she ~ed to be excused; we ~ed to see him 6. (H) ("to request") she ~ed us to come to the concert 7. (L; subj.) ("to request") the family ~ed that the story not be/should not be printed 8. (O; can be used with one object) ("to pose") he ~ed (her) a question (also possible is: he ~ed a question of her) 9. (Q; may have an object) ("to inquire of") he ~ed (his son) point-blank where he was going; she ~ed wistfully how she might help 10. (misc.) to ~ for trouble

askance *adv.* to look ~ at

asking *n.* (colloq.) for the ~ (it's yours for the ~)

ask out *v.* (D; tr.) to ~ to (to ask smb. out to lunch)

asleep *adj.* 1. to be fast, sound ~ 2. to fall ~ 3. (misc.) ~ at the switch ("negligent, not alert")

aspect *n.* ["view"] ["side"] 1. a frightening; grim; humorous; serious ~ (the humorous ~ of the situation) 2. from an ~ (from this ~) 3. in an ~ (in all ~s)

aspersion *n.* to cast ~s on

aspirant *n.* an ~ for; to (an ~ to the throne)

aspiration *n.* (formal) 1. high, lofty, noble ~s 2. an ~ to (~s to independence) 3. ~ to + inf. (she has ~s to study medicine)

aspire *v.* (formal) 1. (d; intr.) to ~ to (to ~ to success) 2. (E) she ~d to become a lawyer

aspirin *n.* 1. to take (an) ~ 2. (misc.) an ~ tablet (he took two ~ tablets; or: he took two ~s)

ass *n.* ["fool"] 1. a pompous ~ 2. to make an ~ of oneself ["donkey"] 3. ~es bray

assail *v.* (formal) 1. to ~ bitterly 2. (D; tr.) to ~ with (to ~ smb. with questions)

assassin *n.* a hired, paid ~

assassination *n.* 1. to attempt; carry out an ~ 2. character; a political ~

assault *n.* 1. (often mil.) to carry out, launch, make; lead an ~ (against, on) (the troops carried out an ~ on the enemy position) 2. (legal) to commit ~ 3. (usu. legal) aggravated; bodily; criminal; indecent, sexual; violent ~ 4. an all-out; armed; military ~ 5. (usu. mil.) by ~ (to take by ~)

assault and battery *n.* (legal) to commit ~

assembly *n.* 1. to convene an ~ 2. a constituent; constitutional; deliberative; general; legislative; national; public ~ 3. (misc.) the freedom, right of ~; unlawful ~

assent I *n.* 1. to give ; nod one's ~ (she gave her ~ to our plan) 2. by common ~ 3. (BE) (the) royal ~

assent II *v.* (formal) (D; intr.) to ~ to (we ~ed to his proposal)

assert *v.* 1. to ~ boldly 2. (L) she ~ed that she was innocent

assertion n. 1. to make an ~ 2. to deny, reject; rebut, refute an ~ 3. a bold; sweeping; unfounded ~ 4. an ~ that + clause (we do not believe his ~ that he is innocent)

assess v. (D; tr.) to ~ at (the value of this property was ~ed at one million dollars)

assessment n. 1. to make an ~ (she made a careful ~ of the situation) 2. a critical; preliminary; realistic ~ 3. a tax ~

asset n. 1. an invaluable, valuable ~ 2. an economic; political ~ 3. an ~ to (she was an invaluable ~ to our firm)

assets n. 1. to realize; unfreeze ~ 2. to mortgage one's ~ 3. to confiscate smb.'s ~ 4. capital; current; financial; fixed; frozen; hidden; intangible; liquid; personal; tangible ~

asseverate v. (formal and rare) (L) they ~ed that they would never surrender

assign v. 1. (A) they ~ed a very difficult mission to us; or: they ~ed us a very difficult mission 2. (D; tr.) to ~ to (headquarters ~ed the soldiers to a different unit; an experienced detective was ~ed to the case; to ~ a painting to a certain century) 3. (esp. BE) (H) we were ~ed to prepare a meal

assignation n. (formal) to make an ~

assignment n. ["task"] ["mission"] 1. to give smb. an ~ 2. to carry out, complete an ~ (the ambassador carried out her ~ brilliantly) 3. a dangerous; difficult, rough, tough ~ 4. an easy ~ 5. an overseas ~ 6. a rush; special ~ 7. an ~ to + inf. (an ~ to guard the president) 8. on ~ ("on a mission") (the correspondent was on ~ in the Far East) ["homework"] (esp. AE) 9. to give, hand out an ~ 10. to do; hand in an ~ (the pupils did their ~) 11. a difficult; easy ~ ["appointment"] (esp. AE) 12. an ~ to (an ~ to a new job)

assimilate v. 1. to ~ completely; easily, readily; rapidly 2. (D; intr., tr.) to ~ into, to (the newcomers tried to ~ into the community; America has ~d millions of immigrants into its way of life) 3. (D; intr.) to ~ with (they did not ~ with the local population)

assimilation n. ~ into, to (their ~ into society was swift)

assist I n. (colloq.) with an ~ from

assist II v. 1. (D; intr., tr.) to ~ at, in, with (the young nurse was ~ing at his first operation; to ~ in the preparation of a report; to ~ with the editing of a manuscript) 2. (formal, rare) (H) to ~ smb. to do smt.

assistance n. 1. to give, offer, provide, render ~ 2. considerable, great, invaluable ~ 3. clerical; legal; technical ~ 4. economic, financial; material; public ~ 5. (AE) directory ~ (BE has *directory enquiries*) 6. ~ in (they received ~ in launching the project) 7. ~ to (economic ~ to developing countries) 8. of ~ (he was of considerable ~ to us) 9.

with (smb.'s) ~ (the project was completed with their ~)

assistant n. 1. a personal ~ (BE; AE has *personal secretary*) 2. a research; teaching ~ 3. a sales, shop ~ (BE) (AE has *salesclerk*) 4. an ~ to (an ~ to the president)

associate I n. 1. a business ~ 2. a close ~ 3. (AE) an Associate in/of Arts

associate II v. 1. to ~ closely 2. (d; intr., refl., tr.) to ~ with (we ~ with all sorts of people; one usually ~s poverty with misery; I ~ myself with their policies)

association n. ["organization"] 1. to form an ~ 2. a bar ~ (AE; BE has *law society*) 3. a building and loan ~/savings and loan ~ (AE; BE has *building society*) 4. a parent-teacher ~ ["connection"] 5. a close ~ 6. an ~ with 7. in ~ with ["connection in the mind"] 8. to bring up, call up, evoke an ~ 9. free ~

assortment n. an odd; rich; wide ~ (of)

assume v. 1. (L) we ~d that he was dead 2. (M) everyone ~d him to be dead

assumed adj. (cannot stand alone) ~ to + inf. (she was ~ to be out of the country)

assumption n. 1. to make an ~ 2. to base an ~ on 3. an erroneous, false, mistaken ~ 4. a reasonable; safe; valid ~ 5. (a) mere; pure ~ 6. an ~ about; of (to make an ~ of guilt) 7. an ~ that + clause (we all made the ~ that the new company would fail) 8. on an ~ (we proceeded on the ~ that he would help)

assurance n. 1. to give an ~ that + clause (he gave every ~ that he would attend) 2. (BE) endowment; life ~ (see the Usage Note for **insurance**) 3. categorical, complete, unconditional ~

assurances n. 1. to give, provide ~ of 2. ~ that + clause (the contractor gave ~ that the work would be completed on time)

assure v. 1. (d; tr.) to ~ of (we ~ed her of our support) 2. (L; must have an object) they ~d us that they would not be late

assured adj. 1. to rest ~ of (you can rest ~ of their safety) 2. to rest ~ that + clause (you can rest ~ that they are safe)

astonish v. 1. to ~ greatly, very much 2. (R) it ~ed me to learn that he was here; it ~ed us that they were able to survive

astonished adj. 1. greatly, very (much) ~ 2. ~ at, by (they were ~ at/by the news of his escape) 3. ~ + inf. (I was ~ to learn of his divorce) 4. ~ that + clause (she was ~ that he had survived)

astonishing adj. 1. ~ to 2. ~ to + inf. (it was ~ to watch them perform) 3. ~ that + clause (it was ~ to everyone that the court had made such a decision)

astonishment n. 1. to express ~ 2. ~ at (he could not conceal his ~ at seeing them together) 3. ~ that + clause (they expressed ~ that I won the election) 4. in ~ (they gaped in ~) 5. to smb.'s ~ (to our ~, they arrived on time)

astound v. (R) it ~ed me to find the country so backward; it ~ed us that they came/should have come

astounded adj. 1. ~ at, by (~ at the news) 2. ~ to + inf. (everyone was ~ to learn of her exploits) 3. ~ that + clause (I was ~ that the mayor had/should have taken bribes)

astounding adj. 1. ~ to + inf. (her performance was ~ to watch) 2. ~ that + clause (it was ~ that an experienced engineer had/should have made such a miscalculation)

astray adv. 1. to lead smb. ~ 2. to go ~

astride adv. (formal) to sit ~ (to sit ~ smb.'s knee)

astute adj. (formal) 1. ~ at (~ at conducting negotiations) 2. ~ to + inf. (it was ~ of you to notice that)

asunder adv. (formal) to rend, tear ~

asylum n. 1. to give, grant ~ to 2. to ask for, seek; receive ~ 3. to deny, refuse smb. ~ 4. political ~ (they were granted political ~)

athlete n. an all-around (AE), all-round; amateur; born; professional; weekend; world-class ~

athletics n. 1. (esp. BE; AE has *track and field*) to go in for ~ 2. intercollegiate ~

atlas n. a dialect, linguistic; geographical; world ~

atmosphere n. 1. to clear the ~ 2. to poison, pollute the ~ 3. a congenial, convivial; cozy; friendly; informal, relaxed; pleasant ~ 4. a carnival; heady ~ 5. a romantic ~ 6. a formal ~ 7. a gloomy; heavy; stifling, stultifying; tense; unpleasant ~ 8. a polluted; rarified ~ 9. the upper ~ 10. (misc.) that restaurant has lots of ~

atom n. to split the ~

atone v. (D; intr.) to ~ for (to ~ for one's sins)

atonement n. 1. to make ~ for 2. (misc.) a day of ~

atrocity n. 1. to commit an ~ 2. a dreadful, grisly, gruesome, heinous, horrible, horrid, monstrous, revolting, vile ~ 3. death-camp; wartime atrocities 4. an ~ against

attach v. 1. (d; refl.) ("to join") to ~ to (she ~ed herself to our group) 2. (D; tr.) ("to fasten") to ~ to (she ~ed an aerial/antenna to the radio; a tag was ~ed to each article) 3. (d; tr.) ("to assign temporarily") to ~ to (the officer was ~ed to headquarters) 4. (d; tr.) ("to ascribe") to ~ to (we ~ed no significance to her statement)

attaché n. an air-force; commercial; cultural; military; naval; press ~

attached adj. 1. deeply, strongly ~ 2. ~ to

attachment n. 1. to feel; form an ~ 2. a close; deep; strong ~ 3. a lasting; lifelong ~ 4. a sentimental ~ 5. an ~ to (to form a lasting ~ to smb.) 6. (BE) on ~ to ("assigned to")

attack I n. ["assault"] (usu. mil.; also fig.) 1. to carry out, make; launch, mount, unleash; lead, spearhead; press an ~ 2. to provoke an ~ 3. to come under ~ 4. to survive, withstand an ~ 5. to blunt;

break up, repel, repulse an ~ 6. an all-out, concerted, full-scale; coordinated; major ~ 7. a preemptive; retaliatory ~ 8. a mock; sneak, surprise ~ 9. an air; seaborne ~ 10. an enemy; terrorist ~ 11. a flank; frontal ~ 12. a nuclear; torpedo ~ 13. an ~ succeeds 14. an ~ fails; fizzles out 15. an ~ against, on (our forces launched an all-out ~ against the enemy) 16. under ~ ["a belligerent action"] (often verbal) 17. to make an ~ 18. a verbal ~ 19. a bitter, blistering, brutal, savage, scathing, sharp, vehement, vicious, violent; scurrilous; unprovoked; wanton ~ 20. an ~ on (he made a blistering ~ on his opponent) 21. (misc.) the leaked document left us open to ~ ["onset of an ailment"] 22. to have an ~ (she had an ~ of hiccups) 23. an acute; fatal; light, slight; recurrent; sudden ~ 24. a heart ~

attack II v. to ~ brutally, savagely, viciously; physically

attempt I n. 1. to make an ~ 2. to foil, thwart an ~ 3. an all-out, concerted, last-ditch; brave, valiant; deliberate ~ 4. a successful ~ 5. a blatant; bold, brazen, daring ~ 6. a botched; clumsy; crude; feeble, halfhearted, weak; premature ~ 7. an abortive, fruitless, futile, vain; ill-fated, unsuccessful ~ 8. repeated ~s 9. a rescue; suicide ~ 10. an ~ against, on (an ~ on smb.'s life) 11. an ~ at (an ~ at being funny) 12. an ~ to + inf. (we made an ~ to get in touch with them) 13. in an ~ (in our ~ to finish the job quickly, we ran out of supplies)

attempt II v. 1. (E) she ~ed to find a job 2. (rare) (G) he ~ed walking 3. (misc.) to ~ smt. in vain

attend v. 1. (BE) (d; tr.) to ~ on (two nurses ~ed on the patient 2. (d; intr.) to ~ to (to ~ to one's duties; to ~ to a customer)

attendance n. ["persons present"] ["number of persons present"] 1. to check (the) ~; to take (the) ~ (in school) 2. average; daily ~ 3. low, poor ~ 4. perfect; regular ~ 5. ~ has gone up; ~ has fallen, gone down ["presence"] 6. ~ at (~ at a ceremony) 7. in ~ (a nurse was in ~) ["misc."] 8. to dance ~ on smb. ("to fawn over smb.")

attendant n. 1. a flight; wedding ~ 2. an ~ to

attention n. ["concentration"] ["notice"] 1. to attract, capture, catch, command, draw, get smb.'s ~ 2. to have, hold, retain smb.'s ~ 3. to call smb.'s ~ to 4. to devote one's ~ to; to focus (one's) ~ on; to give one's ~ to; to pay ~ (to); to turn one's ~ to 5. to bring smt. to smb.'s ~ 6. to distract, divert smb.'s ~ 7. to escape smb.'s ~ 8. close; meticulous; minute; rapt; studious; undivided ~ (this matter will require your undivided ~) 9. ~ to (meticulous ~ to detail) 10. for, to smb.'s ~ (this package was left here for your ~) 11. (misc.) she gave the matter her undivided ~; it came to my ~ that she was very ill; they were the center of ~ ["position of attention"] (usu. mil.) 12. to call smb. to ~ (the sergeant called his platoon to ~); to come to, snap to ~; to stand at ~; or: to stand at the position of ~; or: (BE) to stand to ~ ["care"] 13. to give ~ to; to lavish ~ on 14. medical ~ (to receive medical ~) 15. individual; personal ~ (the manager gave me her personal ~; I lavished my individual ~ on him)

attentive *adj.* ~ to (~ to our needs)

attest *v.* (formal) (d; intr.) to ~ to (several witnesses can ~ to her good character)

attire *n.* 1. casual; civilian; formal ~ 2. in ~ (in formal ~)

attitude *n.* 1. to adopt, assume, strike, take an ~ 2. a cheerful; conciliatory; constructive; flexible; friendly; positive; realistic ~ 3. a respectful; reverent ~ 4. a casual; devil-may-care; frivolous; hands-off; irreverent; nonchalant; wait-and-see ~ 5. a conservative; liberal ~ 6. a cavalier; condescending, patronizing; holier-than-thou ~ 7. a bad, belligerent, defiant, surly; disrespectful; hostile; inflexible, rigid, uncompromising; negative; scornful ~ 8. an ~ about; of; to, towards (to assume an ~ of defiance towards all authority) 9. an ~ that + clause (I didn't like his ~ that he deserves special treatment)

attorney *n.* (esp. AE) 1. to hire, retain an ~ 2. a defense; district (AE; BE has *public prosecutor*); prosecuting ~ 3. an attorney-at-law 4. (CE) an Attorney General 5. (CE) a power of ~

attract *v.* (D; tr.) to ~ to (a crowd was ~ed to the scene of the accident)

attracted *adj.* ~ to (he was ~ to her)

attraction *n.* ["charm"] 1. to feel an ~ to 2. to hold an ~ for 3. an irresistible, strong; physical, sexual ~ (she felt a strong ~ to him) ["something that attracts"] 4. a box-office; chief, main, major; public; scenic; tourist ~ 5. (misc.) the center of ~

attractive *adj.* 1. physically; sexually ~ 2. ~ to (the offer is very ~ to us)

attributable *adj.* ~ to (the fire was ~ to carelessness)

attribute *v.* (d; tr.) to ~ to (we ~ this saying to Shakespeare; they ~d their success to hard work)

attrition *n.* 1. a rate of ~ 2. by, through ~ (the staff will be reduced by ~) 3. (misc.) a war of ~

attune *v.* (D; refl., tr.) to ~ to (you will have to ~ your ears to this type of music)

atypical *adj.* ~ of (such behavior was ~ of him)

auction *n.* 1. to have, hold an ~ 2. an ~ takes place 3. to put smt. up for ~ 4. a public ~ 5. at (an) ~; by ~ (we bought these items at an ~; they sold their house by ~)

audacious *adj.* ~ to + inf. (it was ~ of her to try that)

audacity *n.* 1. to demonstrate, show ~ 2. sheer ~ 3. the ~ to + inf. (he had the ~ to ask for an increase in salary)

audible *adj.* barely, scarcely ~

audience *n.* ["interview"] 1. to give, grant an ~ 2. to have, receive an ~ (with) 3. to seek an ~ with 4. a private ~ (with) 5. at an ~ ["group of spectators"] 6. to attract, draw an ~ 7. to captivate, electrify, grip, move, stir, sway, turn on an ~ (to electrify an ~ = to turn on an ~ = to turn an ~ on) 8. an appreciative, attentive, enthusiastic, receptive, responsive; friendly; sympathetic ~ 9. a cold, passive, unresponsive; hostile; unsympathetic ~ 10. a capacity; large, wide; mass; standing-room-only ~ 11. a captive; select ~ 12. a live; studio ~ 13. an ~ applauds, cheers 14. an ~ boos, hisses, hoots 15. (misc.) the speaker was being heckled and she turned on the ~ ("she attacked the audience")

USAGE NOTE: In formal BE one can have *an ~ of the Queen*; in AE and ordinary BE one has *an ~ with the Queen*

audit *n.* 1. to carry out, conduct an ~ 2. an annual, yearly; external; internal; tax ~

audition I *n.* 1. to give smb. an ~ 2. to have, hold ~s

audition II *v.* 1. (D; intr., tr.) to ~ for (he ~ed for the role of the butler; they ~ed her for a part in the school play) 2. (E) she ~ed to play Juliet

auditorium *n.* 1. a main ~ 2. in an ~

augur *v.* (formal) this ~s well for the future

aura *n.* 1. to have an ~ about 2. a glittering ~ (of)

auspices *n.* under the ~ of smt. (under the ~ of the mayor's office)

austerity *n.* 1. to practice ~ 2. strict; wartime ~

authenticate *v.* (D; tr.) to ~ as (the painting was ~ed as genuine)

authenticity *n.* 1. to establish, prove; vouch for the ~ of smt. 2. to doubt, question the ~ of smt.

author *n.* an anonymous; beginning; classic; contemporary; established, famous, noted, recognized, well-known; prolific; rising; talented; young ~

authorities *n.* ["officials"] civil, civilian; government; local; military; occupation ~

authority *n.* ["control"] ["power"] 1. to assert, demonstrate, show; assume, establish; delegate; exercise, exert, use, wield; have; invoke ~ 2. to give up, relinquish, yield ~ 3. to challenge, defy; deny, reject; rebel against; undermine; usurp ~ 4. absolute, complete, full, supreme, unquestioned ~ 5. parental ~ 6. ~ for; over (he assumed ~ for overseas operations; a commanding officer has complete ~ over her personnel) 7. in ~ (who was in ~?) 8. of ~ (a figure, man, woman of ~; there was an air of ~ about her) 9. under smb.'s ~ (these employees are under my ~) ["legal power"] ["authorization"] 10. to abuse, overstep one's ~ 11. legal; ministerial; presidential; reviewing (mil.); royal ~ 12. by, on smb.'s ~ (by whose ~ were these funds spent? she did it on her own ~) 13. the ~ to + inf. (the police had the ~ to conduct a search) ["expert"] ["source"] 14. to cite, invoke an ~ 15. an appropriate, competent, reliable; indisputable, irrefutable, unimpeachable, unquestioned; leading, respected ~; the greatest living ~ 16. an ~ on (an outstanding ~ on chess) 17. on ~ (to have smt. on good ~; we have it on the highest ~ that the meeting has been cancelled) ["government office"] 18. health authorities; a port ~; school authorities

authorization *n.* 1. to give, grant ~ 2. to receive ~ 3. to revoke smb.'s ~ 4. official ~ 5. ~ for; from 6. (the) ~ to + inf. (we received ~ to begin demolition) 7. with; without ~

authorize *v.* 1. (H) the director ~d us to work in the laboratory 2. (K) she ~d his entering the vault

authorized *adj.* 1. (usu. does not stand alone) ~ to + inf. (we are not ~ to enter the restricted area)

authorship *n.* to dispute; establish ~ (to establish the ~ of an ancient manuscript)

automate *v.* to ~ fully

automatic *adj.* fully ~

automatic pilot *n.* 1. to engage, switch on; disengage, switch off the ~ 2. on ~

automobile *n.* (AE) to drive, operate; park an ~ (see **car** 2-11)

autonomy *n.* 1. to grant ~ 2. to enjoy, have ~ 3. to seek ~ 4. full; local ~

autopsy *n.* to do, perform an ~ on

autumn *n.* in (the) ~

auxiliary *n.* 1. (grammar) a modal ~ 2. (BE) a nursing ~

avail I *n.* (formal) ["aid"] 1. of little ~ 2. to no ~

avail II *v.* (formal) 1. (d; intr.) ("to help") to ~ against (nothing could ~ against the enemy attack) 2. (d; refl.) ("to make use") to ~ of (she ~ed herself of the offer)

available *adj.* 1. easily, readily ~ 2. to make oneself ~; to make smt. ~ 3. ~ to (the information is ~ to anyone) 4. ~ for (are you ~ for a meeting tomorrow?) 5. ~ from 6. ~ to + inf. (is there anyone ~ to replace her?)

avalanche *n.* 1. to set off, trigger an ~ 2. an ~ strikes

avenge *v.* (D; refl.) to ~ on, upon (to ~ oneself on an enemy)

avenue *n.* ["opportunity"] 1. to explore, pursue every ~ 2. an ~ to (an ~ to success) ["street"] 3. in (BE), on (AE) an ~

aver *v.* (formal) (L) he ~red that he was innocent

average *n.* 1. to calculate, work out an ~ 2. (misc.) above ~; below ~; on ~/(AE) on the ~ she works seven hours a day; (AE) he finished school with a B ~

average out *v.* (d; intr., tr.) to ~ at, to (snowfall ~s out in this part of the country at/to twenty inches a year)

averse *adj.* (formal) ~ to (I would not be ~ to taking a drink)

aversion *n.* (formal) 1. to feel, have; take an ~ to 2. a deep, deep-rooted, distinct, marked; natural; pet ~ 3. an ~ to (an ~ to animals)

avert *v.* 1. (D; tr.) to ~ from (he ~ed his eyes from the scene of the accident) 2. (misc.) the accident was narrowly ~ed

aviation *n.* civil; military ~

avid *adj.* (formal) (usu. does not stand alone) ~ for (~ for fame)

avoid *v.* 1. to ~ narrowly; studiously 2. (G) she managed to ~ being punished 3. (misc.) to ~ at all costs

avow *v.* (formal) 1. to ~ openly, publicly 2. to ~ solemnly 3. (L) they ~ed that they had been wrong 4. (M or N; used with a noun) he ~ed himself (to be) a socialist

avowal *n.* 1. to make an ~ 2. an open, public ~ 3. a solemn ~ 4. an ~ to + inf. (his public ~ to reduce inflation was forgotten) 5. an ~ that + clause (she made a solemn ~ that she would never reveal the secret)

await *v.* to ~ eagerly

awake I *adj.* 1. wide ~ 2. ~ to (~ to the danger of inflation) 3. (misc.) to lie ~

awake II *v.* 1. (D; intr.) to ~ from (she awoke from a deep sleep) 2. (d; intr.) to ~ to (I awoke to bright sunlight) 3. (E) they awoke to find the house in flames

awaken *v.* 1. see **awake II** 2. (d; tr.) to ~ to (to ~ smb. to a sense of duty)

awakening *n.* 1. a rude, sudden ~ 2. a sexual ~ 3. a spiritual ~

award I *n.* 1. to confer, grant, make, present an ~ 2. to accept an ~ 3. to earn, receive, win an ~ 4. a posthumous ~ 5. (BE) a pay ~ 6. the ~ went to the best student 7. an ~ for

award II *v.* 1. (A) the judges ~ed the prize to her; or: the judges ~ed her the prize 2. (D; tr.) to ~ for (to ~ a prize for research)

aware *adj.* 1. acutely, keenly, painfully, very (much), well ~ 2. (cannot stand alone) ~ of (they were ~ of the difficulties) 3. ~ that + clause (he was ~ that the deadline had passed)

awareness *n.* 1. growing, heightened ~ 2. public ~ 3. ~ that + clause (there is a general ~ that smoking is harmful)

awash *adj.* ~ with

away *adv.* 1. far ~ 2. ~ from (he is ~ from home)

awe I *n.* 1. to inspire ~ in (he inspired ~ in everyone) 2. to hold smb. in ~ 3. deep ~ 4. in ~ of (to stand in ~ of smb.)

awe II *v.* (D; tr.) to ~ into (to ~ smb. into silence)

awful *adj.* (colloq.) 1. ~ about (I feel ~ about it) 2. ~ for (the situation is ~ for all of us) 3. ~ to + inf. (it was ~ to work there = it was ~ working there) 4. ~ that + clause (it's ~ that they were/should have been reprimanded because of my mistake)

awkward *adj.* 1. ~ at 2. ~ with (he is ~ with children) 3. (BE) ~ for (Monday is ~ for me) 4. ~ to +

inf. (it is ~ to discuss such matters in public = it is ~ discussing such matters in public)

AWOL *adj.* to be; go ~

awry *adj.*, *adv.* to go ~ (our plans have gone ~)

ax, axe *n.* 1. to swing, wield an ~ 2. (misc.) to get the ~ ("to be dismissed"); to have an ~ to grind ("to seek personal advantage")

axiom *n.* 1. to lay down an ~ 2. an ~ that + clause (we accept the ~ that a straight line is the shortest distance between two points)

axiomatic *adj.* ~ that + clause (it is ~ that everyone should pay a fair share of taxes)

axis *n.* on an ~ (to rotate on an ~)

B

babble I *n.* childish; confused; incessant ~

babble II *v.* 1. to ~ ceaselessly, incessantly; incoherently 2. (B) he ~d a few words to her 3. (D; intr.) to ~ about

babe *n.* 1. a ~ in arms ("a small infant; an inexperienced person") 2. a ~ in the woods ("a naive person")

babel *n.* 1. above the ~ (his voice was heard above the ~) 2. a ~ of tongues; voices

baboon *n.* a troop of ~s

baby *n.* 1. (of a woman) to have a ~ 2. (of a woman) to carry, expect a ~ (a pregnant woman carries a ~ for nine months; to carry a ~ to term) 3. (of a mother) to breast-feed, nurse, suckle a ~ 4. (of a midwife, nurse, doctor) to deliver a ~ 5. (of a clergyman) to baptize a ~ 6. to change a ~ ("to change the baby's diaper/nappy") 7. to calm, comfort, hush a ~ 8. to lull; put; rock a ~ to sleep 9. to diaper (AE); swaddle a ~ 10. to wean a ~ 11. to bubble (AE), burp a ~ 12. a blue; full-term; newborn; premature; stillborn; test-tube ~ 13. a ~ babbles, coos; bawls; cries; whimpers 14. a ~ burps; drools; teethes; throws up 15. a ~ crawls, creeps; toddles 16. (misc.) a bouncing ~ boy; girl

baby carriage *n.* (AE) to push, wheel a ~ (BE has *pram*)

baby-sit *v.* (D; intr.) to ~ for (who ~s for you?)

bachelor *n.* 1. a confirmed; eligible ~ 2. (misc.) a ~ of arts; a ~ of science

back I *adj., adv.* 1. ~ to (things are ~ to normal) 2. far, way ~ (~ back in the eighteenth century) 3. (misc.) to go ~ on one's promise/word ("to fail to keep one's promise")

back II *n.* ["part of the body opposite to the front"] 1. to turn one's ~ to smb.; (usu. fig.) to turn one's ~ on smb. 2. to arch one's ~ (the cat arched its ~) 3. a broad ~ 4. on one's, smb.'s ~ (to lie on one's ~; a heavy bag was on his ~) 5. (misc.) the small of the ~; to have a bad ~; to stand ~ to ~; they stood with their ~s to the door ["rear part"] 6. at, in the ~ (of) (a room at the ~ of the house; we sat in the back of the car) 7. from the ~ ["area behind smt."] 8. at the, (AE) in ~ of (BE: a garden at the ~ of the house = AE: a yard in ~ of the house) ["misc."] 9. he did it behind my ~ ("he did it without my knowledge"); at/in the ~ of one's mind ("subconsciously"); to break one's ~ ("to work very hard"); to get one's ~ up ("to balk at smt."); get off my ~ (colloq.) ("leave me alone"); if you scratch my ~, I'll scratch yours (colloq.) ("if you help me, I'll help you"); to have one's ~ to the wall ("to be in a desperate position"); to break the ~ of a job ("to do most of a job"); to put one's/some

(AE) ~ into one's work ("to make a maximum physical effort"); who will sit in ~? (AE)

back III *v.* 1. (D; tr.) ("to support") to ~ against (the independents will ~ us against the majority party) 2. (D; tr.) to ~ for (we will ~ her for public office) 3. (d; intr., tr.) ("to move") to ~ into (to ~ into a garage; she ~ed the car into the driveway) 4. (d; intr., tr.) to ~ out of (he ~ed out of the driveway; to ~ a car out of a garage) 5. (D; intr.) ("to withdraw") to ~ out of (they ~ed out of the deal)

backache *n.* 1. to have ~ (BE)/ a ~ (AE) 2. (a) chronic, nagging, persistent ~

back away *v.* (D; intr.) to ~ from

backbone *n.* ["courage"] 1. ~ for 2. the ~ to + inf. (will he have the ~ to tell the truth?)

back burner *n.* to put smt. on the ~ ("to delay consideration of smt.")

backchat *n.* (BE) see **backtalk**

backdate *v.* (D; tr.) to ~ to (to ~ an agreement to the beginning of the year)

back down *v.* (D; intr.) to ~ from (they had to ~ from their demands)

back door *n.* to get in by, through the ~ (usu. fig.) ("to accomplish smt. by devious means")

backdrop *n.* 1. to provide a ~ for 2. a ~ to (the ~ to the hearings was complex) 3. against a ~ of

backer *n.* 1. to secure ~s (for a project) 2. a financial; powerful ~

back formation *n.* (ling.) a ~ from (*to burgle* is a ~ from *burglar*)

background *n.* ["smb.'s experience, past"] 1. to have a ~ (in) (what sort of ~ does she have?) 2. to check smb.'s ~ 3. a broad; narrow; rich, well-rounded; specialized ~ 4. a deprived, disadvantaged; middle-class; privileged; working-class ~ 5. smb.'s academic, educational; cultural; ethnic; political; religious; social ~ 6. a ~ for (to have the right ~ for a job) ["rear part of a picture, scene"] 7. against, on a ~ (against a dark ~) ["surroundings"] 8. an appropriate, fitting ~ 9. a ~ to (the music served as a ~ to the recitation of poetry) ["a less important position"] 10. to relegate smb. to the ~ 11. in the ~ (to keep, remain, stay in the ~) 12. into the ~ (to fade into the ~) ["history, past"] 13. an historical ~ 14. a ~ of, to (do you know the ~ to this case?)

backing *n.* 1. to gain, have, secure, win ~ 2. to lose ~ (the project has the ~ of the government 3. financial ~ 4. ~ for (financial ~ for a project)

backlash *n.* 1. to create, provoke, stir up (a) ~ 2. ~ against

backlog *n.* 1. to accumulate, build up a ~ 2. to reduce a ~

back off v. (D; intr.) to ~ from (to ~ from one's demands)

backpack v. (P; intr.) to ~ across the continent; to ~ through Europe

backseat n. to take a ~ to smb. (she will not take a ~ to anyone)

backstroke n. to do, swim the ~

backtalk n. (AE) (colloq.) don't give me any ~! (BE has *backchat*)

backtrack v. (D; intr.) to ~ from

backup n. ["substitute"] a ~ for, to

back up v. 1. (D; intr.) to ~ to (he ~ed up to the loading platform) 2. (D; tr.) to ~ with (they backed us up with a generous contribution)

backwards adv. 1. to go ~; to step ~; to walk ~ 2. to put smt. in ~ 3. (misc.) to bend over ~ (usu. fig.)

backwater n. a cultural ~

bacon n. 1. crisp; lean; smoked; streaky (BE) ~ 2. a rasher of ~ 3. (misc.) to bring home the ~ ("to succeed"); (BE) to save smb.'s ~ ("to rescue smb. from a difficulty")

bacteria n. 1. to grow ~ 2. non-pathogenic; pathogenic; virulent ~ 3. a colony of ~

bad I adj. 1. ~ for (smoking is ~ for your health) 2. ~ to + inf. (it's ~ to lie) 3. ~ that + clause (it's too ~ that he was not able to attend the meeting) 4. (misc.) the meat went ~; to feel ~ about smt.; to go from ~ to worse; not ~ ("quite good"); not half ~ ("rather good"); that's (just) too ~ ("nothing can be done about that")

bad II n. 1. (colloq.) to be in ~ with smb. ("to be on bad terms with smb.") 2. to go from ~ to worse

bad form n. (esp. BE) ~ to + inf. (it's ~ to be late)

badger v. 1. (D; tr.) to ~ into (they ~ed me into buying a new car) 2. (D; tr.) to ~ with (to ~ smb. with questions) 3. (H) they ~ed me to buy a new car

baffle v. 1. to ~ completely 2. (R) it ~d me that they rejected our offer

bag n. ["suitcase"] 1. to pack, unpack one's ~s 2. to check; label one's ~s ["container"] ["pouch"] 3. an air ~ (that inflates within a car on impact) 4. a barracks; duffel, kit (BE); flight; garment; musette (AE); overnight ~ 5. a carrier (BE); clutch; shopping; shoulder ~ 6. a jiffy ("padded bag used for mailing"); paper; plastic ~ 7. a sleeping ~ 8. a body ~ 9. an ice ~ 10. (BE) a sponge ~ ("bag for toilet articles") 11. (AE) a grab ~ (BE has *lucky dip*) 12. a tea ~ ["leather ball"] 13. (AE) a punching ~ (BE has *punch ball*) ["misc."] 14. in the ~ ("assured of success")

baggage n. 1. to check; claim one's ~ 2. excess ~ 3. unclaimed ~ 4. a piece of ~ 5. (misc.) (fig.) emotional; ideological; intellectual ~

bagpipes n. 1. to play the ~ 2. ~ skirl, wail

bail I n. 1. to grant, set ~ 2. to post, put up, stand ~ for; (colloq.) to go ~ for 3. to make, raise ~ 4. to

deny, refuse smb. ~ 5. to forfeit, jump, skip ~ 6. on ~ (to free/release smb. on ~; to be set free on a thousand dollars ~)

bail II v. 1. (AE) (d; intr.) ("to parachute") to ~ out of (to ~ out of an airplane) 2. (D; tr.) ("to remove") to ~ out of (~ water out of a boat) 3. (d; tr.) ("to help") to ~ out of (to ~ smb. out of trouble)

bailiwick n. in one's own ~

bait n. 1. to hold out, offer; put out, set out ~ 2. to nibble at; swallow, take the ~ 3. to rise to the ~ 4. tempting ~

bake v. (C) he ~d a cake for us; or: he ~d us a cake

bakery n. at, in a ~ (she works at/in a ~)

balance I n. 1. to strike a ~ between 2. to keep, maintain; recover, regain one's ~ 3. to lose one's ~ 4. to disturb, upset the ~; to throw smt. off ~ 5. to tip the ~ in smb.'s favor 6. a delicate ~ 7. (bookkeeping) a trial ~ 8. a bank; credit; debit ~ 9. a foreign-trade, trade ~ 10. a favorable; unfavorable ~ (a favorable ~ of trade) 11. the strategic ~ 12. (misc.) to hang in the ~ ("to be uncertain"); on ~ ("all in all")

balance II v. (d; tr.) to ~ against; with (to ~ one argument against the other)

balanced adj. evenly ~

balance of power n. 1. to hold the ~ 2. to change; tip; upset the ~

bale (BE) see **bail II** 1

balk v. (D; intr.) to ~ at (he ~ed at the price)

Balkans n. in the ~

ball I n. ["game"] 1. (AE) to play ~ ["spherical object used in a sport"] 2. to bat; bounce; catch; drop; fumble; hit; kick; pass; pitch; throw, toss a ~ 3. a ~ bounces 4. the ~ is dead ("the ball does not bounce") 5. a baseball; basketball; beach; bowling; cue ~; football; golf; medicine; ping-pong; tennis ~; volleyball 6. (BE) a punch ~ (AE has *punching bag*) ["spherical mass"] 8. a cotton ~ 9. a wrecker's ~ 10. in a ~ (to curl up in a ~) ["glass object used in fortune telling"] 11. a crystal ~ ["misc."] 12. to get, set, start the ~ rolling ("to begin an activity"); (colloq.) on the ~ ("efficient"); (AE; colloq.) to play ~ with ("to cooperate with")

ball II n. ["formal dance"] 1. to have, organize a ~ 2. a costume; fancy-dress; inaugural; masked ~ 3. at a ~ (to dance at a ~) 4. (misc.) (colloq.) to have a ~ ("to enjoy oneself")

ballad n. 1. to compose a ~ 2. to perform a ~ 3. a folk; lewd, ribald ~

ballast n. 1. to take on ~ 2. to drop ~

ballet n. 1. to dance, perform; stage a ~ 2. classical; folk ~; (a) water ~

balloon I n. 1. to fly; launch a ~ 2. to blow up, inflate; deflate; pop a ~ 3. a ~ bursts 4. a ~ comes down, drops; floats; goes up, rises 5. a barrage; captive; hot-air; observation ~ 6. (fig.) a trial ~ (to send up a trial~)

balloon II *v.* (d; intr.) to ~ into (to ~ into a scandal)

ballot *n.* 1. to cast a ~ 2. to invalidate a ~ 3. an absentee; open; secret; straw; void ~ 4. a ~ against; for 5. by ~ (to vote by secret ~) 6. on a ~ (our candidate's name is on the ~ in every state)

ballot box *n.* 1. to stuff the ~es 2. at the ~ (the issue will be decided at the ~)

balm *n.* 1. to apply (a) ~ 2. a healing, soothing ~

bamboozle *v.* (colloq.) ("to trick") 1. (D; tr.) to ~ into 2. (D; tr.) to ~ out of

ban I *n.* 1. to impose, place, put a ~ on 2. to lift a ~ from 3. a (nuclear) test ~ 4. a wartime ~ 5. a ~ on

ban II *v.* 1. (D; tr.) to ~ from (they were ~ned from attending) 2. (K) the police ~ned their demonstrating in the park

banana *n.* 1. to peel a ~ 2. a green; ripe; rotten ~ 3. a bunch of ~s

band I *n.* ["group of musicians"] 1. to conduct, lead; form a ~ 2. a brass; concert; dance; jazz; klezmer; marching; military; ragtime; regimental; rock; school; string ~ 3. a big ~ 4. a ~ marches; performs, plays 5. (misc.) to strike up the ~ ["group"] 6. a predatory; roving ~ 7. a ~ of marauders

band II *n.* ["ring"] 1. a wedding ~ ["range of wavelengths"] 2. a wave ~ 3. a citizens ~ (or: CB) ["circular strip"] 4. a brake; elastic (BE), rubber ~

bandage *n.* 1. to apply, put on; change a ~ 2. to wrap a ~ (around); to roll a ~ 3. to remove a ~ 4. to loosen; tighten a ~

Band-Aid (T) *n.* (esp. AE) BE has *Elastoplast* (T) to apply, put on a ~

bandit *n.* a masked ~

band together *v.* (D; intr., refl.) to ~ against (the liberals ~ed together against the new legislation)

bandwagon *n.* ["attractive cause"] to climb aboard/on, jump aboard/on the ~

bandy *v.* to ~ words with smb.

bang I *n.* 1. with a ~ (the door slammed with a ~) 2. (misc.) (AE) to go over with a ~ ("to be successful")

bang II *v.* 1. (d; intr.) to ~ against, at; into; on (she ~ed on the door; I ~ed into the wall) 2. (D; tr.) to ~ against, on (he ~ed his head on the low ceiling)

bang away *v.* (colloq.) (D; intr.) ("to shoot") to ~ at (we ~ed away at the enemy plane)

bang down *v.* (D; intr., tr.) to ~ on (he ~ed his fist down on the drum; she ~ed down on the table)

banish *v.* 1. (D; tr.) to ~ for (they were ~ed for supporting a free press) 2. (D; tr.) to ~ from; to (she was ~ed from the country)

banister *n.* to slide down a ~ (BE also has *to slide down the bannisters*)

banjo *n.* to play; pluck; strum a ~

bank I *n.* ["financial establishment"] 1. to charter; establish a ~ 2. a central; commercial; credit; export-import; investment; land; national, people's,

state; merchant (BE); reserve; savings ~ 3. a drive-in ~ 4. a ~ closes, collapses, fails 5. at, in a ~ (she works at/in a ~) ["fund held in a gambling game"] 6. to break the ~ ["place of storage"] 7. a blood; corneal, eye; data; organ; soil; sperm; tissue ~ 8. a citation ~ (for dictionaries)

bank II *v.* 1. (d; intr.) to ~ on ("to rely on") (we were ~ing on your support) 2. (D; intr.) to ~ with ("to conduct financial operations with") (I ~ with the local branch)

bank III *n.* ["shore"] 1. a rugged; sloping; steep ~ 2. a river ~ 3. on a ~ 4. (misc.) the ~s were flooded

bank IV *n.* ["row"] ["tier"] an elevator (AE) ~

banker *n.* an international; investment; merchant (BE) ~

banking *n.* 1. electronic; international ~ 2. (misc.) where do you do your ~?

bank on *v.* 1. (d.; intr.) to ~ for (they are ~ing on the government for funds) 2. (E) I was ~ing on them to help

bankrupt *adj.* 1. morally ~ 2. to go ~ 3. to declare smb. ~

bankruptcy *n.* to declare, go into, file for, petition for ~

banner *n.* 1. to plant; unfurl; wave a ~ 2. a ~ flutters, waves 3. a regimental ~ 4. (fig.) under a ~

banns *n.* ["declaration of an impending marriage"] to publish, read the ~

banquet *n.* 1. to arrange, give, have, hold a ~ 2. to cater a ~ 3. an elaborate, lavish, sumptuous ~ 4. a farewell; formal; state; wedding ~ 5. a ~ for 6. at a ~

banter *n.* 1. to exchange ~ with 2. good-natured, light; witty ~

baptism *n.* 1. to administer ~; to perform a ~ 2. to accept, receive, undergo ~ 3. (misc.) (to undergo) a ~ of fire

baptize *v.* (N; used with a noun) they ~d him Joseph

bar I *n.* ["counter or place where drinks are sold"] 1. to manage, operate, run a ~ 2. to tend (AE) ~ 3. to stop at a ~ (on the way home); to drink at a ~; to drop into a ~ 4. a cash (AE); open ("free") ~ 5. a cocktail; public (BE); saloon (BE) ~ 6. a coffee (BE); salad; snack ~ 7. a gay; singles ~ ["barrier"] 8. a color ~ 9. a ~ to (a ~ to success) ["barrier in a law court"] 10. at the ~ (the prisoner at the ~; to be tried at the ~) 11. before the ~ (of justice) ["the profession of barrister, trial lawyer"] 12. to be admitted, (esp. BE) called to the ~ 13. (esp. BE) to read for the ~ ["metal strip used as a barrier"] 14. behind ~s ("in prison") (he was put behind ~s) ["strip used in gymnastics"] 15. a horizontal ~ 16. parallel ~s 17. on the ~ (to work out on the ~) ["handrail used by ballet dancers"] 18. at the ~ (to warm up at the ~) ["metal strip used in a suspension system"] 19. a torsion ~ ["lever on a typewriter"] 20. a space ~ ["oblong piece"] 21. a candy; chocolate ~ ["musical measure"] 22. to hum; play; sing a few ~s

bar II v. 1. (D; tr.) ("to exclude") to ~ from (he was ~red from the competition) 2. (K) ("to forbid") they ~red his participating

barb n. ["critical remark"] 1. to aim, sling ~s at 2. a ~ stings

barbarism, barbarity n. 1. to demonstrate, display ~ 2. outright, unmitigated, utter ~ 3. an act of ~ (to commit an act of ~)

barbarous adj. ~ to + inf. (it was ~ of them to treat prisoners in that manner)

barbecue I n. ["party at which barbecued meat is served"] 1. to have a ~ 2. at a ~ 3. a backyard ~

barbecue II v. (C) she ~d a steak for me; or: she ~d me a steak

barbed wire, (AE) **barbwire** n. to string ~

barbell n. 1. to clean; lift; press a ~ 2. an adjustable ~

barber n. at the ~'s

barbershop n. (esp. AE) at, in a ~ (he is at/in the ~)

bare I adj. 1. ~ of (the hills were ~ of vegetation) 2. (misc.) to lay smt. ~

bare II v. (B) she ~d her soul to us

barefoot adv. to go, walk ~

bargain I n. ["agreement"] 1. to drive; make, strike; seal a ~ 2. to meet one's end of a ~ 3. a hard ~ (she drives a hard ~) 4. a ~ with (we struck a ~ with them) 5. a ~ to + inf. (they made a ~ not to cut prices) ["advantageous purchase"] 6. to find, get a ~ 7. to hunt for a ~ 8. to shop for ~s 9. a good, real ~ ["misc."] 10. to make the best of a bad ~ ("to do one's best in a difficult situation"); in (AE), into (BE) the ~ ("in addition, along with")

bargain II v. 1. ("to negotiate") to ~ shrewdly 2. (D; intr.) ("to negotiate") to ~ for; over; with (we ~ed with them for the property) 3. (d; intr.) to ~ for, on (AE) ("to count on") (I wasn't ~ing on any trouble; it was more than I had ~ed for)

bargaining n. collective; plea ~

barge I n. 1. to drive; float; tow a ~ 2. to load; unload a ~

barge II v. 1. (d; intr.) to ~ into (she ~d into the room) 2. (P; intr., tr.) they ~ed out of the restaurant; he ~d his way past the guard; she ~d through the crowd

barge in v. (D; intr.) to ~ on (to ~ on a conversation)

baritone n. to sing ~

bark I n. ["covering of a tree"] ~ peels

bark II n. ["the sound made by a dog"] 1. to let out a ~ 2. a furious; loud, noisy ~

bark III v. 1. to ~ furiously 2. (B) the sergeant ~ed an order to his squad 3. (D; intr., tr.) to ~ at (the dog ~ed at the jogger; the general ~ed a command at her staff) 4. (misc.) "Do it!" he ~ed

barn n. a car ~ (AE; BE has *waggon shed*)

barnacle n. 1. ~s cling (to the bottom of a ship) 2.

(misc.) to cling like a ~

barnstorm v. (P; intr.) to ~ around the country; to ~ through the whole state

barometer n. 1. an aneroid; mercury ~ 2. a ~ is steady; falls; rises

baron n. ["magnate"] a cattle; coal; drug; media; oil; press; robber; steel ~

barracks n. 1. (AE) to GI the ~ 2. (AE) to police (up) the ~ 3. army; disciplinary; police ~ 4. restricted to ~

barrage n. 1. to lay down a ~ 2. to lift a ~ 3. an artillery; rolling ~ 4. an advertising; propaganda ~

barred adj. ~ to (esp. AE) (the street was ~ to traffic)

barrel n. 1. to tap a ~ 2. a beer ~ 3. (misc.) (colloq.) to have smb. over a ~ ("to have placed smb. in a difficult position")

barricade n. 1. to erect, place, set up a ~ 2. to storm a ~ 3. to remove, take down a ~ 4. a barbed-wire ~ 5. a ~ against

barrier n. 1. to erect, place, put up, set up a ~; to form a human ~ 2. to overcome; take a ~ (the horse took the ~ easily) 3. to break down; break through; remove a ~ 4. the sonic, sound ~ (to break the sound ~) 5. a crash (BE); crush (BE), police ~ 6. a cultural; ethnic; language; racial; religious; social ~ (to break a racial ~) 7. a trade ~ 8. a ~ between 9. a ~ to (a ~ to progress)

barter I n. 1. to engage in ~ 2. ~ between; for; with

barter II v. 1. (D; intr., tr.) to ~ for (to ~ furs for tobacco) 2. (D; intr.) to ~ with

base I n. ["center of operations"] 1. to establish, set up a ~ 2. to close (down) a ~ 3. an advanced, forward; home; main ~ 4. an air, air-force; army; military; missile; naval ~ 5. an enemy ~ 6. (misc.) a power ~; a ~ of operations ["goal"] (esp. AE) (baseball) 7. to reach; touch (a) ~ 8. to steal a ~ 9. (misc.) (colloq.) she couldn't get to first ~ with them ("she couldn't even begin to achieve any success with them"); (AE; colloq.) to touch ~ with ("to make contact with") ["collection"] 10. a database ["basic ingredient"] 11. an oil ~ ["foundation"] 12. a solid ~

base II v. (d; tr.) to ~ on, upon (we ~d our conclusions on facts)

baseball n. ["game"] 1. to play ~ 2. night ~ ["ball"] 3. to pitch a ~

basement n. 1. (AE) a finished; full ~ 2. (esp. AE) a bargain ~ (in a department store) 3. in a ~

bash I n. (slang) (BE) ["attempt"] to have a ~ at smt.

bash II v. (D; tr.) to ~ against (he ~ed his head against the door)

bashful adj. ~ about; with

basic adj. ~ to

basics n. back to (the) ~

basic training n. (mil.) to go through, take ~

basin *n.* 1. a river; tidal; yacht ~ 2. a handbasin (BE), washbasin, wash-hand (BE) ~

basis *n.* 1. to be, form, provide a ~ for 2. a trial ~ 3. a firm, solid, sound; shaky ~ 4. a first-name ~ 5. a scientific ~ 6. a ~ for, of 7. on a ~ (on a solid ~; she was promoted on the ~ of her accomplishments; to be paid on an hourly ~; to be on a first-name ~)

bask *v.* to ~ in (to ~ in the sunshine; to ~ in the adulation of one's followers)

basket *n.* ["receptacle"] 1. to make, weave a ~ 2. a laundry, linen (BE); picnic; sewing; wastebasket (AE), wastepaper ~ 3. a wicker ~ ["goal in basketball"] 4. to make, score, shoot, sink a ~ 5. to shoot at the ~ 6. to miss the ~

basketball *n.* ["game"] 1. to play ~ ["ball used in the game of basketball"] 2. to dribble; pass a ~

bass *n.* 1. to sing ~ 2. a deep ~

bat I *n.* ["club"] 1. to swing a ~ 2. a baseball; cricket; table-tennis ~ ["one's turn batting"] 3. (AE) at ~ (who's at ~?) ["misc."] 4. (colloq.) (BE) at full ~ ("very fast"); (AE) right off the ~ ("immediately")

bat II *n.* ["flying mammal"] 1. ~s fly at night 2. (misc.) as blind as a ~

batch *n.* 1. a fresh ~ (of dough) 2. in ~es

bath *n.* 1. to give (the baby) a ~ 2. to have (BE), take a ~ 3. to draw, run a ~ 4. (BE) a swimming ~ ("an indoor swimming pool") 5. a cold; hot; warm ~ 6. a sitz; steam, Turkish; whirlpool ~ 7. a sunbath 8. a sunken ~ 9. (misc.) a blood ~ ("slaughter")
USAGE NOTE: In BE, one meaning of *bath* is "bathtub".

bathe *v.* (D; tr.) to ~ in (she ~d her bruises in lukewarm water)

bathed *adj.* ~ in (~ in sunshine)

bather *n.* a sun ~

bathing *n.* sun ~

bathing suit *n.* (esp. AE) a one-piece; two-piece ~

bathroom see the Usage Note for **room**

baton *n.* 1. (in a relay race) to pass the ~ 2. (of a drum major or majorette) to twirl a ~ 3. (of an orchestra conductor) to raise a ~ 4. a police ~ 5. (in music) under the ~ of

battalion *n.* to command a ~ (a major commands a ~)

batter I *n.* ["mixture for baking"] 1. to mix; pour; stir (a) ~ 2. pancake ~

batter II *v.* 1. (D; intr., tr.) to ~ against, on (the wind ~ed the boat against the rocks) 2. (D; tr.) to ~ into (he ~ed his opponent into submission) 3. (D; tr.) to ~ to (to ~ smt. to pieces)

batter III *n.* ["one whose turn it is to bat"] (baseball) a leadoff ~

battering *n.* to take a ~

battery *n.* ["a group of cells that store and furnish current"] 1. to charge; recharge a ~ 2. to discharge, run down a ~ 3. an alkaline; flashlight

(AE), torch (BE); storage ~ 4. a ~ charges (itself) 5. a ~ discharges, runs (itself) down 6. a ~ is dead, flat (BE) ["artillery unit"] 7. to command a ~ (a captain commands a ~) 8. an anti-aircraft; missile ~

battle I *n.* 1. to do, give, join ~ 2. to fight; lose; win a ~ 3. to break off, terminate a ~ 4. a bloody; fierce, pitched, raging ~ 5. a constant; running ~ 6. a decisive; losing; uphill ~ (engaged in a losing ~) 7. a legal ~ 8. an historic ~ 9. a land; naval ~ 10. a political ~ 11. a ~ royal 12. a ~ rages 13. a ~ against; among, between; for, over; with (they fought a ~ among themselves for domination of the market; the ~ against inflation; to join ~ with smb.; a ~ between two strong adversaries) 14. a ~ to + inf. (it was a real ~ to win the election) 15. at a ~ (at the ~ of Gettysburg) 16. in ~ (to be killed in ~)

battle II *v.* (D; intr.) to ~ against, with; for, over

battlefield *n.* on the ~ (to die on the ~)

battleship *n.* a pocket ~

battle station *n.* to take up one's ~

batty *adj.* (slang) ["crazy, mad"] 1. to drive smb. ~ 2. to go ~ over

baulk (esp. BE) see **balk**

bay I *n.* 1. to hold, keep at ~ 2. to bring to ~

bay II *n.* ["compartment"] a loading ~

bay III *v.* (D; intr.) to ~ at; for (the hounds were ~ing at the fox; the mob was ~ing for blood)

bayonet *n.* 1. to thrust a ~ into (smb.'s body) 2. to fix; unfix ~s

bazaar *n.* 1. a charity; church ~ 2. at a ~

bazooka *n.* to fire; operate a ~

be *v.* 1. (E; usu. in the past) he was never to see his family again; she was to become famous 2. (S) to ~ a teacher; to ~ happy 3. (misc.) you are to be/ appear in court at two o'clock

beach *n.* 1. an isolated; private; public; sandy ~ 2. at; on the ~

beachhead *n.* to establish; hold; secure a ~

beacon *n.* 1. a homing; landing; radar; radio; rotating ~ 2. (BE) a Belisha ~ ("a light marking a pedestrian crossing") 3. a ~ to (to serve as a ~ to others)

bead *n.* ["front sight"] to draw a ~ on

beads *n.* 1. (rel.) to count, say one's ~ 2. to string ~ 3. (rel.) prayer ~ 4. a string of ~

beam I *n.* ["shaft of light"] 1. to direct, shine a ~ at 2. a high; low ~ (on a car) 3. a ~ from; to ["signal"] 4. a laser; radar; radio ~ 5. (also fig.) off the ~; on the ~ ["piece of wood"] 6. a balance ~

beam II *v.* 1. (B) they ~ed the program to the countries of Central America 2. (AE) (d; tr.) to ~ at (the sales campaign was ~ed at young professionals) 3. (D; intr.) to ~ with (to ~ with joy)

beam down *v.* (D; intr.) to ~ on

bean *n.* 1. broad; French (BE), haricot (BE), kidney; green; lima; navy; pinto; runner (BE), string; soya (AE also has *soybean*); wax ~s 2. coffee ~s 3. baked ~s 4. (misc.) to spill the ~s (slang) ("to reveal a secret"); to use the old ~ (slang) ("to use one's head"); full of ~s (slang) ("mistaken") (AE); . ("full of energy") (BE)

bear I *n.* 1. the black; brown; grizzly; koala; Kodiak; polar ~ 2. a teddy ~ 3. ~s hibernate 4. a young ~ is a cub

bear II *v.* 1. (formal) (A; the omission of *to* is rare) ("to carry") the servants were ~ing food to the guests 2. (A; used without *to*) ("to give birth to") she bore him two children 3. (d; intr.) ("to pertain") to ~ on (these facts ~ on the case) 4. (d; intr.) ("to move") to ~ to (we had to ~ to the right; or we had to ~ right) 5. (d; intr.) ("to have patience") to ~ with (please ~ with me for a few minutes) 6. (E; preceded by: can — cannot — can't) ("to stand, tolerate") she can't ~ to watch them suffer 7. (G; often used with: can — cannot — can't) ("to stand, tolerate") he can't ~ being alone; her words ~ repeating 8. (K) ("to stand, tolerate") I cannot ~ his behaving in that manner 9. (O; can be used with one inanimate object) ("to feel") she ~s them a grudge; he ~s (us) no ill will 10. (P; refl.) ("to behave") she bore herself with dignity 11. (misc.) to bring to ~ on (she brought her influence to ~ on the legislators; she can't ~ it when they suffer)

beard *n.* 1. to grow; have a ~ 2. to shave off; trim one's ~ 3. to stroke one's ~ 4. a bushy, heavy, rough, thick; scraggly, unkempt; tough ~ 5. a light, sparse; neat, trim ~

bear down *v.* (d; intr.) to ~ on (our destroyers bore down on the enemy carrier)

bearing *n.* ["relation"] 1. to have a ~ on (that fact has no ~ on the case) 2. a direct ["position"] 3. to take a ~ on (we took a ~ on the hill) ["carriage"] ["manner"] 4. a dignified; military; proud, regal, royal ~ ["machine part that supports"] 5. to burn out a ~ 6. a ball; roller; wheel ~ ["charge on a coat of arms"] 7. a heraldic ~

bearings *n.* ["orientation"] 1. to get one's ~ 2. to lose one's ~

bear up *v.* (D; intr.) to ~ against, under (to ~ under pressure)

beast *n.* ["qualities of an animal"] 1. to bring out the ~ in smb. ["animal"] 2. a rare; wild ~ 3. a ~ of burden; a ~ of prey

beat I *n.* ["a regularly traversed round"] 1. to patrol, walk one's ~ 2. to cover one's ~ 3. a police officer's ~ 4. on one's ~ ["rhythm"] 5. to follow the ~ 6. to miss, skip a ~ 7. on a ~ (to come in on the ~ of three) 8. an irregular; regular, steady ~ 9. to a ~ (to dance to the ~ of the music) ["unit of rhythm"] 10. a ~ to (four ~s to a measure)

beat II *v.* 1. ("to hit") to ~ brutally, mercilessly, savagely, severely, viciously 2. (sports) ("to de-

feat") to ~ decisively, easily; narrowly; soundly; by ten points 3. (d; intr., tr.) ("to strike") to ~ against (the bird beat its wings against the bars of its cage; the waves ~ against the rocks) 4. (D; tr.) ("to defeat") to ~ at (she beat me at chess) 5. (D; tr.) ("to strike") to ~ for (to ~ a prisoner for disobedience) 6. (d; tr.) ("to inculcate") to ~ into (to ~ facts into smb.'s head) 7. (d; tr.) ("to hammer") to ~ into (to ~ swords into plowshares) 8. (d; tr.) ("to strike") to ~ into, to (to ~ smb. into submission; to ~ smb. to death) 9. (d; intr.) ("to strike") to ~ on (smb. was ~ing on the door) 10. (d; tr.) ("to extract") to ~ out of (they beat a confession out of him) 11. (colloq.) (D; tr.) ("to arrive ahead of") to ~ to (I'll ~ you to the car!) 12. (N; used with an adjective) ("to strike") they beat him unconscious 13. (colloq.) (R) ("to astound") it ~s me that they turned down the invitation

beat down *v.* 1. (D; intr.) to ~ on (the sun beat down on us mercilessly) 2. (BE) (D; tr.) ("to persuade to reduce a price") to ~ to (I beat them down to ten pounds)

beating *n.* 1. to give smb. a ~ 2. to get, take a ~ 3. a bad, brutal, good, merciless, savage, severe, vicious ~ (he got a good ~)

beat out *v.* (D; tr.) to ~ for (we beat them out for the title by ten points)

beat up *v.* (AE; slang) (d; intr.) to ~ on ("to beat") (to ~ on smb.)

beautiful *adj.* ~ to + inf. (it was ~ to watch)

beauty *n.* ["a beautiful person or thing"] 1. a dazzling, raving, striking ~ 2. a bathing ~ ["good looks"] 3. to enhance ~ 4. dazzling, striking, wholesome ~ ["attractiveness"] 5. natural; scenic ~ 6. of ~ (a work of great ~)

beauty contest *n.* 1. to hold, stage a ~ 2. to enter a ~

beaver *n.* 1. a colony of ~s 2. (misc.) an eager ~ ("a zealous person")

beaver away *v.* (colloq.) (BE) (D; intr.) ("to work hard") to ~ at

beck *n.* to be at smb.'s ~ and call

beckon *v.* 1. (D; intr.) to ~ to (he ~ed to her) 2. (D; intr.) to ~ with (she ~ed me with her finger) 3. (H) she ~ed me to follow 4. (P; tr.) he ~ed me over

become *v.* 1. (d; intr.) to ~ of (what became of her?) 2. (formal) (R) it doesn't ~ you to speak like that 3. (S) she became a teacher; to ~ depressed

becoming *adj.* ~ to (that tie is not ~ to you)

bed *n.* ["article of furniture for sleeping"] 1. to make, make up a ~ 2. to unmake a ~ 3. to go to ~ with (she went to ~ with a heating pad)

USAGE NOTE: *to go to bed with smb.* means "to have sexual intercourse with smb." 4. to be, lie, stay in ~; to lie; sit on a ~ 5. to get out of ~ 6. to put smb. to ~ (to put the children to ~) 7. to take to one's ~ ("to remain in bed because of illness") 8. a double; king-size; queen-size; single; twin ~ 9. a bunk; camp (BE); folding; hospital; rollaway; sofa; truckle (BE), trundle (AE) ~ 10. a water ~ 11. an unmade ~ 12. a feather ~ ("a feather mattress") ["ground at the bottom of a body of water"] 13. a river ~ ["plot of ground"] 14. a flower ~

bedeck v. (D; tr.) to ~ with

bedfellow n. odd, strange, unlikely ~s (politics make strange ~s)

bedlam n. 1. ~ breaks out 2. absolute, complete, sheer, utter ~

bedroom n. a master; spare ~

bedside n. at smb.'s ~

bedsore n. 1. to develop, get a ~ 2. to prevent a ~

bedtime n. it's past my ~

bee I n. ["insect"] 1. to keep ~s 2. a bumblebee; honeybee; killer; queen; worker ~; social; solitary ~s 3. ~s buzz, hum; sting; swarm 4. a cluster; colony; swarm of ~s 5. (misc.) as busy as a ~

bee II n. (esp. AE) ["meeting to work or compete"] a quilting; sewing; spelling; spinning ~

beef I n. 1. to boil; braise; broil (AE), grill; cook; roast; stew ~ 2. chipped; corned; salt (BE) ~ 3. ~ Wellington 4. baby; prime ~ 5. a side of ~
USAGE NOTE: Corned beef in the US is not the same as corned beef in GB.

beef II v. (D; intr.) ("to complain") to ~ about

beef up v. (D; tr.) to ~ with (to ~ a proposal with concrete data)

beeline n. ["shortest route"] to make a ~ for ("to go directly toward")

beep I n. to give a ~

beep II v. (D; tr.) to ~ at

beer n. 1. to drink; guzzle, swig, swill ~ 2. to brew ~ 3. cold; light; strong ~ 4. near ~ 5. (soft drinks) ginger; root ~ 6. draft ~ 7. a barrel; bottle; can; glass; keg; mug, stein of ~ 8. ~ on tap

beet n. 1. (a) sugar ~ 2. (misc.) as red as a ~ (AE; BE has: as red as a beetroot)

beetle off v. (BE; slang) ("to hurry") (P; intr.) to ~ to London; to ~ home (the variants *beetle, beetle along, beetle away* also occur)

beg v. 1. to ~ humbly 2. (D; intr.) to ~ for (to ~ for mercy) 3. (formal) (d; tr.) to ~ of (I must ~ a favor of you) 4. (E) they ~ged to be allowed to go; I ~ to differ 5. (H) they ~ged her to help 6. (L; subj.) he ~ged that his family be/should be spared 7. (misc.) to go ~ging ("to be unwanted") (those jobs went ~ging)

begging n. to live by ~

begin v. 1. (D; intr., tr.) to ~ as (to ~ as a clerk; to ~ a new career as a teacher) 2. (D; intr.) to ~ by, with (they began by saying a prayer; or: they began with a prayer) 3. (d; intr.) to ~ on (they began on a new case) 4. (E) she began to work 5. (G) she began working

beginner n. an absolute, complete, rank ~

beginning n. 1. to make a ~ 2. to mark a ~ 3. an

auspicious, promising; fresh, new ~ 4. at, in the ~ 5. from (the) ~ (from ~ to end; from the very ~)

begrudge v. (O; can be used with one inanimate object) he ~s us our success

beguile v. (formal) 1. (D; tr.) to ~ into (he ~d me into lending him money) 2. (D; tr.) to ~ out of 3. (D; tr.) to ~ with (to ~ children with stories)

behalf n. in (AE), on smb.'s ~
USAGE NOTE: Some purists maintain that in AE *in smb.'s behalf* means "for smb.'s benefit", whereas *on smb.'s behalf* means "as smb.'s representative".

behave v. 1. to ~ appropriately; normally; responsibly; well 2. to ~ badly, poorly; inappropriately; irresponsibly; strangely 3. (d; intr.) to ~ like (he ~d like a gentleman) 4. (D; intr.) to ~ towards (how did they ~ towards you?)

behavior, behaviour n. 1. to exhibit ~ (to exhibit strange ~) 2. appropriate; diplomatic; disciplined; exemplary; good; model; modest; normal; responsible ~ 3. inappropriate; inconsiderate; inexcusable; obsequious; unacceptable; unbecoming; undignified; undiplomatic; undisciplined; unethical; unruly; unsportsmanlike ~ 4. abnormal; antisocial; asocial; bad; criminal; delinquent; disruptive ~ 5. infantile; irresponsible; willful ~ 6. irrational; neurotic; odd, strange; unorthodox ~ 7. promiscuous; provocative; scandalous ~ 8. sullen; suspicious ~ 9. ~ towards 10. on one's ~ (to be on one's best ~) 11. a code; pattern of ~ 12. (misc.) she got time off for good ~ (in prison)

behest n. at smb.'s ~

behind adv., prep. 1. to fall, lag ~ 2. to remain, stay ~ 3. to leave ~ 4. close ~ 5. ~ by (our team is ~ by two points) 6. ~ in, with (he's ~ with his payments) 7. (misc.) to be solidly ~ smb. ("to support smb. wholeheartedly")

beholden adj. (cannot stand alone) ~ for; to (we are ~ to nobody for anything)

behoove (AE), **behove** (BE) v. (R) (formal) it ~s them to help the needy; it ill ~s you to speak like that

being n. 1. to bring into ~; to come into ~ 2. a celestial; divine; extraterrestrial; human; living; mortal; rational; supernatural ~ 3. the Supreme Being

belch I n. 1. to emit, give, let out a ~ 2. to stifle, suppress a ~

belch II v. (d; intr.) to ~ from (smoke ~ed from the chimney)

belief n. 1. to cling to; express; hold a ~ 2. to shake smb.'s ~ 3. to give up, relinquish, renounce one's ~ 4. an ardent, firm, sincere, strong, unshakable; basic; deep-rooted ~ 5. an erroneous, false, mistaken; fanatical ~ 6. a popular; unpopular ~ 7. a personal; prevalent, widespread ~ 8. political; religious ~s 9. a ~ in (nothing will shake his ~ in ghosts) 10. a ~ that + clause (it is their firm ~ that the earth is flat) 11. beyond ~ 12. in the ~ that... 13. (misc.) against one's ~s

believe *v.* 1. to ~ firmly, sincerely, strongly; mistakenly 2. (D; intr.) to ~ in (to ~ in ghosts) 3. (D; tr.) to ~ of (I can't ~ it of him) 4. (L) we ~ that she will come 5. (M) they all ~ the story to be true 6. (misc.) I ~ so; I ~ not; it is widely ~d that...; ~ it or not; you would not ~ how much she has improved!

believer *n.* 1. an ardent, firm, great, sincere, staunch, strong; true ~ 2. a ~ in (he's no ~ in miracles)

bell *n.* 1. to cast a ~ 2. to ring, sound a ~ 3. to answer the ~ (in boxing) 4. a church; door ~ 5. a diving ~ 6. wedding ~s 7. a ~ chimes, clangs, peals, rings, sounds, tolls 8. (misc.) (boxing) to come out for the ~; to ring a ~ ("to remind smb. of smt.")

belligerency *n.* 1. to demonstrate, display, exhibit ~ 2. a state of ~ 3. ~ towards

belligerent *adj.* ~ towards

bellow *v.* 1. (B) he ~ed a command to his platoon 2. (D; intr., tr.) to ~ at (the sergeant was ~ing orders at her squad) 3. (L) he ~ed that he would fight any man at the bar

bellows *n.* 1. to operate, use ~ 2. a pair of ~

bellyache *v.* (slang) (D; intr.) ("to complain") to ~ about

belong *v.* 1. (d; intr.) ("to deserve to be") to ~ in (he ~s in jail) 2. (d; intr.) to ~ to ("to be owned by") (the book ~s to her) 3. (d; intr.) to ~ to ("to be a member of") (to ~ to an organization) 4. (d; intr.) ("to be appropriate") to ~ under (this item ~s under a different heading) 5. (d; intr.) to ~ with (these books ~ with the works on history)

belongings *n.* smb.'s earthly; personal ~

below I *adv.* 1. to go ~ 2. down ~ 3. far, way, well ~

below II *prep.* ~ in (to be ~ smb. in rank)

belt I *n.* ["band"] 1. to buckle, fasten one's ~ 2. (also fig.) to tighten one's ~ 3. to loosen; unbuckle, undo, unfasten one's ~ 4. a lap, safety, seat, shoulder; life ~ 5. a fan ~ 6. a money ~ 7. a cartridge; Sam Browne ~ 8. a garter (AE), suspender (BE) ~ 9. a conveyor; endless ~ 10. (usu. fig.) below the ~ ("unfairly") ["zone"] (AE) 11. the Bible; corn; cotton; green (BE) ~ ["symbol of expertise in judo or karate"] 12. a black; brown; white ~ ["misc."] 13. under one's ~ ("experienced, lived through")

belt II *v.* (colloq.) (O) I ~ed him one

bench *n.* ["judge's seat"] 1. from the ~ (a reprimand from the ~) 2. on the ~ (who will be on the ~ during her trial?) ["places in Parliament"] (BE) 3. the backbenches; crossbenches; frontbench(es); government ~es; opposition ~es ["place where reserve players sit"] 4. (esp. AE) on the ~ (he spent ten minutes on the ~) ["table"] 5. a carpenter's; work ~ ["long seat"] 6. a park ~

bench warrant *n.* to issue a ~

bend I *n.* 1. to make a ~ (the river makes a ~) 2. a horseshoe; sharp; slight ~ 3. a knee ~ 4. (misc.) (colloq.) (BE) round the ~ ("mentally unsound")

bend II *v.* 1. (D; tr.) to ~ into; out of (she bent the bar into the right shape; the steering wheel is bent out of shape) 2. (D; intr., tr.) to ~ to (the road ~s to the right; she cannot ~ them to her will) 3. (misc.) she bent down and picked up the book; they bent over backwards to please ("they made every effort to be helpful")

bender *n.* (colloq.) ["drunken spree"] to go on a ~

benediction *n.* 1. to give, offer, pronounce the ~ 2. to pronounce a ~ over

beneficial *adj.* 1. ~ for, to (~ to health) 2. ~ to + inf. (it would be ~ to keep abreast of developments in Asia)

beneficiary *n.* 1. to name a ~; to name smb. (as) (a) ~ 2. a chief, main, principal ~

benefit I *n.* 1. to derive, get, reap (a) ~ from 2. to have a ~ (she had the ~ of a good education) 3. a death; fringe; sickness (BE); supplementary (BE); tax ~ 4. a mutual; tangible ~ 5. to be of ~ to 6. for, to smb.'s ~ (for our mutual ~) 7. (misc.) to give smb. the ~ of the doubt; without ~ of clergy

benefit II *v.* (D; intr.) to ~ from (we all ~ed from her success)

benefits *n.* 1. to provide ~ 2. to collect; reap ~ 3. to withhold ~ 4. disability; fringe; health-care; old-age; retirement; strike; survivors' (AE); unemployment; veterans'; workers' ~

benevolent *adj.* ~ towards

bent I *adj.* ["determined"] 1. (cannot stand alone) ~ on (he was ~ on getting himself hurt; ~ on mischief) ["curved"] 2. ~ double

bent II *n.* ["propensity"] 1. to have; show a ~ for 2. to follow one's (own) ~ 3. an artistic; decided; natural; peculiar ~

bequeath *v.* (formal) (A) she ~ed her fortune to him; or: she ~ed him her fortune

bequest *n.* 1. to leave, make a ~ 2. a ~ to

berate *v.* (D; tr.) to ~ for

bereavement *n.* in one's ~

bereft *adj.* (cannot stand alone) ["stripped"] ~ of (~ of all hope; ~ of one's senses)

USAGE NOTE: In the meaning "having recently lost a dear one", the form *bereaved* is used—the bereaved parents.

berry *n.* to pick ~ies

berserk *adj.* to go ~

berth *n.* 1. to make up a ~ 2. a lower; sleeping; upper ~ 3. (misc.) to give smb./smt. a wide ~ ("to avoid smb./smt.")

beseech *v.* (formal) (H) to ~ smb. to show mercy

beset *adj.* (cannot stand alone) ~ by, with (~ by doubts)

beside *prep.* to be ~ oneself with (he was ~ himself

with grief)

besiege v. (D; tr.) to ~ with (to ~ smb. with questions)

besotted adj. ~ with (~ with drink)

best I adj. 1. ~ to + inf. (it is ~ not to speak of it in public) 2. ~ that + clause; subj. (it is ~ that she say/should say nothing to the press)

USAGE NOTE: In BE the following constructions also occur — it is best that she says/said nothing to the press.

best II adv. see **better II** 1

best III n. 1. to do, give; try one's (level) ~ 2. to make the ~ (of smt.) 3. to get the ~ (of smb.) 4. to look one's ~ 5. to bring out the ~ in smb. 6. one's level ~ 7. next, second ~ 8. one's ~ to + inf. (she tried her ~ to finish the job on time) 9. at ~ (at ~, our team may win five matches) 10. at one's ~ (she is not at her ~ in the morning) 11. for the ~ (it turned out for the ~; to hope for the ~; it's all for the ~) 12. in the ~ of (he's not in the ~ of health) 13. in one's Sunday ~ 14. to the ~ of (to the ~ of my ability) 15. (misc.) (colloq.) (AE) give my ~ to your family

bestir v. (formal) (H; refl.) we must ~ ourselves to get there on time

bestow v. (formal) (d; tr.) to ~ on, upon (to ~ an honor on smb.)

bet I n. 1. to lose; make; win a ~ 2. to place a ~ on 3. to accept, take a ~ 4. a good, safe, sure ~ 5. a side ~ 6. a ~ that + clause (she made a ~ that her team would win) 7. on a ~ (he did it on a ~) 8. (misc.) to hedge one's ~s ("to protect oneself by placing several bets")

bet II v. 1. (D; intr., tr.) to ~ on (he bet on that horse; he bet a month's salary on that horse) 2. (L; may have an object) I bet (her) that it would snow 3. (O; can be used with one, two, or three objects) we bet ten pounds; we bet him ten pounds; we bet him ten pounds that it would rain

betake v. (formal and obsol.) (P; refl.) he betook himself to the fair

betray v. (B) the informer ~ed them to the police

betroth v. (B) they were ~ed to each other at an early age

betrothal n. 1. to announce a ~ 2. a ~ to

better I adj. 1. any; far, much; a little; somewhat ~ (is she any ~ today?) 2. ~ at (he is ~ at tennis than at squash) 3. ~ for (the new job is much ~ for me) 4. ~ to + inf. (it is ~ to give than to receive; it is ~ for us to leave early) 5. ~ that + clause; subj. (it's ~ that she go/should go alone)

USAGE NOTE: In BE, the following constructions also occur it's better that she goes/went alone. 6. (misc.) he is no ~ than a common thief

better II adv. 1. he had ~ do it; they had ~ come early 2. to be ~ off

better III n. 1. to get the ~ of smb. 2. to expect;

think ~ of smt. 3. for the ~ (a change for the ~; to take a turn for the ~)

betting n. off-track; parimutuel (AE), totalizator (BE) ~

between adv. 1. in ~ 2. few and far ~

beverage n. 1. an alcoholic; carbonated; intoxicating; non-alcoholic ~ 2. cold; hot ~s

beware v. (D; intr.; only in the imper.) ~ of (~ of the dog!)

bewildered adj. ~ to + inf. (she was ~ to find them gone)

bewildering adj. ~ to + inf. (it was ~ for them to contemplate all the possibilities)

bewilderment n. in ~

beyond adv. 1. far, way, well ~ 2. (misc.) above and ~ the call of duty

bias I n. ["prejudice"] 1. to demonstrate, display, exhibit, have, show (a) ~ 2. to root out ~ 3. deep-rooted, strong; personal ~ 4. racial; religious; sexual ~ 5. a ~ against; for, in favor of; towards ["diagonal line"] 6. on the ~ (to cut on the ~)

bias II v. (D; tr.) to ~ against; in favor of (their upbringing ~ed them against all foreigners)

biased adj. 1. strongly ~ 2. ~ against; in favor of; towards

Bible n. the Holy ~

bibliography n. 1. to compile, make up a ~ 2. an annotated; comprehensive; exhaustive; select, selective ~

bicentenary n. to celebrate, mark, observe a ~

bicentennial (esp. AE) see **bicentenary**

bicker v. (D; intr.) 1. to ~ constantly, incessantly 2. to ~ about, over; with

bickering n. 1. constant, incessant ~ 2. ~ about, over 3. ~ between; with

bicycle n. 1. to pedal, ride a ~ 2. to get on, mount; get off a ~ 3. an exercise, stationary; racing ~ 4. by ~ (to go somewhere by ~)

bid I n. ["bidding of an amount"] 1. to enter, file, make, put in, submit a ~ 2. to call for, invite ~s 3. to raise one's ~ 4. to consider, entertain a ~ 5. to accept; reject, turn down a ~ 6. to recall a ~ 7. an opening; sealed ~ 8. a (hostile) takeover ~ 9. the highest; lowest ~ 10. a ~ for, on (she made a ~ on the painting) ["attempt"] 11. to make a ~ 12. a desperate ~ 13. a ~ for (she made a ~ for the nomination) 14. a ~ to + inf. (he made a ~ to regain his former influence) 15. in a ~ (in a ~ for power; in their ~ to take over the company, they made many enemies)

bid II v. 1. (D; intr.) to ~ against 2. (D; tr.) to ~ for (she bid twenty pounds for the vase) 3. (D; intr.) to ~ for (AE), on (to ~ on a contract)

bid III v. 1. (formal) (A) she bade farewell to them; or: she bade them farewell 2. (obsol.) (H) to ~ smb. to do smt. 3. (obsol.) (I) to ~ smb. do smt.

bidder n. the highest; lowest ~

bidding *n.* ["offering of bids"] 1. to close; open the ~ 2. competitive; spirited ~ ["request"] 3. to do smb.'s ~ 4. at smb.'s ~

big *adj.* ["kind"] ["good"] (colloq., ironical) 1. ~ of (that's ~ of you) 2. ~ to + inf. (it was ~ of you to do that) ["older"] 3. a ~ boy; brother; girl; sister ["very powerful"] 4. ~ business; government; labor

bigamy *n.* to commit; practice ~

bigot *n.* a fanatical, narrow-minded, vicious; religious ~

bigoted *adj.* 1. strongly ~ 2. ~ against 3. ~ to + inf. (it was ~ to say that)

bigotry *n.* 1. to arouse, stir up ~ 2. to demonstrate, display, show ~ 3. fanatical, ingrained, narrow-minded, vicious; religious ~ 4. ~ against

big time *n.* to get into, reach the ~

bike *n.* to ride a ~ (see **bicycle**)

bilk *v.* (esp. AE) (D; tr.) to ~ out of (they ~ed us out of the money)

bill I *n.* ["proposed law"] 1. to amend; draft; introduce, propose; oppose; pass; support a ~; to sign a ~ into law 2. to move; railroad a ~ through a legislature 3. to quash, reject, vote down; veto a ~ 4. to shelve a ~ 5. an appropriations; revenue, tax ~ ["banknote"] (AE) 6. to break, change; pass a ~ 7. a counterfeit; dollar ~ 8. marked ~s ["statement of money owed"] ["debt"] 9. to run up a ~ 10. to itemize; submit a ~ 11. to foot (colloq.), pay; pick up; settle a ~ 12. a hospital, medical; hotel; telephone; utility (electric; gas; water) ~ 13. a ~ falls due, matures 14. (misc.) to put smt. on smb.'s ~ ["poster"] 15. to post, stick (BE) a ~ (post no ~s!) ["misc."] 16. to fill, fit the ~ ("to meet all requirements")

bill II *v.* 1. (D; tr.) ("to describe") to ~ as (she was ~ed as a leading expert) 2. (D; tr.) ("to charge") to ~ for (the doctor did not ~ them for the visit) 3. (H) ("to cast"); ("to announce") he was ~ed to appear as Hamlet

billet *n.* an officers' ~

billiards *n.* to play ~

billing *n.* ["prominence in advertising, promotion"] 1. to get, receive ~ 2. advance; star, top ~ (to get top ~)

bill of health *n.* ["approval"] 1. to give smb. a clean ~ 2. to get, receive; have a clean ~

bill of sale *n.* to make up, prepare a ~

bin *n.* 1. (BE) a dustbin, litter, rubbish ~ 2. a storage ~

bind I *n.* ["trouble"] ["dilemma"] 1. a double ~ 2. in a ~

bind II *v.* 1. (D; tr.) ("to put together") to ~ in (to ~ a book in leather) 2. (D; tr.) ("to tie") to ~ to (they bound him to a post) 3. (D; tr.) ("to require") to ~ to (to ~ smb. to secrecy) 4. (H) ("to require") the contract ~s you to pay interest 5. (misc.) to ~

together

binder *n.* ["deposit of money"] (esp. AE) 1. to place, put down a ~ on ["holder for sheets of paper"] 2. a loose-leaf; ring ~ ["broad bandage"] (AE) 3. to apply a ~ 4. an abdominal; breast; straight ~

binding I *adj.* 1. legally ~ 2. ~ on, upon (the agreement is ~ on you)

binding II *n.* ["fastening of the sections of a book"] 1. a handsome; leather ~ 2. in a ~ (the book is in a leather ~) ["narrow strip of fabric"] 3. to sew on, tack on a ~

bind over *v.* (legal) 1. (D; tr.) to ~ to (she was bound over to the grand jury) 2. (BE) (H) she was bound over to keep the peace

binge I *n.* (colloq.) ["a drunken spree"] 1. to go on a (weekend) ~ ["unrestrained activity"] 2. a shopping ~

binge II *v.* (d; intr.) to ~ on (to ~ on sweets)

binoculars *n.* 1. to adjust, focus; train ~ on 2. high-powered, powerful ~ 3. a pair of ~ 4. (misc.) to watch smt. through ~

biography *n.* an authorized; critical; unauthorized ~

biology *n.* marine; molecular ~

bird *n.* 1. game; land; migratory; tropical; wading; water; woodland ~s 2. ~s of passage; ~s of prey 3. (usu. fig.) a rare ~ 4. ~s chirp, twitter, warble; sing 5. ~s flap their wings; fly; migrate; soar 6. ~s build nests; flock together; molt 7. a covey; flock of ~s 8. (misc.) to ring ~s (for scientific purposes); a ~ in the hand ("smt. already possessed"); ~s of a feather ("people with similar characteristics, tastes, and standards"); as free as a ~ ("absolutely free"); to kill two ~s with one stone ("to accomplish two goals with one action")

bird call *n.* to do, imitate a ~

birdwatching *n.* to go in for, take up ~ (as a hobby)

birth *n.* ["bringing, coming into life"] 1. to give ~ (she gave ~ to twins) 2. to announce; register a ~ 3. a breech; caesarean; live, viable; multiple; normal; premature ~; stillbirth 4. at ~ (she weighed seven pounds at ~) ["origin"] 5. by ~ (he's Spanish by ~) 6. of ~ (of noble ~)

birth control *n.* to practice ~

birthday *n.* 1. to attain (formal), have, reach a ~ 2. to celebrate, mark a ~ 3. at, on a ~ (on her tenth ~) 4. happy ~! (to wish smb. a happy ~)

birth pangs *n.* to endure, suffer ~

birthrate *n.* 1. a falling; high; low; rising; stable ~ 2. the crude ~

birthright *n.* a natural ~

biscuit *n.* 1. to bake ~s 2. a sweet ~ (BE; AE has *cookie*) 3. a cream ~ (BE; AE has *sandwich cookie*) 4. baking-powder; soda; tea ~s 5. (misc.) to take the ~ ("to be the best or worst") (BE; CE has *to take the cake*)

bishop *n.* 1. to ordain a ~ 2. an Anglican, Episcopal; Catholic; Orthodox ~

bison *n.* a herd of ~

bit I *n.* ["share"] 1. to do one's ~ ["small piece, small amount"] 2. a tiny ~ 3. (misc.) every ~ ("all, entirely"); ~ by ~ ("little by little"); he's a ~ of a snob ("he is something of a snob"); she's not the least ~ upset ("she's not at all upset"); wait a ~ ("wait a little"); to blow to ~s ("to destroy completely") ["misc."] 4. (AE) two ~s ("twenty-five cents")

bit II *n.* ["mouthpiece on a horse's bridle"] 1. to chafe, champ at the ~ (also fig.) 2. to take the ~ (between one's teeth) (also fig.)

bitch *v.* (slang; vulgar) (D; intr.) to ~ about (they're always ~ing about the food)

bitchy *adj.* (slang; vulgar) ["nasty"] ~ about

bite I *n.* ["act of biting"] ["result of biting"] 1. to have, take a ~ (she took a ~ out of the apple) 2. an animal; dog; insect; mosquito; snake ~ ["ability to bite"] 3. a powerful ~ (the large dog has a powerful ~) ["snack"] 4. to grab, have a ~ (to eat) 5. a quick ~ ["request for a loan"] (colloq.) 6. to put the ~ on smb. ["amount of money deducted"] (colloq.) 7. to take a ~ from, out of (the wage tax takes quite a ~ from his paycheck)

bite II *v.* 1. (D; intr.) to ~ at (also fig.) (to ~ at the bait) 2. (D; intr.) to ~ into, on (she bit into the apple)

bitter I *adj.* ~ about, over (he was ~ about his lot)

bitter II *n.* to take the ~ (with the sweet)

bitterness *n.* 1. to feel ~ 2. a touch of ~ 3. ~ about, over; towards

bivouac *n.* 1. to go on; set up a ~ 2. to be on ~

bizarre *adj.* ~ that + clause (it was ~ that we ran/should have run into each other in such a remote corner of the world)

blab *v.* 1. (B) she ~bed smt. to him 2. (D; intr.) to ~ about

blabber *v.* (D; intr.) to ~ about

black *n.* ["profit"] 1. in the ~ (to operate in the ~) ["sign of mourning"] 2. to wear ~ ["dark color"] 3. coal, jet ~ ["misc."] 4. to put smt. down in ~ and white ("to write smt. down")

blackboard *n.* to clean, wash; erase (esp. AE) a ~ 2. to write on the ~ 3. at the ~ (two pupils were at the ~) 4. (misc.) to send a pupil to the ~

blacklist *n.* on a ~

black magic *n.* to practice ~

blackmail I *n.* 1. to commit ~ 2. emotional ~ (to use emotional ~)

blackmail II *v.* (D; tr.) to ~ into (to ~ smb. into doing smt.)

black market *n.* on the ~ (to buy smt. on the ~)

black-marketing, black-marketeering *n.* to engage in, to go in for ~

blackout *n.* ["extinguishing or concealment of all lights, as during wartime"] 1. to impose, order a ~ 2. to observe a ~ ["suppression of news"] 3. to impose, order a ~ 4. to lift a ~ 5. to violate a ~ 6. a media; news ~ ["period of unconsciousness"] 7. to have a ~

bladder *n.* 1. to empty one's ~ 2. a full ~

blade *n.* 1. to sharpen a ~ 2. a blunt, dull; sharp ~ 3. a rotary ~ 4. a razor ~

blame I *n.* 1. to ascribe, assign, attribute (the) ~ to smb. 2. to lay, pin, place, put the ~ on smb.; to lay the ~ at smb.'s door 3. to assess; fix the ~ 4. to shift the ~ to smb. (else) 5. to assume, bear, take; get the ~ for (she took the ~ for my mistake) 6. to absolve smb. of ~ for 7. the ~ falls on smb.

blame II *v.* 1. to ~ unfairly, unjustly 2. (D; tr.) to ~ for (they ~d her for the accident) 3. (d; tr.) to ~ on (they ~d the accident on her; they ~d the fire on defective wiring) 4. to be to ~ for (I am not to ~ for the mistake)

blanch *v.* 1. (D; intr.) to ~ at (he ~ed at the sight of the mutilated corpse) 2. (D; intr.) to ~ with (to ~ with fear)

blank I *adj.* to go ~ (my mind went ~)

blank II *n.* ["empty space"] 1. to fill in the ~s (as on a questionnaire) 2. (misc.) my mind was a complete ~ ["blank cartridge"] 3. to fire a ~ ["misc."] 4. to draw a ~ ("to achieve no result")

blanket *n.* 1. a bath; electric; receiving; saddle; sheet ~ 2. a security ~ (also fig.)

blasé *adj.* ~ about (they were very ~ about winning first prize)

blaspheme *v.* (D; intr.) to ~ against (to ~ against God)

blasphemous *adj.* ~ to + inf. (it was ~ of them to speak in that manner)

blasphemy *n.* to commit; utter (a) ~ against

blast I *n.* ["explosion"] 1. to set off a ~ ["gust of wind"] 2. an icy ~ ["verbal attack"] 3. to issue a ~ against 4. a vicious, withering ~ ["misc."] 5. (at) full ~ (the work was proceeding at full ~)

blast II *v.* (D; tr.) to ~ through (a tunnel was ~ed through the rock)

blather I *n.* ["nonsense"] 1. sheer, utter ~ 2. ~ about

blather II *v.* (D; intr.) to ~ (on) about

blaze I *n.* 1. to control; fight a ~ 2. to extinguish, put out a ~

blaze II *v.* (D; intr.) to ~ with (her eyes ~d with anger)

blaze away *v.* (D; intr.) to ~ at (to ~ at the enemy)

blazes *n.* go to ~! ("damn you!")

bleach *n.* liquid ~

bleachers *n.* (AE) to sit in the ~

bleed *v.* 1. to ~ profusely, uncontrollably 2. (fig.) (D; intr.) to ~ for (my heart ~s for him) 3. (D; intr.) to ~ from (to ~ from the nose) 4. (N; used with an adjective) to ~ smb. white 5. (misc.) to ~ to death

bleeding *n.* 1. to staunch, stem, stop (the) ~ 2.

heavy, profuse, uncontrollable ~ 3. internal; menopausal ~ 4. ~ from (~ from the rectum)

blemish *n.* a minor; ugly ~

blench *v.* (D; intr.) ("to flinch") to ~ at (he ~ed at the sight)

blend *v.* 1. to ~ together (their voices ~ together well) 2. (d; intr., tr.) to ~ into (to ~ into the crowd) 3. (D; intr., tr.) to ~ with (water does not ~ with oil)

blend in *v.* (D; intr.) to ~ with (she ~ed in with the crowd)

bless *v.* 1. (D; tr.) to ~ for (she ~ed me for my help) 2. (D; tr.) to ~ with (we are ~ed with good health)

blessing *n.* 1. to give, make, pronounce, say a ~ over 2. to chant a ~ 3. to give one's ~ to; to bestow one's ~ on 4. to ask for God's ~ 5. a divine; priestly ~; God's ~ 6. a ~ for, to (it was a ~ for us) 7. a ~ that + clause (it was a ~ that we didn't have to make the trip) 8. (misc.) a mixed ~; a ~ in disguise; to count one's ~s; to ask a ~ (before a meal)

blight *n.* 1. to cast, put a ~ on, upon 2. a potato ~ 3. urban ~ 4. a ~ on (a ~ on one's honor)

blind I *adj.* ["sightless"] 1. legally; totally ~ 2. (misc.) as ~ as a bat; ~ in one eye ["blinded"] (cannot stand alone) 3. ~ to (~ to danger) 4. ~ with (~ with rage)

blind II *v.* (D; tr.) to ~ to (his infatuation ~ed him to her faults)

blind III (BE) see **window shade**

blindness *n.* color; congenital; night; snow ~

blinds *n.* 1. to adjust; draw; lower; raise the ~ 2. venetian ~

blind spot *n.* to have a ~

blink I *n.* (colloq.) to be on the ~ ("to be out of order")

blink II *v.* (D; intr.) to ~ at ("to show surprise") (she didn't even ~ at his outrageous proposal)

bliss *n.* 1. to enjoy ~ 2. complete, pure, sheer, total, utter ~ 3. connubial, domestic, marital, nuptial, wedded ~ 4. ~ to + inf. (it was ~ to be without a telephone = it was ~ being without a telephone) 5. a state of ~

blister *n.* 1. to open a ~ 2. a fever ~ (AE; CE has *cold sore*) 3. a ~ bursts; forms

blizzard *n.* 1. a raging; winter ~ 2. a ~ rages; strikes 3. a ~ blows itself out

bloc *n.* 1. (obsolescent) the Communist; eastern; NATO; Soviet ~ 2. a military; trade, trading; voting ~

block *n.* ["interruption"] ["obstacle"] 1. (Am. football) to throw a ~ at smb. 2. a mental ~ (when it comes to word games, I have a mental ~) 3. (med.) a heart; nerve; saddle ~ 4. a stumbling; writer's ~ ["street"] ["city square"] (AE) 5. a city ~ (the building occupies an entire city ~) 6. around the ~; in, on a ~ (they went around the ~; they live in this ~) ["big building"] (BE) 7. a council ~ 8. an office;

tower ~ ("a high-rise apartment house") 9. (misc.) a ~ of flats ["platform, work surface"] 10. a butcher's; chopping; headsman's ~ ["auctioneer's platform"] 11. the auction ~ 12. on the ~ ("being auctioned") ["group"] ["bloc"] 13. a trade ~ ["rectangular unit used in construction"] 14. a building; cinder; concrete ~ ["support"] ["brace"] 15. a starting ~ (for a runner) ["section of text"] (computers) 16. to copy; delete; end; move a ~ ["misc."] 17. a chip off the old ~ ("a child who resembles a parent"); to knock smb.'s ~ off ("to punch smb.")

blockade *n.* 1. to impose; maintain a ~ 2. to break (through); lift; run a ~ 3. an economic; naval ~ 4. a ~ against; on

blocks *n.* (esp. AE) to play with ~ (BE has *bricks*)

blonde *n.* a natural; platinum ~

blood *n.* 1. to draw, let ~ 2. to cough (up), spit (up); lose; shed, spill ~ 3. to staunch the flow of ~ 4. to donate, give; type ~ 5. blue; pure; royal ~ 6. whole ~ 7. hot ("fiery") ~ 8. ~ cakes; circulates; clots, coagulates, congeals, curdles; flows, runs; oozes, seeps; spurts (~ spurted from the wound) 9. (fig.) smb.'s ~ boils; freezes; runs cold 10. (fig.) ~ tells 11. by ~ (related by ~) 12. of ~ (of royal ~) 13. (misc.) to be, run in the ~ ("to be hereditary "); in cold ~ ("without feeling"); to draw first ~ ("to score the first victory"); fresh, new, (esp. BE) young ~ ("new personnel"); old ~ ("old personnel"); (colloq.) tired ~ ("rundown condition of the body"); there is bad ~ between them ("they are feuding"); ~ is thicker than water ("one's family is more important than anyone else"); to make smb.'s ~ run cold ("to terrify smb."); to make smb.'s ~ boil ("to arouse smb.'s anger")

blood cell *n.* a red; white ~

blood count *n.* 1. to do a ~ (on) 2. to have a ~ (done)

blood pressure *n.* 1. to monitor; take smb.'s ~ 2. elevated, high; labile; low; normal ~

blood test *n.* 1. to do a ~ (on) 2. to have a ~ (done)

bloodshed *n.* 1. to cause ~ 2. to avert, prevent ~

blood transfusion *n.* 1. to administer, do, give a ~ 2. to get, have a ~

blood vessel *n.* 1. a constricted; occluded ~ 2. a ~ bursts

bloom *n.* 1. to come into ~ 2. full ~ 3. in ~ (the tulips are in full ~)

bloomer (BE) see **blooper**

blooper *n.* (colloq.) (AE) ["blunder"] 1. to commit, make a ~ 2. a prize ~

blossom I *n.* in ~ (the trees are in ~)

blossom II *v.* (D; intr.) to ~ into (their friendship ~ed into true love)

blot *n.* 1. to leave a ~ 2. an ink ~ 3. a ~ on (his actions left a ~ on our name)

blotter *n.* ["blotting paper"] 1. a ~ absorbs (ink, water) ["record"] 2. a police ~

blouse *n.* a full; peasant; see-through ~

blow I *n.* 1. to deal, deliver, strike a ~ (he dealt us a severe ~) 2. to heap, rain ~s on smb. 3. to come to ~s; to exchange ~s 4. to take a ~ (the boxer took several ~s to the head) 5. to cushion, soften; deflect, parry, ward off; dodge a ~ 6. a crippling, crushing, decisive, hard, heavy, knockout, powerful, resounding, severe, staggering, telling, terrible ~ 7. a bitter, cruel, devastating ~ 8. a fatal, mortal ~ 9. a glancing, light ~ 10. a body ~ 11. indiscriminate ~s (to rain indiscriminate ~s on one's victims) 12. a low ("illegal") ~ (also fig.) 13. an exchange of ~s 14. a ~ against, at (to strike a ~ against poverty) 15. a ~ for (to strike a ~ for freedom) 16. a ~ on, to (a ~ on the head; he took a ~ to the chin; a ~ to one's hopes) 17. a ~ to + inf. (it was a bitter ~ to learn of their treachery) 18. under ~s (to reel under crushing ~s)

blow II *v.* 1. to ~ hard (the wind was ~ing hard) 2. (A; usu. without *to*) she blew him a kiss 3. (d; tr.) to ~ into (the explosion blew him into the water) 4. (D; tr.) to ~ off (the wind blew the papers off the table) 5. (D; intr.) to ~ on (~ on the soup: it's too hot) 6. (N; used with an adjective) the wind blew the door shut 7. (misc.) the tank was blown to bits; the ship was blown off course; (slang) he blew ("came") into town

blowout *n.* ["flat tire"] 1. to have a ~ 2. to fix a ~

blow up *v.* ("to enlarge") (D; tr.) to ~ by (to ~ a photograph by twenty percent)

bludgeon *v.* 1. (d; tr.) ("to force by beating") to ~ into (to ~ smb. into doing smt.) (also fig.) 2. (misc.) to ~ smb. to death

blue *n.* ["color"] 1. dark; light; navy; royal ~ ["something colored blue"] 2. a patch of ~ ["symbol of belonging to a team at Oxford or Cambridge"] (BE) 3. to get, win one's ~ ["misc."] 4. out of the ~ ("unexpectedly"); a bolt from/out of the ~ ("smt. unexpected")

blueprint *n.* 1. to draw up, make a ~ 2. a ~ for; of (fig.: a ~ for peace)

blues *n.* 1. to sing the ~ (usu. fig.: "to complain") 2. to have the ~ ("to be sad")

bluff I *n.* ["false threat"] 1. to call smb.'s ~ ("to challenge smb. to carry out a false threat") 2. to fall for smb.'s ~ ("to be deceived by a false threat")

bluff II *v.* 1. (D; tr.) to ~ into; out of (they ~ed him into making concessions) 2. to be caught ~ing

blunder I *n.* 1. to commit, make a ~ 2. an awful, colossal, costly, egregious, fatal, glaring, grave, monumental, serious, stupid, terrible ~ 3. a tactical ~ 4. a ~ to + inf. (it was a ~ to invite them)

blunder II *v.* 1. (d; intr.) to ~ on, upon ("to happen on") 2. (P; intr.) ("to wander") they ~ed into the wrong room; she ~ed across the road

blurt out *v.* 1. (B) he ~ed out the rumor to his friends 2. (L; to) she ~ed out that she was engaged 3. (Q; to) she ~ed out where she had been

blush I *n.* 1. a deep ~ 2. (misc.) at first ~ ("at first sight"); in the first ~ of youth ("as a youth")

blush II *v.* 1. to ~ deeply; readily 2. (D; intr.) to ~ at (to ~ at the very suggestion) 3. (D; intr.) to ~ for, with (he ~ed with shame) 4. (E) I ~ to think of what I said

boar *n.* a wild ~

board *n.* ["ship's deck"] ["train"] ["airplane"] 1. to be on ~; to go on ~ ["commission"] 2. an advisory; draft (AE); editorial; executive; liquor-control (AE); parole; school; zoning ~ 3. on a ~ (to serve on a ~) 4. (misc.) a ~ of directors; a ~ of education; a ~ of governers; a ~ of trustees ["footboard"] 5. a running ~ (on a car) ["flat piece of wood or other material"] 6. a baseboard (AE), skirting (BE) ~ 7. a bulletin (AE), notice (BE) ~ 8. a checkerboard (AE), draughtboard (BE); chessboard; dart ~ 9. a cutting; diving; drawing; ironing ~ 10. an emery ~ ["misc."] 11. an electronic bulletin ~; a sounding ~; across the ~ ("for everyone")

boarder *n.* to have, keep (AE), take in ~s

boards *n.* (esp. AE) ["qualifying examination"] 1. to pass; take one's ~ 2. college; state ~

boast I *n.* 1. to make a ~ 2. an empty, idle, vain; proud ~ 3. ~ that + clause (it was their ~ that they had seen all of the new plays)

boast II *v.* 1. to ~ idly; proudly 2. (D; intr.) to ~ about, of; to (to ~ of one's success) 3. (L; to) she ~ed (to the reporters) that she would win the race

boastful *adj.* ~ about, of

boat *n.* 1. to pilot; row; sail; steer a ~ 2. to launch, lower a ~ 3. to board, get into, get on, get onto; take a ~ 4. to disembark from, get off a ~ 5. to overturn, swamp, upset a ~ 6. an assault ~; gunboat; lifeboat; mosquito, PT (AE; BE has *MTB*); patrol; torpedo ~ 7. a fishing ~; rowboat (AE), rowing (BE) ~; sailboat (AE), sailing (BE) ~; steamboat 8. a flying ~ 9. a ~ goes, sails; heaves; leaks; pitches; rolls; sinks 10. by ~ (to cross a river by ~) 11. in; on a ~ 12. (misc.) to be in the same ~ ("to be in the same circumstances"); to miss the ~ ("to let an opportunity slip by"); to push the ~ out (BE; colloq.) ("to make a special effort, esp. to celebrate"); to rock the ~ ("to cause a disruption")

bobsled, bobsleigh *n.* to ride a ~; to race on ~s

bode *v.* these events ~ well for us

body *n.* ["substance"] ["firmness"] 1. to give ~ to ["group"] ["unit"] 2. an advisory; deliberative; elected; governing; legislative; student ~; the ~ politic 3. in a ~ (they presented their petition in a ~) ["physical object"] 4. a foreign ~ (to remove a foreign ~ from one's eye) 5. a gaseous; liquid; solid ~ 6. a celestial, heavenly ~ ["corpse"] 7. to bury; cremate; embalm; exhume a ~ 8. a bloated; dead; decomposing ~ ["physical structure of a person"] 9. to build up, condition, strengthen one's ~ 10. to sell one's ~ (as a prostitute) 11. a healthy; unhealthy ~ 12. (colloq.) the ~ beautiful ["misc."] 13. to keep ~ and soul together ("to have just enough to live on")

bodyguard *n.* a personal ~

bog *n.* a peat ~

bogged down *adj.* to be; get ~ in (they got ~ in the swamp)

boggle *v.* (d; intr.) to ~ at (the mind ~s at the idea)

boil I *n.* ["state of boiling"] 1. to bring to a (AE)/to the (BE) ~ (bring the milk to a ~) 2. to come to a (AE)/to the (BE) ~ (the water must first come to the ~)

boil II *v.* 1. to ~ gently; hard 2. (C) he ~ed an egg for her; or: he ~ed her an egg 3. (D; intr.) to ~ with (to be ~ing with rage)

boil III *n.* ["furuncle"] 1. to lance a ~ 2. a ~ comes to a head 3. to apply hot compresses to a ~

boil down *v.* 1. (d; intr.) to ~ to (it all ~s down to one simple fact) 2. (D; tr.) to ~ to (she ~ed the whole story down to one paragraph)

boiler *n.* a ~ bursts, ruptures; cracks

boiling-point *n.* to reach (the) ~

boil over *v.* (D; intr.) to ~ into (the situation ~ed over into a real crisis)

bold *adj.* (often used humorously) to be so ~ as to + inf. (may I be so ~ as to ask how old you are?)

boldface *n.* to print, set in ~

bolshy *adj.* (colloq.) (BE) ["rebellious"] ~ about

bolt I *n.* 1. a lightning ~ 2. (misc.) like a ~ from/out of the blue ("unexpectedly"); to shoot one's ~ ("to make a final effort"); to make a ~ for the door ("to run towards the door")

bolt II *v.* 1. ("to attach") (D; tr.) to ~ to (they ~ed the computer to the floor 2. ("to run") (P; intr.) she ~ed down the corridor 3. (misc.) to ~ down one's food ("to eat too fast")

bomb *n.* 1. to detonate, explode, set off; fuse a ~ 2. to drop a ~ 3. to plant a ~ 4. to deactivate, defuse a ~ 5. to dispose of an unexploded ~ 6. an atom, atomic, fission, nuclear; cobalt; fusion, hydrogen; neutron ~ 7. a clean; dirty ~ 8. a buzz; cluster; fragmentation; high-explosive; incendiary; nail; napalm; petrol (esp. BE); pipe; plastic; smoke ~ 9. a car; letter ~ 10. a time ~ 11. a smart ("guided") ~ 12. a ticking ~ (usu. fig.) 13. (AE) a cherry ~ ("a type of firecracker") 14. a ~ explodes, goes off; drops, falls 15. (misc.) (colloq.) (BE) to go like a ~ ("to be very successful")

bombard *v.* (D; tr.) to ~ with (we ~ed them with letters of protest)

bombardment *n.* 1. to conduct a ~ 2. air; constant; intensive ~ 3. under ~ (under constant ~)

bomber *n.* 1. a dive-bomber; fighter; heavy; light; long-range; medium ~ 2. an enemy ~ 3. a suicide ~

bombing *n.* 1. area; around-the-clock; carpet; dive;

indiscriminate, random; pin-point, precision; saturation; shuttle; strategic; tactical ~ 2. a terrorist ~ (a wave of terrorist ~s)

bombshell *n.* ["sensation"] to drop a ~

bomb threat *n.* 1. to receive; send a ~ 2. an anonymous ~

bond I *n.* ["certificate"] 1. to issue a ~ 2. to cash (in), redeem a ~ 3. a debenture; development; government; junk; long-term; municipal; negotiable; savings; serial; treasury; war ~ (to invest money in treasury ~s) ["tie"] ["link"] 4. to forge, form; strengthen a ~ (of friendship) with 5. a close, firm, strong; solemn; spiritual ~ (strong family ~s) 6. a ~ between ["fetters"] 7. to break; cast off one's ~s ["guarantee"] ["obligation"] 8. to set ~ (the judge set ~ for him at two thousand dollars) 9. to furnish, post a ~ 10. to forfeit a ~ ["storage under supervision, as of imported goods"] 11. in ~; out of ~ (to place goods in ~; to take goods out of ~)

bond II *v.* (D; tr.) ("to cause to adhere") to ~ to ("to ~ wood to glass")

bondage *n.* 1. to sell into ~ 2. to hold in ~ 3. to deliver from ~ 4. in ~ to

bond issue *n.* to float a ~

bone *n.* ["part of a skeleton"] 1. to set a (broken) ~ 2. to break, fracture a ~ 3. brittle ~s 4. a (broken) ~ knits 5. to the ~ (chilled/frozen to the ~) ["complaint"] (colloq.) 6. to have a ~ to pick with smb. ["misc."] 7. to make no ~s about smt. ("to be frank about smt."); to feel smt. in one's ~s ("to have a premonition about smt.")

boner *n.* (slang) (AE) ["blunder"] to commit, pull a ~

bone up *v.* (colloq.) (AE) (D; intr.) to ~ on (she had to ~ on her French)

bonfire *n.* 1. to build, light, make a ~ 2. to sit (a)round a ~ 3. a blazing, roaring ~

bonnet (BE) see **hood**

bonus *n.* 1. to give, pay a ~ 2. to get, receive a ~ 3. an annual; Christmas; cost-of-living; special ~ 4. (misc.) as an added ~ you get a free gift

boo *v.* (D; tr.) to ~ off (the actor was ~ed off the stage)

booby trap *n.* 1. to set a ~ 2. to set off, trigger a ~ 3. to deactivate a ~ 4. a ~ explodes, goes off

book I *n.* 1. to author, write; co-author; revise a ~ 2. to edit; proofread a ~ 3. to dedicate, inscribe a ~ 4. to bring out, publish, put out; copyright; reprint; translate a ~ 5. to review a ~ 6. to pirate; plagiarize a ~ 7. to ban; censor a ~ 8. to bind a ~ 9. to set a ~ in type 10. to charge, check a ~ out of a library 11. to renew a ~ (borrowed from a library) 12. to shelve; stack ~s (in a library) 13. a children's; comic ~; cookbook (AE), cookery (BE) ~; phrase; prayer ~ 14. a guide ~; handbook; illustrated; picture; reference ~; schoolbook; telephone ~; text-

book 15. a bank; check (AE), cheque (BE); pass ~
16. a library ~ 17. a rare ~ (our library has a rare ~
collection) 18. (colloq.) the Good Book ("the
Bible") 19. a ~ appears, comes out, is published
20. a ~ goes out of print; a ~ is sold out; a ~ goes
through several printings 21. a ~ about, on (a ~
about computers) 22. (misc.) to make ~ ("to make
or accept bets"); a closed ~ ("an obscure matter,
person"); ("a completed event, condition"); an
open ~ ("an accessible subject, person"); (slang)
to throw the ~ at smb. ("to punish an accused
person severely"); to go by the ~ ("to adhere
strictly to regulations"); in my ~ ("in my opinion")
book II v. (esp. BE) 1. (C) she ~ed a seat for me; or:
she ~ed me a seat 2. (D; intr., tr.) to ~ through to
(can we ~ a ticket through to Berlin?) 3. (misc.)
(CE) ~ed solid, fully ~ed
bookcase n. built-in ~s
bookends n. a pair of ~
booking n. (esp. BE) 1. to make a ~ 2. to cancel a ~
bookkeeping n. 1. to do the ~ 2. double-entry;
single-entry ~
booklet n. a ~ about, on
books n. ["financial records"] 1. to keep (the) ~ 2. to
audit, go over, inspect; balance the ~
book up v. to ~ fully, solid (the hotel is ~ed up solid
= the hotel is fully ~ed up)
boom n. 1. a sonic ~ 2. a baby; business, economic;
postwar; wartime ~ 3. a ~ in (a ~ in property
values) 4. (misc.) to lower the ~ on ("to attack")
boomerang I n. 1. to throw a ~ 2. a ~ always returns
boomerang II v. (D; intr.) to ~ on (the project ~ed
on them)
boon n. a ~ to (a ~ to science)
boor n. an insufferable ~
boost n. 1. to give (smb.) a ~ 2. a big; much-needed
~ 3. a ~ in (a ~ in prices) 4. a ~ to (a ~ to their
morale)
boot I n. see the Usage Note for **trunk**
boot II n. ["dismissal"] (colloq.) 1. to get the ~ (for)
(he got the ~ for sloppy work) 2. to give smb. the ~
(for) (they gave him the ~ for being late)
boot III v. (P; tr.) she ~ed the ball over the fence
booth n. an information; listening; phone, telephone; polling, voting; projection ~
boots n. 1. to lace up; put on; take off; unlace
(one's) ~ 2. bovver (BE; slang; worn by young
rowdies); hip; leather; riding; rubber; walking ~ 3.
a pair of ~ 4. (misc.) to lick smb.'s ~ ("to be overly
subservient to smb."); to die with one's ~ on ("to
die while still active")
bootstraps n. to pull oneself up by one's (own) ~
("to emerge from poverty through one's own efforts")
booty n. 1. to capture, seize, take ~ 2. war ~
border I n. 1. to draw, establish, fix a ~ 2. to cross;
slip across a ~ 3. to guard, patrol a ~ 4. a closed;

common; disputed; fixed; open; recognized; un-
guarded ~ 5. a ~ between; with 6. across, over a ~
(to smuggle goods across a ~) 7. along; at, on a ~
8. as far as, up to the ~ (she drove me as far as the
~) 9. (misc.) north of the ~; south of the ~
border II v. (d; intr.) 1. to ~ on, upon (to ~ on the
absurd) 2. (d; tr.) to ~ with (to ~ a dress with lace)
borderline n. 1. a ~ between 2. on the ~
bore I n. 1. a crashing, frightful, insufferable, utter
~ 2. a ~ to + inf. (it's a ~ to work on this project
every day = it's a ~ working on this project every
day)
bore II n. (esp. BE) ["wave"] a tidal ~
bore III v. 1. (D; intr., tr.) ("to dig") to ~ into (her
eyes ~d into me; they ~d an opening into the mine
shaft) 2. (D; intr., tr.) ("to dig") to ~ through (to ~
a hole through a board) 3. (D; tr.) ("to weary") to ~
to (he ~d us to death/to tears)
bored adj. 1. ~ to (~ to death/to tears) 2. ~ with; BE
also has, esp. in children's language: ~ of (~ with
life) 3. (misc.) he was ~ doing nothing; she was ~
stiff
boredom n. 1. to relieve (the) ~ 2. complete, sheer,
utter; deadly; outright; plain ~ 3. out of ~ (he
started drinking again out of ~)
boring adj. ~ to + inf. (it was ~ to sit there without
anything to do)
born adj. 1. ~ into (~ into wealth) 2. ~ of (~ of poor
parents) 3. ~ to (~ to wealth; ~ to illiterate parents)
4. ~ to + inf. (he was ~ to rule) 5. (misc.) ~ free; ~
lucky; as (if) to the manner ~ ("as if accustomed to
smt."); Mark Twain was ~ Samuel Clemens
borrow v. 1. to ~ heavily (English has ~ed heavily
from many languages) 2. (D; intr., tr.) to ~ from
(she ~ed a book from me; they are always ~ing
from us) 3. (D; tr.) to ~ from; into (the word was
~ed from English into German)
borrowing n. a ~ from (a ~ from French)
bosom n. 1. an ample ~ 2. (formal) in the ~ (in the ~
of one's family) 3. (misc.) to take smb. into/to
one's ~
boss n. 1. an absolute, undisputed ~ 2. a straw ~
("one who has little authority; an assistant fore-
man or forewoman") 3. a party, political ~
both determiner, pronoun ~ of (we saw ~ of them)
USAGE NOTE: The use of the preposition of is
necessary when a pronoun follows. When a noun
follows, two constructions are possible—we saw
both of the students; we saw both (the) students.
bother I n. 1. a ~ to (he was a ~ to everyone) 2. a ~
to + inf. (it was no ~ to take care of them) 3. (BE) a
spot of ~ 4. (esp. BE) he had a lot of ~ finding our
house
bother II v. 1. (D; intr., tr.) to ~ about, with (she
didn't ~ me about/with the details) 2. (E; usu. in
neg. sentences) he didn't ~ to shave; don't ~ to get
up 3. (G; usu. in neg. sentences) he didn't ~ get-

ting up 4. (R) it ~ed me (to learn) that she had not been promoted

bottle *n.* ["container for liquids"] 1. to break; cork; empty; fill; open, uncork; rinse a ~ 2. a baby (AE); feeding (BE), nursing (AE) ~ 3. a hot-water ~ 4. a Thermos (T) ~ (AE; BE has *Thermos flask*) 5. a disposable, no-deposit, no-return; plastic; returnable, reusable ~ ["alcohol"] 6. to take to the ~ ("to begin to drink to excess") 7. to hit the ~ ("to drink to excess") 8. over a ~ ("while drinking") ["courage"] 9. to have a lot of ~ 10. the ~ to + inf. (she hasn't got the ~ to do it)

bottleneck *n.* 1. to form, produce a ~ 2. to be caught, trapped in a ~; to hit a ~ 3. to eliminate a ~ 4. a ~ in

bottom *n.* 1. (usu. fig.) to scrape the ~ of the barrel ("to use one's last resources") 2. (fig.) to hit ("reach") ~ 3. to sink to the ~; to touch ~ 4. a double, false ~ 5. a ~ to (there's a false ~ to the suitcase) 6. at, on the ~ (at the ~ of the well; we never could find out what was at the ~ of the affair) 7. (misc.) to get to the ~ of an affair ("to clear up a matter"); ~s up! ("drink up!"); from the ~ of my heart ("very sincerely"); the ~ has dropped out of the market ("prices have fallen dramatically on the stock market"); to hit rock ~ ("to sink into complete failure")

bottom out *v.* (D; intr.) to ~ at (their stock ~ed out at fifty dollars a share

bough *n.* 1. a slender ~ 2. ~s sway in the breeze

boulevard *n.* 1. a wide ~ 2. along; on a ~

bounce I *n.* 1. a ~ to (there's a ~ to his walk) 2. on the ~ (to catch a ball on the ~; to hit a ball on the first ~)

bounce II *v.* 1. to ~ high 2. (d; intr.) to ~ out of (she ~d out of the chair) 3. (d; intr.) to ~ to (he ~d to his feet) 4. (P; intr., tr.) (the ball ~ed across the street; she ~ed the baby on her knee) 5. (misc.) to ~ up and down (she ~d the ball up and down)

bounce back *v.* (D; intr.) to ~ from (our team ~d back from its defeat)

bound I *adj.* ["headed"] (cannot stand alone) 1. ~ for (~ for London) 2. homeward; outward ~

bound II *adj.* ["covered"] ~ in (the book was ~ in leather)

bound III *adj.* ["sure"] (cannot stand alone) ~ to + inf. (she is ~ to find out)

bound IV *adj.* ["required"] 1. duty ~ 2. legally; morally ~ 3. ~ to + inf. (she is legally ~ to report the incident to the police)

bound V *n.* ["jump, leap"] in, with a ~ (with one ~ he was out of the room)

bound VI *v.* ("to border") (formal) (D; tr.) to ~ on, to (Germany ~s France on the east)

bound VII *v.* ("to jump; to run") (P; intr.) she ~ed out of the room; he ~ed across the field

boundary *n.* 1. to draw, fix, set; extend; mark;

redraw a ~ 2. to form a ~ 3. a common; national ~ 4. a ~ between 5. (misc.) to overstep the ~aries of good taste; the ~ runs along the river

bounds *n.* 1. to set the ~ 2. out of ~ (to) 3. beyond, outside the ~ (beyond the ~ of good taste) 4. within ~ 5. (misc.) to know no ~ (her generosity knew no ~)

bound up *adj.* (cannot stand alone) ["connected"] ~ in; with (~ in one's work; her future is ~ with this firm)

bounty *n.* 1. to offer; pay a ~ 2. to put a ~ on (smb.'s head) 3. a cash ~ 4. a ~ for

bouquet *n.* a wedding ~

bout *n.* ["a period of time"] to have a ~ of (depression, drinking, the flu)

bow I /bau/ *n.* ["bending of the head or body"] 1. to give, make; take a ~ (the envoy made a ~ on entering the throne room; the actor took his ~) 2. a courtly; low ~ 3. a ~ to ["debut"] 4. to make one's ~ (he made his ~ as Hamlet)

bow II *v.* 1. ("to bend the head or body") to ~ politely 2. (D; intr.) ("to bend the head or body") to ~ before; to (to ~ before an emperor; to ~ politely to one's host; to ~ to the inevitable) 3. (d; intr.) to ~ out of ("to abandon") (to ~ out of politics) 4. (misc.) to ~ and scrape ("to be obsequious")

bow III /bou/ *n.* ["device for shooting arrows"] 1. to draw a ~ (in order to shoot an arrow); to release a ~ ["decorative ribbon"] 2. to wear a ~ (in one's hair) ["knot"] 3. to tie a ~; to tie in a ~

bow down /bau/ *v.* (D; intr.) to ~ before, to

bowels *n.* 1. to move one's ~ 2. loose ~

bowl *n.* ["dish, vessel"] 1. a cereal; fruit; mixing; punch; salad; soup; sugar (AE); washing-up (BE) ~ ["championship football game"] (AE) 2. the Cotton; Rose; Sugar ~ ["region"] (esp. AE) 3. a dust; rice ~

bowling *n.* 1. to go in for ~ 2. to go ~

bowling alley *n.* at a ~ (she works at a ~)

bow out *v.* (D; intr.) ("to give up") to ~ as (he had to ~ as a contender) (see also **bow II** 3)

bow tie /bou/ *n.* 1. to tie a ~ 2. to undo, untie a ~

box I *n.* 1. a cigar; jewelry; lunch ~; shoebox; spice ~; toolbox; window ~ 2. a post-office ~ 3. a safe-deposit, safety-deposit ~ 4. a poor ~ (in a church) 5. a ballot ~ 6. a suggestion ~ 7. a letter (BE) ~, mailbox (AE), pillar (BE) ~ 8. a call (BE); phone (BE) ~ 9. a signal ~ (BE; AE has *signal tower*) 10. a fire-alarm ~ 11. a black ~ ("electronic recording device") 12. (ice hockey) a penalty ~ 13. a witness ~ (BE; AE has *witness stand*) 14. a music (AE), musical (BE) ~ 15. a prompt (BE), prompter's (AE) ~ 16. a shooting ~ (BE; CE has *hunting lodge*) 17. a jury; press ~ (for journalists) 18. (BE) a Christmas ~ ("a Christmas gift") 19. (slang) (BE) on the ~ ("on television")

box 40

box II v. 1. (D; intr.) to ~ against (to ~ against a worthy opponent) 2. (D; intr.) to ~ for (to ~ for the title)

boxer n. 1. a clean; dirty ~ 2. ~s box; break; clinch 3. (misc.) to knock out a ~

boxing n. to go in for ~

boy n. 1. an altar; barrow (BE; CE has *street vendor*); chorus; college (esp. AE); delivery; messenger; office; stock ~ 2. a best ~ ("assistant gaffer on a TV or film set") 3. a ball ~ (who retrieves tennis balls) 4. (AE; southern) a good old (ole) ~ ("a good fellow") 5. a little, small; mere ~ 6. a whipping ~ ("a scapegoat") 7. a blue-eyed (BE), fair-haired (AE) ~ ("a favorite") 8. (BE) a back-room ~ ("a scientist")
USAGE NOTE: The meaning "non-white servant", now obsolete, is considered offensive. The AE use of *boy* in the meaning of "black male", now obsolete, is also considered offensive. (See also the Usage Note for **girl**.)

boycott n. 1. to declare; impose a ~ 2. to lift a ~ 3. a consumer; economic, trade; secondary ~ 4. a ~ of, on (they imposed a ~ on all imports; they lifted their ~ of imports)

boyfriend n. a steady ~

brace I n. 1. to wear a ~ 2. a back; leg; shoulder ~

brace II v. 1. (D; intr., refl.) to ~ for (to ~ for an attack) 2. (E; refl.) she ~d herself to hear what the doctor would say

bracelet n. 1. to wear a ~ 2. a chain; charm; diamond; gold; silver ~

braces (BE) see **suspenders**

bracket n. ["support"] 1. to put up ~s (on a wall) ["mark used to enclose"] 2. to enclose (a word) in ~s; to put (a word) into ~s 3. to close ~s 4. angle, broken; round; square ~s ["group with similar characteristics"] 5. an age; income; tax ~

brag v. 1. (D; intr.) to ~ about, of; to 2. (L; to) they ~ged (to us) that they had outwitted their rivals

braid I n. ["threads"] 1. gold; silver ~ ["length of hair"] 2. in a ~ (they wore their hair in ~s)

braid II v. (D; tr.) (esp. AE) to ~ into (to ~ one's hair into pigtails)

brain n. 1. to have a (good) ~ 2. to overtax; tax; use one's ~ 3. to rack one's ~(s) over (she racked her ~ over the problem) 4. to pick smb.'s ~(s) 5. (colloq.) on the ~ (he has nothing but rock music on the ~)

brains n. 1. to blow one's ~ out ("to shoot oneself through the head") 2. the ~ to + inf. (does he have enough ~ to figure it out?)

brainstorm n. ["sudden bright idea"] (AE) to have a ~ (see the Usage Note for **wave I**)

brake I n. 1. to apply, step on a ~/the ~s; to pump the ~s; to put on the ~s; to jam on/slam on the ~s 2. to ride the ~s ("to use the brakes excessively") 3.

(fig.) to put a ~ on (the government put a ~ on plans for expansion) 4. to release, take off a ~/the ~s 5. an air; coaster; disk; electric; emergency; foot; hand; hydraulic; mechanical; power ~ 6. the ~s jammed, locked; faded; failed; held, worked; screeched

brake II v. to ~ gently; hard; suddenly

branch n. ["division"] 1. the executive; judicial; legislative ~ (of the government) 2. a local ~ ["limb of a tree"] 3. to trim ~es 4. overhanging ~es

branch off v. (D; intr.) to ~ from (the spur ~es off here from the main line)

branch out v. 1. (D; intr.) to ~ from; into; to (our firm has ~ed out into various industries) 2. (misc.) to ~ on one's own

brand I n. 1. to put a ~ on (an animal) 2. a name, popular ~

brand II v. 1. (d; tr.) to ~ as (he was ~ed as a traitor) 2. (N; used with a noun) to be ~ed a traitor

brash, brassy adj. ~ to + inf. (it was ~ of him to demand more)

brass n. (colloq.) ["officers"] 1. air-force; army; navy; Pentagon ~ 2. the top ~ ["daring; effrontery"] 3. the ~ to + inf. (she had the ~ to ask for a raise)

brass tacks n. to get down to ~ ("to get down to business")

brat n. (colloq.) 1. a spoiled ~ 2. an Army ~ ("child of an Army family")

bravado n. 1. sheer ~ 2. an act of ~

brave adj. ~ to + inf. (it was ~ of you to do that)

bravery n. to demonstrate, display, exhibit, show; inspire ~

brawl n. 1. a barroom, drunken; street ~ 2. a ~ between

breach n. ["violation"] 1. to commit a ~ (of etiquette, of the peace) 2. an egregious, flagrant ~ 3. a security ~ 4. in ~ of 5. (misc.) (a) ~ of contract ["gap"] 6. to effect, make a ~ (in enemy lines) 7. to close, seal off a ~ 8. to fling oneself, throw oneself into the ~ 9. a ~ in (a ~ in the defenses) ["break in friendly relations"] 10. to cause a ~ (between) 11. to heal a ~ (between)

bread n. ["baked food"] 1. to bake ~ 2. to butter; slice; toast ~ 3. to break ~ with ("to eat with") 4. fresh; moldy; stale ~ 5. black; brown; corn; dark; enriched; leavened; rye; sliced; unleavened; wheat; white; whole meal (BE), whole wheat (AE) ~ 6. a crust; loaf; piece, slice of ~ ["living"] 7. to earn one's daily ~ 8. (misc.) to take the ~ out of smb.'s mouth

breadth n. 1. (formal) in ~ (it is ten feet in ~) 2. (misc.) by a hair's ~ (fig.)

break I n. ["dash"] 1. to make a ~ (for safety) ["escape"] 2. a mass; prison ~ ["interruption"] 3. to make a ~ 4. a clean ~ 5. a ~ in, with (a ~ in the conversation; to make a ~ with tradition) ["rest"]

6. to have (esp. BE), take a ~ 7. a coffee; commercial; lunch; news; station (AE); tea (esp. BE) ~ 8. during, on a ~ ["opportunity"] (colloq.) 9. to give smb. a ~ ["good fortune"] 10. to get a ~ 11. a lucky; unexpected ~ 12. a tax ~

break II v. 1. (B) ("to communicate") I had to ~ the news to them 2. (D; intr.) ("to curl and fall") to ~ against, on (the waves were ~ing against the rocks) 3. (d; intr.) ("to dash") to ~ for (to ~ for cover) 4. (d; intr.) ("to take time") to ~ for (they broke for lunch) 5. (d; intr.) ("to enter forcibly") to ~ into (burglars broke into the house) 6. (d; intr.) ("to begin") to ~ into (to ~ into song) 7. (D; intr., tr.) ("to split") to ~ into (to ~ a chair into pieces) 8. (d; tr.) ("to cure") to ~ of (in time he was broken of his drug habit) 9. (D; intr., tr.) ("to split off") to ~ off (to ~ a branch off a tree) 10. (D; tr.) ("to crack") to ~ on (she broke a tooth on a bone) 11. (d; intr.) ("to escape") to ~ out of (two prisoners broke out of jail; our troops broke out of the encirclement) 12. (d; intr.) ("to penetrate") to ~ through (to ~ through enemy lines) 13. (d; intr.) ("to end relations") to ~ with (I broke with them) 14. (D; tr.) ("to cut off") to ~ with (she broke all ties with her friends) 15. (misc.) to ~ free (from), loose (from); to ~ smb. on the wheel

break away v. (D; intr.) to ~ from (he broke away from his captors)

breakdown n. 1. to have, suffer a ~ (he had a nervous ~) 2. a complete; emotional, mental, nervous ~ 3. a ~ in (a ~ in communications)

break down v. 1. (D; intr., tr.) to ~ into (to ~ a substance into its components) 2. (misc.) to ~ in tears

breaker n. a circuit ~

break even v. (D; intr.) to ~ with

breakfast I n. 1. to eat, have ~ 2. to make, prepare ~ 3. a continental; cooked (BE), English (BE), full, hot; nutritious, wholesome; substantial ~ 4. at ~ (what did you discuss at ~?) 5. for ~ (to eat eggs for ~) 6. (misc.) to have ~ in bed; bed and ~ (as in a tourist home)

breakfast II v. (D; intr.) to ~ on (to ~ on scrambled eggs and toast)

break free v. (D; intr.) to ~ from

break-in n. to commit a ~

break in v. 1. (D; intr.) to ~ from; through (the thieves broke in from the roof; we broke in through the door) 2. (D; intr.) to ~ on (he broke in on their conversation) 3. (D; intr.) to ~ with (she broke in with an inane remark)

breaking n. (the crime of) ~ and entering

breaking point n. 1. to reach ~ (BE)/the ~ (AE) 2. to push smb. to ~ (BE)/the ~ (AE)

break loose v. (D; intr.) to ~ from

break off v. (D; intr.) to ~ from (they broke off from the main wing of the party)

breakout n. 1. to organize a ~ (from prison) 2. to achieve, effect a ~ (from an enemy encirclement) 3. a prison ~

break out v. 1. (D; intr.) to ~ in (he broke out in a rash; to ~ in a cold sweat) 2. (misc.) (Am. football) the back broke out in/into the open

breakthrough n. 1. to achieve, effect, make a ~ 2. a dramatic, major, significant ~ 3. a medical; scientific ~

break through v. (D; intr.) to ~ to (they broke through to the encircled unit)

breakup n. a marital ~

break up v. 1. (D; intr., tr.) to ~ into (they broke up the estate into small lots; our party broke up into several splinter groups) 2. (colloq.) (D; intr.) to ~ with (he broke up with his girlfriend) 3. (misc.) ~ it up! ("stop fighting/congregating and separate!")

breast n. 1. to beat one's ~ 2. to put a (newborn) infant to (the) ~ 3. (of an infant) to take the ~ 4. a pigeon ~ ("a deformity of the chest") 5. (cul.) chicken; turkey ~(s) 6. (misc.) to make a clean ~ of smt. ("to confess smt.")

USAGE NOTE: *chicken breast* and *turkey breast* are raw or cooked; *breast of chicken* and *breast of turkey* are cooked.

breaststroke n. to do, swim the ~

breath n. 1. to draw, take a ~ 2. to catch; hold one's ~ 3. to get one's ~ back 4. to gasp, struggle for ~ 5. to lose one's ~ 6. a deep; long; short ~ (she took a deep ~) 7. out of, short of ~ ("breathless") 8. bad ~ (smokers often have bad ~) 9. (misc.) to spare, save one's ~ ("to avoid a futile conversation"); to waste one's ~ ("to speak in vain"); to take smb.'s ~ away ("to astonish smb."); in the same ~ ("at the same time"); to one's dying/last ~ ("to the end of one's life"); under one's ~ ("in a whisper"); with bated ~ ("with the breath held, in suspense")

breathe v. 1. to ~ deeply 2. (d; tr.) to ~ into (she ~d new life into the project) 3. (D; intr.) to ~ through (to ~ through one's nose) 4. (misc.) to ~ in; to ~ out

breather n. ["rest"] to have (BE), take a ~

breathing n. 1. deep; heavy, labored, noisy; irregular; regular, steady ~ 2. (ling.) rough; smooth ~

breathtaking adj. ~ to + inf. (it was ~ to watch the acrobats perform)

breeches n. riding ~

breed n. 1. a ~ apart 2. a dying; hardy; new; rare ~

breeder n. a cattle, livestock; horse; poultry; sheep ~

breeding n. 1. cattle, livestock; horse; poultry; sheep ~ 2. selective ~ 3. of ~ (a person of good ~)

breeding ground n. a ~ for (poverty is an ideal ~ for crime)

breeze I n. ["light wind"] 1. a ~ blows, comes up 2. a balmy, fresh, gentle, light, soft; cool; sea ~ ["easy task"] (colloq.) 3. a ~ to + inf. (it was a ~ to get him to agree = it was a ~ getting him to agree) ["misc."] 4. (colloq.) (AE) to bat, shoot the ~ ("to chat")

breeze II v. (P; intr.) she ~d through the finals; he ~d into the room; they ~d to an easy victory

brew I n. (a) home ~

brew II v. (C) she ~ed some tea for us; or: she ~ed us some tea

brew-up n. (BE) ["making tea"] to have a ~

bribe I n. 1. to give, offer a ~ 2. to accept, take a ~ 3. to refuse, turn down a ~

bribe II v. 1. (D; tr.) to ~ into (to ~ smb. into collusion) 2. (D; tr.) to ~ with (they ~d him with a free vacation) 3. (H) they ~d him to overlook the violation

brick n. (colloq.) (BE) ["blunder"] to drop a ~

brickbats n. ["insults"] to hurl ~ at

bricks n. 1. to make ~ 2. to burn, fire ~ 3. to lay ~ (a bricklayer lays ~) 4. to point ~ 5. see **blocks**

bride n. 1. to take a ~ 2. a ~ takes a husband 3. a beautiful, lovely ~ 4. a child; war ~ 5. a bride-to-be; a future ~ 6. (misc.) ~ and groom

bridge I n. ["structure carrying a roadway over smt."] 1. to build, construct, erect a ~ 2. to throw a ~ across a river 3. to cross a ~ 4. an arch; Bailey; bascule; cantilever; covered ~; drawbridge; footbridge; pontoon; railroad (AE), railway (BE); suspension; toll; truss ~ (to raise a drawbridge) 5. a jet ~ (at an airport) 6. a ~ collapses 7. a ~ across, over; between (a ~ across a river) 8. (misc.) our planes knocked out the enemy ~ ["partial denture"] 9. to make; put in a ~ ["part of a ship"] 10. on the ~ (the captain was on the ~)

bridge II n. ["card game"] 1. to play ~ 2. auction; contract; duplicate ~ 3. (misc.) to win a game; rubber; trick (when playing ~)

bridgehead n. 1. to establish a ~ 2. to develop, enlarge a ~

bridle I n. to put on a ~

bridle II v. (D; intr.) to ~ at (she ~d at her friend's nasty remark)

brief I n. ["summary of a legal case"] 1. to draw up; file a ~ ["brevity"] 2. in ~ ["misc."] 3. to hold no ~ for ("not to be in favor of")

brief II v. (D; tr.) to ~ smb. about, on (he had to ~ his lawyer on the case)

briefing n. 1. to give smb. a ~ 2. to get, receive a ~ 3. a press ~ 4. a ~ about, on

brigade n. 1. a bucket; fire ~ (BE; AE has *fire department*) 2. (misc.) a brigadier (BE)/brigadier general (AE) commands a ~

brilliant adj. ~ + inf. (it was ~ of him to find a solution so quickly)

brim I n. to the ~ (to fill smt. to the ~)

brim II v. (D; intr.) to ~ with (she was ~ming with enthusiasm)

brim over v. (D; intr.) to ~ with (to ~ with enthusiasm)

bring v. 1. (A) ("to carry") she brought word to them; or: she brought them word 2. (C) ("to carry") he brought a book for me; or: he brought me a book 3. (d; tr.) ("to present") to ~ before (to ~ a proposal before a committee) 4. (d; tr.) ("to summon") to ~ before (he was brought before the court) 5. (d; tr.) ("to carry") to ~ from; into (she brought the chairs into the house from the porch) 6. (d; tr.) ("to move") to ~ into (he brought everything into the open) 7. (d; tr.) to ~ on ("to cause") (he brought trouble on himself) 8. (d; intr.) ("to move") to ~ through (excellent nursing care brought him through the crisis) 9. (D; tr.) ("to carry") to ~ to (he brought wine to the party) 10. (d; tr.) to ~ to ("to cause to reach") (to ~ water to a boil; her speech brought the crowd to its feet; we must ~ him to his senses; to ~ smb. to life) 11. (d; tr.) to ~ within ("to cause to reach") (another few feet will ~ them within range) 12. (H; no passive) ("to induce") we could not ~ him to share our views; she could not ~ herself to read the letter 13. (J) ("to cause to come") his last-minute appeal brought them rushing to his aid 14. (P; tr.) ("to carry") they brought the sofa down the stairs; we brought the drinks over to the table 15. (misc.) to ~ a child into the world

bring around v. (AE) (D; tr.) ("to convince") to ~ to (she brought them around to our point of view)

bring back v. 1. (A) she brought the book back to me; she brought me back the book 2. (C) bring back some coffee for me; or: bring me back some coffee 3. (D; tr.) to ~ from (she brought the books back from Europe) 4. (D; tr.) ("to return") to ~ to (to ~ smb. back to life)

bring down v. 1. (D; tr.) ("to carry") to ~ from; to (they brought the computer down from the bedroom to the basement) 2. (D; tr.) ("to cause to come down") to ~ on (the artillery spotter brought down fire on the enemy tanks; his book brought down the wrath of the authorities on his head) 3. (D; tr.) ("to reduce") to ~ to (they finally brought the price down to a reasonable figure)

bring home v. (D; tr.) ("to make known") to ~ to (the bombing brought the war home to the civilian population)

bring in v. (D; tr.) ("to include") to ~ on (we must ~ them in on our plans)

bring out v. 1. (D; intr.) ("to evoke") to ~ in (the crisis brought out the best in her) 2. (D; tr.) ("to move") to ~ from; into (to ~ everything into the open; she brought out everything from the closet into the bedroom)

bring over v. (D; tr.) ("to move") to ~ to (the incident brought them over to our side)

bring round v. (CE) see **bring around**

bring together v. (D; tr.) ("to unite") to ~ for (we brought them together for negotiations)

bring up v. 1. (B) I didn't want to ~ the subject to her at that time 2. (d; tr.) to ~ against ("to confront with") (the drought brought us up against serious difficulties) 3. (D; tr.) ("to educate") to ~ as (they were brought up as atheists) 4. (D; tr.) ("to raise") to ~ for (to ~ up a question for discussion) 5. (D; tr.) to ~ on, with ("to inculcate with") (they brought the children up on stories about the Old West) 6. (D; tr.) ("to lift") to ~ to (we brought their proficiency up to the required level) 7. (H) ("to educate, rear") our parents brought us up to respect others 8. (misc.) her scream brought us up short ("her scream startled us")

brink n. 1. to bring to, drive to the ~ (of ruin) 2. at, on; to the ~ (he teetered on the very ~ of disaster; at the ~ of war)

brinkmanship, (AE) **brinksmanship** n. to practice ~

bristle v. 1. (D; intr.) to ~ at (he ~d at the remark) 2. (D; intr.) to ~ with (she ~d with anger)

broach v. 1. (B) I would like to ~ the subject to him 2. (D; tr.) to ~ with (I didn't want to ~ the matter with her)

broadcast I n. 1. to carry a ~ 2. to beam a ~ to 3. to record, tape a ~ 4. to jam a ~ 5. a live; local; news; radio ~

broadcast II v. 1. to ~ live 2. (B) they ~ the news to the local population every day 3. (N; used with an adjective) they broadcast the interview live

broadside n. to fire a ~ at

brochure n. an advertising; travel ~

brogue n. 1. to speak (in, with) a ~ 2. a heavy, incomprehensible, thick ~

broil v. (AE) (C) he broiled a few steaks for us; or: he broiled us a few steaks (see also **grill II**)

broiled adj. (AE) charcoal ~

broke adj. (colloq.) ["having no money"] 1. to go ~ 2. flat, stone (AE), stony (BE) ~

broker n. 1. to act as a ~ for 2. a commodity; insurance; marriage; real-estate (AE; BE has *estate agent*) ~3. (AE) a power ~ 4. an honest ~

bromide n. (colloq.) ["platitude"] a (tired, old) ~ about

bronco n. 1. to ride a ~ 2. to break a ~ 3. a bucking ~

Bronx cheer n. (AE) to give, let out a ~

brood v. (D; intr.) to ~ about, on, over

brook n. a babbling ~

broth n. beef; chicken; clear ~

brother n. 1. a big, elder, older; kid (colloq.), little, younger; twin ~ 2. a foster; half ~; stepbrother 3. a brother-in-law 4. a blood; lay; soul ~ 5. a ~ to (he was like a ~ to us) 6. (misc.) Big Brother ("government that exercises complete control")

brouhaha n. ["fuss"] a ~ over

brow n. 1. to knit, wrinkle one's ~ 2. to mop one's ~

browbeat v. (D; tr.) to ~ into; out of (they could not

~ him into confessing)

browse v. 1. (D; intr.) ("to feed, as of cattle") to ~ on (to ~ on leaves) 2. (D; intr.) ("to examine leisurely") to ~ through (to ~ through books)

browser n. a web ~

bruise I n. 1. a minor ~ 2. (misc.) cuts and ~s

bruise II v. to ~ easily

bruised adj. badly ~

bruit about, abroad v. (formal) (L) it was ~ed about that she had resigned

brunt n. to bear, take the ~ (our battalion bore the ~ of the attack)

brush I n. 1. to apply a ~ to 2. a bottle; clothes ~; hairbrush; nailbrush; paintbrush; scrub (AE), scrubbing (BE); shaving ~; toothbrush; upholstery ~

brush II v. 1. (d; intr.) to ~ against (she ~ed against the table) 2. (d; intr.) to ~ by, past (she ~ed by me) 3. (d; tr.) to ~ from, out of (she ~ed the crumbs out of her handbag) 4. (d; tr.) to ~ off (he ~ed the crumbs off the table) 5. (N; used with an adjective) she ~ed her coat clean

brush III n. ["brief unpleasant encounter"] 1. to have a ~ with (to have a ~ with the authorities) 2. a close ~ (a close ~ with the law)

brush-off n. ["snub"] to give smb. the ~

brush up v. 1. (d; intr.) to ~ against (to ~ against a wall) 2. (D; intr.) to ~ on (to ~ on one's Latin)

brusque adj. ~ with

brutal adj. ~ to + inf. (it was ~ of him to do that)

brutality n. 1. to demonstrate, display, exhibit ~ 2. extreme ~ 3. police ~ 4. an act of ~ 5. ~ to, towards, with

bubble I n. 1. to blow ~s 2. to prick a ~ 3. to burst a ~ 4. a ~ bursts 5. air; soap ~s

bubble II v. (D; intr.) to ~ with (to ~ with enthusiasm)

bubble over v. (D; intr.) to ~ with (the children were ~ling over with excitement)

bubbling adj. ~ with (~ with enthusiasm)

buck I n. (colloq.) ["responsibility"] to pass the ~

buck II v. (colloq.) (AE) 1. (d; intr.) to ~ against ("to oppose") (to ~ against the system") 2. (D; intr.) ("to make an all-out effort") to ~ for (to ~ for a promotion)

bucket n. 1. a coal; fire; ice; water ~ 2. a metal; wooden ~ 3. an empty; full ~ 4. (misc.) (colloq.) to kick the ~ ("to die"); a drop in the ~ ("an insignificant amount"); the rain came down in ~s ("it was raining very hard")

buckle I n. 1. to fasten a ~ 2. to undo, unfasten a ~ 3. a brass ~

buckle II v. (D; refl., tr.) ("to fasten") to ~ into (she ~ed the baby into the seat)

buckle III v. (D; intr.) ("to collapse") to ~ under (to ~ under severe pressure)

buckle down v. (colloq.) (D; intr.) to ~ to (to ~ to

work)

bud *n*. ["cell embedded in the tongue"] 1. a taste ~ ["early stage"] 2. to come into ~ 3. to nip in the ~ ["the early stage of a flower"] 4. a ~ opens 5. in ~ (the roses are in ~)

buddy *n*. a bosom, good, great; old ~

budge *v*. (D; intr.) to ~ from (she would not ~ from the spot)

budget I *n*. 1. to draw up a ~ 2. to submit a ~ 3. to balance a ~ 4. to adhere to; keep, remain within a ~ 5. to exceed ; stretch a ~ 6. to cut, reduce, slash a ~ (to slash a ~ by ten percent) 7. an annual; defense; family, household; federal (AE), national; itemized; municipal; state; tight ~ 8. an item in, on a ~ 9. below, within; over (a) ~ (to stay within ~)

budget II *v*. 1. (d; intr.) to ~ for (they ~ed for a new copying machine) 2. (D; tr.) to ~ for (we ~ed a thousand dollars for new books)

buff *n*. ["the bare skin"] 1. in the ~ 2. (BE) to strip to the ~ ["devotee"] 3. a computer; film, movie; history; jazz; opera, theater ~

buffalo *n*. a herd of ~

buffer *n*. 1. to act as a ~ against; between 2. (misc.) a ~ state; zone; (BE) an old ~ ("an old man")

buffet I *n*. a cold ~

buffet II *v*. to be ~ed from pillar to post ("to be forced to go to many places")

buffoon *n*. to play the ~

bug I *n*. ["listening device"] 1. to install a ~ 2. to remove, tear out a ~ ["illness"] (colloq.) 3. to pick up a ~ 4. a ~ is going around ["defect"] (colloq.) 5. to iron out the ~s

bug II *v*. (colloq.) 1. (D; tr.) ("to annoy") to ~ about (he was ~ging me about the money I owed him) 2. (H) ("to urge") they kept ~ging me to buy a new car

bugle *n*. 1. to blow, play a ~ 2. a ~ sounds

build I *n*. ["figure"] a heavy; medium; powerful; slight; slim; stocky; sturdy ~

build II *v*. 1. (C) they built a new library for us; or: they built us a new library 2. (D; tr.) to ~ around (to ~ a plot around a true story) 3. (D; tr.) to ~ from, of, out of (they built a boat out of wood) 4. (D; tr.) to ~ into (he built cupboards into the walls) 5. (D; intr., tr.) to ~ on (to ~ on earlier success; to ~ a relationship on trust) 6. (D; tr.) to ~ onto (the shed was built onto the garage) 7. (D; tr.) to ~ out of (they built a boat out of wood) 8. (d; intr.) to ~ to (the music was ~ing to a climax)

building *n*. 1. to build, erect, put up; renovate a ~ 2. to demolish, raze, tear down a ~ 3. to gut a ~ (fire gutted the ~) 4. a dilapidated, gutted, ramshackle, tumbledown ~ 5. a low; tall (less frequently: *high*) ~ 6. an adjoining ~ 7. an apartment (AE); government; office; parliament; public; school ~ 8. a listed (BE) ~

buildup *n*. 1. an arms, military; gradual ~ 2. (misc.)

during the ~ to the invasion

build up *v*. 1. (D; tr.) to ~ as (they built her up as a contender for the nomination) 2. (D; tr.) to ~ into (they built him up into a huge success) 3. (D; intr.) to ~ to (the tension built up to a climax)

built *adj*. 1. heavily, powerfully, solidly, strongly ~ 2. ~ around (the whole story was ~ around one character) 3. ~ into (quality was ~ into their products) 4. ~ on (her conclusions were ~ on solid data) 5. (misc.) jerry ("cheaply") ~; purpose ~ (BE)

bulb *n*. ["light bulb"] 1. to change, put in, screw in (US) a ~ 2. to take out, unscrew (US) a ~ 3. a ~ blows out; burns out 4. an electric; frosted; incandescent; light; three-way ~ 5. the glare of a ~ ["tuber"] 6. a crocus; tulip ~

bulge *v*. (D; intr.) to ~ with (her suitcase was ~ing with presents)

bulk I *n*. in ~ (to sell smt. in ~)

bulk II *v*. to ~ large (the case ~ed large in his thoughts)

bull I *n*. ["adult male of a bovine animal"] 1. a ~ charges 2. a ~ bellows; gores ["nonsense"] (colloq.) 3. to shoot the ~ (AE) ["misc."] 4. to take the ~ by the horns ("to confront a problem boldly"); like a ~ in a china shop ("in a rough, crude, or clumsy manner")

bull II *n*. ["letter"] a papal ~

bulldoze *v*. to ~ through (they ~d their way through all obstacles)

bulldozer *n*. to operate a ~

bullet *n*. 1. to shoot a ~ 2. a plastic; real; rubber; stray; tracer ~ 3. a ~ flies, whistles, whizzes (through the air) 4. a ~ ricochets 5. a ~ lodges somewhere (the ~ lodged in her shoulder) 6. a hail, volley of ~s 7. (misc.) to bite the ~ ("to perform a very unpleasant task")

bulletin *n*. 1. to issue a ~ about 2. an all-points ~ 3. a daily; news ~ 4. the ~ that + clause (we heard the ~ that the dam had burst)

bullfight *n*. to hold, stage a ~

bullion *n*. gold; silver ~

bull's eye *n*. to hit; score a ~

bully I *n*. (colloq.) a big ~

bully II *v*. (D; tr.) to ~ into (they ~ied him into doing it)

bulwark *n*. a ~ against

bum *v*. (colloq.) (AE) (D; tr.) to ~ off (he ~med a cigarette off me)

bump I *n*. to hit a ~ (in the road)

bump II *v*. 1. (d; intr.) to ~ against, into (she ~ed into me) 2. (D; tr.) to ~ against, on (she ~ed her arm against the table) 3. (colloq.) (AE) (D; tr.) ("to remove without warning") to ~ from (he was ~ed from the flight) 4. (d; intr.) to ~ into ("to meet by chance") (when she went to town, she ~ed into an old friend)

bumpkin *n*. a country ~

bump up v. (d; intr.) (esp. AE) to ~ against (he ~ed up against me)

bum's rush n. (AE) (colloq.) to give smb. the ~ ("to eject smb.")

bum steer n. (colloq.) (AE) ["poor guidance"] 1. to give smb. a ~ 2. to get a ~

bun n. ["knot of hair that resembles a bun"] 1. in a ~ (she wore her hair in a ~) ["type of pastry"] 2. a cinnamon, sticky; hamburger ~

bundle I n. (slang) ["a large amount of money"] to cost; make a ~

bundle II v. (d; tr.) to ~ into (they ~d the children into the car and left)

bundle off v. (D; tr.) to ~ to (we ~d the children off to school)

bundle up v. (D; intr., refl., tr.) to ~ against; in (they ~d up in warm coats against the cold)

bungle v. to ~ appallingly, badly, completely (they completely ~d the job; they ~d the job badly)

bunk n. (slang) (BE) to do a ~ ("to disappear")

buoy n. 1. to anchor a ~ 2. a bell; breeches; life ~

burden I n. 1. to bear, carry, shoulder a ~ 2. to impose, place a ~ on smb. 3. to alleviate, lift, lighten, relieve a ~ 4. to share a ~ 5. to distribute a ~ equitably 6. a crushing, heavy, onerous ~ 7. a financial; tax ~ 8. a ~ on, to (he became a ~ to his family) 9. (misc.) it was a heavy ~ to bear

burden II v. (D; tr.) to ~ with (she didn't want to ~ us with her problems)

bureau n. a better-business (AE); credit; farm; information; missing-persons; news; service; speakers'; travel; weather ~ (AE; BE has *the met, meteorological office*)

bureaucracy n. a bloated, overgrown, swollen; government ~

burglar n. a cat ~

burglar alarm n. see **alarm**

burglary n. to commit (a) ~

burial n. 1. a decent ~ (she didn't even have a decent ~) 2. a ~ takes place (the ~ took place at sea)

buried adj. 1. ~ underground 2. ~ in, under (~ under a pile of paperwork)

burn I n. 1. to get, have, receive a ~ 2. to suffer from a ~ 3. a brush, friction; cigarette ~ 4. a first-degree; second-degree; third-degree ~ 5. a mild, minor, superficial; moderate; severe ~ 6. (misc.) (esp. AE) a slow ~ ("increasing fury")

burn II v. 1. to ~ brightly; furiously 2. (d; refl.) to ~ into (the incident ~ed itself into my memory) 3. (D; intr., tr.) to ~ to (to ~ to the ground; he ~ed the meat to a crisp; the wood ~ed to ashes; she was ~ed to death) 4. (D; intr.) (often fig.) to ~ with (his cheeks ~ed with shame; they were ~ing with curiosity to hear the latest gossip; he was ~ing with passion) 5. (E) I am ~ing to tell you the news 6. (N; used with an adjective) to ~ smb. alive 7. (misc.) to ~ smb. at the stake; she ~ed her hand on the stove;

the fire ~ed out of control

burned, burnt adj. badly, severely ~

burner n. 1. to light, turn on; turn off a ~ 2. a Bunsen; charcoal; gas; oil ~ 3. (misc.) to put smt. on the back ~ ("to postpone action on smt.")

burnout n. (colloq.) (AE) ["exhaustion"] to experience, suffer ~

burn up v. (slang) (AE) (R) it ~ed me up that she was not promoted

burp n. 1. to let out, make a ~ 2. a loud, noisy ~

burrow v. (P; intr., tr.) to ~ a hole into the ground; to ~ one's way out of a dungeon; to ~ through a wall; to ~ under a building

bursary n. (BE) 1. to award a ~ 2. to receive a ~

burst I n. ["series of shots"] 1. to fire a ~ at ["outbreak"] 2. a sudden ~ 3. in ~s ["misc."] 4. she finally finished the job in/with a sudden ~ of energy

burst II v. 1. (d; intr.) to ~ into (the mob burst into the room; to ~ into flames; to ~ into tears) 2. (d; intr.) to ~ out of (to ~ out of a room) 3. (D; intr.) to ~ with (to ~ with pride; the granaries are ~ing with grain) 4. (E) she was ~ing to tell everyone the news

burst in v. (D; intr.) to ~ on, upon (we burst in on them without warning)

burst out v. (G) they burst out laughing

burton n. (slang) (BE) to go for a ~ ("to be lost; to be broken; to be killed; to fail")

bury v. 1. (d; refl., tr.) to ~ in (he ~ied himself in his work) 2. (N; used with an adjective) they ~ied him alive

bus I n. 1. to drive a ~ 2. (as a passenger) to board, get on; catch a ~; get off a ~; to go, travel by ~; to miss a ~; to ride a ~; to ride in/on a ~; to take a ~ 3. a city; double-decker; local; long-distance (AE; BE has *coach*); school; sightseeing ~ 4. the ~es are not running today 5. by ~ (they came by ~)

bus II v. (D; tr.) to ~ to (to ~ children to school)

bush n. 1. to prune, trim a ~ 2. (misc.) to beat about/ (AE) around the ~ ("to speak indirectly")

bushel n. by the ~ (to sell by the ~)

business n. ["commerce"] ["trade"] 1. to conduct, do, transact; drum up ~ (to do ~ with smb.) 2. to lose ~ 3. to go into ~; to go out of ~ 4. big; small ~ 5. a mail-order ~; show ~; the travel ~ 6. retail; wholesale ~ 7. (AE) a land-office ("brisk") ~ (to do a land-office ~ in real estate) 8. ~ drops off; picks up 9. ~ is brisk, booming, flourishing, thriving 10. ~ is bad; slack; slow; ~ is at a standstill 11. in ~ (to be in ~ for oneself; what ~ are you in? we are in the real estate ~) 12. on ~ (to travel on ~) ["firm"] 13. to build up; establish, launch, open a ~ 14. to manage, operate, run a ~ 15. to buy into; buy out; take over a ~ ["work"] 16. to get down to ~ 17. to go about one's ~ 18. to talk ~ ["affairs"] 19. to mind one's own ~ 20. bad; dirty; funny;

(colloq.) monkey ~ 21. company; personal; unfinished; urgent ~ ["cause"] 22. to have ~ to + inf. (he had no ~ to interfere = he had no ~ interfering) ["misc."] 23. to know one's ~ ("to be competent in one's field"); to state one's ~ ("to explain what one is doing"); to mix ~ with pleasure ("to combine work and recreation"); to mean ~ ("to be serious about achieving one's ends"); to give smb. the ~ (AE) ("to deceive smb."); it's none of your ~ ("the matter doesn't concern you")

busing *n.* (US) forced; school; voluntary ~

bust *n.* (slang) ["arrest"] 1. to make a ~ 2. a drug, drugs (BE) ~

bustle off *v.* (D; intr., tr.) to ~ to (she ~ed the children off to school)

busy I *adj.* 1. ~ at, with (the children were ~ with their homework) 2. to be ~ doing smt. (she was ~ getting dinner ready) 3. to keep ~; to keep smb. ~ (they keep ~ helping out at the crisis center; we kept the children ~ cutting out pictures) 4. (misc.) I'm sorry: the line/number is ~

busy II *v.* 1. (d; refl.) to ~ by, with (he busied himself with various jobs) 2. (J; refl.) (she busied herself doing various jobs)

butcher *n.* a family ~ (BE) ("a butcher's business run by a single family"); ("a butcher's business that sells retail rather than wholesale")

butt I *n.* a cigarette; rifle ~

butt II *v.* 1. (d; intr.) to ~ against 2. (colloq.) (d; intr.) to ~ into (to ~ into smb.'s business)

butter *n.* 1. to churn; cream; make ~ 2. to spread ~ (on bread) 3. apple (AE); cocoa; peanut; prune; salted; sweet, unsalted; whipped ~ 4. fresh; rancid ~ 5. a knob (BE), lump (BE); pat; stick of ~ 6. in ~ (to fry in ~)

butterfly *n.* 1. to collect ~flies 2. a ~ flits from flower to flower 3. (misc.) a social ~ ("one who leads an active social life")

butter up *v.* (colloq.) (d; intr.) to ~ to (he keeps ~ing up to the boss)

butt in *v.* (colloq.) (D; intr.) to ~ on (to ~ on a conversation)

button *n.* ["fastener"] 1. to sew on a ~ 2. to do up; undo one's ~s 3. to lose a ~ 4. to rip off, tear off a ~ 5. a ~ comes off (my ~ came off) ["push button"] 6. to press, push a ~ 7. a panic (colloq.); push ["badge"] (AE) 8. a campaign ~ ["misc."] 9. right on the ~ ("exactly correct")

buy I *n.* (colloq.) ["purchase"] a good ~

buy II *v.* 1. (C) we bought a book for her; or: we bought her a book 2. (D; tr.) to ~ for (she bought a hat for twenty dollars) 3. (D; tr.) to ~ from (she bought her car from a local dealer) 4. (d; intr.) to ~ into (to ~ into a business) 5. (misc.) to ~ as is ("to purchase with no guarantee of quality"); to ~ retail; to ~ wholesale; to ~ at a reasonable price

buy back *v.* (D; tr.) to ~ from

buyer *n.* 1. a prospective ~ 2. a ~ for (they found a ~ for the building)

buying *n.* impulse; panic ~

buzz I *n.* (colloq.) ("telephone call") to give smb. a ~

buzz II *v.* 1. (D; intr.) to ~ for (to ~ for one's secretary) 2. (D; intr.) to ~ with (to ~ with activity) 3. (P; intr.) insects were ~ing through the air; photographers were ~ing around the entrance

buzzer *n.* 1. to press, sound a ~ 2. at the ~ (at the ~, stop work immediately!)

bye *n.* (sports) to draw a ~

by-election see **election**

bygones *n.* to let ~ be ~

bylaws *n.* 1. to draft, draw up ~s 2. to amend, change; approve (the) ~

bypass *n.* ["operation"] 1. a coronary, heart ~ ["road"] 2. to take the ~

byplay *n.* ~ between

bystander *n.* an innocent ~

C

cab *n.* 1. to call for; flag down; get; hail; hire; take a ~ 2. to drive a ~ (for a living) 3. a radio ~ 4. by ~; in a ~ (to go somewhere by ~)

cabbage *n.* 1. red; savoy; white ~ 2. boiled ~ 3. a head of ~ 4. (AE) corned beef and ~

cabin *n.* ["compartment"] 1. a first-class; second-class ~ 2. a pressurized ~ (of an airplane) ["small house"] 3. a log ~

cabinet *n.* ["case"] ["cupboard"] 1. a built-in; china; display; kitchen ~ 2. a file (AE), filing ~ ["body of advisors"] 3. the president's ~ 4. a coalition; kitchen ("informal") ~ 5. a shadow ~ ("members of the opposition party who will form the next cabinet") 6. a ~ meets 7. (misc.) a ~ minister (not US); a ~ reshuffle ["cabinet meeting"] (BE) 8. to hold a ~ 9. in ~ (to take a decision in ~)

cable I *n.* ["wire"] 1. to lay, string ~ 2. a submarine ~; a transatlantic ~ 3. an electric, power; telegraph; telephone ~ 4. a ~ snaps 5. a coil of ~ ["cablegram"] 6. to send a ~ 7. to get, receive a ~ 8. a ~ from; to

cable II *v.* 1. (A) we ~d the message to them; or: we ~d them the message 2. (d; intr., tr.) to ~ for (they ~d for immediate delivery) 3. (H) we ~d them to return home immediately 4. (L; may have an object) she ~d (us) that the manuscript had arrived 5. (Q; may have an object) they ~d (us) where to meet

cablegram *n.* 1. to send a ~ 2. to get, receive a ~ 3. a ~ from; to

cache *n.* an arms ~

cadence *n.* (usu. mil.) 1. to count ~ 2. in ~

cadet *n.* 1. an air-force; military; naval; police ~ 2. (slang) (AE) a space ~ ("an absent-minded person")

cadge *v.* (rare) 1. (D; intr.) to ~ for (to ~ for food) 2. (D; tr.) to ~ from, off (to ~ meals from friends)

caesarean, caesarean section *n.* 1. to do, perform a ~ on 2. to have a ~ 3. (misc.) to be born/delivered by ~

café *n.* a sidewalk; transport ~ (BE; AE has *truck stop*)

cafeteria *n.* a school ~

cage *n.* 1. a birdcage 2. a bank teller's (AE) ~

cagey *adj.* (colloq.) ["sly"] ~ about

cahoots *n.* (esp. AE) in ~ with ("in partnership with")

cajole *v.* 1. (d; tr.) (with an inanimate object) to ~ from (she ~d some money from him) 2. (d; tr.) (with an animate object) to ~ into (he ~d me into signing over the property)

cake *n.* 1. to bake; frost (esp. AE), ice a ~ 2. a birthday; wedding ~ 3. (a) chocolate; Christmas (BE); coffee ~; fruitcake; honey; Madeira (BE), sponge; marble; pound; white ~ 4. a layer ~ 5. a piece, slice of ~ 6. (misc.) a piece of ~ ("smt. very easy to do"); to take the ~ ("to be the best or worst"); to go/sell like hot cakes ("to be bought up very quickly")

caked *adj.* ~ in, with (~ with blood)

calamity *n.* 1. to avert; ward off a ~ 2. to survive a ~ 3. a ~ befalls smb. 4. a crushing, dire, grave, great; national ~ 5. a ~ for

calculate *v.* 1. (d; intr.) to ~ on (we ~d on a large crowd) 2. (L) we ~d that the trip would take two days 3. (Q) they ~d where the meteor would hit

calculated *adj.* 1. ill; well ~ 2. (usu. does not stand alone) ~ to + inf. (his actions were ~ to provoke his opponents)

calculations *n.* 1. to do, make, perform ~ 2. mathematical; precise ~

calculator *n.* 1. to use, operate a ~ 2. an electronic; pocket ~

calculus *n.* ["mathematical method"] 1. differential; integral; vector ~ ["deposit formed in an organ of the body"] 2. a biliary; renal; urinary ~

calendar *n.* ["chart that shows the days and months"] 1. the Chinese; Gregorian; Islamic, Muslim; Hindu; Jewish; Julian; Roman ~ 2. a lunar; solar ~ 3. a perpetual ~ 4. a desk; wall ~ ["schedule"] 5. to clear one's ~ 6. a court; school; social ~ 7. a crowded, full ~ 8. on a ~ (what's on your ~ this week?)

calf *n.* 1. a ~ bleats 2. in ~ (the cow was in ~) 3. (misc.) the meat of the ~ is veal

caliber, calibre *n.* ["diameter of the barrel of a weapon"] 1. heavy; light ~ ["quality"] 2. high; low ~ 3. of a certain ~ (there are few workers left of her ~)

calibration *n.* precise ~

calisthenics, callisthenics *n.* 1. to do, perform ~ 2. daily; group, mass ~

call I *n.* ["appeal"] ["summons"] 1. to issue a ~ for (the government issued a ~ to the populace for voluntary contributions) 2. to answer, heed, respond to a ~ (to answer the ~ of duty) 3. a clarion ~ 4. a curtain ~ (the actor had five curtain ~s) 5. a ~ for (we heard a ~ for help) 6. a ~ to (a ~ to arms) 7. at smb.'s beck and ~ ["visit"] 8. to make, pay a ~ on smb. 9. to make a ~ at a place (the ships made ~s at several ports) 10. a business; courtesy; port; professional ~ 11. a house ~ (my doctor makes house ~s) (esp. AE; BE prefers *home visit*) ["invitation"] 12. to accept, answer a ~ ["telephone call"] 13. to give smb. a ~ 14. to make, place a ~ to smb. 15. to answer; get; receive; return; take;

transfer a ~ (who will take her ~?) 16. to put a ~ through (the operator put my ~ right through) 17. a telephone ~ 18. a business; conference; emergency; wake-up ~ 19. a collect (AE), reversed-charge (BE), transferred-charge (BE); dial-direct (AE), direct-dialled (BE); operator-assisted (BE); ordinary (BE), station-to-station (AE); personal (BE, old-fashioned), person-to-person ~ 20. an international; local; long-distance, toll (AE), trunk (BE, old-fashioned); toll-free (AE) ~ 21. an anonymous; crank; threatening ~ 22. a ~ from; to ["signal"] 23. a bugle ~ ["reading aloud"] 24. a roll ~ ["duty"] 25. on ~ (which nurse is on ~?) ["need"] 26. a ~ for (there is no ~ for such behavior) 27. a ~ to + inf. (there was no ~ to complain) ["formation"] (AE) (usu. mil.) 28. sick ~ (to go on sick ~) ["misc."] 29. a close ~ ("a narrow escape")

call II v. 1. (C) ("to summon") she ~ed a taxi for me; or: she ~ed me a taxi 2. (d; intr.) ("to visit") to ~ at (the ship will ~ at several ports) 3. (d; intr.) to ~ for ("to fetch") (I'll ~ for you at two o'clock) 4. (d; intr.) to ~ for ("to require") (the position ~s for an experienced engineer) 5. (d; intr.) to ~ for ("to seek") (to ~ for help) 6. (d; intr., tr.) ("to order by telephone") to ~ for (they ~ed the pharmacy for aspirin) 7. (d; tr.) ("to summon") to ~ into (she was ~ed into the room) 8. (D; intr.) to ~ on ("to visit") (several friends ~ed on us) 9. (slang) (AE) (d; tr.) to ~ on ("to reprimand") (the boss ~ed me on my sloppy writing) 10. (d; tr.) ("to summon") to ~ out of (she was ~ed out of town on business) 11. (D; intr.) ("to shout") to ~ to (she ~ed to me to help her) 12. (d; tr.) ("to summon") to ~ to (to ~ smb. to account; to ~ smt. to mind; the chair ~ed the delegates to order; to be ~ed to the bar) 13. (H) ("to summon") they ~ed her to testify 14. (N; used with a noun or adjective) ("to describe as or name") she ~ed him a stuffed shirt; I would ~ it a disgrace; I ~ that mean; they ~ him Bill; he is ~ed Bill 15. (O) ("to describe as") to ~ smb. a bad name 16. (misc.) (esp. AE) ("to telephone") to ~ collect; long-distance; she ~ed from the office

call away v. 1. (D; tr.) to ~ from (she was ~ed away from her desk) 2. (misc.) they were ~ed away on business

call down v. 1. (D; tr.) ("to summon") to ~ on, upon (to ~ the wrath of God on smb.'s head) 2. (D; intr.) ("to shout") to ~ to (he ~ed down to us from the roof)

call for v. (H) they ~ed for him to resign

call in v. 1. (D; intr.) ("to visit") to ~ at, on (she ~ed in at our place this morning; the doctor ~ed in on her patient) 2. (D; intr.) ("to telephone") to ~ to; with (he ~ed in to the chat show/talk show; she ~ed in with a comment) 3. (s) ("to report by telephone") to ~ sick

call on v. 1. (D; tr.) to ~ for (to ~ a pupil for an answer) 2. (H) the mayor ~ed on the people to remain calm

callous adj. 1. ~ to (~ to suffering) 2. ~ to + inf. (it was ~ of him to say that)

call out v. 1. (D; intr.) to ~ for (to ~ for help) 2. (D; intr., tr.) ("to shout") to ~ to (he ~ed smt. out to me)

call over v. (D; tr.) to ~ to (I ~ed him over to our table)

call up v. 1. (D; tr.) to ~ for (they were ~ed up for military service) 2. (D; intr.) ("to shout") to ~ from; to (she ~ed up to us from the basement) 3. (D; tr.) to ~ on (to ~ smt. on a computer screen 4. (D; intr., tr.) to ~ on (to ~ smb. on the telephone) 5. (D; tr.) to ~ to (she was ~ed up to the podium) 6. (H) he was ~ed up to serve in the army

call upon v. see **call on**

calm I adj. to keep, remain, stay ~

calm II n. 1. to shatter the ~ 2. a dead, perfect; uneasy ~ 3. (misc.) the ~ before the storm; the government appealed for ~

calories n. 1. to count ~ 2. to burn ~ 3. empty ~ (in junk food)

calumny n. to heap ~ on

camel n. an Arabian, one-humped; Bactrian, two-humped ~

camera n. ["photographic apparatus"] 1. to load a ~ 2. an automatic; box; miniature ~ 3. a cine (BE), motion-picture (AE), movie (AE); television, TV; video ~ 4. a security ~ 5. off ~ ("not being filmed") 6. on ~ ("being filmed") 7. (misc.) to face the ~ (in order to be photographed); the ~s are ready to roll (in a film studio); candid ~ ("taking pictures of people without their knowledge") ["judge's chamber"] 8. in ~ (the trial was held in ~; the case was heard in ~)

cameraman, camerawoman n. a motion-picture (AE); television ~

camouflage n. 1. to use, utilize ~ 2. natural ~ 3. by ~ (to conceal by ~)

camp n. 1. to make, pitch, set up ~ 2. to break, strike ~ 3. an army; boot; training ~ 4. a prisoner-of-war, POW, PW (AE) ~ 5. a labor; work ~ 6. a displaced-persons, DP; refugee; repatriation ~ 7. a concentration; detention; internment ~ 8. a day; overnight; summer ~ 9. a trailer ~ (AE; BE has *caravan park, caravan site*) 10. (misc.) the enemy; rival ~

campaign I n. 1. to launch, mount, orchestrate, organize a ~ 2. to carry on, conduct, wage a ~ 3. to intensify a ~ 4. an active, aggressive, all-out, hard-fought, relentless, vigorous; whirlwind ~ 5. a feeble, weak ~ 6. an advertising; membership; publicity, public-relations ~ 7. an election, political; whistle-stop; write-in ~ 8. an anti-smoking; educational ~ 9. a local; national, nationwide ~ 10. a smear; whispering ~ 11. a military ~ 12. the ~ got off to a good start; the ~ fizzled 13. a ~ against; for (the ~ against smoking; a ~ for equal rights) 14. a ~ to + inf. (they launched a ~ to curb alcoholism)

campaign II v. 1. to ~ actively, aggressively, vigorously 2. (D; intr.) to ~ against; for 3. (E) they were ~ing to reduce teenage smoking

camp bed (BE) see cot 1, 2

camper n. (esp. AE) a summer ~ (person)

campus n. (esp. AE) 1. a college, university ~ 2. off; on ~ (to live on ~)

can I n. 1. (AE) an ash, garbage, trash ~ (BE has *dustbin*) 2. a beer; milk; watering ~ 3. a tin ~

can II v. (F) she ~ work (see the Usage Note for **able**)

Canadian n. a French ~

canal n. 1. to build, construct, dig a ~ 2. to dredge a ~ 3. an irrigation ~ 4. (anat.) the alimentary ~

canard n. 1. to circulate, spread a ~ 2. an absurd, preposterous ~

canary n. a ~ sings

cancer n. 1. to develop ~ 2. breast; cervical; colon, colorectal; lung; rectal; skin; stomach ~ 3. inoperable; metastatic; terminal ~ 4. ~ metastasizes; spreads

candid adj. 1. ~ about 2. ~ with

candidacy, candidature n. 1. to announce, file (AE) one's ~ 2. to withdraw one's ~

candidate n. 1. to nominate; put up a ~ (for office) 2. to adopt (BE), choose, select; endorse a ~ 3. (BE) to de-select a ~ ("to decline to select or retain a party candidate") 4. a handpicked; write-in ~ 5. an independent; party; third-party ~ 6. a leading; strong; successful; victorious ~ (a successful ~ for admission to the university; a victorious ~ for the party's nomination) 7. a defeated; unsuccessful; weak ~ 8. a ~ for (a ~ for the presidency) 9. a ~ runs for, stands for (BE) office 10. (misc.) (esp. AE) a slate of ~s

candle n. 1. to dip ~s 2. to light a ~ 3. to blow out, extinguish, snuff out a ~ 4. the ~ was burning; was flickering; was going out; was sputtering 5. a wax ~ 6. a household; votive ~ 7. the flame of a ~ 8. (misc.) to burn the ~ at both ends ("to dissipate one's energy by doing too many things both by day and by night"); not to hold a ~ to smb. or smt. ("to be far inferior to smb. or smt.")

candlelight n. by ~ (to read by ~)

candlestick n. 1. brass; silver ~s 2. a pair of ~s

candor n. 1. complete; disarming ~ 2. the ~ to + inf. (she had enough ~ to tell them the truth)

candy n. (esp. AE) 1. chocolate; cotton; hard ~ 2. a box; piece of ~ (BE has *sweets*)

cane n. ["walking stick"] 1. to carry; twirl a ~ ["plant"] 2. sugar ~ ["stick used for punishment"] (old-fashioned) 3. to get the ~

cannibalism n. to engage in, practice ~

cannon n. 1. to fire a ~ 2. to aim a ~ at; to train a ~

on 3. to load a ~ 4. a ~ booms, roars; fires 5. a water ~ (the police trained a water ~ on the mob) 6. (misc.) ~ fodder; (colloq.) a loose ~ ("a dangerously unpredictable person")

canoe I n. 1. to paddle a ~ 2. by ~ (to cross a river by ~)

canoe II v. (P; intr.) to ~ along a river bank; to ~ across a lake

canon n. ["dogma"] 1. to establish, lay down a ~ ["round"] (mus.) 2. to sing a ~

canter n. ["speed of a horse"] at a ~ (to set off at a ~)

cap n. ["container holding an explosive charge"] 1. a percussion ~ ["head covering"] 2. to place, put a ~ on one's head 3. a peaked; skull ~ 4. a bathing; shower ~ 5. a forage (BE), garrison; overseas; service ~ 6. a baseball ~ 7. (BE) a cricket; rugby ~ (showing that the wearer is a member of a national team) 8. (misc.) to wear (a) ~ and gown (at graduation); (fig.) a thinking ~ ["ceiling"] 9. to place a ~ on (to place a ~ on public spending) ["lid"] 10. to put on, screw on a ~ 11. to screw off, take off, unscrew a ~ ["misc."] 12. the polar ice-cap

capability n. 1. to demonstrate, display, show one's ~ties 2. a defense; first-strike; military; nuclear ~ 3. the ~ to + inf. (the ~ to win) 4. beyond; within one's ~ties

capable adj. 1. perfectly, truly ~ 2. ~ of (he is ~ of anything)

capacity n. ["ability to hold"] 1. to ~ (filled to ~) 2. lung ~ 3. seating; storage ~ 4. a ~ of (a ~ of twenty gallons) ["ability"] 5. intellectual, mental ~ 6. smb.'s earning ~ 7. a ~ for (a ~ for making friends) 8. the ~ to + inf. (she has the ~ to go all the way to the top) 9. beyond one's ~; within one's ~ ["ability to produce"] 10. plant; productive ~ (our country's productive ~) 11. full, peak ~ 12. at ~ (to operate at peak ~) ["function"] 13. an administrative; advisory; professional; supervisory ~ 14. an official; unofficial ~ 15. in a ~ (she acted in an advisory ~; in his ~ as legal advisor, he helped us a great deal)

cape n. ["piece of land"] 1. to round a ~ 2. on a ~

caper n. 1. to cut a ~ 2. a childish ~

capital n. ["wealth"] 1. to borrow; raise ~ 2. to invest, put up; tie up ~ 3. to sink ~ into 4. to withdraw ~ 5. borrowed; circulating, working; fixed, permanent; foreign; idle ~ ["gain"] 6. to make ~ out of smt. 7. political ~ (they made political ~ out of the incident) ["official seat of government"] 8. to establish a ~ 9. a national; provincial; state ~ 10. foreign; world ~s ["main center"] 11. a diamond; fashion; film ~ (where is the film ~ of the world?)

capitalize v. (d; intr.) to ~ on (to ~ on smb.'s mistakes)

capital punishment n. 1. to impose; introduce ~ 2.

to abolish ~

capitulate *v.* (D; intr.) to ~ to (to ~ to the enemy)

capricious *adj.* ~ to + inf. (it was ~ of you to act in that manner)

capsule *n.* 1. a space; time ~ 2. a seed ~

captain *n.* 1. (AE) a bell ~ 2. a group (BE); ship's; team ~ 3. (AE) a precinct ~ (in the police) 4. (mil.) a ~ commands a company or battery 5. (misc.) ~s of industry ("leading industrialists")

captive *adj.* to hold smb. ~; to take smb. ~ (they held us ~ for several weeks)

captivity *n.* 1. to hold in ~ 2. to take into ~ 3. to release from ~ 4. (misc.) to breed wild animals in ~

capture *v.* to ~ smt. on film

car *n.* ["automobile, motorcar"] 1. to drive, operate; run; start; steer a ~ 2. to bring a ~ to a stop; to stop a ~ 3. to back a ~ (she backed the ~ into the garage) 4. to ride in a ~ 5. to go, travel by ~ 6. to hire (BE), rent a ~ 7. to break in (AE), run in (BE) a (new) ~ 8. to fix, repair; service; tune up; winterize a ~ 9. to jack up; park; road-test a ~ 10. to register a ~ 11. to smash up, total, wreck; strip a ~ 12. an antique; veteran (BE); vintage ~ 13. an electric ~ 14. a luxury; passenger; sports ~ 15. a racing; stock ~ 16. an armored; command; scout ~ 17. a Panda (BE), patrol, police, prowl (AE), squad; unmarked (police) ~ 18. a getaway ~ 19. an estate ~ (BE; AE has *station wagon*) 20. a new; secondhand, used ~ 21. a company ~ 22. a ~ runs; starts 23. a ~ breaks down; stalls 24. (misc.) to take a ~ in for service; to fill a ~ up with gasoline/petrol ["vehicle that moves on rails"] 25. (on a train) (esp. AE; BE also has *carriage, wagon/waggon, van*) a baggage (AE; BE has *luggage van*); box (AE); cattle; club, lounge, parlor; dining, restaurant (BE); first-class (AE; BE has *first-class carriage*); flat; freight (AE; BE has *goods wagon*); mail (BE has *mail van*); railroad (AE; BE has *railway carriage*); sleeping; tank ~ 26. a streetcar; trolley ~ (AE; BE has *tram*) 27. a cable ~ 28. (misc.) to uncouple railroad/railway ~s

carbon *n.* activated; radioactive ~

card *n.* 1. a business, calling, visiting ~ 2. a filing; index (AE); record (BE) ~ 3. a library (esp. AE); membership; press ~ 4. a time ~ 5. a banker's (BE), cheque (BE); cash (esp. BE), credit (AE) (used at a cash machine); charge (esp. BE), credit (used for making purchases) ~ 6. a boarding ~ (for boarding a plane) 7. a report ~ (AE; BE has *school report*) 8. a boxing; race (BE), racing (AE) ~ 9. a flash ~ (used as a teaching aid) 10. a high; low; playing; trump (also fig.); wild (also fig.); winning ~ 11. an anniversary; birthday; Christmas; confirmation; Easter; get-well; graduation; greeting (AE); greetings (BE); Hanukkah; New Year's; sympathy; thank-you ~ 12. a postcard (CE), postal (AE) ~ 13. (misc.) a drawing ~ ("smb. or smt. that attracts large audiences")

cards *n.* 1. to play ~ 2. to have, play a game of ~ 3. to cut; deal; shuffle the ~ 4. playing ~ 5. a deck (AE), pack of ~ 6. (misc.) to stack the ~ ("to prearrange conditions to one's own advantage"); to hold all the ~ ("to be in a strong negotiating position"); to be in (AE), on (BE) the ~ ("to be destined by fate"); to lay, put one's ~ on the table ("to reveal one's position"); to play one's ~ right ("to negotiate skillfully")

care I *n.* ["caution"] 1. to exercise, take ~ 2. great, meticulous, painstaking, scrupulous, (the) utmost ~ 3. ~ to + inf. (she took ~ to avoid catching cold) 4. ~ that + clause (take ~ that you don't get involved) 5. with ~ (to handle smt. with ~) ["solicitude"] ["maintenance"] ["keep"] 6. to provide ~ for 7. to take ~ of 8. to entrust smb./smt. to smb.'s ~; to put smb. in smb.'s ~ 9. (tender) loving; parental ~ 10. child; day; foster ~ (day ~ for children) 11. in smb.'s ~ (the children were left in my ~) ["health maintenance and medical care"] 12. to provide ~ for 13. to get, receive ~ 14. dental; health; medical; nursing ~ 15. antenatal (BE), antepartal, prenatal (AE); coronary; postnatal, postpartum ~ 16. emergency; extended; intensive; long-term; primary (health); special ~ (this patient requires intensive nursing ~) 17. custodial; domiciliary; hospice; respite ~ 18. in-patient; out-patient ~ 19. managed ~ 20. under smb.'s ~ (under a doctor's ~) 21. (misc.) a coronary-care unit; an intensive-care unit ["misc."] 22. in ~ of ("at smb.'s address")

care II *v.* 1. (D; intr.) ("to be interested") to ~ about (she doesn't ~ about our opinions) 2. (D; intr.) ("to like") to ~ about, for (he ~s about us; she ~s a lot for you; would you ~ for some more coffee?) 3. (d; intr.) ("to take care of") to ~ for (she ~s for her elderly mother) 4. (E) ("to want") I don't ~ to attend

career *n.* 1. to carve out, make a ~ (for oneself) 2. to enter on; launch a ~ 3. to abandon, give up one's ~ 4. to cut short smb.'s ~ (the accident cut short her ~) 5. a brilliant, distinguished; checkered (AE), chequered (BE); colorful; promising; successful; turbulent ~ 6. an academic; diplomatic; literary; military; political; professional; public; stage ~ 7. a ~ as (to carve out a ~ as a diplomat) 8. a ~ in (she made a ~ for herself in politics) 9. (misc.) her ~ took off

careful *adj.* 1. ~ about, of (a good writer is ~ about details) 2. ~ in (to be ~ in negotiating a new trade agreement) 3. ~ with (we must be ~ with dynamite) 4. ~ to + inf. (she was ~ to avoid controversy) 5. ~ that + clause (she was ~ that everything was/would be completed on time) 6. (misc.) be ~ driving home

careless *adj.* 1. ~ about, in, of, with (~ about one's

appearance) 2. ~ to + inf. (it was ~ of you to leave the door unlocked)

carelessness *n.* ~ about, in, with

caress I *n.* a gentle, loving ~

caress II *v.* to ~ gently, lovingly

cargo *n.* 1. to carry, haul (a) ~ 2. to load, take on; stow; transfer ~ 3. to unload ~ 4. contraband; general ~ 5. (misc.) a ~ plane; ship

caricature *n.* ["an ironic representation"] 1. to draw a ~ of 2. a bold, striking ~ ["travesty"] 3. a ~ of the truth

carnage *n.* senseless, terrible ~

carol I *n.* 1. to sing a ~ 2. a Christmas ~

carol II *v.* to go ~ing

carp *v.* (D; intr.) to ~ about; at

carpet *n.* 1. to beat a ~ 2. to lay a ~ 3. to take up a ~ (the ~ must be taken up and cleaned) 4. (misc.) to roll out the red ~ for smb. ("to give smb. a warm reception"); a flying, magic ~; to call smb. on the ~ ("to call smb. to account for her/his actions")

carpeting *n.* ["floor covering"] 1. fitted (BE), wall-to-wall ~ ["severe reprimand"] (BE) 2. to give smb. a ~

carriage *n.* ["vehicle"] 1. see **baby carriage** 2. a railway ~ (BE; AE has *railroad car*) 3. a horse-drawn ~ ["support"] 4. a gun; typewriter ~ ["bearing"] 5. an erect; proud ~

carriageway *n.* a dual ~ (BE; AE has *divided highway*)

carried away *adj.* ["enthusiastic"] to get ~ (with)

carrier *n.* 1. an aircraft; escort; personnel; troop ~ 2. a letter, mail ~ (AE; CE has *postal worker*) 3. a common, public ~ ("a transport service used by the public") 4. a chronic ~ (of a disease)

carrot *n.* 1. diced ~s 2. a bunch of ~s

carry *v.* 1. (B) she ~ied the books to me 2. (d; tr.) to ~ from; to (we ~ied the table from the door to the center of the room) 3. (d; tr.) to ~ into (~ the chairs into the house) 4. (D; tr.) to ~ on (colloq.), with (I never ~ cash on/with me) 5. (d; tr.) to ~ out of (we ~ied the books out of the room) 6. (d; tr.) to ~ through (her cheerful disposition ~ied her through the crisis) 7. (P; refl.) she ~ies herself well 8. (misc.) to ~ to excess, to an extreme ("to go/take too far")

carry about, around *v.* (D; tr.) to ~ with (I don't want to carry that thing around with me)

carry back *v.* (B) he ~ied the books back to her; the memory ~ied me back to my youth

carry down *v.* (D; tr.) to ~ from; to (they ~ied the chair down from the attic to the basement)

carry forward *v.* (D; tr.) to ~ to (the figures must be ~ied forward to the next page)

carry on *v.* 1. (D; intr.) ("to complain") to ~ about (he is always ~ing on about his colleagues) 2. (D; intr.) ("to continue") to ~ with (~ with your work) 3. (D; intr.) ("to have an affair") to ~ with (the boss

is ~ying on with one of the new employees) 4. (BE) (G) to ~ talking

carry-over *n.* a ~ from; to (a ~ from the past)

carry over *v.* 1. (D; tr.) to ~ from; to (~ these figures over to the next page; to ~ a tradition from one generation to another) 2. (D; intr., tr.) to ~ into (she does not let her personal prejudices ~ into her professional life; she does not ~ her personal prejudices into her professional life)

cart *n.* 1. to draw, pull; push a ~ 2. a ~ creaks; lumbers 3. a shopping ~ (AE; BE has *trolley*) 4. (misc.) to put the ~ before the horse ("to do in the wrong order"); to upset the apple ~ ("to ruin smb.'s plans")

carte blanche *n.* 1. to give smb. ~ 2. to get, have ~ 3. ~ to + inf. (she had ~ to invest his money)

cartel *n.* 1. to form a ~ 2. to break up a ~ 3. a drug (CE), drugs (BE); international, multinational; oil ~

cartilage *n.* (a) torn ~

cart off *v.* (D; tr.) to ~ to (they ~ed him off to jail)

cartoon *n.* 1. to draw a ~ 2. an animated; political ~ 3. a strip ~ (BE; CE has *comic strip*)

cartridge *n.* a blank; practice; ruptured; spent ~

cartwheel *n.* to do, turn a ~

carve *v.* 1. (C) he ~d an ornament for me; or: he ~d me an ornament 2. (D; tr.) to ~ from, out of (to ~ a figure from ivory) 3. (d; intr.) to ~ in (to ~ in wood) 4. (D; tr.) to ~ into (she ~d the wood into a statue)

carve out *v.* (D; tr.) to ~ for (she ~d out a new career for herself)

carve up *v.* (D; tr.) to ~ into (they ~d up the region into three areas)

carving *n.* an ivory; wood ~

case I *n.* ["legal action"] ["argument"] 1. to hear, try a ~ (the court will not hear this ~) 2. to dismiss, throw out a ~ (the judge dismissed the ~) 3. to take a ~ (the lawyer agreed to take the ~) 4. to build; prepare a ~ (we can build a strong ~ with the available data) 5. to make (out), present, state a ~ (she made out a convincing ~ for her client; he presented a good ~ for the new legislation) 6. to argue, plead a ~ (the lawyer argued the ~ skillfully) 7. to rest one's ~ ("to cease introducing evidence") (the defense lawyer rested her ~) 8. to lose; win a ~ 9. to decide; settle a ~ (they persuaded their client to settle the ~ out of court) 10. an airtight, ironclad, open-and-shut, watertight; clear, convincing, prima facie; strong ~ 11. a benchmark, landmark ~ 12. a borderline; weak ~ 13. a court ~ 14. a pending; test ~ 15. a civil; divorce ~ 16. a criminal; murder ~ 17. a ~ goes to trial 18. a ~ against (we had an airtight ~ against him) 19. (misc.) to strengthen a ~; to weaken a ~; the president took her ~ to the people; the first recorded ~ under the new law; to have a good ~

("to have a convincing argument"); is there a ~ for capital punishment? ("can capital punishment be justified?") ["crime, felony"] 20. to break, clear up, crack, solve a ~ (the detective broke the ~) 21. to investigate, work on a ~ (the police worked on the ~ for a year) ["instance, occurrence, example"] 22. to cite a ~ 23. an attested; authenticated; clear; open-and-shut ("easily settled") ~ 24. a borderline; doubtful; hypothetical ~ 25. a celebrated; classic; similar; special; typical ~ 26. an extreme, flagrant; isolated, rare ~ 27. (med.) an acute; advanced; bad; chronic; hopeless; lingering; mild; terminal ~ 28. in a certain ~ (in this ~; in any ~; in ~ of emergency) 29. (misc.) to be the ~ ("to be so"); a ~ in point ("a pertinent case") ["inflectional form"] 30. to govern, take a ~ (certain Russian verbs take the dative ~) 31. the ablative; accusative; dative; genitive; instrumental; locative; nominative; oblique; prepositional; vocative ~ ["misc."] 32. as the ~ may be; in ~ it rains/should rain; a basket ~ ("smb. without arms or legs or who is in a completely hopeless situation")

case II n. ["container"] ["cover"] an attaché; display; jewelry; packing; pillow ~; suitcase; watch ~

case III n. ["type of print"] lower; upper ~

case history n. 1. to get, take a ~ (on) 2. a detailed ~

caseload n. 1. to carry, have a ~ 2. to increase; reduce smb.'s ~ 3. a heavy; light ~ (the social worker carries a heavy ~)

cash I n. 1. to pay (in) ~ 2. to run out of ~ 3. out of, short of ~ 4. cold, hard; loose; ready; spare ~ 5. petty ~ 6. (misc.) she never carries ~; ~ on the barrel (esp. AE)/on the nail (BE) ("pay now in cash"); ~ on delivery ("pay when the order is delivered")

cash II v. (D; tr.) to ~ for (she ~ed the money order for me)

cash in v. (colloq.) (d; intr.) to ~ on (to ~ on one's sudden popularity)

casino n. a gambling ~

casserole n. 1. to do, make a ~ 2. a meat; vegetable ~

cassette n. a blank ~

cast I n. ["set of performers"] 1. to head a ~ 2. to select a ~ 3. an all-star, star-studded ~ 4. a supporting ~ ["rigid dressing of gauze"] (med.) 5. to put a ~ on (to put a ~ on a leg) 6. a plaster ~

cast II v. 1. (D; tr.) ("to assign to a role") to ~ as (he was cast as Hamlet) 2. (d; tr.) ("to throw") to ~ on, over (his actions have cast doubts on our entire campaign)

cast about, around v. (d; intr.) to ~ for ("to seek") (to ~ for a solution)

caste n. 1. a warrior ~ 2. a ~ system

cast in v. to ~ one's lot with smb. ("to join forces with smb.")

casual adj. ~ about (she was very ~ about winning the prize)

casualties n. 1. to inflict ~ on 2. to incur, suffer, take ~ 3. to report ~ 4. heavy, serious; light ~ (to inflict heavy ~ on the enemy) 5. civilian; military; traffic ~

cat n. 1. to neuter a ~; to spay a (female) ~ 2. an alley; stray ~ 3. an Angora; Burmese; feral; marmalade (BE); Persian; Siamese; tabby ~ 4. ~s arch their backs; meow (AE), miaow (BE); purr; scratch 5. a young ~ is a kitten 6. a male ~ is a tomcat 7. (misc.) to let the ~ out of the bag ("to reveal a secret"); to play ~ and mouse with ("to toy with")

catalog, catalogue n. 1. to compile, make up a ~ 2. an author; card; subject ~ 3. a college, school, university ~ (esp. AE; BE has *prospectus*) 4. a mail-order ~ 5. a museum ~

catapult v. (P; intr., tr.) he was ~ed to fame; she ~ed out of obscurity into the limelight

cataract n. (med.) 1. to develop, get, have a ~ 2. to remove a ~

catastrophe n. 1. to suffer a ~ 2. to avert a ~ 3. to survive a ~ 4. an environmental; financial; major, overwhelming ~ 5. a ~ for, to (the fire was a ~ to everyone)

catch I n. ["hook"] 1. to fasten a ~ 2. a safety ~ ["smt. caught"] 3. to bring in, land a ~ (the fishermen landed a good ~) 4. the ~ of the day; the day's ~ ["act of catching"] 5. to make a running ~ (as in baseball or cricket) ["children's game"] 6. to play ~ ["disadvantage"] 7. a ~ that + clause (the ~ is that the pay is low)

catch II v. 1. to ~ red-handed, in the act 2. (C) she caught a small fish for me; or: she caught me a small fish 3. (d; tr.) to ~ by (she caught him by the arm) 4. (D; tr.) to ~ from (she caught a cold from her brother) 5. (D; intr., tr.) to ~ in (the kite caught in a tree) 6. (D; intr., tr.) to ~ on (his shirt caught on a nail; he caught his shirt on a nail) 7. (D; tr.) to ~ with (the police caught them with the stolen goods) 8. (J) we caught him stealing 9. (colloq.) (esp. BE) (O) she caught him one in the eye 10. (misc.) we caught him at a bad time; we caught her unawares

catch on v. 1. (D; intr.) to ~ to ("to comprehend") (he caught on to what I said immediately) 2. (D; intr.) ("to become popular") to ~ with (to ~ with the public)

catch up v. 1. (D; intr.) to ~ on (to ~ on one's correspondence) 2. (D; intr.) to ~ to (AE), with (I'll ~ with you later; BE also has: I'll ~ you up later)

catechism n. (rel.) to learn; recite the ~

categorize v. 1. (D; tr.) to ~ according to, by (the books were ~d by language) 2. (D; tr.) to ~ as (she was ~d as a liberal)

category *n.* 1. to establish, set up a ~ 2. to assign to, put into a ~ 3. a main, major ~ 4. to fall into, fit into a ~ 5. a separate; special ~; a ~ of its own (such phenomena belong in a ~ of their own)

cater *v.* (d; intr.) to ~ for (BE), to (to ~ to all tastes) USAGE NOTE: In BE *cater to* is rare and typically pejorative, meaning "to pander to".

cater-cornered, catty-cornered *adj., adv.* (AE) ~ to

catering *n.* to do (the) ~ (who is going to do the ~?)

catheter *n.* (med.) to change; insert; irrigate; remove a ~

Catholicism *n.* Anglo-Catholicism; Roman ~

cattle *n.* 1. to breed; raise, rear (BE) ~ 2. to drive; graze; herd; round up ~ 3. to brand; rustle ~ 4. beef; dairy; prize ~ 5. ~ graze 6. several head of ~; a herd of ~ 7. young ~ are calves 8. female ~ are cows 9. male ~ are bulls

catty *adj.* (colloq.) ["malicious"] ~ about

catty-cornered see **cater-cornered**

caucus *n.* 1. to form; (esp. AE) hold a ~ 2. a party; trade-union (BE) ~

caught *adj.* to be, get ~ (we were ~ in the rain; the kite got ~ in the tree)

caught up *adj.* ["involved"] ~ in (~ in radical movements)

cause I *n.* ["movement"] ["objective"] 1. to advance, champion, fight for, further, help, promote a ~ 2. to serve a ~ 3. to advocate, espouse, plead a ~ 4. to take up a ~ 5. a common; good, just, noble, righteous, worthwhile, worthy ~ (to make common ~ with smb.) 6. a lost ~ ["reason"] 7. to give; show ~ for 8. (legal) probable ~ 9. a deep-rooted, root, underlying; immediate; leading, major; primary; secondary; ultimate ~ 10. natural ~s (to die of natural ~s) 11. (a) ~ for (there is no ~ for alarm) 12. ~ to + inf. (to find ~ to rejoice; there is no ~ to complain; she had good ~ to be disappointed)

cause II *v.* 1. (C) we ~d them a lot of trouble; or: we ~d a lot of trouble for them 2. (H; no passive) the incident ~d me to reflect

caution I *n.* 1. to exercise, use ~ 2. due; extreme, great ~ 3. ~ in (you should exercise ~ in dealing with them) 4. with ~ (to proceed with ~) 5. (misc.) to fling/hurl/throw ~ to the winds; to sound a note of ~; a word of ~; to err on the side of ~

caution II *v.* 1. (D; tr.) to ~ about, against (they ~ed us against drinking the water) 2. (H) she ~ed us not to go 3. (L; may have an object) they ~ed (us) that we should not drink the water

cautious *adj.* 1. ~ about, of (he was ~ about committing himself; she was ~ of strangers) 2. ~ in (~ in using firearms) 3. ~ with (be ~ with them)

cavalry *n.* 1. to commit ~ 2. heavy; light ~

cave *n.* 1. to explore a ~ 2. a deep ~

cave in *v.* (D; intr.) to ~ to (they finally ~d in to our demands)

cavil *v.* (formal) (D; intr.) to ~ at

cavity *n.* 1. to fill a ~ (in a tooth) 2. the abdominal; chest; oral ~

cease I *n.* without ~

cease II *v.* 1. (E) the old empire has ~d to exist 2. (G) the company has ~d trading

cease-fire *n.* 1. to broker, mediate, negotiate a ~ 2. to declare; sign; work out a ~ 3. to honor, observe a ~ 4. to break, violate a ~ 5. a temporary ~ 6. the ~ has gone into effect; the ~ is holding

cede *v.* (A) France ~d the territory to them; or: France ceded them the territory

ceiling *n.* ["upper limit"] 1. to place, put, set a ~ (on prices) 2. to lower; raise a ~ 3. to abolish, lift a ~ (on prices) 4. a high; low ~ 5. a price; rent ~ 6. a glass ~ ("invisible ceiling") ["top of a room"] 7. a high; low ~ ["misc."] 8. (slang) to hit the ~ (AE; CE has *roof*) ("to lose one's temper")

celebrate *v.* 1. to ~ formally; joyously; noisily; officially; privately; publicly; quietly; solemnly 2. (misc.) to ~ in style

celebrated *adj.* 1. ~ as (~ as a painter) 2. ~ for (~ for scientific research)

celebration *n.* 1. to have, hold a ~ 2. a joyous; noisy ~ 3. a private; quiet ~ 4. a centenary (esp. BE), centennial (esp. AE); formal; official; public; religious; solemn ~

celebrity *n.* ["famous person"] 1. a film, Hollywood; international; literary; local; national; visiting ~ 2. (misc.) a host of ~ties

celery *n.* 1. crisp ~ 2. a bunch; stalk of ~

celibacy *n.* 1. to practice ~ 2. (misc.) to make/take a vow of ~

cell *n.* ["cubicle, small room"] 1. a jail, prison; monk's; nun's; padded ~ ["small mass of protoplasm"] 2. to form a ~ 3. a blood; cancer; egg; germ; nerve; sperm ~ ["receptacle containing electrodes and an electrolyte"] 4. a dry; photoelectric; primary; voltaic ~ ["smallest unit of an organization"] 5. to form a ~ 6. a local; party ~

cellar *n.* a cyclone, storm (AE); wine ~

cellophane *n.* to wrap smt. in ~

cement I *n.* 1. to mix; pour ~ 2. Portland ~ 3. ~ sets

cement II *v.* to ~ smt. in, into place; to ~ smt. together

cemetery *n.* 1. a military; national ~ 2. at, in a ~ (she works at/in the ~; to be buried in a ~)

censor I *n.* a government; military ~

censor II *v.* (D; tr.) ("to remove") (AE) to ~ from (the figures were ~ed from the report)

censorship *n.* 1. to impose, introduce ~ 2. to exercise, practice ~ 3. to abolish, lift ~ 4. rigid, strict ~ 5. film; government(al); military; press ~ 6. ~ of, over

censure I *n.* 1. bitter, strong; public ~ 2. to come under ~ 3. (misc.) a vote of ~

censure II *v.* 1. to ~ bitterly, strongly 2. (D; tr.) to ~

as (they were ~d as traitors) 3. (D; tr.) to ~ for (the senator was ~d for income tax evasion)

census *n.* 1. to conduct, take a ~ 2. a national; traffic (BE) ~ 3. at, in a ~ (at the last ~)

cent *n.* (colloq.) (AE) not to have a red ~ ("to have no money at all")

center I centre *n.* ["middle"] 1. dead ~ 2. at, in the ~ (at the ~ of a circle) ["central point"] 3. a storm ~ (also fig.) 4. at, in a ~ (at the ~ of operations; right in the ~ of activity) ["location where an activity takes place; focus of activity"] 5. an amusement; leisure (BE); sports ~ 6. a community; senior-citizen; social ~ 7. a cultural; literary; music ~ 8. a civic; conference; convention ~ 9. a service; shopping ~ 10. a birthing (AE), childbearing (AE); crisis; day-care; health; medical ~ 11. a research; science ~ 12. a banking; business, commercial; fashion; financial; industrial; manufacturing; trade; wine-producing ~ 13. a communications; information ~ 14. a job (BE) ~ 15. a remand (BE) ~ 16. (mil.) a separation ~ 17. (fig.) a nerve; storm ~ 18. a national; world ~ ["group of nerve cells"] 19. a nerve ~ ["political position"] 20. to move (away) from the ~; to move to the ~ 21. left of ~; right of ~

center II centre *v.* (d; intr., tr.) to ~ around, on, round (BE) upon (attention ~ed on their opening statements)

USAGE NOTE: Some purists reject *to center around/round* as incorrect or illogical.

center stage *n.* 1. to take ~ 2. at ~

central *adj.* (cannot stand alone) ~ to (such values are ~ to our way of life)

century *n.* 1. from; to a ~ (from the fifth to the tenth ~) 2. in a ~ (in the ninth ~) 3. over, through the ~ries 4. (misc.) at the turn of the ~

cereal *n.* 1. to cook, make (AE), prepare ~ 2. breakfast; cooked, hot (AE); dry ~ 3. a bowl of ~ (see also **porridge**)

ceremony *n.* ["formal act"] 1. to conduct, hold, perform a ~ 2. to participate in a ~ 3. to attend a ~ 4. an awards; flag-raising; graduation; inaugural; initiation; swearing-in; welcoming; wreath-laying ~ 5. a funeral; marriage, wedding; religious (to perform a religious ~) ~ 6. a formal; solemn; special ~ 7. a private; public ~ 8. a closing; opening ~ 9. at a ~ ["formality"] 10. to stand on ~ 11. appropriate; great ~ 12. with ~ (with appropriate ~) 13. without ~ (they all pitched in without ~)

certain *adj.* 1. to make ~ 2. absolutely, completely, totally; almost, nearly; quite; very ~ 3. far from ~ 4. for ~ 5. ~ about, of (we were ~ of his support) 6. ~ to + inf. (she is ~ to agree) 7. ~ that; where; who + clause (it is ~ that they will sign the contract; make ~ that all doors are locked; are you ~ that you turned the gas off? are you ~ where the ceremony will be held? are you ~ who will deliver the speech?)

certainly *adv.* 1. almost ~ 2. (misc.) ~ not

certainty *n.* 1. to express ~ 2. absolute, dead; mathematical; moral ~ 3. ~ of (there is no ~ of success) 4. ~ that + clause (there is no ~ that an agreement will be reached) 5. with ~ (to state with ~) 6. (misc.) to know smt. for a ~

certificate *n.* 1. to issue a ~ 2. to cash (in) a ~ 3. a baptismal; birth; death; marriage; medical ~ 4. a money-market; savings; stock; tax-free; treasury ~ 5. a gift ~ 6. a teaching ~ (you cannot teach in this state without a teaching ~) 7. (BE) a school ~

certification *n.* 1. to grant ~ 2. to receive ~ 3. ~ as (he was granted ~ as a kindergarten teacher) 4. ~ in (she has her ~ in critical care nursing)

certify *v.* 1. (D; tr.) to ~ as (he has been ~fied as a critical care nurse; the psychiatrist ~fied him as insane) 2. (D; tr.) to ~ in (she has been ~fied in physical training) 3. (L) she ~fied that it was a true copy 4. (M) can you ~ this to be a true copy? 5. (N; used with an adjective) he was ~fied insane

certitude *n.* 1. absolute, complete, utter ~ 2. ~ that + clause (it is with ~ that I can attest to her good character)

chafe *v.* (d; intr.) to ~ at, under (to ~ at the delay; to ~ under restrictions)

chaff *n.* to separate the (wheat from the) ~ (by threshing or winnowing) (also fig.)

chagrin *n.* 1. to express; feel ~ 2. deep, profound ~ 3. ~ at (to feel ~ at being rejected) 4. ~ that + clause (she expressed her ~ that the bill had been voted down) 5. to smb.'s ~ (to my great ~, the plan did not work)

chagrined *adj.* 1. ~ at (~ at being rejected) 2. ~ to + inf. (she was ~ to learn of the outcome) 3. ~ that + clause (we are ~ that the meeting cannot take place)

chain I *n.* ["series of metal links"] 1. to keep (a dog) on a ~ 2. to put ~s on (the tires of a car) 3. to wear a (gold) ~ (around one's neck) 4. a bicycle; tire ~ 5. a ~ clanks, jangles 6. a link in a ~ ["measuring instrument"] 7. an engineer's; surveyor's ~ ["shackles"] 8. in ~s (the prisoners were in ~s) ["group of associated enterprises"] 9. a department-store; hotel; restaurant ~ ["type of locking device"] 10. to put the ~ on the door ["misc."] 11. to form a human ~; to pull the ~ (BE) ("to flush the toilet"); the food ~ ("the hierarchy of living beings in which each one feeds on the one below")

chain II *v.* (D; tr.) to ~ to (to ~ a dog to a fence)

chair *n.* ["piece of furniture for sitting"] 1. a camp (BE), folding; cane; deck; easy; high; occasional; reclining; rocking; swivel ~ ["professorship"] 2. to endow; establish a ~ 3. to be appointed to, get, receive a ~ 4. to have, hold, occupy a ~ 5. to give up, relinquish a ~ 6. a university ~ ["position of chairperson"] 7. (esp. BE) to occupy; take the ~ 8. a rotating; temporary ~ ["chairperson"] 9. to address one's questions to the ~ [misc.] 10. an electric ~ ("a device for executing criminals")

chairman *n.* 1. a department(al) ~ 2. ~ of the board USAGE NOTE: BE also has *department head, head of (the) department* (in an educational institution); in order to promote non-sexist language, the terms *chair* or *chairperson* are used more and more in place of *chairman* or *chairwoman*.

chairperson see **chairman** 1

chairwoman see **chairman** 1

chalet *n.* a Swiss ~

chalk *n.* 1. to write with ~ (on a blackboard) 2. a piece, stick (BE) of ~

chalkboard *n.* (AE) see **blackboard**

chalk up *v.* 1. (d; tr.) to ~ against (to ~ ten victories against two defeats) 2. (D; tr.) to ~ for (to ~ another victory for our team) 3. (d; tr.) to ~ to (to ~ smt. up to experience/lack of experience)

challenge I *n.* ["dare"] 1. to issue, send a ~ 2. to mount, pose a ~ (to) 3. to accept, respond to, take up a ~ (from) 4. to face, meet a ~; rise to a ~ 5. a direct; formidable, real, serious ~ 6. a ~ to (it was a ~ to our very existence) 7. a ~ to + inf. (it was a ~ just to survive) ["demand for identification"] (usu. mil.) 8. to give the ~ (the sentry gave the ~) ["objection to a prospective juror"] (legal) 9. a peremptory ~ (to use one's peremptory ~)

challenge II *v.* 1. (D; tr.) to ~ for (I ~d her for the championship) 2. (D; tr.) to ~ on (to ~ the government on its policies) 3. (D; tr.) to ~ to (to ~ smb. to a duel) 4. (H) he ~d me to fight

challenger *n.* 1. to take on a ~ 2. a formidable, strong; serious ~

chamber *n.* ["hall used by a legislative body"] 1. the lower; upper ~ 2. an assembly; council; parliamentary; senate ~ ["room"] ["compartment"] 3. a gas; torture ~ 4. a combustion; decompression ~ ["misc."] 5. to hold a trial in ~s (without spectators or the press)

chameleon *n.* ~s change their color

champ *v.* 1. (d; intr.) to ~ at (to ~ at the bit) 2. (E) they were ~ing to get home

champagne *n.* 1. to drink; quaff; sip ~ 2. a bottle; glass of ~

champion *n.* a defending; national; world ~

championship *n.* ["position of a champion"] 1. to hold; win a ~ 2. to regain; retain a ~ 3. to give up, lose, relinquish a ~ 4. an individual; national; team; world ~

championships *n.* ["contest"] 1. to hold ~ 2. (the) national; world ~

chance I *n.* ["opportunity"] ["possibility"] 1. to have, stand a ~ of (she has a good ~ of success; he doesn't have a/the ghost of a ~) 2. to give smb. a ~ 3. to let a ~ slip by; to miss one's ~; to pass up a ~ 4. a fighting; good; strong ~ 5. an even, fifty-fifty; fair; sporting ~ (he has an even ~ of being elected)

6. a faint, fat (colloq.), outside, poor, slight, slim, small ~ 7. a last; only ~ 8. little ~ (there is little ~ of that happening) 9. a ~ against (she doesn't stand a ~ against such strong competitors) 10. a ~ at, for, of (a ~ for success) 11. a ~ to + inf. (she had a ~ to visit her family) 12. a ~ that + clause (there is no ~ that she will win) ["luck"] 13. to take a ~ on ("to try one's luck at") 14. to leave smt. to ~ 15. pure, sheer ~ 16. a lucky ~ 17. by ~ (it was by pure ~ that we met) ["misc."] 18. (the) ~s are that they will not come

chance II *v.* 1. (d; intr.) to ~ on, upon ("to find by chance") (to ~ upon a rare item) 2. (formal) (E) ("to happen") I ~d to be there when they arrived

chandelier *n.* a crystal ~

change I *n.* ["alteration"] ["transition"] 1. to bring about, effect, make a ~ 2. to propose a ~ 3. to undergo (a) ~ 4. an abrupt, quick, sudden ~ 5. a complete, dramatic, drastic, great, major, marked, momentous, profound, radical, significant, striking, sweeping ~ 6. a discernible, visible ~ 7. a long overdue, (much) needed, welcome ~ 8. (a) little, minor, slight ~ (we noticed a slight ~ in her condition; there was little ~ in his condition) 9. cultural; economic; political; social ~ 10. a ~ occurs, takes place 11. a ~ for (a ~ for the better) 12. a ~ from; into, to (the ~ from spring to summer) 13. a ~ in, of (a ~ of direction; a ~ of heart; a ~ of pace; a ~ in the weather; ~s in personnel; a ~ of diet; the ~ of seasons) 14. for a ~ (let's eat out for a ~) ["money returned"] ["metal coins"] 15. to count out; give; make ~ for (can you give me ~ for a pound?) 16. to count; get one's ~ 17. to keep the ~ 18. loose; small; spare ~ 19. (misc.) could you spare a little ~, sir? ["change of clothing"] 20. to make a ~ 21. a quick ~ (to make a quick ~)

change II *v.* 1. to ~ beyond all recognition; to ~ completely, drastically, greatly, radically; suddenly 2. (C) ("to exchange") could you ~ a dollar for me? or: could you ~ me a dollar? 3. (D; intr.) ("to transfer") to ~ for (we must ~ at the next station for Chicago) 4. (D; tr.) ("to exchange") to ~ for (to ~ dollars for pounds) 5. (D; intr.) ("to put on different clothes") to ~ for (to ~ for dinner) 6. (D; intr., tr.) ("to be transformed; to transform") to ~ from; into (the disease ~d him from an athlete into an invalid; to ~ dollars into pounds) 7. (D; intr., tr.) ("to transfer") to ~ from; to (we must ~ from the local to an express; she ~d the appointment to Monday) 8. (D; intr.) ("to put on different clothes") to ~ into (to ~ into smt. less formal) 9. (D; intr., tr.) ("to turn into") to ~ to (the light ~d to green; my mood ~d from despair to hope) 10. (D; tr.) ("to exchange") to ~ with (I would not want to ~ places with her)

change back *v.* 1. (d; intr.) to ~ from; to (they ~d back to peacetime production) 2. (d; intr.) to ~ into

(we ~d back into casual wear)

changeover *n.* 1. a complete, radical, thorough, total ~ 2. a ~ from; to (a ~ from a peacetime to a war economy)

change over *v.* (d; intr.) to ~ from; to (the country ~d over to a war economy; to ~ to the decimal system)

changer *n.* a coin; record ~

channel I *n.* 1. to change ~s 2. a cable; television, TV ~

channel II *v.* 1. (D; tr.) to ~ into (we had to ~ their energy into useful activities) 2. (D; tr.) to ~ towards (we must ~ our efforts towards worthy goals)

channels *n.* 1. diplomatic; military; (the) regular, usual ~ 2. through ~ (he sent his request for transfer through regular ~; to go through ~) 3. (misc.) ~ of communication

chaos *n.* 1. to cause, create ~ 2. complete, total, utter ~ 3. economic; political; social ~ 4. ~ ensues, results 5. a state of ~

chap *n.* (colloq.) a decent, fine, good, nice ~

chapel *n.* ["place of worship"] 1. (a) hospital; military; prison; ship's ~ 2. interdenominational, nondenominational ~ ["Nonconformist place of worship"] (BE) (used as an adjective) 3. are you church or ~?

chaperon, chaperone I *n.* to serve as a ~ (to serve as a ~ at a dance)

chaperon, chaperone II *v.* (D; tr.) to ~ to (we will ~ the students to the theater)

chaplain *n.* a college, university; hospital; military; prison; school; ship's ~

chapter *n.* 1. a closing ~ 2. an introductory, opening ~ 3. a ~ about, on 4. (misc.) a closed ~ (in one's life) ["smt. that belongs to the past"]; to quote ~ and verse ("to cite the exact source or give lots of details")

character *n.* ["personality"] ["behavior"] 1. to build, form, mold smb.'s ~ 2. smb.'s moral; true ~ 3. an excellent, fine, good; impeccable, irreproachable, stainless, unblemished; upright ~ 4. a firm, strong ~ 5. a lovable ~ 6. a bad, disreputable, unsavory ~ 7. a weak ~ 8. the national ~ (their recent actions are not in keeping with their national ~) 9. of ~ (a person of good ~) 10. (misc.) defamation of ~ ["person in a fictitious work"] 11. to play, portray a ~ 12. to create; delineate, depict, draw; develop a ~ 13. to kill off a ~ 14. a fictitious; historical ~ 15. a leading, main, major, principal; minor, supporting ~ 16. in ~; out of ~ (his behavior was in ~ with his upbringing; her actions were out of ~) ["person, esp. dubious or eccentric"] 17. a colorful; curious, strange, weird; unforgettable ~ 18. a dangerous; disreputable, seedy, shady; suspicious; tough; underworld ~ ["letter, figure"] 19. to form, trace; write ~s 20. Arabic; Chinese; cunei-

form; Cyrillic; Greek; Hebrew; Latin; mathematical; special ~s ["nature, special quality"] 21. to have a ~ of its/one's own 22. an official; political; subversive; unofficial ~ (the statements were of a political ~) 23. (misc.) this is a quaint town with a lot of ~

characteristic I *adj.* 1. ~ of 2. ~ to + inf. (it was ~ of them to answer their correspondence promptly)

characteristic II *n.* 1. a distinctive, marked; distinguishing, identifying; dominant, outstanding; unique ~ 2. a family; individual; national ~ 3. facial; physical ~s

characterize *v.* (d; tr.) ("to describe") to ~ as (he can be ~d as a fanatic/as fanatical)

charades *n.* to play ~

charcoal *n.* 1. to burn ~ 2. activated ~

charge I *n.* ["accusation"] 1. to bring, file, level, make a ~; to prefer, press ~s 2. to concoct, cook up, fabricate, trump up a ~ (they trumped up various ~s against her) 3. to prove, substantiate a ~ 4. to answer; face a ~ (of) 5. to dismiss, throw out a ~ (the judge dismissed all ~s) 6. to drop, retract, withdraw a ~ 7. to deny; refute; repudiate a ~ 8. a baseless, fabricated, false, trumped-up; frivolous ~ 9. a civil; criminal ~ 10. a ~ against smb. (to bring a ~ of forgery against smb.) 11. a ~ that (he denied the ~ that he had taken bribes) 12. on a ~ of (he was arraigned on a ~ of embezzlement; to be arrested on various ~s) ["attack"] 13. to lead; make a ~ against 14. to sound the ~ 15. to fight off, repel, repulse a ~ 16. a bayonet; cavalry; infantry ~ ["explosive"] 17. to set off a ~ 18. a depth ~ ["responsibility"] 19. to place, put smb. in ~ of smt. 20. to take ~ of smt. 21. to be in ~ of smt. ["custody"] 22. in smb.'s ~ (the child was in my ~) ["cost"] ["price"] 23. to make a ~ 24. to reverse, transfer (BE) (the) ~s (when telephoning) 25. an exorbitant, unreasonable; reasonable ~ 26. an admission; carrying; cover; minimum; service ~; interest ~s; shipping ~s 27. a ~ against, to (a ~ to smb.'s account) 28. a ~ for (there will be no ~ for installation) 29. (misc.) free of ~ ["infusion of stored energy"] 30. to give (a battery) a ~ 31. an electric; quick; slow ~ ["thrill"] (slang) 32. to give smb. a big ~ 33. to get a ~ out of smt. 34. an emotional ~ ["instructions"] 35. to give one's ~ (the judge gave her ~ to the jury) 36. a ~ to (the judge's ~ to the jury)

charge II *v.* 1. ("to ask in payment") to ~ double 2. (D; intr.) ("to rush") to ~ across (they ~d across the field) 3. (D; intr.) ("to rush") to ~ at, towards (the bull ~d at us) 4. (d; intr.) ("to ask payment") to ~ for (they didn't ~ for it) 5. (D; intr., tr.) to ~ for ("to ask in payment") (they ~d ten dollars for shipping our books; he ~s by the hour for laying a carpet) 6. (d; intr.) ("to rush") to ~ into; out of (to ~ into a room) 7. (D; tr.) to ~ out of ("to borrow from") (to

~ a book out of a library) 8. (D; tr.) ("to impose as an obligation") to ~ to (~ it to my account) 9. (D; tr.) ("to accuse") to ~ with (he was ~d with murder) 10. (D; tr.) ("to suffuse") to ~ with (the air was ~d with tension) 11. (D; tr.) ("to assign") to ~ with (our agency has been ~d with the responsibility of gathering all pertinent information) 12. (L) ("to accuse") they ~d that he had cheated them 13. (O; may be used with one object) ("to ask payment") she ~d (me) fifty dollars for her services; how much did he ~? did they ~ you? they ~d me three hundred dollars rent

chargeable *adj.* ~ to

charge ahead *v.* (D; intr.) to ~ with (they ~d ahead with the project)

charged *adj.* 1. emotionally; highly ~ 2. ~ with (emotion)

charisma *n.* 1. to have ~ 2. personal ~ 3. of great ~

charitable *adj.* 1. ~ towards 2. ~ to + inf. (it was ~ of her to say that)

charity *n.* 1. to dispense, distribute, give ~ to 2. to bestow ~ on, upon 3. to accept; receive ~ 4. to ask for, beg for, plead for ~ 5. an act of ~ 6. ~ for (~ for the needy) 7. (misc.) (proverb) ~ begins at home

charm I *n.* ["amulet"] 1. to wear a ~ 2. a good-luck, lucky ~ ["attractive quality"] 3. to turn on, use one's ~ 4. to exude, ooze ~ 5. to have, possess ~ 6. to lend ~ to 7. great, irresistible; natural; particular, special; unfailing ~ 8. the ~ to + inf. (she has enough ~ to win anyone over) ["misc."] 9. it works like a ~ ("it works perfectly")

charm II *v.* (D; tr.) to ~ into (she ~ed him into agreeing)

charmed *adj.* ~ to + inf. (I would be ~ to accept your invitation)

charmer *n.* 1. (to be) a real ~ 2. a snake ~

charming *adj.* 1. ~ to (she is ~ to everyone) 2. ~ to + inf. (it was ~ to watch them)

chart I *n.* 1. to compile a ~ 2. an aeronautical; bar; clinical; eye; flip; flow; genealogical; pie; statistical; wall ~

chart II *v.* (D; tr.) to ~ for (he has ~ed a difficult course for us)

charter *n.* 1. to apply for a ~ 2. to take out a ~ 3. to grant a ~ 4. to revoke a ~ 5. a ~ to + inf. (the company was granted a ~ to trade in the occupied territory)

chary *adj.* 1. ~ about (~ about doing smt.) 2. ~ of (~ of strangers)

chase I *n.* 1. to give ~ to 2. to abandon, give up the ~ 3. a car; police ~ 4. a wild-goose ~ 5. in ~ of (in full ~) 6. (misc.) (AE) to lead smb. a merry ~ (BE has *to lead smb. a merry dance*)

chase II *v.* 1. (d; intr.) to ~ after (to ~ after fame) 2. (D; tr.) to ~ from, out of (~ the dog out of our yard!) 3. (P; intr., tr.) they ~d the children into the barn; the police ~d the suspect through the park;

we ~d across the field into the station

chaser *n.* 1. a submarine ~ 2. (misc.) (colloq.) an ambulance ~ (esp. AE) ("a lawyer who seeks clients among accident victims"); whiskey with a beer ~ ("whiskey served with a glass of beer")

chasm *n.* 1. to bridge a ~ 2. a deep; gaping, yawning ~ 3. a ~ between

chat I *n.* 1. to have a ~ 2. a friendly, nice, pleasant; little ~ 3. a ~ about; with (we had a pleasant ~ with them about our new grandchild) 4. a ~ between

chat II *v.* (D; intr.) to ~ about; to (BE), with

chatter I *n.* constant, endless, idle, incessant ~

chatter II *v.* 1. ("to talk fast") to ~ constantly, endlessly, incessantly 2. (D; intr.) ("to talk fast") to ~ about 3. (D; intr.) ("to click") to ~ from, with (his teeth were ~ing with the cold)

chauvinist *n.* a male ~

cheap *adj.* 1. (colloq.) dirt ~ 2. to come ~ (those new cars don't come ~) 3. ~ to + inf. (it's not ~ to live in the city; it is ~er to live in the south than in the north) 4. (misc.) to hold life ~

cheat I *n.* 1. a downright; notorious ~ 2. a tax ~

cheat II *v.* 1. (D; intr., tr.) to ~ at (to ~ at cards) 2. (D; intr.) to ~ on ("to be unfaithful to") (to ~ on one's wife) 3. (D; tr.) to ~ out of (he ~ed us out of our money) 4. (misc.) to ~ on an examination

check I *n.* ["order to a bank"] (BE has *cheque*) 1. to issue, make out, write (out) a ~ to 2. to draw a ~ against one's account; to draw a ~ on a bank 3. to cancel; cash; clear; deposit; honor; present a ~ 4. to cover a ~ (by making a deposit) 5. to endorse; negotiate; sign a ~ 6. to pass a (bad) ~; to kite a ~ (AE) ("to write a bad ~"); to raise ("increase fraudulently") a ~ 7. to stop payment of, on a ~ 8. a bad ("not covered"); blank; cashier's; certified; crossed (BE) ~; Eurocheque; negotiable; traveler's ~ 9. a ~ bounces; clears 10. by ~ (to pay by ~) ["verification"] ["control"] 11. to conduct, do, make, run a ~ of, on 12. a background; bed; loyalty; safety, security; spot ~ (to run a background ~ on all new employees) ["endangered position of the king"] (chess) 13. to give ~; to put into ~ 14. to discover ~ 15. discovered; perpetual ~ 16. in ~ (your king is in ~) ["bill in a restaurant"] (AE) 17. to pay the ~, pick up the ~ ["token of ownership, of a right"] (esp. AE) 18. a baggage; claim; hat ~ 19. a rain ~ ["blocking of an opponent"] (ice hockey) 20. a board; body; hook ~ ["restraint"] 21. to hold, keep in ~

check II *v.* 1. (D; intr.) to ~ into ("to verify") (to ~ into smb.'s story) 2. (d; intr.) to ~ into ("to register at") (to ~ into a hotel) 3. (d; intr.) to ~ on ("to verify") (to ~ on smb.'s story) 4. (d; intr.) to ~ out of ("to announce one's departure from") (to ~ out of a hotel) 5. (d; tr.) to ~ out of ("to borrow from") (she ~ed the book out of the library) 6. (D; intr.) to ~ through ("to look through") (to ~ through the files) 7. (esp. AE) (d; tr.) to ~ through to ("to register as far as") (she ~ed her suitcase through to Chicago) 8. (D; intr.) ("to verify") to ~ with (I'll ~ with the porter)

checkbook *n.* 1. to balance a ~ 2. to reconcile a ~ with (a bank statement)

checkers *n.* (AE) (BE has *draughts*) 1. to play ~ 2. Chinese ~ (BE has *Chinese chequers*)

check in *v.* (D; intr.) to ~ at (to ~ at a hotel)

checking account *n.* (AE) (BE has *current account*) to balance a ~ (every month)

checklist *n.* 1. to compile, make up a ~ 2. to go down, go through a ~

check out *v.* (D; tr.) ("to borrow") to ~ from (she ~ed out a book from the library)

checkpoint *n.* at a ~ (we were stopped at a ~)

checkup *n.* 1. to do, give a ~ (the doctor gave me a thorough ~) 2. to have a ~ (I had a ~ at the hospital yesterday) 3. an annual; periodic ~ 4. a careful; thorough ~ 5. a general; regular ~

check up *v.* (D; intr.) to ~ on (to ~ on smb.'s story)

cheek *n.* ["side of the face"] 1. to puff (out) one's ~s 2. burning, flushed; dimpled; chubby, full, rounded; hollow, sunken; pale; rosy, ruddy ~s ["impudence"] (colloq.) 3. the ~ to + inf. (she had the ~ to phone me at home) ["misc."] 4. to turn the other ~ ("to refuse to respond to an attack or insult"); with tongue in ~ ("not seriously")

cheekbones *n.* high, prominent ~

cheeky *adj.* (colloq.) ["impudent"] ~ to + inf. (it was ~ of her to phone you at home)

cheer I *n.* ["rallying cry"] ["cry of approval"] 1. to give, shout a ~ (let's give him three ~s) 2. to draw a ~ (her performance drew ~s) 3. to acknowledge the ~s (of the crowd) 4. a jubilant; loud, resounding, ringing, rousing ~ 5. (AE) a school ~ (let's give the school ~!) 6. a ~ rang out; a ~ went up ["good mood"] 7. Christmas; good ~ 8. of ~ (to be of good ~)

cheer II *v.* 1. to ~ enthusiastically, loudly 2. (D; intr.) to ~ for (they ~ed loudly for their team) 3. (misc.) they ~ed themselves hoarse

cheerful *adj.* ~ about (they are ~ about the future)

cheese *n.* 1. to slice ~ 2. cream; grated; grilled (AE), toasted (BE); hard; mild; processed; semi-soft; sharp; smoked; soft ~ 3. a piece, slice of ~ 4. (misc.) (colloq.) say ~! ("smile"!)

chemistry *n.* ["science that deals with substances"] 1. analytical; inorganic; organic; physical ~ ["personal feelings"] (colloq.) 2. personal ~; the right; wrong ~ 3. the ~ between

cheque (BE) see **check I**, 1-10

chequebook (BE) see **checkbook**

chess *n.* 1. to play ~ 2. (misc.) a ~ game; match; a ~ master

chest *n.* ["thorax"] 1. to beat; throw out one's ~ (with pride) 2. a barrel ~ ["box"] 3. a hope (AE;

BE has *bottom drawer*); ice; medicine; silver; tool; treasure ~

chestnuts *n.* 1. to roast ~ 2. (misc.) to pull smb.'s ~ out of the fire ("to extricate smb. from an unpleasant situation")

chew *v.* 1. (D; intr.) to ~ on (to ~ on bread) 2. (d; intr.) to ~ through (the mouse ~ed through the wall) 3. (D; intr., tr.) to ~ with (she had difficulty ~ing the steak with her new dentures)

chewing gum *n.* a piece; stick of ~

chic I *adj.* ["fashionable"] ~ to + inf. (it's very ~ to give up smoking)

chic II *n.* 1. an indefinable ~ 2. designer; radical ~

chick *n.* 1. to hatch ~s 2. ~s cheep 3. a brood, clutch of ~s

chicken I *n.* 1. ~s cluck 2. a brood of ~s 3. a young ~ is a chick 4. a female ~ is a hen 5. a young, female ~ is a pullet 6. a male ~ is a cock (esp. BE)/ rooster (esp. AE) 7. a young, male ~ is a cockerel (esp. BE); a male, castrated ~ is a capon 8. (as food) baked; barbecued; broiled (AE), grilled; fried; roast; stewed ~ 9. (misc.) to count one's ~s before they are hatched ("to rejoice prematurely")

chicken II *v.* (colloq.) (d; intr.) to ~ out of ("to abandon") (to ~ out of an agreement)

chickenpox *n.* to catch (the) ~, come down with (the) ~, get (the) ~

chide *v.* (D; tr.) to ~ for

chief *n.* 1. an Indian ~ 2. a fire (AE); police (AE) ~ 3. a tribal ~

chieftain *n.* a clan; tribal ~

child *n.* 1. to adopt; bear, give birth to, have a ~ (she had four children) 2. to carry a ~ (a mother carries a ~ for nine months) 3. to beget; conceive a ~ 4. to bring up, raise, rear a ~ 5. to feed; nurse; wean a ~ 6. to indulge, pamper, spoil a ~ 7. to toilet-train, train a ~ 8. to acknowledge a ~ (as one's own) 9. to marry off one's ~ 10. an adopted; dependent; foster; illegitimate (old-fashioned); only; unwanted ~ 11. a mischievous; problem (old-fashioned) ~ 12. a pampered, spoiled ~ 13. a good, well-behaved ~ 14. a bright, gifted, intelligent ~ 15. a precocious; young ~ 16. a handicapped (old-fashioned); retarded (old-fashioned) ~ 17. a flower ~ (of the 1960s); a latchkey (who comes home to an empty house) ~ 18. a happy; loving; well-cared for ~ 19. an abused, mistreated; disadvantaged; neglected ~ 20. a ~ develops, grows (into adulthood) 21. (misc.) to be with ~ (old-fashioned) ("to be pregnant"); to bus children (to school)

childbirth *n.* 1. natural; prepared ~ 2. in ~ (she died in ~)

childhood *n.* 1. to spend one's ~ (somewhere) 2. smb.'s second ~ 3. a happy; repressed; unhappy ~ 4. in smb.'s ~ (in smb.'s early ~) 5. since ~

childish *adj.* ~ to + inf. (it was ~ of him to do that)

child's play *n.* (colloq.) ["easy task"] 1. ~ to (that's

~ to her) 2. ~ to + inf. (it was ~ to solve that riddle)

chill I *n.* 1. (fig.) to cast a ~ on, over 2. to catch; feel a ~ 3. to take the ~ off (take the ~ off the milk) 4. (misc.) there was a (sudden) ~ in our relations; her words sent a ~ through me

chill II *v.* 1. (C) ~ a glass for me; or (rare): ~ me a glass 2. (misc.) ~ed to the bone

chills *n.* 1. to have, get the ~ 2. (misc.) to send ~ up and down smb.'s spine ("to frighten smb.")

chime in *v.* (D; intr.) to ~ with (to ~ with one's opinion)

chimes *n.* 1. to sound ~ 2. organ ~ 3. ~ sound

chimney *n.* 1. smoke goes up a ~ 2. smoke comes out of a ~ 3. ~s belch smoke 4. the ~ draws well 5. a tall ~

chin *n.* 1. a double; smooth ~ 2. a glass ("weak") ~ (of a boxer) 3. (misc.) to keep one's ~ up ("not to become discouraged"); to take it on the ~ ("to suffer a misfortune courageously")

china *n.* ["porcelain"] 1. bone; fine ~ 2. a set of ~

chink *n.* a ~ in smb.'s armor ("a weak point")

chip *n.* ["thin slice"] (AE) 1. a potato ~ (BE has *crisp*) ["semiconductor body"] 2. a computer; integrated-circuit; silicon ~ ["misc."] 3. a bargaining ~ ("smt. that can be used to win concessions"); a ~ off the old block ("a child who resembles its parent"); to have a ~ on one's shoulder ("to harbor resentment")

chip away *v.* (d; intr.) to ~ at (to ~ at a rock; the police kept ~ping away at their alibi)

chip in *v.* 1. (D; intr.) to ~ for (they all ~ped in for a present) 2. (D; intr.) to ~ with (we all ~ped in with our suggestions)

chips *n.* ["gambling tokens"] to cash in one's ~ (also fig.) ("to die")

chisel *v.* 1. (D; tr.) ("to shape with a chisel") to ~ from, out of (to ~ smt. from wood) 2. (d; tr.) to ~ into (to ~ wood into smt.) 3. (colloq.) (D; tr.) to ~ out of ("to cheat out of") (he ~ed me out of my money)

chiseled, chiselled *adj.* ["shaped"] finely ~

chitchat *n.* idle ~

chivvy *v.* (colloq.) (BE) ("to nag") 1. (d; tr.) to ~ into (she ~vied me into going) 2. (H) I ~vied them to help

chloroform *n.* to administer, give ~ to

chock-full *adj.* (colloq.) ~ of

chocolate *n.* ["candy, sweet"] 1. bitter; bittersweet; dark; milk ~ 2. a bar of ~ ["beverage"] 3. hot ~ 4. a cup; mug of ~

choice *n.* 1. to exercise, make a ~ 2. to have a ~ 3. a good, happy, intelligent, judicious, wise ~ (she made a good ~) 4. first; second ~ (we had first ~) 5. a bad, poor, sorry, unwise, wrong ~ 6. a careful; difficult ~ 7. a wide ~ (you have a wide ~ of colors) 8. (a) free; individual; limited ~ (to exercise individual ~) 9. a ~ among, between; in; of (a

~ between two jobs; did you have any ~ in the matter? a ~ of colors) 10. by ~ (we did it by ~) 11. (misc.) we have a difficult ~ to make; take your ~; freedom of ~; Hobson's ("no") ~; they had no ~ but to agree; we had little ~ in the matter

choir *n.* 1. to form; lead a ~ 2. to sing in a ~ 3. a church; school ~

choke I *n.* (on a car) 1. to pull out; push in the ~ 2. an automatic; manual ~

choke II *v.* 1. (D; intr.) to ~ on (to ~ on a bone) 2. (d; intr.) to ~ with (to ~ with emotion) 3. (misc.) to ~ to death

choked *adj.* ["blocked"] ~ with (~ with weeds)

choked up *adj.* 1. (all) ~ about (they were all ~ about their friend's loss) 2. (all) ~ with (~ with emotion)

cholera *n.* 1. to contract, get ~ 2. (misc.) a ~ epidemic

cholesterol *n.* 1. to cut down on ~ 2. high; low in ~

chomp *v.* see **champ**

choose *v.* 1. to ~ carefully, judiciously; to ~ at random 2. (C) ~ a book for me; or: ~ me a book 3. (D; intr.) to ~ among, between, from (to ~ between two offers) 4. (D; tr.) to ~ as (they chose her as their spokesperson) 5. (D; intr., tr.) to ~ by (to ~ by lot; to ~ by tossing a coin) 6. (D; tr.) to ~ for (~ a book for me) 7. (D; tr.) to ~ from (they chose us from a large number of candidates) 8. (E) she chose to remain at home 9. (H) they chose me to serve as their representative

choosing *n.* of one's own ~

choosy (also **choosey**, AE) *adj.* (colloq.) ~ about

chop I *n.* ["cut of meat"] 1. a chump (BE); lamb; mutton; pork; veal ~ ["blow"] 2. a karate ~

chop II *v.* 1. (C) ~ some wood for me; or: ~ me some wood 2. (D; tr.) to ~ into (to ~ smt. into bits) 3. (D; tr.) to ~ off (he ~ped a branch off the tree)

chop off *v.* (D; tr.) to ~ from (she ~ped off a branch from the tree)

chopper *n.* a food; meat ~

chopsticks *n.* to use ~

chop up *v.* 1. (C) ~ some wood for me; or (colloq.): ~ me up some wood 2. (D; tr.) to ~ into (he ~ped the log up into firewood)

chord I *n.* ["combination of three or more musical notes"] 1. to play ~s 2. a dominant; major; minor ~

chord II *n.* ["feeling, emotion"] 1. to strike, touch a ~ 2. a popular; responsive, sensitive, sympathetic ~ (to strike a responsive ~)

chores *n.* 1. to do one's ~ 2. daily; domestic, household; routine ~

chortle *v.* 1. (D; intr.) to ~ about, over 2. (D; intr.) to ~ with (to ~ with glee)

chorus *n.* ["group of singers"] 1. a female; male; mixed ~ ["simultaneous utterance"] 2. to join in, swell the ~

chowder *n.* (AE) clam; corn; fish ~

christen v. (N; used with a noun) they ~ed the child Joseph

christening n. to perform a ~

Christian n. a born-again; devout; evangelical; fundamentalist; good; practicing ~

Christmas n. 1. to celebrate ~ 2. to wish smb. a Merry ~ 3. (a) Happy (BE), Merry ~ (to you)! 4. a white ~ 5. at, for, on ~ (we'll get together at ~) 6. on ~ day; on ~ eve

Christmas tree n. to decorate, trim a ~

chronicle n. 1. to keep a ~ 2. a daily; monthly; weekly ~ 3. (misc.) a ~ of events

chuck v. (colloq.) 1. (A) ~ the ball to me; or: ~ me the ball 2. (P; tr.) he ~ed the newspaper into the can 3. (misc.) she ~ed the child under the chin

chuckle I n. 1. to give, let out; have a ~ (we had a good ~) 2. a hearty ~ 3. a ~ about, over

chuckle II v. 1. (D; intr.) to ~ about, at, over 2. (D; intr.) to ~ to (to ~ to oneself) 3. (D; intr.) to ~ with (to ~ with glee)

chuffed adj. (BE) (colloq.) ("happy, pleased") ~ about, at

chum n. (colloq.) a childhood; old; school ~

chummy adj. (colloq.) ["friendly"] ~ with

chum up v. (D; intr.) to ~ with

church n. 1. to consecrate, dedicate a ~ 2. to attend, go to ~ 3. the Catholic; Christian; (Eastern) Orthodox; Protestant; Uniate ~ 4. the Anglican; Baptist; Christian Science; Congregational; Episcopal; Lutheran; Mennonite; Methodist; Mormon; Presbyterian; Seventh Day Adventist; Unitarian ~ 5. an evangelical; fundamentalist ~ 6. (esp. GB) an established ("official"); free ("Nonconformist") ~ 7. (esp. GB) The Church of England; Ireland; Scotland 8. a parish ~ 9. at, in ~ 10. (misc.) to enter, go into the ~ ("to become a member of the clergy")

churlish adj. ~ to + inf. (it would be ~ to offer such petty criticism)

cider n. hard (AE); sweet ~
USAGE NOTE: In GB, cider is typically alcoholic; in the US it is usually non-alcoholic.

cigar n. 1. to light (up); puff on; smoke a ~ 2. a Havana ~

cigarette n. 1. to have; light (up); puff on, smoke a ~ 2. to roll a ~ (he used to roll his own ~s) 3. to extinguish, put out, stub out a ~ 4. a live ~ 5. a filter-tip; king-size; low-tar; mentholated ~ 6. a carton; pack (AE); packet (BE) of ~s

cinch n. (colloq.) ["certainty"] 1. (AE) a ~ to + inf. (she's a ~ to be elected) 2. ~ that + clause (it's a ~ that he'll win)

cinders n. to spread ~ (on a snow-covered road)

cinema n. (BE) 1. to go to the ~ 2. at, in the ~ (she was known for her work in the ~)

cipher n. ["code"] 1. to break, solve a ~ 2. in ~

circle n. ["circular geometric figure"] 1. to describe, draw a ~ 2. to square a ~ (to square a ~ is impossible) 3. the Antarctic; Arctic; polar ~ (at the Arctic ~) 4. the great ~ (on the earth's surface) 5. a traffic ~ (AE; BE has *roundabout*) 6. (sports) the center ~; the winner's ~ (at a racecourse/racetrack) 7. the area; circumference; diameter; radius of a ~ ["group resembling the figure of a circle"] 8. to form a ~ 9. to join a ~ (she joined the ~ of dancers) ["group"] 10. academic; artistic; literary; professional ~s 11. business, financial; court; diplomatic; official; political; ruling ~s 12. exclusive, select; high ~s (to move in the highest ~s) 13. informed, well-informed ~s 14. a charmed ("exclusive"); close, closed, inner, intimate, narrow; wide ~ (a close ~ of friends) 15. a quilting; sewing ~ 16. a family ~ 17. in a ~ (in our ~ of friends; in informed ~s) ["cycle"] 18. to come full ~ ["misc."] 19. a vicious ~ ("an insoluble, never-ending problem"); to go around in ~s ("to keep coming back to the starting point without finding a solution"); a dress ~ ("the first row of raised seats in a theater")

circuit n. ["path of an electric current"] 1. to break; close a ~ 2. a closed; electrical; integrated; printed; short ~ ["route traveled by a judge on tour"] 3. to make a ~ (the judge makes a ~ every year) 4. on ~ (the judge was on ~) ["series of similar events"] 5. the chat-show (BE), talk-show (AE); lecture; rodeo ~

circuit breaker n. to trip a ~

circular n. 1. to send out a ~ 2. to distribute ~s

circulate v. 1. (D; intr., tr.) to ~ among (the host ~d among the guests; to ~ the memo among the staff members) 2. (D; intr., tr.) to ~ through (blood ~s through the body)

circulation n. ["distribution"] 1. to put into ~ (to put more money into ~) 2. to take out of ~; to withdraw from ~ (to withdraw old banknotes from ~) 3. (an) enormous, large, wide; general, unrestricted ~ (this magazine has attained a wide ~) 4. (a) national, nationwide ~ 5. (a) limited, restricted, small ~ 6. in; out of ~ (this money is no longer in ~) 7. (misc.) this journal has a ~ of one hundred thousand ["movement"] 8. blood ~; or: ~ of the blood 9. good, healthy, normal ~ 10. abnormal, poor ~

circumcision n. 1. to do, perform a ~ (on) 2. to undergo ~

circumference n. in ~ (ten feet in ~)

circumspect adj. ~ about; in

circumstances n. 1. favorable; unfavorable ~ 2. adverse, difficult, trying; desperate; tragic ~ 3. reduced, straitened ~ 4. extenuating, mitigating ~ 5. compelling; exceptional, special ~ 6. suspicious ~ (he was apprehended under very suspicious ~) 7. unforeseen ~ 8. a combination of ~ 9. due to ~ (our absence was due to ~ beyond our control) 10. in, under ~ (in certain ~, I would agree; she will not go under any ~; they lived in difficult ~)

circus *n.* 1. to present, put on a ~ 2. to go to the ~ 3. a three-ring; traveling ~ 4. at a ~ 5. (misc.) a three-ring ~ ("hectic activity")

citation *n.* ["attestation"] 1. the earliest ~ (of the use of a word) 2. a ~ from ["summons"] 3. to issue a ~ for 4. a contempt ~ 5. a ~ to + inf. (she received a ~ to appear in court) ["mention of meritorious performance"] (AE) (mil.) 6. to write smb. up for a ~ 7. to receive a ~ (for bravery) (BE has *to be mentioned in dispatches*) 8. a unit ~

cite *v.* 1. (B) she ~d an interesting passage to us 2. (D; tr.) to ~ as (to ~ smt. as an example) 3. (D; tr.) to ~ for (to ~ smb. for bravery) 4. (misc.) to be ~d in divorce proceedings

citizen *n.* 1. a law-abiding; eminent, leading, prominent; respectable, solid, upright, upstanding ~ 2. a senior ~ 3. a private; second-class ~ 4. a native-born (esp. AE); naturalized, new ~

citizenry *n.* an informed ~

citizenship *n.* 1. to grant ~ 2. to apply for ~ 3. to acquire, receive ~ 4. to revoke smb.'s ~ 5. to give up, renounce one's ~ 6. dual ~

city *n.* 1. to govern, manage (AE), run a ~ 2. a big; capital; cosmopolitan; densely populated; garden (BE), planned; major; port; provincial ~ 3. twin ~ties 4. (the) central; inner ~ 5. a beleaguered; open ~ (during wartime) 6. in a ~ (to live in the ~) (see the Usage Note for **town**)

civil *adj.* 1. ~ to (he wasn't even ~ to his guests) 2. (formal) ~ to + inf. (it was ~ of them to offer their help)

civil action *n.* (legal) to bring a ~ (against)

civil disobedience *n.* 1. (to lead) a campaign of ~ 2. an act of ~

civil disorder *n.* 1. to foment, incite, stir up ~ 2. to put down ~

civilian *n.* an innocent; unarmed ~

civilities *n.* to exchange ~

civilization *n.* 1. to introduce; spread ~ 2. to create a ~ 3. to destroy, stamp out (a) ~ 4. an advanced ~ 5. ancient; modern ~ 6. (misc.) the cradle of ~

civil unrest *n.* see **civil disorder**

clad *adj.* ["clothed"] 1. fully; lightly, scantily; partially ~ 2. smartly ~ 3. ~ in (~ in brown)

claim I *n.* 1. to enter, file, lodge, make, put forward, put in, submit a ~ (she filed a ~ for compensation) 2. to authenticate, back up, establish, press, substantiate a ~ 3. to lay ~ to; to stake, stake out a ~ to 4. (esp. AE) to jump ("steal") smb.'s ~ 5. to contest; disallow, dismiss, reject; discredit; dispute a ~ 6. to forfeit; give up, relinquish, renounce, waive, withdraw a ~ 7. to adjudicate; settle a ~ (they settled their ~ out of court) 8. a legal; legitimate; moral; rightful; undisputed ~ 9. an excessive, extravagant, unreasonable ~ 10. an outstanding; prior ~ 11. a fraudulent; specious;

unsubstantiated, unsupported ~ 12. competing, conflicting, rival ~s 13. a disability; insurance ~; pay ~ (BE) 14. a ~ against; for; on; to (she submitted a ~ for damages against the other driver; there are many ~s on my time; he has no ~ to the estate; a ~ to fame) 15. a ~ that + clause (the ~ that he could reduce taxes proved to be false)

claim II *v.* 1. (E) she ~s to own this property 2. (L) he ~s that he was cheated

claimant *n.* a ~ to (a ~ to the estate)

clam *n.* baked ~s

clamber *v.* (P; intr.) to ~ into/onto a bus

clamor, clamour I *n.* 1. an insistent; loud; public ~ 2. a ~ against; for (a ~ against new taxes)

clamor, clamour II *v.* 1. (d; intr.) to ~ for (to ~ for justice) 2. (E) they were ~ing to see the senator

clamp *v.* (d; tr.) to ~ on, upon (to ~ controls on interest rates)

clampdown *n.* a ~ on

clamp down *v.* (D; intr.) to ~ on (to ~ on pickpockets)

clan *n.* a ~ gathers

clang *n.* a metallic ~

clanger *n.* (colloq.) (BE) ("blunder") to drop a ~

clank *v.* to ~ shut

clap I *v.* ("to put") 1. (d; tr.) to ~ into (to ~ smb. into jail) 2. (d; tr.) to ~ on; over (to ~ a muzzle on a dog; she ~ped her hand over her mouth) 3. (d; tr.) to ~ to (he ~ped his hand to his mouth)

clap II *v.* ("to applaud") to ~ loudly

clarification *n.* 1. to provide; seek ~ 2. additional, further ~

clash I *n.* 1. an angry; bitter; bloody; violent ~ 2. an armed; border ~ 3. a ~ between (there was a violent ~ between the two rivals) 4. a ~ with (a ~ with the police)

clash II *v.* 1. (D; intr.) ("to argue") to ~ over 2. (D; intr.) ("to struggle") to ~ with (the demonstrators ~ed with the police) 3. (D; intr.) ("not to match") to ~ with (red ~es with green)

clasp I *n.* a tie ~

clasp II *v.* (d; tr.) to ~ to (she ~ed the baby to her bosom)

class I *n.* ["lesson"] 1. to conduct, hold, teach (a) ~; to give, meet one's ~ 2. to schedule; reschedule a ~ 3. to attend, go to ~; to audit a ~ (AE); to sit in on a ~; take a ~ 4. to cut (esp. AE); miss a ~ 5. to call off, cancel; dismiss a ~ 6. an advanced; beginners'; intermediate ~ (to sit in on an advanced English ~) 7. a ~ in modern drama 8. in ~ (she was in ~ when the message came) ["group"] 9. to form a ~ 10. the educated; leisure; lower; middle; privileged; ruling ~; underclass; upper; working ~ 11. (BE) the chattering ~es 12. a social ~ 13. (misc.) out of one's ~ ("outclassed"); in a ~ of one's own ("unsurpassed"); ~ conflict/struggle ["division of travelers"] 14. business; cabin; economy; first;

second; third; tourist ~ (to travel first-class) ["group of pupils, students graduating together"] (AE) 15. the freshman; junior; senior; sophomore ~

class II see **classify** 1-4

classification *n.* 1. to make a ~ 2. an arbitrary ~

classify *v.* 1. (D; tr.) to ~ according to (the children were ~fied according to age) 2. (D; tr.) to ~ among, under, with 3. (D; tr.) to ~ as (she was ~fied as fit for service; the documents were ~fied as top-secret) 4. (D; tr.) to ~ by (to ~ books by subject) 5. (D; tr.) to ~ into (to ~ the candidates into groups) 6. (N; used with an adjective) to ~ information confidential

clatter *v.* (P; intr.) the cart ~ed over the cobblestones

clause *n.* ["group of words with a subject and predicate"] 1. a conditional; coordinate; dependent, subordinate; independent, main; nominal, noun; nonrestrictive; relative; restrictive; verbless ~ ["provision"] ["article"] 2. (esp. AE) a grandfather ~ ("a clause that exempts those already engaged in an activity prohibited by new legislation") 3. an escalator; penalty ~ 4. a most-favored-nation ~

claw I *n.* 1. to get, sink one's ~s into 2. to retract one's ~s (cats retract their ~s) 3. sharp ~s 4. nonretractile; retractile ~s

claw II *v.* 1. (d; intr.) to ~ at (the cat ~ed at my hand) 2. (misc.) to ~ one's way to the top

claw back *v.* (BE) (D; tr.) to ~ from (to ~ some of the payment from the government)

clay *n.* 1. to knead, model, shape, work ~ 2. to bake; temper ~ 3. modeling; potter's ~ 4. a lump of ~

clean I *adj., adv.* 1. immaculately, spotlessly ~; squeaky-clean 2. to keep smt. ~ 3. (misc.) to come ~ ("to confess"); we're ~ out of food ("we're completely out of food")

clean II *v.* 1. (d; tr.) to ~ from, off (she ~ed the dirt off her shoes) 2. (D; tr.) to ~ out of (the store was ~ed out of cigarettes)

clean break *n.* to make a ~ (with)

clean breast *n.* to make a ~ of smt.

cleaner *n.* ["device"] 1. a pipe; vacuum ~ ["person"] 2. a street; window ~

cleaning *n.* 1. to do the ~ 2. dry ~ 3. a spring; thorough ~

cleanliness *n.* personal ~

cleanse *v.* 1. to ~ thoroughly 2. (D; tr.) to ~ of (to ~ one's thoughts of sin)

cleansing *n.* 1. a thorough ~ 2. ethnic ~

clean up *v.* 1. (D; intr.) to ~ after (he had to ~ after the children) 2. (colloq.) (AE) (D; intr.) ("to make a profit") to ~ on (to ~ on a deal)

clear I *adj.* 1. abundantly, crystal, perfectly; fairly; painfully ~ 2. (cannot stand alone) ~ about (are you ~ about the situation?) 3. ~ from (the answer is

~ from these facts) 4. ~ of (the roads were ~ of snow; to keep ~ of trouble) 5. ~ to (the situation is ~ to everyone) 6. ~ that + clause (it was ~ that they would not come; the teacher made it ~ that discipline would be maintained) 7. (misc.) it is ~ why she came; it is not ~ how he was able to do it; it is not ~ whether they will attend

clear II *n.* ["uncoded language"] 1. in the ~ (to send a message in the ~) ["blameless state"] 2. in the ~ (the investigators decided that she was in the ~)

clear III *v.* 1. (D; tr.) ("to authorize"); ("to prepare") to ~ for (to ~ an article for export; our plane was ~ed for takeoff; to ~ the decks for action) 2. (D; tr.) ("to remove") to ~ from (to ~ the snow from the driveway) 3. (D; tr.) ("to free") to ~ of (to ~ a harbor of mines; to ~ smb. of guilt; to ~ land of trees) 4. (d; intr.) to ~ off ("to clean") (~ off the table so that we can eat) 5. (d; intr.) to ~ off ("to leave") (~ off my land or I'll call the police) 6. (colloq.) (d; intr.) to ~ out of ("to leave") (to ~ out of town) 7. (d; tr.) ("to remove") to ~ out of (to ~ things out of a cupboard) 8. (D; tr.) ("to get authorization for") to ~ with (to ~ a shipment with the authorities; ~ your plan with headquarters) 9. (H) ("to authorize") we were ~ed to land

clearance *n.* ["act of clearing away"] 1. slum ~ ["authorization"] 2. to get, receive; give ~ for 3. customs ~ 4. ~ to + inf. (the control tower gave the pilot ~ to land) ["space between parts"] 5. valve ~ ["certification of eligibility for access to classified material"] 6. to give; receive ~ 7. (a) security ~

clearinghouse *n.* a ~ for (a ~ for information)

clear off *v.* (D; intr.) ("to leave") to ~ of (AE) (~ of my property!)

cleavage *n.* ["division"] a sharp ~ between (a sharp ~ developed between the two factions)

cleave *v.* (formal) (d; intr.) ("to cling") to ~ to (to ~ to old customs)

cleaver *n.* a butcher's; meat ~

clemency *n.* 1. to grant; show ~ 2. to beg for, seek ~ 3. to deny ~

clerk I *n.* 1. a booking ~ (BE; AE has *ticket agent*) 2. (AE) (in a hotel) a desk, room ~ 3. a bank (BE); cipher, code; city (AE), town; court; filing; mail, postal ~; salesclerk (AE; BE has *shop assistant*); shipping; stockroom ~ 4. a junior; senior ~

clerk II *v.* (AE) (D; intr.) (legal) to ~ for (the budding lawyer was ~ing for a prominent judge)

clever *adj.* 1. ~ at, in (she is ~ at arranging furniture) 2. ~ with (he is ~ with his hands) 3. ~ to + inf. (it was ~ of her to think of that)

cliché *n.* 1. a well-worn ~ 2. (misc.) to speak in ~s

click *v.* 1. (on a computer) (D; intr.) to ~ onto 2. (colloq.) (D; intr.) ("to be successful") to ~ with (the new show ~ed with the public)

client *n.* to serve a ~

clientele *n.* 1. to build up, establish a ~ 2. an exclusive, fashionable, select; international ~

cliff *n.* 1. to climb, scale a ~ 2. a rugged; sheer, steep ~

climate *n.* 1. a friendly, hospitable; hostile, inhospitable; invigorating ~ 2. an arctic, frigid; cold; continental; damp; dry; equatorial; hot; humid; maritime; Mediterranean; mild, moderate, temperate; severe; subtropical; tropical; warm; wet ~ 3. (fig.) an economic; political; social ~ 4. (misc.) a change of ~; to create a friendly ~

climax I *n.* 1. to come to, reach a ~ 2. to bring smt. to a ~; to work up to a ~ 3. to mark a ~ 4. a dramatic, thrilling ~ 5. a sexual ~ 6. a ~ to (the ~ to our efforts)

climax II *v.* (d; intr.) to ~ in, with (the convention ~ed with the candidate's acceptance speech)

climb I *n.* an arduous, difficult, hard; easy; gradual; rough, rugged; steep; tortuous ~

climb II *v.* 1. (d; intr.) to ~ aboard (to ~ aboard a raft) 2. (d; intr.) to ~ down (to ~ down a hill) 3. (d; intr.) to ~ into (the children ~ed into their beds) 4. (d; intr.) to ~ onto, upon (the child ~ed onto her mother's lap) 5. (d; intr.) to ~ out of (to ~ out of a pit) 6. (d; intr.) to ~ over (to ~ over a fence) 7. (D; intr.) to ~ to (to ~ to the top) 8. (D; intr.) to ~ up (to ~ up a hill)

climb-down *n.* (BE) ["retreat"] a ~ from (a ~ from an untenable position)

climb down *v.* 1. (D; intr.) to ~ from (to ~ from a tree) 2. (BE) (D; intr.) ("to retreat") to ~ from (to ~ from an untenable position)

climber *n.* 1. a mountain ~ 2. a social ~

climb up *v.* (D; intr.) to ~ to (she ~ed up to the top)

clinch *n.* in a ~

cling *v.* 1. to ~ tenaciously 2. (d; intr.) to ~ to (to ~ to one's possessions; to ~ to old customs; they clung to the floating wreckage; he clung to my arm) 3. (misc.) to ~ together

clinic *n.* 1. to hold a ~ 2. an abortion; animal; antenatal, prenatal; dental; diagnostic; family-planning; mental health; outpatient; postpartum; special; speech; walk-in; well-child (AE) ~ 3. at, in a ~ (she works at the ~)

clip I *n.* ["device to hold cartridges"] 1. to insert a ~ 2. a cartridge ~ ["device that fastens"] 3. a paper; tie ~

clip II *n.* (colloq.) ["speed"] at a ~ (to move at a fast ~)

clip III *v.* 1. (esp. AE) (D; tr.) to ~ from (to ~ articles from a newspaper) 2. (d; tr.) to ~ to (to ~ one page to another) 3. (N; used with an adjective) she ~ped his hair short

clipper *n.* 1. a nail ~ 2. a barber's ~s 3. a coupon ~ ("one whose income is derived from stocks and bonds")

clipping *n.* 1. a newspaper, press ~ (AE; BE has *press cutting*) 2. fingernail; toenail ~s

clique *n.* a military; ruling ~

cloak I *n.* ["cover"] under a ~ (under a ~ of anonymity)

cloak II *v.* (d; tr.) to ~ in (~ed in secrecy)

cloakroom see the Usage Note for **room**

clock I *n.* 1. to regulate, set; wind a ~ 2. to advance a ~; or: to put, set, turn a ~ ahead/forward (by one hour) 3. to put, set, turn a ~ back (by ten minutes) 4. an alarm; digital; cuckoo; electric; grandfather; wall ~ 5. a time ~ 6. a biological ~ 7. a ~ is fast; right; slow 8. a ~ gains time; goes, runs; keeps time; loses time; runs down; stops; tells (the) time 9. a ~ strikes the hour 10. the dial; face; hands of a ~ 11. (misc.) to watch the ~ ("to wait impatiently for the end of the working day"); to work around the ~ ("to work without rest"); to work against the ~ ("to strive to meet a deadline"); the ~ ran out ("the allotted time expired"); to stop the ~ ("to suspend play in a game so that the clock stops running")

clock II *v.* 1. (D; tr.) ("to time") to ~ at (he was ~ed at a record speed) 2. (J) he was ~ed doing seventy miles an hour

clockwise *adj., adv.* 1. to go ~ 2. to turn (smt.) ~

clockwork *n.* (misc.) to go, work like ~ ("to work perfectly"); as regular as ~ ("completely regular")

clog *v.* (D; tr.) to ~ with (the pipe was ~ged with leaves)

close I *adj., adv.* /klous/ ["near"] 1. ~ to (~ to tears; we live ~ to town; ~ to the truth) ["stingy"] (colloq.) 2. ~ with (~ with one's money) ["secretive"] 3. ~ about (~ about one's past) ["on intimate terms"] 4. ~ to, with (~ with one's parents) ["misc."] 5. to see smt. ~ to (BE), up; they were sitting ~ together

close II *n.* /klouz/ ["finish"] 1. to bring to a ~ 2. to come to, draw to a ~ ["end of a letter"] 3. the complimentary ~ (of/to a letter)

close III *v.* /klouz/ 1. (d; intr.) to ~ about, around, round ("to encircle") (night ~d around us) 2. (D; intr., tr.) to ~ for (to ~ a store for renovations; the shop ~s for lunch) 3. (d; intr.) to ~ on ("to get near to") (the police were ~ing on the fugitive) 4. (D; tr.) ("to shut") to ~ on (she ~d the door on him) 5. (D; tr.) ("to shut") to ~ to (they ~d their eyes to the truth) 6. (d; intr.) to ~ with ("to engage") (to ~ with the enemy) 7. (d; intr., tr.) ("to finish") to ~ with (they ~d the concert with a march) 8. (N; used with an adjective) ("to shut") she ~d the door tight 9. (s) stocks ~d strong; weak

closed *adj.* 1. ~ for (~ for repairs) 2. ~ to (the road was ~ to traffic; ~ to the public)

close in *v.* /klouz/ 1. (D; intr.) to ~ for ("to approach and prepare for") (to ~ for the kill) 2. (D; intr.) to ~ on ("to bring to bay") (the police ~d in on the fugitive)

closemouthed *adj.* ~ about

closeness *n.* ~ to

close off *v.* (D; tr.) to ~ from (they were completely ~d off from the outside world)

closet *n.* ["cupboard"] (esp. AE) 1. a china; clothes; linen; walkin ~ ["toilet"] (esp. BE) (old-fashioned) 2. a water ~ ["misc."] 3. to come out of the ~ (about smt.) ("to come out into the open about smt.")

closeted *adj.* ~ with (he was ~ with the mayor for an hour)

clot *n.* 1. to form a ~ 2. to dissolve a ~ 3. a blood ~ 4. a ~ forms

cloth *n.* 1. to dye; weave ~ 2. homespun ~ 3. a drop ~ 4. a loin ~ 5. a bolt; piece; strip of ~

clothe *v.* 1. (D; tr.) to ~ in (~d in wool) 2. (misc.) fully; partially ~d

clothes *n.* 1. to change; put on; wear (one's) ~ 2. to take off (one's) ~ 3. to iron; launder, wash; mend ~ 4. baby; maternity; night; summer; swaddling; warm; winter ~ 5. elegant, fashionable; new; plain; old ~ 6. castoff; secondhand, used; shabby ~ 7. civilian ~ 8. in ~ (the soldier was in civilian ~)

clothesline *n.* to put up, string; take down a ~

clothing *n.* 1. to put on; wear (one's) ~ 2. to take off (one's) ~ 3. heavy; light; outer; protective; warm ~ 4. summer; winter ~ 5. custom-made, tailor-made; ready-to-wear; trendy ~ 6. castoff; secondhand, used; shabby ~ 7. an article, item of ~ 8. (misc.) to model ~

cloture *n.* (AE) to apply, impose, invoke ~

cloud *n.* 1. to disperse ~s (the strong wind dispersed the ~s) 2. cirrus; cumulus; dark; grey; heavy; thick; high; scattered; threatening; white ~s 3. rain, storm ~s; thunderclouds 4. a mushroom; radioactive ~ 5. ~s form; gather 6. ~s scud across the sky 7. (misc.) under a ~ (of suspicion); the gathering ~s of war; in the ~s ("absorbed in one's fantasies"); to seed ~s (to produce rain); to cast a ~ over ("to cause gloom")

cloudburst *n.* a sudden ~

cloudy *adj.* partly ~ (in weather forecasts)

clout *n.* (colloq.) (esp. AE) ["influence"] ["power"] 1. to have, wield ~ 2. political ~ (he has a great deal of political ~)

clover *n.* ["plant"] 1. a four-leaf ~ ["prosperity"] 2. in ~ ("in luxury")

clown I *n.* 1. to act, play the ~ 2. a circus ~

clown II *v.* (D; intr.) to ~ with

club I *n.* ["association"] 1. to form, organize a ~ 2. to join a ~ 3. to break up, disband a ~ 4. an exclusive; private ~ 5. a book; debating; fan; glee; weight watchers'; working-men's (BE) ~ 6. an athletic; country; tennis; yachting ~ 7. a ~ breaks up, disbands 8. a Christmas ~ (esp. AE) ("type of savings account to provide money for the purchase of Christmas presents"); a savings ~ ["piece of wood"] 9. a golf; Indian ~ 10. a set of golf ~s

["misc."] 11. join the ~! ("we are in the same situation!"); (BE) in the ~ ("pregnant") (see the Usage Note for **team**)

club II *v.* ("to beat") to ~ smb. to death

clue *n.* 1. to discover, find, uncover a ~ 2. to follow up a ~ 3. to have a ~ (the police don't have any ~s) 4. to furnish, provide, supply; leave a ~ 5. an important, key, vital ~ 6. a ~ (as) to (the police had no ~ to her identity) 7. (misc.) he doesn't have a ~ ("he's totally ignorant/insensitive")

clue in *v.* (colloq.) (D; tr.) to ~ on ("to inform about")

clumsy *adj.* 1. ~ at (he's ~ at sports) 2. ~ of (that was ~ of her) 3. ~ with (to be ~ with one's hands) 4. ~ to + inf. (it was ~ of you to make a mistake like that)

cluster I *n.* a consonant ~

cluster II *v.* 1. (d; intr.) to ~ around (the crowd ~ed around the entrance) 2. (P; intr.) they ~ed (together) in small groups

clutch I *n.* ["device for engaging and disengaging a transmission"] 1. to engage, (esp. AE) throw in the ~ ("to release the clutch pedal") 2. to work the ~ 3. to disengage the ~ ("to depress the clutch pedal") 4. to ride the ~ ("to keep the clutch pedal partially depressed") 5. the ~ slips ["crisis"] (AE) 6. in a ~ (to count on smb. in a ~)

clutch II *v.* 1. (d; intr.) to ~ at (to ~ at a branch) 2. (d; tr.) to ~ to (she ~ed her children to her breast) 3. (misc.) to ~ at a straw ("to consider any possibility")

clutches *n.* ["power"] 1. to fall into smb.'s ~ 2. in smb.'s ~ (in the ~ of the enemy)

cluttered *adj.* ~ with (the room was ~ with old newspapers)

coach I *n.* ["trainer of an athlete or team"] 1. a basketball; crew; fencing; football; soccer; swimming; tennis; track-and-field; volleyball ~ ["trainer of a performer or troupe"] 2. a drama; voice ~ ["long-distance bus"] (esp. BE) 3. to go, travel by ~ ["airplane"] (esp. AE) 4. an air ~

coach II *v.* 1. (D; tr.) to ~ for (to ~ a team for a championship match) 2. (D; tr.) to ~ in 3. (misc.) she ~ed the team to victory

coal *n.* 1. to mine, produce ~ 2. to burn, use ~ 3. to shovel ~ (into a furnace) 4. anthracite, hard; bituminous, soft; brown ~ 5. hot, live ~s (to cook meat over hot ~s) 6. ~ burns 7. a chunk, lump of ~; a bed of ~s 8. (misc.) to rake smb. over the ~s ("to criticize smb. harshly")

coalesce *v.* (D; intr.) to ~ into

coalition *n.* (pol.) 1. to form a ~ 2. to break up, disband, dissolve a ~ 3. a ~ breaks up, falls apart 4. a political ~ 5. (AE) a rainbow ~ ("a multiethnic political coalition") 6. a broadly based, umbrella ~ ("a group consisting of many diverse elements") 7. a ~ among, between, of

coast I *n.* 1. a forbidding, inhospitable; rugged ~ 2. off a ~ (a ship sank right off the ~) 3. along, on the ~ (there are many fishing towns on the ~) 4. (AE) on the Coast ("on the Pacific Coast of the US") (he's out on the Coast) 5. (misc.) the ~ is clear ("there is no danger in sight"); from ~ to ~

coast II *v.* (P; intr.) ("to move effortlessly") they ~ed down the hill; they ~ed to an easy victory

coastline *n.* a broken, irregular, jagged; rugged ~

coat *n.* ["sleeved outer garment"] 1. to have a ~ on, wear a ~ 2. to take off one's ~ 3. an all-weather; fur; fur-lined; mink ~; overcoat; raincoat; sheepskin; spring; trench; winter; zip-lined ~ ["layer of paint, varnish, etc."] 4. to apply, put on a ~ (we had to put on a second ~)

coated *adj.* ~ in, with

coating *n.* 1. an outer; protective ~ 2. a thick; thin ~

coat of arms *n.* a family ~

coattails *n.* to hang on smb.'s ~ ("to be totally dependent on smb. else's success")

coax *v.* 1. (D; tr.) to ~ into; out of (she ~ed me into going) 2. (H) he ~ed me to do it

cobwebs *n.* (colloq.) ["confusion"] to blow away, clear, sweep (away) the ~ (from one's brain)

cocaine *n.* to freebase; shoot; smoke; snort; take; use ~

cock *n.* ["rooster"] (esp. BE) 1. ~s crow, go cock-a-doodle-doo ["valve"] 2. a ball ~

cocktail *n.* 1. to make, mix, prepare; sip a ~ 2. fruit ~; a prawn (BE), shrimp (AE) ~ 3. a champagne ~

cocoon *n.* to make, spin a ~

code *n.* ["cryptographic system"] 1. to design, make up a ~ 2. to break, crack, decipher a ~ 3. a binary; secret ~ 4. the Morse ~ 5. in ~ (to send a message in ~) ["body of laws, principles"] 6. to establish, formulate, lay down a ~ 7. a civil; criminal, penal ~; a ~ of justice 8. an ethical, moral ~; a ~ of ethics 9. a building; sanitary ~ 10. a dress ~ ["system of symbols"] 11. an area (AE), dialling (BE) ~ 12. a postal ~ (BE), postcode (BE), zip (AE) ~ 13. a bar ~ ("symbols that are read by a computer") 14. the genetic ~

codicil *n.* (legal) 1. to draw up a ~ 2. a ~ to (a will)

coequal *adj.* (formal) ~ with

coerce *v.* 1. (D; tr.) to ~ into (to ~ smb. into doing smt.) 2. (H) (rare) he was ~d to sign

coercion *n.* under ~ (to do smt. under ~)

coeval *adj.* (formal) ["contemporary"] ~ with

coexist *v.* 1. to ~ peacefully 2. (D; intr.) to ~ with

coexistence *n.* 1. peaceful ~ 2. ~ with

coffee *n.* 1. to brew; grind; make; percolate; strain ~ 2. to drink, have ~ 3. to stir ~ (with a spoon) 4. to grow ~ 5. strong; weak ~ 6. black; white (BE) ~, ~ with cream 7. decaffeinated; fresh; hot; iced; instant; Irish; Turkish ~ 8. a cup of ~; one ~; or: one cup of ~; two ~s; or: two cups of ~ (bring us two cups of ~) 9. (misc.) the ~ is brewing; I had a ~/a

cup of ~

coffin *n.* to lower a ~ into a grave

cogitate *v.* (formal) (D; intr.) to ~ about, on

cognate *adj.* ~ to, with (Dutch is ~ to English and German)

cognizance *n.* (formal) ["notice"] to take ~ of

cognizant *adj.* (formal) (cannot stand alone) ~ of (~ of the danger)

cohabit *v.* (D; intr.) to ~ with

coherence *n.* 1. to lack ~ 2. ~ between

cohesion *n.* ~ among, between

coil I *n.* an induction; primary ~

coil II *v.* 1. (d; intr., refl.) to ~ (a)round (the snake ~ed around its victim) 2. (d; intr., refl.) to ~ into (to ~ into a ball)

coin *n.* 1. to mint, strike ~s 2. to jingle ~s 3. to drop, put a ~ (into a slot) 4. to spin a ~; or: to flip, throw, toss a ~ (in order to decide an issue) (they tossed a ~ to decide who would go first) 5. to collect ~s 6. antique; copper; counterfeit; gold; metal; rare; silver; valuable ~s 7. ~s clink, jingle 8. (misc.) common ~ ("smt. that is widely known"); to pay back in the same ~ ("to treat smb. as he or she has treated others")

coincide *v.* (D; intr.) to ~ in; with (they ~ with each other in their views)

coincidence *n.* 1. mere, pure, sheer ~ 2. an amazing; happy; interesting; odd, strange; remarkable ~ 3. a ~ that + clause (it was pure ~ that we were seated together) 4. by ~ (we ended up in the same town by sheer ~)

coincidental *adj.* 1. purely ~ 2. ~ with 3. ~ that + clause (it was purely ~ that we were seated together)

cold I *adj.* ["of a low temperature"] 1. biting, bitter, bitterly, extremely, freezing ~ (it was bitter ~) 2. ~ to (~ to the touch) ["unfriendly"] 3. ~ towards

cold II *n.* ["low temperature"] 1. biting, bitter, extreme, intense, severe ~ 2. the ~ has let up 3. (misc.) to come in out of the ~; to go out into the ~ ["illness"] 4. to catch (a) ~; to come down with, contract, get, (BE) go down with a ~ 5. to have; nurse a ~; to suffer from a ~ 6. to fight off, shake off, throw off a ~ 7. a bad, severe; lingering; slight ~ 8. the common ~; a chest; head ~ ["misc."] 9. to be left out in the ~ ("to be slighted")

cold cream *n.* to apply ~

cold feet *n.* (colloq.) ["reluctance"] at the last minute he got ~ and withdrew from the deal

cold light *n.* ["clear view"] in the ~ of reality

cold shoulder *n.* (colloq.) ["snub"] to give smb. the ~

cold turkey *n.* (colloq.) ["abrupt cessation of the use of drugs or other harmful substances"] to go ~

collaborate *v.* (D; intr.) to ~ in, on; with (to ~ on a project with smb.)

collaboration *n.* 1. close ~ 2. international ~ 3. in ~ with

collaborator *n.* a wartime ~ (historical and pejorative)

collapse I *n.* 1. (an) economic ~ 2. an emotional, mental, nervous ~ 3. a complete, total, utter ~ (he was in a state of total ~)

collapse II *v.* 1. (d; intr.) to ~ from, with (to ~ from exhaustion) 2. (d; intr.) to ~ under (the weight of smt.)

collar *n.* 1. to turn down; turn up a ~ 2. a button-down; clerical; high; stand-up; starched; stiff; turndown ~ 3. (misc.) hot under the ~ ("very angry")

collate *v.* (D; tr.) to ~ with (to ~ one edition with another edition)

collateral *n.* 1. to put up ~ for 2. to offer, put up, use smt. as ~ for

collect *v.* 1. (D; intr.) to ~ around (a crowd ~ed around them) 2. (D; intr., tr.) to ~ for (to ~ for charity; to ~ money for a good cause) 3. (D; tr.) to ~ from (to ~ money from one's colleagues) 4. (D; intr.) to ~ on (to ~ on one's insurance)

collection *n.* 1. to take up a ~ (of money) 2. to break up a ~ 3. an art; coin; private; stamp ~ 4. a priceless ~

collective *n.* a workers' ~

collector *n.* 1. an art; coin; rare-book; stamp ~ 2. a tax; ticket; toll ~ 3. (AE) a garbage, trash ~ (BE has *dustman*) 4. an ardent, avid, keen (BE), serious ~

college *n.* 1. to go to ~ 2. to apply for admission to (a) ~ 3. to enroll, matriculate at (a) ~; to enter (a) ~ 4. to finish, graduate from ~ 5. to put smb. through ~ ("to pay for smb.'s college education") 6. to drop out of; fail out of (AE), flunk out of (AE; slang) ~ 7. a business (AE); community (AE); junior (AE); technical (BE) ~; a College of Further Education (BE) 8. a war ~ 9. (US) the Electoral College 10. at, in ~ (she's away at ~; he made many friends when he was in ~)
USAGE NOTE: One says *to go to college*, but *to go to a good college* (see the Usage Note for **university**)

collide *v.* 1. to ~ head-on 2. (D; intr.) to ~ with (they ~d with another ship)

collision *n.* 1. to cause a ~ 2. to avoid a ~ 3. a head-on; midair ~ 4. a near ~ 5. a ~ between; with (the ~ between the ships was caused by fog)

collocate *v.* (D; intr.) to ~ with (some verbs ~ with certain nouns)

collocation *n.* a grammatical; lexical ~

colloquy *n.* (formal) a ~ between

collude *v.* 1. (D; intr.) to ~ in; with (to ~ with smb. in doing smt.) 2. (E) to ~ with smb. to do smt.

collusion *n.* 1. ~ between 2. in ~ with

colon *n.* (med.) the ascending; descending; transverse ~

colonel *n.* 1. a chicken (AE; slang), full; lieutenant ~ 2. a ~ commands a regiment

colony *n.* 1. to establish a ~ 2. to disband a ~ 3. a Crown Colony 4. an artists'; leper; nudist; penal ~ 5. an ant ~

color, colour I *n.* ["hue"] 1. a bright, brilliant; contrasting; dark; dull; garish, gaudy, loud; harsh; matching; natural; neutral; pastel; rich; soft; subdued; vivid; warm ~ 2. (usu. fig.) glowing ~s (to picture smt. in glowing ~s) 3. complementary; primary; secondary ~s 4. ~s clash; fade; match 5. in ~ (in natural ~) 6. a combination of ~s; a riot of ~ 7. (misc.) with illustrations in full ~ ["features"] 8. local ~ ["paint"] 9. oil; water ~s 10. a ~ runs ["vividness"] 11. to add, lend ~ (to a story) ["complexion"] 12. to change ~ ("to become pale; to blush") 13. (misc.) the fresh air brought the ~ back to his cheeks ["misc."] 14. off ~ ("not proper") (AE)

color, colour II *v.* 1. (D; intr., tr.) to ~ with (she ~ed the pictures with a yellow crayon 2. (N; used with an adjective) she ~ed her hair red

coloring, colouring *n.* artificial; natural; protective ~

color line, colour line *n.* ["social boundary between races of different color"] to cross the ~

colors, colours *n.* ["banner, flag"] 1. to display, show the ~ 2. to salute; troop the ~ 3. to dip; haul down, strike the ~ 4. college; regimental; school ~ ["armed forces"] 5. to be called to the ~ ["character"] 6. to show one's ~ 7. smb.'s true ~ ["misc."] 8. to come through with flying ~ ("to score an impressive success"); under false ~ ("passing oneself off as another"); to ride under the ~ of a certain stable

column *n.* ["series of articles"] 1. to write a ~ 2. a fashion; gossip; social, society; sports; syndicated ~ (as in a newspaper) 3. a daily; weekly ~ ["feature of a journal, magazine, or newspaper"] 4. advertising (esp. BE) ~s; correspondence (esp. BE) ~s; a personal ~ ["list of numbers"] 5. to add up a ~ ["shaft"] 6. a steering ~ (on a car) 7. (med.) the spinal, vertebral ~ ["row"] 8. a tank ~ ["misc."] 9. a fifth ~ ("enemy supporters behind one's own lines")

columnist *n.* 1. a sports; syndicated ~ 2. a fifth ~ ("an enemy agent operating behind one's own lines")

coma *n.* 1. to fall, go, lapse, slip into a ~ 2. to be in a ~ 3. to come out of a ~ 4. a deep; irreversible ~

comb *n.* 1. a fine-tooth/(BE) fine-toothed ~ (usu. fig.) (we went through the documents with a fine-tooth~) 2. she ran a ~ through her hair

combat *n.* 1. to engage in, go into ~ 2. to break off ~ 3. close, hand-to-hand; deadly, fierce, mortal ~ 4. ~ against; between; with 5. in ~ (killed in ~)

combination *n.* 1. a rare; strange; winning ~ 2. (ling.) a fixed, recurrent; free ~; word ~s 3. in ~ with

combine *v.* 1. (D; intr., tr.) to ~ against (to ~ forces against a common enemy) 2. (D; intr., tr.) to ~ into (they ~d all the pieces into a whole) 3. (D; intr., tr.) to ~ with (hydrogen ~s with oxygen; to ~ initiative with caution; to ~ business with pleasure)

combo *n.* (colloq.) a jazz ~

combustion *n.* 1. to produce ~ 2. internal; spontaneous ~

come *v.* 1. (d; intr.) to ~ across ("to meet by chance") (to ~ across an old friend) 2. (d; intr.) to ~ after ("to follow") (the intermission ~s after the first act) 3. (d; intr.) to ~ after ("to pursue") (the police came after him) 4. (d; intr.) to ~ around ("to turn") (to ~ around the corner) 5. (d; intr.) to ~ around ("to circle") (to ~ around the mountain) 6. (d; intr.) to ~ as ("to be") (it came as a surprise) 7. (d; intr.) to ~ at ("to attack") (he came at me with a knife) 8. (d; intr.) to ~ before ("to appear") (to ~ before the court) 9. (d; intr.) to ~ between ("to alienate; to separate") (to ~ between two friends) 10. (d; intr.) to ~ by, into ("to acquire") (she came by quite a bit of property; he came into a large inheritance) 11. (d; intr.) to ~ down ("to descend") (to ~ down the stairs) 12. (d; intr.) to ~ for ("to pick up") (she came for her book) 13. (d; intr.) to ~ for ("to participate") (to ~ for lunch; to ~ for a walk) 14. (d; intr.) to ~ from ("to originate") (she ~s from a different country; milk ~s from cows) 15. (d; intr.) to ~ into ("to enter") (to ~ into being; to ~ into use; to ~ into focus; to ~ into the open; to ~ into view) 16. (d; intr.) to ~ of ("to result") (this is what ~s of being so careless) 17. (d; intr.) to ~ off ("to fall off") (the knob came off the door) 18. (d; intr.) to ~ on, upon ("to meet") (to ~ upon a stranger; to ~ upon a shocking scene) 19. (d; intr.) to ~ on ("to begin"); ("to enter") (to ~ on duty; to ~ on the scene) 20. (d; intr.) to ~ out of ("to leave") (he came out of the room) 21. (d; intr.) to ~ over ("to affect") (what has come over you?) 22. (d; intr.) to ~ to ("to amount") (the bill came to twenty dollars) 23. (d; intr.) to ~ to ("to arrive at"); ("to reach") (the incident came to their attention; to ~ to grief; success came to her early; he came to his senses; it came to our knowledge that...; to ~ to terms; to ~ to the point; to ~ to a halt) 24. (D; intr.) to ~ to ("to be due") (he got what was ~ing to him) 25. (d; intr.) to ~ to ("to happen") (no harm came to them) 26. (d; intr.) to ~ to ("to be remembered by") (her name finally came to me) 27. (d; intr.) to ~ to ("to regard") (when it ~s to politics) 28. (d; intr.) to ~ under ("to fall") (to ~ under the jurisdiction of a court; to ~ under suspicion; to ~ under smb.'s influence; to ~ under fire) 29. (d; intr.) to ~ up ("to ascend") (to ~ up the stairs) 30. (d; intr.) to

~ with ("to be accompanied by") (the car ~s with power brakes) 31. (E) ("to occur") if it came to be known that...; to ~ to pass ("to happen") 32. (E) ("to begin") they finally came to consider me a friend 33. (G) ("to approach") the children came running 34. (P; intr.) ("to occur in a certain order") Tuesday ~s after Monday; January ~s before February 35. (s) to ~ true; the dressing came undone 36. (misc.) what will ~ ("become") of him? the years to ~; to ~ on strong ("to try to make a very strong impression"); to ~ into a fortune ("to inherit or acquire a fortune"); the case never did ~ before the court; he had it ~ing ("he deserved his punishment"); (BE) (colloq.) don't ~ the innocent victim with me!

come about *v.* (L) how did it ~ that you were late?

come across *v.* 1. (d; intr.) to ~ as ("to appear") (she came across as hostile) 2. (colloq.) (d; intr.) to ~ with ("to make available") (he finally came across with the money)

come after *v.* (D; tr.) ("to attack") to ~ with (she came after me with a knife)

come along *v.* (D; intr.) to ~ for (she came along for the ride)

come around *v.* (D; intr.) ("to change") to ~ to (she finally came around to our viewpoint)

come at *v.* (D; tr.) ("to attack") to ~ with (he came at me with an knife)

come away *v.* ("to leave") 1. (D; intr.) to ~ from (I came away from the meeting with a strange feeling) 2. (d; intr.) to ~ with (he came away with a favorable impression)

comeback *n.* ["recovery"] 1. to attempt, try; make, stage a ~ 2. a successful; unsuccessful ~ ["retort"] 3. a snappy ~

come back *v.* 1. (d; intr.) to ~ at ("to react") (to ~ at smb. with a wisecrack) 2. (D; intr.) ("to return") to ~ from (they came back from their honeymoon last week) 3. (D; intr.) ("to return") to ~ to (they came back to their hometown; the details are ~ing back to me)

come by *v.* (D; intr.) ("to drop in") to ~ for (to ~ for a drink)

come clean *v.* (D; intr.) ("to admit") to ~ about (he came clean about the bribe)

comedian *n.* an alternative (BE) ("anti-establishment"); nightclub; radio; stand-up; TV ~

comedown *n.* a ~ to + inf. (it's a ~ to work at such a low salary)

come down *v.* 1. (BE) (D; intr.) to ~ from ("to leave") (to ~ from Oxford) 2. (d; intr.) to ~ from ("to originate from") (this statue has come down to us from the fifteenth century) 3. (d; intr.) to ~ on ("to treat") (the teacher came down hard on him for missing class) 4. (d; intr.) to ~ to ("to amount to") (it ~s down to the same old thing) 5. (d; intr.) to ~ with ("to catch, develop") (to ~ with a cold)

comedy *n.* alternative (BE); black; light; musical; situation; slapstick ~

come forth, come forward *v.* (D; intr.) to ~ with ("to present") (to ~ with new evidence)

come in *v.* 1. (D; intr.) ("to enter") to ~ by, through (to ~ by the front door) 2. (d; intr.) to ~ for ("to be subjected to") (to ~ for criticism) 3. (D; intr.) to ~ on ("to join") (to ~ on a project) 4. (d; intr.) to ~ on ("to encounter unexpectedly") (he came in on an ugly scene) 5. (s) to ~ handy; my horse came in third

come on *v.* (colloq.) 1. (d; intr.) to ~ as ("to appear") (he ~s on as a radical) 2. (d; intr.) to ~ to ("to show sexual interest in smb.") (he came on to her) 3. (misc.) to ~ strong ("to attempt to impress or attract")

come out *v.* 1. (d; intr.) to ~ against ("to oppose") (to ~ against a proposal) 2. (d; intr.) to ~ for, in favor of ("to support") (to ~ for a bill) 3. (d; intr.) to ~ for ("to try out for") (are you ~ing out for the team?) 4. (d; intr.) to ~ with ("to make known; to publish") (to ~ with a new book; to ~ with the truth) 5. (L) it came out that he had cheated 6. (P; intr.) ("to end up, result") to ~ on top ("to be victorious") 7. (s) the pictures came out fine 8. (misc.) to ~ in spots ("to be covered with spots as a result of illness"); they came out from behind the bushes; she meant it as a compliment, but it came out as an insult

come over *v.* 1. (D; intr.) ("to come") to ~ as (she came over as a tourist) 2. (D; intr.) ("to come") to ~ from (they came over from Europe) 3. (D; intr.) to ~ to ("to approach, join") (she came over to our table; they came over to our side) 4. (D; intr.) ("to come") to ~ with (their ancestors came over with the Pilgrims) 5. (BE) (s) ("to begin to feel") to ~ (all) faint; (all) nervous

come round see **come around**

come through *v.* (D; intr.) to ~ with ("to provide") (he finally came through with the money)

come up *v.* 1. (d; intr.) to ~ against ("to meet") (to ~ against opposition) 2. (D; intr.) to ~ for ("to be brought up for") (the question finally came up for discussion) 3. (d; intr.) to ~ to ("to reach") (the water came up to our knees; their proposal did not ~ to our standards) 4. (d; intr.) to ~ to ("to approach") (he came up to me and introduced himself) 5. (d; intr.) to ~ with ("to produce") (she came up with a good idea) 6. (misc.) to ~ to expectations; to ~ in the world; to ~ from/through the ranks; the new project came up as a topic for discussion

comeuppance *n.* (colloq.) ["well-deserved misfortune"] to get one's ~

comfort *n.* 1. to bring, give, provide ~ 2. to derive, get ~ from 3. to find, take; seek ~ in (she finds ~ in helping others) 4. to enjoy the ~s (of life) 5. cold,

little ~ 6. creature ~s; spiritual ~ 7. a ~ to (they were a great ~ to their parents) 8. a ~ to + inf. (it was a ~ to know that they were safe) 9. in ~ (to live in ~)

comfortable *adj.* 1. to feel ~ 2. to make smb. ~ 3. ~ with (are you ~ with this decision?) 4. ~ to + inf. (it is ~ to sit here in the shade = it is ~ sitting here in the shade)

comforter *n.* (AE) a down ~

comforting *adj.* ~ to + inf. (it was ~ to be sure of their support)

coming *n.* 1. the Second Coming 2. with the ~ (of summer)

comma *n.* 1. to place, put in a ~ 2. inverted ~s (BE; CE has *quotation marks*)

command I *n.* ["authority"] ["control"] 1. to assume, take (over) ~ 2. to exercise ~ 3. to give up, relinquish; lose one's ~ 4. firm ~ 5. ~ of, over (he assumed ~ of the regiment) 6. in ~ of (he was put in ~ of the task force; who will be placed in ~ of the division?) 7. under smb.'s ~ (we were under her ~) 8. the chain of ~ ["headquarters"] 9. the high, supreme ~ 10. a unified ~ ["order"] 11. to carry out, execute; give, issue a ~ 12. a ~ that + clause; subj. (we obeyed their ~ that prisoners be/ should be treated properly) 13. at smb.'s ~ (at his ~ we opened fire) ["military unit"] 14. a combat; military ~ ["mastery"] 15. fluent, perfect ~ (fluent ~ of a language)

command II *v.* 1. (H) he ~ed his men to fire 2. (L; subj.) the captain ~ed that the company fall in/ should fall in

commandant *n.* (mil.) the ~ of the Marine Corps; the ~ of a military/service school

commander *n.* 1. a lieutenant; naval ~ 2. a battalion; camp; company; division; regimental; supreme ~ 3. a ~ commands a unit

commandment *n.* (rel.) 1. to keep the ~s 2. to violate a ~ 3. the Ten Commandments

commemoration *n.* in ~ of

commence *v.* (formal) 1. (D; intr.) to ~ by, with (we'll ~ by reading/with a reading of the minutes of the last meeting) 2. (G) (mil.) ~ firing!

commencement exercises *n.* (AE) to attend; hold ~

commend *v.* 1. to ~ highly 2. (formal) (B) I ~ him to you 3. (D; tr.) to ~ for (she was ~ed for bravery) 4. (D; tr.) to ~ on (she ~ed him on his performance)

commendable *adj.* ~ to + inf. (it is ~ of you to help others)

commendation *n.* 1. to receive a ~ 2. to present a ~ 3. a ~ for (a ~ for bravery)

commensurable *adj.* ~ to, with

commensurate *adj.* ~ to, with (a reward ~ with the results achieved)

comment I *n.* ["observation"] ["remark"] 1. to have, make, pass a ~ (on); to have a ~ to make (on) 2. an appropriate, fitting; favorable; incisive; perceptive, shrewd; revealing ~ 3. a casual; passing ~ 4. an ironic, wry ~ 5. a cryptic; inappropriate; off-the-record ~ 6. a caustic, critical, derogatory, sarcastic, scathing, unfavorable; nasty, vicious; provocative; trenchant ~ 7. (a) ~ about, on (there was no ~ about the incident in the press) 8. (a) ~ from (there was no ~ from the other party) 9. a ~ that + clause (her ~ that she would retire soon was greeted with dismay) 10. without further ~; no ~! ["gossip"] ["talk"] 11. to arouse, cause, evoke ~ 12. considerable; critical, scathing; favorable; unfavorable ~ (the incident evoked considerable ~ in the capitals of Europe)

comment II v. 1. (D; intr.) to ~ about, on 2. (L) she ~ed that she was very happy to be a guest in their country

commentary n. 1. to give a ~ 2. a play-by-play, running; political ~ 3. a ~ on 4. (misc.) a sad ~ (on the world situation)

commentator n. 1. a news; radio; sports; TV ~ 2. a ~ on (a ~ on political affairs)

commerce n. 1. to carry on, engage in ~ 2. to develop, expand ~ 3. international; interstate; overseas ~ 4. ~ among; between; with (to carry on ~ with the countries of Central America) 5. (misc.) a Chamber of Commerce

commercial n. ["paid spoken advertisement"] a radio; TV ~

commiserate v. (d; intr.) to ~ on; with (I ~ with you on your misfortune)

commissar n. a political ~

commission I n. ["committee"] ["council"] 1. to appoint, establish, set up a ~ 2. to chair a ~ 3. to disband a ~ 4. a fact-finding; investigating; joint; planning; roving ~ 5. (misc.) (GB) a Royal Commission ["certificate conferring rank"] (usu. mil.) 6. to award, confer a ~ 7. to earn, win a (battlefield) ~ 8. to resign one's ~ 9. a battlefield ~ ["fee"] 10. to charge; pay a ~ 11. to get, earn a ~ 12. to deduct; divide a ~ 13. a ~ for, on 14. on ~ (to work on ~) ["operating condition"] 15. to be; go out of ~ 16. to put out of ~ (the storm put all power lines out of ~) ["task"] (formal) 17. to accept, get, receive a ~ 18. to execute a ~ 19. a ~ to + inf. (a ~ to serve)

commission II v. 1. (D; tr.) to ~ as (she was ~ed as a captain) 2. (H) she ~ed an artist to paint her portrait 3. (N; used with a noun) she was ~ed a second lieutenant

commissioner n. 1. a high ~ for (the high ~ for occupied territories) 2. a fire; health; police; water ~ 3. a county; township ~ 4. (GB) the Canadian High Commissioner in London

commit v. 1. (D; refl.) ("to devote") to ~ to (to ~ oneself to a cause) 2. (D; tr.) ("to assign") to ~ to (to ~ funds to a project) 3. (D; tr.) ("to confine") to ~ to (to ~ smb. to a mental hospital; ~ted to prison)

4. (d; tr.) ("to place") (to ~ a child to a relative's care; to ~ a poem to memory; to ~ one's thoughts to paper) 5. (H; usu. refl.; no passive) ("to pledge") he ~ted himself to support her parents

commitment n. ["promise"] 1. to have; make a ~ 2. to affirm, honor, meet a ~ 3. a firm; prior ~ 4. a ~ to + inf. (he made a ~ to pay off his debts) 5. a ~ that + clause (they reaffirmed their ~ that they would help) ["devotion"] 6. to demonstrate, display, show ~ 7. an all-out, total; deep, passionate ~ 8. (a) ~ to (~ to a cause)

committed adj. 1. deeply, firmly, totally, wholeheartedly ~ 2. ~ to (~ to his principles) 3. ~ to + inf. (they are ~ to help us; or, more usu.: they are ~ to helping us)

committee n. 1. to appoint, establish, form, organize, set up a ~ 2. to chair; sit on a ~ 3. to disband a ~ 4. an ad-hoc; advisory; budget; congressional; credentials; executive; finance; grievance; legislative; nominating; planning; program; select; special; standing; steering; strike; watchdog; ways-and-means ~; a ~ of the whole 5. a ~ on (a ~ on problems of the elderly) 6. on a ~ (who is serving on the ~?) 7. (misc.) to report a bill out of ~

commodity n. 1. to trade in ~ties 2. a basic; farm; marketable; staple ~

common I adj. 1. quite; very ~ 2. (cannot stand alone after a noun) ~ to (a heritage ~ to both our peoples) 3. ~ to + inf. (it is quite ~ for the trains to be late; it is ~ to read of strikes)

common II n. 1. in ~ with 2. to have in ~ (they have a lot in ~)

commonplace I adj. ~ to + inf. (it was ~ for them to travel abroad)

commonplace II n. 1. to state a ~ 2. to exchange ~s (about; with) 3. a ~ to + inf. (it's a ~ to say that people should work hard)

common sense n. 1. to apply, exercise, show, use; have ~ 2. the ~ to + inf. (he had the ~ to remain silent) 3. (misc.) good; plain ~ (just plain good old ~)

common touch n. to have; lose the ~

commotion n. 1. to cause, create, make, raise a ~ 2. a great ~ 3. a ~ subsides 4. a ~ about, over 5. in a state of ~

commune v. (d; intr.) to ~ with (to ~ with nature)

communicate v. 1. to ~ clearly; officially; unofficially 2. to ~ online 3. (B) she tried to ~ her thoughts to her children 4. (D; intr.) to ~ by, in, through (to ~ by/in code; to ~ through signals) 5. (D; intr.) to ~ with (to ~ with one's parents)

communication n. ["message"] 1. to address, direct, send (all) ~s (to a certain place) 2. to receive a ~ 3. a direct; official; personal; privileged ("confidential") ~ 4. a ~ from; to ["act, means of communicating"] 5. to establish ~ 6. to cut off ~s 7. mass ~s 8. online; radio; two-way ~ 9. ~ between; with (to establish ~ with the rescue team; to cut off all ~s with the mainland) 10. in ~ (with) (she has been in ~ with her family) 11. (misc.) a means of ~; open lines of ~; a breakdown in ~

communication cord n. (BE) to pull a ~ (AE has *emergency cord*)

communion n. ["sharing"] 1. in ~ (with) ["a Christian sacrament, the Eucharist"] 2. to administer, give ~ 3. to receive; take ~ 4. Holy Communion

communiqué n. 1. to issue a ~ 2. a joint ~ 3. an official ~ 4. a ~ about, on (they issued a ~ on the results of the conference)

community n. ["group of persons with common interests"] 1. an (the) academic, college, university; business; gay; intelligence ~; the international ~; a (the) religious; scientific ~ ["group of persons who live together"] 2. a close-knit ~ 3. a life-care (AE); retirement ~ 4. (AE) a bedroom ~ (BE has *dormitory town*) 5. (misc.) a pillar of the ~

commute I n. (colloq.) ["ride to work"] 1. an easy; long ~ 2. a ~ from; to

commute II v. 1. (D; intr.) ("to travel regularly") to ~ between; from; to (to ~ between two cities; to ~ from the suburbs to the city) 2. (D; tr.) ("to change") to ~ to (the Governor ~d his death sentence to life imprisonment)

commuter n. 1. a suburban ~ 2. a ~ between; from; to

compact n. (formal) ["agreement"] 1. to make a ~ with 2. a ~ between; with 3. a ~ to + inf. (we made a ~ not to discuss the matter further)

companion n. 1. smb.'s boon; close, constant, inseparable ~ 2. smb.'s life; traveling ~ 3. a ~ for, to (she worked as a ~ to an elderly woman)

company n. ["military unit consisting of several platoons"] 1. to command a ~ (a captain commands a ~) 2. to deploy; form a ~ 3. a cannon; headquarters; infantry ~ ["companionship"] 4. to keep (smb.) ~; to seek smb.'s ~ 5. to part ~ with 6. good, pleasant ~ 7. (good) ~ for (the children were good ~ for us) ["guests"] 8. to expect; have; invite ~ (we enjoy having ~) ["associates"] ["association"] ["gathering of persons"] 9. to keep ~ with 10. mixed ~ (don't use that word in mixed ~) 11. (colloq.) bad, fast ~ ("reckless, wild associates") (he runs around in/with fast ~) 12. present ~ ("those present") (present ~ excepted) 13. in ~ (to behave appropriately in ~; in ~ with others) ["firm"] 14. to manage, operate, run a ~ 15. to establish, form a ~ 16. a finance; holding; insurance; investment; joint-stock; multinational; pharmaceutical; shipping; transport (esp. BE), transportation (esp. AE) ~ 17. an opera; repertory (esp. BE), stock (AE); theatrical ~ 18. (BE) a (public) limited ~ (AE prefers *corporation*) 19. a ~ fails, goes bankrupt ["fire-fighting unit"] (esp. AE) 20. an engine, hose; ladder ~

comparable adj. ~ to, with

compare I n. beyond; without ~

compare II v. 1. to ~ advantageously, favorably; unfavorably 2. (d; intr.) to ~ to, with (these roads cannot ~ with ours) 3. (d; tr.) to ~ to, with (how would you ~ this wine with a good French wine?) USAGE NOTE: The construction *to compare x to y* usually means "to claim a similarity between x and y" (to compare New York to a beehive). The construction *to compare x with/and y* usually means "to discuss similarities and differences between x and y" (to compare New York with/and London).

comparison n. 1. to draw, make a ~ 2. to bear, stand ~ 3. to defy ~ 4. a favorable; unfavorable ~ 5. a ~ between; to, with (there is no ~ between them; she made a ~ of our literature to/with theirs; I would like to draw a ~ between recent events and those of the 1930s) 6. beyond ~ 7. by, in ~ (with) (her works suffer by ~) USAGE NOTE: Note that there can be a difference in prepositions between *a comparison of New York to a beehive* and *a comparison of New York with/and London*. See the Usage Note for **compare II**. The preposition *between* can be used in both meanings — *a comparison between New York and a beehive* and *a comparison between New York and London*.

compartment n. 1. a glove ~ 2. a first-class; second-class; sleeping ~ 3. a watertight ~ 4. (in a refrigerator) a freezer; ice ~

compartmentalize v. (D; tr.) to ~ into

compass n. ["device for navigation"] 1. to box the ~ 2. to read a ~ 3. a magnetic; mariner's ~ ["limit, range"] 4. beyond; within the ~ (beyond the ~ of the court's jurisdiction)

compassion n. 1. to arouse ~ 2. to demonstrate, display, show; feel, have ~ 3. deep, great, profound, strong ~ 4. ~ for 5. out of, with ~ (to act out of ~)

compassionate adj. ~ towards

compatibility n. ~ between, with

compatible adj. 1. perfectly ~ 2. ~ with

compel v. (H) to ~ smb. to do smt.

compelled adj. ~ to + inf. (she felt ~ to offer an apology)

compensate v. 1. (d; intr.) ("to make up for") to ~ for (I cannot ~ for my past failings) 2. (D; tr.) ("to reimburse") to ~ for (to ~ smb. for damages)

compensation n. 1. to authorize, grant; make, pay; offer ~ 2. to deny, refuse ~ 3. to claim; seek ~ 4. to get, receive ~ 5. adequate, appropriate ~ 6. unemployment; workmen's (AE) ~ 7. ~ for (~ for the damage suffered) 8. in ~ for (she received a cash award in ~ for the lost suitcase)

compete v. 1. (d; intr.) to ~ against, with (that store ~s with us) 2. (D; intr.) to ~ for (to ~ for first prize)

3. (D; intr.) to ~ in (to ~ in a contest) 4. (E) they are ~ting to corner the market

competence *n.* ["ability"] 1. to acquire, gain ~ 2. (ling.) communicative; linguistic ~ 3. ~ as (her ~ as an interpreter is well known) 4. ~ for (does she have the necessary ~ for the position?) 5. ~ in (~ in English) 6. the ~ to + inf. (do they have the ~ to cope with the job?) ["jurisdiction"] (legal) 7. beyond, outside; within the ~ (the matter lay within the ~ of the court)

competent *adj.* 1. highly; very ~ 2. ~ as (he is ~ as a teacher) 3. ~ at, in (she is ~ in her field) 4. ~ to + inf. (she is ~ to teach history; ~ to stand trial)

competition *n.* ["rivalry"] ["opposition"] 1. to come up against ~, to face ~ 2. to offer, provide ~ 3. to undercut, undersell the ~ 4. bitter, close, fierce, formidable, heavy, intense, keen, stiff, strong, tough; cutthroat, unfair, unscrupulous ~ 5. fair; free, unfettered; healthy ~ 6. ~ among, between; with (stiff ~ among several firms) 7. ~ for (~ for control of the market) 8. ~ to + inf. (there was bitter ~ to control the market) 9. in ~ with ["contest"] ["match"] 10. to hold, stage a ~ 11. to enter a ~ 12. a gymnastics; high-diving; speed-skating ~ 13. (an) open ~ 14. a ~ for (a ~ for the championship)

competitive *adj.* 1. fiercely, highly, keenly, very ~ 2. ~ with (to be ~ with the best)

competitor *n.* a formidable, keen, strong; unscrupulous ~

compilation *n.* 1. to do, make a ~ 2. a ~ from (various sources)

compile *v.* (D; tr.) to ~ from (to ~ a dictionary from various sources)

complacency *n.* ~ about; towards

complacent *adj.* 1. to become, get, grow ~ 2. ~ about; towards

complain *v.* 1. to ~ bitterly, loudly, vociferously; constantly 2. (D; intr.) to ~ about, of; to (I ~ed to the manager about the service; she ~ed of indigestion) 3. (L; to) she ~ed (to the manager) that there was no hot water

complainer *n.* a chronic ~

complaint *n.* 1. to bring, file, lodge, make, register, swear out a ~ 2. to express, voice a ~ 3. to accept, act on, respond to a ~ 4. to disregard, ignore; reject a ~ 5. a bitter, loud, vociferous ~ 6. a formal, official; justified; legitimate ~ 7. a frivolous; unjustified ~ 8. a ~ about; with (she filed a ~ about the service with the manager) 9. a ~ against (they lodged a ~ against me) 10. a ~ to (our ~ to the dean was ignored) 11. a ~ that + clause (they rejected his ~ that proper procedures had not been followed) 12. (misc.) grounds for/(a) cause for ~; a flood of ~s

complement *n.* 1. a full; perfect ~ 2. (naval) a ship's ~ ("crew") 3. (grammar) a predicate ~ 4. a ~ to

(white wine is a perfect ~ to fish)

complementary *adj.* ~ to

complete I *adj.* ~ with (a turkey dinner ~ with all the trimmings)

complete II *v.* (G) she has just ~d writing her second novel

completion *n.* 1. to approach, near ~ 2. on ~ of (on ~ of this dictionary we will need a rest)

complex *n.* ["bad feelings or repressed desires"] 1. to have a ~ about 2. to give smb. a ~ (about) 3. an Electra; Oedipus ~ 4. a guilt; persecution ~ 5. an inferiority; superiority ~ ["large system"] 6. the military-industrial ~ 7. an apartment (AE); housing; shopping; sports ~

complexion *n.* ["skin, esp. on smb.'s face"] 1. a clear; dark; fair; flawless; florid, ruddy; good; healthy; light, pale; pasty; sallow; smooth ~ ["aspect"] 2. to put a new ~ on smt. 3. a political ~ (the political ~ of the new administration)

complexity *n.* of (great) ~

compliance *n.* 1. ~ with (~ with the law) 2. in ~ with (in ~ with regulations)

complication *n.* 1. to cause ~s 2. to avoid; prevent ~s (to prevent the ~s of pregnancy) 3. ~s arise, set in

complicity *n.* 1. ~ between; with 2. ~ in (a crime)

compliment I *n.* ["praise"] 1. to pay smb. a ~ 2. to lavish, shower ~s on 3. to return a ~ 4. to accept a ~; to take smt. as a ~ 5. to angle for, fish for ~s 6. to bandy ~s 7. a backhanded, dubious, left-handed; nice, pretty; sincere ~ 8. a ~ on; to (she paid him a nice ~ on his success; her remarks were meant as a ~ to your achievements)

compliment II *v.* (D; tr.) to ~ on (I ~ed him on his performance)

complimentary *adj.* 1. highly ~ 2. ~ about

compliments *n.* ["greetings"] 1. to convey, present, send one's/smb.'s ~ 2. (misc.) with the author's ~; with the ~ of the management; my ~ to the chef

comply *v.* (D; intr.) to ~ with (to ~ with the law; to ~ with smb.'s request)

component *n.* a basic, essential, key, main, principal ~

comport *v.* (formal) (P; refl.) to ~ oneself with dignity; to ~ oneself well

compose *v.* 1. (B) to ~ an ode to an emperor 2. (D; tr.) to ~ for (to ~ a symphony for a special concert)

composed *adj.* ["consisting"] (cannot stand alone) ~ of (the team was ~ of seasoned players) (see the Usage Note for **comprised**)

composer *n.* a classical; major; minor; popular ~

composition *n.* ["essay"] 1. to do, write a ~ (on) ["piece of music"] 2. to perform, play a ~

composure *n.* 1. to keep, retain; recover, regain one's ~ 2. to lose one's ~ 3. with great ~

compound I *n.* ["mixture"] a chemical; organic ~

compound II *n.* ["enclosure"] an embassy; factory;

prison ~

comprehend v. 1. (L) she did not ~ that he would not return 2. (Q) I could not ~ why he would not agree

comprehensible adj. 1. ~ to 2. (misc.) it was not ~ to me why they refused to come

comprehension n. 1. to defy, elude ~ 2. reading ~ 3. beyond ~ 4. (misc.) she gaped at me with (a) dawning ~

comprehensives n. ["comprehensive examination"] (AE) to take one's ~

compress I n. 1. to apply a ~ to 2. a cold; dry; hot; wet ~

compress II v. (D; tr.) to ~ into (to ~ a whole paragraph into two sentences)

comprised adj. ["consisting"] (cannot stand alone) ~ of

USAGE NOTE: Some purists prefer *composed of* to *comprised of.*

compromise I n. 1. to agree (BE), agree on, agree to, arrive at, come to, reach, work out a ~ 2. to reject a ~ 3. an acceptable, reasonable ~ 4. a ~ between; on; with (we reached a ~ on the payment)

compromise II v. (D; intr.) to ~ on, over; with (they ~d on certain items with us)

comptroller n. the Comptroller General (AE)

compulsion n. 1. to feel a ~ 2. (a) moral ~ 3. a ~ to + inf. (he felt no ~ to do it) 4. under ~ (to give in under ~)

compulsory adj. 1. ~ for 2. ~ to + inf. (it was ~ to register)

compunction n. 1. to feel, have; show ~ 2. ~ about (she felt no ~ about making us wait) 3. without ~ (he violated the law without the slightest ~)

computer n. 1. to boot up; reboot a ~ 2. to operate, use a ~ 3. to switch on, turn on a ~ 4. to switch off, turn off a ~ 5. to program a ~ 6. an analog; desktop; digital; electronic; general-purpose; handheld; home; laptop; mainframe ~; microcomputer; minicomputer; parallel; personal; serial ~ 7. the ~ is down ("the computer is not functioning") 8. the ~ is up ("the computer is functioning") 9. a ~ bombs (AE), crashes; freezes up 10. by ~ (the book was typeset by ~) 11. on a ~ (to run a program on a ~)

comrade n. 1. a fallen ~ 2. a ~ in arms 3. an old ~

con v. (colloq.) ("to trick") 1. (D; tr.) to ~ into (to ~ smb. into doing smt.) 2. (D; tr.) to ~ out of (he ~ned me out of my money)

conceal v. 1. (D; tr.) to ~ from 2. (Q) they tried to ~ how they did it

concede v. 1. (B) he finally ~d the election to his opponent 2. (L; to) she ~d (to us) that she had been mistaken

conceded adj. (cannot stand alone) ~ to + inf. (this painting is ~ to be her best work)

conceit n. insufferable, overwhelming ~

conceivable adj. 1. barely, hardly ~ 2. ~ that + clause (it is ~ that they knew about it beforehand)

conceive v. 1. (d; intr.) to ~ of (can you ~ of such cruelty?) 2. (L) I could not ~ that he would do such a thing 3. (Q) I could not ~ how he could have done that

conceive of v. (d; intr.) to ~ as (to ~ life as a struggle)

concentrate v. (D; intr., tr.) to ~ on (to ~ all our efforts on solving the problem)

concentration n. 1. to disrupt, disturb smb.'s ~ 2. deep, intense ~ 3. ~ on 4. in ~ (in deep ~) 5. (misc.) smb.'s powers of ~

concept n. 1. to formulate, frame a ~ 2. to grasp, understand a ~ 3. an abstract ~ 4. the ~ that + clause (the ~ that trade lessens international tensions is valid)

conception n. ["concept"] 1. to have a ~ (you have no ~ of the problems we must face) 2. a clear; vague ~ 3. the ~ that + clause (the ~ that the superpowers must fight is dangerous) ["becoming pregnant or being conceived"] 4. to prevent ~ 5. at ~

conceptualize v. (d; tr.) to ~ as (the author ~d the war as a crusade)

concern I n. ["interest"] ["apprehension"] 1. to arouse, cause, give ~ 2. to express, voice; show ~ 3. to feel; share ~ 4. (a) deep, grave, serious; major; paramount; primary ~ (there is grave ~ about the national debt) 5. (a) growing; overriding; widespread ~ 6. (a) common; particular ~ (we share a common ~ over the problems of pollution) 7. (a) national ~ 8. (a) public ~ 9. considerable, utmost ~ (this is a matter of utmost ~ to all of us; they have expressed considerable ~ about the growing crime rate) 10. an object of ~ 11. ~ about, for, over, with (~ about debts; ~ for the children; ~ over the future) 12. ~ to + inf. (~ to know the truth) 13. ~ that + clause (to express ~ that they might fail) 14. of ~ to (the matter was of deep ~ to us) 15. in one's ~ (in their ~ over the debt) 16. out of ~ (she did it out of ~ for her family) ["firm"] 17. to manage a ~ 18. (misc.) a going ("successful") ~

concern II v. 1. (d; refl.) to ~ oneself about, over, with (she ~ed herself with the problem of illiteracy) 2. (misc.) to whom it may ~

concerned adj. 1. deeply, gravely, greatly ~ 2. about, for, over; with (~ about safety) 3. (esp. BE) ~ to + inf. (~ to know your decision) 4. ~ that + clause (we are ~ that they might have missed the train) 5. (misc.) as far as I'm ~

USAGE NOTE: The phrases *concerned about*, *concerned over* and less frequently, *concerned for*, mean "worried about" (concerned about your safety). The phrase *concerned with* means "interested in" (concerned with establishing the truth).

concert n. ["musical program"] 1. to give, hold,

stage a ~ 2. to cancel a ~ 3. a band; live; orchestral; pop; (BE) prom, promenade; rock; subscription ~ 4. at a ~ (we met at the ~) ["harmony, agreement"] 5. in ~ (with) ("together") (to work in ~; voices raised in ~)

concerto *n.* 1. to compose, write a ~ 2. to perform, play a ~ 3. a piano; violin ~ 4. a ~ for (a ~ for piano and orchestra)

concession *n.* ["yielding"] 1. to grant, make a ~ 2. a ~ to ["right to conduct business"] 3. to grant; receive a ~ 4. a parking; refreshment ~ 5. a ~ to + inf. (their firm received a ~ to prospect for oil)

conclave *n.* ["meeting"] a party ~

conclude *v.* 1. (d; intr., tr.) to ~ by, with (she ~d the meeting by asking us to pray; to ~ a concert with a rousing march) 2. (D; tr.) to ~ from (what did they ~ from the evidence?) 3. (L) we ~d that he would not come

conclusion *n.* 1. to arrive at, come to, draw, reach a ~ 2. to jump, leap to a ~ 3. to bring to a ~ 4. a correct; logical; reasonable, tenable, valid ~ 5. a foregone; inescapable, inevitable ~ 6. an erroneous, false, invalid, wrong; hasty ~ 7. a ~ that + clause (their ~ that war is inevitable is disturbing) 8. at the ~ (at the ~ of the concert) 9. in ~ (in ~, I repeat that war is wrong)

concoction *n.* (colloq.) to whip up a ~

concomitant *adj.* (formal) ~ with

concord *n.* (formal) in ~ with

concordance *n.* ["list of words"] 1. to compile a ~ 2. a ~ to ["harmony"] 3. in ~ with

concordat *n.* (rel.) 1. to conclude, draw up a ~ 2. a ~ between; with

concrete *n.* 1. to pour ~ 2. to set smt. in ~ 3. prestressed; ready-mix; reinforced ~ 4. ~ sets 5. a slab of ~

concur *v.* (formal) ("to agree") 1. to ~ completely, fully, wholeheartedly 2. (D; intr.) to ~ in (to ~ in supporting a cause) 3. (D; intr.) to ~ with (to ~ with an opinion; to ~ with smb.) 4. (L) we ~ that the practice should be halted

concurrence *n.* 1. complete, full, unanimous ~ 2. ~ in 3. in ~ with 4. with the ~ of

concurrent *adj.* ~ with

concussion *n.* 1. to get, have, receive, sustain a ~ 2. a mild; severe; slight ~

condemn *v.* 1. to ~ bitterly, harshly, roundly, strongly; unfairly, unjustly 2. (D; tr.) to ~ as (they were ~ed as traitors) 3. (D; tr.) to ~ for (he was ~ed for stealing a horse) 4. (D; tr.) to ~ to (to ~ smb. to death; ~ed to hard labor) 5. (H) he was ~ed to spend the rest of his life in prison

condemnation *n.* 1. to issue a ~ 2. (a) bitter, harsh, scathing, strong; sweeping, universal; unfair, unjust ~

condense *v.* (D; tr.) to ~ from; into (you must ~ your paper into a few paragraphs)

condescend *v.* (formal) 1. (d; intr.) to ~ to (to ~ to cheating) 2. (E) to ~ to mingle with the workers

condescending *adj.* ~ to (~ to one's juniors)

condition I *n.* ["requirement"] 1. to impose, lay down, set (down) state, stipulate a ~ 2. to accept a ~ 3. to fulfill, meet, satisfy a ~ 4. a basic, essential ~ 5. a strict ~ 6. a ~ for (they imposed strict ~s for the use of the car) 7. on ~ that + clause; subj. (she will join us on ~ that you also be there) ["state of repair"] 8. (a) bad, poor, terrible ~ 9. (an) excellent, good, mint, peak, perfect, tip-top ~ 10. operating, running ~ 11. in ~ (our house is in good ~; his car is in running ~; the roads are in terrible ~) ["good health"] ["fitness"] 12. to get into ~ 13. in ~; out of ~ (he never exercises and is out of ~) ["state of health"] 14. excellent; good ~ 15. fair, satisfactory; stable ~ 16. bad, critical, poor; serious; weakened ~ 17. ~ to + inf. (she is in no ~ to drive) 18. in ~ (the patient was in critical ~) ["ailment"] 19. an acute; chronic; degenerative; disabling; untreatable ~ 20. a heart; lung; skin ~ ["misc."] 21. to endure the human ~

condition II *v.* 1. (D; refl.) to ~ for 2. (formal) (D; tr.) to ~ on 3. (D; tr.) to ~ to (~ed to life in the jungle) 4. (H) to ~ smb. to do smt.

conditional *adj.* ~ on

conditioned *adj.* ~ to + inf. (the dog was ~ to attack at a certain signal)

conditioner *n.* a hair; skin ~

conditions *n.* ["circumstances"] 1. favorable; normal; optimal; stable ~ 2. abnormal; adverse; appalling; deplorable, pitiful, squalid; difficult; primitive; repressive; unfavorable; unstable ~ 3. driving; housing; living; sanitary; working ~ 4. economic; political; social ~ 5. weather ~ (if weather ~ permit) 6. in ~ (they live in squalid ~) 7. under ~ (to work under difficult ~)

condole *v.* (BE) (d; tr.) to ~ with smb. (on smt.) (to ~ with smb. on the death of a parent)

condolences *n.* 1. to convey, extend, express, offer send ~ 2. to accept ~ 3. heartfelt, sincere ~ 4. ~ on (I conveyed our sincere ~ to them on the death of their mother)

condone *v.* 1. (G) I don't ~ coming late to work 2. (K) I don't ~ his coming late to work

conducive *adj.* (cannot stand alone) ~ to (exercise is ~ to good health)

conduct I *n.* 1. appropriate; chivalrous; ethical; irreproachable; professional; proper ~ 2. disorderly; improper; inappropriate, unbecoming; unethical; unprofessional ~ 3. (mil.) bad; dishonorable (AE); good ~; ~ unbecoming an officer 4. (misc.) a code of ~

conduct II *v.* 1. (d; refl.) to ~ like (he ~ed himself like a good soldier) 2. (P; refl.) to ~ oneself with dignity 3. (formal) (P; tr.) she was ~ed into the conference room; they ~ed us through the museum

conductor *n.* ["substance that conducts"] 1. a lightning ~ ["person who collects fares"] (BE) 2. a bus ~ ["director"] 3. a guest; orchestra ~

cone *n.* 1. an ice-cream ~ 2. a fir; pine ~

confederacy *n.* 1. to enter, join; form a ~ 2. a ~ among, between; with

confederate *v.* (D; intr.) to ~ with

confederation *n.* 1. to enter, join; form a ~ 2. a ~ among, between; with 3. a loose, weak ~

confer *v.* 1. (D; intr.) ("to converse") to ~ about; with (we will ~ with them about this matter) 2. (D; tr.) ("to bestow") to ~ on (to ~ an award on smb.)

conference *n.* 1. to convene, organize a ~ 2. to have, hold a ~ 3. to attend a ~ 4. an annual ~ 5. an international ~ 6. a news, press; peace; staff (AE); summit ~ 7. a ~ between 8. a ~ on (to hold a ~ on disarmament) 9. at a ~ (you'll see her at the press ~) 10. in ~ (he is in ~ and cannot come to the telephone)

confess *v.* 1. to ~ frankly, honestly; publicly; voluntarily, willingly 2. (B) he ~ed his crime to the police 3. (D; intr.) to ~ to (to ~ to a crime; to ~ to the police; he ~ed to cheating on the exam) 4. (L; to) he ~ed (to us) that he had lied

confession *n.* 1. to make; sign a ~ 2. to extort, extract, force a ~ from; to beat a ~ out of (the police beat a ~ out of him) 3. to repudiate, retract, take back, withdraw a ~ 4. a deathbed; forced; full; public; voluntary ~ 5. (rel.) to hear smb.'s ~ 6. (rel.) to go to ~ 7. a ~ that + clause (he made a public ~ that he had accepted bribes)

confetti *n.* to sprinkle, throw ~

confide *v.* 1. (B) he ~d his secret to us 2. (d; intr.) to ~ in (she ~s in her sister) 3. (L; to) she ~d (to us) that she was about to retire

confidence *n.* ["trust"] ["reliance"] 1. to enjoy, have; gain, win smb.'s ~ 2. to inspire, instill ~ in smb. 3. to have; place one's ~ in smb. 4. to take smb. into one's ~ 5. to shake; undermine smb.'s ~ 6. to betray smb.'s ~ 7. absolute, every, perfect, supreme ~ (I have absolute ~ in her ability) 8. public ~ 9. ~ in (my ~ in him was shaken) 10. (misc.) your ~ in her is misplaced; a vote of ~/of no ~ ["secrecy"] ["secret"] 11. to exchange ~s 12. to violate a ~ 13. strict ~ 14. in ~ (she told it to me in strictest ~) ["belief in one's own ability"] ["firm belief"] 15. to express; gain; have ~ 16. to exude, ooze, radiate ~ (he just oozes ~) 17. to bolster, boost smb.'s ~ 18. to shake; undermine smb.'s ~ 19. buoyant, unbounded ~ 20. the ~ to + inf. (he doesn't have enough ~ to proceed on his own) 21. ~ that + clause (nothing could shake her ~ that she would succeed) 22. (misc.) self-confidence

confident *adj.* 1. supremely ~ 2. ~ about, in 3. ~ of (~ of success) 4. ~ that + clause (she was ~ that she would succeed)

confidential *adj.* 1. highly, strictly ~ 2. to keep smt. ~

confidentiality *n.* 1. to maintain ~ 2. to violate ~ 3. strict ~

confine *v.* (D; refl., tr.) to ~ to (~d to bed; ~d to quarters; the lecturer ~d herself to one topic; ~ yourself to the facts)

confinement *n.* ["imprisonment"] ["being confined"] 1. solitary ~ (they put him in solitary ~) 2. ~ to (~ to quarters) 3. in ~ (in solitary ~) ["lying-in"] (obsol.) 4. in ~ (before the birth of a child)

confines *n.* beyond; within the ~ (impossible within the ~ of the system)

confirm *v.* 1. (L) the president ~ed that a summit conference would take place 2. (Q) she did not ~ when she would arrive 3. (misc.) to ~ in writing

confirmation *n.* 1. official; unofficial ~ 2. ~ that + clause (we have received ~ that she will attend) 3. in ~ of

confiscate *v.* (D; tr.) to ~ from

conflagration *n.* a major ~

conflict I *n.* 1. to provoke a ~ 2. to come into ~ with 3. to avert, avoid a ~ 4. to resolve a ~ 5. (an) armed, military; cultural; direct; ethnic; religious ~ 6. (a) bitter ~ 7. (a) ~ about, over; among, between; with (a ~ between neighboring countries over their common border; a ~ with one's relatives about the terms of a will) 8. in (a) ~ with (their stories are in ~ with each other)

conflict II *v.* (D; intr.) to ~ with (your version ~s with mine)

confluence *n.* at a ~ (the city lies at the ~ of three rivers)

conform *v.* (D; intr.) to ~ to, with (to ~ to specifications)

conformance *n.* in ~ with

conformity *n.* 1. strict ~ 2. ~ to 3. in ~ with

confront *v.* (D; tr.) to ~ about, over; with (to ~ a prisoner with a witness)

confrontation *n.* 1. to have; provoke a ~ 2. to avert, avoid a ~ 3. an armed, military; direct ~ 4. a bitter ~ 5. a ~ about, over; among, between; with

confuse *v.* (d; tr.) to ~ with (I always ~ him with his brother)

confused *adj.* 1. easily; very ~ 2. ~ about, over 3. to become, get ~ 4. ~ to + inf. (I was ~ to learn of his latest decision)

confusing *adj.* ~ to + inf. (it was ~ to listen to the testimony)

confusion *n.* 1. to cause, create; lead to ~ 2. to avoid; clear up ~ 3. ~ arises; reigns 4. to throw into ~ (their unexpected arrival threw our plans into ~) 5. complete, general, mass, total, utter ~ 6. ~ about, over; between 7. in ~ (to withdraw in utter ~; in the ~ they escaped) 8. a scene; state of ~ (it was a scene of utter ~)

congestion *n.* 1. traffic ~ 2. nasal; lung, pulmonary

~

conglomerate *n.* a financial; industrial; multinational ~

congratulate *v.* 1. to ~ heartily, sincerely, warmly 2. (D; refl., tr.) to ~ on, upon (to ~ smb. on her/his promotion)

congratulations *n.* 1. to extend, offer ~ on 2. deepest, heartiest, hearty, sincere, warm, warmest ~ 3. ~ on, upon (my warmest ~ on your promotion!) 4. ~ to (~ to you on your promotion)

congress *n.* 1. to convene, hold a ~ 2. an annual; biennial; international; party ~ 3. (misc.) an act of Congress

congruence *n.* (formal or technical) (in) ~ with

congruent *adj.* (formal or technical) ~ to, with

congruity *n.* (formal) ~ with

congruous *adj.* (formal) ~ to, with

conjecture I *n.* (formal) ["guess"] 1. to make a ~ 2. pure ~ 3. a ~ about 4. a ~ that + clause (her ~ that the election would be a landslide proved to be true) 5. (misc.) it is a matter for/of ~ whether they can still win

conjecture II *v.* (formal) (L) ("to guess") the press ~d that a summit conference would take place

conjugation *n.* ["verb forms"] an irregular; regular ~

conjunction *n.* ["connecting word"] 1. a coordinating; subordinating ~ ["cooperation"] ["coincidence"] 2. in ~ with

connect *v.* 1. to ~ closely, intimately; loosely 2. (d; intr.) to ~ to, with (this bus is supposed to ~ with a train) 3. (D; tr.) to ~ to, with (are you ~ed with this firm? to ~ a TV set to an antenna)

connection, connexion *n.* ["association"] 1. to establish, make a ~ 2. to break, sever a ~ 3. a close, intimate; direct; loose, tenuous ~ 4. a foreign; international ~ 5. a ~ between; to; with (there was no ~ between the two phenomena; to have a ~ with smb.) 6. in a certain ~ (in this ~; in ~ with the other matter) ["acquaintance"] ["tie"] 7. business; professional; social ~s ["transfer during a trip"] 8. to make; miss a ~ ["linking of two telephones"] 9. to get a ~ ["link, linking"] 10. a faulty; loose ~ ["misc."] 11. to have ~s ("to have influential supporters"); to use one's ~s

connect up *v.* (D; tr.) to ~ to, with (to ~ a telephone up to the exchange)

connexion (BE) see **connection**

connive *v.* 1. (D; intr.) to ~ at; in; with (to ~ in cheating smb.) 2. (E) they ~d (with each other) to cheat her

conquest *n.* 1. to make a ~ 2. to consolidate; extend one's ~s 3. military; world ~

conscience *n.* 1. to appeal to; arouse, stir smb.'s ~ 2. to have a ~ 3. to have smt. on one's ~ 4. to ease, salve one's ~; to wrestle with one's ~ 5. a clear; guilty ~ (to have a guilty ~) 6. a matter of ~ 7.

(misc.) in all ~ (CE), in good ~ (AE), in all good ~ (AE); pangs of ~

conscientious *adj.* ~ about (she is ~ about her work)

conscious *adj.* 1. fully ~ 2. (cannot stand alone) ~ of (~ of danger) 3. ~ that + clause (she became ~ that everyone was staring at her)

consciousness *n.* ["conscious state"] 1. to lose; recover, regain ~ ["awareness"] 2. to raise smb.'s ~ 3. class; political; social ~ ["misc."] 4. (the) stream of ~

conscript *v.* 1. (D; tr.) to ~ for (to ~ troops for national defense) 2. (D; tr.) to ~ into (to ~ youths into the armed forces)

conscription *n.* 1. to introduce ~ 2. military; universal ~

consecrate *v.* 1. (D; tr.) to ~ as (he was ~d as archbishop) 2. (d; tr.) to ~ to (she ~d her life to helping the poor) 3. (N; used with a noun) he was ~d archbishop

consecration *n.* ~ to

consensus *n.* 1. to reach a ~ 2. a general ~ 3. (a) ~ among; on 4. a ~ that + clause (there is a general/general ~ among the experts that we should abstain)

consent I *n.* 1. to give one's ~ to 2. to refuse, withhold one's ~ 3. common; general; informed; mutual; parental; tacit; unanimous ~ 4. by ~ (by mutual ~) 5. (misc.) the age of ~

consent II *v.* 1. (D; intr.) to ~ to (to ~ to a proposal) 2. (E) she ~ed to help

consequence *n.* ["importance"] 1. of ~ (to) (a matter of some ~) ["result"] 2. in ~ of

consequences *n.* ["results"] 1. to have ~ for 2. to accept, bear, face, suffer, take the ~ 3. dire, disastrous; grave, serious ~ 4. far-reaching, fateful; inevitable; unforeseeable; unforeseen ~

conservation *n.* 1. energy; forest; soil; water; wildlife ~ 2. (the) ~ of natural resources

conservative I *adj.* 1. deeply ~ 2. ~ in (~ in one's views)

conservative II *n.* a diehard, dyed-in-the-wool; political ~

consider *v.* 1. ("to regard") to ~ favorably 2. (D; tr.) ("to regard"); ("to examine") to ~ as (we ~ed him as a possible candidate) 3. (D; tr.) ("to regard as a candidate") to ~ for (he cannot be ~ed for the job) 4. (G) ("to contemplate") she ~ed resigning 5. (L) ("to take into account") you must ~ that she has been here only one month 6. (M) ("to believe") we ~ her to be our friend 7. (N; used with an adjective, noun, past participle) ("to believe") we ~ her qualified; we ~ her a genius; we ~ed him a possible candidate 8. (Q) ("to contemplate") they ~ed where to hide the money

USAGE NOTE: Note the contrasts between *consider as* and *consider* in the following text — In her book she considers ("examines") Shakespeare as a playwright and as a poet. She considers ("believes") Shakespeare (to be) both a great playwright and a great poet. However, she considers ("believes") Shakespeare (to be) even greater as a playwright than as a poet.

considerate *adj.* 1. ~ of (he was ~ of everyone) 2. ~ towards 3. ~ to + inf. (it was ~ of her to do that)

consideration *n.* ["thought"] ["concern"] 1. to give ~ to (to give some ~ to a matter) 2. to show ~ for 3. to take smt. into ~ 4. to deserve; require ~ (the matter requires careful ~) 5. careful; due; serious ~ 6. a major; minor; overriding ~ 7. financial; humanitarian; personal ~s 8. for smb.'s ~ (I submit the enclosed proposal for your ~) 9. in ~ of (in ~ of past services) 10. on careful ~ of 11. out of ~ for smb. 12. under ~ (the matter is under ~) 13. with ~ for (with due ~ for your feelings, we must reject your request) ["fee"] 14. for a ~ (for a modest ~, he'll do anything)

consign *v.* 1. (B) they ~ed the shipment to us 2. (d; tr.) to ~ to (the paintings were ~ed to our care)

consignment *n.* ["a sale allowing the dealer to return unsold merchandise"] to sell; ship on ~

consist *v.* 1. (d; intr.) to ~ of ("to be composed of") (our state ~s of thirty counties) 2. (formal) (d; intr.) to ~ in ("to be equivalent to") (freedom ~s in the absence of oppressive laws)

consistent *adj.* 1. ~ in (she is ~ in her support of our party) 2. ~ with (~ with our principles)

consistory *n.* (usu. rel.) to convoke, hold a ~

consolation *n.* 1. to afford, offer ~ 2. (of) ~ to (that will be a great ~ to us; that should be of some ~ to you; that is of no ~ to me) 3. a ~ to + inf. (it's a ~ to know that they are safe = it's a ~ knowing that they are safe) 4. a ~ that + clause (our only ~ was that no one was hurt seriously) 5. (misc.) a word of ~

console *v.* 1. (D; tr.) to ~ on (to ~ smb. on the loss of a loved one) 2. (d; refl.) to ~ with (I ~d myself with the thought that the situation could be worse)

consommé *n.* 1. clear ~ 2. a bowl; cup of ~

consonance *n.* in ~ with

consonant I *adj.* (formal) ~ with

consonant II *n.* 1. to articulate, pronounce a ~ 2. a dental; double, geminate; final; guttural; hard; labial; liquid; palatal; soft; unvoiced; velar; voiced ~ 3. (misc.) a ~ cluster

consort *v.* (formal) (d; intr.) to ~ with

consortium *n.* to form, organize a ~

conspicuous *adj.* 1. ~ for, in 2. (misc.) to be ~ by one's absence

conspiracy *n.* 1. to hatch, organize a ~ 2. to crush; foil; uncover a ~ 3. (a) criminal ~ 4. a ~ against; with 5. a ~ to + inf. (a ~ to overthrow the government) 6. (misc.) a ~ of silence

conspire *v.* 1. (D; intr.) to ~ against; with 2. (E) they ~d to overthrow the government

constable *n.* (BE) ["police officer"] a chief ~

consternation *n.* 1. to cause ~ 2. to express; feel ~ 3. in ~ 4. to smb.'s ~ (to our ~, the current was turned off)

constituent *n.* (ling.) an immediate; ultimate ~

constitute *v.* (S; used with a noun) this ~s a problem

constitution *n.* ["basic law"] 1. to adopt, establish; ratify a ~ 2. to draw up, frame, write a ~ 3. to preserve, safeguard a ~ 4. to abrogate; amend, change a ~ 5. to violate a ~ 6. a written; unwritten ~ ["physical makeup"] 7. a feeble, frail; iron, rugged, strong ~

constitutional *adj.* ~ to + inf. (it is not ~ to censor the press)

constitutionality *n.* to challenge, question, test; establish the ~ (of a law)

constituency *n.* a core ~

constrain *v.* (formal) (H) to ~ smb. to do smt.

constrained *adj.* (formal) (cannot stand alone) ~ to + inf. (we were ~ to act)

constraint *n.* ["restriction"] 1. to impose, place, put a ~ on, upon 2. financial; legal ~s ["compulsion"] 3. under ~ (to act under ~)

construct I *n.* a theoretical ~

construct II *v.* (D; tr.) to ~ of, out of (the house is ~ed of wood)

construction *n.* ["building industry"] 1. in ~ (he is in ~) ["act of building"] 2. shoddy; solid, sturdy ~ 3. commercial; modular; residential ~ 4. of ~ (buildings of shoddy ~) 5. under ~ (the new skyscraper is under ~) ["interpretation"] 6. to put a ~ on (he put the wrong ~ on my statement) ["syntactic phrase"] 7. an absolute; idiomatic ~

construe *v.* 1. (d; tr.) to ~ as (he ~d the statement as a threat) 2. (M) I ~d his speech to be a warning

consul *n.* a ~ general; an honorary ~

consulate *n.* a ~ general

consult *v.* 1. (D; tr.) to ~ about, on; with (to ~ with smb. about a problem) 2. (D; tr.) to ~ about, on (to ~ smb. about smt.)

consultant *n.* 1. a business; legal; medical; nursing; political ~ 2. a ~ for, on; to (a ~ to the president on foreign policy) 3. (med.) a ~ in

consultation *n.* 1. to have, hold ~s 2. ~s about, on; with 3. in ~ with (they solved the problem in ~ with several experts)

consulting *n.* online ~

consumed *adj.* ~ with (~ with guilt)

consumption *n.* 1. conspicuous; mass ~ 2. fuel ~ 3. (misc.) unfit for human ~

contact *n.* ["being together"] ["connection"] 1. to come in, into ~; to establish, make ~ 2. to maintain, stay in ~ 3. to bring into ~ 4. to avoid; break off; lose ~ 5. (electrical) to break ~ 6. close, intimate; direct; eye; face-to-face; indirect; physical ~ 7. radar; radio; telephone ~ (the control tower was in radar ~ with the plane) 8. ~ between; with (to establish ~ with one's relatives; to stay in ~ with friends) 9. in ~ (have they been in ~?) 10. on ~ (the bomb exploded on ~ with the ground) 11. a point of ~ ["acquaintance"] ["tie"] 12. to have ~ (with) 13. business; cultural; personal; professional; international; social ~s

contagious *adj.* extremely, highly, very ~

container *n.* a metal; plastic ~

contaminate *v.* (D; tr.) to ~ by, with (to ~ smb. with smt; a wound ~d by bacteria)

contamination *n.* radioactive ~

contemplate *v.* (G) he ~d resigning

contemplation *n.* 1. quiet; silent ~ 2. lost in ~

contemporaneous *adj.* (formal) ~ with

contemporary *adj.* ~ with

contempt *n.* ["scorn"] 1. to demonstrate, display, show; have ~ for 2. bitter, deep, profound, total, unmitigated, utter ~ 3. ~ for 4. beneath ~ 5. in, with ~ (I looked at them with ~) ["disrespect"] (usu. legal) 6. to hold in ~ (to hold smb. in ~ of court) ("to accuse smb. of disrespect for a court") 7. civil; criminal ~

contemptible *adj.* ~ to + inf. (it was ~ of him to behave like that)

contemptuous *adj.* ~ of (he was ~ of all authority)

contend *v.* (formal) 1. (D; intr.) ("to compete") to ~ for; with (to ~ for a position) 2. (L) ("to claim") he ~ed that he had been cheated

contender *n.* 1. a formidable, leading, main, serious, strong; likely ~ 2. a presidential ~ 3. a ~ for (the leading ~ for the heavyweight crown)

content I *n.* 1. ~ with (they were ~ with their lot) 2. ~ to + inf. (she was not ~ to remain at home)

content II *n.* to one's heart's ~ ("to one's complete satisfaction")

content III *v.* (formal) (d; refl.) to ~ with (to ~ oneself with a simple life)

contention *n.* ["argument"] 1. to rebut, refute; reject a ~ 2. to substantiate, support a ~ 3. a ~ about 4. a bone of ~ ("something contentious") 5. a ~ that + inf. (it is his ~ that taxes are too low) ["competition"] 6. in ~ (for); (with) (which teams are in ~ for the title?)

contents *n.* 1. to divulge the ~ (of a letter) 2. a table of ~

contest I *n.* 1. to have, hold, organize, stage a ~ 2. to judge a ~ 3. to enter a ~ 4. to lose; win a ~ 5. a bitter, hard-fought; close; one-sided ~ 6. a beauty; public-speaking ~ 7. a ~ among, between; for

contest II *v.* to ~ bitterly

contestant *n.* a ~ for

contested *adj.* bitterly, closely, hotly, vigorously ~

context *n.* 1. a historical ~ 2. in; out of ~; within a ~ (to cite a passage out of ~)

contiguous *adj.* ~ to, with

continent *n.* on a ~

contingency *n.* 1. to provide for every ~ 2. a ~ arises 3. an unforeseen ~

contingent *adj.* (pompous) (cannot stand alone) ~ on, upon (the time of his arrival is ~ on the weather)

continuance *n.* ["adjournment"] (legal) (AE) to grant a ~

continue *v.* 1. to ~ unabated 2. (D; intr.) to ~ as (she will ~ as chairperson) 3. (D; intr.) to ~ by (she ~d by citing more facts) 4. (D; intr.) to ~ with (she ~d with her work) 5. (E) they ~d to write 6. (G) they ~d writing 7. (misc.) to be ~d

continuity *n.* 1. to break the ~ 2. ~ between (there was no ~ between the first and second acts)

continuum *n.* 1. to constitute, form a ~ 2. the health-illness ~ 3. along a ~ 4. a ~ from; to

contorted *adj.* ~ with (her face was ~ with rage)

contraband *n.* 1. to smuggle ~ 2. to seize ~ 3. ~ of war

contraception *n.* 1. to practice, use ~ 2. a method of ~

contraceptive *n.* a chemical; oral; vaginal ~

contract I *n.* 1. to conclude, sign; enter into; land (colloq.); negotiate; ratify a ~ 2. to carry out, execute; honor a ~ 3. to draft, draw up, write (up) a ~ 4. to assign (after bidding), let; award a ~ 5. to abrogate, cancel, repudiate a ~ 6. to breach, break, violate a ~ 7. a binding; exclusive; legal, valid; void ~ 8. an oral, verbal; written ~ 9. (colloq.) (AE) a sweetheart ~ ("an agreement favorable to the employer that was reached without the participation of the union members") 10. (AE) a yellow-dog ~ ("a contract that obligates the workers not to join a union") 11. a marriage ~ 12. a ~ for; with 13. a ~ to + inf. (they landed a ~ to build a bridge) 14. under ~ to, with (that player is under ~ with our team) 15. (misc.) (a) breach of ~; to put out a ~ on smb. ("to arrange to have smb. murdered")

contract II *v.* 1. (d; intr.) to ~ for; with (the city ~ed for a new library with their firm) 2. (E) the firm ~ed to construct the bridge

contract III *v.* ("to shorten") (D; intr., tr.) to ~ to (in spoken English, "it is" often ~s/is often ~ed to "it's")

contractions *n.* to time (labor) ~

contractor *n.* a building; defense; electrical; general; plumbing ~; a sub-contractor

contract out *v.* (D; tr.) to ~ to (the work was ~ed out to several local firms)

contradict *v.* to ~ flatly

contradiction *n.* 1. an apparent; basic; direct; flat, outright; glaring; inherent ~ 2. a ~ between 3. in ~ to, with (his words and his deeds are in ~ to/with each other) 4. (misc.) a ~ in terms

contradictory *adj.* ~ to

contradistinction *n.* (formal) in ~ to

contraption *n.* (colloq.) to build, put together, slap together a ~

contrary I *adj.* (cannot stand alone) ~ to (his actions are ~ to the rules)

contrary II *n.* 1. on the ~ (does your back feel any better? on the ~, it feels much worse) 2. to the ~ (I will come next month unless you write to the ~)

contrast I *n.* 1. to present a ~ 2. a harsh, sharp, stark, startling; marked, striking, vivid ~ 3. a favorable; unfavorable ~ 4. a ~ between, to, with 5. by ~ (with) 6. in ~ (to) (in ~ to their neighbors, they live modestly) 7. (misc.) for (the sake of) ~

contrast II *v.* 1. to ~ sharply 2. to ~ favorably; unfavorably 3. (D; intr., tr.) to ~ with (their deeds ~ with their promises)

contravention *n.* (formal) in ~ of (to act in ~ of international law)

contribute *v.* 1. (D; tr.) to ~ for (we ~d clothing for the flood victims) 2. (D; intr., tr.) to ~ to, towards (to ~ to charity; she ~d a week's salary to the relief fund)

contribution *n.* ["donation, gift"] 1. to make a ~ (to) 2. to send in a ~ 3. a charitable; in-kind; monetary; voluntary ~ 4. a big, generous, large; small, token ~ (to make a generous ~ to charity) ["accomplishment, presentation"] 5. to make a ~ (to) 6. a brilliant, great, notable, outstanding, remarkable; important; invaluable, key; major, significant, substantial; minor, modest; valuable ~ (she made an outstanding ~ to science) 7. a ~ to, towards

contributor *n.* ["one who gives money"] 1. an anonymous; generous; major; regular ~ 2. a ~ to (a generous ~ to charity) ["one who contributes scholarly works"] 3. a prolific; regular ~ 4. a ~ to (a regular ~ to a journal)

contrition *n.* 1. to show ~ 2. to express; feel ~ 3. (often rel.) an act of ~ 4. ~ for

contrive *v.* (E) she somehow ~d to arrange a meeting

control *n.* 1. to establish; exercise, exert, wield; gain, have; retain ~ (over) 2. to assume, take ~ of 3. to bring smt. under ~ (the fire was finally brought under ~) 4. to wrest ~ from 5. to lose; relinquish ~ of (she lost ~ of the car) 6. absolute, complete; close, strict; full ~ (to exert strict ~ over smt.) 7. lax, loose; remote ~ 8. government; parental ~ 9. air-traffic; flight; mission ~ 10. arms; gun ~ 11. birth; communicable-disease ~ 12. cost; quality ~ 13. damage; fire; flood ~ 14. emissions; pest ~ 15. stress; thought ~ 16. price; rent; wage ~ 17. ~ of, over (to establish ~ over prices) 18. in ~ (of) (she was in full ~ of the situation) 19. beyond, out of ~ (the car went out of ~; the fire got out of ~) 20. under ~ (the fire was finally brought under ~; keep them under ~; the area was placed under the ~ of the military)

controlled *adj.* tightly ~

controller *n.* an air-traffic, flight ~

controls *n.* ["restrictions"] 1. to impose, introduce ~ (on) 2. to tighten ~ (on) 3. to lift, remove ~

(from) 4. to relax ~ (on) 5. price; rent; wage ~ ["regulating instruments"] 6. to take over the ~ (the copilot took over the ~) 7. dual ~ 8. at the ~

controversial *adj.* bitterly, highly, very ~

controversy *n.* 1. to arouse, cause, fuel, generate, stir up (a) ~ 2. to settle a ~ 3. a bitter, fierce, furious, heated, lively ~ 4. a ~ dies down; flares up 5. a ~ about, over 6. a ~ between, with

convalesce *v.* (D; intr.) to ~ from

convalescence *n.* a lengthy, long ~

convenience *n.* ["comfort"] 1. a ~ to + inf. (it's a great ~ to live in town = it's a great ~ living in town) 2. at smb.'s ~ (answer at your earliest ~) ["device that adds to comfort"] 3. modern ~s 4. the latest ~s 5. (BE) a public ~ ("a public toilet")

convenient *adj.* 1. mutually ~ 2. ~ for (will Tuesday be ~ for you?) 3. ~ to + inf. (it is very ~ to have the bus stop so close = it is very ~ having the bus stop so close) 4. ~ that + clause (it's very ~ that he can drive you to work)

convent *n.* to enter a ~ ("to become a nun")

convention *n.* ["assembly"] ["conference"] 1. to have, hold a ~ 2. an annual; national; party; political ~ ["agreement"] 3. a copyright ~ ["practice, tradition"] 4. to defy, flout ~ 5. a longstanding ~ 6. ~ dictates (that we eat three meals a day) 7. by ~

conventional *adj.* ~ in (one's tastes)

converge *v.* (d; intr.) to ~ on, upon; towards (to ~ on the speaker's platform)

conversant *adj.* (cannot stand alone) ["familiar"] 1. fully, thoroughly ~ 2. ~ with (~ with procedures)

conversation *n.* ["talk"] 1. to begin, strike up; carry on, have, hold a ~ 2. to make ~ (we had little in common, and it was difficult to make ~) 3. to bug, monitor, tap a ~ 4. to hog, monopolize; liven up, stimulate a ~ 5. to break off, end, finish, terminate; interrupt a ~ 6. (an) animated, lively; boring, dull; intimate; light; serious ~ 7. (a) private; telephone ~ 8. (a) ~ lags; picks up 9. fragments, scraps, snatches of (a) ~ (we overheard scraps of their ~) 10. (a) ~ about; with 11. in ~ (she was in ~ with a friend) ["sexual intercourse"] (legal) 12. criminal ~ ("adultery")

conversations *n.* ["negotiations"] 1. to hold ~ 2. to break off ~ 3. ~ about; with

converse *v.* 1. to ~ fluently (to ~ fluently in a foreign language) 2. (D; intr.) to ~ about; with

conversion *n.* ["change"] 1. condo; loft ~ 2. a ~ from; into, to ["a score made by a kick or pass after a goal has been scored"] (Am. football, rugby) 3. to make a ~ ["adoption of a new religion"] 4. to undergo ~ 5. a religious ~ 6. a ~ from; to

convert I *n.* 1. to gain a ~ 2. a ~ to (a ~ to Buddhism)

convert II *v.* 1. (AE) (D; intr.) ("to change one's religion") to ~ from; to (they ~ed from Buddhism to Hinduism) 2. (D; intr., tr.) ("to change"); ("to change smb.'s religion") to ~ from; into, to (to ~ smb. to Islam; the plant ~ed to microchip production; they ~ed their money from marks into pounds; to ~ a barn into a garage)

converter *n.* a catalytic ~

convertible *adj.* 1. freely ~ 2. ~ into, to (~ into hard currency)

convey *v.* 1. (B) ("to give") ~ my best wishes to them 2. (D; tr.) ("to transfer") to ~ from; to (the title to the property was ~ed from them to you) 3. (Q) ("to explain") she tried to ~ how she felt

conveyance *n.* ["vehicle"] a public ~

convict I *n.* an escaped ~

convict II *v.* (D; tr.) to ~ of (he was ~ed of murder)

conviction *n.* ["strong belief"] 1. to carry ~ (his story carries ~) 2. a burning, deep, firm, strong, unshakeable; lifelong; personal; religious ~ 3. a ~ about 4. a ~ that + clause (she expressed her firm ~ that television was harmful to children) 5. by ~ (a pacifist by ~) 6. (misc.) to have the courage of one's ~s ["guilty verdict"] 7. to get, win a ~ (the prosecutor got ten ~s last year) 8. to overturn a ~ (the appeals court overturned the ~) 9. a previous ~ 10. a ~ for (a previous ~ for embezzlement)

convince *v.* 1. (D; tr.) to ~ of (he ~d me of his sincerity) 2. (esp. AE) (H) we ~ed ("persuaded") her to stay home 3. (L; must have an object) he ~d everyone that he was honest

convinced *adj.* 1. absolutely, completely, firmly, thoroughly ~ 2. ~ that + clause (we are ~ that our project will succeed)

convocation *n.* ["assembly"] 1. to hold a ~ ["assembly of graduates of a university"] (GB) 2. a member of ~

convoy *n.* 1. to form a ~ 2. a naval ~ 3. in; under ~ (to travel in ~)

convulsed *adj.* ~ in, with (~ in/with laughter)

convulsions *n.* to go into, have ~

cook I *n.* 1. the chief, head ~ 2. (AE) a short-order ~

cook II *v.* (C) ~ some vegetables for us; or ~ us some vegetables

cooker *n.* ["pot"] 1. a pressure ~ (also fig.) ["stove"] (BE) 2. an electric; gas ~

cookie *n.* AE; BE has *(sweet)* biscuit 1. to bake ~s 2. a chocolate-chip; homemade; sandwich ~ (CE) a fortune ~

cooking *n.* 1. to do the ~ 2. home; home-style ~ 3. (BE) good, plain (English) ~

cookout *n.* (esp. AE; CE has *barbecue*) to have a ~

cool I *adj.* ["calm"] 1. to keep, remain, stay ~ ["indifferent"] ["unfriendly"] 2. ~ to, towards (she was ~ to the idea)

cool II *n.* (slang) ["composure"] to blow, lose; keep one's ~

cool III *v.* (D; tr.) to ~ to (boil the mixture and then ~ it to room temperature)

coolant *n.* to add ~

coolness *n.* ["indifference"] ~ to, towards

coop *n.* 1. a chicken ~ 2. (misc.) (colloq.) to fly the ~ ("to escape")

cooperate *v.* 1. to ~ closely; fully 2. (D; intr.) to ~ in, on; with (to ~ in/on a project with smb.)

cooperation *n.* 1. close; wholehearted ~ 2. ~ between; in, on; with (~ on a project with another university) 3. in ~ with (their dictionary was published in ~ with the Ministry of Education) 4. with smb.'s ~ 5. (misc.) to enlist smb.'s ~

cooperative, co-op, coop *n.* 1. to set up a ~ 2. a consumers'; farmers'; housing; producers'; workers' ~

coop up *v.* (D; tr.) to ~ in; with (we were ~ed up in a small room)

coordinate *v.* 1. to ~ carefully; closely 2. (D; tr.) to ~ with (we must ~ our operations with theirs)

coordination *n.* 1. close ~ 2. ~ among, between; with

cop *v.* (colloq.) (esp. AE) (D; intr.) to ~ out of ("to renege on") (to ~ out of a responsibility)

cope *v.* (D; intr.) to ~ with (to ~ with difficulties)

cop out *v.* (colloq.) (esp. AE) ("to renege") to ~ on (to ~ on a responsibility)

copulate *v.* (D; intr.) to ~ with

copy I *n.* ["reproduction"] 1. to make, run off a ~ 2. to Xerox (T) a ~ 3. to print ~pies (the publisher decided to print ten thousand ~pies of the book) 4. to inscribe a ~ (the author inscribed a ~ of her book for him) 5. (a) clean, fair ~; hard ("readable") ~ (from a computer); a rough; true ~ 6. a backup; blind; carbon; extra; master ~; photocopy; top (BE) ("original"); Xerox (T) ~ ["manuscript"] ["draft of material to be printed"] 7. to edit ~ ["issue, publication"] 8. an advance; back; complimentary, presentation ~ ["news"] 9. to make good ~ ("to be newsworthy")

copy II *v.* 1. (D; tr.) to ~ for (please ~ the article for me) 2. (D; tr.) to ~ from, out of (she ~ied the paragraph from the encyclopedia)

copybook *n.* (BE) to blot one's ~ ("to ruin one's reputation")

copyright *n.* 1. (of a copyright office) to grant, register a ~ 2. (of an author, publisher) to apply for; claim; have, hold, own; secure a ~ 3. to infringe a ~ 4. an ad-interim; full-term; statutory ~ 5. a ~ expires, runs out 6. a ~ on (a book) 7. under ~

cord *n.* 1. to pull (on) a ~ 2. to tie a ~ (around smt.) 3. a telephone ~ 4. a communication (BE), emergency (AE); electric (AE; BE has *flex*); extension ~ 5. a spinal; umbilical ~ 6. a length, piece of ~

cordial *adj.* ~ to, towards

cordon *n.* ["protective ring of police, soldiers"] 1. to form a ~ 2. to throw a ~ around (an area)

cords *n.* the vocal ~

core *n.* 1. the hard ~ 2. at the ~ (at the ~ of the problem) 3. to the ~ (rotten to the ~) 4. (misc.) to get to the ~ of a matter

cork *n.* to pop, remove a ~

corn *n.* ["maize"] (esp. AE) 1. to grow, raise; husk, shuck (AE) ~ 2. hybrid; Indian; sweet; young ~ 3. an ear; kernel of ~ 4. (misc.) ~ on the cob

corner *n.* 1. to round, turn; take a ~ 2. a blind; tight ~ 3. (also fig.) around the ~ (they live around the ~; to go around the ~; prosperity is just around the ~) 4. at, on a ~ (of a street) 5. in the ~ (of a room) 6. (misc.) the four ~s of the earth; I could see her out of the ~ of my eye; (boxing) a neutral ~; to cut ~s ("to do something the easiest and quickest way"); forced into a ~ ("crowded into a difficult position"); to establish a ~ on the market ("to monopolize the market")

cornerstone *n.* to lay a ~

corollary *n.* a ~ to

coronary *n.* 1. to have a ~ 2. a massive ~

coronation *n.* to have, hold a ~

corporal *n.* a lance ~

corporation *n.* 1. to establish, form, set up a ~ 2. to manage, run a ~ 3. to dissolve a ~ 4. (BE) a public ~ 5. a multinational ~

corps *n.* 1. the diplomatic; officer; press ~ 2. an army ~ 3. the Air Corps; the Marine Corps

corpse *n.* 1. to bury, inter; lay out a ~ 2. to dig up, exhume a ~ 3. a ~ decays, decomposes, rots

corpus *n.* (ling.) 1. to collect, gather a ~ 2. a closed; spoken; written ~

corpuscle *n.* a red; white ~

correct *adj.* ["true"] 1. ~ in (you are ~ in thinking that he is foolish) 2. ~ to + inf. (it would be ~ to say that we have committed a blunder) 3. ~ that + clause (is it ~ that he has resigned?) 4. (misc.) politically ~ (also PC)

correction *n.* 1. to make a ~ 2. to mark ~s (in a text)

correctness *n.* political ~ (also PC)

correlate *v.* (d; intr., tr.) to ~ with (to ~ one set of data with another set)

correlation *n.* 1. (a) close, high, strong ~ 2. a ~ between; with

correspond *v.* 1. ("to be similar") to ~ approximately, roughly; closely; exactly 2. (D; intr.) ("to be equal") to ~ to (what German word ~s to *hound*?) 3. (BE) (D; intr.) ("to be in harmony") to ~ with (his actions do not ~ with his words) 4. (D; intr.) ("to write") to ~ about; with (they have been ~ing with each other about this matter for years)

correspondence *n.* ["exchange of letters"] 1. to carry on, conduct; enter into (a) ~ 2. to break off, end (a) ~ 3. business, commercial; personal ~ 4. ~ about; between; with 5. in ~ with (to be in ~ with smb. about smt.) ["conformity"] 6. close ~ 7. ~ between (~ between theory and practice)

correspondent *n.* a diplomatic; foreign; special; war ~

corresponding *adj.* ~ to

corridor *n.* 1. an air; long; narrow; winding ~ 2. a ~ across; between; through

corruption *n.* 1. to expose ~ 2. moral; political ~ 3. (misc.) bribery and ~; graft and ~ (AE)

corsage *n.* to pin a ~ on

cortex *n.* the cerebral ~

cosigner *n.* a ~ for, of (a ~ for a promissory note)

cosmetics *n.* to apply, put on; use ~

cost I *n.* 1. to bear the ~ 2. to defray the ~ 3. to drive up the ~ 4. to pay ~s 5. to spare no ~ 6. to cut, reduce ~s 7. to estimate; put, set a ~ at (he put the ~ at one hundred dollars) 8. to cover, meet; split the ~ 9. advertising; court; direct; fixed; indirect; overhead; production ~s (who will pay the court ~s?) 10. a high ~ (the high ~ of energy) 11. a unit ~ 12. at a certain ~ (at any ~; at all ~s; at the ~ of his health; at a terrible ~; at no ~ to the taxpayer) 13. the ~ in (the ~ in time was considerable)

cost II *v.* 1. (O; may be used with one inanimate object) it cost us ten dollars; it cost ten dollars 2. (P; with an animate object) his blunder cost us dearly 3. (misc.) it ~s (us) fifty thousand dollars a year to maintain this house

co-star *v.* (D; intr.) to ~ with

cost-effective *adj.* ~ to + inf. (it would not be ~ to hire temporary workers)

costly *adj.* ~ to + inf. (it is ~ to run an air conditioner all day)

costume *n.* 1. an academic; bathing (BE), swimming (BE) ~ 2. (a) folk, national, traditional; Halloween; period ~ (they were all in national ~)

cot *n.* ["folding bed"] (AE; BE has *camp bed*) 1. to open up, unfold a ~ 2. a folding ~ ["child's bed"] (BE) 3. see **crib I**

cottage *n.* a country; summer; thatched; weekend ~

cotton I *n.* 1. to gin; grow; pick; plant ~ 2. (AE) absorbent ~ (CE has *cotton wool*) 3. pure, one hundred percent ~ 4. a bale; reel (BE); wad of ~

cotton II *v.* (colloq.) (d; intr.) ("to take a liking") to ~ to

cotton on *v.* (colloq.) (BE) (D; intr.) ("to understand") to ~ to

cotton up *v.* (colloq.) (esp. AE) (d; intr.) ("to try to ingratiate oneself") to ~ to

couch I *n.* 1. to lie on a ~ 2. a studio ~

couch II *v.* (formal) (D; tr.) to ~ in (to ~ a request in tactful language)

cough I *n.* 1. to develop a ~ 2. to have a ~ 3. to suppress a ~ 4. a bad, heavy, nasty; croupy; dry; hacking, persistent; smoker's ~

cough II *v.* to ~ loudly

coughing *n.* a fit of ~

could *v.* (F) he ~ not attend the meeting

council *n.* 1. to convene, convoke a ~ 2. a city (AE), local (BE); county; district; executive; student; township (AE) ~ 3. The Privy Council (GB)

counsel I *n.* ["advice"] 1. to give, offer, provide ~ 2.

to take ~ (from) 3. sage, wise ~ 4. ~ about, concerning ["lawyer"] 5. (a) legal ~ 6. ~ for (~ for the defense; ~ for the prosecution) ["misc."] 7. to keep one's own ~ ("to keep one's plans secret")

counsel II v. 1. (D; tr.) to ~ about, in, on 2. (D; tr.) to ~ against (I ~ed him against going) 3. (H) he ~ed us to wait

counseling, counselling n. bereavement; family; guidance; marriage; pastoral; vocational ~

counselor, counsellor n. ["adviser"] 1. a bereavement; family; guidance; marriage; pastoral; vocational ~ 2. a ~ to (a ~ to the ambassador)

count I n. ["act of counting"] ["total, tally"] 1. to do, make, take a ~ 2. to keep ~ of 3. to lose ~ of 4. (boxing) to go down for the ~ ("to be counted out"); to take a ~ of ten; to get up at/on the ~ of nine 5. an accurate, correct ~ 6. a final, last ~; the latest ~ 7. a blood; cell; pollen; sperm ~ 8. a body ~ 9. the ~ stands at... 10. at a certain ~ (there were fifty at the latest ~) 11. by smb.'s ~ (by my ~) ["issue"] 12. on a certain ~ (on all ~s) ["charge, accusation"] 13. on a certain ~ (he was guilty on all ~s)

count II v. 1. (d; intr.) ("to be taken into account") to ~ against (your previous convictions will ~ against you) 2. (d; tr.) ("to consider") to ~ among (I always ~ed her among my friends) 3. (d; intr., tr.) ("to be regarded; to regard") to ~ as (the draw ~s as a victory; we ~ed the draw as a victory) 4. (d; intr.) ("to be valued") (his opinion ~s for very little) 5. (d; intr.) ("to rely") to ~ for; on, upon (she ~ed on us for help; she ~ed on us to help her) 6. (D; intr.) ("to name numbers") to ~ from; to (to ~ from one to ten) 7. (D; intr.) ("to be taken into account") to ~ towards (do associate members ~ towards a quorum?) 8. (N; refl., tr.; used with an adjective) ("to consider") we must ~ ourselves lucky (to have escaped)

countdown n. 1. a final ~ 2. a ~ from; to (the ~ to zero has begun)

count down v. (D; intr.) to ~ to (to ~ to zero)

countenance I n. (biblical) a forbidding, stern: radiant, shining ~

countenance II v. 1. (G) they will not ~ cheating on the exam 2. (K) I will not ~ his doing that

counter I adj., adv. to act, be, go, run ~ to (that runs ~ to all our traditions)

counter II n. ["surface, table over which business is conducted"] 1. a bargain; notions (AE) ~ 2. a check-in; check-out; ticket ~ 3. a lunch ~ 4. at a ~ ["misc."] 5. over the ~ ("through a broker's office"); ("without a prescription"); under the ~ ("illicitly")

counter III v. 1. (D; intr.) to ~ by (they ~ed by calling in the police) 2. (D; intr., tr.) to ~ with (she ~ed with an even stronger argument; they ~ed our proposal with one of their own) 3. (L) she ~ed that

her advice had not been heeded

counter IV n. ["instrument"] 1. to set a ~ 2. a crystal; Geiger ~

counterattack n. 1. to launch, make a ~ 2. a ~ against (see also **attack I**, 1)

counterbalance n. a ~ to

counterblow n. 1. to deal, deliver a ~ 2. a ~ against, to

countercharge n. 1. to bring, file, make a ~ 2. a ~ against (see also **charge I**, 1)

counterclaim n. 1. to bring, enter, make a ~ 2. a ~ against (see also **claim I**, 1-2)

counterclockwise adj., adv. (AE) to go ~; to turn (smt.) ~ (BE has *anticlockwise*)

counterespionage n. 1. to conduct ~ 2. ~ against (see also **espionage**)

counterfeit n. a crude; skillful ~

counterintelligence n. to conduct ~ (see also **intelligence** 7-8)

countermeasures n. 1. to take ~ 2. ~ against

counteroffensive n. 1. to launch, undertake a ~ 2. to go over to the ~ 3. a ~ against

counteroffer n. to make a ~ (see also **offer I**, 2-3)

counterpart n. 1. to have a ~ in 2. a ~ of, to

counterplot n. 1. to hatch a ~ 2. a ~ against (see also **plot I**, 1-6)

counterpoint n. ["accompanying melody"] 1. double; single; triple ~ 2. in ~ to ["contrasting element"] 3. to provide a ~ to; to serve as a ~ to

counterproductive adj. ~ to + inf. (it is ~ to raise so many objections)

counterproposal n. to make, offer a ~ (see also **proposal** 1-3, 8-9)

counterpunch n. to deliver, throw a ~ (see also **punch I**, 1)

counterrevolution n. 1. to foment, stir up a ~ 2. to carry out; organize a ~ 3. a ~ against (see also **revolution** 1-4, 6)

countersign n. to give the ~

countersuit n. (legal) 1. to bring a ~ 2. a ~ against (see also **suit I**, 1-4)

counterweight n. a ~ to (her realism serves as a ~ to his hysteria)

country n. ["nation"] 1. to govern, rule, run a ~ 2. a civilized ~ 3. a foreign ~; smb.'s mother ~; smb.'s native ~ 4. a host; neighboring ~ 5. a democratic; developing; foreign; industrialized; occupied; third-world; underdeveloped ~ ["rural area"] 6. the back ~ 7. open; rough, rugged ~ (in open ~) 8. in the ~ (to live in the ~) ["misc."] 9. (BE) to go to the ~ ("to call a general election")

count up v. (d; intr.) to ~ to (the child could ~ to twenty)

coup n. ["successful action"] 1. to pull off, score a ~ 2. an attempted; bloodless; military ~ (see also **coup d'état**)

coup de grace n. ["finishing blow"] to administer,

deliver, give the ~ (to)

coup d'état *n.* ["sudden overthrow of a government"] 1. to carry out, stage a ~ 2. an attempted ~ 3. a bloodless; bloody; military ~

couple I *n.* a childless; courting; elderly; engaged; loving; married; newlywed; odd; unmarried; young ~

couple II *v.* (D; tr.) to ~ to, with (to ~ a dining car to a train)

coupled *adj.* ~ with (poverty ~ with unemployment can lead to crime)

couplet *n.* a heroic; rhyming ~

coupon *n.* 1. to detach; redeem a ~ 2. (misc.) to clip ~s ("to profit from stocks and bonds")

courage *n.* 1. to demonstrate, display, show; have (the) ~ 2. to gather (up), get up, muster, pluck up, screw up, summon up, work up (the) ~ 3. to draw, take ~ (from) 4. to take ~ to + inf. (it takes ~ to tell the truth) 5. dauntless, great, immense, indomitable, sheer; moral; physical ~ 6. an act of ~ 7. the ~ to + inf. (he lacked the ~ to do it) 8. of ~ (a person of great ~) 9. (misc.) to have the ~ of one's convictions; take ~ and press on

courageous *adj.* ~ to + inf. (it was ~ of her to volunteer)

courier *n.* 1. to dispatch a ~ 2. a diplomatic; motorcycle ~ 3. a ~ to 4. by ~ (the message came by ~)

course I *n.* ["organized program of study"] 1. to conduct, do (esp. BE), give, offer, teach a ~ 2. to do (esp. BE), take a ~ 3. to audit (AE), sit in on a ~ 4. to enroll for, register for, sign up for a ~ 5. to fail; pass a ~; to take a ~ pass-fail (AE) 6. to complete; drop; drop out of; withdraw from a ~ 7. to introduce; organize, plan a ~ 8. to cancel a ~ 9. a demanding, difficult, rigorous; easy, gut (AE; colloq.) ~ 10. an advanced; beginning, elementary, introductory; intermediate ~ 11. (at a university) a core; crash; elective; graduate, postgraduate (esp. BE); intensive; interdisciplinary; laboratory; lecture; noncredit; pass-fail; remedial; required; survey; undergraduate ~ 12. a correspondence; day-release (BE); extension; makeup; refresher ~ 13. a ~ covers, deals with, treats a subject (our history ~ covered the nineteenth century) 14. a ~ in, on (she took a ~ in mathematics; they offered a ~ on lexicography) ["itinerary"] ["path"] 15. to chart, map out, mark out, plot a ~ 16. to follow, pursue, take a ~ (the law must take its ~) 17. to set ~ for (we set ~ for the nearest port) 18. to alter, change ~ (it's not good to change ~ in midstream) 19. to stay the ~ ("to persist until the end") 20. to run its ~ (the disease ran its expected ~) 21. a collision; middle; natural; zigzag ~ (events took their natural ~) 22. a ~ of action (to pursue a ~ of action) 23. off ~; on ~ (our ship was right on ~; to be on a collision ~; the plane was off ~; the sailboat was blown off ~)

["playing area"] 24. a golf ~; racecourse (esp. BE) ["training area"] 25. an obstacle ~ ["period"] 26. in the ~ of (in the ~ of an investigation; in the ~ of time; in due ~; in the ordinary ~ of events) ["training area, race"] 27. to do, run a ~ 28. an assault (BE), obstacle; training ~ (the trainees ran the obstacle ~) ["part of a meal"] 29. a first; main ~ ["misc."] 30. of ~ ("naturally") (see the Usage Note for **track**)

course II *v.* (d; intr.) to ~ through (the blood ~d through her veins)

court *n.* ["place where justice is administered"] 1. to adjourn; dismiss (a) ~ 2. to go to ~ (over); take smb. to ~ (over) 3. to clog the ~s (with frivolous litigation) 4. an appeals (esp. BE), appellate; circuit; city, municipal; county; crown (BE); district (AE); federal (US); high; higher; lower; magistrate's; superior; supreme ~ 5. a criminal; domestic relations, family; juvenile; orphans'; probate; small-claims; traffic; trial ~ 6. a night; police ~ 7. a kangaroo ("irregular"); moot ~ 8. a ~ of appeal(s); a ~ of common pleas; a ~ of domestic relations; a ~ of law; a ~ of original jurisdiction; a ~ of inquiry (BE) 9. a ~ adjourns; convenes 10. a ~ holds (that), rules (that) 11. in ~ (to testify in ~; in open ~) 12. out of ~ (to settle a case out of ~) ["sovereign's residence"] 13. to hold ~ (now usu. fig.) 14. at ~ (at the ~ of Louis XIV) ["homage"] 15. to pay ~ to smb. ["sports arena"] 16. a badminton; basketball; clay (for tennis); grass (for tennis); handball; indoor; outdoor; squash; tennis; volleyball ~ ["motel"] (obsol.) (AE) 17. a motor, tourist ~

courteous *adj.* 1. ~ to, towards, with (she is ~ to everyone) 2. ~ to + inf. (it was ~ of him to do that) 3. (misc.) kind and ~

courtesy *n.* 1. to display, extend, show ~ (they showed us every ~) 2. common; unfailing ~ 3. professional; senatorial (US) ~ 4. an act of ~ 5. ~ to, towards (it was done as a ~ to you) 6. the ~ to + inf. (he didn't have the ~ to answer my letter) 7. by ~ of 8. (misc.) she did me the ~ of remaining silent; a basket of fruit was delivered to our door ~ of the management

courthouse *n.* (esp. AE; CE has *court*) a county; federal; state ~

court martial I *n.* 1. to hold a ~ 2. to try smb. by ~ 3. a drumhead; general; special; summary ~

court martial II *v.* (D; tr.) to ~ for (he was ~ed for desertion)

courtship *n.* a whirlwind ~

cousin *n.* 1. a distant; first; second ~; a first ~ once removed 2. a ~ of, to (she is a first ~ to the countess) 3. (colloq.) kissing ("friendly") ~s

covenant I *n.* a ~ between

covenant II *v.* (BE) 1. (E) he ~ed to pay the interest 2. (L) she ~ed that she would pay the bill

Coventry *n.* (esp. BE) to send to ~ ("to ostracize")

cover I *n.* ["shelter"] ["concealment"] 1. to seek; take ~ 2. to break ~ 3. (colloq.) to blow smb.'s ~ ("to give smb. away") 4. ~ from (~ from enemy fire) 5. under ~ (under ~ of darkness) ["covering"] 6. cloud ~ 7. a dust; mattress; pillow ~ 8. between, under the ~s (the children were huddled under the ~s) ["defense"] 9. air; protective ~ ["front"] 10. a ~ for (the whole operation was a ~ for foreign agents) ["envelope"] 11. under separate ~ ["binding"] 12. a back; front ~ 13. a book; magazine ~ 14. from ~ to ~ (to read a book from ~ to ~) 15. on the ~ (her picture was on the ~ of the magazine)

cover II *v.* 1. ("to report on") to ~ live (the event will be ~ed live by/on TV) 2. (D; refl., tr.) ("to protect") to ~ against (this policy will ~ you against flood damage) 3. (d; intr.) to ~ for ("to substitute for; to protect") (to ~ for a friend) 4. (D; tr.) ("to place over") to ~ with (to ~ a child with a blanket)

coverage *n.* ["insurance"] 1. to provide ~ against, for 2. comprehensive, full ~ ["reporting"] 3. to give; receive ~ 4. complete, extensive, full, wide; front-page ~ (the story received wide ~) 5. live; media; newspaper; television ~

covered *adj.* ~ in, with (~ in blood)

covering *n.* a light ~ of (snow)

cover-up *n.* a ~ for

cover up *v.* 1. (D; intr.) to ~ for ("to protect") (she ~ed up for me when I made that blunder) 2. (D; tr.) to ~ with ("to place over") (she ~ed up the child with a blanket)

covetous *adj.* ~ of

cow I *n.* 1. to milk a ~ 2. a dairy, milch (old fashioned) ~ 3. ~s calve; low, moo 4. a ~ chews its cud 5. the meat of the ~ is beef 6. a young ~ is a calf 7. (misc.) (colloq.) holy ~! (AE); silly ~! (BE)

cow II *v.* (D; tr.) to ~ into (to ~ smb. into making concessions)

coward *n.* an abject, dirty ~

cowardice *n.* 1. to display, show ~ 2. abject, rank; moral ~ 3. (misc.) an act of ~; a streak of ~

cowardly *adj.* ~ to + inf. (it was ~ of them to behave like that)

coy *adj.* ~ about; with (don't be ~ with me about your past record)

cozen *v.* (formal) 1. (d; tr.) to ~ into 2. (d; tr.) to ~ from, out of (to ~ smb. out of his money)

cozy up *v.* (colloq.) (AE) (D; intr.) to ~ to

CPR (cardiopulmonary resuscitation) *n.* to do ~ on smb.

crab I *n.* ["rower's defective stroke"] to catch a ~

crab II *v.* (colloq.) ("to complain") (D; intr.) to ~ about

crack I *n.* ["remark"] (colloq.) 1. to make a ~ (about) 2. a dirty, nasty ~ 3. a ~ that (her ~ that you are always late was unjustified) ["moment"] 4. at

the ~ of dawn ["attempt"] 5. to have a ~ at (let's have a ~ at it) ["hole"] 6. to peer through a ~ ["misc."] 7. she opened the window just a ~

crack II *v.* 1. (N; used with an adjective) she ~ed it open 2. (P; intr., tr.) she ~ed the eggs into a bowl; to ~ under the strain; his voice ~ed with emotion; she ~ed her head against the wall

crackdown *n.* 1. to launch a ~ 2. a ~ on (a ~ on drunk drivers)

crack down *v.* (D; intr.) to ~ on (to ~ on drug dealers)

cracked up *adj.* (colloq.) (cannot stand alone) ["reputed"] ~ to be (this hotel is not all/what it's ~ to be)

cracker *n.* ["dry biscuit"] 1. (esp. AE) a graham; soda; unsalted ~ 2. (BE) a cream ~

cracking *adj.* (colloq.) to get ~ ("to start working on smt.")

crackpot *n.* (colloq.) a ~ to + inf. (he was a ~ to do it)

cradle *n.* 1. to rock a ~ 2. (misc.) from the ~ to the grave ("during smb.'s whole life")

craft *n.* ["occupation"] 1. to ply, practice a ~ 2. to learn, master a ~ ["boat"] 3. a landing ~ 4. (in plural) pleasure; small ~

crafted *adj.* artfully, beautifully; carefully, skillfully ~

craftsman, craftswoman *n.* a master ~

USAGE NOTE: Note also the term *craftsperson*.

cram *v.* 1. (D; intr.) ("to study hastily") to ~ for (to ~ for an exam) 2. (d; tr.) ("to jam") to ~ into (to ~ one's things into a suitcase) 3. (D; tr.) to ~ with (the basement was ~med with debris) 4. (misc.) to ~ a suitcase full of clothes

cramp *n.* 1. to get a ~ (esp. AE)/get ~ (BE) 2. stomach ~(s); writer's ~ 3. (BE) seized with ~

cramped *adj.* ~ for (space)

cranberry *n.* to pick ~ries

crane *n.* to operate a ~

crank *n.* ["handle"] to turn, use a ~

crap game *n.* (AE) a floating ~

craps *n.* (AE) to play, shoot ~

crash I *n.* ["sudden noise"] 1. a loud, resounding ~ ["violent accident"] 2. a plane ~ (to survive a plane ~) ["sudden collapse"] 3. a stockmarket ~

crash II *v.* 1. (d; intr.) to ~ against (waves ~ against the rocks) 2. (d; intr., tr.) to ~ into (the car ~ed into a pole) 3. (d; intr.) to ~ through (the car ~ed through the barrier) 4. (d; intr.) to ~ to (to ~ to the floor) 5. (misc.) the plane ~ed in flames

crass *adj.* ~ to + inf. (it was ~ of him to ask how much you earn)

crater *n.* a bomb ~

crave *v.* 1. to ~ strongly 2. (d; intr.) to ~ for (to ~ for peace and quiet)

USAGE NOTE: The phrase *to crave for smt.* is synonymous with *to crave smt.*

craving n. 1. to feel, have a ~ 2. a powerful, strong ~ 3. a ~ for 4. a ~ to + inf. (a strong ~ to be free)

craw n. ["crop of a bird or insect"] to stick in smb.'s ~ ("to be distasteful to smb.")

crawl I n. ["swimming stroke"] 1. to do, swim the ~ ["act of crawling"] (also fig.) 2. at a ~ (traffic moved at a ~) 3. to a ~ (traffic slowed to a ~)

crawl II v. 1. (d; intr.) to ~ into (to ~ into a hole) 2. (d; intr.) to ~ out of (to ~ out of the ruins) 3. (d; intr.) to ~ with (the city is ~ing with reporters) 4. (P; intr.) to ~ under the bed; she ~ed across the floor; they ~ed from under the ruins

crawl out v. (D; intr.) to ~ from under (to ~ from under the ruins)

crayon n. colored; wax ~s

craze n. 1. the current, latest, newest ~ 2. the ~ swept the country 3. a ~ for

crazed adj. ~ with (anger)

crazy adj. (colloq.) ["infatuated"] 1. (cannot stand alone) ~ about (he is ~ about her) ["foolish"] 2. ~ to + inf. (it was ~ of her to do that; she was ~ to drive without headlights) ["insane"] 3. to drive smb. ~; to go ~

cream n. ["component of milk"] 1. to whip ~ 2. clotted (BE); double (BE), whipping; ice; single (BE); sour, soured (BE); whipped ~ ["cosmetic"] 3. to apply ~ 4. cleansing; cold; face; hand; moisturizing; shaving; skin; vanishing ~ ["misc."] the ~ of the crop ("the very best")

crease n. 1. to iron out, remove, smooth down the ~s 2. a sharp ~

create v. ("to appoint") (BE) (N; used with a noun) he was ~d duke

creature n. 1. living ~s 2. a ~ of habit

credence n. 1. to attach, give, lend ~ to 2. to gain ~

credentials n. 1. to establish; present one's ~ (as) 2. to evaluate; examine smb.'s ~ 3. excellent, impeccable, sound ~

credibility n. 1. to establish (one's) ~ (as) 2. to lose one's ~ 3. to damage, undermine smb.'s ~ 4. (misc.) a ~ gap

credit I n. ["time given for payment"] 1. to allow, give, extend, offer ~ (this store does not give ~) 2. to deny, refuse smb. ~ 3. consumer ~ 4. on ~ (to buy smt. on ~) 5. (misc.) a line of ~ ["recognition"] ["honor"] 6. to do ~ to; to reflect ~ on (her work does ~ to her teachers = her work does her teachers ~) 7. to claim (the) ~ for; to get, take (the) ~ for (he took ~ for my work) 8. to deserve ~ (for) 9. to give smb. ~ for (I give her ~ for being so sensible) 10. a ~ to (they are a ~ to their parents) 11. ~ that + clause (it was to her ~ that she never gave up) 12. to smb.'s ~ (to her ~, she was never late for work; she has a dozen publications to her ~) ["sum allowed, deducted"] 13. an energy (AE); tax ~ ["recognition that a student has completed a course or unit of study"] 14. to earn, get, receive;

transfer ~ (for a course) 15. advanced ~

credit II v. 1. (D; tr.) to ~ to (to ~ an amount to smb.'s account) 2. (d; tr.) to ~ with (to ~ smb. with common sense; to ~ an account with fifty dollars)

credit card n. 1. to issue a ~ 2. (misc.) to put a purchase on one's ~

creditor n. to pay off one's ~s

credo n. a ~ that + clause (it is our ~ that everyone is equal)

credulity n. to strain, stretch smb.'s ~

creed n. 1. to adhere to a ~ 2. a political; religious ~ 3. a ~ that + clause (it is our ~ that we must help the poor) 4. (misc.) all races and ~s

creep v. 1. (d; intr.) to ~ into (to ~ into a hole) 2. (d; intr.) to ~ out of (an insect crept out of the pipe) 3. (P; intr.) to ~ across the floor; the baby crept around the room 4. (misc.) to ~ on all fours; to ~ out from under a bush

creeps n. (colloq.) ["fear"] it gives me the ~

creep up v. (D; intr.) to ~ on (he crept up on me in the dark)

creepy adj. (colloq.) ["weird"] ~ about (there is smt. ~ about him)

crescendo n. 1. to reach a ~, rise to a ~ 2. a deafening; rising ~

crest n. ["top"] 1. to ride (on) the ~ of a wave (to ride the ~ of a wave of popularity) 2. at the ~ ["heraldic device"] 3. a family ~

crew n. ["group working together"] 1. a camera; ground; gun; road; skeleton; stage; tank; TV; work; wrecking ~ ["ship's personnel"] 2. a ship's ~ 3. a ~ mutinies 4. in a ~ ["rowing team"] (AE) 5. a varsity ~ 6. to go out for ~ [misc.] 7. a motley ~ ("a disparate group")

crib I n. (AE) 1. to assemble, put up a ~ 2. to dismantle a ~ (BE has *cot*)

crib II v. (colloq.) (D; intr., tr.) ("to plagiarize") to ~ from

cricket I n. ["game"] 1. to play ~ ["fair play"] (colloq.) 2. ~ to + inf. (it's not ~ to cheat at cards)

cricket II n. ["insect"] ~s chirp

crier n. a town ~

crime n. 1. to commit, perpetrate a ~ 2. to combat; deter; eradicate, stamp out, wipe out; prevent ~ 3. to solve a ~ 4. an atrocious, brutal, heinous, horrendous, horrible, infamous, outrageous, unspeakable, vicious, violent ~ 5. a copycat ~; (a) white collar ~ 6. (an) economic ~; (a) hate ~ (AE); a victimless ~; a war ~ 7. a daring; major, serious; minor, petty; perfect ~ 8. inner-city; juvenile ~; street ~ 9. a ~ of passion 10. organized ~ 11. a ~ against (a ~ against humanity) 12. a ~ to + inf. (it was a ~ to butcher French like that) 13. a ~ that + clause (it is a ~ that so many people go to bed hungry) 14. (misc.) to investigate a ~; to report a ~ (to the police); many ~s go unreported; it's a ~ how/the way he behaves!

criminal I *adj.* ~ to + inf. (it was ~ of him to do that) 2. ~ that + clause (it is ~ that he is/should be allowed to remain in this country)

criminal II *n.* 1. to apprehend, arrest, catch a ~; to bring a ~ to justice; to punish a ~ 2. to pardon; parole; release a ~ 3. to rehabilitate a ~ 4. a born; common; dangerous; desperate; habitual, hardened, inveterate, vicious; infamous, notorious; master; petty; war ~ 5. a band, gang of ~s

crimp *n.* (colloq.) (AE) ["obstacle"] to put a ~ in

cringe *v.* 1. (D; intr.) to ~ at (to ~ at one's mistake) 2. (D; intr.) to ~ before (to ~ before one's superiors) 3. (D; intr.) to ~ with (to ~ with embarrassment)

crisis *n.* 1. to cause, lead to, precipitate, provoke, stir up a ~ 2. to aggravate, worsen a ~ 3. to avert, forestall a ~ 4. to deal with, defuse, overcome, resolve, settle a ~; to face a ~; to ride out, weather a ~ 5. an acute, grave, serious; impending; mounting ~ 6. a cabinet; constitutional; international; national ~ 7. an economic, financial, fiscal; energy; political ~ 8. a family; food; housing; identity; mid-life; personal ~ 9. a ~ deepens; eases 10. a ~ over (there was a ~ over the budget deficit) 11. a ~ in (the ~ in health care) 12. in a ~

crisp *n.* burned to a ~

criterion *n.* 1. to adopt, establish; apply a ~ 2. to meet, satisfy criteria 3. a reliable, valid ~

critic *n.* 1. a harsh, severe, unkind; impartial, unbiased; outspoken ~ 2. an art; drama, theater; film; literary; music; social ~ 3. (misc.) an armchair ~

critical *adj.* ["criticizing"] 1. sharply, very ~ 2. ~ of (he was ~ of my work) ["indispensable"] (AE) 3. ~ for, to (~ to our work) 4. ~ that + clause; subj. (it is ~ that the work be/should be completed on time)

criticism *n.* 1. to arouse, provoke, stir up ~ 2. to come in for; draw ~ 3. to express, offer ~; to level ~ at 4. to accept, take, tolerate ~ 5. to react to, respond to ~ 6. to reject ~ 7. to temper one's ~ 8. to subject smb./smt. to ~ 9. constructive; fair; mild; sober; valid ~ 10. nitpicking, petty; unfair ~ 11. adverse, biting, damaging, devastating, harsh, hostile, scathing, severe, sharp, strong, sweeping, swingeing (BE), unsparing, withering ~ 12. literary; textual ~ 13. (the) higher; lower ~ (of the Bible) 14. (misc.) the barbs of ~; beneath ~

criticize *v.* 1. to ~ bitterly, harshly, severely, sharply, strongly; fairly; unfairly; widely 2. (D; tr.) to ~ for (to ~ smb. for sloppy work)

critique *n.* to give, present a ~

crop I *n.* ["produce grown by farmers"] 1. to grow; plant a ~ 2. to gather, harvest, reap a ~ 3. to bear, yield a ~ 4. to rotate ~s 5. to dust, spray ~s 6. a bountiful, bumper, fine, record ~ 7. a poor; subsistence ~ 8. a cash; fodder; staple ~ 9. a ~ fails ["stick"] 10. a riding ~

crop II *v.* (N; used with an adjective) they ~ped the grass short

cropper *n.* (colloq.) ["failure"] to come a ~ ("to fail")

croquet *n.* to play ~

croquettes *n.* chicken; salmon ~s

cross I *adj.* ["irritable"] ~ at, with (~ at smt.; ~ with smb.)

cross II *n.* ["symbol of the Christian religion"] 1. to die on the ~ (said of Jesus Christ) 2. to make the sign of the ~ 3. (misc.) to bear one's ~ ("to bear a heavy burden") ["figure of a cross"] 4. to make one's ~ (in place of a signature) ["mixture"] 5. a ~ between (a ~ between a peach and a plum)

cross III *v.* 1. (D; intr., tr.) ("to go") to ~ from; to (they ~ed from one bank of the river to the other; we ~ed the valley from one ridge to the other) 2. (d; tr.) to ~ off (to ~ a name off a list) 3. (D; tr.) ("to crossbreed") to ~ with (to ~ one breed with another)

cross-country *adv.* to go, travel ~

cross-examination *n.* 1. to conduct, do a ~ 2. to subject smb. to ~ 3. a rapid-fire ~ 4. under ~

cross-examine *v.* 1. to ~ sharply; unmercifully 2. (D; tr.) to ~ about, on

cross fire *n.* 1. to be caught in a ~ 2. to subject to ~ 3. exposed to ~

crossing *n.* 1. to make a ~ 2. a rough; smooth ~ 3. a border ~ 4. a grade (AE); level (BE); pedestrian, pelican (BE), zebra (BE); railroad (AE), railway (esp. BE) ~ 5. a transoceanic ~ 6. at a ~ (at the border ~) 7. on a ~ (hit by a car on a pedestrian ~)

cross over *v.* (D; intr.) to ~ into, to (she ~ed over to the other lane)

cross-purposes *n.* at ~ (to work at ~)

cross-refer *v.* (D; intr., tr.) to ~ between; from; to

cross-reference *n.* 1. to make a ~ 2. a ~ from; to

crossroads *n.* at a ~ (also fig.)

crossword (BE) see **crossword puzzle**

crossword puzzle *n.* (esp. AE) to do, work (out) a ~

crow I *n.* 1. ~s caw 2. (misc.) as the ~ flies ("in a straight line"); to eat ~ (AE) ("to be placed in a humiliating position")

crow II *v.* (colloq.) ("to exult") (d; intr.) to ~ about, over (to ~ about one's success; to ~ over an enemy's misfortune)

crowd I *n.* ["throng"] 1. to attract, draw a ~ 2. to disperse a ~ 3. an angry, hostile, unfriendly; cheering, friendly; enormous, huge, tremendous; overflow ~ 4. a ~ collects, gathers; disperses, melts away, thins out; roars 5. a ~ mills, swarms (around the entrance) ["audience"] 6. a capacity ~ ["group"] 7. a bad; fast, wild ~; the wrong ~ (to run around with a fast ~; she got in with the wrong ~)

crowd II *v.* 1. (d; intr.) to ~ around (to ~ around the entrance) 2. (d; intr.) to ~ into, to (to ~ into a small room) 3. (d; tr.) to ~ off, out of (they ~ed me off the road) 4. (d; intr.) to ~ through (they ~ed through the turnstiles) 5. (misc.) to ~ together

crowded *adj.* ~ with (the streets were ~ with tourists)

crown I *n.* ["part of a tooth"] 1. to put a ~ on (a tooth) ["monarch's headdress"] 2. to wear a ~ ["boxing title"] 3. to lose; win the (heavyweight) ~

crown II *v.* 1. (d; tr.) to ~ with (their efforts were ~ed with success) 2. (N; used with a noun) they ~ed him king

crucial *adj.* 1. ~ for, to (these negotiations are ~ for/to the future of our firm) 2. ~ that + clause; subj. (it is ~ that this matter remain/should remain secret; BE has *remains secret*)

crude *adj.* ~ to + inf. (it was ~ of him to say that)

cruel *adj.* 1. ~ to, towards (~ to animals) 2. ~ to + inf. (it was ~ of him to say that)

cruelty *n.* 1. to display, show ~ 2. consummate, deliberate, wanton ~ 3. mental ~ 4. an act of ~ 5. ~ to, towards (~ to animals)

cruise I *n.* 1. to go on, set off on, take a ~ 2. an extended, long; pleasure; round-the-world, world; shakedown; short ~ 3. a ~ along; around (to take a ~ around the world) 4. a ~ from; to 5. a ~ through 6. on a ~

cruise II *v.* (P; intr.) to ~ along the coast; to ~ around the world; to ~ through the coastal waters

cruiser *n.* a battle; converted; guided-missile; heavy; light; medium ~

crumble *v.* (D; intr.) to ~ into

crunch *n.* (colloq.) ["shortage"] 1. an energy; financial ~ ["showdown"] (colloq.) 2. if it comes to the ~

crusade I *n.* 1. to conduct; launch a ~ 2. to embark on; engage in; go on; join a ~ 3. a one-man, one-woman ~ 4. a holy; moral ~ 5. a ~ against; for (a ~ against smoking) 6. a ~ to + inf. (they launched a ~ to ban smoking)

crusade II *v.* 1. (D; intr.) to ~ against; for (to ~ against smoking) 2. (E) they ~d to ban smoking

crush I *n.* ["infatuation"] (colloq.) 1. a schoolboy; schoolgirl; youthful ~ 2. a ~ on (to have a ~ on smb.)

crush II *v.* 1. (d; intr.) to ~ against (the mob ~ed against the barriers) 2. (D; tr.) to ~ into (to ~ a substance into powder) 3. (misc.) to ~ smb. to death

crust *n.* ["impudence"] (colloq.) the ~ to + inf. (she had the ~ to ask for a raise)

crutch *n.* 1. to walk on, with ~es 2. a pair of ~es

cry I *n.* 1. to give, raise (formal), utter a ~ 2. an anguished, plaintive; bloodcurdling; heartrending; loud, lusty; piercing; rallying; shrill ~ 3. a battle, war ~ 4. a ~ for (a ~ for help) 5. (misc.) a far ~ from ("very far from"); to have a good ~

cry II *v.* 1. to ~ bitterly; loudly 2. (D; intr.) ("to weep") to ~ at (they cried bitterly at the sad news)

3. (d; intr.) ("to appeal") to ~ for (to ~ for justice) 4. (d; intr.) ("to weep") to ~ for, with (to ~ for joy; to ~ with grief) 5. (d; intr.) ("to weep") to ~ over (to ~ over one's bad luck) 6. (d; intr.) to ~ to ("to complain to") (don't come ~ing to me) 7. (L; to) ("to shout") she cried loudly to us that the house was on fire 8. (misc.) to ~ wolf ("to give a false alarm"); to ~ one's eyes out; to ~ over spilled/spilt milk ("to complain in vain"); she cried herself to sleep; to ~ on smb.'s shoulder ("to seek sympathy from smb.")

cry out *v.* 1. (d; intr.) ("to appeal") to ~ against; for (to ~ against injustice; to ~ for equal rights) 2. (D; intr.) ("to scream") to ~ in (to ~ in pain) 3. (d; intr., tr.) ("to shout") to ~ to (he cried out to us to stop) 4. (L; to) ("to shout") she cried out (to us) that the rain was coming through the roof

crystal *n.* 1. ~ glitters, sparkles 2. fine ~

crystallize *v.* (D; intr.) to ~ into (their ideas finally ~d into a feasible project)

cube *n.* a bouillon (AE), stock (BE); ice; sugar ~

cube root *n.* to calculate, find, extract the ~

cucumber *n.* 1. to peel; slice a ~ 2. (misc.) (as) cool as a ~

cud *n.* a cow chews its ~

cuddle up *v.* 1. (D; intr.) to ~ to (the twins ~d up to each other) 2. (misc.) to ~ together

cudgels *n.* ["support"] to take up the ~ for

cue *n.* ["signal"] 1. to give the ~ 2. to take one's ~ from smb. 3. to miss the ~ 4. a ~ to + inf. (it was my ~ to enter the room) 5. on ~

cuff *n.* 1. a French; trouser (AE) ~ 2. (misc.) (esp. AE) on the ~ ("on credit")

cull *v.* (D; tr.) to ~ from

culminate *v.* (d; intr.) to ~ in; with (to ~ in victory; to ~ with an appeal for unity)

cult *n.* 1. to join a ~ 2. a cargo; fertility; religious ~

cultivation *n.* under ~

culture *n.* ["pattern of activites, values, and artifacts of a society"] 1. to develop a ~ 2. (an) ancient; ethnic; human; material; modern; pop; primitive; tribal ~ ["enlightenment"] ["good taste"] 3. to bring ~ to 4. to disseminate, foster, spread ~ ["vocational training"] (AE) 5. beauty ~ ["cultivation of living material in a media"] 6. to do, grow a ~ 7. a tissue ~

cunning I *adj.* ~ to + inf. (it was ~ of them to do that)

cunning II *n.* to show ~

cup *n.* ["prize"] 1. to lose; win a ~ 2. a challenge; world ~ ["small drinking vessel"] 3. to drain, empty one's ~ 4. a coffee; drinking; paper; plastic ~; teacup 5. (misc.) to be in one's cups ("to be drunk")

cupboard *n.* 1. an airing (BE); built-in; kitchen ~ 2. (usu. fig.) a bare ~

cupid *n.* to play ~ (to)

curb *n.* ["restraint"] a ~ on

curd *n.* soybean (AE), soya bean (BE) ~

cure I *n.* 1. to effect, provide, work a ~ 2. a certain, known, sure; complete; magical; miraculous; spontaneous ~ 3. a rest; water ~ 4. a ~ for (there is no known ~ for this disease)

cure II *v.* (D; tr.) to ~ of (to ~ smb. of a disease)

curfew *n.* 1. to clamp a ~ on; impose a ~ (they imposed a ~; the military government clamped a ~ on the town) 2. to lift a ~ 3. to observe a ~ 4. to violate a ~ 5. a midnight ~

curiosity *n.* 1. to arouse, excite, pique, whet (one's) ~ 2. to satisfy one's ~ 3. (a) healthy; idle; intellectual; natural; unquenchable ~ 4. ~ about 5. out of ~ (he did it out of ~)

curious *adj.* ["eager to know"] 1. ~ about (~ about smb.'s past) 2. ~ to + inf. (I would be ~ to know what really happened) ["odd"] 3. ~ that + clause (it is ~ that she didn't remember the incident)

curl *v.* (D; intr., tr.) to ~ around (the roots ~ed around the water pipes; she ~ed her finger around the doorknob)

curls *n.* 1. natural ~ 2. in ~ (she wears her hair in ~)

curl up *v.* 1. (D; intr.) to ~ in, into (to ~ into a ball) 2. (D; intr.) to ~ with (she ~ed up with a good book)

currency *n.* ["paper money"] 1. to issue; print ~ 2. to call in, withdraw ~ 3. to devalue (a) ~ 4. (a) blocked; convertible, hard; foreign; local; nonconvertible, soft, weak; stable, strong ~ 5. (misc.) they were paid in local ~ ["general use"] 6. to enjoy, have ~ (to enjoy wide ~)

current *n.* ["flow of electricity"] 1. to switch on, turn on the ~ 2. to switch off, turn off the ~ 3. alternating; direct; electric; high-tension; low-tension; oscillating ~ ["flow"] 4. an air; underwater ~ 5. a powerful, strong; treacherous ~ 6. against; with the ~

curriculum *n.* 1. to draw up, design a ~ 2. a college, university; school ~ 3. a basic, core; national (BE) ~ 4. a ~ in (the ~ in engineering)

curry *n.* 1. hot, mild ~ 2. fish; meat; vegetable ~

curse I *n.* 1. to pronounce, put a ~ on, upon smb. 2. to utter a ~ 3. to lift a ~ 4. a bitter ~ 5. under a ~

curse II *v.* 1. to ~ bitterly 2. (D; tr.) to ~ for (she ~d him for his clumsiness) 3. (D; tr.) to ~ with (he has been ~d with poor health)

cursor *n.* to move a ~ (on a computer)

curt *adj.* ~ with (the hotel clerk was ~ with the guests)

curtain *n.* 1. to draw; lower; raise a ~ 2. (in the theater) to ring down; ring up the ~ 3. a drop; shower; stage, theater ~ 4. a lace; net ~ 5. (fig.) a bamboo; iron ~ 6. (in the theater) the ~ goes up, rises; comes down, drops, falls (see also **curtains**)

curtain call *n.* to get, have; take a ~

curtains *n.* ["drapes"] 1. to hang, put up ~ 2. to close, draw; draw, open the ~ 3. a pair of ~ ["ruin"] (colloq.) 4. ~ for (it will be ~ for him if he loses his job)

curtsy, curtsey I *n.* 1. to bob, give, make a ~ 2. a deep ~

curtsy, curtsey II *v.* (D; intr.) to ~ to (to ~ to the Queen)

curve I *n.* ["bend, esp. in a road"] 1. to make a ~ (the road makes a ~ to the right) 2. to take a ~ (in a car) 3. a hairpin, horseshoe; sharp ~ 4. a ~ in (there was a ~ in the road) ["distribution indicated by a line, used in mathematics and statistics"] 5. to plot a ~ ("to locate a curve by plotted points") 6. (teaching) to grade (AE), mark on a ~ 7. a bell, bell-shaped, normal distribution ~ ["misc."] 8. (baseball and fig; AE) to throw smb. a ~

curve II *v.* 1. to ~ sharply 2. (D; intr.) to ~ to (to ~ to the right) 3. (P; intr.) the missile ~d through the air

cuss *v.* (D; intr.) to ~ at (he ~ed at the other drivers)

custody *n.* ["guardianship"] 1. to award, grant ~ 2. to gain, get, receive, win; have; take ~ (of) 3. to lose ~ (of) 4. joint ~ ["arrest"] 5. to take smb. into ~ 6. remanded in ~ 7. police; protective ~ 8. in ~ ("under arrest") (held in ~)

custom *n.* 1. to establish a ~ 2. to cherish, observe, practice; preserve a ~ 3. to defy ~ 4. (a) local ~ 5. an ancient, old; barbaric; native; pagan; quaint; religious; social; time-honored, traditional; tribal ~ 6. a ~ dies out 7. a ~ to + inf. (it is not our ~ to break the law) 8. a ~ that + clause (it is an old ~ that men tip their hats when greeting smb.) 9. by ~

customary *adj.* 1. ~ for 2. ~ to + inf. (it is ~ for diners to tip the waiter)

customer *n.* 1. to attract ~s 2. to serve, wait on a ~ 3. an irate; prospective; regular, steady; satisfied ~ 4. a cash ~ 5. (misc.) an odd, tricky ("a strange person"); an ugly ~ ("a violent person")

customs *n.* 1. to clear, get through, go through, pass through ~ (we got through ~ very quickly) 2. to clear, get smt. through ~ (we got the toys through ~ without difficulty) 3. to declare smt. at ~

cut I *n.* ["wound made by smt. sharp"] 1. to bandage a ~ 2. a clean; deep; nasty; superficial ~ ["reduction"] 3. to make; take a ~ 4. a budget; pay; personnel, staff; spending; tax ~ 5. a ~ in (we had to take a ~ in pay) ["haircut"] 6. a crew ~

cut II *v.* 1. ("to gash") to ~ deeply 2. ("to slice") to ~ easily (the meat ~s easily) 3. (C) ("to slice") ~ a piece of cake for me; or: ~ me a piece of cake 4. (d; intr.) ("to go") to ~ across (to ~ across a field) 5. (D; tr.) ("to reduce") to ~ by; from; to (they cut expenses by five percent; taxes were cut from eight percent to six percent) 6. (D; tr.) ("to sever") to ~ from, off (to ~ a branch from a tree; he was cut from the team (AE); she cut a thin slice from the loaf; ~ the crust off the bread) 7. (d; intr.) ("to slice") to ~ into (she cut into the cake) 8. (D; tr.)

("to slice") to ~ into (he cut the meat into small pieces) 9. (D; intr.) ("to break into, interrupt") to ~ into (to ~ into a conversation; work ~s into my leisure time) 10. (D; refl.) ("to gash") to ~ on (she cut herself on a knife) 11. (D; tr.) ("to remove") to ~ out of (she was cut out of the will) 12. (d; intr.) ("to go") to ~ through (they cut through the woods; let's ~ through this building) 13. (D; tr.) to ~ with (to ~ meat with a knife) 14. (N; used with an adjective) ("to trim") she cut her hair short 15. (misc.) to ~ smb. short ("to interrupt smb."); to ~ smb. to the quick ("to insult smb. deeply"); to ~ smt. to pieces; to ~ smt. in half

cut ahead, cut in front *v.* (d; intr.) to ~ of ("to cut off") (the other runner cut ahead of her; they cut in front of us)

cut away *v.* (D; tr.) to ~ from

cutback *n.* a ~ in (a ~ in production)

cut back *v.* (D; intr.) to ~ on (to ~ on smoking)

cut down *v.* 1. (D; intr.) to ~ on (to ~ on smoking) 2. (misc.) to ~ smb. down to size ("to deflate smb.'s ego")

cut in *v.* 1. (D; intr.) to ~ on (he cut in on me when I was dancing) 2. (slang) (D; tr.) to ~ on (he cut me in on the deal)

cutlet *n.* a lamb (BE); mutton (BE); veal; vegetarian ~

cut off *v.* 1. (C) ("to slice") he cut off a slice for me; or: he cut me off a slice 2. (D; tr.) ("to separate") to ~ from (we were cut off from civilization)

cut out I *adj.* ["suited"] 1. ~ for (she wasn't ~ for this job 2. ~ to + inf. (I wasn't ~ to be an administrator)

cut out II *v.* 1. (D; tr.) to ~ from, of (to ~ an article out from the newspaper) 2. (G) she had to ~ driving after dark

cutter *n.* 1. a cookie (AE); paper ~ 2. (a pair of) wire ~

cutting *n.* a press ~ (BE; AE has *press clipping*)

cutting edge *n.* ["leading edge"] at the ~ (of)

cut up *v.* (D; tr.) to ~ into (to ~ smt. up into pieces)

cyberspace *n.* 1. in ~ 2. welcome to ~!

cycle *n.* 1. to complete a (full) ~ 2. to go through, pass through a ~ 3. a business; economic; estrous (AE), oestrous (BE); life; menstrual ~ 4. (as on a washing machine) a delicate; normal; permanent-press; spin ~ 5. in ~s (some epidemics occur in ~s)

cynical *adj.* ~ about (~ about smb.'s motives)

cynicism *n.* bitter ~

cypher (esp. BE) see **cipher**

cyst *n.* to remove a ~

czar *n.* (colloq.) (AE) ["a person with great power"] (often pejorative) a drug; financial; gambling; shipbuilding ~ (BE spelling is *tsar*)

D

dab *v.* 1. (d; intr.) to ~ at (to ~ at one's eyes with a handkerchief) 2. (d; tr.) to ~ on (she dabbed some lotion on her face)

dabble *v.* (d; intr.) to ~ at, in, with (to ~ in politics; to ~ at painting)

dagger *n.* 1. to draw a ~ 2. to plunge a ~ into (smb.) 3. (misc.) to look ~s at ("to look angrily at")

daisy *n.* 1. to pick ~sies 2. (misc.) as fresh as a ~

dally *v.* 1. (D; intr.) ("to be slow") to ~ over (to ~ over one's work) 2. (d; intr.) ("to play") to ~ with (to ~ with the idea of studying abroad)

dam *n.* 1. to build, construct, erect a ~ 2. a hydroelectric; storage ~ 3. a ~ bursts

damage I *n.* ["harm"] 1. to cause, do ~ to; to inflict ~ on 2. to suffer, sustain ~ 3. to repair, undo ~ 4. to assess the ~ 5. grave, great, extensive, heavy, incalculable, irreparable, serious, severe; lasting, permanent; widespread ~ 6. light, slight ~ 7. environmental; fire; flood; material; property; structural ~ 8. brain ~ (irreversible brain ~) 9. ~ from (~ from the fire) 10. ~ to (was there much ~ to the car? the ~ done to the house was extensive; to do grave ~ to smb.'s reputation)

damage II *v.* 1. to ~ badly, irreparably, severely 2. easily ~d

damages *n.* ["compensation"] 1. to award ~ (the court awarded ~) 2. to claim; sue for ~ 3. to pay; receive, recover ~ 4. compensatory; exemplary; punitive; nominal ~ 5. ~ for 6. in ~ (to award one thousand dollars in ~)

damn I *n.* (colloq.) ["small amount"] it isn't worth a ~; not to give a (tinker's) ~ (CE; BE also has *tinker's curse* or *tinker's cuss*); (I don't give a ~ for their opinions!)

damn II *v.* (D; tr.) to ~ for (they were ~ed for their sins)

damnation *n.* eternal ~

damnedest, damndest *n.* (colloq.) ["utmost"] to do, try one's ~ (to do smt.)

damper *n.* ["deadening influence"] to put a ~ on

dance I *n.* 1. to do, perform a ~ (with) 2. to have a ~ with (may I have the next ~?) 3. to sit out a ~ 4. to give, hold a ~ (they held a dinner ~) 5. (the) classical ~; modern ~ 6. a barn; dinner; formal; school ~ 7. a circle, round; country; folk; line; square; sword; tap; tribal; war ~ 8. to go to a ~ 9. at a ~ (they met at a ~) 10. (misc.) (BE) to lead smb. a merry ~ (AE has *to lead smb. a merry chase*)

dance II *v.* 1. (D; intr.) to ~ to (to ~ to the music of a rock group) 2. (D; intr.) to ~ with 3. (P; intr., tr.) he ~d her around the room; they were ~cing through the park 4. (misc.) to ~ for, with joy; to ~ to smb.'s tune ("to conform to smb.'s wishes"); to

~ attendance on smb. ("to satisfy smb.'s every whim")

dancer *n.* a ballet; ballroom; belly; exotic; folk; tap; taxi ~

dancing *n.* aerobic; ballroom, social; belly; break; circle, round; country; folk; line; square; tap ~

dander *n.* ["temper"] (colloq.) to get one's ~ up

danger *n.* 1. to constitute, pose, represent; create (a) ~ 2. to expose to ~ 3. to confront; court; face; sense (a) ~ 4. to flirt with ~ 5. to avert (a) ~ 6. (an) acute, deadly, extreme, grave, mortal; immediate, imminent, impending; real ~ 7. (legal) a clear and present ~ 8. a ~ to (a ~ to national security) 9. a ~ that + clause (there was a ~ that fire would break out) 10. in ~ (our lives were in ~; the building is in imminent ~ of collapsing) 11. out of ~

dangerous *adj.* 1. extremely ~ 2. ~ for 3. ~ to (it's ~ to your health) 4. ~ to + inf. (it's ~ for children to play in the street) 5. ~ that + clause (it's ~ that so many people have guns)

dangle *v.* 1. (d; intr.) to ~ from (his keys ~d from a chain) 2. (d; tr.) to ~ before, in front of (to ~ bait in front of smb.)

dare I *n.* 1. to take a ~ 2. on a ~ (she did it on a ~)

dare II *v.* 1. (E) I don't ~ to protest 2. (F) I ~ not protest (formal); I don't ~ protest; she didn't ~ open her mouth; how ~ you speak to me like that? 3. (H) he ~d me to sue him

USAGE NOTE: Some purists believe that *I don't dare protest* is an incorrect blend of *I don't dare to protest* and *I dare not protest*.

daring *adj.* ~ to + inf. (it was ~ to attempt the climb at night)

dark I *adj.* 1. pitch ("completely") ~ 2. (misc.) to get, grow ~

dark II *n.* ["darkness"] 1. after; before ~ 2. in the ~ (to grope for the door in the ~) 3. (misc.) the child is afraid of the ~ ["ignorance"] 4. to keep smb. in the ~

darkness *n.* 1. complete, pitch, total ~ 2. ~ falls 3. in (the) ~

darn *n.* (colloq.) ["small amount"] not to give a ~ (I don't give a ~!)

dart I *n.* ["pointed object"] 1. to throw a ~ (at) 2. a poisoned ~ ["rush"] 3. to make a ~ (for) (he made a sudden ~ for the door)

dart II *v.* 1. (d; tr.) to ~ at (to ~ a glance at smb.) 2. (P; intr.) the children ~ed into the room; the hare ~ed along the edge of the clearing

darts *n.* to play ~

USAGE NOTE: A singular verb is used with this noun—*darts is a popular game*.

dash I *n.* ["rush"] 1. to make a ~ for (to make a ~ for safety) 2. a frantic, mad ~ 3. in a ~ (I'm in a ~ to catch the next train)

dash II v. (P; intr., tr.) when the rain started, we ~ed for cover

data n. 1. to access; feed in, input, key in; process; retrieve; store ~ 2. to cite; collect, gather; evaluate; transfer ~ 3. to plot ~ (on a map) 4. biographical; scientific; statistical ~ 5. comparative; concrete; raw; solid ~

USAGE NOTE: Purists insist on *these data are available* and consider *this data is available* to be incorrect.

database n. 1. to compile, create a ~ 2. to link ~s 3. a central; incomplete; online ~

date I n. ["time"] 1. to announce; fix, set a ~ 2. to bring (smb.) up to ~ 3. to bear a ~ (the letter bears no ~) 4. a significant ~ (in history) 5. a closing; cutoff; due; expiration, expiry (BE); opening; target ~ 6. at a certain ~ (the meeting will be held at a later ~; at a future ~) 7. on a certain ~ (on this ~ in history) 8. to ~ (how many have returned their invitations to ~?) ["rendezvous, meeting"] 9. to have; make a ~ (I made a ~ to see them) 10. to go out on a ~ 11. to break a ~ 12. a blind; double ~ 13. a ~ with ["misc."] 14. out of ~; to go out of ~; up to ~; to bring a dictionary up to ~

date II v. (d; intr.) to ~ from (this custom ~s from the seventeenth century)

date back v. (d; intr.) to ~ to (the temple ~s back to the tenth century)

dateline n. the international ~ (to cross the international ~)

dating n. carbon ~

daub v. 1. (d; tr.) to ~ on, onto (to ~ paint on the ceiling) 2. (D; tr.) ~ with (to ~ walls with mud)

daughter n. 1. to adopt a ~ 2. to marry off a ~ 3. an older; only; younger ~ 4. an adopted; foster ~; stepdaughter 5. a daughter-in-law 6. a ~ to (she was like a ~ to me)

dawdle v. (D; intr.) ("to waste time") to ~ over

dawn I n. 1. (formal) ~ breaks 2. at (the crack of) ~

dawn II v. 1. (s) the day ~ed cloudy 2. (misc.) it ~ed on me that the following day would be her birthday; it finally ~ed on us what must be done

day n. 1. a bright, sunny; chilly, cool; clear, fine, nice; cloudy; cold; dreary, gloomy; foggy; hot, stifling; rainy; warm ~ 2. an eventful, field, memorable, red-letter ~ (we had a field ~ criticizing their report) 3. the appointed ~; a fast; holy; opening; visiting; wedding; working ~ (opening ~ of the baseball season) 4. ~ breaks, dawns 5. by ~ (London by ~) 6. by the ~ (to be paid by the ~) 7. during the ~ (the store was open during the ~) 8. for a ~ (we are going to town for the ~) 9. from ~ to ~ (from one ~ to the next) 10. in a ~ (we cannot do the whole job in a ~; back in the old ~s) 11. on a certain ~ (on the following ~; on New Year's Day;

on Friday) 12. within several ~s (within ten ~s) 13. (misc.) ~ after ~; ~ and night ("all the time"); D-day ("a day on which a significant event is scheduled to begin"); to take a ~ off; ~ in, ~ out; to carry, save, win the ~ ("to be victorious"); the other ~ ("recently"); his ~s are numbered ("he will die soon"); the dog ~s ("the hot days of July and August"); halcyon ~s; the good old ~s; it was a big ~ ("successful"; "important") ~ for our team; to take one ~ at a time; judgment ~; on the ~ (BE; colloq.) ("when the time comes"); it is early ~s yet (BE) ("it is too soon to tell what will develop")

USAGE NOTE: The collocation *by day* contrasts with *by night* (London by day is very different from London by night). (See the Usage Note for **night**.)

daybreak n. at ~

daydream I n. a ~ about, of

daydream II v. 1. (D; intr.) to ~ about 2. (L) she was always ~ing that she would get rich

daylight n. in broad ~

daylights n. (colloq.) ["insides"] 1. to beat, knock the (living) ~ out of smb. ["wits"] 2. to scare the (living) ~ out of smb.

daytime n. in the ~

daze n. in a ~ (he's always in a ~)

dazed adj. ~ at (~ at the sight of the carnage)

dead I adj. ["having died"] 1. to drop ~ (of a heart attack) 2. brain; clinically ~ 3. ~ on arrival (also DOA) 4. (misc.) to be left for ~; to play ~ ["unresponsive"] 5. (cannot stand alone) ~ to (he was ~ to the world) 6. (misc.) (as of a telephone) to go ~

dead II n. ["the deceased"] 1. to bury the ~ 2. to honor the ~ 3. the war ~ 4. (misc.) to rise from the ~; the quick and the ~

dead III n. ["period of greatest quiet"] in the ~ of (the) night

dead end n. to arrive at, come to, reach a ~

dead heat n. to end in a ~

dead horse n. (colloq.) ["a topic that has been exhausted"] to beat, flog a ~

deadline n. 1. to establish, set a ~ 2. to meet a ~ 3. to extend a ~ 4. to miss a ~ 5. to work against, to (BE) a ~ 6. a ~ for (the ~ for this job is tomorrow)

deadlock n. 1. to end in (a) ~, reach a ~ 2. to break a ~ 3. a ~ between; over

deadlocked adj. ~ over

dead set adj. ["resolutely"] ~ against; on

deadwood n. (also fig.) 1. to cut away, cut out the ~ 2. to get rid of, remove the ~

deaf adj. 1. partially; profoundly, stone ~ 2. (cannot stand alone) ~ to (they were ~ to all our pleas)

deafness n. 1. to cause ~ 2. congenital ~ 3. partial; profound ~

deal I n. ["transaction"] 1. to close, wrap up (colloq.); to cut (colloq.), do (BE), make (AE), strike a ~ with (we closed the ~ with them yesterday) 2. a business; done; shady ~ ["treatment"] 3. a fair, square; raw (colloq.), rotten (colloq.), rough (colloq.) ~ (she got a raw ~ from her boss) ["arrangement"] 4. a package ~ ["amount"] 5. a good, great ~ (of) ["misc."] 6. (colloq.) a big ~ ("an impressive matter"); it means a great ~ to her ("it is very important to her"); it's no big ~ ("it's not so important")

deal II v. 1. (formal) (A) he dealt a deathblow to the enemy; or: he dealt the enemy a deathblow 2. (d; intr.) to ~ in (they ~ in furs) 3. (d; intr.) to ~ with (we ~ with many customers; to ~ with complaints; I'll ~ with the children later; this chapter ~s with the problem of inflation)

dealer n. 1. an antique(s); art; book; car; drug; junk ~ 2. a reputable ~ 3. a ~ in (a ~ in rare books)

dealership n. an automobile (AE), car ~

dealing n. insider ~

dealings n. ["business"] 1. business; straight; underhanded ~ 2. ~ with (I have had ~ with them)

deal out v. (B) she dealt out the cards to the other players

deal with v. (D; intr.) to ~ as (they dealt with me as an equal)

dear adj. 1. (cannot stand alone) ~ to (this project is ~ to my heart) 2. (misc.) to hold (smb.) ~

death n. 1. to cause ~ 2. to face ~; to meet one's ~ 3. to feign ~ 4. to cheat, escape ~ 5. to mourn smb.'s ~ 6. to announce; register smb.'s ~ 7. (an) accidental; agonizing; certain, sure; heroic; instant, instantaneous; lingering; living; natural; painful; sudden, unexpected; tragic; untimely; violent; wrongful ~ (to die a natural ~; to meet a violent ~) 8. brain ~ 9. (a) cot (BE), crib (AE) ~ 10. ~ by (~ by drowning; fire; firing squad; hanging; lethal injection) 11. at smb.'s ~ (at her ~ the estate was broken up) 12. to ~ (beaten; burnt; choked; frozen; put; shot; starved; stoned; trampled to ~) 13. (fig.) bored; frightened to ~ 14. (misc.) a fight to the ~; a ~ in the family; (sports) sudden ~ ("an overtime period ending when the first point or goal is scored"); ~ to tyrants!; in ~ as in life; till ~ us do part

deathbed n. on one's ~

deathblow n. to deal a ~ (they dealt the enemy a ~)

death knell n. to sound, toll the ~

death penalty n. 1. to introduce the ~ 2. to abolish the ~

death row n. on ~

debar v. (formal) (d; tr.) to ~ from (he was ~red from practice)

debatable adj. ~ whether + clause (it is ~ whether smoking should be officially banned)

debate I n. 1. to conduct, have, hold; chair, moderate a ~ 2. to encourage; provoke, spark (AE)/spark off (BE) (a) ~ 3. an acrimonious, bitter, heated, sharp, stormy ~ 4. a lively, spirited ~ 5. a campaign; parliamentary; public ~ 6. (a) formal ~ (in formal ~) 7. a ~ about, on, over; between; with 8. (misc.) a matter for ~

debate II v. 1. to ~ heatedly, hotly 2. (D; intr.) to ~ about, on (to ~ about disarmament) 3. (D; intr.) to ~ with 4. (G) (esp. BE) Parliament ~d disarming 5. (Q) we ~d how to do it

debit I n. (BE) direct ~ (to pay by direct ~)

debit II v. ("to charge") 1. (D; tr.) to ~ against, to (to ~ a purchase against smb.'s account; to ~ an amount to smb.'s account) 2. (D; tr.) to ~ with (~ her account with the entire amount)

debris n. to clear ~

debt n. 1. to contract, incur, run up; owe a ~; to get into, go into ~ 2. to collect, recover a ~ 3. to discharge, pay (off), settle; wipe out; work off; write off a ~ 4. to cancel; repudiate a ~ 5. a bad; outstanding, unsettled ~; mounting ~s 6. a business; foreign; gambling; personal, private ~ 7. the national ~ 8. in ~ for; to (he is in ~ to me for a large sum) 9. out of ~ (to stay out of ~) 10. (misc.) a ~ of honor; a ~ of gratitude; deep(ly) in ~

debut n. 1. to make one's ~ (to make one's ~ in society) 2. a professional; stage ~ 3. a ~ as (to make one's ~ as an actor)

decadence n. 1. to fall into ~ 2. moral ~

decant v. (D; tr.) ("to pour") to ~ from; to

decay n. 1. to fall into ~ 2. dental, tooth ~ 3. radioactive ~ 4. environmental; inner-city, urban ~ 5. moral ~

decease n. (formal and legal) upon smb.'s ~

deceit n. 1. to practice ~ 2. to expose ~ 3. a web of ~

deceitful adj. ~ to + inf. (it was ~ of you to say such things behind her back)

deceive v. 1. (D; tr.) to ~ about (she ~d them about her intentions) 2. (D; refl., tr.) to ~ into (to ~ smb. into doing smt.)

decency n. 1. common; human ~ 2. the ~ to + inf. (he didn't even have the ~ to call) 3. (misc.) to observe the ~cies; a spark of ~

decent adj. ~ to + inf. (it was ~ of her to help us)

deception n. 1. to practice ~ 2. to see through (a) ~ 3. (a) cruel; deliberate ~ 4. by, through ~ (to obtain smt. by ~)

decide v. 1. to ~ unanimously 2. (d; intr.) ("to make a decision") to ~ against (to ~ against buying a car) 3. (legal) (d; intr.) to ~ against; for ("to find for") (the jury ~d for the plaintiff) 4. (D; intr.) ("to choose") to ~ between (it was difficult to ~ between the two) 5. (d; intr.) to ~ on ("to choose in favor of") (we have ~d on a new computer) 6. (E) ("to choose") we ~d to stay home 7. (H) (BE) what finally ~d you to do it? 8. (L) ("to make a decision") she ~d that the children would stay home 9. (Q) ("to make a decision") we could not ~ where to go

decision n. ["act of deciding"] 1. to arrive at, come

to, make, reach, take (BE) a ~ 2. (esp. legal) to affirm, uphold; appeal (AE), appeal against; hand down (AE), render a ~ 3. (esp. legal) to overrule, reverse a ~ 4. to defer; reconsider a ~ 5. a big, momentous; crucial; fateful; landmark (esp. legal); weighty ~ 6. a clear-cut; ethical; fair; favorable; good, sensible, wise; just ~ 7. a collective, joint; unanimous ~ 8. a final; firm; irreversible, irrevocable ~ 9. an agonizing, difficult; arbitrary; hasty, rash, snap ~ 10. a bad, poor, unwise; unfair, unjust; unfavorable ~ 11. a court; majority; split ("divided") ~ 12. a ~ about, on 13. a ~ to + inf. (we made the ~ to accept their offer) 14. the ~ that + clause (we applauded the ~ that taxes would be cut) 15. (misc.) early ~ (AE; used in the process of admitting students to universities) ["decisiveness"] ["firmness"] 16. to lack ~ 17. of ~ (a man, woman of ~)

deck n. ["pack of playing cards"] (AE) 1. to cut; shuffle a ~ 2. to stack a ~ ("to arrange cards dishonestly") (also fig.) ["floor on a ship"] 3. to swab a ~ 4. an aft, after; flight; lower; main; poop; promenade ~; sundeck; upper ~ 5. on ~ (she was on the lower ~; I went up on ~) 6. (misc.) (usu. fig.) clear the ~s for action! ["device for tape recordings"] 7. a tape ~

deck out v. (D; refl., tr.) to ~ in (~ed out in their Sunday best)

declaration n. 1. to issue, make a ~ 2. a solemn; unilateral; written ~ 3. a currency; customs ~

declare v. 1. (B) he ~d his love to her 2. (D; tr.) to ~ against, on (to ~ war on another country) 3. (L; to) the president ~d that the situation would improve 4. (M) the court ~d the law to be unconstitutional 5. (N; used with a noun, adjective, past participle) the court ~d the law unconstitutional; the government ~d him persona non grata

declension n. an adjective; noun; strong; weak ~

decline I n. 1. to go into, sink into, suffer a ~ 2. a gradual; sharp; steady; steep ~ 3. a ~ in (a ~ in trade) 4. in (a) ~ (trade is in ~) 5. into (a) ~ (trade fell/went into ~) 6. on the ~ (trade is on the ~)

decline II v. 1. (D; tr.) (grammar) to ~ for (to ~ a noun for case) 2. (E) she ~d to address the delegates

decorate v. 1. (D; tr.) ("to give a medal to") to ~ for (to ~ a soldier for valor) 2. (D; tr.) ("to adorn") to ~ with (to ~ a room with flowers) 3. (misc.) tastefully ~d

decoration n. ["medal"] 1. to award a ~ 2. (AE) to write smb. up for a ~ 3. a ~ for (she was awarded a ~ for bravery)

decorations n. ["ornaments"] 1. to put up ~ 2. Christmas ~ 3. elaborate; festive; party ~

decorator n. 1. an interior ~ 2. (BE) a painter and ~

decorum n. 1. to display ~ 2. proper; strict ~ 3. (misc.) to behave with ~

decouple v. (D; tr.) ("to separate") to ~ from

decoy v. (D; tr.) to ~ into (they ~ed us into a corner)

decrease I n. 1. a gradual; moderate; sharp; slight; steady; substantial ~ 2. a ~ in 3. on the ~ (crime is on the ~)

decrease II v. (D; intr., tr.) to ~ from; to (the nurse ~d the dosage from four to two)

decree I n. 1. to issue a ~ 2. to rescind, revoke a ~ 3. a consent (legal); divorce; executive; government; royal ~ 4. (GB) a ~ absolute; a ~ nisi 5. a ~ that + clause; subj. (we had to obey the ~ that beards be/should be shaved off) 6. by ~ (by royal ~)

decree II v. (formal) 1. (L; may be subj.) the government ~d that a new tax be/should be imposed; the government ~d that it was illegal to traffic in furs 2. (N) the court ~d the law unconstitutional

decry v. (formal) 1. (D; tr.) to ~ as (to ~ drinking as sinful) 2. (K) she decried their gambling and drinking

dedicate v. (d; refl., tr.) to ~ to (she ~d her life to science; the book was ~d to her husband; they ~d themselves to helping the poor)

dedication n. 1. to demonstrate, display, show ~ 2. complete, great, total ~ 3. ~ to (~ to the cause of freedom) 4. ~ to + inf. (they had the ~ to continue their research in spite of the obstacles)

deduce v. 1. (D; tr.) to ~ from (what can we ~ from these figures?) 2. (L) on the basis of the evidence we ~d that he was guilty 3. (Q) the police were able to ~ where the fugitive was hiding

deduct v. (D; tr.) to ~ from (to ~ a tax from one's wages)

deductible adj. ~ from

deduction n. ["subtracting"] ["deducting"] 1. to make a ~ (from) 2. to make; take a ~ for (income tax purposes) 3. a ~ for; from (our employer makes a ~ from our salary for the income tax) ["conclusion"] 4. to make a ~ 5. an illogical; logical ~ 6. a ~ about 7. the ~ that + clause (these events confirm my ~ that he was to blame)

deed I n. ["something done"] 1. to do, perform a ~ 2. a brave, daring, heroic; chivalrous; good, kind; great, illustrious, noble, praiseworthy ~ 3. a dirty (colloq.); evil, foul, wicked ~ 4. in word and ~ ["legal instrument of transfer"] 5. to transfer a ~ 6. a title ~ 7. a ~ to (to hold a ~ to property) 8. by ~ (to transfer property by ~)

deed II v. (AE) (B) ("to transfer") he ~ed the property to his daughter

deem v. (formal) 1. (M) we ~ed her to be worthy of support 2. (N; used with an adjective, noun) we ~ her worthy of support 3. (misc.) we ~ed it proper that she should be supported

deep adj. 1. ~ in (~ in thought; ~ in the forest) 2. (misc.) the well was forty feet ~; ~ down she is a good person

deep water n. ["trouble"] (colloq.) in ~

deer *n.* 1. a herd of ~ 2. a young ~ is a fawn 3. a female ~ is a doe 4. a male ~ is a buck, stag 5. the meat of a ~ is venison

default I *n.* 1. a ~ on (a ~ on one's mortgage payments) 2. by ~ (to win by ~) 3. in ~ of (anything better)

default II *v.* (D; intr.) to ~ on (to ~ on a debt)

defeat I *n.* 1. to inflict (formal) a ~ on 2. to meet, suffer (a) ~ (at smb.'s hands) 3. to go down in, to ~ 4. to invite ~ 5. to accept, admit, concede ~ 6. a crushing, decisive, disastrous, humiliating, overwhelming, resounding, total, utter; ignominious, shameful ~ 7. in ~ (they were resourceful in ~)

defeat II *v.* 1. to ~ decisively, roundly, resoundingly, soundly 2. to ~ narrowly 3. (D; tr.) to ~ by (they were ~ed by three goals to one)

defect I *n.* 1. to correct a ~ 2. a glaring ~ 3. a minor ~ 4. a birth, congenital; character; hearing; mechanical; mental; physical; speech; structural ~ 5. a ~ in (there was a ~ in the transmission)

defect II *v.* ("to desert") 1. (D; intr.) to ~ from (to ~ from the army) 2. (D; intr.) to ~ to (to ~ to the enemy)

defection *n.* 1. a ~ from (a ~ from the party) 2. a ~ to (a ~ to the West)

defective *adj.* ~ in

defence (BE) see **defense**

defenceless (BE) see **defenseless**

defend *v.* 1. to ~ staunchly, strongly, vigorously 2. (D; refl., tr.) to ~ against, from (she ~ed herself against the attack) 3. (G) we cannot ~ drinking on the job 4. (K) I cannot ~ his drinking on the job

defendant *n.* to arraign a ~

defender *n.* 1. a public ~ ("a lawyer who represents poor people at public expense") 2. a staunch ~ (of smt.)

defense, defence *n.* 1. to conduct, organize, put up a ~ 2. to breach, overwhelm smb.'s ~s 3. an adequate; airtight, impenetrable; heroic; inadequate, weak; strong, vigorous; stubborn ~ 4. civil; national ~ 5. military ~s 6. (sports) a one-on-one; zone ~ 7. a legal ~ 8. a ~ against 9. a ~ that + clause (her ~ that she was provoked was not accepted) 10. in ~ of 11. (misc.) (sports) in (BE), on (AE) ~; (legal) the ~ rests; to spring to smb.'s ~

defenseless, defenceless *adj.* ~ against (~ against any attack)

defense pact, defence pact *n.* a mutual ~

defensive I *adj.* ~ about (they were very ~ about their party's record on tax reform)

defensive II *n.* on the ~ (to put smb. on the ~)

defer *v.* 1. (D; intr.) to ~ in; to (he ~red to his partner in everything) 2. (D; tr.) to ~ until (the trial was ~red until the prisoner's recovery) 3. (formal) (G) we ~red going 4. (formal) (K) we ~red our going

deference *n.* 1. to show ~ to 2. blind; due ~ (with due ~) 3. in, out of ~ to 4. with all ~ to (with all ~ to

you, I think you are wrong)

deferential *adj.* ["respectful"] ~ to

defiance *n.* ["resistance"] 1. to show ~ 2. to glare in ~ 3. ~ against, towards (~ towards all authority) 4. in ~ of (to act in ~ of one's parents) 5. an act of ~

defiant *adj.* ~ towards

deficiency *n.* ["defect"] ["inadequacy"] 1. a hearing; iron; mental; mineral; vitamin ~ 2. a major, serious; minor, slight ~ 3. (a) ~ in ["incomplete work"] (as in school) (AE) 3. to make up a ~

deficient *adj.* ~ in

deficit *n.* 1. to run, show a ~ 2. to make up; reduce a ~ 3. a budget; operating; trade ~ 4. a ~ in

define *v.* 1. to ~ clearly 2. (D; tr.) to ~ as (we can ~ *burnout* as *exhaustion*)

defined *adj.* ["outlined, delineated"] 1. clearly, sharply ~; well-defined 2. ~ against (sharply ~ against a light background)

definite *adj.* 1. ~ about (she was ~ about it) 2. ~ that + clause (is it ~ that they will sign the contract?)

definition *n.* 1. to formulate, give, provide, write a ~ 2. a dictionary; formulaic; referential; synonym ~ 3. a clear ~ 4. by ~

deflect *v.* (D; tr.) to ~ from; into; onto

defraud *v.* (D; tr.) to ~ of (he ~ed them of their money)

deft *adj.* ~ at (she is ~ at dealing with administrators)

defy *v.* (H; passive is rare) she ~fied them to prove her guilty

degenerate *v.* (D; intr.) to ~ from; into

degradation *n.* in ~ (to live in ~)

degrading *adj.* ~ to + inf. (it was ~ to work in such conditions)

degree *n.* ["academic title"] 1. to award a ~ to; to confer a ~ on 2. to do (BE), earn, get, receive, take a ~ 3. an academic; college (AE), university ~ 4. an advanced, graduate, postgraduate (esp. BE); first (BE), undergraduate ~ 5. an earned (AE); honorary ~ 6. an associate; bachelor's; doctoral, doctor's; honours (BE); master's ~ 7. (BE) a good ~ ("a first or upper second at a British university") 8. a ~ from; in (to take a ~ in history; she got her ~ from Cambridge) ["extent"] ["level"] 9. to achieve a ~ (to achieve a high ~ of proficiency) 10. a great, high, large; greater, higher; lesser, lower; low, slight ~ 11. to a ~ (to a high ~) ["form of an adjective or adverb"] 12. the comparative; positive; superlative ~ ["misc."] 13. by ~s ("gradually"); (BE; colloq.) to a ~ ("to a very high degree"); to the nth ~

deign *v.* (formal or humorous) (E) she ~ed to be interviewed

dejected *adj.* 1. very ~ 2. ~ to + inf. (he was ~ to learn that he had failed the examination)

dekko *n.* (slang) (BE) ["look"] to have a ~ at

delay I *n.* 1. to brook no ~ 2. an agonizing; intermi-

nable, long; unavoidable; unexpected, unforeseen ~ 3. a ~ in (she apologized for the ~ in answering)
delay II *v.* 1. (G) we ~ed sending the telegram 2. (K) he ~ed my calling the police
delaying action *n.* to fight a ~
delegate I *n.* 1. a party ~ 2. a ~ at large 3. a ~ from; to (a ~ from the south to the convention)
delegate II *v.* 1. (B) he ~d his responsibilities to a deputy 2. (H) she was ~d to represent us
delegation *n.* 1. to head a ~ 2. an official; unofficial ~ 3. a ~ from; to
delete *v.* (D; tr.) to ~ from (to ~ smt. from a dossier)
deleterious *adj.* ~ to
deletion *n.* 1. to make a ~ 2. a ~ from (she made a ~ from the text)
deliberate I *adj.* ~ in (~ in one's speech)
deliberate II *v.* 1. (D; intr.) to ~ about, on, over 2. (rare) (Q) we ~d where to meet
deliberations *n.* ~ about
delicacy *n.* 1. extreme, great ~ 2. a matter of extreme ~
delight I *n.* 1. to feel ~; to take ~ in (they took ~ in watching the children play) 2. great, intense, sheer ~ 3. ~ at 4. a ~ to + inf. (it was a ~ to watch such fine acting) 5. ~ that + clause (they expressed their ~ that they had been invited) 6. to smb.'s ~ (to my great ~, our guests arrived on time) 7. with ~ (they accepted our invitation with great ~)
delight II *v.* 1. (d; intr.) to ~ in (to ~ in the beauties of nature) 2. (D; tr.) to ~ with (they ~ed the children with their funny stories) 3. (R) it ~ed me (to learn) that you can attend
delighted *adj.* 1. ~ at, by, with 2. ~ to + inf. (we'll be ~ to come) 3. ~ that + clause (I'm ~ that you were able to visit us)
delightful *adj.* ~ to + inf. (it was ~ to swim in the heated pool)
delinquency *n.* 1. juvenile ~ 2. (AE) ~ in
delinquent I *adj.* (AE) ~ in (~ in paying one's rent)
delinquent II *n.* a juvenile; tax (AE) ~
delirious *adj.* ~ with
delirium *n.* in a ~
deliver *v.* 1. (B) they ~ed the merchandise to us 2. (D; tr.) to ~ from; into (~ us from evil; they ~ed us into enemy hands) 3. (pompous) (D; refl.) to ~ of (to ~ oneself of an opinion) 4. (D; tr.) to ~ to (they ~ed the circular to each house; the limousine ~s you to your door) 5. (misc.) to ~ on a promise (esp. AE); to ~ by hand; she was ~ed of a baby girl
deliverance *n.* (formal) ~ from (~ from captivity)
delivery *n.* ["act of delivering"] ["bringing"] 1. to make a ~ (to) 2. to accept, take ~ (of) 3. an emergency ~; (an) overnight; prompt ~ (we guarantee prompt ~) 4. general (AE) ~ (BE has *poste restante*); mail (esp. AE), postal (AE); recorded (BE); rural-free (AE); special ~ 5. a ~ to 6. on ~ (payment on ~) 7. (misc.) door-to-door ~ (they

offer door-to-door ~) ["childbirth"] 8. a breech; caesarean; normal ~ ["manner of speaking or throwing"] 9. an effective ~
delude *v.* 1. (D; refl., tr.) to ~ into 2. (L; refl.) don't ~ yourself that she loves you
deluge *v.* (d; tr.) to ~ with (we were ~d with offers)
delusion *n.* 1. to cherish, cling to a ~ 2. a ~ that + clause (he was under the ~ that he would inherit money) 3. under a ~ (to labor under a ~) 4. (misc.) ~s of grandeur
delve *v.* 1. to ~ deeply 2. (d; intr.) to ~ for (to ~ for information) 3. (d; intr.) to ~ into (to ~ into the background of a case)
demand I *n.* ["urgent request"] 1. to make a ~; to state one's ~s 2. to meet, respond to, satisfy a ~; to give in to, yield to a ~ 3. to ignore; reject a ~ 4. to drop, give up a ~ 5. an excessive, exorbitant, unrealistic; final; moderate, modest, reasonable; non-negotiable ~ 6. union; wage ~s 7. a ~ for; on (a ~ for compensation; to make ~s on smb.'s time) 8. a ~ that + clause; subj. (they rejected our demand that no one be/should be punished) 9. at, on ~ (payment on ~) ["desire for a commodity"] 10. to create a ~ 11. to meet, satisfy a ~ 12. (a) brisk, enormous, great, heavy, strong; growing, increased, increasing ~ 13. (a) limited, little ~ 14. consumer; popular; public ~ 15. ~ drops off, falls off; increases, rises 16. a ~ for (there is a brisk ~ for home computers) 17. by ~ (by popular ~) 18. in ~ (small cars are in great ~) ["misc."] 19. the law of supply and ~
demand II *v.* 1. (D; tr.) to ~ from, of (to ~ an apology from smb.) 2. (E) she ~s to be informed of everything 3. (L; subj.) we ~ed that he help/should help us
demanding *adj.* ~ of (she is very ~ of her employees)
demarcation *n.* a ~ between (lines of ~ between the two zones)
demean *v.* (formal) (D; refl.) ("to degrade") to ~ by (I will not ~ myself by cheating on the examination)
demeaning *adj.* 1. ~ to (is charity ~ to its recipients?) 2. ~ to + inf. (it is ~ to be kept waiting so long)
demeanor *n.* a cheerful, friendly; unfriendly ~
demerit *n.* a ~ for (a ~ for being late)
demise *n.* ["death"] on, upon smb.'s ~
demobilization *n.* on, upon ~
democracy *n.* a constitutional; parliamentary; representative ~
Democrat *n.* (US) a registered ~
demon *n.* to exorcise a ~
demonstrable *adj.* clearly ~
demonstrate *v.* 1. to ~ convincingly 2. (B) ("to explain by showing") they ~d the new invention to us 3. (D; intr.) ("to protest by marching") to ~

against (the students ~d against the government) 4. (D; intr.) ("to display support by marching") to ~ for, in favor of (to ~ for lower taxes) 5. (L; to) ("to prove by showing") we ~d (to them) that a new computer would save considerable time 6. (Q; to) ("to explain by showing") she ~d (to him) how the computer works

demonstration n. ["explanation"] 1. to give, put on a ~ 2. a practical ~ ["protest"] 3. to mount, organize, stage a ~ 4. to break up, quell a ~ 5. an antinuclear; peace; political ~ 6. a disorderly, violent; non-violent, orderly, peaceful ~ 7. a mass; organized; spontaneous; staged ~ 8. a public; student ~ 9. a ~ against ["expression of support"] 10. to mount, organize, stage a ~ 11. a ~ for, in favor of, in support of 12. (misc.) they marched as/in a ~ of support

demote v. (D; tr.) to ~ from; to (he was ~d to the rank of corporal)

demur I n. (formal) without ~ (they accepted without ~)

demur II v. (formal) (D; intr.) ("to object") to ~ at, to (to ~ at a proposal)

den n. 1. a lion's ~ 2. a gambling; opium ~; a ~ of iniquity; a ~ of thieves

denial n. ["refusal, rejection"] 1. to issue a ~ 2. a categorical, emphatic; flat; outright; strenuous, strong, vehement; unqualified ~ 3. a ~ that + clause (they issued a ~ that their firm had been involved) ["a psychological process"] 4. in (a state of) ~

denomination n. ["group"] 1. a religious ~ (to belong to a religious ~) ["unit of money"] 2. large; small ~s (the store did not accept currency in large ~s)

denominator n. 1. to find the least (math.)/lowest (math. or fig.) common ~ 2. a common ~

denounce v. 1. to ~ angrily, bitterly; openly, publicly; roundly, strongly 2. (B) to ~ smb. to the police 3. (D; tr.) to ~ as (to ~ smb. as an illegal alien) 4. (G) they ~d drinking in the strongest possible terms 5. (K) she ~d his drinking

density n. 1. population; traffic ~ 2. high; low ~

dent n. 1. to make, put a ~ in (he made a ~ in the door; to make a ~ in the backlog of work) 2. to hammer out, remove, straighten out a ~

denture n. 1. a partial ~ 2. complete, full ~s 3. a set of ~s

denude v. (D; tr.) to ~ of (the hillside was ~d of trees)

denunciation n. 1. to issue, make a ~ 2. an angry, bitter, scathing, strong, vehement; sweeping ~

deny v. 1. to ~ angrily; categorically, emphatically, fervently, flatly, strongly, vehemently 2. (A; usu. used without to) he ~ies himself nothing; they were ~ied admittance; to ~ smb. bail; Everton's defence ~ied Liverpool the winning goal; he ~ies

nothing to his family; or: he ~ies his family nothing 3. (G) she ~ied knowing anything 4. (L; to) she ~ied that she had been there 5. (rare) (M) he ~ied it to be the case

deodorant n. 1. to apply, put on (a) ~ 2. to use (a) ~ 3. (a) cream; roll-on; spray; stick; underarm ~

depart v. 1. (D; intr.) to ~ for (to ~ for London) 2. (D; intr.) to ~ from (our train ~s from platform seven)

department n. ["division of a school, of a university"] 1. to chair, run a ~ 2. a strong; weak ~ 3. an accounting; anthropology; astronomy; biology; chemistry; classics; economics; English; French; geology; German; history; Italian; linguistics; mathematics; music; nursing; philosophy; physics; political science; psychology; Slavic, Slavonic; sociology; Spanish ~ 4. the chair (esp. AE), head (esp. BE) of a ~ ["division of a company or government"] 5. an accounting; finance; fire (AE) (BE has *fire brigade*); health; personnel; police; recreation; sanitation; service ~ ["division of a hospital"] 6. a casualty (BE), emergency (AE) ~

departure n. 1. to be, mark, represent a ~ from (this marks a ~ from established procedures) 2. a sudden ~ 3. a ~ for 4. a ~ from; to 5. (misc.) a point of ~

depend v. 1. to ~ entirely, heavily, solely; partly (on) 2. (d; intr.) to ~ on, upon (she ~s on her parents)

dependence n. 1. drug ~ 2. ~ on, upon

dependency n. 1. a colonial ~ 2. alcohol; drug ~

dependent adj. ~ for; on, upon (he is ~ on his parents for support)

depend on, depend upon v. 1. (D; intr.) to ~ for (to ~ smb. for advice) 2. (H) you can ~ her to be there

depict v. 1. (B) they ~ed the situation to us in great detail 2. (d; tr.) to ~ as (he was ~ed as a traitor) 3. (J) the artist ~ed him strolling through a garden

deplete v. (D; tr.) to ~ of

deplorable adj. 1. ~ to + inf. (it was ~ to live under such conditions = it was ~ living under such conditions) 2. ~ that + clause (it is ~ that such corruption exists/should exist)

deplore v. 1. to ~ deeply, strongly, thoroughly 2. (G) we ~ taking drugs 3. (K) we ~ their taking drugs

deport I v. (formal) ("to behave") 1. (d; refl.) to ~ like (he ~ed himself like a gentleman) 2. (P; refl.) to ~ oneself well

deport II v. (D; tr.) ("to send out of the country") to ~ from; to

deportation n. (a) mass ~

depose v. (D; tr.) to ~ from

deposit I n. ["money put into a bank account"] 1. to make a ~ 2. a demand; direct; minimum; time ~ 3. on ~ (the money was on ~ in a bank) ["down payment"] 4. to give, leave a ~; to put a ~ down on 5. to forfeit, lose one's ~

deposit II *v.* 1. (D; tr.) to ~ in (to ~ money in a bank) 2. (D; tr.) to ~ with (she ~ed the funds with her lawyer)

deposition *n.* (legal) 1. (of a witness) to make a ~ 2. (of a lawyer) to defend; notice; take a ~ 3. a sworn ~ 4. a ~ that (he made a ~ that he had witnessed the accident)

deposits *n.* 1. rich ~ 2. coal; gold; mineral; oil; ore ~ (rich ~ of ore)

depot *n.* an ammunition; arms; bus; freight (AE), goods (BE); fuel; supply ~

depreciate *v.* 1. (D; intr.) to ~ by (to ~ by ten percent) 2. (D; intr.) to ~ in (to ~ in value)

depress *v.* (formal) (R) it ~ed everyone that no progress was made during the negotiations

depressed *adj.* 1. deeply, very ~ 2. ~ about, at, over; by (~ at the bad news) 3. ~ to + inf. (she was ~ to learn of her illness)

depressing *adj.* 1. deeply, profoundly, very ~ 2. ~ to + inf. (it is ~ to read the headlines) 3. ~ that + clause (it's ~ that so many young people use drugs)

depression *n.* ["low economic activity"] 1. to cause a ~ 2. a major, severe; minor ~ 3. an economic ~ 4. (misc.) the Great Depression (of the 1930s) ["dejection"] 5. to cause ~ 6. to suffer from ~ 7. (a) chronic; clinical; deep, severe, total; postnatal, postpartum ~ (he was in a state of total ~) 8. a bout of ~

depressor *n.* a tongue ~

deprivation *n.* to suffer ~

deprive *v.* (d; tr.) to ~ of (to ~ smb. of everything)

depth *n.* ["distance from top to bottom"] ["distance from front to back"] 1. in ~ (the river is thirty feet in ~) ["place at the bottom of a body of water"] 2. to a ~ (the water froze to a ~ of two feet) 3. to reach a ~ (the divers reached great ~s) ["capability"] 4. beyond, out of one's ~ ["worst part"] 5. in the ~s (in the ~s of the Depression) ["misc."] 6. in ~ ("thoroughly"); to plumb the ~s of smt. ("to get to the root of smt."); in the ~s of despair; to lack ~ ("to be superficial")

depth charge *n.* to drop a ~

depute *v.* (formal) (esp. BE) 1. (B) ("to assign") (he ~d the bookkeeping to me while he was away) 2. (H) ("to appoint as deputy, to delegate") to ~ smb. to do smt.

deputize *v.* 1. (esp. AE) (D; tr.) ("to appoint") to ~ as (he ~d me as his assistant) 2. (esp. BE) (D; intr.) to ~ for ("to replace") (to ~ for smb. as secretary) 3. (AE) (H) ("to appoint as deputy") to ~ smb. to do smt.

deputy *n.* 1. to swear in a ~ 2. to act as (a) ~ 3. a special ~ 4. a ~ for

deranged *adj.* mentally ~

derelict *adj.* ~ in (~ in one's duty)

derision *n.* 1. to arouse, provoke ~ 2. an object of ~ 3. (misc.) hoots of ~

derivation *n.* of a certain ~ (words of Latin ~)

derive *v.* 1. (d; intr.) ("to come") to ~ from (many words ~ from Latin) 2. (D; tr.) ("to trace") to ~ from (to ~ a word from a Latin root) 3. (D; tr.) ("to receive") to ~ from (to ~ pleasure from music)

derogatory *adj.* ~ of, to, towards

descend *v.* 1. (d; intr.) to ~ from ("to come down from") (do you know from whom you are ~ed?) 2. (D; intr.) to ~ into ("to go into") (to ~ into a cave) 3. (d; intr.) ("to swoop down") to ~ on, upon (the guerrillas ~ed on the village) 4. (d; intr.) ("to stoop") to ~ to (to ~ to a life of petty crime)

descendant *n.* a direct, lineal ~

descended *adj.* (cannot stand alone) 1. directly ~ 2. ~ from (~ from a royal family)

descent *n.* ["origin"] 1. to trace smb.'s ~ 2. direct ~ 3. ~ from 4. of a certain ~ (of mixed ~) ["decline"] 5. a gradual, steep ~ ["visit, influx"] 6. a ~ on, upon (a sudden ~ of tourists on a resort) ["coming down"] 7. to make a ~ into

describe *v.* 1. to ~ graphically; minutely; vividly; in detail 2. (B) she ~d the scene to us 3. (D; refl., tr.) to ~ as (he was ~d as being very cruel) 4. (G) she ~d living under the occupation 5. (K) she ~d in detail their living under the occupation 6. (Q; to) he ~d (to us) how we should proceed

description *n.* 1. to give, provide a ~ 2. to answer to a ~ (he answers to the ~ of the escaped convict) 3. to beggar, defy ~ 4. an accurate, correct, exact; clear, graphic; matter-of-fact, objective ~ 5. a glowing; lively, picturesque, vivid ~ 6. a blow-by-blow; detailed, full, lengthy, thorough; firsthand ~ 7. a brief, short; superficial ~ 8. a job ~ 9. of a certain ~ (a person of that ~ was seen here yesterday) 10. (misc.) beyond ~

desensitize *v.* (D; tr.) to ~ to (to ~ smb. to suffering)

desert I *n.* 1. to reclaim a ~ 2. a trackless ~ 3. (fig.) a cultural; intellectual ~ 4. in a ~

desert II *v.* 1. (D; tr.) to ~ for (to ~ the stage for Hollywood) 2. (D; intr.) to ~ from (he ~ed from his regiment) 3. (D; intr.) to ~ to (to ~ to the enemy)

desertion *n.* a ~ from (~s from the army have increased)

deserts *n.* ["reward"] ["punishment"] to get one's just ~

deserve *v.* 1. to ~ richly 2. (E) she ~d to win 3. (G) he ~d being recommended for a decoration 4. (misc.) to ~ better (of); to ~ ill of; to ~ well of

deserving *adj.* 1. richly ~ 2. ~ of (~ of help)

design I *n.* ["plan"] 1. a creative ~ 2. software ~ 3. a ~ for (a ~ for a new library) ["intention"] 4. by ~ (was it by accident or by ~?)

design II *v.* 1. (C) he ~ed a beautiful house for us; or: he ~ed us a beautiful house 2. (d; tr.) to ~ as 3.

(d; tr.) to ~ for (~ed for recreational purposes)

designate I *adj.* (placed after a noun) a minister ~

designate II *v.* 1. (D; tr.) to ~ as (the state was ~d as a disaster area) 2. (H) we ~d him to serve as our delegate 3. (N; used with a noun) the state was ~d a disaster area

designation *n.* a ~ as

designed *adj.* (cannot stand alone) 1. ~ for (~ for use in cold climates) 2. ~ to + inf. (the equipment is ~ to operate at any altitude)

designer *n.* an aircraft; dress; fashion; graphic; interior; software ~

designs *n.* ["evil intentions"] 1. to have, harbor ~ against, on, upon (to have ~ on smb.'s money) 2. sinister ~

desirable *adj.* 1. ~ to + inf. (it is ~ to wait) 2. ~ that + clause; subj. (it is ~ that you be/should be there by two o'clock)

desire I *n.* 1. to arouse, create, whet (a) ~ 2. to evince, express, voice a ~ 3. to feel, have a ~ 4. to satisfy a ~ 5. to repress, stifle, suppress a ~ 6. (an) ardent, blind, burning, deep, earnest, fervent, insatiable, intense, keen, overwhelming, passionate, strong; sincere; unfulfilled ~ 7. animal; sexual ~s 8. a ~ for 9. a ~ to + inf. (a ~ to excel) 10. a ~ that + clause; subj. (it was her ~ that the estate be/should be divided evenly)

desire II *v.* 1. to deeply, fervently, strongly ~ 2. (E) she ~s to remain neutral in the dispute 3. (formal) (H) to ~ smb. to do smt. 4. (formal) (L; subj.) I ~ that he be present

desirous *adj.* (formal) 1. (cannot stand alone) ~ of (~ of fame) 2. ~ that; subj. (he is ~ that you be/should be there)

desist *v.* (formal) (D; intr.) to ~ from (to ~ from further litigation)

desk *n.* ["counter"] 1. (in a hotel) a front (AE), reception (BE) ~ 2. at the ~ (I'll meet you at the front ~) ["department"] 3. an information ~ 4. (at a newspaper) a city; copy ~ ["table for writing"] 5. to clear one's ~ 6. a cluttered ~ 7. a rolltop; writing ~

USAGE NOTE: In AE *city desk* means "local news desk"; in BE it means "financial news desk".

desolation *n.* complete, utter ~

despair I *n.* 1. to overcome ~ 2. bitter, deep, sheer, total, utter ~ 3. the depths of ~ 4. in ~ (in utter ~) 5. out of ~ (to do smt. out of ~) 6. (misc.) to drive smb. to ~

despair II *v.* 1. to ~ deeply 2. (D; intr.) to ~ of (to ~ of success)

despatch (BE) see **dispatch I, II**

desperate *adj.* ~ for (~ for help)

desperation *n.* 1. an act of ~ 2. in ~

despicable *adj.* ~ to + inf. (it was ~ of him to desert his family)

despise *v.* 1. to ~ utterly 2. (D; tr.) to ~ for (I ~d him

for his cowardice) 3. (K) I ~ his refusing to accept responsibility

despoil *v.* (formal) (D; tr.) to ~ of

despondent *adj.* ~ about, over

despot *n.* an absolute; benevolent; enlightened ~

destination *n.* 1. to reach one's ~; to arrive at one's ~ 2. smb.'s final, ultimate ~

destine *v.* 1. (d; tr.) to ~ for 2. (H) fate ~d her to go far in life

destined *adj.* (cannot stand alone) 1. ~ for (the shipment is ~ for New York) 2. ~ to + inf. (she was ~ from birth to become president)

destiny *n.* 1. to achieve, fulfill one's ~ 2. to decide, shape smb.'s ~ 3. (historical) Manifest Destiny 4. ~ to + inf. (it was her ~ to make an important medical discovery) 5. ~ that + clause (it was my ~ that I would never return)

destitute *adj.* ~ of (~ of feeling)

destitution *n.* in ~ (to die in ~)

destroyer *n.* a tank ~

destruction *n.* 1. to carry out ~ (with a human subject: the soldiers carried out the total ~ of the village) 2. to cause ~ (with any subject: the flood caused great ~) 3. complete, mass, total, utter; wanton; widespread ~ (weapons of mass ~)

destructive *adj.* ~ of

detach *v.* (D; tr.) to ~ from (the officer was ~ed temporarily from her unit)

detail I *n.* ["small part"] ["minute treatment"] 1. to bring up, cite; disclose; fill in; furnish, give; go into (the) ~s 2. to go into ~ (you don't need to go into great ~) 3. to work out (the) ~s 4. an essential, important; mere, minor; technical ~ (can you fill in the technical ~s?) 5. (a) gory, graphic, grisly, gruesome, harrowing, lurid, revolting, sordid, unsavory; meticulous, microscopic, minute; petty ~ (they went into lurid ~; they brought up petty ~s; the newspapers reported the gruesome ~s; he described the event in graphic ~; only the police knew the sordid ~s of the crime) 6. (a) ~ about (they discussed the important ~s about the campaign) 7. in ~ (to treat a topic in minute ~) 8. (misc.) spare me the ~s ["detachment"] (usu. mil.) 9. to form a ~ 10. a fatigue, work ~

detail II *v.* ("to assign") 1. (D; tr.) to ~ for (to ~ a unit for fatigue duty) 2. (H) they ~ed us to investigate the charges

detain *v.* 1. to ~ forcibly 2. (D; tr.) to ~ for (he was ~ed for questioning)

detained *adj.* unavoidably ~

detection *n.* 1. to avoid, escape ~ 2. early ~

detective *n.* an amateur; house (obsol.); private ~

detector *n.* a lie; metal; mine; smoke ~

detention *n.* in ~ (he was kept in ~ for two hours)

deter *v.* (D; tr.) to ~ from

detergent *n.* (a) biodegradable; laundry; liquid; synthetic ~

deterioration *n.* 1. continuing; marked; steady ~ 2. a ~ in (I noted a ~ in her condition)

determination *n.* ["decisiveness"] 1. to show ~ 2. dogged, fierce, firm, great, grim, iron, sheer, unflinching, unyielding ~ ["firm intention"] 3. to express one's ~ 4. to shake smb.'s ~ 5. ~ to + inf. (I admire her ~ to succeed) ["judicial decision"] 6. to come to a ~ (of a case) 7. the final ~ (of a case)

determine *v.* 1. (E) he ~d to learn English (more usu. is: he is ~d to learn English) 2. (L) the police ~d that no crime had been committed 3. (Q) we must ~ where the conference will take place

determined *adj.* 1. very ~ 2. ~ to + inf. (she is ~ to finish law school) 3. ~ that + clause (they were ~ that everyone would receive food)

deterrent *n.* 1. an effective, powerful ~ 2. a nuclear ~; the ultimate ~ 3. a ~ against, to

detest *v.* 1. (G) he ~s working 2. (K) we ~ his constantly lying

detestable *adj.* ~ to + inf. (it is ~ to speak like that; it was ~ of them to do that)

detour *n.* 1. to set up a ~ 2. to follow, make, take a ~ 3. a ~ around

detract *v.* (d; intr., tr.) to ~ from (the scandal will not ~ from his fame)

detriment *n.* 1. a ~ to 2. to the ~ of

detrimental *adj.* ~ to (smoking is ~ to health)

devastation *n.* 1. to cause ~ 2. complete, total, utter, widespread ~ 3. (misc.) the terrorists left a trail of ~

develop *v.* 1. to ~ fully; rapidly; slowly 2. (D; intr.) to ~ from; into (to ~ from a child into an adult)

developed *adj.* highly ~

developer *n.* a property (BE); real-estate (AE) ~

development *n.* ["advancement, change, maturation"] 1. arrested; economic; historical; intellectual; physical ~ 2. the latest ~s; recent ~s; technological ~s 3. a dramatic, exciting; interesting; new, recent; surprising ~ 4. a ~ in (recent ~s in physics) 5. (misc.) a stage of ~; a stage in the ~ of ["large housing project"] 6. a housing ~ 7. (BE) a ribbon ~ ("line of similar buildings constructed along roads leading out of a town")

deviate *v.* 1. to ~ sharply; slightly 2. (D; intr.) to ~ from

deviation *n.* 1. a marked, sharp; slight ~ 2. (statistics) a standard ~ 3. a ~ from

device *n.* 1. a contraceptive; intrauterine (IUD) ~ 2. a laborsaving; timesaving ~ 3. a detonating; explosive; incendiary; thermonuclear ~ 4. a literary; mnemonic; rhetorical; stylistic ~ 5. a flotation; listening ~ 6. a ~ for 7. a ~ to + inf. (it was a ~ to mislead the voters) 8. (misc.) left to one's own ~s ("on one's own; unaided")

devil *n.* ["spirit of evil"] 1. go to the ~! ("damn you!") 2. the ~ incarnate ["severe reprimand"] (esp. AE) 3. to catch the ~ ["fellow"] (colloq.) 4. a lucky; poor ~ ["disturbed state"] 5. (in) a ~ of a mess ["misc."] 6. where the ~ did she go? speak of the ~! there'll be the ~ to pay! he's a little ~!

devoid *adj.* (cannot stand alone) ~ of (~ of any redeeming features)

devolution *n.* ~ to (the ~ of power to local government)

devolve *v.* (formal) 1. (d; intr.) ("to be transferred") to ~ on, upon (his duties ~d on his deputy) 2. (D; tr.) ("to transfer") to ~ to (to ~ authority to local government)

devote *v.* 1. to ~ oneself completely, entirely 2. (D; refl., tr.) to ~ to (she ~d herself to her work; we must ~ a lot of time to this project)

devoted *adj.* 1. blindly, completely, deeply, entirely, thoroughly, utterly, very ~ 2. ~ to (~ to one's family)

devotee *n.* a ~ of (a ~ of the theater)

devotion *n.* 1. to demonstrate, display, show ~ 2. to inspire ~ (from) 3. absolute, blind, complete, deep, great, selfless, slavish, thorough, undying, unflagging, unstinting, unswerving, utter ~ 4. religious ~ 5. ~ to (blind ~ to the cause; ~ to one's duty) 6. with ~ (to serve with ~)

devour *v.* to ~ eagerly, ravenously

dexterity *n.* 1. to demonstrate, display, show ~ 2. great; intellectual; political; manual ~ 3. ~ in (she showed great political ~ in handling the problem)

dexterous, dextrous *adj.* ~ with (~ with one's hands)

diabetes *n.* to develop ~

diagnose *v.* (D; tr.) to ~ as (they ~d her illness as diabetes)

diagnosis *n.* 1. to make a ~ 2. to confirm a ~ 3. (med.) (a) differential ~ 4. a ~ that + clause (further studies confirmed the ~ that the tumor was benign)

diagonal I *adj.* ~ to

diagonal II *n.* on the ~ (to cut on the ~)

diagram *n.* to draw a ~

dial I *n.* to turn a ~

dial II *v.* to ~ direct, directly (she ~led London direct)

dialect *n.* 1. to speak (in) a ~ 2. a local, regional; social; standard ~ 3. in ~ (the stories were written in ~)

dialing, dialling *n.* direct ~

dialogue *n.* 1. to enter into a ~ (with); to have a ~ with 2. a constructive, fruitful, meaningful ~ 3. a ~ between; with

diameter *n.* in ~ (the circle is ten inches in ~)

diamond *n.* 1. to cut; grind; polish; set a ~ 2. a cut; flawless, perfect; industrial; rare; rough, uncut ~ 3. a ~ sparkles 4. (misc.) a baseball ~; a ~ in the rough (AE), a rough ~ (BE) ("a person who is kinder and/or more intelligent than he/she appears to be")

diaper *n.* (AE) 1. to change, put on a ~ 2. cloth;

disposable ~s (BE has *nappy*)

diaphragm *n.* ["contraceptive device"] to insert, put in; remove, take out a ~

diarrhea, diarrhoea *n.* 1. to come down with, get; have ~ 2. severe ~ 3. an attack of ~

diary *n.* 1. to keep a ~ 2. a personal ~

diatribe *n.* 1. to utter a ~ 2. to launch into a (long) ~ 3. a bitter ~ 4. a ~ against

dice *n.* 1. to play ~ 2. to roll, throw (the) ~ 3. loaded ~ 4. a roll of the ~ 5. a pair of ~ 6. (misc.) (esp. AE; colloq.) no dice! ("I do not agree!")

dichotomy *n.* 1. an absolute; growing ~ 2. a ~ between

dicker *v.* to ~ about, over; for; with

dictate *v.* 1. (D; intr., tr.) to ~ to (she was ~ing to her secretary; the conqueror ~s terms to the conquered) 2. (L; can be subj.) the financial crisis ~d that we begin/should begin immediately 3. (Q; to) they ~d (to us) how everything would be done

dictation *n.* 1. to give ~ 2. to take ~ 3. to transcribe ~

dictator *n.* an absolute; benevolent; brutal; military; ruthless ~

dictatorship *n.* 1. to establish, set up a ~ 2. to overthrow a ~ 3. an absolute; benevolent; brutal; military; ruthless ~ 4. (to live) under a ~

diction *n.* clear ~

dictionary *n.* 1. to compile, write a ~ 2. to expand; revise; update a ~ 3. to consult, use a ~ 4. an abridged, desk; bilingual; biographical; college (AE), collegiate (T); combinatorial, combinatory; concise; dialect; etymological; general-use, general-purpose; historical; learner's, learners'; medical; monolingual; multilingual; multivolume; names; orthographic, spelling; pronouncing; pocket; reverse; technical; unabridged ~ 5. a ~ of abbreviations; collocations; foreign words; personal names; place names; quotations; synonyms

diddle *v.* 1. (esp. BE) (colloq.) (D; intr.) ("to cheat") to ~ out of 2. (AE) (D; intr.) ("to fool around") to ~ with

die I *n.* the ~ is cast (fig.)

die II *v.* 1. to ~ heroically; instantly; suddenly (he ~d heroically at the front) 2. (d; intr.) to ~ by (to ~ by the sword; to ~ by one's own hand) 3. (d; intr.) to ~ for (to ~ for one's beliefs) 4. (colloq.) (d; intr.) (only in the progressive) to ~ for ("to want") (she's dying for a cup of coffee) 5. to ~ from, of (he died of tuberculosis; to ~ of natural causes) 6. (colloq.) (E) (only in the progressive) ("to want") she's dying to find out 7. (S) she ~d happy; he ~d a poor man; (legal) to ~ intestate 8. (misc.) to ~ a horrible death; to ~ in action/battle; to ~ in one's sleep; (fig.) to ~ laughing; rumors ~ hard

diet *n.* 1. to be on, follow, stick to a ~ 2. to go on a ~ 3. to prescribe a ~; to put smb. on a ~ 4. a balanced, healthy, well-balanced ~ 5. a crash; special; star-

vation; therapeutic ~ 6. a bland; high-calorie; high-carbohydrate; high-fiber, high-fibre; high-protein; liquid; low calorie; low-carbohydrate; low-cholesterol; low-fat; low-residue; low-salt, low-sodium; salt-free; soft ~ 7. a reducing, slimming (esp. BE) ~ 8. a macrobiotic; vegan, vegetarian ~ 9. (misc.) a steady ~ (she was on a steady ~ of parties)

differ *v.* 1. to ~ considerably, greatly, markedly, radically, sharply, widely; slightly 2. (D; intr.) to ~ about, in, on, over 3. (D; intr.) to ~ from (this arrangement ~s from the one I had in mind) 3. (D; intr.) to ~ with (I ~ with you on that point)

difference *n.* 1. to make a ~ 2. to tell the ~ 3. to have; reconcile, resolve, settle, thrash out ~s 4. to set aside ~s 5. to air ~s 6. to split the ~ ("to take an average") 7. a considerable, great, huge, marked, striking, vast ~ 8. an essential, fundamental; noticeable, perceptible; significant ~ 9. an irreconcilable; radical ~ 10. an insignificant, little, minor, slight; subtle; superficial ~ 11. ~s among; a ~ between; from 12. a ~ in (a ~ in age) 13. a ~ to (that makes no ~ to me) 14. (misc.) a world of ~ ("a considerable difference")

different *adj.* 1. basically, completely, entirely, totally, widely; quite; radically ~ 2. ~ in (they are quite ~ in outlook) 3. ~ from, than (esp. AE), to (BE)

USAGE NOTE: Some purists consider only *different from* to be correct. Note that, as prepositions, *from, than, to* can all introduce full clauses (different from/than/to what we thought), but only *than* can, as a conjunction, become part of a clause (different than we thought).

differential *n.* 1. a pay; price ~ 2. a ~ between

differentiate *v.* 1. (d; intr.) to ~ between 2. (d; tr.) to ~ from (to ~ right from wrong)

differentiation *n.* to make a ~ between

differing *adj.* widely ~

difficult *adj.* 1. ~ for (typing is ~ for me) 2. ~ to + inf. (it is ~ to please him = he is ~ to please = he is a ~ person to please = pleasing him is ~; it is ~ to translate this book = this book is ~ to translate = this is a ~ book to translate; it is ~ for me to translate such material = such material is ~ for me to translate)

difficulty *n.* 1. to cause, create, make, present ~ties (for) 2. to come across, encounter, experience, face, get into, have, meet, run into ~ties 3. to clear up, overcome, resolve, surmount a ~ 4. (a) grave, great, insurmountable, serious, severe ~ 5. economic, financial; learning; personal; technical ~ties 6. a ~ arises 7. ~ in (she has ~ in breathing = she has ~ breathing) 8. ~ties about, over; with (we had ~ties with them about the price) 9. in ~ (he is in serious ~) 10. (misc.) many ~ties face us

diffident *adj.* ~ about

diffuse *v.* (formal) (D; tr.) to ~ through, throughout (~d through the air)

dig I *n.* (colloq.) ["excavation"] 1. to go on a ~ 2. an archeological ~ ["poke"] 3. to give smb. a ~ in (the ribs) ["critical remark"] 4. (colloq.) to have, take a ~ at smb.

dig II *v.* 1. (D; intr.) to ~ for ("to search for") (to ~ for gold) 2. (d; intr.) ("to delve, search") to ~ into (to ~ into a report; he dug into his own pocket) 3. (d; intr., tr.) ("to jab") to ~ into (his elbow was ~ging into my ribs; he dug his spurs into the sides of the horse) 4. (D; intr., refl., tr.) ("to move earth" and fig.) to ~ into (they dug themselves into a hole) 5. (D; intr., refl., tr.) ("to free, liberate" and fig.) to ~ out of (they dug themselves out of a hole) 6. (D; intr., tr.) ("to move, move earth" and fig.) to ~ through, under (to ~ a tunnel through a mountain; they had to ~ through a lot of red tape; they dug under the street)

dignified *adj.* ~ to + inf. (it is not ~ to beg for money)

dignify *v.* (D; tr.) to ~ by, with (I would not ~ that shack by calling it a hotel; she did not ~ his comment with a response)

dignitary *n.* a local; visiting ~

dignity *n.* 1. to have, possess ~ 2. to maintain one's ~ 3. the ~ to + inf. (does he have enough ~ to cope with a hostile press?) 4. (misc.) to live in ~; to die in/with ~; to behave with ~; beneath smb.'s ~; a person of great ~

digress *v.* (D; intr.) to ~ from

digression *n.* ["act of digressing"] 1. a ~ from ["digressive remarks"] 2. a ~ on (he launched into a ~ on the need for more power plants)

dilate *v.* (d; intr.) ("to speak or write in detail") (formal) to ~ on, upon (to ~ upon a subject)

dilatory *adj.* (formal) ~ in (they were ~ in acting on your complaint)

dilemma *n.* 1. to confront; face; have a ~ 2. to resolve a ~ 3. an ethical, moral ~ 4. a ~ about, over 5. in a ~ 6. (misc.) on the horns of a ~

diligence *n.* 1. (legal) due ~ 2. the ~ to + inf. (does she have enough ~ to finish the job on time?)

diligent *adj.* ~ about; in (~ in one's work)

dillydally *v.* (D; intr.) to ~ over; with

dilute *v.* (D; tr.) to ~ with (to ~ the punch with water)

dimension *n.* ["importance"] 1. to add, introduce; assume, take on a ~ (the issue assumed serious ~s) 2. (misc.) a problem of international ~s ["measurement"] (can be fig.) 3. a third ~ 4. in a ~ (in two ~s) 5. (misc.) time has been referred to as the fourth ~

diminish *v.* (d; intr.) to ~ in (to ~ in value)

din *n.* ["noise"] 1. to make a ~ 2. an infernal ~ 3. above, over the ~

dine *v.* 1. (D; intr.) to ~ on ("to eat") (to ~ on steak)

2. (D; intr.) to ~ with 3. (misc.) to ~ at home; to ~ in; to ~ out

dining *n.* congregate ~

dinner *n.* 1. to eat, have ~ 2. to cook, make, prepare ~ 3. to give a ~ 4. a formal; TV ~ 5. at, during ~ 6. for ~ (what will we have for ~?)

dint *n.* by ~ of (by ~ of hard work)

dip I *n.* ["short swim"] 1. to have (BE), take (esp. AE) a ~ ["a soft food"] 2. a cheese ~ ["drop"] 3. to make a ~ (the road makes a ~) 4. a sharp ~ 5. (misc.) there is a sharp ~ in the road up ahead

dip II *v.* 1. ("to drop") to ~ sharply (the road ~s sharply) 2. (d; intr.) ("to drop, fall") to ~ below (the sun ~ped below the horizon) 3. (d; tr.) ("to lower") to ~ into (she ~ped her pen into the ink) 4. (d; intr.) to ~ into ("to withdraw from") (to ~ into one's savings)

diphtheria *n.* to come down with, contract, get; have; prevent ~

diploma *n.* 1. to award, confer, present a ~ 2. to earn; receive a ~ 3. a college; high-school (AE) ~ 4. a ~ in (a ~ in Applied Linguistics)

diplomacy *n.* 1. to rely on, resort to ~ 2. dollar; gunboat; high-level; media; public; quiet; shuttle ~

diplomat *n.* a career, professional; foreign ~

diplomatic *adj.* ~ to + inf. (it was not ~ to make such demands)

diplomatic immunity *n.* 1. to grant ~ 2. to claim; have ~ 3. to withdraw ~

direct *v.* 1. (d; tr.) ("to point") to ~ against, at (they ~ed the attacks against the enemy's seaports) 2. (d; tr.) ("to address") to ~ at, to (the remark was ~ed at you) 3. (D; tr.) ("to guide") to ~ to (can you ~ me to the post office?) 4. (d; tr.) ("to aim") to ~ to, towards (our efforts were ~ed towards the elimination of poverty) 5. (H) ("to order") she ~ed us to remain silent 6. (L; subj.) ("to order") the government ~ed that supplies be/should be/were (BE) sent to the flooded areas

direction *n.* ["course"] 1. to change ~ 2. the opposite; right; wrong ~ 3. an anticlockwise (BE), counterclockwise (AE); clockwise ~ 4. from; in a ~ (from the opposite ~; in the ~ of London; in a clockwise ~; a step in the right ~) 5. a sense of ~ ["supervision"] 6. under smb.'s ~ ["guidance"] 7. to give ~ to

directions *n.* ["instructions"] 1. to give, issue ~ 2. to follow; read (the) ~ 3. clear; explicit, precise, specific ~ 4. ~ for; to (~ for using the printer; they gave us ~ to the palace) 5. ~ that + clause; subj. (she gave ~ that her estate be given/should be given to charity)

directive *n.* 1. to issue a ~ 2. a ~ about; against 3. a ~ that + clause; may be used with the subj. (the government issued a ~ that all firearms be/must be/should be handed in)

director *n.* 1. an acting; managing ~ 2. athletic (AE); funeral; music; program ~ 3. a casting; film, movie (esp. AE) ~ 4. a board of ~s

directorate *n.* interlocking ~s

directory *n.* a business; city; classified; telephone ~

dirge *n.* a funeral; mournful ~

dirt *n.* 1. in the ~ (to play in the ~) 2. a speck of ~ 3. (misc.) to hit the ~ ("to fall to the ground"); to dig up ~ about smb. ("to seek and find negative information about smb.")

dirty linen *n.* to wash one's ~ in public ("to air one's problems in public")

disability *n.* 1. to have a ~ 2. a learning; mild; moderate; physical; serious, severe ~ (children with learning ~ties)

disabled *adj., n.* learning; physically ~ (learning ~ children; help for the learning ~)

disabuse *v.* (D; tr.) to ~ of

disadvantage *n.* 1. to have, suffer a ~ 2. to offset, outweigh a ~ 3. an added; decided; distinct ~ 4. a ~ for, to 5. a ~ to + inf. (it was a ~ not to have a car available = it was a ~ not having a car available) 6. at a ~ (that places/puts me at a decided ~) 7. to smb.'s ~ (many factors worked to our ~)

disadvantaged *adj.* culturally; economically; educationally; physically ~

disadvantageous *adj.* 1. ~ for; to 2. ~ to + inf. (it would be ~ for us to delay)

disagree *v.* 1. to ~ bitterly, profoundly, sharply; completely, totally, utterly 2. (D; intr.) to ~ about, on, over; with 3. (of food) to ~ with (the sauce ~d with me)

disagreeable *adj.* ~ to

disagreement *n.* 1. to express a ~ 2. to have a ~ (with) 3. to resolve, settle a ~ 4. a bitter, marked, serious, sharp; slight; total ~ 5. a ~ among, between, with 6. a ~ about, on, over 7. in ~ with 8. (misc.) both sides are (locked) in total ~ over the terms of a settlement

disappear *v.* 1. to ~ completely 2. (D; intr.) to ~ from (to ~ from view) 3. (D; intr.) to ~ in, into (they ~ed into the darkness)

disappearance *n.* 1. a mysterious; sudden ~ 2. a ~ from

disappoint *v.* 1. to ~ bitterly, deeply 2. (R) it ~ed everyone that she did not win the prize

disappointed *adj.* 1. bitterly, deeply, greatly, very ~ 2. ~ about, at, in, with (~ at/with the results; I was deeply ~ in/with him) 3. ~ to + inf. (she was ~ to learn that she had failed the course) 4. ~ that + clause (we are ~ that you will not be able to attend)

disappointing *adj.* 1. deeply, very ~ 2. ~ to + inf. (it is ~ to analyze the results) 3. ~ that + inf. (it's ~ that so few showed up)

disappointment *n.* 1. to express; feel ~ 2. (a) bitter, cruel, deep, great, keen, profound ~ 3. ~ about, at, over (she felt deep ~ at not getting the job) 4. a ~ from

for, to (his refusal was a bitter ~ to the whole staff) 5. ~ that + clause (he expressed keen ~ that the hearing had been postponed) 6. to smb.'s ~ (to our great ~, it started to rain)

disapproval *n.* 1. to express; indicate, show (one's) ~ 2. public; strong ~ 3. (misc.) a chorus of ~; a note of ~; a show of ~

disapprove *v.* 1. to ~ completely, strongly, thoroughly, utterly 2. (D; intr.) to ~ of (they ~d strongly of my proposal)

disarmament *n.* general, universal; multilateral; nuclear; phased; unilateral ~

disarray *n.* 1. complete, sheer, total, utter ~ 2. in ~ (to break up in total ~) 3. (misc.) a state of ~; to throw a meeting into ~

disassociate, dissociate *v.* (D; refl.) to ~ from
USAGE NOTE: Some purists prefer *dissociate.*

disaster *n.* 1. to cause (a); to invite ~ 2. to experience, meet, suffer (a) ~ 3. to court ~ 4. to spell ~ (for) 5. to cope with; recover from (a) ~ 6. to avert (a) ~ 7. a major, terrible, tragic, unmitigated, unqualified ~ 8. a near ~ 9. an ecological; environmental; impending; national; natural ~ 10. (a) ~ strikes

disastrous *adj.* 1. ~ for, to 2. ~ to + inf. (it would be ~ for us not to wait)

disbar *v.* (D; tr.) to ~ from (to ~ from practice)

disbelief *n.* 1. complete, total, utter; mock ~ 2. in ~ (to shake one's head in ~)

disburse *v.* (B) to ~ funds to the states

disc *n.* ["tag"] (BE) (mil.) 1. an identification ~ ["recording"] 2. to cut a ~ (see **disk**) 3. a compact ~ (also CD); laser ~ (see also **disk**)

discern *v.* (formal) 1. (L) they soon ~ed that he was lying 2. (Q) they could not ~ who was telling the truth

discharge I *n.* 1. a dishonorable; general; honorable; medical; undesirable ~ (from the armed forces) 2. a ~ from (a ~ from a hospital)

discharge II *v.* 1. (D; tr.) to ~ for (to ~ an employe for stealing) 2. (D; tr.) to ~ from (to ~ smb. from hospital/from a hospital) 3. (D; tr.) to ~ into (to ~ waste into a river)

disciple *n.* an ardent, devoted; fanatical ~

discipline I *n.* ["control; training"] 1. to enforce, keep; establish; maintain ~ 2. to crack down on violations of ~ 3. to ease up on, relax ~ 4. to undermine ~ 5. to violate ~ 6. firm, harsh, iron, rigid, severe, stern, strict ~ 7. lax, loose, slack ~ 8. military; party ~ 9. ~ breaks down 10. the ~ to + inf. (they didn't have enough ~ to cope with the job) ["branch of learning"] 11. an academic ~

discipline II *v.* 1. (D; tr.) to ~ for 2. (H; usu. refl.) (she ~d herself to exercise every day)

disciplined *adj.* highly, very ~

disclaimer *n.* 1. to bear a ~ 2. to issue, publish a ~ 3. a ~ about

disclose v. 1. (B) the authorities finally ~d the facts to the press 2. (L; to) the report ~d that she had served time in prison

disclosure n. 1. to make a ~ (to) 2. a financial; full; public; sensational, startling ~ 3. a ~ that + clause (the ~ that he had been in prison ruined his chances for public office)

discomfort n. 1. to cause ~ 2. to bear; experience; put up with ~ 3. to alleviate ~ 4. acute; physical ~

disconcert v. (formal) (R) it ~ed us (to learn) that they had refused our offer

disconcerting adj. 1. ~ to + inf. (it is ~ to watch them make one mistake after the other) 2. ~ that + clause (it is ~ that so many pupils have dropped out of school)

disconnect v. (D; tr.) to ~ from

disconsolate adj. ~ about, at, over

discontent n. 1. to cause, stir up ~ 2. deep; outspoken; public; widespread ~ 3. ~ about, at, over, with 4. (misc.) murmurs of ~; rumblings of ~

discontinue v. (G) she ~d paying rent

discord n. 1. to arouse, foment, generate, stir up; spread ~ 2. domestic, family, marital ~ 3. bitter; widespread ~ 4. ~ among, between 5. ~ in (~ in smb.'s family relationships) 6. (misc.) a note of ~

discount n. 1. to give a ~ 2. a cash ~ 3. a ~ on (to give a ~ on all purchases) 4. at a ~ (she sold it at a ~)

discourage v. (D; tr.) to ~ from

discouraged adj. 1. deeply, very ~ 2. ~ at, about, over 3. ~ to + inf. (we were ~ to see that many students had failed)

discouragement n. deep ~

discouraging adj. 1. deeply, very ~ 2. ~ to + inf. (it is ~ to read the newspapers) 3. ~ that + clause (it's ~ that so little progress has/should have been made in banning nuclear weapons)

discourse I n. ["connected speech"] 1. (grammar) direct; indirect ~ ["speech, talk"] (formal) 2. to deliver a ~ (on, upon)

discourse II v. (formal) (D; intr.) to ~ on, upon

discourteous adj. 1. ~ to 2. ~ to + inf. (it was ~ of him to say that)

discourtesy n. 1. to show ~ 2. (a) grave ~

discover v. 1. (J) I ~ed them swimming in our pool 2. (L) we ~ed that he can cook 3. (rare) (M) we ~ed him to be a good cook 4. (Q) I never have ~ed how it works

discovery n. ["finding"] 1. to make a ~ 2. a dramatic; exciting, startling, world-shaking 3. a scientific ~ 4. a ~ that + clause (we made the exciting ~ that exercise can be fun) ["pretrial disclosure of facts"] (legal) 5. to conduct ~

discredit n. 1. to bring ~ on, to 2. a ~ to (they are a ~ to our family) 3. to smb.'s ~

discreet adj. 1. ~ in 2. ~ to + inf. (it was not ~ of you to say that)

discrepancy n. 1. a glaring, striking, wide ~ 2. a ~ between; in

discretion n. 1. to exercise, show, use ~ in 2. complete, full, wide ~ 3. parental; viewer ~ 4. ~ to + inf. (she has full ~ to make decisions) 5. at one's ~ (to act at one's own ~) 6. with; without ~ (to proceed with ~) 7. (misc.) the soul of ~

discriminate v. 1. (D; intr.) to ~ against; in favor of (to ~ against minorities) 2. (d; intr.) to ~ among, between 3. (d; tr.) to ~ from (to ~ right from wrong)

discrimination n. 1. to practice ~ 2. to subject smb. to ~ 3. age; racial; religious; reverse; sex ~ 4. blatant; outright ~ 5. ~ against; in favor of

discus n. to throw the ~

discuss v. 1. (D; tr.) to ~ with (to ~ smt. with smb.) 2. (Q) we ~ed how we would do it

discussion n. 1. to arouse, provoke, stir up (a) ~ 2. to have; lead a ~ 3. to be up for; bring smt. up for ~; to come up for ~ 4. an animated, brisk, heated, lively, spirited; brief; candid, frank, open; lengthy, long; quiet, peaceful; serious ~ 5. a group; panel; round-table ~ (to lead a panel ~) 6. a ~ about, of 7. open for, open to ~ 8. under ~ (their case is now under ~) 9. (misc.) the point of a ~

discussions n. 1. to have, hold; schedule ~ 2. to curtail, end, terminate ~ 3. high-level; preliminary ~ 4. ~ among, between; with 5. ~ about

disdain I n. 1. to have; show ~ 2. ~ for (to have the greatest ~ for smt.)

disdain II v. (esp. BE) (formal) 1. (E) she ~ed to speak with them 2. (G) they ~ed watching TV

disdainful adj. ~ of; towards

disease n. 1. to come down with, contract; have a ~ 2. to carry; spread, transmit (a) ~ 3. to cure; prevent (a) ~ 4. to combat, fight; conquer, eradicate, stamp out, wipe out (a) ~; to bring a ~ under control 5. a common; rare ~ 6. a mild; serious ~ 7. a deadly; debilitating, wasting, degenerative; fatal; incurable, untreatable ~ 8. an acute; chronic ~ 9. an acquired; congenital; hereditary ~ 10. a communicable, contagious, infectious; sexually transmitted, social, venereal; tropical ~ 11. caisson; (a) deficiency; heart; (an) industrial, occupational; kidney; (a) skin ~ 12. Addison's; Alzheimer's; Hodgkin's; Legionnaire's ~ 13. foot-and-mouth, hoof-and-mouth ~ 14. a ~ spreads 15. the outbreak of a ~

disembark v. (D; intr.) to ~ from

disengage v. (D; refl., intr., tr.) to ~ from

disentangle v. (D; refl., tr.) to ~ from

disfavor, disfavour n. 1. to fall into ~ with 2. in ~ 3. (misc.) to look with ~ on

disfigured adj. badly ~

disgorge v. (D; tr.) to ~ into (the sewer ~d waste material into the river)

disgrace I n. 1. to bring; suffer ~ 2. (a) deep; public

~ 3. a ~ to (they are a ~ to their family) 4. a ~ to + inf. (it was a ~ to behave like that = it was a ~ behaving like that) 5. a ~ that + clause (it's a ~ that these roads are so poorly marked) 6. in ~ (he quit in ~ over the bribe)

disgrace II v. (D; refl., tr.) to ~ by (she ~d herself by getting drunk)

disgraceful adj. 1. ~ to + inf. (it was ~ to behave like that = it was ~ behaving like that) 2. ~ that + clause (it was ~ that he got/should have got/should have gotten drunk on duty)

disgruntled adj. ~ at, over, with

disguise I n. 1. to assume a ~ 2. to shed, throw off a ~ 3. a clever ~ 4. in ~

disguise II v. 1. thinly ~d 2. (D; refl., tr.) to ~ as (he was ~d as a waiter)

disgust I n. 1. to express; feel ~ 2. complete, deep, great, utter ~ 3. ~ at, with 4. in ~ (he left in great ~) 5. to smb.'s ~ (to my ~ I discovered that...)

disgust II v. 1. to ~ completely, thoroughly 2. (R) it ~ed everyone that they had taken bribes

disgusted adj. 1. completely, thoroughly, totally, utterly, very ~ 2. ~ at, with 3. ~ to + inf. (she was ~ to see him drunk) 4. ~ that + clause (I am ~ that he is absent again)

disgusting adj. 1. ~ to + inf. (it was ~ to watch) 2. ~ that + clause (it's ~ that the crime rate is so high)

dish n. ["food served in a dish"] 1. a favorite; main; side ~ ["container for food"] 2. a chafing; serving ~ ["antenna"] 3. a satellite ~

disharmony n. 1. to stir up ~ 2. ethnic; racial; religious ~

dishearten v. (formal) (R) it ~ed all of us (to learn) that she had been dismissed

disheartened adj. 1. ~ at 2. ~ to + inf. (he was ~ to learn of the bad news)

disheartening adj. 1. ~ to + inf. (it is ~ to read the daily press) 2. ~ that + clause (it was ~ that so few passed/should have passed the test)

dishes n. ["dirty containers, cutlery, and utensils left after a meal"] 1. to do, wash; dry; rinse; stack the ~ 2. dirty ~ ["containers for holding food"] 3. plastic ~ 4. a set of ~

USAGE NOTE: BE usu. uses to wash up rather than to do, wash the dishes.

dishonest adj. 1. intellectually; morally ~ 2. ~ in (to be ~ in one's dealings) 3. ~ to + inf. (it is ~ to lie about one's age)

dishonor, dishonour n. 1. to bring ~ on, to 2. a ~ to (they are a ~ to their country)

dish out v. (B) he was ~ing out food to the women

dishwasher n. 1. to load, stack; empty, unload a ~ 2. an automatic ~

disillusioned adj. ~ about, at; with

disinclined adj. (cannot stand alone) ~ to + inf. (he seems ~ to put up resistance)

disk n. ["structure in a spinal column"] 1. to slip

("dislocate") a ~ 2. a slipped ~ ["flat plate for computer storage"] 3. to back up; format; insert a ~; to copy onto a ~ 4. a back-up; fixed, hard; floppy; magnetic; optical ~

USAGE NOTE: BE prefers the spelling disc for 1 and 2. See **disc**

diskette n. see disk 3

dislike I n. 1. to take a ~ to 2. to have; show a ~ for, of 3. an active, cordial, deep, hearty, strong, violent; instant; instinctive; mutual ~

dislike II v. 1. to ~ deeply, very much 2. (G) he ~s going to the opera 3. (K) we ~ his hanging around with that crowd

dislodge v. (D; tr.) to ~ from (the doctor ~d the bone from her throat)

disloyal adj. ~ to

disloyalty n. to demonstrate, show ~ to

dismay I n. 1. to express; feel ~ 2. ~ at, with 3. in, with ~ (to moan in ~) 4. to smb.'s ~ (to my great ~, she was absent again)

dismay II v. (formal) (R) it ~ed me to learn of her actions; it ~ed us that the project had been canceled

dismayed adj. 1. ~ at, with 2. ~ to + inf. (he was ~ to see that he had a flat tire)

dismaying adj. ~ to + inf. (it is ~ to contemplate the results of their incompetence)

dismiss v. 1. to ~ curtly, summarily; lightly; out of hand 2. (D; tr.) to ~ as (he was ~ed as incompetent) 3. (D; tr.) to ~ for (I was ~ed for being late) 4. (D; tr.) to ~ from (she was ~ed from her job) 5. (misc.) (BE; cricket) the bowler ~ed the next batsman for six runs

dismissal n. 1. an abrupt, curt; summary ~ 2. a ~ from

dismount v. (D; intr.) to ~ from

disobedience n. 1. blatant; willful ~ 2. civil ~ 3. ~ to (~ to orders)

disobedient adj. ~ to

disorder n. ["lack of order"] 1. to throw into ~ 2. in ~ (to retreat in ~) ["riot"] 3. violent ~s 4. ~s broke out 5. civil; public ~ ["illness"] 6. a brain; circulatory; digestive; mental; minor; nervous; personality; respiratory; stomach ~

disoriented adj. ~ about, as to (~ as to time and place)

disparity n. 1. a considerable, great, wide ~ 2. a ~ between, in

dispatch I n. ["news item"] ["message"] 1. to file; send a ~ 2. to dateline a ~ 3. a ~ from; to 4. a ~ that + clause (we read her ~ that war had been declared) 5. (misc.) (BE; mil.) mentioned in ~es (for bravery in combat) ["promptness"] 6. with great ~

dispatch II v. 1. (D; tr.) to ~ from; to (the message was ~ed from battalion headquarters to each company) 2. (rare) (H) he was ~ed to carry the message

dispensation n. 1. to give, grant (a) ~ 2. to obtain;

request (a) ~ (from) 3. (a) papal; royal; special ~ 4. a ~ to + inf. (they obtained a ~ to travel abroad)

dispense v. 1. (B) to ~ charity to the needy; to ~ equal justice to all 2. (d; intr.) to ~ with (to ~ with the formalities)

dispenser n. a cash; coffee; drinks (BE); soap ~

dispersed adj. widely ~

displace v. (D; tr.) to ~ as (she was ~d as champion)

display I n. 1. to make, put on a ~ (to make a vulgar ~ of one's wealth) 2. to put smt. on ~ 3. a dazzling, imposing, impressive; lavish, ostentatious, spectacular; modest; public; vulgar ~ (to make a public ~ of grief; to put on a dazzling ~ of one's skill) 4. a firework (BE), fireworks (AE) ~ 5. a graphic ~ (of a computer) 6. on ~ (the new models were on ~)

display II v. (B) he ~ed his ignorance to everyone

displeased adj. ~ about, at, with

displeasure n. 1. to incur smb.'s ~ 2. to feel; show; voice one's ~ with 3. to smb.'s ~

disposal n. ["availability"] 1. to have at one's ~ (I had a huge car at my ~) 2. to place, put smt. at smb.'s ~ 3. at smb.'s ~ ["elimination"] 4. bomb; garbage; sewage; waste ~ ["device used to grind up garbage"] 5. a garbage ~; or: a garbage-disposal unit

dispose v. 1. (d; intr.) to ~ of ("to deal with") (to ~ of the opposition) 2. (d; intr.) to ~ of ("to get rid of") (to ~ of the rubbish) 3. (formal) (H) ("to incline") what ~d him to do it?

disposed adj. (formal) ["inclined"] (cannot stand alone) 1. ~ to, towards (he seems well ~ towards us) 2. ~ to + inf. (she is ~ to accept our offer)

disposition n. ["inclination"] 1. a ~ to + inf. (a ~ to argue) ["personality"] 2. a bland; buoyant, cheerful, genial, happy, lively, pleasant, sunny; mild; nervous; sour, unpleasant ~

dispossess v. (D; tr.) to ~ of (they were ~ed of their wealth)

disproportionate adj. ~ to

dispute I n. 1. to stir up a ~ about 2. to adjudicate; arbitrate; resolve, settle a ~ (to settle a ~ out of court) 3. an acrimonious, bitter, heated, sharp ~ 4. a public ~ 5. a border; industrial, labor; international; jurisdictional; legal; pay; territorial ~ 6. a ~ about, over; with 7. in ~ (this point is in ~; labor is in ~ with management) 8. in a ~ (he is in a ~ with his insurance company)

dispute II v. 1. to ~ hotly 2. (D; intr.) (esp. BE) to ~ about, over; with (they are always ~ting with each other over politics) 3. (L) I do not ~ that he was there

disqualification n. 1. to lead to, result in ~ 2. ~ for (the incident led to her ~ for cheating) 3. ~ from (it resulted in his ~ from the contest)

disqualify v. 1. (D; tr.) to ~ for (the athlete was ~fied for taking drugs) 2. (D; tr.) to ~ from

disregard I n. 1. to show ~ 2. (a) blatant, callous,

complete, flagrant, total; reckless; willful ~ 3. ~ for 4. in ~ of (in total ~ of the regulations)

disregard II v. 1. to ~ completely 2. (K) we cannot ~ his coming late to work so often

disrepair n. 1. a state of ~ 2. in ~ (the building is in ~) 3. to fall into ~

disrepute n. 1. to fall into ~ 2. to bring smt. into ~ 3. to hold smb. in ~

disrespect n. 1. to show ~ 2. to intend, mean no ~ 3. deep, profound ~ 4. ~ for (I meant no ~ for your traditions)

disrespectful adj. 1. ~ to 2. ~ to + inf. (it was ~ of them to say that)

disruption n. 1. to cause (a) ~ 2. (a) complete, total; widespread ~ 3. ~ in

dissatisfaction n. 1. to express, voice; feel ~ 2. deep, keen, profound; growing; widespread ~ 3. ~ about, at, over, with (they expressed deep ~ with working conditions) 4. ~ among (~ among the workers)

dissatisfied adj. ~ with

dissension n. 1. to cause, sow, stir up; introduce ~ 2. (a) deep; growing; widespread ~ 3. ~ among, between 4. rumblings of ~

dissent I n. 1. to express ~ 2. to brook (formal), tolerate no ~ 3. to squash, stifle ~ 4. political; strong ~ 5. ~ from 6. (misc.) rumblings of ~; voices of ~

dissent II v. (D; intr.) to ~ from

dissertation n. 1. to defend; do, write a ~ (to write a ~ under smb.'s supervision) 2. to supervise a ~ 3. (esp. AE) a doctoral ~ 4. a ~ about, on

USAGE NOTE: AE prefers a *doctoral dissertation, master's thesis*; BE prefers a *doctoral thesis, master's dissertation/master's essay*.

disservice n. 1. to do smb. a ~ 2. a ~ to

dissident n. a political ~

dissimilar adj. ~ to

dissimilarity n. a ~ between

dissociate v. (D; refl., tr.) to ~ from (we ~d ourselves from his views) (see the Usage Note for **disassociate**)

dissolve v. 1. (D; intr., tr.) to ~ in (to ~ sugar in water) 2. (misc.) to ~ in/into laughter

dissonance n. cognitive ~ ("the holding of incompatible beliefs simultaneously")

dissuade v. (D; tr.) to ~ from

distance I n. 1. to cover; run; travel; walk a ~ 2. to keep a ~ (to keep a safe ~ between cars) 3. to close the ~ between 4. a discreet; good, great, long, vast; safe; short ~ (we traveled a short ~) 5. commuting; driving; hailing; shouting; striking; walking ~ (it's within easy walking ~) 6. (a) braking, stopping ~ 7. a ~ between; from; to (the ~ between New York and London is about three thousand miles; the ~ from Philadelphia to Chicago is less than eight hundred miles) 8. at a ~ (at a discreet ~; we spotted them at a ~ of two hundred yards) 9. from a ~ (I spotted her from a ~) 10. in the ~ (the city was visible in the ~) (misc.) 11. to keep one's ~ ("to not allow familiarity"); a short ~ away; quite a ~; some ~ (they are still some ~ apart)

distance II v. (D; refl.) to ~ from

distant adj. ~ from

distaste n. 1. to develop; express; feel; show (a) ~ 2. (a) strong ~ 3. (a) ~ for 4. with ~

distasteful adj. 1. ~ to (his behavior was ~ to everyone) 2. ~ to + inf. (it was ~ for me to have to enforce discipline)

distil, distill v. (D; tr.) to ~ from; into (to ~ whiskey from grain)

distinct adj. ~ from

distinction n. ["differentiation"] 1. to draw, make a ~ 2. to blur a ~ 3. a clear-cut; fine; obvious; subtle ~ 4. a class ~ 5. a ~ between ["eminence"] ["superiority"] 6. to enjoy, have, hold a ~ (he holds the dubious ~ of being the first person to break the new speed limit) 7. a doubtful, dubious ~ 8. of ~ (an artist of ~) 9. with ~ (to serve with ~)

distinctive adj. ~ of

distinguish v. 1. (d; intr.) to ~ among, between 2. (d; refl.) to ~ as (she ~ed herself as a painter) 3. (d; refl.) to ~ by (he ~ed himself by running five marathons) 4. (D; tr.) to ~ from (to ~ good from evil) 5. (d; refl.) to ~ in (they ~ed themselves in the fine arts)

distinguishable adj. 1. clearly, plainly ~ 2. ~ from

distinguished adj. ~ for

distortion n. a crude, gross, grotesque; deliberate; malicious; willful ~

distract v. (D; tr.) to ~ from (the music ~ed them from their studies)

distraction n. 1. to drive smb. to ~ 2. a ~ from (it was a ~ from their daily routine)

distraught adj. ~ about, at, over, with

distress I n. 1. to cause ~ 2. to feel; suffer ~ 3. to alleviate, ease ~ 4. deep, great, profound ~ 5. economic, financial ~ 6. emotional, mental, psychological; physical ~ 7. ~ at, over, with 8. in ~ (they were in deep ~ over their loss) 9. to smb.'s ~ (to our ~, her condition did not improve)

distress II v. 1. to ~ deeply 2. (R) it ~ed me (to read) that a new epidemic had broken out

distressed adj. 1. deeply ~ 2. ~ about, at, by, over, with (~ at the news) 3. ~ to + inf. (I was deeply ~ to learn of your loss)

distressing adj. 1. deeply, very ~ 2. ~ to + inf. (it is ~ to listen to the news) 3. ~ that + clause (it is ~ that nations constantly quarrel)

distribute v. 1. to ~ equitably, fairly; evenly; inequitably, unfairly; unevenly; widely 2. (B) the instructor ~d the test papers to the students 3. (D; tr.) to ~ among (to ~ food among the poor)

distribution n. 1. (an) equitable, fair; even; inequi-

table, unfair; uneven; wide ~ 2. (math.) normal ~ 3. (ling.) complementary ~ 4. ~ among (the ~ of surplus food among the needy)

district n. 1. the business (esp. AE); financial; red-light; tenderloin (AE); theater ~ 2. a congressional; health; postal; school; voting ~

distrustful adj. ~ of

disturb v. (R) it ~ed me (to read) that a new epidemic had broken out

disturbance n. 1. to cause, create, make a ~ 2. to quell, put down a ~ 3. a minor ~

disturbed adj. 1. emotionally, mentally, psychologically ~ 2. seriously, severely ~ 3. ~ about, at, by, over 4. ~ to + inf. (I am ~ to learn of this latest incident)

disturbing adj. 1. ~ to + inf. (it is ~ to find evidence of widespread corruption) 2. ~ that + clause (it's ~ that so few people vote)

disuse n. to fall into ~

ditch n. 1. to dig a ~ 2. a deep; shallow ~ 3. an antitank; drainage ~

dither I n. in a ~ (about, over)

dither II v. (D; intr.) to ~ about, over

ditty n. 1. to sing a ~ 2. a popular ~

dive I n. 1. to make a ~ (at) 2. to go into a ~ (the plane went into a ~) 3. a swallow (BE), swan (AE) ~ 4. a back; headfirst; high ~ 5. a crash ~ (of a submarine) 6. a power ~ (of a plane) 7. a ~ for (they made a ~ for the ditch) 8. a ~ from; into 9. (misc.) (colloq.) to take a ~ ("to lose a boxing match deliberately")

dive II v. 1. to ~ headfirst 2. (D; intr.) to ~ for (to ~ for pearls; to ~ for cover) 3. (D; intr.) to ~ from; into (she ~d into the pool from the high diving board) 4. (D; intr.) to ~ off (he ~d off the boat) 5. (P; intr.) he ~d under the bed; she ~d to a depth of thirty feet; they ~d over the side of the boat

diverge v. 1. to ~ markedly, sharply, widely 2. (D; intr.) to ~ from

divergence n. 1. (a) marked, sharp, wide ~ 2. a ~ between (there was a sharp ~ between their views) 3. a ~ from (they found a wide ~ from the norm)

diversion n. ["amusement"] 1. a favorite; popular ~ ["turning"] 2. a ~ from; to (a ~ of traffic from the damaged bridge to an alternate route) ["distraction"] 3. to create a ~ 4. a welcome ~

diversity n. cultural; ethnic; multicultural; religious ~

divert v. (D; tr.) to ~ from; to

divest v. (formal) (d; refl., tr.) to ~ of (they ~ed themselves of all stocks and bonds)

divide I n. 1. a continental ~; (in North America) the Great Divide 2. (fig.) the great ~ ("death") (to cross the great ~) 3. a ~ between

divide II v. 1. to ~ equally, evenly 2. (D; tr.) to ~ among, between; with (to ~ profits among the partners) 3. (D; tr.) to ~ by (to ~ six by three) 4. (D;

tr.) to ~ from (the channel ~s the island from the mainland) 5. (D; intr., refl., tr.) to ~ into (they ~d the loot into equal shares; to ~ three into six) 6. (misc.) to ~ in half

divided *adj.* 1. deeply, sharply; hopelessly ~ 2. ~ on, over (they are sharply ~ over the choice of a new chairperson)

dividend *n.* ["sum divided among stockholders"] 1. to declare a ~ 2. (also fig.) to pay a ~ 3. a share, stock (esp. AE) ~ 4. a handsome, large ~

divide off *v.* (D; tr.) to ~ into (the room was ~d off into three alcoves by a partition)

divide up *v.* (D; tr.) to ~ among, between; into (they ~d up the profits into equal shares)

dividing line *n.* 1. to draw a ~ between 2. to cross the ~ 3. a thin ~

divisible *adj.* ~ by; into

division *n.* ["mathematical operation of dividing"] 1. to do ~ 2. long; short ~ ["major military unit"] 3. an airborne; armored; infantry; motorized ~ ["classification"] 4. to make a ~ 5. an arbitrary ~ 6. (BE; sports) first ~; second ~; etc. (our club is in the second ~ of the league) ["dividing"] 7. a deep; equal; equitable; sharp; unequal ~ 8. cell ~ 9. ~ among; between ["type of voting"] (BE) 10. to force a ~

divisor *n.* a common ~

divorce *n.* 1. to file for, sue for ~ 2. to get, receive a ~ 3. to grant a ~ 4. a messy ~; (a) no-fault ~; an uncontested ~; (a) ~ by mutual consent 5. (misc.) a ~ settlement

divorced *adj.* ~ from (he was ~d from his wife)

divulge *v.* 1. (B) to ~ information to the press 2. (L; to) they ~d (to us) that the stock had already been sold 3. (Q; to) they did not ~ (to us) where the money was hidden

dizzy *adj.* 1. ~ from (~ from the rays of the sun) 2. ~ with (~ with success)

do *v.* 1. (C) ("to perform") she did a favor for me; or: she did me a favor 2. (d; tr.) to ~ about ("to help improve") (what can we ~ about his schoolwork?) 3. (d; tr.) to ~ about, with ("to deal with, treat") (what should we ~ about/with students who fail?) 4. (d; intr.) to ~ by ("to treat") (the firm did very well by her when she retired) 5. (BE) (d; intr.) to ~ for ("to act as housekeeper for") (she does for me twice a week) 6. (colloq.) (BE) (d; intr.) to ~ for ("to ruin") (that long hike nearly did for me) 7. (d; tr.) to ~ for ("to make arrangements for") (what did you ~ for light when the electricity was turned off?) 8. (D; tr.) to ~ for ("to help") (what can I ~ for you?) 9. (d; tr.) to ~ out of ("to cheat out of") (they did him out of his inheritance) 10. (d; tr.) to ~ to ("to inflict on") (what did they do to her?) 11. (d; tr.) to ~ to, with ("to change") (what have they done to the center of the city? what have you done with your hair?) 12. (d; tr.) to ~ with ("to use for")

(what should we ~ with this old typewriter?) 13. (d; tr.) to ~ with ("to concern") (their suggestion has nothing to ~ with the problem) 14. (d; intr.) to ~ without ("to manage without") (we had to ~ without fresh fruit) 15. (G; only in the perfect) he is (AE)/has (CE) done talking 16. (P; intr.) ("to fare") she is ~ing very well; he is ~ing nicely; our business is ~ing very well financially 17. (misc.) you did well to tell me; she could ~ with a long vacation

USAGE NOTE: In the meaning "to fare", the verb *do* can have a medical meaning — the patient is doing well after the operation; mother and child are doing well after a difficult delivery.

do away *v.* (d; intr.) to ~ with ("to eliminate") (they did away with that department several years ago)

dock I *n.* ["basin for ships"] 1. to go into ~ 2. a dry, floating ~ 3. at, on a ~; in (a) ~ (there was labor trouble down on the ~s; the ship was in ~)

dock II *v.* 1. (D; intr.) to ~ at (the ship ~ed at Portsmouth) 2. (D; intr.) to ~ with (the spaceship ~ed with the satellite)

dock III *n.* ["place for the accused in a court"] to put smb. in the ~

dock IV *v.* (D; tr.) ("to deduct, take") to ~ from (they ~ed ten dollars from her wages)

docket *n.* ["agenda"] on the ~

doctor *n.* 1. a family ~ 2. a witch ~ 3. a barefoot ~ ("an auxiliary medical worker in a rural area, esp. in China") 4. ~s prescribe medication 5. ~s see; treat (their) patients 6. (misc.) to see ("consult") a ~; a spin ~ ("one who puts a special interpretation on events")

doctorate *n.* 1. to award, grant a ~ 2. to earn; get, obtain, receive; have, hold a ~ 3. an earned (AE); honorary ~ 4. a ~ in (a ~ in physics)

doctrine *n.* 1. to apply; preach a ~ 2. to establish a ~ 3. to disprove a ~ 4. (a) sound ~ 5. a basic; defense; religious ~ 6. a ~ that + clause (it was their basic ~ that nothing was better than free trade)

document *n.* 1. to draw up; issue; sign a ~ 2. to file; store ~s 3. (esp. AE) to notarize a ~ 4. to classify; declassify a ~ 5. to falsify; forge a ~ 6. to shred ~s 7. a classified; confidential; historic; legal; official; restricted; secret; top-secret ~ 8. an authentic ~ 9. a ~ about, concerning

documentary *n.* 1. to film a ~ 2. to show a ~ 3. a ~ about, on

documentation *n.* 1. to provide ~ for 2. adequate, appropriate, proper; inadequate, insufficient, weak; strong ~

dodge I *n.* a tax ~

dodge II *v.* 1. (D; intr.) to ~ behind (to ~ behind a door) 2. (rare) (G) he ~d serving in the armed forces

dodger *n.* ["evader"] a draft; tax ~

dog *n.* 1. to breed; keep ~s 2. to walk a ~ (on a leash)

3. to muzzle a ~ 4. (AE) to curb one's ~ 5. a mad, rabid; stray; vicious; wild ~ 6. a bird (AE), gun (BE); Eskimo; guard (BE); guide, seeing-eye; hunting ~; lapdog (also fig.); pet; police; sheep; sniffer (esp. BE); toy ~; watchdog; working ~ 7. ~s bark; bite; growl; howl; salivate; snap; snarl; wag their tails; whine; yelp 8. a pack of (wild) ~s 9. a young ~ is a pup(py) 10. a female ~ is a bitch 11. (misc.) a lucky ~ ("a lucky person"); a running ~ ("a lackey"); a ~'s life ("a wretched existence"); to work like a ~ ("to work very hard")

USAGE NOTE: In CE a *police dog* is one used by the police; in AE it can also mean a breed of dog called a *German shepherd* in AE and an *Alsatian* in BE.

dogfight *n.* ["aerial combat"] to engage in a ~

doghouse *n.* ["disfavor"] (colloq.) in the ~

dogma *n.* (an) economic; political; religious ~

dogmatic *adj.* ~ about

doily *n.* a lace; linen; paper ~

doing *n.* 1. that took some ~! ("that required great effort") 2. that's none/not of my ~!

doldrums *n.* (colloq.) ["stagnation"] in the ~

dole *n.* (colloq.) (BE) ["unemployment insurance"] on the ~ (to be on the ~; to go on/sign on the ~)

dole out *v.* (B) she ~d out some food to the children

doll *n.* a china; Kewpie (T); paper; rag ~

dollar *n.* 1. a half; silver ~ 2. a falling; rising; strong; weak ~ (the international markets experienced difficulties with the falling ~) 3. (misc.) the ~ was strong against the franc

doll up *v.* (colloq.) (D; refl., tr.) to ~ for (she ~ed herself up for the party)

dolphin *n.* 1. a school of ~s 2. a young ~ is a calf 3. a female ~ is a cow 4. a male ~ is a bull

domain *n.* ["sector"] the public ~ (in the public ~)

dominance *n.* 1. ~ in 2. ~ over 3. under smb.'s ~

dominion *n.* ~ over

domination *n.* 1. world ~ 2. ~ over 3. under smb.'s ~

donate *v.* 1. (B) she ~d her books to the library 2. (D; tr.) to ~ for (to ~ money for a charity)

donation *n.* 1. to make a ~ 2. to send in a ~ 3. a charitable; voluntary ~ 3. a big, generous, large, sizable; small ~ 4. a ~ to

done *adj.* 1. ~ with (we're ~ with the chores) 2. (BE) to have ~ with (we've ~ with the plates) 3. (misc.) after that hike, I'm ~ for ("I'm completely exhausted")

donkey *n.* ~s bray, go heehaw, heehaw

donor *n.* 1. an anonymous; generous ~ 2. a blood; organ ~

doom I *n.* 1. to seal smb.'s ~ 2. to go to, meet one's ~ 3. impending ~ 4. (misc.) the crack of ~; a sense of ~ hung over us

doom II *v.* (D; tr.) to ~ to (that will ~ him to oblivion)

doomed *adj.* 1. ~ to (~ to failure) 2. ~ to + inf. (she is ~ to eke out a miserable existence)

door *n.* 1. to hang a ~ 2. to bar, bolt; close, shut; lock; open; slam; unlock a ~ 3. to break down, force a ~ 4. to knock at, on a ~ 5. to answer the ~ 6. the ~ is ajar; bolted; closed; locked; open; unlocked 7. a back; double; French (AE; BE has *French window*); front, main; revolving; screen; side; sliding; stage; storm (esp. AE) ~ 8. a ~ closes, shuts; creaks, squeaks; opens; slams shut 9. a ~ to (the ~ to this room is never locked) 10. at the ~ (who is at the ~?) 11. (misc.) behind closed ~s ("in secret"); they live next ~ to us; to sell from ~ to ~; to close the ~ on any compromise ("to rule out the possibility of any compromise"); at death's ~ ("almost dead"); to show smb. the ~ ("to ask smb. to leave")

doorbell *n.* 1. to ring a ~ 2. to answer a ~ 3. a ~ rings

doornail *n.* (misc.) as dead as a ~

doorstep *n.* at, on smb.'s ~ ("very close")

doorway *n.* 1. (fig.) the ~ to (the ~ to freedom) 2. in the ~ (she stood in the ~)

dope *n.* ["drugs"] (colloq.) to take ~

doped up *adj.* (colloq.) 1. ~ on (~ on pills) 2. ~ with (~ with medication)

dormancy *n.* a state of ~

dormant *adj.* to lie, remain, stay ~

dose *n.* 1. to administer, give a ~ 2. to measure out a ~ 3. to receive; take a ~ 4. a fatal, lethal ~ 5. a heavy, massive, strong ~ 6. a light, small, weak ~ 7. (misc.) she received a massive ~ of radiation; in small ~s

dosed up *adj.* ~ with (she was ~ with cough medicine)

dossier *n.* to have; keep a ~ on smb.

dot *n.* 1. a tiny ~ 2. (misc.) on the ~ ("precisely")

dotted *adj.* ~ with

dotage *n.* to be in one's ~

dote *v.* (d; intr.) to ~ on, upon (she ~s on her grandchildren)

dotted line *n.* to sign on the ~ ("to agree to smt. by signing a document")

double I *n.* ["accelerated pace"] 1. at, on (esp. AE) the ~ ["betting"] 2. the daily ~

double II *v.* (D; intr.) ("to do smt. additional") to ~ as (the gardener ~d as the chauffeur)

double back *v.* (P; intr.) she ~d back towards the park

double-date *v.* (colloq.; esp. AE) (D; intr.) to ~ with

double fault *n.* (tennis) to commit a ~

double figures *n.* in ~ (inflation was in ~)

doubles *n.* (tennis) 1. to play ~ 2. ladies' (BE), women's; men's; mixed ~

double take *n.* (colloq.) ["delayed reaction"] to do a ~

double up *v.* 1. (D; intr.) ("to share living accommodations") to ~ with 2. (misc.) to ~ in pain

doubt I *n*. 1. to plant; raise (a) ~ (her proposal raised serious ~s in my mind) 2. to cast ~ on 3. to feel ~; to entertain, harbor, have ~s about 4. to express, voice (a) ~ 5. to clear up, dispel, resolve a ~ 6. (a) deep, serious, strong; gnawing; lingering; reasonable; slight ~ 7. ~s appear, arise 8. a ~ about, of 9. (a) ~ that + clause (he expressed serious ~ that he could finish the job on time) 10. beyond (a shadow of) a ~; without a ~ 11. in ~ (the result was never in serious ~) 12. (misc.) to give smb. the benefit of the ~; (colloq.) there is no ~ about it: she's the best

USAGE NOTE: Some purists recommend that *whether* or the more informal *if* be used with the noun *doubt*, especially in the meaning "uncertainty"—she expressed doubt (about/as to) whether they would finish on time ("she was not certain whether they would finish on time"). In the meaning of "disbelief", the conjunction *that* is common—she expressed doubt that they would finish on time ("she did not believe that they would finish on time"). Note that in interrogative sentences the use of *that* prevails—is there any doubt that they will finish on time? In negative sentences the conjunction *that* must be used—there is no doubt that they will finish on time.

doubt II *v*. 1. to ~ strongly, very much 2. (L) I ~ that (if, whether) she will want to participate

USAGE NOTE: See the Usage Note for **doubt I**. Thus, to express "uncertainty", one can say—she doubted whether they would finish on time. To express "disbelief", one can say—she doubted that they would finish on time. In negative sentences, only *that* is used—she doesn't doubt that they will finish on time.

doubtful *adj*. 1. ~ about, of 2. ~ that (if, whether) + clause (it's ~ that she will be present)

USAGE NOTE: See the Usage Note for **doubt I**. Thus, to express "uncertainty", one can say—it is/ I am doubtful whether they will finish on time. To express "disbelief", one can say—it is/I am doubtful that they will finish on time.

dough *n*. 1. to knead, mix, roll (out), work ~ 2. flaky; firm; stiff ~ 3. ~ rises

doughnuts *n*. 1. to make ~ 2. glazed; jelly ~

dove *n*. 1. a gentle ~ 2. ~s coo

dovetail *v*. (D; tr., intr.) ("to fit") to ~ into, with

down I *adj*. (colloq.) ["angry"] ~ on (he's ~ on us)

down II *adv*. 1. ~ against (the dollar was ~ against the pound) 2. (misc.) ~ on one's luck; we were ~ to our last five dollars; (BE) the fault is ~ to you; ~ with tyranny!

downfall *n*. 1. to bring about smb.'s ~; to lead to smb.'s ~ 2. to head for a ~

downgrade *v*. (D; tr.) to ~ to (the embassy was ~d to a legation)

downhill *adv*. to go ~ (also fig.)

download *v*. (D; tr.) to ~ to (to ~ a program to a computer)

down payment *n*. 1. to make a ~ 2. a ~ on

downpour *n*. 1. a brief; steady; sudden; torrential ~ 2. caught in a ~

downsizing *n*. corporate ~

downstairs *adv*. to come; go; run ~

downturn *n*. 1. a modest, slight ~ 2. a sharp ~ 3. a ~ in (there was a sharp ~ in the economy) 4. (misc.) the economy took a slight ~

dowry *n*. to provide a ~ for

dozen *n*. 1. a baker's; round ~ 2. by the ~ (they're cheaper by the ~)

draft I *n*. ["rough copy"] 1. to make, prepare a ~ 2. a final, polished; first, preliminary, rough; working ~ ["conscription"] (AE) 3. to introduce the ~ 4. to avoid, dodge, evade; resist the ~ ["current of air"] 5. to feel; sit in a ~ ["order for payment"] 6. to honor a ~ 7. a bank ~ 8. a ~ for; on (a ~ on the Paris branch of our bank for one thousand pounds) ["drawing of liquid"] 9. on ~ (beer on ~)

USAGE NOTE: BE prefers the spelling *draught* in senses 5 and 9.

draft II *v*. (AE) 1. (D; tr.) ("to conscript") to ~ into (to ~ young people into the army) 2. (H) they ~ed her to serve as their delegate

draft in *v*. (BE) (H) see **draft II** 2

drag I *n*. ["puff"] 1. to have, take a ~ (on a cigarette) ["obstacle"] 2. a ~ on (a ~ on the economy) ["street"] (colloq.) 3. the main ~ ["women's clothing worn by a male transvestite"] (slang) 4. in ~ 5. (misc.) a ~ queen

drag II *v*. 1. (d; intr.) ("to search at the bottom of a lake, river, sea") to ~ for (to ~ for a body) 2. (D; tr.) ("to search") to ~ for (they ~ged the lake for the body) 3. (d; intr.) ("to draw deeply") to ~ on (to ~ on a pipe) 4. (P; tr.) ("to pull, tug") they ~ged the tables into the garden; to be ~ged into a war; we ~ged the old sofa out of the house; they ~ged the logs through the forest; they ~ged him (over) to the door

drag down *v*. (usu. fig.) (D; tr.) to ~ into (to ~ smb. down into the gutter)

dragnet *n*. 1. to cast a ~ (to apprehend a criminal) 2. a police ~

dragoon *v*. (d; intr.) ("to coerce") to ~ into

drag over *v*. (D; tr.) ("to pull") to ~ to (they ~ged her over to the car)

drain I *n*. 1. to clean out, clear, unblock, unclog a ~ 2. to block, clog a ~ 3. (misc.) a brain ~; supporting them is a ~ on our resources; to go down the ~ ("to be lost")

drain II *v*. 1. (d; intr.) to ~ from (the blood ~ed from his face when he heard the news) 2. (D; tr.) to ~ of (~ the tank of all water) 3. (N; used with an adjective) they ~ed the swamps dry 4. (P; intr., tr.) they ~ed the liquid into the basin; they ~ed the water out of the basement; the liquid ~ed through a porous layer 5. (s) the swamp eventually ~ed dry

drama n. 1. a courtroom ~; docudrama; epic; historical; television ~ 2. high ~ 3. a ~ unfolds

dramatics n. 1. to study ~ 2. amateur ~

drape v. 1. (D; intr., tr.) to ~ around, over (she ~d her scarf around her shoulders) 2. (D; tr.) to ~ in, with (he was ~d in a sheet)

drapes n. (AE; CE has *curtains*) 1. to hang ~ 2. to close, draw; draw, open the ~ 3. window ~ 4. a pair of ~

draught (BE) see **draft I** 5, 9

draughts n. (BE) see **checkers**

draw I n. ["act of drawing a weapon"] 1. on the ~ (quick on the ~) (also fig.) 2. (misc.) to beat smb. to the ~ ["lottery"] (esp. BE) 3. to hold a ~ (AE has *drawing*) 4. a prize ~ ["misc."] 5. the luck of the ~ ("pure chance")

draw II v. 1. (C) ("to sketch") ~ a picture for me; or: ~ me a picture 2. (misc.) to ~ freehand 3. (D; tr.) to ~ against, on ("to take from") (to ~ a check/cheque against an account) 4. (D; intr.) ("to pick a number at random") to ~ for (to ~ for a prize) 5. (D; tr.) ("to remove") to ~ from, out of (to ~ money from an account; to ~ water from a well) 6. (D; tr.) ("to elicit") to ~ from (to ~ applause from an audience) 7. (d; tr.) ("to bring") to ~ into (to ~ smb. into a quarrel) 8. (d; intr.) ("to move") to ~ into (the train was ~ing into the station) 9. (d; intr.) ("to puff") to ~ on (to ~ on a pipe) 10. (d; intr.) to ~ on, upon ("to take from") (to ~ on one's reserves; to ~ on an account) 11. (D; tr.) ("to attract") to ~ to (to ~ smb.'s attention to smt.) 12. (d; intr.) ("to move") to ~ to (to ~ to a close 13. (D; intr., tr.) to ~ with (our team drew with the visitors) 14. (J) "to sketch") the artist drew them looking out at the sea 15. (N; used with an adjective) ("to pull") ~ the rope tight 16. (misc.) he drew a gun on his opponent

draw ahead v. (D; intr.) to ~ of (she drew ahead of the other runners)

draw alongside v. (D; intr.) to ~ of (he drew alongside of our car)

draw away v. (D; intr.) to ~ from ("to increase the distance from") (the leader drew away from the pack)

drawback n. 1. a major ~ 2. a ~ to

draw back v. (D; intr.) to ~ from (she drew back from the edge of the cliff)

drawbridge n. to lower; raise a ~

drawer n. 1. to close, push in a ~ 2. to open, pull out a ~ 3. a bottom; top ~ 4. (misc.) a chest of ~s

drawing n. ["picture"] 1. to do, make a ~ 2. a rough ~ ["representation by lines"] 3. mechanical ~ 4. (a) freehand; line ~ ["lottery"] (esp. AE) 5. to hold a ~ (BE has *draw*)

drawing board n. ["planning stage"] 1. on the ~ 2.

(misc.) back to the ~

drawl n. 1. a Southern ~ 2. (to speak) in, with a ~

draw off v. (D; tr.) to ~ from (they drew off some coolant from the radiator)

draw up v. 1. (D; intr.) to ~ to (he drew up to the entrance) 2. (misc.) he drew himself up to his full height; she drew up even with us

dread I n. 1. to have a ~ of smt. 2. to fill smb. with ~; to strike ~ into smb. 3. to live in ~ of smt.

dread II v. 1. (rare) (E) I ~ to see him again 2. (G) she ~s going to the dentist

dreadful adj. 1. ~ to + inf. (it is ~ to contemplate the possibility of another war) 2. ~ that + clause (it's ~ that there may be another war)

dream I n. ["image seen while sleeping"] 1. to have a ~ 2. to interpret ~s 3. a bad; odd; recurring; wet; wild ~ 4. a ~ about, of ["hope"] ["goal"] 5. to achieve, realize one's ~s 6. a childhood; visionary; wild ~ 7. a ~ comes true 8. a ~ of 9. a ~ to + inf. (it was his ~ to become a teacher) 10. a ~ that + clause (it was only a ~ that she might be elected) 11. beyond smb.'s wildest ~s

dream II v. 1. (D; intr.) to ~ about, of 2. (L) she never ~ed that she would someday write dictionaries

dreary adj. it was very ~ to do the same job every day = it was very ~ doing the same job every day

dredge v. (D; intr., tr.) to ~ for (to ~ a river for a missing swimmer)

drenched adj. ~ in, with (they were ~ in perspiration)

dregs n. the ~ of society

drenched adj. 1. thoroughly ~ 2. ~ to (we were ~ed to the skin)

dress I n. ["attire"] 1. casual, informal; evening, formal; native, traditional ~ 2. improper; proper ~ 3. in ~ (in informal ~) ["woman's frock"] 4. a casual; cocktail; evening (esp. BE); low-cut; maternity; party; summer ~ 5. a ~ is long; short; tight 6. a ~ fits (well) 7. in a ~ (she was in a summer ~) ["women's garment for sleeping"] (BE) 8. a night-dress (CE has *nightgown*)

dress II v. 1. to ~ casually, informally; conservatively; elegantly, smartly; lightly; neatly; warmly 2. (d; intr., tr.) to ~ as (he was ~ed as a sailor) 3. (d; intr.) to ~ for (to ~ for dinner) 4. (d; intr.) to ~ in (to ~ in black) 5. (D; tr.) to ~ with (to ~ a salad with oil and vinegar) 6. (misc.) to get ~ed; poorly ~ed; well ~ed; (mil.) ~ right!

dressing n. ["bandage"] 1. to apply, put on a ~ (to apply a ~ to a wound) 2. to change, replace; remove a ~ 3. a sterile ~ 4. a ~ comes off ["sauce"] 5. (a) salad ~ ["misc."] 6. window ~ ("smt. presented to show only the favorable aspects")

dressing down n. ["scolding"] 1. to give smb. a ~ 2. to get, receive a ~

dress up v. 1. (D; intr., tr.) to ~ as (he ~ed up as a

cowboy; they ~ed her up as a ballerina) 2. (D; intr.) to ~ for (she got ~ed up for the party)

dribble I n. (basketball) a double ~

dribble II v. (P; intr., tr.) she ~d the ball across the court; the milk ~d down my shirt

drier see **dryer**

drift I n. ["pile"] 1. a deep ~; a snowdrift ["movement"] 2. a ~ to, towards (a ~ to the right) ["meaning"] (colloq.) 3. to get the ~

drift II v. 1. (d; intr.) to ~ into (to ~ into a life of crime) 2. (D; intr.) to ~ with (to ~ with the current) 3. (P; intr.) the boat ~ed down the river; we ~ed from town to town; to ~ out to sea; to ~ towards shore 4. (misc.) to ~ apart; to ~ aimlessly

drift away v. (D; intr.) to ~ from

drift back v. (D; intr.) to ~ to (the strikers ~ed back to work)

drill I n. ["boring tool"] 1. to operate, use a ~ 2. a dentist's; electric, power; hand; pneumatic; rotary ~ ["exercise"] 3. to conduct a ~ 4. (mil.) close-order; rifle ~ 5. an air-raid; civil-defense; evacuation; fire ~

drill II v. 1. (D; intr.) ("to prospect") to ~ for (to ~ for oil) 2. (D; tr.) ("to train") to ~ in (to ~ students in pronunciation) 3. (d; tr.) ("to instill") to ~ into (to ~ discipline into cadets)

drink I n. 1. to fix (esp. AE), make, mix a ~ 2. to pour a ~ 3. to down; have, take; nurse a ~ 4. a cold, cool; fizzy (BE) ("sparkling"); hot; potent, stiff, strong; still (BE) ("not sparkling"); warm; weak ~ 5. a mixed; soft ~ 6. over a ~ (we had a nice chat over a ~) 7. (misc.) to drown one's sorrows in ~; to buy a round of ~s; he took to ~ in his old age

drink II v. 1. (d; intr.) to ~ from, out of (I always ~ tea from a glass) 2. (d; intr.) to ~ to (let's ~ to good health) 3. (D; tr.) to ~ to (to ~ a toast to smb.) 4. (misc.) to drink heavily; to ~ one's whiskey neat/straight; to ~ oneself to death; to ~ smb. under the table

drinker n. a hard, heavy; light, moderate ~

drinking n. 1. excessive; hard, heavy; social ~ 2. a ~ bout

drip I n. 1. a steady ~ 2. an intravenous; saline ~ 3. on a ~ (they put her on a saline ~)

drip II v. 1. (D; intr.) to ~ from (the water was ~ping from the tap) 2. (D; intr.) to ~ with 3. (P; intr., tr.) water ~ped over me; oil ~ped onto the road; she was ~ping the juice all over the floor

drive I n. ["trip in a vehicle"] 1. to go for, go on, have (BE), take a ~ 2. an easy ~ (it's an easy half hour ~ to their place) 3. a test ~ ["campaign"] 4. to initiate, launch a ~ (for) (to launch a ~ for flood relief) 5. a charity; economy; fund-raising; membership; recruiting ~ 6. a ~ to + inf. (they launched a ~ to raise funds for charity) ["energy"] 7. the ~ to + inf. (does she have enough ~ to finish the job?) ["impulse"] 8. a basic; sex ~ ["type of propul-

sion"] 9. a chain; disk; fluid; four-wheel; front-wheel; rear-wheel ~ (see also **driveway**)

drive II v. 1. to ~ fast; slow 2. (d; intr.; used with -ing forms) to ~ at ("to suggest") (what is she ~ving at?) 3. (d; tr.) to ~ from, out of ("to force") (to ~ an invader out of a country; they drove her out of office; the noise drove me out of my mind) 4. (d; tr.) ("to direct") to ~ through; with (to ~ a nail through a wall with a hammer) 5. (d; tr.) to ~ to ("to bring to") (to ~ smb. to despair) 6. (H) ("to force") he was driven by necessity to steal 7. (N; used with an adjective) ("to make") he drove me crazy 8. (P; intr., tr.) ("to go; transport") I drove across town; she drove me past the station; who ~s the children to school? we drove through the park

drive away v. (D; intr., tr.) to ~ from (we drove away from their house)

drive down v. (D; intr.) to ~ to (let's ~ to the waterfront)

drive home v. 1. (B) to ~ a point home to smb. 2. (L; to) he could not ~ (to her) that we cannot afford a new car 3. (Q; to) we must ~ (to him) where the difficulties lie

drive over v. (d; intr., tr.) ~ to (we drove over to their house)

driver n. 1. a bus; cab, taxi; limousine; lorry (BE), truck; mule; tractor ~ 2. (BE) an engine ~ (AE has *engineer*) 3. a learner (BE), student (AE) ~ 4. a drunk, drunken; hit-and-run; reckless ~ 5. a careful, cautious, defensive, safe; designated ~ 6. a backseat ~

driver's license n. (AE) 1. to issue; revoke; suspend a ~ 2. to apply for; get, obtain; lose a ~ (BE has *driving licence*)

driveway n. (esp. AE; BE prefers *drive*) 1. to pave, surface a ~ 2. to share a ~ 3. a ~ between (a ~ between two houses)

driving n. 1. to do the ~ 2. careful, defensive, safe; careless, reckless ~ 3. city; highway (AE), motorway (BE); turnpike (AE) ~ 4. rush-hour; stop-and-go ~ 5. drink-driving (BE), drunk (esp. AE), drunken (esp. AE) ~ 6. (misc.) ~ under the influence (also DUI)

driving licence n. (BE) see **driver's license**

drool v. (colloq.) (D; intr.) ("to show pleasure") to ~ over (they were ~ing over their new grandchild)

drop I n. ["fall"] 1. an abrupt, sudden; sharp; sheer ~ 2. a ~ in (a sharp ~ in the interest rate) ["depository"] 3. a mail ~

drop II v. 1. (A; used without *to*) ("to communicate") ~ me a line when you get there; I ~ped her a hint 2. (d; intr.) ("to lag") to ~ behind (he ~ped behind the other runners) 3. (D; intr., tr.) ("to fall; to let fall") to ~ from (the book ~ped from her hand; his name was ~ped from the list) 4. (d; intr., tr.) ("to fall; to let fall") to ~ into (the stone ~ped into the water; I ~ped a coin into the slot) 5. (D; tr.)

("to let fall") to ~ on (she ~ped a book on the floor) 6. (d; intr.) to ~ out of ("to abandon") (to ~ out of school) 7. (d; intr.) to ~ out of ("to disappear") (to ~ out of sight) 8. (D; intr.) ("to fall") to ~ to (prices ~ped to the lowest point in a year; everyone ~ped to the ground) 9. (misc.) to ~ dead

drop behind v. (D; intr.) to ~ in (to ~ in one's work)

drop by v. (D; intr.) to ~ for (to ~ for a drink)

drop down v. 1. (D; intr., tr.) to ~ from (the apples ~ped down from the tree; she ~ped the apples down from the tree) 2. (D; tr.) to ~ to (I'll ~ this down to you)

drop in v. 1. (D; intr.) to ~ for (I'll ~ for a visit) 2. (D; intr.) to ~ on (~ on me at any time)

drop off v. 1. (D; tr.) ("to leave") to ~ at (could you ~ the books at the library? could you ~ me off at the station?) 2. (misc.) to ~ (to sleep)

droppings n. animal ~

drops n. (med.) 1. to instil, put in ~ 2. cough; ear; eye; knockout; nose ~

drought n. a prolonged; severe ~

droves n. in ~ (the tourists came in ~)

drowsiness n. to induce ~

drown v. 1. ("to drench") (D; tr.) to ~ in, with (to ~ the meat in ketchup) 2. (misc.) to ~ one's sorrows in drink

drubbing n. ["beating"] 1. to give smb. a ~ 2. to take a ~ (our team took a ~) 3. a severe ~

drudgery n. sheer ~

drug n. 1. to administer, give; inject; prescribe a ~ 2. to take a ~ 3. to ban; test a ~ 4. a dangerous, toxic; mild; potent, powerful, strong; weak ~ 5. an addictive; habit-forming; hallucinogenic; non-addictive ~ 6. a generic; nonprescription, over-the-counter; prescription; proprietary ~ 7. an anti-inflammatory; miracle, wonder; sulfa (AE); sulpha (BE) ~ 8. a ~ wears off 9. (misc.) a ~ on the market ("smt. for which there is little demand"); a ~ addict; a ~ dealer/pusher

drug abuse n. to combat ~

drugs n. 1. to do (colloq.), take, use ~ 2. to deal, peddle, push, sell, traffic in (illicit) ~ 3. hard; soft ~ 4. illegal, illicit ~ 5. on ~ (to be on ~)

drugstore n. (esp. AE; BE has *chemist's*) at, in a ~ (he works at/in a ~)

drum I n. ["percussion instrument"] 1. to beat, play a ~ 2. a bass ~; kettledrum; snare ~ 3. muffled ~s 4. the ~s roll ["cylinder"] 5. a brake ~ ["container"] 6. an oil ~

drum II v. 1. (d; tr.) to ~ into (to ~ smt. into smb.'s head) 2. (P; intr.) the rain was ~ming against the windows; she was ~ming on the table with her fingers

drum up v. (D; tr.) to ~ for (he ~med up some business for us)

drunk I adj. 1. blind, dead, roaring, stinking ~ 2. to get ~ on (he got ~ on cheap wine) 3. ~ with (~ with

power)

drunk II n. to roll ("rob") a ~ (colloq.)

drunkard n. an habitual ~

dry I adj. 1. bone ~ 2. to go, run ~ (the well ran ~)

dry II v. (D; refl., tr.) to ~ with (he dried himself with a towel)

dryer n. 1. to turn on a ~ 2. to turn off a ~ 3. to unload a ~ 4. a clothes ~ 5. a hair ~ 6. (misc.) is the ~ running? the ~ is off/on

dry off v. (D; refl., tr.) to ~ with (she dried the children off with a towel)

dry run n. (esp. AE) to do, have a ~ (BE prefers *dummy run*)

dub I v. (N; used with a noun) ("to name") they ~bed him *Bud*

dub II v. (D; tr.) ("to provide with a new sound track") to ~ into (to ~ a film into English)

dubious adj. 1. ~ about, of 2. ~ if, that, whether + clause (it's ~ if they'll come)

duck I n. 1. ~s quack; waddle 2. a young ~ is a duckling 3. a male ~ is a drake 4. (misc.) to take to smt. like a ~ (takes) to water ("to adapt to smt. quickly and easily")

duck II v. 1. (d; intr.) to ~ out of ("to evade") (to ~ out of an obligation) 2. (P; intr.) ("to move") we ~ed into the nearest building; she ~ed behind the partition; the children ~ed under the table

ducking n. 1. to give smb. a ~ 2. to get a ~

dudgeon n. ["indignation"] in high ~

due I adj. 1. (cannot stand alone) ~ for (~ for a promotion) 2. (cannot stand alone) ~ to (her absence was ~ to illness) 3. to come, fall ~ (the note has fallen ~) 4. ~ to + inf. (the train is ~ to arrive at ten o'clock)

USAGE NOTE: Purists prefer to use *due to* as an adjectival predicate phrase modifying the subject—her absence was due to illness. Otherwise, *because of* or *owing to* is preferred—she was absent because of illness; owing to illness she was absent.

due II n. ["recognition"] to give smb. her/his ~

duel I n. 1. to have, fight a ~ (over) 2. to challenge smb. to a ~ 3. a ~ between 4. a ~ to the death

duel II v. 1. (D; intr.) to ~ over 2. (D; intr.) to ~ with

due process n. (legal) 1. to observe ~ 2. (misc.) by ~ of law

dues n. 1. to pay ~ 2. annual; membership ~ (BE also has *membership fees*)

duet n. 1. to play; perform; sing a ~ 2. a piano ~

dukes n. (colloq.) ["fists"] to put up one's ~

dumb adj. ["stupid"] (colloq.) (esp. AE) 1. to play ~ 2. ~ to + inf. (it was ~ of you to say that) ["mute"] 3. to strike smb. ~

dumbfounded adj. 1. completely ~ 2. ~ at, by (~ at the news) 3. ~ to + inf. (he was ~ to learn that his wife had left him) 4. ~ that + clause (we were ~ that she refused the offer)

dumbstruck see **dumbfounded**

dummy run (BE) see **dry run**

dump I n. ["place for dumping"] (esp. AE) 1. a garbage, trash ~; the town ~ (BE prefers *refuse tip*) ["dilapidated place"] (colloq.) 2. a real ~ (this town is a real ~) ["storage area"] 3. an ammunition; supply ~

dump II v. 1. (slang) (esp. AE) to ~ on ("to project bad experiences or feelings on") (I have enough troubles of my own—don't ~ on me) 2. (P; tr.) they ~ed their bags on the floor; the company was ~ing waste products into the river

dumping ground n. a ~ for

dumps n. down in the ~ ("dejected")

dun v. (D; tr.) to ~ for (to ~ smb. for payment)

dune n. a sand ~

dungarees n. a pair of ~

dunk v. (D; tr.) to ~ in (to ~ doughnuts in coffee)

dupe I n. an innocent ~

dupe II v. (D; tr.) to ~ into (he was ~d into signing)

duplicate n. 1. to make a ~ 2. in ~

duplicity n. ~ in

duration n. 1. (a) long; moderate; short ~ 2. of a certain ~ (of short ~) 3. for the ~ (of the war)

duress n. under ~ (to sign a confession under ~)

dusk n. at ~

dust I n. 1. to collect, gather; raise ~ 2. fine, powdery ~ 3. coal; cosmic; gold; radioactive; volcanic ~ 4. a cloud; layer; particle, speck of ~ 5. ~ collects; settles 6. (misc.) from ~ to ~

dust II v. 1. (D; tr.) to ~ for (to ~ smt. for fingerprints) 2. (D; tr.) to ~ with (to ~ smt. with insecticide)

duster see the Usage Note for **eraser**

dusting n. a light ~ (of snow)

duty n. ["obligation"] ["service"] 1. to assume, take on a ~ 2. to carry out, discharge, do, perform one's ~ 3. to relieve smb. of her/his ~ties; to suspend smb. from her/his ~ties 4. to shirk one's ~ 5. an ethical, moral; legal; professional ~ 6. a painful, unpleasant; pleasant ~ 7. a ceremonial; civic; official; patriotic; public ~ 8. supervisory ~ties 9. (esp. mil.) active; combat; detached; fatigue; guard; light; noncombatant; overseas; sea; special; temporary ~ (to see active ~) 10. a ~ to (a ~ to one's country) 11. a ~ to + inf. (physicians have a ~ to report such cases) 12. on ~; off ~ (who was on ~ yesterday? when do you get/go off ~? she was never on active ~) 13. (misc.) (a) dereliction of ~; a sense of ~; in (the) line of ~; ~ calls ["tariff"] ["tax"] 14. to impose a ~ on 15. to pay (a) ~ on 16. to lift a ~ from 17. to exempt smt. from ~ 18. customs; excise ~ties 19. (BE) (obsol.) (a) death ~ (CE has *inheritance tax*)

duty bound adj. ~ to + inf. (we are ~ to help out financially)

dwell v. (d; intr.) to ~ on (to ~ on a question; to ~ on one's personal problems)

dweller n. a cave; city; cliff; country; lake; town ~

dwindle v. (D; intr.) to ~ (away) to (to ~ to nothing)

dye I n. 1. to apply ~ to 2. natural; synthetic; vegetable ~s 3. (a) ~ fades; takes

dye II v. (N; used with an adjective, noun) she ~d the dress (a lovely shade of) blue

dynamite n. 1. ~ explodes 2. a stick of ~ 3. (misc.) (fig.) political ~

dynasty n. 1. to establish, found a ~ 2. to overthrow a ~ 3. a ~ rules

dysentery n. 1. to come down, go down (BE) with, get ~; have ~ 2. an attack of ~ 3. amebic ~

E

each *determiner, pronoun* ~ of (~ of them)
USAGE NOTE: The use of the preposition *of* is necessary when a pronoun follows. When a noun follows, two constructions are possible—we saw each student; we saw each of the students.

eager *adj.* 1. ~ for (~ for success) 2. ~ to + inf. (she's ~ to help) 3. (formal; esp. BE) ~ that + clause (we were ~ that they should participate)

eagerness *n.* 1. ~ to + inf. (we appreciate his ~ to help) 2. (misc.) in their ~ to please, they went too far

eagle *n.* 1. a bald; golden ~ 2. ~s scream; soar 3. a young ~ is an eaglet

ear *n.* 1. to perk up (AE), prick up; wiggle one's ~s 2. to pierce smb.'s ~s 3. a musical ~ 4. the inner; middle; outer ~ 5. smb.'s ~s perk up (AE), prick up; ring 6. an ~ for (to have an ~ for music) 7. by ~ (to play music by ~) 8. (misc.) to be all ~s ("to listen attentively"); to lend an ~ to ("to pay attention to"); to turn a deaf ~ to ("to pay no attention to"); to fall on deaf ~s ("to be disregarded"); a cauliflower ~ ("an ear deformed by repeated blows"); to have smb.'s ~ ("to have access to smb. who is superior in rank"); to box smb.'s ~s ("to strike smb. on the ears"); the loud music grated on our ~s; up to one's ~s in debt ("heavily in debt"); to play it by ~ ("to improvise"); her ~s were burning ("she felt that others were talking about her")

earache *n.* to have an ~ (esp. AE), to have ~ (BE)

eardrum *n.* a perforated ~

earful *n.* 1. to give smb. an ~ 2. to get an ~ (from)

earliest *n.* at the ~

early *adj.* the train was five minutes ~

earmark *v.* 1. (d; tr.) to ~ for (money has been ~ed for the new library) 2. (H) money has been ~ed to go to the new library

earmarks *n.* ["characteristics"] to have all the ~ of

earmuffs *n.* 1. to put on ~ 2. a pair of ~

earn *v.* (C) his accomplishments ~ed respect for him; or: his accomplishments ~ed him respect

earnest I *adj.* ~ about

earnest II *n.* 1. in (deadly) ~ 2. in ~ about

earnings *n.* annual, yearly; average; gross; net, take-home ~

earphones *n.* 1. to put on ~ 2. to plug in ~ 3. a pair, set of ~

earplug *n.* 1. to insert, put in an ~ 2. to remove, take out an ~ 3. a pair of ~s

earrings *n.* 1. to wear ~ 2. to put on ~ 3. a pair of ~

earshot *n.* in, within; out of ~

earth *n.* 1. to circle; orbit the ~ 2. the ~ revolves around the sun; rotates on its axis 3. on (the) ~ (is there more land or more water on ~?) 4. a clod, clump, lump of ~ 5. (misc.) down to ~ ("practical"); who on ~ would ever do that? what on ~ is that?

earthquake *n.* 1. to record an ~ 2. a devastating, destructive; light; strong, severe ~ 3. an ~ strikes (a severe ~ struck the area) 4. the magnitude of an ~ 5. an ~ measures six on the Richter scale

earwax *n.* to remove ~

ease I *n.* 1. at ~ (to put smb. at ~; ill at ~) 2. at ~ with (she feels at ~ with us) 3. (formal) for ~ in (for ~ in sleeping) 4. with ~ (he can lift a hundred pounds with great ~) 5. (misc.) (mil.) (to stand) at ~

ease II *v.* 1. (N; used with an *adj.*) they ~d the door shut 2. (P; refl., tr.) they ~d the piano through the window; they ~d their way toward the exit

easement *n.* ["right of way"] (legal) to grant an ~

ease up *v.* (D; intr.) to ~ on (you should ~ on your workers: you've been pushing them too hard)

east I *adj., adv.* 1. directly, due, straight ~ 2. ~ of (~ of the city) 3. (misc.) to face; go, head ~; northeast by ~; southeast by ~

east II *n.* 1. from the ~; in the ~; to the ~ 2. (AE) back ~ ("in the eastern part of the US") 3. (BE) out ~ ("in, to Asia") 4. the Far East; the Middle East; the Near East
USAGE NOTE: The *Far East* refers to the countries of eastern Asia. The *Middle East* refers to the countries of the eastern Mediterranean. The *Near East* is now generally an old-fashioned synonym of the preceding term; formerly it referred to the Balkans and the Ottoman Empire.

Easter *n.* at; for ~ (all the children came home for ~)

easy *adj.* ["not difficult"] 1. fairly; very ~ 2. ~ for (that job was ~ for her) ["lenient"] 3. (cannot stand alone) ~ on (you are too ~ on the children; go ~ on him: he's been sick) ["showing moderation"] 4. (cannot stand alone) ~ on (go ~ on the hot peppers) ["not difficult"] 5. (cannot stand alone) ~ to + inf. (this book is ~ to translate = it is ~ to translate this book = this is an ~ book to translate; Bob is ~ to please = it is ~ to please Bob; it is not ~ to be a parent = it is not ~ being a parent; it is ~ for you to say that)

easy street *n.* on ~ (to be on ~) ("to be well off")

eat *v.* 1. to ~ heartily, voraciously 2. (d; intr.) to ~ into, through (acid ~s into metal) 3. (d; intr.) to ~ out of (our cat ~s out of its own dish) 4. (d; intr., tr.) to ~ with (to ~ with one's fingers) 5. (misc.) let's ~ in/out this evening

eat away *v.* (d; intr.) to ~ at (the waves ~ at the shore)

eater *n.* a big, heavy; compulsive; fussy, picky; light ~

eavesdrop *v.* (D; intr.) to ~ on (to ~ on a conversation)

ebb *n.* 1. at a low ~ 2. on the ~ (the tide is on the ~)

eccentric *adj.* 1. ~ in (~ in one's habits) 2. ~ to + inf. (she thought it was ~ to go swimming at night)

echelon *n.* 1. (mil.) the forward; rear ~ 2. the higher, top, upper; lower ~s of society

echo I *n.* 1. to produce an ~ 2. to hear an ~ 3. an ~ sounds

echo II *v.* (P; intr.) the news ~ed around the world; the park ~ed to the sounds of the children; the courtroom ~ed with the shouts of the spectators; their screams ~ed through the corridors

eclipse *n.* ["obscuring of the moon or sun"] 1. a full, total; lunar; partial; solar ~ ["dimming of smb.'s influence"] 2. to go into ~ 3. in ~

ecology *n.* deep; human, social ~

economical *adj.* ["inexpensive"] ~ to + inf. (it's more ~ to go by bus = it's more ~ going by bus)

economics *n.* supply-side; trickle-down ~

economize *v.* (D; intr.) to ~ on (to ~ on fuel)

economy *n.* ["frugality"] 1. to practice ~ 2. strict ~ ["economic structure"] 3. a capitalist, free-market; national; peacetime; planned; wartime ~ 4. an ailing, shaky, weak; sluggish; sound, stable, strong ~ ["the science of economics"] 4. political ~

ecstasy *n.* 1. pure, sheer; religious ~ 2. in ~ about, over 3. (misc.) a look of ~; they went into ~sies over the new furniture

ecstatic *adj.* ~ about, at, over (~ at being selected)

edge I *n.* ["margin, border"] (also fig.) 1. a cutting; jagged, ragged; sharp ~ 2. at, by, near, on an ~ (she stood at the ~ of the crater) ["advantage"] (colloq.) 3. to have, hold an ~ on, over 4. an ~ on (to gain a competitive ~ on smb.) ["misc."] 5. to take the ~ off smb.'s appetite ("to satisfy smb.'s appetite partially"); to be on ~ ("to be tense")

edge II *v.* 1. (d; tr.) to ~ out of (to ~ smb. out of a job) 2. (P; intr., tr.) to ~ one's way through a crowd; she ~d towards the door

edge up *v.* ~ (D; intr.) to ~ to (she ~d up to the counter)

edgy *adj.* (colloq.) ["nervous"] ~ about

edict *n.* 1. to issue an ~ 2. to recall, rescind an ~ 3. a royal; solemn ~ 4. an ~ that + clause (the government issued an ~ that all prisoners should be released)

edification *n.* for smb.'s ~ (I said that for your ~)

edition *n.* 1. to bring out, publish an ~ (to bring out a new ~) 2. (of a book, dictionary) an abridged; annotated; corrected; critical; deluxe; enlarged, expanded; first; hardback; limited; paperback; revised; thumb-indexed; unabridged; unexpurgated; variorum ~ 3. (of a newspaper) a city; home;

evening; final; morning; special ~ 4. (misc.) (BE) an omnibus ~ ("the rebroadcast of the week's episodes of a soap opera or of a series"); the ~ went through three printings

editor *n.* 1. a city ~ 2. a copy (esp. AE) ~, subeditor (esp. BE); fashion; managing; news; political; senior; society; technical ~; editor-in-chief

USAGE NOTE: In AE, *city editor* means "local news editor"; in BE it means "London financial editor".

editorial *n.* 1. to write an ~ 2. an ~ about

editorship *n.* under the ~ of

educate *v.* 1. (D; tr.) to ~ about, in, on; for, to (~d about one's responsibilities) 2. (H) to ~ smb. to do smt.

educated *adj.* highly, well; poorly ~

education *n.* 1. to give, provide an ~ 2. to get, obtain, receive an ~ 3. to complete one's ~ 4. compulsory; formal; free ~ 5. private; public (AE), state (BE) ~ (private ~ is costly; funds for public ~ are scarce) 6. (BE) a public school ~ 7. elementary (esp. AE), primary; higher, tertiary (BE); secondary ~; a college (AE), university ~ 8. adult (AE), continuing, further (BE) ~ 9. health; physical; sex ~ 10. in-service; pre-professional; professional; vocational ~ 11. remedial; special ~ 12. a broad, general; liberal ~; (a) progressive ~ 13. the ~ to + inf. (does she have enough ~ to cope with the job?)

eel *n.* 1. a conger; electric ~ 2. (misc.) as slippery as an ~

effect *n.* ["result"] ["influence"] 1. to have, produce an ~ on 2. to heighten an ~ 3. to take ~ (the drug took ~) 4. to feel an ~ (I feel the ~ of the narcotic) 5. to mar; negate, nullify; sleep off the ~ (of smt.) 6. a beneficial, good, salutary; desired ~ (her calm manner had a salutary ~ on the children) 7. a dramatic; exhilarating; hypnotic ~ 8. a calculated; cumulative; deterrent; far-reaching; long-term; net, overall; practical; profound ~ 9. a limited, marginal; minimal; short-term ~ 10. an adverse, bad, deleterious, harmful; chilling; crippling; damaging, deadening, disastrous ~ 11. a domino; retroactive; ripple ("gradually spreading") ~ 12. an environmental; greenhouse ("warming of the earth's surface") ~ 13. a halo ("overly favorable judgment based on irrelevant factors"); knock-on (BE) ("additional") ~ 14. a placebo; side ~ 15. an ~ wears off 16. to good; little; no; some ~ ["operation"] 17. to put into ~ (to put new regulations into ~) 18. to come into, go into, take ~ (when does the new law take ~?) 19. in ~ (the ordinance is still in ~) ["desired impression"] 20. for ~ (she said that purely for ~) ["meaning"] 21. to the ~ (he said smt. to the ~ that he might be late; words to that ~) ["reality"] ["practice"] 22. in ~

effective *adj.* 1. ~ against (~ against the common cold) 2. ~ in (~ in fighting forest fires) 3. ~ to + inf. (it would be more ~ not to respond to the charges)

effects *n.* ["belongings"] 1. household; personal ~ ["impressions"] 2. sound; special ~ ["results"] 3. to counteract the ~ (of) 4. ill ~ (they experienced no ill ~)

efficiency *n.* 1. to improve, increase, promote ~ 2. to impair ~ 3. fighting; maximum, peak ~ 4. ~ in (~ in combating absenteeism) 5. (misc.) at peak ~

efficient *adj.* 1. ~ at, in (she was very ~ at getting things done; they were very ~ in reducing waste) 2. ~ to + inf. (it is not ~ to hire poorly trained workers)

effigy *n.* to burn; hang smb. in ~

effort *n.* 1. to make, put forth an ~ 2. to concentrate; intensify; redouble one's ~s 3. to devote one's ~s to 4. to spare no ~ 5. to foil, stymie, thwart smb.'s ~s 6. an all-out, bold, concerted, conscious, furious, gallant, great, Herculean, heroic, massive, maximum, painstaking, sincere, strenuous, studious, superhuman, valiant ~ 7. a collaborative, joint, united ~ 8. an abortive; desperate; frantic; minimal; useless, vain ~ 9. ceaseless, unceasing; unsparing, untiring; wasted ~s 10. a team ~; the war ~ 11. an ~ to + inf. (they made an all-out ~ to finish the work on time) 12. with a certain ~ (it was only with great ~ that we could do the job)

effrontery *n.* the ~ to + inf. (he had the ~ to demand more money)

egg *n.* 1. to fertilize; hatch; incubate; lay ~s 2. to beat, whisk (BE); boil; crack; fry; poach an ~ 3. to candle ~s 4. an addled, bad, rotten ~; fresh ~ 5. a boiled; coddled; devilled; fried; hard-boiled; poached; raw; Scotch (BE); scrambled; shirred (AE); soft-boiled ~ 6. a clutch of ~s 7. the white of an ~; the yolk of an ~ 8. (misc.) a bad/rotten ~ ("a bad person"); a good ~ ("a good person"); to have ~ on one's face ("to be in an embarrassing position"); (BE) to teach one's grandmother to suck ~s ("to try to tell smb. smt. that they already know")

egg on *v.* (H) to ~ smb. on to do smt.

egg whites *n.* to beat, whip, whisk ~

ego *n.* 1. to bolster, boost, flatter smb.'s ~ 2. to bruise, deflate smb.'s ~ 3. an enormous, inflated, overbearing ~ 4. an alter ~

either *determiner, pronoun* ~ of (~ of the two; ~ of them)

USAGE NOTE: The use of the preposition *of* is necessary when *two* or a pronoun follows. When a noun follows, the following constructions are used—either student will know the answer; either of the students will know the answer.

eject *v.* (D; intr., tr.) to ~ from (to ~ from a disabled plane; they were ~ed from the room for disorderly conduct)

elaborate *v.* (D; intr.) to ~ on

Elastoplast (T) *n.* (BE) see **Band-Aid**

elated *adj.* 1. ~ about, at, over (~ at the good news) 2. ~ to + inf. (they were ~ to hear the news)

elbow I *n.* 1. tennis ~ ("an elbow that hurts because of excessive exercise") 2. at smb.'s ~ ("close to smb.") 3. (misc.) to rub ~s with smb. ("to have contact with smb."); (BE, colloq.) to give smb. the ~ ("to end a relationship with smb.")

elbow II *v.* (P; tr.) they ~ed me out of the way; he ~ed his way up to the front; she ~ed her way through the crowd

elbow grease *n.* ["great effort"] 1. to use ~ 2. to put ~ into smt.

elbowroom *n.* 1. to give smb. ~ 2. to have ~ 3. ~ for

elders *n.* 1. to respect one's ~ 2. the church; village ~

elect *v.* 1. to ~ unanimously 2. (D; tr.) to ~ as (she was ~ed as vice-president) 3. (D; tr.) to ~ to (he was ~ed to the state legislature) 4. (formal) (E) he ~ed to become a physician 5. (H) she was ~ed to represent us 6. (N; used with a noun) the nation ~ed her vice-president

elected *adj.* democratically; popularly ~

election *n.* 1. to hold, schedule an ~ 2. to call for ~s 3. to carry, win an ~ 4. to decide, swing an ~ (her last speech swung the ~ in her favor) 5. to concede; lose an ~ 6. to fix, rig an ~ 7. a close, hotly contested; rigged ~ 8. a free; general; local; national; primary; runoff ~ 9. smb.'s ~ to (her ~ to the senate was welcome news) 10. at, in an ~ (she was defeated in the last ~) 11. (misc.) ~ fever ("excitement before an election"); (BE) the runup to an ~ ("the pre-election period")

electrical appliance *n.* 1. to plug in an ~ 2. to unplug an ~

electrician *n.* to call (in) an ~

electricity *n.* 1. to generate; induce ~ 2. to conduct ~ 3. to hook up, turn on the ~ 4. to cut off, disconnect, turn off the ~ 5. static ~ 6. ~ flows 7. (misc.) the ~ is off; the ~ is on; the ~ went off; the ~ came on/went on

electrocardiogram *n.* 1. to do; have an ~ 2. to read an ~

elegance *n.* 1. faded; sheer ~ 2. sartorial ~

element *n.* ["component"] 1. a basic, essential, key, vital ~ ["group"] 2. a foreign ~ 3. diverse; extremist, radical ~s 4. criminal; rowdy, unruly; subversive; undesirable ~s ["substance"] 5. ~s combine 6. chemical ~s ["natural environment"] 7. in one's ~; out of one's ~ ["factor"] 8. the human ~ ["misc."] 9. to brave the ~s ("to go out in bad weather")

elephant *n.* 1. a rogue ("wild") ~ 2. ~s trumpet 3. a herd of ~s 4. a young ~ is a calf 5. a female ~ is a cow 6. a male ~ is a bull

elevate *v.* (formal) (D; tr.) to ~ to (to ~ smb. to the peerage)

elevation *n.* ["height"] 1. at a certain ~ (at an ~ of two thousand meters) ["raising"] 2. smb.'s ~ to (her ~ to the presidency)

elevator *n.* ["device for raising and lowering people and freight"] (AE for 1-6; BE has *lift*) 1. to operate an ~ 2. to call; take an ~ (we took the ~ to the tenth floor) 3. a down; express; self-service; up ~ 4. a freight (AE) ~ 5. a service ~ 6. a bank of ~s ["storage building"] 7. a grain ~

elicit *v.* (D; tr.) to ~ from

eligibility *n.* 1. ~ for 2. ~ to + inf. (~ to vote)

eligible *adj.* 1. ~ for (~ for promotion) 2. ~ to + inf. (she is ~ to vote)

eliminate *v.* (D; tr.) to ~ from

elimination *n.* 1. ~ from 2. (misc.) by the process of ~

elite *n.* a cultural; intellectual; party; power; social ~

elixir *n.* the ~ of life; the ~ of youth

elk *n.* 1. a herd of ~ 2. a female ~ is a cow 3. a male ~ is a bull
USAGE NOTE: The European *elk* is the North American *moose*. The North American *elk* resembles the European *red deer*, but is larger.

elope *v.* (D; intr.) to ~ with (she ~d with her childhood sweetheart)

eloquence *n.* 1. flowery ~ 2. ~ about

eloquent *adj.* 1. to wax ~ 2. ~ about

E-mail, e-mail I *n.* 1. to send (an) ~ (to) 2. to get, receive (an) ~ (from) 3. by ~ (to send a message by ~) 4. to be on ~, to have ~

E-mail, e-mail II *v.* (A) they ~ed a message to me; or: they ~ed me a message (see also **fax II**)

emanate *v.* (d; intr.) to ~ from

emancipate *v.* (D; tr.) to ~ from (to ~ serfs from bondage)

emancipation *n.* 1. political ~ 2. ~ from

embankment *n.* 1. a high, steep ~ 2. a railroad, railway ~

embargo *n.* 1. to enforce; impose an ~ 2. to place, put an ~ on 3. to lift, remove an ~ from 4. an arms; trade ~ 5. an ~ against, on 6. under ~

embark *v.* 1. (D; intr.) to ~ for (to ~ for France) 2. (d; intr.) to ~ on, upon (to ~ on a new career)

embarrass *v.* 1. to ~ deeply 2. (R) it ~ed him to be caught cheating

embarrassed *adj.* 1. deeply, very ~ 2. financially ~ 3. ~ about, at, over 4. ~ to + inf. (he was ~ to see his name in print) 5. ~ that + clause (he was ~ that he was caught cheating)

embarrassing *adj.* 1. ~ to + inf. (it was ~ to fail the exam) 2. ~ that + clause (it's ~ that our streets are so dirty)

embarrassment *n.* 1. to cause ~ 2. to feel ~ 3. acute; deep ~ 4. ~ about, at, over (we felt ~ about the diclosure) 5. an ~ to (his outburst was an ~ to his family) 6. to smb.'s ~ (to my ~, she accepted the invitation)

embassy *n.* 1. a foreign ~ 2. at, in an ~ (she works at/in the ~)

embed *v.* 1. to ~ deeply; firmly 2. (D; refl., tr.) to ~ in

embellish *v.* (D; tr.) to ~ with (she ~ed her story with a few lurid details)

embers *n.* 1. burning; hot; live ~ 2. dying ~ 3. the glow of (burning) ~

embezzle *v.* (D; intr., tr.) to ~ from

embezzlement *n.* 1. to commit (an act of) ~ 2. ~ from

emblazoned *adj.* 1. ~ across, on 2. ~ with

emblem *n.* a national ~

emblematic *adj.* ~ of

embodiment *n.* a living ~ (of an ideal)

embody *v.* (D; tr.) to ~ in

embolden *v.* (formal) (H) what ~ed him to make the attempt?

embolism *n.* an air; cerebral; coronary; pulmonary ~

emboss *v.* (D; tr.) 1. to ~ on 2. to ~ with

embrace I *n.* a loving, tender, warm; passionate; tight ~

embrace II *v.* to ~ tenderly, warmly

embroider *v.* 1. (D; tr.) to ~ for (she ~ed a towel for me) 2. (D; tr.) to ~ on; with

embroil *v.* (D; refl., tr.) to ~ in

embroiled *adj.* ~ in; with

embryo *n.* 1. to implant an ~ 2. a human ~ 3. an ~ develops

emerge *v.* 1. (d; intr.) to ~ as (he ~d as the leading contender) 2. (D; intr.) to ~ from (the sun ~d from behind the clouds; to ~ from the shadows) 3. (L) it ~d that she was an heiress 4. (s) they ~d unscathed

emergency *n.* 1. to cause, create; declare an ~ 2. a grave, serious; life-and-death; life-threatening; national ~ 3. a state of ~ 4. in case of an ~ (esp. AE); in (the event of) an ~

emergency cord *n.* (AE) to pull an ~ (BE has *communication cord*)

emigrate *v.* (D; intr.) to ~ from; to

eminence *n.* 1. to achieve, win ~ 2. of ~ (a person of great ~)

eminent *adj.* 1. ~ as (she was ~ as a painter) 2. ~ in

emissary *n.* 1. a peace; personal ~ 2. an ~ to

emission *n.* 1. to control; test ~s 2. sulfur (AE), sulphur ~s 3. a nocturnal ~ 4. the sun's ~s

emit *v.* (D; tr.) to ~ into (to ~ smoke into the air)

emotion *n.* 1. to stir up, whip up ~(s) 2. to display, show; express ~ 3. to contain, control, curb, suppress ~ 4. deep, sincere, pent-up; strong ~(s) 5. conflicting, mixed ~s 6. with ~ (to speak with deep ~) 7. (misc.) her voice broke with ~

empathize *v.* (D; intr.) to ~ with

empathy *n.* 1. to feel; show ~ 2. ~ with

emphasis *n.* 1. to lay, place, put ~ on 2. great, particular, special ~

emphasize *v.* 1. (B) she ~d its importance to me 2. (L) I ~d that everyone should come on time

emphatic *adj.* ~ about, in

empire *n.* 1. to govern, rule an ~ 2. to build, build up; consolidate an ~ 3. to break up an ~ 4. a business; colonial; commercial; industrial; publishing ~

emplacement *n.* an antiaircraft; concealed; gun ~

employ I *n.* (to be) in smb.'s ~

employ II *v.* 1. to ~ gainfully 2. (D; tr.) to ~ as (she was ~ed as a programmer) 3. (H) to ~ smb. to solve a problem

employee *n.* 1. to engage (esp. BE), hire (esp. AE), take on an ~ 2. to dismiss, fire, lay off, sack (colloq.) an ~; (BE) to make an ~ redundant 3. a government; white-collar ~ 4. a full-time; part-time ~ 5. a fellow ~

employer *n.* an equal-opportunities (BE), equal-opportunity (AE) ~

employment *n.* 1. to give, provide ~ 2. to find; look for, seek ~ 3. casual (BE); full-time; part-time; seasonal; steady ~ 4. ~ peaks; rises 5. ~ is down; up 6. ~ as (to find ~ as a mechanic)

empower *v.* (H) to ~ smb. to do smt.

empty I *adj.* ~ of (~ of meaning)

empty II *v.* 1. (D; tr.) ("to remove from") to ~ from, out of (she ~tied the grain from the sacks) 2. (d; intr.) ("to flow") to ~ into (the Danube ~ties into the Black Sea) 3. (D; tr.) ("to remove from") to ~ of (she ~tied the briefcase of its contents) 4. (P; tr.) ("to put") she ~tied the cakes onto the plate; I ~tied all the toys into the bin

enable *v.* (H) to ~ smb. to do smt.

enamored *adj.* 1. deeply ~ 2. ~ of, with

encase *v.* (D; tr.) to ~ in

enclose *v.* (D; tr.) to ~ in; with

encore *n.* 1. to do; play; sing an ~ 2. an ~ to

encounter *n.* 1. to have an ~ (with) 2. a brief, fleeting; casual; chance; close ~ 3. an ~ between; with

encourage *v.* 1. to ~ warmly 2. (D; tr.) to ~ in (I ~d them in their work) 3. (H) she ~d me to leave 4. (K) who ~d his taking drugs? 5. (R) it ~d me (to learn) that they had promised to help

encouraged *adj.* 1. ~ at, by (~ at the news) 2. ~ to + inf. (I was ~ to see such excellent results)

encouragement *n.* 1. to give, offer, provide ~ 2. to find ~ in 3. warm ~ 4. ~ to

encouraging *adj.* 1. ~ to + inf. (it is ~ to read that illiteracy is declining) 2. ~ that + clause (it's ~ that the inflation rate has dropped)

encroach *v.* (d; intr.) to ~ on, upon (to ~ on smb.'s territory)

encrusted *adj.* ~ in, with

encumber *v.* (D; tr.) to ~ with

encyclopedia, encyclopaedia *n.* 1. to compile an ~ 2. (humorous) a walking ~

end I *n.* ["finish"] 1. to bring smt. to an ~; to come to the ~ of smt.; put an ~ to smt.; to reach the ~ of (a story) 2. a violent ~ (she met with a violent ~) 3. at an ~ (her career was at an ~) 4. at the ~ (at the ~ of the word) 5. by the ~ (by the ~ of the year) 6. to the ~ (to the bitter ~) 7. (misc.) he met his ~ in a shootout with the police ["side"] 8. the deep; shallow ~ (of a pool) 9. the far, opposite ~ 10. from ~ to ~; from (the) beginning to (the) ~ ["purpose"] 11. to accomplish, achieve one's ~s ["misc."] 12. to be on the receiving ~ ("to be a recipient"); to make ~s meet ("to manage to get along on one's income"); to the ~s of the earth ("to the most remote parts of the earth"); in the ~ ("finally"); for hours on ~ ("for long periods of time")

end II *v.* 1. (d; intr., tr.) to ~ by (he ~ed his remarks by quoting Lincoln) 2. (d; intr.) to ~ in (the word ~s in a consonant; to ~ in a draw; to ~ in disaster) 3. (D; intr., tr.) to ~ with (we ~ed our meal with a nice dessert)

endear *v.* (D; refl., tr.) to ~ to (she ~ed herself to everyone)

endeavor, endeavour *v.* (formal) (E) he ~ed to remain calm

endemic *adj.* ~ among, in, to

ending *n.* 1. a happy; sad; storybook; surprise ~ (to have a happy ~) 2. (grammar) a feminine; grammatical; inflectional; masculine; neuter; plural ~

endorsement *n.* ["approval"] 1. to give one's ~ 2. to get, receive smb.'s ~ 3. to seek smb.'s ~ 4. to withdraw one's ~ 5. a full; official; strong; qualified; unqualified ~

endow *v.* 1. to ~ richly 2. (d; tr.) to ~ with

endowment *n.* to provide an ~ for

end up *v.* 1. (d; intr.) to ~ as (she ~ed up as governor of the state) 2. (d; intr.) to ~ by (she ~ed up by going to law school) 3. (d; intr.) to ~ in (to ~ in a draw; to ~ in a free-for-all) 4. (d; intr.) to ~ with (I ~ed up with the estate) 5. (G) he ~ed up robbing banks 6. (S) she ~ed up governor of the state; to ~ rich

endurance *n.* 1. to test smb.'s ~ 2. physical ~ 3. the ~ to + inf. (does she have enough ~ to run the entire distance?) 4. beyond ~ 5. (misc.) smb.'s powers of ~

endure *v.* 1. (G) she cannot ~ seeing hungry children 2. (K) I cannot ~ his weeping 3. (misc.) to ~ to the bitter end

enema *n.* 1. to administer, give an ~ 2. to get, have an ~

enemy *n.* 1. to conquer, overcome, rout an ~ 2. to confront, engage, face an ~ 3. to have an ~; to make an ~ (of) 4. an arch, avowed, bitter, deadly, implacable, insidious, irreconcilable, mortal, relentless, sworn, vicious; formidable, powerful ~ 5. a common, mutual; natural; political; secret ~ 6. a public ~ (public ~ number one) 7. (misc.) to be one's own worst ~

energy *n.* ["capacity"] 1. to apply one's ~ (to); to

expend one's ~ (on) 2. to devote one's ~ to 3. to direct (one's) ~ to, towards; redirect one's ~ (to, towards) 4. to dissipate; sap smb.'s ~ 5. boundless, limitless, unflagging; latent; misguided ~ 6. a burst of ~ 7. the ~ to + inf. (does she have the ~ to get all of these jobs done?) ["usable power"] 8. to provide ~ for 9. to consume ~ 10. to conserve ~ 11. to harness ~ (to harness solar ~) 12. atomic, nuclear; kinetic; solar ~ 13. sources of ~ 14. (misc.) an ~ crisis

enforce v. to ~ rigidly, strictly, stringently

enforcement n. 1. rigid, strict, stringent ~ 2. law ~

engage v. 1. (D; tr.) to ~ as (to ~ smb. as a guide) 2. (d; intr., tr.) to ~ in (to ~ in sports; to ~ smb. in conversation) 3. (d; intr.) to ~ with (the first gear ~s with the second) 4. (esp. BE) (H) we ~d him to drive us round the city

engaged adj. ["busy"] 1. actively; directly ~ 2. ~ in, on (esp. BE) (we are ~ in compiling a dictionary) ["betrothed"] 3. to get ~ 4. ~ to (Bill is ~ to Betty) ["hired"] 5. (esp. BE) ~ to + inf. (she was ~ to work in public relations)

engagement n. ["betrothal"] 1. to announce an ~ 2. to break (off) an ~ 3. an ~ to (her ~ to him was announced in the local paper) ["appointment"] ["obligation"] 4. to cancel an ~ 5. a luncheon; previous, prior; social; speaking ~ ["battle"] 6. to break off an ~ 7. a naval ~

engine n. ["motor"] 1. to crank, start; gun, race; jump-start; operate, run; rev up an ~ 2. to lubricate; repair; service; tune up an ~ 3. to cut, kill, turn off; start (up); warm up an ~ 4. an air-cooled; aircraft; diesel; donkey; electric; internal-combustion; jet; radial; reciprocating; rocket; rotary; steam; turbojet; V-8; valve-in-head ~ 5. a cold ~ (don't drive fast on a cold ~) 6. an ~ functions, runs, works; idles; starts; warms up 7. an ~ backfires; breaks down; dies, fails, stalls; floods; gets overheated; knocks, sputters 8. an ~ burns gasoline (AE), petrol (BE) 9. an ~ runs on electric power; solar energy ["vehicle"] 10. a fire ~

engineer n. ["skilled specialist in a branch of engineering"] 1. a chemical; civil; electrical; flight; graduate; highway; marine; mechanical; metallurgical; mining; operating; sanitary; systems; transportation ~ ["driver"] 2. a locomotive ~ (AE; BE has engine driver) ["technician"] 3. an operating; radio; sound ~

engineered adj. (cannot stand alone) ~ to + inf. (~ to last for a century)

engineering n. chemical; civil; electrical; genetic; highway; human; hydraulic; marine; mechanical; metallurgical; sanitary; systems; traffic; transportation ~

English n. 1. American; Australian; Basic; Black; British; Canadian; Common, World; Indian; Middle; Modern; New Zealand; Old; South Afri-

can ~ 2. BBC; colloquial; current; idiomatic; the King's, the Queen's; Shakespearean; standard ~ 3. spoken; written ~ 4. broken, fractured; nonstandard; pidgin; substandard ~ 5. in fluent; good; plain ~

engrave v. 1. (d; refl., tr.) to ~ on (the events ~d themselves on my memory) 2. (D; tr.) to ~ with

engrossed adj. 1. deeply ~ 2. ~ in, with (~ in one's work)

engulf v. (D; tr.) to ~ in

enigma n. an ~ to

enjoin v. (formal) 1. (d; tr.) ("to forbid") to ~ from 2. (d; tr.) ("to order") to ~ on (to ~ a duty on smb.) 3. (H) ("to order") to ~ smb. to obey the law

enjoy v. 1. to ~ enormously, greatly, immensely, very much 2. (G) she ~s swimming 3. (K) they ~ his singing 4. (misc.) to ~ oneself

enjoyable adj. 1. highly, very ~ 2. ~ to + inf. (it is ~ to swim in the ocean)

enjoyment n. 1. to give, provide ~ 2. to derive, get ~ from 3. full, great ~

enlarge v. 1. (D; tr.) ("to make larger") to ~ by (to ~ a photograph by ten percent) 2. (D; tr.) ("to make larger") to ~ into, to (to enlarge an office into a conference room) 3. (d; intr.) to ~ on, upon ("to discuss in detail")

enlargement n. to make an ~ (of a photograph)

enlighten v. (D; tr.) to ~ about, on (can you ~ me on this subject?)

enlightening adj. 1. thoroughly, very ~ 2. ~ to + inf. (it was ~ to read the old newspaper accounts of the incident)

enlist v. 1. (D; intr.) to ~ for (to ~ for three years) 2. (D; intr.) to ~ in (to ~ in the army) 3. (H) we ~ed them to help

enlistment n. 1. to extend one's ~ 2. ~ in (~ in the Peace Corps)

enmeshed adj. (cannot stand alone) ~ in, with (~ in legal details)

enmity n. 1. to stir up ~ 2. to incur smb.'s ~ 3. (a) bitter; longstanding ~ 4. ~ against, towards; among, between

enough adj., determiner, pronoun 1. ~ for (that's ~ for me) 2. ~ to + inf. (it's ~ to know that they are safe; we've had ~ excitement to last a lifetime) 3. ~ of (~ of them) USAGE NOTE: 1. The use of the preposition of is necessary when a pronoun follows. When a noun follows, the use of of the limits the meaning—we have seen enough documentaries; we have seen enough of the documentaries that we discussed earlier. 2. Enough money is more common than money enough.

enquire (BE) see **inquire**

enquiries n. (BE) (to assist in finding telephone numbers) 1. directory ~ (AE has directory assistance or information) 2. international ~ (AE has *international information*)

enquiry (BE) see **inquiry**

enrage *v.* (R) it ~d me (to learn) that he had embezzled company funds

enraged *adj.* 1. ~ at, by, over 2. ~ to + inf. (she was ~ to learn that her friends had left without her) 3. ~ that + clause (she was ~ that her friends had left without her)

enroll, enrol *v.* 1. (D; intr., tr.) to ~ as (she ~ed as a special student) 2. (D; intr., refl., tr.) to ~ for, in (to ~ for a course; to ~ students in a course)

enrollment, enrolment *n.* 1. (a) heavy, large; light, small ~ 2. open ("unrestricted") ~ 3. ~ for, in (the ~ in several courses went up)

en route *adv.* ~ from; to (they are ~ to London)

ensconced *adj.* (cannot stand alone) 1. comfortably; firmly; safely; snugly ~ 2. ~ in (snugly ~ in an easy chair)

ensemble *n.* a brass; string; woodwind ~

enshrined *adj.* ~ in (these rights are ~ in the constitution)

ensnare *v.* (D; tr.) to ~ in (~d in red tape)

ensue *v.* (D; intr.) to ~ from

ensure *v.* (formal) 1. (A; usu. used without *to*) the present contract cannot ~ you a job 2. (K) I cannot ~ his being on time 3. (L) no one can ~ that he'll come

entail *v.* 1. (G) it ~s moving to another city 2. (K) this job would ~ your learning how to use a computer

entangle *v.* (D; tr.) to ~ in, with

entanglement *n.* 1. a barbed-wire ~ 2. ~ in, with

enter *v.* 1. (D; intr.) ("to come in") to ~ by (to ~ by the rear door) 2. (D; intr., tr.) ("to enroll") to ~ for (BE), in (to ~ smb. for/in a contest; they ~ed their horse for/in the race; I've ~ed for/in the mile run) 3. (d; intr.) to ~ into ("to participate in") (to ~ into negotiations) 4. (D; tr.) ("to put into") to ~ into (to ~ data into a computer) 5. (D; intr.) to ~ on, upon ("to begin") (to ~ on a new career)

enterprise *n.* ["ownership"] 1. free; private ~ ["undertaking"] 2. to embark on, start an ~ 3. a joint ~ 4. a commercial ~ ["initiative"] 5. of ~ (a person of great ~)

entertain *v.* (D; tr.) to ~ with (to ~ children with funny stories)

entertaining I *adj.* ~ to + inf. (it's ~ to watch people in a restaurant)

entertaining II *n.* ["acting as a host"] to do ~ (they do very little ~)

entertainment *n.* 1. to provide ~ 2. adult; live; private; public ~ 3. ~ to + inf. (it was pure ~ to watch them dance) 4. to smb.'s ~ (to everyone's ~, she showed up in a clown's costume) 5. ~ for

enthralling *adj.* ~ to + inf. (it was ~ to watch the ballet)

enthuse *v.* (colloq.) (D; intr.) to ~ about, over

enthusiasm *n.* 1. to arouse, drum up, kindle, stir up, whip up ~ 2. to demonstrate, display, show; radiate ~ 3. to blunt, dampen smb.'s ~ 4. to feel ~ 5. to lose ~ 6. boundless, contagious, great, infectious, unbounded, unbridled, unflagging, wild ~ 7. ~ grows, mounts, rises 8. ~ wanes 9. ~ for 10. the ~ to + inf. (they had enough ~ to continue the campaign in spite of the difficulties)

enthusiastic *adj.* 1. very, wildly; less than ~ 2. ~ about, at, over (she was less than ~ about my plan)

entice *v.* 1. (D; tr.) to ~ into (to ~ smb. into a life of crime) 2. (D; tr.) to ~ with (they ~d the children with candy) 3. (H) the display ~d them to enter the shop

entice away *v.* (D; tr.) we could not ~ the children away from the cakes

entirety *n.* in its ~

entitle *v.* 1. (d; tr.) to ~ to (your years of service ~ you to a pension) 2. (H) to ~ smb. to do smt. 3. (N) ("to name") they ~d the book "Our Tradition"

entitled *adj.* (cannot stand alone) ["having the right"] 1. ~ to (she is fully ~ to benefits) 2. ~ to + inf. (we are ~ to attend all concerts free) ["named"] 3. ~ + noun (the book is ~ "Our Tradition")

entrance *n.* 1. to gain ~ (to) 2. to make an/one's ~ 3. a back, rear; front, main; service; side ~ 4. a dramatic, grand, triumphal ~ (to make a grand ~) 5. an ~ from; into, to (the ~ to this building) 6. at an ~ (wait for me at the ~) 7. (misc.) we were refused ~; she always makes a late ~; the police sealed off the ~ to the building

entranced *adj.* ~ at, by, over, with

entrap *v.* (D; tr.) to ~ in, into

entreat *v.* (formal) (H) to ~ smb. to do smt.

entree *n.* ["access"] to gain; have ~ into, to

entrenched *adj.* 1. deeply, firmly ~ 2. ~ in

entrepreneur *n.* an independent; private ~

entrust *v.* 1. (B) he ~ed his money to me 2. (d; tr.) to ~ with (she ~ed me with her watch)

entrusted *adj.* (cannot stand alone) ~ with

entry *n.* ["headword and definition"] (in a dictionary) 1. to give, include an ~ 2. a main; run-on ~; sub-entry 3. at, in, under an ~ ["act of entering"] 4. to make an ~ (to make a triumphal ~; to make an ~ in a diary) 5. to gain ~ to (they gained ~ to his apartment) 6. to allow, grant; refuse ~ (they refused us ~ into the country) 7. forced, illegal ~ (of a burglar) 8. an ~ into (she announced her ~ into the presidential race; our ~ into the war) ["bookkeeping procedure"] 9. to make an ~ for 10. double; single ~ ["participation in a contest"] 11. to submit an ~ (to) 12. a winning ~

entry blank, entry form *n.* 1. to fill in, fill out (esp. AE) an ~ 2. to send in, submit an ~ for

entwine *v.* (D; refl., tr.) to ~ around (the vines ~d themselves around the tree)

enumerate *v.* (B) to ~ the facts to smb.

enunciate *v.* 1. to ~ clearly 2. (B) she ~d her theory to her colleagues

envelop *v.* (D; intr.) to ~ in

envelope *n.* 1. to address; seal an ~ 2. a pay ~ (AE; BE has *pay packet*) 3. a self-addressed; stamped; window ~

USAGE NOTE: AE has *stamped self-addressed envelope*; BE has *stamped addressed envelope (SAE)*.

envious *adj.* ~ of

environment *n.* 1. to clean up the ~ 2. to preserve, protect the ~ 3. to pollute the ~ 4. a clean, healthy ~ 5. a polluted, unhealthy ~ 6. a friendly, pleasant ~ 7. a hostile, unfriendly ~ 8. a social; working ~

envisage *v.* 1. (d; tr.) to ~ as (we ~ this dictionary as a handbook for serious students) 2. (G) she had not ~d marrying him 3. (J) we could not ~ them cooperating 4. (K) I hadn't ~d his staying away so long 5. (L) we had not ~d that the situation would get so bad 6. (Q) I could not ~ how it could have happened

envision *v.* (AE) see **envisage**

envoy *n.* 1. to dispatch, send an ~ 2. a peace; personal; special ~ 3. an ~ to (our ~ to Paris)

envy I *n.* 1. to arouse, stir up ~ (of) 2. to feel ~ 3. to show ~ 4. out of ~ (she did it out of ~) 5. ~ at, of, towards 6. (misc.) an object of ~; consumed/green with ~

envy II *v.* (O) they ~ us our new house

epic *n.* 1. a folk; historical; Hollywood ~ 2. an ~ about

epicenter, epicentre *n.* at the ~

epidemic *n.* 1. to touch off, trigger an ~ 2. to contain, control an ~ 3. an ~ breaks out, strikes; rages; spreads 4. a cholera; flu; measles; typhoid; typhus ~

epigram *n.* to compose; deliver an ~

epilepsy *n.* to have ~

epilogue *n.* an ~ to

episode *n.* a dramatic; funny, humorous; thrilling; touching; tragic ~

epithet *n.* 1. to hurl ~s at 2. a harsh, offensive, vicious, vile ~

epoch *n.* 1. to mark; usher in an ~ 2. a glacial; revolutionary ~

equal I *adj.* 1. ~ in (~ in price) 2. ~ to, with (one kilometer is ~ to five eighths of a mile; ~ to the occasion)

equal II *n.* an ~ in (to have no ~ in political cunning)

equal III *v.* 1. (D; tr.) to ~ as (no one could ~ her as a dancer) 2. (D; tr.) to ~ in

equality *n.* 1. to achieve, attain ~ 2. racial; religious; sexual; social; total ~ 3. ~ among, between; with (~ between the sexes) 4. ~ in (~ in pay) 5. ~ of (~ of opportunity)

equanimity *n.* 1. to maintain; regain one's ~ 2. to disturb, upset smb.'s ~ 3. with ~ (to react with ~ to upsetting news)

equate *v.* (D; tr.) to ~ to, with (one should not ~ wealth with happiness)

equation *n.* 1. to formulate, state an ~ 2. to reduce; solve, work (esp. AE) an ~ 3. a differential; first-degree; identical; integral; linear; quadratic; simple ~; an ~ in one unknown; an ~ in two unknowns 4. (misc.) the human ~

equator *n.* above; at, on; below the ~

equidistant *adj.* ~ between; from

equilibrium *n.* 1. to establish; maintain; restore smb.'s ~ 2. to lose one's ~ 3. to disrupt, disturb, upset the ~ 4. in (a state of) ~

equinox *n.* the autumn, autumnal; spring, vernal ~

equip *v.* 1. (d; tr.) to ~ for; with 2. (H) her training ~ped her to cope with the new job

equipment *n.* 1. to install, set up; operate; test ~ 2. to maintain; repair ~ 3. audiovisual; camping; electronic; firefighting; military; office; sports ~ 4. heavy; light ~ 5. (the) ~ for (~ for road construction) 6. the ~ to + inf. (do you have enough ~ to do the job?)

equipped *adj.* 1. badly, ill; well ~ 2. ~ for; with 3. ~ to + inf. (our hospital is ~ to handle emergency cases)

equity *n.* ["supplementary system of justice"] in ~ (a suit in ~)

equivalent I *adj.* ~ in; to

equivalent II *n.* an approximate; exact ~

equivocal *adj.* ~ about

era *n.* 1. to introduce, usher in an ~ 2. the Christian, Common; Roman ~ 3. a bygone ~; the horse-and-buggy ~ 4. in an ~ (in the Roman ~) 5. (misc.) the beginning of a new ~; the end of an ~ (her farewell performance marked the end of an ~)

USAGE NOTE: The abbreviation CE (*Common Era*) is used by some non-Christians instead of AD. Thus, 1920 CE equals 1920 AD, and 100 BCE equals 100 BC.

erase *v.* (D; tr.) to ~ from

eraser *n.* a blackboard; ink ~

USAGE NOTE: In BE an *eraser* is usu. called a *rubber*; a *blackboard eraser* may be called a *duster*.

erect *adj.* to hold oneself ~; to stand ~

erosion *n.* 1. gradual, slow; severe ~ 2. beach; glacial; soil; wind ~

errand *n.* 1. to do, run an ~; to go on an ~ 2. personal ~s 3. a fool's ("useless") ~ 4. an ~ for (could you run an ~ for me?) 5. (misc.) an ~ of mercy

erroneous *adj.* ~ to + inf. (it's ~ to assume that the press always prints the truth)

error *n.* 1. to commit, make an ~ 2. to compound an ~ 3. to correct, rectify an ~ 4. to admit to (making) an ~ 5. a cardinal, costly, egregious, flagrant, glaring, grievous, gross, major, serious; fatal ~ 6. a minor, slight ~ 7. a clerical; grammatical; printer's, typographical; programming; textual; typing ~ 8. a human; tactical ~ 9. (statistics) (a) random ~ 10. an ~ in (an ~ in judgment) 11. an ~ to + inf. (it was an ~ to invite them) 12. by, through ~ (her name was omitted by ~) 13. in ~ (she was in ~) 14. (misc.) a margin of ~; by trial and ~

erudition *n.* 1. to display; flaunt one's ~ 2. great ~

erupt *v.* (D; intr.) to ~ in, into (the demonstrations ~ed into violence)

eruption *n.* 1. a volcanic ~ 2. a skin ~

escalate *v.* (D; intr.) to ~ into (the local war ~d into a major conflict)

escalator *n.* 1. to take an ~ 2. a down; up ~

escapade *n.* a childish, schoolboy; wild ~

escape I *n.* ["act of escaping"] 1. to organize, plan, plot an ~ 2. to make an ~; to make good one's ~ 3. to foil, thwart an ~ 4. a daring, dramatic; hairbreadth, narrow ~ 5. an ~ from (an ~ from prison) 6. (misc.) they had a narrow ~ ["misc."] 7. a fire ~ ("an emergency staircase")

escape II *v.* 1. (D; intr.) to ~ from; to (to ~ from the police) 2. (G) a famous actor cannot ~ being recognized 3. (s) to ~ unhurt
USAGE NOTE: *To escape from the police* means "to escape from police custody". *To escape the police* means "to elude the police without being caught".

escort I *n.* 1. to provide an ~ for 2. an armed; fighter; motorcycle; police ~ 3. an ~ for 4. under ~

escort II *v.* 1. (D; tr.) to ~ from; to 2. (P; tr.) the president was ~ed through the city; they were ~ed out of the building

escrow *n.* 1. to place, put in ~ 2. to hold, keep in ~

escutcheon *n.* 1. an armorial ~ 2. (misc.) (humorous) a blot on smb.'s ~

espionage *n.* 1. to conduct, engage in ~ 2. industrial; military ~

esprit de corps *n.* 1. to develop (an) ~ 2. (a) strong ~

essay *n.* 1. to write an ~ about, on 2. a critical; literary ~ (see the Usage Note for **dissertation**)

essence *n.* 1. the very ~ of smt. 2. in ~ 3. of the ~ (time is of the ~)

essential *adj.* 1. ~ for; to 2. ~ to + inf. (it is ~ to work hard) 3. ~ that + clause; subj. (it is ~ that all students be/should be present)

essentials *n.* the bare, basic ~

establish *v.* 1. (d; refl., tr.) to ~ as (the press ~ed him as the leading contender) 2. (L) the police ~ed that she was innocent 3. (Q) the police ~ed how the crime was committed

establishment *n.* 1. an educational; financial; political ~ 2. (misc.) to fight the Establishment ("to struggle against the established order")

estate *n.* 1. to administer, manage an ~ 2. a country

~ 3. (BE) a housing ~ 4. (BE) an industrial ~ 5. (misc.) to come into an ~ ("to inherit smt.")

esteem I *n.* 1. to hold smb. in high ~ 2. to fall; rise in smb.'s ~ 3. high ~

esteem II *v.* to ~ greatly, highly

estimate I *n.* 1. to give, make; submit an ~ (the contractors had to submit ~s) 2. (colloq.) (esp. AE) a ballpark ("approximate") ~ 3. an approximate, rough; conservative; long-range; preliminary; realistic; short-range; written ~ 4. an ~ that + clause (it's my ~ that the interest rate will drop by two percent) 5. at an ~ (at a rough ~) 6. by smb.'s ~ (by my ~)

estimate II *v.* 1. (d; tr.) to ~ at (we ~d the cost at five hundred dollars) 2. (BE) (d; intr.) to ~ for (to ~ for the repairs) 3. (L) I ~ that we'll arrive at about two o'clock 4. (M) we ~ the cost to be five thousand dollars 5. (Q) we could not ~ how much damage had been caused

estimation *n.* in smb.'s ~ (in my ~ the situation is not critical)

estranged *adj.* ~ from (he was ~ from his wife)

estrangement *n.* (an) ~ between; from

etch *v.* 1. to ~ sharply 2. (D; tr.) to ~ into (sharply ~ed into my memory)

etched *adj.* ~ in (~ in my memory)

ether *n.* under ~

ethic *n.* the work ~

ethical *adj.* ~ to + inf. (it is not ~ to plagiarize)

ethics *n.* 1. business; medical; professional ~ 2. a code of ~

etiquette *n.* 1. to prescribe ~ 2. courtroom; diplomatic; legal; medical; military; professional; social ~ 3. the rules of ~ 4. (misc.) a breach of ~

etymology *n.* 1. to ascertain, determine, trace an ~ 2. (a) folk ~ (the professor explained the origin of the word as a/by folk ~)

Eucharist *n.* to celebrate; give; receive, take the ~

eulogy *n.* 1. to deliver a ~ (for) 2. a touching ~

euphemism *n.* a ~ for

euphoria *n.* a feeling; state of ~

evacuate *v.* (D; tr.) to ~ from; to (the civilians were ~d from the city to the country)

evacuation *n.* 1. to carry out an ~ 2. a mass ~ 3. an ~ from; to

evade *v.* (G) they ~ paying taxes by subterfuge

evaluate *v.* (D; tr.) to ~ as (he was ~d as unfit for military service)

evaluation *n.* 1. to make an ~ 2. a critical; fair, objective; realistic ~

evasion *n.* draft (AE); tax ~

eve *n.* 1. Christmas Eve; New Year's Eve (on New Year's Eve) 2. on the ~ (on the ~ of the revolution)
USAGE NOTE: In AE *Christmas Eve* means the "night before Christmas"; in BE it can also mean "the entire day before Christmas".

even *adj.* 1. to get ~ with smb. ("to take revenge on

smb.") 2. (misc.) to break ~ (when betting)

evening *n.* 1. in the ~; (AE) ~s (he works in the ~; or AE: he works ~s) 2. on a certain ~ (on that evening)

event *n.* 1. an auspicious; major; outstanding; significant ~ 2. a dramatic; earth-shaking, earth-shattering; sensational; spectacular; world-shaking ~ 3. a disastrous; tragic ~ 4. a historical; literary ~ 5. a gala; social; solemn ~ 6. a sporting ~ 7. a media ~ (to stage a media ~) 8. a blessed ~ ("a birth") (old-fashioned) 9. the main ~ 10. current ~s 11. (sports) track-and-field ~s 12. an ~ occurs, takes place 13. in the ~ that + clause (in the ~ that they come/should come) 14. in an ~ (in the ~ of fire; in any ~) 15. (misc.) the media sometimes manipulate ~s; a chain of ~s; in the normal course of ~s; in either ~; in all ~s

ever *adv.* 1. ~ so much 2. hardly ~; if ~; rarely/seldom if ~

evict *v.* (D; tr.) to ~ from

eviction *n.* 1. to face ~ 2. (an) ~ from

evidence *n.* 1. to furnish, give, introduce, produce, provide ~ 2. to collect, gather ~ 3. to dig up, find, turn up, unearth ~ 4. to piece together ~ 5. to fabricate, falsify, trump up ~ 6. to plant ~ (on smb.) 7. to tamper with ~ 8. to conceal; destroy; suppress; withhold ~ 9. to corroborate (the) ~ 10. to turn King's (BE), Queen's (BE), state's (AE) ~ 11. ample, strong, substantial; clear, cogent, compelling, convincing; conclusive; concrete, hard; incontestable, indisputable, irrefutable, undeniable, unquestionable; reliable, trustworthy; satisfactory ~ 12. direct; documentary; material; prima facie; statistical ~ 13. admissible; anecdotal; circumstantial; forensic; hearsay; inadmissible; scientific ~ 14. damaging; inconclusive; telltale ~ 15. (the) ~ indicates, points to, suggests 16. a body of ~ 17. a piece; scrap, shred of ~ 18. ~ against; for, in favor of 19. ~ that + clause (the lawyer produced conclusive ~ that the accused could not have been at the scene of the crime) 20. in ~ (they were very much in ~) 21. (misc.) the bulk of the ~

evident *adj.* 1. ~ to 2. ~ that + clause (it is ~ that she will be elected)

evil I *adj.* ~ to + inf. (it is ~ to kill)

evil II *n.* 1. to do ~ 2. to root out ~ 3. an unmitigated ~ 4. a necessary ~ 5. (misc.) the lesser of two ~s; ~ incarnate

evocative *adj.* (formal) (cannot stand alone) ~ of

evolution *n.* 1. a gradual; historical ~ 2. an ~ from; into, to

evolve *v.* (d; intr.) to ~ from, out of; into

exact I *adj.* ~ in; with

exact II *v.* (formal) (D; tr.) to ~ from (to ~ tribute from the population)

exaggerate *v.* to ~ greatly, grossly

exaggerated *adj.* greatly, grossly, highly ~

exaggeration *n.* 1. a gross ~ 2. ~ to + inf. (it is an ~ to claim that inflation has been controlled)

exam *n.* ["test"] 1. see **examination** 2. (colloq.) (AE) to ace an ~

examination *n.* ["test"] ["set of questions"] 1. to administer, conduct, give an ~ 2. to draw up, make up, prepare, set (BE) an ~ 3. to invigilate (BE), monitor, proctor (AE), supervise an ~ 4. to do (BE), sit (BE), take an ~ 5. to fail, flunk (AE; colloq.); pass an ~ 6. a difficult, stiff; easy ~ 7. a bar; civil-service; state-board (AE) ~ 8. a comprehensive; doctoral; master's ~ 9. an end-of-term (BE); final; makeup ~ 10. an essay; multiple-choice; open-book; true-false ~ 11. an oral; written ~ 12. a competitive; entrance; external (BE); placement; qualifying ~ 13. an ~ in, on (an ~ in physics; an ~ on irregular verbs) ["inspection"] ["scrutiny"] 14. to do, make an ~ 15. to have, undergo a (physical) ~ 16. a careful, close, complete, in-depth, thorough; cursory, perfunctory, superficial ~ 17. a physical ~ (the doctor did a thorough physical ~ of/on the patient) 18. on ~ (on close ~ of the facts, she discovered that...) 19. under ~

examination paper *n.* 1. to mark an ~ 2. to hand in an ~

examine *v.* 1. to ~ carefully, closely, thoroughly 2. (D; tr.) to ~ for (to ~ a car for defects) 3. (D; tr.) to ~ in, on (to ~ students in physics; I was ~d on irregular verbs)

examiner *n.* 1. a bank; medical ~ 2. an external; internal ~

example *n.* 1. to cite, give, provide an ~ 2. to set an ~ (for) 3. to make an ~ of 4. to follow smb.'s ~ 5. a classic; concrete; extreme; glaring, striking; illustrative; impressive; inspiring; perfect; prime, shining; textbook; typical ~ 6. an ~ for, to 7. (misc.) to lead by personal ~

exasperate *v.* (R) it ~s me that they never keep their promises

exasperated *adj.* 1. ~ about, at, by, over, with 2. ~ to + inf. (she was ~ to find nobody at home) 3. ~ that + clause (she was ~ that she found nobody at home)

exasperating *adj.* 1. ~ to 2. ~ to + inf. (it is ~ to teach in a school like that one) 3. ~ that + clause (it's ~ that we cannot find any spare parts)

exasperation *n.* 1. ~ at (~ at bureaucrats) 2. in ~ (in her ~, she slammed the door)

ex cathedra *adv.* to speak ~

excavations *n.* to carry out archeological ~

exceed *v.* (D; tr.) to ~ in (to ~ smb. in productivity)

excel *v.* (D; intr.) to ~ at, in (to ~ at sports)

excellence *n.* ~ at, in

exception *n.* ["exclusion"] 1. to make an ~ for 2. to grant an ~ 3. an ~ to (an ~ to the rule) 4. with an ~ (everything is fine with the ~ of one item; with few

~s) 5. (misc.) without ~ ["objection"] 6. to take ~ to (she took strong ~ to what he said)

excerpt I *n.* 1. to quote an ~ 2. an ~ from

excerpt II *v.* (D; tr.) to ~ from (to ~ a passage from a work)

excess *n.* 1. in ~ of 2. to ~ (to drink to ~)

exchange I *n.* ["act of exchanging"] 1. to agree to; make an ~ 2. a cultural ~ 3. a hostage; prisoner-of-war ~ 4. in ~ (for) 5. an ~ between ["place where items are bought or sold"] 6. a commodity; corn (BE), grain (AE); farmers'; post (AE); stock ~ ["central office"] 7. an employment (BE), labour (BE); telephone ~ ["argument"] 8. to have an ~ (about) 9. an angry, heated ~ (of words) (they had an angry ~ about the new proposal) ["currency"] 10. foreign ~

USAGE NOTE: The BE terms *employment exchange* and *labour exchange* have been largely superseded by *employment office* and *Job Centre.*

exchange II *v.* 1. (D; tr.) to ~ for (I ~d the defective tire for a good one) 2. (D; tr.) to ~ with (to ~ places with smb.)

exchange rate *n.* 1. to set an ~ 2. to apply an ~ 3. a fixed; floating ~

excited *adj.* 1. ~ about, at, over (to get ~ about smt.) 2. ~ to + inf. (she was ~ to learn the news) 3. ~ that + clause (we were ~ that they were coming)

excitement *n.* 1. to arouse, cause, create, stir up ~ 2. to feel ~ 3. to buzz, throb with ~ 4. considerable, great, intense; mounting ~ 5. ~ builds (to a climax); dies down; mounts, rises 6. ~ about, at, over 7. in ~ 8. (misc.) a tingle, tremor of ~

exciting *adj.* ~ 1. to + inf. (it's ~ to read adventure stories) 2. ~ that + clause (it was ~ that they all came to my party)

exclaim *v.* (formal) 1. (BE) (D; intr.) to ~ at (she ~ed at his appearance in shorts) 2. (L) he ~ed that he was innocent

exclude *v.* (D; tr.) to ~ from

exclusion *n.* 1. ~ from 2. to the ~ of (they watched her to the ~ of everyone else)

exclusive *adj.* 1. mutually ~ 2. ~ of

excommunication *n.* to decree, order, pronounce (an) ~

exculpate *v.* (formal) (D; tr.) to ~ from

excursion *n.* 1. to go on an ~ 2. an ~ to

excursus *n.* an ~ into

excuse I *n.* 1. to find; have; make; make up an ~ for 2. to accept an ~ 3. to reject an ~ 4. an acceptable, good, satisfactory, valid; convincing; perfect; plausible ~ 5. a feeble, flimsy, lame, poor, unacceptable, unsatisfactory, weak ~ 6. a convenient; glib; ready-made ~ 7. an ~ for (an ~ for being late) 8. an ~ to + inf. (it was just an ~ to leave early) 9. an ~ that + clause (they accepted the ~ that I had been ill) 10. (misc.) a poor ~ for smt.; to make one's ~s ("to explain one's absence")

excuse II *v.* 1. (D; tr.) to ~ as (he was ~d as physically unfit for duty) 2. (D; tr.) to ~ for (to ~ smb. for coming late) 3. (D; tr.) to ~ from (he was ~d from drill; BE also has: he was ~d drill) 4. (G) we will never ~ taking innocent hostages 5. (K) please ~ my arriving late

ex-directory *adj.* (BE) to go ~ ("to have one's number removed from the telephone book")

execute *v.* 1. (D; tr.) to ~ as (he was ~d as a deserter) 2. (D; tr.) to ~ for (she was ~d for murder)

execution *n.* 1. to carry out an ~ 2. a mass; public; summary ~ 3. ~ by (~ by firing squad)

executive *n.* a business; chief; corporate; senior ~

exempt I *adj.* ~ from

exempt II *v.* (D; tr.) to ~ from

exemption *n.* 1. to claim an ~ 2. to grant an ~ 3. a draft (AE); tax ~ 4. an ~ for (he received an ~ for his elderly parents) 5. (an) ~ from (an ~ from the draft)

exercise I *n.* ["bodily exertion"] 1. to engage in, go in for ~; to take (BE) ~ 2. to get ~ (she gets plenty of ~ at her job) 3. to do ~s 4. (a) hard, strenuous, vigorous; regular ~ 5. (an) aerobic; body-building; flexibility; isometric; relaxation; remedial; setting-up; warming-up ~ 6. physical ~ 7. a form of ~ (brisk walking is an excellent form of aerobic ~) ["practice drill"] 8. oral; written ~s (as in a language textbook) ["misc."] 9. an ~ in futility ("an unsuccessful attempt")

exercise II *v.* to ~ hard, strenuously, vigorously; regularly

exercised *adj.* ["upset"] ~ about, over

exercises *n.* ["ceremony"] (esp. AE) 1. to hold ~ 2. commencement, graduation ~

exertion *n.* physical; strenuous ~

exhausted *adj.* completely, totally ~

exhaustion *n.* 1. heat; nervous; total ~ 2. a state of ~

exhibit I *n.* ["exhibition"] (AE) 1. to have, hold, mount, organize, put on an ~ 2. to close; open an ~ 3. an art; photo; traveling ~ 4. on ~ ["piece of evidence shown in court"] (legal) 5. ~ A

exhibit II *v.* (B) she ~ed her paintings to the public

exhibition *n.* 1. to have, hold, mount, organize, put on an ~ 2. to close; open an ~ 3. an art; international; photo; trade; traveling ~ 4. (esp. BE) on ~ 5. (misc.) to make an ~ of oneself (by behaving badly)

exhilarating *adj.* ~ to + inf. (it's ~ to climb mountains)

exhort *v.* 1. (D; tr.) to ~ to (to ~ smb. to action) 2. (H) to ~ students to work harder

exile I *n.* ["forced absence"] 1. to send smb. into ~ 2. to go into ~ 3. ~ from (her ~ from her homeland lasted many years) 4. from ~ (they have returned from ~) 5. in ~ (to live in ~) ["person forced to leave"] 6. a political ~

exile II *v.* (D; tr.) to ~ from; to

exist *v.* (D; intr.) to ~ on (to ~ on bread and water)

existence *n.* 1. to lead a certain ~ (to lead a drab ~) 2. to eke out a (miserable) ~ 3. a drab, miserable; hand-to-mouth, precarious ~

exit I *n.* 1. to make an/one's (she made a hasty ~) 2. (in a plane) an emergency; tail; window; wing ~ 3. an emergency; fire ~ 4. an ~ from; to 5. at an ~ (she waited for me at the ~) 6. (misc.) the police sealed off the ~; no ~!

USAGE NOTE: *Exit* is CE; however, BE often uses the notice *Way Out.*

exit II *v.* (D; intr.) to ~ from; to (to ~ to the system on a computer)

exodus *n.* 1. a mass ~ (there is a mass ~ from Paris every August) 2. an ~ from; to

exonerate *v.* (D; tr.) to ~ from

exorcise *v.* (D; tr.) to ~ from

expand *v.* 1. (D; tr.) ("to make larger") to ~ by (they ~ed the dictionary by twenty percent) 2. (D; intr., tr.) ("to become larger") ("to make larger") to ~ into (to ~ an article into a book) 3. (d; intr.) to ~ on, upon ("to explain in detail") (to ~ on a topic)

expanse *n.* a broad, vast, wide; open ~

expatiate *v.* (formal) (d; intr.) to ~ on, upon ("to discuss in detail")

expatriate *v.* (formal) (D; tr.) to ~ from; to

expect *v.* 1. (D; tr.) to ~ from, of (we ~ed more from him) 2. (E) she ~s to leave tomorrow 3. (H) we ~ed them to wait 4. (L) I ~ that the weather will be nice 5. (misc.) I ~ not; I ~ so

expectancy *n.* life ~

expectation *n.* 1. in ~ of 2. an ~ that + clause (it was our ~ that they would come early)

expectations *n.* 1. to come up to, live up to, meet ~ 2. to exceed, surpass ~ 3. to fall short of ~ 4. great, high ~ 5. ~ for (they had great ~ for their daughter) 6. beyond ~ (to succeed beyond all ~) 7. (misc.) contrary to ~ (contrary to all ~s, she did not come)

expedient *adj.* ~ to + inf. (sometimes it is ~ to make concessions)

expedition *n.* 1. to launch, mount, organize; lead; send an ~ 2. to go on an ~ 3. an archeological; scientific ~ 4. a hunting; mountain-climbing ~ 5. a military; punitive ~ 6. an ~ into, to (to lead an ~ to the Amazon) 7. (misc.) a fishing ~ ("an attempt to obtain information")

expel *v.* (D; tr.) to ~ from (to ~ a child from school)

expend *v.* (D; tr.) to ~ for, on (to ~ considerable funds on a new skating rink)

expenditure *n.* 1. to curb, curtail, cut down (on), reduce ~s 2. a capital ~ 3. public ~s 4. an ~ for, on

expense *n.* 1. to incur, run up an ~ 2. to go to great ~; to spare no ~; to put smb. to great ~ 3. to curb, curtail, cut down (on), reduce ~s 4. to spare no ~ 5. to cover, defray ~s 6. to reimburse ~s 7. to share ~s 8. (a) business; entertainment; funeral; household; incidental; legal; living; operating; out-of-pocket; overhead; personal; tax-deductible; traveling ~(s) 9. at smb.'s ~ (at my ~; at government ~; at great ~, they sent their children to college)

expense account *n.* 1. to be on, have an ~ 2. to pad an ~

expensive *adj.* ~ to + inf. (it's more ~ to live in the city than in the country)

experience *n.* ["practice"] ["participation"] 1. to acquire, gain, gather, get ~ (from) 2. to have ~ (in) 3. broad, extensive, wide; direct, firsthand; hands-on; practical; previous; relevant ~ 4. an educational, learning ~ 5. ~ to + inf. (they don't have enough ~ to do the job) 6. by, from ~ (to know from previous ~) ["adventure"] ["event"] 7. to have; share an ~ (I had quite an ~) 8. a bitter, painful, terrible, traumatic, unpleasant ~ 9. a frightening, hair-raising, harrowing, terrifying, unnerving ~ 10. an enlightening, ennobling, rewarding; interesting; memorable, unforgettable; pleasant ~ 11. a common ~

experienced *adj.* ~ at, in

experiment I *n.* 1. to carry out, conduct, do, perform, run; replicate an ~ (on) 2. a control; controlled ~ 3. a chemistry; laboratory; physics ~ 4. an ~ fails; succeeds; works 5. an ~ in (an ~ in communal living)

experiment II *v.* (D; intr.) to ~ on, upon, with

expert I *adj.* ~ at, in

expert II *n.* 1. to call in, consult an ~ 2. an acknowledged, recognized ~ 3. a demolition; efficiency; foreign-policy; legal; self-styled; technical ~ 4. an ~ at, in, on (an ~ at troubleshooting; an ~ in computer science)

expertise *n.* 1. to display ~ 2. technical ~ 3. ~ in 4. the ~ to + inf. (does she have the ~ to do the job?)

expiration *n.* at, on the ~ (what will she do at the ~ of her term in office?)

explain *v.* 1. to ~ briefly; clearly; fully; satisfactorily 2. (B) she ~ed the problem to me 3. (L; to) he ~ed (to us) that the examination would take place later 4. (Q; to) he ~ed (to us) why he was late

explanation *n.* 1. to give, offer, provide an ~ 2. to accept an ~ 3. to demand an ~ 4. to owe smb. an ~ 5. a brief, concise, simple, succinct; clear, lucid; convincing; rational; satisfactory; unsatisfactory ~ 6. an ~ for; of 7. an ~ that + clause (they accepted her ~ that she had been unavoidably detained)

expletive *n.* ~ deleted

explicit *adj.* 1. sexually ~ 2. ~ about

explode *v.* (D; intr.) to ~ in, with (to ~ with rage)

exploit I *n.* 1. to perform an ~ 2. a daring; fantastic; heroic ~

exploit II *v.* to ~ ruthlessly

exploitation *n.* 1. commercial ~ 2. ruthless ~

exploration *n.* space; underwater ~

explore *v.* to ~ carefully, gingerly (they had to ~ this possibility very gingerly)

explorer *n.* a brave; intrepid ~

explosion *n.* 1. to set off, touch off an ~ 2. a deafening, loud; powerful; tremendous ~ 3. a nuclear ~ 4. a population ~ 5. an ~ ripped through the laboratory

explosive *n.* 1. to set off an ~ 2. to plant an ~ 3. to sniff out ~s 4. (a) high; plastic ~

exponent *n.* ["champion"] a leading ~ (a leading ~ of reform)

export I *n.* 1. a chief, leading, major ~ 2. an ~ from, to

export II *v.* (D; intr., tr.) to ~ from; to (we ~ to many countries; they ~ tractors from the West Coast to several Asian countries)

expose *v.* 1. (D; tr.) to ~ as (she was ~d as an impostor) 2. (D; refl., tr.) to ~ to (to ~ smb. to danger; ~d to the elements)

exposition *n.* 1. to hold an ~ 2. an international, world ~

expostulate *v.* (formal) (D; intr.) ("to argue") to ~ about, on; with

exposure *n.* ["being exposed"] 1. ~ to (~ to the elements) 2. of ~ (to die of ~) ["time during which film is exposed"] 3. a double; time ~ ["baring one's private parts"] 4. indecent ~ ["location in relation to the sun"] 5. a southern ~ (a house with a southern ~) ["publicity"] 6. wide ~

expound *v.* (formal) 1. (B) she ~ed her theory to her colleagues 2. (d; intr.) to ~ on (to ~ on one's favorite subject)

express I *n.* ["fast train"] 1. see **train I**, 3 ["special postal service"] (BE) 2. by ~ (to send a letter by ~)

express II *v.* 1. to ~ clearly; forcefully 2. (B) he ~ed his sympathy to the bereaved family 3. (BE) (D; tr.) ("to squeeze") (formal) to ~ from, out of (to ~ juice from an orange) 4. (D; refl., tr.) to ~ in (to ~ oneself in good English) 5. (Q) I cannot ~ how grateful I am

expression *n.* ["making known"] ["showing"] 1. to give ~ to (she tried to give ~ to her feelings) 2. to find ~ in (he finds ~ in his painting) ["phrase"] 3. a colloquial; common; elliptical; figurative; fixed; hackneyed, trite; idiomatic; old-fashioned; technical ~ ["look"] 4. an amused; happy; pleasant ~ 5. a blank; bored; deadpan ~ 6. a silly, vacuous ~ 7. a puzzled, quizzical ~ 8. a grim; grave; serious; intense ~ 9. an angry; pained ~ (she had a pained ~ on her face)

expressive *adj.* ~ of

expropriate *v.* (D; tr.) to ~ from (to ~ land from the absentee owners)

expulsion *n.* ~ from

expunge *v.* (D; tr.) to ~ from

expurgate *v.* (D; tr.) to ~ from

extend *v.* 1. (A) ("to convey") they ~ed a warm welcome to us; or: (esp. AE) they ~ed us a warm welcome 2. (d; intr.) ("to reach") to ~ beyond (the forest ~s beyond the border) 3. (d; intr.) ("to reach") to ~ from; to (the border ~s to the river) 4. (D; tr.) ("to prolong") to ~ from; to (we ~ed the fence to the edge of our property) 5. (d; intr.) ("to continue") to ~ into (the cold wave ~ed into March) 6. (d; intr., tr.) ("to spread") to ~ over (their power ~s over the whole country) 7. (P; intr.) ("to stretch") the plateau ~s for many miles

extension *n.* ["increase in time allowed"] 1. to grant an ~ 2. to ask for, request; get, receive an ~ ["branch"] (AE) 3. a university ~ ["misc."] 4. by ~ ("consequently")

extent *n.* 1. the full ~ (the full ~ of the damage) 2. to a certain ~ (to a great ~; they were emaciated to such an ~ that they required special treatment)

exterior *n.* a calm; forbidding, stern ~ (a soft heart under a stern ~)

extermination *n.* complete, total ~

external *adj.* ~ to (formal)

extinguisher *n.* a fire ~

extol, extoll *v.* (D; tr.) to ~ as (they were ~ed as heroes)

extort *v.* (D; tr.) to ~ from (to ~ money from merchants)

extortion *n.* 1. to commit; practice ~ 2. to pay ~

extract I *n.* ["substance extracted"] 1. almond; lemon; vanilla ~ ["excerpt"] 2. an ~ from (an ~ from a book)

extract II *v.* (D; tr.) to ~ from (to ~ information from smb.)

extraction *n.* ["origin"] of a certain ~ (a family of Irish ~)

extradite *v.* (D; tr.) to ~ from; to

extradition *n.* 1. to ask for, request, seek (smb.'s) ~ 2. to grant (smb.'s) ~ 3. to deny (smb.'s) ~ 4. to contest, fight, oppose ~ 5. to waive ~ ("to agree to be extradited")

extraneous *adj.* ~ to

extraordinary *adj.* ~ that (it was ~ that no one reported the incident to the police)

extrapolate *v.* (D; intr., tr.) to ~ from, on the basis of

extravagance *n.* ~ in

extravagant *adj.* ~ in, with (~ in spending their father's money)

extreme *n.* 1. to go to an ~ (to go from one ~ to the other) 2. at an ~ (at the other ~) 3. in the ~ ("extremely") 4. (misc.) to carry to an ~

extremist *n.* a political; religious ~

extremities *n.* ["limbs"] the lower; upper ~

extricate *v.* (D; refl., tr.) to ~ from (she ~d herself from a difficult situation)

extrinsic *adj.* (formal) ~ to

exude *v.* (d; intr.) to ~ from

exult *v.* (D; intr.) to ~ at, in, over

exultation *n.* ~ at, in, over

eye *n.* ["organ of sight"] 1. to blink; close, shut;

open; roll; squint one's ~s 2. to avert; drop, lower; lift, raise one's ~s 3. to rest; strain one's ~s 4. to clap (BE; colloq.), lay, set one's ~s on smt. ("to see smt.") 5. to keep one's ~s open, peeled, skinned (BE) ("to be watchful") 6. the naked ~ (the meteor could be seen with the naked ~) 7. bloodshot; bulging; glassy; sunken ~s 8. bright, clear ~s 9. ~s blaze; blink; shine, sparkle; tear, water; twinkle 10. a pair of ~s 11. in one's ~s (tears were in his ~s; fear could be seen in their ~s) ["vision, sight"] 12. good, strong; weak ~s 13. an eagle ~ ("keen sight") ["area around the eyes"] 14. (also fig.) a black ~ (to give smb. a black ~) ["look, glance"] 15. to cast an ~ on smt.; to run one's ~ over smt.; to fix one's ~ on smt. 16. to take one's ~s off (they could not take their ~s off Hannah) 17. an anxious; critical; sharp, watchful, weather; suspicious ~ 18. a jaundiced ~ ("an envious, hostile look") 19. (of one who flirts) bedroom ("seductive") ~s; a roving, wandering ~ (he has a roving ~) 20. curious, prying; piercing ~s ["attention"] ["interest"] ["observation"] 21. to catch smb.'s ~ 22. to open smb.'s ~s (to the truth) 23. to close, shut one's ~s (to the truth); to turn a blind ~ to smt. ("to let smt. pass as if unnoticed") 24. to have, keep an ~ on smt. ("to keep smt. under observation") 25. to have, keep an ~ out for smt. ("to watch for smt. attentively") 26. the public ~ (to be constantly in the public ~) 27. with an ~ to (with an ~ to public opinion) ["judgment"] ["viewpoint"] 28. a good, keen ~ 29. an ~ for (she has a good ~ for distances) 30. to the trained ~ 31. in smb.'s ~s (in the ~s of the law, she is innocent until proved guilty) ["perception"] ["apprecia-

tion"] 32. to open smb.'s ~s to smt. 33. an ~ for (an ~ for beauty; to have an ~ for a good bargain) ["device that detects"] 34. an electric ~ ["detective"] (colloq.) 35. a private ~ ["prosthesis for an eye"] 36. an artificial, glass ~ ["misc."] 37. an ~ for an ~ ("an equivalent retaliation"); to feast one's ~s on smt. ("to look at smt. with great pleasure"); to give smb. the ~ ("to flirt with smb.") or ("to give smb. a visual signal"); to make ~s at smb. ("to look lovingly at smb."); to see ~ to ~ with ("to agree with"); the mind's ~ ("imagination or memory"); the evil ~ ("a look intended to inflict harm"); his ~ fell on a bargain ("he discovered a bargain"); under the teacher's watchful ~; easy on the ~s ("pretty"); more than meets the ~ ("more than is seen"); to look someone in the ~ ("to look at someone directly"); before one's ~s; without batting an ~ (AE) ("while remaining calm")

eyebrow n. 1. to pluck, tweeze one's ~s 2. bushy, thick ~s 3. (misc.) to lift, raise an ~ ("to express one's surprise")

eyeglasses n. (AE: CE has *glasses*) a pair of ~

eyelash n. 1. to flutter one's ~s ("to flirt") 2. (misc.) without batting an ~ (AE) ("while remaining calm") see **eyelid** 3

eyelid n. 1. drooping ~s 2. the lower; upper ~ 3. (misc.) without batting an ~ (esp. BE) ("while remaining calm") see **eyelash** 2

eye shadow n. to apply, put on ~

eyesight n. failing, poor, weak; keen; perfect ~

eyeteeth n. to cut one's ~ on smt. ("to become knowledgeable while doing smt.")

eyewitness n. an ~ to (there was an ~ to the crime)

F

fable *n.* a ~ about

fabric *n.* ["material"] 1. to weave a ~ 2. a cotton; rayon; silk; synthetic; woolen; wrinkle-free ~ ["structure"] 3. a basic; social ~ (the basic ~ of the country)

fabrication *n.* a complete, outright, total ~; (a) pure ~

face I *n.* ["grimace"] 1. to make, pull (BE) a ~ (at) ["prestige"] 2. to save ~ 3. to lose ~ ["front part of the head"] 4. to press one's ~ (against a window) 5. (fig.) to show one's ~ (he didn't dare show his ~) 6. to powder one's ~ 7. a beautiful, lovely, pretty; handsome; ruddy; ugly ~ 8. an oval; round ~ 9. a familiar; strange ~ 10. (misc.) to come/meet ~ to ~; to bring ~ to ~; to look smb. in the ~; I would never say that to her ~; to laugh in smb.'s ~; ~ down ["expression"] 11. an angry; long; sad; serious ~ 12. a happy; funny ~ (to make a funny ~) 13. a poker, straight ~ (to keep a straight ~) 14. a ~ lights up (her face lit up) ["makeup"] (colloq.) 15. to put one's ~ on ["misc."] 16. in the ~ of serious difficulties ("facing serious difficulties"); on the ~ of it ("judging by appearances"); to disappear from the ~ of the earth; to fly in the ~ of smt. ("to disregard, contradict"); to fall flat on one's ~ (usu. fig.)

face II *v.* 1. to ~ squarely 2. (d; tr.) to ~ with (to ~ smb. with irrefutable evidence) 3. (G) I could not ~ going there alone 4. (P; intr.) to ~ east; to ~ towards the back of the room

face up *v.* (d; intr.) to ~ to (to ~ to reality)

face value *n.* (to take smt.) at ~

facial *n.* 1. to do a ~ 2. to get, have a ~

facilitate *v.* (formal) 1. to ~ greatly 2. (K) their help will ~ our finishing the job on time

facilities *n.* ["installations"] 1. to provide ~ for 2. ample; excellent; modern ~ 3. outmoded; poor; run-down ~ 4. airport; port; public; storage; transportation ~ (our city has excellent port ~) 5. dining, eating; hotel; recreational ~ 6. daycare; educational; medical; public health; research ~ 7. ~ for

facility *n.* ["skill"] 1. a ~ for, in, with (to have a ~ for languages) ["installation"] 2. to operate a ~ 3. (AE) a correctional ~ ("a prison")

facsimile *n.* in ~

fact *n.* ["something that is true"] 1. to ascertain, establish a ~ 2. to check, confirm, verify a ~ 3. to cite, present; collect, gather, get, marshal (the) ~s 4. to classify; evaluate, interpret (the) ~s 5. to face (the) ~s 6. to stick to the ~s 7. to distort, twist; embellish, embroider (the) ~s 8. to ignore a ~ 9. an

accepted, demonstrable, established; cold, dry, hard, incontestable, incontrovertible, indisputable, irrefutable, proven, undeniable, unquestionable ~ 10. a basic, essential, pertinent; historical; little-known; statistical; well-known ~ 11. the bare ~s 12. a ~ that + clause (it's a ~ that some officials are corrupt) ["reality"] 13. to distinguish ~ from fiction 14. in ~ ["misc."] 15. a question of ~; the ~s of life; as a matter of ~

faction *n.* a contending; extremist; opposing; rebel ~; warring ~s

factor I *n.* 1. a contributing; critical, crucial, deciding, determining, essential, important, key, major ~ 2. (math. and fig.) a common ~ 3. (meteorology) a wind-chill ~ 4. a safety ~ 5. a genetic ~ 6. a ~ in

factor II *v.* (d; tr.) to ~ into (they ~ed the effects of taxation into their policy recommendations)

factory *n.* 1. to manage, operate, run a ~ 2. to open a ~ 3. to close, shut down a ~ 4. an automobile (AE); clothing; munitions; shoe; textile ~ 5. at, in a ~ (she works at/in a ~)

faculties *n.* ["capacities"] 1. smb.'s mental ~ 2. her ~ were failing 3. (misc.) in possession of one's ~

faculty *n.* ["division of a university"] (esp. BE; CE has *school*) 1. a ~ of arts and sciences; education; law; medicine; science ["teaching staff"] (esp. AE; BE prefers *staff*) 2. on the ~ (she is on the ~) 3. a college, university; school ~ 4. the standing ("permanent") ~ ["ability"] 5. a ~ for (a ~ for learning languages)

fad *n.* 1. the latest, newest ~ 2. a passing ~

faddism *n.* food ~

fade *v.* 1. (d; intr.) (usu. fig.) to ~ from, out of (to ~ from the picture) 2. (d; intr.) to ~ into (to ~ into obscurity) 3. (misc.) (AE) to ~ in the stretch ("to drop out of contention near the end of a contest")

fail I *n.* without ~

fail II *v.* 1. to ~ completely; dismally, miserably 2. (D; intr.) to ~ in (to ~ in business) 3. (D; tr.) to ~ in, on (to ~ a student in/on an examination) 4. (E) she ~ed to comprehend the seriousness of the situation

failing *n.* a common ~

failure *n.* 1. to experience ~ 2. an abject, complete, dismal, hopeless, ignominious, miserable, outright ~ 3. a box-office; business; crop ~ 4. heart; kidney; respiratory ~ 5. an engine; mechanical; power ~ 6. a ~ to + inf. (the patient's ~ to respond to treatment was discouraging) 7. (misc.) doomed to ~; to end in ~

faint I *adj.* to feel ~ from (she felt ~ from lack of air)

faint II *n.* 1. to fall into a ~ 2. a dead ~ (to fall into a dead ~)

faint III *v.* (D; intr.) to ~ from (to ~ from loss of blood)

fair I *adj.* ["just"] 1. perfectly, scrupulously ~ 2. ~ to, with (he's ~ to his employees) 3. ~ to + inf. (it's ~ to say that she deserved the promotion) 4. ~ that + clause (it's not ~ that our application was rejected) ["of medium quality"] 5. ~ at, in (she's ~ at mathematics) 6. (misc.) ~ to middling ("not too bad")

fair II *n.* an annual; book; county ~; funfair (BE); health; livestock; state (US); trade; world's ~

fair game *n.* ~ for

fairness *n.* 1. ~ in (we expect ~ in their judgment) 2. in ~ to (in ~ to her, we should give her another chance)

faith *n.* ["firm belief, trust"] 1. to have ~ (in); to place, put one's ~ in 2. to lose ~ (in) 3. to shake; test smb.'s ~ (in) 4. (an) abiding, enduring, steadfast; blind; deep, strong, unshakable; implicit; simple ~ 5. on ~ (to accept on ~) ["fidelity to one's promises"] 6. to break; keep ~ with 7. to demonstrate, show good ~ 8. in good ~; in bad ~ (she acted in good ~) ["religion"] 9. to adhere to, practice a ~ 10. to abjure, recant, renounce one's ~ 11. the true ~ (brought up in the true ~) 12. by ~ (she is a Buddhist by ~)

faithful I *adj.* ~ in; to

faithful II *n.* (plural) the party ~

faithfulness *n.* ~ to

fake *v.* (esp. AE) (usu. sports) (d; tr.) to ~ out (to ~ an opposing player out of position)

fall I *n.* ["dropping, coming down"] 1. to have, take a ~ 2. to break a ~ 3. a bad, nasty ~ (she had a bad ~ and broke her ankle) 4. a free ~ (of a parachutist) 5. a sharp, steep; sudden ~ 6. a ~ from (a ~ from a horse; a ~ from grace) 7. a ~ in (a sudden ~ in prices) ["autumn"] (AE) 8. an early; late ~ 9. in (the) ~ (we have a lot of rain in the ~)

fall II *v.* 1. ("to drop") to ~ flat, headlong; short 2. (d; intr.) to ~ behind ("to lag") (to ~ behind the others) 3. (D; intr.) ("to drop") to ~ down (to ~ down the stairs) 4. (d; intr.) to ~ for ("to be tricked") (we fell for their sales pitch) 5. (colloq.) (d; intr.) to ~ for ("to become infatuated with") (he fell for her) 6. (D; intr.) ("to drop") to ~ from (to ~ from a tree; to ~ from grace) 7. (d; intr.) ("to come"); ("to drop") to ~ into (to ~ into disfavor; to ~ into disrepute; to ~ into place; to ~ into a trap) 8. (d; intr.) ("to be divided") to ~ into (to ~ into three categories) 9. (D; intr.) ("to drop") to ~ off (to ~ off a table) 10. (D; intr.) ("to drop") to ~ on (to ~ on one's back; the stress ~s on the last syllable) 11. (d; intr.) ("to come") to ~ on (the holiday fell on a Monday) 12. (d; intr.) ("to come"); to ~ on ("to attack") (the soldiers fell on the refugees and killed them) 13. (d; intr.) ("to drop") to ~ out of (to ~ out of bed; to ~ out of favor) 14. (d; intr.) ("to drop") to ~ over

(she fell over the side of the ship) 15. (D; intr.) ("to drop") to ~ through (to ~ through a hole in the ice) 16. (formal) (d; intr.) ("to devolve") to ~ to (the responsibility fell to us; it fell to me to break the news) 17. (D; intr.) ("to drop") to ~ to (he fell to his knees; the book fell to the floor; her voice fell to a whisper) 18. (D; intr.) ("to be defeated") to ~ to (the city fell to the enemy) 19. (d; intr.) ("to drop") ("to come") to ~ under (to ~ under a train; to ~ under smb.'s influence) 20. (S) to ~ due; to ~ silent; she fell ill; we fell victim to their sales pitch 21. (misc.) to ~ apart; to ~ asleep; to ~ foul of the law; to ~ in love with smb.; to ~ in battle; to ~ on hard times; to ~ to pieces; to ~ into step; to ~ through the cracks ("to be neglected through error or omission")

fallacious *adj.* (formal) ~ to + inf. (it's ~ to assume that they will agree)

fallacy *n.* 1. a ~ to + inf. (it's a ~ to assume that he will help) 2. a ~ that (it's a ~ that all politicians are corrupt)

fall back *v.* 1. (D; intr.) to ~ into (to ~ into an easy chair) 2. (D; intr.) to ~ on, to (the troops fell back to their defensive positions)

fall behind *v.* (D; intr.) to ~ in, with (to ~ with the rent)

fall down *v.* to ~ on the job

fall in *v.* 1. (d; intr.) to ~ with ("to join") (to ~ with the wrong crowd) 2. (d; intr.) to ~ with ("to agree") (she fell in with their suggestion)

falling out *n.* (colloq.) ["quarrel"] to have a ~ with

fall on *v.* (E) it fell on me to break the news

fallout *n.* 1. radioactive ~ 2. ~ from (also fig.)

fall out *v.* 1. (D; intr.) ("to quarrel") to ~ with (to ~ with smb.) 2. (misc.) the platoon fell out on the company street

fallow *adj.* ["uncultivated"] to lie ~ (the field lay ~)

fall short *v.* (D; intr.) to ~ of (they fell short of their goal)

fall to *v.* (G) he fell to brooding

false *adj.* to ring ~

false front *n.* ["deceptive manner"] to put up a ~

falsehood *n.* 1. to tell, utter a ~ 2. an absolute, downright, utter ~

false start *n.* to make a ~

falsetto *n.* to sing ~

falter *v.* (D; intr.) to ~ in (to ~ in one's determination)

fame *n.* 1. to achieve, attain, win ~ 2. to seek ~ 3. international; national; undying ~ 4. (misc.) at the height of one's ~

familiar *adj.* ["known"] 1. ~ to (is this area ~ to you?) 2. (misc.) all too ~ ["acquainted"] 3. thoroughly ~ 4. ~ with (are you ~ with the details?)

familiarity *n.* 1. to demonstrate, display, show ~ (with) 2. thorough ~ 3. ~ with

familiarize *v.* (d; refl., tr.) to ~ with (she had to ~

herself with the facts of the case)

family *n*. ["social unit traditionally consisting of parents and children"] 1. to start a ~ 2. to clothe; feed; raise; support a ~ 3. the close, immediate; extended; nuclear ~ 4. a good ("respected") ~ (she comes from a good ~) 5. a blended; dysfunctional; single-parent; two-income ~ 6. the royal ~ 7. the head of a ~; a member of a ~ 8. in the ~ (poor vision runs in the ~) 9. (misc.) ~ planning ("birth control"); (old-fashioned) in the ~ way ("pregnant") ["group of related languages"] 10. a language ~

family style *adv*. (esp. AE) to serve (a meal) ~

famine *n*. 1. ~ strikes (~ struck several provinces) 2. widespread ~ 3. (misc.) a potato ~

famous *adj*. 1. ~ as (he is ~ as an actor) 2. ~ for (the city is ~ for its museums)

fan I *n*. ["electrical device for cooling"] 1. to turn on; turn off a ~ 2. a ceiling; electric; exhaust (AE), extractor (BE) ~ ["paper or cloth fan"] 3. to wave a ~

fan II *n*. ["admirer"] ["supporter"] 1. an ardent, avid ~ 2. (AE) a ~ roots (for a team)
USAGE NOTE: In CE one can be a *fan* of a certain sport—a football fan. In CE one can also be a fan of a certain team—a Dodger fan, Manchester United fan. In BE, however, one would usu. be called a *supporter* of a team.

fanatic *n*. 1. a dangerous ~ 2. a fitness; religious; sports ~ 3. a ~ to + inf. (he had to be a ~ to do that)

fancy I *n*. 1. to take a ~ to 2. to catch, strike, take (BE), tickle smb.'s ~ 3. a passing ~ 4. a flight of ~

fancy II *v*. 1. (d; tr.) ("to like") to ~ as (I don't ~ him as an actor) 2. (G) ("to like") I don't ~ going there 3. (G) ("to imagine") just ~ winning first prize 4. (L) ("to imagine") she ~cied that she heard footsteps 5. (N) (BE) ("to imagine") when she was young she ~cied herself an Olympic swimmer

fanfare *n*. 1. to sound a ~ 2. with great ~

fangs *n*. an animal bares its ~

fan out *v*. to ~ in all directions

fantasize *v*. (D; intr.) to ~ about

fantastic *adj*. ["very good"] (colloq.) ~ to + inf. (it's ~ to work with them = it's ~ working with them)

fantasy *n*. 1. to act out a ~ 2. to indulge in ~ 3. a childhood; sexual ~ 4. a ~ about 5. (misc.) (to live in) a world of ~/~ world

far *adj., adv*. 1. ~ from (~ from the city; the problem is ~ from being solved) 2. by ~, ~ and away (she is by ~ the better player) 3. (misc.) ~ away; ~ beyond; ~ into (the future); ~ and wide; so ~ so good; to go ~ on one's connections; ~ be it from me to criticize, but..
USAGE NOTE: The phrases *by far* and *far and away* mean "very much"—she is by far/far and away the better player. In nonstandard BE the two

phrases can be blended to produce *by far and away*.

farce *n*. 1. a ~ about 2. a ~ to + inf. (it was a ~ to conduct a trial under such conditions = it was a ~ conducting a trial under such conditions)

fare I *n*. ["payment for transportation"] 1. to charge; pay a ~ 2. a full; half; reduced ~ 3. at a ~ (at a reduced ~) ["food"] 4. simple ~

fare II *v*. (formal) (P; intr.) she ~d well in the big city

farewell *n*. 1. to make one's ~s 2. to bid smb. ~ 3. a fond; sad; tearful ~ 4. a ~ to

farm *n*. 1. to manage, operate, run, work a ~ 2. a chicken, poultry; dairy; sheep; stock; stud; truck (AE) ~ 3. a collective; cooperative; private ~ 4. on a ~ (to work on a ~)

farmer *n*. a dirt (AE); tenant ~

farming *n*. 1. to be engaged in ~ 2. chicken; dairy; poultry; sheep; stock; collective; truck (AE) ~ 3. collective; cooperative ~ 4. subsistence ~

farmland *n*. to cultivate, work ~

farm out *v*. (B) the work was ~ed out to several associates

farsighted *adj*. ~ to + inf. (it was ~ of her to buy up this property)

farsightedness *n*. the ~ to + inf. (they had enough ~ to provide for their old age)

fascinated *adj*. 1. ~ at, by, with (~ at the spectacle of a rocket launching) 2. ~ to + inf. (I was ~ to learn of their work)

fascinating *adj*. 1. ~ to + inf. (it's ~ to listen to her) 2. ~ that + clause (it's ~ that migratory birds never get lost)

fascination *n*. 1. to have, hold a ~ for (the Himalayas have/hold a special ~ for climbers) 2. a morbid; special ~ 3. ~ at, over, with

fashion I *n*. ["vogue"] 1. a ~ 2. to come into ~; to go out of ~ 3. contemporary, current ~(s); the latest ~(s) 4. high ~ 5. in ~ (big hats are no longer in ~) 6. out of ~ ["manner"] 7. in a ~ (she behaved in a strange ~)

fashion II *v*. 1. (D; tr.) to ~ from, out of (to ~ a pipe out of clay) 2. (d; tr.) to ~ into (to ~ clay into a pipe)

fashionable *adj*. ~ to + inf. (it is now very ~ to recycle)

fashion show *n*. to hold, organize a ~

fast I *adv*. 1. to hold ~ to (they held ~ to their beliefs) 2. to stand ~

fast II *n*. 1. to observe a ~ 2. to break a ~

fasten *v*. (D; tr.) 1. to ~ onto, to (to ~ a corsage to a lapel) 2. (D; tr.) to ~ with (to ~ one's hair with a clip)

fastidious *adj*. ~ about (~ about one's appearance)

fast lane *n*. (life) in the ~

fast one *n*. (colloq.) ["trick"] to pull a ~ (on)

fast-talk *v*. (colloq.) (D; tr.) to ~ into; out of (to ~

smb. into doing smt.)

fat *n.* 1. to skim off; trim (away) the ~ 2. animal; vegetable ~ 3. polyunsaturated; saturated ~ 4. deep; excess ~ (to fry in deep ~) 5. subcutaneous ~ 6. (misc.) (colloq.) to live off the ~ of the land ("to live very well"); to chew the ~ ("to chat")

fatal *adj.* 1. ~ for, to (that move was ~ to his career) 2. ~ to + inf. (it would be ~ to hesitate)

fatalities *n.* 1. to cause ~ 2. highway (AE), motorway (BE), traffic ~

fate *n.* 1. to decide, seal smb.'s ~ 2. to tempt ~ 3. to meet, suffer a ~ (they both suffered a similar ~) 4. (a) bitter, cruel ~ 5. blind, inexorable ~ 6. a quirk, stroke, twist of ~ 7. ~ to + inf. (it was our ~ never to meet again) 8. (misc.) ~ decreed that we would win the lottery; a cruel ~ befell them

fated *adj.* (formal) 1. ~ to + inf. (they were ~ never to meet) 2. ~ that + clause (it was ~ that they should never meet again)

father *n.* 1. an expectant (AE); proud ~ 2. an adoptive; biological; foster; lone (BE); single ~; stepfather 3. a father-in-law 4. a ~ to (he was like a ~ to them) 5. (misc.) the city ~s; a founding ~

fatigue *n.* 1. to feel ~ 2. battle, combat; mental ~ 3. metal ~ 4. a state of ~ (she was in a state of complete ~)

faucet *n.* (AE) 1. to turn on a ~ 2. to turn off a ~ 3. a ~ drips, leaks 3. a leaky ~ 4. a cold-water; hot-water ~ (CE has *tap*)

fault I *n.* 1. to find ~ with 2. to correct a ~ 3. to overlook smb.'s ~s 4. a grievous; human ~ 5. a ~ that + clause (it was not my ~ that he was late) 6. at ~ (we were all at ~) 7. through smb.'s ~ 8. to a ~ (she is fastidious to a ~)

fault II *v.* (D; tr.) ("to blame") to ~ for

faux pas *n.* 1. to commit, make a ~ 2. a grave, serious ~

favor I favour *n.* ["friendly act, service"] 1. to do, grant (smb.) a ~ 2. to perform a ~ (for smb.) 3. to return a ~ 4. a special ~ ["approval"] ["liking"] 5. to win smb.'s ~ 6. to curry ~ with 7. to vie for smb.'s ~ 8. to find, gain ~ with; to find ~ in smb.'s eyes 9. to lose ~ 10. universal ~ 11. in ~ with 12. out of ~ (with) (to fall out of ~) 13. to look with ~ on smt. ["support"] 14. to come out in ~ of 15. in ~ of (these facts speak in ~ of his acquittal; we are in ~ of reform) 16. in smb.'s ~ (the odds are in her ~)

favor II favour *v.* 1. (D; tr.) to ~ smb. over smb. else 2. (formal) (D; tr.) to ~ with (she will now ~ us with a song) 3. (G) he ~s raising taxes

favorable, favourable *adj.* ~ for, to

favored, favoured *adj.* 1. heavily ~ 2. ~ to + inf. (our team is heavily ~ to win)

favorite, favourite *n.* 1. a heavy, strong; odds-on ~ 2. a ~ with 3. to play ~s

favoritism, favouritism *n.* 1. to show ~ 2. strong ~

favors, favours *n.* ["small gifts"] 1. party ~ ["sexual privileges"] 2. to grant one's ~ to smb.; to bestow one's ~s on

fawn *v.* (d; intr.) to ~ on, over

fax I *n.* 1. to send a ~ (to) 2. to get, receive a ~ (from) 3. by ~ (to send a document by ~)

fax II *v.* 1. (A) we ~ed a message to them; or: we ~ed them a message 2. (d; intr., tr.) to ~ for (we ~ed for immediate delivery) 3. (H) we ~ed them to return home immediately 4. (L; may have an object) she ~ed (us) that the manuscript had been lost 5. (Q; may have an object) they ~ed (us) where to meet

faze *v.* (L; must have an object) it did not ~ me at all that she declined the offer

fear I *n.* 1. to arouse, instill, kindle ~ 2. to express; feel; show ~ (she felt ~ for their safety) 3. to confirm one's (worst) ~s 4. to allay, calm, dispel ~ 5. to overcome ~ 6. (a) grave, mortal, strong; groundless; idle; inarticulate; lingering; morbid; sudden ~ 7. ~ that + clause (there are ~s that no compromise can be worked out) 8. for ~ of (he lied for ~ of being punished) 9. in ~ of (he is in ~ of his life) 10. out of ~ (he did it out of ~) 11. (misc.) to strike ~ into smb.'s heart

fear II *v.* 1. to ~ greatly, very much 2. (d; intr.) to ~ for (I ~ for his safety) 3. (E) I ~ to think what may happen 4. (K) he ~s my getting involved 5. (L) we ~ that we will not be able to attend

fearful *adj.* 1. ~ of 2. ~ that + clause (they were ~ that the river would flood)

feasible *adj.* ~ to + inf. (it was not ~ to build a bridge at that point)

feast I *n.* 1. to give; have a ~ 2. a royal, sumptuous; wedding ~

feast II *v.* (formal) (D; intr., tr.) to ~ on, upon (to ~ on steak and potatoes; to ~ one's eyes on beautiful scenery)

feat *n.* 1. to accomplish, perform a ~ 2. a brave, heroic; brilliant, notable, noteworthy, outstanding, remarkable ~ (to perform a remarkable ~) 3. no mean, small ~ (it was no mean ~ to get him to agree)

feather *n.* 1. to pluck ~s (from a chicken) 2. (misc.) as light as a ~ ("very light"); a ~ in smb.'s cap ("a symbol of accomplishment"); to smooth smb.'s ruffled ~s ("to calm smb.")

feature I *n.* ["quality"] 1. a characteristic, distinctive, distinguishing; notable; noteworthy, salient; special; typical ~ 2. a redeeming ~ ["contour"] ["line"] 3. coarse; prominent; sharp; striking ~s 4. delicate, fine; regular; soft ~s ["main film"] 5. a double ~ ("a program consisting of two films in a movie theater") ["special item"] 6. an optional ~ (we chose several optional ~s for our new car)

feature II *v.* (D; tr.) to ~ as (she was ~d as a dancer)

federate *v.* (D; intr., tr.) to ~ into; with

federation *n.* 1. to form a ~ 2. a ~ among, between

fed up *adj.* ~ about, of (BE), with

fee *n.* 1. to charge a ~ 2. to pay a ~ 3. to split ~s (as of lawyers, doctors) 4. to waive one's ~ 5. a fat, large; flat; nominal ~ 6. an administrative; admission, entrance; contingency; laboratory; membership; registration ~ 7. a ~ for (a ~ for service) 8. for a ~ (for a nominal ~)

feed *v.* 1. (A) they fed erroneous information to us; or: they fed us erroneous information 2. (d; tr.) to ~ into, to (to ~ data into a computer) 3. (D; intr.) to ~ on (certain animals ~ on insects) 4. (d; tr.) to ~ with (they fed us with erroneous information)

feedback *n.* 1. to give, provide ~ 2. to get, receive ~ 3. ~ from (we welcome ~ from our customers) 4. negative; positive ~ 5. ~ concerning, on

feeding *n.* breast; communal; forced; intravenous ~

feel I *n.* 1. (colloq.) to have a (good) ~ for 2. to get the ~ of (the new car) 3. I like the ~ of (this fabric)

feel II *v.* 1. ("to believe") to ~ deeply, keenly, strongly 2. (D; intr.) ("to have an opinion") to ~ about (how do you ~ about this problem?) 3. (d; intr.) ("to grope") to ~ (around) for (he felt around in his pockets for his keys) 4. (colloq.) (d; intr.) to ~ for ("to sympathize with") (I ~ for them) 5. (D; tr.) ("to experience") to ~ for (to ~ pity for smb.) 6. (I) ("to sense") he could ~ his heart beat 7. (J) ("to sense") he could ~ his heart beating 8. (L) ("to believe") we ~ that you should return home 9. (Q) I could not ~ where the swelling was 10. (s) to ~ comfortable; I ~ cheated; to ~ sorry about smt.; to ~ good ("happy"); to ~ fine/well ("healthy"); to ~ bad ("unwell") or ("sad") 11. (BE) (S) I ~ such a fool 12. (misc.) it ~s good to be on vacation; it felt nice to swim in the heated pool; she felt proud of her children; to ~ bad/badly ("sad") about smt.; (esp. BE) I ~ rather poorly today (see also **feel like**)

feeler *n.* ["probe"] to put out, throw out a ~

feeling *n.* ["emotional reaction"] 1. to arouse, inspire, stir up ~ ["appreciation"] 2. to develop a ~ for (to develop a ~ for classical music) ["sentiment"] ["sensation"] 3. to express; show; vent one's ~s 4. to experience, have a ~ 5. to harbor ~s (to harbor warm ~s of friendship towards smb.) 6. to bottle up, repress; hide, mask one's ~s 7. to lose ~ (he lost all ~ in his foot) 8. a deep, strong; eery, strange; friendly, tender, warm; gloomy, sad; hostile; intangible; intense; queasy; satisfied; sick; sinking; sneaking; uneasy ~ 9. (colloq.) a gut ("instinctive") ~ 10. smb.'s innermost, intimate; pent-up ~s 11. hard ~s (we have no hard ~s) ("we are not angry") 12. a ~ that + clause (I had an eery ~ that I had been there before) ["attitude"] ["opinion"] 13. definite; strong ~s (we have strong ~s about this matter) 14. popular ~ (popular ~ was running against the president) 15. ~s about, on (to have definite ~s on a subject) ["sensitivity"] 16. to

hurt smb.'s ~s 17. delicate, sensitive ~s ["premonition"] 18. a ~ that + clause (I had a ~ that she would show up)

feel like *v.* 1. (G) she ~s like resting 2. (S; used only with nouns) to ~ a fool; it ~s like satin; it ~s like rain 3. (misc.) (esp. AE) it ~s like it's going to rain

feel up *v.* (d; intr.) to ~ to ("to feel capable of") (do you ~ to a drive to town?)

feint *n.* 1. to make a ~ 2. a ~ to (the right)

fellow *n.* ["scholar"] ["fellowship holder"] 1. a research; senior; teaching ~ ["man"] 2. a fine, good; honest; nice, regular (AE); young ~

fellowship *n.* ["stipend; support for studies"] 1. to award, grant; establish a ~ 2. to apply for; to receive, win a ~ 3. a graduate, postgraduate (esp. BE); postdoctoral ~ ["community of interest"] 4. to foster, promote (good) ~ 5. to enjoy good ~ 6. close, strong, warm ~ 7. ~ with 8. a sense of ~

felony *n.* 1. to commit, perpetrate a ~ 2. to compound a ~ ("to waive prosecution in return for compensation")

feminist *n.* an ardent, dedicated; moderate; radical ~

fence I *n.* 1. to build, erect, put up a ~ 2. a high; low ~ 3. a barbed-wire; chain-link; picket; rail; snow; wrought-iron ~ 4. a ~ around; between 5. (misc.) to mend ~s ("to set things right"); on the ~ ("uncommitted"); to straddle the ~ ("to be uncommitted")

fence II *v.* (d; intr.) ("to vie") to ~ for (the drivers were ~cing for position)

fence off *v.* (D; tr.) to ~ from (the yard was ~d off from the street)

fend *v.* to ~ for oneself

fender *n.* (AE) a dented ~ (BE has *wing*)

ferment *n.* 1. intellectual; political; social ~ 2. in ~ (the country was in ~)

ferry I *n.* 1. to board; take a ~ 2. by ~ (to cross a river by ~)

ferry II *v.* 1. (d; tr.) to ~ across (to ~ troops across a river) 2. (P; tr.) we have to ~ the children to and from school

fertilization *n.* in vitro ~

fertilizer *n.* 1. to spread ~ 2. artificial; chemical; natural ~

fervor, fervour *n.* 1. great ~ 2. evangelical; messianic; patriotic; religious ~ 3. with ~ (she spoke with great ~)

festival *n.* 1. to hold a ~ 2. a dance; drama; film; folk; harvest; music; religious ~

festoon *v.* (D; tr.) to ~ with (the hall was ~ed with lights)

fetch *v.* (C) please ~ my pipe for me; or: please ~ me my pipe

fête *n.* (esp. BE) 1. to hold a ~ 2. a church; village ~

fetish *n.* 1. to make a ~ of smt. (they made a ~ of good grooming) 2. (esp. BE) to have a ~ about

(smt.)

fettle *n.* they were in fine ~

fetus, foetus *n.* 1. to abort a ~ 2. a viable ~

feud I *n.* 1. to stir up a ~ 2. a bitter, deadly, internecine ~ 3. a blood; family; personal ~ 4. a ~ between, with 5. a ~ about, over

feud II *v.* (D; intr.) to ~ about, over; with

fever *n.* ["elevated temperature of the body"] 1. to come down with, develop a ~ 2. to have, run a ~ 3. a burning; constant; high; intermittent; mild, slight; recurrent; remittent ~ 4. a ~ breaks, subsides ["disease or condition"] 5. glandular; hay; relapsing; rheumatic; Rocky Mountain spotted; scarlet; trench; typhoid; undulant; yellow ~

fever pitch *n.* 1. to reach (a) ~ 2. at (a) ~

few I *determiner, pronoun* 1. relatively ~ 2. ~ in number 3. a ~ of (we saw a ~ of them)
USAGE NOTE: The use of the preposition *of* is necessary when a pronoun follows. Compare the following constructions with nouns—we saw very few (of the) students; we saw (only) a few ("several") (of the) students.

few II *n.* 1. (a) precious, very ~ 2. quite a ~ 3. (misc.) to have a ~ too many ("to drink too much"); ~ and far between ("rare"); just a ~, only a ~

fiasco *n.* 1. to end in a ~ 2. a complete, total, utter ~

fib *n.* to tell a ~

fiber, fibre *n.* 1. artificial, synthetic; coarse; cotton; rayon; wool ~ 2. optical ~ (for the electronic transmission of information) 3. nerve ~ 4. (fig.) moral ~

fiction *n.* 1. pure ~ (her story was pure ~) 2. light; popular; romantic; science ~

fiddle I *n.* 1. to play the ~ 2. (AE; colloq.) a bass ~ (CE has *double bass*) 3. (BE; colloq.) on the ~ ("cheating") 4. (misc.) as fit as a ~ ("very healthy")

fiddle II *v.* (d; intr.) ("to fool around") to ~ with (he kept ~ling with his computer)

fiddle around *v.* (D; intr.) ("to fool around") to ~ with (she was ~ling around with the controls)

fidelity *n.* ["loyalty"] 1. to pledge, swear ~ 2. ~ to ["quality of electronic reproduction"] 3. high ~

fidget *v.* (D; intr.) to ~ with

field *n.* ["cultivated area"] 1. to cultivate; plow; till, work a ~ 2. a corn; rice; wheat ~ 3. in a ~ (farmers were working in the ~s) ["area used for athletic events"] 4. to take the ~ 5. a baseball; football; soccer (BE often has *pitch*) ~ 6. on the ~ (how many players were on the football ~?) ["area used as a landing strip"] 7. a flying, landing ~ 8. on the ~ ["area used for practical work"] 9. to work (out) in the ~ ["unbroken expanse"] ["space"] 10. an open ~ 11. a battlefield 12. a visual ~ ["area producing a natural resource"] 13. a coal; gold; oil ~ ["space in which electric lines of force are present"] (physics) 14. an electromagnetic, mag-

netic; gravitational ~ ["area of activity"] 15. in a ~ (in the ~ of science) 16. in smb.'s ~; outside (of) smb.'s ~ (her works are outside of my ~) ["misc."] 17. on the ~ of honor; (esp. AE) to play the ~ ("to avoid committing oneself")

field day *n.* ["a great success"] to have a ~ (they had a ~ with the reporters)

field glasses *n.* to focus, train ~ on

fieldwork *n.* to do ~

Fifth *n.* (colloq.) (AE) ["the Fifth Amendment, protecting witnesses against self-incrimination"] to invoke, plead, take the ~

fight I *n.* ["struggle"] 1. to pick, provoke, start a ~ (he picked a ~ with me) 2. to put up, wage a ~ (to wage a ~ against corruption) 3. to get into a ~ (to get into a ~ with a neighbor about the property line) 4. to lose; win a ~ 5. to break up, stop a ~ 6. a bitter, desperate, fierce, hard, stubborn; last-ditch ~ (to put up a last-ditch ~) 7. a clean, fair; dirty, unfair ~ 8. a ~ to the death; a ~ to the finish 9. a fist ~ 10. a ~ breaks out, starts; rages 11. a ~ about, over; against; among, between; for; with (a ~ for justice; a ~ between local politicians) 12. a ~ to + inf. (we joined the ~ to reduce waste) ["boxing match"] 13. to hold, stage; promote a ~ 14. to fix a ~ ("to influence the results of a ~ illegally") 15. a clean; dirty; grudge ~ 16. a championship, title ~ 17. (misc.) the big ~ (everyone was talking about the big ~)

fight II *v.* 1. to ~ bravely, heroically; clean; desperately, hard, stubbornly; dirty, unfairly; fair, fairly 2. (D; intr., tr.) to ~ about, over; against; among; for; with (he was always ~ing with his neighbors about the noise; Great Britain fought with Turkey against Russia; they are always ~ing among themselves; the United States fought a war with Mexico over their common border; the war was fought for a just cause; the dogs were ~ing over a bone) 3. (D; intr.) to ~ like (they fought like heroes) 4. (E) to ~ to win 5. (misc.) to ~ to the finish; to ~ with one's fists

fight back *v.* 1. (D; intr.) to ~ against, at (to ~ at terrorism) 2. (misc.) to ~ in self-defense

fighter *n.* ["pugilist"] 1. a clean; dirty ~ ["fighting aircraft"] 2. a long-range; medium-range ~ ["misc."] 3. a firefighter

fighting *n.* 1. to step up the ~ 2. bitter, fierce, hard, heavy; hand-to-hand ~ 3. clean; dirty ~ 4. street ~ 5. (the) ~ breaks out; escalates; rages 6. (the) ~ dies down

fight on *v.* to ~ to the very end

figure I *n.* ["impression"] ["appearance"] 1. to cut a (fine) ~ ("to make a strong impression") 2. a conspicuous, dashing, fine, handsome, imposing, striking, trim ~ (to cut a dashing ~) 3. a ridiculous, sorry ~ ["person"] ["personage"] 4. a familiar; key, leading; national; prominent, well-known;

public ~ 5. a political; religious; underworld ~ 6. a father; mother; parental ~ ["number"] 7. to bandy ~s 8. to round down (esp. BE); to round off (esp. AE); to round up (esp. BE) ~s 9. approximate, ball-park (esp. AE; colloq.), round; available; exact; official; reliable ~s 10. in ~s (in round ~s) ["form"] 11. a symmetrical ~ 12. (misc.) to do a ~ eight/a ~ of eight (BE) (as in ice skating)

figure II *v.* 1. (d; intr.) ("to play a role") to ~ in (she ~d prominently in history) 2. (colloq.) (esp. AE) ("to estimate") (L) we ~d that he would arrive at around two o'clock 3. (colloq.) (esp. AE) (M) ("to estimate") I ~d him to be worth a few hundred thousand

figure on *v.* (colloq.) (esp. AE) (G) ("to intend") I ~d on staying a few days

figure out *v.* (colloq.) 1. (L) he ~d out that we could not possibly get there on time 2. (Q) she could not ~ how to do it

filch *v.* (D; tr.) (colloq.) ("to steal") to ~ from

file I *n.* ["dossier"] ["folder"] 1. to make up, open, start a ~ 2. to keep a ~ 3. to close a ~ 4. official ~s 5. a confidential ~ 6. a vertical ~ 7. a ~ on (to keep a ~ on smb.) 8. on ~ (these documents are kept on ~) ["collection of data in a computer"] 9. to access; copy; create, open; delete, erase; download; edit; print; save a ~ 10. a batch; data; text ~

file II *v.* 1. (D; intr.) ("to apply") to ~ for (to ~ for divorce) 2. (D; tr.) ("to submit") to ~ with (she ~d an application with several employment agencies)

file III *n.* ["row"] 1. single ~ 2. in single ~

file IV *v.* ("to move in a line") 1. (d; intr.) to ~ by, past (to ~ past a coffin) 2. (d; intr.) to ~ into; out of (to ~ into an auditorium; the jury ~d out of the courtroom)

file V *n.* ["tool for smoothing surfaces"] a nail ~

file VI *v.* ("to smooth or shape") (N) she ~d her nails smooth

filibuster I *n.* to carry on, conduct, engage in a ~

filibuster II *v.* (D; intr.) to ~ against

filing *n.* ["storage of data"] to do ~

fill I *n.* ["what is necessary to satisfy"] to drink; eat; have one's ~ (to have one's ~ of trouble)

fill II *v.* 1. (D; tr.) to ~ to (the auditorium was ~ed to capacity; to ~ to overflowing) 2. (D; intr., tr.) to ~ with (the lecture hall ~ed with people; to ~ a hole with sand)

fill-in *n.* ["replacement or substitute"] a ~ for (she is a ~ today for the regular announcer)

fill in *v.* 1. (D; intr.) to ~ for ("to replace") (to ~ for a friend) 2. (D; tr.) to ~ on ("to inform") (to ~ smb. in on the details) 3. (D; tr.) ("to make full") to ~ with (to ~ a hole with dirt)

filling *n.* (dental) 1. to put in; replace a ~ 2. to cement a ~ 3. to lose a ~ 4. a broken, cracked ~ 5. a permanent; temporary ~ 6. a ~ breaks, cracks; chips; falls out

fill up *v.* ("to make full") (D; tr.) to ~ with (to ~ the car with gas/petrol)

film *n.* ["cinema picture, motion picture"] 1. to cut, edit; direct; make, produce, shoot a ~ (the ~ was shot on location) 2. to distribute; promote; release; show a ~ 3. to ban; censor a ~ 4. to rate; review a ~ 5. to see, take in, watch a ~ 6. an action; adventure; gangster; travel ~ 7. a documentary; educational; instructional; propaganda; training ~ 8. a children's ~ 9. an adult, blue (BE), erotic, pornographic, X-rated ~ 10. a black-and-white; color; colorized ~ 11. a feature; silent; sound; television, TV ~ 12. (misc.) (BE) to work in ~s ("to work in the film industry"); to act in a ~

USAGE NOTE: In a theater, one *sees a film*; on a home TV, one *watches a film* or *sees a film*. ["roll of material used to take photographs"] 13. to insert, load; remove; rewind; wind ~ 14. to develop; expose ~ 15. to splice ~ 16. black-and-white; color; fast ~ 17. 8-millimeter; 16-millimeter; 35-millimeter ~ 18. a roll of ~ 19. (misc.) to capture smt. on ~

filter I *n.* 1. to pass smt. through a ~ 2. a cloth; dust; oil; sand ~

filter II *v.* 1. (d; intr.) to ~ into (foreign influence began to ~ into the country) 2. (d; intr.) to ~ out of (they slowly ~ed out of the room) 3. (d; intr.) to ~ through (sunlight ~ed through the drapes)

filter down *v.* (D; intr.) to ~ to (news slowly ~ed down to us)

filter through *v.* (D; intr.) to ~ to (reports have started to ~ to headquarters)

filth *n.* in ~ (to live in ~)

fin *n.* a caudal; dorsal; pectoral; pelvic ~

finale *n.* the grand ~

finals *n.* ["final examinations"] 1. to sit (BE), take one's ~ ["last competition"] 2. to get into, reach the ~

finance *n.* high; public ~

financing *n.* deficit; private; public ~

find I *n.* 1. an archeological ~ 2. an important; lucky; rare ~

find II *v.* 1. (C) ~ an interesting book for me; or: ~ me an interesting book 2. (legal) (d; intr.) ("to decide") to ~ against; for (to ~ for the plaintiff) 3. (D; tr.) ("to discover") to ~ for (have you found a suitable candidate for the job?) 4. (J) ("to discover") we found her working on her book 5. (L) ("to discover") we found that she was always ready to help 6. (M) ("to discover") we found London to be a fascinating city 7. (N; used with an adjective, past participle) we found London fascinating; to ~ smb. wanting; the soldiers found the village destroyed; she was found guilty by the jury 8. (Q) we could not ~ where the money was hidden 9. (misc.) we found it difficult to believe

finding *n.* 1. a preliminary ~ 2. (a) ~ that + clause (it was the court's ~ that no crime had been committed) 3. (misc.) to rubber-stamp a committee's ~s

find out *v.* 1. (D; intr.) to ~ about (we found out about the accident yesterday) 2. (D; intr.) to ~ for (she found out about the concert for me) 3. (D; intr., tr.) to ~ from (we found it out from the reporter) 4. (L) we found out that the train would be late 5. (Q) I finally found out how to operate the new computer

fine I *adj.* ~ to + inf. (it's ~ to reduce taxes, but the deficit will be increased)

fine II *n.* 1. to impose, issue, levy a ~ on smb. 2. (colloq.) to slap a ~ on smb. 3. to draw, receive; pay a ~ 4. a big, heavy, hefty, stiff ~ 5. a small ~ 6. a mandatory ~ 7. a ~ for (a ~ for illegal parking)

fine III *v.* 1. (D; tr.) to ~ for (to ~ smb. for illegal parking) 2. (O; can be used with one animate object) the police ~d him twenty dollars; the police ~d him

finery *n.* ["showy clothing"] in all one's ~ (dressed up in all their ~)

finger I *n.* 1. to drum, tap one's ~s 2. to point a ~ at 3. (usu. fig.) to snap one's ~s (I jump when she snaps her ~s) ("I obey her commands without question") 4. an accusing; warning ~ (to point an accusing ~ at smb.) 5. a forefinger, index ~; little; middle; ring; trigger ~ 6. (misc.) she ran her ~s through her hair; to get one's ~s burned ("to bear unpleasant consequences"); to prick a ~; she jammed her ~ in the door; to lay a ~ on smb. ("to harm smb."); I can't lay/put my ~ on what is wrong ("I cannot discover what is wrong"); to count on one's ~s; to keep one's ~s crossed ("to hope for smt."); to lift a ~ ("to make an effort"); to have one's ~ in smt. ("to be involved in smt."); the ~ of suspicion points at/to you ("you are under suspicion"); to have smb. wrapped around one's little ~ ("to have smb.'s complete devotion")

finger II *v.* (colloq.) (D; tr.) ("to identify") to ~ as (he was ~ed as one of the escaped convicts)

fingernails *n.* 1. to cut, trim; file; manicure smb.'s ~ 2. to bite, chew one's ~

fingerprints *n.* 1. to leave ~ 2. take smb.'s ~ 3. telltale ~ 4. a set of ~ (the police got a clean set of ~) 5. (misc.) to dust for ~; the ~ had been carefully wiped off

fingertips *n.* at one's ~ (to have information at one's ~)

finicky *adj.* ~ about

finish I *n.* ["end"] 1. a close; photo ~ 2. at the ~ 3. to the ~ (to fight to the ~) ["polish"] 4. a dull; glazed; glossy; matte ~

finish II *v.* 1. (D; intr., tr.) to ~ by, with (they ~ed their performance by singing a song/with a song; are/have you ~ed with your work?) 2. (G) they ~ed working at four o'clock 3. (s) to ~ last

finish line, (BE) **finishing line** *n.* to cross; reach the ~

finish up *v.* 1. (D; intr., tr.) to ~ by, with (we ~ed up the year with no profit; they ~ed up by scrubbing the floor) 2. (G) she ~ed up buying two suits instead of one 3. (s) they ~ed up bankrupt

fire I *n.* ["destructive burning"] 1. to set, start a ~ 2. to set ~ to (they set ~ to the barn) 3. to catch ~ (the house caught ~) 4. to contain; douse, extinguish, put out; fight; stamp out a ~ 5. to bring a ~ under control 6. a raging, roaring ~ 7. a brush; chemical; electrical; forest ~ 8. a ~ breaks out; burns; rages (out of control); smoulders; spreads (the ~ burned out of control for two hours) 9. a ~ goes out 10. on ~ (the house was on ~) ["burning, combustion"] 11. to build, kindle a ~, lay the (BE) ~; light, make a ~ 12. to fuel; poke, stir; stoke a ~ 13. to bank; douse, extinguish, put out a ~ 14. a ~ burns; goes out; smoulders 15. (misc.) the ~ is out; the glow of a ~ ["shooting"] 16. to commence, open ~ (to open ~ on the enemy) 17. to exchange ~ (with the enemy) 18. to call down ~ on 19. to attract, draw ~ 20. to return ~ 21. to cease ~ (cease ~!) 22. to hold one's ~ 23. concentrated, fierce, heavy, murderous; rapid ~ 24. cross; friendly; harassing; hostile; incoming; interdictory ~ 25. artillery; automatic; machine-gun; rifle; semiautomatic; small-arms ~ 26. under ~ (also fig.) 27. (misc.) (directly) in the line of ~; a baptism of ~ ["misc."] 28. to play with ~ ("to take a risk"); to fight ~ with ~ ("to use extreme measures as a counterattack"); to set the Thames (BE)/the world on ~ ("to be very successful")

fire II *v.* 1. to ~ point-blank 2. (B) the quarterback ~d a pass to an end 3. (D; intr., tr.) to ~ at (he ~d at me; he ~d his pistol at me) 4. (D; intr., tr.) to ~ into (he ~d his pistol into the air; to ~ into a crowd) 5. (D; tr.) to ~ with (they ~d me with enthusiasm)

fire alarm *n.* 1. to set a ~ 2. to activate, set off, trigger a ~ 3. a ~ goes off, rings, sounds

fire away *v.* (D; intr.) to ~ at (to ~ at the enemy)

fire back *v.* (D; intr.) to ~ at

firecracker *n.* 1. to light, set off a ~ 2. to shoot off ~s 3. a ~ goes off

fire drill *n.* 1. to conduct, hold a ~ 2. at a ~

fired up *adj.* ["excited"] (all) ~ about, with

fire extinguisher *n.* 1. to train a ~ (on a fire) 2. to operate a ~ 3. to recharge a ~

fire sale *n.* to hold a ~

fireside *n.* by the ~ (to sit by the ~)

fireworks *n.* 1. to set off, shoot off ~ 2. a spectacular display of ~

firing line *n.* ["line from which soldiers fire their weapons"] in (BE), on (AE) the ~ (also fig.)

firm I *adj.* ["competitive, strong"] 1. ~ against (the pound was ~ against the dollar) ["strict"] 2. ~ with (~ with the children)

firm II *n.* ["company"] 1. to establish; manage, operate, run a ~ 2. an advertising; business; law, legal; manufacturing; shipping ~ 3. a reputable ~ 4. in a ~ (she works in a reputable ~)

first *adj., n.* 1. to come in ~ (in a race) 2. the ~ to + inf. (she was the ~ to arrive) 3. among the ~ 4. at ~

first aid *n.* 1. to administer, give ~ 2. to get ~

first-class *adv.* to travel ~

first strike *n.* 1. to carry out, make a ~ 2. (misc.) a first-strike capability

fish I *n.* 1. to catch (a) ~ 2. baked; broiled (AE), grilled; dried; filleted; fresh; freshwater; fried; frozen; saltwater; smoked ~ 3. tropical ~ 4. ~ bite at bait; swim 5. a school, shoal of ~ 6. (misc.) to drink like a ~ ("to drink excessive amounts of alcohol"); an odd, queer ~ ("a strange person"); a cold ~ ("an unfriendly person")

fish II *v.* 1. (d; intr.) to ~ for (to ~ for compliments) 2. to go ~ing

fish around *v.* (D; intr.) to ~ for (to ~ for information)

fish fry *n.* to have a ~

fishing *n.* 1. to go ~ 2. to go in for ~ 3. to do some ~ 4. deep-sea ~

fishy *adj.* (colloq.) ~ about (there is smt. ~ about them)

fission *n.* binary; nuclear ~

fist *n.* 1. to make a ~ 2. to clench; raise; shake one's ~ 3. a tight ~ 4. (misc.) an iron ~ ("a harsh policy"); a mailed ~ ("a threat of armed force")

fisticuffs *n.* to engage in ~

fit I *n.* ["emotional reaction"] 1. to have, throw a ~ ["misc."] 2. by ~s and starts ("in irregular bursts of activity")

fit II *adj.* ["qualified"] ["physically capable"] 1. physically ~ 2. ~ for (~ for duty; ~ for human consumption) 3. ~ to + inf. (he is not ~ to work) 4. to keep ~ ["suitable"] 5. to see, think ~ to + inf. (they saw ~ to employ smb. else) 6. (misc.) ~ for a king/queen

fit III *n.* ["manner of fitting"] a good; loose; perfect; snug, tight ~

fit IV *v.* 1. to ~ together 2. (D; tr.) to ~ for (to ~ a customer for a new suit; to ~ smb. for glasses) 3. (D; intr.) to ~ into (everything fit into the suitcase) 4. (d; tr.) to ~ into (she was able to ~ all the books into one carton)

USAGE NOTE: In BE the past and past participle of *fit* are usu. *fitted*. AE usu. has *fit* when the verb cannot be used in the passive form—the tailor fitted the customer carefully (CE); the suit was fitted carefully by the tailor (CE); the suit fit me a year ago (AE).

fit in *v.* (D; intr.) to ~ with ("to blend in") (she fit right in with our crowd)

fitness *n.* 1. physical ~ 2. ~ for

fit out *v.* 1. (d; tr.) to ~ as (the ship was ~ted out as a

tender) 2. (d; tr.) to ~ for (the expedition was ~ted out for a long trip) 3. (d; tr.) to ~ with (the bus was ~ted out with new air conditioning)

fitting I *adj.* 1. ~ to + inf. (it is ~ to pay tribute to the early pioneers) 2. ~ that + clause; may take subj. (it is ~ that she be/should be honored; it is ~ that she was honored)

fitting II *n.* ["small part"] 1. an electrical; female; gas; male ~ ["trying on of a garment"] 2. to go for a ~ 3. (misc.) a ~ room

fix I *n.* (colloq.) ["difficult situation"] 1. to be in a ~ 2. a fine, nice, pretty ~ ["injection of a narcotic"] (slang) 3. to get; need a ~

fix II *v.* 1. (AE) (C) ("to prepare") ~ a drink for me; or: ~ me a drink 2. (d; tr.) to ~ on (she ~ed her gaze on him) 3. (colloq.) (esp. AE) (E) ("to get ready") they're ~ing to eat

fixation *n.* ["obsession"] a ~ about, on, with (to have a ~ on smt.)

fixing *n.* 1. price ~ 2. (misc.) (colloq.) a turkey with all the ~s

fixture *n.* a lighting; plumbing; shop (esp. BE), store (esp. AE) ~

fix up *v.* 1. (d; tr.) (colloq.) to ~ with ("to match with") (to ~ smb. up with a good job; my friends ~ed me up with her)

flag *n.* 1. to display, fly; hang out; hoist, raise, run up, unfurl; wave a ~ 2. to dip, lower a ~; to strike the ~ 3. a garrison; national ~ 4. the white ~ ("symbol of surrender") 5. a ~ flaps, flies, flutters, waves (the ~ was flying at half-mast) 6. under a ~ (the ship sailed under the Panamanian ~) 7. (misc.) to show/wave the ~ ("to demonstrate one's patriotism"); (under) a ~ of truce; to register a ship under a ~ of convenience

flair *n.* 1. to develop; have; show a ~ for 2. a distinctive ~

flak *n.* ["criticism"] (colloq.) to catch; come in for, run into; take ~ (he took a lot of ~ for that one)

flame *n.* 1. (also fig.) to kindle a ~ 2. (fig.) to fan, stir the ~s (of racism) 3. to burst into ~(s) 4. a clear; open ~ 5. a ~ burns 6. in ~s (to go up in ~s; the house was in ~s) 7. (misc.) an (the) eternal ~; the Olympic ~; an old ~ ("an old love"); a wall of ~

flank *n.* 1. to turn ("go around") a ~ (to turn the enemy's ~) 2. on a ~ (on the left ~) 3. (misc.) a ~ attack

flap *n.* (slang) ["commotion"] 1. a political ~ 2. in a ~ about, over

flare I *n.* 1. to light; shoot up a ~ 2. to set out, set up a ~ (they set up ~s along the runway) 3. a parachute ~

flare II *v.* (d; intr.) to ~ into (to ~ into violence)

flare up *v.* 1. (D; intr.) to ~ at (to ~ at the slightest provocation) 2. (D; intr.) to ~ in (to ~ in anger)

flash I *n.* 1. a blinding ~ 2. an electronic ~ (for a camera) 3. a hot ~ (AE; BE has *hot flush*) 4. a news

~ 5. in a ~ ("quickly")

flash II v. 1. (usu. B; rarely A) ("to convey by light") they ~ed a signal to the crew 2. (d; intr) ("to pass") to ~ across, through (an old memory ~ed across my mind; a thought ~ed through my mind) 3. (D; tr.) ("to shine") to ~ at (the driver ~ed his lights at us) 4. (d; intr.) ("to come suddenly") to ~ into (a brilliant idea ~ed into her mind) 5. (D; intr.) ("to glow") to ~ with (her eyes ~ed with anger)

flashback n. a ~ to (a ~ to smb.'s childhood)

flashlight n. (AE; BE has *torch*) 1. to turn on a ~ 2. to shine, train a ~ on 3. to turn off a ~

flash point n. to reach a ~

flask n. 1. a Thermos (T) (BE), vacuum (BE) ~; AE has *Thermos* (T) *bottle* 2. a hip ~

flat I adj. ["flavorless, stale"] 1. to go ~ (the beer has gone ~) ["extended at full length"] 2. (also fig.) to fall ~ (as an actor he fell ~) 3. (also fig.) she fell ~ on her face ["exact"] 4. she ran a mile in seven minutes ~

flat II n. ["deflated tire"] (esp. AE; BE prefers *flat tyre* or *puncture*) 1. to get; have a ~ 2. to change; fix a ~ ["apartment"] (esp. BE) 3. to rent a ~ from 4. to let a ~ to 5. to furnish; redecorate; renovate a ~ 6. a council; furnished; garden; high-rise; service; studio; unfurnished ~ (AE has *apartment*) 7. converted; purpose-built ~s 8. a block of ~s (AE has *apartment building/apartment house*)

flatter v. 1. (D; refl.) to ~ on (to ~ oneself on one's knowledge of history) 2. (D; tr.) to ~ smb. about, on

flattered adj. 1. ~ at, by (~ at the invitation) 2. ~ to + inf. (she was ~ to be invited) 3. ~ that + clause (we were ~ that she came to visit us)

flattering adj. 1. ~ to + inf. (it is ~ to be interviewed on TV) 2. ~ that + clause (it's ~ that we've been chosen)

flattery n. to resort to, use ~

flavor, flavour I n. ["characteristic quality"] 1. to impart a ~ to 2. a colloquial; foreign; old-world ~ ["taste"] 3. a bitter; delicate; pleasant; strong; tart ~ 4. an artificial; natural ~

flavor, flavour II v. (D; tr.) to ~ with (to ~ the punch with orange syrup)

flaw n. 1. a fatal ~ 2. a ~ in (there's a ~ in your reasoning)

flea n. ~s bite

flee v. (D; intr.) to ~ from; to

fleece v. (D; tr.) to ~ of

fleet I adj. ~ of foot

fleet II n. ["group of ships"] 1. a fishing ~ 2. a ~ sails 3. (misc.) a ~ calls at a port; the ~ is in

flesh n. 1. to mortify the ~ 2. proud ~

flesh out v. (D; tr.) to ~ with (to ~ a report with greater detail)

flexibility n. 1. to demonstrate, show ~ 2. ~ in; towards 3. the ~ to + inf. (she has enough ~ to cope with the job)

flexible adj. 1. ~ about 2. ~ in; towards

flick v. (D; intr.) to ~ through ("to go through quickly") (to ~ through a report)

flier n. see **flyer**

flies (BE) see **fly III**

flight I n. ["flying"] ["airplane"] 1. to catch, take; miss a ~ 2. to cancel; delay; overbook a ~ 3. a chartered; coast-to-coast; connecting; cross-country; direct; domestic; international; maiden; manned; nonstop; reconnaissance; round-the-world; scheduled; shakedown; solo; space; test; suborbital; supersonic; unmanned ~ 4. a bumpy, rough; smooth ~ 5. a ~ from; to (a ~ from Philadelphia to Frankfurt) 6. a ~ over (a ~ over the South Pole) 7. in ~ (at that moment the plane was in ~ over the Mediterranean) 8. on a ~ (on the ~ to Chicago)

flight II n. ["fleeing"] 1. to take ~ 2. to put to ~ (their army was put to ~) 3. full, headlong ~ (the enemy was in full ~)

flinch v. (D; intr.) to ~ from

fling I n. (colloq.) ["attempt"] 1. to have a ~ at smt. ["period of self-indulgence"] 2. to have a last ~

fling II v. 1. (d; tr.) to ~ at (to ~ a stone at smb.) 2. (d; tr.) to ~ to (they flung their rifles to the ground) 3. (N; used with an adjective) we flung the doors open 4. (P; tr.) they flung their hats into the air; she flung her coat across the room; to ~ caution to the winds

flip v. 1. (slang) (D; intr.) ("to lose one's mind") to ~ over (he ~ped over her) 2. (d; intr.) to ~ through ("to go through quickly") (to ~ through an article)

flirt I n. an incorrigible; terrible ~

flirt II v. (D; intr.) to ~ with

flirtation n. to carry on, engage in a ~ with

flit v. (P; intr.) bees ~ from flower to flower; the idea ~ted into her brain

float v. (P; intr., tr.) they ~ed the logs downstream; we ~ed across the lake; she ~ed to the surface

flock I n. to tend a ~ (of sheep)

flock II v. (P; intr.) the crowd ~ed around the speaker; customers ~ed into the store; to ~ together

floe n. an ice ~

flood I n. 1. a flash; raging ~ 2. the ~ inundated; struck (several cities) 3. a ~ subsides

flood II v. 1. (d; intr.) to ~ into (refugees ~ed into the city 2. (D; tr.) to ~ with (to ~ the market with cheap goods)

flood level n. to reach, rise to ~

floodlight n. to focus; shine a ~ on

floodwaters n. 1. raging; rising ~ 2. ~ recede, subside

floor n. ["story"] 1. the bottom; first; ground; lower; main; second; top; upper ~ 2. on a ~ (on the second ~) ["lower surface of a room"] 3. to mop; scrub; sweep; wash; wipe a ~ 4. to buff; polish;

wax a ~ 5. a dirt (AE), earth (BE); inlaid; parquet; tile; wooden ~ 6. on a ~ (he was sleeping on the ~) ["right to speak"] 7. to ask for; get, take the ~ 8. to give smb. the ~ 9. to yield the ~ ["place where members sit"] 10. to clear the ~ 11. from the ~ (a motion was made from the ~) ["misc."] 12. the ocean ~

USAGE NOTE: In AE the *first floor* and the *ground floor* are usually the same. In BE, the *first floor* is the floor above the *ground floor*.

flop I *n.* 1. a commercial; complete, total ~ 2. a ~ as (she was a complete ~ as an actress)

flop II *v.* 1. (D; intr.) to ~ as (she ~ped as a stage actress) 2. (P; intr.) his head ~ped to the side

flora *n.* 1. intestinal ~ 2. (misc.) ~ and fauna ("plants and animals")

floss *n.* 1. dental ~ 2. candy ~ (BE; AE has *cotton candy*)

flour *n.* 1. to mix ~ with 2. to sift ~ 3. bleached; cake; enriched; self-rising (AE), self-raising (BE); unbleached; white ~ 4. (BE) corn ~ (AE has *cornstarch*)

flow I *n.* 1. to regulate a ~ 2. to cut off; staunch, stem, stop the ~ (of blood) 3. a smooth; steady ~ 4. a cash ~ 5. a lava ~ 6. a ~ from; to (the ~ of traffic from the suburbs to the city)

flow II *v.* 1. (D; intr.) to ~ from, out of (water ~ed from the pipe) 2. (D; intr.) to ~ from; to (the river ~s from east to west) 3. (D; intr.) to ~ into, to (rivers ~ into the sea) 4. (P; intr.) traffic ~ed across town; blood ~s through the body; tears ~ed down her cheeks; the river ~s east

flower *n.* ["plant"] 1. to grow; plant ~s 2. to pick, pluck; water ~s 3. to arrange ~s 4. a fragrant ~ 5. artificial; cut; dried; pressed ~s 6. (US) a state ~ 7. ~s bloom; fade, wither, wilt 8. (misc.) a bouquet; spray of ~s

flu *n.* 1. to come down with (the); have (the) ~ 2. intestinal ~ 3. a strain of ~ (virus) 4. an attack, bout; outbreak; touch of (the) ~

fluctuate *v.* 1. (D; intr.) to ~ between 2. (D; intr.) to ~ with (his mood ~s with the weather)

fluctuation *n.* ~ in (the daily ~ in commodity prices)

fluency *n.* 1. to acquire ~ 2. to demonstrate, display ~ 3. ~ in (~ in a foreign language) 4. ~ to + inf. (she has enough ~ to order a meal in English)

fluent *adj.* ~ in (~ in English)

fluids *n.* 1. (med.) to force; measure; restrict; withhold ~ 2. to drink, take ~ 3. to retain ~ 4. body; clear; cold; hot ~

fluke *n.* (colloq.) ["stroke of luck"] 1. a pure ~ 2. by a ~ (he won by a ~)

flunk *v.* (colloq.) (esp. AE) (D; intr.) to ~ out of (he ~d out of school)

flurry *n.* 1. a brief; sudden ~ 2. a snow ~

flush I *adj.* ["even"] 1. ~ with (~ with the ground) ["rich in"] 2. ~ with (~ with funds)

flush II *n.* ["a rush of blood"] 1. a hot ~ (BE; AE has *hot flash*) ["excitement"] 2. the first ~ (of success)

flush III *v.* (D; intr.) ("to become red") to ~ with (to ~ with pride)

flush IV *v.* 1. (d; tr.) ("to get rid of") to ~ down (she ~ed the poison down the toilet) 2. (d; tr.) ("to chase") to ~ from, out of (they were ~ed from their hiding place) 3. (d; tr.) ("to remove") to ~ out of (to ~ the waste products out of one's body)

flute *n.* to play the ~

flutter *n.* ["confused state"] in a ~

flux *n.* ["constant change"] 1. in ~ 2. a state of ~ (the market is in a state of ~)

fly I *n.* 1. to shoo away the flies 2. to swat a ~ 3. a fruit; tsetse ~ 4. flies buzz; fly

fly II *v.* 1. (D; intr.) to ~ across, over (to ~ across the ocean) 2. (d; intr.) to ~ at ("to attack") 3. (D; intr., tr.) ("to travel by plane") ("to pilot") to ~ from; to (she flew from New York to London; he flew his private plane to Florida) 4. (d; intr.) to ~ into ("to arrive by plane") (to ~ into Chicago) 5. (d; intr.) to ~ into ("to go into") (to ~ into a rage) 6. (d; intr.) to ~ out of ("to depart by plane") (to ~ out of Chicago) 7. (P; intr., tr.) to ~ south; they flew the equipment over to Tokyo 8. (misc.) to ~ blind ("to ~ a plane solely with the help of instruments"); to ~ high ("to be elated or successful"); to ~ nonstop; to ~ in the face of tradition ("to defy tradition"); to ~ off the handle ("to become angry")

fly III *n.* (AE; BE has *flies*) ["opening on trousers"] 1. to close, do up (BE), zip (up) one's ~ 2. to open, unzip one's ~

fly down *v.* (D; intr.) to ~ to the islands

flyer *n.* ["small advertising circular"] to distribute ~s (in the neighborhood) (also *flier*)

fly in *v.* (D; intr.) to ~ from (they flew in from London)

flying *n.* blind; formation; instrument; stunt ~

flying colors, flying colours *n.* ["success"] to come through with ~

flying start *n.* to get off to a ~

flyover (BE) see **overpass**

foam *v.* to ~ at the mouth

fob off *v.* (colloq.) 1. (D; tr.) ("to get rid of by deceit") to ~ as (he ~bed the painting off as a genuine Cezanne) 2. (D; tr.) ("to get rid of by deceit") to ~ on (to ~ cheap merchandise on customers) 3. (BE) (D; tr.) ("to deceive") to ~ with (to ~ customers with cheap merchandise)

focus I *n.* 1. to bring smt. into ~ 2. in ~; out of ~

focus II *v.* (D; intr., tr.) to ~ on (we must ~ our attention on two major problems)

fodder *n.* 1. cannon ~ 2. ~ for

foe *n.* 1. a bitter, implacable; formidable ~ 2. a political ~ 3. (misc.) to vanquish a ~

foetus (BE) see **fetus**

fog n. 1. (a) dense, heavy, thick; light; patchy ~ 2. a ground ~ 3. a ~ burns off, clears, dissipates, lifts 4. a patch of ~ 5. (misc.) in a ~ ("bewildered")

foible n. a human ~

foil I n. ["thin metallic covering"] aluminium (BE), aluminum (AE); gold; silver ~; tinfoil

foil II n. ["comparison"] to act as a ~ for, to

foist v. (d; tr.) to ~ on (they ~ed their problems on us)

foist off v. (D; tr.) to ~ on (to ~ inferior merchandise on a customer)

fold I n. ["group"] 1. in the ~ (they are all back in the ~ now) 2. to return to the ~ 3. to welcome smb. back into the ~

fold II v. 1. to ~ double, in half 2. to ~ neatly 3. (D; tr.) to ~ into (she ~ed the newspaper into a hat)

folder n. a manila ~

fold up v. (D; intr., tr.) to ~ into (the bed ~s up into the wall)

foliage n. 1. dense ~ 2. autumn ~

follow v. 1. to ~ blindly; faithfully 2. to ~ close behind, closely 3. (d; intr.) to ~ in (to ~ in smb.'s footsteps) 4. (L) it ~s from what has been said that he cannot be considered for the job 5. (P; tr.) she ~ed me out of the room; they ~ed us through town

follower n. a devoted, faithful ~

following n. ["followers"] 1. to attract a ~ 2. a devoted, faithful, loyal; large ~

follow through v. (D; intr.) ("to continue") to ~ with

follow-up n. 1. to do a ~ on (the reporter did a ~ on her first story) 2. a ~ to (this letter is a ~ to our telephone conversation)

follow up v. 1. (D; intr.) to ~ on (to ~ on a story) 2. (D; intr., tr.) to ~ with (we should ~ with a letter)

folly n. 1. sheer ~ 2. ~ to + inf. (it was ~ to persist)

fond adj. (cannot stand alone) ~ of (she is ~ of him)

fondness n. 1. to display, show (a) ~ for 2. (a) great ~ 3. (a) ~ for

font n. ["bowl"] a baptismal ~

food n. 1. to cook, prepare; heat; reheat ~ 2. to bolt, gulp (down); chew; digest; eat; swallow; taste ~ 3. appetizing, delicious, tasty; exotic; gourmet; plain; spicy ~ 4. nourishing, nutritious, wholesome ~ 5. coarse; fine; heavy; light; rich; simple ~ 6. canned (AE), tinned (BE); frozen ~ 7. kosher; soul (AE) ~ 8. health; junk ~ 9. ~ spoils 10. scraps of ~ 11. (misc.) ~ for thought

fool I n. 1. to play the ~ 2. to make a ~ of smb. 3. a big; complete; doddering (old); poor; silly; stupid; utter; young ~ 4. a ~ to + inf. (I was a ~ to trust him)

fool II v. 1. (D; tr.) to ~ into (she ~ed them into investing their money) 2. (D; intr.) to ~ with

fool about (BE) see **fool around**

fool around v. (D; intr.) to ~ with (don't ~ with fire)

foolhardy adj. ~ to + inf. (it was ~ of him to try)

foolish adj. ~ to + inf. (it was ~ to take the test without preparation; he was ~ to try)

foolishness n. ~ to + inf. (it was ~ to do it)

fool's paradise n. to live in a ~

foot n. ["lower extremity of a leg"] 1. to stamp; tap one's ~ 2. to shuffle one's feet 3. to get to, rise to one's feet 4. to set ~ on (she has never set ~ on foreign soil) 5. bare feet; flat feet 6. in one's stocking feet 7. at smb.'s feet (the dog lay at their feet) 8. on ~ (they came on ~) 9. (misc.) to drag one's feet ("to move very slowly") or ("to refuse to act"); fast/light/quick on one's feet; to put one's best ~ forward ("to attempt to make a good impression"); to put one's ~ down ("to say 'no' firmly"); to get a ~ in the door ("to make an initial step"); underfoot ("beneath one's feet"); to put one's ~ in one's mouth ("to make an inappropriate statement"); she always lands on her feet ("she always manages to get out of difficulty"); to stand on one's own two feet ("to show independence") ["bottom, end"] 10. at the ~ of (at the ~ of the bed) ["unit of measurement equalling twelve inches"] 11. a cubic; square ~

football n. 1. to play ~ 2. a ~ game (AE), match (BE) 3. association ~ ("soccer") 4. a political ~ ("an issue debated by politicians")

foot fault n. (tennis) to commit a ~

foothold n. 1. to establish, gain, get, secure, win a ~ 2. a firm; precarious ~

footing n. 1. to keep one's ~ 2. to lose one's ~ 3. an equal; firm, secure, solid, sure; unequal ~ 4. a friendly; war ~ 5. on a certain ~ (to be on a friendly ~ with smb.; to place a country on a war ~)

footnote n. a ~ to (the ~s to a chapter)

footprint n. to leave a ~ (in the snow)

footrace n. to run a ~

footsie n. (slang) ["collusion" (AE)] ["footplay"] to play ~ with

footstep n. 1. to dog smb.'s ~s 2. to follow in smb.'s ~s 3. heavy; light ~s

footwork n. fancy ~ (as of a boxer)

forage v. (D; intr.) to ~ for (to ~ for food)

foray n. 1. to make a ~ 2. a bold ~ 3. a ~ into

forbear v. (formal, rare) 1. (d; intr.) to ~ from (to ~ from any predictions) 2. (E) she forbore to make any commitments

forbid v. 1. to ~ categorically, expressly, outright 2. (H) she has forbidden him to smoke in her presence; I ~ you to take the car

force I n. ["compulsion"] ["violence"] 1. to apply, resort to, use ~ 2. to renounce (the use of) ~ 3. armed; brute; deadly; lethal; physical ~ 4. moral; spiritual ~ 5. by ~ ["military power"] 6. to marshal, muster, rally one's ~s 7. to join ~s against; with 8. allied, friendly ~s 9. enemy, hostile ~s 10. armed, military; ground; naval; nuclear; security

~s (strong naval ~s began to shell the enemy positions) 11. an air ~ 12. an expeditionary; guerrilla; occupation; peacekeeping; task ~ (a naval task ~) 13. a show of ~ ["organized body, group"] 14. a labor, work; police; sales; task ~ 15. in full ~ (the police were out in full ~) ["energy"] ["power"] 16. to spend its/one's ~ (the storm has spent its ~) 17. centrifugal; centripetal ~ 18. a driving; explosive; irresistible; magnetic; motivating ~ 19. the vital ~ ("basic force") ["effect"] 20. in ~ (the regulation is still in ~)

force II v. 1. (d; tr.) to ~ into (they ~d their way into the building) 2. (d; tr.) to ~ off (we were ~d off the road) 3. (d; refl., tr.) to ~ on (she tried to ~ her views on us) 4. (d; tr.) to ~ through (to ~ one's way through a crowd) 5. (H) they ~d her to sign 6. (N; used with an adjective) he ~d the door open

foreboding n. 1. a gloomy ~ 2. a ~ that + clause (I have a ~ that there will be a bad storm)

forecast I n. 1. to do, make a ~ 2. a long-range; short-range; weather ~ (to give the weather ~)

forecast II v. (L) she forecast that an earthquake would occur

foreclose v. (D; intr.) to ~ on (they will ~ on us) ("they will foreclose our mortgage")

foredoomed adj. ~ to (~ to failure)

forefront n. in the ~

foreground n. in the ~

forehead n. a high; low ~

foreign adj. ~ to

forerunner n. ["precursor"] a ~ of, to

foresee v. 1. (K) nobody could ~ his running away 2. (L) he foresaw that prices would drop 3. (Q) who can ~ what should be done?

foresight n. the ~ to + inf. (he had the ~ to provide for the education of his children)

forest n. 1. to clear, cut down; denude a ~ 2. a dense, thick; impenetrable; luxuriant; primeval; virgin ~ 3. a broadleaf; coniferous; deciduous; evergreen; (tropical) rain ~ 4. a national; state (US) ~ 5. the ~ stretches for miles

foretell v. 1. (L) no one could have foretold that they would end up here 2. (Q) no one can ~ where they will end up

forethought n. the ~ to + inf. (she had the ~ to save money)

forewarn v. 1. (D; tr.) to ~ about, of 2. (L) we were ~ed that there would be a hurricane

foreword n. a ~ of, to

forfeit v. (B) he ~ed the game to his opponent

forge v. (d; intr.) ("to move ahead") to ~ into the lead

forge ahead v. (D; intr.) to ~ with (they were ~ing ahead with their grandiose plans)

forgery n. 1. to commit ~ 2. a clever; crude; skillful ~

forget v. 1. to ~ completely, utterly 2. (D; intr.) to ~

about (she forgot about the concert) 3. (E) I forgot to call 4. (G; usu. in neg. and interrogative constructions) the children will never ~ visiting this park 5. (K) the audience will not ~ your singing this role 6. (L) don't ~ that we are going out this evening 7. (Q) a person never ~s how to swim

USAGE NOTE: The sentence *she forgot to buy a newspaper* means that she did not buy a newspaper. The sentence *she forgot about buying a newspaper* may mean either that she did not buy a newspaper or that she bought a newspaper but does not remember buying it.

forgetful adj. ~ of (he has become ~ of things)

forgive v. 1. (D; tr.) to ~ for (to ~ smb. for a mistake) 2. (biblical) (O; may be used with one object) ~ us our sins

forgiveness n. to ask for, beg, seek smb.'s ~

fork n. ["pronged device"] 1. a tuning ~ ["division into branches"] 2. at a ~ in the road ["implememt for eating"] 3. a carving; dinner; salad ~

fork over v. (colloq.) (B) we had to ~ our savings to our creditors

form I n. ["printed document"] 1. to fill in (esp. BE), fill out (esp. AE), fill up (obsol. BE) a ~ 2. to hand in, submit a ~ 3. an application; entry; requisition; tax ~ ["shape"] ["manner"] 4. to assume, take (on) a ~ (to assume human ~) 5. an abridged, condensed; comprehensive; concise; convenient, handy; revised ~ 6. in a ~ (the book came out in abridged ~; we reject fraud in any ~; a fiend in human ~) ["grammatical element"] 7. a bound; colloquial; combining; diminutive; free; inflectional; negative; obsolete; plural; positive; singular; surface; underlying; verbal ~ ["behavior"] 8. bad; good, proper ~ (it's bad ~ to come late to a formal reception) ["condition"] 9. bad; excellent, good; superb ~ 10. in (certain) ~ (she was in superb ~ today — she didn't lose a single match) ["good condition"] 11. in (AE), on (BE) ~ (I'm not in ~ today) 12. off ~ ["table giving information"] 13. a racing ~ ["secondary school class"] (BE) 14. in a ~ (in the fourth ~)

form II v. 1. (D; tr.) to ~ from, out of (they ~ed an army out of rabble) 2. (d; tr.) to ~ into (to ~ chopped beef into patties)

formal adj. ~ with (he is always ~ with his colleagues)

formalities n. 1. to complete, go through the ~ 2. bureaucratic; legal ~ 3. the usual ~

format n. a set; suitable ~

formation n. ["arrangement of troops, ships, aircraft"] 1. to break ~ 2. close; tight ~ 3. battle ~ (drawn up in battle ~) 4. in ~ (to fly in close ~) ["structure"] ["grouping"] 5. a cloud; rock ~ 6. (ling.) a back ~

formula n. ["milk mixture for infant feeding"] (AE) 1. to make up, prepare ~ ["symbolic representation"] ["method"] 2. to devise a ~ 3. a chemical; mathematical; scientific ~ 4. a ~ for 5. a ~ to + inf. (a ~ to settle the strike)

form up *v.* (D; intr.) to ~ in (to ~ in three ranks)

fort *n.* 1. a strong ~ 2. a ~ falls; holds out 3. (misc.) to hold (down) the ~ ("to bear responsibility in the absence of others")

fortify *v.* 1. (D; tr.) to ~ against 2. (D; refl., tr.) to ~ with (he ~ied himself with a shot of whiskey)

fortitude *n.* 1. to demonstrate, display, show ~ 2. (humorous) intestinal ~ ("great courage") 3. moral ~ 4. the ~ to + inf. (they had enough ~ to finish the job) 5. with ~ (they underwent their ordeal with great ~)

fortress *n.* 1. to besiege; storm, take a ~ 2. an impenetrable, impregnable; strong ~ 3. a ~ falls; surrenders; holds out

fortunate *adj.* 1. ~ in (we are ~ in having such a nice house) 2. ~ to + inf. (she is ~ to have influential friends) 3. ~ that + clause (it is ~ that we can all meet tomorrow)

fortune *n.* ["wealth"] 1. to accumulate, amass, make a ~ 2. to come into, inherit a ~ 3. to seek one's ~ 4. to dissipate, run through, spend, squander; lose a ~ 5. an enormous, large, vast ~ 6. a family ~ 7. (misc.) it cost me a small ~ to repair our car ["luck"] 8. to try one's ~ 9. the (good) ~ to + inf. (they had the good ~ to find a suitable house quickly) 10. (good) ~ that + clause (it was our good ~ that it did not rain) 11. ~ smiled on us 12. a stroke of good ~ ["fate"] 13. to tell smb.'s ~

forum *n.* 1. to conduct, hold a ~ 2. an open, public ~ 3. a ~ about, on

forward *v.* 1. (usu. B; occasionally A) they always ~ my mail to me 2. (D; tr.) to ~ from; to (to ~ letters to a new address; the books were ~ed from Amsterdam to Tokyo)

foul I *adv.* 1. see **afoul** 2. to fall ~ of (to fall ~ of the law)

foul II *n.* 1. to commit a ~ 2. an intentional, professional (BE); personal; team; technical ~ 3. a ~ against (she committed a ~ against the other guard)

foul III *v.* (esp. basketball) (D; intr.) to ~ out of (to ~ out of a game)

foul out *v.* (esp. basketball) (D; intr.) to ~ on (he ~ed out on five personals)

foul play *n.* ["violence"] 1. to meet with ~ 2. to rule out; suspect ~

found *v.* (D; tr.) to ~ on (our country was ~ed on certain principles)

foundation *n.* ["underlying base"] 1. to lay; shore up a ~ 2. to undermine a ~ 3. a firm, solid, sound, strong ~ 4. a shaky; weak ~ 5. the ~ (of a building) settles ["an endowed institution"] 6. a charitable, philanthropic; educational ~

fountain *n.* 1. a drinking, water ~ 2. (esp. AE) a

soda ~

fours *n.* ["two hands and two feet"] on all ~

fox *n.* 1. an arctic, white; desert; red; silver ~ 2. a ~ barks; yelps 3. a young ~ is a cub, pup 4. a female ~ is a vixen 5. (misc.) as sly as a ~; a wily ~ (usu. fig.)

fraction *n.* 1. to reduce a ~ 2. a common; complex, compound; decimal; improper; irreducible; partial; proper; simple, vulgar ~

fracture *n.* 1. to reduce, set a ~ 2. a compound; compression; greenstick; hairline; simple; stress ~ 3. multiple ~s

frailty *n.* human ~

frame I *n.* a bicycle; mirror; picture; window ~

frame II *v.* (D; tr.) ("to incriminate wrongly") to ~ for (she was ~d for murder)

framework *n.* 1. a conceptual; theoretical ~ 2. within a ~

franchise *n.* ["the right to vote"] 1. to exercise one's ~ ["the license to sell a product or services in a certain area"] 2. to grant a ~ 3. to get; have, hold a ~ 4. to withdraw a ~

frank *adj.* 1. brutally, perfectly ~ 2. ~ about; with (she was ~ with us about everything)

frankness *n.* 1. disarming ~ 2. ~ about; with

frantic *adj.* ~ about, over

fraternity *n.* (US) 1. to pledge a ~ ("to agree to join a fraternity") 2. a college ~ (see also **sorority**)

fraternize *v.* (D; intr.) to ~ with

fratricide *n.* to commit ~

fraud *n.* 1. to commit ~; to perpetrate (a) ~ 2. to expose (a) ~ 3. mail; vote ~

fraudulent *adj.* ~ to + inf. (it was ~ to claim an exemption of that type)

fraught *adj.* (cannot stand alone in AE) ~ with (the situation was ~ with danger)

fray *n.* to enter, join the ~

frayed *adj.* ~ at the edges

frazzle *n.* burnt to a ~ ("completely burnt"); worn to a ~ ("completely worn out")

freak *n.* a ~ of nature

freak out *v.* (slang) (D; intr., tr.) to ~ on (to ~ on drugs)

free I *adj.* 1. ~ from, of (~ from pain; ~ of debt) 2. ~ for (are you ~ for dinner?) 3. ~ with (~ with advice) 4. ~ to + inf. (I am ~ to accept your invitation) 5. (misc.) to set smb. ~

free II *v.* 1. (D; tr.) to ~ from 2. (H) the new schedule ~d me to spend more time with the children

freedom *n.* 1. to gain, secure, win ~ 2. to give, grant ~ (to) 3. to abridge, curtail; deny (a) ~ 4. academic; political; religious ~ 5. ~ of action; of assembly; of inquiry; of movement; of the press; of religion, worship; of speech 6. ~ from (~ from want) 7. the ~ to + inf. (we have the ~ to do what we want)

free-for-all *n.* to join in a ~

free hand *n.* ["freedom of action"] 1. to give smb. a ~ 2. to get; have a ~ 3. a ~ to + inf. (she had a ~ to do whatever she wanted)

free throw *n.* (basketball) to make a ~

free will *n.* 1. to exercise one's ~ 2. of one's own ~

freeze I *n.* ["frost"] ["freezing"] 1. a deep, hard ~ ["freezer"] (BE) 2. a deep ~ ["fixing at a certain level"] 3. to impose a ~ 4. a nuclear; price; wage ~ 5. a ~ on

freeze II *v.* 1. to ~ hard, solid (it froze hard last night) 2. (D; tr.) to ~ out of (to ~ smb. out of a conversation) 3. (D; intr.) to ~ to ~ (his exposed skin froze to the metal; to ~ to death)

freezer *n.* 1. to defrost a ~ 2. a home ~ 3. (misc.) a ~ compartment (in a refrigerator)

freight *n.* ["goods, cargo"] 1. to carry; handle; load; ship ~ ["freight train"] (colloq.) (AE) 2. to hop, jump ("board") a ~

French *n.* Canadian ~ (natives of Quebec speak Canadian ~)

French toast *n.* to make ~

frenzy *n.* 1. a wild ~ 2. in a ~ (in a ~ of despair) 3. (misc.) to work oneself up into a ~

frequency *n.* ["number of repetitions"] 1. alarming; great, high; low ~ 2. with ~ (with alarming ~) ["number of periodic waves per unit of time"] (physics) 3. high; low; medium; ultrahigh ~ 4. a radio ~ 5. on a ~

fresco *n.* to paint a ~

fresh I *adj.* ["recent"] ["new"] ~ from, out of (~ out of school)

fresh II *adj.* (colloq.) (AE) ["bold"] ["impudent"] ~ with (don't get ~ with me)

freshener *n.* an air, room ~

fret *v.* 1. (D; intr.) to ~ about, over 2. (misc.) to ~ and fume

friction *n.* 1. to create, generate, produce ~ 2. ~ among, between; with (there has been some ~ between the union and management)

friend *n.* 1. to be; make a ~ 2. to be; make ~s (with smb.) 3. a bosom, close, good, intimate, old; faithful, fast, loyal, staunch, strong, true; lifelong ~ 4. a mutual; personal; special ~ 5. a fair-weather; false ~ 6. inseparable ~s 7. a pen ~ (BE; CE has *pen pal*) 8. a ~ to (she was a good ~ to us) 9. (misc.) my good ~

friendliness *n.* ~ to, towards

friendly *adj.* 1. ~ of (that was ~ of you) 2. ~ to, towards, with 3. ~ to + inf. (it was ~ of him to offer his help) 4. (misc.) user-friendly

friendship *n.* 1. to cement, develop, form, make, strike up a ~ 2. to cherish, cultivate a ~ 3. to promote (international) ~ 4. to break up, destroy a ~ 5. a close, firm, intimate, lasting, strong, warm; lifelong; long; special ~ 6. the bonds of ~ 7. (a) ~ among, between; with

fright *n.* 1. to give smb. a ~ 2. (esp. BE) to take ~ at

smt. 3. a nasty; sudden ~ 4. stage ~ 5. in, with ~ (to scream with ~)

frighten *v.* 1. (d; tr.) to ~ into (to ~ smb. into submission) 2. (d; tr.) to ~ out of (to ~ smb. out of doing smt.) 3. (misc.) to ~ smb. to death

frightened *adj.* 1. ~ about, at, by, of (~ at the very thought; ~ of the dark) 2. ~ to + inf. (she was ~ to see a stranger approach) 3. (misc.) to be ~ out of one's wits; to be ~ to death

frightening *adj.* 1. ~ to + inf. (it's ~ to contemplate such a possibility) 2. ~ that + clause (it's ~ that a war could break out at any time)

frightful *adj.* see **frightening**

fringe *n.* 1. the lunatic ~ 2. on the ~s (of society)

fringe benefits *n.* to get; provide ~

fritter away *v.* (D; tr.) to ~ on (to ~ one's time away on trifles)

frivolous *adj.* ~ to + inf. (it was ~ of him to make such an accusation)

frog *n.* 1. a grass; green; wood ~ 2. ~s croak; jump 3. an immature ~ is a tadpole 4. (misc.) to have a ~ in one's throat ("to be hoarse")

front I *adv.* to face ~

front II *n.* ["front line"] (mil.) 1. at, on the ~ (the war correspondents spent two days at the ~; there has been no activity on this ~) ["area of activity"] 2. the home; political ~ 3. on a ~ (on a broad ~; on the home ~) ["advanced part"] 4. at the ~ of; in ~ of ["movement"] ["campaign"] 5. a popular; united ~ (to present a united ~) ["boundary"] (meteorology) 6. a cold; occluded; stationary; warm ~ ["walk, road along a body of water"] (BE) 7. a river; sea ~ 8. along a ~ (to walk along the sea ~) 9. on a ~ (is there a hotel on the sea ~?) ["behavior"] 10. to put on, put up a ~ 11. a bold, brave, brazen ~ (to put on a bold ~) ["facade"] 12. a ~ for (the store was a ~ for illegal drug sales) ["misc."] 13. up ~ ("in advance"; "frankly")

front III *v.* 1. (d; intr.) to ~ for (to ~ for the mob) 2. (d; intr.) to ~ on, onto (our building ~s on the main road)

frontage *n.* 1. lake; ocean; river ~ 2. ~ on

frontier *n.* 1. to advance, extend, push back, roll back a ~ (to extend the ~s of science) 2. to cross a ~ 3. on a ~ 4. a ~ between

front line *n.* at, in, on the ~

frost *n.* 1. a bitter, hard, heavy, severe; light, slight ~ 2. eternal ~, permafrost 3. ~ forms 4. a touch of ~

froth *v.* to ~ at the mouth

frown I *n.* 1. to wear a ~ 2. an angry; perpetual ~

frown II *v.* 1. (D; intr.) to ~ at ("to look with displeasure at") (the teacher ~ed at the noisy children) 2. (d; intr.) to ~ on, upon ("to disapprove of") (they ~ on all forms of affection in public) 3. (misc.) to ~ with displeasure

frozen *adj.* ~ hard, solid, stiff

frugal *adj.* (formal) ~ of (esp. BE), with (~ of one's

money)

frugality *n.* (formal) to practice ~

fruit *n.* 1. to grow ~ 2. (also fig.) to bear ~ (not all trees bear ~) 3. to pick, pluck ~ (off a tree) 4. ripe; unripe ~ 5. fresh; luscious; young ~ 6. citrus; tropical ~ (our country exports citrus ~) 7. (fig.) forbidden ~ 8. candied, glazed; canned (AE); tinned (BE); dried; fresh; frozen ~ 9. (misc.) (fig.) the ~s of one's labor

fruitcake *n.* (misc.) (colloq.) as nutty as a ~ ("completely insane")

fruition *n.* 1. to bring smt. to ~ 2. to come to ~

fruitless *adj.* ~ to + inf. (it is ~ to try)

frustrated *adj.* 1. ~ in (she was ~ in her attempts to help) 2. ~ to + inf. (he was ~ to find no support among his friends) 3. ~ that + clause (they were ~ that they could find no support)

frustrating *adj.* 1. ~ to + inf. (it's ~ for me to work in a place like that) 2. ~ that + clause (it is ~ that so few people support this worthy cause)

frustration *n.* 1. to express one's ~ 2. to vent one's ~ on 3. deep; mounting ~ 4. ~ builds up, mounts 5. ~ about, at, over, with

fry *v.* (C) ~ an egg for me; or: ~ me an egg

fry-up *n.* (colloq.) (BE) ["frying of foods"] 1. to do, have a ~ ["dish of fried foods"] 2. to do, make, prepare a ~

fudge *v.* (D; intr.) ("to hedge") to ~ on (to ~ on an issue)

fuel *n.* 1. to take on ~ 2. to run out of ~ 3. to conserve, save ~ 4. aviation; high-octane; jet; leaded; liquid; nuclear; solid; unleaded ~ 5. fossil; synthetic ~s 6. (misc.) (usu. fig.) to add ~ to the fire

fugitive *n.* 1. to track down a ~ 2. a ~ from (a ~ from justice)

fulfillment, fulfilment *n.* 1. to find; seek ~ (in) 2. personal ~ (a sense of personal ~) 3. partial ~ (of the requirements for a doctoral degree)

full *adj.* 1. ~ of (the tank was ~ of water) 2. ~ to the brim

fulminate *v.* (D; intr.) to ~ against

fumble I *n.* to make a ~

fumble II *v.* 1. to ~ blindly 2. (d; intr.) ("to grope") to ~ for (he was ~ling in his pocket for the key) 3. (d; intr.) to ~ with ("to handle clumsily") (she was ~ling with the lock)

fumble about, fumble around *v.* (D; intr.) to ~ for (she ~d around in her pocket for a pencil)

fume *v.* 1. (D; intr.) to ~ about, at, over (to ~ at the delay) 2. (D; intr.) to ~ with (she was ~ming with annoyance) (see also **fret**)

fumes *n.* 1. to emit, give off ~ 2. to inhale ~ 3. cigar; cigarette; gas ~ 4. noxious, toxic ~

fun *n.* 1. to have ~ (we had a lot of ~) 2. to make ~ of smb.; to poke ~ at smb. 3. to spoil the ~ 4. clean, good, harmless ~ 5. ~ to + inf. (it was ~ to go on

the roller coaster = it was ~ going on the roller coaster) 6. for, in ~ (to play for ~) 7. (misc.) let's go for the ~ of it; it was so much ~/such ~

function I *n.* ["characteristic action"] 1. to fulfill, perform a ~ 2. a grammatical ~ 3. the bodily ~s ["mathematical correspondence"] 4. an exponential; inverse; linear; trigonometric ~ ["social event"] 5. to attend a ~ 6. an annual; official; public; social ~

function II *v.* 1. to ~ properly 2. (d; intr.) to ~ as (this valve ~s as a safety device)

fund *n.* 1. to establish, set up a ~ 2. to administer, manage a ~ 3. an inexhaustible ~ 4. a consolidated (BE); contingency, emergency; pension; relief; secret; sinking; slush (colloq.); strike; trust ~ 5. a mutual ~ (AE; BE has *unit trust*)

fundamental *adj.* ~ to

funded *adj.* federally ~

funding *n.* 1. to approve ~ 2. to cut off, terminate, withdraw ~ 3. federal; state ~

funds *n.* 1. to allocate, allot ~ 2. to disburse, pay out ~ 3. to raise ~ 4. federal; local; public; state ~ 5. matching ~ 6. private ~ 7. limited; unlimited ~ 8. (stamped on a check) insufficient ~ (AE; BE has *refer to drawer*) 9. ~ dry up, run out 10. the ~ to + inf. (we have the ~ to complete the work)

funeral *n.* 1. to conduct; hold a ~ 2. to attend a ~ 3. a military; state ~ 4. at a ~

funfare *n.* (BE) at a ~

funk *n.* ["depressed state"] (colloq.) a blue ~ (in a blue ~)

funnel I *n.* to pour smt. through a ~

funnel II *v.* (B) to ~ arms to the partisans

funny *adj.* (colloq.) ["strange"] ["interesting"] 1. ~ about (there's smt. ~ about that affair) 2. ~ to + inf. (it's ~ to watch how people order in a restaurant = it's ~ watching how people order in a restaurant) 3. ~ that + clause (it's ~ that they didn't call)

funny bone *n.* to tickle smb.'s ~

fur *n.* 1. to wear (a) ~ 2. (misc.) the ~ started to fly ("a violent discussion began")

furious *adj.* 1. ~ about, at, over smt. 2. ~ at (esp. AE) with smb. 3. ~ to + inf. (he was ~ to learn that his pay check had been lost) 4. ~ that + clause (she was ~ that the information had been leaked)

furlough *n.* (esp. AE) on ~

furnace *n.* 1. to stoke a ~ 2. a blast; coal; coke; gas; hot-air; oil; open-hearth ~

furnish *v.* 1. to ~ elegantly; luxuriously; plainly, sparsely; tastefully 2. (B) to ~ supplies to the refugees 3. (D; tr.) ("to provide") to ~ for (to ~ blankets for the refugees) 4. (D; tr.) ("to provide") to ~ with (can you ~ us with the necessary information?) 5. (D; tr.) ("to supply with furniture") to ~ with (they ~ed the room with very expensive tables, chairs, and drapes)

furniture *n.* 1. to arrange ~ 2. to upholster ~ 3.

antique; colonial; modern; period ~ 4. garden, lawn, outdoor, patio; office; street (BE) ~ 5. secondhand, used; unfinished (esp. AE) ~ 6. an article, piece, stick of ~

furor, furore *n.* to create a ~

furrow *n.* 1. to make, turn a ~ 2. an even, straight ~

furtherance *n.* in ~ of

fury *n.* 1. to vent one's ~ on, upon 2. to fly into a ~ 3. blind; elemental; pent-up; savage, unbridled ~

fuse I *n.* ["tube, wick used to set off an explosive charge"] 1. to light a ~ 2. a slow ~ (also fig.)

fuse II *n.* ["safety device"] 1. to blow, blow out (esp. AE) a ~ 2. to change a ~ 3. a safety ~ 4. a ~ blows, blows out (esp. AE) 5. (misc.) to blow a ~ ("to get very angry")

fuse III *n.* (AE) ["detonating device"] 1. to arm, set a ~ 2. a contact; delayed; percussion; proximity; time ~ (AE also has **fuze**)

fuse IV *v.* (D; intr.) to ~ with

fusion *n.* nuclear ~

fuss I *n.* 1. to kick up, make, put up, raise a ~ 2. a ~ about, over 3. (misc.) (BE) to make a ~ of smb.

fuss II *v.* 1. (D; intr.) to ~ about, over 2. (D; intr.) to ~ with

fussy *adj.* ~ about

futile *adj.* ~ to + inf. (it's ~ to speculate about what might have been = it's ~ speculating about what might have been)

futility *n.* an exercise in ~

future *n.* 1. to foretell, predict the ~ 2. to plan (out) the ~ 3. to face the ~; to look forward to the ~; to look into the ~ 4. a bleak; dismal; uncertain ~ 5. a bright, promising, rosy ~ 6. the distant; unforeseeable ~ 7. the foreseeable; immediate, near ~ 8. a ~ for (there is no ~ for them here) 9. for; in the ~ (in the near ~) 10. (BE) in ~ ("from now/then on") (be more careful in ~) 11. (misc.) what will the ~ bring?

fuze (AE) see **fuse III**

G

gadfly *n.* ["annoying person"] a ~ to (the reporter was a constant ~ to the government)

gadget *n.* 1. a ~ for (they have a ~ for everything) 2. a ~ to + inf. (a ~ to clean windows)

gaff *n.* (slang) (BE) to blow the ~ ("to reveal a secret")

gaffe *n.* ["blunder"] to commit, make a ~

gag I *n.* (colloq.) ["joke"] as, for a ~ (she did it as/ for a ~)

gag II *v.* (D; intr.) to ~ on (to ~ on food)

gaga *adv.* (colloq.) ["enthusiastic"] to go ~ over smt.

gage see **gauge**

gain I *n.* 1. to make ~s (in recent years minority groups have made considerable political ~s) 2. to consolidate one's ~s 3. to nullify a ~ 4. a considerable, enormous, notable, substantial, tremendous ~ 5. a personal; tangible ~ 6. (an) economic, financial; political ~ 7. ill-gotten ~s 8. (economics) capital ~s

gain II *v.* 1. (D; tr.) to ~ from (to ~ independence from the homeland) 2. (D; intr.) to ~ in ("to acquire") (to ~ in experience) 3. (D; intr.) to ~ on ("to move faster than") (the police were ~ing on the fugitive; to ~ on one's pursuers)

gait *n.* 1. a shambling; steady; unsteady ~ 2. at a certain ~ (at a steady ~)

gale *n.* 1. a heavy, raging, severe, strong ~ 2. a sudden ~ 3. a ~ blows itself out; blows up; rages; subsides

gall I *n.* (colloq.) ["impudence"] 1. unmitigated ~ 2. the ~ to + inf. (he had the ~ to sue for damages)

gall II *v.* (R) it ~ed her that they were not invited

gallant *adj.* ~ to + inf. (it was ~ of him to say that)

gallantry *n.* to display ~

gallery *n.* 1. an art; fresco ~ 2. a press; public; visitors' ~ 3. a shooting ~ 4. (misc.) to play to the ~ ("to attempt to attract public attention")

galling *adj.* 1. ~ to 2. ~ to + inf. (it's ~ to watch him deceive everyone)

gallon *n.* an imperial ~

gallop *n.* 1. to break into a ~ 2. at a ~ (at full ~)

gallows *n.* to be sent to the ~

galvanize *v.* (d; tr.) to ~ into (to ~ smb. into action)

gambit *n.* (chess) 1. to play a ~ 2. to accept; decline a ~ 3. an opening ~

gamble *v.* 1. (D; intr.) to ~ at (to ~ at cards) 2. (D; intr.) ("to risk") to ~ on (to ~ on smb.'s cooperation) 3. (D; intr.) to ~ with (to ~ with smb.'s future)

gambler *n.* a compulsive, inveterate; professional ~

gambling *n.* 1. to ban; legalize ~ 2. compulsive; illegal; legal; offshore; organized ~

game I *adj.* ["ready, willing"] 1. ~ for (are you ~ for

a hike?) 2. ~ to + inf. (are you ~ to go for a swim?)

game II *n.* ["contest, match"] 1. to have, play a ~ 2. to lose; win a ~ 3. (AE) to call ("cancel") a (baseball) ~ 4. to throw ("purposely lose") a ~ 5. a close; crucial; fair ~ 6. a bowl (Am. football); championship; home; practice; wild-card (Am. professional football) ~ ["form of recreation"] 7. to play a ~ 8. a ball; board; card; children's; computer; numbers; parlor; video; word ~ 9. a ~ of cards; a ~ of chance; a ~ of skill ["deception"] 10. to see through smb.'s ~ 11. (AE) a con, confidence ~ ["tactic, strategy"] 12. a waiting ~ 13. a cat-and-mouse ~ ["hunted animals"] 14. to hunt; stalk ~ 15. big; small ~ 16. (fig.) fair ~ ("a legitimate object of attack") (to be fair ~ for smb.) 17. (misc.) a ~ preserve, refuge ["prostitution"] (colloq.) (BE) 18. on the ~ ["misc."] 19. the mating ~ (see the Usage Note for **match**)

games *n.* ["competition"] ["maneuvers"] 1. to hold ~ 2. war ~ 3. the Commonwealth; Olympic; summer; winter ~

gamut *n.* 1. to run the ~ from; to 2. the whole ~ (her performance ran the whole ~ from outstanding to terrible)

gander *n.* (colloq.) ["look"] to have, take a ~ at

gang *n.* 1. to form a ~ 2. to join a ~ 3. to break up, bust (up) a ~ 4. a chain; section; street; work ~ 5. an inner-city; juvenile ~

gangrene *n.* ~ sets in

gang up *v.* 1. (d; intr.) to ~ against, on 2. (d; intr.) to ~ with

gaol (BE) see **jail I, II**

gap *n.* 1. to leave a ~ 2. to bridge, close, fill, narrow a ~ 3. to widen a ~ 4. an unbridgeable, wide, yawning ~ 5. a communications; credibility; culture; generation; gender; trade ~ 6. a ~ between 7. a ~ in

gape *v.* (D; intr.) to ~ at

garage *n.* 1. (esp. AE) a parking ~ 2. (misc.) to park a car in a ~

garage sale *n.* (AE) to have, hold a ~

garb I *n.* 1. ceremonial; everyday; formal, official ~ 2. in (formal) ~

garb II *v.* (d; refl.) to ~ in (they ~ed themselves in colorful costumes)

garbage *n.* (esp. AE) 1. to collect, pick up the ~ 2. to dispose of; dump ~

garden *n.* 1. to lay out; plant a ~ 2. to maintain a ~ 3. to water; weed a ~ 4. a botanical; formal; herb; market (BE); rock; rose; sunken; terraced; vegetable; zoological ~ (see the Usage Note for **yard I**)

gardening *n.* 1. to do, go in for ~ 2. landscape;

market (BE) ~

garlic *n.* 1. a clove of ~ 2. a whiff of ~

garment *n.* a foundation ~

garnish *v.* (D; tr.) to ~ with (to ~ a salad with parsley)

gas *n.* ["accelerator"] 1. to step on the ~ ["combustible gaseous mixture"] 2. to connect; light, turn on the ~ 3. to cut off, disconnect; turn off the ~ 4. coal; natural ~ ["substance dispersed through the air to disable the enemy"] 5. mustard; nerve; poison, toxic; tear ~ ["misc."] 6. laughing ~ ("nitrous oxide") (see also **gasoline**)

gash *n.* 1. to make a ~ 2. a deep, nasty ~

gasket *n.* to blow a ~ (colloq.) ("to lose one's temper")

gasoline *n.* (AE) high-octane; leaded; lead-free, unleaded; premium; regular ~ (BE has *petrol*)

gasp I *n.* 1. to emit, give, let out a ~ 2. an audible ~ 3. a ~ for (a ~ for breath) 4. (misc.) the last ~ ("the last effort")

gasp II *v.* 1. (d; intr.) to ~ at, in, with ("to express surprise at") (they ~ed at our offer; she ~ed in amazement) 2. (D; intr.) ("to breathe with difficulty") to ~ for (to ~ for breath)

gas range *n.* 1. to light, turn on a ~ 2. to turn off a ~

gate *n.* 1. to close, shut; open a ~ 2. the back; front; main ~ 3. a ~ closes, shuts; opens 4. a starting ~ (at a racetrack) 5. at a ~ 6. (misc.) passengers for flight ten proceed to ~ five; (AE) (colloq.) to give smb. the ~ ("to reject smb."); (AE) (colloq.) to get the ~ ("to be dismissed")

gateway *n.* a ~ to (the ~ to the west)

gather *v.* 1. (d; intr.) ("to assemble") to ~ around (they ~ed around the speaker) 2. (d; tr.) ("to conclude") to ~ from (I ~ from the expression on your face that you don't like the proposal) 3. (L) ("to conclude") I ~ that you don't like him

gathering *n.* a family; public; social ~

gauge *n.* ["measuring device"] 1. a fuel; oil; pressure; rain; tire-pressure; water; wind ~ ["distance between rails"] 2. broad, wide; narrow; standard ~

gauntlet I *n.* ["challenge"] 1. to throw down the ~ 2. to pick up, take up the ~

gauntlet II *n.* ["ordeal"] to run a ~ (to run the ~ of reporters)

gavel I *n.* 1. to rap a ~ 2. a rap of the ~

gavel II *v.* (d; tr.) to ~ into (he ~led the protesters into silence)

gawk *v.* (colloq.) (D; intr.) to ~ at

gawp *v.* (BE) (D; intr.) to ~ at

gaze I *n.* 1. to avert; fix; lower one's ~ 2. an admiring; intense, rapt, steady, unblinking; penetrating, piercing; wistful ~

gaze II *v.* 1. to ~ intently 2. (d; intr.) to ~ at 3. (d; intr.) to ~ into (to ~ into the distance; she ~d into my eyes)

gear I *n.* ["toothed wheel as part of a transmis-

sion"] 1. to change (BE), shift ~(s) 2. to reverse ~s 3. to strip ~s 4. bottom (BE), low; high (AE), top (BE); reverse ~ 5. a worm ~ 6. ~s clash, grind; jam, lock, stick; mesh 7. in ~; out of ~ ["equipment"] 8. fishing; hunting; riot; skiing ~ ["clothing"] (colloq.) (BE) 9. trendy ~

gear II *v.* (d; tr.) to ~ to (the whole economy is ~ed to the tourist trade)

gear up *v.* (d; intr., tr.) to ~ for (we are ~ing up for increased production)

gem *n.* (colloq., fig.) 1. an absolute ~ ("smb. or smt. extraordinary") 2. a ~ of an idea ("an excellent idea")

gender *n.* 1. grammatical ~ 2. (the) feminine; masculine; neuter ~ (many languages have no neuter ~) 3. (misc.) ~ neutral

gene *n.* 1. to transfer, transplant ~s 2. to cut; splice ~s 3. a defective; dominant; recessive ~

general I *adj.* in ~ ("generally")

general II *n.* 1. a brigadier (US); commanding; four-star; lieutenant; major ~ 2. (US) a ~ of the Army

generality *n.* 1. a broad, sweeping; vague ~ 2. (to speak) in ~ties

generalization *n.* 1. to make a ~ 2. a broad, sweeping; valid ~ 3. a ~ about 4. a ~ that + clause (it is a valid ~ that exercise promotes good health)

generalize *v.* 1. (D; intr.) to ~ about 2. (D; intr.) to ~ from (to ~ from several specific cases)

general quarters *n.* to sound ~

generation *n.* 1. the baby boom/baby boomer; coming, future, next; new; older; present; younger ~ 2. future; past ~s 3. a lost ~ 4. (misc.) a ~ gap; from ~ to ~

generosity *n.* 1. to demonstrate, display, show ~ 2. great, lavish, magnanimous, unstinting ~ 3. (misc.) to abuse smb.'s ~

generous *adj.* 1. ~ in; to; with (~ with money) 2. ~ to + inf. (it was ~ of her to contribute such a large sum)

genial *adj.* ~ towards

genitalia *n.* (plural) female; male ~

genius *n.* ["great mental capacity, ability"] 1. to demonstrate, show ~ 2. an inventive; rare ~ 3. a spark, stroke of ~ ["ability"] 4. a ~ for (he has a ~ for getting into trouble) ["person of great mental capacity, ability"] 5. an artistic; budding; inventive; mathematical; mechanical; military; musical ~ 6. a rare; real ~ 7. a ~ at (she is a ~ at mathematics) 8. a ~ to + inf. (she was a ~ to think of that)

genocide *n.* to commit, perpetrate ~

gentle *adj.* ~ with

gentleman *n.* 1. a complete, perfect, real, true ~ 2. a country ~ 3. (misc.) every inch a ~; a ~ of the old school

gentry *n.* the landed; local ~

gen up *v.* (slang) (BE) (D; intr., refl., tr.) ("to inform") to ~ about, on (they ~ned me up on the situation)

geography *n.* dialect, linguistic; economic; physical; political ~

geometry *n.* descriptive; Euclidean; plane; projective; solid ~

germ *n.* ["microorganism"] 1. ~s multiply 2. (some) ~s cause disease

germane *adj.* ~ to (~ to the discussion)

German measles *n.* ["rubella"] to catch, come down with ~

gestation *n.* 1. (a) period of ~ 2. in ~

gesticulate *v.* 1. to ~ angrily, frantically, wildly 2. (D; intr.) to ~ with (to ~ with one's arms)

gesture I *n.* 1. to make a ~ 2. to use ~s 3. an angry; derogatory; obscene; rude ~ 4. an empty, meaningless; frantic; habitual ~ 5. a bold; defiant ~ 6. a haughty, imperious ~ 7. a conciliatory; friendly; humane, kind ~ 8. a glorious, grand, grandiose, magnificent, noble ~

gesture II *v.* 1. (D; intr.) to ~ to (the teacher ~d to the pupil to stop talking) 2. (D; intr.) to ~ with (to ~ with one's hand)

get *v.* 1. (B) ("to deliver") I have to ~ a message to her 2. (C) ("to obtain") she got a newspaper for me; or: she got me a newspaper 3. (d; intr., tr.) to ~ across, over ("to cross"); ("to cause to cross") (to ~ across a bridge; the general finally got his troops across the river) 4. (d; intr.) to ~ after ("to exert pressure on") (you'll have to ~ after them if they keep making noise) 5. (d; intr.) to ~ around ("to evade") (we cannot ~ around the regulations) 6. (d; intr.) to ~ at ("to suggest") (what are you ~ting at?) 7. (d; intr.) to ~ at ("to reach") (I hope that the children cannot ~ at the medicine; you're safe here: your enemies cannot ~ at you; to ~ at the truth) 8. (esp. AE) (d; intr.) to ~ behind ("to support") (we must ~ behind her campaign) 9. (d; intr.) to ~ between ("to try to separate") (never ~ between fighting dogs) 10. (D; tr.) ("to receive") to ~ for (what did you ~ for your birthday? she got one hundred dollars for her sewing machine; she got five years for larceny) 11. (d; tr.) ("to obtain, receive") to ~ from, out of (she got the truth out of him; he ~s pleasure from smoking) 12. (d; intr., refl., tr.) to ~ in, into ("to enter"); ("to cause to enter") (to ~ into trouble; to ~ oneself into debt; to ~ smb. into trouble; to ~ into a car; to ~ into a fight) 13. (d; intr.) to ~ into ("to affect") (what got into him?) 14. (d; intr.) to ~ off ("to leave") (to ~ off a train) 15. (d; intr.) to ~ on ("to enter") (to ~ on a train) 16. (d; intr.) to ~ on ("to affect") (to ~ on smb.'s nerves) 17. (d; tr.) to ~ on ("to cause to enter") (he finally got the whole group on the train) 18. (d; intr.) to ~ onto ("to enter") (she could not ~ onto the train) 19. (d; intr.) to ~ onto ("to take up for discussion") (we got onto a very inter-

esting topic) 20. (colloq.) (esp. AE) (d; intr.) to ~ onto ("to become aware of") (we finally got onto her schemes) 21. (d; intr., tr.) to ~ out of ("to leave"); ("to extricate"); ("to extricate oneself from") (to ~ out of a car; I got him out of trouble; to ~ out of trouble; when did he ~ out of prison?) 22. (d; intr.) to ~ over ("to overcome") (you'll have to ~ over your fear of speaking in public) 23. (d; intr.) to ~ over ("to recover from") (has she got/gotten over the shock?) 24. (d; intr.) to ~ past ("to slip by") (we got past the guard) 25. (d; intr.) ("to be unnoticed") to ~ past (the error got past him) 26. (d; intr., tr.) to ~ past ("to cause to pass") to ~ through (to ~ through a door; we could not ~ the piano through the window) 27. (d; intr.) to ~ to ("to reach") (to ~ to a telephone; to ~ to the point; we got to the theater late) 28. (colloq.) (d; intr.) to ~ to ("to affect") (her pleas got to me) 29. (colloq.) (d; intr.) to ~ to ("to bribe") (they got to the mayor himself) 30. (d; tr.) ("to deliver") to ~ to (to ~ smb. to a hospital) 31. (d; intr.) to ~ within ("to come") (don't ~ within range of the enemy artillery) 32. (E) ("to succeed in") if you can ~ to see her, you may receive some help; if you ~ to know her, you'll like her 33. (colloq.) (E; used in the perfect tense) ("to be obliged to") she's got to finish the work by tomorrow 34. (G) ("to begin") he finally got going 35. (H; no passive) ("to bring about") she finally got the television to work; I got a gardener to cut the grass 36. (J; more usu. is H) ("to bring about") she finally got the television working 37. (N; used with an adjective, past participle) ("to make") we got our tools ready; he got us involved; try to ~ them interested 38. (P; intr.) ("to arrive") he finally got home 39. (s) ("to become") to ~ angry; to ~ drunk; to ~ loose; to ~ rid of; to ~ even with smb. 40. (S) (BE) you are ~ting a big girl now 41. (misc.) to ~ cracking ("to start moving"); to ~ in touch with smb.; to ~ nowhere ("to be unsuccessful"); to ~ somewhere ("to score a success")

USAGE NOTE: In AE, the past participle of *to get* is usu. *gotten*—they'd gotten everything ready. In BE, it is *got*—they'd got everything ready. (Note that *ill-gotten gains* is CE.) However, CE does use *have got*: *he's got work*; *I've got to go*. Only BE uses *had got* to form the past tense of this construction—*I'd got to do it yesterday* "I had to do it yesterday". BE also has *he'd got work* "he had work".

get across *v.* (B) ("to make clear") she tried to ~ her ideas across to us

get after *v.* (H) ("to induce") you'll have to ~ him to trim the bushes

get ahead *v.* (d; intr.) to ~ of ("to occupy a position in front of") (try to ~ of him)

get along *v.* 1. (D; intr.) ("to manage") to ~ on (we

cannot ~ on his salary) 2. (D; intr.) ("to relate") to ~ with (how does she ~ with her brother?)

get around v. 1. (d; intr.) ("to find time") to ~ to (we finally got around to answering our correspondence) 2. (L) it got around that she was resigning

getaway n. 1. to make (good) one's ~ 2. a quick ~

get away v. 1. (D; intr.) ("to escape") to ~ from (to ~ from one's pursuers) 2. (D; intr.) ("to escape") to ~ with (the thieves got away with the loot) 3. (d; intr.) to ~ with ("to succeed in") (they didn't ~ with their scheme)

get back v. 1. (d; intr.) ("to get revenge") to ~ at; for (we got back at him for his insult) 2. (D; intr.) ("to return") to ~ from (we got back from our trip early) 3. (D; tr.) ("to receive") to ~ from (we got the money back from him; they got back a lot of money from their investment) 4. (D; intr.) ("to come back, return") to ~ to (I got back to New York yesterday; I'll ~ to you) 5. (d; intr.) to ~ to ("to resume") (to ~ to work)

get behind v. (D; intr.) ("to be late") to ~ in, with (to ~ with one's payments)

get by v. 1. (D; intr.) ("to manage") to ~ on (to ~ on very little) 2. (D; intr.) ("to manage") to ~ with (we'll have to ~ with one car)

get clear v. (D; intr.) to ~ of

get down v. 1. (D; intr.) ("to dismount") to ~ from (to ~ from a horse) 2. (D; tr.) ("to bring down") to ~ from (she got the book down from the shelf) 3. (d; intr.) to ~ to ("to begin"); ("to take up") (to ~ to work; to ~ to details)

get in v. ("to join") 1. (d; intr.) to ~ on (to ~ on the act) ("to participate in"); (to ~ on the ground floor) ("to join at the very beginning") 2. (d; intr.) to ~ with (to ~ with the wrong crowd) 3. (misc.) to ~ out of the rain; to ~ a word in edgeways/edgewise

get off v. 1. to ~ lightly 2. (B) we got a letter off to them yesterday 3. (d; intr.) to ~ to ("to begin with") (to ~ to a good start) 4. (D; intr.) ("to escape") to ~ with (he got off with a light sentence; to ~ with a few scratches)

get on v. 1. (d; intr.) ("to fare") to ~ at (she is ~ting on well at her job) 2. (D; intr.) ("to advance") to ~ in (to ~ in years) 3. (d; intr.) ("to continue") to ~ with (to ~ with one's work) 4. (esp. BE) (d; intr.) ("to get along") to ~ with (how does she ~ with her brother?)

get out of v. (G) I couldn't ~ doing it

get over v. (D; intr.) ("to pass") to ~ to (to ~ to the other side)

get round (BE) see **get around**

get through v. 1. (B) ("to deliver") (she finally got the message through to them) 2. (D; intr.) ("to reach") to ~ to (we could not ~ to her) 3. (D; intr.) ("to finish") (esp. AE) to ~ with (we must ~ with our work)

get-together n. to have a ~

get together v. 1. (d; intr.) to ~ on ("to agree on") (we finally got together on a compromise) 2. (D; intr.) ("to meet") to ~ with (we got together with some friends last night)

get-up n. ["outfit"] an elaborate ~

get up v. 1. (colloq.) (BE) (d; refl., tr.) ("to dress up") to ~ as, like (she got herself up as a ballerina for the party) 2. (D; intr.) ("to rise") to ~ from (to ~ from the table)

ghastly adj. ~ to + inf. (it was ~ of him to say that)

ghetto n. an inner-city, urban ~

ghost n. ["apparition"] 1. to see a ~ 2. to exorcise a ~ 3. a ~ appears 4. to believe in ~s

gibe I n. a ~ about, at

gibe II v. (D; intr.) to ~ at

gift n. ["present"] 1. to give, present a ~ to 2. to bear ~s for, to 3. to heap, lavish, rain ~s on 4. to exchange ~s with 5. an extravagant, lavish; generous; outright ~ 6. a farewell; graduation; shower (AE); wedding ~ 7. to unwrap; wrap a ~ ["talent"] 8. to have a ~ for 9. a ~ for (a ~ for languages)

gifted adj. 1. highly, very; intellectually; musically; physically ~ 2. ~ with

giggle I n. 1. to get, have the ~s 2. an infectious; nervous; silly ~ 3. an attack of the ~s 4. (misc.) (colloq.) (BE) as a ~ ("as a prank")

giggle II v. (D; intr.) to ~ at

gimmick n. an advertising, promotional; election; sales ~

girder n. a steel ~

girdle n. 1. a tight ~ 2. a panty ~

girl n. 1. a career; chorus; college (esp. AE); dancing; flower; office; pinup; stock; working ~ 2. a ball ~ (who retrieves tennis balls) 3. a call ~ ("prostitute who can be summoned by telephone") USAGE NOTE: It can be offensive to call a woman a *girl*. Thus, *career woman* and *working woman* are considered by many to be more acceptable than *career girl* and *working girl*. (See the Usage Note for **woman**.) In some circles, *working girl* can be a euphemism for *prostitute*. In addition, the former use of *girl* in the meaning of "black female" is considered offensive. (See also the Usage Note for **boy**.)

girlfriend n. a steady ~

giro n. ["system of transferring money"] (BE) by ~ (to transfer money by ~)

girth n. to measure the ~ of

gist n. (colloq.) ["main meaning"] to get the ~ of

give v. 1. (A) she gave the book to me; or: she gave me the book 2. (D; tr.) to ~ for (she gave money for a new health center) 3. (H) she gave us to understand that she would attend 4. (misc.) they gave generously of their time

giveaway n. (colloq.) ["unintentional revelation"] a dead ~

give away v. 1. (B) ("to donate") she gave all her

money away to the poor 2. (D; tr.) ("to betray") to ~ to (they gave him away to the police) 3. (Q) ("to betray") they did not ~ where the money was hidden

give back v. (usu. B; sometimes A) she gave the money back to us

give in v. (D; intr.) ("to yield") to ~ to (we had to ~ to their demands)

given adj. (cannot stand alone) ~ to (~ to exaggeration)

give out v. (B) we gave the food out to those who needed it

give over v. 1. (D; refl.) ("to abandon oneself") to ~ to (to ~ oneself over to grief) 2. (esp. BE) (D; tr.) ("to turn over") to ~ to (the building was given over to the youth club) 3. (colloq.) (BE) (used in the imper.) (G) ("to stop") ~ hitting the child

give up v. 1. (B) ("to yield") he gave up his seat to a man on crutches 2. (D; intr.) ("to lose hope") to ~ on (we have given up on her) 3. (D; refl., tr.) ("to turn over") to ~ to (the murderer gave himself up to the police) 4. (G) ("to stop") she gave up attempting to influence them 5. (misc.) they were given up for dead

give way v. (d; intr.) ("to yield") to ~ to (reason gave way to hysteria)

glad adj. 1. ~ about, of 2. ~ to + inf. (I will be ~ to help) 3. ~ that + clause (we are ~ that they are coming)

glance I n. 1. to cast, dart, shoot; steal a ~ at 2. to exchange ~s 3. an admiring; amused; imploring; shy; wistful ~ 4. a casual, cursory, fleeting, passing ~ 5. a knowing; meaningful, significant; penetrating, probing, searching ~ 6. a conspiratorial; furtive; quizzical; sidelong; stolen, surreptitious; suspicious ~ 7. a disapproving, indignant; hostile; withering ~ 8. at a ~ (I recognized her at a ~)

glance II v. 1. ("to look") to ~ admiringly; casually; furtively, surreptitiously; imploringly; indignantly; knowingly; meaningfully; quizzically; shyly; suspiciously 2. (d; intr.) ("to look") to ~ at 3. (d; intr.) ("to look") to ~ down (she ~d down the list) 4. (d; intr.) ("to ricochet") to ~ off (the rock ~d off the window)

gland n. 1. the pituitary; prostate; thyroid ~ 2. the adrenal; ductless, endocrine; eccrine, sweat; lachrymal; lymph; mammary; salivary ~s 3. swollen ~s

glare I n. 1. in the ~ (in the ~ of publicity) 2. the ~ of headlights

glare II v. 1. (D; intr.) ("to stare") to ~ at 2. (d; intr.) ("to shine") to ~ into (the sun ~d into my eyes)

glass n. ["transparent substance"] 1. to blow, make ~ 2. clear, translucent; cut; ground; plate; safety; sheet; stained ~ 3. a pane, sheet; piece, sliver, splinter of ~ ["tumbler"] ["container"] 4. to drink a ~ (of water) 5. to drain; fill a ~ 6. to raise one's ~

(to give a toast) 7. to clink, touch ~es (when giving a toast) 8. a champagne; cocktail; drinking; shot; water; wine ~ 9. a measuring ~ ["optical instrument"] 10. a magnifying ~

glasses n. ["spectacles"] 1. to put on; take off; wear ~ 2. to be fitted for ~ 3. dark, sun; reading ~ 4. a pair of ~ ["binoculars"] 5. field; opera ~ ["misc."] 6. to see life through rose-colored ~ ("to see only the good in life")

gleam I n. 1. a faint ~ 2. a wild ~ (there was a wild ~ in his eyes)

gleam II v. (D; intr.) to ~ with

glean v. (D; tr.) to ~ from

glee n. 1. to express ~ 2. with ~ (to dance with ~)

glide v. (P; intr.) to ~ across enemy lines; to ~ through the air

glider n. 1. to fly a ~ 2. to launch; tow a ~ 3. a ~ flies; glides; soars

glimmer I n. a faint, pale, slight, weak ~

glimmer II v. (D; intr.) to ~ with (the heavens ~ed with stars)

glimpse n. 1. to catch a ~ of 2. a brief, fleeting ~ 3. a ~ into (a ~ into the life of a coal miner)

glint v. (D; intr.) to ~ with

glisten v. (D; intr.) to ~ with

glitch n. (slang) ["mishap"] an unexpected ~

glitter v. 1. (D; intr.) to ~ in (to ~ in the sunlight) 2. (D; intr.) to ~ with

gloat v. (D; intr.) to ~ over

globe n. 1. to circle, girdle the ~ 2. around the ~

gloom n. 1. to express ~ 2. (an) all-pervading, deep, unrelieved ~ 3. ~ about, over (to express ~ over the situation)

gloomy adj. ~ about, over

glorious adj. ~ to + inf. (it would be ~ to live in a peaceful world)

glory I n. 1. to achieve, win ~ 2. to bring ~ to 3. to reflect ~ on 4. crowning; eternal, everlasting ~ 5. military ~ 6. a blaze of ~ 7. ~ to (eternal ~ to our heroes!) 8. in (one's/smb.'s) ~ (to bask in smb.'s ~; to be in one's ~) 9. (misc.) to restore smt. to its former ~; covered in, with ~

glory II v. (d; intr.) to ~ in (to ~ in one's triumph)

gloss I n. ["luster"] 1. to give smt. a ~ 2. a high ~

gloss II v. (d; intr.) to ~ over ("to cover up") (to ~ over one's mistakes)

glove n. 1. boxing; kid; lace; leather; rubber; suede; work ~s 2. an oven ~ (esp. BE; AE has *pot holder*) 3. a pair of ~s 4. (misc.) to fit like a ~ ("to fit perfectly")

glow I n. 1. to cast, emit a ~ 2. an eerie ~ 3. a bright; dim; soft; warm ~

glow II v. 1. to ~ brightly; dimly 2. (D; intr.) to ~ with (to ~ with pride)

glower v. (D; intr.) to ~ at

glued adj. (cannot stand alone) ~ to (he was ~ to his TV set; her eyes were ~ to the door)

glum *adj.* ~ about

glut I *n.* a ~ on the market

glut II *v.* (D; refl., tr.) to ~ with (to ~ the market with cheap goods)

glutton *n.* a ~ for punishment

gnaw *v.* 1. (d; intr.) to ~ (away) at 2. (D; intr.) to ~ through (the rodents ~ed through the wood)

go I *n.* (colloq.) ["attempt"] 1. a ~ at (let's have a ~ at it) ["misc."] 2. to make a ~ of it ("to get along"); always on the ~

go II *v.* 1. to ~ fast; slow 2. (d; intr.) ("to proceed") to ~ about (to ~ about one's business) 3. (d; intr.) to ~ across ("to cross") (to ~ across a river) 4. (d; intr.) to ~ after ("to follow") (this piece of the puzzle ~es after that one) 5. (d; intr.) to ~ after, at ("to seek to reach") (the dog went after the intruder; she went after the job) 6. (d; intr.) to ~ against ("to be opposed to"); ("to be unfavorable to") (this ~es against my principles; to ~ against the grain; the war began to ~ against them) 7. (d; intr.) to ~ around ("to circle") (they went around the block) 8. (d; intr.) to ~ before ("to precede") (this piece of the puzzle ~es before that one) 9. (d; intr.) to ~ beyond ("to exceed") (to ~ beyond the call of duty) 10. (d; intr.) to ~ by ("to travel") (to ~ by car) 11. (d; intr.) ("to pass") to ~ by (to ~ by smb.'s house) 12. (d; intr.) to ~ by ("to follow") (to ~ by the rules) 13. (d; intr.) ("to be known") to ~ by (he used to ~ by another name) 14. (d; intr.) to ~ down ("to descend") (to ~ down a hill) 15. (d; intr.) ("to leave") to ~ for (to ~ for a drive; to ~ for a walk; to ~ for the doctor) 16. (d; intr.) ("to be spent") to ~ for (half our money ~es for food) (see also 27) 17. (d; intr.) ("to be sold") to ~ for (the painting went for a hundred dollars) 18. (d; intr.) to ~ for ("to attack") (he went straight for me; to ~ for the jugular) 19. (d; intr.) ("to try") to ~ for (she went for first prize) 20. (d; intr.) to ~ for ("to concern") (what he said ~es for you too) 21. (colloq.) (d; intr.) to ~ for ("to like") (I could ~ for her; we could ~ for a drink) 22. (d; intr. ("to move") to ~ from; to (to ~ from the sublime to the ridiculous) 23. (d; intr.) to ~ into ("to enter") (to ~ into town; to ~ into the army; to ~ into detail; five ~es into ten twice) 24. (d; intr.) to ~ off ("to leave") (to ~ off duty; the train went off the tracks; to ~ off the air) 25. (d; intr.) to ~ on ("to leave") (to ~ on a trip) 26. (colloq.) (d; intr.) to ~ on ("to judge by"); ("to rely on") (we must ~ on the assumption that he'll agree; we don't have much to ~ on) 27. (esp. BE) (d; intr.) to ~ on ("to be spent for") (half our money ~es on food) (see also 16) 28. (d; intr.) to ~ out of ("to leave") (to ~ out of the house; to ~ out of business) 29. (d; intr.) to ~ over ("to examine") (to ~ over the books) 30. (d; intr.) to ~ over ("to cross") (they went over the mountain) 31. (d; intr.) to ~ through ("to be sold out in") (the dictio-

nary went through three printings) 32. (d; intr.) ("to pass") to ~ through (to ~ through a red light; to ~ through a door; to ~ through channels) 33. (d; intr.) to ~ through ("to endure") (she went through a lot) 34. (d; intr.) to ~ through ("to spend, squander") (he went through his inheritance in six months) 35. (d; intr.) to ~ through ("to repeat") (to ~ through the main points again) 36. (d; intr.) to ~ through ("to conduct") (to ~ through a ceremony) 37. (d; intr.) to ~ through ("to examine") (to ~ through the books) 38. (d; intr.) ("to travel") to ~ to (we went to Alaska) 39. (d; intr.) ("to move") to ~ to (she went to the door) 40. (d; intr.) to ~ to ("to attend") (to ~ to school; to ~ to college) 41. (d; intr.) to ~ to ("to be received by") (the estate went to her; first prize went to my cousin) 42. (d; intr.) to ~ to ("to reach") (this road ~es to town; the railway ~es to the border) 43. (d; intr.) ("to move") to ~ towards (she went towards the exit) 44. (d; intr.) to ~ towards ("to be designated for") (our contributions went towards setting up a shelter for the homeless) 45. (d; intr.) to ~ up ("to ascend") (to ~ up a hill) 46. (d; intr.) to ~ with ("to date"); ("to be a companion to") (Jim ~es with Nancy) 47. (d; intr.) ("to combine") ("to match") to ~ with (which verb ~es with that noun? does this blouse ~ with that skirt?) 48. (d; intr.) to ~ without ("to get along without") (to ~ without water) 49. (E) ("to intend, plan") we are ~ing to see them 50. (G) to ~ shopping 51. (s) to ~ unnoticed; everything went wrong 52. (misc.) to ~ abroad; to ~ bad ("to be corrupted"); ("to turn sour"); to ~ bankrupt; to ~ to bed; to ~ begging ("to be in little demand"); to ~ broke ("to run out of money"); (BE) to ~ to the country ("to call a general election"); to ~ easy on smb. ("to treat smb. leniently"); to ~ to great expense ("to spend a great deal"); to ~ to extremes; to ~ out of one's mind; to ~ native ("to behave like the natives"); to ~ overboard ("to exaggerate"); to ~ to pieces ("to disintegrate"); to ~ to press ("to be printed"); to ~ to sea ("to become a sailor"); to ~ steady (with) (esp. AE) ("to be a boyfriend or girlfriend of"); to ~ to trial (the case went to trial); to ~ to waste ("to be wasted"); to ~ wrong ("to be corrupted"); to ~ from bad to worse ("to become much worse"); she has a lot ~ing for her ("she has many advantages"); cows ~ "moo"

go about *v.* (G) they went about seeking new customers

goad *v.* 1. (D; tr.) to ~ into (to ~ smb. into doing smt.) 2. (D; tr.) to ~ with (she kept ~ing him with insults) 3. (H) he kept ~ing me to fight

go-ahead *n.* 1. to give smb. the ~ 2. to get the ~ 3. the ~ to + inf. (we got the ~ to proceed with the investigation)

go ahead *v.* 1. (D; intr.) to ~ of (she went ahead of me) 2. (D; intr.) ("to proceed") to ~ with (to ~ with one's plans)

goal *n.* 1. to set a ~ 2. to achieve, attain, reach, realize a ~ 3. (sports) to kick, make, score a ~ 4. (sports) to nullify a ~ 5. an immediate; realistic; ultimate ~ 6. a long-range, long-term ~ 7. a short-range, short-term ~ 8. (sports) a disputed; field; winning ~ 9. (BE) (soccer) an own ~ ("a goal scored by a player against his own team")

goal line *n.* to cross; reach the ~

go along *v.* 1. (D; intr.) to ~ for ("to participate") (to ~ for the ride) 2. (D; intr.) to ~ with ("to agree to") (to ~ with a compromise)

go around *v.* (d; intr.) ("to keep company") to ~ with (they were ~ing around with undesirable characters)

goat *n.* 1. to keep (BE), raise (esp. AE) ~s 2. a mountain ~ 3. ~s bleat 4. a flock, herd of ~s 5. a young ~ is a kid 6. a female ~ is a doe or nanny goat 7. a male ~ is a buck or billy goat 8. (misc.) to get smb.'s ~ ("to irritate smb.")

go away *v.* (D; intr.) to ~ for (to ~ for a rest)

go back *v.* 1. (d; intr.) ("to renege") to ~ on (to ~ on one's promise) 2. (D; intr.) ("to return") to ~ to (he went back to his home) 3. (d; intr.) ("to date back") to ~ to (this painting ~es back to the seventeenth century)

God *n.* 1. to bless; praise; pray to; worship ~ 2. to believe in ~ 3. (misc.) in praise of ~; thank ~! ~ forbid! for ~'s sake! almighty ~/~ almighty

go down *v.* 1. (d; intr.) ("to become known") to ~ as; in (to ~ in history as a great ruler) 2. (D; intr.) ("to descend") to ~ into (to ~ into a mine) 3. (d; intr.) ("to descend") to ~ to (to ~ to the river) 4. (BE) (d; intr.) ~ with ("to catch, develop") (to ~ with measles) 5. (misc.) to ~ to defeat; they went down with their ship; (BE) last year he went down from Cambridge ("he left Cambridge last year"); (esp. BE) her speech went down well with them

godsend *n.* 1. a real ~ 2. a ~ to

godspeed *n.* (old-fashioned) to bid, wish smb. ~

go forward *v.* (d; intr.) ("to proceed") to ~ with (to ~ with one's plans)

goggle *v.* (D; intr.) to ~ at

go in *v.* 1. (d; intr.) ("to occupy oneself") to ~ for (to ~ for gardening) 2. (d; intr.) ("to join") to ~ with ("to join") (he agreed to ~ with them)

going *n.* ["progress"] rough, slow ~ (to face rough ~)

going-over *n.* ["beating"] ["inspection"] 1. to give smb./smt. a ~ 2. to get a ~ 3. a good ~ (to get a good ~)

gold *n.* 1. to mine; pan; prospect for ~ 2. to strike ~ (also fig.) ("to discover smt. valuable") 3. pure, solid ~ 4. a (rich) vein of ~ 5. a bar of ~ 6. (misc.) as good as ~ ("very good")

gold standard *n.* 1. to adopt the ~ 2. to go off the ~

golf *n.* 1. to play ~ 2. clock (BE); miniature ~ 3. a round of ~ (to play a round of ~)

golf ball *n.* to drive; putt a ~

gong *n.* to sound a ~

gonorrhea *n.* to catch, contract, get; have ~

good I *adj.* 1. any ~ (is he any ~ at chess?) 2. ~ at, in (she is ~ at/in mathematics) 3. ~ for (exercise is ~ for you; this ticket is ~ for a month) 4. ~ to (he is ~ to his parents) 5. ~ with (he is ~ with his hands) 6. ~ to + inf. (it's ~ to be home again; it was ~ of you to come) 7. ~ that + clause (it's ~ that we don't have to work tomorrow) 8. (misc.) for ~ ("forever"); she is ~ about baby-sitting ("she doesn't mind babysitting"); they made ~ their escape ("they succeeded in escaping")

good II *n.* ["something useful"] 1. to do ~ 2. the common; highest ~ ["positive qualities"] 3. to bring out the ~ in smb. ["favor"] 4. in ~ with smb. ["favorable result"] 5. to come to no ~ ["restitution"] 6. to make ~ (for) ["benefit, help"] 7. to do smb. ~ (a rest will do you a world of ~; it will do you ~ to take a vacation) ["misc."] 8. to be up to no ~ ("to be plotting mischief")

goodbye *n.* to say; wave ~ (to)

good offices *n.* through smb.'s ~

goods *n.* 1. to order ~ 2. to send, ship ~ 3. to sell; stock ~ 4. capital; consumer; dry (esp. AE), soft (esp. BE); durable; manufactured; piece, yard (AE) ~ 5. damaged; shoddy; stolen ~ 6. (misc.) to have the ~ on (colloq.) ("to have evidence against"); smb.'s worldly ~; to deliver the ~ ("to keep one's word")

good time *n.* ["enjoyment"] to have a ~

good turn *n.* ["good deed"] to do (smb.) a ~

goodwill *n.* 1. to display, show ~ 2. to promote ~ 3. international ~ 4. a gesture, sign, token of ~

go off *v.* (D; intr.) ("to leave") to ~ with (she went off with my pen)

go on *v.* 1. (d; intr.) ("to continue") to ~ about (to ~ about one's business) 2. (d; intr.) ("to continue") to ~ as (she went on as chairperson) 3. (D; intr.) ("to perform") to ~ as (to ~ as Hamlet) 4. (d; intr.) ("to advance") to ~ to (to ~ to greater accomplishments) 5. (D; intr.) ("to continue") to ~ with (they went on with their work) 6. (E) ("to advance") she went on to become dean 7. (G) ("to continue") he went right on typing

goose *n.* 1. geese cackle, honk 2. a flock, gaggle of geese 3. a young ~ is a gosling 4. a male ~ is a gander

goose bumps, gooseflesh, goose pimples *n.* to get ~

go out *v.* 1. (D; intr.) ("to leave") to ~ for (to ~ for a walk) 2. (esp. AE) (D; intr.) ("to try out") to ~ for (to ~ for a team) 3. (BE) (d; intr.) to ~ to ("to emigrate") (she went out to New Zealand) 4. (D; intr.) ("to go steady") to ~ with (Olga has been ~ing out with Joe) 5. (G) they went out drinking every night 6. (misc.) our hearts ~ to the bereaved ("we have deep sympathy for the bereaved"); to ~ into the world ("to become independent")

go over v. 1. (d; intr.) ("to pass") to ~ from; to (let's ~ from this side of the room to the other side of the room; to ~ to the attack) 2. (d; intr.) to ~ to ("to desert to") (to ~ to the enemy) 3. (misc.) her speech went over well ("her speech was a success")

Gordian knot n. to cut the ~

gorge v. (D; refl.) to ~ on, with (to ~ oneself on sweets)

gorilla n. a band of ~s

gospel, Gospel n. 1. to preach; spread the ~ 2. to believe in the ~ 3. the ~ truth

gossip I n. 1. to spread ~ 2. (BE) to have a ~ (with) 3. common; idle; juicy; malicious, vicious; silly ~ 4. a piece, tidbit (AE), titbit (BE) of ~ 5. ~ about 6. ~ that + clause (have you heard the ~ that he intends to resign?)

gossip II v. (D; intr.) to ~ about; with

go through v. (d; intr.) ("to proceed") to ~ with (to ~ with one's plans)

goulash n. Hungarian ~

go up v. 1. (d; intr.) to ~ against ("to oppose") (to ~ against a formidable foe) 2. (D; intr.) ("to rise") to ~ by (prices went up by ten percent) 3. (d; intr.) to ~ to ("to approach") (she went up to him and said something) 4. (D; intr.) ("to ascend") to ~ to (to ~ to the top) 5. (BE) to ~ to (to ~ to London; to ~ to university) 6. (misc.) to ~ north

governess n. a ~ for, to (she served as a ~ to three small children)

government n. 1. to form a ~ 2. to head; operate, run a ~ 3. to recognize a (new) ~ 4. to bring down, overthrow, topple; destabilize, subvert; dissolve; seize a ~ 5. (a) clean; corrupt; stable; strong; unstable; weak ~ 6. a caretaker; civil; coalition; interim; military; provisional; puppet; shadow ~ 7. an authoritarian, autocratic; communist; conservative; democratic; dictatorial, totalitarian; liberal; parliamentary; reactionary; socialist ~ 8. (a) central; federal; local; municipal; national; provincial ~ 9. a student ~ 10. a ~ falls 11. under a ~ (to live under a democratic ~) 12. (misc.) (BE) ~ and opposition; the ~ benches

USAGE NOTE: In BE, the noun *government* may be used with either a singular or plural verb. In AE, this noun is always used with a singular verb.

governor n. 1. to appoint; elect smb. ~ 2. a deputy, lieutenant; military ~ 3. a ~ general

gown n. an academic; dressing; evening (AE); formal; hospital ~; nightgown; wedding ~

grab v. 1. (C) ~ a few for me; or: ~ me a few 2. (d; intr.) to ~ at (she ~bed at my arm) 3. (d; tr.) to ~ by (he ~bed me by the shoulder) 4. (d; intr.) to ~ for (she ~bed for his pistol)

grabs n. (colloq.) up for ~ ("readily available to anyone")

grace I n. ["short prayer"] 1. to say ~ ["sense"] ["decency"] 2. the ~ to + inf. (she had the good ~ to concede defeat) ["favor"] 3. divine ~ 4. to fall from ~ 5. by the ~ of God 6. in smb.'s good ~s 7. (rel.) a state of ~ ["willingness"] 8. with bad; good ~ ["attractiveness"] 9. effortless ~ ["feature"] 10. a saving ~

grace II v. (d; tr.) to ~ with (she ~d us with her presence)

gracious adj. 1. ~ to, towards (she is ~ to all) 2. ~ to + inf. (it was ~ of him to make the offer)

gradation n. 1. (ling.) vowel ~ 2. a ~ in

grade I n. ["mark, rating"] (esp. AE) 1. to make out ~s; to give a ~ 2. to get, receive a ~ 3. an excellent; high; failing; fair, mediocre; low; passing ~ 4. (a student's) average; top ~s (she got top ~s in all her exams) ["standard"] 5. to make the ~ 6. a high; low; medium; prime ~ ["degree of descent, rise"] 7. a slight; steep ~

grade II v. 1. to ~ high; low 2. to ~ on a curve

graduate I n. 1. a college (AE), university; high-school (AE) ~ 2. a ~ in (a ~ in medicine)

graduate II v. 1. (D; intr., tr.) to ~ from (to ~ from college) 2. (D; intr.) to ~ in (to ~ in law) 3. (misc.) to ~ with honors, cum laude

graduate studies n. to pursue ~

graduate work n. to do ~

graduation n. 1. a college; high-school (AE) ~ 2. ~ from (~ from college)

graduation ceremonies, graduation exercises n. to hold ~

graffiti n. 1. to deface walls with ~ 2. to remove ~

graft I n. ["act of grafting, inserting"] 1. to do a ~ 2. a bone; skin ~ 3. a (skin) ~ takes ["bribes"] (AE) 4. ~ and corruption ["work"] (colloq.) (BE) 5. hard ~

graft II v. (D; tr.) to ~ on to, onto

grain n. ["food plants"] 1. to grow ~ 2. to store ~ ["texture"] 3. a fine; rough; smooth ~ 4. (to go) against the ~; with the ~ ["misc."] 5. to take smt. with a ~ of salt ("to be skeptical about smt.")

grammar n. 1. comparative; descriptive; functional; generative; historical; normative; prescriptive; structuralist; systemic; transformational ~ 2. (misc.) it's bad ~ to say *ain't*

grand adj. see **great**

grandeur n. delusions of ~

grant I n. 1. to award, give a ~ 2. to apply for a ~ 3. to receive a ~ (from) 4. a block; cash; categorical (AE); federal (AE); government; matching; research ~ 5. a ~ for (a ~ for research on folklore) 6. a ~ to + inf. (we received a ~ to attend the conference)

grant II v. 1. (A) the government ~ed a pension to her; or: the government ~ed her a pension 2. (L; may have an object) I ~ (you) that this is true 3.

(formal) (M) I ~ this to be true

granted *adj.* 1. to take smb. for ~ ("to assume that smb. will agree, cooperate") 2. to take smt. for ~ ("to assume that smt. is certain to happen") 3. (misc.) ~ that it's true, so what?

grapefruit *n.* 1. pink; seedless; white ~ 2. (misc.) half a ~; a ~ section

grapes *n.* 1. to pick ~ 2. to press ~ 3. seedless; sweet ~ 4. a bunch of ~ 5. (usu. fig.) sour ~

grapevine *n.* ["circulation of rumors, gossip"] by, on, through the ~ (to hear news through the ~)

graph *n.* 1. to draw a ~ 2. a bar ~

graphics *n.* computer; media ~

grapple *v.* 1. (d; intr.) to ~ for (they ~d for the key) 2. (d; intr.) to ~ with (to ~ with a problem)

grasp I *n.* ["comprehension"] 1. to have a good ~ (of a subject) 2. a firm; thorough ~ 3. an intuitive ~ ["reach"] 4. to slip from smb.'s ~ 5. beyond smb.'s ~ 6. within smb.'s ~

grasp II *v.* 1. (d; intr.) to ~ at, for 2. (D; tr.) to ~ by (to ~ smb. by the arm) 3. (L) they finally ~ed that it was true 4. (Q) they could never ~ how to do it

grass *n.* 1. to cut, mow; water the ~ 2. high, tall ~ 3. a blade; tuft of 4. (misc.) keep off the ~!

grasshopper *n.* 1. ~s jump, leap 2. ~s chirp

grass on *v.* (slang) (BE) (D; tr.) ("to inform on") to ~ to (he ~ed on them to the police)

grate *v.* (D; intr.) to ~ on (the noise ~s on my ears)

grateful *adj.* 1. deeply; everlastingly ~ 2. ~ for; to (I am ~ to you for your help) 3. ~ to + inf. (we were ~ to be alive) 4. ~ that + clause (I'm ~ that you can help)

gratification *n.* 1. to express ~ 2. deep, profound ~ 3. instant ~ 4. smb.'s ~ at

gratified *adj.* 1. ~ at, by, over, with (~ at the outcome) 2. ~ to + inf. (we were ~ to learn that our proposal has been accepted) 3. ~ that + clause (I am ~ that they kept their word)

gratifying *adj.* 1. ~ to + inf. (it was ~ to see the results of the exam) 2. ~ that + clause (it was ~ that she lived to see the fruits of her labor)

gratitude *n.* 1. to express; feel; show ~ 2. deep, profound, sincere, undying; eternal, everlasting ~ 3. ~ for (she expressed her ~ for our help) 4. ~ to (she felt eternal ~ to him for his help) 5. in, with ~ to (we are making this contribution in ~ to all of you)

grave *n.* 1. to dig a ~ 2. to desecrate a ~ 3. a common, mass; pauper's; unmarked; watery ~ 4. at a ~ (to pray at a ~) 5. (misc.) a gravedigger; from (the) cradle to (the) ~

graveside *n.* 1. at a ~ (to pray at a ~) 2. (misc.) a ~ service

gravitate *v.* (d; intr.) to ~ to, towards

gravity *n.* ["seriousness"] 1. to grasp the ~ (of a situation) ["weight"] 2. specific; zero ~ 3. the center; force of ~

gravy *n.* thick; watery ~

gray (AE) see **grey**

graze *v.* (d; intr.) to ~ against (he ~d against the table)

grease *n.* 1. to cut, dissolve ~ 2. axle ~ 3. a spot of ~

great *adj.* (colloq.) 1. ~ at (she's ~ at improvising) 2. ~ to + inf. (it was ~ of you to help; it was ~ to see everyone again = it was ~ seeing everyone again) 3. ~ that + clause (it was ~ that we could finally meet)

great divide *n.* to cross the ~ ("to die")

great guns *n.* (colloq.) to go ~ ("to have great energy")

greatness *n.* to achieve ~

great one *n.* (colloq.) ["enthusiast"] a ~ for (he's a ~ for telling fibs)

greed *n.* 1. to demonstrate, display ~ 2. insatiable ~ 3. ~ for 4. consumed with ~

greedy *adj.* 1. ~ for 2. ~ to + inf. (it was ~ of them to eat up all the candy)

Greek *n.* (colloq.) it was (all) ~ to me ("it was incomprehensible to me")

green I *v.* 1. to turn ~ (of a traffic light) 2. (cannot stand alone) ~ with (envy)

green II *n.* ["color"] 1. (a) bright; dark; light ~ ["green light"] 2. on ~ (turn on ~ only)

green light *n.* ["permission to continue"] 1. to give smb. the ~ 2. to get the ~

greet *v.* 1. to ~ warmly 2. (D; tr.) to ~ with (they were ~ed with cheers) 3. (misc.) to ~ with open arms ("to welcome warmly")

greeting *n.* 1. to extend a ~ 2. to respond to a ~ 3. a cordial, friendly, sincere, warm; enthusiastic ~ 4. an official ~

greetings *n.* 1. to exchange ~ 2. to extend, send ~ 3. to receive ~ 4. to return ~ 5. cordial, friendly, sincere, warm, warmest; enthusiastic ~ 6. official ~ 7. holiday, season's ~ (see also **regards**)

grenade *n.* 1. to launch; lob, throw a ~ 2. a hand; percussion; rifle ~ 3. (misc.) to pull the pin on a ~

grey *n.* dark; light ~

gridlock *n.* (esp. AE) 1. to cause ~ 2. (misc.) ~ paralyzed the western end of the city

gridlocked *adj.* (AE) hopelessly ~ (traffic was hopelessly ~)

grief *n.* 1. to cause ~ 2. to express; feel, suffer ~ 3. to come to ~ 4. to ease smb.'s ~ 5. bitter, deep, inconsolable, overwhelming, profound ~ 6. ~ at, over 7. of ~ (to die of ~) 8. (misc.) good ~! ("exclamation expressing mild dismay")

grievance *n.* 1. to air, vent a ~ 2. to file, submit a (formal) ~ 3. to hear a ~ (the committee heard the ~) 4. to harbor, nurse a ~ 5. to redress; settle a ~ 6. a justified, legitimate, valid; unjustified ~ 7. a ~ against

grieve *v.* 1. to ~ deeply 2. (D; intr.) to ~ for, over 3. (R) it ~d me (to learn) that she had been severely injured

grill I *n.* 1. a charcoal ~ 2. mixed ~

grill II *v.* ("to broil") (C) ~ a hamburger for me; or: ~ me a hamburger

grill III *v.* ("to question") 1. to ~ mercilessly, relentlessly 2. (D; tr.) to ~ about (he was ~ed about his role in the swindle)

grimace I *n.* to give, make a ~

grimace II *v.* (D; intr.) to ~ in, with (to ~ with pain)

grin I *n.* 1. to flash a ~ 2. a broad; contagious, infectious; foolish, silly; sardonic; sheepish ~ 3. (misc.) wipe that silly ~ off your face!

grin II *v.* 1. to ~ broadly 2. (D; intr.) to ~ at 3. (D; intr.) to ~ with (to ~ with pleasure)

grind I *n.* ["boring activity"] the daily ~

grind II *v.* 1. (C) ~ a pound of coffee for me; or: ~ me a pound of coffee 2. (D; tr.) to ~ into (to ~ wheat into flour) 3. (N: used with an adjective) I ground the coffee very fine 4. (misc.) to ~ to a halt; she ground her heel into the dirt

grind away *v.* (colloq.) (D; intr.) ("to work hard") to ~ at (to ~ at one's studies)

grinder *n.* 1. a coffee ~ 2. (AE) a meat ~ (BE has *mincing machine, mincer*)

grip *n.* ["grasp"] ["hold"] 1. to get a ~ on; to strengthen one's ~ on 2. to lose one's ~ 3. to loosen, relax, release; tighten one's ~ 4. a firm, iron, strong, tight, vise-like; loose, weak ~ ["control"] 5. to get a ~ on oneself 6. to lose one's ~ 7. in the ~ of (in the ~ of a general strike) ["device that grips"] 8. a hair ~ (BE; AE has *bobby pin*) ["stagehand"] 9. a first, key ~

gripe I *n.* (colloq.) ["complaint"] 1. a legitimate ~ (he has a legitimate ~) 2. a ~ about 3. a ~ that + clause (her ~ is that she is not treated fairly)

gripe II *v.* (colloq.) 1. (D; intr.) ("to complain") to ~ about, at 2. (L; to) he kept ~ing to everyone that he was not paid enough

grips *n.* to come to, get to (esp. BE) ~ with smt. ("to confront")

grist *n.* ~ for (AE), to (BE) smb.'s mill ("smt. used to good advantage")

grit *n.* ["courage, perseverance"] (colloq.) 1. to display, show ~ 2. true ~ 3. the ~ to + inf. (they had enough ~ to hold out in the face of real hardship)

groan I *n.* 1. to emit, give, heave, let out, utter a ~ 2. a loud ~

groan II *v.* 1. (D; intr.) to ~ about, over (to ~ over new taxes) 2. (D; intr.) to ~ in, with (to ~ with frustration) 3. (d; intr.) to ~ under (the table ~ed under the weight of the food) 4. (L) he ~ed that he had been shot 5. (misc.) to ~ under the weight of oppression

groom *v.* 1. (d; tr.) to ~ as (she was ~ed as our next candidate) 2. (d; tr.) to ~ for (to ~ smb. for the presidency) 3. (H) they were ~ing her to assume the presidency

grooming *n.* good; immaculate ~

groove *n.* 1. (stuck) in a ~ 2. to fit into a ~ 3. to slide along a ~

grope *v.* 1. to ~ blindly 2. (D; intr.) to ~ for (to ~ for one's keys) 3. (P; intr., tr.) to ~ around (in the dark); they ~d their way along the corridor

grotesque *adj.* ~ to + inf. (it was ~ of him to come dressed like that)

ground *n.* ["contested area"] 1. to gain ~ on 2. to hold, stand one's ~ 3. to give ~ 4. to lose, yield ~ ["soil"] ["terrain"] 5. firm, hard, solid; frozen; high; soft; swampy ~ 6. hallowed, holy ~ 7. on the ~ ["interest"] 8. common ~ (to find common ~ with smb.) ["area used for a specific purpose"] 9. a burial; camping; dumping ~; fairground; hunting; parade; picnic ~; playground; proving; recreation (BE) ~ ["area of knowledge"] 10. to cover, go over ~ (we covered the same ~ yesterday) ["misc."] 11. to break ~ ("to begin building"); to break new ~ ("to explore smt. new"); to get off the ~ ("to get started"); from the ~ up ("from the very beginning"); on delicate ~ ("in a situation that demands great tact"); to get off the ~ ("to get started"); on dangerous ~ ("exposed to danger"); on safe ~ ("in safety"); on shaky ~ ("without a firm basis"); smb.'s favorite stamping ~ ("smb.'s favorite spot"); (to occupy) the moral high ~

grounded *adj.* (usu. does not stand alone) ~ in (she is well ~ in grammar)

ground floor *n.* to be in on/get in on the ~ ("to be part of an undertaking from the beginning")

grounding *n.* ["training"] 1. to receive a (good) ~ (in) 2. a ~ in (a good ~ in physics)

ground rules *n.* to establish, lay down the ~

grounds *n.* ["basis, foundation"] 1. to give smb. ~ 2. ample; solid ~ 3. moral ~ 4. for (~ for divorce) 5. ~ to + inf. (we had sufficient ~ to sue; there were no ~ to deny bail) 6. on ~ (on what ~?) ["sediment"] 7. coffee ~ ["area used for a specific purpose"] 8. hospital ~ 9. on the (hospital) ~

groundwork *n.* to do, lay the ~ for

ground zero *n.* at ~ (a camp was set up at ~)

group I *n.* 1. an affinity; age; family; social ~ 2. an ethnic, minority; special-interest; splinter ~ 3. a peer; pressure ~ 4. a control; discussion; encounter ~ 5. (music) a pop; rock ~ 6. (BE) a ginger ~ ("a group of activists") 7. (medical) a blood ~

group II *v.* 1. (d; intr.) to ~ around (the scouts ~ed around their leader) 2. (d; tr.) to ~ by (the children were ~ed by age) 3. (d; tr.) to ~ into (the teams were ~ed into two leagues) 4. (d; tr.) to ~ under (to ~ several types under one heading)

grouse *v.* (D; intr.) to ~ about

grove *n.* an olive; orange ~

grovel *v.* 1. (D; intr.) to ~ to (she will not ~ to anyone) 2. (misc.) to ~ at smb.'s feet; to ~ in the dirt

grow *v.* 1. (D; intr.) to ~ by (the city grew by ten percent) 2. (d; intr.) ("to develop") to ~ from (oaks ~ from acorns) 3. (d; intr.) ("to develop") to ~ into (the small shop grew into a large firm) 4. (colloq.) (d; intr.) to ~ on ("to become likable") (the strange new sculpture just ~s on you) 5. (d; intr.) to ~ out of ("to become too large for") (the children grew out of their clothes) 6. (d; intr.) ("to develop") to ~ out of (the city grew out of a small village) 7. (d; intr.) ("to develop") to ~ to (to ~ to adulthood; to ~ to one's full height) 8. (E) ("to begin") we grew to love them 9. (s) ("to become") to ~ longer; old; older; taller (in the autumn/fall the days ~ longer) USAGE NOTE: The verb *grow* "to become" often suggests a gradual process rather than a sudden change. Compare *it grew cold* (gradually) and *it turned cold* (suddenly).

growl *v.* 1. (B) he ~ed a few words to us 2. (D; intr.) to ~ at (the dog ~ed at the jogger) 3. (L; to) he ~ed (to us) that he would be late

growth *n.* 1. to foster, promote, stimulate ~ 2. to arrest, inhibit, retard, stifle, stunt ~ 3. rapid; untrammeled; zero ~ 4. economic; population ~ (zero population ~) 5. (med.) a benign, non-cancerous, non-malignant; cancerous, malignant; inoperable ~ (to remove a malignant ~) 6. (biology) cell ~ 7. ~ in 8. (misc.) a scraggly ~ (of beard)

grow up *v.* (E) she grew up to be an able politician

grub *v.* (d; intr.) ("to rummage") to ~ for (to ~ for food)

grudge *n.* 1. to bear, harbor, have, hold, nurse a ~ 2. a bitter; deep-seated ~ 3. a ~ against

grumble *v.* 1. to ~ constantly 2. (D; intr.) to ~ about, at, over; to (to ~ at new taxes) 3. (L; to) they ~d (to us) that the decision was not fair

grumbler *n.* a chronic, constant ~

grumbling *n.* chronic, constant ~

grumpy *adj.* (colloq.) ~ about

grunt I *n.* to give, let out, utter a ~

grunt II *v.* 1. (B) she ~ed a few words to them 2. (L; to) he ~ed (to her) that he would get up later 3. (misc.) to ~ and groan

guarantee I *n.* ["assurance of quality"] 1. to give, offer, provide a ~ 2. a written ~ 3. a ~ against (a ~ against mechanical defects) 4. under ~ (the car is still under ~) ["assurance, pledge"] 5. to give a ~ 6. a firm ~ 7. a ~ that + clause (we have a firm ~ that the work will be finished on time)

guarantee II *v.* 1. to ~ fully 2. (A; usu. without *to*) we cannot ~ you regular hours 3. (D; tr.) to ~ against (to ~ a new car against rust) 4. (D; tr.) to ~ for (to ~ a washing machine for one year) 5. (H) it's ~d to last five years 6. (L) she can ~ that you will be satisfied 7. (formal) (M) the owner ~d the coins to be genuine

guard I *n.* ["group of sentries"] ["sentry"] 1. to call out the ~ 2. to mount, post the ~ 3. to change,

relieve the ~ 4. an advance; armed; color; honor; palace; police; rear; security ~ (they slipped past the palace ~) 5. under ~ ["guard duty"] 6. to stand ~ over 7. on ~ (to go on ~) ["militia"] 8. a home ~ ["police officer"] ["auxiliary police officer"] 9. (AE) a crossing ~ 10. a prison ~ (AE; BE has *warder, wardress*) (see the Usage Note for **warden**) ["alertness"] ["readiness to fight"] 11. off ~; on ~ (to be caught off ~) 12. to put smb. on their ~ 13. to keep one's ~ up 14. to let one's ~ down ["protective article of clothing"] 15. a knee; nose; shin ~

guard II *v.* 1. to ~ closely (the player was ~ed closely by her opponent) 2. (d; intr.) to ~ against (to ~ against catching cold) 3. (D; tr.) to ~ against (to ~ an embassy against intruders) 4. (D; tr.) to ~ from (to ~ smb. from harm)

guardian *n.* 1. to appoint smb. ~ 2. (often fig.) a self-appointed ~ 3. a legal ~

guerrilla *n.* 1. an armed ~ 2. (misc.) a ~ band

guess I *n.* 1. to have (esp. BE), hazard, make, take (AE), venture a ~ 2. an educated, informed, shrewd; lucky; random, wild; rough ~ 3. a ~ that + clause (it is only a ~ that she will be appointed)

guess II *v.* 1. to ~ shrewdly; wildly 2. (D; intr.) to ~ at (to ~ at smb.'s age) 3. (L) I could not have ~ed that she would be late 4. (Q) ~ where the money is 5. (misc.) to keep smb. ~ing; (AE) I ~ she's late; I ~ not; I ~ so

guesswork *n.* (I got the answer) by pure ~

guest *n.* 1. to greet, welcome; introduce a ~ 2. to have ~s (for dinner) 3. a dinner; wedding; weekend ~ 4. an invited; welcome ~ 5. an unexpected; uninvited; unwelcome ~ 6. a paying; regular ~ (at a hotel)

guff *n.* (colloq.) ["back talk"] to take ~ (I will not take any of your ~)

guffaw *n.* 1. to emit, give, let out a ~ 2. a loud ~

guidance *n.* 1. to offer ~ to; to provide ~ for 2. to seek ~ 3. friendly; parental; spiritual; vocational ~ 4. under smb.'s ~

guide I *n.* ["guidebook"] 1. a handy; pocket ~ 2. a ~ to (this handbook is a good ~ to London) ["person who guides"] 3. a tour ~

guide II *v.* (P; tr.) to ~ smb. around a city; she ~ed us out of the congested area

guidelines *n.* 1. to draw up, establish ~ for 2. to adhere to, follow ~ 3. to ignore; violate ~ 4. flexible; rigid ~

guilt *n.* 1. to establish, prove smb.'s ~ 2. to bear (the) ~ for 3. to admit; expiate one's ~ 4. collective ~ 5. (misc.) ~ by association; the burden of ~

guiltless *adj.* ~ of

guilt trip *n.* (slang) to lay a ~ on smb.

guilty *adj.* 1. to find; pronounce ~ of (the jury found him ~ of murder) 2. to feel ~ about smt. 3. ~ of 4. (misc.) to plead ~; to plead not ~; ~ as charged

guinea pig *n.* to serve as a ~; to be used as a ~

guise *n.* in, under the ~ of (under the ~ of friendship)

guitar *n.* 1. to play (a/the) ~ 2. to pluck, strum a ~ 3. an acoustic; electric, steel; Hawaiian ~

gulf *n.* 1. a wide, yawning ~ 2. a ~ between (a wide ~ between generations)

gull *v.* (old fashioned) ("to trick") 1. (D; tr.) to ~ into 2. (D; tr.) to ~ out of

gulp *n.* 1. to take a ~ 2. at, in a ~ (she swallowed the whole spoonful at one ~)

gum *n.* 1. to chew ~ 2. bubble; chewing ~ 3. a stick of ~

gumption *n.* (colloq.) ["courage"] the ~ to + inf. (will she have enough ~ to refuse?)

gun I *n.* 1. to aim; fire; point a ~ at 2. to turn a ~ on smb. 3. to draw a ~ (on) 4. to hold a ~ on smb. 5. to hold a ~ to smb.'s head 6. to load; unload a ~ 7. (artillery) to lay ("adjust") a ~ 8. to carry, pack (AE, colloq.) a ~ 9. to silence an enemy ~ 10. to spike ("make unusable") a ~ 11. an antiaircraft; antitank; BB; burp (colloq.), submachine, Tommy (colloq.); field; heavy; machine; ray; riot ~; shotgun; starter's; stun; zip (AE) ~ 12. a grease; spray ~ 13. a ~ fires, goes off; jams; misfires 14. (misc.) to jump the ~ ("to start too early"); to stick to one's ~s ("to staunchly defend one's position"); a smoking ~ ("dramatic proof")

gun II *v.* (d; intr.) to ~ for ("to search for with a gun") (also fig.)

gunfire *n.* 1. heavy, murderous ~ 2. under ~

gung ho *adj.* (slang) ["enthusiastic"] ~ about

gunpoint *n.* to hold smb. at ~

gunpowder *n.* 1. smokeless ~ 2. a grain of ~

gurgle *v.* (B) the baby ~d a few sounds to us

gush *v.* 1. (d; intr.) to ~ from (a column of oil ~ed from the ground) 2. (d; intr.) to ~ over (they were ~ing over their new grandchild)

gusher *n.* ["oil well from which oil gushes"] to hit a ~

gush forth *v.* (D; intr.) to ~ from

gust *n.* fitful; strong ~s (the wind was blowing in fitful ~s)

gusto *n.* with ~ (with great ~)

gutless *adj.* (colloq.) ~ to + inf. (it was ~ of him to lie)

guts *n.* (colloq.) 1. the ~ to + inf. (he doesn't have the ~ to do it) 2. (misc.) to hate smb.'s ~ ("to hate smb. very much")

gutter *n.* (fig.) 1. to get down into the ~ 2. to drag smb. down into the ~

guy *n.* (colloq.) 1. a great, nice, regular (AE) ~ 2. a bad; good ~

USAGE NOTE: In AE *you guys* (colloq.) can now be used in speaking not only to a group of men, but also to a group of men and women, and even to a group of women only.

gymnastics *n.* to do ~

gyp *v.* (slang) (D; tr.) to ~ out of (he ~ped me out of my share)

gyrate *v.* 1. ~ wildly 2. (D; intr.) to ~ to (the young people were ~ting wildly to the music)

H

habeas corpus *n.* (to obtain; seek) a writ of ~

habit *n.* ["custom"] ["usual manner"] 1. to acquire, develop, form, pick up; have a ~ 2. to make a ~ of smt. 3. to fall into, get into a ~ 4. to break, shake a ~; to get out of a ~; (slang) to kick the ~ 5. to break smb. of a ~ 6. an annoying; bad; deplorable; strange ~ 7. an entrenched, fixed, ingrained; incurable ~ 8. a filthy; nasty; repulsive ~ 9. a good ~ 10. irregular; regular ~s 11. a ~ of (he has a bad ~ of interrupting people) 12. by force of ~ 13. in the ~ of (she is in the ~ of getting up early) 14. out of ~ (I did it out of ~) ["costume"] 15. a monk's; nun's; riding ~

habitat *n.* a natural ~

habits *n.* ["customs"] drinking; eating; sleeping; work ~

habituated *adj.* ~ to (they became ~ to drugs early in life)

hack I *n.* ["hireling"] a party ~

hack II *v.* 1. ("to chop") (d; intr.) to ~ at (to ~ at a tree) 2. (computers) (d; intr.) ("to penetrate") to ~ into (to ~ into secret files) 3. (misc.) they ~ed their way through the forest; to ~ (a body) to pieces

hack away *v.* (D; intr.) ("to chop away, reduce") to ~ at (to ~ at the dense undergrowth; to ~ at the work force)

hacking *n.* computer ~

hackles *n.* ["anger"] to raise smb.'s ~

haemorrhage (BE) see **hemorrhage**

haggle *v.* (D; intr.) to ~ about, over; with

hail *v.* 1. (C) ("to summon") ~ a taxi for me; or: ~ me a taxi 2. (esp. AE) (d; intr.) to ~ from ("to be from") (where do you ~ from?) 3. (D; tr.) ("to proclaim") to ~ as (she was ~ed as a heroine) 4. (rare) (N; used with a noun) ("to name") to ~ smb. emperor

hailstones *n.* ~ fall

hair *n.* 1. to brush; comb; curl ~ 2. to backcomb (BE), tease (AE); braid, plait; do; set; style ~ 3. to cut; trim ~ 4. to blowdry, dry; shampoo, wash ~ 5. to color, dye, tint ~ 6. to part one's ~ (he parts his ~ in the middle, and I part mine on the side) 7. to stroke smb.'s ~ 8. to lose, shed one's ~ (people lose their ~; animals shed their ~) 9. braided, plaited; curly; dry; kinky; normal; oily; straight; wavy ~ 10. bobbed, short; long; thick; thinning ~ 11. unmanageable, unruly ~ 12. dark; light ~ 13. black; blond; brown; dark; grey; light; red; white ~ 14. body; facial; pubic ~ 15. ~ falls out; grows 16. a single ~ 17. a curl, lock; strand of ~ 18. a head; shock of ~ (he has a thick head of ~) 19. (misc.) how does she wear her ~? to tear one's ~ out ("to become extremely agitated"); to split ~s

("to nitpick"); to get in smb.'s ~ ("to annoy smb."); to let one's ~ down ("to lose one's inhibitions"); by a ~ ("by a small margin")

haircut *n.* 1. to get a ~ 2. to give smb. a ~ 3. a short ~

hairline *n.* a receding ~

hair's breadth *n.* 1. (to miss) by a ~ 2. (to come) within a ~ (of)

half *determiner, pronoun* 1. (in telling time) ~ past the hour (it's ~ past four) 2. ~ of (~ of them) 3. (misc.) it's not ~ bad ("it's fairly good"); to go halves ("to divide smt. evenly")

USAGE NOTE: The use of the preposition *of* is necessary when a pronoun follows. When a noun follows, the *of* may be omitted—half (of) the students; half (of) the audience. However, compare—she spent half (of) the money; she spent her half of the money. Note the constructions—a half hour, half an hour.

half-mast *n.* at ~ (the flags were flying at ~)

half price *n.* at ~ (to admit children at ~)

halftime *n.* at ~ (the band performed at ~)

halfway *adj., adv.* 1. ~ between 2. (misc.) to meet smb. ~ ("to compromise with smb.")

hall *n.* 1. a city, town; concert; dance; entrance; lecture; mess; music; pool; study ~ 2. (BE) in ~ (at a university) (to dine; live in ~)

hallucination *n.* 1. to have ~s 2. a drug-induced ~

halo *n.* a ~ (a)round (the sun, moon)

halt *n.* 1. to call a ~ (to smt.) 2. to bring smt. to a ~ 3. to come; grind, screech to a ~ 4. an abrupt; complete; grinding, screeching ~

halter *n.* to put a ~ on an animal

ham *n.* 1. baked; cured; honey-roast (BE), sugar-cured (AE); smoked ~ 2. a slice of ~

hamburger *n.* to grill a ~

hammer I *n.* 1. to swing a ~ 2. (sports) to throw the ~ 3. a drop ~ 4. to come under the (auctioneer's) ~ ("to be sold at auction")

hammer II *v.* 1. (d; intr.) to ~ at (to ~ at enemy positions) 2. (D; tr.) to ~ into (to ~ a nail into a wall; to ~ an idea into smb.'s head)

hammer and tongs *adv.* to go at smb. ~ ("to attack smb. with great energy")

hammer away *v.* (d; intr.) to ~ at (to ~ at a compromise; to ~ at the enemy)

hamper *v.* (D; tr.) to ~ in

hand I *n.* ["part of the arm below the wrist"] 1. to shake smb.'s ~; to shake ~s (with smb.) 2. to clasp, grab, grasp; press; pump; take smb.'s ~ 3. to hold; join ~s 4. to lay one's ~s on 5. to cup; fold one's ~s 6. to clap one's ~s 7. to wring one's ~s 8. to lower; raise one's ~ 9. bare; delicate; dishpan (esp. AE);

gentle ~s (he grasped the hot metal with his bare ~s) 10. a pair of ~s 11. by ~ (to do smt. by ~) 12. by the ~ (to lead smb. by the ~; take smb. by the ~) 13. ~s off; ~s up ["help"] ["active participation"] 14. to give, lend smb. a ~ 15. to lift a ~ (he would not lift a ~ to help) 16. to have a ~ in 17. a guiding; helping ~ (to lend a helping ~) 18. a ~ at, in, with (give me a ~ with the dishes) ["worker"] 19. a factory, mill (BE); hired; ranch ~ ["specialist"] 20. an old ~ (at smt.) ["pointer on a clock"] 21. an hour; minute; second, sweep-second ~ ["ability"] 22. to try one's ~ at smt. ["control"] 23. to get out of ~ 24. to take smb. in ~ 25. a firm; iron ~ ["pledge of betrothal"] (formal) 26. to ask for smb.'s ~ ["cards held by a player"] (also fig.) 27. to show, tip one's ~ 28. to have, hold a ~ 29. a good, strong; losing; weak; winning ~ (she held a strong ~) ["possession"] ["ownership"] 30. to fall into smb.'s ~s 31. to change ~s 32. enemy; private; safe ~s (the documents fell into enemy ~s; the files were in safe ~s) ["source"] 33. at first ~ ("directly") 34. at second ~ ("indirectly") ["viewpoint"] 35. on one (AE), on the one ~ ("from one viewpoint"); on the other ~ ("from the other viewpoint") ["closeness"] 36. at, on ~ (near at ~) ["applause"] 37. to give smb. a ~ 38. to get, receive a ~ 39. a big ~ (they got a big ~ after their performance) ["misc."] 40. do you have a free ~? ("are you free to help?"); we had a free ~ in this matter ("we were able to function in this matter without any restrictions"); she is good with her ~s ("she has great manual dexterity"); a show of ~s ("a vote taken by raising hands"); to lay a ~ on smb. ("to harm smb."); from ~ to mouth ("barely existing"); to have one's ~s full ("to be very busy"); to eat out of smb's ~ ("to be subservient to smb."); to force smb.'s ~ ("to compel smb. to act"); to throw up one's ~s ("to give up"); to wash one's ~s of smt. ("to shed all responsibility for smt."); with a heavy ~ ("crudely"); to suffer at smb.'s ~s; with clean ~s ("innocent"); to go ~ in ~ ("to go together"); to win ~s down ("to win easily"); all ~s on deck! ("all sailors on deck"); to have time on one's ~s ("to have free time"); to have worthless property on one's ~s ("to be burdened by worthless property"); ~ in glove with ("conspiring with")

hand II *v.* 1. (A) ~ the salt to me; or: ~ me the salt 2. (misc.) you have to ~ it to her! ("you must give her credit!")

hand back *v.* (usu. B; occ. A) she ~ed the documents back to me

handball *n.* 1. to play ~ 2. team ~

handbook *n.* a ~ for (a ~ for beginners)

handbrake *n.* 1. to put the ~ on 2. to release the ~

handcuff *v.* (D; tr.) to ~ to (the prisoner was ~ed to the bars)

handcuffs *n.* 1. to put (the) ~ on smb. 2. to remove ~

hand down *v.* 1. (D; tr.) to ~ from; to (to ~ a tradition to the next generation; to ~ old clothes from one child to the next) 2. (misc.) she ~ed it down to me from the shelf

handicap *n.* ["assigned advantage or disadvantage"] 1. to assign, give; have a ~ ["hindrance"] 2. to overcome a ~ 3. a physical ~ 4. a ~ to 5. under a ~

hand in *v.* (B) to ~ homework to the teacher

handle I *n.* ["part grasped by the hand"] 1. to turn a ~ 2. (BE) a starting ~ 3. (to pick up smt.) by the ~ ["misc."] (colloq.) 4. to fly off the ~ ("to lose one's temper"); to get a ~ on smt. ("to comprehend smt.")

handle II *v.* to ~ carefully; to ~ with care

handler *n.* a baggage; food ~

handling *n.* 1. delicate; gentle; tactful ~ (the matter requires delicate ~) 2. careless, inept; rough ~ 3. special ~ (by the post office)

hand on *v.* (D; tr.) to ~ to (to ~ traditions to the next generation)

hand organ *n.* to grind, play a ~

handout *n.* (colloq.) ["alms"] 1. to give smb. a ~ 2. to ask for a ~

hand out *v.* (B) to ~ food to the needy

hand over *v.* (B) to ~ a criminal to the police

handpicked *adj.* 1. ~ for 2. ~ to + inf. (she was ~ to do the job)

handrail *n.* 1. to grasp a ~ 2. to hold on to a ~

handshake *n.* 1. a cordial, warm; firm ~ 2. (misc.) a golden ~ ("a gift presented to smb. who is retiring")

handspring *n.* to do, turn a ~

handstand *v.* to do a ~

handwriting *n.* 1. to decipher smb.'s ~ 2. clear, legible; illegible ~ 3. (misc.) (AE) to see the ~ on the wall (for CE, see **writing** 5) ("to see impending failure")

handy *adj.* 1. to have, keep smt. ~ 2. ~ at; with (she's ~ with tools) 3. ~ for (this tool is ~ for various jobs) 4. ~ to + inf. (it's ~ to have a pharmacy so close = it's ~ having a pharmacy so close) 5. (misc.) to come in ~

hang I *n.* (colloq.) ["knack"] to get the ~ of smt.

hang II *v.* 1. ("to be suspended"); ("to fall") to ~ limp; loose, loosely 2. (colloq.) (d; intr.) to ~ around ("to frequent") (to ~ around a bar) 3. (D; intr.) ("to be suspended") to ~ by (to ~ by a thread) (see also 16) 4. (D; tr.) ("to execute by hanging") to ~ for (he was ~ed for murder ~) 5. (d; intr.; tr.) ("to be suspended; to suspend") to ~ from (flags hung from the windows; to ~ a flag from a window) 6. (d; intr.) ("to cling") to ~ on (to ~ on smb.'s arm) 7. (d; intr.) to ~ on, upon ("to listen closely to") (they hung on every word) 8. (d; intr.) to ~ on ("to depend on") (the outcome ~s on the results of the election) 9. (d; intr.) to ~ on ("to be

oppressive") (time ~s on their hands) 10. (d; intr., tr.) ("to be suspended"); ("to suspend") to ~ on (she hung the picture on the wall) 11. (d; intr.) ("to cling") to ~ onto (he hung onto my arm) 12. (colloq.) (d; intr.) to ~ onto ("to keep, retain") (we intend to ~ onto this property; they hung onto their customs) 13. (d; intr.) ("to lean") to ~ out of (to ~ out of a window) 14. (d; intr.) ("to be suspended") to ~ over (the coat was ~ing over the chair; the threat of war hung over the country) 15. (d; tr.) ("to drape, suspend") to ~ over (she hung the wet towel over the tub) 16. (misc.) her paintings were ~ing in the museum; to ~ by a thread ("to be in a critical situation"); to ~ in the balance ("to be undecided")
USAGE NOTE: The past and past participle of *hang* are *hung* or *hanged*. The form *hanged* is more usual in the sense "killed by hanging". In other senses the form *hung* is usual.

hang around v. (colloq.) ("to spend time") 1. (D; intr.) to ~ at (they ~ at the senior citizens club) 2. (d; intr.) to ~ with (he likes to ~ with the boys down at the bar)

hang back v. (D; intr.) to ~ from (to ~ from giving information)

hang down v. (D; intr.) to ~ from; to (to ~ from a branch)

hanger n. a coat ~

hang on v. 1. (D; intr.) to ~ to ("to grasp") (to ~ to the rail) 2. (D; intr.) to ~ to ("to keep") (to ~ to one's privileges) 3. (misc.) to ~ for dear life; (BE) to ~ like grim death

hangout n. (colloq.) ["gathering place"] a ~ for

hang out v. (slang) (D; intr.) ("to spend time") to ~ with (to ~ with one's friends)

hangover n. 1. to have a ~ 2. to sleep off a ~

hang-up n. (colloq.) ["worry"] to have a ~ about

hang up v. (D; intr.) to ~ on (she hung up on me) ("she broke off her telephone conversation with me")

hanker v. (colloq.) 1. (d; intr.) to ~ after, for ("to want") (to ~ for a good steak) 2. (E) ("to want") she ~ed to go south

hankering n. (colloq.) 1. a ~ after, for 2. a ~ to + inf. (a ~ to travel)

happen v. 1. (d; intr.) to ~ on, upon (we ~ed on an old ruin) 2. (D; intr.) to ~ to (what ~ed to you?) 3. (E) she ~ed to be there when we arrived 4. (L) it (so) ~ed that they were out when we got there

happiness n. 1. to bring ~ (to) 2. find; seek ~ 3. to wish smb. ~ 4. personal ~ 5. a feeling, glow of ~

happy adj. 1. deliriously ~ 2. ~ about; at; with 3. (colloq.) ~ for (we are ~ for them) 4. ~ to + inf. (I'll be ~ to attend the meeting; she'll be ~ to work here = she'll be ~ working here) 5. ~ that + clause (they are very ~ that the proposal was accepted)

harangue I n. to deliver, launch into a ~

harangue II v. (D; tr.) to ~ about (she always ~s the children about their untidy rooms)

harassment n. 1. to engage in ~ 2. to subject to ~ 3. police; sexual ~

harbor, harbour n. 1. to clear; dredge a ~ 2. to blockade; mine a ~ 3. an artificial; natural ~ 4. a safe ~ (also fig.)

hard I adj. ["demanding"] 1. (cannot stand alone) ~ on (she's very ~ on herself) ["difficult"] 2. ~ to + inf. (this book is ~ to translate = it is ~ to translate this book = it is a ~ book to translate; she is ~ to understand = it is ~ to understand her; it is ~ to get them to participate = it is ~ getting them to participate) 3. ~ for (this job will be ~ for me; it is ~ for us to concentrate) ["misc."] 4. to play ~ to get ("to pretend to be uninterested in an invitation or proposal"); ~ of hearing

hard II adv. ~ at (~ at work)

hardened adj. (cannot stand alone) ~ to (~ to suffering)

hard labor n. at ~ (he was sentenced to three years at ~)

hard line n. (pol.) to adopt, take; follow a ~ (on)

hard-pressed adj. ~ to + inf. (we were ~ to find justification for our actions)

hard put adj. ["facing difficulties"] ~ to + inf. (she was ~ to pay her rent)

hardship n. 1. to bear, endure, face, suffer, undergo ~ 2. to overcome a ~ 3. severe, unrelieved ~ 4. a ~ to + inf. (it was a real ~ for her to get to work on time)

hard time n. (colloq.) 1. to give smb. a ~ ("to make things difficult for smb.") 2. (misc.) we had a ~ finding her; to fall on ~s

hard up adj. (colloq.) ("in need of") ~ for (they are ~ for new ideas)

hardware n. 1. computer ~ 2. military ~

hark back v. (d; intr.) ("to revert") to ~ to (to ~ to the old days)

harm n. 1. to cause, do ~ 2. to undo ~ 3. to come to ~ 4. considerable, grave, great, immeasurable, irreparable, severe ~ 5. (actual/BE; grievous) bodily ~ 6. ~ in; to (there is no ~ in doing that; was any ~ done to the children?) 7. ~ to + inf. (it will not do you any ~ to try again) 8. (misc.) to mean no ~; out of ~'s way; (esp. AE) in ~'s way

harmful adj. 1. ~ to (~ to one's health) 2. ~ to + inf. (it's ~ to smoke)

harmless adj. 1. ~ to 2. ~ to + inf. (it's ~ to daydream)

harmonica n. (esp. AE) to play a ~

harmonize v. (D; intr.) to ~ with

harmony n. ["concord, agreement"] 1. to achieve; maintain ~ 2. close; perfect ~ 3. ethnic; marital; racial; religious ~ 4. in ~ (with) ["congruity"] (ling.) 5. vowel ~

harness I n. in ~ ("at work")

harness II *v.* (D; tr.) to ~ to (to ~ horses to a coach)

harp I *n.* to play the ~

harp II *v.* (d; intr.) to ~ on (to keep ~ing on the same old theme)

harpoon *n.* to hurl, throw; shoot a ~

harsh *adj.* ~ to, with (he's too ~ with the children)

harvest *n.* 1. to bring in, reap a ~ 2. an abundant, bountiful, bumper, rich; poor ~ 3. (fig.) a bitter ~

hash I *n.* ["failure, mess"] to make a ~ of smt.

hash II *v.* (colloq.) (AE) (d; intr.) to ~ over ("to discuss") (to ~ over a question)

hassle I *n.* ["struggle"] a ~ to + inf. (it was a ~ to get a visa = it was a ~ getting a visa)

hassle II *v.* (D; tr.) to ~ about, over; with

haste *n.* 1. to make ~ ("to hurry") 2. with unseemly ~ 3. in ~ (they acted in great ~) 4. (misc.) in their ~ to leave, they forgot their keys

hasten *v.* (E) he ~ed to apologize

hat *n.* 1. to don, put on a ~ 2. to doff, take off; tip a ~ 3. to have a ~ on, to wear a ~ 4. a bowler; cowboy, stetson, ten-gallon; top ~ 5. a fur; panama; straw ~ 6. a cardinal's ~ 7. (misc.) to pass the ~ ("to collect money"); to hang up one's ~ ("to retire"); to take one's ~ off to smb. ("to congratulate smb.; to feel respect for smb."); to talk through one's ~ ("to say foolish things"); to throw one's ~ in/into the ring ("to enter a political campaign"); to keep smt. under one's ~ ("to keep smt. confidential"); at the drop of a ~ ("without hesitation")

hatch *n.* 1. to batten down the ~es 2. an escape ~

hatchet *n.* to bury the ~ ("to make peace")

hate I see **hatred**

hate II *v.* 1. to ~ bitterly, deeply, intensely, profoundly, utterly 2. (E) he ~s to work 3. (G) she ~s going to school 4. (J) he ~s people watching when he practices 5. (K) she ~s his staying out late 6. (misc.) (colloq.) I'd ~ (for/AE) you to think that it was intentional; she ~s it when people watch her

hateful *adj.* 1. ~ to 2. ~ to + inf. (it was ~ of him to say that)

hatred *n.* 1. to arouse, incite, stir up ~ 2. to instill ~ 3. to incur ~ 4. to develop; express; feel; show ~ 5. abiding, bitter, blind, deep, deep-rooted, implacable, intense, profound, violent, virulent ~ 6. ~ for, towards 7. consumed with, filled with ~

hat trick *n.* to do a ~

haul I *n.* ["distance"] a long; short ~ (also fig.)

haul II *v.* (D; tr.) to ~ from; to (to ~ coal from the mines to the city)

haul off *v.* (D; tr.) to ~ to (they were all ~ed off to jail)

haul up *v.* (D; tr.) to ~ before (to ~ smb. up before a magistrate)

haunt *n.* a favorite; quiet ~

have *v.* 1. (d; tr.) ("to keep") to ~ about (BE), around (it's dangerous to ~ a gun around the house) 2. (d; tr.) to ~ against ("to consider as grounds for rejection, dislike") (I ~ nothing against him) 3. (D; tr.) to ~ for ("to consume") (what are we ~ing for dinner?) 4. (colloq.) (d; tr.) to ~ on ("to possess evidence against") (you ~ nothing on me) 5. (d; tr.) to ~ on ("to wear") (to ~ a sweater on) 6. (d; tr.) to ~ on ("to be busy with") (I don't ~ anything on tonight) 7. (E) ("to be obligated") we ~ to leave 8. (H) I ~ a great deal/nothing/something to say to her; I ~ nothing to wear; we ~ smt. to tell you; I ~ a job to do 9. (esp. AE) ("to cause") he had a gardener cut the grass (CE also has: he got a gardener to cut the grass); she had her research assistant look up the information; (CE) what would you have me do? 10. (J) we soon had them all laughing 11. (N; used with an adjective; past participle) ("to consume"); ("to cause") I'll have my martini dry; we had a meal sent up to our room; they had the building torn down; he had his hair cut; she had her tonsils removed 12. (misc.) he had two children by his first wife; to ~ one's tonsils out; to ~ it in for smb. ("to have a grudge against smb."); she had a strange thing happen to her ("a strange thing happened to her"); he had it coming (to him) ("he deserved it"); I had it out with them ("we had a very frank discussion"); she had her handbag stolen ("her handbag was stolen")

haven *n.* 1. a safe; tax ~ 2. a ~ for

havoc *n.* to play, raise, wreak ~ with

hay *n.* 1. to make ~ 2. to bundle, gather, stack ~ 3. a haystack 4. a bale of ~; a wisp of ~ 5. (misc.) (AE; colloq.) to hit the ~ ("to go to sleep")

haymaker *n.* (colloq.) ["punch"] to throw a ~

hayride *n.* to go on a ~

haywire *adj.* (colloq.) to go ~ ("to be ruined")

hazard *n.* 1. a health; fire; occupational; safety ~ 2. a ~ to (a ~ to health)

hazardous *adj.* 1. ~ to (~ to one's health) 2. ~ to + inf. (it is ~ to work at that height = it is ~ working at that height)

haze *n.* 1. a light ~ 2. the ~ lifts

hazy *adj.* ~ about (she's ~ about the details)

head I *n.* ["upper part of the body"] 1. to nod; shake one's ~ 2. to bare; bow; drop, duck, hang, lower; lift, raise; move; poke, stick; scratch; toss; turn one's ~ (to scratch one's ~ in amazement; to poke one's ~ around the corner) 3. to hold one's ~ high ("to be proud") 4. from ~ to foot ["length of a horse's head"] 5. by a ~ (our horse won by a ~) ["poise"] 6. to keep; lose one's ~ 7. a cool, level ~ (to keep a level ~) ["person"] 8. to count ~s 9. per ~ (to charge two dollars per ~) ["brain"] 10. to use one's ~ 11. to cram, fill, stuff smb.'s ~ (with nonsense) 12. a clear ~ 13. to have a ~ for (figures) 14. (misc.) it never entered my ~ that they would not support the proposal ["climax"] 15. to bring smt. to a ~ 16. to come to a ~ (the boil came to a ~; when will the crisis come to a ~?) ["front part"] 17. at the ~ (of a column) ["leader"] 18. a titular ~ 19. (misc.) crowned ~s (of state) ["chairperson"] (esp. BE) 20. (the) department ~, (the) ~ of (the) department (AE usu. has *chair, chairperson*) ["misc."] 21. a thick ~ of hair; success went to his ~ ("his success made him conceited"); ~ over heels ("completely"); ~s up ("watch out"); to get smt. through one's ~ ("to finally comprehend smt."); to hang one's ~ in shame ("to be greatly embarrassed"); to be ~ and shoulders above smb. ("to be greatly superior to smb."); to keep one's ~ above water ("to barely survive"); over smb.'s ~ ("incomprehensible"); out of one's ~ ("delirious"); to make ~ or tail of ("to comprehend"); to put ~s together ("to collaborate"); prejudice reared its ugly ~ ("prejudice appeared"); he took it into his ~ to leave ("he suddenly decided to leave"); success turned her ~ ("she was spoiled by success"); to bury one's ~ in the sand ("to isolate oneself from reality"); to have a swelled, swollen (BE) ~ ("to be conceited"); to bang/beat/knock one's ~ against a stone wall ("to be cruelly frustrated")

head II *v.* 1. (d; intr.) ("to go") to ~ for (to ~ for the city; to ~ for a downfall) 2. (P; intr., tr.) they ~ed (their boat) east; to ~ out of town; to ~ for the west coast; they were ~ing towards the city

headache *n.* 1. to get; have a ~ 2. a bad, racking, severe, splitting; migraine; sick; slight ~ 3. the noise gave her a ~

head back *v.* 1. (D; intr.) to ~ from (to ~ from the theater) 2. (D; intr.) to ~ to, towards (to ~ towards home)

head count *n.* to do, have, make, take a ~

heading *n.* 1. a chapter ~ 2. under a ~

headlights *n.* 1. to turn on the ~ 2. to turn off the ~ 3. to dim, dip (BE) the ~ 4. (misc.) (in) the glare of the ~

headline *n.* 1. to carry a ~ 2. banner; front-page; screaming ~s 3. in (banner) ~s 4. the story made the ~s

headlock *n.* ["wrestling hold"] to get, put; have a ~ on smb.

headquarters *n.* 1. to set up ~ 2. supreme ~ 3. an army; corps; military; police ~ 4. at ~

headstand *n.* to do a ~

headstart *n.* to have a ~ on, over

headway *n.* to gain, make ~ against; with

heal *v.* (D; tr.) to ~ of (she was ~ed of her illness)

healer *n.* a faith ~

healing *n.* faith ~

health *n.* ["condition of the body and mind"] 1. to enjoy good ~ 2. to maintain; promote (good) ~ 3. to recover, regain one's ~ 4. to risk; ruin, undermine smb.'s ~ 5. bad, broken, delicate, deteriorat-

ing, failing, feeble, fragile, frail, ill, poor ~ 6. good; robust; excellent ~ 7. holistic; mental; physical ~ 8. for one's ~ (she swims for her ~; smoking is bad for one's ~) 9. in a certain ~ (they are in good ~) 10. (misc.) the state of smb.'s ~ ["science of protecting the health of the community"] 11. community, public; occupational ~ ["misc."] 12. (here's) to your (good) ~!

health care *n.* 1. to deliver, provide ~ 2. holistic ~

health insurance *n.* 1. national ~ 2. compulsory; voluntary ~

healthy *adj.* ["promoting health"] 1. ~ for (smoking is not ~ for you) ["safe"] (colloq.) 2. ~ to + inf. (it's not ~ to walk there at night = it's not ~ walking there at night)

heap I *n.* 1. a compost; dump; scrap ~ 2. in; on a ~ (everything was piled up in a ~)

heap II *v.* 1. (d; tr.) to ~ on, upon (to ~ gifts on smb.) 2. (D; tr.) to ~ with (she ~ed my plate with food)

hear *v.* 1. (d; intr.) ("to learn") to ~ about, of (we have heard of her; have you heard about the earthquake?) 2. (d; intr.) ("to receive word") to ~ from (I have not heard from him about this matter) 3. (I) ("to perceive by ear") I heard them go out 4. (J) ("to perceive by ear") we heard them coming up the stairs 5. (L) ("to learn") we have heard that he is in town 6. (N; used with a past participle) ("to listen to") we heard the aria sung in Italian 7. (Q) ("to learn") we heard why she left

hearing *n.* ["perception of sounds"] 1. acute, keen ~ 2. defective, impaired ~ 3. hard of ~ 4. ~ impaired ["session of a committee, court"] 5. to conduct, hold a ~ 6. a fair, impartial; open ~ (he got a fair ~) 7. Congressional ~s 8. an administrative; court; judicial; pre-trial; public ~ 9. at a ~ (to testify at a ~)

heart *n.* ["organ that circulates the blood"] 1. to transplant a ~ 2. a bad, weak; good, healthy, strong ~ 3. an artificial ~ 4. a ~ beats; fails, stops; palpitates, throbs; pounds, thumps; pumps blood ["the heart as the center of emotion"] 5. to gladden; harden smb.'s ~ 6. to break; steal, win smb.'s ~ my ~ aches, bleeds (for her); my ~ is broken; my ~ skips a beat 7. from the ~ (to speak from the ~) 8. in one's ~ (in my ~ I know that she is right) ["disposition"] 10. a cold, cruel, hard; good, kind, soft, tender, warm; stout ~ (she has a kind ~); a ~ of gold ["liking"] 11. to have a ~ for (she has no ~ for this type of work) 12. after one's own ~ (he's a man after my own ~) ["sympathy"] 13. to have a ~ (have a ~ and lend me some money) ["essence"] 14. to get to the ~ of smt. 15. at ~ (he's not bad at ~) ["feeling"] 16. to have a change of ~ 17. a heavy; light ~ 18. with a (heavy) ~ ["courage"] 19. to take ~ from (he took ~ from her example) 20. to lose ~ 21. a brave; faint ~ 22. my ~ sank 23. the ~ ~

to + inf. (I didn't have the ~ to tell her) ["memory"] 24. by ~ (to know a poem by ~) ["resolve"] 25. to set one's ~ (on doing smt.) 26. a change of ~ ["misc."] 27. a bleeding ~ ("one who always supports the underdog"); to eat one's ~ out ("to brood"); to lose one's ~ to ("to fall in love with"); from the bottom of one's ~ ("sincerely"); to have one's ~ in the right place ("to have good intentions"); to do smb.'s ~ good ("to make one happy"); with all one's ~ ("wholeheartedly"); to take smt. to ~ ("to take smt. seriously"); the way to smb.'s ~ ("how to please smb."); my ~ was not in it ("I did not really want to do it")

heart attack n. 1. to have a ~ 2. a fatal; massive; mild; severe; sudden ~

heartbroken adj. 1. ~ about, at, over (~ over a friend's death) 2. ~ to + inf. (she was ~ to learn of the verdict) 3. ~ that + clause (I'm ~ that he cannot come)

heart failure n. congestive; massive ~

heartless adj. ~ to + inf. (it was ~ of her to say that)

heartstrings n. ["deep feelings"] to tug at smb.'s ~

heat I n. ["warmth"] 1. to conduct; generate, produce; radiate ~ 2. to absorb ~ 3. to alleviate the ~ 4. blistering, extreme, great, intense, oppressive, scorching, stifling, sweltering, unbearable ~ 5. dry; penetrating; radiant; red; white ~ 6. animal; body ~ 7. ~ emanates from (an oven) 8. (misc.) the body loses ~ ["excitement"] 9. in the ~ (of battle) ["estrus, sexual excitement"] 10. in (AE), on (BE) ~ (the bitch was in ~) ["heating system"] 11. to raise, turn up; turn on the ~ 12. to lower, turn down; turn off the ~ 13. electric; gas; steam ~ ["preliminary race, race"] 14. to run a dead ~ 15. a qualifying ~ ["pressure"] (colloq.) 16. to put the ~ on (the police were putting the ~ on him)

heat II v. 1. (C) ~ some water for me; or: ~ me some water 2. (D; tr.) to ~ to (she ~ed the oven to two hundred degrees)

heater n. 1. to turn on; turn up the ~ 2. to turn down; turn off the ~ 3. an electric; gas; hot-water, immersion (BE); kerosene (AE); paraffin (BE); oil; radiant; space ~

heating n. central; forced-air; space ~

heave v. 1. (P; tr.) ("to throw") they ~d the trash into the pit 2. (misc.) as we were ready to leave, our friends hove into view

heave-ho n. (colloq.) ["ejection"] to give smb. the (old) ~

heaven n. 1. to go to ~ 2. in ~ 3. (misc.) in seventh ~ ("in a state of bliss"); to move ~ and earth ("to make a maximum effort"); for ~'s sake

hedge n. ["row of shrubs"] 1. to crop, trim a ~ ["protection against loss"] 2. a ~ against (a ~ against inflation)

hedged adj. (esp. BE) ~ about/round with (the project was ~ round with many restrictions)

heed n. to pay ~ to; to take ~ of

heedful adj. (cannot stand alone) ~ of (~ of advice)

heedless adj. (cannot stand alone) ~ of (~ of danger)

heel n. ["tyrannical oppression"] 1. under the (iron) ~ (under the ~ of the occupier) ["misc."] 2. to turn on one's ~ ("to turn away abruptly"); smb.'s Achilles' ~ ("smb.'s vulnerable point"); (BE) down at ~ ("shabby")

heels n. 1. to click one's ~ 2. built-up; high, stiletto; low ~ 3. to be at, on smb.'s ~ ("to follow smb. closely") 4. (misc.) to cool/kick (BE) one's ~ ("to be kept waiting"); to dig in one's ~ ("to be stubborn; to resist"); (esp. AE) down at the ~ ("shabby"); to drag one's ~ ("to move slowly"); to kick up one's ~ ("to be very lively"); to show one's ~ ("to flee"); to take to one's ~ ("to flee"); hard on smb.'s ~ ("close to smb.");

hegemony n. 1. to have ~ over 2. under smb.'s ~

height n. 1. to attain, reach a ~; to rise to a ~ 2. to clear; scale a ~ 3. a dizzy, precipitous, vertiginous ~ 4. dizzying ~s 5. one's full ~ (she rose to her full ~) 6. a ~ above; below (at a ~ of two hundred feet above sea level) 7. at a ~ (at the ~ of one's success; to fly at a ~ of ten thousand feet) 8. in ~ (ten feet in ~) 9. (misc.) to adjust the ~ of a table; to achieve new ~s

heir n. 1. to fall ~ (to fall ~ to a large estate) 2. an ~ apparent; an ~ presumptive 3. an immediate; rightful ~ 4. ~ to

USAGE NOTE: The form *heiress* is used in some combinations as, for example, *heiress to a large fortune*.

heirloom n. a family; priceless ~

helicopter n. 1. to fly, pilot a ~ 2. an attack ~ (see also **airplane**)

hell n. (colloq.) ["the netherworld"] 1. go to ~! 2. to be in ~ ["scolding"] 3. to catch, get ~ 4. to give smb. ~ ["great suffering"] 5. to go through ~ 6. sheer, unmitigated, unspeakable ~ 7. ~ to + inf. (it was ~ to work there = it was ~ working there) ["misc."] 8. to beat (the) ~ out of smb. ("to give smb. a good thrashing"); to wait till ~ freezes over ("to wait forever"); living there was was ~ on earth ("it was terrible to live there"); a ~ of a team ("an excellent team"); for the ~ of it ("for no real reason"); to be ~ on ("to be harmful to"); (BE; slang) bloody ~

hell-bent adj. (cannot stand alone) ["determined"] 1. ~ for, on (~ on balancing the budget) 2. ~ to + inf. (~ to balance the budget)

hello n. 1. to say ~ (to) 2. a big ~ (they gave me a big ~)

helm n. 1. to take (over) the ~ 2. at the ~

helmet n. 1. a crash, safety; football; pith, sun ~ 2. a steel ~

help I n. 1. to give, offer, provide ~ 2. to call for, seek ~ 3. to cry for, plead for ~ 4. a big ~ (to) (she was a big ~ to us) 5. (a) great, invaluable, tremendous; little ~ 6. of ~ (to) (she was of great ~ to us; they were of little ~ to me) 7. (misc.) ~ wanted (as in a newspaper advertisement); domestic ~; (BE) a home ~ (AE has *home health aide*)

help II *v.* 1. (D; tr.) ("to assist") to ~ across (we ~ed them across the street) 2. (D; tr.) ("to assist") to ~ in, with (we ~ed them in their work; she ~ed me with the translation) 3. (D; tr.) ("to assist in moving") to ~ into; off; out of (~ them into the house; ~ her off the train; ~ him out of the car) 4. (D; tr.) ("to assist") to ~ through (they ~ed us through the crisis) 5. (D; refl., tr.) ("to serve oneself") to ~ to (she ~ed herself to the dessert) 6. (D; tr.) ("to serve") to ~ to (can I ~ you to some food?) 7. (E) they ~ed to cook the meal 8. (esp. AE) (F) ("to assist") she ~ed move the furniture 9. (G; often used with: cannot — can't — couldn't) ("to keep from") we couldn't ~ laughing 10. (H) she ~ed us to move the furniture 11. (esp. AE) (I) she ~ed us move the furniture 12. (misc.) I couldn't ~ but laugh

helpful *adj.* 1. ~ in; to (she's been very ~ to us) 2. ~ of (that was very ~ of you) 3. ~ to + inf. (it's always ~ to be well-informed; it was ~ of you to do that)

helping *n.* a generous; second ~

helping hand *n.* to give, lend (smb.) a ~

helpless *adj.* 1. ~ against (we were ~ against the invasion) 2. ~ to + inf. (they were ~ to prevent an opposition victory)

help off *v.* (d; tr.) to ~ with (he ~ed me off with my coat)

help on *v.* (d; tr.) to ~ with (she ~ed me on with my jacket)

help out *v.* 1. (D; intr., tr.) to ~ by (she ~ed out by listing all the items alphabetically) 2. (D; intr., tr.) to ~ with (she ~ed me out with some good advice) 3. (misc.) she ~s them out in her own way

helter-skelter *adv.* to flee ~

hem *n.* 1. to let down, let out, lower a ~ 2. to raise, take up a ~ 3. to pin up a ~ 4. to straighten a ~

hemisphere *n.* 1. the eastern; northern; southern; western ~ 2. the left; right ~ (of the brain)

hemline *n.* to lower; raise a ~

hemmed in *adj.* ~ on all sides

hemorrhage *n.* 1. a brain, cerebral; internal ~ 2. a massive ~

hen *n.* 1. ~s cackle, cluck 2. ~s lay eggs

hepatitis *n.* infectious; serum ~

herbs *n.* dried; fresh; medicinal ~

herd I *n.* 1. to drive; round up a ~ 2. to tend a ~ 3. a dairy ~ 4. (misc.) to ride ~ on ("to control"); to follow the ~ ("to go along with the crowd"); the common ~ ("the great mass of people")

herd II *v.* (P; tr.) the prisoners were ~ed into the compound; the children were ~ed out of the class-

room; the tourists were ~ed through the exhibit

here *adv.* from ~

hereafter *n.* in the ~

heresy *n.* 1. to be guilty of ~; to commit ~ 2. to preach ~ 3. ~ to + inf. (it was ~ to talk like that)

heritage *n.* 1. to cherish one's ~ 2. to repudiate one's ~ 3. a priceless, proud, rich ~ 4. a cultural; family; national; religious ~

hernia *n.* a hiatal; inguinal ~

hero *n.* 1. a conquering; folk; local; military, war; national; popular; unsung ~ 2. a ~ to (when she returned, she was a ~ to her followers)

heroic *adj.* ~ to + inf. (it was ~ of them to oppose the invader)

heroin *n.* to do (colloq.), inject, shoot (colloq.), shoot up (with) (colloq.), smoke ~

heroine *n.* see **hero**

heroism *n.* to demonstrate, display ~

herpes *n.* 1. to come down with, contract, get ~ 2. genital ~

hesitancy *n.* 1. to show ~ 2. ~ about, in

hesitant *adj.* 1. ~ about (they are ~ about signing a contract) 2. ~ to + inf. (they are ~ to sign a contract)

hesitate *v.* 1. (D; intr.) to ~ over (to ~ over a choice) 2. (E) she ~d to act; do not ~ to call me

hesitation *n.* 1. to show ~ 2. (a) momentary, slight ~ 3. ~ about, in (I have no ~ about throwing him out)

het up *adj.* (slang) ["excited"] to get (all) ~ about, over

hew *v.* (d; intr.) ("to adhere") (AE) to ~ to (to ~ to the party line)

hex *n.* (AE) to put a ~ on smb.

heyday *n.* ["most successful period"] 1. to have one's ~ 2. in one's ~

hiatus *n.* a brief ~

hiccups *n.* 1. to get; have the ~ 2. to get rid of the ~ 3. an attack of (the) ~

hide I *n.* 1. to tan a ~ 2. (misc.) to save smb.'s ~ ("to rescue smb."); to tan smb.'s ~ ("to spank smb.")

hide II *v.* 1. (D; intr.) to ~ behind (to ~ behind a legal technicality) 2. (D; intr., tr.) to ~ from

hide-and-seek *n.* to play ~

hideaway *n.* a secret ~

hideous *adj.* ~ to + inf. (it was ~ to watch)

hideout *n.* a secret ~

hide out *v.* to ~ from (to ~ from the police)

hiding I *n.* ["concealment"] 1. to go into ~ 2. to come out of ~ 3. in ~

hiding II *n.* (colloq.) ["a beating"] 1. to give smb. a ~ 2. to get a ~ (he got a good ~ for his misbehavior)

hierarchy *n.* 1. to rise in the ~ 2. an academic; church; corporate; military; ruling ~

high I *adj.* 1. ~ in (~ in iron) 2. (misc.) ~ up; (colloq.) to get ~ on (a drug)

high II *n.* ["acme"] 1. to reach a ~ 2. an all-time ~ ["state of euphoria"] (slang) 3. to reach a ~ 4. to be

highball *n.* ["type of drink"] to make, mix a ~

highhanded *adj.* ~ to + inf. (it was ~ of him to remove the equipment without permission)

high horse *n.* (colloq.) ["arrogance"] to get on one's ~

highness *n.* (her, his, your) royal ~; their royal ~es

high point *n.* to reach the ~ (in/of smb.'s career)

high-pressure *v.* (D; tr.) to ~ into (she was ~d into signing)

high road *n.* ["direct route"] to take the ~ (to)

high school *n.* (esp. AE) 1. to enter ~ 2. to graduate from ~ 3. (to be) at, in ~

high sign *n.* (esp. AE) ["signal"] 1. to give smb. the ~ 2. to get the ~

high time *n.* 1. ~ to + inf. (it's ~ to leave) 2. ~ that + clause (it's ~ that they left)

high treason *n.* to commit ~

highway *n.* 1. (AE) a divided ~ (BE has *dual carriageway*) 2. a limited-access ~ 3. on the ~ 4. the ~ to 5. (misc.) the Information Highway

hijack *v.* (D; tr.) to ~ to (they were ~ed to an unknown country)

hijacking *n.* 1. to carry out, commit a ~ 2. to foil, thwart a ~

hike I *n.* 1. to go on; organize a ~ 2. a long; short ~ (they went on a long ~) 3. an overnight ~ (as of Boy Scouts)

hike II *v.* (P; intr.) they ~d to town on foot; we ~d around the village; the scouts ~d over the mountain

hill *n.* 1. to climb up, go up; come down a ~ 2. rolling ~s; a steep ~ 3. in the ~s (to live in the ~s) 4. on a ~ (the house stood on a ~) 5. the top of a ~ 6. (misc.) (colloq.) to take to the ~s ("to take refuge in the hills")

hilt *n.* ["limit"] to the ~

hinder *v.* 1. (D; tr.) to ~ from 2. (D; tr.) to ~ in

hindrance *n.* a ~ to

hindsight *n.* with (the benefit of) ~

hinge *v.* (d; intr.) ("to depend") to ~ on, upon

hint I *n.* 1. to drop, give a ~ 2. to take a ~ 3. a broad, obvious; delicate, gentle, subtle; helpful ~ 4. the merest, slightest ~ 5. a ~ about, of (a ~ about the answer; a ~ of suspicion) 6. a ~ that + clause (she dropped a ~ that she would retire soon) 7. at a ~ (they fled at the first ~ of trouble)

hint II *v.* 1. (d. intr.) to ~ at 2. (L; to) he ~ed (to us) that an agreement had been reached

hip *n.* 1. to shake, sway, wiggle one's ~s 2. (misc.) they stood with their hands on their ~s

hire I *n.* for ~

hire II *v.* 1. (D; tr.) to ~ as (to ~ smb. as a guide) 2. (esp. BE) (D; tr.) to ~ from (to ~ a car from an agency) (AE usu. uses *to rent*) 3. (H) we ~d her to mow our lawn

hired *adj.* ~ to + inf. (he was ~ to work as a gardener)

hire out *v.* (D; refl., tr.) to ~ as; to (he ~d himself out as a mercenary to the highest bidder)

hire purchase *n.* (BE) on ~ (to buy smt. on ~)

hiss *v.* 1. (D; intr.) to ~ at (the crowd ~ed at the delay) 2. (D; tr.) to ~ off (they were ~ed off the stage)

history *n.* 1. to make ~ 2. to trace the ~ of smt. 3. to distort; revise, rewrite ~ 4. to go down in ~ as (he went down in ~ as a tyrant) 5. ancient; medieval; modern; past; recorded ~ 6. cultural; military; natural ~ 7. a case; family; life; medical; personal; social ~ 8. (an) oral ~ 9. a ~ of (she had a long ~ of drug abuse) 10. in, throughout ~ (people have struggled for freedom throughout recorded ~) 11. (misc.) ~ repeats itself; a page in ~; the nurse did/got/took the patient's ~

hit I *n.* ["blow that strikes the target"] 1. to score a ~ 2. to take a ~ (our ship took several direct ~s) 3. a direct ~ ["success"] (colloq.) 4. to make a ~ with (she made quite a ~ with the audience) 5. a big, smash ~

hit II *v.* 1. ("to strike") to ~ hard 2. (d; tr.) ("to strike") to ~ against, on (he hit his head on the ceiling) 3. (d; intr.) to ~ at ("to attack") (the press hit hard at governmental corruption) 4. (slang) (AE) (d; tr.) to ~ for ("to request") (he hit me for twenty dollars) 5. (D; tr.) ("to strike") to ~ in, on, over (to ~ smb. in the face; she hit me on the hand) 6. (slang) (AE) ("to make sexual overtures to") to ~ on smb. 7. (d; intr.) to ~ on, upon ("to discover") (they finally hit on an acceptable compromise) 8. (BE) (O; can be used with one animate object) ("to strike") he hit me a hard blow 9. (P; tr.) she hit the ball over the net; the batter hit the ball into the bleachers

hit back *v.* (D; intr.) to ~ at

hitch I *n.* (colloq.) ["obstacle"] ["stoppage"] 1. a slight; technical ~ 2. a ~ in (there's been a slight ~ in our plans) 3. without a ~ (it went off without a ~) ["period of military service"] (esp. AE) 4. to do a ~ 5. to sign up for another ~

hitch II *v.* (d; tr.) to ~ to (to ~ horses to a cart)

hitch up *v.* (D; tr.) to ~ to (to ~ horses to a cart)

hit off *v.* to ~ it off with smb. ("to get along well with smb.")

hit out *v.* (D; intr.) to ~ against, at (they ~ against their political rivals)

hitter *n.* (esp. AE; baseball and fig.) 1. a designated ~ 2. a leadoff; pinch ~

hit up *v.* (slang) (AE) (d; tr.) ("to request") to ~ for (he hit me up for a loan)

hoax *n.* 1. to perpetrate a ~ 2. to play a ~ on smb. 3. a literary ~

hobble *v.* (P; intr.) she ~d across the street; they ~d into the room

hobby *n.* to have, pursue, take up a ~

hobnob *v.* (d; intr.) to ~ with

hock *n.* (colloq.) in ~ ("pawned")

hockey *n.* 1. to play ~ 2. field (AE); ice ~

hoist *v.* (d; tr.) to ~ onto, to (the workers were ~ed onto the roof)

hold I *n.* ["grip"] 1. to catch, get, grab, lay, seize, take ~ of 2. to keep ~ of 3. to loosen, relax; lose, relinquish one's ~ (of) 4. to tighten one's ~ 5. a firm, strong ~ 6. a ~ on ["type of wrestling grip"] 6. to break a ~ ["control, domination"] 7. to consolidate; have; maintain; tighten a ~ 8. to loosen; relinquish one's ~ 9. a firm, strong, tight ~ 10. a ~ on, over (they refused to relinquish their ~ over this area; they thought they had a ~ on us) ["waiting"] 11. on ~ (the plan is on ~ until next year; when I called him, he put me on ~; I cannot leave the phone because I'm still on ~)

hold II *v.* 1. ("to keep") to ~ high (to ~ one's head high; also fig.) 2. ("to keep, support") to ~ tight, tightly 3. (d; tr.) to ~ against ("to take into account") (we will not ~ your past blunders against you; they held his criminal record against him) 4. (D; tr.) to ~ by ("to keep, support") (to ~ smb. by the hand) 5. (d; tr.) to ~ in ("to regard") to ~ smb. in contempt; to ~ smb. in high esteem) 6. (d; intr.) to ~ onto ("to seize and cling to") (~ onto my arm) 7. (d; intr.) ("to adhere") to ~ to (to ~ to the terms of a contract) 8. (d; tr.) ("to make smb. comply") to ~ to (they held us to the terms of the contract) 9. (d; tr.) ("to restrict") to ~ to (we held the visiting team to a tie) 10. (d; intr.) ("to agree") to ~ with (I don't ~ with his ideas) 11. (formal) (L) ("to assert") we ~ that these truths are self-evident 12. (M) ("to consider") we ~ him to be responsible 13. (N; used with an adjective) ("to consider"); ("to keep") to ~ smb. responsible; she held the ladder steady; they ~ life cheap

hold III *n.* ["interior of a ship below decks"] in the ~

hold back *v.* 1. (D; tr.) ("to keep") to ~ from (lack of education held him back from promotion) 2. (d; intr.) to ~ with (to ~ with one's reserves)

holder *n.* 1. a candle; cigarette; napkin ~ 2. (AE) a pot ~

hold forth *v.* (D; intr.) ("to give an opinion") to ~ about, on (to ~ about various matters)

holdings *n.* ["investments"] 1. to diversify one's ~ 2. far-flung ~

hold off *v.* (G) to ~ making a decision

hold out *v.* 1. (B) ("to offer") they didn't ~ much hope to us; to ~ a helping hand to smb. 2. (D; intr.) to ~ against ("to resist") (they held out against the enemy for a month) 3. (D; intr.) to ~ for ("to demand") (they held out for better terms) 4. (d; intr.) to ~ on ("to keep information from") (don't ~ on me) 5. (D; intr.) to ~ to ("to persevere") to ~ to (to ~ to the end)

holdover *n.* a ~ from (a ~ from the old days)

hold up *v.* 1. (d; tr.) to ~ as (to ~ as an example) 2. (esp. AE) (D; intr.) to ~ on (they had to ~ on their travel plans) 3. (d; tr.) to ~ to (to ~ smt. up to ridicule)

hole *n.* 1. to bore; burrow; dig; drill; make a ~ 2. to fill (in), plug a ~ 3. a deep; gaping, yawning ~ 4. a rabbit; watering ~ 5. a bullet ~ 6. (misc.) to pick ~s in smt. ("to find flaws in smt."); to poke a ~ in smb.'s argument; (golf) to shoot a ~ in one; we're five hundred dollars in the ~ ("we owe five hundred dollars that we cannot pay")

hole up *v.* (colloq.) (D; intr., tr.) to ~ in (they were ~d up in an old farmhouse)

holiday *n.* ["day set aside for the suspension of business, labor"] 1. to celebrate, observe a ~ 2. a bank (BE), legal (AE); public; national; religious ~ ["period of rest"] (esp. BE; AE prefers *vacation*) 3. to have, take a ~ 4. to go on ~ 5. a summer ~ 6. a ~ from 7. on ~ (she was away on ~) ["misc."] 8. a busman's ~ ("a holiday spent in doing one's usual work") (see the Usage Note for **vacation**)

holler *v.* (colloq.) (esp. AE) 1. (B) she ~ed a few words to him 2. (D; intr., tr.) to ~ at (they ~ed at the children)

hollow *v.* (d; tr.) to ~ out of (to ~ a canoe out of a log)

holocaust *n.* a nuclear ~

holster *n.* a shoulder ~

holy orders *n.* ["ordination"] to receive, take ~

holy water *n.* to sprinkle ~

homage *n.* 1. to pay ~ to 2. in ~ to

home *n.* ["establishment providing care or service"] 1. to manage, operate, run a ~ 2. a convalescent; funeral (AE); nursing; remand (BE); rest; retirement ~ ["residence"] 3. to build; establish a ~ 4. to provide a ~ for 5. to make one's ~ at, in 6. an ancestral; childhood; country; mobile; summer; winter ~ 7. (a) ~ for, to (San Francisco was ~ to them for years) 8. at ~ (make yourself at ~; she is never at ~; AE also has: she is never ~) ["family"] 9. a broken; foster; good ~ ["misc.] 10. to romp ~ ("to score an easy victory"); she is at ~ in Greek literature; to go ~

USAGE NOTE: In many instances *home* is used as an adverb—to go home, to get home from work, etc.

home in *v.* (D; intr.) to ~ on (to ~ on a target)

home page *n.* (computers) to create; view; visit a ~

home run *n.* (AE; baseball and fig.) ["hit that allows the batter to score a run"] to hit a ~

homesick *adj.* 1. to get ~ 2. ~ for

home straight (BE), **homestretch** *n.* to come into the ~

home visit *n.* to go on, make a ~

homework *n.* 1. to do, prepare ~ 2. to assign, set (BE) ~ 3. to hand in ~ 4. to correct; grade, mark ~

(a teacher corrects ~)

homicide *n.* 1. to commit ~ 2. justifiable ~

homily *n.* 1. to deliver a ~ 2. a ~ about, on

hone *v.* 1. (D; tr.) to ~ to (to ~ smt. to a point) 2. (misc.) finely ~d

honest *adj.* 1. ~ about; with (be ~ about this matter with us) 2. ~ to + inf. (it's not ~ to keep lost property)

honesty *n.* 1. to impugn smb.'s ~ 2. ~ in 3. in all ~ (in all ~, do you believe him?) 4. the ~ to + inf. (she had the ~ to report the bribe)

honey *n.* 1. to gather ~ 2. (misc.) as sweet as ~

honeycombed *adj.* (cannot stand alone) ~ with

honeymoon *n.* 1. to go on one's ~ 2. to spend one's ~ (they spent their ~ in Hawaii) 3. a second ~ 4. (misc.) the ~ is over (usu. fig.)

honk *v.* (D; intr.) to ~ at

honor I honour *n.* ["respect"] ["credit"] 1. to bring, do ~ to (she brought ~ to her family) 2. an ~ to (he is an ~ to his school) 3. in smb.'s ~; in ~ of (to give a reception in smb.'s ~) ["distinction"] ["recognition"] 4. to win (an) ~ 5. to bestow, confer an ~ on 6. a dubious; great, high ~ 7. an ~ that + clause (it was a great ~ that we were chosen) 8. (to graduate) with ~s 9. (misc.) she did us the ~ of attending our party ["privilege"] 10. to have the ~ (may I have the ~ of your company?) 11. an ~ to + inf. (it was an ~ to serve with you) ["integrity"] ["reputation"] 12. to stake one's ~ on smt. 13. one's word of ~; an affair of ~ 14. on one's (word of) ~ ["rite"] 15. to do the ~s ("to serve as host") 16. military ~s (to be buried with full military ~s) ["misc."] 17. a (military) guard of ~

honor II honour *v.* 1. (D; tr.) to ~ as (she was ~ed as a community leader) 2. (D; tr.) to ~ by; with

honorable, honourable *adj.* ~ to + inf. (it is not ~ to deceive them with false promises)

honorarium *n.* to pay; receive an ~

honor bound, honour bound *adj.* ~ to + inf. (we were ~ to get the job done on time)

honored, honoured *adj.* 1. deeply, greatly, highly 2. ~ to + inf. (he was ~ to be invited) 3. ~ that + clause (I am ~ that you have decided to offer me the position)

hood *n.* (AE) ["cover over a car engine"] to check under the ~ (of a car) (BE has *bonnet*)

hoodwink *v.* 1. (D; tr.) to ~ into 2. (D; tr.) to ~ out of

hoof *n.* 1. a cloven ~ 2. hoofs clatter 3. on the ~ (to buy cattle on the ~)

hook *n.* ["curved piece of metal, wood"] 1. a crochet; meat; pruning ~ 2. (misc.) to hang a coat on a ~; to leave the phone off the ~ ["blow delivered with bent arm"] 3. to deliver a ~ (he delivered a right ~ to his opponent's jaw) ["piece of metal or plastic used to catch fish"] 4. to bait a ~ ["misc."] (slang) 5. off the ~ ("relieved of responsibility")

hooked *adj.* (slang) ["addicted"] ~ on (~ on drugs)

hookey, hooky *n.* (colloq.) (AE) to play ~ ("to play truant")

hooks and eyes *n.* ["type of fastening"] 1. to fasten; unfasten ~ 2. to sew on ~

hookup *n.* 1. a satellite ~ 2. a ~ with

hook up *v.* 1. (D; tr.) to ~ to (to ~ a telephone up to the cable) 2. (D; intr.) to ~ with ("to join")

hoop *n.* to roll a ~

hoopla *n.* (slang) (AE) ["bustle, noise, fuss"] the ~ subsides

hoot I *n.* (colloq.) ["slightest care"] not to give a ~

hoot II *v.* 1. (D; intr.) ("to shout") to ~ at (they ~ed at me to get moving) 2. (misc.) they ~ed her off the stage

hop I *n.* ["short flight"] 1. a short ~ 2. a ~ from; to (it's a short ~ from Detroit to Cleveland)

hop II *v.* 1. (d; intr.) to ~ into (the children ~ped into their nice warm beds) 2. (d; intr.) to ~ out of (to ~ out of a chair) 3. (P; intr.) the children ~ped across the puddle; to ~ onto a bus

hope I *n.* 1. to arouse, inspire, stir up ~ 2. to build up, raise smb.'s ~s 3. to get smb.'s ~s up 4. to express, voice a ~ 5. to cherish, entertain, nurse a ~ 6. to cling to a ~ 7. to pin, place, put one's ~s on 8. to crush, dash, deflate, shatter; thwart smb.'s ~s 9. to abandon, give up, lose ~ 10. an ardent, fervent, fond; devout; pious; sincere ~ 11. a real; realistic, reasonable ~ 12. a dim, faint, slender, slight; false, idle, illusory, vain; unrealistic, unreasonable ~ 13. high ~ 14. ~s are fulfilled, realized 15. ~s crumble, fade 16. a flicker, glimmer, ray, spark of ~ 17. ~ for; in; of (~ for better times; we had high ~s for her) 18. a ~ that + clause (it was our ~ that they would settle near us; there was little ~ that she would be elected) 19. in, with the ~ (we returned to the park in the ~ of finding her wallet) 20. beyond, past (all) ~

hope II *v.* 1. to ~ fervently, sincerely, very much 2. (D; intr.) to ~ for (to ~ for an improvement) 3. (E) she ~s to see them soon 4. (L) we ~ that you are comfortable 5. (misc.) I ~ so; I ~ not; here's ~ing

hopeful I *adj.* 1. ~ of 2. ~ that + clause (we are ~ that they will agree)

hopeful II *n.* a presidential; young ~

hopeless *adj.* 1. ~ at (he's ~ at balancing his checkbook) 2. ~ to + inf. (it's ~ to expect her to help)

hopper *n.* (AE) ["container for bills that are being considered"] a legislative ~

hopscotch *n.* to play ~

horizon *n.* 1. (fig.) to broaden, expand one's ~s 2. above; below the ~ 3. on the ~ (to appear on the ~)

hormone *n.* a female; growth; male; sex ~

horn *n.* ["device on a car"] 1. to blow, honk, sound, toot a ~ 2. ~s blare, blow 3. a ~ gets stuck ["musical instrument"] 4. to play a ~ 5. an English (AE); French ~ ["misc."] 6. on the ~s of a dilemma ("in a dilemma"); to lock ~s with ("to come into conflict with"); to take the bull by the ~s ("to confront a problem boldly"); (AE) to blow/toot one's own ~ ("to boast")

hornet n. ~s sting

hornet's nest n. ["angry reaction"] to stir up a ~

horn in v. (D; intr.) to ~ on ("to interrupt")

Horn of Africa n. in, (esp. AE) on the ~

horoscope n. to read smb.'s ~

horrible adj. 1. ~ to (she was ~ to her workers) 2. ~ to + inf. (it is ~ to work there = it is ~ working there) 3. ~ that + clause (it's ~ that he was fired)

horrid adj. 1. ~ to 2. ~ to + inf. (it was ~ of you to tease them like that = you were ~ to tease them like that)

horrified adj. 1. ~ at, by (~ at the prospect of losing one's job) 2. ~ to + inf. (she was ~ to learn the news) 3. ~ that + clause (we were ~ that she had been chosen)

horrify v. (R) it ~fied us (to learn) that their house had burned down

horrifying adj. ~ to + inf. (it is ~ to contemplate that possibility)

horror n. 1. to express; feel ~ 2. to have a ~ of 3. indescribable, unspeakable, sheer ~ 4. ~ at (she expressed her ~ at the crime) 5. in ~ (to scream in ~) 6. to smb.'s ~ (to his ~, the bus caught fire) 7. (misc.) a scream, shriek of ~

horror-stricken, horror-struck adj. 1. ~ at 2. ~ + inf. (we were ~ to learn that the students had been hurt)

horse n. ["animal"] 1. to mount; ride; walk a ~ 2. to lead a ~ by the bridle 3. to dismount, get off a ~ 4. to bridle; curry; groom; harness; hobble; saddle; shoe a ~ 5. to break (in) a ~ 6. to breed, raise; train a ~ 7. a cart (BE), draft (AE), dray; race; saddle; thoroughbred; wild ~; a workhorse (usu. fig.) 8. ~s bolt; canter; gallop; rear; shy; trot 9. ~s neigh; snicker; whinny 10. an unbroken ~ bucks 11. a herd of (wild) ~s; a pair; team of ~s 12. a young ~ is a foal 13. a female ~ is a mare 14. a male ~ is a stallion; a castrated male ~ is a gelding 15. a young female ~ is a filly 16. a young male ~ is a colt ["padded block"] (gymnastics) 17. a pommel, side (AE); vaulting ~ ["misc."] 18. to back the wrong ~ ("to support the losing side"); to beat/flog a dead ~ ("to discuss an issue that has already been settled"); from the ~'s mouth ("from an original source"); to hold one's ~s ("to behave more carefully"); a ~ of a different color ("an entirely different matter"); on one's high ~ ("behaving arrogantly"); to eat like a ~ ("to eat a great deal"); to work like a ~ ("to work very hard"); to play the ~s ("to bet on horse races"); to look a gift ~ in the mouth ("to be very critical of a gift")

horse around v. (colloq.) (D; intr.) to ~ with

horseback n. 1. to ride ~ 2. on ~

hose n. ["flexible tube"] 1. to play, train a ~ on 2. a

fire; garden; rubber; water ~ ["stockings"] 3. mesh ~; pantyhose (AE); stretch; support ~

hospitable adj. ~ to, towards

hospital n. 1. to establish, found a ~ 2. to manage, run a ~ 3. to be admitted to ~ (BE)/to be admitted to the/a ~ (AE), to enter ~ (BE)/to enter the/a ~ (AE), to go into, to ~ (BE)/to go into, to the/a ~ (AE) 4. to be discharged from ~ (BE), to leave ~ (BE)/to be discharged from the/a ~ (AE), to leave the/a ~ (AE) 5. a base; evacuation; field; military; station; veterans ~ 6. a children's; general; mental ~ 7. a city, municipal; community, non-profit; cottage (BE); private, proprietary (AE); state; teaching ~ 8. at, in a ~ (she works at/in a ~) 9. in ~ (BE)/in the/a ~ (AE) (she's ill and has been in/in the ~ for a week)

USAGE NOTE: In BE, the phrases *to go to hospital, to be in hospital* mean "to be hospitalized"; in AE one says *to go to the/a hospital, to be in the/a hospital*. But: *she went to the hospital to visit her mother* is CE.

hospitality n. 1. to extend, offer, show ~ 2. to enjoy; repay smb.'s ~ 3. to abuse smb.'s ~ 4. cordial, warm; lavish ~

host n. 1. to play ~ to (who will play ~ to our foreign guests?) 2. to act as ~ 3. a congenial, gracious ~ 4. a chat show (BE), talk show (AE) ~ 5. ~ to (which city will be ~ to the next World's Fair?)

hostage n. 1. to take smb. ~ 2. to seize, take ~s 3. to hold smb. (as a) ~ (they were held ~) 4. to exchange ~s 5. to free, liberate ~s

hostel n. a youth ~

hostess n. 1. see **host** (1, 2, 3, 4) 2. an air (BE), airline (AE) ~ 3. a dance-hall; nightclub ~

USAGE NOTE: In AE, the term *flight attendant* has almost completely replaced *airline hostess*.

hostile adj. 1. openly ~ 2. ~ to, towards

hostilities n. ["war"] 1. to begin, open ~ 2. to end; suspend ~ 3. impending ~ 4. ~ begin, break out, erupt; cease, end 5. an outbreak of ~ 6. ~ between

hostility n. 1. to arouse, stir up ~ 2. to display, show ~ 3. to express; feel ~ 4. (a) bitter, deep, profound; open; veiled ~ 5. ~ against, to, towards 6. ~ between

hot adj. 1. boiling, burning, piping, scalding, steaming; unbearably; uncomfortably ~ 2. (misc.) ~ on smb.'s heels/trail ("close behind smb. being pursued")

hot cakes n. to go, sell like ~ ("to sell quickly and in large numbers")

hotel n. 1. to manage, operate, run a ~ 2. a deluxe, five-star, luxury; first-class; four-star; posh, swanky (colloq.); three-star ~ 3. a run-down, seedy ~ 4. at, in a ~ (she works at/in a ~) 5. (misc.) to check in, register at a ~; to check out of a ~

hot line n. 1. to establish, set up a ~ 2. a ~ between 3. a ~ links heads of state

hot pursuit *n.* in ~ (they crossed the border in ~ of the terrorists)

hot water *n.* ["trouble or difficulty"] 1. to be in ~ 2. to get into ~

hound I *n.* ["hunting dog"] 1. a pack of ~s 2. (esp. BE) to ride to ~s, to follow the ~s ("to hunt on horseback with dogs") 3. ~s bay ["enthusiast"] 4. autograph ~s

hound II *v.* 1. (d; tr.) to ~ from, out of (they ~ed her out of office) 2. (d; tr.) to ~ into (to ~ smb. into doing smt.) 3. (H) they kept ~ing me to get a haircut

hour *n.* 1. to show, tell the ~ (my watch shows the minute and ~) 2. a solid ("full") ~ (the police grilled him for three solid ~s) 3. an ungodly ("very early"); ("very late") ~ (she called at an ungodly ~) 4. the decisive ~; or: the ~ of decision 5. the cocktail ~ 6. business, office, working; peak; visiting ~s (during peak ~s more trains run) 7. flexible; irregular; regular ~s (she keeps regular ~s) 8. the rush ~ (traffic is very heavy during the rush ~) 9. at a certain ~ (at the appointed ~; we had to get up at an ungodly ~) 10. by the ~ (to pay workers by the ~) 11. during, in, on a certain ~ (during the lunch ~; in one's ~ of need) 12. in, inside, within an ~ (she'll be here in an ~, or BE: in an ~'s time) 13. on the ~ ("every hour") 14. (BE) out of ~s (I cannot see you out of normal working ~s) 15. (misc.) they spent many happy ~s playing cards; to keep late ~s ("to go to bed late"); one's finest ~ ("the noblest period in one's life"); after ~s ("after work"); (a) happy ~ ("period in which a bar sells alcoholic drinks at a reduced price"); H-hour/zero hour ("time at which a significant event is scheduled to begin")

house *n.* ["building"] ["home"] 1. to build, put up a ~ 2. to redecorate, refurbish, remodel, renovate a ~ 3. to demolish, raze, tear down a ~ 4. to rent a ~ from smb. 5. to let (BE), rent (out) a ~ to smb. 6. (BE) to move ~ 7. a dilapidated, ramshackle ~ 8. an apartment (AE); council (BE) ~ 9. a detached; one-family, single; ranch (AE); row (AE); terraced (BE); semidetached; town ~ 10. a country; manor (esp. BE); summer ~ 11. a brick; clapboard (AE); weatherboard; frame; prefabricated ~ 12. a lodging (esp. BE), rooming (AE) ~ 13. a haunted ~ 14. (AE) a fraternity; sorority ~ ["housekeeping"] 15. to clean ~ 16. to keep ~ for smb. ["theater"] 17. to bring the ~ down ("to win thunderous approval") 18. an empty; full, packed ~ (to play to a packed ~) 19. an opera ~ ["chamber of a legislative body"] 20. a lower; upper ~; both ~s of Congress ["firm"] 21. a banking; clearing ~ 22. a discount; mail-order; pharmaceutical; publishing ~ 23. a gambling ~ 24. a slaughterhouse ["place providing a public service"] 25. a boarding; halfway; safe; settlement ~ ["bar"] (BE) 26. a free; public; tied ~

["shelter"] 27. a reptile ~ (at a zoo) ["misc."] 28. a ~ of correction/detention ("a prison"); a disorderly ~ ("a brothel"); (AE) a station ~ ("a police station"); drinks are on the ~ ("drinks are served free"); (an) open ~ ("informal hospitality"); an open ~ (AE)/show ~ (BE) ("a residence being sold or rented out that is open for inspection")

house arrest *n.* to place, put smb. under ~

house call *n.* (esp. AE) to make ~s

household *n.* 1. to establish, set up a ~ 2. to run a ~ 3. (the) head of (a) ~

housekeeping *n.* 1. to set up ~ 2. to do ~ 3. light ~

housewarming *n.* to have a ~

housework *n.* 1. to do ~ 2. light ~

housing *n.* council (BE), public (AE); fair (AE), open (AE); low-cost, low-income; off-campus; student; subsidized; substandard ~

hovel *n.* a miserable, wretched ~

hover *v.* 1. (d; intr.) to ~ around (we ~ed around our guide) 2. (d; intr.) to ~ between (to ~ between life and death) 3. (d; intr.) to ~ over (the fear of a new war ~ed over us)

howl I *n.* to give, let out a ~

howl II *v.* 1. (D; intr.) to ~ at 2. (D; intr.) to ~ with (to ~ with pain)

howler *n.* ["blunder"] to make a ~

Hoyle *n.* according to ~ ("according to the rules")

hub *n.* ["focal point"] at the ~ (at the ~ of activity)

huddle I *n.* 1. to go into a ~ 2. in a ~

huddle II *v.* (P; intr.) to ~ around a fire; to ~ together

hue *n.* to raise a ~ and cry

huff *n.* (to leave) in a ~

hug I *n.* 1. to give smb. a ~ 2. an affectionate, loving; bear; big; tight ~ (she gave him a big bear ~)

hug II *v.* to ~ tightly

hum *v.* 1. (usu. B; occ. A) ~ the tune to me 2. (D; tr.) to ~ for (to ~ a song for smb.) 3. (D; intr.) to ~ with (the town was ~ming with activity)

human *adj.* ~ to + inf. (it's only ~ to seek a better life)

humane *adj.* ~ to + inf. (it's not ~ to treat people like that)

humanity *n.* ["quality of being humane"] 1. to display ~ 2. common ~ ["the human race"] 3. a crime against ~

humble *v.* (D; refl.) to ~ before (to ~ oneself before God)

humble pie *n.* (forced) to eat ~

humiliate *v.* to ~ deeply

humiliating *adj.* 1. ~ to + inf. (it is ~ to take orders from him) 2. ~ that + clause (it's ~ that we may not make our own decisions)

humiliation *n.* 1. to suffer ~ 2. abject; bitter; deep; public ~

humility *n.* 1. to demonstrate, display, show ~ 2. in,

with ~ (she recognized her responsibility with deep ~)

humor, humour *n.* ["something funny"] 1. bitter, caustic; black; gallows ~ 2. deadpan, dry, straight; sly, wry; subtle ~ 3. earthy; infectious; irrepressible; slapstick ~ 4. a sense of ~ 5. a dash, trace, vein of ~ ["mood"] 6. (a) bad, ill (esp. BE); good ~ (she's in good ~ today) 7. a ~ to + inf. (he's in no ~ to be fooled with) 8. in a certain ~ (in bad ~)

hump *n.* ["fit of depression"] (colloq.) (BE) 1. it gives me the ~ ("it depresses me") 2. I got; had the ~ ["worst part"] (colloq.) 3. over the ~

hunch *n.* (colloq.) ["feeling"] ["suspicion"] 1. to play a ~ ("to act on the basis of a hunch") 2. a ~ that (I have a ~ that she will not come) 3. on a ~ (she did it on a ~)

hunger I *n.* 1. (formal) to allay, alleviate, appease one's ~ 2. to satisfy one's ~; to gratify one's ~ (fig.) 3. (a) gnawing, ravenous ~ 4. a ~ for (~ for knowledge) 5. of ~ (to die of ~)

hunger II *v.* 1. (d; intr.) to ~ after, for 2. (E) to ~ to know the truth

hungry *adj.* 1. (cannot stand alone) ~ for (~ for news) 2. to be, feel; get; go ~

hunker down *v.* (D; intr.) ("to settle down") to ~ for (to ~ for the night)

hunt I *n.* 1. to organize, stage a ~ 2. to go on a ~ 3. a ~ for (a ~ for big game; the ~ for a new director)

hunt II *v.* 1. (D; intr.) to ~ for (to ~ for big game) 2. (misc.) to ~ high and low

hunter *n.* a bargain; big-game; bounty; fortune; head; souvenir ~

hurdle *n.* 1. to clear, overcome, take a ~ 2. to hit, knock down a ~ 3. (the) high; low ~s

hurl *v.* 1. (d; refl., tr.) to ~ at (to ~ oneself at the enemy; to ~ insults at smb.) 2. (misc.) to ~ oneself into the fray

hurrah *n.* the last ~ ("a last attempt")

hurricane *n.* 1. a severe, violent ~ 2. a ~ hits, strikes (the ~ struck several cities) 3. a ~ blows itself out 4. the eye of a ~

hurry I *n.* 1. in a ~ 2. a ~ to + inf. (we were in a ~ to finish)

hurry II *v.* 1. (E) he ~ried to respond to her letter 2. (P; intr.) to ~ across the road; to ~ towards the school; to ~ to the scene

hurry back *v.* (D; intr.) to ~ to (she ~ried back to her desk)

hurt I *adj.* ["insulted"] 1. deeply, very ~ ["injured"] 2. badly, seriously; slightly ~

hurt II *v.* 1. to ~ badly, seriously; deeply; slightly 2. (R) it ~s me to cough; it ~s me to see her ruin her life

hurtful *adj.* (formal) ~ to

hurtle *v.* (d; intr.) to ~ through the air (a large rock came ~ling through the air)

husband *n.* 1. to divorce; leave one's ~ 2. a common-law; cuckolded; estranged ~; ex-husband, former; faithful; henpecked; jealous; philandering, unfaithful ~ 3. (misc.) she had two children by her first ~

husbandry *n.* animal ~

hush *n.* 1. a ~ fell (over the crowd) 2. a deathly ~

hustings *n.* ["route of an election campaign"] to go out on the ~

hustle I *n.* (slang) ["quick movement"] to get a ~ on (AE)

hustle II *v.* (P; tr.) the police ~d the prisoner into a cell

hut *n.* 1. a bamboo; thatched ~ 2. a Nissen (BE), Quonset (AE) ~

hutch *n.* a rabbit ~

hydrant *n.* 1. to open, turn on a ~ 2. to turn off a ~ 3. a fire ~

hyena *n.* 1. a brown; laughing; spotted; striped ~ 2. a ~ howls 3. a clan, pack of ~s

hygiene *n.* 1. to practice (good) ~ 2. dental; feminine; field; industrial; mental; personal; sexual; social ~

hygienist *n.* a dental, oral ~

hymen *n.* to rupture a ~

hymn *n.* 1. to chant, sing a ~ 2. a rousing; solemn ~ 3. a ~ to (a ~ to freedom)

hypersensitive *adj.* ~ about, to

hypertension *n.* essential; malignant; mild; severe ~

hypnosis *n.* 1. to induce, produce ~ 2. to put smb. under ~ 3. under ~

hypnotism *n.* to practice ~

hypocrisy *n.* 1. to display ~ 2. sheer ~ 3. ~ to + inf. (it was sheer ~ to criticize the other political party about its tax policy)

hypocritical *adj.* 1. ~ about 2. ~ to + inf. (it was ~ of her to make the offer)

hypothesis *n.* 1. to advance, formulate, propose, put forth/forward a ~ 2. to confirm; test a ~ 3. to accept; reject a ~ 4. a null; working ~ 5. the ~ that + clause (she advanced the ~ that the disease was spread by rodents)

hypothesize *v.* 1. (D; intr.) to ~ about 2. (L) they ~d that the disease was spread by rodents

hysterectomy *n.* 1. to do, perform a ~ (on) 2. to have a ~

hysteria *n.* 1. to produce ~ 2. mass ~ 3. an attack, fit of ~

hysterical *adj.* ~ about

hysterics *n.* 1. to have ~ 2. a fit of ~ (to have a fit of ~) 3. in ~ (about, over) (her jokes had us in ~)

I

ice *n.* 1. to form, make, produce ~ 2. to melt ~ 3. hard; thick ~ 4. cracked; crushed ~ 5. dry ~ 6. black; pack ~ 7. ~ forms; melts 8. a patch; sheet of ~ 9. on the ~ (to slip on the ~) 10. (misc.) to break the ~ ("to create a more relaxed atmosphere"); to cut no ~ (with) ("to have no effect on"); on thin ~ ("in a dangerous situation"); on ~ ("in reserve"); (a) water ~

iceberg *n.* 1. to hit, strike an ~ (the ship struck an ~) 2. (misc.) (fig.) the tip of the ~

icebox *n.* (colloq.) (AE) to raid the ~ ("to eat heartily esp. during the night")

ice cap *n.* the polar ~

ice cream *n.* 1. to make ~ 2. hand-dipped ~ 3. chocolate; strawberry; vanilla ~

icicle *n.* an ~ forms; hangs down

icon *n.* to paint an ~

I. D. see **identification** 4

idea *n.* 1. to come up with, conceive, get, hit upon; develop; have an ~ 2. to consider, explore, entertain, toy with an ~ 3. to communicate, disseminate ~s 4. to market, package an ~ 5. to implement an ~ 6. to endorse, espouse, favor an ~ 7. to dismiss, drop, reject an ~ 8. a bright, brilliant, clever, good, great, ingenious; logical ~ 9. a fresh, new, novel ~ 10. a clear; fixed; general; main ~ 11. a daring; grandiose ~ 12. an approximate, rough; vague ~ 13. the faintest, slightest ~ (she didn't have the faintest ~ of what I meant) 14. an old, outmoded, stale, warmed-over ~ 15. an absurd, bad, crackpot, crazy, fantastic, far-fetched, foolish, wild; desperate; silly, simplistic, stupid; strange ~ 16. an ~ about 17. an ~ to + inf. (it was her ~ to have a party) 18. the ~ that + clause (I had no ~ that she would attend the meeting) 19. (misc.) he didn't get the ~ ("he did not understand"); an association of ~s

ideal I *adj.* ~ for

ideal II *n.* 1. to attain; realize an ~ 2. a lofty, noble ~; high ~s

idealistic *adj.* ~ about

identical *adj.* ~ to, with (his hat is ~ to mine)

identification *n.* ["process of identifying"] 1. to make an ~ 2. (a) positive ~ 3. a means of ~ ["document"] 4. to carry; show ~

identify *v.* 1. to positively ~ 2. (B) she ~fied the intruder to the police 3. (D; refl., tr.) to ~ as; to (he ~fied himself as an old friend of the family; she ~fied him to the police as the intruder) 4. (D; tr.) to ~ by (the police ~ fied her by her fingerprints) 5. (d.; intr., refl., tr.) to ~ with (she always ~fies with the underdog; he didn't want to be ~fied with the liberals)

identity *n.* 1. to establish smb.'s ~ 2. to conceal; reveal one's ~ 3. to assume smb.'s ~ 4. mistaken ~ (it was a case of mistaken ~)

ideology *n.* to embrace; espouse an ~

idiocy *n.* 1. congenital ~ 2. ~ to + inf. (it was sheer ~ for him to arrive late)

idiot *n.* 1. a blithering, blooming, blundering, confounded, driveling ~ 2. the local, village ~ 3. an ~ to + inf. (he was an ~ to agree)

idiotic *adj.* ~ to + inf. (they were ~ to do that)

idle *adj.* 1. to lie, remain, stand ~ (the machinery stood ~ for a month) 2. to be left ~

idol *n.* 1. to worship an ~ 2. (fig.) a fallen; matinee; national; popular ~

idolize *v.* (D; tr.) to ~ as (she was ~d as a movie star)

ignition *n.* (in a car) 1. to switch on, turn on the ~ 2. to switch off, turn off the ~

ignorance *n.* 1. to betray, demonstrate, display, show ~ 2. blissful ~ 3. abysmal, appalling, blatant, complete, crass, profound, total ~ 4. ~ about; of 5. in ~ (of) (I was in complete ~ of the facts; in my ~, I believed that there were tigers in Africa)

ignorant *adj.* 1. blissfully ~ 2. ~ in; of (~ of the facts)

ignore *v.* 1. to ~ completely, totally 2. (K) you'll have to ~ their talking so loud

ilk *n.* ["kind"] of a certain ~

ill *adj.* 1. to be taken ~ 2. to become, fall, get; feel ~ 3. chronically; critically, dangerously, desperately, gravely, seriously; incurably, terminally ~ 4. emotionally; mentally; physically ~ 5. ~ with (she is ~ with a tropical disease) 6. (misc.) ~ at ease ("uncomfortable"); the situation bodes ~ for the future; it makes me ~ to smell that sewage; it ~ becomes (BE)/behooves (AE) you to say such things

ill-advised *adj.* ~ to + inf. (you would be ~ not to invite both of them)

ill-disposed *adj.* (formal) (cannot stand alone) ~ to, towards (they are ~ towards me)

illegal *adj.* 1. ~ for (smoking is ~ for minors) 2. ~ to + inf. (it is ~ to drive while intoxicated)

ill feeling *n.* 1. to foment, stir up ~ 2. to bear, harbor ~ 3. ~ against 4. ~ over (there was a great deal of ~ stirred up over the appointment)

illiteracy *n.* 1. to eliminate, stamp out ~ 2. functional; widespread ~

illiterate *n.* a functional ~

illness *n.* 1. to get over an ~ 2. to come down with, develop an ~ 3. to succumb to an ~ 4. (an) acute; sudden ~ 5. (a) chronic; lingering 6. (a) minor; slight ~ 7. (a) catastrophic; grave, major, serious ~ 8. (a) fatal; incurable, untreatable; terminal ~ 9.

mental ~ 10. (misc.) the management; treatment of an ~

illogical *adj.* 1. ~ of 2. ~ to + inf. (it's of us ~ to assume that)

ills *n.* economic; social ~

illuminating *adj.* ~ to + inf. (it was ~ to read the candidate's earlier speeches)

illusion *n.* 1. to create, give, produce an ~ 2. to cherish, harbor, have an ~ 3. to dispel, shatter an ~ 4. an optical ~ 5. an ~ about 6. an ~ to + inf. (it's an ~ to think that...) 7. an ~ that + clause (it is an ~ that appeasement will deter an aggressor) 8. under an ~

illustrate *v.* 1. (D; tr.) to ~ with (she ~d her lectures with slides) 2. (L) their report ~d that their profits were falling 3. (Q; to) the incident ~d (to us) where we had gone wrong

illustration *n.* ["example"] 1. to give, offer, provide an ~ 2. by way of ~ ["picture"] 3. to draw an ~ 4. a graphic ~

illustrative *adj.* ~ of (~ of one's views)

ill will *n.* 1. to stir up ~ 2. to bear, feel, harbor ~ towards smb. 3. ~ about, over; between

image *n.* ["position, standing"] 1. to project an ~ 2. to bolster, improve smb.'s ~ 3. a public; tarnished ~ ["picture"] 4. (computers) to digitize an ~ 5. a clear ~ 6. a mental ~ (I have a clear, mental ~ of that place) 7. a mirror ~ ["misc."] 8. a spitting ~ (a spitting ~ of George Washington); to be created in the ~ of God; a graven ~; a virtual ~ (computers)

imagery *n.* poetic; vivid ~

imagination *n.* 1. to capture, excite, fire smb.'s ~ 2. to have (an) ~ 3. to show, use one's ~ 4. to lack ~ 5. to defy, stagger, stir smb.'s ~ 6. an active, fertile, lively, vivid; creative ~ 7. a feeble; wild ~ 8. a figment; stretch of smb.'s ~ 9. the ~ to + inf. (does she have the ~ to figure out what happened?) 10. in one's ~ 11. (misc.) by no stretch of the ~; it is pure ~ on your part; to leave nothing to the ~

imagine *v.* 1. (d; tr.) to ~ as (can you ~ her as an actress?) 2. (G) I can't ~ going to the party without an invitation 3. (J) can you ~ me becoming a teacher? 4. (K) it is difficult to ~ his marrying anyone 5. (L) I ~ that they will be delighted to hear from you 6. (N; used with an adjective, noun, past participle) can you ~ him president? 7. (Q) can you ~ how thrilled I was?

imbalance *n.* 1. to correct, redress an ~ 2. a trade ~ 3. an ~ between

imbecile *n.* an ~ to + inf. (he was an ~ to sign a contract with them)

imbecilic *adj.* ~ to + inf. (it was ~ to do that)

imbed see **embed**

imbued *adj.* (cannot stand alone) 1. deeply, profoundly, thoroughly ~ 2. ~ with (~ with a fighting spirit)

imitation *n.* 1. to do, give an ~ of smb. 2. a pale ~ 3.

in ~ of

imitative *adj.* (formal) ~ of

immaterial *adj.* 1. wholly ~ 2. ~ to 3. (misc.) it is ~ whether she attends or not; it is ~ how or when they get here

immature *adj.* 1. emotionally; mentally; physically ~ 2. ~ for (she is ~ for her age) 3. to + inf. (it was ~ of her to do that)

immaturity *n.* to display ~

immerse *v.* 1. to ~ deeply 2. (D; refl., tr.) to ~ in (she ~d herself in the water; ~d in one's work)

immersion *n.* 1. total ~ 2. ~ in (total ~ in one's work)

immigrant *n.* 1. an illegal; legal ~ 2. an ~ from; to (~s to Canada)

immigrate *v.* (D; intr.) to ~ from; into, to (to ~ into a country)

immigration *n.* 1. illegal; legal ~ 2. a flood; wave of ~ 3. ~ from; into, to

immodest *adj.* ~ to + inf. (it was ~ of me to say that)

immoral *adj.* ~ to + inf. (it's ~ to steal)

immune *adj.* ["exempt"] 1. ~ from (~ from prosecution; her prestige made her ~ from criticism) ["unaffected"] 2. ~ to (~ to a disease; her self-confidence made her ~ to criticism)

immunity *n.* ["resistance to disease"] 1. to acquire, develop; have ~ 2. to confer, give ~ (this shot will give you ~ for about twelve months; that vaccine will confer lifelong ~) 3. acquired; natural ~ 4. active; passive ~ 5. ~ against ["exemption; special status"] 6. to grant ~ to 7. to have ~ 8. diplomatic ~ (to have diplomatic ~) 9. ~ from (~ from prosecution)

immunization *n.* 1. to carry out a (mass) ~ against 2. active; passive ~

immunize *v.* (D; tr.) to ~ against (the children have been ~d against polio)

impact I *n.* 1. to have, make an ~ on, upon 2. to lessen, soften the ~ 3. (a) considerable, strong; cumulative; great; lasting; profound ~ 4. (a) dramatic; emotional; favorable ~ 5. (an) environmental ~ 6. on ~ (the pole collapses on ~)

impact II *v.* (esp. AE) (d; intr.) to ~ on, upon

impaired *adj.* hearing; visually ~

impairment *n.* (a) hearing; memory; mental; physical; speech; visual ~

impale *v.* (D; tr.) to ~ on, upon (the driver was thrown from the car and ~d on a fence)

impart *v.* (B) to ~ knowledge to students

impartiality *n.* 1. to demonstrate, display, show ~ 2. ~ in

impasse *n.* 1. to reach an ~ 2. to break an ~ 3. at an ~ (negotiations were at an ~)

impatience *n.* 1. to display, show ~ 2. ~ with 3. ~ to + inf. (we noted their ~ to begin)

impatient *adj.* 1. ~ at, with (~ at the delay; ~ with children) 2. ~ for (I was ~ for the trip to start) 3. ~

to + inf. (we were ~ to leave)

impeach *v.* (D; tr.) to ~ for (to ~ smb. for taking bribes)

impediment *n.* 1. a speech ~ 2. an ~ to (an ~ to progress)

impel *v.* (formal) 1. (d; tr.) to ~ into, to 2. (H) to ~ smb. to do smt.

impelled *adj.* (cannot stand alone) ~ to + inf. (she felt ~ to intercede)

imperative I *adj.* 1. ~ to + inf. (it is ~ to act now) 2. ~ that + clause; subj. (it is ~ that you be/should be present)

imperative II *n.* 1. a moral ~ 2. an ~ that + clause; subj. (it is a moral ~ that no concessions be/should be made)

imperceptible *adj.* ~ to (~ to the touch)

imperfection *n.* a slight ~

impersonation *n.* to do, give an ~

impertinence *n.* the ~ to + inf. (he had the ~ to demand a raise)

impertinent *adj.* 1. ~ to 2. ~ to + inf. (it was ~ of him to behave like that)

impervious *adj.* ~ to (~ to criticism)

impetuous *adj.* ~ to + inf. (it was ~ of her to do that)

impetus *n.* 1. to give, provide an ~ 2. to gain ~ 3. a fresh ~ 4. a powerful, strong ~ 5. an ~ to 6. an ~ to + inf. (there was no ~ to work harder)

impinge *v.* (formal) (d; intr.) to ~ on, upon (to ~ on smb.'s rights)

impingement *n.* an ~ on, upon

implant I *n.* a breast; heart; kidney ~

implant II *v.* 1. to ~ deeply 2. (d; tr.) to ~ in (to ~ respect for democracy in the younger generation)

implicate *v.* (D; tr.) to ~ in (to ~ smb. in a scandal)

implication *n.* 1. to have an ~ 2. a derogatory, negative; serious; significant; subtle ~ 3. an ~ for 4. an ~ that + clause (I resent your ~ that my work is unsatisfactory) 5. by ~ 6. (misc.) to realize the full ~s of smt.

implicit *adj.* 1. ~ in (~ in the contract) 2. ~ that + clause (it is ~ in our agreement that she will be a partner)

implore *v.* (formal) (H) they ~d her to help

imply *v.* (L; to) she ~lied (to us) that she knew more than she had told the reporters

impolite *adj.* 1. ~ to 2. ~ to + inf. (it is ~ to interrupt someone who is speaking; it was ~ of them not to respond)

import I *n.* an ~ from; into, to (~s from abroad)

import II *v.* (D; tr.) to ~ from; into (to ~ goods from abroad)

importance *n.* 1. to acquire, assume ~ 2. to attach, attribute ~ to 3. (a) considerable, great, overriding, paramount, primary, prime, utmost, vital ~ (the matter assumed paramount ~) 4. minor, secondary ~ 5. ~ for, to 6. of ~ (it was a question of great ~ to us)

important *adj.* 1. vitally ~ 2. ~ for (irrigation is ~ for farming) 3. ~ to (winning the contest was very ~ to her) 4. ~ to + inf. (it is ~ to study hard) 5. ~ that + clause; subj. (it is ~ that everyone attend/should attend/BE: attends)

importune *v.* (formal) 1. (D; tr.) to ~ for 2. (H) to ~ smb. to do smt.

impose *v.* 1. (D; intr., refl.) to ~ on, upon ("to take advantage of") (to ~ on smb.'s good nature; don't ~ yourself on them) 2. (D; tr.) ("to levy") to ~ on (to ~ a new tax on cigarettes)

imposition *n.* an ~ on

impossible I *adj.* 1. almost, practically, quite, virtually, well-nigh ~ 2. physically ~ 3. ~ for (it's ~ for me to help) 4. ~ to + inf. (it is ~ to predict the future) 5. ~ that + clause (it's ~ that she would refuse such an invitation)

impossible II *n.* 1. to attempt the ~ 2. to do the ~

impractical *adj.* ~ to + inf. (it's ~ to live in one city and work in another)

imprecation *n.* (formal) 1. to utter an ~ 2. an ~ against

impregnate *v.* (d; tr.) to ~ with

impress *v.* 1. to ~ deeply; favorably 2. (D; tr.) to ~ as (she ~ed me as a scholar) 3. (d; tr.) to ~ on, upon (he tried to ~ on them the importance of being punctual) 4. (D; tr.) to ~ with (she ~ed me with her grasp of the subject) 5. (R) it ~ed me that they cooperated so willingly

impressed *adj.* 1. easily ~ 2. deeply, greatly, highly, strongly, very ~

impression *n.* ["effect"] 1. to convey, create, give an ~ 2. to make an ~ on, upon 3. a deep, indelible, lasting, profound, strong, vivid ~ (they made a lasting ~ on the visitors) 4. an excellent, favorable, good ~ 5. an erroneous, false, inaccurate, wrong ~ (they created an erroneous ~ of their capabilities) 6. a bad, unfavorable ~ 7. a first ~ 8. an ~ that + clause (she conveyed the false ~ that her family was wealthy) ["opinion"] 9. to form, get, gain, have an ~ 10. an accurate; fleeting; general; personal ~ (I got only a fleeting ~ of her performance) 11. an excellent, favorable, good ~ 12. an erroneous, false, inaccurate, wrong ~ (we formed an erroneous ~ of their abilities) 13. a bad, unfavorable ~ 14. a first ~ 15. an ~ that + clause (we had the false ~ that her family was wealthy) 16. under an ~ (I was under the ~ that you would come) ["mark"] 17. to make, take an ~ of a key ["imitation"] 18. to do an ~ (the comedian does humorous ~s)

imprint I *n.* 1. to bear an ~ (to bear the ~ of genius) 2. to leave one's ~ on 3. an indelible ~ 4. (misc.) published under the ~ of a vanity press

imprint II *v.* (d; refl., tr.) to ~ in, on, upon (the scene ~ed itself on their minds)

imprison *v.* (D; tr.) to ~ for (to ~ smb. for fraud)

imprisonment *n.* life ~

improbable *adj.* 1. highly ~ 2. ~ that + clause (it's highly ~ that she'll accept the invitation)

improper *adj.* 1. ~ for 2. ~ to + inf. (it was ~ to do that)

impropriety *n.* crass ~

improve *v.* 1. to ~ greatly, noticeably, significantly, very much; gradually, slowly; rapidly 2. (D; intr.) to ~ in (she has ~d in English) 3. (d; intr.) to ~ on, upon (I cannot ~ on her performance) 4. (misc.) to ~ with age

improvement *n.* 1. to bring about an ~ 2. to show (an) ~ 3. a considerable, decided, definite, distinct, great, marked, noticeable, significant, substantial; gradual, slow; minor, slight; rapid ~ 4. an ~ in, of (an ~ in her work; an ~ of service) 5. an ~ on, over, upon (this edition is an ~ over the previous one)

improvisation *n.* to do an ~

improvise *v.* (D; intr., tr.) to ~ on (to ~ on a given subject)

imprudent *adj.* ~ to + inf. (it was ~ of them to speculate on the stock exchange)

impudence *n.* 1. brazen ~ 2. the ~ to + inf. (he had the ~ to breach the contract)

impudent *adj.* ~ to + inf. (it was ~ of her to answer like that; she was ~ to answer like that)

impulse *n.* ["driving force"] 1. to feel an ~ 2. to curb, repress, resist an ~ 3. an irresistible; sudden ~ 4. an ~ to + inf. (he felt an irresistible ~ to buy a new TV set) 5. on, under (an) ~ (to act on ~) ["stimulus"] 6. to convey, transmit an ~ 7. an electrical; nerve ~

impunity *n.* with ~ (to act with ~)

impute *v.* (formal) (d; tr.) to ~ to (to ~ base motives to smb.)

in I *adv.* (colloq.) 1. ~ for ("facing") (they are ~ for trouble) 2. ~ with ("on intimate terms with") (they are ~ with highly influential people)

in II *n.* (colloq.) ["influence"] to have an ~ with smb.

in III *prep.* ~ smb. to + inf. (it's not ~ me to lie; she doesn't have it ~ her to break her word)

inability *n.* ~ to + inf. (her ~ to pay caused trouble)

inaccessible *adj.* ~ to (~ to students)

inaccuracy *n.* 1. a glaring ~ 2. ~ in

inaccurate *adj.* 1. completely; somewhat ~ 2. ~ in 3. ~ to + inf. (it is ~ to say that she was dismissed)

inadequate *adj.* 1. completely, grossly, totally, woefully ~ 2. ~ for; to (the supply of water is ~ for the trip; ~ to the occasion) 3. ~ to + inf. (the supply is ~ to meet the demand)

inadvisable *adj.* ~ to + inf. (it was ~ to delay)

inapplicable *adj.* ~ to

inappropriate *adj.* 1. ~ for, to (~ to the occasion) 2. ~ to + inf. (it is ~ for you to wear shorts at a formal reception) 3. ~ that + clause; subj. (it is ~ that she be/should be present)

inattention *n.* ~ to (~ to detail)

inattentive *adj.* ~ to

inaudible *adj.* ~ to

inaugurate *v.* (D; tr.) to ~ as (to be ~d as president)

inauguration *n.* 1. to have, hold an ~ (for) 2. the presidential ~

incantation *n.* to chant, intone, utter an ~

incapable *adj.* (cannot stand alone) ~ of (she is ~ of cheating)

incarnation *n.* (in) a previous ~

incense *n.* to burn ~

incensed *adj.* 1. greatly, highly, very ~ 2. ~ about, at, over 3. ~ to + inf. (she was ~ to learn of the accusation) 4. ~ that + clause (she was highly ~ that they failed to invite her)

incentive *n.* 1. to give, offer, provide an ~ 2. to have an ~ 3. a powerful, strong ~ 4. a tax ~ 5. an ~ for 6. an ~ to (an ~ to increased investment) 7. an ~ to + inf. (they have no ~ to work harder)

inception *n.* at; from; since smt.'s ~

incest *n.* to commit ~

inch I *n.* 1. to contest, fight for every ~ of one's land 2. a cubic; square ~ 3. every ~ ("to the utmost degree") (she is every ~ a champion) 4. within an ~ ("almost") (he was beaten within an ~ of his life) 5. (misc.) ~ by ~; to miss smt. by ~es

inch II *v.* (P; intr.) to ~ forward slowly; to ~ towards the goal; to ~ along a corridor

incidence *n.* a high; low ~ (a high ~ of crime)

incident I *adj.* (formal) (cannot stand alone) ~ to (the risks ~ to military service)

incident II *n.* 1. to cause, give rise to, provoke an ~ 2. to cover up, suppress an ~ 3. an amusing, funny, humorous; curious; nasty, painful, ugly, unpleasant; pleasant; strange; touching ~ 4. a border; diplomatic; international ~ 5. an ~ occurs, takes place 6. without ~ (the ceremony was held without ~)

incidental *adj.* ~ to (problems ~ to growing up)

incision *n.* 1. to make an ~ 2. a deep ~ 3. an ~ into

incisors *n.* central; lateral ~

incite *v.* 1. (D; tr.) to ~ to (to ~ workers to rebellion) 2. (H) to ~ the populace to riot

incitement *n.* ~ to (~ to riot)

inclination *n.* 1. to feel an ~ 2. a natural; strong ~ 3. an ~ for, to, towards 4. an ~ to + inf. (the carburetor has an ~ to flood)

incline *v.* (esp. BE) 1. (d; intr.) to ~ to, towards (he ~s to laziness) 2. (d; tr.) to ~ to (it ~d me to anger) 3. (E) I ~ to believe that she is innocent 4. (H) the news ~d me to leave at once

inclined *adj.* (cannot stand alone) 1. academically; artistically; intellectually; mechanically; musically; romantically ~ 2. ~ to + inf. (I am ~ to agree)

include *v.* (D; tr.) to ~ among, in (to ~ smb. in a list of candidates; who was ~d among the guests?)

inclusive *adj.* ~ of

incognito *adj.*, *adv.* to go, travel; remain ~
incognizant *adj.* ~ of
income *n.* 1. to earn an ~ 2. to have an ~ 3. to generate (an) ~ 4. an annual, yearly; monthly; weekly ~ 5. a gross; net; taxable ~ 6. an earned; unearned ~ 7. a fixed; independent ~ 8. a good, high, sizeable ~ 9. a limited, low ~ 10. (an) ~ from (~ from investments) 11. per capita ~ 12. beyond one's ~ (they live beyond their ~) 13. on a certain ~ 14. within one's ~ (to live within one's ~)
incommensurable *adj.* ~ with
incommensurate *adj.* ~ to, with
incommunicado *adv.* to hold smb. ~
incompatibility *n.* ~ with
incompatible *adj.* 1. mutually ~ 2. ~ with
incompetence *n.* ~ at, in
incompetent *adj.* 1. grossly, hopelessly, totally ~ 2. ~ at, in 3. ~ to + inf. (he is ~ to judge)
incomplete *n.* ["academic deficiency"] to make up an ~ (the student had to make up three ~s)
incomprehensible *adj.* 1. ~ to 2. ~ that + clause (it is ~ that they were admitted to the program)
inconceivable *adj.* 1. ~ to 2. ~ that + clause (it is ~ that she could be considered for the job)
incongruous *adj.* 1. ~ with 2. ~ that + clause (it was ~ that those two bitter rivals should be playing on the same team)
inconsiderate *adj.* 1. ~ of (he's ~ of her feelings) 2. ~ to + inf. (it was ~ of you to say that)
inconsistency *n.* ~ in
inconsistent *adj.* ~ in; with
inconvenience I *n.* 1. to cause ~ 2. to put up with (an) ~ 3. (a) considerable, great; minor, slight; temporary ~ 4. an ~ for 5. an ~ to + inf. (it's an ~ to have to shop so far from home)
inconvenience II *v.* (H) I hope that it will not ~ you to stop by tomorrow
inconvenient *adj.* 1. ~ for 2. ~ to + inf. (it is ~ to meet tomorrow)
incorporate *v.* (D; tr.) to ~ into
incorrect *adj.* 1. ~ in 2. ~ to + inf. (it's ~ to say that she is a good administrator)
increase I *n.* 1. a considerable, dramatic, large, sharp, significant, sizable, substantial; gradual; moderate; slight; steady ~ 2. a cost-of-living; pay; rate ~ 3. an ~ in (an ~ in coal consumption) 4. on the ~
increase II *v.* 1. (D; intr., tr.) to ~ by (production ~d by ten percent) 2. (D; intr., tr.) to ~ from; to (the physician ~d the dosage from one to four) 3. (D; intr., tr.) to ~ in (the guards were ~d in number)
incredible *adj.* ~ that + clause (it was ~ that nobody paid/should have paid attention to the new invention)
increment *n.* an ~ in (an ~ in salary)
incriminate *v.* (D; tr.) to ~ in
inculcate *v.* 1. (D; tr.) to ~ in, into (to ~ ideas in the

minds of young people) 2. (d; tr.) to ~ with (they were ~d with radical ideas)
incumbent I *adj.* (cannot stand alone) ~ on, upon + to + inf. (it's ~ on you to warn them)
incumbent II *n.* to unseat an ~
incursion *n.* 1. to make an ~ 2. an armed ~ 3. an ~ into (to make an ~ into neutral territory)
indebted *adj.* 1. deeply, heavily ~ 2. (cannot stand alone) ~ for; to (we are ~ to her for her help)
indecent *adj.* ~ to + inf. (it was ~ of him to do that)
indecision *n.* ~ about, over
indecisive *adj.* ~ about
indefinite *adj.* ~ about
indelicate *adj.* 1. highly, very ~ 2. ~ to + inf. (it was highly ~ of her to raise that matter in public)
indemnification *n.* to pay ~ for
indemnify *v.* (D; tr.) to ~ for
indemnity *n.* 1. to pay an ~ 2. double ~ 3. an ~ for
indent *v.* (BE) (d; intr.) ("to request officially") to ~ for; on (we had to ~ on the company for new computers)
indentation *n.* to make an ~
independence *n.* 1. to achieve, gain, win ~ from 2. to assert, declare one's ~ from 3. to grant ~ 4. to lose one's ~ 5. financial; political ~
independent *adj.* 1. fiercely, very ~ 2. financially ~ 3. ~ from, of
index *n.* ["alphabetical list"] 1. to compile, do, make an ~ 2. an author; cumulative; subject ~ 3. an ~ to (an ~ to a book) ["indicator"] 4. a consumer-price, cost-of-living; price ~ 5. an ~ to (an ~ to economic progress) ["ratio of one dimension to another"] 6. a cephalic; cranial; facial ~
indexed *adj.* ~ to (pensions ~ to inflation)
Indian *n.* an American ~
USAGE NOTE: To somebody from Canada or the United States, a primary meaning of *Indian* is "American Indian". To somebody from other English-speaking countries, the primary meaning is "somebody from India". Note that a *West Indian* is always somebody from the West Indies. In contemporary usage, *American Indian* is being replaced by *Native American*.
indicate *v.* 1. to ~ clearly 2. (B) she ~d her reasons to us 3. (L; to) they ~d (to us) that they would sign the contract 4. (Q; to) they ~d (to us) why they would sign
indication *n.* 1. to give an ~ 2. a clear ~ 3. every; no ~ 4. an ~ that + clause (there is every ~ that she will recover)
indicative I *adj.* ~ of
indicative II *n.* (grammar) in the ~ (the verb was in the ~)
indict *v.* (D; tr.) to ~ for (to ~ smb. for murder)
indictment *n.* (usu. legal) 1. to hand up (AE), issue, present, return an ~ 2. to waive (the) ~ 3. to quash an ~ 4. (fig.) a stinging, swingeing (BE); sweeping

~ (of) 5. an ~ against 6. an ~ for 7. on ~ (to try a case on ~)

indifference *n.* 1. to affect, feign ~ 2. to display, show ~ 3. complete; marked; studied ~ 4. ~ about, concerning 5. ~ to, towards 6. with ~ 7. (misc.) it's a matter of complete ~ to me whether or not she comes

indifferent *adj.* 1. to remain ~ 2. ~ about, concerning 3. ~ to, towards

indigenous *adj.* ~ to

indigestion *n.* 1. to cause ~ 2. to give smb. ~ (pickles give me ~) 3. to get; have; suffer from ~ 4. acute, severe; chronic ~ 5. an attack, touch of ~

indignant *adj.* 1. ~ about, at, over 2. ~ that + clause (we were ~ that the performance was canceled) 3. (misc.) to wax ~ (over smt.)

indignation *n.* 1. to arouse ~ (in smb.); to fill smb. with ~ 2. to express; feel, show ~ 3. burning; deep; helpless; public; righteous ~ 4. ~ about, at, over (to feel ~ at gross injustice) 5. to smb.'s ~

indignity *n.* 1. to inflict an ~ on 2. to suffer ~ties

indiscreet *adj.* 1. ~ in 2. ~ to + inf. (it was ~ of her to say that)

indiscretion *n.* 1. to commit an ~ 2. a youthful ~

indiscriminate *adj.* ~ in

indispensable *adj.* ~ for, to (~ to life)

indisposed *adj.* (formal) ~ to + inf. (she appears ~ to go)

indisputable *adj.* ~ that + clause (it is ~ that the evidence was tampered with)

indistinguishable *adj.* ~ from

individualism *n.* rugged ~

individuality *n.* to express one's ~

indoctrinate *v.* (D; tr.) to ~ against; in; with

indoctrinated *adj.* ~ to + inf. (they were ~ to believe that their culture was superior)

indoctrination *n.* ~ against; in; with

indoors *adv.* to be; come; go; stay ~

induce *v.* (H) we could not ~ her to come

inducement *n.* 1. to give, offer, provide; have an ~ 2. a strong ~ 3. a financial, monetary ~ 4. an ~ to 5. an ~ to + inf. (we had no ~ to work harder)

induct *v.* (D; tr.) to ~ into (to ~ smb. into an official position); (esp. AE: to ~ smb. into the armed forces)

induction *n.* ~ into

indulge *v.* (d; intr., refl., tr.) to ~ in (to ~ in the luxury of a nice warm bath; he ~s her in everything)

indulgence *n.* 1. to grant an ~ 2. to ask for smb.'s ~ 3. ~ to, towards

indulgent *adj.* ~ to, towards

industry *n.* 1. to build up, develop (an) ~ 2. (an) ~ springs up 3. a basic, key ~ 4. a cottage; defense; service; high-tech ~ 5. heavy; light ~ 6. the aerospace; aircraft; automobile (esp. AE), motor-manufacturing (BE); building, construction; coal; computer; cosmetics; dairy; film; food; machine-tool; meat-packing; pharmaceutical; shipbuilding; steel; textile; tourist, travel; trucking (esp. AE) ~ 7. a smokestack ("old, obsolete") ~ 8. (misc.) government often regulates ~; a branch of ~

ineffective *adj.* ~ against

inefficiency *n.* 1. gross ~ 2. ~ in

inefficient *adj.* 1. grossly, hopelessly, very ~ 2. ~ to + inf. (it's ~ to set up two offices)

inelegant *adj.* ~ to + inf. (it was ~ to phrase the request in that manner)

ineligibility *n.* ~ for

ineligible *adj.* 1. ~ for 2. ~ to + inf. (she is still ~ to vote)

inept *adj.* ~ at, in

ineptitude *n.* 1. to demonstrate, display ~ 2. ~ at, in

inequality *n.* 1. gross ~ 2. ~ between 3. ~ in

inertia *n.* 1. sheer ~ 2. through ~

inevitable *adj.* ~ that + clause (it was ~ that she would find out)

inexcusable *adj.* 1. ~ to + inf. (it was ~ of him to blurt that out) 2. ~ that + clause (it is ~ that she was left out)

inexperienced *adj.* ~ at, in

infallibility *n.* 1. papal ~ 2. ~ in

infallible *adj.* ~ in

infancy *n.* ["first stage"] in one's ~ (the industry was still in its ~)

infant *n.* 1. to breast-feed, nurse, suckle an ~ 2. to bubble, burp an ~ 3. to wean an ~ 4. a newborn; premature ~ 5. (misc.) ~ mortality (see also **baby** 7-9, 13-15)

infanticide *n.* to commit ~

infantile *adj.* ~ to + inf. (it was ~ to behave like that)

infantry *n.* light; motorized; mountain ~

infatuated *adj.* ~ with

infatuation *n.* ~ with

infect *v.* (D; tr.) to ~ (to ~ with) they were ~ed with an unidentified virus

infection *n.* 1. to cause; pass on, spread, transmit (an) ~ 2. to prevent (an) ~ 3. to treat an ~ 4. ~ an acute; chronic; deep; latent; localized; minor, slight; superficial; primary; secondary; serious, severe; systemic ~ 5. (an) ~ sets in; spreads

infer *v.* 1. (D; tr.) to ~ from (to ~ a conclusion from the facts) 2. (L) I ~ that my proposal has been accepted 3. (Q) we had to ~ what she meant

inference *n.* 1. to draw, make an ~ from 2. an invalid; valid ~ 3. an ~ that + clause (we made the ~ that she had been wrongly accused) 4. by ~

inferior *adj.* 1. ~ in (~ in rank) 2. ~ to (he felt ~ to them)

inferiority *n.* 1. intellectual; social ~ 2. a feeling of ~ 3. ~ to

inferiority complex *n.* to have, suffer from an ~ (about)

inferno *n.* a blazing, raging, roaring ~

infest *v.* (D; tr.) to ~ with (their clothing was ~ed with lice)

infidelity *n.* 1. conjugal, marital ~ 2. ~ to (~ to one's ideals)

infighting *n.* 1. political ~ 2. ~ among, between

infiltrate *v.* (D; intr.) to ~ into

infiltration *n.* ~ into; through (enemy ~ into our lines)

infinitive *n.* 1. to split an ~ 2. a split ~

infinity *n.* to ~

inflame *v.* (D; tr.) to ~ with (they were ~d with enthusiasm for their cause)

inflammable *adj.* highly, very ~

inflammation *n.* 1. to cause (an) ~ 2. a mild; severe ~ 3. (an) ~ subsides

inflation *n.* 1. to cause ~ 2. to bring down, control, curb, reduce ~ 3. creeping; double-digit; galloping, high, rampant, runaway, uncontrolled ~ 4. the rate of ~ (the rate of ~ stands at three percent)

inflection, inflexion *n.* a falling; rising ~

inflexibility *n.* ~ in

inflexible *adj.* ~ in

inflict *v.* (D; tr.) to ~ on, upon (to ~ heavy losses on the enemy)

influence I *n.* 1. to exert, have ~ on; to exercise ~ over 2. to use one's ~ 3. to wield ~ 4. to bring ~ to bear 5. to flaunt one's ~ 6. (colloq.) to peddle ~ 7. to consolidate, strengthen one's ~ 8. to counteract, curb, neutralize smb.'s ~ 9. (a) bad, baleful, baneful, negative; pernicious; undue; unwholesome ~ 10. (a) beneficial, good, positive, salutary; calming; civilizing; leavening; moderating ~ 11. (a) considerable; far-reaching; lasting; major; powerful, profound, strong ~ 12. (a) direct; indirect ~ 13. (a) cultural; moral ~ 14. an ~ for (an ~ for good) 15. ~ on; with 16. the ~ to + inf. (they have enough ~ to get the bill passed) 17. under smb.'s ~; under the ~ of (to come under smb.'s ~; to drive under the ~ of alcohol) 18. (misc.) outside ~s; a sphere of ~; an ~ peddler (AE), pedlar

influence II *v.* 1. to ~ deeply, profoundly, strongly 2. (D; tr.) to ~ in 3. (H) who ~d her to do that?

influential *adj.* ~ in

influx *n.* an ~ from; into

inform *v.* 1. (D; tr.) to ~ about, of (we ~ed them of the incident) 2. (d; intr.) to ~ against, on (he ~ed on his accomplices) 3. (L; must have an object) she ~ed them that she would soon come 4. (Q; must have an object) the thief ~ed the police where the money was hidden

informal *adj.* ~ with (she's ~ with everyone)

informant *n.* a native ~

information *n.* 1. to disseminate, furnish, give, offer, provide ~ 2. to collect, dig up, find, gather; extract ~ 3. to classify ~ 4. to disclose, divulge, leak ~ 5. to declassify ~ 6. to feed ~ (into a

computer) 7. to access; retrieve ~ (from a computer) 8. to save; store ~ (in a computer) 9. to cover up, suppress, withhold ~ 10. classified, confidential; detailed; firsthand; inside; misleading; reliable; secondhand; secret ~ 11. (AE) long-distance ~ (BE has *long-distance enquiries, trunk enquiries*) 12. ~ about, on 13. ~ that + clause (we have ~ that she has returned to this country) 14. for smb.'s ~ (for your ~)

informative *adj.* ~ to + inf. (it was ~ to read the latest statistics)

informed *adj.* 1. to keep smb. ~ 2. ~ about, of

informer *n.* 1. to turn ("become") ~ 2. a police ~

inform on *v.* (D; tr.) to ~ to (he ~ed on them to the police)

infraction *n.* 1. to commit an ~ 2. a major; minor ~

infringe *v.* (d; intr.) to ~ on, upon (to ~ on smb.'s rights)

infringement *n.* an ~ of, on (an ~ of smb.'s rights)

infuriate *v.* (R) it ~d me (to read) that he had been indicted

infuriated *adj.* 1. ~ about, at, over; with 2. ~ to + inf. (he was ~ to find his seat occupied)

infuriating *adj.* 1. ~ to + inf. (it's ~ to pay such prices for inferior merchandise) 2. ~ that + clause (it's ~ that these items are so expensive)

infuse *v.* 1. (d; tr.) to ~ into (to ~ new life into the troops) 2. (d; intr.) to ~ with (the stock market was ~d with optimism)

infusion *n.* 1. an herbal ~ 2. an intravenous ~ 3. an ~ into (an ~ of new resources into a project)

ingenious *adj.* ~ to + inf. (it was ~ of her to solve the problem so quickly)

ingenuity *n.* 1. to exercise; show ~ 2. human ~ 3. the ~ to + inf. (she had the ~ to succeed where everyone else had failed)

ingot *n.* a gold ~

ingrained *adj.* 1. deeply ~ 2. ~ in

ingratiate *v.* (D; refl.) to ~ with (she ~d herself with the boss)

ingratitude *n.* 1. to demonstrate, display, show ~ 2. base, rank ~ 3. ~ to, towards

ingredients *n.* 1. to combine ~ (in baking) 2. basic, essential; principal ~ 3. the ~ for, of 4. (misc.) the book has all the ~ of a best-seller

inhale *v.* to ~ deeply

inhere *v.* (formal) to ~ in

inherent *adj.* ~ in, to

inherit *v.* (D; tr.) to ~ from (to ~ a fortune from an uncle)

inheritance *n.* to claim one's ~ 2. to come into an ~

inhibit *v.* (D; tr.) to ~ from

inhibitions *n.* 1. to have ~ (about) 2. to lose one's ~

inhospitable *adj.* 1. ~ to 2. ~ to + inf. (it is ~ to turn a stranger away)

inimical *adj.* (formal) ~ to (actions ~ to the maintenance of friendly relations between our countries)

iniquity *n.* a den of ~

initiate *v.* (d; tr.) to ~ into (to ~ students into the mysteries of linguistics)

initiation *n.* 1. to conduct, hold an ~ 2. an ~ into (an ~ into a fraternity)

initiative *n.* 1. to demonstrate, display, exercise, show ~ 2. to take the ~ (in) 3. to stifle ~ 4. to lose the ~ 5. private ~ 6. the ~ to + inf. (does she have enough ~ to get this job done?) 7. on one's (own) ~ (she made the decision on her own ~)

inject *v.* 1. (D; tr.) to ~ into (to ~ a note of humor into the proceedings) 2. (D; tr.) to ~ with (they were ~ed with a new drug)

injection *n.* 1. to administer, give an ~ 2. to get an ~ 3. a lethal ~ 4. a hypodermic; intradermal; intramuscular; intravenous; subcutaneous ~ 5. an ~ against, for 6. by ~ (to take a drug by ~) 7. (misc.) an ~ of new money into a business

injudicious *adj.* (formal) ~ to + inf. (it was ~ of you to speak to the press)

injunction *n.* 1. to grant, hand down (AE), issue an ~ 2. to deliver an ~ 3. to get; seek an ~ 4. an ~ against (an ~ against picketing) 5. a permanent; temporary ~ 6. an ~ to + inf. (an ~ to prevent picketing) 7. an ~ that + clause; subj. (the court issued an ~ that picketing not take/should not take place)

injure *v.* to ~ badly, critically, seriously, severely; slightly

injurious *adj.* ~ to

injury *n.* 1. to inflict (an) ~ on 2. to receive, suffer, sustain an ~ 3. to escape ~ 4. a fatal; minor, slight; serious, severe ~ 5. bodily ~; an internal ~; multiple ~ries 6. an ~ to (an ~ to the head) 7. (misc.) to add insult to ~

injustice *n.* 1. to do smb. an ~ 2. to commit an ~ 3. to redress, remedy an ~ 4. (a) blatant, gross, rank ~ 5. an ~ to

ink *n.* 1. indelible; India (AE), Indian (BE); invisible; marking; permanent; printer's; secret; washable ~ 2. ~ smudges 3. a blob, blot, drop, spot of ~

inkling *n.* 1. to give smb. an ~ 2. to have an ~ 3. the faintest, slightest ~ 4. an ~ about, of 5. an ~ that + clause (I didn't have the slightest ~ that he was ill)

inlaid *adj.* ~ with (~ with silver)

inland *adv.* to go, travel ~

inmate *n.* a prison ~

inn *n.* a country; roadside, wayside ~

innate *adj.* ~ in

inner city *n.* to redevelop, revitalize the ~

innocence *n.* 1. to establish, prove, show smb.'s ~ 2. to assert, maintain, protest one's ~ 3. (misc.) an air of (injured) ~; (in) wide-eyed ~

innocent *adj.* ~ of

innovation *n.* 1. a daring; major; radical ~ 2. an ~ in

innuendo *n.* 1. to cast, make an ~ 2. an ~ about 3. an ~ that + clause (she made an ~ that he had a prison record)

inoculate *v.* (D; tr.) 1. to ~ against (to ~ a dog against rabies) 2. (D; tr.) to ~ with (they were ~d with a vaccine)

inoculation *n.* 1. to give an ~ 2. to get, have, receive an ~ 3. an ~ against (an ~ against tetanus)

input I *n.* 1. ~ into, to 2. (misc.) the ~ of our customers is welcome

input II *v.* (D; tr.) to ~ into (to ~ data into a computer)

inquest *n.* 1. to conduct, hold an ~ 2. a coroner's; formal ~ 3. an ~ into

inquire *v.* 1. (D; intr.) to ~ about, after; into 2. (formal) (D; intr.) to ~ of (may I ~ of you where the meeting is?) 3. (Q) he ~d where we were to meet
USAGE NOTE: In BE, the spelling *enquire* is also used—we enquired about her health.

inquiry *n.* 1. to conduct, hold, make; launch an ~ 2. a discreet; exhaustive, thorough; official; private; public ~ 3. an ~ about (to make ~ries about a matter) 4. an ~ about, into (an official ~ into the incident was launched)
USAGE NOTE: The noun *inquiry* can mean "question" or "investigation". In BE, the spelling *enquiry* has been recommended for the meaning "question"—an enquiry about her health. Compare—an official inquiry into the incident.

inquisition *n.* 1. to carry out, conduct an ~ 2. a cruel, senseless ~

inquisitive *adj.* ~ about

inroads *n.* 1. to make ~ 2. deep ~ 3. ~ in, into, on, upon (to make ~ on the freedom of the press)

insane *adj.* 1. criminally ~ 2. to go ~ 3. ~ to + inf. (it was ~ of him to risk everything)

insanity *n.* 1. (legal) to plead ~ 2. outright, pure, sheer ~ 3. (legal) temporary ~ 4. ~ to + inf. (it was sheer ~ to steal the money)

inscribe *v.* 1. (D; tr.) to ~ for (to ~ a book for smb.) 2. (D; tr.) to ~ in (to ~ one's name in a book) 3. (D; tr.) to ~ with (she ~d the book with her name)

inscription *n.* 1. to bear, have an ~ 2. to decipher an ~

insecticide *n.* to spray, spread, use an ~

insects *n.* 1. ~ bite; crawl, creep; fly 2. a swarm of (flying) ~

insecure *adj.* ~ about; in

insecurity *n.* 1. financial; job ~ 2. a feeling of ~

insemination *n.* artificial ~

insensibility *n.* 1. to display, show ~ 2. ~ to

insensible *adj.* 1. (BE) ~ of 2. ~ to

insensitive *adj.* 1. ~ to (~ to the feelings of others) 2. ~ to + inf. (it was ~ of her to bring that up)

insensitivity *n.* 1. to display, show ~ 2. ~ to

inseparable *adj.* ~ from

insert *v.* (D; tr.) to ~ into (to ~ a new sentence into a paragraph; to ~ a key into a lock)

inside I *adv.* ~ out ("with the inner surface facing

out"); ("thoroughly") (to know a subject ~ out)
USAGE NOTE: The compound preposition *inside of* can refer to time or space. Referring to time, it is colloq. CE—to finish a job inside (of) an hour; referring to space, it is colloq. AE—inside (of) a building.

inside II *n.* (colloq.) ["confidential information"] (AE) 1. to have the ~ on ["position of trust"] 2. to be on the ~

insight *n.* 1. to gain; have (an) ~ into 2. to give, offer, provide (an) ~ 3. a deep, profound; new ~ 4. the ~ to + inf. (she had the ~ to predict what would happen) 5. (misc.) a person of great ~

insignia *n.* military; royal ~

insignificance *n.* to fade, pale into ~

insinuate *v.* 1. (d; refl.) ("to ingratiate") to ~ into (to ~ oneself into smb.'s good graces) 2. (L; to) ("to suggest") she ~ (to us) that her partner had embezzled funds

insinuation *n.* 1. to make an ~ (to) 2. an ~ about 3. an ~ that + clause (she didn't like his ~ that she had cheated)

insist *v.* 1. to ~ absolutely, definitely, positively; stubbornly 2. (D; intr.) to ~ on (they ~ on more money; she ~ed on coming with us) 3. (L; can be used with the subj.) she ~ed that everyone attend/should attend he ~ed that the accused was innocent

insistence *n.* 1. dogged, firm, stubborn ~ 2. ~ on (~ on an increase in salary) 3. ~ that + clause; can be subj. (we resent your ~ that the debt be/should be paid at once) 4. at smb.'s ~

insistent *adj.* 1. ~ on, upon 2. ~ that + clause; subj. (~ that the debt be/should be paid)

insolence *n.* 1. to display, show ~ 2. gross ~ 3. the ~ to + inf. (they had the ~ to file a complaint)

insolent *adj.* 1. ~ in (~ in their manner) 2. ~ to, towards 3. ~ to + inf. (it was ~ of them to demand special treatment)

insoluble *adj.* ~ in (water)

insolvency *n.* to force into ~

insomnia *n.* to suffer from ~

inspect *v.* to ~ closely, thoroughly; perfunctorily; visually

inspection *n.* 1. to carry out, conduct, make an ~ 2. a careful, close, thorough; cursory, perfunctory, superficial; on-site; visual ~ 3. a technical ~ 4. on ~ (on closer ~ the money turned out to be counterfeit) 5. (misc.) the troops were getting ready for ~

inspector *n.* 1. a customs; fire; health; mine; police; safety ~ 2. the ~ general

inspiration *n.* 1. a great ~ 2. to give, offer, provide ~ 3. to derive, draw ~ from 4. to find ~ in 5. divine ~ 6. ~ comes (from many sources) 7. a flash, spark of ~ 8. an ~ for (what provided the ~ for the statue?) 9. an ~ to (her example was an ~ to young people) 10. the ~ to + inf. (what gave him the ~ to

do it?)

inspire *v.* 1. (D; tr.) to ~ in; with (the latest consumer reports do not ~ confidence in that product; her recent speeches ~d her followers with hope) 2. (D; tr.) to ~ to (the leaders set out to ~ the rank and file to greater productivity) 3. (H) to ~ smb. to do smt.

inspiring *adj.* ~ to + inf. (it was ~ to watch)

instability *n.* economic; emotional; political ~

install *v.* 1. (d; tr.) to ~ as (to ~ smb. as president) 2. (P; refl.) they ~ed themselves in front of the TV; the protesters ~ed themselves at the entrance

installations *n.* military; naval; port ~

installment, instalment *n.* 1. to pay an ~ 2. monthly; quarterly ~s 3. in ~s (the book came out in ~s; to pay in ~s)

installment plan *n.* (AE) on the ~ (to buy smt. on the ~) (BE has *hire purchase*)

instance *n.* ["example"] 1. to cite, give an ~ 2. an isolated, rare ~ 3. for ~ 4. in an ~ (in rare ~s; in a few isolated ~s)

instant *n.* 1. at a certain ~ (at that ~ I realized who had planned the whole scheme) 2. (misc.) for an ~; in an ~

instigate *v.* (H) (esp. BE) to ~ smb. to do smt.

instigation *n.* at smb.'s ~

instill, instil *v.* 1. to ~ deeply, firmly 2. (D; tr.) to ~ in, into (to ~ respect for the law in the younger generation)

instinct *n.* 1. to arouse an ~ 2. to follow one's (own) ~s 3. a basic; destructive; herd; human; killer; maternal; natural ~ 4. animal; predatory ~s 5. an unerring ~ 6. an ~ for 7. the ~ to + inf. (nothing can destroy the ~ to survive) 8. by ~

institute *n.* 1. a research ~ 2. an ~ for (an ~ for theoretical research) 3. at, in an ~ (to work at/in an ~)

institution *n.* 1. to endow; support an ~ 2. a charitable; educational; financial; penal; philanthropic; political; private; social; state-supported ~ 3. a heavily endowed ~ 4. (misc.) an ~ of higher learning; the ~ of marriage

instruct *v.* 1. (D; tr.) ("to teach") to ~ in (to ~ soldiers in field hygiene) 2. (H) ("to order") she ~ed us to begin work at once 3. (L; must have an object) ("to inform") we have been ~ed that the matter has been settled by our lawyers 4. (Q; must have an object) ("to order") we were ~ed where to meet

instruction *n.* 1. to conduct, give, provide ~ 2. to take ~ (before converting to a religion) 3. advanced; beginning, elementary; bilingual; intermediate; remedial ~ 4. computer-assisted ~ 5. ~ in (to provide advanced ~ in mathematics)

instructions *n.* 1. to give, issue ~ 2. to leave ~ (for smb.) 3. to get, receive; have ~ 4. to carry out, follow ~ 5. to await (further) ~ 6. verbal; written ~

7. clear, explicit, precise ~ 8. specific ~ 9. ~ for 10. ~ to + inf. (we had ~ to report to her) 11. ~ that + clause; subj. (she left ~ that her estate be/should be divided evenly) 12. on ~ (we acted on your ~)

instructive *adj.* ~ to + inf. (it will be ~ to analyze the results)

instructor *n.* an ~ in, of (an ~ in physics)

instrument *n.* ["implement"] 1. a blunt; delicate; sharp ~ 2. surgical ~s 3. ~s of torture 4. an ~ for (an ~ for good) ["device for producing a musical sound"] 5. to tune, tune up an ~ 6. to play an ~ 7. a brass; musical; percussion; stringed; wind; woodwind ~ ["misc."] 8. pilots study their ~s before taking off

instrumental *adj.* (cannot stand alone) ~ in (her help was ~ in tracking down the criminal)

insubordinate *adj.* ~ to

insubordination *n.* 1. gross, rank ~ 2. ~ to (~ to authority)

insufficient *adj.* 1. ~ for; in 2. ~ to + inf. (it's ~ to cite only one example)

insulate *v.* (D; tr.) to ~ against, from

insulation *n.* ~ against, from

insult *n.* 1. to fling, hurl, shout an ~ at 2. to swallow, take an ~ 3. to avenge an ~ 4. a gratuitous; imaginary; nasty, vicious ~ 5. an ~ to (an ~ to smb.'s intelligence) 6. (misc.) to trade ~s; a stream of ~s; to add ~ to injury

insulted *adj.* 1. deeply ~ 2. ~ to + inf. (I was ~ to have been overlooked)

insurance *n.* 1. to provide ~ for 2. to sell, write ~ 3. to underwrite ~ 4. to carry; take out ~ (our firm carries fire ~) 5. to cancel; renew ~ 6. accident; automobile (AE), motor (BE), motor-car (BE); collision; flight; marine; travel ~ 7. disability; health; hospitalization; life, whole life (esp. AE); major-medical (AE); medical ~ 8. fire; flood; hurricane ~ 9. homeowner's; property; title ~ 10. group; liability (AE), third party (BE); no-fault; term (esp. AE) ~ 11. comprehensive; compulsory; voluntary ~ 12. (GB) National Insurance 13. social; unemployment ~ 14. ~ against; on (~ against loss from flood; ~ on one's personal effects) 15. (misc.) an ~ policy

USAGE NOTE: BE has traditionally distinguished between *insurance* (to provide compensation for what may happen) and *assurance* (to provide compensation for what will happen); thus—*fire insurance* and *life assurance*. However, nowadays, *life insurance* is also used in BE.

insure *v.* 1. (D; refl., tr.) to ~ against; for (to ~ one's home against loss from fire; to ~ one's life for fifty thousand dollars) 2. (L) their support ~d that the project would receive financial backing

USAGE NOTE: In AE, the verb *insure* may be used as a synonym of *ensure*.

insured *adj.* fully; heavily ~

insurrection *n.* 1. to foment, stir up an ~ 2. to crush, put down, quell, suppress an ~

insusceptible *adj.* ~ to

integrate *v.* (D; intr., tr.) to ~ into; with

integration *n.* 1. economic; racial; school; token ~ 2. ~ into

integrity *n.* 1. to display, show; have ~ 2. great ~ 3. territorial ~ 4. the ~ to + inf. (he had the ~ not to accept bribes) 5. (misc.) a person of ~

intellect *n.* 1. to appeal to the ~ 2. (a) keen, sharp, superior ~ 3. of ~ (a person of keen ~)

intelligence *n.* ["ability to comprehend, learn"] 1. to demonstrate, exhibit, show; have, possess ~ 2. great, high, keen; limited; low; normal; outstanding, remarkable ~ 3. native, natural ~ 4. (computers) artificial ~ 5. the ~ to + inf. (she had the ~ to see through their scheme) 6. of a certain ~ (a person of considerable ~) ["information"] 7. to collect, gather ~ 8. classified; combat, military; industrial; secret ~ 9. ~ that + clause (we have ~ that there will be an attack soon)

intelligent *adj.* ~ to + inf. (it would not be ~ to provoke her)

intelligible *adj.* ~ to

intend *v.* 1. (d; tr.) ("to design") to ~ as (it was ~ed as a joke) 2. (d; tr.) ("to design") to ~ for (the book is ~ed for children) 3. (E) ("to plan") she ~s to file suit 4. (G) ("to plan") what do you ~ doing? 5. (BE) (H) ("to want") we ~ them to do it 6. (L; subj.) ("to want") we never ~ed that she get/should get involved

intended *adj.* (cannot stand alone) ~ for (this dictionary is ~ for serious students)

intent I *adj.* (cannot stand alone) ~ on, upon (she is ~ on getting the job done quickly)

intent II *n.* 1. criminal ~ 2. ~ to + inf. (with ~ to kill) 3. by ~ 4. (misc.) for (esp. AE), to all ~s and purposes ("practically"); (legal) loitering with ~ (to commit a crime)

intention *n.* 1. to announce, declare, state one's ~ 2. to make one's ~s clear 3. every; no ~ (she has every ~ of accepting the invitation) 4. bad, evil; good; honorable ~s 5. the ~ to + inf. (have you heard of her ~ to resign?)

interact *v.* (d; intr.) to ~ with

interaction *n.* ~ among, between; with

interactive *adj.* ~ with

interbreed *v.* (D; intr.) to ~ with

intercede *v.* 1. (D; intr.) to ~ for; with (to ~ with the authorities for smb.) 2. (misc.) to ~ on smb.'s behalf

interchangeable *adj.* 1. freely ~ 2. ~ with

intercom *n.* on, over, through, via the ~

intercourse *n.* 1. to have ~ with 2. anal; oral; sexual ~ 3. social ~ 4. ~ among, between; with

interest I *n.* ["concern"] ["curiosity"] 1. to arouse, drum up, excite, generate, kindle, pique, spark, stimulate, stir up; revive ~ (in) 2. to hold smb.'s ~ 3. to demonstrate, display, evince, exhibit, express, have, manifest, show ~ 4. to pursue an ~ (he pursued his ~ in historical research) 5. to take an ~ in (she took a keen ~ in the project) 6. to lose ~ (in) (they lost all ~ in sports) 7. an academic; active; passing; vested ~ 8. a burning, consuming, deep, great, intense, keen, lively, profound, serious, strong ~ 9. broad, wide; common, mutual; general; narrow; universal, widespread ~s 10. human ~ (this story has a lot of human ~) 11. personal; popular ~ 12. the national; (the) public ~ 13. ~ drops off, flags, wanes; peaks; picks up 14. a conflict of ~(s) 15. ~ in (to show no ~ in financial matters) 16. ~ to + inf. (it's in/to our ~ to have stable prices) 17. in smb.'s ~ (to act in one's own best ~) 18. in a certain ~ (in the national ~; in the public ~) 19. in the ~(s) of (in the ~s of safety; in the ~s of our organization) 20. of ~ (to) (this story will be of ~ to us; these new developments are of local ~ only) 21. to smb.'s ~ (see 16) ["money paid for the use of money"] 22. to bear, earn, pay, yield ~ 23. to draw; receive ~ 24. to lose ~ 25. to add; calculate; charge; compound ~ 26. compound; simple ~ 27. ~ accrues (to an account) 28. ~ on (~ on a loan; six percent ~ is paid on all accounts) 29. at a certain (rate of) ~ (at six percent ~) 30. (misc.) to return a high rate of ~ ["share"] 31. to own an ~ (in a business) 32. a half ~ (see also **interests**)

interest II v. 1. to ~ greatly, very much 2. (D; tr.) to ~ in (could I ~ you in this project?)

interested adj. 1. deeply, greatly, highly, keenly, very much ~ 2. ~ in (we are ~ in politics) 3. ~ to + inf. (you will be ~ to know that an agreement has been reached)

interesting adj. 1. highly, very ~ 2. ~ for; to 3. ~ to + inf. (~ to watch = it's ~ to watch him) 4. ~ that + clause (it's ~ that the incident was not reported in the newspapers)

interests n. ["stakes, investments"] 1. to have ~ (to have ~ throughout the world) 2. to advance, further, promote smb.'s ~ 3. to defend, guard, look after, protect one's ~ 4. to serve smb.'s ~ (it serves their ~ to have stability in the area) 5. far-flung; international; worldwide ~ 6. ~ clash; coincide ["groups having a common concern"] 7. banking; business, commercial; shipping ~ 8. competing; controlling; special; vested ~

interface I n. an ~ between; with

interface II v. (D; intr., tr.) to ~ with (to ~ a machine with a computer)

interfere v. (D; intr.) to ~ between (BE), with; in USAGE NOTE: In BE, *to interfere with smb.* often means "to molest smb. sexually".

interference n. 1. to brook, stand for, tolerate no ~ 2. unwarranted ~ 3. military; outside ~ 4. ~ in, with 5. (misc.) (esp. Am. football) to run ~ for

interim n. in the ~

interior n. in the ~ (the situation in the ~ of the country was critical)

interject v. (D; tr.) to ~ into

interjection n. an ~ into (the ~ of new issues into a campaign)

interlace v. (d; tr.) to ~ with

interlard v. (formal) (d; tr.) to ~ with (to ~ a speech with quotations from the bible)

interlibrary loan n. to borrow, get a book through ~

interlink v. (D; tr.) to ~ with (the systems are ~ed with each other)

interlude n. 1. a romantic ~ 2. a musical ~ 3. a brief ~

intermarriage n. ~ between, with

intermarry v. (D; intr.) to ~ with (to ~ with the local population)

intermediary n. 1. an ~ between (an ~ between the warring groups) 2. through an ~

intermingle v. (d; intr.) to ~ with (to ~ with the crowd)

intermission n. an ~ between USAGE NOTE: In AE, *intermission* has the meaning "pause between parts of a theatrical performance". In BE, *interval* is used in this meaning.

Internet n. 1. to surf the ~ 2. to join the ~ 3. on the ~

internship n. (AE) to serve one's ~

interplay n. ~ among, between

interpolate v. (D; tr.) to ~ into

interpose v. (D; refl., tr.) to ~ among, between

interpret v. 1. (B) I had to ~ the passage to them 2. (d; tr.) to ~ as (they ~ed his response as an admission of guilt) 3. (D; intr., tr.) to ~ for (to ~ for foreign visitors) 4. (H) they ~ed her response to be an admission of guilt

interpretation n. 1. to make an ~ 2. to put a certain ~ on (they put a completely different ~ on his behavior) 3. a broad, free, liberal, loose; strict ~ (of the law)

interpreter n. 1. to serve (smb.) as an ~ 2. to communicate, speak through an ~ 3. a conference; court; simultaneous ~

interpreting n. conference; simultaneous ~

interrogation n. 1. to conduct an ~ 2. a police ~ 3. under ~

interrogator n. 1. to serve as an ~ 2. a prisoner-of-war ~

interrogatory n. (legal) to file; serve an ~

intersect v. (d; intr.) to ~ with (this street ~s with the main road)

intersection n. 1. a busy; dangerous ~ 2. at an ~

intersperse v. (P; tr.) to ~ anecdotes throughout a speech

intertwine v. (D; intr.) to ~ with

interval n. ["space of time between events"] 1. a brief, short; irregular; regular ~ 2. a lucid ~ 3. at a certain ~ (at regular ~s) ["distance"] ["gap"] 4. to maintain an ~ (the proper ~ should be maintained between vehicles) 5. an ~ between (see the Usage Note for **intermission**)

intervene v. 1. (D; intr.) to ~ between 2. (D; intr.) to ~ in; with (to ~ in smb.'s affairs; to ~ with the authorities)

intervention n. 1. armed, military; government ~ 2. medical; nursing; surgical ~ 3. divine ~

interview I n. 1. to conduct an ~ 2. to give, grant an ~ 3. to have, hold an ~ (the dean of admissions had/held ~s with prospective students; the prospective students had ~s with the dean of admissions after they toured the campus) 4. an exclusive; job; personal; taped; telephone; television, TV ~ 5. an ~ for; with (to have an ~ with the personnel director for a job)

interview II v. (D; tr.) to ~ about; for (to ~ smb. for a job)

interwoven adj. ~ with

intestate adj. to die ~

intestine n. the large; small ~

intimacy n. ~ between; with

intimate I adj. ~ with

intimate II v. 1. (B) (formal) she ~d her wishes to us 2. (L; to) they ~d (to us) that an agreement would be worked out soon 3. (Q; to) they would not ~ (to us) how the problem could be solved

intimation n. 1. to give an ~ 2. ~ that + clause (there was no ~ that she would retire)

intimidate v. (D; tr.) to ~ into (to ~ smb. into doing smt.)

into prep. (colloq.) ["interested in; involved in"] she is ~ classical music; when did you get ~ relaxation?

intolerable adj. 1. ~ to 2. ~ to + inf. (it's ~ to allow hardened criminals to roam our streets) 3. ~ that + clause (it is ~ that such excesses are allowed)

intolerance n. ["lack of tolerance"] 1. to display, show ~ 2. to stir up ~ against 3. racial; religious ~ ["sensitivity"] 4. ~ to (drugs)

intolerant adj. ~ of

intonation n. a falling; rising ~

intoxication n. a state of ~

intransigence n. ~ about

intransigent adj. ~ about

intrigue I n. 1. to carry on, engage in (an) ~ 2. petty; political ~ 3. a hotbed; web of ~ 4. an ~ against

intrigue II v. 1. (d; intr.) to ~ against; with (to ~ against the government) 2. (R) it ~d me (to learn) that she resigned

intrigued adj. ~ to + inf. (I was ~ to learn that she had resigned)

intrinsic adj. ~ in, to

introduce v. 1. (B) she ~d me to her friends 2. (D; tr.) to ~ into (to ~ new methods into an industry) 3. (d; tr.) to ~ to (to ~ students to the elements of

computer science)

introduction n. 1. to make an ~ 2. to serve as an ~ 3. a formal ~ 4. an ~ into, to (an ~ to a book) 5. (misc.) a letter of ~

introductory adj. (formal) ~ to

intrude v. 1. (D; intr.) to ~ into 2. (D; intr.) to ~ on, upon (to ~ on smb.'s privacy)

intrusion n. 1. to make an ~ 2. an unwarranted; unwelcome ~ 3. an ~ into (to make an ~ into enemy territory) 4. an ~ on, upon (an ~ on my time) 5. (misc.) pardon my ~

intuit v. (esp. BE) (L) she ~ed that the meeting would support her

intuition n. 1. an ~ that + clause (I had an ~ that something was wrong) 2. by ~ (by ~, she sensed what was wrong)

inundate v. (D; intr.) to ~ with (we were ~d with requests)

inure v. (formal) (d; tr.) to ~ to (to ~ smb. to hardship; ~d to danger)

invalid v. (BE) 1. (d; tr.) to ~ home 2. (d; tr.) to ~ out of (to be ~ed out of the army)

invaluable adj. ~ for, to

invasion n. 1. to carry out; launch, mount an ~ 2. to repel, repulse an ~ 3. an enemy ~

invective n. 1. to hurl ~/~s at 2. bitter; coarse, vulgar ~ 3. a stream, torrent of ~/~s 4. ~ against

inveigh v. (formal) (d; intr.) to ~ against

inveigle v. (d; tr.) to ~ into; out of (to ~ smb. into doing smt.)

invention n. 1. to come up with an ~ 2. to patent, register an ~ 3. to market, promote an ~ 4. a brilliant, ingenious ~

inventory n. 1. to make an ~ (of); to take (an) ~ (of) 2. (AE) to reduce (an) ~ (by having a sale) 3. an annual ~ 4. closed for ~

invest v. 1. ("to place money or resources") to ~ heavily 2. (D; intr., tr.) ("to place money or resources") to ~ in (to ~ heavily in municipal bonds; to ~ surplus funds in stocks) 3. (formal) (d; tr.) ("to entrust") to ~ with (to ~ smb. with authority)

invested adj. (formal) (cannot stand alone) ~ with (~ with broad powers)

investigation n. 1. to carry out, conduct, make; launch an ~ 2. a cursory, perfunctory; full, painstaking, thorough; impartial; ongoing; pending ~ 3. a criminal; internal; police ~ 4. an ~ into, of (to launch an ~ into charges of corruption) 5. on, upon ~ (on closer ~ we discovered the cause of the fire) 6. under ~ (the incident is under ~)

investigator n. a government; private ~

investment n. 1. to make an ~ 2. a good, lucrative, profitable; safe; solid, sound ~ 3. a bad, poor; risky ~ 4. capital; heavy; long-term; overseas ~s 5. an ~ in (~s in oil stocks)

investor n. a heavy; large; small; speculative ~

invidious adj. (formal) ~ to + inf. (it is ~ to deprive

workers of health insurance)

invigorating *adj.* ~ to + inf. (it's ~ to swim in the sea)

invisible *adj.* 1. ~ from (the house was ~ from the road) 2. to (~ to the naked eye)

invitation *n.* 1. to extend, issue, send an ~ 2. to send out ~s 3. to get, receive an ~ 4. to accept an ~ 5. to decline, refuse, spurn, turn down an ~ 6. a cordial, kind; formal; informal; open, standing; personal ~ 7. an ~ to (an ~ to a party) 8. an ~ to + inf. (she has received an ~ to attend the reception) 9. at smb.'s ~ (they came at my ~) 10. by ~ (participation is by ~ only) 11. (misc.) in that dormitory an unlocked drawer is an open ~ to theft

invite *v.* 1. to ~ cordially (everyone is cordially ~d) 2. (D; tr.) to ~ to (we ~d them to our party) 3. (H) they ~d us to participate

invite over *v.* (D; tr.) to ~ for; to (we ~d them over to our place for a drink)

invite out *v.* (D; tr.) to ~ for (they ~d us out for dinner)

invocation *n.* to offer, pronounce the ~

invoice I *n.* 1. to issue; make out; pay; process; send an ~ 2. a duplicate; original ~

invoice II *v.* (D; tr.) to ~ for (we ~d them for the full amount)

involve *v.* 1. (D; tr.) to ~ in; with (to ~ smb. in a project; we were ~d with the technical details) 2. (G) that assignment would ~ traveling a great deal 3. (K) that job would ~ my traveling a great deal

involved *adj.* 1. deeply; directly; emotionally ~ (with) 2. ~ in; with (I got her ~ in the planning; to become ~ with smb.)

involvement *n.* 1. an emotional ~ 2. (a) direct ~ 3. ~ in; with

invulnerable *adj.* ~ to

inward *adv.* ~ bound

IQ *n.* 1. to test smb.'s ~ 2. to have a certain ~ (she has an ~ of 130) 3. an average, normal; high; low ~ 4. an ~ of (an ~ of one hundred; the ~ of a genius) 5. (misc.) an ~ test

irate *adj.* ~ about

ire *n.* to arouse, incur, rouse smb.'s ~

irk *v.* (R) it ~s her to have to get up so early; it ~s me that they get all the credit

irksome *adj.* (formal) 1. ~ to + inf. (it is ~ to listen to his constant complaints) 2. ~ that + clause (it is ~ that she refuses to resign)

iron *n.* ["type of metal"] 1. to mine; smelt ~ 2. cast; corrugated; crude; pig; scrap; wrought ~ ["device for pressing clothes"] 3. to plug in an ~ 4. to unplug an ~ 5. to pass, run an ~ over a shirt 6. a cool; hot ~ 7. an electric; steam ~ ["rodlike device used for branding"] 8. a branding ~ ["tool used to apply solder"] 9. a soldering ~ ["instrument used to curl hair"] 10. a curling ~ ["hook"] 11. a climbing; grappling ~ ["utensil for making waffles"] 12.

a waffle ~ ["misc."] 13. to have several ~s in the fire ("to be involved in several activities at the same time"); to strike while the ~ is hot ("to act at the proper moment")

ironic, ironical *adj.* ~ that + clause (it's ~ that the weakest student in mathematics was/should have been elected class treasurer)

ironing *n.* to do the ~

irons *n.* ["shackles"] 1. to clap, put smb. into ~ 2. in ~

irony *n.* 1. bitter ~ 2. dramatic; tragic ~ 3. a touch of ~ 4. an ~ that + clause (it was a tragic ~ that he was killed in a traffic accident after the war)

irrational *adj.* ~ to + inf. (it was ~ to react in that manner)

irreconcilable *adj.* ~ with

irregular *adj.* grossly, highly, very ~

irregularity *n.* 1. a gross ~ 2. ~ in (an ~ in the accounts)

irrelevant *adj.* 1. ~ to 2. ~ to + inf. (it's ~ to cite such outdated evidence) 3. ~ that + clause (it's ~ that she was out of town)

irrespective *adj.* ~ of

irresponsible *adj.* ~ to + inf. (it was ~ of him to speak to reporters)

irreverent *adj.* 1. ~ of 2. ~ to + inf. (it would be ~ to whistle during a religious ceremony)

irritant *n.* an ~ to

irritate *v.* 1. to ~ greatly, very much 2. (R) it ~d me (to learn) that she had been promoted

irritated *adj.* 1. ~ at (~ at being awakened so early) 2. ~ to + inf. (he was ~ to see her dancing with someone else)

irritating *adj.* 1. ~ to + inf. (it's ~ to see them waste so much time) 2. ~ that + clause (it's ~ that he got off so easy)

irritation *n.* ["anger"] 1. to express, show; feel ~ 2. to conceal, hide one's ~ 3. ~ at, with 4. ~ that + clause (she could not hide her ~ that she had not been invited) ["sore"] 5. to relieve, soothe an ~

irrupt *v.* (D; intr.) to ~ in; into (to ~ in a frenzied demonstration)

irruption *n.* an ~ into

island *n.* 1. a desert, uninhabited; tropical ~ 2. a safety (AE), traffic ~ 3. on an ~

isolate *v.* (D; refl., tr.) to ~ from

isolated *adj.* ~ from

isolation *n.* in ~ (to live in ~)

isotope *n.* a radioactive ~

issue I *n.* ["number of a journal"] 1. to bring out, publish an ~ 2. a back; current; special; thematic ~ 3. an ~ comes out, is published ["question"] 4. to bring up, raise an ~ 5. to address; confront; deal with, face; debate; discuss; explore; straddle an ~ 6. to settle an ~ 7. to avoid, evade, sidestep; skirt an ~ 8. a basic; collateral, side ~ 9. a burning; dead; sensitive; substantive ~ 10. a contentious, controversial, debatable, thorny; divisive ~ 11. an environmental; moral; political; social ~ 12. a global; local; national ~ 13. at ~ (the point at ~) 14. (misc.) to avoid the ~; to confuse the ~; to force the ~; to make an ~ of smt.; to take ~ with smb. on smt. ("to disagree with smb. about smt.") ["children"] 15. without ~ (to die without ~)

issue II v. 1. (B) ("to distribute") the army ~d new rifles to the troops 2. (formal) (d; intr.) ("to come") to ~ from (blood ~d from the wound; smoke ~d from the chimneys) 3. (BE) (d; tr.) to ~ with (the pupils were ~d with new textbooks)

it *pronoun* of ~ (they made a mess of ~; to have had a hard time of ~)

italics *n.* to put smt. into ~

itch I *n.* ["itchy feeling"] 1. to relieve; scratch an ~ 2. ["wish"] (colloq.) an ~ to + inf. (she has an ~ to go out west)

itch II *v.* (colloq.) (usu. used in the progressive) 1. (d; intr.) to ~ for (to be ~ing for a fight) 2. (E) he's ~ing to get into action

itching *n.* 1. to cause ~ 2. to alleviate, relieve (the) ~

itchy *adj.* to feel ~ all over

item *n.* 1. a luxury ~ 2. a budget ~ 3. a collector's ~ (BE also has *collector's piece*) 4. a news ~ 5. ~ by ~ (she answered all objections ~ by ~) 6. (misc.) an ~ of importance

itinerary *n.* 1. to plan (out), prepare an ~ 2. a tentative ~ 3. according to an ~

ivy *n.* 1. ~ climbs 2. (misc.) (US) poison ~

J

jab I *n.* ["short punch"] 1. to throw a ~ 2. a left; right ~ 3. a ~ to (a left ~ to the head) ["injection"] (BE) 4. a flu ~

jab II *v.* 1. (D; intr.) to ~ at (he ~bed at the other boxer with his left) 2. (D; tr.) to ~ in (she ~bed me in the ribs) 3. (d; tr.) to ~ into (she ~bed a knife into the roast)

jabber *v.* (D; intr.) to ~ about

jack *n.* (esp. BE) (colloq.) ["human being"] every man ~

jackal *n.* a pack of ~s

jackass *n.* a damned; stupid ~

jacket *n.* ["garment for the upper body"] 1. a battle (AE); bulletproof (BE); dinner; donkey (BE); field; flak; life; pea; smoking; sport (AE), sports ~ ["cover"] 2. (AE) a record ~ 3. a dust ~ ("cover for a book") ["potato skin"] 4. to bake potatoes in their ~s

jackpot *n.* 1. to win the ~ 2. to hit the ~ (also fig.)

jacks *n.* to play (a game of) ~

jag *n.* (colloq.) ["state of intoxication"] 1. to have a ~ on ["spell"] 2. a crying ~

jail I *n.* 1. to go to ~ (he went to ~ for his crime) 2. to be sent to ~ (she was sent to ~ for shoplifting) 3. to serve time in ~ 4. to break ~; to break out of ~

jail II *v.* (D; tr.) to ~ for (to be ~ed for murder; to be ~ for life)

jailbreak *n.* 1. to attempt; make a ~ 2. a daring; mass ~

jam I *n.* ["food made by boiling fruit with sugar"] 1. to spread ~ (on bread) 2. apricot; gooseberry; grape; peach; plum; (red) raspberry; strawberry ~

jam II *n.* ["blockage"] 1. a log; traffic ~ ["difficult situation"] 2. (to be) in a ~

jam III *v.* 1. to ~ full 2. (D; tr.) to ~ in (she ~med her fingers in the door; or: she got her fingers ~med in the door) 3. (d; intr., tr.) to ~ into (they all tried to ~ into the small room; he ~med everything into one suitcase) 4. (d; tr.) to ~ on (she ~med a hat on his head) 5. (D; tr.) to ~ with (the street was ~med with traffic) 6. (N; used with an adjective) to ~ smt. tight

jam-packed *adj.* ~ with

jar I *n.* ["jolt"] 1. to feel a ~ 2. a slight ~

jar II *v.* 1. (d; intr.) to ~ against ("to strike") (I ~red against the table) 2. (d; intr.) to ~ on ("to irritate") (the noise ~red on my nerves) 3. (d; intr.) ("to clash") to ~ with 4. (N; used with an adjective) to ~ a tooth loose

jar III *n.* ["container"] 1. a biscuit (BE), cookie (AE) ~ 2. an earthenware; glass; Mason (esp. AE); plastic; stone ~

jargon *n.* 1. to speak in, use ~ 2. computer; legal; medical; military; professional, technical, trade ~

jaunt *n.* ["pleasure trip"] 1. to go on a ~ 2. a ~ through; to

javelin *n.* to hurl, throw the ~

jaw I *n.* 1. to move one's ~ (his ~ was broken and he could not move it) 2. to set one's ~ (she set her ~ in determination) 3. to dislocate one's ~ 4. the lower; upper ~ 5. (misc.) to snatch victory from the ~s of defeat

jaw II *v.* (colloq.) 1. (AE) (D; intr.) ("to speak angrily") to ~ about; at 2. (BE) (D; intr.) ("to chat") to ~ about

jealous *adj.* 1. bitterly, blindly, violently ~ 2. ~ of

jealousy *n.* 1. to arouse, cause ~ 2. to feel ~ 3. bitter, blind; fierce; groundless, unfounded; petty ~ 4. professional ~ 5. a fit of ~ 6. ~ towards

jeans *n.* 1. blue (AE); cut-off; designer ~ 2. a pair of ~

jeer *v.* (D; intr.) to ~ at

jelly *n.* ["food made from boiled fruit juice"] apple; blackberry; cherry; red currant; grape; mint; peach; plum; quince; strawberry ~

jeopardy *n.* 1. to place, put (smb.) in ~ 2. (legal) double ~ 3. in ~ (our lives were in ~)

jerk *n.* ["sudden movement"] with a ~ (the train started with a ~)

jest I *n.* (formal) 1. an idle ~ 2. in ~ (that was said in ~)

jest II *v.* (formal) (D; intr.) to ~ about; with

jester *n.* a court ~

jet I *n.* 1. to fly, pilot a ~ 2. to travel by ~ 3. a jumbo ~ (see also **airplane** 1, 2)

jet II *v.* (P; intr.) ("to fly by jet") to ~ around the world; to ~ across the country; to ~ from New York to London

jewel *n.* 1. to mount a ~ 2. crown; precious; priceless ~s

jewelry, jewellery *n.* 1. antique; costume; imitation; junk ~ 2. a piece of ~

jibe I *n.* see **gibe I**

jibe II *v.* see **gibe II**

jibe III *v.* (colloq.) (esp. AE) (D; intr.) ("to agree") to ~ with (her story doesn't ~ with yours)

jiffy *n.* (colloq.) ["short time"] in a ~

jig *n.* to dance, do; play a ~

jigsaw (BE) see **jigsaw puzzle**

jigsaw puzzle *n.* (AE) to do, put together a ~

jingle *n.* 1. to compose, make up a ~ 2. to hum a ~ 3. an advertising; rhyming ~

jinx *n.* (colloq.) (esp. AE) to put a ~ on smb.

jitters *n.* (colloq.) ["panic"] 1. to get; have the ~ 2.

to give smb. the ~ 3. a case of the ~ (she had a bad case of the ~)

job *n.* ["task"] 1. to do; finish a ~ 2. to take on a ~ 3. a backbreaking; difficult, hard; dirty; time-consuming ~ 4. odd ~s (he does odd ~s) 5. a ~ to + inf. (it was quite a ~ to find him = it was quite a ~ finding him) ["employment"] 6. to find, get, land, take; have a ~ (she got a ~ addressing envelopes; I have a ~ as a receptionist) 7. to apply for a ~ 8. to hunt for, look for a ~ 9. to hold, hold down a ~ 10. to give up, quit; resign from a 11. to lose a ~ 12. a cushy, easy, soft; desk ~ 13. a demanding ~ 14. a dead-end; menial ~ 15. a full-time; part-time; proper (esp. BE); steady; summer; temporary ~ 16. a ~ in (he took a ~ in construction) 17. at a ~ (she was working at two ~s) 18. on the ~ (he is always on the ~) (also fig.) 19. (misc.) to be-tween ~s; my ~ pays well; right now she is out of a ~; they all walked off the ~ in protest ["criminal act"] (colloq.) 20. to do, pull a ~ 21. an inside ~ ["misc."] 22. a snow ~ (AE) ("deceit"); a put-up ~ ("a prearranged scheme"); he really did a ~ on his opponent ("he inflicted a crushing defeat on his opponent")

USAGE NOTE: In colloq. BE, *on the job* can also mean "having sex".

jockey I *n.* a disc (BE), disk (AE) ~

jockey II *v.* 1. (D; intr.) to ~ for (to ~ for position) 2. (d; tr.) to ~ into (to ~ smb. into position)

jog *v.* (P; intr.) to ~ across the park; we ~ged around the track

jogging *n.* 1. to go in for ~ 2. (misc.) to go ~

join *v.* 1. (D; tr.) to ~ for (would you ~ us for a drink?) 2. (d; intr.) to ~ in (they all ~ed in singing the national anthem) 3. (D; tr.) to ~ in (to ~ smb. in a drink) 4. (D; tr.) to ~ to, with (to ~ one wire to another; they all ~ed hands with each other; to ~ forces with one's allies) 5. (D; intr.) to ~ with (we must ~ with them in fighting tyranny)

join in *v.* 1. (D; intr.) to ~ as (she ~ed in as a volunteer) 2. (D; intr.) to ~ with

joint *n.* 1. (med.) to dislocate a ~ 2. (anatomical) an elbow; hip; knee; shoulder ~ 3. (med.) an arthritic; painful ~ 4. (technical) a ball-and-socket; mortise; riveted; toggle; universal; welded ~ 5. (misc.) (slang) to case a ~ ("to inspect a place before robbing it") (also fig.)

join together *v.* (D; intr.; tr.) ~ in; with (to ~ in worship)

join up *v.* (D; intr.) to ~ with (we'll ~ with you in the next town)

joke I *n.* 1. to crack, tell a ~ 2. to ad-lib a ~ 3. to play a ~ on 4. to carry a ~ too far 5. to take a ~ (he can't take a ~) 6. to make a ~ of smt. 7. to get ("under-stand") a ~ 8. a clean; funny; harmless ~ 9. an old, stale; private; standing ~ 10. a practical; sick ~ 11. a blue (BE), coarse, crude, dirty; obscene, off-

color, smutty ~ 12. a ~ falls flat 13. the butt, object of a ~ 14. the point of a ~ 15. a ~ about 16. (colloq.) no ~ to + inf. (it's no ~ to oppose smb. like her = it's no ~ opposing smb. like her) 17. (misc.) as a ~; to turn smt. into a ~; the ~ was on me

joke II *v.* (D; intr.) to ~ about; with (I was ~ing with her about her latest escapade)

joker *n.* 1. a practical ~ 2. (cards) ~s wild; a ~ in the pack (also fig.)

joking *n.* ~ apart, aside

jolt I *n.* ["shock"] 1. to give smb. a ~ 2. to get, receive a ~ 3. to feel a ~ 4. a severe ~ 5. a ~ to (it was a ~ to her pride) 6. with a ~ (I woke up with a ~)

jolt II *v.* 1. (D; tr.) to ~ into (they were ~ed into action by the shocking news 2. (D; tr.) to ~ out of (she was finally ~ed out of her depression)

josh *v.* (colloq.) (D; tr.) to ~ about

jostle *v.* 1. (d; intr.) to ~ for (to ~ for position) 2. (d; intr.) to ~ with (the children were ~ling with each other)

journal *n.* ["diary"] 1. to keep a ~ ["magazine"] 2. to publish, put out a ~ 3. to edit a ~ 4. to subscribe to, take (old-fashioned; esp. BE) a ~ 5. a learned, professional, scholarly; trade ~

journalism *n.* advocacy; check book; investigative; yellow ~

journey I *n.* 1. to embark on, go on, set off on, start on a ~ 2. to make, undertake a ~ 3. to break, interrupt a ~ (we broke our ~ to Nairobi at Cairo) 4. an arduous; long; perilous; pleasant; safe; senti-mental; short; tiring ~ (we had a pleasant ~) 5. a round-the-world ~ 6. a leg, stretch of a ~ 7. a ~ across; around; from; into; through; to 8. on a ~ (they were on a ~ to Europe) 9. (misc.) have a safe ~!

journey II *v.* (P; intr.) to ~ across the desert; to ~ around the world

joust *v.* (D; intr.) ("to compete") 1. to ~ for (to ~ for position) 2. to ~ with

jowls *n.* heavy ~

joy *n.* 1. to express; feel ~ 2. to find, take ~ 3. to burst with; radiate ~ 4. boundless, deep, great, indescribable, ineffable, overwhelming, pure, sheer, unbounded ~ 5. ~ at, in (they found ~ in helping others) 6. a ~ to (such children are a ~ to their parents) 7. a ~ to + inf. (it was a ~ to behold) 8. (a) ~ that + clause (she could not hide her ~ that everyone was safe) 9. for, with ~ (to dance with ~; to jump for ~) 10. to smb.'s ~ (to our ~, our friends will be able to come)

joyful *adj.* ~ about, over

joyride *n.* to go for, on a ~

jubilant *adj.* ~ about, at, over (they were ~ over their victory)

jubilation *n.* 1. to express; feel ~ 2. ~ about, at, over

(~ over a victory)

jubilee *n.* 1. to celebrate a ~ 2. a diamond; golden; silver ~

Judaism *n.* Conservative; Liberal (BE), Progressive (BE); Orthodox; Reform ~
USAGE NOTE: *Liberal Judaism* and *Progressive Judaism* in Great Britain are approximately equivalent to *Reform Judaism* in North America. *Reform Judaism* in Great Britain is approximately equivalent to *Conservative Judaism* in North America.

judge I *n.* 1. a fair, impartial; harsh, severe; lenient ~ 2. a hanging ("severe") ~ 3. a circuit; district; itinerant; trial ~ 4. (sports) a field ~ 5. (mil.) a ~ advocate; a ~ advocate general 6. a panel of ~s

judge II *v.* 1. to ~ fairly, impartially; harshly, severely, sternly; leniently 2. (d; intr.) to ~ by, from (~ging by appearances; to ~ from the facts) 3. (colloq.) (L) we ~ that she is the best candidate 4. (M) I ~ her to be about twenty years old 5. (N; used with an *adj.*) the project was ~d impractical 6. (Q) we cannot ~ whether she is guilty

judgment, judgement *n.* 1. to display, exercise, show ~ (she always exercises good ~) 2. to form, make a ~ 3. to hand down (AE), pass, pronounce, render ~ on 4. to sit in ~ on 5. to defer, reserve, suspend ~ 6. bad, poor; good, sound; impaired; sober ~ (to display poor ~) 7. a moral; snap; value ~ 8. a ~ against; for 9. a ~ that + clause (I repeat my ~ that he was to blame) 10. in smb.'s ~ (in my ~, she is not guilty) 11. (misc.) an error of ~; use your own ~; I agreed against my better ~

judiciary *n.* the federal (US) ~

judicious *adj.* (formal) ~ to + inf. (it would be ~ to remain silent)

juggle *v.* (D; intr.) to ~ with (they shouldn't be ~ling with the figures)

jugular *n.* ["jugular vein"] to go for the ~ (colloq.) ("to attempt to finish off")

juice *n.* 1. digestive, gastric ~s 2. apple; fruit; grape; grapefruit; lemon; orange; pineapple; tomato; vegetable ~

jump I *n.* 1. to clear, take a ~ (on horseback) 2. to make a ~ (with a parachute) 3. (sports) the broad (AE), long; high; ski; triple ~ 4. (sports) a water ~ 5. a delayed (parachute) ~ 6. (basketball) the center ~ 7. a quantum ~ 8. a ~ from; to 9. a ~ in (a ~ in profits) 10. (misc.) to get the ~ on smb. ("to anticipate smb.")

jump II *v.* 1. (d; intr.) to ~ across (to ~ across a stream) 2. (d; intr.) to ~ at ("to be eager for") (she ~ed at the chance) 3. (d; intr.) to ~ for, with (to ~ for joy) 4. (d; intr.) to ~ from, off (he ~ed off the roof) 5. (d; intr.) to ~ from; to (to ~ from one topic to another) 6. (d; intr.) ("to leap") to ~ into; onto (the child ~ed into bed; the dog ~ed onto the sofa) 7. (d; intr.) to ~ on ("to attack") (he ~ed on his

opponent) 8. (d; intr.) to ~ out of (to ~ out of a window) 9. (d; intr.) to ~ over (to ~ over a fence) 10. (d; intr.) to ~ to (to ~ to one's feet) 11. (d; intr.) ("to rush") to ~ to (to ~ to conclusions; to ~ to smb.'s defense) 12. (misc.) to ~ down smb.'s throat ("to berate smb."); to ~ up and down (for joy)

jump clear *v.* (D; intr.) to ~ of (she ~ed clear of the wreckage)

jump down *v.* (D; intr.) to ~ from; to (he ~ed down from the roof)

jump off *v.* (d; intr.) to ~ from; to (she ~ed off to a good start)

jump up *v.* 1. (D; intr.) to ~ from (to ~ from one's seat) 2. (D; intr.) to ~ on, onto, to (to ~ onto the table) 3. (D; intr.) to ~ out of (she ~ed up out of her chair)

jumpy *adj.* (colloq.) ["nervous"] ~ about

junction *n.* at a ~

juncture *n.* ["transition"] 1. (ling.) close; open; terminal ~ ["situation"] 2. a critical ~ 3. at a certain ~ (we were at a critical ~)

jungle *n.* ["tropical forest"] 1. a dense; teeming; tropical ~ ["dangerous place"] 2. an asphalt, concrete; blackboard ~

junior I *adj.* 1. ~ in (~ in rank) 2. ~ to (he is ~ to me by three years)

junior II *n.* ~ by (he is my ~ by four years)

junket *n.* (esp. AE) ["pleasure trip"] 1. to go on a ~ 2. a fact-finding ~ 3. a ~ to (the legislators went on a ~ to Hawaii)

junta *n.* 1. a military; revolutionary; ruling ~ 2. by ~ (government by ~)

jurisdiction *n.* 1. to have ~ 2. local ~ 3. original; primary ~ (a court of original ~) 4. ~ over (to have ~ over a case) 5. outside; under, within a ~ (that case is under the ~ of this court) 6. (misc.) to fall within the ~ of a court; to accept (or reject) the ~ of a court

jurisprudence *n.* analytical; medical ~

juror *n.* 1. to challenge; dismiss a (prospective) ~ 2. to suborn a ~ 3. an alternate (AE); prospective ~

jury *n.* 1. to convene, empanel, swear in a ~ 2. to charge, instruct; sequester a ~ (the judge charged the ~) 3. to dismiss a ~ 4. to fix ("corrupt"), tamper with a ~ 5. to serve on a ~ 6. a hung ("deadlocked") ~ 7. a grand (US); petit; trial ~ 8. a blue-ribbon (AE) ("special") ~ 9. a ~ deliberates 10. a ~ arrives at, comes to, reaches a verdict 11. (misc.) the ~ is still out ("the jury is still deliberating"); the ~ is still out on him ("a final decision has still not been reached concerning him"); (a) trial by ~; a ~ of one's peers

jury trial *n.* to waive a ~

just *adj.* ~ to, towards

justice *n.* ["rules of law"] ["administration of law"] 1. to administer, dispense, mete out, render ~ 2. to obstruct ~ 3. to deny; pervert (the course of) ~ 4. to temper ~ with mercy 5. divine; poetic ~ 6. frontier (AE); summary ~ 7. ~ prevails 8. a miscarriage; parody, travesty of ~ 9. to bring (a criminal) to ~ 10. (misc.) the scales of ~; ~ is blind (fig.) ["recognition, appreciation"] 11. to do ~ to (her portrait does not do ~ to her/her portrait does not do her ~) 12. in ~ to ["judge"] 13. an associate (esp. US); chief (esp. US) ~; Lord Chief Justice (GB) ["magistrate"] 14. a traffic court ~; a ~ of the peace USAGE NOTE: The plural of *Lord Chief Justice* is *Lords Chief Justice*.

justification *n.* 1. to find ~ for 2. in ~ of

justified *adj.* 1. completely, fully, totally ~ 2. ~ in (are we ~ in assuming that she will attend?)

justify *v.* 1. (B) can you ~ your actions to me? 2. (G) nothing ~fies cheating on an exam 3. (K) what ~fied her being late?

jut out *v.* 1. (D; intr.) to ~ from; over (the balcony ~s out over the swimming pool) 2. (D; intr.) to ~ into (to ~ into the sea)

juxtapose *v.* (D; tr.) to ~ with

juxtaposed *adj.* ~ with

juxtaposition *n.* in ~ with

K

kangaroo *n*. 1. ~s hop, jump, leap 2. (Australian) a mob of ~s 3. a young ~ is a joey

kayak *n*. to paddle a ~

keel *n*. on an even ~ ("well-balanced")

keel over *v*. (D; intr.) to ~ from (to ~ from the heat)

keen *adj*. ["very interested"] (esp. BE) 1. ~ on (she's ~ on music; he's ~ on her) ["eager"] (BE) 2. ~ to + inf. (she is ~ to pass the examination)

keep I *n*. ["maintenance"] to earn one's ~

keep II *v*. 1. (D; tr.) ("to have") to ~ about (esp. BE), around (do you ~ a screwdriver around the house?) 2. (d; intr.) to ~ after ("to keep persuading") (~ after the children to clean up) 3. (d; tr.) to ~ at ("to hold") (she kept them at their studies) 4. (d; tr.) ("to hold") to ~ for (the librarian will ~ the book for you) 5. (d; intr., refl.) to ~ from ("to refrain") (she could not ~ from talking) 6. (d; tr.) ("to conceal") to ~ from (to ~ a secret from smb.) 7. (d; tr.) ("to hold back"); ("to prevent") to ~ from (the rain kept us from going; don't ~ her from her work) 8. (d; tr.) ("to hold") to ~ in (to ~ smb. in ignorance; to ~ a car in a garage) 9. (d; intr.) ("to remain") to ~ off (~ off the grass) 10. (d; tr.) ("to hold") to ~ off (~ the children off the street) 11. (d; intr.) ("to remain") to ~ out of (~ out of my way; I kept out of their quarrel) 12. (d; tr.) ("to hold") to ~ out of (~ the guests out of the house) 13. (d; intr.) ("to be confined") to ~ to (she kept to her room) 14. (d; intr.) ("to continue") to ~ to (to ~ to the right) 15. (D; tr.) ("to reserve") to ~ to (to ~ a secret to oneself) 16. (G) ("to continue") she kept reading 17. (J) ("to cause") he kept us waiting 18. (N; used with an adjective, noun, past participle) ("to maintain"); ("to hold") she kept us busy; they kept him prisoner; the fire kept us warm; she kept the children amused with her stories 19. (s) ("to remain") to ~ quiet; to ~ warm 20. ("misc.") to ~ (to the) right

keep abreast *v*. 1. (d; intr.) ("to be informed") to ~ of (she kept abreast of the news) 2. (D; tr.) ("to inform") to ~ of (they kept me abreast of the latest developments)

keep ahead *v*. (D; intr.) ("to remain in front") to ~ of (he kept ahead of his rivals)

keep aloof *v*. (D; intr.) to ~ from ("to remain at a distance from") (she kept aloof from the others)

keep away *v*. (D; intr., tr.) to ~ from (he kept away from us; she kept the dogs away from the children)

keep back *v*. (D; tr.) to ~ from (they kept her back from the crowd)

keep clear *v*. (D; intr., tr.) to ~ of (~ of him; they kept the roads clear of snow)

keeping *n*. ["care"] 1. in ~ (in safe ~) ["confor-

mity"] 2. in ~ with (in ~ with regulations) 3. out of ~ with

keep on *v*. (G) ("to continue") she kept on working

keep up *v*. (D; intr.) to ~ with ("to remain on the same level with") (I ran to ~ with the others; she worked hard to ~ with the other students)

keg *n*. a powder ~

kelter (BE) see **kilter**

ken *n*. ["understanding"] beyond; within one's ~

kettle *n*. 1. to put a ~ up to boil 2. (esp. BE) to put a ~ on ("to prepare tea or coffee") 3. a teakettle 4. a ~ boils; whistles 5. (misc.) (colloq.) a fine ~ of fish ("a mess")

kettledrum *n*. to play a ~

key I *n*. ["device for turning the bolt of a door"] 1. to duplicate; make a ~ 2. to insert, put in a ~ 3. to turn a ~ 4. to fit, match a ~ 5. a duplicate; master; skeleton ~ 6. ~s dangle (on a chain) 7. a bunch of ~s 8. a ~ to (a ~ to a door) ["solution"] 9. a ~ to (to hold the ~ to a mystery; a ~ to the exercises in a textbook) ["system of notes"] (mus.) 10. a high; low; major; minor ~ 11. in a (certain) ~ (played in the ~ of C) 12. off ~ ["button on a keyboard"] 13. to press, strike a ~ 14. to jam a ~ 15. (on a typewriter) a backspace; dead; shift ~ 16. (on a computer) a control; escape; function, soft; return ~ ["device for turning on the ignition in a car"] 17. an ignition ~

key II *v*. see **keyed**

keyboard *n*. 1. a computer; typewriter ~ 2. a piano ~ 3. a standard ~

keyed *adj*. (esp. BE) (cannot stand alone) ~ to (~ to the needs of our armed forces; our plants are ~ to producing civilian aircraft)

keyed up *adj*. ["psychologically ready"] ~ about; for, over (~ for the big game)

keyhole *n*. to look through, peep through a ~

keypunch *n*. to operate a ~

keystone *n*. a ~ of, to (the ~ to success is hard work)

kibosh *n*. (colloq.) ["end"] to put the ~ on smt.

kick I *n*. ["blow delivered with the foot"] 1. to give smb. a ~ 2. a nasty, vicious ~ 3. a ~ in (a ~ in the groin) 4. (football, rugby) a drop ~ 5. (soccer) a free; penalty ~ ["thrill"] (slang) 6. to get a ~ out of smt. ["strong effect"] (slang) 7. to have a ~ (this vodka has a ~ to it)

kick II *v*. 1. (colloq.) (d; tr.) to ~ out of ("to expel") (he was ~ed out of school) 2. (P; tr.) they ~ed sand in my face; she ~ed the ball over the fence

kick off *v*. (slang) (d; intr.) to ~ by; with ("to begin") (they ~ed off the conference with a cocktail party)

kicks *n*. (colloq.) ["thrill"] (just) for ~ (they did it for ~)

kid *v.* (colloq.) (D; tr.) ("to tease good-naturedly") to ~ about (they ~ded him about his paunch)

kid around *v.* (colloq.) (D; intr.) ("to fool") to ~ with

kid gloves *n.* to treat smb. with ~ ("to treat smb. with great deference or mildness")

kidney *n.* 1. to transplant a ~ 2. an artificial; floating ~

kill I *n.* 1. to make a ~ (the lion made the ~) 2. at the ~ (to be in at the ~) 3. (misc.) to close in/go in/move in for the ~

kill II *v.* 1. to ~ (smb.) outright 2. (usu. mil.) ~ed in action 3. (colloq.) (R) it just ~s me to think about the money we lost

killer *n.* ["murderer"] 1. a copycat; multiple, serial; psychopathic ~ 2. a ~ strikes

killing *n.* ["putting to death"] 1. (a) mercy ~ ["large profit"] (colloq.) 2. to make a ~

kilter *n.* ["order"] out of ~

kin *n.* next of ~ (to notify the next of ~)

kind I *adj.* 1. ~ of (that was very ~ of you) 2. ~ to (~ to animals) 3. ~ to + inf. (it was ~ of you to help us)

kind II *n.* ["sort"] 1. of a ~ (of all ~s; of several ~s; two of a ~) ["same manner"] 2. in ~ (to be paid back in ~; to respond in ~) ["goods"] 3. in ~ (to pay smb. back in ~)

kindergarten *n.* to attend, go to (a) ~

kindly *adv.* ["readily"] to take ~ to ("to accept readily")

kindness *n.* ["quality of being good, kind"] 1. to display, show ~ 2. human ~ 3. ~ to, towards 4. out of ~ (she did it out of ~) 5. an act of ~ 6. (misc.) the milk of human ~ ["good, kind act"] 7. to do smb. a ~ 8. to repay, return a ~

kind of *adv.* (colloq.) ["somewhat"] she ~ of hinted that she might come; it was ~ nice

king *n.* 1. to crown a ~ 2. to crown; proclaim smb. ~ 3. to depose, dethrone a ~ 4. (chess) to checkmate a ~ 5. a despotic; popular; strong; weak ~ 6. a ~ ascends, mounts the throne 7. a ~ reigns 8. a ~ abdicates 9. (misc.) to toast the ~

kingdom *n.* the animal; mineral; plant, vegetable ~

king's evidence *n.* (BE) to turn ~ (see also **queen's evidence, state's evidence**)

kink *n.* ["imperfection"] to iron out the ~s

kinship *n.* 1. to feel (a) ~ with smb. 2. (a) ~ between, with

kiosk *n.* a telephone ~ (BE; CE has *telephone booth*)

kiss I *n.* 1. to blow; throw; give (smb.) a ~ 2. to steal a ~ 3. an affectionate; fervent; passionate; French; goodnight; loving, tender ~ 4. a ~ on (a ~ on the cheek) 5. (misc.) the ~ of death; (BE) the ~ of life ("mouth-to-mouth resuscitation") (AE has *cardiopulmonary resuscitation* or *CPR*)

kiss II *v.* 1. to ~ passionately; tenderly 2. (D; tr.) to

~ on (she ~ed the baby on the cheek) 3. (O; can be used with one animate object) (she ~ed him goodnight)

kit *n.* ["equipment"] 1. a first-aid; instruction; mess; sewing; shaving; survival ~ ["clothing and equipment"] (BE) 2. camping; travelling ~ 3. (misc.) (mil.) a ~ bag

kitchen *n.* a communal; field; fitted (BE); soup ~

kite *n.* 1. to fly a ~ 2. (misc.) (AE; colloq.) go fly a ~! ("go away")

kith *n.* ["friends and relatives"] ~ and kin

kitty *n.* ["fund, pool"] in the ~ (how much is in the ~?)

knack *n.* ["skill"] 1. to get; have the ~ of smt. 2. an uncanny ~ 3. a ~ for, of (she has a ~ for getting into trouble; she has the ~ of getting what she wants) 4. a ~ to (there's a ~ to baking a good cake)

knee I *n.* 1. to bend one's ~s 2. to dislocate; wrench one's ~ 3. a trick ("defective") ~ 4. ~s buckle 5. (fig.) at smb.'s ~ (she learned the language at her mother's ~) 6. (usu. fig.) on bended ~ (s) 7. (misc.) to drop/fall to one's ~s; to get down on one's ~s

knee II *v.* (D; tr.) to ~ in (he ~d his opponent in the stomach)

kneel *v.* 1. (D; intr.) to ~ before 2. (misc.) to ~ in prayer

knell *n.* to sound, toll the ~

knife *n.* ["instrument for cutting"] 1. to draw, pull a ~ 2. to brandish, wield a ~ 3. to plunge a ~ into smb. 4. to pull a ~ (on smb.) 5. to stab smb. with a ~ 6. to sharpen a ~ 7. a blunt, dull; sharp ~ 8. a bowie; boy-scout; clasp; hunting ~; penknife, pocketknife 9. a bread; butcher (esp. AE), butcher's (esp. BE); butter; carving; electric; fish; kitchen; paring; steak ~ 10. a flick (BE; AE has *switchblade*); sheath; trench ~ 11. a paper (BE; AE has *letter opener*) ["surgery"] (old-fashioned) 12. under the ~ (she was under the ~ for two hours)

knight *n.* 1. to dub, make smb. a ~ 2. a ~'s wife is a lady

knighthood *n.* to bestow, confer a ~ on, upon

knit *v.* (C) ~ a scarf for me; or: ~ me a scarf

knitting *n.* ["action of knitting"] 1. to do ~ ["one's own business"] (colloq.) (esp. AE) 2. to mind, stick to, tend to one's (own) ~

knob *n.* 1. to turn, twist a ~ 2. a control ~

knock I *n.* ["thumping noise"] 1. engine ~ 2. a gentle; loud ~ 3. a ~ at, on (a ~ at/on the door) ["blow"] (colloq.) 4. hard ~s (she has taken some hard ~s in her life)

knock II *v.* 1. ("to rap") to ~ gently; loudly 2. (colloq.) (d; intr.) ("to wander") to ~ about, around (he ~ed around the western part of the state for a few months) 3. (d; intr., tr.) ("to strike") to ~ against (she ~ed her head against the ceiling) 4. (D; intr.) ("to rap") to ~ at, on (to ~ at/on the door) 5. (d; tr.) ("to pound") to ~ into (to ~ some sense into smb.'s head) 6. (d; tr.) to ~ off ("to fell") (he ~ed me off my feet) 7. (d; tr.) ("to remove") to ~ out of (the impact ~ed two teeth out of his mouth) 8. (d; tr.) to ~ to (she ~ed him to the ground) 9. (N; used with an adjective) ("to render by striking") to ~ smb. unconscious 10. (P; tr.) ("to render by striking") she ~ed me down 11. (misc.) ~ it off! (slang) ("stop!")

knock down v. (colloq.) (BE) (D; tr.) ("to persuade to reduce a price") to ~ to (I ~ed him down to ten pounds)

knockout n. 1. to score a ~ 2. a technical ~

knot n. 1. to tie; tighten a ~ 2. to loosen; undo, untie a ~ 3. the Gordian ~ (to cut the Gordian ~) 4. a loose; tight ~ 5. a bowline; granny; reef, square ~ 6. (misc.) tied up in ~s

know I n. in the ~ (about)

know v. 1. (D; intr.) to ~ about, of (we knew about the incident) 2. (D; tr.) to ~ as (I knew her as a colleague) 3. (d; tr.) to ~ by (to ~ smb. by name; I knew her by sight only) 4. (d; tr.) to ~ from ("to be able to differentiate") (the little child doesn't ~ a dog from a cat) 5. (H; only in the past and perfect) I've known him to lose his temper 6. (BE) (I; only in the past and perfect) I've known him lose his temper 7. (L) we ~ that they will come 8. (formal) (M) I ~ him to be a fool 9. (Q) she ~s how to drive 10. (misc.) to ~ smt. for a fact ("to know smt. to be true"); to ~ smt. by heart; to ~ smt. inside out/to ~ smt. backwards and forwards; you should ~ better; she always ~s best; to ~ for certain/for sure; to ~ smt. like the back of one's hand; (colloq.) she ~s better than to stay out late

know-how n. 1. the necessary ~ (he doesn't have the necessary ~ for the job) 2. technical ~ 3. the ~ to + inf. (she has the ~ to do the job)

knowing n. there is no ~ (what they will do)

knowledge n. 1. to acquire, accumulate, gain ~ 2. to absorb, assimilate, soak up ~ 3. to have ~ (of a subject) 4. to broaden, deepen one's ~ 5. to brush up (on) one's ~ (of a subject) 6. to demonstrate, display, show ~ 7. to communicate, disseminate; impart ~ 8. to flaunt, parade one's ~ 9. to deny (all) ~ (of smt.) 10. detailed; extensive; profound, thorough ~ 11. rudimentary; slight, superficial ~ 12. direct; inside, intimate; intuitive; practical ~ 13. (a) fluent; reading; speaking; working ~ (to have fluent ~ of English; to have reading/a reading ~ of several languages) 14. common ~ 15. (formal) carnal ~ (to have carnal ~ of) 16. ~ about, of 17. the ~ to + inf. (she has enough ~ about the subject to write a good book) 18. the ~ that + clause (it is common ~ that he has spent time in prison) 19. to smb.'s ~ (to my ~, she has never been here) 20. to come to smb.'s ~ (it came to our ~ that she had left town) 21. (misc.) to the best of one's ~; a person of great ~

knowledgeable adj. ~ about

known adj. 1. internationally; nationally; well; widely ~ 2. ~ as (~ as a patron of the arts) 3. ~ for (~ for being witty) 4. ~ to (~ to everyone) 5. (cannot stand alone) ~ to + inf. (she is ~ to frequent that bar; she is ~ to be a patron of the arts) 6. ~ that + clause (it is ~ that she has a criminal record) 7. (misc.) better/otherwise ~ as (Samuel Clemens, better ~ as Mark Twain)

knuckle n. 1. to rap smb. on, over the ~s 2. to bruise; scrape one's ~ 3. to crack one's ~s 4. brass ~s (AE; CE has *knuckle duster*)

knuckle down v. (D; intr.) to ~ to (to ~ to work)

knuckle under v. (D; intr.) ("to submit") to ~ to (to ~ to an aggressor)

kowtow v. (d; intr.) to ~ to ("to fawn over") (to ~ to the boss)

kudos n. (colloq.) ["praise"] 1. to earn, win ~ 2. ~ to smb. for smt. (~ to our mayor for reducing taxes) 3. (BE) to get ~ for

L

label I *n.* ["sticker"] 1. to affix, attach, put on, stick on; sew on a ~ 2. to bear, carry, have a ~ 3. to remove, take off a ~ 4. an adhesive, gummed ~ 5. a brand; designer; manufacturers'; union ~ (on a garment) ["descriptive phrase in a dictionary entry"] 6. to apply, use a ~ 7. a field; regional; stylistic; temporal; usage ~ ["recording company"] 8. for, on, under a ~ (on which ~ was the song recorded?) ["misc."] 9. to pin a ~ on smb. ("to assign smb. to a category"); a warning ~

label II *v.* 1. (d; tr.) to ~ as (he was ~ed as a delinquent) 2. (D; tr.) to ~ with (all items should be ~ed with a price) 3. (N; used with an adjective, noun) her story was ~ed false/a hoax

labeled *adj.* clearly ~

labor I labour *n.* ["work"] 1. to do, perform ~ 2. backbreaking; manual, physical; menial; painstaking; productive; sweated (BE), sweatshop; skilled; unskilled ~ 3. a division of ~ 4. (misc.) a ~ of love ["servitude"] 5. forced; hard; slave ~ (he got ten years at hard ~; democratic countries forbid forced ~; slave ~ has been outlawed) ["work force"] 6. casual (BE); child; migrant; organized; seasonal; skilled; unskilled ~ ["giving birth"] 7. to induce ~ 8. to go into ~ 9. difficult, prolonged, protracted; easy; false ~ 10. in ~ (she was in ~ for five hours)

labor II labour *v.* 1. (d; intr.) to ~ as (to ~ as a migrant worker) 2. (d; intr.) to ~ under (to ~ under a misconception)

laboratory *n.* 1. a chemistry; crime; experimental; language; physics; research ~ 2. at, in a ~

laborer, labourer *n.* 1. a common; day; immigrant; itinerant; skilled; unskilled ~ 2. (BE) an agricultural labourer (CE has *farm worker*) 3. (BE) a casual labourer (AE has *transient worker*)

lace I *n.* delicate; exquisite; fine ~

lace II *v.* 1. (d; intr.) to ~ into ("to attack verbally") (they ~d into her for being late) 2. (D; tr.) to ~ with ("to add to") (they ~d the punch with rum)

laceration *n.* a deep; minor, superficial; severe ~

lack I *n.* for ~ of (for ~ of fuel, their planes were grounded)

lack II *v.* (D; intr.) to ~ for (formal) (we don't ~ for anything)

lacking *adj.* 1. badly, completely, sadly, totally, utterly ~ 2. ~ in (~ in common sense)

lacquer *n.* to apply ~

lad *n.* 1. a young ~ 2. (BE) a bit of a ~

ladder *n.* ["framework with rungs for climbing"] 1. to put up a ~ 2. to steady a ~ 3. to lean a ~ (against a wall) 4. to climb, go up, mount a ~ 5. to come down, descend a ~ 6. an aerial; extension; rope ~ 7. an accommodation ~ (over the side of a ship) ["unraveled stitches in a stocking"] (BE; CE has *run*) 8. to get, have a ~ (in) ["path"] 9. the ~ to success ["hierarchy"] 10. a career ~; the social ~

laden *adj.* 1. fully, heavily ~ 2. ~ with

lady *n.* 1. a leading; young ~ 2. the first ~ ("wife of the President or of a state governor") 3. a bag ~ ("a destitute woman living on the streets") 4. (misc.) the first ~ of the American theater

lag I *n.* 1. a cultural; time ~ 2. jet ~

lag II *v.* 1. to ~ badly 2. (D; intr.) to ~ behind; in (she ~ged behind the others) 3. (D; intr.) to ~ by (their party was ~ging by ten points in the polls)

lag behind *v.* 1. (D; intr.) to ~ by (their party was ~ging behind by ten points in the polls) 2. (D; intr.) to ~ in (to ~ in one's work)

laid up *adj.* ~ with (~ with the flu)

lake *n.* 1. a deep; dry ~ 2. an artificial ~ 3. at, on a ~ (they have a summer bungalow at/on a ~)

lam *n.* (slang) ["flight"] on the ~ (she took it on the ~) ("she fled")

lamb *n.* 1. a sacrificial ~ 2. ~s bleat 3. a leg of ~; a shoulder of ~ 4. (misc.) as gentle as a ~; like a ~ to (the) slaughter

lamb chops *n.* 1. to broil (AE), grill ~ 2. a rack of ~

lame *adj.* 1. ~ in (~ in one leg) 2. to go ~

lament I *n.* 1. a bitter ~ 2. a ~ for

lament II *v.* 1. to ~ bitterly, deeply 2. (D; intr.) to ~ over

lamented *adj.* the late ~ (smb.)

lamp *n.* 1. to plug in a ~ 2. to turn on a ~ 3. to light a ~ 4. to unplug a ~ 5. to turn off a ~ 6. an arc; bedside; floor (AE), standard (BE); gooseneck; table; wall ~ 7. a reading; safety ~; sunlamp; ultraviolet ~ 8. an electric; fluorescent; incandescent; neon ~ 9. a kerosene (AE), paraffin (BE); oil; spirit ~

lance *n.* to throw a ~

land I *n.* ["soil"] ["ground"] 1. to clear ~ (to clear ~ of trees and brush) 2. to cultivate (the), work the ~; irrigate; reclaim (the) ~ 3. to redistribute (the) ~ 4. arable; barren; fertile; grazing; marginal ~ 5. private; public ~ 6. a plot of ~ ["solid surface of the earth"] 7. to raise, sight ~ (from a ship) 8. to reach ~ 9. dry ~ 10. a body of ~ 11. by ~ (to travel by ~) 12. on (the) ~ ["rural area"] 13. to go back to the ~ ["country"] ["domain"] 14. smb.'s native ~ 15. a promised ~ (we were in the promised ~) ["area"] 16. no man's ~ (in no man's ~) ["misc."] 17. the Holy Land

land II *v.* 1. (d; intr., tr.) to ~ in ("to get involved"; "to involve") (he ~ed in trouble; such behavior ~ed her in trouble) 2. (colloq.) (O) ("to punch") she ~ed him one in the eye

landfill *n.* a sanitary ~

landing *n.* ["coming down to earth"] 1. to make a ~ 2. a belly; blind; bumpy; crash; emergency; forced; hard; instrument; pancake; three-point ~ 3. a safe; smooth; soft ~ 4. a parachute ~ ["level part of a staircase"] 5. on a ~

landing gear *n.* 1. to raise, retract a ~ 2. to let down, lower a ~ 3. a retractable ~

landlord *n.* an absentee; slum ~

landowner *n.* a big, large ~

landscape *n.* 1. a beautiful, magnificent, picturesque ~ 2. a bleak, gloomy ~ 3. a desert; lunar ~ 4. (misc.) the political ~

land up *v.* 1. (d; intr.) to ~ in (he ~ed up in Moscow) 2. (s) they ~ed up penniless; she ~ed up drifting from job to job

lane *n.* 1. to change, shift ~s 2. to cross over into, get over into the other ~ 3. the fast (also fig.); inside; outside; passing; slow ~ 4. (BE) the nearside ("left"); offside ("right") ~ 5. an air; sea; shipping ~ 6. in a ~ (we like life in the fast ~)

language *n.* ["linguistic system of communication"] 1. to use a ~ 2. to plan; standardize a ~ 3. to acquire, master; learn, study a ~ 4. to speak (in) a ~ 5. to butcher, murder a ~ 6. to enrich; purify a ~ 7. (the) spoken; written ~ 8. smb.'s first, native; second ~ 9. a cognate; foreign; international; world; national; official; universal ~ 10. colloquial, informal; formal; idiomatic; (a) literary, (a) standard; (a) nonstandard; nontechnical; substandard; technical ~ 11. an ancient; artificial; classical; creolized; dead, extinct; living; modern; natural; trade ~ 12. an agglutinative; inflecting; isolating; synthetic; tone ~ 13. an object, target; source; working ~ 14. sign ~ (to communicate in sign ~) ["style of speaking or writing"] 15. to use (a) ~ 16. biblical; elegant; flowery; rich ~ 17. everyday, plain, simple; polite ~ 18. abusive; bad, coarse, crude, dirty, foul, nasty, obscene, offensive, street, unprintable, vile, vulgar; blunt, explicit; rough, strong, vituperative ~ 19. children's; diplomatic; men's; women's ~ ["system of signs, symbols used by a computer"] 20. an assembly; computer, machine, programming; high-level ~ ["misc."] 21. ~ acquisition; ~ learning; ~ maintenance; ~ teaching; body ~

languish *v.* (D; intr.) to ~ in (to ~ in prison)

lantern *n.* 1. to light a ~ 2. to shine a ~ on 3. a battery-operated; kerosene (AE), paraffin (BE); propane ~ 4. a ~ flashes; gleams; shines

lap I *n.* ["complete circuit around a track"] 1. to do; drive; run a ~ (they are running the last ~ of the race) 2. on a ~ (they are on the last ~) 3. (misc.) (BE) ~ of honour/(AE) victory ~; how many ~s do they have to go? ["part of the body from the knees to waist of a sitting person"] 4. in, on smb.'s

~ (the little girl sat in her mother's ~) 5. (misc.) in the ~ of the gods ("with an uncertain future")

lap II *v.* 1. to ~ gently 2. (d; intr.) to ~ against (the waves ~ped against the sides of the boat)

lapse I *n.* 1. a momentary, temporary; occasional ~ (of memory) 2. a linguistic ~ 3. a ~ in (a ~ in judgment)

lapse II *v.* (d; intr.) to ~ into (to ~ into a coma)

larceny *n.* 1. to commit ~ 2. aggravated; grand; petty; simple ~

lard I *n.* to render ~

lard II *v.* (formal) (d; tr.) to ~ with (to ~ a speech with biblical references)

larder *n.* a full, well-stocked ~

large *n.* 1. at ~ ("uncaptured") (the prisoner was still at ~) 2. an assemblywoman at ~ ("an assemblywoman who represents several or all districts") 3. by and ~ ("in general")

lark I *n.* ["prank"] 1. as a ~ 2. for a ~ (he did it just for a ~)

lark II *n.* ["type of bird"] 1. ~s sing, warble 2. a bevy of ~s 3. (misc.) as happy as a ~

lash *v.* 1. (d; intr.) to ~ against (the rain ~ed against the roof) 2. (d; intr.) to ~ at, into (the speakers ~ed into the government) 3. (d; tr.) to ~ into (to ~ a crowd into a fury) 4. (d; tr.) to ~ to (to ~ the cargo to the deck)

lash back *v.* (D; intr.) to ~ against, at (to ~ at one's critics)

lash out *v.* (D; intr.) to ~ against, at

lasso *n.* 1. to throw a ~ 2. to catch with a ~

last I *adj., adv.* 1. to come in ~ (in a race) 2. the ~ to + inf. (she was the ~ to finish)

last II *n.* 1. to breathe one's ~ 2. (misc.) she was the ~ to arrive; to see the ~ of smb.; at ~; at long ~

last III *v.* 1. (d; intr.) to ~ from; to, until (the meeting ~ed from one to three) 2. (P; intr.) the examination ~ed two hours; the food will ~ (us) (for) a week; the meeting ~ed (for) an hour

last rites *n.* 1. to administer, give, perform (the) ~ 2. to receive (the) ~

last word *n.* to get in, have the ~ (she had the ~ in the argument)

latch *v.* (colloq.) (d; intr.) to ~ onto (since he didn't know anyone else, he ~ed onto us)

late *adj.* 1. ~ for (she was ~ for class) 2. ~ in (we were ~ in filing our tax return; I was ~ in getting up) 3. ~ with (they are ~ with the rent) 4. of ~ ("recently") 5. (misc.) the train was five minutes ~

later *adv.* ~ on

latest *n.* 1. the ~ about (have you heard the ~ about the elections?) 2. at the ~ (they will arrive tomorrow at the ~)

lathe *n.* 1. to operate a ~ 2. a turret; vertical ~

lather *n.* ["sweating"] 1. to work oneself into a ~ ["foam"] 2. to work up a ~

latitude *n.* ["freedom of action"] 1. to allow smb. ~

in (we are allowed quite a bit of ~ in selecting our subjects) ["distance measured in degrees north or south of the equator"] 2. high; low ~s 3. at a ~ (at a ~ of ten degrees north)

laudable *adj.* (formal) ~ to + inf. (it was ~ of you to help them)

laugh I *n.* 1. to get a ~ (the joke got a big ~) 2. to stifle, suppress a ~ 3. a belly; derisive; forced; hearty, loud; infectious; sardonic; subdued ~ 4. (misc.) to have the last ~ on smb.; to do smt. for a ~/for ~s

laugh II *v.* 1. to ~ aloud, out loud; hard; loud; uproariously 2. (D; intr.) to ~ about ("to show one's amusement by laughing") (everyone ~ed about the incident) 3. (D; intr.) to ~ at ("to respond to smt. funny by laughter") (to ~ at a joke) 4. (D; intr.) to ~ at ("to show one's derision for") (they ~ed at our efforts; she ~ed at our warnings) 5. (d; tr.) to ~ out of ("to drive out by laughter") (he was ~ed out of court) 6. (N; used with an adjective) he ~ed himself hoarse 7. (misc.) to ~ up one's sleeve ("to laugh secretly"); to burst out ~ing

laughingstock *n.* 1. to make a ~ of smb. 2. to be; become a ~

laughter *n.* 1. to cause, provoke ~ 2. to burst into ~ 3. contagious, infectious; convulsive; derisive; hearty, loud, raucous, uproarious; hysterical; sardonic; subdued ~ 4. a burst, fit, gale, roar; ripple of ~; peals of ~ 5. (misc.) to double up with ~; to roar with ~; canned ~

launch *v.* 1. (D; tr.) ("to fire") to ~ against, at (the missiles were ~ed against enemy targets) 2. (d; intr.) to ~ into ("to begin") (to ~ into a tirade)

launcher *n.* a missile; rocket ~

laundry *n.* ["clothes, linens that are to be washed or have been washed"] 1. to do (the) ~ 2. to dry; fold; iron; sprinkle the ~ 3. clean; dirty ~ ["establishment for washing clothes, linens"] 4. a self-service ~ 5. at, in a ~ (they work at a ~)

laurels *n.* 1. to gain, reap, win ~ 2. to rest on one's ~

lava *n.* 1. to spew ~ (volcanoes spew ~) 2. molten ~ 3. ~ flows

lavish I *adj.* ~ in, with (~ with praise; ~ in donating money to charity)

lavish II *v.* (d; tr.) to ~ on (to ~ gifts on smb.)

law *n.* ["statute, regulation"] 1. to administer, apply, enforce, uphold a ~ 2. to adopt, enact, pass; draft; promulgate a ~ 3. to obey, observe a ~ 4. to interpret a ~ (courts interpret ~s) 5. to annul, repeal, revoke a ~; to declare a ~ unconstitutional (US) 6. to break, flout, violate a ~ 7. to challenge, test; cite; strike down a ~ (in the courts) 8. a fair, just; stringent; unfair ~ 9. a blue (US); ex post facto; federal (US); lemon (US); shield (US); state (US); sunset (US); sunshine (US); sus (GB); unwritten; zoning ~; the licensing ~s (GB) 10. a ~ against; on (there is no ~ against fishing) 11. a ~

that + clause (there is a ~ that all income must be reported) 12. (misc.) dietary ~s; Congress makes ~s ["body of statutes, regulations"] 13. to administer, apply, enforce, uphold the ~ 14. to obey the ~ 15. to interpret the ~ (courts interpret the ~) 16. to break; flout the ~ 17. case; common; constitutional; parliamentary; statutory ~ 18. civil; criminal; military ~ 19. administrative; antitrust; business, commercial; contract; corporate ~ 20. copyright; environmental; family, marriage; immigration; international; labor; maritime; patent; tax ~ 21. canon; Islamic; Mosaic; Roman ~ 22. the supreme ~ (of the land) 23. according to the ~ 24. against; outside; within the ~ (it is against the ~ to smoke in an elevator) 25. by ~ ["jurisprudence"] ["lawyer's profession"] 26. to practice ~ 27. to study ~ ["principle"] 28. Mendel's; Newton's; Parkinson's; periodic ~ 29. the ~ of diminishing returns; the ~ of gravity; the ~ of motion; the ~ of supply and demand; the ~ of the jungle (also fig.) ["misc."] 30. to take the ~ into one's own hands; to lay down the ~; (BE) to go to ~; in the eyes of the ~; (AE) an attorney at ~; everyone is equal under the ~; the letter of the ~; the spirit of the ~; a higher ("divine") ~; natural ~

law and order *n.* 1. to establish; keep, maintain; restore ~ 2. a breakdown in/of ~

lawful *adj.* ~ to + inf. (is it ~ to hunt deer in this state?)

lawn *n.* 1. to mow, trim a ~ 2. to sprinkle, water a ~

lawn mower *n.* to operate, work a ~

lawsuit *n.* 1. to bring, file, institute; lose; settle; win a ~ 2. a class-action; frivolous ~ 3. a ~ against; over

lawyer *n.* 1. to hire, retain a ~ 2. a practicing ~ 3. a civil-rights; corporation; criminal; defense ~; (esp. AE) trial ~ (BE prefers *barrister*) 4. (AE) a Philadelphia ("shrewd") ~ 5. (humorous; often mil.) a barrack-room (esp. BE), guardhouse (esp. AE) ~ ("a soldier who claims to know all about military law"); a jailhouse ~ (AE)

lax *adj.* 1. ~ about (they are ~ about their appearance) 2. ~ in (the police were ~ in enforcing the law)

laxative *n.* 1. to take a ~ 2. to prescribe a ~ 3. an effective; mild; strong ~ 4. a ~ works

lay *v.* 1. (N; used with an adjective) ("to render"); ("to place") she laid her soul bare; they laid the boards bare 2. (colloq.) (O; can be used with two objects followed by a clause) ("to bet") he laid me ten dollars that it would not rain 3. (P; tr.) ("to place") we laid the books on the table 4. (misc.) to ~ oneself open to ridicule; to ~ ten dollars on a horse to win

layer *n.* 1. the bottom; outer; top ~ 2. an even; thin; uneven ~ 3. a protective ~ 4. the ozone ~ 5. in ~s (to dress in ~s)

lay off *v.* 1. (D; tr.) to ~ from (she was laid off from her job at the factory) 2. (G) he laid off smoking

layout *n.* ["design"] 1. an artist's; typographer's ~ 2. page ~

layover *n.* a ~ between (a ~ between planes)

leach out *v.* (D; tr.) ("to separate") to ~ from

lead I /liyd/ *n.* ["position in front"] ["leading position"] 1. to assume, take a/the ~ in 2. to build up, increase one's ~ 3. to hold, maintain a/the ~ 4. to follow smb.'s ~ 5. to give up, lose, relinquish the ~ 6. a comfortable, commanding ~ 7. a ~ over (she built up a commanding ~ over her closest rivals) 8. in the ~ ["principal role"] 9. to play the ~ (in a play) 10. the female; male ~ ["clue"] 11. to run down, track down a ~ 12. the police have no ~s 13. a good, promising ~ ["leash"] (BE) 14. see **leash** 1, 2 ["cord"] (BE) 15. an extension; television ~

lead II /liyd/ *v.* 1. (D; tr.) ("to guide") to ~ against (to ~ troops against the enemy) 2. (D; tr.) ("to guide") to ~ by (to ~ smb. by the hand; to ~ a horse by the bridle) 3. (d; intr.) ("to go") to ~ from; to (the path ~s from the house to the river; all roads ~ to Rome) 4. (d; tr.) ("to guide") to ~ from; to (she led the group from the bus to the auditorium) 5. (D; tr.) to ~ in (to ~ the students in a cheer) 6. (d; intr.) ("to guide") to ~ into (the prisoners were led into the courtroom) 7. (d; tr.) ("to guide") to ~ off; onto (she led the team off the field) 8. (d; tr.) ("to guide") to ~ out of (the fire fighters led them out of the burning building) 9. (d; tr.) ("to guide") to ~ through (to ~ smb. through the fog) 10. (d; intr.) to ~ to ("to result in") (the infection led to gangrene; these evening courses will ~ to an academic degree) 11. (d; intr.) ("to begin") to ~ with (the boxer led with a left jab) 12. (H) ("to induce") what led her to resign? I was led to believe that she would accept our offer 13. (P; intr., tr.) ("to go") ("to guide") the road ~s nowhere; she led them over the mountain across the border 14. (misc.) to ~ smb. a merry chase (AE) = to ~ smb. a merry/pretty dance (BE)

lead back *v.* (D; intr., tr.) ("to return") to ~ from; to (the road ~s back to town; she led us back from the road to the starting point)

lead down *v.* 1. (d; intr.) ("to go") to ~ from; to (the path ~s down from the village to the main road) 2. (d; tr.) ("to guide") to ~ from; to (they led us down from the mountain to the river)

leader *n.* 1. a born, natural; decisive, strong; undisputed; weak ~ 2. (in a legislature) a floor; majority; minority; opposition; party ~ 3. a labor; military; political; troop ~ 4. a squadron ~ 5. a ~ in

leadership *n.* 1. to assume, take on, take over the ~ 2. to exercise, provide ~ 3. to relinquish, surrender ~ 4. firm, strong ~ 5. collective; party; political ~ 6. ~ in

lead off *v.* (D; intr.) ("to begin") to ~ with (she led off with a lively song)

lead up *v.* 1. (d; intr.) ("to go up") to ~ from; to (the path ~s up from the beach to the top of the hill) 2. (d; intr.) to ~ to ("to precede and cause") (can you describe the events that led up to your decision?) 3. (D; tr.) ("to guide") to ~ from; to (she led us up from the beach to the top of the hill)

leaf I *n.* 1. a bay; tea ~ 2. gold ~ 3. autumn; deciduous leaves 4. leaves fall; rustle; turn (the leaves were turning yellow) 5. (misc.) to turn over a new ~ ("to make a fresh start"); to take a ~ from smb.'s book ("to follow smb.'s example")

leaf II *v.* (d; intr.) to ~ through ("to look through superficially") (to ~ through a book)

leaflet *n.* propaganda ~s (to drop propaganda ~s over enemy lines)

league *n.* ["alliance"] 1. to form a ~ 2. in ~ with ["group of teams"] 3. to form a ~ 4. (esp. Am. baseball) a big, major; bush (colloq.), minor ~; (soccer) the premier ~ ["level"] 5. in the same ~; out of one's ~

leak I *n.* 1. to spring a ~ 2. to plug, stop a ~ 3. a ~ in (a ~ in a pipe) 4. (misc.) a security ~

leak II *v.* 1. (B) ("to divulge") they ~ed the news to the press 2. (d; intr.) ("to enter by flowing") to ~ into (water ~ed into the basement) 3. (D; intr.) ("to escape by flowing") to ~ out of (the oil ~ed out of the tank) 4. (D; intr.) ("to be divulged") to ~ to (the news ~ed to the press)

leak out *v.* 1. (D; intr.) to ~ to (the news ~ed out to the press) 2. (L; to) it ~ed out (to the press) that the president's trip had been cancelled

lean *v.* 1. (d; intr.) to ~ across, over (to ~ across a table) 2. (d; intr., tr.) to ~ against, on (to ~ against a wall; to ~ on a desk) 3. (d; intr.) to ~ out of (to ~ out of a window) 4. (d; intr.) to ~ to (to ~ to one side) 5. (d; intr.) ("to tend") to ~ to, towards (they are now ~ing to our position) 6. (misc.) in the end we had to ~ on them ("we finally had to exert pressure on them"); to ~ over backwards to help smb. ("to make a maximum effort to help smb.")

leaning *n.* 1. a strong ~ 2. a ~ towards (to have a strong ~ towards political conservatism)

lean on *v.* 1. (d; intr.) ("to rely on") to ~ for (they had to ~ their friends for help) 2. (colloq.) (H) we had to ~ him to pay

leap I *n.* 1. a giant, great; quantum ~ 2. a ~ forward 3. (misc.) by ~s and bounds

leap II *v.* 1. (d; intr.) to ~ at ("to be eager for") (to ~ at an opportunity) 2. (P; intr.) ("to jump") to ~ across a barrier; to ~ over a fence; to ~ into the bus 3. (misc.) to ~ to smb.'s defense ("to defend smb. with enthusiasm")

leap down *v.* (D; intr.) to ~ from (to ~ from a tree)

leapfrog I *n.* to play ~

leapfrog II *v.* (d; intr.) to ~ from; to (American forces ~ged from one island to another)

learn *v.* 1. (d; intr.) to ~ about, of 2. (d; intr.) to ~ by (to ~ by experience) 3. (D; intr., tr.) to ~ from (to ~ from experience; she ~ed everything from me) 4. (E) she is ~ing to drive 5. (L) we have ~ed from them that he has found a job 6. (Q) they are ~ing how to dance

learning *n.* 1. book (colloq.); cognitive; higher; language; programmed ~ 2. (misc.) a seat of ~

lease I *n.* 1. to hold a ~ (on) 2. to take (out) a ~ (on) 3. to lose; renew a ~ 4. to cancel a ~ 5. mining; (off-shore) oil ~s 6. a long; short ~ 7. a ~ expires, runs out 8. a ~ on 9. under (a) ~ (to hold land under ~) 10. (misc.) a new ~ of (BE), on (AE) life ("a new chance to lead a happy life")

lease II *v.* 1. (usu. B; occ. A) to ~ property to smb. 2. (D; tr.) to ~ as (they ~d the building as a warehouse) 3. (D; tr.) to ~ from (to ~ property from smb.)

lease out *v.* (B) to ~ property to smb.

leash *n.* ["strap"] 1. to slip ("get free of") a ~ 2. on a ~ (to walk a dog on a ~) ["control"] ["restraint"] 3. to hold in ~ 4. to strain at the ~ ("to attempt to cast off controls")

least *n.* at; at the; at the very; in the; not in the ~

leather *n.* composition; genuine; imitation; patent; saddle ~

leave I *n.* ["period of absence from duty, work"] 1. to give, grant a ~ 2. to extend smb.'s ~ 3. to go on ~; to take a ~ 4. to overstay one's ~ 5. to cancel smb.'s ~ 6. (an) annual; compassionate; maternity; paternity; research; sabbatical; shore; sick; terminal ~ 7. (a) ~ of absence 8. on ~ (she was on maternity ~) (see the Usage Note for **vacation**) ["permission"] (formal) 9. to ask ~ (to do smt.) 10. to give ~ (to do smt.) 11. by smb.'s ~ ["departure"] (formal) 12. to take ~ of ["misc."] 13. to take ~ of one's senses ("to act irrationally")

leave II *v.* 1. (A) ("to bequeath") he left his estate to her; or: he left her his estate 2. (C) ("to entrust") she left the report for me; or: she left me the report 3. (D; intr.) ("to depart") to ~ for (they have left for London) 4. (D; tr.) ("to abandon") to ~ for (she left her comfortable home for a rugged life in the desert; he was left for dead on the battlefield; to ~ Paris for London) 5. (D; intr.) ("to depart") to ~ from (they left from the main station) 6. (d; tr.) to ~ out of ("to omit") (we had to ~ this paragraph out of the text) 7. (d; tr.) ("to abandon") to ~ to (we left them to their own devices; I ~ the decision to your judgment; to ~ nothing to the imagination) 8. (d; tr.) ("to cause to remain") to ~ with (they left the children with her mother; she left her books with us) 9. (H) ("to take leave of") we left them to muddle through on their own; they were left to fend for themselves 10. (J) ("to abandon") I left him working in the garden 11. (N; used with an adjective, past participle, noun) ("to cause to be in a certain state or condition") they left the fields fallow; the film left me cold; the flood left them homeless; ~ me alone; the enemy left the countryside devastated; the war left her an orphan 12. (P; tr.) ("to forget") I left my books at home 13. (misc.) it ~s nothing to be desired; we left this decision up to her

leave of absence *n.* see **leave I** 1-8

lecture I *n.* ["formal talk"] 1. to deliver, give a ~ 2. to attend; follow ("understand") a ~ 3. a public ~ 4. a ~ about, on 5. at a ~ ["reprimand"] 6. to give smb. a ~ (about smt.)

lecture II *v.* 1. (D; intr.) ("to discuss formally") to ~ about, on 2. (D; tr.) ("to reprimand") to ~ for (she ~d the boys for being late) 3. (d; intr.) ("to discuss formally") to ~ to (to ~ to advanced students)

lecturer *n.* 1. a senior ~ (BE) 2. a ~ in, on (a ~ in English) (see the Usage Note for **professor**)

lectureship *n.* a ~ in

leech *n.* to apply ~es to

leer *v.* (D; intr.) to ~ at

leery *adj.* ~ about, of

leeway *n.* to allow, give, provide ~ (they gave him more ~)

left I *adv.* to bear, go, turn ~

left II *n.* ["left side"] 1. to keep to the ~ 2. on the ~; to the ~ ["radical, leftist groups"] 3. the extreme, far, radical ~ ["punch delivered with the left hand"] 4. to deliver, throw a ~ 5. a hard, stiff ~ 6. a ~ to (a ~ to the head) ["turn to the left"] (colloq.) 7. to take a ~ 8. to make a sharp ~

leftovers *n.* 1. to eat up; use up ~ 2. to warm up ~

left-winger *n.* an extreme ~

leg *n.* ["limb"] 1. to bend; cross; kick; lift, raise; lower; spread; straighten; stretch one's ~s 2. a game, gammy (BE) ("lame") ~ 3. an artificial, wooden ~ 4. (an animal's) front; hind ~s 5. (misc.) he doesn't have a ~ to stand on ("he has no defense"); to pull smb.'s ~ ("to deceive smb. playfully"); on one's last ~s ("near collapse"); to get a ~ up on smt. (AE; slang) ("to be in command of a situation"); to stretch one's ~s ("to exercise one's legs") ["part"] 6. the last ~ (of a race)

legacy *n.* 1. to hand down a ~ 2. a lasting ~ 3. a ~ to

legal *adj.* ~ to + inf. (is it ~ to own a pistol in this state?)

legend *n.* ["inscription"] ["wording"] 1. to bear a ~ ["myth, story"] 2. a ~ arises 3. a living; local; popular ~ 4. a ~ to (her exploits were a ~ to millions) ["notable person"] 5. to be, become a ~ (in one's own lifetime)

legislation *n.* ["statutes, laws"] 1. to adopt, enact, pass; draft; introduce ~ 2. to veto; vote down ~ 3. to abrogate, repeal; rescind ~ 4. emergency; enabling; progressive; remedial; social ~ 5. a piece of ~ 6. ~ against; for (they introduced a piece of ~ against the new tax)

legislature *n.* 1. to convene a ~ 2. to disband, dismiss, dissolve a ~ 3. a bicameral ~ 4. a state ~ (US) 5. before a ~ (new proposals coming before the ~)

legitimacy *n.* 1. to confirm; establish the ~ (of smt.) 2. to challenge, question the ~ (of smt.)

legitimate *adj.* ~ to + inf. (is it ~ to pose such questions?)

legwork *n.* (colloq.) to do the ~

leisure *n.* at smb.'s ~

lemon *n.* to squeeze a ~

lend *v.* 1. (A) she lent the money to him; or: she lent him the money 2. (d; refl.) to ~ to ("to be suitable for") (it ~s itself to satire) (see the Usage Note for **loan II**)

length *n.* 1. full ~ 2. at ~ (she described each event at great ~) 3. in ~ (ten feet in ~) 4. (misc.) to keep smb. at arm's ~ ("to keep smb. at a certain distance"); to go to great ~s to do smt. ("to make a great effort to do smt."); the horse won by two ~s; to travel the ~ and breadth of the country

leniency *n.* 1. to show ~ 2. ~ to, towards, with

lenient *adj.* ~ to, towards, with

lens *n.* 1. to grind a ~ 2. a concave; convex; crystalline; telephoto, telescopic; wide-angle; zoom ~ 3. contact; corrective ~es 4. plastic ~es; thick ~es

leopard *n.* 1. a snow ~ 2. a young ~ is a cub 3. a female ~ is a leopardess

leprosy *n.* 1. to develop, get ~ 2. to have, suffer from ~

lesion *n.* an open ~

less *adv., n.* 1. a bit, little ~ 2. no ~ than 3. much ~

lesson *n.* ["instruction"] 1. to give ~s 2. to take ~s (to take ~s in English) 3. to study one's ~s ["something that should be known"] 4. to learn a ~ (she learned a ~ from that experience) 5. to teach smb. a ~ 6. a moral; object; valuable ~ 7. a ~ in (to teach smb. a ~ in good manners) 8. a ~ to (let that be a ~ to you)

let *v.* 1. (esp. BE; CE has *to rent out*) (B) ("to give the use of in return for payment") they ~ rooms to students 2. (I) ("to allow") we cannot ~ them go 3. (misc.) to ~ smb. alone; ~ us continue for awhile; to ~ smb. off a bus; to ~ smb. on a bus; to ~ the air out of a tire; I don't have five dollars, ~ alone ten dollars; to ~ oneself go ("to relax"; "to neglect oneself")

let drop *v.* (L) she let drop that she planned to retire

lethargy *n.* (in) a state of ~

let in *v.* 1. (D; refl., tr.) to ~ for ("to cause") (you'll ~ yourself in for a lot of trouble if you take her in as a partner) 2. (d; tr.) to ~ on ("to share") (to let smb. in on a secret)

let off *v.* 1. to ~ lightly 2. (D; tr.) ("to release") to ~ with (he was let off with a small fine)

let on *v.* 1. (D; intr.) to ~ about ("to reveal") (she did not ~ about her promotion) 2. (L; to) ("to indi-

cate") he let on (to the accused) that he could be bribed

let out *v.* (esp. BE) (B) to ~ rooms to students (see also

rent out)

let's (verbal form) (F) ~ continue; ~ go

letter *n.* ["written message"] 1. to type; write a ~ 2. to mail, post (BE), send; seal a ~ 3. to get, receive; open, unseal a ~ 4. to answer, reply to, respond to a ~ 5. to drop, put a ~ into a mailbox (AE), letter box (BE) 6. to certify; register; trace a ~ 7. to take (down), transcribe a ~ 8. to dictate a ~ 9. to deliver; forward a ~ 10. a brief; detailed; long; rambling ~ 11. an anonymous; business; chain; cover; fan; follow-up; form; love; open; pastoral; personal; poison-pen; threatening ~ 12. an airmail; certified; dead; express; registered; special-delivery ~ 13. the ~s crossed in the mail (esp. AE), post (BE) 14. a ~ about 15. a ~ from; to (we received a ~ from her about the incident) 16. in a ~ ["unit of an alphabet"] 17. a block; capital, large, upper-case; lower-case, small ~ ["first letter of the name of a school, college denoting membership on a sports team"] (AE) 18. to earn, win one's ~ 19. a school ~ ["misc."] 20. to follow instructions to the ~; to follow the ~ of the law

lettuce *n.* 1. to shred ~ 2. crisp ~ 3. bib; cos (BE), romaine (AE); iceberg; leaf ~ 4. a head of ~

letup *n.* a ~ in (there was no ~ in the bickering)

let up *v.* (D; intr.) ("to ease up") to ~ on (she should ~ on the children)

leukemia, leukaemia *n.* 1. to develop ~ 2. to have ~ 3. to suffer from ~ 4. acute ~

level I *adj.* ~ with (to draw ~ with; ~ with the street)

level II *n.* ["height"] ["plane"] 1. to reach a ~ 2. a high; low; record ~ 3. an energy; poverty; subsistence ~ 4. eye; ground; sea; water ~ 5. the federal (US), national; international; local; state (US) ~ 6. at, on a ~ (at sea ~; at the highest ~s; on the international ~) ["instrument for determining a horizontal plane"] 7. a spirit ~

level III *v.* 1. (d; tr.) to ~ against (to ~ charges against smb.) 2. (D; tr.) to ~ to (the village was ~ed to the ground) 3. (colloq.) (d; intr.) to ~ with ("to tell the truth to") (she ~ed with me)

level best *n.* to do one's ~

lever *n.* 1. to pull; push a ~ 2. a gear ~ (BE; AE has *gearshift*)

leverage *n.* 1. to apply; wield ~ 2. political ~ (they have no political ~)

levy I *n.* to impose a ~ (on)

levy II *v.* (D; tr.) to ~ on (to ~ a tax on rum)

lexicon *n.* to compile a ~

liability *n.* 1. to accept, acknowledge, assume, incur, take on a ~ 2. to exempt smb. from ~ 3. full; limited ~ 4. a ~ for (we assumed full ~ for our children's debts)

liable adj. ["legally obligated"] 1. ~ for; to (she is ~ to them for her children's debts) ["likely"] 2. (cannot stand alone) ~ to + inf. (she is ~ to show up at any time)

liaise v. (BE) (D; intr.) ("to mediate") to ~ between; with

liaison n. ["communication"] 1. to establish; maintain ~ 2. a ~ between; with ["love affair"] 3. to enter into a ~ with 4. to have a ~ with

liar n. an abject, compulsive, congenital, consummate, incorrigible, inveterate, outright, pathological ~

lib n. (colloq.) gay; women's ~ (see **liberation** 1)

libel n. 1. to commit ~ 2. (a) ~ against, on

liberal I adj. ~ in; with

liberal II n. a bleeding-heart; knee-jerk; staunch ~

liberate v. (D; tr.) to ~ from

liberation n. 1. gay; women's ~ 2. ~ from

liberties n. ["undue familiarity"] to take ~ with

liberty n. ["freedom"] 1. to gain ~ 2. individual, personal; political; religious ~ 3. civil ~ties ["permission"] 4. to take the ~ (of doing smt.) (may I take the ~ of reminding you of your promise? I took the ~ of opening your package) ["authorized absence"] (AE) (naval) 5. on ~ ["misc."] 6. are you at ~ to give us any information?

library n. 1. to accumulate, build up a ~ 2. to computerize a ~ 3. a children's; circulating, lending; free, municipal, public; law; mobile; music; reference; rental; research; school; university ~ 4. at, in (she works at/in the ~)

license I licence n. 1. to grant, issue a ~ 2. to apply for; receive; renew a ~ 3. to revoke; suspend a ~ 4. a driver's (AE), driving (BE); dog; hunting; liquor (esp. AE); marriage; state (esp. US) ~ 5. poetic ~ 6. a ~ to + inf. (we had a ~ to sell beer) 7. under ~ (the product is made under foreign ~)

license II licence v. (H) she is ~d to practice nursing

lick v. 1. (d; intr.) to ~ against, at (the flames ~ed at the roof of the next house) 2. (N; used with an adjective) she ~ed the plate clean

licking n. ["beating"] 1. to give smb. a (good) ~ 2. to get a ~

lid n. ["cover"] 1. to cover smt. with a ~ 2. to put a ~ on smb. 3. to take off a ~ ["curb"] 4. to clamp, clap, put a ~ on smt.

lie I n. ["falsehood"] 1. to tell a ~ 2. to give the ~ to ("to prove to be false") 3. a bald-faced, barefaced, blatant, brazen, deliberate, downright, monstrous, outright, transparent, whopping ~ 4. a white ~ 5. a pack, tissue, web of ~s 6. (misc.) to live a ~ ("to conceal the truth about oneself")

lie II v. ("to tell a falsehood") 1. to ~ flatly, outright 2. (D; intr.) to ~ about; to (he lied to the judge about the accident)

lie III v. 1. ("to be") to ~ ahead 2. ("to be in a reclining position") to ~ flat; still 3. (d; intr.) ("to

be") to ~ with (responsibility lies with the president) 4. (P; intr.) ("to be located") to ~ in bed; Mexico ~s to the south 5. (s) to ~ fallow (the field lay fallow) 6. (misc.) to ~ in wait for; to ~ awake; to ~ low

lie-detector test n. 1. to administer, give a ~ 2. to subject smb. to a ~ 3. to take a ~ 4. to fail; pass a ~

lie down v. (misc.) to take smt. lying down ("to accept smt. without protest"); to ~ on the job ("to work very little")

lien n. ["legal claim"] 1. to put, slap (esp. AE; colloq.) a ~ on smt. 2. to have a ~ on smt.

lie to v. (D; intr.) to ~ about (she ~d to me about the incident)

lieutenant n. 1. a first; flight (GB); second ~ 2. a ~ junior grade (US)

life n. 1. to lead a ~ (to lead a busy ~) 2. to prolong; save; spare a ~ 3. to devote one's ~ (to smt.) 4. to live, spend one's ~ (doing smt.) 5. to give, lay down, sacrifice; lose; risk one's ~ 6. to claim, snuff out, take a ~ (she took her own ~; the accident claimed many lives) 7. to ruin smb.'s ~ 8. to bring; restore smb. to ~ 9. to come to; to take on ~ (the statue took on ~ in the sculptor's skilled hands) 10. an active; busy, hectic; exciting ~ 11. a charmed; full; good; happy; idyllic ~ 12. an easy; peaceful, quiet, serene; sheltered; simple ~ 13. an ascetic, austere; cloistered; monastic ~ 14. a difficult, hard, miserable, tough; dull; lonely, solitary; unhappy ~ 15. a dissipated, dissolute; stormy, turbulent ~ 16. a long; short ~ 17. daily, everyday; modern ~ 18. campus (esp. AE); city; country, rural; suburban; village ~ 19. civilian; political; public ~ (in civilian ~ the sergeant was a teacher) 20. (a) nomadic ~ (the hunters led a nomadic ~) 21. smb.'s family; home; love; married; personal; private; sex; social ~ (to lead a hectic social ~; married ~ seemed to agree with them; in private ~ she was very easygoing) 22. animal; bird; human; marine; plant ~ 23. (in) adult ~ 24. the shelf ~ (of smt. being sold in a store) 25. in ~ (early in ~) 26. (misc.) in the prime of ~; the facts of ~; the accused got ~ ("the accused was sentenced to life imprisonment"); to show signs of ~; (to hang on) for dear ~ ("with all one's energy"); not on your ~ ("not for anything in the world"); to start a new ~; to make a new ~ for oneself; to breathe/infuse (new) ~ into smt.; to bring back to ~; to stake one's ~ on smt.; a way of ~; to pester the ~ out of smb.; a matter of ~ and death; a ~ of ease; full of ~; (slang) get a ~! ("don't be so obsessive!") ("do smt. new, useful, constructive!")

lifeboat n. 1. to launch, lower a ~ 2. to swamp a ~ (the ~ was swamped in the surf) 3. (misc.) to take to the ~s

life insurance n. to take out ~ on

life jacket n. 1. to inflate a ~ 2. to put on a ~

lifeline *n.* ["rope used to save a life"] 1. to throw smb. a ~ ["vital route"] 2. to cut a ~ 3. a ~ to

life sentence *n.* 1. to give smb. a ~ (for murder) 2. to get, receive a ~

lifestyle *n.* 1. to have a certain ~ 2. an alternate (AE), alternative; luxurious; ostentatious; sedentary; simple ~

life support *n.* on ~ (the patient was on ~)

lifetime *n.* 1. to devote a ~ (to smt.) 2. during, in one's ~ 3. (misc.) to last a ~; the chance, opportunity of a ~

lift I *n.* ["device for raising and lowering people and freight"] (BE; AE has *elevator*) 1. to operate a ~ (a liftboy or liftman operates a ~) 2. to take a ~ (we took the ~ to the tenth floor) 3. a service ~ (see also **elevator** 1-6) ["conveyor suspended from a cable"] 4. a chair, ski ~ ["ride"] (colloq.) 5. to bum; get a ~ (from smb.) 6. to give smb. a ~ ["boost, inspiration"] (colloq.) 7. to get a ~ (from smb. or smt.) 8. to give smb. a ~ (your words of encouragement gave us a real ~)

lift II *v.* 1. (D; tr.) ("to raise") to ~ from (she did not ~ her head from the TV set) 2. (d; tr.) ("to steal") to ~ from (the material was ~ed from smb.'s dissertation) 3. (D; tr.) ("to raise") to ~ out of (they ~ed the crates out of the hold) 4. (misc.) the jet ~ed off the runway

lift down *v.* (D; tr.) to ~ from; to (they ~ed the trunk down from the shelf to the floor)

lift up *v.* (D; tr.) to ~ from; to (he ~ed the child up from the floor to the bed)

ligament *n.* to strain; tear a ~

light I *adj.* 1. to make ~ of ("to attach little importance to") 2. ~ of foot

light II *n.* ["illumination"] ["source of brightness"] 1. to put on, switch on, turn on a ~ 2. to shine, throw a ~ on smt. 3. to cast, shed ~ on smt. 4. to dim; extinguish, switch off, turn off, turn out a ~ 5. to dim the ~s, turn the ~s down; to turn the ~s up 6. a blinding; bright, strong; harsh ~ 7. a dim, dull, faint; soft ~ 8. moonlight; sunlight 9. an electric; klieg; landing; neon; overhead; pilot; strobe; traffic; warning ~ 10. (on a car) a backup (AE), reversing (BE); brake; dome; instrument; parking ~; taillight 11. a ~ flashes; flickers; glows, shines; goes on; the ~s are on 12. a ~ goes off; goes out; the ~s are off; out 13. ~ travels (very fast) 14. (BE) the ~s have fused ("a fuse has blown") 15. by the ~ of (to read by the ~ of a candle) ["traffic light"] 16. to go through a (red) ~ 17. the ~ changes, switches (to green/red) 18. against a ~ (to cross against the ~) 19. at a ~ (to stop at a ~) ["flame used to light a cigarette"] 20. to give smb. a ~ ["flame on a stove"] (AE) 21. a low ~ (cook it on/over a low ~) ["misc."] 22. in ~ of (esp. AE), in the ~ of ("in view of"); in the harsh ~ of reality; a guiding ~ ("one who sets an example"); to see the ~ ("to compre-

hend the truth"); to bring smt. to ~ ("to make smt. known"); to come to ~ ("to become known"); she wanted to see her name in ~s ("she wanted to succeed on the stage and become famous"); the northern ~s; the southern ~s

light III *v.* 1. (d; intr.) to ~ into ("to attack") (he lit into his opponent) 2. (D; intr.) to ~ on, upon ("to come across") (to ~ on a rare dictionary) 3. (C) ~ a cigarette for me; or: ~ me a cigarette

light bulb see **bulb** 1-4

lighter *n.* a cigarette ~

lighting *n.* 1. dim; good; poor; soft ~ 2. artificial; electric; fluorescent ~ 3. diffused; direct; indirect ~

lightning *n.* 1. ball; forked; heat, sheet ~ 2. ~ flashes; strikes 3. a bolt, flash, streak, stroke of ~

light out *v.* (colloq.) (esp. AE) (D; intr.) to ~ for ("to leave for")
USAGE NOTE: The past and past participle of this verb are usu. *lit out*—she lit out for home.

light up *v.* (D; intr.) to ~ with (her face lit up with pleasure)

like I *prep.* (colloq.) ~ to + inf. (it was ~ them to be late)

like II *v.* 1. to ~ a great deal, a lot, very much 2. (E) he ~s to read 3. (G) she ~s reading 4. (H; no passive) (often with the conditional) I'd ~ him to go; I ~ people to tell me the truth; I'd ~ you to go; AE also has, slightly colloq.: I'd ~ for you to go; CE has: what I'd ~ is for you to go 5. (M) we ~ our friends to be honest 6. (N; used with an adjective) I ~ my steak rare
USAGE NOTE: The verb *like* can be used with *it* + clause—I like it when you smile; I'd like it if you smiled.

likelihood *n.* 1. every; great; little ~ 2. a good, strong ~ 3. ~ that + inf. (there is every ~ that she'll come) 4. in all ~

likely *adj.* 1. (cannot stand alone) ~ to + inf. (she is ~ to show up; it is not ~ to snow) 2. ~ that + clause (it is ~ that there will be more rain)

liken *v.* (D; tr.) ("to compare") to ~ to (her estate could be ~ed to a fortress)

likeness *n.* 1. to catch a ~ (the artist caught the ~) 2. to bear a ~ 3. a living; striking, uncanny; strong; true ~ 4. a family ~ 5. a ~ between; to

likewise *adv.* to do ~

liking *n.* 1. to take a ~ to 2. to develop; have a ~ for 3. to smb.'s ~ (that is not to my ~)

limb *n.* 1. to stretch one's ~s 2. an artificial ~ 3. the lower; upper ~s 4. (misc.) out on a ~ ("in a precarious position")

limbo *n.* in ~ (in political ~)

limelight *n.* 1. to get, have, hold the ~ 2. to hog the ~ 3. to be in the ~ ("to have high public visibility")

limit I *n.* 1. to impose, place, put, set a ~ on 2. to disregard, exceed a ~ 3. to reach a ~ (she reached the ~ of her endurance) 4. an age; credit; speed; term; time; weight ~ 5. a ~ on; to 6. within ~s 7. (misc.) to push smb. to the ~

limit II v. (D; refl., tr.) to ~ to (she had to ~ herself to twenty minutes)

limitations n. 1. to put ~ on 2. budgetary, financial ~ 3. within certain ~

limited adj. 1. ~ in (~ in resources) 2. ~ to

limits n. 1. (AE) city ~ 2. (AE) (esp. mil.) off ~ (to); on ~ (to) (the bar was put off ~ to all military personnel) 3. beyond; within (reasonable) ~

limo n. ["limousine"] (colloq.) a stretch ~

limousine n. 1. to hire; take a ~ 2. an airport; bulletproof ~

limp n. 1. to have a ~ 2. a decided, marked, pronounced; slight ~

line I n. ["long, thin mark"] 1. to draw a ~ 2. a broken; dotted; solid, unbroken ~ 3. a contour; crooked; curved; diagonal; straight; wavy; zigzag ~ 4. a fine, thin; heavy, thick ~ 5. a horizontal; parallel; perpendicular; vertical ~ ["row of people waiting; queue"] 6. to form a ~ 7. (AE) to buck ("push into") a ~ 8. to get in; into ~; to stand, wait in ~ 9. a check-in; checkout; chow ~ 10. a ~ forms ["row"] 11. to form a ~ 12. a picket; police; receiving ~ ["row of characters"] 13. to indent; insert a ~ 14. (fig.) to read between the ~s ["unit of text"] 15. to deliver a ~ 16. to go over, rehearse; memorize one's ~s (the actors had to rehearse their ~s several times) 17. to fluff one's ~s 18. a dull; witty ~ (there isn't a dull ~ in the whole play) ["route"] 19. to introduce a (new) ~ 20. to discontinue a ~ 21. a branch; feeder; main ~ 22. a bus; commuter; high-speed; steamship; streetcar (AE), tram (BE) ~ 23. supply ~s (to cut enemy supply ~s) ["path"] 24. to follow a ~ (to follow a ~ of reasoning; to follow the ~ of least resistance) ["telephone connection"] 25. to get a ~; to give smb. a ~ 26. the ~ is busy, engaged (BE), tied up (esp. AE) 27. the ~ is free, open 28. the ~ goes dead 29. an outside; party ("shared"); private ~ 30. a helpline (BE), hot ~ (a helpline for desperate people; a hot ~ for missing children) 31. on the ~ (to stay on the ~) ["note"] 32. to drop smb. a ~ ["information"] 33. to get a ~ on smb. ["type of merchandise"] 34. to carry; handle; introduce a ~ 35. to discontinue, drop a ~ 36. a complete, full ~ ["policy"] 37. to adhere to, follow, hew to (AE), pursue, take a ~ 38. a firm, hard; official; party ~ (to hew to the official ~) ["flattering talk"] (colloq.) 39. to feed, give, hand smb. a ~ ["wire"] ["pipe"] ["conduit"] 40. a fuel; oil; sewage; steam; telegraph; telephone ~ 41. high-voltage; power ~s (the power ~s are down) ["boundary"] 42. (AE) a city; county; state; township ~ 43. a dividing; snow; squall; tree ~ 44. (sports) a base; end; foul; goal; service ~; sideline 45. at, on a ~ (at the goal ~; on the base ~; on the sidelines) ["established position along a front"] ["boundary"] (mil.) 46. to hold a ~ 47. a battle; cease-fire; firing; front ~ 48. (the) enemy ~s (behind enemy ~s) 49. at, on a ~ (on the cease-fire ~) ["conveyor belt"] 50. an assembly, production ~ (to work on an assembly ~) ["occupation"] ["field of interest"] 51. what ~ are you in? ["contour"] 52. the ~s of a ship ["limit"] 53. to hold the ~ (on prices) 54. to draw the ~ ("to set a limit") ["turn"] ["order"] 55. in ~ for (she is next in ~ for promotion) ["alignment"] 56. in ~; out of ~ (the wheels are out of ~) ["conformity"] 57. to toe the ~ 58. to bring smb. into ~; to keep smb. in ~ 59. to get into ~; to get out of ~ 60. in ~ with (in ~ with your stated policy) ["cord, device for catching fish"] 61. to cast a ~ 62. to reel in; reel out a ~ 63. a fishing ~ ["rope"] 64. to throw a ~ to smb. (who is in the water) 65. a plumb ~ ["division"] 66. to cross a ~ 67. a color ~ ["tendency"] 68. along, on certain ~s (along modern ~s) ["dynasty"] 69. to establish, found a ~ 70. an unbroken ~ ["distinction"] 71. a fine, nebulous, thin ~ between ["misc."] 72. the bottom ~ ("the final result"); to be on the firing ~ ("to be at the center of activity"); to sign on the dotted ~ ("to sign an agreement"); a credit ~ ("amount of credit allowed"); to walk a straight ~; to put smt. on the ~ ("to risk smt."); to lay it on the ~ ("to speak candidly"); in the ~ of duty; top of the ~ ("best quality"); on ~ ("in operation"); to go online ("to become linked to a computer network"; see also **online**)

line II v. (D; tr.) to ~ with (she ~d the shelf with paper)

lineage n. 1. to trace smb.'s ~ 2. an ancient; royal ~

lined up adj. 1. ~ for (~ for inspection) 2. ~ in (~ in columns; ~ in a row)

linen n. 1. to change the (bed) ~ 2. fresh ~ 3. bed; fine; pure; table ~

liner I n. ["steamship"] a cruise; luxury; ocean; passenger; transatlantic ~

liner II n. ["lining"] a helmet ~

lineup n. 1. a police ~ (AE; BE has *identification parade*) 2. (AE) to be in a ~ (as a suspect) 3. (sports) a starting ~

line up v. 1. (D; intr.) to ~ behind (to ~ behind the table) 2. (D; intr., tr.) to ~ for (the teacher ~d the pupils up for roll call) 3. (D; intr., tr.) to ~ in (to ~ in three ranks) 4. (D; intr., tr.) to ~ with (to ~ one thing up with another)

linger v. (d; intr.) to ~ over ("to take one's time with") (don't ~ over your coffee)

lingo n. (colloq.) ["language, dialect"] 1. to speak the ~ 2. to understand the ~ 3. the local ~

linguistics n. applied; comparative; computational; contrastive; descriptive; general; generative; historical ~; psycholinguistics; sociolinguistics; structural; transformational ~

liniment *n.* to apply, rub in ~

lining *n.* 1. a brake; coat ~ 2. a zip-in ~ 3. (misc.) a silver ~ ("the bright side of a problem")

link I *n.* 1. to establish, forge, form a ~ 2. to sever a ~ 3. a direct ~ 4. a close; strong; weak ~ 5. a connecting; rail; road ~ 6. the missing ~ 7. a cuff ~ 8. a ~ between; to, with (he has ~s to the underworld)

link II *v.* 1. to ~ closely; inextricably 2. to ~ electronically 3. (D; tr.) to ~ to, with (these events are ~ed to each other)

linkage *n.* (a) ~ between, to, with

links *n.* ["golf course"] (out) on the ~

link-up *n.* a ~ between; to; with

link up *v.* (D; intr.) to ~ to, with (we ~ed up with their forces on the Danube)

linoleum *n.* inlaid ~

lion *n.* 1. a mountain ~ 2. ~s prowl; roar 3. a pride of ~s 4. a young ~ is a cub 5. a female ~ is a lioness 6. (misc.) the ~ is the king of beasts

lip *n.* 1. to curl; lick; move; part; pucker; purse; round one's ~s 2. to press one's ~s to (she pressed her ~s to the baby's forehead) 3. chapped; dry; moist ~s 4. thick; thin ~s 5. the lower; upper ~ 6. from smb.'s (own) ~s (I heard it from her ~s) 7. on one's ~s (she died with a prayer on her ~s) 8. on everyone's ~s (her name was on everyone's ~s) 9. (misc.) to bite one's ~ ("to restrain oneself"); to moisten one's ~s; to lick/smack one's ~s ("to anticipate or remember with pleasure"); to keep a stiff upper ~ ("to refuse to become discouraged"); don't give me any of your ~ ("don't be impudent with me"); to seal smb.'s ~s ("to induce smb. to remain silent"); to read ~s

lip service *n.* ["meaningless promise"] to pay ~ to

lipstick *n.* to apply, put on; remove, wipe off ~

liquid *n.* 1. (a) clear; cloudy; thick ~ 2. (a) dishwashing (AE), washing-up (BE) ~

liquor *n.* ["alcoholic drinks"] (esp. AE) 1. to ply smb. with ~ 2. to hold one's ~ 3. hard, strong; intoxicating ~ 4. malt ~

list I *n.* ["catalog, roll"] 1. to compile, draw up, make (up) a ~ 2. to head a ~ 3. to go down, read down a ~ 4. the dean's ~ (AE); a reading ~ 5. an alphabetical ~; checklist; shopping ~ (to go down a checklist) 6. a guest; mailing; waiting ~ 7. the honours ~ (GB) (she hoped that her name would be in the honours ~) 8. a short ~ (of candidates) 9. a casualty ~ (a daily casualty ~ was posted) 10. a danger ~ (esp. BE) (she rang the hospital to find out if her mother was still on the danger ~) 11. a wish ~ (we were asked to draw up a wish ~ for the new project) 12. on a ~ (she was third on the ~; high on the ~ of priorities) 13. (misc.) at the bottom of a ~; at the top of a ~

list II *v.* ("to include") 1. (d; intr.) to ~ among (to be ~ed among the casualties) 2. (d; refl., tr.) to ~ as (she ~ed herself as an independent voter; he was ~ed as missing) 3. (d; tr.) to ~ under (the new journals are ~ed under acquisitions)

list III *n.* ["tilt"] a ~ to (a ~ to starboard)

list IV *v.* (D; intr.) ("to tilt") to ~ to (to ~ to starboard)

listen *v.* 1. to ~ attentively, carefully, closely, intently 2. (d; intr.) to ~ for (to ~ for a signal) 3. (D; intr.) to ~ to (to ~ to advice)

listener *n.* a good, sympathetic ~

listen in *v.* (D; intr.) to ~ on, to (to ~ on smb.'s conversation)

listen out *v.* (D; intr.) to ~ for

listen to *v.* 1. (esp. AE) (I) we ~ed to them sing 2. (J) we ~ed to them singing

listing *n.* an exclusive ~ (of a property being sold)

list price *n.* (to sell smt.) at ~

lists *n.* ["combat arena"] to enter the ~

lit *adj.* brightly; dimly ~ (a dimly ~ street)

litany *n.* 1. a boring; long ~ 2. (misc.) a ~ of complaints (we had to listen to their ~ of complaints)

literacy *n.* 1. to spread ~ 2. adult; computer ~

literate *adj.* 1. fully; highly ~ 2. computer ~ 3. ~ in

literature *n.* 1. to produce (a) ~ 2. (an) extensive, voluminous ~ 3. belletristic; classical; contemporary; great; modern; professional; promotional; pulp ~ 4. comparative ~ 5. a body of ~ (a considerable body of ~) 6. ~ about, on (there was extensive ~ on the topic) 7. (misc.) to keep abreast of the ~; to review the ~ (when beginning a research project)

litigation *n.* 1. to initiate, start ~ 2. ~ against; over; with 3. in ~ (the case was in ~)

littered *adj.* ~ with (the streets were ~ with old newspapers)

little *adv., n.* 1. precious ~ 2. ~ by ~ ("gradually") 3. ~ to + inf. (we had ~ to say) 4. (misc.) a ~ bit; a ~ closer; a ~ further; a ~ longer; a ~ shorter

liturgy *n.* to chant; offer; recite the ~

live I /layv/ *adv.* ["directly"] to come ~ (this telecast is coming to you ~ from Wimbledon; you can catch her ~ in concert this evening)

live II /liv/ *v.* 1. to ~ comfortably; dangerously; high; simply 2. to ~ long 3. (d; intr.) to ~ by ("to adhere to") (to ~ by certain principles) 4. (d; intr.) ("to exist") to ~ for (they ~ only for their children) 5. (d; intr.) to ~ in (to ~ in fear; to ~ in luxury; to ~ in poverty) 6. (d; intr.) ("to subsist") to ~ off, on (they ~ on her salary; you cannot ~ on love alone; to ~ off one's parents) 7. (D; intr.) ("to survive") to ~ to (she ~d to ninety) 8. (d; intr.) ("to cohabit") to ~ with (they ~ with each other) 9. (colloq.) (d; intr.) to ~ with ("to tolerate") (can you ~ with this arrangement?) 10. (E) she ~d to regret her decision; he ~d to be ninety 11. (P; intr.) ("to reside") to ~ in the country 12. (misc.) they ~ beyond their means ("they spend more than they earn"); to ~ from hand to mouth ("to eke out a bare living"); to ~ from day to day ("to be concerned only with the present"); to ~ together ("to cohabit"); long ~ the King/Queen!

livelihood *n.* 1. to earn one's ~ 2. to lose one's ~

livestock *n.* to graze; keep ~

live up *v.* 1. (d; intr.) to ~ to ("to satisfy") (to ~ to expectations) 2. (misc.) (colloq.) to ~ it up ("to enjoy oneself ostentatiously")

livid *adj.* ~ with (~ with rage)

living *n.* ["livelihood"] 1. to earn, get (BE), make a ~ (she makes a good ~ by selling cars) 2. to eke out (colloq.); scrape (esp. BE) a ~ (to eke out a precarious ~) 3. a comfortable, decent, good; honest ~ (to earn a comfortable ~) 4. (misc.) what do you do for a ~? ["manner of existence"] 5. communal; gracious; high; suburban ~ 6. a cost; standard of ~

living room *n.* a sunken ~

load I *n.* 1. to carry, transport a ~ 2. to lessen, lighten a ~ (also fig.) 3. to dump, shed a ~ 4. a heavy; light ~ 5. a capacity, maximum, peak ~ 6. a caseload; teaching ~; workload 7. (misc.) to take a ~ off smb.'s mind

load II *v.* 1. (D; tr.) to ~ into, onto (to ~ coal into a ship) 2. (d; tr.) to ~ to (to ~ a ship to full capacity) 3. (D; tr.) to ~ with (to ~ a ship with coal)

load down *v.* (D; tr.) to ~ with

load up *v.* (D; tr.) to ~ with

loaf *n.* 1. a fish; meat ~ 2. a ~ of bread

loan I *n.* 1. to float, negotiate, raise a ~ 2. to give, make; offer a ~ 3. to get, receive, take out a ~ 4. to secure; underwrite a ~ 5. to pay off, repay a ~ 6. to call in a ~ 7. an interest-free; long-term; low-interest; short-term ~ 8. interlibrary ~ (she got the book on/through interlibrary ~) 9. a ~ to 10. on ~ from; on (the painting was on ~ to the National Gallery from the Louvre)

loan II *v.* (A) she ~ed the money to me; *or:* she ~ed me the money

USAGE NOTE: When *to loan* means "to lend officially", it is CE—the Louvre has loaned a painting to the National Gallery. When it means "to lend", it is esp. AE—she loaned me the money.

loanword *n.* 1. to adopt a ~ 2. a ~ from (a ~ from French)

loath *adj.* (pompous or lit.) (cannot stand alone) ~ to + inf. (we are ~ to summon the authorities)

loathe *v.* 1. to ~ deeply, intensely 2. (G) he ~s working

loathing *n.* 1. deep, intense ~ 2. ~ for, of 3. with ~

lob *v.* 1. (D; tr.) to ~ at, to (to ~ a ball at smt.) 2. (D; tr.) to ~ over (she ~bed the ball over the net)

lobby I *n.* ["pressure group"] 1. an education; environmental; farm; labor; oil ~ ["large hall"] 2. a hotel; theater ~ 3. in the ~ (let's meet in the ~)

lobby II *v.* 1. to ~ actively; hard 2. (D; intr.) to ~

against; for (to ~ against higher taxes; to ~ for a bill) 3. (H) we ~bied our delegate to support the proposal

locate *v.* 1. (P; tr.) ("to place") we ~d our firm in Florida 2. (P; intr.) (esp. AE) ("to move") our firm is going to ~ in California

location *n.* 1. to pinpoint a ~ 2. a central; exact ~ 3. at a ~ (at an undisclosed ~) 4. on ~ (to shoot a film on ~)

lock I *n.* 1. to force; pick a ~ 2. a combination; deadbolt; double; mortise; safety; secure; time ~ 3. a Chubb (T); Yale (T) ~ 4. under ~ and key ("locked up securely")

lock II *v.* 1. (d; intr.) to ~ on, onto ("to sight and track") (to ~ onto a target) 2. (d; tr.) to ~ out of (they were ~ed out of their room)

locked *adj.* ["bound"] (cannot stand alone) ~ in (~ in mortal combat)

locket *n.* a gold; silver ~

locomotive *n.* 1. to drive a ~ 2. a diesel; electric; steam ~

locusts *n.* 1. ~ swarm 2. a swarm of ~

lodge I *n.* ["house"] 1. a hunting; ski ~ ["organization, society"] 2. a fraternal; Masonic ~ ["motel"] (AE) 3. a motor ~

lodge II *v.* 1. (D; tr.) to ~ against; with (to ~ a complaint against a neighbor with the police) 2. (d; intr.) to ~ in (the bullet ~d in his shoulder)

lodger *n.* to take in ~s

lodgings *n.* to find; look for, seek ~

log I *n.* ["record"] ["diary"] 1. to keep a ~ 2. a captain's; ship's ~ ["piece of timber"] 3. to float ~s (down a river) 4. to split a ~; to saw a ~ in two ["misc."] 5. to sleep like a ~ ("to sleep very soundly")

log II *v.* (d. intr.) to ~ into, onto (to ~ onto a computer system)

logarithm *n.* a common; natural ~

loggerheads *n.* at ~ with ("in disagreement with")

logic *n.* 1. to apply, use ~ 2. clear; cold; incontrovertible; irrefutable; simple ~ 3. false, specious, spurious ~ 4. deductive; formal; inductive; symbolic ~ 5. ~ in (there is no ~ in their policy)

logical *adj.* 1. ~ to + inf. (it is ~ to assume that they will attend) 2. ~ that + clause (it's only ~ that we should go in one car)

logjam *n.* 1. to break (up), clear a ~ 2. (fig.) (esp. AE) a legislative ~

loins *n.* ["power"] to gird one's ~ ("to prepare oneself for a difficult task")

lollipop *n.* to lick, suck a ~

lonely *adj.* ~ for

lonesome *adj.* (AE) ~ for

long I *adj.* (colloq.) ["strong"] ~ on (~ on common sense)

long II *adv.* 1. ~ after; ago 2. ~ before

long III *n.* 1. before ~ (our guests will arrive before

~) 2. for ~ (they will not be here for ~)

long IV *v.* 1. (d; intr.) to ~ for (to ~ for peace) 2. (E) she ~ed to return home; I ~ed for them to return

long chalk (BE) see **long shot**

long-distance *adv.* to call, telephone ~

long division *n.* to do ~

long face *n.* to make, pull (BE) a ~

long haul see **long run**

longing *n.* 1. to feel, have a ~ 2. a secret ~ 3. a ~ for

longitude *n.* at a ~ (at a ~ of ten degrees west)

long run *n.* ["long-range outlook"] in, over the ~

long shot *n.* ["slight chance"] not by a ~ (AE) ("absolutely not")

long way *n.* 1. we took the ~ home 2. a ~ from; to (it's a ~ from our house to the station)

look I *n.* ["glance"] ["expression"] 1. to get, have, take a ~ (at) (we got a good ~ at their new car) 2. to dart, shoot, throw a ~ (at) 3. to sneak, steal a ~ (at) 4. to give smb. a ~ 5. to get, receive a ~ (from) 6. an adoring, loving, tender ~ (she got an adoring ~ from her mother) 7. a close, hard; curious, inquiring, searching; eloquent, meaningful; knowing; penetrating, pensive, thoughtful; piercing; rapt; significant; steady ~ (we must take a close ~ at their proposal) 8. a come-hither, inviting, provocative ~ 9. a blank, distant, faraway, vacant; strange ~ (she had a faraway ~ in her eyes) 10. an anxious, worried; pleading ~ (he shot a pleading ~ at the teacher) 11. a bemused, puzzled, quizzical; bewildered; skeptical; troubled ~ (she gave the instructor a bewildered ~) 12. a disapproving, stern; grim; icy; scathing; sharp; withering ~ 13. an angry; baleful; belligerent; dirty, nasty, vicious; furtive, shifty, sinister; hostile; resentful; sour; sullen; suspicious ~ (she gave us a dirty ~) 14. a second ~ (to take a second ~ at smt.) ["appearance"] 15. a tailored ~ 16. a haggard; hungry; lean ~ 17. a curious, strange ~ 18. a guilty; innocent ~ ["misc."] 19. by, from the ~(s) of it, the situation is serious

look II *v.* 1. (d; intr.) to ~ after ("to watch") (to ~ after the children) 2. (D; intr.) to ~ around ("to watch") (to ~ around the corner) 3. (D; intr.) to ~ at ("to examine") (to ~ at a painting) 4. (D; intr.) to ~ for ("to seek") (to ~ for a job) 5. (d; intr.) to ~ into ("to investigate") (to ~ into a complaint) 6. (d; intr.) to ~ like ("to resemble") (this horse ~s like a winner; BE also has: this horse ~s a winner) 7. (d; intr.) ("to appear") to ~ like (it ~s like rain = it ~s as if/as though it will rain) 8. (D; intr.) ("to watch") to ~ out (AE), out of (to ~ out of a window) 9. (d; intr.) to ~ over ("to watch") (to ~ over a wall) 10. (d; intr.) to ~ through ("to direct one's gaze through") (to ~ through a telescope) 11. (d; intr.) to ~ through ("to examine") (to ~ through one's files) 12. (d; intr.) to ~ to ("to turn to") (to ~ to one's parents for help) 13. (d; intr.) to ~ to ("to

appear") (how does this ~ to you?) 14. (s) she ~s terrible 15. (misc.) to ~ smb. squarely in the eye; to ~ from one to the other; to ~ one's age; to ~ everywhere; to ~ all over; to ~ high and low; to ~ under the bed

look about (BE) see **look around**

look ahead *v.* (D; intr.) to ~ to (to ~ to a bright future)

look around *v.* (d; intr.) to ~ for ("to seek") (to ~ for a job)

look at *v.* 1. (AE) (I) ~ him jump 2. (J) ~ him jumping

look away *v.* (D; intr.) to ~ from (I ~ed away from the stage)

look back *v.* (D; intr.) to ~ at, on (to ~ at the past year)

look down *v.* 1. (d; intr.) to ~ at; from ("to direct one's gaze down at") (to ~ at the beach from the balcony of the hotel) 2. (d; intr.) to ~ on ("to despise") (to ~ on all forms of corruption)

look forward *v.* (d; intr.) to ~ to (to ~ to spring; to ~ to a meeting with eager anticipation; I ~ to going)

look in *v.* (D; intr.) to ~ on (to ~ on the children)

look on *v.* 1. to ~ favorably; unfavorably 2. (D; tr.) to ~ as (we ~ her as a friend) 3. (D; intr., tr.) to ~ with (they ~ed on the new project with favor)

lookout *n.* 1. to post a ~ 2. to keep a (sharp) ~ for 3. on the ~

look out *v.* 1. (d; intr.) to ~ for ("to watch for") (the police were ~ing out for burglars) 2. (d; intr.) to ~ for ("to protect") (to ~ for one's own interests) 3. (d; intr.) to ~ on, onto, over ("to face") (our windows ~ onto the square)

look round (BE) see **look around**

looks *n.* ["appearance"] good ~

look to *v.* (d; intr.) to ~ for ("to turn to") (to ~ to one's friends for help)

look up *v.* 1. (d; intr.) ("to stare") to ~ at (we ~ed up at the skyscraper) 2. (d; intr.) to ~ to ("to respect") (children ~ to their parents)

look upon see **look on**

loom I *n.* a hand; power ~

loom II *v.* 1. (P; intr.) a ship ~ed out of the fog 2. (misc.) to ~ large (her possible candidacy ~ed large in the future plans of the party)

loop *n.* 1. to make a ~ 2. to loop the ~ (in an airplane) 3. (misc.) to throw smb. for a ~ ("to shock smb.")

loophole *n.* 1. to find a ~ 2. to close, plug a ~ 3. a tax ~ 4. a ~ in

loose I *adj.* 1. to cut (smb.) ~ 2. to let, set, turn (smb.) ~ 3. to come; work ~

loose II *n.* on the ~

loose end *n.* (BE) at a ~ (see **loose ends**, 2)

loose ends *n.* 1. to clear up the ~ 2. (AE) at ~ ("with no definite obligations")

looting *n.* 1. to engage in ~ 2. widespread ~ 3. an

outbreak of ~

lope *v.* (P; intr.) she ~d through the park

lord I *n.* 1. to worship the Lord 2. a feudal ~; a warlord 3. (misc.) a Law Lord (GB); Good Lord!

lord II *v.* to ~ it over smb. ("to flaunt one's superiority over smb.")

lorry *n.* (BE) 1. to drive, operate a ~ (CE has *truck*) 2. an articulated ~ (AE has *trailer truck*) 3. a breakdown ~ (AE has *tow truck*) 4. a tipper ~ (AE has *dump truck*) 5. a dustbin ~ (AE has *garbage truck*)

lose *v.* 1. (D; intr., tr.) to ~ to (our team lost to them by three points; we lost the match to them) 2. (O) his errors lost him the match

lose out *v.* 1. (D; intr.) to ~ on (to ~ on a deal) 2. (D; intr.) to ~ to (she lost out to her rival)

loser *n.* a bad, poor, sore; born; good ~

loss *n.* 1. to inflict ~es on (our forces inflicted heavy ~es on the enemy) 2. (sports) to hand smb. a ~ (they handed our team its first ~ of the season) 3. to incur, suffer, sustain, take ~es (to take heavy ~es) 4. to cut; make up, offset, recoup, replace a ~ (to recoup one's gambling ~es) 5. to make good a ~ 6. to report a ~ (to the police) 7. heavy; light ~es 8. a great; irredeemable, irreparable, irreplaceable, irretrievable; sad; total ~ 9. a hearing; heat; memory; weight ~ 10. a net ~ 11. a ~ in (a ~ in weight) 12. a ~ to (an irreplaceable ~ to our nation) 13. at a ~ (to be at a ~ for words) 14. (misc.) ~es in dead and wounded

lost *adj.* 1. irretrievably; totally ~ 2. to get ~ (the small child got ~) 3. ~ to (~ to the world) 4. (misc.) (slang) get ~! ("go away!"); ~ at sea; ~ in thought

lot *n.* ["one's fortune"] 1. to cast, throw in one's ~ with 2. a happy; hard, sorry, unhappy ~ 3. smb.'s ~ to + inf. (it fell to her ~ to break the sad news) ["object used in deciding by chance"] 4. by ~ (to choose by ~) ["plot of ground"] (esp. AE) 5. an empty, vacant ~ 6. a parking ~ (AE; BE has *car park*) 7. a used-car ~ ["large amount"] 8. a whole ~ (of) 9. (misc.) we had a ~ to talk about; we have a ~ of work to do; ~s of money

lotion *n.* 1. to apply, rub in (a) ~ 2. an after-shave; body; hand; skin; suntan ~

lots *n.* to cast, draw ~

lottery *n.* 1. to hold a ~ 2. to win a ~ 3. a daily; weekly ~ 4. a national; state ~

loud *adv.* to count out ~

loudspeaker *n.* (to speak) over, through a ~

lounge I *n.* 1. a cocktail ~ 2. a sun ~ (BE; AE has *sun porch*) 3. a transit ~ (at an airport) 4. a VIP ~ (at an airport)

lounge II *v.* (P; intr.) she enjoys ~ing around the pool

lour see **lower I**

louse *n.* a plant; wood ~

lousy *adj.* (slang) ~ to + inf. (it's ~ to be without

work = it's ~ being without work)

lout *n.* a drunken; stupid ~

love I *n.* ["deep affection"] 1. to inspire ~ for 2. to declare, express one's ~ for smb. 3. blind; calf (esp. BE); puppy; cupboard (BE); deep, profound, sincere, true; platonic; romantic; undying; unrequited ~ 4. ~ for, of (~ for one's country; to have no ~ for smb.) 5. for, out of ~ (to do smt. for ~) 6. to be in ~ (with smb.) (to be head over heels in ~ with smb.; deeply/hopelessly/madly in ~) 7. to fall in; out of ~ (with smb.) 8. (misc.) ~ at first sight ["expression of deep affection"] 9. to give; send one's ~ (give them our ~) ["sexual activity"] 10. to make ~ (to, with) ("to have intercourse") 11. free ~

love II *v.* 1. to ~ blindly; dearly; deeply; madly; passionately; really, very much (I would dearly ~ to see them again) 2. (E) she ~s to swim 3. (G) she ~s swimming 4. (N; used with an adjective) she ~s her steak rare 5. (misc.) (colloq.) I ~ it when you smile; I'd ~ (for; AE) you to come over and see our new TV = what I'd ~ is for you to come over and see our new TV

lovely *adj.* (colloq.) 1. ~ to + inf. (it was ~ of you to arrange this party; it was ~ to see you again = it was ~ seeing you again) 2. ~ that + clause (it was ~ that you could come)

lover *n.* 1. to take a ~ 2. to jilt, reject a ~ 3. a great; lousy (colloq.) ~ 4. (misc.) an art; music; nature ~

low I *adj.* ["lacking"] (cannot stand alone) ~ in, on (she is ~ in funds; they were ~ on ammunition)

low II *n.* 1. to hit, reach an all-time ~ 2. an all-time; new ~

lowdown *n.* to get; have the ~ on smb.

lower I /lau-/ *v.* (D; intr.) ("to frown") to ~ at

lower II /lou-/ *v.* 1. (D; tr.) to ~ by (he ~ed the bar by ten inches) 2. (D; tr.) to ~ to (they ~ed supplies to the stranded miners; she ~ed her voice to a whisper; they ~ed the flag to half-mast)

low profile *n.* to keep, maintain a ~

loyal *adj.* 1. steadfastly ~ 2. ~ to

loyalty *n.* 1. to command, inspire ~ 2. to demonstrate, show ~ 3. to pledge, swear ~ 4. blind; deeprooted, steadfast, strong, unquestioned, unshakable, unswerving ~ 5. party ~ 6. divided ~ties 7. ~ to (unswerving ~ to one's friends)

lozenge *n.* a cough; fruit; throat ~

luck *n.* ["success"] ["good fortune"] 1. to bring ~ 2. to try one's ~ (at smt.) 3. to press, push one's ~ 4. pure, sheer ~ 5. to wish smb. ~ 6. beginner's; dumb ~ 7. smb.'s ~ holds; improves, turns; runs out 8. a bit, stroke of ~ 9. ~ at, in, with (~ at gambling) 10. the ~ to + inf. (she had the good ~ to hold the winning ticket; it was pure ~ to find him = it was pure ~ finding him) 11. ~ that + clause (it was sheer ~ that we met) 12. in; with ~ (you are in ~ to find them at home) 13. down on one's ~; out of ~ ["fate"] ["chance"] 14. to trust to ~ 15. to try one's ~ (at smt.) 16. bad, hard, tough ~ 17. good; pure, sheer ~ (we had bad ~) 18. the ~ to + inf. (we had the bad ~ to get there at the wrong time) 19. ~ that + clause (it was bad ~ that he broke his leg) 20. (misc.) she had a run of bad ~

lucky adj. 1. ~ at, in, with (~ at cards; ~ in love) 2. ~ for (that was ~ for you) 3. ~ to + inf. (you are ~ to be alive) 4. ~ that + clause (it's ~ that we got here early)

ludicrous adj. 1. ~ to + inf. (it's ~ to dress like that) 2. ~ that + clause (it's ~ that we have to show our pass each time)

lug v. (P; tr.) she ~ged the boxes into the other room; we will have to ~ the equipment upstairs

luggage n. 1. to check, register (esp. BE) one's ~ 2. (esp. AE) to check one's ~ through (to the final destination) 3. to claim one's ~ 4. carry-on, hand ~ 5. personalized ~ 6. unclaimed ~ 7. a piece of ~

lukewarm adj. ["halfhearted"] 1. ~ about, to (~ about a proposal; ~ to an idea) ["tepid"] 2. ~ to (~ to the touch)

lull I n. 1. a momentary, temporary ~ 2. a ~ in (a momentary ~ in the fighting)

lull II v. 1. (d; tr.) to ~ into (to ~ smb. into a false sense of security) 2. (d; tr.) to ~ to (to ~ a child to sleep)

lullaby n. to hum; sing a ~ to

lumbar puncture n. to do, perform a ~

lumber I n. (AE) green; seasoned ~ (CE has *timber*)

lumber II v. (P; intr.) the bear ~ed through the forest

lumber III v. (colloq.) (BE) (D; tr.) ("to burden") to ~ with (I've been ~ed with all their problems)

lump n. 1. to bring a ~ to one's throat 2. the doctor discovered a ~ in her breast

lump together v. (D; tr.) to ~ with (they ~ed all of the workers together with the managers)

lumps n. (colloq.) ["punishment"] to take one's ~

lunacy n. 1. sheer ~ 2. ~ to + inf. (it was ~ to climb that mountain)

lunatic n. a ~ to + inf. (he was a ~ to try that)

lunch I n. 1. to eat (esp. AE), have ~ 2. a brown-bag (AE); business, working; light; school; set (esp. BE) ~ 3. a box; picnic ~ 4. at ~ (they were all at ~) 5. for ~ (we had a salad for ~)

lunch II v. (D; intr.) to ~ on

lunchtime n. at ~ (we'll meet at ~)

lung n. 1. an iron ~ 2. congested ~s 3. a collapsed ~ 4. (misc.) they were screaming at the top of their ~s

lunge I n. 1. to make a ~ 2. a ~ at, for, towards

lunge II v. (D; intr.) to ~ at, for, towards

lurch I n. ["sudden movement"] to give a ~ (the stricken ship gave a ~)

lurch II v. (P; intr.) he ~ed towards me

lurch III n. ["vulnerable position"] in the ~ (to leave smb. in the ~)

lure v. (P; tr.) to ~ smb. into a trap; he was ~d to his death

lure away v. (D; tr.) to ~ from; to (she was ~d away from her comfortable rural home to the big city)

lurk v. (P; intr.) to ~ in the shadows

lust I n. 1. to arouse, rouse ~ 2. to feel ~ 3. to gratify, satisfy one's ~ 4. blood; insatiable, unquenchable; unbridled ~ 5. ~ for (~ for power)

lust II v. (d; intr.) to ~ after, for

luster, lustre n. ["glory"] 1. to add ~ to 2. to take on a new ~

luxuriate v. (D; intr.) to ~ in (to ~ in newly acquired wealth)

luxury n. 1. to enjoy (a) ~ (to enjoy the ~ of a hot bath) 2. to afford a ~ (can we afford the ~ of a second car?) 3. pure, sheer; unaccustomed ~ 4. ~ to + inf. (it was sheer ~ to relax on the beach = it was sheer ~ relaxing on the beach) 5. in ~ (they lived in ~; to wallow in ~) 6. (misc.) in the lap of ~

lyre n. to play the ~

lyrical adj. ~ about, over (to wax ~ about the scenery)

M

mace *n.* ["staff used as a symbol of authority"] a ceremonial ~

machete *n.* to brandish, wield a ~

machine *n.* 1. to operate, run, use, work a ~ 2. to shut down a ~ 3. an adding, calculating ~ 4. an answering; video-game ~ 5. a cash, money access (AE); cigarette; slot (BE), vending ~ 6. a composing, linotype, typesetting; copy, copying, duplicating; fax ~ 7. a heart-lung; X-ray ~ 8. an earth-moving; milking; milling; sanding; sewing; threshing; washing ~ 9. a voting ~ 10. a mincing ~ (BE; AE has *meat grinder*) 11. a fruit (BE), slot (AE); pinball ~ (to play a pinball ~) (BE also has *pintable*) 12. a party; political ~ 13. a ~ functions, runs; breaks down

machine gun *n.* 1. to fire, operate a ~ 2. a heavy; light; medium ~ 3. an air-cooled; water-cooled ~ 4. a ~ jams

machine-gun nest *n.* to clean out, wipe out a ~

machinery *n.* ["machines"] 1. to install; operate, run ~ 2. to maintain; repair ~ 3. farm; heavy ~ ["apparatus"] 4. administrative; law-enforcement; propaganda ~ 5. ~ for (~ for negotiations)

mad *adj.* ["infatuated"] (colloq.) 1. (cannot stand alone) ~ about (they are ~ about each other) ["angry"] (colloq.) 2. hopping ~ 3. to get ~ 4. ~ at (she's ~ at him; to get ~ at smb.) ["insane"] 5. stark raving ~ 6. to go ~ 7. to drive smb. ~ 8. ~ with (~ with pain) 9. ~ to + inf. (he was ~ to try it)

maddening *adj.* 1. ~ to + inf. (it's ~ to have to wait here) 2. ~ that + clause (it's ~ that they never answer the telephone)

made *adj.* (cannot stand alone) ~ from, of, out of; with

USAGE NOTE: Compare these examples, which illustrate general tendencies—1. *a stew can be made with vegetables* (vegetables are not the only ingredient). 2. *a stew can be made of/out of vegetables; a chair can be made of/out of wood; shoes are usually made of/out of leather* (only one major substance or ingredient is used). 3. *synthetic rubber can be made from petroleum; paper can be made from wood* (the basic substance has been greatly changed). (see **make II**)

made-to-order *adj.* ~ for

madness *n.* 1. sheer, utter ~ 2. ~ to + inf. (it was sheer ~ to do it)

magazine *n.* ["supply depot"] 1. a powder ~ ["journal"] 2. an alumni (esp. AE); fashion; glossy (esp. BE); illustrated; popular ~

maggots *n.* crawling with ~

magic *n.* 1. to perform; work ~ (on) 2. black; white

~ 3. pure, sheer ~ 4. by ~ (the medicine worked as if by ~)

magistrate *n.* a police (esp. AE); stipendiary (BE) ~

magnanimity *n.* 1. to display, show ~ towards 2. great ~

magnanimous *adj.* 1. ~ towards 2. ~ to + inf. (it was ~ of you to make the offer)

magnate *n.* a coal; industrial; shipping; steel; tobacco ~

magnet *n.* a ~ attracts iron

magnetism *n.* animal; personal; physical; sheer ~

magnitude *n.* 1. considerable, great ~ 2. of a certain ~ (of considerable ~)

magpie *n.* ~s chatter

maid *n.* ["female servant"] a chambermaid; housemaid; kitchen ~; lady's ~; parlormaid

mail I *n.* (esp. AE; BE usu. has *post* for 1-5, 8-9) ["letters"] ["postal system"] 1. to address; send out (the) ~ 2. to deliver the ~ 3. to forward; sort (the) ~ 4. incoming; outgoing; return ~ 5. airmail; certified; domestic; express; first-class; foreign; franked; registered; second-class; special-delivery; surface; third-class ~ 6. fan; hate; junk ~ 7. (esp. AE) a piece of ~ 8. by return ~ (BE has *by return of post*) 9. in the ~ (our letters crossed in the ~) 10. (misc.) electronic ~, E-mail; voice ~

mail II *v.* (esp. AE; BE usu. has *post*) 1. (A) she ~ed the package to me; or: she ~ed me the package 2. (D; tr.) to ~ from; to (the letter was ~ed from Oregon to Pennsylvania) (for BE see **post II**)

mail III *n.* ["armor"] chain ~

main *n.* ["main pipe, duct"] 1. an electric; gas; sewer; water ~ 2. the water ~ burst

mainland *n.* 1. from; to the ~ 2. on the ~

mainstream *n.* 1. in the ~ (of politics) 2. outside the ~

maintain *v.* (L) she ~s that the accusation is groundless

maintenance *n.* 1. preventive; routine ~ 2. building; health; road ~

majesty *n.* ["sovereign"] 1. Her; His; Your Majesty; Their Majesties ["grandeur"] 2. in all its ~

major I *n.* ["academic specialization"] (AE) 1. to give, offer a ~ (our department gives a literature ~) 2. a ~ in (our department offers a ~ in literature) ["student who is specializing"] (AE) 3. a ~ in (she is a ~ in English; or: she is an English ~) ["officer"] 4. a ~ commands a battalion

major II *v.* (AE) (d; intr.) ("to specialize") to ~ in (to ~ in Russian) (BE has *to read Russian*)

majority *n.* ["number of votes greater than half"] (CE); ["greater number of votes"] (BE) 1. to get, receive a ~ 2. to have, hold a ~ (the Democrats have a slim ~ in the House) 3. a clear; great; large; overwhelming, vast ~ 4. a bare, narrow, slender, slim, small ~ 5. an absolute ~ (BE; AE has *majority*) 6. a (relative) ~ (BE; AE has *plurality*) 7. a simple; two-thirds; working ~ 8. by a ~ (to win by an overwhelming ~) 9. (misc.) the silent ~ (i.e., those who have moderate or conservative views but do not voice them); in a ~ (in the ~ of cases) ["full legal age"] 10. to attain, reach one's ~

USAGE NOTE: Compare the verbs in the following constructions—the majority of the (two hundred) votes were for peace; a majority of two hundred votes was enough to win.

make I *n.* (colloq.) ["search for gain or sexual favors"] on the ~ (he's always on the ~)

make II *v.* 1. (A) ("to propose") she made an offer to us; or: she made us an offer 2. (C) ("to prepare") ~ an omelet for me; or: ~ me an omelet 3. (d; intr.) to ~ for ("to head for") (she made for the exit; the ship made for the open sea) 4. (d; intr.) to ~ for ("to lead to") (willingness to compromise ~s for success in negotiations) 5. (D; tr.) ("to provide") to ~ for (to ~ room for smb.) 6. (D; tr.) ("to create") to ~ from, of, out of (to ~ butter from cream; she made a table out of wood; tires can be made from/of/out of synthetic rubber) 7. (d; tr.) ("to transform") to ~ into (to ~ a novel into a film; the experience made her into a skeptic) 8. (slang) (AE) (d; intr.) to ~ like ("to imitate") (to ~ like a clown) 9. (d; tr.) to ~ of ("to interpret") (what do you ~ of their offer?) 10. (d; tr.) ("to create") to ~ of, out of (to ~ a fool of smb.; the army made a man out of him; she made a good husband out of him) 11. (D; tr.) ("to create") to ~ with (you ~ a stew with meat and vegetables) 12. (I) ("to cause"); ("to force") she made the children clean their room; we made them wait; the police could not ~ him talk; your problems ~ mine seem unimportant 13. (N; used with an adjective, noun, past participle) ("to cause to become") the news made us happy; the rough sea made them seasick; we made our position clear; he made me his deputy; she could not ~ herself understood 14. (S; used with nouns) ("to prove to be") she made a good deputy 15. (misc.) (AE; colloq.) he finally made colonel ("he was finally promoted to the rank of colonel"); the story made all the papers; we made the station just in time; we made it to the party on time; the ship barely made it to port; she made it to the top; to ~ good one's escape

USAGE NOTE: When pattern I is put into the passive, *to* is inserted—they were made to wait. (see the Usage Note for **made**)

make away see **make off**

make believe *v.* (L) let's ~ that we are on a space ship

make do *v.* (D; intr.) to ~ with ("to manage with") (we'll have to ~ with this stove; we'll have to ~ with this old car)

make off *v.* (d; intr.) to ~ with ("to steal and take away") (the thieves made off with the silverware)

make out *v.* 1. (colloq.) ("to have success") (D; intr.) to ~ with (how did you ~ with the new boss?) 2. (misc.) he ~s himself out to be very important; she is not so bad as she is made out to be

make over *v.* 1. (B) ("to transfer legally") she made the bonds over to me 2. (D; tr.) ("to create") to ~ from; into (she made the boy's jacket over from her father's coat; she took the old dress and made it over into a skirt)

maker *n.* 1. an auto ~; filmmaker; policymaker 2. (misc.) to meet one's ~ ("to die and go to heaven")

makeup *n.* ["cosmetics"] 1. to apply, put on; use ~ 2. to remove ~

make up *v.* 1. (D; refl., tr.) ("to change one's appearance") to ~ as (he made himself up as an old man) 2. (D; tr.) ("to create") to ~ into (she took the fabric and made it up into curtains) 3. (d; intr.) to ~ for ("to recoup") (to ~ for lost time) 4. (colloq.) (d; intr.) to ~ to ("to gain favor with") (you should try to ~ to your boss) 5. (D; intr.) ("to become reconciled") to ~ with (she made up with her sister) 6. (misc.) I couldn't take the children for a treat today, but I promised to ~ it up to them next week

making *n.* ["evolution"] 1. in the ~ (a revolution in the ~) ["creation"] 2. not of a person's own ~ (the problem is not of my ~)

makings *n.* ["potential"] to have the ~ of (she has all the ~ of a good orator)

maladjustment *n.* an emotional ~

malady *n.* (lit.) a fatal; serious; strange ~

malaise *n.* a general; spiritual ~

malaria *n.* 1. to come down with, develop ~ 2. to eradicate, stamp out ~

malarkey *n.* (slang) ["nonsense"] (just) plain; pure, sheer ~

malevolence *n.* 1. pure, sheer ~ 2. out of ~ (he did it out of sheer ~)

malformation *n.* a congenital ~

malice *n.* 1. to bear ~ towards 2. (legal) with ~ aforethought

malicious *adj.* ~ towards

mall *n.* 1. a pedestrian; shopping ~ 2. at a ~ (she works at a shopping ~)

malpractice *n.* legal; medical; professional ~

mammals *n.* the higher; lower ~

man *n.* 1. an average; fat; grown; handsome; middle-aged; old; short; tall; thin; ugly; wise; young ~ 2. Cro-Magnon; Heidelberg; Java; Neanderthal; Peking; Piltdown ~; primitive ~ 3. a divorced; family; married; single ~ 4. a betting, gambling; con, confidence; fancy (esp. BE); hatchet; hit (esp. AE); ladies'; marked; organization; party (pol.); professional; Renaissance; right-hand; self-made; straight; straw ~ (AE; BE has *man of straw*); yes-man 5. an anchorman; businessman; leading ~; liftman (BE); maintenance ~; newspaperman; rewrite; stunt ~; weatherman 6. a moving (AE), removal (BE) ~ 7. a second-story ~ (AE; CE has *cat burglar*) 8. (pol.) (AE) an advance ~ 9. enlisted men (AE; BE has *other ranks*) 10. a university ~ (BE; AE has *college graduate*) 11. a lollipop ~ (BE; CE has *crossing guard*) 12. a best ~ (at a wedding) 13. to a ~ ("everyone") 14. (misc.) he's a ~ of his word; ~ is mortal; (esp. BE) every ~ jack ("every man"); a dirty old ~ (pejor.) ("an immoral man"); a medicine ~; the ~ of the year; a ~ of letters; a ~ of action; a ~ of the world

manage v. 1. (D; intr.) ("to cope") to ~ on (they ~ on very little) 2. (colloq.) (D; intr.) ("to cope") to ~ with (we cannot ~ with our present income) 3. (D; intr.) ("to cope") to ~ without (we cannot ~ without a car) 4. (E) ("to succeed") she somehow ~d to see him

management n. 1. efficient; poor ~ 2. middle; senior, top ~ 3. under ~ (under new ~)

manager n. 1. an assistant; bank; branch; business; campaign; city; credit; general; hotel; office; sales; service; stage ~ 2. a baseball ~
USAGE NOTE: For other sports *coach* is used.

mandate I n. ["order"] 1. to seek; win a ~ 2. to have a ~ 3. to carry out a ~ 4. a clear ~ 5. a ~ to + inf. (we had a ~ to eliminate illiteracy) 6. under a ~ (to do smt.) ["assignment to administer an area"] 7. a ~ over 8. under (a) ~

mandate II v. (formal) 1. (H) the president is ~d to carry out the laws 2. (esp. AE) (L; subj.) the constitution ~s that the president carry out the laws

mandated adj. federally ~ (US)

mandatory adj. ~ to + inf. (it is ~ to pay all traffic fines within ten days)

mane n. a horse's; lion's ~

maneuver I manoeuvre n. 1. to carry out, conduct, execute a ~ 2. (mil.) to conduct, hold ~s 3. a brilliant, clever; military; political; tactical ~ 4. on ~s (they were on ~s for two weeks)

maneuver II manoeuvre v. 1. (d; intr.) to ~ for (to ~ for position) 2. (d; tr.) to ~ into (we ~ed them into a compromise) 3. (d; tr.) to ~ out of (the player was ~ed out of position)

mangle v. to ~ beyond recognition

manhole n. an open ~

manhood n. to reach ~

manhunt n. 1. to carry out, conduct; launch, organize a ~ 2. a ~ for

mania n. 1. to have a ~ 2. a ~ for

maniac n. a homicidal; raving ~

manicure n. 1. to give smb. a ~ 2. to get a ~

manifest n. 1. a plane's; ship's ~ 2. on a ~

manifestation n. a clear ~

manifesto n. 1. to draft, draw up; issue a ~ 2. an election (BE); party (esp. BE); political ~

manner n. 1. a charming; cheerful, lively; friendly; gentle, mild; gracious ~ 2. a courteous, polite; debonair; elegant, grand, polished, suave ~ 3. a casual, hit-or-miss, offhand, relaxed; intriguing ~ 4. a businesslike; dignified; forthcoming; matter-of-fact; professional; statesmanlike ~ 5. a stern, unsmiling ~ 6. an awkward; sheepish ~ 7. a cursory; flippant; slipshod, sloppy; supercilious ~ 8. an affected; cloying; ingratiating, servile, unctuous; pretentious; prim ~ 9. an abrupt, brusque; aggressive; arrogant, cavalier, imperious, overbearing; hostile ~ 10. a boorish; coarse, crude, rude, uncouth; obnoxious; rude; sullen, surly; taciturn ~ 11. bad; good ~s 12. table ~s 13. (a doctor's) bedside ~ 14. in a certain ~ (she was businesslike in her ~; in the grand ~; in an awkward ~; everything was done in a well organized ~) 15. (misc.) to the ~ born ("as if so from birth"); in a ~ of speaking ("as it were"); to mind one's ~s ("to behave properly")

manoeuvre (BE) see **maneuver**

mansion n. (US) a governor's ~

manslaughter n. 1. to commit ~ 2. involuntary; voluntary ~

mantle n. ["symbol of authority"] to assume; inherit; wear the ~ (of power)

manual n. an instruction; laboratory; owner's; teacher's ~

manufacturer n. an aircraft; automobile (AE), motorcar (BE); clothing; computer; drug; furniture; radio; shoe; television ~

manure n. 1. to spread ~ 2. a heap, pile of ~

manuscript n. 1. to edit; proofread; revise a ~ 2. to submit a ~ (for publication) 3. to accept; reject a ~ 4. an authentic; unpublished ~ 5. an illuminated ~ 6. (misc.) the original ~ dates back/goes back to the fifteenth century

many determiner, pronoun 1. a good, great ~ 2. ~ of (~ of them)
USAGE NOTE: The use of the preposition *of* is necessary when a pronoun follows. When a noun follows, the use of *of the* limits the meaning—we saw many students; we saw many of the students whom we had met earlier.

map n. 1. to draw; trace a ~ 2. to consult; read a ~ 3. a large-scale; small-scale ~ 4. a contour; dialect; military; Ordnance-Survey (GB); relief; road; street; strip; weather ~ 5. on a ~ (to find a village on a ~) 6. (misc.) to put a place on the ~ ("to make a place well-known"); to wipe smt. off the ~ ("to destroy smt.")

map out v. (d; tr.) to ~ for (to ~ a future for one's children)

marathon n. 1. to organize, stage a ~ 2. to run a ~ 3.

marry off

a dance ~

marauder *n.* a band of ~s

marble *n.* a slab of ~

marbles *n.* 1. to play ~ 2. a game of ~ 3. (misc.) (colloq.) to lose one's ~ ("to lose one's mind")

march I *n.* ["procession"] 1. to join; lead a ~ 2. a death; forced; hunger ~ 3. a peace ~ 4. a ~ from; into, to 5. on the ~ (science is on the ~) ["music that accompanies marching"] 6. to compose; play; strike up a ~ 7. a funeral; military; wedding ~ 8. a lively, rousing, stirring ~ ["misc."] 9. to steal a ~ on smb. ("to outwit smb.")

march II *v.* 1. (d; intr.) to ~ against (to ~ against the enemy) 2. (D; intr., tr.) to ~ from; to (the battalion ~ed from the barracks to the parade ground) 3. (d; intr., tr.) to ~ into (the troops ~ed into town) 4. (d; intr.) to ~ on, to, towards (to ~ on the next town) 5. (P; intr., tr.) to ~ along the road; to ~ the students out of the room

march down *v.* (d; intr., tr.) to ~ to (the teacher said that if we didn't behave, she would ~ us down to the principal's office)

marching orders *n.* ["notice of dismissal"] (colloq.) (BE) to give smb. her/his ~ (AE has *walking papers*)

march off *v.* (D; intr., tr.) to ~ to (they were ~ed off to prison)

march on *v.* (D; intr.) to ~ to (the troops ~ed on to the next town)

mare *n.* a brood, stock ~

margarine *n.* 1. to spread ~ 2. vegetable ~

margin *n.* 1. to adjust; set a ~ (when typing) 2. to justify a ~ (in setting type, in word processing) 3. a close, narrow, slender, slim, small ~ 4. a comfortable, decisive, handsome, large, wide; safe ~ 5. by a ~ (they won by a slim ~) 6. in, on a ~ (to make notes in the ~s) 7. (misc.) a ~ of error; a ~ of safety; a profit ~

marihuana, marijuana *n.* 1. to grow ~ 2. to smoke ~

marina *n.* a municipal, public ~

marine *n.* a mercantile (BE), merchant (AE) ~

marionette *n.* to manipulate a ~

mark I *n.* ["sign, symbol"] 1. to make one's ~ ("to make a cross in place of a signature") 2. an accent, stress; diacritical; exclamation (BE; AE has *exclamation point*); punctuation; question; quotation ~ 3. (mil.) a hash ~ 4. a laundry ~ ["impression, imprint"] 5. to leave, make one's ~ (they will leave their ~ on history) 6. a distinguishing; high-water; indelible ~ ["target"] 7. to find, hit the ~ (the bullet found its ~) 8. to miss; overshoot the ~ 9. to fall short of the ~ 10. off the ~, wide of the ~ ["skin blemish"] 11. a strawberry ~ (esp. BE; CE has *birthmark*) ["victim"] 12. an easy ~ ["starting line of a race"] 13. on your ~s! ["misc."] 14. to toe the ~ ("to adhere to the rules"); to bear the ~ of Cain;

the actress won high ~s for her performance (see also **grade I** 1-4)

mark II *v.* 1. (D; tr.) to ~ as (these items were ~ed as acceptable) 2. (d; tr.) to ~ for (~ed for death) 3. (K) this birthday ~s his coming of age 4. (N; used with an adjective) she ~ed the documents secret

mark down *v.* (D; tr.) to ~ from; to (the instructor ~ed her down from A to B)

marker *n.* ["IOU"] (colloq.) (AE) to call in a ~

market *n.* ["store, shop"] ["group of shops or stalls"] 1. a fish; food ~; hypermarket (BE); meat ~; supermarket 2. a farmers'; flea; open-air ~ 3. at a ~ (to shop at the ~) ["place where trade is conducted"] 4. to open a new ~ 5. a commodity; money; stock ~ 6. a free, open; overseas; spot ~ 7. on; onto a ~ (to buy oil on the spot ~; to put a new product on the ~; a new computer has just come out on the ~) ["stock market"] 8. to play the ~("to speculate") 9. to depress the ~ 10. a bear ("falling"); bull ("rising") ~ 11. the ~ is active; sluggish 12. the ~ is firm, steady; rising; up 13. the ~ is depressed; down; falling 14. the ~ rallies; slumps 15. the ~ closes strong; weak 16. the ~ opens strong; weak ["supply of goods, services"] 17. to capture, corner, monopolize a ~ 18. to flood, glut a ~ 19. the housing; labor ~ 20. a buyer's; seller's ~ ["demand"] 21. to create a ~ 22. to study the ~ 23. to depress a ~ 24. a ~ for (there is no ~ for large cars) 25. in the ~ for (we're in the ~ for a new house) 26. a drug on the ~ ("smt. for which there is little demand") ["trade"] 27. the bond; commodities; securities; stock; used-car; wheat ~

marketplace *n.* in the ~

marksman, markswoman *n.* a crack, expert, skilled ~

markup *n.* a ~ on (their ~ on merchandise was small)

marmalade *n.* orange ~

marriage *n.* 1. to enter into a ~ 2. to announce a ~ 3. to consummate a ~ 4. to arrange a ~ 5. to solemnize a ~ 6. to propose ~ 7. to annul a ~ 8. to break up, dissolve a ~ 9. a good, happy, stable ~ 10. a bad, unhappy; broken ~ 11. an arranged; civil; common-law; communal; group; morganatic; open; proxy; secret; trial ~ 12. an interfaith; interracial; mixed ~ 13. a ~ breaks up, collapses, dissolves 14. a ~ of convenience 15. a ~ into (a family) 16. a ~ to (smb.) 17. (misc.) to give (one's child) in ~

marriage ceremony *n.* to perform a ~

married *adj.* 1. happily ~ 2. to get ~ (to)

marrow *n.* 1. bone ~ 2. vegetable ~ (BE; AE has *squash*)

marry *v.* 1. (D; intr.) to ~ for (to ~ for love) 2. (d; intr.) to ~ into (to ~ into a good family) 3. see **marry off**

marry off *v.* (D; tr.) to ~ to

marshal *n*. an air; field ~

marshmallow *n*. to roast, toast ~s

martial law *n*. 1. to declare, impose, invoke ~ 2. to rescind; suspend ~ 3. under ~ (the area was placed under ~)

martini *n*. 1. to fix (esp. AE), make, mix a ~ 2. a dry ~

martyr *n*. 1. to make a ~ (of smb.) 2. a ~ to (a ~ to tyranny) 3. (misc.) to burn a ~ at the stake; to play the ~

martyrdom *n*. to suffer ~

marvel I *n*. 1. to achieve, do, work ~s 2. a ~ to 3. a ~ that + clause (it's a ~ to me that he received the award)

marvel II *v*. 1. (d; intr.) to ~ at (to ~ at smb.'s skill) 2. (L) (esp. BE) I ~ that she arrived on time

marvelous, marvellous *adj*. 1. absolutely, quite (esp. BE) ~ 2. ~ to + inf. (it's ~ to have a day off = it's ~ having a day off; it was ~ of you to help) 3. ~ that + clause (it's ~ that we could see each other again)

mascara *n*. 1. to apply, put on ~ 2. to remove, wipe off ~

mask *n*. 1. to put on; wear a ~ 2. to take off a ~ 3. a death; gas; oxygen; ski; stocking; surgical ~

masquerade *v*. (D; intr.) to ~ as (to ~ as a police-man)

mass I *n*. ["body of matter"] 1. a shapeless; sticky ~ 2. a land ~ 3. a critical ~ 4. a dense ~ (of smoke) 5. (med.) a fixed; hard; irregular; movable; nodular; palpable ~

mass II *n*. ["celebration of the Eucharist"] 1. to celebrate, offer, say (a, the) ~ 2. to attend, go to, hear ~ 3. (a) high; low; nuptial; pontifical; requiem; solemn; votive ~ 4. a ~ for

massacre *n*. 1. to carry out, perpetrate a ~ 2. a brutal ~

massage *n*. 1. to give (smb.) a ~ 2. to get a ~ 3. a back; body; facial; therapeutic ~

mast *n*. 1. a tall ~ 2. (to fly) at half ~ 3. (misc.) (lit.) before the ~ ("at sea as a sailor")

master I *n*. 1. to find one's ~ ("to find one who is superior") 2. a question ~ (BE; AE has quizmaster) 3. (chess) a grand ~ 4. a past ~ 5. a ~ at, of (a ~ of deceit)

master II *v*. to ~ completely, thoroughly

masterpiece *n*. 1. to create a ~ 2. an enduring ~ 3. a literary ~

mastery *n*. 1. to demonstrate, display, show ~ 2. to achieve, acquire ~ 3. (a) complete; thorough ~ 4. ~ of; over (~ of one's subject; ~ over other people)

mat *n*. 1. to weave a ~ 2. a bath; exercise; place; prayer; welcome ~

match I *n*. ["slender piece of wood that catches fire when struck"] 1. to light, strike a ~ 2. to light, put, set a ~ to 3. a safety ~ 4. a book; box of ~es 5. (misc.) children should not play with ~es

match II *n*. ["marriage"] ["marriage partner"] 1. to make a ~ 2. a good ~ 3. a ~ for ["contest"] 4. to promote, stage a ~ 5. a championship; crucial; play-off; return; test (BE) ("international cricket or rugby") ~ 6. a football ~ (esp. BE; AE has *football game*) 7. a boxing; chess; cricket; fencing; golf; hockey; polo; tennis; wrestling ~ 8. a ~ between; with (a wrestling ~ between two strong competitors) ["equal competitor"] 9. to meet one's ~ 10. no ~ for (he proved to be no ~ for me; I was no ~ for her) 11. smb.'s ~ in (she was more than my ~ in ability) ["pair"] 12. a good; perfect ~ 13. a ~ for

USAGE NOTE: When two teams compete before spectators, BE usu. has *match* (a football match); AE usu. has *game* (a football game). However, when the team game is of North American origin, BE often uses *game* too (a basketball game). A *chess match* is CE.

match III *v*. 1. (D; tr.) to ~ against, with ("to pit against") (she was ~ed against a formidable opponent) 2. (D; tr.) ("to equal") to ~ in (no one can ~ him in speed and agility) 3. (D; tr.) to ~ with ("to find the equivalent of") (she wants to ~ this candlestick with a similar one)

matched *adj*. ideally ~

matchmaker *n*. a professional ~

match up *v*. (D; intr.) to ~ to, with (he doesn't ~ to his opponent)

mate I *n*. ["petty officer"] (naval) 1. a boatswain's; first; machinist's ~ ["junior partner"] 2. (BE) a plumber's ~ 3. (US; pol.) smb.'s running ~

mate II *v*. (D; intr., tr.) to ~ with (zebras don't ~ with donkeys; to ~ a donkey with a mare)

material I *adj*. ~ to (this evidence is ~ to our case)

material II *n*. ["data"] 1. to collect, gather ~ 2. source ~ 3. ~ about, on (to gather ~ about the case) 4. ~ for (to gather ~ for a dictionary) ["matter"] 5. building ~ 6. radioactive; raw; synthetic ~ 7. promotional; reading; reference ~ 8. writing ~s 9. packing ~ ["cloth"] 10. a piece, swatch of ~

materialism *n*. dialectical; historical ~

materialize *v*. (d; intr.) to ~ out of (a figure ~d out of the shadows)

mathematics *n*. applied; elementary; higher; pure ~

matrimony *n*. 1. holy ~ (they were united in holy ~) 2. the state of ~

matron *n*. 1. a dignified ~ 2. a ~ of honor (at a wedding)

matter I *n*. ["affair"] 1. to deal with, pursue, take up a ~ 2. to discuss a ~ 3. to arrange a ~ 4. to clear up, settle, straighten out a ~ 5. to complicate; simplify a ~ 6. to give a ~ (attention, thought) (we have given this ~ considerable thought) 7. to not mince ~s ("to express oneself candidly") 8. to drop a ~; to let a ~ drop 9. a business; personal, private ~ 10. a complex, complicated; delicate ~ 11. an important, pressing, serious, weighty ~ 12. a petty, trifling, trivial; simple ~ 13. no easy, no laughing ~ (it's no easy ~ to find a house in this city = it's no easy ~ finding a house in this city; being accused of assault is no laughing ~) 14. ~s came to a head 15. a ~ for (a ~ for conjecture; a ~ for speculation) 16. a ~ of (a ~ of grave importance) 17. in ~s of (in ~s of finance) 18. (misc.) as a ~ of fact ("really"); to take ~s into one's own hands; the fact of the ~ is that...; a ~ of record (legal); for that ~ ("concerning that"); a ~ of a few minutes; a ~ of personal opinion; a ~ of some urgency; a ~ of life and death; the crux/heart of the ~; no ~ how she tries, she gets no credit; you look so sad — what's the ~? you haven't done this properly — what's the ~ with you? ["material"] ["substance"] 19. printed; reading; subject ~ 20. gaseous; liquid; organic; solid; vegetable ~ 21. gray ~ ("brains") 22. the front ~ (of a book)

matter II v. 1. (D; intr.) to ~ to (her financial status doesn't ~ to us) 2. (L; to) it doesn't ~ (to us) that we are not rich 3. (Q; to) it does not ~ where I work

mattress n. 1. a firm; soft ~ 2. a double, full; king-size; queen-size; single, twin ~ 3. an air ~

mature adj. 1. emotionally; mentally; physically ~ 2. ~ for (she is ~ for her age)

maturity n. 1. to reach ~ 2. full ~

maxim n. a ~ that + clause (it is a valid ~ that competition increases productivity)

maximum n. 1. to set a ~ 2. at a ~ (excitement was at its ~)

may v. 1. (F) she ~ still show up 2. (misc.) we ~ as well give in; ~ we wish you a Happy New Year! (see also **might II**)

mayhem n. to commit ~

meadow n. in a ~

meal I n. ["repast"] 1. to cook, fix (esp. AE; colloq.), prepare a ~ 2. to put together, slap together, whip together a ~ 3. to eat, have; enjoy a ~ 4. to make a ~ of (to make a ~ of soup) 5. to order; serve a ~ 6. to skip a ~ 7. a big, heavy; decent, hearty, solid, square; hot; sumptuous ~ (to have a square ~) 8. a light, small; simple; skimpy ~ 9. a main ~ (the main ~ of the day) ["misc."] 10. (BE; colloq.) to make a ~ of smt. ("to behave as if smt. easy were difficult")

meal II n. ["ground seeds"] Indian ~ (BE; CE has *cornmeal*)

mean I adj. 1. ~ about (he was very ~about the loan) 2. ~ with (esp. BE) 3. ~ to (he's ~ to everyone) 4. ~ to + inf. (it was ~ of her to say that)

mean II n. ["mathematical value"] 1. to find a ~ 2. an arithmetic; harmonic ~ ["middle point"] 3. a golden ~

mean III v. 1. (A; usu. used without *to*) she meant them no harm 2. (d; tr.) to ~ as (it was meant as a favor) 3. (d; tr.) to ~ for (his remark was meant for

you) 4. (D; tr.) to ~ to (her words meant nothing to me) 5. (E) I meant to write 6. (H) we never meant you to go without us 7. (L) she really meant that she wanted us to leave 8. (S) *Hund* ~s "dog"; waiting longer ~s driving after dark 9. (misc.) they never knew what it meant to be hungry; she ~s what she says

meander v. (P; intr.) the brook ~s through the valley

meaning n. 1. to distort, twist; misconstrue a ~ 2. an accepted; basic; clear; connotative; double, equivocal; figurative; hidden, obscure; literal ~ 3. grammatical; lexical; referential ~ 4. a shade of ~ 5. in a ~ (in the accepted ~ of the word)

meaningful adj. ~ to (the ceremony was very ~ to all those who came)

meaningless adj. ~ to (the lecture was ~ to all those who did not understand the language)

meanness n. 1. ~ to 2. out of ~ (she did it out of ~)

means n. ["method"] 1. fair; foul ~ 2. an effective ~ 3. by any ~ 4. by ~ of (the roof is held in place by ~ of steel cables) 5. (misc.) the end does not justify the ~; a ~ to an end ["resources"] ["wealth"] 6. independent; moderate ~ 7. the ~ to + inf. (do they have the ~ to buy such a large house?) 8. according to, within one's ~ (to live within one's ~) 9. beyond one's ~ (to live beyond one's ~) 10. of ~ (a person of moderate ~) ["misc."] 11. by all ~ ("yes, of course"); by no ~ ("in no way")

meant adj. (cannot stand alone) ["destined"] 1. ~ for (they were ~ for each other) ["intended"] 2. ~ to + inf. (her remark was ~ to be a compliment) ["supposed"] (colloq.) (BE) 3. ~ to + inf. (Brighton is ~ to be lovely in summer)

meantime, meanwhile n. in the ~

measles n. 1. to catch, come down with, get (the) ~ 2. an epidemic; outbreak of ~ 3. a case of ~

measure I n. 1. a cubic; dry; liquid; metric; square ~ 2. a tape ~ 3. in a certain ~ (in large ~) 4. (misc.) for good ~ ("as smt. extra"); made to ~ ("custom-made"); to take smb.'s ~ ("to evaluate smb.") (see also **measures**)

measure II v. 1. (d; tr.) to ~ against (to ~ one's accomplishments against smb. else's) 2. (D; tr.) to ~ for (to ~ smb. for new shoes) 3. (P; intr.) the room ~s twenty feet by ten

measurement n. 1. to take a ~; to take smb.'s ~s 2. exact ~s 3. a metric ~ 4. a scientific ~ 5. chest; waist ~s

measures n. 1. to carry out, take ~ 2. farsighted; interim; stopgap, temporary ~ 3. corrective; precautionary, preventive, prophylactic; safety, security ~ 4. emergency; extraordinary ~ 5. draconian; drastic, harsh, stern, stringent, tough; extreme, radical ~ 6. coercive; compulsory; punitive ~ 7. ~ to + inf. (we took ~ to insure their safety) 8. ~ against (to take ~ against smuggling)

measure up *v.* (D; intr.) to ~ to (he didn't ~ to his opponent)

meat *n.* 1. to barbecue; broil (AE), grill; cook; cure; fry; roast; sear; stew ~ 2. to carve, cut; slice ~ 3. dark; red; white ~ 4. fatty; lean ~ 5. raw; tender; tough ~ 6. halal; kosher ~ 7. canned (AE), tinned (BE); fresh; frozen ~ 8. boned; chopped (AE), ground (AE), minced (BE); soup ~ 9. ~ goes bad, spoils 10. a slice of ~

meat grinder *n.* (AE) to pass meat through a ~ (BE has *mincer*)

mecca *n.* 1. a tourist ~ 2. a ~ for (the mall was a ~ for shoppers)

mechanic *n.* an automobile (AE), motorcar (BE); master ~

mechanics *n.* celestial; fluid; quantum ~

mechanism *n.* 1. to activate, trigger a ~ 2. a defense; escape; fail-safe; survival ~

medal *n.* 1. to award, give a ~ 2. to earn, get, win a ~ 3. to strike ("make") a ~ 4. a bronze; gold; silver ~ (as a prize) 5. a ~ for (to earn a ~ for bravery)

meddle *v.* (D; intr.) to ~ in; with (don't ~ in their affairs)

media *n.* 1. the electronic; local; mass; national; news ~ 2. in the ~ (the elections were covered in the local ~)

mediate *v.* (D; intr.) to ~ between (to ~ between the warring parties)

mediation *n.* 1. to offer ~ 2. to go to ~ 3. ~ between

mediator *n.* 1. to appoint a ~ 2. a government ~ 3. a ~ between

Medicaid *n.* (US) on ~ (the family had to go on ~)

Medicare *n.* (US) on ~ (we will be on ~ next year)

medication *n.* 1. to take (a) ~ 2. to administer, dispense, give (a) ~ 3. to order; prescribe (a) ~ 4. to put smb. on ~ 5. to discontinue (a) ~ 6. to take smb. off ~ 7. (an) effective; mild; potent, strong ~ 8. (an) intramuscular; intravenous; oral; parenteral; topical ~ 9. to be on ~ for (she is now on ~ for high blood pressure)

medicine *n.* ["method, science of treating disease"] 1. to practice ~ 2. to study ~ 3. aerospace, space; aviation; military; sports; tropical ~ 4. community, social; industrial, occupational; preventive ~ 5. family; internal; physical ~ 6. clinical; forensic, legal ~ 7. molecular; nuclear ~ 8. allopathic; ayurvedic; holistic; homeopathic; osteopathic ~ 9. alternative, complementary (BE), fringe (BE); folk; traditional ~ 10. defensive ~ 11. socialized (esp. AE) ~ 12. veterinary ~ ["remedy"] 13. to take (a) ~ (to take ~ for a cold) 14. to prescribe (a) ~ 15. a cough; nonprescription, over-the-counter; patent; proprietary ~ 16. strong ~ (also fig.) 17. ~ for ["punishment"] (colloq.) 18. to take one's ~ ("to accept one's punishment")

meditate *v.* 1. to ~ deeply 2. (D; intr.) to ~ on, upon

meditation *n.* 1. to go in for, practice ~ 2. transcen-

dental ~ 3. deep, profound ~ 4. (deep) in ~

medium *n.* ["middle degree"] 1. a happy ~ 2. a ~ between (a ~ between two extremes) ["system"] 3. a ~ of instruction ["means"] 4. by, through a ~ (to be transmitted through the ~ of air)

meet I *n.* (esp. AE) (sports) 1. to hold, organize a ~ 2. a dual; swim, swimming; track; track-and-field ~

meet II *v.* 1. (D; intr., tr.) to ~ for (we met them for dinner) 2. (d; intr.) to ~ with ("to encounter") (to ~ with approval; they met with an accident) 3. (esp. AE) (d; intr.) to ~ with ("to have a meeting with") (our negotiators will ~ with them tomorrow) 4. (misc.) to ~ smb. halfway ("to compromise with smb.") to ~ face to face; to ~ head-on

meeting *n.* 1. to call, convene; open a ~ 2. to attend a ~ 3. to arrange, organize, schedule a ~ 4. to have, hold a ~ 5. to chair, conduct, preside over a ~ 6. to adjourn; break up; close a ~ (they close their ~s with a prayer) 7. to call off, cancel; postpone; reschedule a ~ 8. to disrupt a ~ (the protesters disrupted the ~ by shouting slogans) 9. a clandestine, secret; closed; emergency; mass; open; private; protest; public ~ 10. a board; business; cabinet; committee; departmental; faculty (esp. AE); prayer; revival; staff; town (US) ~ 11. an athletics ~ (BE; AE has *track meet*) 12. a race ~ (BE; AE has *racing card*) 13. a ~ between, of 14. at; in a ~ (I saw her at the ~; she's in a ~ and cannot be disturbed) 15. (misc.) to call a ~ to order; a chance ~

meet up *v.* (AE) (D; intr.) to ~ with

megaphone *n.* (to speak) through a ~

melody *n.* 1. to hum; play; sing a ~ 2. a haunting ~

melon *n.* 1. a juicy; ripe; tasty ~ 2. a honeydew ~; watermelon 3. a slice of ~

melt *v.* (d; intr.) to ~ into (to ~ into the crowd)

member *n.* 1. to recruit new ~s 2. an active; associate; card-carrying; charter (AE), founder (BE); full; honorary; life; paid-up; ranking; sustaining ~ 3. a corresponding ~ (of an academy) 4. (misc.) to admit new ~s into an organization

membership *n.* 1. to apply for ~ 2. to renew one's ~ 3. to grant ~ 4. to deny, refuse ~ (to smb.) 5. to drop, resign one's ~ 6. closed; open ~ 7. (an) agency, institutional; associate; full; honorary; individual; life; permanent; temporary ~ 8. a ~ lapses 9. ~ in (AE), of (BE) (~ in/of an organization)

membrane *n.* 1. mucous ~ 2. ~s rupture (her ~s ruptured too early in labor)

memo *n.* 1. to write out, write up a ~ 2. an interoffice; office ~ 3. a ~ from; to (see also **memorandum**)

memoirs *n.* to publish; write one's ~

memorandum *n.* 1. to draw up, prepare a ~ 2. to send around a ~ (in an office) 3. to initial a ~ 4. a confidential, secret; diplomatic; interoffice; official; private ~ 5. a ~ about, on 6. a ~ from; to

memorial *n.* 1. to build, erect, put up a ~ 2. to unveil a ~ 3. a war ~ 4. a ~ to

memory *n.* ["power of recalling"] 1. to jog, refresh smb.'s ~ 2. to commit smt. to ~ 3. to slip smb.'s ~ (the date has slipped my ~) 4. to lose one's ~ 5. a bad, poor; good; infallible; long; photographic; powerful; retentive; short ~ (my cousin has a long ~) 6. (med.) long-term; short-term; visual ~ 7. a ~ for (a good ~ for names) 8. (to speak) from ~ 9. (misc.) a lapse of ~ ["something recalled, recollection"] 10. to bring back, call up, conjure up, dredge up, evoke, stir up a ~ (the incident evoked painful ~ies) 11. to blot out, bury, suppress a ~ 12. bitter; bittersweet; dim, vague; enduring; fond, happy, pleasant; haunting, poignant; painful, sad, unpleasant ~ries ["collective remembrance"] 13. to honor, perpetuate, revere, venerate smb.'s ~ 14. a blessed, sacred ~ 15. in ~ of (to erect a monument in smb.'s ~) 16. in living ~ 17. of blessed, sacred ~ 18. (misc.) dedicated to smb.'s ~ ["capacity for storing information in a computer"] 19. (a) random-access; read-only; virtual ~

menace I *n.* 1. to constitute a ~ 2. a ~ to

menace II *v.* (D; tr.) to ~ with (to ~ smb. with reprisals)

mend *n.* on the ~ ("improving")

mending *n.* invisible ~

menopause *n.* to go through ~

mentality *n.* a siege ~

mental note *n.* to make a ~ (of smt.)

mention I *n.* 1. to make ~ of 2. to deserve ~ 3. honorable ~ (conferred in a contest for an accomplishment of merit that does not win a prize) 4. special ~ (her work deserves special ~ at this time) 5. at the ~ (at the very ~ of his name I shuddered)

mention II *v.* 1. (B) she ~ed the book to me 2. (D; tr.) to ~ as (she was ~ed as a possible candidate) 3. (K) he failed to ~ my being late twice last week 4. (L; to) they ~ed (to her) that they would bring a guest 5. (Q; to) she forgot to ~ where we should meet 6. (misc.) to ~ smb. by name

mentor *n.* a ~ to (who is the ~ to the young prince?)

menu *n.* ["bill of fare"] 1. to bring a ~ (the waiter brought the ~) 2. on a ~ (what's on the ~?) ["list of commands for a computer program"] 3. an edit; main; print ~

mercenary *n.* a foreign ~

merchandise *n.* 1. to buy, purchase; order ~ 2. to flog (BE, colloq.), hawk, sell ~ 3. to ship ~ 4. to carry (a line of) ~ 5. first-class, high-quality ~ 6. assorted; general ~ 7. defective, inferior, shoddy ~

merciful *adj.* 1. ~ to, towards 2. ~ + inf. (it was ~ of her to offer help)

merciless *adj.* ~ to; towards

mercy *n.* 1. to have ~ on 2. to show ~ to, towards 3.

to beg for, implore (smb.'s) ~ 4. to throw oneself on smb.'s ~ 5. divine; infinite ~; smb.'s tender ~cies (ironic) 6. at smb.'s ~ 7. (misc.) we turned him over to the tender ~cies of the student court

merge *v.* 1. to ~ gradually; imperceptibly 2. (D; intr., tr.) to ~ into (to ~ several small companies into one large one) 3. (D; intr., tr.) to ~ with (our bank ~d with theirs)

merger *n.* 1. to carry out, effect a ~ 2. a ~ between, of; with

merit *n.* 1. intrinsic ~ 2. relative ~s 3. according to, on (the basis of) ~ (to decide a case on its ~s) 4. of ~ (their case is of dubious ~)

merry-go-round *n.* 1. to ride (on) a ~ 2. to get on a ~ 3. to get off a ~

mesh *v.* (D; intr.) to ~ with (the gears ~ with each other)

mess I *n.* ["untidy condition"] (may be fig.) 1. to make a ~ (they made a ~ of the project) 2. to leave a ~ 3. to clean away, clean up, clear away, clear up, straighten out, straighten up, sweep out, sweep up a ~ 4. a complete, terrible, unsightly, utter ~ 5. in a ~ (to leave things in an utter ~) ["dining hall"] (mil.) 6. an enlisted (AE); officers' ~ 7. at, in a ~ (they always eat at the company ~)

mess II *v.* (colloq.) 1. (d; intr.) to ~ in (don't ~ in their affairs) 2. to ~ with (don't ~ with him)

mess about (BE) see **mess around**

message *n.* 1. to convey; relay; send, transmit a ~ 2. to deliver; leave a ~ 3. to get, receive a ~ 4. to intercept a ~ 5. to garble; scramble; unscramble a ~ 6. a clear; coded; cryptic, secret; garbled; urgent ~ 7. an E-mail ~ (she sent me an E-mail ~) 8. (on a computer) an error ~ 9. a ~ from; to (they received an urgent ~ from their partner) 10. a ~ to + inf. (we got a ~ to meet them at the restaurant) 11. a ~ that + clause (we received a ~ that we were to return at once) 12. in a ~ 13. (misc.) to get the ~ ("to grasp the situation"); a divine ~ (from God)

mess around *v.* (colloq.) (AE) (D; intr.) to ~ with

messenger *n.* to dispatch a ~

Messiah *n.* to await the ~

metabolism *n.* 1. to disturb, upset smb.'s ~ 2. basal ~

metal *n.* 1. to pour ~ 2. scrap ~ (to recycle scrap ~) 3. (a) base; ferrous; heavy; nonferrous; precious ~ 4. molten; sheet ~ 5. ~ corrodes, rusts

metamorphose *v.* (D; intr., tr.) to ~ into

metamorphosis *n.* 1. to undergo ~ 2. a ~ into

metaphor *n.* a mixed ~

mete out *v.* (B) to ~ justice to everyone

meter I metre *n.* ["verse rhythm"] ["arrangement of syllables"] 1. anapaestic, anapestic; dactylic; heroic; iambic; trochaic ~ ["unit of length"] 2. a cubic; square ~

meter II *n.* ["instrument for measuring"] 1. to read a ~ (she came to read the gas ~) 2. an electric;

exposure; gas; parking; postage; water ~ (she parked her car at a parking ~)

method n. 1. to apply, employ, use a ~ 2. to adopt; devise a ~ 3. to give up, scrap a ~ 4. an antiquated, obsolete; crude; devious; infallible, sure; modern, up-to-date; orthodox, traditional; refined, sophisticated; sound; unorthodox ~ 5. the case; deductive; empirical; inductive; scientific; Socratic ~ 6. unscrupulous (business) ~s 7. the audiovisual; direct, oral; grammar-translation ~ (of foreign language instruction); the tutorial ~ (of instruction) 8. teaching ~s 9. the rhythm ~ (of contraception) 10. a ~ for; in, to (a ~ for learning languages; there is a definite ~ in her manner of interrogation) 11. a ~ to + inf. (they devised a ~ to extract the ore)

methodical adj. ~ in (~ in one's work)

methodology n. (a) teaching ~

meticulous adj. ~ about, in (she is ~ in her dress)

mettle n. 1. to prove, show one's ~ 2. to put smb. on her/his ~

mezzanine n. (AE) ["first rows of a balcony in a theater"] in the ~

mickey, Mickey Finn n. (slang) ["a drink to which a strong drug or narcotic has been added"] to slip smb. a ~

microcosm n. in ~ (the whole nation in ~)

microphone n. 1. to hook up, set up a ~ 2. to speak into, through a ~ 3. a concealed, hidden; throat ~

microscope n. 1. a compound; electron; optical ~ 2. under a ~ (they examined the tissue under the ~)

midair n. in ~ (the planes collided in ~)

middle n. 1. in the ~ (in the ~ of the last century; in the ~ of the room) 2. (misc.) to split smt. down the ~

middle ground n. 1. to find (a) ~ 2. (a) ~ between (they could find no ~ between the opposing sides)

midmorning n. at ~

midnight n. at ~

midnight oil n. (colloq.) to burn the ~ ("to work or study late at night")

midpoint n. 1. to reach a ~ 2. at (the) ~

midriff n. 1. to expose one's ~ 2. a bare ~

midsemester n. (AE) at ~

midst n. in the ~ of

midstream n. 1. to reach ~ 2. in ~ (also fig.)

midway adj., adv. ~ between; through

midyear n. at ~

mien n. (lit.) an impassive; proud ~

miffed adj. (colloq.) 1. ~ at 2. ~ that + clause (she was ~ that he came so late)

might I n. 1. armed, military ~ 2. with all one's ~

might II v. 1. (F) I ~ do that 2. (misc.) we ~ as well go; they ~ have been here earlier (see also **may**)

migraine n. 1. a severe ~ 2. an attack of ~

migrate v. 1. (d; intr.) to ~ between 2. (D; intr.) to ~ from; to

migration n. 1. internal; mass ~ 2. annual ~ (the

annual ~ of birds) 3. ~ from; to

mildew n. ~ forms

mile n. 1. a land, statute; nautical, sea ~ 2. (misc.) to miss by a ~ ("to miss by a great deal")

mileage n. 1. to get ~ (I get good ~ with this small car; to get good ~ out of tires) 2. (misc.) the press got a lot of ~ out of the scandal

mileometer (BE) see **odometer**

milestone n. 1. to reach a ~ (usu. fig.) 2. (misc.) a ~ in human history

military n. 1. to call in the ~ 2. to serve in the ~

military service n. compulsory, universal; voluntary ~

militate v. (d; intr.) to ~ against (see the Usage Note for **mitigate**)

militia n. 1. to call out, mobilize the ~ 2. to serve in the ~ 3. a citizen ~

milk I n. 1. to boil ~ 2. to express ~ 3. curdled, sour; fresh ~ 4. attested (BE), certified; chocolate; condensed; evaporated; fermented; fortified; fresh; homogenized; long-life (BE); low-fat; non-fat; pasteurized; powdered; raw; reconstituted; skim (AE), skimmed (esp. BE); UHT (BE); whole ~ 5. cow's; ewe's; sheep's; goat's ~ 6. coconut ~ 7. ~ curdles, turns sour 8. a gallon; half-gallon; half-pint; pint; quart of ~ 9. a bottle; carton; cup; glass of ~

milk II v. 1. (D; tr.) to ~ from, of, out of (to ~ information from smb.; to ~ a company of thousands of dollars) 2. (N; used with an adjective) to ~ smt. dry

mill I n. ["machine for grinding"] 1. a coffee; pepper ~ ["factory"] 2. a flour; lumber; paper; rolling; steel; textile ~ ["place where results are achieved in a quick, routine way"] 3. a diploma; divorce; marriage; propaganda; rumor ~ ["misc."] 4. to go through the ~ ("to acquire experience under difficult conditions")

mill II v. (d; intr.) to ~ about, (a)round (to ~ around the entrance)

millstone n. ["heavy burden"] to have a ~ around one's neck

mime n. 1. to act a play in ~ 2. (misc.) the art of ~

mincemeat n. to make ~ of ("to defeat decisively")

mincer n. (BE) AE has meat grinder

mind I n. 1. to make up one's ~ 2. to make up one's ~ to do smt. 3. to broaden, cultivate, develop one's ~ 4. to speak one's ~ 5. to change one's ~ 6. to bear, have, keep (smt.) in ~ (please bear this request in ~; they had (it) in ~ to leave before dawn; keep in ~ that you have to leave early in the morning; bear in ~ that the deadline is tomorrow) 7. to bring, call smt. to ~ 8. to keep one's ~ on smt. 9. to put, set one's ~ to smt. 10. to ease one's ~, set one's ~ at ease 11. to take one's ~ off smt. 12. to cross, enter one's ~ (it never crossed my ~ to telephone; it crossed my ~ that the store would be closed at five o'clock; that possibility never entered my ~) 13. to come to ~ (some names come readily to ~) 14. to know one's own ~ 15. to slip one's ~ (it slipped my ~ that I had an appointment) 16. to lose one's ~ 17. an analytical, brilliant, disciplined, keen, logical, nimble, quick, sharp ~ 18. a clear, sound, uncluttered ~ 19. an inquiring, inquisitive, open, scientific ~ (to keep an open ~; to have an inquiring ~) 20. a closed, narrow, one-track ~ 21. a deranged, dirty, sick, twisted, unbalanced, unsound, warped ~ 22. in one's ~ (in one's right ~; in one's subconscious ~) 23. on one's ~ (what's on your ~?) 24. out of one's ~ (to go out of one's ~) 25. (misc.) I have half a ~ to vote for smb. else ("I may well vote for smb. else"); to give smb. a piece of one's ~ ("to state one's views to smb. very bluntly"); a meeting of (the) ~s; we were all of the same ~ ("we all had the same opinion"); a state of ~; it was a load off my ~ ("I felt relieved"); to be of sound ~; the noise drove me out of my ~

mind II *v.* 1. (G) I don't ~ waiting; would you ~ opening the window? 2. (J) would you ~ me opening the window? 3. (K) he didn't ~ their smoking; would you ~ my opening the window? 4. (L) do you ~ that he is late? 5. (Q) (esp. BE) ~ how you go! 6. (misc.) never ~ about that; would you ~ (it) if I opened the window?

minded *adj.* (BE) ~ to + inf. (the Prime Minister is ~ to ask for a vote of confidence)

mindful *adj.* (cannot stand alone) ~ of (~ of one's responsibilities)

mindless *adj.* ~ of (~ of any danger)

mind's eye *n.* in one's ~

mine I *n.* ["excavation from which minerals are taken"] 1. to open (up); operate, run, work a ~ 2. to close down a ~ 3. a coal; copper; diamond; gold; iron; lead; salt; silver; tin; zinc ~ 4. an abandoned; open-cast (BE), open-pit (AE), strip (AE) ~ 5. (misc.) the ~ was worked out ["explosive charge"] 6. to arm; lay a ~ 7. to hit, strike a ~ 8. to detonate, set off a ~ 9. to clear, remove, sweep ~s 10. to defuse; detect; disarm a ~ 11. a ~ blows up, explodes 12. an antipersonnel; antitank; contact; drifting, floating; land; magnetic; pressure; submarine ~

mine II *v.* (D; intr.) to ~ for (to ~ for coal)

minerals *n.* metallic; nonmetallic; rock ~

mingle *v.* (D; intr.) to ~ with

miniature *n.* in ~

minimal pair *n.* (ling.) to constitute, represent; produce a ~

minimum *n.* 1. a bare; irreducible ~ 2. at a ~

mining *n.* open-cast (BE), open-pit (AE), strip (AE); shaft ~

minister I *n.* 1. to accredit a ~ 2. a ~ plenipotentiary; a ~ without portfolio 3. a cabinet; chief; foreign; prime ~ 4. a ~ from; to

minister II *v.* (d; intr.) to ~ to (to ~ to smb.'s needs)

ministry *n.* ["organized religion"] 1. to enter the ~ 2. a lay ~ ["a government department"] (UK) 3. a defence; foreign; health ~, etc. (or: a ~ of defence; foreign affairs; health, etc.)

minor I *n.* 1. to serve ~s (this bar does not serve ~s) 2. an emancipated ~

minor II *v.* (AE) (d; intr.) to ~ in (to ~ in French) ("to have French as a secondary subject")

minority *n.* 1. an ethnic; religious ~ 2. in a ~ (we were in the ~; in a ~ of cases)

minuet *n.* to dance; play a ~

minus see **plus** 2

minute *n.* ["sixtieth part of an hour"] 1. in a ~ (she'll be here in a ~) ["instant"] 2. the last ~ (at the last ~) ["present time"] 3. this ~ 4. (esp. BE) at the ~ (she's not here at the ~) 5. up to the ~

minutes *n.* ["official record"] 1. to keep, take ~ 2. to accept, approve; correct; read the ~ 3. to reject the ~

miracle *n.* 1. to accomplish, perform, work a ~ 2. a ~ to + inf. (it will take a ~ to save them) 3. a ~ that + clause (it's a ~ that she was not killed) 4. by a ~ (we survived by a ~) 5. (misc.) a ~ worker

miraculous *adj.* ~ that + clause (it's ~ that they were rescued)

mirage *n.* 1. to see a ~ 2. a ~ appears; disappears

mire *n.* (to be stuck) in the ~

mired *adj.* to get ~ (in the mud)

mired down (esp. AE) see **mired**

mirror *n.* 1. to hang a ~ 2. a full-length; hand; pocket; rearview; sideview (AE), wing (BE); two-way ~

mirth *n.* 1. to provoke ~ 2. general ~

misapprehension *n.* 1. (to labor) under a ~ 2. a ~ that + clause (we were laboring under the ~ that we would receive help)

miscalculate *v.* to ~ badly

miscalculation *n.* 1. to make a ~ 2. to correct a ~ 3. a bad, glaring, serious ~ 4. a ~ about

miscarriage *n.* ["abortion"] 1. to have a ~ ["failure"] 2. a gross ~ (of justice)

mischief *n.* 1. to cause, do, make; mean; plot, stir up ~ 2. to be up to, get into ~ 3. malicious ~ 4. out of ~ (to stay out of ~; to keep children out of ~) 5. full of ~ 6. up to ~ 7. (misc.) there was ~ brewing

misconception *n.* 1. a common; general, popular ~ 2. a ~ that + clause (it's a common ~ that one can lose weight by exercise alone)

misconduct *n.* gross; professional; serious; sexual ~

miscount *n.* to make a ~

misdeed *n.* 1. to commit a ~ 2. to rectify a ~ 3. a glaring ~

misdemeanor, misdemeanour *n.* to commit a ~

miserable *adj.* 1. ~ about, over (I feel ~ about it) 2. ~ to + inf. (it is ~ to work there = it is ~ working there)

misery n. 1. to cause ~ 2. to alleviate, relieve ~ 3. abject, acute, deep; sheer, untold ~ 4. ~ to + inf. (it was sheer ~ to live there = it was sheer ~ living there) 5. in ~ (to live in ~)

misfit n. a social ~

misfortune n. 1. to have, suffer (a) ~ 2. the ~ to + inf. (she had the ~ to get there at the wrong moment)

misgivings n. 1. to have ~ about 2. to express one's ~ 3. ~ that + clause (we had ~ that he would back out of the agreement)

mishap n. (formal) 1. to have a ~ 2. a ~ befell us 3. without ~ (we completed the project without ~)

misinformation n. 1. to give, peddle, plant, spread ~ 2. to correct ~ 3. ~ about

misinformed adj. 1. badly, grossly ~ 2. ~ about

misjudge v. to ~ badly, completely

mislead v. 1. (D; tr.) to ~ about (we were misled about this matter) 2. (D; tr.) to ~ into (he was misled into a life of crime)

misleading adj. 1. grossly, very ~ 2. ~ to + inf. (it is ~ to cite only certain sources)

mismanagement n. gross ~

misnomer n. a ~ to + inf. (it's a ~ to call this village a city)

mispronounced adj. commonly, frequently ~

misread v. (D; tr.) to ~ as (they misread me as a liberal)

misrepresent v. (D; tr.) to ~ as (the press ~ed them as revolutionaries)

misrepresentation n. gross ~

miss I n. 1. a clean; near ~ 2. (colloq.) (BE) to give smt. a ~ ("not to do smt.")

miss II v. 1. to ~ terribly, very much (she ~es her family very much) 2. to ~ narrowly (he narrowly ~ed being hit by a car) 3. (D; intr.) to ~ about (what do you ~ most about home? 4. (G) I ~ walking in the park; we ~ going to church every week

missed adj. deeply, sorely ~

missile n. 1. to fire, launch; guide a ~ 2. to intercept a ~ 3. an air-to-air; air-to-ground, air-to-surface; antiaircraft, ground-to-air, surface-to-air; antimissile; ballistic; cruise; ground-to-ground, surface-to-surface; guided; intercontinental ballistic; intermediate-range, medium-range; long-range, strategic; nuclear; short-range, tactical; submarine-launched ~

missing adj. 1. ~ from (~ from a group) 2. (misc.) ~ in action (mil.); to turn up ~

missing link n. a ~ between

mission n. ["task"] 1. to accomplish, carry out, perform a ~ 2. to undertake a ~ 3. (mil.) to fly a ~ 4. (usu. mil.) to abort, cancel, scratch, scrub a ~ 5. a bombing; combat; dangerous; military; search-and-destroy; suicide ~ 6. a rescue ~ 7. a training ~ 8. a diplomatic; fact-finding; goodwill; pioneer-

ing; trade ~ 9. on a ~ (they went on a goodwill ~ to Asia) 10. a ~ to + inf. (our ~ was to work out a trade agreement) 11. (misc.) ~ impossible (often humorous) ["group sent to perform a task"] 12. a diplomatic; military; trade ~ 13. a ~ from; to (a trade ~ to Africa)

missionary n. 1. a foreign; medical ~ 2. a ~ from; to

miss out v. (D; intr.) to ~ on (to ~ on a profitable deal)

misstatement n. 1. to make a ~ 2. a ~ about

mist n. 1. (a) dense, heavy, thick ~ 2. (a) fine, thin ~ 3. (a) ~ clears, lets up, lifts, rises

mistake I n. 1. to make a ~ 2. to correct, rectify a ~ 3. to excuse, forgive a ~ 4. to admit one's ~ 5. a bad, big, costly, dreadful, ghastly, glaring, serious, terrible, tragic ~ 6. a fatal; foolish; minor, slight ~ 7. ~s happen, occur 8. ~s abound (on every page) 9. a ~ about; in (we made a ~ about that; she made a ~ in counting on their help) 10. a ~ to + inf. (it was a ~ to appoint her = it was a ~ appointing her) 11. by ~ (to do smt. by ~)

mistake II v. (d; tr.) to ~ for (he mistook me for my brother)

mistaken adj. 1. ~ about; in 2. ~ for (she was ~ for her sister)

mistletoe n. ["Christmas decoration"] 1. to hang the ~ 2. to stand under the ~ ("to indicate one's willingness to be kissed, during the Christmas season") 3. a sprig of ~

mistrial n. (legal) to declare a ~

mistrust n. 1. to arouse ~ 2. deep, profound ~ 3. ~ between; of; towards

mistrustful adj. ~ of

misunderstanding n. 1. to cause, give rise to, lead to a ~ 2. to have a ~ (with) 3. to clear up, resolve a ~ 4. a ~ about, over; between

mitigate v. (d; intr.) (substandard) to ~ against ("to militate against")

mitt n. ["glove"] 1. an oven ~ (AE) 2. (baseball) a catcher's; first baseman's ~

mix I n. ["mixture"] a cake; cement; pancake; soup ~

mix II v. 1. (C) ~ a nice drink for me; or: ~ me a nice drink 2. (D; intr., tr.) to ~ with (he doesn't ~ with people like that; she ~ed the brandy with wine)

mixed up adj. 1. ~ in (~ in a scandal) 2. ~ with (she got herself ~ with criminals)

mixer n. ["informal dance, party"] (AE) 1. to give, hold a ~ ["device for mixing"] 2. a cement, concrete; electric ~ ["person who mixes socially"] 3. a good; poor ~

mix-up n. 1. to cause a ~ 2. a ~ about, in, over

mix up v. (D; tr.) to ~ with (he always ~es me up with my brother)

moan I n. 1. to emit a ~ 2. a barely audible, feeble, weak; loud ~

moan II v. 1. to ~ feebly; loudly 2. (D: intr.) to ~

about, over (to ~ over new taxes) 3. (D; intr.) to ~ with (to ~ with pain) 4. (L; to) she ~ed that she had a splitting headache

mob I *n.* 1. to inflame, stir up a ~ 2. to control, subdue a ~ 3. to disperse a ~ 4. an angry; undisciplined, unruly, wild ~ 5. a ~ disperses; gathers; runs amok, runs wild

mob II *v.* (D; tr.) to ~ for (fans were ~bing her for her autograph)

mobile *adj.* highly; upwardly ~

mobility *n.* upward ~

mobilization *n.* 1. to order (a) ~ 2. to carry out ~ 3. full, general; partial ~

mobilize *v.* 1. (D; intr., tr.) to ~ for (we are ~zing our party for the campaign) 2. (H) we are ~zing voters to participate in the election

mockery *n.* 1. to make a ~ of 2. a mere ~

mock-up *n.* ["model"] to do, prepare a ~

mode *n.* ["fashion"] 1. the latest ~ ["the setting of equipment"] 2. (a tape recorder) in play-back; recording ~ 3. (a space craft) in re-entry ~ 4. an access; insert ~ (on a computer)

model I *n.* 1. to take as a ~ 2. to pose; serve as a ~ 3. a role ~ 4. an artist's; fashion; photographer's ~ 5. a scale; working ~ 6. (of a car) a deluxe; economy; late ~ 7. a ~ for

model II *v.* 1. (d; refl., tr.) to ~ after, on (the academy was ~ed after a British public school) 2. (d; intr., tr.) to ~ in (to ~ in clay) 3. (d; tr.) to ~ into; out of (the children ~ed toys out of clay)

moderate *adj.* ~ in (they were ~ in their demands)

moderation *n.* 1. to display, show ~ 2. ~ in (~ in the consumption of alcohol) 3. in ~ (to drink in ~)

modest *adj.* 1. ~ about (she was ~ about her achievements) 2. ~ in

modesty *n.* 1. to affect; display, show ~ 2. false ~ (without false ~) 3. ~ about 4. in all ~

modification *n.* 1. to make a ~ in 2. to undergo ~s 3. extensive; slight ~s 4. behavior ~ 5. a ~ in, to (there will be several ~s to the plan before it goes into effect)

modifier *n.* a dangling (esp. AE); noun ~

modulation *n.* frequency ~ (FM)

module *n.* a command; lunar; service ~

modus operandi *n.* to establish, work out a ~

modus vivendi *n.* to establish, reach, work out a ~

mogul *n.* a media; movie; television ~

moisture *n.* to absorb, soak up ~

molar *n.* 1. to cut a ~ 2. an impacted ~ 3. a first; second; third ~

mold I mould *n.* ["furry growth"] to gather ~

mold II mould *n.* 1. a jello (AE), jelly (BE); plaster ~ 2. in a ~ (to be cast in a ~) 3. (misc.) to break out of a ~

mold III mould *v.* 1. (D; tr.) to ~ from, in, out of (to ~ a figure in/out of clay) 2. (D; tr.) to ~ into (she ~ed the clay into a figure

mole *n.* ["burrowing insectivore"] 1. ~s burrow ["spy"] 2. to plant a ~

molestation *n.* child; sexual ~

moment *n.* 1. to savor the ~ 2. an appropriate, suitable; auspicious, opportune; critical, crucial; embarrassing, inappropriate, inopportune; propitious; solemn ~ 3. a rash ~ (in a rash ~) 4. the psychological, right ~ ("the most favorable time") 5. a ~ for (this is a ~ for rejoicing) 6. a ~ to + inf. (this is the ~ to act) 7. at a ~ (at that ~) ("then"); (at the/this ~) ("now") 8. for the ~ (for the ~ let us drop this subject) 9. in a ~ (she'll be here in a ~; in a crucial ~ of smb.'s life) 10. (misc.) there's never a dull ~

momentum *n.* 1. to gain, gather ~ 2. to lose ~

monarch *n.* an absolute; constitutional ~

monarchy *n.* 1. to establish, set up a ~ 2. to overthrow a ~ 3. an absolute; constitutional; hereditary; limited ~

money *n.* 1. to coin; make, produce; print ~ 2. to counterfeit ~ 3. to circulate ~ 4. to earn, make ~ 5. to bank; change; deposit; draw, withdraw ~ (to deposit ~ in a bank; to withdraw ~ from a bank) 6. to contribute, donate; put up ~ (to donate ~ to a worthy cause) 7. to collect, raise; refund, return ~ 8. to owe; save; spend; tie up ~ 9. to lose; squander, throw away, waste ~ (they threw away their ~ on worthless investments) 10. to borrow; lend, (esp. AE) loan ~ 11. to invest ~ in; to put ~ into (they invested their ~ in stocks and bonds; they put her ~ into municipal bonds) 12. (colloq.) to sink (a lot of) ~ into (a venture) 13. to launder (illegally acquired) ~ 14. counterfeit; earnest; easy; hush; marked; paper; pin, pocket, spending; prize; seed; tight ~ 15. blood; conscience ~ 16. tax ~ (politicians should not waste tax ~) 17. (esp. AE) mad ~ ("small amount of money carried for emergency use or for impulse buying") 18. ~ for (I have ~ for the rent) 19. for ~ (to do smt. for ~) 20. out of ~ (we are out of ~) 21. (misc.) to have ~ to burn ("to have a great deal of money"); that was ~ well-spent

money order *n.* (esp. AE) 1. to make out a ~ 2. to send a ~ 3. to cash a ~

monitor I *n.* 1. an electronic; heart ~ 2. a video ~ (for a computer)

monitor II *v.* to ~ closely

monkey *n.* 1. a howler; rhesus; ring-tailed; spider ~ 2. a horde, troop of ~s 3. (misc.) (colloq.) to make a ~ (out) of smb. ("to make a fool of smb.")

monkey about (BE) see **monkey around**

monkey around *v.* (colloq.) (AE) (D; intr.) to ~ with

monkey wrench *n.* ["disruption"] (colloq.) (esp. AE) to throw a ~ into smt. ("to disrupt smt.")

monogamy *n.* to practice ~

monologue, monolog *n.* to recite a ~

mononucleosis *n.* infectious ~ (CE also has *glandu-*

lar fever)

monopoly *n.* 1. to establish, gain a ~ 2. to have, hold a ~ 3. to break (up) a ~ 4. a government, state ~ 5. a ~ of, on, over 6. (misc.) to play Monopoly (T)

monotone *n.* in a ~

monotonous *adj.* ~ to + inf. (it is ~ to watch television every day = it is ~ watching television every day)

monotony *n.* to break, relieve the ~

monstrous *adj.* 1. ~ to + inf. (it is ~ to preach hatred) 2. ~ that + clause (it's ~ that innocent children throughout the world go hungry)

month *n.* 1. a lunar ~ 2. last; next; this ~ 3. by the ~ (she is paid by the ~) 4. for a ~ (he'll be here for a ~) 5. in a ~ (they will arrive in a ~; esp. BE: they will get here in a ~'s time) 6. in a certain ~ (in the ~ month of May) 7. in, to (colloq.) a ~ (there are four weeks in a ~)

monument *n.* 1. to build, erect, put up a ~ 2. an ancient; historic, historical; literary; national ~ 3. a ~ to

mooch *v.* (slang) (AE) 1. (D; tr.) ("to beg for") to ~ from, off (he ~ed a cigarette from me) 2. (d; intr.) ("to sponge") to ~ off of, on (to ~ on one's friends)

mood I *n.* ["state of mind"] 1. a cheerful; ebullient; festive, holiday; genial, good, happy, jovial, joyful ~ 2. a mellow; nostalgic; pensive; tranquil ~ 3. a melancholy; solemn, somber ~ 4. an angry; bad, foul; bellicose; bilious; defiant; resentful; sullen ~ 5. in a ~ (in a good ~) 6. a ~ changes 7. a ~ for (I'm not in a ~ for TV) 8. a ~ to + inf. (I'm not in a ~ to read)

mood II *n.* ["verb form"] the conditional; imperative; indicative; subjunctive ~

moon I *n.* 1. the ~ revolves around the earth 2. a crescent; full; gibbous; half; harvest; new; quarter ~ 3. the ~ wanes; waxes 4. the ~ comes out 5. on the ~ (astronauts have walked on the ~)

moon II *v.* (D; intr.) to ~ over

moonlight *n.* 1. by ~ 2. in the ~

moonlight flit *n.* (colloq.) (BE) ["moving without paying one's rent, debts"] to do a ~

moor *v.* (D; tr.) to ~ to (to ~ a boat to a pier)

moose *n.* 1. a band, herd of ~ 2. a young ~ is a calf 3. a female ~ is a cow 4. a male ~ is a bull (see the Usage Note for **elk**)

mop I *n.* a dry, dust, wet ~

mop II *v.* 1. (D; tr.) to ~ from (to ~ the sweat from one's brow) 2. to ~ with (to ~ a floor with a cloth) 3. (N; used with an adjective) we ~ped the floor clean

moped *n.* to ride a ~

moral *n.* a ~ to (there's a ~ to the story)

morale *n.* 1. to boost, lift, raise ~ 2. to keep up ~ 3. to destroy, undermine ~ 4. high; low ~

moral fiber, moral fibre *n.* the ~ to + inf. (does she

have the ~ to adhere to principle?)

morality *n.* private; public; sexual ~

moralize *v.* (D; intr.) to ~ about, on, over, upon

morals *n.* 1. to protect, safeguard (public) ~ 2. to corrupt smb.'s ~ 3. lax, loose; strict ~ 4. public ~

morass *n.* to get bogged down in a ~

moratorium *n.* 1. to declare a ~ 2. to lift a ~ 3. a ~ on

morbid *adj.* ~ about (don't be ~ about the future)

more *determiner, pronoun* 1. ~ to + inf. (we have ~ to do) 2. ~ of (~ of them)

USAGE NOTE: The use of the preposition *of* is necessary when a pronoun follows. When a noun follows, the use of *of the* limits the meaning—we drank more wine; we drank more of the wine that you brought yesterday.

mores *n.* cultural; sexual; social ~

morgue *n.* 1. a city (esp. AE); newspaper ~ 2. at, in a ~ (to work in a ~)

morning *n.* 1. early; late ~ 2. in the ~; (AE) ~s (she works in the ~; or AE: she works ~s) 3. from ~ (from ~ to night) 4. on a ~ (on a cold ~ last month; on the ~ of July 20)

moron *n.* (colloq.) 1. an utter ~ 2. a ~ to + inf. (I was a ~ to accept his offer)

Morse code *n.* 1. to tap out, use (the) ~ 2. to send (a message) in ~

morsel *n.* a choice, juicy, tasty ~

mortality *n.* infant; maternal ~

mortal *n.* a mere ~

mortar *n.* ["type of cannon"] 1. a trench ~ ["bowl"] 2. a ~ and pestle

mortgage *n.* 1. to give; hold a ~ (the local bank gave us a twenty-year ~; the bank holds our ~) 2. to get, receive; take out a ~ on (we got a twenty-year ~ from the bank) 3. to pay off a ~ 4. to finance; foreclose; refinance a ~ 5. a chattel; conventional; first; second ~

mortification *n.* 1. deep ~ 2. to smb.'s ~ (to my everlasting ~)

mortified *adj.* ["embarrassed"] 1. deeply ~ 2. ~ to + inf. (I was ~ to learn that my account was overdrawn) 3. ~ that + clause (we were ~ that our manuscript was rejected)

mortuary *n.* at, in a ~

Moses *n.* holy ~! (esp. AE; colloq.)

Moslem see **Muslim**

mosquito *n.* 1. ~s bite; fly; hum 2. ~s carry, spread disease

most *determiner, n., pronoun* 1. to get the ~ (out of life) 2. to make the ~ (of one's opportunities) 3. ~ of (~ of them) 4. at (the) ~

USAGE NOTE: The use of the preposition *of* is necessary when a pronoun follows. When a noun follows, the following constructions are used—most American wine comes from California; most of the wines that we import come from Europe; we like most students; we like most of the students who study in this department.

motel *n.* to check into; out of a ~

mothballs *n.* ["protective storage"] 1. to put into ~ (to put ships into ~) 2. to take out of ~

mother *n.* 1. an expectant; nursing ~ 2. a lone (BE), single; unwed; welfare; working ~ 3. an adoptive; biological, birth, natural; foster ~; stepmother; surrogate ~ 4. a mother-in-law 5. a ~ to (she was like a ~ to them) 6. (misc.) a den ~; a ~ superior

motif *n.* 1. a guiding ~ 2. a ~ runs through a work

motion I *n.* ["proposal"] 1. to make a ~ 2. to second a ~ 3. to accept, adopt, carry, pass a ~ 4. to defeat, reject, vote down a ~ 5. to consider, entertain, vote on a ~ 6. (AE) to table a ~ ("to postpone voting on a proposal") 7. (BE) to table a ~ ("to call for a vote on a proposal") 8. to withdraw a ~ 9. the ~ carried, passed 10. a ~ to + inf. (she made a ~ to adjourn) 11. a ~ that + clause; subj. (she made a ~ that debate be/should be stopped) 12. on a ~ (on my ~ they brought up the question of admitting new members) ["movement"] 13. to set smt. in ~ 14. harmonic; perpetual ~ ["misc."] 15. to go through the ~s ("to pretend to do smt.")

motion II *v.* 1. (d; tr.) to ~ into; out of (she ~ed us into the room) 2. (D; intr.) to ~ to (she ~ed to us) 3. (H) he ~ed (to) us to come closer

motivate *v.* (H) what ~d her to leave home?

motivated *adj.* highly, strongly ~

motivation *n.* 1. strong ~ 2. the ~ to + inf. (she has the ~ to master English)

motive *n.* 1. to establish, find a ~ 2. to doubt, question, suspect smb.'s ~s 3. altruistic; honorable; noble ~s; the highest ~s (to have nothing but the highest ~s) 4. base, dishonorable, sinister; selfish; ulterior ~s 5. the profit ~ 6. an underlying ~ 7. a ~ behind, for (the police could not find a ~ for the murder) 8. a ~ to + inf. (she had no ~ to commit the crime)

motor I *n.* 1. to start a ~ 2. to turn off a ~ 3. an outboard ~ 4. a ~ runs, works; stalls (see also **engine** 1-9)

motor II *v.* (d; intr.) to ~ to (they ~ed to town)

motorbike *n.* 1. to ride a ~ 2. to ride on a ~ (as a passenger)

motorcar *n.* (BE) to drive; park a ~ (see **car** 1-11)

motorcycle *n.* 1. to drive, ride a ~ 2. to ride on a ~ (as a passenger)

motor scooter *n.* to drive, ride a ~

motor vehicle *n.* 1. to operate a ~ 2. to register a ~

motorway (BE) see **highway**

motto *n.* 1. to coin a ~ 2. a school; state ~

mound *n.* 1. a burial ~ 2. (baseball) (AE) to take the ~

mount *n.* an engine ~

mountain *n.* 1. to climb, go up, scale a ~ 2. to come down, go down a ~ 3. high; rugged; snow-capped, snow-clad, snow-covered ~s 4. block; folded; volcanic ~s 5. a chain, range of ~s 6. down; over; up a ~ 7. (misc.) the elevation, height of a ~; to make a ~ out of a molehill ("to exaggerate"); the peak, top of a ~

mounted *adj.* ["astride"] 1. ~ on (~ on a fine horse) ["fixed"] 2. ~ on (the specimens were ~ed on a poster)

mourn *v.* (D; intr.) to ~ for, over

mourning *n.* 1. to declare, proclaim (a period of) ~ 2. to go into ~ 3. deep ~ 4. national ~ 5. in ~ for 6. a sign of ~

mouse I *n.* ["a small rodent"] 1. to catch mice 2. a field; house; meadow; white ~ 3. mice gnaw; scamper; squeak 4. (misc.) as quiet as a ~

mouse II *n.* ["a device on a computer"] to click; move; use a ~

moustache, mustache *n.* 1. to grow a ~ 2. to shave off; trim a ~ 3. to finger, twist one's ~ 4. a drooping; handlebar ~

mouth *n.* 1. to close, shut; open one's ~ 2. to cram, stuff one's ~ (with food) 3. to rinse one's ~ (out) 4. at the ~ (of a cave; river) 5. (misc.) (colloq.) a big ~ ("a gossip"); to shoot off one's ~ ("to talk too much"); to make smb.'s ~ water ("to create a desire or appetite in smb."); to keep one's ~ shut ("to remain silent")

mouthful *n.* (colloq.) ["something true"] 1. to say a ~ ["a mouth full of food"] 2. to swallow a ~

mouth off *v.* (colloq.) (D; intr.) to ~ about (he kept ~ing off about his troubles)

mouthpiece *n.* ["spokesperson"] 1. to act, serve as a ~ for 2. smb.'s official ~

move I *n.* ["act"] 1. to make a ~ (who will make the first ~?) 2. a false ~ (one false ~ would be costly) 3. a bold; brilliant, clever, shrewd, smart, wise; decisive ~ 4. a ~ to + inf. (they made a ~ to settle the dispute) ["moving of a piece as in chess, checkers"] 5. to make a ~ 6. a brilliant; stupid, wrong ~ 7. an opening ~ (also fig.) ["act of moving"] 8. a ~ to (our firm's ~ to the Coast) 9. (misc.) (colloq.) to get a ~ on ("to go faster"); on the ~

move II *v.* 1. ("to stir") to ~ deeply, profoundly 2. ("to change the position of") to ~ bodily 3. (d; intr.) ("to request") to ~ for (to ~ for a new trial) 4. (D; intr., tr.) ("to change or cause to change one's position, place of residence, place of work") to ~ from; into; to; out of (let's ~ from this table to that one; they ~d from the city to the suburbs; the firm is ~ving to California; let's ~ the chair from/out of this room to that one; he ~d his family from/out of an old house into a new apartment; we are ~ving our main office from/out of the city to a small town) 5. (D; intr.) ("to act") to ~ on (to ~ on a matter) 6. (D; tr.) ("to stir") to ~ to (she was ~d to tears) 7. (d; intr.) ("to change one's position") to ~ towards (to ~ towards the exit) 8. (E) ("to propose") the committee ~d to block her nomination 9. (H) ("to induce") what ~d her to make such a gesture? 10. (L; subj.) ("to propose") she ~d that the resolution be/should be approved 11. (P; intr.) ("to circulate") she ~s in the best society; to ~ among the elite; to ~ near the very top of power

move ahead v. (D; intr.) to ~ of (to ~ of the pack)

move away v. (D; intr.) to ~ from (to ~ from the city)

move in v. 1. (d; intr.) ("to close in") to ~ for (to ~ for the kill) 2. (D; intr.) to ~ on ("to close in on") (the police ~d in on the fugitives) 3. (D; intr.) to ~ on ("to establish control of") (organized crime was ~ving in on the industry) 4. (D; intr.) to ~ on, with ("to take up residence with") (her relatives wanted to ~ with her)

movement n. ["organized effort to attain a goal"] 1. to launch a ~ 2. to support a ~ 3. to oppose; suppress a ~ 4. a civil-rights; consumer; feminist; women's; labor; mass; peace; political; radical, revolutionary; resistance; social ~ 5. a ~ against; for; towards (the ~ for equal pay) ["division of a musical composition"] 6. to perform; play a ~ ["military maneuver"] 7. a pincers ~ ["move"] 8. a downward; upward ~ 9. deft, dextrous; graceful; rhythmic ~ 10. awkward; erratic; jerky; uncoordinated ~s 11. a ~ towards ["evacuation"] 12. a bowel ~ (to have a bowel ~)

move on v. (D; intr.) to ~ to (to ~ to the next town)

move up v. 1. (D; intr.) to ~ into, to (she has ~d up to the position of general manager) 2. (D; intr.) to ~ through (to ~ through the ranks)

movie n. (esp. AE) ["film"] 1. to make, produce a ~ 2. to direct a ~ 3. to see, watch a ~ 4. (CE) a home ~

USAGE NOTE: One usually *watches* a movie on a home TV, and *sees* a movie in a theater or at home. See also **film** 1-12.

movies n. (AE) ["cinema"] 1. to go to the ~ 2. silent ~ 3. at the ~

mower n. 1. to operate, work a ~ 2. a hand; lawn; power ~

much determiner, n., pronoun 1. to make ~ of smt. 2. ~ of (we did not believe ~ of what we heard; he isn't ~ of an artist) 3. ~ to + inf. (she has ~ to say; we have ~ to learn) 4. (misc.) ~ as we want to help USAGE NOTE: The use of the preposition *of* is necessary when a pronoun follows—we did not believe much of what we heard. When a noun follows, the use of *of the* limits the meaning—much sorrow is caused by drug abuse; much of the sorrow that is caused by drug abuse could be avoided.

muck n. ["mess"] (colloq.) (BE) to make a ~ of smt.

muck about v. (colloq.) (BE) to ~ with ("to mess around with")

mucus n. 1. to cough up; secrete ~ 2. nasal ~

mud n. ["wet earth"] 1. to spatter ~ 2. ~ oozes, squishes 3. a layer of ~ 4. (misc.) to spatter smb. with ~; to wallow in the ~ ["malicious charges"] 5. to sling, throw ~ at smb.

muddle n. ["confusion"] 1. to make a ~ of smt. 2. in a ~

mufti n. ["civilian clothes"] in ~

mug n. a beer; shaving ~

mulct v. (D; tr.) ("to defraud") to ~ of (to ~ smb. of her/his money)

mule n. 1. to drive; ride a ~ 2. ~s bray 3. a team of ~s 4. (misc.) as stubborn as a ~

mull over v. (Q) we ~ed over whether to accept the proposal

multiplication n. to do ~

multiply v. (D; tr.) to ~ by (to ~ five by ten)

mum adj. 1. to keep, remain ~ 2. ~ about 3. (misc.) ~'s the word

mumble v. 1. (B) she ~d smt. to me 2. (D; intr., tr.) to ~ about (he ~d smt. about his job) 3. (L; to) he ~d (to us) that he would get up later

mumps n. to catch, come down with the ~

munch away v. (D; intr.) to ~ at (they were ~ing away at their sandwiches)

murder n. ["homicide"] 1. to commit ~ 2. a brutal, cold-blooded, grisly, heinous, savage, vicious, wanton ~ 3. an attempted; premeditated; ritual ~ 4. (AE) (a) first-degree; second-degree ~ 5. mass ~ 6. multiple, serial ~s ["ruinous influence"] (colloq.) 7. ~ on (the rainy weather has been ~ on business) ["great hardship"] 8. it was ~ standing out in the cold

murderer n. a cold-blooded, vicious; mass ~

murmur I n. ["complaint"] 1. to let out a ~ (she didn't let out a ~) 2. without a ~ ["abnormal sound"] (med.) 3. a heart ~

murmur II v. 1. to ~ gently, softly 2. (D; intr., tr.) to ~ to (she ~ed smt. to him) 3. (L; to) she ~ed to us that she wanted to leave

muscle n. 1. to contract; flex, tense; move; pull, strain; relax; wrench a ~ 2. to develop one's ~s 3. bulging ~s 4. involuntary; smooth; striated; voluntary ~s 5. ~s ache; contract

muscle in v. (colloq.) (D; intr.) to ~ on (to ~ on smb.'s territory)

muse v. (D; intr.) to ~ about, over, upon

museum n. 1. an art (esp. AE; BE prefers *art gallery*); children's; ethnographic; public; science; wax ~ 2. at, in a ~ (to work at a ~)

mushroom I n. 1. to pick ~s 2. an edible ~

mushroom II v. (D; intr.) to ~ from; into, to

music n. 1. to compose, write ~ 2. to arrange ~ 3. to perform, play ~ 4. to put, set smt. to ~ 5. to read ~ 6. background; canned; piped; incidental; light; soft, sweet ~ 7. bluegrass; country; hillbilly; folk; western ~ 8. ballet; band; chamber; classical; dance; instrumental; klezmer; orchestral; organ ~

9. funky; gospel; march, martial; modern; popular; rock; sacred; serious; soul ~ 10. choral; vocal
~ 11. sheet ~ 12. a piece of ~ 13. (fig.) ~ to (what
she said was ~ to my ears) 14. to ~ (to dance to the
~ of a big band) 15. (misc.) to face the ~ ("to
accept one's punishment")

musical *n.* 1. to produce, stage a ~ 2. a Broadway ~

musical chairs *n.* to play ~

musician *n.* an accomplished; natural; strolling ~

Muslim *n.* a Black; Shiite; Sunni ~

muslin *n.* bleached; unbleached ~

must *v.* 1. (F) we ~ go 2. (misc.) I really ~ go; you
surely ~ know; they ~ have left

mustache see **moustache**

muster I *n.* to pass ~

muster II *v.* 1. (d; tr.) to ~ into (to ~ smb. into the
army) 2. (d; tr.) to ~ out of ("to discharge from")
(to be ~ed out of the army)

mutation *n.* 1. to induce a ~ 2. a gene; genetic ~

mute *adj.* to stand ~ ("to remain silent during an
arraignment")

mutiny I *n.* 1. to foment, incite, stir up; organize a ~
2. to crush, put down, quell a ~ 3. a ~ breaks out

mutiny II *v.* (D; intr.) to ~ against

mutter *v.* 1. (B) she ~ed a few words to us 2. (D;
intr.) to ~ about 3. (L; to) she ~ed (to him) that she
would catch up later

mysterious *adj.* ~ about (~ about one's past)

mystery *n.* 1. to pose a ~ (her disappearance poses a
real ~) 2. to clear up; solve, unravel a ~ 3. an
unsolved ~ 4. a murder ~ 5. a ~ deepens 6. a ~ to (it
was a ~ to me) 7. (misc.) cloaked, shrouded,
wrapped in ~; a veil of ~

mystified *adj.* 1. ~ to + inf. (she was ~ to find her
watch gone) 2. ~ that + clause (we were ~ that they
did not show up)

mystifying *adj.* 1. ~ to 2. ~ that + clause (it's ~ that
the matter was never investigated)

myth *n.* 1. to create; perpetuate a ~ 2. to debunk,
dispel; explode a ~ 3. a popular ~ 4. a ~ that +
clause (we dispelled the ~ that their army was
invincible)

N

nadir *n.* 1. to reach a ~ 2. at a ~

nag *v.* 1. (D; intr.) to ~ at (he kept ~ging at her) 2. (D; tr.) to ~ into (they ~ged him into buying a new car) 3. (H) he kept ~ging her to buy a new sofa

nail I *n.* ["tapered piece of metal"] 1. to drive, hammer a ~ (he drove a ~ into the board) 2. to remove a ~ 3. a loose ~ 4. (misc.) as hard/tough as ~s; to hit the ~ on the head ("to describe smt. succinctly and correctly") ["horny substance growing at the ends of fingers and toes"] 5. to cut, pare, trim; do; file; manicure; paint, polish one's ~s 6. to break, split a ~ 7. to bite; chew one's ~s 8. a fingernail; toenail

nail II *v.* 1. (D; tr.) to ~ to (she ~ed the plaque to the wall) 2. (P; tr.) she ~ed the boards together

naive *adj.* 1. ~ of (that was ~ of you) 2. ~ to + inf. (it's ~ to trust everyone; you are ~ to believe them)

naked *adj.* 1. stark ~ 2. (misc.) to walk around ~

naked eye *n.* to the ~ (visible to the ~)

name I *n.* ["appellation"] 1. to adopt, assume, take; bear; change; use a ~ 2. to give smb. a ~ 3. to call smb. a (bad) ~ 4. to immortalize smb.'s ~ 5. to invoke God's ~ 6. to sign one's ~ 7. an assumed; code; legal; personal; professional; proper; stage ~ (she took a stage ~ when she began her acting career) 8. a Christian (esp. BE), first, given (AE); family ~, surname; maiden; married; middle ~ (she uses her middle ~) 9. a bad, dirty; fancy; pet ~ 10. a geographic ~ 11. a brand, proprietary, trade ~ 12. a file ~ 13. a common, vernacular ("not technical") ~ 14. a ~ for (there is no ~ for such conduct) 15. by ~ (to know smb. by ~) 16. in ~ (she is the chairperson in ~ only) 17. in smb.'s ~ (the book was charged out in your ~) 18. under a ~ (under an assumed ~) ["reputation"] 19. to make a ~ (for oneself) 20. to clear one's ~ 21. to besmirch, smear smb.'s (good) ~ 22. to give smb. a bad ~ 23. a bad; big; good ~ (she is a big ~ in fashion) ["misc."] 24. to drop ~s ("to boast of one's connections"); to name ~s; in the ~ of the law

name II *v.* 1. (d; tr.) to ~ after, for (AE) (Hannah was ~d after her great-grandmother) 2. (d; tr.) to ~ as (she was ~d as the winner) 3. (H) (esp. AE) they ~d me to head the commission 4. (N; used with a noun) she was ~d winner of the contest

name-calling *n.* to engage in, go in for, resort to ~

nameless *adj.* to remain ~

nap *n.* 1. to have, take a ~ 2. an afternoon; morning ~

napkin *n.* 1. to fold a ~ 2. to tuck a ~ (under one's chin) 3. a cocktail; dinner; linen; paper ~

nappy (BE) see **diaper**

narcosis *n.* 1. to produce (a state of) ~ 2. (a) ~ wears off 3. under ~

narcotics *n.* to smuggle ~ (into a country)

narrate *v.* (B) she ~d her story to us

narration *n.* a graphic; gripping ~

narrow down *v.* (D; tr.) to ~ to (the choice was ~ed down to a few candidates)

narrow-minded *adj.* ~ to + inf. (it was ~ of her to say that)

nasal passages *n.* blocked, congested ~

nasty *adj.* 1. ~ about (they were very ~ about the whole incident) 2. ~ to (he is ~ to everyone) 3. ~ to + inf. (it was ~ of them to do that)

nation *n.* 1. to build; establish a ~ 2. a civilized; developing; friendly; independent; industrial; peace-loving; sovereign ~ 3. belligerent, warring ~s 4. across the ~ (there were strikes across the ~) 5. (misc.) a member ~ (of the UN)

national *n.* ["citizen"] a foreign ~

national anthem *n.* to play; sing; strike up the ~

National Guard *n.* (US) to call out; federalize the ~

nationalism *n.* 1. to foster ~ 2. extreme; rampant ~

nationhood *n.* to achieve ~

native *adj.* 1. ~ to (this flower is ~ to our state) 2. (misc.) to go ~ ("to behave like the local population when in a foreign country")

natter *v.* (colloq.) (BE) (D; intr.) ("to chatter") to ~ about; to (to ~ on to smb. about smt.)

natural I *adj.* 1. (AE) ~ to (that comes ~ to me) 2. ~ to + inf. (it's ~ to want a nice car) 3. ~ that + clause (it's perfectly ~ that children love/should love ice cream)

natural II *n.* (colloq.) ["person who seems to be destined for success"] 1. a ~ for (she is a ~ for this kind of job) 2. a ~ to + inf. (she's a ~ to win the election)

nature *n.* ["character, quality"] 1. an impetuous; placid ~ 2. human ~ (it's only human ~ to want to live well) 3. second ~ (that is almost second ~ to me) 4. smb.'s true ~ 5. by ~ (she is friendly by ~) 6. in smb.'s ~ (it was not in her ~ to complain) 7. of a certain ~ (wounds of a serious ~) ["physical universe"] 8. to harness (the forces of) ~ 9. (misc.) mother ~; a freak of ~; back to ~; let ~ take its course; to appeal to smb.'s better ~

naught *n.* (lit.) 1. to come to ~ 2. all for ~

naughty *adj.* 1. ~ of 2. ~ to + inf. (it was ~ to do that)

nausea *n.* 1. to bring on, cause ~ 2. to experience ~ (he experiences ~ when he rides in car) 3. a wave of ~ (she felt a wave of ~ come over her; a wave of ~ came over her)

nauseated *adj.* to feel ~

nauseating *adj.* 1. ~ to 2. ~ to + inf. (it was ~ to watch them)

nauseous *adj.* 1. to become, feel ~ 2. to make smb. ~

USAGE NOTE: Some purists still claim that *nauseous* means only "nauseating". In fact, most speakers now use it as a synonym of *nauseated*.

navigation *n.* celestial; electronic ~

navigate *v.* (d; intr.) to ~ by (to ~ by the stars)

navy *n.* 1. a merchant ~ (BE; AE has *merchant marine*) 2. the Royal Navy; the US Navy 3. in the ~ (to serve in the ~)

near *adv.* ~ to (she came ~ to winning the title)
USAGE NOTE: When *near* is a preposition, it is not used in the collocation *near to*. Compare *close to*: the golf links are close to/near the station.

nearer, nearest *adj., adv.* ~ to (the park is nearer to our hotel than it is to yours; which bus stop is nearest to Times Square?)

nearness *n.* ~ to

neat *adj.* ~ in (~ in one's habits)

necessary *adj.* 1. absolutely ~ 2. ~ for; to 3. ~ to + inf. (it is ~ to sleep) 4. ~ that + clause; subj. (it is ~ that we all be/should be there)

necessitate *v.* 1. (G) the promotion would ~ living abroad 2. (K) going to college would ~ his moving to the city

necessity *n.* 1. to obviate a ~ 2. an absolute, dire; military ~ 3. the bare; daily ~ties 4. a ~ arises 5. a ~ for 6. a ~ to + inf. (there is no ~ to leave so early) 7. of ~ (you will of ~ remain silent) 8. (misc.) the ~ties of life

neck I *n.* 1. to crane one's ~ 2. to twist, wring smb.'s ~ 3. (to have) a stiff ~ 4. (misc.) to save one's ~; it's a pain in the ~; what are you doing in this ~ of the woods? the two leading competitors are ~ and ~; to risk one's ~ ("to risk one's life"); to break one's ~ trying to do smt. ("to make a maximum effort to get smt. done"); to stick one's ~ out ("to expose oneself to danger"); by a ~ ("by a close margin"); up to one's ~ in work ("swamped with work"); ~ and ~ ("even")

neck II *v.* (colloq.) (D; intr.) ("to hug and kiss") to ~ with

neckline *n.* a high; low, plunging; sweetheart ~

necktie *n.* (AE) 1. to put on; wear a ~ 2. to tie a ~ 3. a loud ~ (CE has *tie*)

need I *n.* 1. to create a ~ 2. to feel, have a ~ 3. to fill, meet; obviate a ~ 4. to satisfy a ~ 5. to minister, tend to smb.'s ~s 6. an acute, compulsive, crying, desperate, dire, pressing, urgent; growing; special ~ 7. a basic, fundamental; personal; unfulfilled, unmet; universal ~ 8. a biological; emotional, psychological; physical; physiological; spiritual ~ 9. bodily; emergency; material ~s 10. a ~ arises 11. a ~ for (there is no ~ for violence) 12. a ~ to + inf.

(there was a pressing ~ to act immediately; there was no ~ for you to go) 13. in ~ (to live in dire ~; badly in ~) 14. in ~ of (badly in ~ of food)

need II *v.* 1. to ~ badly, desperately, sorely 2. (D; tr.) to ~ for (we ~ you for this job) 3. (E) we all ~ to work 4. (F; in neg. and occ. in interrogative sentences) she ~ not work; or: she doesn't ~ to work; ~ she go? or: does she ~ to go? 5. (G) the house ~s painting 6. (H) she ~s smb. to help her 7. (N; used with a past participle) I ~ my coat mended
USAGE NOTE: The sentence *she needn't have gone* implies that she did go (though there was no need for her to go). The sentence *she didn't need to go* does not indicate if she went or not.

needed *adj.* badly, much ~

needle I *n.* 1. to thread a ~ 2. a darning; hooked; knitting; sewing ~ 3. a gramophone (BE), phonograph (AE) ~ 4. a hypodermic ~ 5. a pine ~ 6. (misc.) a ~ in a haystack ("smt. that is impossible to find")

needle II *v.* 1. (D; tr.) to ~ about (she was ~ling him about his blunder) 2. (D; tr.) to ~ into (~d me into losing my temper)

needlepoint *n.* to do ~

needless *adj.* ~ to + inf. (it is ~ to worry)

needlework *n.* to do ~

negative *n.* ["exposed film"] 1. to develop; make a ~ ["phrase that rejects"] 2. in the ~ (to reply in the ~) ["expression that contains negation"] 3. a double ~

neglect I *n.* 1. benign; complete, gross, total; willful ~ 2. child, parental ~ 3. a state of ~

neglect II *v.* 1. to ~ completely, totally; willfully 2. (E) she ~ed to pay the fine

neglectful *adj.* 1. completely, totally ~ 2. ~ of

negligence *n.* 1. contributory; criminal; gross; rank; willful ~ 2. (legal) gross; ordinary; slight ~ 3. ~ in; towards

negligent *adj.* 1. grossly ~ 2. ~ about; in

negotiate *v.* 1. (D; intr.) to ~ about, over 2. (D; intr.) to ~ for 3. (D; intr.) to ~ with (we ~d with them for release of the prisoners; to ~ with smb. about a common border) 4. (E) we ~d with them to release the hostages 5. (misc.) to ~ from a position of strength

negotiation *n.* under ~ (the treaty is still under ~)

negotiations *n.* 1. to conduct; enter into, open ~ 2. to renew, resume ~ 3. to break off ~ 4. delicate; direct; high-level; top-level; marathon, round-the-clock; secret ~ 5. contract; diplomatic; peace ~ 6. successful ~ 7. fruitless, unsuccessful ~ 8. ~ succeed 9. ~ break down, collapse 10. ~ between, with 11. ~ for 12. (misc.) ~ are deadlocked over several points

negotiator *n.* a management; union ~

neighbor I neighbour *n.* 1. a next-door ~ 2. a ~ to (she was a good ~ to us)

neighbor II neighbour *v.* (esp. BE) (D; intr.) to ~ on

neighborhood, neighbourhood *n.* 1. a friendly; good, nice, pleasant ~ 2. a changing ~ 3. a bad, rough, tough ~ 4. an ethnic; residential ~ 5. the immediate ~ (all of our friends live in the immediate ~) 6. in a ~ (we live in a nice ~)

neighborly, neighbourly *adj.* ~ to + inf. (it was ~ of you to do that)

neither *determiner, pronoun* ~ of (~ of the two; ~ of them)
USAGE NOTE: The use of the preposition *of* is necessary when *two* or a pronoun follows. When a noun follows, two constructions are possible—neither student knew the answer; neither of the students knew the answer.

nelson *n.* ["type of wrestling hold"] a full; half ~

nemesis *n.* to meet one's ~

neologism *n.* to coin a ~

nerve *n.* ["assurance"] ["gall"] (colloq.) 1. to display, have ~ 2. the ~ to + inf. (she had the ~ to ask for another day off) ["self-confidence"] 3. to lose one's ~ ["sensitivity"] 4. a raw ~ (his remark hit a raw ~) ["band of nervous tissue"] 5. the cranial ~s

nerves *n.* ["nervousness"] 1. an attack; bundle of ~ ["mental state"] 2. to fray, frazzle smb.'s ~; to get on smb.'s ~ 3. to calm, settle, steady one's ~ 4. frayed, frazzled, jangled; steady; strong; taut; weak ~ ["misc."] 5. to have ~ of steel ("to be very strong emotionally"); my ~ are shot; a war of ~

nervous *adj.* 1. to make smb. ~ 2. ~ about, of (BE) (we were ~ about the recent reports of local violence)

nest *n.* 1. to build, make a ~ 2. a machine-gun ~ 3. (misc.) to feather one's ~ ("to enrich oneself); a hornets' ~ ("an angry reaction")

nest egg *n.* ["money set aside as a reserve"] to accumulate; set aside a (little) ~

nestle *v.* 1. (d; intr., tr.) to ~ against (the children ~d against their mother) 2. (P; intr.) the small village ~d in the green hills

nestle up *v.* (d; intr.) to ~ against, to (the children ~d up to their mother)

net *n.* 1. to weave a ~ 2. to cast, spread a ~ 3. (computers) to surf the ~ (see also **Internet**) 4. a butterfly; fishing; mosquito ~ 5. a life (AE), safety (also fig.) ~ 6. in a ~ (to catch fish in a ~)

netting *n.* mosquito; wire ~

nettles *n.* ~ sting

network I *n.* 1. an old-boy; old-girl ~ 2. a communications; computer; road ~ 3. (computers) a local area ~ (LAN) 4. national ~ (of radio, TV stations) 5. over a ~ (over a national ~)

network II *v.* (D; intr., tr.) to ~ with (the computers were ~ed with each other; to ~ with the right people)

neurosis *n.* mild; severe ~

neurotic *adj.* ~ about

neutral I *adj.* ~ in (~ in a dispute)

neutral II *n.* ["position of disengaged gears"] in ~ (to run an engine while in ~)

neutrality *n.* 1. to maintain, observe ~ 2. to declare one's ~ 3. armed; strict ~

new *adj.* 1. ~ at; in (I'm ~ at this) 2. ~ to (this procedure is ~ to us) 3. brand ~

newcomer *n.* a ~ to

new ground *n.* to break ~

new leaf *n.* to turn over a ~ ("to make a fresh start")

news *n.* ["new information"] 1. to announce, give, report; break, spring; cover the ~ 2. to spread (the) ~ 3. to censor; control; cover up, suppress (the) ~ 4. to color, distort, twist (the) ~ 5. good, welcome, wonderful; interesting ~ 6. unexpected ~ 7. earthshaking, earth-shattering, sensational, shocking, startling, worldshaking ~ 8. bad, devastating, grim ~ 9. local; international; national; political ~ 10. the latest ~ (have you heard the latest ~?) 11. ~ spreads, travels 12. a bit, item, piece of ~; a ~ item 13. ~ about, of (~ about the earthquake; is there any news of them?) 14. the ~ that + clause (have you heard the ~ that the border has been closed?) ["newscast"] 15. to hear, listen to; turn on; watch the ~ 16. the late; morning; nightly ~ (on TV) 17. on the ~ (we heard that item on the late ~) 18. (misc.) to make (the) ~ ("to be newsworthy")

news conference *n.* to broadcast; hold; schedule; televise a ~

newspaper *n.* 1. to edit; get out, publish, put out; print a ~ 2. to deliver ~s 3. to subscribe to a ~ 4. a local; national (esp. BE) 5. a daily; evening; morning; weekly ~ 6. a school ~ 7. a ~ comes out, is published 8. (misc.) to make the ~s ("to be printed in the newspapers"); a ~ proprietor (BE), publisher (AE)

New Year *n.* 1. to greet, ring in, usher in the ~ 2. to wish smb. a Happy New Year

next *adj., adv.* 1. (cannot stand alone) ~ to (there's a newsstand ~ to the hotel) 2. (misc.) ~ of kin; ~ in line

nibble *v.* (D; intr.) to ~ at, on (the children were ~ling at pretzels; to ~ on cheese)

nibble away *v.* (D; intr.) to ~ at, on

nice *adj.* 1. ~ to, with (she's ~ to the children) 2. ~ to + inf. (it's ~ just to sit and relax = it's ~ just sitting and relaxing; she is ~ to work with = it is ~ to work with her = it is ~ working with her = she is a ~ person to work with; it was ~ of you to come) 3. ~ that + clause (it's ~ that we could all get together) 4. (misc.) it's ~ and hot

niche *n.* ["position"] 1. to carve out a ~ (she has carved out a ~ for herself in her field) 2. to occupy a ~ (she occupies a special ~ in her field)

nick *n.* (misc.) in the ~ of time ("precisely when needed")

nickname v. (N; used with a noun) he was ~d *Butch*

niggle v. (D; intr.) to ~ about, over (to ~ over every sentence)

nigh adv. (old-fashioned) ["near"] ~ on, onto, unto (~ onto ten years)

night n. 1. to have; spend a ~ (we had a restless ~; we spent the ~ working on the report) 2. a clear; moonlit; starlit ~ 3. a dark, murky; moonless; overcast; stormy ~ 4. a restless, sleepless ~ 5. an early; late ~ 6. a first, opening ~ (of a play) 7. a wedding ~ 8. last; tomorrow ~; tonight 9. ~ falls 10. at ~ (to work at ~; late at ~) 11. by ~ (London by ~) 12. for a ~ (to put smb. up for the ~) 13. on a certain ~ (on the ~ of December first; on that ~) 14. all through, throughout the ~ 15. (misc.) to bid, wish smb. good ~; to say good ~ to smb.; (AE) to work ~s; in the dead of (the) ~

USAGE NOTE: The collocation *at night* is usu. used with verbs (she works at night) and contrasts with *during the day*. The collocation *by night* is usu. used with nouns (London by night) and contrasts with *by day*. (see the Usage Note for **day**)

nightcap n. ["last drink of the night"] 1. to have a ~ 2. (misc.) to invite smb. in for a ~; to join smb. in a ~

nightclub n. at, in a ~ (to work at/in a ~)

nightfall n. at ~

nightingale n. ~s sing, warble

nightlight n. a ~ glows dimly

nightmare n. 1. to have a ~ 2. a horrible, terrible ~ 3. a ~ about

nightshift n. 1. to work the ~ 2. (to work) on the ~

nighttime n. in the ~

nip I n. ["stinging cold"] (there is) a ~ in the air

nip II v. (colloq.) (BE) (P; intr.) ("to move quickly") she ~ped out and bought some bread

nipples n. cracked; sore, tender ~

nitpick v. (colloq.) (D; intr.) to ~ at

nitty-gritty n. (colloq.) ["essence"] to get down to the ~

no n. ["negative response"] 1. they would not take ~ for an answer 2. to say ~ 3. an emphatic ~ 4. (a) ~ to (a request)

noble adj. ~ to + inf. (it was ~ of him to make the sacrifice)

nobody pronoun we had ~ to talk to = we had ~ that we could talk to

nod I n. ["movement of the head"] 1. to give a ~ 2. an affirmative, approving ~ 3. a ~ to 4. (misc.) a ~ of approval; (BE) the proposal was approved/ passed on the ~ (without the need for a vote) ["awarding of a decision"] (usu. sports) 5. to get the ~

nod II v. 1. (D; intr., tr.) to ~ at, to (when she entered the room, she ~ded to us) 2. (misc.) to ~ in agreement

node n. a lymph ~

noise n. 1. to make, produce (a) ~ 2. to cut (AE; colloq.), cut down (on), reduce the ~ 3. (a) background; extraneous ~ 4. (a) constant, persistent; deafening; loud; shrill; strange ~ 5. a ~ abates, dies down

noise about, noise abroad v. (L) it was ~d about that he was retiring

noises n. ["signs, indications"] (colloq.) to make all the right ~

nominate v. 1. (D; tr.) to ~ as (she was ~d as our candidate) 2. (D; tr.) to ~ for (to ~ smb. for the presidency) 3. (H) they ~d her to serve as chairperson

nomination n. 1. to place, put smb. (smb.'s name) in ~ 2. to get, win a ~ 3. to accept; reject a ~ 4. a ~ for; to (a ~ to a committee)

nominative n. (grammar) the ~ absolute

nonconformity n. ~ in; to; with

none determiner, n., pronoun ~ of (~ of them)

USAGE NOTE: The use of the preposition *of* is necessary when a pronoun follows. When a noun follows, the use of *of the* limits the meaning; *no* replaces *none* when the meaning is not limited— we saw none of the students whom we had discussed earlier; we drank none of the wine that you brought; we saw no students; we drank no wine.

nonexistent adj. virtually ~

nonsense n. 1. to speak, talk ~ 2. to brook, put up with, tolerate no ~ 3. (colloq.) (AE) to cut (out) the ~ 4. complete, outright, perfect, pure, sheer, total, utter ~ 5. ~ to + inf. (it was sheer ~ to trust them) 6. (misc.) (BE) to make ~ (a) of ("to spoil") (the recession made a ~ of our plans for expansion)

nonsensical adj. ~ to + inf. (it's ~ to trust her)

nook n. 1. a cozy ~ 2. a breakfast ~ 3. (misc.) every ~ and cranny

noon n. 1. high ~ 2. at ~ 3. from ~ (to evening)

no one see **nobody**

noose n. 1. to tighten a ~ around (they tightened the ~ around his neck) 2. a hangman's ~

norm n. ["standard"] 1. to establish, set a ~ 2. to deviate from the ~ ["average"] 3. above; below the ~

normal I adj. 1. ~ to + inf. (it's ~ to want a steady job) 2. ~ that + clause (it's only ~ that we should expect equal pay)

normal II n. 1. above; below ~ 2. (misc.) back to ~

north I adj., adv. 1. directly, due, straight ~ 2. ~ of (~ of the city) 3. up ~ 4. (misc.) to face; go, head ~; northeast by ~; northwest by ~

north II n. 1. magnetic; true ~ 2. from the ~; in the ~; to the ~

northeast I adj., adv. 1. ~ of (to be ~ of the city) 2. (misc.) to go, head ~; north by ~

northeast II n. from; in; to the ~

North Pole n. at the ~

northwest I adj., adv. 1. ~ of (to be ~ of the city) 2.

(misc.) to go, head ~; north by ~

northwest II *n.* from; in; to the ~

nose I *n.* 1. to blow; powder; wipe one's ~ 2. to pick one's ~ 3. an aquiline, Roman; bulbous; pug, snub, turned-up ~ 4. a blocked-up, stuffed-up; bloody; running, runny ~ (the child has a runny ~) 5. through the ~ (to breathe through the ~) 6. a ~ bleeds; runs 7. (misc.) to bury one's ~ in a book ("to become absorbed in a book"); to count ~s ("to count those present"); to cut off one's ~ to spite one's face ("to harm one's own interests"); to lead smb. by the ~ ("to order smb. around"); to pay through the ~ ("to pay an exorbitant price"); to keep one's ~ out of smb. else's business; to poke, stick one's ~ into smb. else's business; to thumb one's ~ at smb. ("to defy smb."); to keep one's ~ to the grindstone ("to work long and hard"); under smb.'s (very) ~ ("in smb.'s plain sight"); to turn up one's ~ at ("to sneer at"); on the ~ (AE; colloq.) ("exactly"); a ~ for scandal ("an ability to ferret out scandal"); by a ~ ("by a small margin"); to follow one's ~ ("to go straight forward"); to tweak ("pinch") smb.'s ; to keep one's ~ clean ("to stay out of trouble"); to follow one's ~ ("to go straight ahead")

nose II *v.* 1. (colloq.) (D: intr.) to ~ into (to ~ into smb.'s affairs) 2. (P; intr., tr.) she ~d the car into the street

nosebleed *n.* 1. to get; have a ~ 2. to stop a ~ 3. a light; severe ~

nose dive *n.* 1. (also fig.) to go into, take a ~ (stocks took a ~) 2. to come out of, pull out of a ~

nostalgia *n.* 1. to feel ~ 2. ~ for

nostrils *n.* flaring, wide ~

nosy, nosey *adj.* (colloq.) ~ about

notable *adj.* ~ for

notch *n.* ["cut"] 1. to make a ~ 2. a ~ in

notch up *v.* (esp. BE) (d; tr.) ("to score") to ~ against (our team has ~ed up seven victories against them)

note I *n.* ["memorandum"] ["record"] 1. to make a ~ of (she made a ~ of the exact time) 2. to take ~ of 3. (BE) a credit ~ (for returned merchandise; AE has *credit slip*) 4. a mental ~ ["short letter"] ["official letter"] 5. to compose, write a ~ 6. to address; deliver a ~ 7. to drop, send smb. a ~ 8. a diplomatic; protest ~ 9. a thank-you ~ 10. a ~ from; to ["musical tone"] 11. to hit, strike; hold a ~ (she hit the high ~ beautifully) 12. a false ~ (also fig.) 13. a high; low ~ 14. (AE) an eighth; half; quarter; whole ~ ["characteristic feature"] 15. to strike a ~ (to strike a sour ~) 16. a festive; fresh; optimistic; positive; triumphant ~ 17. a personal ~ 18. a discordant; false; jarring; negative; pessimistic; sour; warning ~ 19. one a ~ (the meeting ended on an optimistic ~) ["comment"] 20. a usage ~ (as in a dictionary) ["document relating to a debt"] 21. to

discount a ~ 22. to hold a ~ 23. to call in a ~ 24. a demand; promissory; treasury ~ 25. a ~ matures ["paper money"] 26. a banknote; pound ~ ["importance"] 27. of ~ (several people of ~ were present; nothing of ~; worthy of ~)

note II *v.* 1. (L) we ~d that she was late again 2. (Q) ~ how it is done

notebook *n.* a loose-leaf ~ (AE)

noted *adj.* 1. duly ~ 2. (cannot stand alone) ~ for (our city is ~ for its fine restaurants)

notes *n.* ["condensed record"] 1. to make, take ~ (on) (our students always take copious ~) 2. (usu. fig.) to compare ~ 3. copious, detailed ~

nothing *n.* 1. to ask (for) ~ (to ask ~ in return) 2. to gain ~ by (we will gain ~ by ignoring the regulations) 3. ~ about (we know ~ about it) 4. ~ to (they are ~ to us) 5. ~ to + inf. (we have ~ to lose) 6. (misc.) to leave ~ to chance; to make ~ of being awarded an honor; we expect ~ of him; you can expect nothing from them; good for ~; ~ doing ("definitely not"); we have ~ that we can discuss; there is ~ between them; it cost next to ~; I got it for next to ~

notice I *n.* ["heed"] 1. to take ~ of 2. to attract ~ 3. to escape ~ 4. scant ~ (to attract scant ~) 5. ~ that + clause (it came to our ~ that she will be retiring) ["sign"] 6. to place, post, put up a ~ ["announcement"] ["notification"] 7. to bring smt. to smb.'s ~ 8. to serve ~ on 9. advance ~ 10. a ~ that + clause (we read the ~ that the water would be turned off for two hours) 11. at, on (AE) short ~ 12. until further ~ ["warning of one's intention to end an agreement"] 13. to give ~ 14. to put smb. on ~ 15. a month's; week's ~ 16. (colloq.) ~ to + inf. (the landlady gave him ~ to move) 17. subject to ~ ["review "] 18. to get rave ~s (the play got rave ~s) ["mention"] 19. a brief ~ 20. a book ~

notice II *v.* 1. (esp. AE) (I) we ~d him leave the house 2. (J) we ~d him leaving the house 3. (L) we ~d that she had left 4. (Q) did you ~ where she went?

notification *n.* 1. to send ~ 2. to get, receive ~ 3. ~ that + clause (we read the ~ that our building had been sold) 4. pending (further) ~

notify *v.* 1. (BE) (B) to ~ a crime to the police 2. (D; tr.) to ~ about, of (we ~fied the police of the incident) 3. (BE) (H) we'll ~ her to draw up a contract 4. (L; must have an object) she ~fied us that she would accept the position 5. (formal) (Q) he will ~ us where we are to meet

notion *n.* 1. to entertain, have a ~ 2. to dispel a ~ 3. an abstract, concrete; foggy, hazy, vague; ludicrous; odd, strange; preconceived; widespread ~ 4. a ~ about, of (she didn't have the slightest ~ of what I meant) 5. a ~ that + clause (we tried to dispel the ~ that benefits would be curtailed)

notoriety *n.* 1. to achieve, gain ~ 2. ~ for (~ for

being corrupt) 3. ~ surrounding (the ~ surrounding the published accounts of bribery in high places)

notorious *adj*. 1. ~ as (he was ~ as an outlaw) 2. ~ for (our town is ~ for its gambling casinos)

noun *n*. 1. to decline, inflect a ~ 2. an abstract; attributive; collective; common; compound; count; mass, uncountable; predicate; proper; verbal ~ 3. a feminine; masculine; neuter ~

nourishment *n*. 1. to get, take ~ 2. to give ~ 3. ~ for

novel *n*. 1. to publish; write a ~ 2. a detective, mystery; historical; romantic ~ 3. (misc.) to make a ~ into a film

novelty *n*. 1. to outgrow smt.'s ~ (it outgrew its ~) 2. a ~ wears off 3. a ~ for, to 4. a ~ to + inf. (it was a ~ to sleep so late)

novice *n*. 1. a rank ~ 2. a ~ at, in

now *adv*. 1. just; right ~ 2. by ~ 3. from ~ on 4. until, up to ~

nowhere *adv*. 1. to get, go ~ (with) ("to fail to arrive at a result") 2. ~ to + inf. (we had ~ to go) 3. (misc.) from, out of ~ (she came from/out of ~ to win the race)

nuance *n*. a delicate, fine, subtle ~

nuclear weapons *n*. to ban; dismantle, scrap ~

nucleus *n*. ["core"] to form a ~

nude *n*. in the ~ (to pose in the ~)

nudge *v*. 1. (d; tr.) to ~ into, towards (they ~d us into a compromise) 2. (H) she ~d me to finish quickly

nugget *n*. a gold ~

nuisance *n*. 1. to cause, create a ~ 2. to make a ~ of oneself 3. a confounded, damned, dreadful ~ 4. a public ~ 5. a ~ to 6. a ~ to + inf. (it was a ~ to move during the semester = it was a ~ moving during the semester) 7. a ~ that + clause (it's a ~ that there's no hot water)

nuisance value *n*. 1. to have a ~ 2. a high ~

null *adj*. (misc.) ~ and void

numb *adj*. 1. to go ~ (my arm went ~) 2. ~ with (~ with cold)

number I *n*. ["symbol indicating quantity"] 1. to round down (esp. BE); to round off (esp. AE); to round up (esp. BE) ~s 2. to square a ~ 3. an even; odd ~ 4. a high; low ~ 5. an algebraic; binary; cardinal; complex; compound; decimal; imaginary; infinite; irrational; mass; mixed; natural; negative; ordinal; positive; prime; quantum; random; whole ~ ["symbol serving to identify smt."] 6. the daily; lucky; winning ~ (of a lottery) 7. a box ~ (as at a post office) 8. the call ~ (of a book) 9. a serial ~ (of a product; of a soldier) 10. a fax; telephone ~ 11. a registration ~ ["quantity"] 12. to decrease, reduce; increase a ~ (to reduce the ~ of traffic accidents) 13. a considerable, goodly, large; enormous, great, untold ~ 14. an approximate, round; certain; growing; small; total ~ 15. in ~ (few in ~) ["telephone number"] 16. to call; dial a ~ 17. an unlisted ~ (AE; BE has *ex-directory listing/num-*

ber) ["issue"] 18. a back ~ ["single selection in a program of entertainment"] 19. to do, perform a ~ ["misc."] 20. to carry a ~ (when adding)

number II *v*. 1. (d; refl., tr.) to ~ among (I ~ her among my friends) 2. (D; tr.) to ~ from; to (we ~ed the tickets from one to five hundred) 3. (d; intr., tr.) to ~ in (our books ~ in the thousands) 4. (S) (esp. BE) our books ~ thousands

numbers *n*. ["form of gambling"] (US) 1. to play the ~ ["large group"] 2. in ~ (there is safety in ~) ["misc."] 3. by the ~ ("done according to specific directions")

numeral *n*. an Arabic; Roman ~

nuptials *n*. (formal or humorous) to officiate at, perform (the) ~

nurse I *n*. 1. a community-health (AE), public-health (AE) ~ (BE is approximately *health visitor*) 2. a community (BE), district (BE), visiting (AE) ~ 3. a geriatric, gerontological; home-health; industrial-health, occupational-health; maternal-child health; medical-surgical; obstetric; operating-room (AE), operating-theatre/theatre (BE); pediatric; psychiatric-mental health; school ~ 4. a graduate (AE); Licensed Practical (AE), State Enrolled (BE); practical; professional; Registered (AE), State Registered (BE) ~ 5. a general-duty; private-duty ~ 6. a head; supervising ~ 7. (misc.) an advanced practice ~; a ~ practitioner (US); a nurse-midwife

nurse II *v*. 1. (d; tr.) to ~ back to (to ~ smb. back to health) 2. (D; tr.) to ~ through (to ~ a patient through an illness)

nursery *n*. 1. a day ~ 2. at, in a ~

nursing *n*. 1. to study ~ 2. community-health, public-health ~ (AE; BE has *health-visitor service*) 3. geriatric, gerontological; home-health; industrial-health, occupational-health; maternal-child health; medical-surgical; obstetric; operating-room (AE), operating-theatre/theatre (BE); pediatric; psychiatric-mental health; school ~ 4. practical; professional ~ 5. general-duty; holistic; primary; private-duty ~ 6. (misc.) advanced practice ~

nut *n*. 1. to crack a ~ 2. to shell ~s 3. (misc.) a hard/tough ~ to crack ("a difficult problem to deal with")

nutrients *n*. basic, essential ~

nuts *adj*. (colloq.) ["infatuated"] 1. ~ about (he's ~ about her) ["crazy"] 2. to go ~

nutshell *n*. (colloq.) ["brief form"] in a ~ (to put smt. in a ~) ("to state smt. very succinctly")

nutty *adj*. (slang) 1. ~ to + inf. (it's ~ to behave like that) 2. (misc.) as ~ as a fruitcake

nuzzle up *v*. (D; intr.) to ~ against; to (the dog ~d up against her)

nylon *n*. 1. sheer ~ 2. a pair of ~s ("a pair of nylon stockings")

O

oaf *n*. a clumsy; stupid ~

oar *n*. to feather; peak ~s

oath *n*. ["solemn promise; solemn promise to tell the truth"] 1. to administer an ~ to smb. 2. to put smb. under ~ 3. to swear, take an ~ (of office) 4. to break, violate an ~ 5. a sacred, solemn ~ 6. a loyalty ~ 7. an ~ to + inf. (she took an ~ to do her duty) 8. an ~ that + clause (I took an ~ that I would obey all regulations) 9. on (BE), under ~ (to testify under ~ to tell the truth) 10. (misc.) to take the Hippocratic ~ ["swearword"] 11. to mutter, utter an ~ 12. a mild; strong ~ 13. a string of ~s

oatmeal *n*. ["porridge"] (esp. AE) 1. to cook, make, prepare ~ 2. a bowl of ~

obedience *n*. 1. to demand, exact ~ from 2. to instill ~ in 3. to pledge, swear ~ to 4. blind, strict, un-questioning ~ 5. ~ to

obedient *adj*. ~ to

obeisance *n*. (formal) ["bow"] 1. to make an ~ (to) 2. a deep ~

obituary *n*. 1. to send in; write an ~ 2. to print, publish an ~ 3. an ~ for 4. (misc.) to read the ~ries

object I *n*. 1. an immovable; inanimate; material; physical ~ 2. a sex ~ 3. (grammar) a direct; indirect ~ 4. (misc.) an ~ of derision; an unidentified flying ~ (= UFO)

object II *v*. 1. to ~ strenuously, strongly, violently 2. (D; intr.) to ~ to (to ~ to new taxes) 3. (L; to) she ~ed that the accusation was based on hearsay

objection *n*. 1. to have; lodge, make, raise an ~ 2. to brush aside; deal with, meet an ~ 3. to overrule; sustain an ~ 4. to withdraw an ~ 5. a valid ~ 6. a serious, strenuous, strong, violent, vociferous ~ 7. (legal) ~ overruled; ~ sustained 8. an ~ to (to raise an ~ to a proposal; we have no ~s to your going) 9. an ~ that + clause (the judge overruled their ~ that illegal evidence had been introduced) 10. over smb.'s ~s (the resolution was adopted over the vociferous ~s of the opposition)

objectionable *adj*. ~ to

objective *n*. 1. to achieve, attain, gain, meet an ~ 2. to formulate, set, state an ~ 3. (mil.) to take an ~ 4. a major, primary; realistic; worthy ~ 5. an eco-nomic; military; political ~ 6. a long-range; short-range ~ 7. the ultimate ~

objectivity *n*. in all ~

objector *n*. a conscientious ~

obligate *v*. (H) what does the agreement ~ us to do?

obligated *adj*. 1. ~ to (I'm ~ to you) 2. ~ to + inf. (she is ~ to pay off all debts by the end of the year)

obligation *n*. 1. to assume, take on an ~ 2. to feel an ~ 3. to discharge, fulfill, meet an ~ 4. to default on

an ~ 5. a contractual; family; legal; moral; social; solemn ~ 6. a military ~ ("required military ser-vice") 7. an ~ to (an ~ to one's parents) 8. an ~ to + inf. (we have an ~ to help them) 9. under (an) ~ (she was under no ~ to reply) 10. without ~

obligatory *adj*. 1. ~ for 2. (formal) ~ on, upon (doing one's duty is ~ on a soldier) 3. ~ to + inf. (in certain countries it is ~ to vote)

oblige *v*. 1. (d; tr.) to ~ by (would you ~ me by not smoking?) 2. (H) the contract ~s us to pay a pen-alty if we finish late

obliged *adj*. 1. ~ to (I'm ~ to you) 2. ~ to + inf. (we are ~ to attend all classes)

obliterate *v*. 1. to ~ completely, entirely, totally, utterly 2. (D; tr.) to ~ from

oblivion *n*. 1. to fall, sink into ~ 2. consigned to ~

oblivious *adj*. (cannot stand alone) ~ of, to (~ of one's surroundings; she was ~ to what was going on)

obnoxious *adj*. 1. ~ to 2. ~ to + inf. (it was ~ of them to do that)

oboe *n*. to play the ~

obscene *adj*. 1. ~ to + inf. (it's ~ to make such a comparison) 2. ~ that + clause (it is ~ that the abuse of women is still tolerated in many parts of the world)

obscenity *n*. to shout ~ties

obscure *adj*. ~ to (the meaning was ~ to me)

obscurity *n*. 1. to emerge from ~ 2. to sink into ~

observance *n*. 1. a religious ~ 2. a solemn, strict ~ (of the rules) 3. in ~ (of a holiday)

observant *adj*. ~ of

observation *n*. ["comment"] 1. to make an ~ 2. an astute, keen, penetrating, shrewd ~ 3. a personal ~ 4. an ~ about 5. an ~ that + clause (she made the astute ~ that the whole matter had been exagger-ated) ["condition of being observed"] 6. to keep; place smb. under ~ 7. close ~ 8. to be under ~ (they were under close ~) ["act of observing"] 9. to make ~s 10. (an) empirical; scientific ~ 11. (misc.) powers of ~

observe *v*. 1. to ~ attentively, carefully, closely 2. (I) we ~d them enter the building 3. (J) we ~d them entering the building 4. (L; to) ("to comment") several commentators have ~d that the rate of inflation has eased 5. (Q) I ~d how it was done

observer *n*. 1. a casual; impartial; keen, perceptive; outside; shrewd; skilled ~ 2. a military ~ 3. a team of ~s

obsess *v*. (D; intr.) (colloq.) to ~ about, over (don't ~ about your appearance)

obsessed *adj*. ~ by, with (~ by greed; ~ with fear)

obsession *n.* an ~ with

obsolescence *n.* built-in; planned ~

obstacle *n.* 1. to constitute, pose, present an ~ 2. to place, put an ~ in the way of smb. 3. to come across, confront, encounter an ~ 4. to clear, overcome, surmount an ~ 5. (of a horse) to take an ~ 6. to remove an ~ 7. a formidable, great, huge; insurmountable ~ 8. an artificial; natural ~ 9. an ~ to (an ~ to progress)

obstinate *adj.* ~ about; in

obstruction *n.* 1. to remove an ~ 2. an intestinal; respiratory ~ 3. an ~ to

obtrude *v.* (formal) (d; intr.) ("to intrude") to ~ on, upon

obvious I *adj.* 1. ~ to (her disappointment was ~ to everyone) 2. ~ that + clause (it's ~ that he is drunk)

obvious II *n.* to state the ~

occasion I *n.* ["opportunity"] 1. to have; take an ~ (to do smt.) 2. a propitious ~ 3. an ~ for 4. an ~ to + inf. (I had no ~ to speak with them; there was no ~ for me to tell her) 5. an ~ arises ["happening"] ["event"] 6. to celebrate; mark, observe an ~ 7. a festive, gala; happy, joyful, joyous ~ 8. an auspicious; fitting; special ~ 9. a memorable; momentous; unforgettable ~ 10. an official; state ~ 11. a sober; solemn ~ 12. on an ~ (on this ~; on numerous ~s) ["challenge"] 13. to rise to the ~ ["reason"] 14. an ~ for (there is no ~ for alarm) ["misc."] 15. on ~ ("sometimes")

occasion II *v.* (rare) (O; can be used with one object) your actions have ~ed (us) a great deal of expense

Occident *n.* in the ~

occlusion *n.* a coronary ~

occupation *n.* ["profession"] 1. to have an ~ 2. a hazardous; profitable, rewarding ~ 3. by ~ (she is a waitress by ~) ["act of occupying"] 4. a military ~ 5. under ~ 6. (misc.) a zone of ~

occupied *adj.* 1. deeply; solely ~ 2. ~ in; with (they are ~ with their own concerns)

occupy *v.* (d; refl., tr.) to ~ with (she ~pied them with minor chores)

occur *v.* ("to come to mind") (d; intr.) to ~ to (an idea ~red to her; it never ~red to me to ask; it suddenly ~red to me that we could ask her for help)

occurrence *n.* a common, daily, everyday, regular, usual; frequent; infrequent; rare, unusual ~

ocean *n.* 1. to cross the ~ (by ship) 2. across the ~ (to fly across the ~) 3. in the ~

o'clock *adv.* at (ten) ~

odd *adj.* 1. ~ to + inf. (it was ~ of her to do that) 2. ~ that + clause (it's ~ that she is not at home)

odds *n.* ["allowance designed to equalize a bettor's chances"] 1. to give, lay ~ 2. to accept, take ~ 3. to buck ("oppose") the ~ ["disadvantages"] 4. to beat the ~ 5. considerable, formidable, great, heavy,

hopeless, insurmountable, long, overwhelming ~ 6. ~ against (all the ~ were against us) 7. against ~ (to struggle against formidable ~; to succeed against all ~) ["advantages"] 8. ~ in favor of ["disagreement"] 9. at ~ over; with ["possibility"] 10. the ~ that + clause (what are the ~ that they will show up?) ["misc."] 11. by all ~ ("without question")

ode *n.* 1. to compose an ~ 2. an ~ to (an ~ to joy)

odious *adj.* ~ to

odometer *n.* (AE) to turn back an ~ (BE has *mileometer*)

odor, odour *n.* ["smell"] 1. to emit, exude, give off, have, produce an ~ 2. to perceive; recognize an ~ 3. a good; pleasant ~ 4. a faint, slight ~ 5. a heavy; persistent; pungent, strong ~ 6. a bad, fetid, foul, rank, unpleasant; musty ~ 7. an ~ emanates from 8. an ~ permeates smt. (an unpleasant ~ permeated the entire room) ["repute"] (BE) 9. in bad; good ~ (with)

off *adv.* ["situated"] 1. badly, poorly; worse ~ 2. better; comfortably; well ~ ["not exact"] 3. far, way ~ 4. ~ in (he's way ~ in his calculations) ["misc."] 5. to have a day ~ ("to be free from work")

off-balance *adj., adv.* caught ~

offend *v.* 1. to ~ deeply, gravely, terribly 2. (D; intr.) to ~ against (to ~ against common decency) 3. (R) it ~ed me deeply that you did not come

offender *n.* a chronic; first; juvenile; sex ~

offense, offence *n.* ["infraction"] 1. to commit an ~ 2. a first; minor, petty, trivial ~ 3. a serious ~ 4. a capital; civil; criminal; impeachable; indictable ~ 5. an ~ against ["feeling of outrage"] 6. to take ~ at (she takes ~ at every remark) ["insult"] (formal) 7. to cause, give ~ 8. an ~ to

offensive I *adj.* 1. ~ to (his actions were ~ to everyone) 2. ~ to + inf. (it's ~ to read such things in the newspaper)

offensive II *n.* 1. to assume, go on, go over to, start (up), take the ~ 2. to launch, mount an ~ 3. to carry out, conduct, undertake an ~ 4. to break off an ~ 5. an economic; military; peace ~ 6. (usu. mil.) a ground; full-scale ~ (their forces launched a full-scale, ground ~) 7. an ~ against (they mounted an economic ~ against the neighboring countries) 8. on the ~ (the candidate went on the ~)

offer I *n.* 1. to make an ~ (she made me an attractive ~) 2. to consider an ~ 3. to accept, agree to an ~ 4. to decline, refuse, reject, spurn, turn down an ~ 5. to withdraw an ~ 6. an attractive, generous; firm; reasonable; tempting ~ 7. a tentative ~ 8. an introductory; job; trial ~ 9. an ~ to + inf. (her ~ to help was accepted gratefully) 10. (BE) on ~ ("available")

offer II *v.* 1. (A) she ~ed the job to me; or: she ~ed me the job 2. (D; refl., tr.) to ~ as (the money was

~ed as an inducement) 3. (D; tr.) to ~ for (to ~ a reward for information; we ~ed them one hundred thousand dollars for the house) 4. (E) they ~ed to compromise

offering *n.* 1. to make an ~ 2. a burnt; peace; sacrificial; votive ~ 3. an ~ to

offer up *v.* 1. (d; tr.) to ~ as (to ~ as a sacrifice) 2. (D; tr.) to ~ for (they ~ed up the child for adoption) 3. (D; tr.) to ~ to (to ~ prayers to God)

office *n.* ["function"] 1. to assume (an) ~ 2. to seek (public) ~ 3. (pol.) to run for (esp. AE), stand for (BE) ~ 4. to hold; take ~ 5. to resign from (an) ~ 6. (pol.) (an) appointive; elective; high; public ~ 7. (pol.) in; out of ~ (our party is out of ~) 8. a term of ~ 9. (misc.) smb.'s good ~s ("smb.'s services as a mediator") ["ministry"] (BE) 10. the Foreign; Home ~ ["place where a function is performed"] 11. to open; set up an ~ 12. to lease; rent an ~ 13. to manage, run an ~ 14. a branch; head, home, main ~ 15. a booking; box, ticket ~ 16. a business; dentist's (AE); doctor's (AE); lawyer's ~ 17. a left-luggage (BE); lost-and-found (AE), lost property (BE) ~ 18. a customs; dead-letter; Met (BE), Meteorological (BE); patent; post; registry (BE) ~ 19. at, in an ~ (she works at our ~)

USAGE NOTE: In North America, doctors and dentists have *offices*; in Great Britain, they have *surgeries*.

office hours *n.* 1. to have, keep ~ 2. after; during; (BE) out of, outside ~

officer *n.* ["person holding a certain rank in the armed forces"] 1. to commission an ~ 2. to promote an ~ 3. to break, demote; cashier, dismiss an ~ 4. a commissioned; non-commissioned; petty; warrant ~ 5. a company-grade (AE); field-grade (AE); junior ~ 6. a commanding; flag; general; high-ranking; ranking; senior; superior; top-ranking ~ 7. a line; staff ~ 8. an air-force; army; military; naval ~ 9. a duty; executive; gunnery; intelligence; liaison ~ 10. ~ of the day; ~ of the deck ["person holding a position of authority"] 11. a correctional (AE); court; juvenile (AE); law-enforcement; peace, police; probation; truant (AE) ~ 12. a customs; revenue (BE) ~ 13. a health; medical; senior nursing (BE) ~ 14. an executive; personnel; public-relations ~ 15. (misc.) a chief executive ~ (CEO); to install newly elected ~s; (GB) a returning ~

official *n.* 1. a high, high-ranking, senior, top-ranking; responsible ~ 2. an appointed; elected ~ 3. a church; public ~ 4. a city; county; federal (US); government; local; state ~ 5. a customs; health; law-enforcement; police; postal ~ 6. (misc.) to bribe an ~

officiate *v.* 1. (D; intr.) to ~ as (she ~d as the chairperson) 2. (D; intr.) to ~ at (to ~ at a ceremony)

offing *n.* in the ~ ("forthcoming")

offspring *n.* to produce ~

ogle *v.* (d; intr.) to ~ at

oil *n.* ["petroleum"] 1. to drill for; hit, strike ~ 2. to pump ~ 3. to produce; refine ~ 4. crude; refined ~ 5. offshore ~ 6. ~ gushes from a well ["lubricant"] 7. to change; check the ~ 8. household; linseed; lubricating; machine; motor ~ ["fatty liquid"] 9. canola (esp. US); coconut; cooking; corn; cottonseed; olive; palm; peanut; safflower; salad; sunflower; vegetable ~ 10. castor; cod-liver; mineral ~ 11. a film of ~ ["misc."] 12. to burn the midnight ~ ("to work very late at night"); ~ and water do not mix

oils *n.* to paint in ~

ointment *n.* 1. to apply, put on, rub in, rub on (an) ~ 2. a soothing ~ 3. a skin ~ 4. (misc.) a fly in the ~ ("smt. that irritates or causes harm")

OK I *adj.* (colloq.) 1. ~ for; with (is this ~ with you? is that ~ for you?) 2. ~ to + inf. (it is ~ to bring your lunch with you)

OK II *n.* (colloq.) ["approval"] 1. to give one's ~ 2. to get the ~ 3. the ~ to + inf. (we got the ~ to continue)

old *adj.* (misc.) she's ten years ~; to grow ~ gracefully; any ~ thing

old age *n.* 1. to live to a ripe ~ 2. extreme; ripe ~ 3. in ~ (in her ~ she took up painting)

old hand *n.* an ~ at (she's an ~ at politics)

O levels *n.* (GB) ["ordinary-level secondary school examinations"] to do, sit, take (one's) ~

olive branch *n.* ["symbol of peace"] 1. to extend, hold out, offer the ~ 2. to accept; decline, reject the ~

Olympic Games *n.* 1. to hold the ~ 2. to host the ~

omelet, omelette *n.* 1. to make an ~ 2. a cheese; mushroom; plain; Spanish; Western ~

omen *n.* 1. a bad; good ~ 2. an ~ for

omission *n.* 1. to correct, rectify an ~ 2. a glaring ~ 3. an ~ from (an ~ from a list)

omit *v.* 1. (D; tr.) to ~ from (she ~ted his name from the list) 2. (E) (esp. BE) he ~ted to explain why he had been late

on *prep.* 1. to have smt. ~ smb. ("to have evidence against smb.") 2. the fire went out ~ me ("the fire went out through no fault of mine") 3. we were ~ to what was happening ("we were aware of what was happening") 4. well ~ in years ("rather old") 5. (misc.) (the) drinks are ~ me ("I will pay for the drinks")

once *adv.* 1. at ~ 2. ~ again, more 3. (misc.) ~ upon a time

one *pronoun* 1. ~ by ~ 2. ~ of (~ of them; ~ of the students)

once-over *n.* (colloq.) ["a look"] to give smb./smt. the ~

online *adv.* ["linked by computer"] 1. to be ~ 2. to

get, go ~ 3. to communicate ~

onslaught *n.* 1. to resist an ~ 2. an enemy; sudden ~

onus *n.* 1. the ~ is on smb. to do smt. (the ~ is on you to get the job done) 2. the ~ lies, rests with smb. (the ~ of proof lies with the police) 3. to put the ~ on smb.

ooze *v.* 1. (d; intr.) to ~ from, out of; into (blood was ~ing from the wound) 2. (d; intr.) to ~ with (to ~ with charm)

open I *adj.* 1. wide ~ 2. ~ for (~ for business) 3. (cannot stand alone) ~ to (~ to the public; I'm ~ to suggestions) 4. (misc.) to lay oneself ~ to criticism

open II *n.* 1. in, into the ~ (to bring smt. out into the ~) 2. (misc.) it is all out in the ~ now ("everything has been revealed")

open III *v.* 1. (D; intr., tr.) to ~ by, with (we ~ed our meeting by singing a song; we ~ed our meeting with a prayer) 2. (D; tr.) to ~ for (to ~ new land for development) 3. (d; intr.) to ~ into, onto, to (the gate ~s into the garden; to ~ onto the terrace; the door ~s to the street) 4. (D; tr.) to ~ to (they ~ed their meetings to the public) 5. (N; used with an adjective) ~ your mouth wide 6. (misc.) does the door ~ in or out? ~ your books at/to (AE) page three

opener *n.* ["device that opens"] 1. a bottle; can (AE), tin (BE) ~ 2. a letter ~ (AE; BE has *paper knife*)

open house *n.* to have, hold (an) ~

opening *n.* ["vacancy"] 1. an ~ for (we have an ~ for an engineer) ["putting into operation"] 2. a grand ~ (the grand ~ of a new supermarket)

open season *n.* 1. to declare ~ (on) 2. an ~ on (an ~ on deer)

open up *v.* (D; intr., tr.) to ~ to (the government has ~ed up the files to the public; he finally ~ed up to the press)

opera *n.* 1. to perform, stage an ~ 2. (a) comic; grand; light ~ 3. a soap ~ 4. a horse ~ ("western film") 5. at the ~

operate *v.* 1. (d; intr.) to ~ against (their troops were ~ing against the guerrillas) 2. (med.) (D; intr.) to ~ for; on (the surgeon ~d on her for appendicitis; she was ~d on for appendicitis)

operating system *n.* to boot up; reboot the ~ (of a computer)

operation *n.* ["surgical procedure"] 1. to perform an ~ 2. to have, undergo an ~ 3. to come through, go through, survive an ~ 4. a delicate; emergency; exploratory; major; minor ~ 5. an ~ for; on (an ~ for the removal of gallstones) ["military or police activity"] 6. to conduct; launch, mount, undertake an ~ 7. covert; guerrilla; joint; large-scale; minesweeping; mopping-up ~s ["state of being functional"] 8. to put into ~ (the plant has been put into ~) 9. in ~ (the factory is in ~) ["project"] 10. a cloak-and-dagger, covert, secret; rescue ~

operations *n.* 1. to conduct ~ 2. combined, joint; drilling; military; mining; mopping-up; naval; offensive; salvage ~ 3. (mil.) a theater of ~

operator *n.* 1. a computer; crane; elevator (AE); ham, radio; machine (AE); radar; switchboard (AE), telephone (AE); tour ~ 2. (colloq.) a slick, smooth ~

opinion *n.* 1. to air, express, give, offer, pass, state, venture, voice an ~ 2. to form an ~ about (I still have not formed an ~ about the candidates) 3. to mold (public) ~ 4. to entertain, have, hold an ~ 5. (legal) (AE) to hand down an ~ (the court handed down an ~) 6. to ask for, seek smb.'s ~ 7. a candid, frank, honest ~ 8. a considered; informed; objective; strong ~ (she has strong ~s about everything) 9. a personal; prevailing, prevalent ~ 10. a negative; positive ~ 11. a contrary, dissenting; opposing ~ 12. a high; low ~ of (he has a high ~ of himself) 13. (an) expert; lay; legal; medical ~ 14. political; popular; public ~ 15. a second ~ (as given by a doctor) 16. shades of ~ 17. an ~ about, on 18. the ~ that + clause (she expressed her ~ that a compromise would be reached) 19. in smb.'s ~ (in my humble ~) 20. of an ~ (she is of the ~ that nothing will help) 21. (misc.) a clash of ~s; a difference of ~

opponent *n.* 1. a formidable, strong; weak ~ 2. (ironic) my worthy ~

opportunity *n.* 1. to grab, seize, take an ~ 2. to afford, give, offer an ~ 3. to find; have an ~ 4. to lose, miss; pass up an ~ 5. a fleeting; lost, missed ~ 6. a golden, once-in-a-lifetime; great ~ (they had a once-in-a-lifetime ~ to visit Europe) 7. ample ~ 8. (an) equal ~ ("government policy of giving all citizens an equal chance") 9. (an) ~ arises 10. an ~ for 11. an ~ to + inf. (we had an ~ to visit our parents) 12. at the first ~ 13. (misc.) ~ knocks ("appears"); a window of ~

USAGE NOTE: The US has *equal-opportunity employers.* The UK has *equal-opportunities employers.*

oppose *v.* 1. to ~ bitterly, resolutely, strongly, vehemently, vigorously 2. (G) they ~ spending the money 3. (K) I ~d his dropping out of college

opposed *adj.* 1. adamantly; diametrically; ideologically; strongly, vehemently ~ 2. ~ to

opposite I *adj.* (BE) ~ to

USAGE NOTE: When *opposite* means "facing", it can be an adjective in BE—her house is opposite to ours. More usu., *opposite* is used as a preposition in both BE and AE—her house is opposite ours. When *opposite* means "diametrically opposed", it is used only in BE as an adjective—her opinions are opposite to ours.

opposite II *n.* 1. a direct, polar ~ 2. an ~ of, to 3. (misc.) ~s attract

opposition *n.* 1. to arouse, stir up ~ 2. to offer, put up ~ 3. to crush, overcome, wear down ~ 4. to come across, encounter, face, meet, run up against ~ 5. to brook no ~ 6. (ling.) to neutralize an ~ 7. bitter, determined, fierce, stiff, strong, unbending, unyielding, vehement ~ 8. growing, mounting ~ 9. ~ hardens, stiffens; wanes, weakens 10. ~ to (~ to new taxes) 11. against, despite, in spite of, over (the) ~ (we adopted the resolution over the ~ of the other party) 12. in ~ to

oppression *n.* under ~ (to live under ~)

opt *v.* 1. (d; intr.) to ~ for 2. (d; intr.) to ~ out of (to ~ out of the conflict) 3. (E) they ~ed to decline the invitation

optimism *n.* 1. to display, radiate, show; express ~ 2. cautious, guarded; eternal, incurable, unflagging ~ 3. ~ about, over

optimist *n.* an eternal, incurable ~

optimistic *adj.* 1. cautiously, guardedly; incurably ~ 2. ~ about, over 3. ~ that + clause (we are ~ that the results will be favorable)

option *n.* 1. to exercise an ~ 2. to take an ~ on 3. an exclusive; first ~ 4. (AE) a local ~ (of a political subdivision) 5. a share; stock ~ 6. an ~ on 7. an ~ to + inf. (they had an ~ to buy the team) 8. (misc.) to have no ~ but to...; to keep one's ~s open

oracle *n.* ["authority"] to consult an ~

orange *n.* 1. to peel; squeeze an ~ 2. a mandarin; navel ~

oration *n.* 1. to deliver an ~ 2. a funeral ~

oratory *n.* 1. eloquent, persuasive, powerful ~ 2. inflammatory, rabble-rousing ~ 3. campaign ~

orbit *n.* 1. to make an ~ around, of, round (the spaceship made five ~s of the moon) 2. to be in; go into ~ 3. in; into ~ (to put a satellite into ~)

orchard *n.* an apple; cherry; peach ~

orchestra *n.* 1. to conduct, direct (esp. AE), lead (esp. AE) an ~ 2. a chamber; dance; philharmonic, symphony; pops; string ~ 3. an ~ performs, plays; tunes up

ordain *v.* 1. (D; tr.) he was ~ed as a priest 2. (formal) (L; subj.) the emperor ~ed that all foreigners be/should be expelled 3. (N; used with a noun) he was ~ed (a) priest

ordeal *n.* 1. to go through, undergo an ~ 2. a dreadful, terrible, terrifying, trying ~ 3. (an) ~ by fire; water

order I *n.* ["request for merchandise or services"] 1. to give, place, put in an ~ 2. to make out, write out an ~ 3. to fill; receive, take an ~ (has the waiter taken your ~?) 4. to cancel an ~ 5. a back; mail; prepublication; rush; shipping; standing ~ 6. a side (esp. AE; in a restaurant) ~ 7. (new) ~s are falling off; are picking up 8. on ~ (the merchandise is on ~) 9. to ~ (made to ~) 10. (misc.) a tall ~ to fill ("a difficult task to carry out") ["command"] 11. to give, hand down (AE), issue an ~ 12. to carry out, execute; obey, take an ~ 13. to cancel, coun-

termand, rescind, revoke; violate an ~ 14. a direct; executive; preservation (BE); specific ~ 15. doctor's; marching; sealed; standing; verbal; written ~s 16. an ~ to + inf. (we received an ~ to attack) 17. an ~ that + clause; subj. (headquarters issued an ~ that the attack be/should be resumed) 18. at, by, on smb.'s ~ (by whose ~ was this done?) 19. under ~s (we were under ~s to remain indoors) ["court decree"] 20. to issue an ~ 21. an affiliation (BE); cease-and-desist; court; gag; maintenance (BE), support (AE); restraining ~ ["association, group"] 22. a cloistered; Masonic; mendicant; monastic; religious; secret ~ ["system"] 23. an economic; pecking; social ~ (he's at the bottom of the pecking ~) ["proper procedure"] 24. (a) point of ~ 25. in ~; out of ~ (the senator was out of ~) 26. to call a meeting to ~ ("to begin a meeting"; "to reestablish proper procedure at a meeting") ["state of peace"] 27. to establish; keep, maintain; restore ~ 28. public ~ ["state in which everything is in its proper place or condition"] 29. to put smt. in/into ~ 30. apple-pie, good, shipshape ~ 31. in; out of ~ (everything is in good ~; this machine is out of ~ again) ["condition"] 32. working ~ (in working ~) ["sequence"] 33. alphabetical; chronological; logical; numerical ~ 34. ascending; descending ~ 35. in; out of ~ (in ~ of importance; in alphabetical ~; these entries are out of ~) ["military formation"] 36. close; extended; open ~ ["instructions to pay"] 37. a money (AE), postal (BE) ~ ["misc."] 38. law and ~; a new ~; a new world ~; an old ~; of the ~ of (BE)/on the ~ of (AE) ("approximately"); research of the highest ~

order II *v.* 1. (C) ~ a copy for me; or: ~ me a copy 2. (D; tr.) to ~ from (to ~ merchandise from a mail-order house) 3. (d; tr.) to ~ from, out of (she ~ed him out of the house) 4. (d; tr.) to ~ off (the referee ~ed the player off the field) 5. (H) the sergeant ~ed his platoon to fall in 6. (L; subj.) the mayor ~ed that free food be/should be distributed 7. (M) the judge ~ed the prisoner to be transferred 8. (esp. AE) (N; used with a past participle) the judge ~ed the prisoner transferred to the county jail 9. (misc.) the doctor ~ed her to bed

ordinance *n.* ["local law"] 1. to adopt, enact, pass an ~ 2. to issue an ~ 3. to apply, enforce an ~ 4. to repeal, rescind, revoke an ~ 5. to obey, observe an ~ 6. to violate an ~ 7. a city, municipal; local; township ~ 8. an ~ that + clause; subj. (the town issued an ~ that all dogs be/should be muzzled)

ordinary *n.* out of the ~

ordnance *n.* naval ~

ore *n.* copper; iron ~

organ *n.* ["part of the body"] 1. body; internal; major; reproductive, sex, sexual; sense, sensory; speech; vital; vocal ~s ["large wind instrument"] 2. to play the ~ 3. a barrel; electronic; hand; pipe;

reed ~ ["publication"] 4. a government; house (esp. BE); official; party ~

organism *n.* 1. a dead; healthy; living ~ 2. a deadly; harmful; infectious ~ 3. microorganisms; minute ~s

organization *n.* 1. to establish, form an ~ 2. to run an ~ 3. to disband, dissolve an ~ 4. a charitable, philanthropic; relief ~ 5. a civic, community; non-governmental; nonprofit, not-for-profit (AE); professional; religious; voluntary ~ 6. a student; women's; youth ~ 7. an international; local; national; state; UN ~ 8. a central; umbrella ~ 9. a government; official ~ 10. a health-maintenance (AE) ~ 11. a profit-making, proprietary (AE) ~ 12. a front ~ for

orgasm *n.* to achieve, have, reach an ~

orgy *n.* 1. to engage in, stage an ~ 2. a drunken ~

Orient *n.* in the ~

orient, orientate *v.* (D; refl., tr.) to ~ to (to ~ oneself to one's surroundings)

orientated, oriented *adj.* ~ towards (~ towards the needs of young consumers)

orientation *n.* ["introduction"] 1. to give, offer smb. (an) ~ to 2. to get, go through, receive (an) ~

origin *n.* 1. to have an ~ in (the problem has its ~s in the nineteenth century) 2. in ~ (the documents were Norse in ~) 3. of ~ (she is of humble ~; the fire was of undetermined ~)

original *n.* in the ~ (to read a text in the ~)

originality *n.* 1. to display, show ~ 2. ~ in

originate *v.* (d; intr.) to ~ from; in; with (the idea ~d with her)

orphan *n.* 1. to be left an ~ 2. a war ~

orthodoxy *n.* (a) rigid, strict ~

oscillate *v.* (D; intr.) to ~ between

Oscar (T) *n.* 1. to receive, win an ~ 2. (misc.) to be nominated for an ~

osmosis *n.* by ~ (to absorb by ~)

ossify *v.* (D; intr.) to ~ into (their ideas ~fied into a rigid orthodoxy)

other *adj.* ["second"] every ~ (I jog every ~ day)

ought *v.* (E) you ~ to help

oust *v.* (D; tr.) to ~ from

out *adj., adv.* ["unconscious"] 1. ~ cold ("completely unconscious") ["intent on"] 2. ~ to + inf. (she is ~ to get revenge) ["gone"] 3. ~ to (~ to lunch) ["misc."] 4. over and ~ (used at the end of a radio message); to turn smt. inside ~; down and ~ ("destitute"); they are ~ for a walk; he is ~ for your money ("he is attempting to get your money")

outage *n.* (AE) ["failure"] a power ~

outbreak *n.* a sporadic ~

outburst *n.* an angry; furious; spontaneous; sudden; violent ~

outcome *n.* 1. to decide the (final) ~ of 2. a probable; successful ~ 3. to evaluate, measure ~s ("to evaluate results")

outcry *n.* 1. to make, raise an ~ 2. an international; public ~ 3. an ~ against; for

outdo *v.* 1. (D; tr.) to ~ in (she outdid them in every field) 2. (misc.) not to be outdone

outdoors *adv.* 1. to be; go ~ 2. (misc.) in the great ~

outgrowth *n.* a direct; indirect ~

outing *n.* to go on an ~

outlay *n.* ["spending of money"] 1. to make ~s for 2. a capital; huge; large; modest; small ~

outlet *n.* ["passage"] 1. an ~ to (an ~ to the sea) ["means of expression"] 2. to find an ~ for (to find an ~ for one's emotions) 3. to provide an ~ for ["retail store"] 4. a factory; retail; sales ~ ["socket"] (AE) 5. an electrical ~

outline I *n.* 1. to draw up, make an ~ 2. a bare; broad, general; dim; rough ~ 3. in ~ (to draw in ~; to present a project in broad ~)

outline II *v.* 1. (B) they ~d the project to us 2. (d; tr.) to ~ against (the ship was ~d against the horizon)

outlook *n.* ["viewpoint"] 1. to have an ~ on (she has a healthy ~ on life) 2. a cheerful, optimistic, positive; healthy ~ 3. a negative, pessimistic ~ 4. in ~ (we are quite similar in ~) ["prospects"] 5. a bright ~ 6. a bleak, dark, dim, dismal, dreary, gloomy ~ 7. the long-range, long-term; short-range, short-term ~ 8. an ~ for (the ~ for the future is bright)

outpost *n.* a military ~

output *n.* 1. to increase, step up ~ 2. to curtail, cut back, reduce ~ 3. annual; daily; industrial; monthly ~

outrage I *n.* ["anger"] 1. to express; feel ~ 2. to spark (AE), spark off (BE), stir up ~ 3. (misc.) a sense of ~ ["offensive act"] 4. to commit an ~ 5. an ~ against (an ~ against public morality) 6. an ~ to + inf. (it was an ~ to take innocent civilians hostage) 7. an ~ that + clause (it was an ~ that her name was omitted)

outrage II *v.* (R) we were ~d (to learn) that she had been arrested

outrageous *adj.* 1. ~ to + inf. (it's ~ to permit such behavior) 2. ~ that + clause (it's ~ that such practices are allowed)

outs *n.* (colloq.) (AE) to be on the ~ with smb. ("to be on bad terms with smb.")

outset *n.* at; from the ~

outside *n.* 1. from the ~ 2. on the ~

outsider *n.* a rank ~

outskirts *n.* on the ~ (of a city)

outspoken *adj.* ~ in (~ in their opposition to new taxes)

outstanding *adj.* ~ in (~ in scientific achievement)

outward *adv.* ~ bound

outweigh *v.* to far ~

ovation *n.* 1. to get, receive an ~ 2. to give smb. an ~ (the audience gave them a thunderous ~) 3. a standing; thunderous, tremendous ~ 4. to an ~ (they walked out on the stage to a thunderous ~)

oven *n.* 1. to light, turn on an ~ 2. to turn off an ~ 3. an electric; gas; microwave; self-cleaning ~ 4. a hot; pre-heated ~

over *adj.* ["finished"] 1. ~ between; with (it's all ~ between them) 2. (misc.) ~ and done with

overboard *adv.* 1. to fall ~ 2. (misc.) man ~! to go ~ over smt. ("to carry smt. to excess")

overcharge *v.* 1. (D; tr.) to ~ by (they ~d us by twenty percent) 2. (D; tr.) to ~ for (they ~d us for the book; we were ~d for it by ten percent)

overcome *v.* 1. (D; tr.) to ~ by (they were overcome by smoke) 2. (D; tr.) to ~ with (I was overcome with emotion)

overcompensate *v.* (D; intr.) to ~ for (he ~s for his poor performance in class by doing extra assignments for the teacher)

overdose I *n.* 1. to give; take an ~ 2. a fatal, lethal; massive ~ 3. a drug ~

overdose II *v.* (D; intr.) to ~ on (to ~ on a medication)

overdue *adj.* long ~

overflow I *n.* 1. to catch the ~ 2. the ~ from

overflow II *v.* 1. (D; intr.) to ~ into (the mob ~ed into the street) 2. (d; intr.) to ~ with (the stadium was ~ing with spectators)

overgrown *adj.* ~ with

overhaul I *n.* ["repairs"] a complete; major; thorough ~ (our car needs a major ~)

overhaul II *v.* to ~ completely; thoroughly

overhear *v.* 1. (I) we overheard him say it 2. (J) they overheard us discussing our plans

overindulge *v.* (D; intr., refl., tr.) to ~ in (we ~d ourselves in the rich pastries)

overindulgence *n.* ~ in

overjoyed *adj.* 1. ~ at (we were ~ at your success) 2. ~ to + inf. (we were ~ to learn the good news) 3. ~ that + clause (we were ~ that you could make it)

overlap *v.* (D; intr.) to ~ with (their territory ~s with ours)

overload I *n.* circuit; sensory ~

overload II *v.* (D; tr.) to ~ with (the ship was ~ed with cargo)

overpass *n.* (esp. AE) an ~ over (an ~ over a road) (BE has *flyover*)

overrated *adj.* vastly ~

overreact *v.* (D; intr.) to ~ to (they ~ed to the news)

overrun *adj.* ~ with (~ with weeds)

overseas *adv.*, *n.* 1. to go, travel ~ 2. (misc.) to return from ~

oversight *n.* 1. an ~ that + clause (it was through an ~ that you were not invited) 2. by, through an ~ (her name was omitted through an ~)

overstocked *adj.* ~ with (~ with merchandise)

overtime *n.* ["extra time worked"] 1. to do, put in, work (five hours) ~ ["extra wage"] 2. to earn ~ 3. to pay ~ 4. on ~ (I was on ~ all week) ["extra period"] (sports) (AE; BE has *extra time*) 5. in ~ 6. a sudden-death ~

overtones *n.* 1. to develop, take on; have ~ 2. political; racial ~ (the dispute took on political ~)

overture *n.* ["musical introduction"] 1. to compose; perform, play an ~ 2. an ~ to ["introductory proposal"] 3. to make an ~; to make ~s to 4. to spurn smb.'s ~s

overview *n.* to give an ~ of

owe *v.* 1. (A) she ~s ten dollars to her sister; or: she ~s her sister ten dollars (the *to* is usu. not used when the indirect object is a pronoun: she owes her ten dollars) 2. (D; tr.) to ~ for, on (we still ~ one hundred dollars for the car) 3. (misc.) we ~ it to our students to grade their papers promptly

owing *adj.* ~ to

owl *n.* ~s hoot

own *determiner, pronoun* 1. to hold one's ~ ("to continue to survive") 2. to come into one's ~ ("to receive recognition") 3. on one's ~ ("independently") 4. of one's ~ (for reasons of one's ~) ("for one's own reasons")

owner *n.* 1. a part ~ 2. the lawful, rightful ~

ownership *n.* collective; communal; joint; private; public; state ~

own up *v.* (colloq.) (D; intr.) ("to confess") to ~ to (she ~ed up to stealing the watch)

ox *n.* 1. oxen bellow 2. a pair; team; yoke of oxen 3. (misc.) as strong as an ~

oxygen *n.* 1. to administer ~; to give smb. ~ 2. to get, receive ~ 3. liquid ~

P

pace I *n.* ["rate of movement"] 1. to set the ~ 2. to keep ~ with 3. to change ~; to slacken the ~ 4. an even, steady ~ 5. a blistering, brisk, fast, rapid; dizzy, frantic, hectic; grueling, killing ~ 6. a slack, slow, sluggish; snail's ("extremely slow") ~ 7. at a certain ~ (at a fast ~) 8. (misc.) a change of ~ (also fig.) ["step"] (esp. mil.) 9. to take a ~ (to take three ~s forward) ["misc."] 10. to put smb. through the ~s ("to subject smb. to a test of skill")
pace II *v.* (P; intr.) she was ~ing back and forth
pacemaker *n.* (med.) 1. to fit smb. with a ~ 2. to insert, put in a ~
pacifier *n.* (AE) to suck on a ~ (BE has *dummy*)
pack I *n.* ["deck of playing cards"] 1. to cut; shuffle a ~ (of cards) ["load, bundle"] 2. a backpack; full field (mil.); parachute ~ ["mass"] 3. an ice ~
pack II *v.* 1. (C) ~ a sandwich for me; or: ~ me a sandwich 2. (d; intr.) to ~ into (they all ~ed into the auditorium) 3. (D; tr.) to ~ into (I ~ed everything into one suitcase) 4. (N; used with an adjective) ~ everything tight
package *n.* 1. to deliver a ~ 2. to address; insure; mail (esp. AE), post (BE); send a ~ 3. to get, receive a ~ 4. to open, unwrap; seal; wrap a ~ 5. a bulky; neat ~ 6. (computers) a software ~ 7. (misc.) a ~ deal
packaging *n.* tamper-proof; tamper-resistant ~
packed *adj.* 1. densely, tightly ~ 2. loosely ~ 3. vacuum ~ 4. ~ with (streets ~ with people)
packet *n.* a pay ~ (BE; AE has *pay envelope*)
packing *n.* ["act of packing"] to do the ~
pack off *v.* (D; tr.) to ~ to (to ~ the children off to camp)
pact *n.* 1. to agree to, make; sign a ~ 2. to denounce a ~ 3. a formal; informal; official ~ 4. a defense; mutual-assistance; nonaggression; trade ~ 5. a ~ between 6. a ~ to + inf. (we had a ~ not to reveal the facts of the case) 7. a ~ that + clause (the two governments signed a ~ that they would jointly defend their borders)
pad *n.* ["cushion"] 1. a heating; heel; knee; shoulder ~ ["piece of material"] 2. a gauze; quilted; scouring ~ ["connected sheets of paper"] 3. a scratch (esp. AE); writing ~ ["airstrip"] 4. a helicopter; launch, launching ~ ["smb.'s residence"] (slang) 5. at smb.'s ~
paddle I *n.* a ping-pong, table-tennis ~
paddle II *v.* (P; intr., tr.) I ~d the canoe across the lake; we ~d down the river
paean *n.* (lit.) ["hymn of praise"] 1. to sing a ~ 2. a ~ to (to sing a ~ to smb.'s glory)
page I *n.* ["leaf of a book, journal, newspaper"] 1. to turn a ~ 2. to turn down a ~ 3. to turn to a certain ~ 4. to cite a (volume and) ~ 5. to set a ~ (in type) 6. a title ~ (in a book) 7. the amusement; editorial; front; society; sports ~ (in a newspaper) 8. on ~ one; turn to ~ five 9. (misc.) you will not find a dull ~ in the whole book; a glorious ~ in our history; it reads like a ~ from real life ["one side of a sheet of paper"] 10. a blank ~ (see also **home page**)
page II *n.* ["youth who serves"] 1. (BE) a hotel ~ 2. (US) a congressional ~
page III *v.* to ~ smb. on, over a loudspeaker
pageant *n.* 1. to put on, stage a ~ 2. a beauty; colorful ~
paid *adj.* badly, poorly; highly, well ~
pail *n.* a garbage (AE); ice; lunch; milk ~
pain I *n.* ["sensation of suffering"] 1. to cause ~ 2. to inflict ~ (on) 3. to exacerbate the ~ 4. to bear, endure, stand, take ~ (she cannot stand ~) 5. to experience, feel, have, suffer ~ (she experienced constant ~) 6. to allay, alleviate, control, deaden, dull, ease, kill, relieve, soothe ~ 7. (an) acute, agonizing, excruciating, great, intense, severe, sharp, unbearable ~ 8. (a) burning, searing; piercing; shooting; stabbing; throbbing ~ 9. a dull; slight ~ 10. (a) chronic, constant, gnawing, intractable, lingering, nagging, persistent, steady ~ 11. (a) recurrent; referred; sudden ~ 12. (an) abdominal, stomach; back; chest; phantom limb; physical ~ (he felt sharp chest ~s and went to see the doctor) 13. ~ appears; disappears, wears off; intensifies 14. a spasm; stab; twinge of ~ 15. a ~ in (she has severe ~s in her back) 16. in ~ (to be in chronic ~) 17. (misc.) the ~ shot through her arm; a high (or low) threshold of ~ ["penalty"] 18. on, under, upon ~ of (mass meetings were forbidden on ~ of death) ["bother"] 19. (colloq.) a ~ to + inf. (it's a ~ to get up so early in the morning = it's a ~ getting up so early in the morning) 20. (misc.) he's a ~ in the neck ("he's a bothersome person"); what a ~!
pain II *v.* 1. to ~ badly, deeply 2. (R) it ~ed me to watch them quarrel; it ~ed me that she did not keep her promise
pained *adj.* (cannot stand alone) ~ to + inf. (I was ~ to learn of his refusal to help)
painful *adj.* 1. ~ for (that experience was very ~ for us) 2. ~ to 3. ~ to + inf. (it's ~ to read of such things)
pains *n.* ["trouble"] 1. to go to, spare no, take ~ to + inf. (she took great ~ to get her message across) ["physical suffering"] 2. (med.) chest; labor ~ 3. (usu. fig.) growing ~ ["misc."] 3. (esp. BE) at ~ to + inf. (The Prime Minister was at ~ to deny the charges)

paint I *n.* 1. to apply, spread ~ (to apply ~ to a surface; to spread ~ evenly) 2. to spray ~ (to spray ~ on a wall) 3. to daub ~ (to daub ~ on a wall) 4. to dilute, thin ~ 5. to mix ~s 6. to remove; scrape ~ 7. exterior; flat; floor; gloss; house; latex; lead-based; metallic; oil-based; wall ~ 8. grease; war ~ 9. wet ~! 10. ~ chips; peels; smears 11. a blob, dab, daub, lick, speck, spot; splash of ~ 12. a coat of ~ (to apply a second coat of ~) 13. a set of (oil) ~s

paint II *v.* 1. (usu. D; C occurs occ.) to ~ for (she ~ed a beautiful portrait for us) 2. (D; tr.) to ~ from (to ~ a scene from life) 3. (d; intr.) to ~ in (to ~ in oils) 4. (J) the artist ~ed them strolling through their garden 5. (N; used with an adjective) to ~ a house white 6. (misc.) to ~ the town red ("to go on a binge")

painter *n.* 1. a house; sign ~ 2. a landscape; portrait ~

painting *n.* 1. to do; restore a ~ 2. to exhibit ~s 3. to authenticate a ~ 4. (a) finger; oil; water-color ~ 5. (an) abstract; representative ~ 6. an original ~ 7. a ~ depicts, portrays, shows (smt.)

pair off, pair up *v.* (D; intr., tr.) to ~ with

pajamas, pyjamas *n.* a pair of ~

pal *n.* a pen ~ (BE also has *pen friend*)

palace *n.* a bishop's (BE); imperial; presidential (not US); royal ~

pal around *v.* (AE) (d; intr.) to ~ with

palatable *adj.* ~ to

palate *n.* 1. a cleft; perforated ~ 2. the hard; soft ~ 3. (misc.) to tickle the ~ ("to be very tasty")

pale I *adj.* ["devoid of color"] 1. deathly ~ 2. to go, turn ~ 3. ~ with (rage)

pale II *v.* 1. (d; intr.) ("to become devoid of color") to ~ at ("to ~ at the sight of blood") 2. (d; intr.) ("to become less important") to ~ before, beside (everything ~d before the possibility of war) 3. (d; intr.) ("to fade") to ~ into (to ~ into insignificance)

pale III *n.* ["prescribed area"] beyond, outside the ~

pall I *n.* ["blanket of gloom"] to cast a ~ over

pall II *v.* (D; intr.) ("to become less attractive") to ~ on, upon (her constant preaching began to ~ on everyone)

palm I *n.* ["part of the hand"] 1. to read smb.'s ~ ("to tell smb.'s fortune") 2. (misc.) to have an itchy ~ ("to have a great desire for money, bribes"); to grease smb.'s ~ ("to bribe smb.")

palm II *n.* a potted; royal ~

palm off *v.* 1. (D; tr.) to ~ as (he ~ed off the copy as an original) 2. (D; tr.) to ~ on (to ~ inferior merchandise on smb.)

palpable *adj.* ~ to

pal up *v.* (d; intr.) to ~ with

pan I *n.* 1. to grease a ~ 2. (AE) a baking; cake ~ (BE has *baking tin; cake tin*) 3. a frying ~ 4. (misc.) to scour (the) pots and ~s

pan II *v.* (d; intr.) to ~ for (to ~ for gold)

panacea *n.* 1. to find a ~ 2. a universal ~ 3. a ~ for

panache *n.* (with) great ~

pancake *n.* 1. to make a ~ 2. (misc.) as flat as a ~

pandemonium *n.* 1. to cause, create, stir up ~ 2. sheer ~ 3. ~ breaks out; reigns; subsides

pander *v.* (d; intr.) to ~ to (to ~ to the worst elements in society)

panegyric *n.* to deliver a ~ 2. a ~ on

panel *n.* ["board"] 1. a control, instrument ~ ["group that discusses or investigates a topic"] 2. to select a ~ 3. to serve on a ~ 4. an impartial ~ 5. an advisory; blue-ribbon (esp. AE), expert; consumer; fact-finding; government ~ 6. a ~ on (a ~ on drug addiction) 7. (misc.) to convene a ~ of judges

panel discussion *n.* to conduct, lead, moderate; hold a ~

paneling, panelling *n.* wood ~

pangs *n.* 1. birth ~ (usu. fig.) 2. ~ of conscience; hunger (she felt ~ of conscience)

panic I *n.* 1. to cause, create ~ 2. to spread ~ 3. to feel ~ at (they felt ~ at the thought of leaving their family) 4. to avert, prevent ~ 5. sheer, total, utter ~ 6. ~ spreads; subsides 7. in a ~ over (they were in a ~ over the news) 8. in ~ (they fled in ~) 9. (misc.) a state of ~

panic II *v.* 1. (D; intr.) to ~ about, at, over (to ~ at the outbreak of fire) 2. (d; tr.) to ~ into (the bad news panicked many into fleeing the city)

panic button *n.* to press, push the ~

panicky *adj.* to get ~ over

pant *v.* (D; intr.) to ~ for (to ~ for breath)

pants *n.* 1. (esp. AE) see **trousers** 2. ski; sweat ~ 3. a pair of ~

paper I *n.* ["lecture, treatise; manuscript for publication"] 1. to deliver, give, offer, present, read a ~ 2. to publish; write a ~ 3. a discussion; invited; working ~ 4. a ~ about, on ["essay; written assignment"] 5. (in a school, at a university) to do, write; hand in a ~ (the pupils did a ~ on the problem of air pollution; the students were required to hand in their ~s by the end of the semester) 6. an examination, test; term ~ 7. a ~ about, on 8. a ~ for (I had to do a ~ for my history course) ["document"] 9. a green (BE); white ~ 10. a position ~ ["negotiable instruments"] 11. commercial; negotiable ~ ["material made from wood pulp"] 12. to recycle (scrap) ~ 13. blank; graph; lined; unlined ~ 14. cigarette; filter; litmus; toilet; wrapping ~ 15. crepe; glossy; manila; tar; tissue; wax, waxed ~ 16. bond; carbon; scrap; scratch (esp. AE); tracing; typing; writing ~ 17. a quire; ream; roll of ~ ["sheet of writing material"] 18. to line ~ 19. a piece, sheet; scrap of ~ 20. on ~ ("in written form") (we got it down on ~) ["newspaper"] 21. to get a ~ out, publish a ~ 22. a daily; school; Sun-

day; trade ~ (see also **newspaper**)
paper II *v.* (N) she ~ed the ceiling white
paperback *n.* in ~ (the book came out in ~)
papers *n.* ["documents"] 1. to draw up ~ 2. to show one's ~ 3. (US) to take out first ~ ("to begin the process of becoming a naturalized citizen") 4. first (US); naturalization; second (US); ship's; working ~ 5. forged ~ ["schoolwork"] 6. to correct, grade (esp. AE), mark ~ ["articles sent by mail"] 7. printed ~ (BE; CE has *printed matter*)
par *n.* ["nominal value"] 1. at ~ ["common level"] 2. on a ~ with ["average"] 3. above, over; below ~ 4. up to ~ (to feel up to ~)
parachute I *n.* 1. to pack a ~ 2. a ~ opens; fails to open
parachute II *v.* 1. (B) we ~d supplies to the stranded climbers 2. (P; intr., tr.) they ~d behind enemy lines; we ~d to safety
parachute jump *n.* to make a ~
parade I *n.* 1. to have, hold, stage a ~ 2. to review a ~ 3. a church (BE); identification (BE; AE has *police lineup*); inaugural; military; sick (BE; AE has *sick call*); ticker-tape ~ 4. at a ~ (we met them at the ~ 5. on ~ (the regiment was on ~)
parade II *v.* (P; intr., tr.) to ~ in front of an audience; to ~ around the room
parade rest *n.* at ~ (the platoon was at ~)
paradise *n.* 1. an earthly ~ 2. sheer ~ 3. ~ to + inf. (it is sheer ~ to relax in the sun)
paradox *n.* a ~ that + clause (it's a ~ that such good friends cannot work together)
paradoxical *adj.* ~ that + clause (it's ~ that we should feel cold in warm weather)
parallel I *adj.* ~ to, with
parallel II *n.* 1. to draw a ~ between; with 2. to find ~s among, between 3. a striking ~ 4. (misc.) without ~ (in history); (esp. BE) her career developed in ~ with his; their accomplishment has no ~
paralysis *n.* 1. to cause, induce ~ 2. complete; creeping; partial; temporary; total ~ 3. infantile ~
paramount *adj.* ~ over
paranoid *adj.* ~ about
paraphernalia *n.* drug ~
paratroops *n.* to commit, deploy; drop ~
parcel *n.* 1. to deliver a ~ 2. to address; insure; mail (esp. AE), post (BE); send a ~ 3. to get, receive a ~ 4. to open, unwrap; seal; wrap a ~
parcel out *v.* 1. (B) she ~ed out the work to us 2. (D; tr.) to ~ among (she ~ed out the assignments among us)
pardon I *n.* 1. to grant a ~ 2. to ask, beg smb.'s ~ 3. a full ~
pardon II *v.* (D; tr.) to ~ smb. for
pare down *v.* (D; tr.) to ~ to (to ~ expenses to the minimum)
parent *n.* 1. to obey one's ~s 2. a loving; permissive; strict; unfit ~ 3. an adoptive; biological, natu-

ral; foster; lone (BE), single ~; stepparent
parentheses *n.* (esp. AE; BE prefers *brackets*) 1. to put smt. in, into ~ 2. between, in ~
parity *n.* ["equality"] 1. to achieve, attain, establish ~ 2. ~ among, between; with ["equivalence in value"] 3. at ~
park I *n.* 1. to lay out a ~ 2. an amusement; safari (BE); theme ~ 3. a city; national; public; state ~ 4. a caravan (BE), trailer (AE) ~ 5. a car ~ (BE; AE has *parking lot*); a multi-storey car ~ (BE; AE has *parking garage*) 6. (BE) a coach; lorry ~ 7. an industrial ~ (AE; BE has *industrial estate*); a science ~ (BE) 8. at, in a ~
park II *v.* (colloq.) ("to deposit with") (d; tr.) to ~ on (AE), with (they ~ed their children on us and went to the theater)
parking *n.* 1. to allow; ban, restrict ~ 2. illegal; legal ~ 3. long-term; short-term ~ 4. (misc.) no ~!
parking meter *n.* at a ~ (we were parked at a ~)
parlance *n.* common; legal ~ (in common ~)
parlay *v.* (esp. AE) (d; tr.) ("to convert") to ~ into (to ~ a small investment into a fortune)
parley I *n.* to hold a ~ with
parley II *v.* (D; intr.) to ~ with
parliament *n.* 1. to convene (a) ~ 2. to adjourn; disband, dismiss, dissolve (a) ~ 3. a bicameral; national; provincial; unicameral ~ 4. a hung; rump ~ 5. a ~ adjourns; convenes, meets; disbands 6. a house of ~ 7. in ~ (to sit in ~) 8. (misc.) an act of ~; to stand for (BE) ~; a member of ~ (in GB abbreviated as MP)
USAGE NOTE: In Great Britain, the Queen or King *opens* (a *session* of) Parliament. After the *State Opening*, Parliament is *in session*. Parliament *sits* until the session is over and then it *rises*.
parlor, parlour *n.* 1. a beauty; funeral; massage ~ 2. a sun ~ (AE; BE has *sun lounge*)
USAGE NOTE: The services offered by a *massage parlor* are often sexual rather than therapeutic.
parody *n.* 1. to compose, write a ~ 2. a ~ of, on
parole I *n.* ["conditional release from prison"] 1. to grant a ~ 2. to violate (one's) ~ 3. early ~ 4. on ~ (to release smb. on ~)
parole II *v.* (D; tr.) to ~ from (to ~ smb. from prison)
part I *n.* ["share"] 1. to do one's ~ ["viewpoint, position"] 2. for, on one's ~ (for my ~, I will say no more) ["participation"] 3. to take ~ (in) 4. an active ~ ["role"] 5. to play a ~ (to play the ~ of Hamlet) 6. to act; dress; look the ~ 7. to learn, memorize, study one's ~; to understudy a ~ 8. a bit; cameo; leading, major; minor; speaking; walk-on ~ (she had a bit ~ in the play) ["element, portion"] 9. to spend a ~ of (they spent the major ~ of their life in England) 10. an essential; important, significant; large, major ~ 11. an insignificant, minor, small ~

~ 12. the (a) better ("greater"); good ("large") ~ (the better ~ of an hour) 13. a component, constituent, integral ~ 14. for the most ~ ("mostly") 15. in ~ ("partly") (in great ~) ["component of a machine"] 16. a defective ~ 17. a moving ~ 18. automobile (AE), (motor)car (BE); spare ~s ["division"] 19. in ~s (a story in five ~s) ["side"] 20. to take smb.'s ~ (in a dispute) 21. (legal) of a ~ (the party of the first ~) ["dividing line in hair"] (AE; BE has *parting*) 22. to have; make a ~ (in one's hair) ["sexual organs"] 23. the private ~s ["area"] 24. a remote ~ (in a remote ~ of the country)

part II *v.* 1. (D; intr.) to ~ as (to ~ as friends) 2. (d; intr., tr.) to ~ from (the children were ~ed from their parents) 3. (d; intr.) to ~ with (she hates to ~ with her money)

partake *v.* (d; intr.) to ~ of (to ~ of food and drink)

partial *adj.* ["fond of"] (colloq.) (cannot stand alone) ~ to

partiality *n.* ["bias"] 1. to show ~ in ["liking"] 2. a ~ for (she shows a ~ for expensive clothes)

participant *n.* 1. an active; reluctant, unwilling; willing ~ 2. a ~ in

participate *v.* 1. to ~ actively; fully 2. (D; intr.) to ~ in

participation *n.* 1. active ~ 2. unwilling; willing ~ 3. audience ~ 4. ~ in

participle *n.* (grammar) an active; dangling (esp. AE), misrelated (BE); passive; past; perfect; present ~

particle *n.* 1. a dust; minute ~ 2. (physics) an alpha; elementary; subatomic ~

particular I *adj.* ~ about (~ about one's appearance)

particular II *n.* ["detail"] 1. in every ~; in all ~s ["misc."] 2. in ~ ("especially")

parting *n.* (BE) see **part I**, 22

partition I *n.* 1. to build, erect, put up a ~ 2. to dismantle, take down a ~ 3. a movable ~ 4. a ~ between

partition II *v.* (D; tr.) to ~ into (the area was ~ed into two countries)

partner *n.* 1. an active; full; junior; senior ~ 2. a business; trading ~ 3. a silent (AE), sleeping (BE) ~ 4. (boxing) a sparring ~ 5. (misc.) a ~ in (~s in crime)

partner up *v.* (BE) (D; tr.) to ~ with

partnership *n.* 1. to form; go into a ~ 2. to break up, dissolve a ~ 3. a ~ between 4. a ~ in 5. in ~ (with)

partridge *n.* a covey of ~s

party *n.* ["social gathering"] 1. to arrange, give, have, throw; host a ~ (for) 2. to attend, go to; crash a ~ 3. to liven up a ~ 4. a birthday; Christmas; New Year's Eve ~ 5. a cocktail; dinner; garden, lawn (AE); tea ~ 6. a coming-out; farewell; going-away ~ 7. a pajama, slumber; surprise ~ 8. a lavish; wild ~ 9. a singles; stag ~ 10. a ~ breaks up (the ~ broke

up at midnight) 11. at a ~ (we had a good time at the ~) ["political organization"] 12. to establish, form a ~ 13. to break up, disband, dissolve a ~ 14. a centrist; conservative; liberal; populist; progressive; radical; reactionary ~ 15. a communist; labor; socialist ~ 16. a left-wing; right-wing ~ 17. the majority; minority; opposition; political; ruling; splinter ~ 18. (misc.) the ~ in power ["litigant"] (legal) 19. an aggrieved; disinterested; guilty; innocent; third ~ 20. the interested ~ties 21. a ~ to (a lawsuit) 22. (misc.) the ~ of the first, second part ["group sent on a mission"] 23. a boarding; landing; raiding; rescue; scouting; search; stretcher; surveying ~ ["participant"] 24. a ~ to (we will not be a ~ to this arrangement)

party line *n.* 1. to follow, hew to (AE) the ~ 2. to deviate from, veer from the ~

pass I *n.* ["permission"] ["leave of absence"] 1. to issue a ~ 2. to cancel, revoke a ~ 3. a boarding; safe-conduct ~ 4. a ~ to (we got a ~ to town) 5. on (a) ~ (they are in the city on ~) ["flight"] 6. to make a ~ (over a target) ["aggressive attempt to become friendly"] 7. to make a ~ (at smb.) ["transfer of a ball, puck"] 8. to complete; throw a ~ 9. to block; intercept a ~ 10. (Am. football) a forward; incomplete; lateral; touchdown ~ ["ticket"] 11. a free ~ 12. a ~ to (we got free ~es to the concert) ["passing grade"] (BE) 13. to get a ~ (in) ["misc."] 14. things came to a pretty ~ ("the situation became very complicated")

pass II *v.* 1. (A) ("to hand"); ("to throw") ~ the sugar to me; or: ~ me the sugar; my teammate ~ed the ball to me; or my teammate ~ed me the ball 2. (D; intr.) to ~ as, for ("to be accepted as") (she can ~ as/for a Russian) 3. (d; intr.) to ~ between ("to be exchanged") (a significant look ~ed between them) 4. (D; intr.) ("to go past") to ~ by (they ~ed by my house) 5. (d; intr.) ("to shift") to ~ from; to (to ~ from one subject to another) 6. (d; intr.) to ~ on, upon ("to judge") (to ~ on the merits of a case) 7. (D; tr.) ("to deliver") to ~ on, upon (the judge ~ed sentence on the accused; to ~ judgment on smb.) 8. (d; intr.) ("to go"); ("to fly") to ~ over (several planes ~ed over our house; to ~ over a bridge) 9. (d; intr.) to ~ over ("to disregard") (they ~ed over her when promotions were handed out) 10. (d; intr.) ("to go") to ~ through (she was just ~ing through town) 11. (d; tr.) ("to insert") to ~ through (he ~ed the cable through the loop; to ~ meat through a grinder) 12. (d; intr.) to ~ to ("to be handed down to") the estate ~ed to the daughter 13. (P; intr.) ("to move") to ~ into history; rumors ~ed around town 14. (s) to ~ unnoticed 15. (misc.) (BE) to be ~ed fit for (service)

pass III *n.* ["passage"] 1. to clear a ~ 2. to block a ~ 3. a mountain ~ 4. a ~ between; over; through (a ~ through the mountains)

passage *n.* ["transit"] 1. to book ~ (on a ship) 2. free ~ ["section"] 3. an obscure ~ (in a text) ["way, channel"] 4. to clear; force a ~ 5. a secret ~ ["channel in the body"] 6. nasal ~s 7. (BE) the back ~ ("the rectum") ["transition"] 8. a ~ from; through; to 9. (misc.) a rite of ~ ["trip"] 10. an outward ~

passageway *n.* a ~ between

pass along *v.* (B) ~ the message along to the others

pass around *v.* (B) ~ the chocolate around to the children

pass down *v.* (d; intr., tr.) to ~ from; to (to ~ a tradition to the next generation; the custom was ~ed down from their ancestors)

passenger *n.* 1. to carry ~s (trains carry many ~s every day) 2. to pick up, take on ~s 3. to drop (off), let off ~s 4. a business-class; first-class; second-class; standard-class (BE); steerage; tourist-class; transit ~ 5. a ~ for (~s for the next flight should go to the last gate)

passing *n.* ["death"] 1. to mourn smb.'s ~ ["misc."] 2. in ~ ("incidentally")

passion *n.* 1. to arouse, excite, inflame, stir up ~ 2. to gratify, satisfy one's ~ 3. to control, curb, restrain one's ~ 4. (an) all-consuming, burning, deep, smoldering; animal, frenzied, wild ~ 5. ~s run high 6. a ~ for (a ~ for gambling) 7. (misc.) to fly into a ~; his eyes blazed with ~

pass off *v.* (d; refl., tr.) to ~ as (he ~ed himself off as a doctor)

pass on *v.* 1. (B) they ~ed the information on to us 2. (d; intr.) to ~ from; to (let's ~ to another topic)

pass out *v.* (B) they ~ed the food out to all who came

pass over *v.* (D; tr.) to ~ for (they ~ed her over for promotion)

passport *n.* 1. to issue; renew a ~ 2. to have, hold a ~ 3. to apply for a ~ 4. to falsify, forge a ~ 5. to stamp, validate a ~ 6. to revoke a ~ 7. a diplomatic; Nansen ~ 8. a false; valid ~ 9. a ~ expires 10. (fig.) a ~ to (a ~ to happiness)

pass round (BE) see **pass around**

password *n.* 1. to give the ~ 2. (computers) to enter, key in the ~

past *n.* ["time preceding the present"] 1. to glorify; recall, recapture the ~ 2. to forget the ~ 3. the distant ~ 4. a colorful, glorious ~ 5. a checkered (AE), chequered (BE); dark, lurid, murky ~ 6. in the ~

paste I *n.* to make, mix a ~

paste II *v.* (D; tr.) to ~ on, to (to ~ a piece of paper on/to the wall)

pastime *n.* the national ~ (in America the national ~ is baseball)

pastry *n.* 1. to bake, make ~ 2. light; puff (BE) ~ 3. (a) Danish ~

pasture *n.* 1. to put smb. out to ~ (usu. fig.) 2. (misc.) to leave for greener ~s

pat I *adj., adv.* (colloq.) (esp. AE) to stand ~ ("to refuse to change")

pat II *n.* to give smb. a ~ (on the back)

pat III *v.* (D; tr.) to ~ on (to ~ smb. on the head)

patch *n.* ["piece of material used to cover a hole"] 1. to sew on a ~ ["insignia"] 2. a shoulder ~ ["plot of ground"] 3. a brier; cabbage; potato ~

patch through *v.* (D; tr.) ("to connect") to ~ to (she ~ed me through to headquarters)

patent *n.* 1. to grant, issue a ~ 2. to apply for; obtain, take out a ~ 3. to hold a ~ 4. to infringe a ~ 5. ~ applied for; pending 6. a ~ expires, runs out 7. a ~ on (she took out a ~ on her invention)

paternity *n.* 1. to establish ~ 2. to acknowledge (one's) ~

path *n.* 1. to beat, blaze, clear, make a ~ (to clear a ~ through a jungle) 2. to cross smb.'s ~ 3. to follow a ~ 4. a beaten ~ 5. a bridle ~ 6. a ~ goes, leads somewhere 7. a ~ from; to (the ~ to success) 8. (misc.) to lead smb. up the garden ~ ("to deceive smb."); to lead smb. down the primrose ~ ("to lead smb. in an ill-advised search for pleasure"); off the beaten ~ ("in an unfamiliar or unusual place")

pathetic *adj.* 1. ~ to + inf. (it was ~ to watch her condition deteriorate day by day) 2. ~ that + clause (it's ~ that he has sunk so low)

pathway *n.* a ~ to

patience *n.* ["quality of being patient"] 1. to display, show ~ 2. to tax, test, try smb.'s ~ 3. to lose one's ~ 4. to run out of ~ 5. endless, inexhaustible, infinite ~ 6. smb.'s ~ wears thin 7. ~ for (with, (she has endless ~ with the children) 8. the ~ to + inf. (do you have the ~ to do this job?) 9. out of ~ with ["card game"] (BE) 10. to play ~ (AE has *solitaire*)

patient I *adj.* ~ in; with

patient II *n.* 1. to cure; handle; treat a ~ 2. to admit a ~ (to a hospital) 3. to discharge a ~ (from a hospital) 4. an ambulatory; hospital ~; inpatient; outpatient; private ~ 5. a cardiac; comatose; mental ~

patio *n.* on a ~ (let's have a drink on the ~)

patriot *n.* an ardent, fervent, staunch; sincere ~

patriotism *n.* 1. to display, show ~ 2. (an) ardent, fervent, staunch, strong; sincere ~

patrol *n.* 1. a border; highway (AE), motorway (BE); military; police; reconnaissance ~ 2. (naval) (a) shore ~ 3. on ~ (they are out on ~)

patron *n.* 1. a regular, steady ~ 2. (misc.) a ~ of the arts

patronage *n.* 1. political ~ 2. under smb.'s ~

patter *v.* (d; intr.) to ~ against, on (the rain was ~ing on the windows)

pattern I *n.* 1. to establish, set a ~ 2. to follow a ~ 3. an intricate; overall; strange; underlying ~ 4. a holding; traffic ~ (our plane was in a holding ~) 5. (ling.) an intonation; speech ~ 6. a behavior; personality ~ 7. a sewing ~ 8. a floral ~

pattern II *v.* (d; tr.) to ~ after, on, upon (we ~ed our road system on theirs)

patty *n.* (esp. AE) a beef; lamb; meat ~

pause *n.* ["temporary stop"] 1. an awkward; long, prolonged; pregnant; short ~ 2. a ~ in ["reason or cause for hesitating"] 3. to give smb. ~

pavement *n.* ["paved surface"] 1. to tear up the ~ (in order to lay pipes) 2. the ~ buckles 3. (misc.) to pound the ~ ("to walk about aimlessly or with determination")

USAGE NOTE: In BE, *pavement* also means "sidewalk".

pawn *n.* a helpless ~

pay I *n.* 1. to boost, raise smb.'s ~ 2. to cut; dock; withhold smb.'s ~ 3. to draw, receive ~ 4. back; disability; equal; incentive; mustering-out (mil.); overtime; severance (AE; BE has *redundancy payment*); retroactive; sick; strike; take-home ~ 5. annual, yearly; daily; hourly; monthly; weekly ~ 6. ~ for (equal ~ for equal work) 7. in smb.'s ~ (he was in the ~ of the enemy)

pay II *v.* 1. to ~ dearly; handsomely, highly, well 2. (A) she paid the money to me; or: she paid me the money 3. (D; intr.) to ~ by, in (to ~ by check; to ~ in cash; to ~ by the hour) 4. (D; intr., tr.) to ~ for (have you paid for the book? I paid ten dollars for this shirt) 5. (D; intr., tr.) to ~ into (we have been ~ing into a pension fund; the money was paid into her account) 6. (d; intr., tr.) to ~ out of (she paid out of her own pocket) 7. (E) it doesn't ~ to economize on essentials 8. (H) he paid us to watch his house

payable *adj.* 1. ~ to (make the check ~ to me) 2. (misc.) ~ at sight; ~ in advance; ~ on demand

pay back *v.* 1. (A) we must pay the money back to her; or we must pay her back the money 2. (D; tr.) to ~ for (she paid me back for the tickets)

paycheck *n.* a monthly; weekly ~

pay dirt *n.* (colloq.) (AE) ["success"] to hit, strike ~

payment *n.* 1. to accept, receive ~ (for) 2. to make (a) ~ (to) 3. to stop ~ (of, on a check) 4. to suspend ~s 5. a cash; down ("initial"); redundancy (BE; AE has *severance pay*); token ~ 6. (an) advance; part, partial; prompt ~ 7. (a) ~ for, on 8. in full ~ (of a bill) 9. (misc.) the balance of ~s

payoff *n.* 1. to make a ~ 2. to get, receive a ~ 3. a political ~ 4. a ~ for

pay out *v.* (B) the benefits have been paid out to the workers

payroll *n.* 1. to meet (esp. AE) a ~ 2. a monthly; weekly ~ 3. on the ~ (how many workers are on the ~?)

peace *n.* 1. to achieve, bring about; promote ~ 2. to make ~ (with) 3. to negotiate (a) ~ with 4. to sue for ~ (with) 5. to impose (a) ~ on 6. to keep, maintain the ~ 7. to break, disturb, shatter, under-

mine the ~ 8. a durable, lasting, permanent ~ 9. a fragile ~ 10. ~ reigns 11. at ~ (with) (we were at ~ with our neighbors) 12. in ~ (to live in ~) 13. (misc.) a breach of the ~; ~ and quiet; a ~ march

peacetime *n.* in ~

peacock *n.* 1. a ~ struts 2. (misc.) as proud as a ~

peak *n.* 1. to reach a ~ 2. to scale the ~ (of a mountain) 3. snow-capped ~s 4. at the ~ (at the ~ of her success)

pearls *n.* 1. to string ~ 2. cultured; imitation; natural ~ 3. a string of ~

peas *n.* 1. to shell, shuck (AE) ~ 2. split ~ 3. (misc.) as like as two ~ in a pod

peck I *n.* (colloq.) ["kiss"] to give smb. a ~ on the cheek

peck II *v.* (d; intr.) to ~ at (to ~ at one's food)

pecker *n.* ["spirits"] ["courage"] (colloq.) (BE) to keep one's ~ up

peculiar *adj.* 1. ~ to 2. ~ that + inf. (it's ~ that he never answers his phone)

pedal I *n.* 1. to depress, step on a ~ 2. an accelerator (BE), gas (AE); brake; clutch ~

pedal II *v.* (P; intr., tr.) she ~ed the bicycle down the hill; they ~ed their way across the state; we were ~ing through town

peddler, pedlar *n.* a drug; influence; itinerant; smut ~

pedestal *n.* 1. to put smb./smt. on a ~ ("to hold smb./smt. in high esteem") 2. on a ~ ("held in high esteem")

pedigree *n.* of (a) certain ~ (of unknown ~)

peek I *n.* to have, take a ~ (at; through)

peek II *v.* 1. (D; intr.) to ~ at (to ~ at the picture) 2. (d; intr.) to ~ into (to ~ into the files) 3. (d; intr.) to ~ under (to ~ under the bed) 4. (P; intr.) to ~ over the bushes; to ~ through the window

peek in *v.* 1. (D; intr.) to ~ at (we ~ed in at the dress rehearsal) 2. (misc.) she ~ed in from behind the bushes

peek out *v.* 1. (D; intr.) to ~ at 2. (D; intr.) to ~ from behind (to ~ from behind the shades) 3. (D; intr.) to ~ from under (to ~ from under the bed)

peel I *n.* an apple; banana; lemon; orange; potato ~ (see the Usage Note for **rind**)

peel II *v.* 1. (C) ~ a banana for me; or: ~ me a banana 2. (D; intr., tr.) to ~ from (he ~ed the bark from the tree; the paper was ~ing from the wall)

peep I *n.* ["sound"] 1. to let out a ~ 2. a ~ out of (we didn't hear a ~ out of her; we haven't had a ~ out of them all day)

peep II *n.* ["look"] to have, take a ~ (at; through)

peep III *v.* ("to look") 1. (D; intr.) to ~ at (to ~ at smb. in the next room) 2. (d; intr.) to ~ into (to ~ into smb.'s dossier) 3. (d; intr.) to ~ under (to ~ under the bed) 4. (P; intr.) to ~ over the bushes; to ~ through the window

peep out *v.* 1. (D; intr.) to ~ at 2. (D; intr.) to ~ from behind (to ~ from behind the blinds) 3. (D; intr.) to ~ from under (to ~ from under the bed)

peer I *n.* (GB) 1. to create, make smb. a ~ 2. a hereditary; life ~ 3. a ~ of the realm

peer II *v.* 1. (d; intr.) to ~ at; through (to ~ at smb. through a window) 2. (d; intr.) to ~ into (to ~ into smb.'s eyes)

peerage *n.* (GB) 1. to elevate, raise smb. to the ~ 2. a hereditary; life ~

peer out *v.* 1. (D; intr.) to ~ at 2. (D; intr.) to ~ from behind (to ~ from behind the curtains) 3. (D; intr.) to ~ from under (to ~ from under a car)

peeve *n.* smb.'s pet ~

peevish *adj.* ["irritable"] ~ about

peg *n.* ["degree, step"] (fig.) 1. to come down a ~ 2. to bring, take smb. down a ~ ["misc."] (BE) 3. (to buy clothing) off the ~ ("ready-made")

peg away *v.* (BE) (D; intr.) ("to work hard") to ~ at (to ~ at one's job)

pelt *v.* (d; tr.) to ~ with (to ~ smb. with rocks)

pelt down *v.* (D; intr.) to ~ on (the rain ~ed down on the roof)

pen I *n.* ["enclosure"] 1. a pig; sheep ~ ["dock"] 2. a submarine ~

pen II *n.* ["device for writing"] 1. a ballpoint; felt-tip (AE), fibre-tip (BE); fountain ~ 2. (misc.) with a stroke of the ~, the new law was enacted

penalize *v.* (D; tr.) to ~ for

penalty *n.* 1. to impose a ~ 2. to pay a ~ (to pay the full ~ for one's mistakes) 3. to rescind a ~ 4. a heavy, severe, stiff, strict; light, mild; maximum; minimum ~ 5. the death ~ 6. a ~ for 7. on, under ~ (of death)

penance *n.* to do, perform ~ for

penchant *n.* a ~ for

pencil *n.* 1. to sharpen a ~ 2. a colored; indelible; lead; mechanical ~ 3. a cosmetic, eyebrow ~ 4. a styptic ~

pendulum *n.* 1. to swing a ~ 2. a ~ swings

penetrate *v.* 1. to ~ deeply 2. (D; intr.) to ~ into (our troops ~d deeply into enemy lines)

penetration *n.* 1. (a) deep ~ 2. (mil.) (a) ~ in depth

penicillin *n.* 1. oral ~ 2. an injection, jab (BE; colloq.), shot of ~ 3. (misc.) a course of ~

penitence *n.* 1. to show ~ (for) 2. true ~ (for)

penitent *adj.* ~ for

pen name *n.* under a ~ (to write under a ~)

pennant *n.* ["baseball championship"] (AE) to lose; win the ~

penny *n.* 1. to pinch ~nies ("to be frugal") 2. (misc.) a pretty ~ ("a large sum of money"); (BE; colloq.) the ~ drops ("somebody finally understands"); (BE; colloq.) to spend a ~ ("to use a toilet")

USAGE NOTE: Seven US *pennies* are worth seven *cents*. Seven UK *pennies* are worth seven *pence*.

pension *n.* 1. to award, grant a ~ 2. to draw, receive

a ~ 3. to revoke a ~ 4. a disability; old-age; survivor's ~ 5. on a ~ (to live on a ~; to retire on a ~) 6. (misc.) a ~ plan

people *n.* 1. average, common, little, ordinary, plain ~ 2. business; city; country; working ~ 3. old; young ~ 4. the chosen ~ 5. the right ~ 6. boat ~ ("destitute refugees traveling in boats")

peopled *adj.* ~ by, with (an imaginary landscape ~ with unforgettable characters)

pepper I *n.* ["spice"] 1. ground ~ (freshly ground ~) 2. black; hot; red; white ~ 3. a dash of ~ ["vegetable"] 4. (a) green; red; sweet; yellow ~ 5. stuffed ~s

pepper II *v.* (d; tr.) ("to shower") to ~ with (she was ~ed with questions)

pep talk *n.* to give a ~ (the coach gave the team a ~)

pep up *v.* (D; tr.) to ~ with (to ~ a dish with unusual spices)

perceive *v.* 1. (d; tr.) to ~ as (I ~d her statement as a threat) 2. (L) we ~d that the situation was critical 3. (Q) they could not ~ what the problem was

percentage *n.* ["profit"] (colloq.) (a) ~ in (there is no ~ in investing more money)

perceptible *adj.* 1. barely ~ 2. ~ to

perception *n.* 1. to have a ~ 2. (a) clear; keen ~ 3. color; depth; extrasensory ~ 4. the ~ that + clause (events confirmed our ~ that she had been treated unfairly)

perceptive *adj.* 1. ~ of (that observation was very ~ of her) 2. ~ to + inf. (it was ~ of them to grasp our meaning)

perceptiveness *n.* the ~ to + inf. (she had the ~ to know what would happen)

perch I *n.* 1. a high ~ 2. from one's ~ 3. (misc.) (colloq.; BE) to fall off one's ~ ("to die")

perch II *v.* (P; intr.) the birds ~ed on the wire

percolate *v.* (P; intr.) ("to pass slowly") the news ~d down to the troops; the water ~d through the sand)

per diem *n.* ["daily allowance for expenses"] 1. to pay (a) ~ 2. to receive (a) ~

perennial *n.* ["flower"] a hardy ~

perfect I *adj.* ~ for (she would be ~ for the job)

perfect II *n.* (grammar) the future; past; present ~

perfection *n.* 1. to achieve, attain, reach ~ 2. sheer ~ 3. the acme of ~ 4. to ~ (cooked to ~)

perfidy *n.* (formal) an act of ~

perform *v.* 1. to ~ in concert; live 2. (D; intr.) to ~ in (to ~ in a play) 3. (D; intr., tr.) to ~ for (to ~ for a live audience; to ~ a concerto for a live audience) 4. (D; intr., tr.) to ~ on (to ~ on the piano; to ~ a concerto on the piano)

performance *n.* ["act of performing"] 1. to deliver, give, put on a ~ 2. to arrange, schedule a ~ 3. to cancel; postpone; reschedule a ~ 4. a breathtaking, brilliant, electrifying, inspired, outstanding, remarkable, spellbinding, superb, wonderful ~ 5. a listless, mediocre, run-of-the-mill; uneven ~ 6. a benefit; cameo; command; farewell; gala; live; premier; public; repeat; request; solo ~ 7. a ~ as, in (her ~ as the mother was inspired) ["functioning of a machine"] 8. (high) engine ~

performer *n.* a star ~

perfume *n.* 1. to dab on, put on, spray on ~ 2. to use, wear ~ 3. to reek of (derog.); smell of ~ 4. (a) heady, strong ~ 5. a bottle of ~ 6. a whiff of ~

perfumed *adj.* ~ with (the air was ~d with the scent of honeysuckle)

peril *n.* 1. to face a ~ 2. to avert a ~ 3. at one's ~ 4. in ~ (our lives were in ~)

perimeter *n.* ["boundary"] 1. (mil.) to guard, protect a ~ 2. on a ~

period *n.* ["portion of time"] 1. a cooling-off; rest; set; trial; waiting ~ 2. an off-peak; peak; transitional ~ 3. an incubation ~ 4. a question-and-answer ~ 5. (sports) an extra ~ 6. for a ~ 7. in a certain ~ (in that ~ of history) ["menstruation"] 8. to have a ~ 9. a monthly ~ ["punctuation mark"] (esp. AE; BE prefers *full stop*) 10. to place, put a ~ (at the end of a sentence)

periodical *n.* 1. to publish, put out a ~ 2. to subscribe, take (BE) a ~ 3. a current ~ (where does the library keep current ~s?) 4. bound ~s

peripheral *adj.* ~ to

periphery *n.* on the ~

periscope *n.* 1. to lower; raise a ~ 2. (as commands) ~ down! ~ up!

perish *v.* (formal) 1. (D; intr.) to ~ by (to ~ by the sword) 2. (D; intr.) to ~ from, of (to ~ from disease) 3. (D; intr.) to ~ in (to ~ in a disaster)

perjury *n.* to commit ~

perm *n.* ["permanent wave"] 1. to give smb. a ~ 2. to get a ~

permeated *adj.* (cannot stand alone) ~ with (~ with idealism)

permissible *adj.* ~ to + inf. (it is not ~ to smoke in the library)

permission *n.* 1. to give, grant ~ 2. to deny, refuse ~ 3. to ask, ask for, request, seek ~ 4. to get; have ~ 5. planning ~ (BE; AE has *building permit*) 6. official; verbal; written ~ 7. ~ for 8. ~ to + inf. (we had ~ to leave early)

permit I *n.* 1. to give, grant a ~ 2. to cancel, rescind, revoke a ~ 3. apply for, request, seek a ~ 3. to have a ~ 4. a building (AE; BE has *planning permission*); work ~ 5. an export; import; travel ~ 6. a ~ to + inf. (they have a ~ to carry a gun)

permit II *v.* 1. (H) they ~ted her to leave 2. (O; can be used with one inanimate object) the doctors ~ two meals a day; the doctors ~ her two meals a day; she ~ted herself one glass of wine

pernickety (esp. BE) see **persnickety**

perpendicular *adj.* ~ to

perpetuity *n.* in ~ ("forever")

perplex *v.* (R) it ~ed me to learn of his decision; it

~ed me that they refused the offer

perplexed *adj.* 1. ~ about, at, by, over 2. ~ to + inf. (we were ~ to learn of your decision) 3. ~ that + clause (we were ~ that they refused the offer)

perplexing *adj.* 1. ~ to + inf. (it was ~ to read so many contradictory accounts of the incident) 2. ~ that + clause (it was ~ that they refused the offer)

persecute *v.* (D; tr.) to ~ for (they were ~d for their religious beliefs)

persecution *n.* 1. to suffer ~ 2. relentless; ruthless ~ 3. political; racial; religious ~

perseverance *n.* 1. to display, show ~ 2. dogged ~ 3. ~ at, in 3. the ~ to + inf. (she had enough ~ to finish)

persevere *v.* (D; intr.) to ~ at, in

persist *v.* (D; intr.) to ~ in, with (to ~ in doing smt.)

persistence *n.* 1. to display, show ~ 2. dogged ~ 3. ~ in 4. the ~ to + inf. (will you have the ~ to stick it out?)

persistent *adj.* 1. doggedly ~ 2. ~ in

persnickety *adj.* (colloq.) (esp. AE) ["fussy"] ~ about

person *n.* 1. a juridical; private; real ~ 2. a displaced; missing ~ 3. (legal) a ~ aggrieved 4. (grammar) the first; second; third ~ 5. in ~ (to appear in ~)

personal history *n.* to record, take down smb.'s ~

personality *n.* ["noted person"] 1. a celebrated; media; TV ~ ["behavioral characteristics"] 2. a charismatic, charming, dynamic, forceful, magnetic, striking ~ 3. a domineering; strong ~ 4. a dual, split; multiple ~ ["misc."] 5. to indulge in ~ties ("to make impolite remarks about people")

personnel *n.* enlisted (AE; BE has *other ranks*); government; indigenous; military; qualified, skilled; support ~

perspective *n.* 1. to put smt. into ~ 2. to put a new ~ on smt. 3. a distorted ~ 4. the proper, right, true; wrong ~ 5. from a ~ (to view a situation from a new ~) 6. in ~ (to look at, see smt. in ~)

perspicacity *n.* the ~ to + inf. (she had enough ~ to see through their schemes)

perspiration *n.* 1. excessive, profuse ~ 2. beads of ~ (ran down my face)

perspire *v.* to ~ freely, profusely

persuade *v.* 1. (D; tr.) to ~ of (we had to ~ them of the need to evacuate their house) 2. (H) we ~d them to leave 3. (L; must have an object) we ~d her that it would be best to wait

persuasion *n.* 1. political ~ 2. (humorous) religious ~ (what is their religious ~?) 3. powers of ~

persuasiveness *n.* the ~ to + inf. (she has enough ~ to convince anyone)

pertain *v.* (d; intr.) to ~ to (these facts ~ to the case)

pertaining *adj.* (cannot stand alone) ~ to

pertinent *adj.* 1. ~ to 2. ~ to + inf. (is it ~ to cite those facts?) 3. ~ that + clause (it is ~ that she knew the defendant personally)

perturb v. (R) it ~ed me (to learn) that she was late again

perturbed adj. 1. ~ about, at, by, over 2. ~ to + inf. (we were ~ to learn of the bad news from the front) 3. ~ that + clause (we were ~ that she was late again)

perturbing adj. 1. ~ to + inf. (it's ~ to read such distortions of fact in the press) 2. ~ that + clause (it is ~ that she still believes such nonsense)

perusal n. a casual, quick; detailed ~ (of smt.)

pervaded adj. (cannot stand alone) ~ with (~ with cynicism)

perverse adj. ~ to + inf. (it was ~ to behave like that)

perversion n. sexual ~

pessimism n. 1. to display ~ 2. to overcome ~ 3. ~ about, at, over

pessimistic adj. ~ about, at, over

pest n. 1. a garden ~ 2. (misc.) he can be a real ~

pester v. 1. (D; tr.) to ~ about, for (he kept ~ing me for his money) 2. (D; tr.) to ~ into (they ~ed me into going) 3. (H) they kept ~ing me to buy a new car

pet n. 1. to have, keep a ~ 2. a household ~ 3. a teacher's ~ 4. (misc.) a ~ animal

petition I n. 1. to circulate, get up a ~ 2. to file, present a ~ 3. to sign a ~ 4. to grant a ~ 5. to withdraw a ~ 6. to deny, reject a ~ 7. a ~ about; against; for

petition II v. 1. (D; intr., tr.) to ~ for (to ~ for a new trial; they ~ed the government for tax relief) 2. (E) they ~ed to have the case retried 3. (H) we have ~ed (the) city council to provide more teachers 4. (formal) (L; subj.) they ~ed that the case be/should be retried

petrol (BE) see **gasoline**

petty adj. ~ to + inf. (it was ~ of him to do that)

phalanx n. ["formation"] to form a (solid) ~

pharmacy n. 1. a hospital ~ 2. at, in a ~ (she works down at the ~)

phase n. 1. to begin, enter; reach a ~ 2. to go through a ~ 3. a closing, final, last ~ 4. a critical, crucial ~ 5. an early; first, initial, new, opening ~ (the war was entering its final ~)

pheasant n. a brace of ~s

phenomenon n. 1. an isolated, rare ~ 2. a natural ~ 3. a common ~ 4. a new ~

philosophical adj. ~ about

philosophize v. (D; intr.) to ~ about

philosophy n. ["belief"] 1. to espouse, have a ~ 2. a homespun; moral; political ~ 3. ~ that + clause (it was her ~ that people should help each other) 4. (misc.) one's ~ of life

phlegm n. to cough up ~

phobia n. to have a ~ (about)

phone I n. 1. to pick up the ~ 2. to slam down the ~

3. a cell, cellular ~ 4. the ~ died on me (see **telephone I**)

phone II v. see **telephone II**

phone book n. see **telephone directory**

phoneme n. (ling.) an independent, separate ~

photo see **photograph I**

photocopy n. to make a ~

photofinish n. (to end) in a ~

photograph I n. 1. to take a ~ 2. to develop; touch up a ~ 3. to blow up, enlarge a ~ 4. to crop a ~ 5. to mount a ~ 6. an aerial; black-and-white; color; family; group; still ~ 7. (misc.) to pose for a ~

photograph II v. (P; intr.) she ~s well

photographer n. an amateur; court; fashion; press; professional ~

photography n. color; still; trick ~

phrase n. 1. to coin; turn a ~ 2. a choice; well-turned ~ 3. a colloquial; illustrative ~ 4. an empty; glib; hackneyed, stock, trite ~ 5. (grammar) a nominal, noun; participial; prepositional; verb ~

physical, physical examinaton n. 1. to do, give a ~ 2. to get, have a ~ 3. to fail; pass a ~ 4. a complete ~

physician n. (esp. AE) 1. an attending; family; house; practicing ~ 2. an allopathic; homeopathic; osteopathic ~ (CE has *doctor*)

physics n. applied; classical, Newtonian; high-energy, particle; nuclear; solid-state; theoretical ~

physique n. a burly, magnificent, muscular, power-ful ~

pianist n. a concert; jazz ~

piano n. 1. to play the ~ 2. to tune a ~ 3. a baby grand; grand; upright ~ 4. (misc.) to perform at the ~; a ~ is in tune or out of tune

piazza n. ["open square"] on a ~

pick I n. ["tool for breaking"] an ice ~

pick II n. (colloq.) ["selection"] 1. to take one's ~ 2. to have one's ~ (of)

pick III v. 1. (C) ("to select") ~ a nice melon for me; or: ~ me a nice melon 2. (d; intr.) to ~ at ("to eat sparingly") (to ~ at one's food) 3. (d; intr.) ("to scratch") to ~ at (to ~ at a scab) 4. (D; tr.) ("to select") to ~ for (she was ~ed for the team) 5. (D; tr.) ("to select") to ~ from, out of (she ~ed this album from our record library) 6. (colloq.) (d; intr.) to ~ on ("to find fault with") (she's always ~ing on me) 7. (H) ("to select") they ~ed me to serve as secretary 8. (N; used with an adjective) the animals ~ed the carcass clean

picketing n. informational; mass ~

picket line n. 1. to form, organize a ~ 2. (esp. AE) to join, walk a ~ 3. to honor a ~ 4. to cross a ~ 5. in, on (AE) a ~

pickings n. (colloq.) ["choice"] easy; lean (AE), slim ~

pickle n. 1. a dill; sour; sweet ~ 2. (BE) mustard ~; ~s and chutney 3. (misc.) in a ~ ("in trouble")

USAGE NOTE: In the United States, a pickle is a pickled cucumber. In Great Britain, the typical pickle is a thick sauce of pickled vegetables.

pick out v. 1. (C) ~ a nice melon for me; or: ~ me out a nice melon 2. (D; tr.) ("to select") to ~ for (we must ~ the best candidate for the job) 3. (H) I ~ed out a nice tie to go with this shirt

pick up v. 1. (d; intr.) to ~ after ("to clean up for") (I was always ~ing up after them) 2. (slang) (d; intr.) to ~ on ("to continue"); ("to become aware of")

picnic n. ["outing with a meal"] 1. to go on, have a ~ ["picnic meal"] (BE) 2. to make; pack a ~ ["plea-sure"] (colloq.) 3. a ~ to + inf. (it's no ~ to work there = it's no ~ working there)

picture I n. ["photograph"] 1. to snap, take a ~ 2. in, on a ~ ["drawing, image, painting"] 3. to draw; paint; retouch a ~ 4. to frame; hang; mount a ~ 5. (BE) an Identikit (T) ~ 6. in a ~ (did you see the animals in the ~?) 7. (misc.) to pose, sit for a ~; as pretty as a ~ ["film"] 8. a motion (AE), moving (esp. AE) ~ 9. in a ~ (who played in that ~?) 10. (esp. BE) to go to the ~s ["description"] 11. to draw, paint a ~ 12. a clear; detailed; gloomy, grim; realistic; rosy; vivid ~ 13. a mental ~ 14. (misc.) (colloq.) to get the ~ ("to comprehend the situa-tion"); to keep/put smb. in the ~ ("to keep smb. informed"); the big, larger ~ ("the overall view")

picture II v. 1. (d; tr.) to ~ as (I cannot ~ her as an actress) 2. (J) can you ~ them leading a demonstra-tion? 3. (Q) can you ~ (to yourself) what they are doing now?

pie n. 1. to bake, make a ~ 2. an apple; blueberry; cherry; lemon-meringue; mince; pecan; pumpkin ~ 3. (AE) ~ a la mode 4. a cottage, shepherd's (BE); meat; pork ~ 5. a piece, slice, wedge of ~ 6. (misc.) as easy as ~

piece n. ["figure used in a game"] 1. chess ~s ["coin"] 2. a fifty-cent; gold; ten-cent ~ ["an artis-tic work"] 3. a collector's ~ (BE; CE has *collector's item*) 4. a conversation ~ 5. a ~ of music ["unit"] 6. by the ~ ["fragment"] 7. to cut, slice smt. into ~s 8. to slice off a ~ of smt. 9. to break into ~s (the vase fell and broke into small ~s; she broke the dish into ~s) 10. ~ by ["misc."] 11. to go to ~s ("to fall apart"); a solid ~ of work ("high-quality work"); to give smb. a ~ of one's mind ("to tell smb. brusquely what one thinks"); to speak one's ~ ("to state one's opinion frankly"); a ~ of news; (BE; colloq.) a nasty ~ of work ("a nasty person"); to pick a theory to ~s ("to disprove a theory")

piecemeal adv. to do smt. ~

piecework n. to do ~

pier n. 1. a loading ~ 2. at, on a ~ (to meet smb. at the ~)

pig n. ["hog, swine"] 1. a sucking (BE), suckling (AE) ~ 2. ~s grunt, oink, squeal 3. a young ~ is a

piglet, shoat (AE) 4. a female ~ is a sow 5. a male ~ is a boar ["glutton"] (colloq.) 6. to make a ~ of oneself ["misc."] 7. as fat as a ~; to buy a ~ in a poke ("to buy, accept smt. with no previous in-spection")

pigeon n. 1. a carrier, homing ~ 2. a clay ~ 3. ~s coo 4. a flight of ~s

piggyback adv. to carry smb. ~ ("to carry smb. on one's shoulders")

pigheaded adj. ~ of (that was ~ of him)

pig out v. (slang) (D; intr.) to ~ on (to ~ on ice cream)

pile I n. ["concrete post"] to sink a ~

pile II n. ["soft raised surface on a rug"] (a) shaggy; smooth; soft; thick ~

pile III n. ["fortune"] (colloq.) 1. to make a ~ ["reactor"] 2. an atomic ~ ["building"] (BE) 3. a stately ~ ["stack"] 4. to put smt. into a ~

pile IV v. 1. (P; intr.) ("to crowd") the children ~d into the car 2. (P; tr.) ("to stack") to ~ wood on the fire 3. (misc.) to ~ books in a stack

pileup n. (colloq.) a traffic ~ (AE)

pilfer v. (D; tr.) to ~ from

pilgrimage n. 1. to go on, make a ~ 2. a ~ to (they went on a ~ to Jerusalem) 3. on a ~

pill n. ["tablet of medicine"] 1. to prescribe a ~ 2. to swallow, take a ~ 3. (colloq.) to pop ~s 4. a head-ache; sleeping ~ ["oral contraceptive"] 5. to take the ~ 6. the morning-after ~ 7. to be on the ~ ["misc."] 8. it was a bitter ~ to swallow ("it was very difficult to experience failure")

pillbox n. to storm; take a ~

pillow n. to fluff up, plump up a ~

pilot I n. ["person who flies aircraft"] 1. an air-force; airline, commercial; bomber; fighter; glider; helicopter; licensed; test ~ ["person who guides ships into and out of a port"] 2. to drop; take on the ~ 3. a harbor ~ ["device for steering"] 4. an automatic ~

pilot II v. (P; tr.) ("to guide") the bill was skillfully ~ed through the Senate; they ~ed the refugees to safety

pin I n. ["metal fastener"] 1. to stick a ~ into smt. 2. a safety; straight ~ 3. a bobby ~ (AE; BE has *hair grip*) 4. a drawing ~ (BE; AE has *thumbtack*) 5. a ~ pricks 6. (misc.) the head of a ~ ["tube-shaped piece of wood"] 7. a rolling ~ ["target in bowl-ing"] 8. to spot ("place") ~s ["support"] 9. to insert, put in a ~ (as in hip surgery) ["misc."] 10. on ~s and needles ("extremely anxious")

pin II v. 1. (D; tr.) ("to trap") to ~ against (~ned against the wall) 2. (D; tr.) ("to trap") to ~ beneath, underneath (he was ~ned beneath the car) 3. (d; tr.) ("to place") to ~ on (we ~ned our hopes on her; to ~ the blame on smb.) 4. (d; tr.) ("to secure") to ~ to (her arms were ~ned to her sides; to ~ a notice to the wall)

pincers *n.* a pair of ~

pinch I *n.* ["painful squeeze"] 1. to give smb. a ~ ["emergency"] (colloq.) 2. at (BE), in (esp. AE) a ~ ["arrest"] (colloq.) 3. to make a ~ ["suffering"] 4. to feel the ~

pinch II *v.* 1. (colloq.) (D; tr.) ("to arrest") to ~ for (~ed for speeding) 2. (D; tr.) ("to squeeze") to ~ in (she ~ed her finger in the door) 3. (D; tr.) ("to squeeze") to ~ on (he ~ed me on the cheek)

pinch-hit *v.* (AE) (from baseball) (D; intr.) to ~ for ("to replace")

pin down *v.* (D; tr.) to ~ to (to ~ smb. down to a specific time)

pine *v.* 1. (d; intr.) to ~ after, for (to ~ for home) 2. (E) they were ~ing to return home

pink I *adj.* tickled ~

pink II *n.* (colloq.) ["good health"] in the ~ (of condition)

pinnacle *n.* 1. to reach a ~ (to reach the ~ of one's power) 2. at a ~ (at the ~ of one's success)

pintable (BE) see **machine** 11

pipe I *n.* ["device for smoking"] 1. to light a ~ 2. to puff on, smoke a ~ 3. to fill one's ~ 4. a peace ~ ["long tube"] 5. to install, lay ~s 6. a drain; exhaust; gas; overflow; sewage; steam; water ~ 7. a ~ bursts; gets blocked; leaks

pipe II *v.* 1. (D; tr.) to ~ from; into, to (to ~ water from a stream to a house) 2. (misc.) to ~ all hands on deck; to ~ an admiral aboard/on board

pipeline *n.* in a ~ (also fig.) (there are several projects in the ~)

pipe up *v.* (colloq.) (D; intr.) to ~ with (she ~d up with the correct answer)

piping *n.* copper; lead; plastic ~

pique *n.* (in) a fit of ~

piracy *n.* 1. to commit ~ 2. air; literary ~; ~ on the high seas 3. an act of ~

pistol *n.* 1. to cock a ~ 2. to aim, point; level a ~ at 3. to fire a ~ (at) 4. to load; unload a ~ 5. to draw, whip out a ~ 6. an automatic; dueling; starting; toy; water ~ 7. the ~ fired, went off; jammed; misfired

pit I *n.* 1. to dig a ~ 2. a bottomless ~ 3. a gravel ~ 4. (misc.) an orchestra ~

pit II *v.* (d; tr.) to ~ against (we were ~ted against a formidable opponent)

pitch I *n.* ["high-pressure sales talk"] (colloq.) 1. to deliver a ~ 2. a sales ~ ["blade angle"] 3. a propeller ~ 4. reverse ~ ["intensity"] 5. a fever; high; low ~ (to reach a fever ~) 6. at a certain ~ (during the last weeks of the campaign, activity was at a high ~) ["throw of a baseball"] 7. to throw a ~ 8. an underhand ~ 9. a wild ~ (to uncork a wild ~) ["playing field"] (BE) 10. a cricket; football ~ 11. off; on the ~ ["musical tone"] 12. to give the ~ 13. a high; low; musical ~ 14. perfect ~ (she has perfect ~)

pitch II *v.* 1. (A) ("to throw") ~ the ball to me; or: ~ me the ball 2. (d; intr.) to ~ into ("to begin to work together enthusiastically") (let's all ~ into this job)

pitch in *v.* (D; intr.) ("to contribute") to ~ with (they ~ed in with a hundred dollars)

pitfall *n.* 1. to avoid a ~ 2. a hidden ~

pitiful *adj.* ~ to + inf. (it's ~ to see such suffering)

pittance *n.* a mere ~

pity *n.* 1. to arouse ~ (in) 2. to feel; show ~ 3. to have, take ~ on smb. 4. ~ for 5. a ~ to + inf. (it's a ~ to see what has happened) 6. a ~ that + clause (it's a ~ that the meeting was canceled) 7. out of ~ (he agreed out of ~ for her children) 8. (misc.) for ~'s sake; a sense of ~

pivot *v.* (d; intr.) to ~ on (the dancer ~ed on the ball of her foot; the future ~s on what we decide now)

placard *n.* to carry a ~

place I *n.* ["space occupied at a table"] 1. to lay (BE), set (esp. AE) a ~ for smb. ["position"] 2. to take smb.'s ~ 3. to change, swap, switch, trade ~s (with) 4. to keep, save smb.'s ~ 5. to give up, relinquish one's ~ 6. to lose one's ~ 7. to fall into ~ 8. (misc.) to know one's ~ (in life); to give up one's ~ in line/in a queue; to occupy a prominent ~ in world literature ["point in space"] 9. a meeting ~ 10. at, in a ~ (at the same old ~) ["dwelling"] 11. at smb.'s ~ (let's meet at your ~) ["appropriate position"] 12. in; out of ~ (everything was in ~) ["seat"] 13. to take one's ~ (they took their ~s) ["standing in a competition"] 14. to take a ~ (she took second ~ in the competition) 15. a ~ goes to (first ~ went to Smith) ["duty, function"] 16. smb.'s ~ to + inf. (it's not my ~ to criticize them) ["stage"] ["step"] 17. in a ~ (in the first ~) ["misc."] 18. to take ~ ("to happen"); to go ~s ("to be successful"); all over the ~ ("everywhere"); in ~ of ("instead of")

place II *v.* 1. (d; tr.) ("to put") to ~ above (to ~ one's family above all other concerns) 2. (d; tr.) ("to put") to ~ at (she ~d her car at our disposal) 3. (d; tr.) ("to present") to ~ before (to ~ evidence before a grand jury) 4. (d; tr.) ("to put") to ~ in (to ~ one's confidence in smb.) 5. (D; tr.) to ~ with ("to find a home for") (to ~ a child with a family) 6. (P; tr.) ("to put") to ~ books on a table 7. (s) she ~d first in the race

placebo *n.* 1. to administer, give a ~ 2. (misc.) a ~ effect

placed *adj.* highly ~

plagiarism *n.* to be guilty of ~

plagiarize *v.* (D; tr.) to ~ from (she ~d the paragraph from a book)

plague I *n.* 1. bubonic ~ 2. a ~ spreads 3. (misc.) to avoid smb. like the ~

plague II *v.* (D; tr.) ("to bother") to ~ with (to ~ smb. with repeated requests)

plain I *adj.* 1. ~ to (the truth is ~ to everybody) 2. ~

to + inf. (the facts are ~ to see) 3. ~ that + clause (it's ~ to everyone that she will never return) 4. (misc.) as ~ as day; or: as ~ as the nose on your face; to make smt. ~

plain II *n.* 1. a broad, vast; coastal ~ 2. on a ~

plain clothes *n.* in ~ (the police officer was in ~)

plan I *n.* 1. to conceive, concoct, devise a ~ 2. to draw up, formulate, map out, work out a ~ 3. to outline a ~ 4. to announce, unveil a ~ 5. to present, propose a ~ 6. to accept, approve a ~ 7. to carry out, execute, implement a ~ 8. to put a ~ into operation 9. to drop, scrub; shelve a ~ 10. to reject, turn down a ~ 11. to foil, frustrate, thwart a ~ 12. a brilliant, ingenious; well-thought-out ~ 13. a feasible; realistic ~ 14. a complicated, elaborate; detailed; grandiose, sweeping ~ 15. an impracticable; impractical; unrealistic ~ 16. a contingency; master; tentative ~ 17. a secret; security ~ 18. a five-year; long-term; short-term ~ 19. (on) the installment ~ (AE; BE has *hire-purchase*) 20. a flight ~ 21. a floor, seating ~ 22. a health ~ ("health insurance"); a pension, retirement ~ 23. an easy-payment ~ 24. travel; wedding ~s (they have announced their wedding ~s) 25. a ~ calls for (smt.) 26. ~s materialize; succeed, work 27. ~s fail 28. a ~ for 29. a ~ to + inf. (the mayor had a ~ to reduce traffic congestion) 30. (misc.) to go according to ~; to make ~s (for a wedding)

plan II *v.* 1. (d; intr.) to ~ for (to ~ for one's old age) 2. (d; intr.) to ~ on (to ~ on early retirement) 3. (E) we ~ to visit them soon 4. (Q) they ~ned very carefully how they would accomplish their mission

plan ahead *v.* (D; intr.) to ~ for (to ~ for retirement)

plane I *n.* ["airplane"] 1. to board, hop, take a ~ 2. to charter a ~ 3. to go by, travel by ~ 4. to catch; miss a ~ 5. to change ~s (we changed ~s in Chicago) 6. to clear a ~ (for landing or takeoff) 7. a cargo; fighter ~ (see also entry for **airplane**)

plane II *n.* ["level surface"] 1. an inclined ~ 2. on a lofty ~

plane III *v.* (N; used with an adjective) to ~ a board smooth

plank *n.* ["board extending from a ship"] to walk the ~ ("to go to one's death") (see the Usage Note for **platform**)

planning *n.* 1. careful; grandiose; long-range, long-term; short-range, short-term ~ 2. central; city; discharge; estate; family; financial; language; town (BE) ~

plan on *v.* (G) we ~ned on spending a month in Europe

plant I *n.* ["shrub, bush"] 1. to grow ~s 2. to water a ~ 3. an annual; biennial; climbing; decorative; exotic; perennial; tropical ~ 4. a ~ grows ["factory"] ["utility"] 5. to manage, operate, run a ~ 6. a nuclear; power; waste-disposal ~ ["buildings"]

["equipment"] 7. (the) physical ~ (of an institution)

plant II *v.* 1. (D; tr.) ("to place secretly") to ~ on (the police ~ed evidence on her) 2. ("to sow") (D; tr.) to ~ with (to ~ a field with rye) 3. (misc.) to ~ an idea in smb.'s head

plantation *n.* a coffee; cotton; rubber; sugar; tea ~

plaque *n.* ["filmy deposit on teeth"] 1. to remove ~ (from teeth) 2. dental ~ 3. ~ accumulates, builds up, forms ["tablet"] 4. to put up; unveil a ~ (in smb.'s honor) 5. a commemorative, memorial ~

plaster I *n.* ["pasty composition"] 1. to apply ~ (to apply ~ to a wall) 2. to daub ~ (to daub ~ on a wall) 3. crumbling, falling ~ 4. ~ comes off, falls off, peels; sets ["pastelike mixture used for healing purposes"] 5. a mustard ~ ["tape"] 6. (BE) (a) sticking ~

plaster II *v.* 1. (d; tr.) ("to cover") to ~ with (they ~ed the walls with posters) 2. (P; tr.) ("to put up") to ~ announcements all over the walls; they ~ed notices on every bulletin board

plastic *n.* laminated ~

plate *n.* ["dish"] 1. a cake; dinner; paper; salad; soup ~ ["denture"] 2. a dental; lower; partial; upper ~ ["tag"] 3. a license (esp. AE), number (BE) ~ ["thin layer"] 4. armor; silver ~ ["container passed around for donations of money"] 5. to pass the ~ 6. a collection ~ ["geological feature"] 7. a tectonic ~

plateau *n.* 1. a high ~ 2. (misc.) to reach a ~ ("to cease making progress")

platform *n.* ["raised stage"] 1. to mount ("ascend") a ~ 2. from a ~ (to speak from a ~) 3. a launching ~ ["flat surface"] 4. from a ~ (trains leave from that ~) ["statement of policies"] (esp. AE; BE prefers *manifesto*) 5. to draft, draw up a ~ 6. to adopt a ~ 7. a party; political ~
USAGE NOTE: A political platform consists of various statements that are called planks.

platitude *n.* 1. to mouth, utter a ~ (he's always mouthing ~s) 2. in ~s (to speak in ~s)

platoon *n.* 1. to form a ~ 2. to deploy a ~ 3. to command a ~ (a lieutenant commands a ~)

plaudits *n.* to earn, receive, win ~

plausible *adj.* 1. ~ to + inf. (it is ~ to assume that they will not accept our invitation) 2. ~ that + clause (it's ~ that most of the voters will not support this referendum)

play I *n.* ["stage presentation"] 1. to direct; do, present, produce, put on, stage; revive; write a ~ 2. to perform; rehearse a ~ 3. to see a ~ 4. to criticize, pan (colloq.); review a ~ 5. an historical; miracle; morality; mystery; nativity; one-act; passion; TV ~ 6. a ~ closes; flops; opens; runs (the ~ ran for two years on Broadway) 7. (misc.) the ~ got rave reviews; the ~ was a (smash) hit ["action, activity"] 8. to bring into ~ (to bring various forces into ~) 9.

to come into ~ ["competition, playing"] 10. fair; foul; rough; team ~ 11. at; in; into; out of ~ (to put the ball into ~; the children were at ~) ["attempt to attract"] (colloq.) 12. to make a ~ for (he made a ~ for her) ["misc."] 13. a ~ on words ("a pun")

play II v. 1. ("to compete") to ~ fair; foul; rough 2. (C) ("to perform") ~ a nice song for me; or: ~ me a nice song 3. (d; intr.) ("to compete") to ~ against (to ~ against a strong opponent) 4. (D; intr.) ("to amuse oneself") to ~ at (she ~s at being a writer) 5. (d; intr.) ("to gamble") to ~ for (to ~ for money) 6. (d; intr.) ("to perform") to ~ for (she ~s for our team) 7. (d; intr.) to ~ for ("to attempt to obtain") (to ~ for time) 8. (d; intr.) to ~ on, upon ("to exploit") (to ~ on smb.'s fears) 9. (d; intr.) to ~ on ("to pun") (to ~ on words) 10. (D; tr.) ("to do, make") to ~ on (they ~ed a joke on us; she ~ed a trick on me) 11. (d; intr.) ("to perform") to ~ to (to ~ to a full house) 12. (esp. tennis) (d; intr.) ("to direct one's strokes") to ~ to (to ~ to an opponent's forehand) 13. (D; intr., tr.) ("to amuse oneself") to ~ with (to ~ with the children; to ~ a game with the children) 14. (L) (esp. in children's language) ("to pretend") let's ~ that I'm the teacher and you're the pupil 15. (O; can be used with one object) ("to oppose in") I'll ~ you a game of cards 16. (s) ("to feign") they ~ed dead 17. (misc.) to ~ smb. for a fool ("to ridicule smb."); to ~ it by ear ("to improvise"); to ~ into smb.'s hands ("to come under smb.'s control")

play about (BE) see **play around**

play along v. (D; intr.) to ~ with (we had to ~ with their various proposals)

play around v. (D; intr.) to ~ with

play back v. (B) she ~ed the tape back to us

player n. ["athlete"] 1. a clean; dirty ~ 2. a key ~ ["electronic instrument"] 3. a cassette; compact disc; record ~ ["participant"] 4. a key; major ~

playground n. 1. (BE) an adventure ~ ("children's playground designed for spontaneous play") 2. a city, municipal, public; school ~

playing n. clean; dirty ~

play off v. (d; tr.) to ~ against ("to set against") (to ~ one side off against the other)

playoffs n. to get into/to the ~

play up v. (d; intr.) to ~ to ("to flatter") (to ~ to the boss)

plea n. 1. to enter, make, put forward a ~ 2. to answer, respond to a ~ 3. to deny, reject a ~ 4. (slang) (esp. AE) to cop a ~ ("to plead guilty to a lesser charge") 5. an ardent, emotional, fervent, impassioned, moving, passionate, tearful; urgent ~ 6. (to enter) a guilty ~; (to enter) a ~ of not guilty; more usu. is: to plead guilty; to plead not guilty 7. a ~ of insanity 8. a ~ for (a ~ for mercy) 9. (misc.) ~ bargaining

plead v. 1. to ~ fervently 2. (D; intr.) to ~ for; with

(to ~ with the judge for mercy; she ~ed with the judge to show mercy) 3. (E) she ~ed to be reunited with her child 4. (legal) to ~ guilty (to a charge) 5. (legal) to ~ not guilty (to a charge)

pleasant adj. 1. ~ to (she is ~ to everyone) 2. ~ to + inf. (it's ~ to lie in the sun = it's ~ lying in the sun; she is ~ to work with = it is ~ to work with her = it is ~ working with her = she is a ~ person to work with)

pleasantry n. to exchange ~tries

please v. 1. to ~ greatly, highly 2. (R) it ~d us to learn of your success; it ~d us greatly that you could accept our invitation 3. (misc.) ~ be seated

pleased adj. 1. greatly, highly, very ~ 2. ~ about, at, by, with 3. ~ to + inf. (we are ~ to be here; I am ~ to meet you) 4. ~ that + clause (she was ~ that the proposal had been accepted)

pleasing adj. ~ to

pleasure n. 1. to afford, give, provide ~ (it gives me great ~ to present the next speaker) 2. to feel; find, have, take ~ in 3. to derive, get ~ from 4. to forgo a ~ 5. (a) genuine, great, real; rare ~ 6. a perverse; vicarious ~ 7. a ~ for (working here is a ~ for me) 8. a ~ to + inf. (it's a ~ to work with them = it's a ~ working with them = they are a ~ to work with; it is a ~ to teach these children = it is a ~ teaching these children = these children are a ~ to teach; it was a ~ for me to teach these children) 9. at smb.'s ~ (to serve at the president's ~) 10. for ~ (she reads history for ~) 11. with ~ (I accept with ~)

plebiscite n. 1. to conduct, hold a ~ 2. a ~ to + inf. (a ~ to determine the status of a territory) 3. (misc.) to decide by ~

pledge I n. 1. to make, take a ~ 2. to give smb. one's ~ 3. to honor, redeem one's ~ 4. to break, violate a ~ 5. a firm; solemn ~ 6. a campaign, election ~ 7. a ~ to + inf. (she made a solemn ~ to contribute fifty pounds) 8. a ~ that + clause (he took a ~ that he would stop smoking) 9. (misc.) to take the ~ ("to vow to stop drinking")

pledge II v. 1. (A) she ~d her support to us; or: she ~d us her support 2. (d; tr.) to ~ as (they ~d their assets as collateral) 3. (D; tr.) to ~ to (she was ~d to secrecy) 4. (E) they ~d to return 5. (H; refl.) they ~d themselves to avenge his death 6. (L; to) he ~d that he would repay the debt within a month

plenty determiner, n., pronoun 1. ~ of (~ of money) 2. ~ to + inf. (she gave us ~ to do) 3. (formal) in ~ (to live in ~) 4. (formal) of ~ (a time of ~)

pliers n. a pair of ~

plod v. 1. (d; intr.) to ~ through ("to go through laboriously") (to ~ through a long reading list) 2. (P; intr.) ("to move") they ~ded slowly along the road

plod away v. (D; intr.) to ~ at (to ~ at one's job)

plot I n. ["conspiracy"] 1. to devise, hatch; weave a ~ 2. to foil, thwart a ~ 3. to expose, uncover a ~ 4.

a cunning, diabolic(al); sinister ~ 5. a ~ against 6. a ~ to + inf. (to expose a ~ to overthrow the government) ["story"] 7. to build, construct the ~ (of a novel) 8. a contrived; intricate ~ 9. a simple ~ 10. a ~ thickens ["piece of ground"] 11. a burial, cemetery; garden ~; a ~ of land

plot II v. 1. (D; intr.) to ~ against (to ~ against the government) 2. (E) they ~ted to overthrow the government 3. (Q) they were ~ting how to obtain the necessary information

plow, plough I n. to pull a ~

plow, plough II v. 1. (d; intr.) to ~ into ("to strike") (the racing car skidded and ~ed into the crowd) 2. (d; intr.) to ~ through ("to go through laboriously") (to ~ through a long reading list; to ~ through a crowd; to ~ through deep snow)

plow back, plough back v. (d; tr.) to ~ into (to ~ all profits into the firm)

ploy n. 1. to resort to, use a ~ 2. a clever, ingenious; cynical ~ 3. a ~ to + inf. (it was a ~ to get money)

pluck I n. ["courage"] 1. to display, show ~ 2. to require, take ~ (standing up to the boss took a lot of ~) 3. the ~ to + inf. (he had enough ~ to stand up to the boss)

pluck II v. 1. (d; intr.) ("to tug") to ~ at 2. (D; tr.) ("to pull") to ~ from (to ~ feathers from a chicken)

plug I n. ["electrical fitting"] 1. to insert, put a ~ into a socket 2. a ~ fits into a socket ["device carrying an electric current"] 3. a spark, sparking (BE) ~ ["word of praise"] (colloq.) 4. to put in a ~ for ["misc."] (colloq.) 5. to pull the ~ ("to cut off a life-support system"); to pull the ~ on smt. ("to put an end to smt.")

plug II v. (d; intr., tr.) to ~ into (the lamp ~s into this socket; to ~ into a computer network)

plug away v. (D; intr.) to ~ at ("to work at laboriously") (to ~ at a job)

plumber n. 1. to call (in) a ~ 2. a master ~

plumbing n. 1. to install ~ 2. indoor ~

plummet v. (d; intr.) to ~ to; towards (to ~ to earth)

plump I adj. pleasingly ~

plump II v. (colloq.) (D; intr.) to ~ for ("to support")

plump down v. (colloq.) (D; refl., tr.) to ~ in, into, on (she ~ed herself down into the chair)

plunge I n. ["risk"] (colloq.) to take the ~

plunge II v. 1. (d; intr.) ("to throw oneself") to ~ from; to (to ~ to one's death from a cliff) 2. (d; intr.) ("to dive") to ~ into ("to rush") to ~ into the water; to ~ into war) 3. (d; tr.) ("to throw"); ("to thrust") to ~ into (the room was ~ed into darkness; to ~ a dagger into smb.'s heart) 4. (d; intr., tr.) ("to throw oneself"; "to thrust") to ~ through (she ~d through the ice; he ~d the spear through the barrier)

plural n. in the ~

plurality n. by a ~ (AE: to win the election by a ~)

plus n. 1. a big ~ (it was a big ~ in her favor) 2. (misc.) to weigh the ~es and the minuses

ply v. 1. (d; intr.) ("to travel") to ~ between (these ships ~ between the two cities) 2. (d; tr.) ("to provide") to ~ with (they plied him with liquor)

pneumonia n. 1. to come down with, contract, develop ~ 2. bronchial; viral ~

poach v. (D; intr.) ("to hunt illegally on smb.'s property") to ~ on, upon (to ~ on smb.'s land)

pocket n. 1. to empty; fill one's ~s 2. to turn out one's ~s 3. to pick smb.'s ~ 4. a back; coat; hip; inside; shirt; side; watch ~ 5. an air ~ 6. (misc.) (BE) in ~ ("with a profit"); out of ~ ("with a loss")

pocketbook n. ["handbag"] (AE) to carry a ~

podium n. 1. to mount a ~ 2. to stand at a ~ 3. from; on a ~

poem n. 1. to compose, write a ~ 2. to memorize; read; recite; scan a ~ 3. a dramatic; epic, heroic; lyric; narrative; prose ~

poet n. 1. the ~ laureate 2. a poet-in-residence

poetry n. 1. to compose, write ~ 2. to memorize; read; recite; scan ~ 3. dramatic; epic, heroic; lyric; narrative; romantic ~

pogrom n. to carry out; instigate; organize a ~

point I n. ["location, position, place, spot"] 1. to arrive at, reach a ~ 2. an assembly; rallying ~ 3. a central; focal; salient; vantage ~ 4. a jumping-off; starting; turning ~ 5. a cutoff; fixed ~ 6. a pressure ~ 7. a vanishing ~ 8. the ~ of no return 9. at a ~ (at that ~ in history) 10. for a ~ (for all ~s said) 11. from; to a ~ (from this ~ to that ~) ["level"] ["degree"] 12. to arrive at, reach a ~ 13. a high; low ~ (she has reached the high ~ of her career) 14. the boiling; freezing; melting ~ 15. the breaking; saturation ~ 16. up to a ~, to a ~ (AE) (to a certain ~ they are right) ["step, stage"] 17. at, on the ~ (they were on the ~ of leaving; the commissioners were at a delicate ~ in the negotiations) ["argument"] ["topic"] 18. to bring up, make, raise a ~ 19. to argue, debate; cover, discuss; emphasize, stress, underscore; explain; illustrate; prove, win; review a ~ 20. to belabor; strain, stretch a ~ 21. to drive, hammer, press a ~ home; to make one's ~; to get a ~ across 22. to concede, yield a ~ 23. a controversial; crucial; fine; major; minor; moot; selling; sore; sticking; subtle; talking; telling ~ 24. a ~ comes up (the same ~ has come up several times) 25. the ~ that + clause (she made the ~ that further resistance was useless) 26. beside the ~ (her remarks were beside the ~) 27. on a ~ (on that ~ we disagree) 28. to the ~ (to speak to the ~; she was brief and to the ~) 29. (misc.) to come to the ~; ~ by ~; a good ("convincing") ~; to have a ~ ("to have a convincing argument") ["core, essence"] 30. to see the ~ (she never did see the ~ of the joke) 31. to come to, to get to the ~ 32. to miss the ~ (we missed the ~ of the story) ["emphasis"] 33. to make a ~ of (he made a ~ of repeating her name several times) ["distinguishing feature"] 34. smb.'s bad, weak; good, strong ~s ["punctuation mark"] 35. a decimal; exclamation (AE) ~ ["scoring unit"] 36. to score a ~ (also fig.); to rack up ~s 37. to shave ~s ("to manipulate the results of a contest for illegal purposes") 38. (esp. tennis) a game; match; set ~ 39. by ~s (to lead by five ~s) 40. (boxing) on ~s (to win on ~s) ["regard"] 41. in ~ of (in ~ of law; in ~ of fact) ["aim, object, purpose, reason"] 42. to get, see the ~ 43. to have a ~ 44. a ~ in (there is no ~ in complaining = there is no ~ complaining) 45. a ~ to (there is no ~ to your going) 46. (misc.) what's the ~? the ~ is that our party cannot win the election ["tapered end"] 47. a sharp ~ (this pencil has a sharp ~) ["socket"] (BE) 48. a cooker; mains; power ~ ["misc."] 49. a ~ of view; at the ~ of a gun; a Brownie ~ (colloq.) ("ingratiation in the eyes of a superior") (to make Brownie ~s); a case in ~ ("a pertinent case"); a ~ of order; the cardinal ~s of the compass

point II v. 1. (D; intr.) to ~ at, to, towards ("to draw attention to") (she ~ed at me) 2. (d; tr.) ("to aim") to ~ at (to ~ a gun at smb.) 3. (D; intr.) to ~ to ("to cite") (they ~ed to poverty as a major problem; the evidence ~s to him as the criminal) 4. (P; intr., tr.) ("to aim, direct") (the needle ~s north; to ~ a boat downstream; she ~ed the muzzle towards the door

pointers n. ["advice"] 1. to give smb. ~ on 2. to ask for; get ~ on

pointless adj. ~ to + inf. (it's ~ to continue the discussion)

point of view n. 1. to have, hold a ~ 2. a fresh; optimistic, positive ~ 3. a negative, pessimistic ~ 4. from the ~ of 5. one's ~; smb.'s ~

point out v. 1. (B) she ~ed out the sights to us 2. (L; to) they ~ed out (to us) that such investments would be risky 3. (Q; to) I ~ed out to them where I work

poise I n. 1. to keep, maintain one's ~ 2. to lose one's ~ 3. the ~ to + inf. (do you have enough ~ to speak without notes?)

poise II v. (D; refl.) ("to brace oneself") to ~ for (she ~d herself for the ordeal)

poised adj. ["ready"] 1. ~ for (~ for action) 2. ~ to + inf. (they were ~ to attack)

poison I n. 1. to administer, give (a) ~ 2. to swallow, take ~ 3. (a) deadly, lethal; slow; strong ~ 4. rat ~ (to spread rat ~)

poison II v. to ~ smb.'s mind against smb.

poison gas n. to use ~ against

poisoning n. blood; food; lead; ptomaine ~

poke I n. ["punch"] (colloq.) to give smb. a ~ (in the eye)

poke II v. 1. (d; intr.) to ~ at ("to jab") (he kept ~ing at me) 2. (D; tr.) ("to jab") to ~ in (to ~ smb. in the ribs) 3. (d; tr.) ("to extend") to ~ out of (to ~ one's

head out of the window) 4. (d; intr., tr.) ("to produce by piercing") to ~ through (to ~ a hole through a wall) 5. (P; tr.) ("to thrust") to ~ one's head through a window 6. (misc.) to ~ fun at smb.

poke about see **poke around**

poke around v. (colloq.) (D; intr.) to ~ in ("to look through") (stop ~ing around in my desk)

poker n. to play ~

polarization n. ~ between

polarize v. (D; intr., tr.) to ~ into (~d into opposing camps)

pole I n. ["long, slender piece of wood, metal"] 1. to put up a ~ 2. a breakaway; fishing; ski; tent; totem ~ 3. a telegraph; telephone (AE); utility (AE) ~

pole II n. ["end of the earth's axis"] 1. the North; South Pole (a camp was set up at the North Pole) 2. a celestial; magnetic ~ ["terminal of a battery"] 3. a negative; positive ~ ["misc."] 4. ~s apart; or: at opposite ~s ("diametrically opposed")

police n. border; campus (US); city, municipal; local; military; mounted; riot; secret; security; state ~

police car n. an unmarked ~

policeman n. 1. a military ~ (abbreviated as *MP*) 2. see **police officer**

police officer n. an off-duty; plainclothes; uniformed ~

policewoman see **police officer**

policy I n. ["plan"] ["principle"] 1. to adopt, establish, formulate, set a ~ 2. to adhere to, follow, pursue a ~ 3. to carry out, implement a ~ 4. to form, make, shape (a) ~ 5. to change, modify, revise (a) ~ 6. to violate (a) ~ 7. a clear, clear-cut; prudent; sound, wise ~ 8. a friendly; open-door ~ 9. a conciliatory; flexible ~ 10. a cautious; deliberate; established, firm, set ~ 11. a controversial; divisive; foolish; ill-conceived; rigid; wait-and-see ~ 12. a scorched-earth ~ 13. a long-range, long-term; short-range, short-term ~ 14. an official; standard ~ 15. an established; written ~ 16. (a) company; personnel ~ 17. (a) domestic; economic; educational; financial, fiscal, monetary; foreign; government, public; military; national; population; social ~ 18. a ~ on, towards 19. a ~ to + inf. (it is our established ~ to treat everyone fairly) 20. a ~ that + clause; subj. (it is company ~ that all workers be/should be paid according to the same criteria)

policy II n. ["contract for insurance"] 1. to take out a ~ 2. to issue, write up a ~ 3. to reinstate a ~ 4. to cancel a ~ 5. an endowment; homeowner's; insurance; lifetime; straight life; term ~ 6. a ~ matures ["contract"] 7. a service ~ (we have a service ~ for all of our major appliances)

polio, poliomyelitis n. 1. to contract, develop; get; have ~ 2. to prevent ~

polish n. ["gloss"] 1. to apply ~ 2. floor; French (BE); furniture; shoe; silver ~ 3. nail ~ (BE has *nail varnish*)

polite adj. 1. ~ to 2. ~ to + inf. (it was not ~ to say that)

politeness n. 1. studied ~ 2. ~ to

politic adj. ["expedient"] ~ to + inf. (it would not be ~ to get involved in their affairs)

political fences n. ["political standing"] to mend one's ~

politician n. an astute, shrewd; crafty, crooked, cunning, scheming, wily; glib; great; hack; honest ~

politics n. 1. to go into ~ 2. to play ~ 3. to talk ~ 4. local, parish-pump (BE); national; partisan, party; pork-barrel; power; practical ~

poll n. 1. to carry out, conduct, take a ~ 2. an exit ~ (taken of voters leaving the voting booths) 3. a straw ("unofficial") ~ 4. a public-opinion ~ 5. a national, nationwide ~ 6. a ~ among, of (to conduct a ~ among students) 7. in a ~ (their strong feelings came out in several ~s)

pollination n. cross ~

polls n. 1. to go to the ~ (in order to vote) 2. the ~ close; open (at a certain time) 3. at the ~ (to be defeated at the ~)

pollution n. 1. to control ~ 2. air; environmental; noise, sound; water ~

polo n. 1. to play ~ 2. water ~

polyandry n. to practice ~

polygamy n. to practice ~

polyp n. 1. to remove a ~ 2. a benign; malignant ~

pomp n. 1. ceremonial ~ 2. ~ and circumstance

pond n. 1. to drain a ~ 2. a stagnant ~ 3. a duck; fish ~

ponder v. 1. (d; intr.) to ~ on, over, upon (to ~ over a problem) 2. (Q) I ~ed how we could finish on time

pontificate v. (D; intr.) to ~ about, on

pony n. 1. to ride a ~ 2. a polo; Shetland ~

pool I n. ["joint enterprise"] 1. to form a ~ 2. a car; stenographic (AE), typing ~ ["group of vehicles"] 3. a motor ~ ["total of money bet by gamblers"] 4. a football ~ (BE has *the pools*) ["billiards"] 5. to play, shoot ~ ["stock, supply"] 6. a gene ~

pool II n. ["basin"] 1. an indoor; outdoor; paddling (BE), wading (AE); swimming ~ ["small body of water"] 2. a deep; shallow; stagnant ~

pools see **pool I** 4

poor adj. 1. ~ at (they are ~ at exploiting their natural resources) 2. ~ in (the country is ~ in natural resources)

pop I adv. (colloq.) to go ~ ("to make a short explosive sound")

pop II v. (P; intr., tr.) we have to ~ into the store for a minute; ~ your head out of the window and see if it's raining; to ~ around the corner

popular adj. 1. ~ as (she was ~ as a nightclub singer) 2. ~ with (~ with teenagers)

popularity n. 1. to acquire, gain, win ~ 2. to enjoy ~ 3. to lose ~ 4. declining; great; growing, increasing ~ 5. ~ declines, slips; grows, increases 6. ~ among, with

populated adj. densely, heavily; sparsely ~

population n. 1. a decreasing, shrinking; dense; excess, overflow; expanding, growing, increasing, rising; sparse; stable; transient ~ 2. an aging; civilian; foreign-born; indigenous; local; native-born; rural; urban ~ 3. (misc.) ~ control; a ~ explosion

porch n. 1. (AE) a back; front ~ (BE uses *veranda*) 2. (AE) a sun ~ (BE has *sun lounge*) 3. (AE) a screened, screened-in ~ (BE uses *veranda*) 4. (BE) a church ~

pore v. (d; intr.) to ~ over ("to examine") (to ~ over a document)

pores n. blocked, clogged, closed; open ~

pornography n. 1. to peddle ~ 2. explicit, hardcore; soft, soft-core ~

porpoise n. 1. a school of ~s 2. a young ~ is a calf 3. a female ~ is a cow 4. a male ~ is a bull

porridge n. (esp. BE) 1. to cook, make ~ 2. (misc.) a bowl of ~; (BE; slang) to do ~ ("to spend time in prison")

port I n. ["harbor"] 1. to clear, leave ~ 2. to come into, make, reach ~ ("to arrive at a port") 3. to call at a ~ 4. a fishing; free; home ~ 5. in; into ~ (to put into ~) 6. (misc.) a ~ of call; a ~ of entry; any ~ in a storm ("whatever help is available")

port II n. ["type of wine"] ruby; tawny; vintage ~

portfolio n. ["a set of shares"] 1. an investment ~ ["position of a government minister"] 2. a minister without ~

portion n. 1. an individual ~ 2. equal ~s

portion out v. (B) they ~ed the food out to the needy

portrait n. 1. to do, paint a ~ 2. to commission a ~ 3. a composite; family; full-length; group ~ 4. (misc.) to pose for, sit for one's ~

portray v. (d; tr.) to ~ as (to ~ smb. as a hero)

pose I n. to assume, strike; hold a ~

pose II v. 1. (d; intr.) to ~ as ("to pretend to be") (to ~ as an expert) 2. (D; intr.) to ~ for ("to serve as a model for") (to ~ for an artist) 3. (misc.) to ~ a threat to smb./smt.

posit v. (formal) (L) her book ~s that the soul and the spirit are distinct

position I n. ["posture"] 1. to assume, take a ~ 2. an awkward, uncomfortable; comfortable ~ 3. a kneeling; lotus; lying; prone; reclining; sitting; squatting; standing; straddle; supine; upright ~ 4. the fetal, foetal ~ ["attitude"] 5. to adopt, assume, take a ~ 6. a controversial; firm; flexible; hostile; radical; strong; uncompromising; untenable; weak ~ 7. an official; unofficial ~ 8. a ~ on (to take a ~ on foreign aid) 9. a ~ that + clause (they took the ~ that further resistance would be useless) ["site"] ["military site"] 10. to attack, overrun, storm a ~ 11. to consolidate; hold, maintain; occupy, take up; regain a ~ 12. to give up, lose, relinquish, surrender, yield a ~ 13. a defensive; dominant; enemy; favorable; fortified; impregnable; key; powerful, strong; unfortified; untenable, vulnerable, weak ~ ["place"] ["situation"] 14. to occupy, take a ~ 15. to jockey for, maneuver for ~ 16. an embarrassing; ludicrous ~ 17. an enviable; high, leading, prominent; responsible; unique ~ (to occupy a prominent ~) 18. a legal; political; social ~ 19. a ~ to + inf. (we may be in a ~ to help you) 20. from a certain ~ (they negotiated from a ~ of strength) 21. in a ~ (she is in a ~ to know) 22. (misc.) a ~ of power; a ~ of strength; a ~ of weakness ["proper place"] 23. in ~ (the players were in ~) 24. out of ~ ["job"] 25. to create a (new) ~ 26. to apply for, look for, seek a ~ 27. to find, get a ~ 28. to fill a ~ 29. to hold, hold down a ~ (she holds a responsible ~ in a law firm) 30. a permanent; temporary ~ 31. a teaching; tenured; tenure-track ~ 32. a government; official ~ 33. a managerial; senior ~ ["misc."] 34. (as in chess) a drawn; losing; winning ~

position II v. 1. (H) they ~ed the bomb to go off when the first car reached the gate 2. (P; refl., tr.) I ~ed myself near the entrance; observers were ~ed along the ridges

positive adj. 1. ~ about, of (we were ~ of the outcome) 2. ~ that + clause (they were ~ that their party would win)

possess v. (H) what ~ed you to do it?

possession n. 1. to gain, get, take ~ of 2. to come into ~ of smt. 3. in ~ of (they are in ~ of valuable documents) 4. in smb.'s ~ (they have in their ~ many priceless antiques)

possessions n. 1. one's earthly; material; personal ~ 2. one's cherished; priceless; valuable ~

possibility n. 1. to consider, entertain; raise a ~ 2. to discount, eliminate, exclude, rule out a ~ 3. a distinct, good, real, strong ~ 4. a remote, slim ~ 5. a ~ of (there is a strong ~ of snow) 6. a ~ that + clause (there's a strong ~ that the concert will be canceled) 7. (misc.) within the realm of ~

possible adj. 1. easily, perfectly, very; humanly ~ 2. ~ for (anything is ~ for them) 3. ~ to + inf. (it is ~ to rent a boat) 4. ~ that + clause (it is ~ that we will be able to attend)

possum n. (colloq.) to play ~ ("to pretend to be asleep")

post I n. ["mail"] 1. (BE) see **mail I** 2. (BE) free ~ 3. (CE) parcel ~ 4. (BE) by return of ~ (AE has by return mail)

post II v. (BE) 1. (A) she ~ed the book to me; or: she ~ed me the book 2. (D; tr.) to ~ from; to (the letter was ~ed from London to Edinburgh) (AE has **mail II**)

post III n. ["station"] 1. a command; listening; observation; trading ~ ["place of duty"] 2. to leave; quit one's ~ 3. at one's ~ (to be asleep at one's ~)

post IV v. 1. (esp. BE) (d; tr.) ("to assign") to ~ to (she was ~ed to Bonn) 2. (P; tr.) ("to place, position") they ~ed him at the gate; I was ~ed near the door

post V n. ["pole"] 1. a starting ~ (at a horse race) 2. (misc.) from pillar to ~ ("from one situation to another without letup"); (BE) to pip at the ~ ("to overtake and defeat at the very end")

postage n. 1. to pay the ~ 2. the return ~ 3. ~ due; ~ for; ~ paid

postcard n. 1. to send a ~ 2. to drop smb. a ~ 3. a picture ~

posted adj. to keep smb. ~

poster n. 1. to mount, put up a ~ 2. to take down a ~ 3. a campaign ~

posterior adj. (formal) ["after, later"] ~ to

posterity n. preserved for ~

postmaster n. the ~ general

postmortem n. to do, hold, perform a ~

postpone v. 1. to ~ indefinitely 2. (D; tr.) to ~ to, until (the concert has been ~d to Wednesday) 3. (G) they ~d leaving because of the weather

postscript n. 1. to add a ~ 2. a ~ to

postulate I n. (formal) a ~ that + clause (his ~ that the area was uninhabited proved to be true)

postulate II v. (formal) (L) they ~d that the collision had been caused by fog

posture I n. 1. to adopt, assume a ~ 2. an erect, upright; good ~ 3. a defense; political ~

posture II v. (D; intr.) ("to pretend") to ~ as

pot I n. 1. (fig.) a melting ~ 2. a pepper ~ (BE; AE has pepper shaker) 3. a chamber ~ 4. a coffeepot; teapot 5. (misc.) to scour ~s and pans; to go to ~ ("to be ruined")

pot II n. (colloq.) ["marijuana"] to smoke ~

potato n. 1. to bake; boil; fry; mash; peel; roast; sauté ~es 2. a baked ~ 3. a sweet ~ 4. chipped (BE), French-fried (AE); mashed; scalloped ~es

potential n. 1. to develop; realize one's ~ 2. to have (great) ~ 3. a ~ for

potion n. a love; magic; sleeping ~

potluck n. ["whatever is offered"] to take ~

potshot n. (colloq.) ["critical remark"] to take a ~ at

potter v. (BE) (d; intr.) to ~ about (to ~ about the house) (AE has putter)

pottery n. to glaze ~

potty adj. (colloq.) (esp. BE) ["infatuated"] ~ about

pouch n. 1. an ammunition; tobacco ~ 2. diplomatic ~ (the letter was sent by diplomatic ~)

poultice n. to apply a ~

pounce v. (d; intr.) to ~ on, upon (the cat ~d on the

mouse)

pound I *n.* ["enclosure"] a dog ~

pound II *v.* 1. (d; intr.) to ~ against, at (to ~ at the door; our artillery was ~ing at the enemy positions) 2. (d; tr.) to ~ into (I've been trying to ~ some facts into their heads) 3. (d; intr.) to ~ on (to ~ on a table)

pour *v.* 1. (C) ~ a cool drink for me; or: ~ me a cool drink 2. (d; intr.) to ~ down (tears ~ed down her cheeks) 3. (d; intr., tr.) to ~ from (blood ~ed from the gaping wound) 4. (d; intr., tr.) to ~ into (water ~ed into the pit) 5. (d; intr., tr.) to ~ out of (oil ~ed out of the tank) 6. (d; tr.) to ~ over (to ~ gravy over meat)

pour out *v.* (D; intr., tr.) to ~ from, of; into, onto, to (the water ~ed out of the tank into the street; she told me to ~ the solution from the large flask; the spectators ~ed out of the stadium onto the parking lot)

pout *v.* (D; intr.) to ~ about

poverty *n.* 1. to breed ~ (illiteracy breeds ~) 2. to alleviate; eliminate, eradicate, wipe out ~ 3. abject, dire, extreme, grinding, severe ~ 4. in ~ (to live in grinding ~)

poverty line *n.* above; below the ~ (many people live below the ~)

powder *n.* 1. to put on ~ 2. baby; dusting; face; talcum ~ 3. baking; curry; garlic ~ 4. bleaching; scouring ~ 5. tooth ~ 6. gunpowder; smokeless ~ 7. (misc.) (slang) to take a ~ ("to run off unexpectedly"); (colloq.) to keep one's ~ dry ("to remain calm")

power *n.* ["authority"] 1. to assume, gain, take; concentrate, consolidate; exercise, have, hold, wield ~ 2. to abuse; seize ~ 3. to relinquish; transfer ~ 4. emergency; executive; political ~ 5. discretionary ~s 6. ~ over (they seized ~ over several provinces) 7. the ~ to + inf. (the prime minister has the ~ to dissolve parliament) 8. in; into ~ (the government in ~; to come into ~) 9. (misc.) the ~ behind the throne ["dominance"] 10. the balance of ~ 11. to have smb. in one's ~ 12. absolute ~ 13. ~ corrupts ["nation"] 14. the great, world ~s; a superpower 15. (the) warring ~s 16. a colonial; foreign; industrial; occupying ~ ["capability"] 17. to develop one's ~s (of observation) 18. bargaining; earning; purchasing ~ 19. curative, healing; recuperative ~ 20. psychic; supernatural ~s 21. in, within smb.'s ~ (it was not within my ~ to help) ["military force, police force"] 22. air; military; naval, sea; police ~ 23. fire ~ ["source of energy"] 24. to turn on the ~ 25. to cut off, turn off the ~ 26. electric; hydroelectric; nuclear; steam; water ~ 27. (misc.) (AE) a ~ outage ["motive force"] 28. under one's own ~ ["exponent"] (math.) 29. to raise to a ~ (to raise five to the third ~)

powerless *adj.* ~ to + inf. (she was ~ to help)

power line *n.* to down a ~ (several ~s were downed during the storm)

power mower *n.* to operate, work a ~

power of attorney *n.* 1. to give, grant a ~ 2. to notarize a ~ 3. to hold a ~ 4. a ~ to + inf. (we had a ~ to conduct her business)

powwow *n.* (colloq.) ["conference"] to hold a ~

pox *n.* ["plague"] a ~ on

practicable *adj.* ["feasible"] ~ to + inf. (it was not ~ to put up a new building there)

practical *adj.* ["realistic"] 1. ~ about; in ["sensible"] 2. ~ to + inf. (it is not ~ to do that)

practice I practise *n.* ["habit"] 1. to make a ~ of smt. 2. a common, normal, standard, usual ~ 3. a local; universal, widespread ~ 4. a ~ to + inf. (it was her ~ to drink a glass of wine every evening) ["exercise"] 5. to have ~ (we have ~ today at four o'clock) 6. target ~ 7. ~ at, in (~ at tying knots) 8. the ~ to + inf. (I've had enough ~ to pass the test) 9. in; out of ~ (since they closed the gym, I've been out of ~) ["professional activity"] 10. to have one's own ~ 11. (a) law, legal; medical; nursing; professional ~ 12. (of doctors) (a) family, general ~ 13. (of doctors) (a) group; private ~ (they went into private ~) 14. a lucrative ~ ["application"] 15. in; into ~ (to put a theory into ~; in theory and in ~) ["method of conducting business"] 16. sharp, unethical, unfair, unscrupulous ~s 17. (esp. AE) fair-trade ~s

USAGE NOTE: In Great Britain, *private practice* refers to a practice that is not under the National Health Service.

practice II practise *v.* 1. (d; intr.) ("to work") to ~ as (to ~ as a lawyer) 2. (D; intr.) ("to drill") to ~ at (to ~ at batting the ball) 3. (D; intr.) to ~ on (you can ~ mouth-to-mouth resuscitation on me) 4. (G) the boy ~d throwing the lasso

practitioner *n.* a family, general; nurse (AE); private ~

prairie *n.* 1. a rolling; treeless; windswept ~ 2. on the ~

praise I *n.* 1. to earn, merit; get, receive, win ~ 2. to bestow, heap, lavish ~ on smb. 3. to give ~ to smb. 4. to sing smb.'s ~s 5. faint; fulsome, unctuous; glowing, high, lavish, strong, unrestrained, unstinting; universal ~ 6. ~ for 7. in ~ of 8. (misc.) a chorus of ~

praise II *v.* 1. to ~ highly, strongly, to the skies 2. (D; tr.) to ~ for

praiseworthy *adj.* (formal) ~ to + inf. (it is ~ to do volunteer work)

pram *n.* (BE) to push, wheel a ~ (AE has *baby carriage, carriage*)

prance *v.* (P; intr.) to ~ around the room

prank *n.* 1. to play a ~ on smb. 2. a childish; cruel, mean, wanton; foolish; harmless; innocent; mischievous ~

prate see **prattle**

pratfall n. ["an embarrassing failure"] to take a ~

prattle v. 1. to ~ endlessly 2. (D; intr.) to ~ (on) about (he ~d on endlessly about his operation)

pray v. 1. to ~ aloud; devoutly, fervently; silently 2. (D; intr.) to ~ for; to (to ~ to God for good health) 3. (E) she ~ed (to God) to be pardoned for her transgressions 4. (L; to) we ~ed (to God) that they would be safe

prayer n. 1. to chant; offer; say; utter a ~ 2. to answer a ~ 3. a devout, fervent, solemn ~ 4. a silent ~ 5. (a) communal; daily; evening; morning ~ 6. a ~ for (to offer a ~ for peace) 7. a ~ that + clause; subj. (our ~ that peace be/should be restored was heard) 8. in ~ (the group was deep in ~ when we entered) 9. (misc.) the answer to all our ~s

preach v. 1. (D; intr.) to ~ about (he's always ~ing about one thing or another) 2. (D; intr.) to ~ against (to ~ against sin) 3. (colloq.) (D; intr.) to ~ at (stop ~ing at me) 4. (D; intr.) to ~ to (to ~ to one's congregation) 5. (L; to) to ~ that the end of the world is near

preacher n. an itinerant; lay ~

preamble n. a ~ to

precaution n. 1. to take ~s 2. elaborate ~s 3. a wise ~ 4. health; safety; security ~s 5. a ~ against 6. a ~ to + inf. (it would be a wise ~ to consult a lawyer)

precedence n. 1. to have, take ~ over 2. to give ~ to

precedent n. 1. to create, establish, set a ~ 2. to cite a ~ 3. to break (a) ~ 4. a dangerous ~ 5. a ~ for 6. without ~

precept n. a ~ that + clause (we adhere to the ~ that all criminals can be rehabilitated)

preceptor n. a ~ to

precinct n. a pedestrian (BE); police (AE); shopping (BE); voting ~

precious adj. ~ to

precipitate v. (d; tr.) to ~ into (to ~ a country into war)

precipitation n. heavy; light ~

precise adj. ~ about; in

precision n. 1. great, utmost; military; surgical; unerring, unfailing ~ 2. ~ in (unfailing ~ in handling the instruments is required for this task) 3. with ~ (it must be done with the utmost ~)

preclude v. (formal) 1. (d; tr.) to ~ from (to ~ smb. from doing smt.) 2. (K) that will ~ our having to do it again

precondition n. to set ~s

precursor n. a ~ of, to

predecessor n. smb.'s immediate ~

predestined adj. (cannot stand alone) 1. ~ to (~ to glory) 2. ~ to + inf. (she was ~ to go far in life) 3. ~ that + clause (it was ~ that they would never meet again)

predicament n. 1. an awkward; dire ~ (to get into an awkward ~) 2. in a ~

predicate v. (d; tr.) ("to base") to ~ on, upon (to ~ a theory on certain facts)

predict v. 1. (K) I ~ed their getting into trouble 2. (L) she ~ed that it would rain 3. (Q) who can ~ how the elections will turn out?

predictable adj. ~ that + clause (it was ~ that their party would win the election)

prediction n. 1. to make a ~ 2. a dire, gloomy, unfavorable ~ 3. a favorable ~ 4. a ~ that + clause (she made a ~ that the crisis would be over soon) 5. a ~ comes true

predilection n. a ~ for

predispose v. (formal) 1. (d; tr.) to ~ to 2. (H) what ~d you to go?

predisposed adj. (cannot stand alone) 1. ~ to (~ to violence) 2. ~ to + inf. (~ to act rashly)

predisposition n. 1. a ~ to, towards 2. a ~ to + inf. (a ~ to act rashly)

predominance n. ~ over

predominant adj. ~ over

predominate v. (D; intr.) to ~ over

preeminence n. ~ in

preeminent adj. ~ in (the visiting athletes were ~ in the high jump)

preen v. (formal) (d; refl.) to ~ oneself on ("to pride oneself on")

preface I n. a ~ to (a ~ to a book)

preface II v. (d; tr.) to ~ with (she ~d her remarks with a personal anecdote)

prefer v. 1. (D; tr.) ("to bring") to ~ against (to ~ charges against smb.) 2. (D; tr.) to ~ to (she ~s fish to meat) 3. (E) we ~ to remain at home 4. (G) I ~red going to a concert 5. (esp. BE) (H; no passive) I'd ~ you to stay out of the dispute 6. (K) I would ~ your staying out of the dispute 7. (L; subj.) she ~s that he not get/should not get involved 8. (M) I ~ my coffee to be hot 9. (N) I ~ my coffee hot 10. (misc.) I (very) much ~ living in the suburbs USAGE NOTE: This verb can be used in several ways to express preference—I prefer walking to riding; I prefer to walk rather than (to) ride; I prefer not to ride.

preferable adj. 1. ~ to 2. ~ to + inf. (it is ~ to remain silent) 3. ~ that + clause; subj. (it is ~ that she go/ should go alone) USAGE NOTE: This adjective can be used in several ways—walking is preferable to riding; it's preferable to walk rather than to ride.

preference n. 1. to give ~ to 2. to demonstrate, display, show; express a ~ 3. a decided; individual; marked; strong ~ 4. (US) (a) veterans' ~ 5. a ~ for (she showed a decided ~ for classical music) 6. in ~ to

prefix v. (d; tr.) to ~ to (to ~ a title to a name)

pregnancy n. 1. to terminate a ~ 2. an ectopic; false; full-term; normal ~

pregnant a. 1. to become, fall (BE), get ~ 2. ~ by

(she got ~ by her husband before he was sent to the front) 3. ~ with (at that time she was ~ with her first child)

prejudice I *n.* ["bias"] 1. to arouse, stir up ~ (against, towards) (to stir up ~ against immigrants) 2. to have, hold (a) ~ 3. to display, show ~ (towards) 4. to break down, eliminate ~ 5. (a) blind, deep, deep-rooted, deep-seated, ingrained, strong ~ 6. race, racial; religious ~ 7. ~ against, towards (AE) ["harm"] 8. without ~ to (without ~ to our claims)

prejudice II *v.* 1. to ~ strongly 2. (D; tr.) to ~ against 3. (misc.) her reputation for honesty ~d me strongly in her favor

prejudicial *adj.* ~ to

preliminary I *adj.* ~ to

preliminary II *n.* a ~ to

prelude *n.* a ~ to

premature *adj.* 1. ~ in (they were ~ in their assessment) 2. ~ to + inf. (it is ~ to celebrate)

première *n.* 1. to give, have, hold, stage a ~ 2. to attend a ~ 3. a film; lavish; world ~

premise *n.* ["proposition"] (logic) 1. the major; minor ~ ["assumption"] 2. the ~ that + clause (her ~ that the results of the election were already decided proved to be true)

premised *adj.* ~ on, upon (their fiscal policy was ~ on the assumption of rising unemployment)

premises *n.* ["property"] on the ~ (to be consumed on the ~)

premium *n.* ["high value"] 1. to place, put a (high) ~ on (she puts a high ~ on punctuality) ["additional sum"] 2. to pay a ~ 3. at a ~ (to sell at a ~) ["fee paid to an insurance company"] 4. an insurance ~ 5. a ~ on a policy (I pay the ~ on my policy every six months)

premonition *n.* 1. to have a ~ 2. a ~ that + clause (she had a ~ that an accident would happen)

preoccupation *n.* a ~ with

preoccupied *adj.* ~ with

preordained *adj.* 1. ~ to + inf. (they were ~ to meet) 2. ~ that + clause; subj. (it was ~ that they meet/should meet/would meet)

preparation *n.* in ~ for (we are resting in ~ for the strenuous journey)

preparations *n.* 1. to make ~ 2. careful, elaborate, thorough ~ 3. ~ for

preparatory *adj.* ~ to

prepare *v.* 1. to ~ carefully, thoroughly 2. (C) I'll ~ a nice supper for you; or: I'll ~ you a nice supper 3. (D; intr., refl., tr.) to ~ for (she was ~ing for the examination; they ~d themselves for unpleasant news; she is ~ing a paper for presentation at the national meeting) 4. (E) they were ~ing to leave 5. (H) parents should ~ children to cope with life

prepared *adj.* 1. ~ for (we were ~ for anything) 2. ~ to + inf. (we are ~ to leave)

preparedness *n.* 1. military ~ 2. (misc.) a state of ~

preposition *n.* a compound; simple ~

preposterous *adj.* ~ to + inf. (it's ~ to speak of such things)

prerequisite I *adj.* (usu. does not stand alone) ~ to

prerequisite II *n.* a ~ for, to

prerogative *n.* 1. to exercise one's ~ 2. the royal ~ 3. smb.'s ~ to + inf. (it's our ~ to order an investigation)

prescribe *v.* 1. (D; tr.) to ~ for (to ~ a remedy for the common cold) 2. (formal) (L; subj.) regulations ~ that a lawyer draw up/should draw up the papers 3. (Q) the court ~d how the money should be spent

prescription *n.* 1. to fill (AE), make up a ~ 2. a ~ for 3. by ~; on a ~ (to obtain a drug on a doctor's ~; by ~ only)

presence *n.* 1. to make one's ~ felt, known ("to make others notice one's presence") 2. a commanding ~ 3. in smb.'s ~

presence of mind *n.* 1. to display; show (great) ~ 2. the ~ to + inf. (she had the ~ to call the police)

present I *n.* ["present time"] 1. at ~ 2. for the ~ ["present tense of a verb"] 3. in the ~

present II *n.* ["gift"] 1. to give smb. a ~ 2. to unwrap; wrap a ~ 3. to make smb. a ~ of smt. 4. an anniversary; birthday; Christmas; graduation; wedding ~ 5. a ~ for

present III *v.* 1. (B) ("to give") they ~ed an award to her 2. (d; tr.) ("to introduce") to ~ as (she was ~ed as a computer expert) 3. (D; tr.) ("to introduce") to ~ to (the new employees were ~ed to the rest of the staff) 4. (d; tr.) to ~ with ("to give a gift to") (he ~ed her with a beautiful bouquet of roses)

presentable *adj.* to make oneself ~

presentation *n.* ["position of a fetus"] (med.) 1. a breech; face ~ ["act of presenting"] 2. to make a ~ (who will make the ~ at the awards ceremony?) ["report"] 3. to give a ~ 4. an oral ~ 5. a ~ on (she gave an oral ~ on her current research)

presentiment *n.* (formal) ["foreboding"] a ~ that + clause (she had a ~ that an accident would happen)

preservative *n.* 1. a food ~ 2. an artificial ~

preserve I *n.* 1. a forest; game, wild-life ~ 2. (BE) see **preserves**

preserve II *v.* 1. (D; tr.) to ~ against, from (to ~ the environment from the ravages of pollution) 2. (D; tr.) to ~ for (we wish to ~ this tradition for our grandchildren)

preserver *n.* a life ~
USAGE NOTE: Especially in AE, *life preserver* means "life belt", "life jacket"; in BE, it means "club used for self-defence".

preserves *n.* ["fruit preserved by cooking with sugar"] apricot; blueberry; cherry; grape; peach; raspberry; strawberry ~

preside *v.* (D; intr.) to ~ at; over

presidency *n.* 1. to gain the ~ 2. to assume the ~ 3. a rotating ~

president *n.* 1. to elect; inaugurate a ~ 2. a vice ~ 3. a former, past; incoming; incumbent; outgoing ~ 4. a ~ elect

press I *n.* ["instrument for crushing, shaping, squeezing"] 1. a cider; cookie (AE); hydraulic; wine ~ ["publishing house"] 2. a university; vanity ~ ["device for printing"] 3. a printing ~ 4. the ~es roll 5. (misc.) to go to ~; hot off the ~; stop the ~es! 6. in ~ (our book is now in ~) ["newspapers, magazines"] ["reporters"] 7. to censor; control; muzzle the ~ 8. a free ~ 9. the foreign; gutter, yellow; local; popular; tabloid ~ ["publicity"] 10. a bad; good ~ (we got a bad ~) ["smoothness of a fabric"] 11. (a) permanent ~ ["aggressive defense used in basketball"] 12. a full-court ~ ["type of lift used by weight lifters"] 13. to do a ~ 14. a bench; military ~

press II *v.* 1. to ~ hard 2. (d; intr., tr.) ("to push") to ~ against (to ~ against a door) 3. (d; intr., tr.) to ~ for ("to urge") (to ~ for reform; to ~ the authorities for information) 4. (D; tr.) ("to shape") to ~ into (to ~ clay into various forms) 5. (d; tr.) ("to place") to ~ into (to ~ all equipment into service) 6. (D; intr.) ("to squeeze") to ~ on (to ~ on a button) 7. (H) ("to urge") they were ~ing me to agree to the compromise 8. (P; intr.) ("to push") the crowd ~ed around the candidate; the fans ~ed into the stadium

press conference *n.* 1. to give, hold; schedule; stage a ~ 2. to televise a ~

pressed *adj.* ~ for time

press on *v.* 1. (D; intr.) to ~ to (the troops ~ed on to the next town) 2. (D; intr.) to ~ with (the police ~ed on with the investigation)

press-up *n.* (BE) to do a ~ (see also **push-up**)

pressure I *n.* 1. to exert, place, put ~ on smb. 2. to bring ~ to bear on smb. 3. to keep up, maintain the ~ on 4. to build up, increase (the) ~ 5. to feel (the) ~ 6. to bear up under, withstand (the) ~ 7. to ease, relieve (the) ~ 8. to face; resist (the) ~ (to resist ~ from extremist groups) 9. enormous, great, heavy, inexorable, intense, maximum, relentless, severe, strong, unrelieved ~ 10. firm; light ~ 11. financial; outside; parental; peer; population; public ~ (to resist public ~) 12. air; blood; oil; water ~ 13. (esp. meteorology) atmospheric; barometric ~ 14. high; low ~ 15. ~ builds up, increases, rises 16. ~ eases, falls 17. ~ for (~ for tax reform) 18. ~ from (to face inexorable ~ from the media) 19. ~ to + inf. (they are putting ~ on her to retire) 20. under ~ (under relentless ~)

pressure II *v.* (AE) 1. (D; tr.) to ~ into (to ~ smb. into doing smt.) 2. (H) to ~ smb. to do smt.

pressurize *v.* (BE) see **pressure II**

prestige *n.* 1. to enjoy, have ~ 2. to gain ~ 3. to damage smb.'s ~ 4. great, high; little, low ~ 5. the

~ to + inf. (does she have enough ~ to get the party nomination?) 6. of ~ (of little ~)

presume *v.* 1. (d; intr.) to ~ on, upon (to ~ upon smb.'s good nature) 2. (E) I will not ~ to give you advice 3. (L) we can ~ that she will return 4. (M) we must ~ her to be innocent 5. (N; used with an adjective) we must ~ her innocent; she must be ~d innocent until proven guilty

presumption *n.* a ~ that + clause (our decision was based on the ~ that they would agree)

presumptuous *adj.* ~ to + inf. (it's ~ of you to make such claims)

presuppose *v.* (L) we ~ that they will accept our offer

presupposition *n.* a ~ that + clause (all of this is based on the ~ that they will agree)

pretence see **pretense**

pretend *v.* 1. (d; intr.) ("to claim") to ~ to (to ~ to expert knowledge in a field) 2. (E) ("to feign"); ("to make believe") she ~ed not to notice; I ~ed to be busy; the children ~ed to be cowboys 3. (L; to) ("to feign"); ("to make believe") she ~ed that she was asleep; they ~ed that they were tourists

pretender *n.* a ~ to (a ~ to a throne)

pretense, pretence *n.* ["simulation"] ["false show"] 1. to make a ~ (he made no ~ of being objective) 2. to see through smb.'s ~ 3. under a ~ (under the ~ of patriotism; under false ~s) 4. without ~ (a person without ~) ["unsupported claim"] 5. to see through smb.'s ~ 6. a ~ that + clause (he saw through the ~ that lower taxes would cause unemployment) ["appearance"] 7. to keep up, maintain a ~ (to maintain some ~ of legality) ["attempt"] 8. a ~ at; of (without any ~ at objectivity)

pretentious *adj.* ~ to + inf. (it was ~ of them to assume that we would attend)

pretext *n.* 1. to find a ~ for 2. a flimsy; mere ~ 3. a ~ to + inf. (it was a ~ to occupy more territory) 4. a ~ that + clause (she refused to attend on the ~ that she would be out of town) 5. on, under a ~ (he would call for help on the slightest ~; under what ~ did she approach them?) 6. (misc.) they start quarreling at the slightest ~

pretty *adj.* to be sitting ~ ("to be well off")

prevail *v.* 1. (D; intr.) to ~ against, over (to ~ against overwhelming odds) 2. (d; intr.) to ~ on, upon smb. to do smt. (they ~ed on me to buy a new television set)

prevent *v.* 1. (D; tr.) to ~ from (nothing can ~ this disease from spreading) 2. (J) (BE) nothing can ~ this disease spreading 3. (K) you cannot ~ their getting married

prevention *n.* 1. (health care) primary; secondary ~ 2. accident; crime; disease; fire ~

preview *n.* 1. to give a ~ 2. a sneak ~ (of a film)

prey I *n.* 1. to fall ~ to 2. easy ~ 3. ~ for; to

prey II *v.* (d; intr.) to ~ on (to ~ on small game)

price I *n.* 1. to fix, set a ~ 2. to place, put a ~ on 3. to quote a ~ 4. (BE) to agree a ~ 5. to drive up; hike (AE; colloq.), increase, mark up, raise ~s 6. to curb, hold down, keep down; freeze; maintain, stabilize ~s 7. to bring down, drive down ~s (the latest news brought down oil ~s) 8. to cut, lower, mark down, reduce, roll back, slash ~s 9. to undercut (smb.'s) ~s 10. to bring, command, fetch, get a ~ (icons bring a high ~) 11. an attractive, fair, moderate, popular, reasonable ~ 12. a bargain, low, reduced ~ 13. an exorbitant, high, inflated, outrageous, prohibitive, steep, stiff ~ 14. an asking; buying, purchase; cost; discount; going; list; market; reduced; regular; resale; retail; sale; selling; unit; wholesale ~ 15. an admission ~ 16. (at an auction) a reserve (esp. BE), upset (esp. AE) ~ 17. ~s drop, fall, go down, plummet, slump 18. ~s go up, rise, shoot up, skyrocket, soar 19. a ~ for (to pay an exorbitant ~ for smt.) 20. a ~ on 21. at a certain ~ (to sell merchandise at reduced ~s) 22. (misc.) what ~ an economic recovery now? (BE) ("what are the chances of an economic recovery now?"); what ~ glory if you die in the trenches? (BE); to put a ~ on smb.'s head ("to post a reward for apprehending or killing smb."); they paid a heavy ~ for their freedom

price II *v.* 1. (D; tr.) to ~ at (they ~d it at five hundred dollars) 2. (D; refl., tr.) to ~ out of (they ~d themselves out of the market) 3. (N) they ~d it too high

price index *n.* a consumer; retail ~

price tag *n.* to put a ~ on smt.

prick I *n.* a pin ~

prick II *v.* (D; refl., tr.) to ~ on (to ~ one's finger on a thorn)

pride I *n.* 1. to take ~ in 2. to hurt smb.'s ~ 3. civic; community; ethnic; fierce, great, strong; injured, wounded ~ (to take great ~ in one's children) 4. the ~ to + inf. (do they have enough ~ to defend their principles?) 5. out of ~ (he refused out of ~) 6. (misc.) to appeal to smb.'s ~; to burst with ~; to pocket, swallow one's ~; to swell with ~; a feeling/ glow of ~; a blow to smb.'s ~

pride II *v.* (d; refl.) to ~ on (to ~ oneself on one's strength)

priest *n.* 1. to ordain a ~ 2. to defrock, unfrock a ~ 3. an Anglican; Catholic; Episcopalian; Hindu; Mormon; Orthodox ~ 4. a high; local, parish ~

priesthood *n.* to enter; leave the ~

primacy *n.* ~ over

primary *n.* ["party election"] (US) 1. to hold a ~ 2. a closed; direct; open; preferential; presidential; runoff ~

prime *n.* 1. to come into, reach one's ~ 2. to pass one's ~ 3. in one's ~ 4. (misc.) past one's ~; to be cut down in one's ~

primed *adj.* 1. ~ for (~ for the big game) 2. ~ to + inf. (we are ~ to begin)

prince *n.* 1. a crown ~ 2. (misc.) a ~ consort; regent

princess *n.* a crown ~

principal *n.* ["an official"] 1. a school ~ ["money invested"] 2. to repay the ~

principle *n.* 1. to establish, formulate, lay down a ~ 2. to apply a ~ 3. to adhere to (a) ~ 4. to betray, compromise one's ~s 5. an abstract; basic, fundamental; general; guiding; moral; sound; strict; underlying ~ 6. high ~s 7. the ~ that + clause (we adhere to the ~ that everyone should be treated fairly) 8. against smb.'s ~s 9. in ~ (to agree in ~) 10. on ~ (on ~, I am opposed to the decision) 11. (misc.) a matter, question; person of ~; she made it a ~ never to be late for work

print I *n.* ["photograph"] 1. to develop; make a ~ ["printed state"] 2. in ~; out of ~ (I have not seen the story in ~; the book is out of ~) ["text of a contract"] 3. the fine, small ~ (people should always read the fine ~) ["printed letters"] 4. clear; fine; large; small ~ ["impression made by type"] 5. dark; light ~

print II *v.* to ~ smt. (in) boldface; in italics; in Roman

printer *n.* ["device for printing computer data"] a daisy wheel; dot-matrix; laser; letter-quality; serial; thermal ~

printing *n.* 1. to put out a ~ (of a book) 2. offset ~ 3. (misc.) the book went through three ~s

prior *adj.* (cannot stand alone) ~ to

priority *n.* 1. to establish, set a ~ 2. to have, take ~ over 3. to give ~ to 4. high; low ~ 5. (a) first, number-one, top ~ 6. (misc.) to reexamine, rethink; reorder, sort out one's ~ties

prise, prize (BE) see **pry** 2, 3

prise off, prize off (BE) see **pry off**

prison *n.* 1. to go, be sent, be sentenced to ~ 2. to keep smb. in ~ 3. to spend time in ~ 4. to release smb. from ~ 5. to be released from ~ 6. to break out of, escape from ~ 7. a maximum-security, minimum-security; open (BE) ~

prisoner *n.* 1. to take smb. ~; to take a ~ (we took many ~s) 2. to hold, keep smb. ~ 3. to free, release a ~ 4. a political ~ 5. a ~ escapes 6. (misc.) a ~ of conscience

prisoner of war *n.* 1. to hold prisoners of war 2. to interrogate prisoners of war 3. to exchange, free, liberate, repatriate prisoners of war

privacy *n.* 1. to disturb, invade, violate smb.'s ~ 2. an invasion of smb.'s ~ 3. in ~ (to do smt. in the ~ of one's home)

private I *n.* in ~ (to do smt. in ~)

private II *n.* ["common soldier"] 1. a buck ~ (AE) 2. (US) a ~ first-class (the British Army has *lance corporal*)

privilege *n.* 1. to award, give, grant a ~ 2. to enjoy, exercise; have a ~ (to enjoy guest ~s) 3. to abuse a

~ 4. to revoke, withdraw; suspend a ~ 5. a class; exclusive; special ~ 6. full; franking; guest; kitchen ~s 7. executive ~ 8. a ~ to + inf. (it was a ~ to work with them = it was a ~ working with them)

privileged *adj.* (usu. does not stand alone) ~ to + inf. (we are ~ to live in a democracy)

privy *adj.* ["having access"] ~ to (they are ~ to secret documents)

prize I *n.* 1. to award, give, present a ~ 2. to distribute ~s 3. to accept; receive, win a ~ 4. to take a ~ (who took first ~?) 5. a booby; consolation; door; first; second; third ~ 6. a ~ goes to (second ~ went to my sister)

prize II (BE) see **pry** 2, 3

prized *adj.* ["valued"] ~ for (this wine is ~ for its bouquet)

pro see **professional**

probability *n.* 1. (a) real, strong ~ 2. little ~ 3. a ~ that + clause (there was little ~ that their party would win the election) 4. in all ~

probable *adj.* 1. hardly ~ 2. highly, very ~ 3. ~ that + clause (it's ~ that she will not arrive until tomorrow; more usu. is: she'll probably not arrive until tomorrow)

probate *n.* 1. to grant ~ 2. to prove a will at ~

probation *n.* 1. to place, put smb. on ~ 2. to release smb. on ~ 3. to violate (the terms of one's) ~ 4. on ~ (he's out on ~ for a year)

probe I *n.* 1. to conduct; launch a ~ 2. an exhaustive, thorough ~ 3. an interplanetary; space ~ 4. a police ~ 5. a ~ into, of (a police ~ into racketeering)

probe II *v.* 1. to ~ deeply, thoroughly 2. (d; tr.) to ~ about, on (to ~ smb. on a matter) 3. (D; intr.) to ~ for (to ~ for weak spots) 4. (D; intr.) to ~ into (to ~ into the facts)

problem *n.* ["unsettled question"] ["source of difficulty"] 1. to cause, create, pose, present a ~ 2. to have a ~ (with) 3. to be, constitute a ~ 4. to address, explore; bring up, raise; confront, face a ~ 5. to attack, come to grips with, deal with, grapple with, tackle a ~ 6. to lick, resolve, settle, solve a ~ 7. to avoid, sidestep a ~ 8. an acute, daunting, difficult, grave, major, pressing, serious; insoluble, insurmountable ~ 9. a complex, complicated, involved, knotty, perplexing, thorny ~ 10. a delicate, ticklish ~ 11. a minor, petty ~ 12. an attitude; drink (BE), drinking (AE); emotional; physical; psychological; social ~ 13. a perennial ~ 14. a ~ arises, comes up 15. a ~ to + inf. (it's a ~ to make ends meet = it's a ~ making ends meet) 16. (misc.) the crux of a ~; to get to the heart of a ~ ["mathematical statement requiring a solution"] 17. to do, solve a ~ 18. a complicated; difficult; easy; simple ~

procedure *n.* 1. to establish a ~ 2. to follow a ~ 3. (a) correct, proper; normal, regular, standard ~ (to follow regular ~s) 4. a complex, complicated; delicate ~ 5. a simple ~ 6. a scientific; surgical ~ 7. (surgery) a major; minor ~ 8. bureaucratic; parliamentary; safety ~s 9. (misc.) a point of ~

proceed *v.* 1. (d; intr.) to ~ against (to ~ against smb. in court) 2. (d; intr.) to ~ from; to (to ~ from New York to Philadelphia) 3. (d; intr.) to ~ with (to ~ with one's research) 4. (E) she ~ed to tell us every detail

proceedings *n.* (often legal) 1. to bring, initiate, institute; conduct ~ against (to initiate legal ~ against a competitor) 2. judicial, legal ~ 3. bankruptcy; criminal; divorce ~ (to institute divorce ~)

proceeds *n.* ["profit"] 1. net ~ 2. the ~ amount to 3. ~ from, of (~ from the sale of surplus property)

process *n.* 1. a creative ~ 2. a democratic; electoral ~ 3. the aging ~ 4. the judicial, legal ~ 5. mental ~es 6. due ~ (she was deprived of due ~)

processing *n.* 1. data; food ~ 2. (computers) batch ~

procession *n.* 1. to lead a ~ 2. a ceremonial; funeral; religious; torchlight; triumphal; wedding ~ 3. in (a) ~ (to march in a ~)

processor *n.* 1. a food ~ 2. a word ~

proclaim *v.* (formal) 1. (L; to) the president ~ed (to the nation) that new currency would be issued 2. (N; used with a noun) the entire state was ~ed a disaster area

proclamation *n.* 1. to issue, make a ~ 2. a ~ that + clause (the government issued a ~ that all prisoners would be pardoned)

proclivity *n.* (formal) 1. a ~ for; to, towards 2. a ~ to + inf. (we noted her ~ to form strong attachments)

procure *v.* 1. (C) (BE) she was unable to ~ a ticket for us; or: she was unable to ~ us a ticket 2. (D; tr.) to ~ for

prod *v.* 1. (D; tr.) to ~ into (to ~ smb. into doing smt.) 2. (H) they kept ~ding me to buy a new car 3. (misc.) to ~ smb. in the ribs

prodigy *n.* a child; infant ~

produce I *n.* ["fruits and vegetables"] 1. farm ~ 2. fresh; perishable ~

produce II *v.* 1. (d; tr.) to ~ as (she ~d several letters as evidence) 2. (D; tr.) to ~ for (to ~ food for export) 3. (D; tr.) to ~ from (to ~ gas from coal)

producer *n.* an executive; film, movie; radio; stage, theater; steel; television, TV ~

product *n.* 1. to market, promote a (new) ~ 2. a by-product; an end, finished; manufactured ~ 3. a waste ~ 4. the gross national ~ (= GNP) 5. (misc.) to endorse a ~

production *n.* ["work presented on the stage, radio, TV, etc."] 1. to put on, stage a ~ 2. a Hollywood; stage, theatrical; TV ~ ["process of producing"] 3. to go into; start up ~ 4. to beef up, boost, increase, speed up, step up ~ 5. to halt, stop ~ 6. to cut back (on), decrease, roll back ~ 7. industrial; mass ~ 8. coal; oil; steel ~ 9. (misc.) the means of ~ ["misc."] 10. (slang) to make a big ~ out of smt. ("to make a big fuss over smt.")

production line *n.* to automate a ~

productive *adj.* ~ of

productivity *n.* high; low ~

products *n.* agricultural; dairy ~

profess *v.* (formal) 1. (E) he ~ed to know nothing about the matter 2. (L) she ~ed that she knew nothing 3. (M; refl.) he ~ed himself to be ignorant of the matter 4. (N; refl.) she ~ed herself ignorant of the matter

profession *n.* 1. to practice a ~ 2. the legal; medical; nursing; teaching ~ 3. by ~ (she's a lawyer by ~)

professional, pro *adj.* and *n.* 1. (usu. sports) to turn ~ (he turned ~ at the age of twenty) 2. a real, true ~ (she is a real ~) ("she does her work seriously and well")

USAGE NOTE: A *professional tennis player* and a *professional golfer* compete for money. A *tennis professional* and a *golf pro* coach for money, usu. at clubs.

professor *n.* 1. (AE) an adjunct; assistant; associate; full ~ 2. (GB) a Regius ~ (appointed by the Crown) 3. a research; visiting ~ 4. a ~ emerita, emeritus; an emerita, emeritus ~ 5. a college (esp. US), university ~ 6. (misc.) an absent-minded ~

USAGE NOTE: We speak of a professor *of* mathematics, but of a lecturer or reader *in* mathematics.

professorship *n.* 1. to get, have, hold a ~ 2. an endowed ~

proficiency *n.* 1. to demonstrate, display ~ 2. to achieve ~ 3. language ~ 4. ~ at, in

proficient *adj.* ~ at, in

profile *n.* ["public exposure"] 1. to have a high ~ 2. to keep, maintain a low ~ ["side view"] 2. in ~

profit I *n.* 1. to clear, earn, make, realize, reap, show, turn a ~ 2. to bring (in), yield a ~ 3. a handsome, juicy, large, tidy; marginal, small; quick ~ 4. an excess, exorbitant, windfall ~ 5. a clear; net; gross ~ 6. ~s fall; rise 7. a ~ on (to make a ~ on a deal) 8. at a ~ (to operate at a ~) 9. (misc.) to share (in) the ~s; ~s were up by ten percent

profit II *v.* (D; intr.) to ~ by, from

profitable *adj.* ~ to + inf. (is it ~ to work this mine?)

profiteer *n.* a black-market; war ~

profuse *adj.* ~ in (~ in one's apologies)

profusion *n.* in ~

prognosis *n.* 1. to make a ~ 2. a favorable; gloomy, unfavorable ~

program I *n.* ["plan"] 1. to chart, draw up; organize a ~ 2. to carry out, implement; evaluate; introduce; launch; phase out, terminate a ~ 3. a crash; long-range; pilot; short-range ~ 4. a building; development; political ~ 5. a ~ to + inf. (to launch a ~ to reduce crime) ["schedule"] 6. on smb.'s ~ (what's on your ~ today?) ["entertainment"] 7. to put on a ~ ["broadcast, telecast"] 8. a call-in (AE), phone-

in (BE); radio; television ~ 9. a ~ comes on; goes off ["coded instructions for a computer"] 10. to boot up; debug; download; execute; load; reboot; run; write a ~ 11. a user-friendly ~ 12. a computer; software; word processing ~ ["academic course of study"] 13. a graduate, postgraduate (esp. BE); honors; training; undergraduate ~ 14. a ~ in (a ~ in linguistics) ["organized activities"] 15. an orientation; outreach; recreation; work-study (AE) ~ ["misc."] 16. a reading ~ (for a dictionary)

USAGE NOTE: The BE spelling is *programme*, except for the computer uses (10-12).

program II *v.* (H) to ~ a computer to store certain information

USAGE NOTE: Except when referring to the computer, the BE spelling is *programme*—to programme an alarm system.

programme see Usage Notes for **program I, II**

programmer *n.* a computer ~

programming *n.* computer ~

progress I *n.* 1. to make ~ 2. to facilitate ~ 3. to block, hinder, impede, obstruct ~ 4. amazing, considerable, good, great; material, significant; rapid; smooth; steady ~ 5. little; slow; spotty ~ 6. economic; scientific; technological ~ 7. ~ in (to make little ~ in solving the problems of air pollution) 8. ~ towards (~ towards peace) 9. in ~ (negotiations are in ~)

progress II *v.* (D; intr.) to ~ from; to (to ~ from the basics to advanced concepts)

progression *n.* an arithmetic; geometric; harmonic ~

prohibit *v.* 1. (D; tr.) to ~ from 2. (rare) (K) you cannot ~ their going out

prohibition *n.* 1. to repeal a ~ 2. a ~ against

project I *n.* ["organized undertaking"] 1. to conceive; draw up a ~ 2. to launch a ~ 3. to carry out a ~ 4. to do a ~ (on) (the children did a ~ on dinosaurs) 5. to shelve a ~ 6. an irrigation; land-reclamation; pilot ("experimental"); public-works; research; water-conservation ~ ["publicly financed housing"] 7. a housing ~ (BE has *council estate, housing estate*)

project II *v.* 1. (D; tr.) to ~ into (to ~ a missile into space) 2. (D; tr.) to ~ onto (to ~ slides onto a screen)

projected *adj.* ~ to + inf. (production is ~ to increase by five percent)

projectile *n.* to fire; launch a ~

projection *n.* ["estimate"] 1. to make a ~ 2. a computer ~ ["system of presenting a map"] 3. an isometric; Mercator ~

projector *n.* 1. to operate, run, work a ~ 2. a cine-projector (BE); film, motion-picture (AE); opaque; overhead; slide ~

proliferation *n.* nuclear ~

prologue *n.* a ~ to

prom *n.* ["formal school dance"] (AE) 1. the junior; senior ~ 2. at the ~ 3. (misc.) to go to the ~; to take smb. to the ~
USAGE NOTE: In BE, *prom* means "a promenade concert".

prominence *n.* 1. to acquire, come to, gain ~ 2. to give ~ to (to give ~ to a story)

prominent *adj.* socially ~

promiscuity *n.* sexual ~

promise I *n.* ["vow"] 1. to make a ~ 2. to fulfill, keep a ~ 3. to break, renege on, repudiate a ~ 4. a broken; empty, false, hollow; rash; vague ~ 5. a sacred, solemn ~ 6. a campaign ~ (politicians sometimes break campaign ~s) 7. a ~ to + inf. (she made a ~ to write every week) 8. a ~ that + clause (they kept their ~ that the debt would be repaid promptly) 9. (misc.) to hold smb. to a ~ ["basis for hope"] 10. to show ~ (the young boxer showed real ~) 11. great, real; little ~ 12. ~ as (he showed great ~ as a boxer) 13. of ~ (a young boxer of ~)

promise II *v.* 1. to ~ solemnly 2. (A) he ~d the book to me; or: he ~d me the book 3.(E) she ~d to return early; it ~s to be an exciting year 4. (H; often used in neg. constructions) he ~d me never to show up late again 5. (L; may have an object) he ~d (me) that he would never show up late again 6. (misc.) (BE) I ~ you ("I assure you")

promissory note *n.* to call in a ~

promote *v.* 1. (D; tr.) to ~ from; to (she was ~d from captain to major) 2. (old-fashioned) (BE) (N; used with a noun) she was ~d major

promotion *n.* ["advancement in rank"] 1. to put smb. in for (a) ~ 2. to recommend smb. for (a) ~ 3. to approve smb. for (a) ~ 4. to approve a ~ 5. to put in for, try for (a) ~ (she put in for ~ to floor supervisor last month; he never tried for a ~) 6. to get, make (AE), win (a) ~ (he finally made his ~ to major; she got a ~ very quickly) 7. a ~ from; to (a ~ from lieutenant to captain; a ~ to the rank of professor) ["furtherance, fostering"] 8. health ~ ["advertising"] 9. prepublication ~ 10. sales ~ 11. in ~ (she is in ~)

prompt I *adj.* 1. ~ at, in (~ in fulfilling one's obligations) 2. ~ to + inf. (~ to respond)

prompt II *v.* (H) what ~ed you to say that?

promptness *n.* ~ at, in

prone *adj.* ["likely"] (cannot stand alone) 1. ~ to (~ to exaggeration) 2. ~ to + inf. (she is ~ to exaggerate)

pronoun *n.* a demonstrative; indefinite; interrogative; personal; possessive; reflexive; relative ~

pronounce *v.* 1. (D; intr., tr.) to ~ after (~ after me) 2. (formal) (M) the physician ~d him to be healthy 3. (N; used with an adjective, noun) she was officially ~d dead; they were ~d husband and wife

pronouncement *n.* 1. to issue, make a ~ 2. a ~ about, on 3. a ~ that + clause (the government

issued a ~ that taxes would be lowered)

pronunciamento *n.* (derog.) 1. to issue, make a ~ 2. a ~ that + clause (they issued a ~ that only their theories would be acceptable)

pronunciation *n.* 1. to acquire a (good) ~ 2. to correct smb.'s ~ 3. a native ~ (of a language) 4. (a) spelling ~ 5. a nonstandard; standard ~ 6. BBC, Received (RP); General American ~

proof *n.* ["conclusive evidence"] 1. to furnish, give, offer, present, produce, provide, show ~ 2. to have ~ 3. ample, clear, conclusive, concrete, convincing, definite, incontestable, incontrovertible, indisputable, irrefutable, living, positive, tangible, undeniable, unquestionable ~ 4. documentary; mathematical; scientific ~ 5. ~ that + clause (the prosecutor furnished convincing ~ that the accused could have been at the scene of the crime) 6. (misc.) the burden of ~ ["composed type"] 7. to correct, read ~ 8. galley; page; reproduction ~s

proofreading *n.* to do (the) ~

prop *v.* 1. (d; tr.) to ~ against (~ a chair against the door) 2. (N; used with an adjective) ~ the window open

propaganda *n.* 1. to engage in, spread ~ 2. to counteract, neutralize ~ 3. enemy; ideological; political; vicious ~ 4. ~ against

propeller *n.* 1. a ~ spins, turns 2. (misc.) the blade of a ~

propensity *n.* (formal) 1. a ~ for (a ~ for exaggerating) 2. a ~ to + inf. (he has a ~ to exaggerate)

proper *adj.* 1. ~ for (their attire is not ~ for this occasion) 2. ~ to + inf. (it is not ~ to enter that restaurant without a jacket) 3. ~ that + clause; subj. (it is ~ that she state/should state her own opinion)

property *n.* ["smt. owned"] 1. to attach; confiscate, seize ~ 2. to buy; develop; inherit; lease; let (esp. BE), rent; sell; transfer ~ 3. to reclaim; recover (stolen) ~ 4. (an) abandoned; beachfront; commercial ~ 5. common; communal; government; individual; joint; movable; personal; private; public; real ~ 6. intellectual ~ 7. community ~ ("property held jointly by two spouses") 8. a piece of ~ ["quality"] 9. (to have) medicinal ~ties

prophecy *n.* 1. to make a ~ 2. to fulfill a ~ 3. a gloomy; self-fulfilling ~ 4. a ~ comes true; proves to be true 5. a ~ about 6. a ~ that + clause (her ~ that we would fail did not come true)

prophesy *v.* 1. (K) no one could ~ your becoming governor 2. (L; to) I ~sied that she would succeed

prophet *n.* 1. a false ~ 2. (rel.) a major; minor ~

propinquity *n.* (formal) ~ to

propitious *adj.* ~ for, to

proportion *n.* 1. (a) direct; inverse ~ 2. in ~ (to) 3. out of ~ to (the punishment was out of ~ to the crime) 4. (misc.) a sense of ~

proportional *adj.* 1. directly; inversely ~ 2. ~ to

proportionate *adj.* ~ to

proportions *n.* ["extent"] 1. to assume, take on ~ 2. astronomical, huge; epic; epidemic; menacing ~ (the outbreak assumed epidemic ~) 3. of certain ~ (of astronomical ~)

proposal *n.* 1. to draw up, make, present, put forth, put forward, submit a ~ 2. to back, support a ~ 3. to accept, adopt a ~ 4. to consider, entertain; receive a ~ 5. to block, kill (colloq.), reject, turn down a ~ 6. to withdraw a ~ 7. a concrete ~ 8. a ~ falls through 9. a ~ for 10. a ~ to + inf. (the committee rejected the ~ to reduce taxes) 11. a ~ that + clause; subj. (they presented a ~ that all workers be/should be given free dental care)

propose *v.* 1. (B) she ~d a new plan to us 2. (D; tr.) to ~ for (to ~ smb. for membership in a club) 3. (D; intr.) to ~ to ("to offer marriage to") 4. (E) I ~ to leave very early 5. (G) she ~d leaving very early 6. (K) she ~d his going in my place 7. (L; subj.; to) we ~d (to them) that she be/should be appointed

proposition *n.* ["unethical, immoral proposal"] (colloq.) 1. to make (smb.) a ~ ["subject, question to be discussed"] 2. the ~ that + clause (we debated the ~ that war should be outlawed) ["business proposal"] 3. an attractive; business ~

proprieties *n.* ["accepted behavior"] to observe the ~

propriety *n.* ["conformity with accepted standards of behavior"] 1. to doubt the ~ of smt. 2. with ~ (to behave with ~)

propulsion *n.* jet; nuclear; rocket ~

prop up *v.* 1. (D; tr.) to ~ against (she ~ped up the chair against the door) 2. (D; refl., tr.) to ~ with (she ~ped herself up with pillows)

pros and cons *n.* 1. to consider, weigh the ~ 2. to debate the ~

prose *n.* 1. to write (in) ~ 2. descriptive ~

prosecute *v.* 1. to ~ vigorously 2. (D; tr.) to ~ for (to ~ smb. for murder)

prosecution *n.* 1. to conduct a ~ 2. to face ~ 3. a vigorous ~ 4. criminal ~ 5. ~ for 6. (AE) the ~ rests 7. (misc.) subject to (criminal) ~

prosecutor *n.* a public ~ (esp BE; AE has *district attorney*)

proseminar *n.* 1. to give, hold a ~ 2. a ~ on

prospect I *n.* ["anticipated outcome"] 1. a bright, rosy; inviting ~ 2. a bleak, grim; daunting; dim ~

prospect II *v.* (D; intr.) to ~ for (to ~ for gold)

prospects *n.* ["chances"] 1. to have ~ for (to have ~ for the future) 2. long-term ~ 3. ~ that + clause (~ are that the situation will improve) ["financial expectations"] 4. with; without ~

prospectus *n.* (BE) a college, university; school ~ (AE uses *catalog*)

prosperity *n.* 1. to create ~ 2. to enjoy ~

prostitution *n.* 1. to engage in ~ 2. to decriminalize, legalize ~ 3. to ban, outlaw ~

prostrate I *adj.* ~ with (~ with grief)

prostrate II *v.* (D; refl.) to ~ oneself before

prostration *n.* heat; nervous ~

protect *v.* (D; tr.) to ~ against, from

protection *n.* 1. to afford, give, offer, provide ~ 2. government; police ~ 3. consumer; environmental ~ 4. ~ against, from 5. under smb.'s ~ (she was placed under our ~)

protective *adj.* 1. overly ~ 2. ~ of, towards

protector *n.* a chest; surge ~

protein *n.* 1. (of food) to furnish, provide ~ 2. (a) complete; incomplete; simple; total ~

protest I *n.* ["complaint"] ["dissent"] 1. to enter, file, lodge, register a ~ 2. to express, voice a ~ 3. to cause, draw, spark (AE), spark off (BE), trigger a ~ 4. to dismiss, reject a ~ 5. a strong, vehement, vigorous; violent (we lodged a strong ~ with their government) 6. a mild; weak ~ 7. a ~ against 8. a ~ that + clause (the court rejected their ~ that due process had not been observed) 9. in ~ (to resign in ~) 10. under ~ (they complied with the order under ~) ["public demonstration of disapproval"] 11. to organize, stage a ~ 12. to put down, quell a ~ 13. an anti-nuclear; anti-war; mass; noisy; political; public ~ 14. a ~ against 15. (misc.) a storm of ~

protest II *v.* 1. to ~ bitterly, strongly, vehemently, vigorously 2. (D; intr.) to ~ about, against (to ~ against a war; AE also has: to ~ a war) 3. (K) (AE) we ~ed his being released 4. (L; to) we ~ed (to the mayor) that taxes were too high

protestation *n.* 1. a ~ against 2. a ~ that + clause (we believe her ~s that she is innocent)

protocol *n.* ["minutes"] ["statement"] 1. to draw up a ~ ["official code of conduct"] 2. to observe; violate ~ 3. court, palace, royal; diplomatic; military ~ 4. ~ demands/requires that + clause (~ demands that they visit/should visit the embassy) 5. (misc.) according to ~; a breach of ~

protrude *v.* (D; intr.) to ~ from

proud *adj.* 1. justly ~ 2. ~ of (~ of one's children) 3. ~ to + inf. (she will be ~ to serve) 4. ~ that + clause (he is ~ that he served in the army) 5. (misc.) to do smb. ~

prove *v.* 1. to ~ conclusively 2. (B) she was able to ~ her innocence to us 3. (E) she ~d to be a good worker 4. (L; to) he ~d (to everyone) that he could cope with the job 5. (M) history ~d her to be right 6. (N; used with an adjective, past participle) the evidence ~d him guilty 7. (Q) she ~d to us how it had been done 8. (s) the rumor ~d true

proverb *n.* 1. a ~ goes, runs 2. a ~ that (there is an old ~ that haste makes waste)

provide *v.* 1. (d; intr.) to ~ for (to ~ for one's family; to ~ for every contingency) 2. (D; tr.) to ~ for, to (to ~ blankets for the refugees; to ~ services to the needy) 3. (d; tr.) to ~ with (they were ~d with the proper equipment; we ~d the refugees with blankets) 4. (L; subj.) this bill ~s that money be/should be allocated for flood control 5. (O) (colloq.) (esp. AE) the phone call ~d her an excuse to leave

providence *n.* divine ~

providential *adj.* (formal) ~ that + clause (it was ~ that we arrived at exactly the same time)

province *n.* 1. an autonomous ~ 2. (esp. in Canada) an inland; maritime ~; the Province of Alberta, Ontario, etc.

proving ground *n.* a ~ for

provision *n.* ["preparations"] 1. to make ~ for 2. financial ~s ["clause in a legal document"] 3. to violate a ~ (of a contract) 4. according to a ~ 5. under a ~ 6. (esp. AE) with a ~ that + clause (I will do it with the ~ that they also contribute)

proviso *n.* 1. to add a ~ 2. with a ~ that + clause; subj. (we will agree to the proposal with the ~ that overtime be/should be paid)

provocation *n.* 1. deliberate; extreme, gross, severe ~ 2. ~ for (there was no ~ for such behavior) 3. at a ~ (he loses his temper at the slightest ~) 4. under ~ (he did use strong language, but only under extreme ~)

provocative *adj.* highly, very ~

provoke *v.* 1. (D; tr.) to ~ into (to ~ smb. into doing smt.) 2. (H) what ~d you to do it?

prowess *n.* 1. to demonstrate, display ~ 2. athletic; military ~ 3. ~ in

prowl I *n.* on the ~

prowl II *v.* (P; intr.) to ~ around the neighborhood; they ~ed through the forest

proximate *adj.* (cannot stand alone) ~ to

proximity *n.* 1. close ~ 2. ~ to 3. in ~ to 4. in the ~ of (a new hotel will be built in the ~ of the airport)

proxy *n.* 1. to get, have, hold smb.'s ~ 2. a ~ to + inf. (he had a ~ to vote for me) 3. by ~ (to vote by ~)

prudent *adj.* ~ to + inf. (it was ~ of you to sell that property)

prudish *adj.* ~ about

pry *v.* 1. (D; intr.) to ~ into (to ~ into smb.'s affairs) 2. (D; tr.) to ~ out of (to ~ information out of smb.) 3. (N; used with an adjective) they pried the door open

USAGE NOTE: For senses two and three, BE uses *prise* or *prize*.

pry off *v.* (AE) (D; tr.) to ~ with (she pried off the top with a crowbar) (BE has *prise off, prize off*)

P.S. *n.* to add a ~ (to)

psalm *n.* to recite a ~

p's and q's *n.* ["manners"] to mind one's ~

pseudonym *n.* 1. to adopt; use a ~ 2. under a ~ (to write under a ~)

psychology *n.* ["science of the mind"] 1. abnormal; applied; behavioral; child; clinical; cognitive; developmental; educational; experimental; general; Gestalt; social ~ ["attitudes"] 2. group; mob ~ ["knowledge of a person's habits, reactions"]

(colloq.) 3. to use ~

psych up *v.* (colloq.) (H; refl.) they ~ed themselves up to do well on the exam

pub-crawl *n.* (esp. BE) to go on a ~

puberty *n.* 1. to reach (the age of) ~ 2. at ~

public *n.* 1. to educate, enlighten the ~ 2. to fool, mislead the ~ 3. the general; great British (BE; humorous); listening; reading; theatergoing; traveling ~ 4. in ~

publication *n.* ["act of publishing"] 1. to begin, start ~ 2. to stop; suspend ~ 3. to ban ~ (the government banned ~ of the newspaper) ["printed work"] 4. a government; official ~

publicity *n.* 1. to give, provide ~ 2. to gain, get, receive ~ 3. to seek ~ 4. to avoid, shun ~ 5. advance; enormous, extensive, wide ~ 6. adverse, bad ~ 7. favorable, good 8. ~ for 9. (misc.) a blaze of ~ (they left for Europe in a blaze of ~)

publicized *adj.* highly, widely ~

public opinion *n.* 1. to arouse, stir up ~ 2. to form, mold ~ 3. to affect, influence, sway, swing; manipulate ~ 4. to express ~ 5. to canvass, poll, probe, sound out ~

public welfare see **welfare**

publishing *n.* desk-top ~

puff I *n.* a powder ~

puff II *n.* to have, take a ~ (on a cigarette)

puff III *v.* 1. (d; intr.) to ~ at, on (to ~ on a pipe; he sat ~ing away at his pipe) 2. (misc.) to ~ smoke into smb.'s face

pull I *n.* ["force"] 1. gravitational ~ ["influence"] (colloq.) 2. to use one's ~ 3. the ~ to + inf. (she had enough ~ to avoid paying the fine)

pull II *v.* 1. to ~ hard 2. (d; intr.) ("to tug") to ~ at (the little boy was ~ing at his father's coat) 3. (AE; colloq.) (d; intr.) to ~ for ("to support") (we were ~ing for the home team; they were ~ing for our team to win) 4. (d; intr.) ("to move") to ~ into (the train ~ed into the station) 5. (d; intr.) to ~ off ("to turn off") (to ~ off the road) 6. (D; tr.) ("to tug") to ~ off (she ~ed the sheets off the bed) 7. (D; intr.) ("to tug") to ~ on (to ~ on a rope) 8. (d; intr.) ("to move") to ~ out of (the train ~ed out of the station; to ~ out of a dive) 9. (d; tr.) ("to lift") to ~ out of (they ~ed her out of the water) 10. (N) ("to tug") she ~ed the rope tight 11. (P; tr.) ("to tug") they ~ed the cart across the field 12. (misc.) to ~ a gun on smb.; (esp. BE) to ~ a door to

pull ahead *v.* (D; intr.) to ~ of (to ~ of the other runners)

pull alongside *v.* (D; intr.) to ~ of (to ~ of the other car)

pull away *v.* (D; intr., tr.) to ~ from (to ~ from the curb; she ~ed the child away from the fire)

pull back *v.* (D; intr.) to ~ from; to (to ~ from the others; to ~ to our original position)

pull down *v.* (D; tr.) to ~ over (she ~ed her hat down

over her eyes)

pulley *n.* a fixed; movable ~

pull over *v.* (D; intr.) to ~ from; to (to ~ to the curb)

pull up *v.* (D; intr.) to ~ to (to ~ to the curb)

pulp *n.* 1. wood ~ 2. to beat smb. to a ~

pulpit *n.* 1. to ascend, mount the ~ 2. from; on the ~ (to denounce wrongdoing from the ~)

pulse *n.* 1. to feel; take ("measure") smb.'s ~ 2. to quicken smb.'s ~ (the excitement quickened his ~) 3. an erratic, irregular, unsteady; normal; rapid; regular, steady; strong; weak ~ 4. a ~ races; slackens, slows

pump I *n.* 1. to prime; work a ~ 2. a bicycle; gasoline (AE), petrol (BE) ~ 3. a centrifugal; heat; stomach; suction; sump ~

pump II *v.* 1. (D; tr.) ("to interrogate") to ~ for (they ~ed her for information) 2. (d; tr.) to ~ into (to ~ investments into a company; to ~ water into a tank) 3. (D; tr.) to ~ out of (to ~ water out of a flooded basement) 4. (N; used with an adjective) we ~ed the basement dry

pun *n.* to make a ~

punch I *n.* ["blow"] 1. to deliver, give, land, throw a ~ 2. to pull ("soften") one's ~es (also fig.) 3. to roll with a ~ 4. a hard; knockout; one-two; rabbit; solid; Sunday ~ 5. a ~ in, on, to (a ~ in the face; a ~ on the nose) ["misc."] 6. to pack a ~ ("to be powerful"); to beat smb. to the ~

punch II *v.* (D; tr.) to ~ in, on (I ~ed him in/on the jaw)

punch III *n.* ["mixed drink usu. consisting of fruit juice, liquor, etc."] 1. to make ~ 2. to spike ("add alcohol to") the ~ 3. to water down the ~ 4. fruit ~

Punch *n.* as pleased as ~ ("very pleased")

punctilious *adj.* ~ about

punctual *adj.* ~ about, in (~ in paying one's rent)

punctuality *n.* ~ in

punctuate *v.* (d; tr.) to ~ with (to ~ one's comments with quotations from the Bible)

punctuation mark *n.* to place, put a ~ somewhere

puncture *n.* (esp. BE) 1. to fix, mend, patch, repair a ~ 2. a slow ~

pundit *n.* a political ~

punish *v.* 1. to ~ cruelly; harshly, severely; lightly, mildly; summarily 2. (D; tr.) to ~ for (they were ~ed harshly for their crime)

punishable *adj.* ~ by (~ by death)

punishment *n.* 1. to administer, mete out ~ to 2. to impose, inflict ~ on 3. to escape ~ 4. to suffer, take ~ 5. cruel, cruel and unusual; harsh, severe, unjust ~ 6. just; light, mild ~ 7. capital; corporal; summary ~ 8. (mil.) company ~ 9. ~ for 10. as, in ~ (for)

pupil I *n.* ["opening in the iris of the eye"] constricted; dilated ~s

pupil II see the Usage Note for **student**

puppet *n.* 1. to manipulate, move a ~ 2. a hand ~

purchase I *n.* ["act of buying"] to make a ~

purchase II *v.* 1. (D; tr.) to ~ for 2. (D; tr.) to ~ from

purge I *n.* 1. to carry out, conduct a ~ 2. a radical, sweeping ~

purge II *v.* 1. (D; tr.) ("to remove") to ~ from (all dissidents were ~d from the party) 2. (D; tr.) ("to cleanse") to ~ of (the party was ~d of all disloyal elements)

purify *v.* (D; tr.) to ~ of

purity *n.* great; moral ~

purple I *adj.* ["livid"] ~ with (~ with rage)

purple II *n.* dark; light ~

purple III *n.* (BE) born to the ~ ("born into the royal family")

purport *v.* (formal) (E) ("to claim") they ~ to be our friends

purported *adj.* (cannot stand alone) ~ to + inf. (they are ~ to be wealthy)

purpose *n.* 1. to accomplish, achieve, fulfill a ~ 2. to serve a ~ 3. to put smt. to a good ~ 4. a lofty, worthy; useful ~ 5. for a ~ (it was done for a good ~; we arranged the meeting for the ~ of preventing a strike) 6. (misc.) for all practical ~s ("in reality"); on ~ ("purposely"); with the express ~ of; to no ~

purse strings *n.* ["finances"] to control, hold the ~

pursuance *n.* (formal) in ~ of (in ~ of one's duties)

pursuant *adj.* (formal) (cannot stand alone) ~ to

pursue *v.* to ~ aggressively; doggedly, patiently, relentlessly

pursuit *n.* ["chase"] 1. dogged, relentless; hot ~ 2. in ~ of (in hot ~ of the terrorists) 3. (misc.) the ~ of happiness ["hobby"] 4. smb.'s favorite ~

purview *n.* to fall outside; under; within the ~ of smt. (this question falls outside the ~ of this investigation)

pus *n.* 1. to discharge ~ 2. ~ forms

push I *n.* ["act of pushing"] 1. to give smb. a ~ (our car was stuck and they gave us a ~) 2. a hard ~ ["advance"] 3. to launch a ~ (the army launched a ~ to reach the sea) 4. a big ~ 5. a ~ to; towards (a ~ to the sea)

push II *v.* 1. ("to shove") to ~ hard 2. (D; intr.) ("to shove") to ~ against (to ~ against the door) 3. (d; intr.) to ~ for ("to urge") (to ~ for reform) 4. (d; intr.) to ~ into ("to force one's way") (to ~ into a crowded bus) 5. (D; tr.) ("to force to move") to ~ into (we ~ed the stalled car into the garage) 6. (d; intr.) ("to press") to ~ on (to ~ on a handle) 7. (d; intr., tr.) to ~ through ("to force one's way through") (to ~ through a crowd; to ~ one's way through a crowd) 8. (d; intr.) ("to move") to ~ to, towards (our troops ~ed towards the next village) 9. (H) ("to urge") to ~ smb. to do smt. 10. (N; used with an adjective) ~ the chair closer 11. (P; tr.) ("to shove") she ~ed the book under the bed; I was ~ed out of the way 12. (misc.) the army was ~ed to the breaking point

push ahead *v.* (D; intr.) to ~ with (they ~ed ahead with their plans)

push down *v.* (D; intr.) to ~ on (to ~ on a lid)

push on *v.* (D; intr.) ("to continue") to ~ to (we ~ed on to the next town)

pushover *n.* ["easy target"] a ~ for

push-up *n.* (esp. AE) to do ~s (see also **press-up**)

push up *v.* (D; intr.) to ~ on (to ~ on a handle)

put I *adj.* (colloq.) ["remaining in one place"] to stay ~

put II *v.* 1. (B) ("to pose") to ~ a question to smb. 2. (d; tr.) ("to place") to ~ before (to ~ a proposal before a committee) 3. (d; tr.) ("to place") to ~ in; into (to ~ milk in/into the refrigerator; to ~ new equipment into service; to ~ a criminal in prison; to ~ money in/into circulation; to ~ a plan into operation; to ~ one's affairs in order; to ~ a theory into practice; to ~ wood into a stove; to ~ sugar in/into tea; to ~ a car into a garage; to ~ words into smb.'s mouth; to ~ one's faith in smb.; ~ yourself in my place; to ~ smb. in a bad mood) 4. (d; intr.) ("to move") to ~ into (the ship put into port) 5. (d; tr.) ("to express") to ~ into (to ~ one's feelings into words) 6. (d; tr.) ("to place") to ~ on (to ~ books on a table; to ~ a stamp on a letter; to ~ smb.'s name on a list; the doctor put the patient on a diet) 7. (d; tr.) ("to bet") to ~ on (to ~ money on a horse) 8. (d; tr.) ("to place") to ~ out of (to ~ an enemy tank out of action) 9. (d; tr.) ("to assign") to ~ to (we put them all to work) 10. (d; tr.) ("to place") to ~ to (she put her fingers to her lips) 11. (d; tr.) ("to set") to ~ to (to ~ words to music) 12. (P; tr.) ("to place") ~ your shoes near the door; ~ the skis next to the fire; ~ the children to bed; ~ your things under the bed; to ~ troops across a river; she put her hand over her mouth; he put his arm around my shoulder 13. (misc.) to ~ a question to a/the vote; to ~ smb. to shame; to ~ smb. to death; to ~ smb. under arrest; to ~ smb. to great expense; to ~ smb. through the paces ("to subject smb. to a test of skill"); the ship put out to sea; I put it ("suggested") to them that the plan should be revised

put ahead *v.* (D; tr.) to ~ by (we put the clocks ahead by one hour)

put aside *v.* (D; tr.) to ~ for (we put aside some money for our future needs)

put down *v.* 1. (d; tr.) ("to consider") to ~ as (we can ~ this trip down as a business expense) 2. (d; tr.) to ~ for ("to enter a pledge for") (I'll ~ you down for five tickets) 3. (BE) (d; tr.) ("to enter") to ~ for (to ~ one's son for Eton) 4. (D; tr.) to ~ on (she put the books down on the table) 5. (d; tr.) ("to attribute")

to ~ to (to ~ a blunder down to inexperience)

put forward *v.* (D; tr.) to ~ by (we put the clocks forward by ten minutes)

put in *v.* (D; tr.) to ~ for ("to submit") (to ~ a claim for damages)

put off *v.* ("to postpone") 1. (D; tr.) to ~ until (she put the trip off until next week) 2. (G) we put off leaving because of the snow

put out *v.* 1. (D; refl.) ("to disturb") to ~ oneself out for (don't ~ yourself out for us) 2. (misc.) to ~ to sea; to ~ to stud

put over *v.* (D; tr.) ("to fob off") to ~ smt. over on smb. (he put his scheme over on the unsuspecting investors)

putter *v.* (AE) (d; intr.) to ~ around (to ~ around the house) (BE has *potter*)

put through *v.* (D; tr.) ("to connect") to ~ to (she was finally put through to her number)

put up *v.* 1. (B) ("to propose") I'll put the idea up to the whole committee 2. (d; tr.) ("to propose") to ~ as (we put her up as a candidate) 3. (old-fashioned) (BE) (d; intr.) ("to stay") to ~ at; with (to ~ at a hotel; to ~ with friends in Exeter) 4. (d; tr.) ("to offer") ("to propose") to ~ for (to ~ smt. up for sale; to ~ smb. up for an award) 5. (d; tr.) ("to provide") to ~ for (she put up the money for the flowers) 6. (D; tr.) ("to give shelter to") to ~ for (to ~ smb. up for a/the night) 7. (d; intr.) to ~ with ("to tolerate") (we will not ~ with such behavior) 8. (H) ("to place") to ~ water up to boil; he put the meal up to cook 9. (misc.) I put her up to it ("I persuaded her to do it")

puzzle I *n.* 1. to do, solve a ~ 2. a crossword ~; jigsaw ~ (AE; BE has *jigsaw*) 3. a ~ to (the whole matter was a ~ to the police) 4. to put the pieces of a ~ together

puzzle II *v.* 1. (d; intr.) to ~ over (to ~ over a problem) 2. (R) it ~d me that they never answered the telephone

puzzled *adj.* 1. ~ to + inf. (we were ~ to learn of her decision) 2. ~ that + clause (we were ~ that she had withdrawn)

puzzlement *n.* in ~ (they looked at us in great ~)

puzzle out *v.* (Q) we finally ~d out where they had hidden the key

puzzling *adj.* 1. ~ to (her behavior was ~ to everybody) 2. ~ to + inf. (it was ~ to see her at that hour) 3. ~ that + clause (it was ~ that she went straight home)

pyjamas (BE) see **pajamas**

pyramid *n.* the food ~

pyre *n.* a funeral ~

Q

quagmire *n.* 1. to get bogged down in a ~ 2. in a ~ of

quail I *n.* a bevy, covey of ~

quail II *v.* (d; intr.) ("to lose courage") to ~ at, before (we ~ed at the thought of getting lost in the forest)

quake *v.* 1. (D; intr.) to ~ at (to ~ at the sight of the apparition) 2. (D; intr.) to ~ with (to ~ with fear) 3. (misc.) we were ~king in our boots

qualification *n.* ["limitation"] 1. with; without ~ 2. a ~ that + clause (we agreed with the ~ that there should be adequate compensation)

qualifications *n.* ["qualities, attributes"] 1. excellent, fine, outstanding, strong ~ 2. the necessary ~ 3. academic; educational; physical; professional ~ 4. the ~ for (she has the ~ for the job) 5. the ~ to + inf. (this engineer has outstanding ~ to build the bridge)

qualified *adj.* 1. eminently, fully, highly, suitably ~; well-qualified 2. poorly ~ 3. ~ as (~ as an engineer) 4. ~ by (~ by education and experience for the position) 5. ~ for (she is highly ~ for the job) 6. ~ to + inf. (he is ~ to pass judgment on this matter)

qualify *v.* 1. (D; intr.) to ~ as (she ~fied as a teacher of the handicapped) 2. (D; intr., tr.) to ~ for (she ~fied for the position; what ~fied him for the job?) 3. (E) he ~fied to teach mathematics 4. (H) what ~fies her to represent us?

quality *n.* ["feature"] 1. admirable; endearing; innate; moral; personal; redeeming ~ties (he has no redeeming ~ties) 2. (misc.) there was a rhapsodic ~ about her playing ["degree of excellence"] 3. excellent, sterling, superb, superior; fine, good, high ~ 4. inferior, low, poor ~ 5. of a certain ~ (of good ~) 6. (misc.) (the) ~ of life

qualms *n.* 1. to feel, have ~ 2. ~ about (I have no ~ about borrowing money) 3. without (any) ~

quandary *n.* 1. a hopeless ~ 2. in a ~ (we were in a hopeless ~) 3. a ~ about, over (they are in a ~ about their finances)

quantity *n.* ["amount"] 1. a considerable, huge, large, vast ~ 2. a sufficient ~ 3. a negligible, small ~ 4. in (large) ~ties ["factor"] 5. an unknown ~

quarantine *n.* 1. to impose, institute a ~ 2. to put smb. in ~ 3. to lift a ~ 4. strict ~ 5. in, under ~ (to place under ~)

quarrel I *n.* 1. to cause, lead to a ~ (their political differences led to a bitter ~) 2. to have, pick, provoke, start a ~ (she picked a ~ with her neighbor) 3. to patch up, settle a ~ 4. a bitter, furious, violent; long-standing; never-ending ~ 5. a domestic, family ~ 6. a ~ breaks out, ensues 7. a ~ about, over; between; with (a bitter ~ broke out between them over the use of the telephone; he had a violent ~ with me about the money that he had borrowed)

quarrel II *v.* 1. to ~ bitterly, furiously, violently 2. (D; intr.) to ~ about, over; with (she ~ed with her neighbor about the noise)

quarry I *n.* ["prey"] 1. to stalk one's ~ 2. to bring one's ~ to bay 3. hunted ~

quarry II *n.* ["open excavation"] 1. to work a ~ 2. an abandoned ~ 3. a marble; stone ~

quarter I *n.* ["mercy"] 1. to give, show ~ (the invaders showed no ~) 2. to ask for; receive ~ ["one fourth"] 3. (in telling time) (a) ~ of (AE), to (the hour) (it was a ~ to five) 4. (a) ~ after (AE), past (the hour) (it is a ~ past five)

quarter II *v.* (esp. mil.) (D; tr.) ("to assign to a lodging place") to ~ on, upon (to ~ troops on the local population)

quarters *n.* ["housing"] 1. to find ~ 2. bachelor; living; officers' ~ 3. cramped ~ 4. ("misc.") confined to ~ ["assigned stations on a ship"] 5. battle, general ~ ["sources"] 6. from certain ~ (from the highest ~) ["misc."] 7. at close ~ ("close together")

quartet *n.* 1. to play a ~ 2. a ~ performs, plays 3. a piano; string; woodwind ~ 4. a barbershop ~

quay *n.* at, on a ~

queasy *adj.* ["uneasy"] ~ about (to feel ~ about smt.)

queen *n.* 1. to crown a ~ 2. to crown; proclaim smb. ~ 3. to depose, dethrone a ~ 4. a despotic; popular; strong; weak ~ 5. a ~ ascends, mounts the throne 6. a ~ reigns 7. a ~ abdicates (a throne) 8. a ~ consort; mother 9. (misc.) to toast the ~; a beauty ~; a drag ~ (colloq. and derog.) ("a male transvestite")

queen's evidence *n.* (BE) to turn ~ (see also **king's evidence, state's evidence**)

queer I *adj.* 1. ~ about (there is smt. ~ about them) 2. ~ to + inf. (it's ~ to be speaking of the heat in January) 3. ~ that + clause (it's ~ that she hasn't arrived yet)

queer II *v.* (colloq.) (d; refl.) ("to put oneself in a bad light") to ~ with (he ~ed himself with all his professors)

query *n.* 1. to put a ~ to 2. to reply, respond to a ~ 3. a ~ about

quest *n.* 1. to set out on a ~ (for) 2. a ~ for 3. in ~ of

question I *n.* ["query"] 1. to ask (smb.) a ~; to ask a ~ of smb. 2. to address, pose, put a ~ to smb. 3. to bring up, raise a ~ 4. to fire, shoot a ~ at 5. to answer, field, reply to, respond to a ~ (the senator fielded all ~s expertly) 6. to beg ("evade") the ~ 7. to parry, sidestep smb.'s ~s 8. a civil ("polite");

relevant; straightforward ~ 9. an academic, hypothetical, rhetorical; debatable, moot ~ 10. a complex; complicated; puzzling ~ 11. a blunt, direct;
pointed; probing ~ 12. an awkward, embarrassing,
sticky, ticklish; irrelevant; leading; loaded, tricky;
thorny; trivial ~ 13. (on an examination) an essay;
multiple-choice; true-false ~ 14. an examination,
test ~ 15. a ~ about, as to, concerning ["matter
being discussed"] 16. to consider, debate, discuss;
look into; raise a ~ 17. to put the ~ ("to vote on the
matter being discussed") 18. a burning; controversial; crucial; explosive; open; vexed (esp. BE) ~
19. (misc.) (colloq.) to pop the ~ ("to propose
marriage") ["doubt"] ["dispute"] 20. to clear up,
resolve a ~ 21. a ~ about, as to, of (there is no ~
about her sincerity) 22. beyond (all) ~ 23. in, into
~ (to come into ~; to call smt. into ~) 24. open to ~
25. without ~ ["misc."] 26. out of the ~ ("impossible"); the ~ of/as to/whether he'll go; there's
some ~ whether he'll go
USAGE NOTE: The sentence *there's no question
that he'll go* is ambiguous. It could mean "there's
no question of him/his going — he'll stay". Or, it
could mean "there's no question but that he'll go
— he'll go".

question II *v.* 1. (D; tr.) to ~ about (the police ~ed
her about her activities) 2. (Q) they ~ed where the
money had gone

questionable *adj.* 1. highly, very ~ 2. (misc.) it's ~
whether she was actually there

questioning *n.* 1. close ("intensive") ~ 2. under ~
(under close ~ by the district attorney)

questionnaire *n.* 1. to draw up, formulate a ~ 2. to
circulate, distribute, hand out, send out a ~ 3. to
answer, complete, fill in, fill out (esp. AE), fill up
(BE; old-fashioned); hand in, return a ~

queue I *n.* (esp. BE) 1. to form a ~ 2. to join; jump
the ~ 3. in a ~ (to stand in a ~)

queue II *v.* see **queue up**

queue up *v.* (esp. BE) (D; intr.) to ~ for (they had to
~ for fresh fruit)

quibble I *n.* a minor ~

quibble II *v.* (D; intr.) to ~ about, over; with (to ~
about trifles)

quick I *adj.* 1. ~ about (be ~ about it) 2. ~ at (~ at

picking up a new language) 3. ~ with (~ with one's
hands) 4. (cannot stand alone) ~ to + inf. (she is ~
to learn; he is ~ to take offense) 5. (misc.) ~ on (~
on one's feet)

quick II *n.* 1. to cut smb. to the ~ ("to offend smb.
gravely") 2. (misc.) the ~ and the dead

quicksand *n.* a bed of ~

quiet I *adj.* to be; keep ~

quiet II *n.* to shatter the ~

quilt *n.* a crazy; down; patchwork ~

quintet *n.* 1. to play, perform a ~ 2. a ~ performs,
plays

quip I *n.* 1. to make a ~ about 2. a ready ~

quip II *v.* 1. (D; intr.) to ~ about; at 2. (L) she ~ped
that being without a telephone for a few days
would be nice

quirk *n.* 1. a strange ~ 2. by a ~ of fate

quit *v.* 1. (D; intr., tr.) to ~ because of, over (he quit
his job because of the bribe) 2. (colloq.) (esp. AE)
(D; intr.) ("to stop") to ~ on (the engine quit on us)
3. (G) (esp. AE) she quit smoking

quits *n.* (colloq.) to call it ~ ("to cease doing smt.")

quiver I *n.* to feel a ~ (of excitement)

quiver II *v.* (D; intr.) to ~ with (to ~ with fear)

quiz I *n.* ["short test"] 1. to draw up, make up a 2.
to give a ~ 3. to take a ~ 4. to fail; pass a ~ 5. a
daily; pop (AE); weekly ~ 5. an oral; unan-
nounced; written ~

quiz II *v.* (D; tr.) to ~ about (the police ~zed the
neighbors about the incident)

quoits *n.* 1. to pitch, play ~ 2. a game of ~

quorum *n.* 1. to constitute, make (up) a ~ 2. to have;
lack a ~

quota *n.* 1. to assign, establish, fix, set a ~ 2. to fill,
fulfill, meet a ~ 3. to exceed one's ~ 4. an import;
production; racial ~

quotation *n.* ["citation"] 1. to give a ~ from 2. a
direct ~ ["estimate of cost"] 3. to give, submit a ~
(for)

quote I *n.* 1. in ~s 2. see **quotation**

quote II *v.* 1. to ~ directly; in full 2. (A) she ~d
several verses to us; or: she ~d us several verses 3.
(d; intr.) to ~ from (she loves to ~ from
Shakespeare) 4. (D; tr.) to ~ from (to ~ a passage
from the Bible)

quotient *n.* an intelligence ~ (IQ)

R

r *n.* 1. to roll, trill an ~ 2. a retroflex; rolled, trilled; uvular ~

rabbi *n.* a chief; Conservative; Liberal (BE), Progressive (BE); Orthodox; Reform ~
USAGE NOTE: See the entry for **Judaism**

rabbit *n.* 1. ~s breed quickly; burrow 2. a ~ warren

rabbit on *v.* (colloq.) (BE) (D; intr.) ("to chatter") to ~ about

rabid *adj.* ["fanatical"] ~ about, on (~ on a certain subject)

rabies *n.* to come down with, get ~

race I *n.* ["group distinguished by certain physical traits"] 1. the Caucasoid; Mongoloid; Negroid ~ 2. the human ~ 3. (misc.) a person of mixed ~

race II *n.* ["contest of speed"] ["competition"] 1. to organize, stage a ~ 2. to drive; row; run a ~ 3. to enter; lose; win a ~ 4. to fix (the results of) a ~ 5. a close, even, hotly contested, tight; grueling; uneven ~ 6. an automobile (AE), motor (esp. BE); boat; cross-country; dog; drag ("acceleration") ~; footrace; horse; long-distance; relay ~ 7. (pol.) a congressional; governor's, gubernatorial; political; presidential; senatorial ~ 8. the arms ~ 9. a ~ against, with; between; for (the ~ for the presidency was run between well qualified candidates; a ~ against time) 10. a ~ to + inf. (the ~ to conquer space) ["misc."] 11. a rat ~ ("very hectic activity")

race III *v.* 1. (D; intr.) to ~ against, with (to ~ against time) 2. (D; intr.) to ~ for (to ~ for a prize) 3. (D; intr., tr.) to ~ to (let's ~ to school; I'll ~ you to the car; we ~d the child to the emergency room) 4. (E) we ~d to get there in time 5. (P; intr., tr.) to ~ through the park; they ~d around the corner; we ~d them down the hill

race up *v.* (D; intr.) to ~ to (they ~d up to the top of the hill)

racialism (BE) see **racism**

racing *n.* auto (AE), motor (esp. BE); flat; harness; horse; stockcar ~

racism *n.* 1. to stamp out ~ 2. blatant, out-and-out; endemic; rampant; vicious, virulent ~

rack I *n.* ["framework, stand"] 1. a bicycle; bomb; clothes; hat; luggage (AE), roof (BE); magazine; rifle; towel ~ 2. a dish (esp. AE), plate (BE) ["instrument of torture"] 3. on the ~

rack II *n.* ["destruction"] to go to ~ and ruin

racked *adj.* 1. ~ by (~ by doubt) 2. ~ with (~ with pain)

racket I *n.* ["noise"] 1. to make a ~ 2. a terrible ~ ["dishonest practice"] 3. to operate, run a ~ 4. a numbers; protection ~

racket II racquet *n.* ["bat used to play tennis, etc."] 1. to swing a ~ 2. to string a ~ 3. a badminton; squash; tennis ~

racketeer *n.* a big-time, notorious; petty ~

radar *n.* to track by ~

radiant *adj.* ~ with (~ with joy)

radiate *v.* (D; intr.) to ~ from

radiation *n.* 1. to emit ~ 2. nuclear ~ 3. harmful ~

radio I *n.* ["radio receiving set"] 1. to plug in; put on, switch on, turn on a ~ 2. to switch off, turn off; unplug a ~ 3. to turn down; turn up a ~ 4. to listen to the ~ 5. an AM; (CB) Citizens' Band; clock; FM; long-wave (esp. UK); portable; medium-wave (esp. BE); shortwave; transistor ~ 6. on, over the ~ (I heard the bad news over the ~) ["radio broadcasting industry"] 7. public ~ 8. (to be) in ~

radio II *v.* 1. (A) we ~ed the message to them; or: we ~ed them the message 2. (d; intr., tr.) to ~ for (they ~ed us for help)

radioactivity *n.* 1. to emit, generate, produce ~ 2. (a) dangerous (level of) ~

radishes *n.* a bunch of ~

radius *n.* 1. a cruising ~ 2. in, within a ~ of (within a ~ of fifty miles)

raffle *n.* 1. to hold a ~ 2. a ~ for

raft *n.* 1. to launch a ~ 2. a life ~ 3. on a ~ (to float on a ~)

rafting *n.* white-water ~

rag I *n.* to chew the ~ (slang) ("to chat")

rag II *v.* (slang) (D; tr.) to ~ about (they ~ged him about his beard)

rage I *n.* ["anger"] 1. to provoke, stir up smb.'s ~ 2. to express; feel ~ 3. to fly into a ~ 4. (a) blind, towering, ungovernable, violent; jealous; sudden ~ 5. a fit, outburst of ~ 6. a ~ against 7. in a ~ 8. (misc.) to quiver with ~ ["fashion"] (colloq.) 9. the latest ~ 10. a ~ for 11. (misc.) it's all the ~

rage II *v.* 1. (D; intr.) to ~ against, at 2. (misc.) to ~ out of control (the fire ~d out of control); the epidemic ~d through the city

ragged *adj.* to run smb. ~

rags *n.* 1. a bundle of ~ 2. (dressed) in ~ 3. (misc.) from ~ to riches ("from poverty to prosperity")

raid *n.* 1. to carry out, conduct a ~ 2. an air; bombing; border; guerrilla; police; retaliatory; suicide ~ 3. a ~ into (a ~ into enemy territory) 4. a ~ on, upon (a ~ on an illegal gambling casino)

rail I *n.* ["barrier, handrail"] 1. at the ~ (to stand at the ~) 2. (to jump) over the ~ 3. (misc.) to hold on to a ~

rail II *v.* (d; intr.) ("to complain") to ~ about, against, at

railroad I *n.* (esp. AE) 1. to manage, operate, run a

~ 2. a double-track; elevated; single-track ~ 3. a transcontinental ~ 4. a ~ from; to 5. on a ~ (they used to work on the ~)

railroad II v. (colloq.) ("to force") 1. (d; tr.) to ~ into (they ~ed us into signing the contract) 2. (d; tr.) to ~ through (to ~ a bill through a legislature)

rails n. 1. to go off, jump the ~ 2. to ride the ~ (see **rod** 5)

railway n. 1. (esp. BE) see **railroad I** 2. a scenic ~ (BE) 3. a cable; cog; light; rack ~ 4. a broad-gauge; narrow-gauge; normal-gauge ~

rain I n. 1. to make, produce ~ 2. to keep the ~ out 3. (a) drenching, driving, heavy, pouring, soaking, torrential; freezing; intermittent; light; steady ~ 4. acid ~ 5. ~ falls; freezes; lets up; pours; starts; stops 6. ~ beats, patters (against the windows) 7. (misc.) the ~ came down in buckets; to get caught in the ~; (BE) it's pouring with ~

rain II v. 1. to ~ buckets, cats and dogs, hard 2. (misc.) tears ~ed down her cheeks; to ~ gifts on smb.

rainbow n. a ~ appears, comes out

rain check n. (esp. AE) ["a deferred offer"] 1. to offer a ~ on 2. to give a ~ on 3. to take a ~ on

rain down v. (D; intr.) to ~ on (confetti ~ed down on the spectators)

raindrops n. ~ fall

rainfall n. 1. to measure ~ 2. annual, yearly; average; heavy; light, low; measurable; normal ~

rain in v. (D; intr.) to ~ on (it was ~ing in on us)

rainwater n. to catch, collect ~ (in a barrel)

raise I n. (AE) 1. to give smb. a ~ (in salary) 2. to deserve; get a ~ 3. a pay ~ 4. an across-the-board; annual ~ (BE has *rise*)

raise II v. 1. (D; tr.) ("to lift") to ~ above (~ your hand above your head) 2. (D; tr.) ("to increase") to ~ by (they ~d their offer by one thousand dollars) 3. (D; tr.) ("to lift") to ~ from; to (to ~ a sunken ship from the bottom of the sea to the surface) 4. (d; tr.) ("to elevate") to ~ to (to ~ smb. to the peerage) 5. (H) ("to bring up") they ~d their children to respect the rights of other people

raising n. consciousness ~

raisins n. seeded; seedless ~

rake v. 1. (D; tr.) to ~ into (to ~ hay into piles) 2. (d; intr.) to ~ through (they ~d through piles of rubbish to find the lost items) 3. (misc.) to ~ smb. over the coals (to criticize smb. severely)

rally I n. ["mass meeting"] 1. to hold, organize, stage a ~ 2. a mass; peace; pep (AE); political; protest ~ ["competition, race between cars"] 3. to have, hold, organize, stage a ~

rally II v. 1. (d; intr., tr.) to ~ around, round (to ~ around a leader) 2. (d; intr., tr.) to ~ for (the commanders ~ied their troops for a counterattack) 3. (d; intr., tr.) to ~ to (they ~ied to the support of their country)

ram I n. a battering ~

ram II v. 1. (d; tr.) to ~ into (to ~ piles into a river bed) 2. (misc.) to ~ smt. down smb.'s throat ("to force smb. to accept smt.")

ramble on v. (D; intr.) ("to talk in a disorganized manner") to ~ about (she ~d on about her childhood)

ramp n. 1. a steep ~ 2. (misc.) to go down a ~; to go up a ~

rampage I n. to go on a ~

rampage II v. (P; intr.) to ~ through the streets; they ~d around the city hall

rampant adj. to run ~ (inflation was running ~)

ramparts n. to storm the ~

ranch n. 1. a cattle; dude ~ 2. at, on a ~ (he works at the ~; to live on a ~)

rancher n. a cattle; sheep ~

rancor, rancour n. 1. to stir up ~ 2. to express; feel; show ~ 3. deep-seated ~ 4. ~ against, towards (to feel ~ towards smb.) 5. with; without ~

random n. at ~ (to choose at ~)

random sample n. to select, take a ~

range I n. ["series of connecting mountains"] 1. a mountain ~ ["distance that a gun fires, can fire"] 2. close, short; long; point-blank ~ 3. artillery; rifle ~ 4. at; from a certain ~ (at close ~) 5. in, within ~ 6. out of ~ ["place where shooting is practiced"] 7. an artillery; firing; rifle; rocket ~ 8. at, on a ~ ["extent, scope"] 9. a narrow; wide ~ 10. within a ~ (within a narrow ~) ["cooking stove"] 11. an electric; gas ~ ["open region on which livestock graze"] 12. to ride the ~ 13. on the ~ ["misc."] 14. a driving ~ (where one practices driving golf balls)

range II v. 1. (d; tr.) ("to align") to ~ against (they were all ~d against us) 2. (d; intr.) ("to extend") to ~ from; to (prices ~ from ten dollars to thirty dollars) 3. (P; intr.) her talk ~d over a wide variety of subjects; the troops ~d through the fields 4. (misc.) prices ~ between eighty and ninety dollars

ranger n. a forest ~

rank I n. ["row"] (esp. mil.) 1. to form a ~ 2. to break ~s (also fig.) 3. (misc.) to come up, rise from the ~s ["position, grade"] 4. to attain; have, hold a ~ (to hold the ~ of captain) 5. to pull (colloq.), use one's ~ 6. to strip of a ~ 7. high; junior; low; senior ~ 8. (mil.) permanent (AE), substantive (BE) ~ 9. (mil.) other ~s (BE; AE has *enlisted personnel*) 10. cabinet ~ 11. by, in ~ (to be seated by ~) 12. of ~ (of cabinet ~; of high ~) ["misc."] 13. to close ~s ("to unite"); a taxi ~ (BE; CE has *taxi stand*); to come up from the ~s ("to work one's way up to a high position"); the ~ and file ("everyone"); to swell the ~s ("to increase the numbers of")

rank II v. 1. to ~ high; low 2. (d; intr., tr.) ("to be rated; to rate") to ~ above (nobody ~s above Shakespeare; we do not ~ anyone above him) 3. (d; intr.) to ~ among (she ~s among our best instructors) 4. (d; intr., tr.) to ~ as (to ~ as an outstanding chess player; we ~ you as our best candidate) 5. (d; intr., tr.) to ~ with (Pushkin ~s with Tolstoy) 6. (misc.) on a scale of one to five we ~ the service four; we ~ the service very high

rankle v. (R) it ~d me that they got all the credit

ransom I n. 1. to pay (a) ~ for 2. to demand; exact a ~ from 3. to hold smb. for ~

ransom II v. (D; tr.) to ~ for (she was ~ed for two million dollars)

rant v. 1. (D; intr.) to ~ about; at 2. (misc.) to ~ and rave

rap I n. (colloq.) ["blame"] 1. to take the ~ for 2. (AE) a bad, bum ~ (she got a bum ~) ("she was punished for smb. else's misdeeds") ["charge"] 3. to beat the ~ 4. on a ~ (he was sent to prison on a murder ~)

rap II v. 1. (d; intr.) ("to strike") to ~ at, on (to ~ on the window) 2. (d; tr.) ("to strike") to ~ over (she ~ped him over the knuckles)

rap III v. (slang) (D; intr.) ("to converse") to ~ about; with

rape n. 1. to commit ~ 2. attempted ~ 3. acquaintance, date; gang; marital; statutory ~ 4. a brutal ~

rapidity n. (with) great, lightning ~

rapids n. 1. to ride, shoot ("pass through") (the) ~ 2. a stretch of ~

rapport n. 1. to develop, establish; have ~ 2. close, good ~ 3. a ~ between, with 4. in ~ with (they worked in close ~ with us)

rapprochement n. to bring about a ~ between; with

rapture n. 1. complete, total, utter ~ 2. ~ about, at, over 3. in ~ over 4. (misc.) to go into ~s over

rare adj. 1. ~ to + inf. (it's ~ to see snow here in September) 2. ~ that + clause (it is ~ that he gets home before dark)

raring adj. (colloq.) ["eager"] (cannot stand alone) ~ to + inf. (we are ~ to go)

rash I adj. ~ to + inf. (it was ~ of her to try that)

rash II n. 1. a diaper (AE), nappy (BE); heat; skin ~ (the baby has heat ~) 2. nettle ~ 3. a ~ breaks out 4. (misc.) to break out in a ~

raspberry n. (colloq.) ["contemptuous noise"] to give smb. the ~

rat I n. 1. a black; brown; water ~ 2. (misc.) to smell a ~ ("to suspect that the truth is not being told"); a dirty ~ ("a contemptible person")

rat II v. (colloq.) (D; intr.) ("to inform") to ~ on; to

rate I n. ["amount in relation to something else"] 1. to fix, set; increase, raise; lower, reduce a ~ 2. a fast; flat; high; low; moderate; slow; steady ~ 3. bargain; reasonable; reduced; regular ~s 4. an accident; birth; crime; death; divorce; dropout; fertility; growth; marriage; morbidity; mortality ~ 5. a base; discount; exchange; group; inflation; interest; mortgage; primary; prime; tax ~ 6. a metabolic; pulse; respiration ~ 7. an annual; hourly;

monthly; seasonal; weekly ~ 8. a ~ falls; rises 9. at a certain ~ (at a steady ~; she borrowed money at a high interest ~) ["misc."] 10. at any ~ ("in any case"); first ~ ("top quality")

rate II v. 1. to ~ high(ly); low 2. (d; intr., tr.) ("to be ranked; to rank") to ~ among (that player is ~d among the very best) 3. (d; intr., tr.) ("to be ranked; to rank") to ~ as (this wine ~s as excellent; she is ~d as one of the best tennis players in the country) 4. (d; intr.) ("to compare") to ~ with (this wine ~s with the very best) 5. (colloq.) (AE) (D; intr.) ("to enjoy a favored status") to ~ with (she really ~s with them) 6. (P; intr., tr.) ("to rank") this restaurant is ~d very highly 7. (GB) (P; tr.) ("to assess for tax purposes") their flat is ~d at eight hundred pounds this year 8. (misc.) on a scale of one to ten, we would ~ this restaurant eight

rather adv. 1. ~ + inf. + than (she would ~ play tennis than watch TV) 2. (colloq.) ~ + clause + than (I would ~ you stayed home than go out in this blizzard; she would ~ you did your homework than watched TV) 3. ~ + inf. (she would ~ not watch TV) 4. ~ + clause (she would ~ you didn't watch TV) 5. (misc.) I prefer to walk ~ than (to) ride; I prefer walking ~ than riding

rating n. ["classification"] ["limit"] 1. a high; low ~ 2. a credit; efficiency; octane; power ~ ["ordinary seaman"] (BE) 3. a naval ~

ratio n. 1. a compression ~ 2. a direct; inverse ~ 3. a ~ between, of; to (at a ~ of three to one)

ration I n. ["fixed allowance"] 1. a daily; monthly; weekly ~ 2. a food; gasoline (AE), petrol (BE) ~

ration II v. 1. to ~ strictly 2. (D; tr.) to ~ to (we were ~ed to ten gallons of gasoline/petrol a month)

rational adj. ~ to + inf. (it is not ~ to expect miracles)

rationalization n. ["excuse"] 1. a mere ~ 2. a ~ for (a ~ for refusing to contribute) 3. a ~ to + inf. (it was a ~ to argue that increased spending would help the economy) 4. a ~ that + clause (their ~ that increased spending is bad has been disproved)

rationing n. 1. to introduce ~ 2. to end, terminate ~ 3. food; gasoline (AE), petrol (BE) ~ 4. emergency; wartime ~

ration out v. (D; tr.) to ~ among, to

rations n. 1. to issue ~ 2. army; emergency; short ~ 3. on ~ (we were on short ~)

rattle I n. ["noise in the throat caused by air passing through mucus"] 1. the death ~ ["device producing a rattling sound"] 2. a baby's ~

rattle II v. (colloq.) (R) it ~d me to realize how close we had been to a real catastrophe

rattled adj. badly ~ (she was badly ~ at the news)

rattlesnake n. a ~ bites, strikes

ravages n. ["destruction"] to repair the ~ (wrought by war)

rave v. (D; intr.) 1. to ~ about, over; to (she was

~ving to us about her grandchild) 2. (D; intr.) to ~ against/at (he was ~ving at the new taxes) 3. (L; to) she kept ~ving to everyone that she had been wronged

ravine n. a deep ~

raw n. ["natural state"] in the ~

ray n. 1. to emit, send forth, send out ~s 2. a cathode; cosmic; death; gamma; infrared; ultraviolet; X ~ 3. heat; light ~s

raze v. (D; tr.) to ~ to (to ~ a building to the ground)

razor n. 1. to hone, set, sharpen a ~ 2. a dull; keen, sharp ~ 3. a double-edged; electric; safety; single-edged; straight ~

reach I n. 1. easy ~ 2. beyond, out of ~ 3. in, within ~ (to bring smt. within ~; within easy ~) 4. (misc.) a boardinghouse ("very long") ~

reach II v. 1. (A; used without to) ("to pass") ~ me the salt 2. (d; intr., tr.) ("to extend") to ~ across, around (she ~ed her hand across the table) 3. (d; intr.) ("to extend one's hand") to ~ for (she ~ed for a cigarette) 4. (d; intr.) ("to extend one's hand") to ~ into (she ~ed into her pocket for her keys) 5. (D; intr.) ("to extend") to ~ to (the rope doesn't ~ to the ground)

reaches n. ["area"] 1. the lower; upper ~ (the upper ~ of the river) 2. vast ~ (the vast ~es of the western plains)

reach out v. 1. (d; intr.) to ~ for ("to attempt to obtain") (to ~ for mutual understanding) 2. (D; tr.) ("to extend") to ~ for (she ~ed out her hand for the change) 3. (d; intr.) to ~ into, to ("to attempt to help") (to ~ to the local community) 4. (D; tr.) ("to extend") to ~ to (~ your hand to me)

react v. 1. to ~ calmly; strongly 2. (D; intr.) to ~ against (to ~ against unfair treatment) 3. (D; intr.) to ~ to (to ~ to a stimulus; to ~ to a provocation) 4. (d; intr.) to ~ with (this medication ~s with aspirin)

reaction n. 1. to cause, provoke, spark, trigger a ~ 2. to encounter, meet with a ~ 3. to have a ~ 4. an enthusiastic; favorable, positive ~ 5. an immediate, instantaneous, quick, spontaneous; instinctive, knee-jerk (usu. fig.); natural, normal ~ 6. an adverse, negative; angry, hostile ~ 7. (a) delayed ~ 8. a strong; weak ~ 9. an allergic; chain; chemical; nuclear; physiological ~ 10. a ~ against, to (a natural ~ to provocation) 11. in ~ to

reactionary n. a die-hard, dyed-in-the wool ~

reactor n. an atomic, nuclear; breeder; fission ~

read v. 1. (A) she read a nice story to the children; or: she read the children a nice story 2. (D; intr.) to ~ about 3. (d; tr.) ("to interpret") to ~ as (this story should be read as a satire) 4. (d; intr., tr.) to ~ for (she used to ~ for the patients in the nursing home; could you ~ that material for me?) 5. (esp. BE) (d; intr.) ("to study") to ~ for (to ~ for a degree; to ~ for the bar) 6. (d; intr.) ("to audition") to ~ for (she will ~ for the role of the ingenue in the new play)

7. (D; intr., tr.) to ~ from; to (she read from page ten to page thirty) 8. (d; tr.) to ~ into ("to attribute") (don't try to ~ anything else into her letter) 9. (d; tr.) ("to enter") to ~ into (to ~ data into a computer) 10. (AE) (d; tr.) to ~ out of ("to exclude") (he was read out of the party) 11. (d; intr.) to ~ through (she read through the book at one sitting) 12. (d; intr.) to ~ to (she loves to ~ to the children) 13. (L) we read that prices would be going up 14. (misc.) to ~ by candlelight; to ~ a language fluently; to ~ between the lines; to ~ aloud, to ~ out loud; the letter ~s like an accusation; the play ~s well; the cablegram ~s as follows...; to ~ a child to sleep; to ~ smb. like a book ("to comprehend smb.'s motives very clearly"); a widely read column; she's widely read in the classics ("she has extensive knowledge of the classics")

read back v. (B) ~ the sentence back to me

reader n. ["one who reads"] 1. an avid, omniverous, voracious ~ 2. a regular ~ (of a newspaper) 3. a copy ~ (AE; BE has subeditor) 4. (rel.) a lay ~ ["university teacher below the rank of professor"] (BE) 5. a ~ in (a ~ in physics) ["practice book for reading"] 6. a basic ~ ["assessor of a dissertation, thesis"] 7. a first; second ~ ["misc."] 8. a publisher's ~ 9. a mind ~ (see the Usage Note for **professor**)

readiness n. 1. combat; tactical ~ 2. ~ for 3. ~ + inf. (her ~ to help was appreciated) 4. (to hold oneself) in ~

reading n. ["act of reading"] 1. extensive; heavy; light; remedial; responsive; serious; solid ~ 2. a dramatic; poetry ~ 3. assigned; background; required; suggested ~(s) (have you done the assigned ~ for the course?) at a ~ (at the first ~) 5. in a ~ (you will not be able to absorb the material in one ~) ["interpretation"] 6. a new ~ of (Shakespeare)

readjust v. (D; intr., refl., tr.) to ~ to

readjustment n. to make a ~ (to)

read out v. (B) she read the instructions out to me

read up v. (d; intr.) to ~ on (to ~ on a subject)

ready I adj. 1. ~ for (~ for any emergency; we are ~ for you to start) 2. ~ with (she is always ~ with an answer) 3. ~ to + inf. (we are ~ to begin) 4. (misc.) to get (smb.) ~ for

ready II n. at the ~

ready III v. 1. (D; refl., tr.) to ~ for (she readied herself for the confrontation) 2. (H) we readied ourselves to face the music

reaffirm v. (L; to) she ~ed (to us) that she would serve as treasurer

realism n. to lend ~ (the sound effects lend ~ to the scene)

realist n. a down-to-earth, hardheaded ~

realistic adj. 1. ~ about 2. ~ to + inf. (is it ~ to

expect such results?)

reality *n.* 1. to become a ~ 2. (the) grim, harsh, sober ~ (the harsh ~ of life) 3. (computers) virtual ~ 4. in ~ 5. (misc.) to accept ~; to deny ~; to face ~

realization *n.* 1. to come to the ~ 2. a full; growing; sudden ~ 3. the ~ that + clause (the ~ that a catastrophe could occur at any time sobered them up)

realize *v.* 1. to ~ fully 2. (L) she ~d that she had been cheated 3. (Q) I ~d how my words had been distorted

realm *n.* in a ~ (in the ~ of science)

reapply *v.* (D; intr.) to ~ for; to (to ~ for admission to a university)

reappoint *v.* 1. (D; tr.) to ~ as (to ~ smb. as chairperson) 2. (D; tr.) to ~ to (to ~ smb. to a committee) 3. (H) to ~ smb. to serve as secretary 4. (N; used with a noun) we ~ed her treasurer

reappraisal *n.* 1. to do, make a ~ 2. an agonizing; careful; objective; thorough ~

rear I *n.* 1. to bring up the ~ 2. at, from, in, to the ~ (the column was attacked from the ~)

rear II *v.* (H) we ~ed our children to help others

reason I *n.* ["cause, justification"] 1. to cite, give a ~ 2. a cogent, compelling, convincing, good, important, plausible, solid, sound, strong, urgent ~ 3. a logical; personal; prime; real; underlying; valid ~ 4. every ~; (a) sufficient ~ 5. a ~ against; behind; for (the real ~ behind their decision was never made public; to have a ~ for not going) 6. a ~ to + inf. (we had every ~ to complain; there is sufficient ~ to be concerned) 7. a ~ that + clause (the ~ that/why she did it is a mystery) 8. by ~ of 9. for a ~ (he quit for personal ~s; for no apparent ~) 10. with ~ (I fear him and with good ~) ["logic"] 11. to listen to; see ~ 12. to stand to ~ ("to be logical") (it stands to ~ that the majority party will be reelected) 13. (misc.) an appeal to ~ ["reasonable limits"] 14. within ~ (I'll do anything for you within ~) ["sanity"] 15. to lose one's ~

reason II *v.* 1. (D; intr.) to ~ with ("to attempt to persuade") (you can't ~ with him) 2. (L) ("to argue") they ~ed that any new proposal would fail

reasonable *adj.* 1. ~ about (let's be ~ about this) 2. ~ of 3. ~ to + inf. (it is not ~ to demand so much from them)

reasoning *n.* 1. cogent, logical, plausible, solid, sound; objective; subjective ~ 2. faulty; shrewd; specious ~ 3. deductive; inductive ~ 4. ~ that + clause (her ~ that the crime had been committed elsewhere proved to be true)

reassign *v.* (D; tr.) to ~ to (to ~ smb. to headquarters)

reassure *v.* 1. (D; tr.) to ~ about, of (they ~d us of their support) 2. (L; must have an object) we ~d them that we would not be late

reassuring *adj.* 1. ~ to + inf. (it is ~ to note that

airport security has been improved) 2. ~ that + clause (it is ~ that airport security has been improved)

rebate *n.* 1. to give a ~ 2. to get, receive a ~

rebel I *n.* a ~ against

rebel II *v.* (D; intr.) to ~ against, at (to ~ against tyranny; they ~led at the thought of getting up before dawn)

rebellion *n.* 1. to foment, stir up a ~ 2. to crush, put down, quash, quell, smash, stifle a ~ 3. open ~ 4. an armed ~ 5. a ~ breaks out 6. a ~ against 7. in ~ (in open ~)

rebound I *n.* 1. (basketball) to grab a ~ 2. (misc.) on the ~ (right after her divorce she married smb. on the ~)

rebound II *v.* (D; intr.) to ~ from (to ~ from a setback)

rebuff *n.* 1. to meet with a ~ 2. a polite; sharp ~

rebuke I *n.* 1. to administer, deliver, give a ~ 2. to draw, receive a ~ 3. a mild; scathing, sharp, stern, stinging ~ 4. a ~ to

rebuke II *v.* 1. to ~ mildly; sharply, sternly 2. (D; tr.) to ~ for (to ~ smb. for sloppy work)

rebuttal *n.* to make, offer a ~

recall I *n.* ["remembrance"] 1. beyond ~ ["memory"] 2. complete, total ~

recall II *v.* 1. ("to remember") to ~ distinctly, vividly; fondly 2. (d; tr.) ("to remember") to ~ as (I ~ him as a very bashful child) 3. (D; tr.) ("to call back") to ~ from; to (to ~ smb. from retirement to active duty) 4. (G) ("to remember") she ~ed seeing him 5. (J) I ~ them visiting us 6. (K) ("to remember") I ~ed their visiting us 7. (L) ("to remember") she ~ed that she had an appointment 8. (Q) ("to remember") I could not ~ where we had agreed to meet

recede *v.* (D; intr.) to ~ from

receipt *n.* ["receiving"] 1. to acknowledge ~ of 2. in ~ of (we are in ~ of your letter) 3. on ~ of ["written acknowledgment of something received"] 4. to give, make out, write out a ~ 5. to get a ~ 6. (esp. US) a return ~ (for registered mail) 7. a ~ for 8. (misc.) box office ~s

receive *v.* 1. to ~ smb. coldly, coolly; favorably; warmly 2. (d; tr.) to ~ as (the astronauts were ~d as conquering heroes) 3. (D; tr.) to ~ from (he ~d a letter from her) 4. (d; tr.) to ~ into (to ~ smb. into a church)

receive back *v.* to ~ into the fold (after many years of wandering, they were ~d back into the fold)

receiver *n.* ["part of a telephone"] 1. to pick up the ~ 2. to hang up, put down, replace a ~ 3. a telephone ~ ["radio"] 4. a shortwave ~ ["one who catches a forward pass"] (Am. football) 5. to hit; spot a ~ (to spot a ~ down the field)

receivership *n.* 1. to put a firm into ~ 2. in ~

reception *n.* ["social gathering"] 1. to give, hold;

host a ~ 2. a diplomatic; formal; informal; official; wedding ~ 3. a ~ for (a ~ for graduating students) 4. at a ~ (we met at the ~) ["reaction, response"] ["greeting"] 5. to get, meet with a ~ 6. to accord, give (smb.) a ~ 7. a cordial, friendly, warm; emotional; enthusiastic; favorable; jubilant; lavish; rousing ~ (they gave us a warm ~; the book received a favorable ~) 8. a chilly, cold, cool; hostile; lukewarm; mixed; unfavorable; unfriendly ~ (their proposal got a mixed ~) ["registration desk in a hotel"] (BE) 9. at ~ (leave your key at ~) ["receiving of broadcasts"] 10. good, strong; poor, weak ~

receptive adj. ~ to (~ to any reasonable offer)

recess n. 1. to take a ~ 2. to declare a ~ 3. a spring; summer; winter ~ 4. in ~ (parliament was in ~)

recession n. 1. a business, economic ~ 2. a major ~ 3. in (a) ~ (the country was in a major ~) 4. (misc.) to come out of a ~; to go into a ~

recipe n. 1. to follow a ~ 2. the ~ calls for, requires 3. a ~ for

recipient n. a worthy ~

reciprocate v. (D; intr.) to ~ by; for; with

reciprocity n. 1. ~ between 2. (misc.) on a basis of ~

recital n. 1. to give a ~ 2. an organ; piano; violin ~

recite v. (B) she ~d her poetry to the audience

reckless adj. ~ to + inf. (it was ~ of them to go out alone at night)

reckon v. 1. (BE) (D; tr.) to ~ among, as (I ~ them among my friends/as my friends) 2. (colloq. in AE) (d; intr.) ("to depend") to ~ on (you can always ~ on my support) 3. (colloq. in AE) (d; intr.) ("to deal") to ~ with (we'll have to ~ with him later) 4. (BE) (E) we ~ to reach our destination before nightfall 5. (colloq.) (L) I ~ we'll have to see them eventually 6. (BE) (M) they ~ her to be a great actress

reckoning n. ["navigation"] 1. dead ~ ["calculations"] 2. by smb.'s ~ (by my ~) 3. (misc.) the day of ~

reclaim v. (D; tr.) to ~ from

reclamation n. land; water ~

recluse n. an aging, elderly; virtual ~

recognition n. 1. to give, grant ~ 2. to achieve, gain, get, receive, win ~ 3. general, universal; growing; international, worldwide; national; official; public; tacit; wide ~ (to receive universal ~) 4. (diplomatic) de facto; de jure ~ 5. ~ for; from (to receive ~ for one's accomplishments from one's colleagues) 6. beyond ~ (burned beyond ~) 7. in ~ of 8. (misc.) to give/show no sign(s) of ~

recognizance n. (legal) on one's own ~ (she was released on her own ~)

recognize v. 1. to ~ officially 2. (D; tr.) to ~ as (she is universally ~d as an authority on the subject) 3. (L) we ~d that the situation was hopeless

recognized adj. 1. generally, universally; officially; widely ~ 2. ~ as (she is still ~ as an authority)

recoil v. 1. (D; intr.) to ~ at, from 2. (misc.) to ~ in horror

recollect v. 1. (G) she could not ~ being there 2. (K) can you ~ my calling you? 3. (L) I ~ that the weather was cold 4. (Q) can anyone ~ how the alarm is deactivated?

recollection n. 1. to have a ~ of 2. a dim, hazy, vague; painful; vivid ~

recommend v. 1. to ~ enthusiastically, highly, strongly 2. (BE) (A) she ~ed a good dictionary to me; or: she ~ed me a good dictionary 3. (AE) (B) she ~ed a good dictionary to me 4. (D; tr.) to ~ as (she was ~ed as a suitable candidate for the job) 5. (D; tr.) to ~ for (to ~ smb. for a job) 6. (G) she ~ed waiting 7. (BE) (H; no passive) I ~ you to buy this book 8. (K) he ~ed their investing in railroad stocks 9. (L; subj.; to) she ~ed (to us) that our trip be/should be postponed

recommendation n. 1. to give smb. a ~ 2. to provide, write a ~ for smb. 3. to make a ~ 4. to act on, carry out, implement; consider a ~ 5. a lukewarm; negative; positive; strong; weak ~ 6. a ~ for 7. a ~ to (her ~ to us was to postpone the trip) 8. a ~ to + inf. (we ignored her ~ to postpone the trip) 9. a ~ that + clause; subj. (we ignored her ~ that our trip be/should be postponed) 10. at, on smb.'s ~ (we hired him on her ~)

recommit v. (D; tr.) ("to confine again") to ~ to (he was ~ted to the mental hospital)

recompense I n. (formal) 1. as (a) ~ (for) 2. in ~ (for)

recompense II v. (formal) (D; tr.) to ~ for

reconcile v. 1. (D; refl., tr.) to ~ to (he had to ~ himself to his fate) 2. (d; tr.) to ~ with (we tried to ~ her with her family; to ~ a checkbook with a bank statement)

reconciliation n. 1. to bring about, effect a ~ 2. a ~ between; with 3. (misc.) in a spirit of ~

reconnaissance n. 1. to carry out, conduct ~ 2. aerial ~ 3. (a) ~ in force

reconstruct v. (D; tr.) to ~ from (to ~ a crime from the evidence)

record I n. ["best performance"] 1. to establish, set a (new) ~ 2. to equal, tie a ~ 3. to beat, better, break, surpass a ~ 4. to hold a ~ 5. an unbroken ~ 6. an attendance; speed ~ 7. an all-time; national; Olympic; world ~ 8. ~s fall ["account of events"] ["file"] 9. to keep; make a ~ (to keep a ~ of events) 10. to close; open up a ~ 11. an accurate; detailed; official; sketchy; verbatim; written ~ 12. a daily; monthly; weekly ~ 13. an historical ~ 14. (a) public ~ (a matter of public ~) 15. a medical; school ~ 16. of; on ~ (the coldest day on ~) 17. (misc.) to set the ~ straight ("to correct a misunderstanding") ["past performance"] 18. to have a ~ 19. a clean, impeccable, spotless, unblemished ~ (when she came to the firm, she had a spotless ~) 20. a brilliant, distinguished, outstanding; excellent; good ~ (she has an excellent academic ~) 21. a mediocre, spotty ~ 22. an academic; safety; service ~ (this airline's safety ~ is impeccable) ["recorded crimes"] 23. to have a ~ (he's been in jail and has a ~) 24. a criminal, police; prison ~ ["publication"] ["public disclosure"] 25. to go on ~ (by; with) 26. for the ~ (was her statement for the ~?) 27. off; on the ~ (what she told the reporters was off the ~) ["grooved disc"] 28. to cut, make a ~ 29. to play a ~ 30. a gramophone (BE), phonograph (AE); long-playing ~

record II v. 1. to ~ live; openly; secretly 2. (D; tr.) to ~ from; on (we ~ed the program from the radio on our new tape recorder) 3. (L) ("to report") the newspapers ~ed that a new era in international cooperation had begun 4. (Q) ("to report") the investigators ~ed how the crime syndicate had been protected

recorder n. a flight; tape; video, video-cassette; voice ~ (see also **tape recorder**)

recording n. 1. to make a ~ 2. to play a ~ 3. a tape; video ~

records n. ["recorded information"] 1. to file; keep ~ 2. to dig up ~ 3. to destroy; falsify ~ 4. accurate ~

recount I n. 1. to do, make a ~ (of votes) 2. to ask for, demand a ~

recount II v. 1. (B) to ~ a story to smb. 2. (Q) she ~ed how it happened

recourse n. 1. to have ~ to 2. without ~ to

recover v. (D; intr., tr.) to ~ from (to ~ from an illness; the police ~ed the missing items from the bottom of the river)

recovery n. 1. to make a ~ 2. a complete; gradual; quick, rapid, speedy; remarkable; slow ~ (the patient made a quick ~) 3. an economic ~ 4. a ~ from 5. (misc.) to wish smb. a speedy ~

recreation n. for ~ (what do you do for ~?)

recriminations n. 1. bitter; mutual ~ 2. without ~

recruit I n. a fresh, green, raw ~

recruit II v. 1. (D; tr.) to ~ for (to ~ volunteers for charitable work) 2. (D; tr.) to ~ from; to (to ~ volunteers from friendly countries; to ~ members to a political party) 3. (H) to ~ mercenaries to serve in the army

recruiter n. an air force; army; marine; navy ~

rectitude n. moral ~

recuperate v. (D; intr.) to ~ from (to ~ from the flu)

recuperation n. 1. ~ from 2. (misc.) smb.'s powers of ~

recur v. (D; intr.) ("to come again to mind") to ~ to (that thought keeps ~ring to me)

recuse v. (esp. US) (D; refl.) to ~ from (the judge ~d herself from the case)

red I adj. 1. (of a traffic light) to turn ~ 2. (misc.) to

turn ~ with embarrassment; as ~ as a beet (AE), beetroot (BE)

red II n. ["color"] 1. (a) bright; dark; light ~ ["red light"] 2. on ~ (no turn on ~) ["debt"] 3. in the ~ (to operate in the ~) ["misc."] 4. to see ~ ("to become furious")

red carpet n. ["warm reception"] to put out, roll out the ~ for smb.

rededicate v. (d; refl., tr.) to ~ to (we must ~ ourselves to our cause)

rededication n. ~ to

redeem v. (D; tr.) to ~ from

redemption n. 1. ~ from 2. beyond, past ~

redeploy v. (D; tr.) to ~ from; to (troops were being ~ed from Europe to Asia)

redeployment n. 1. large-scale ~ (the large-scale ~ of troops) 2. ~ from; to

redevelopment n. urban ~

red-faced adj. ~ with (~ with shame)

red light n. 1. to go through, jump (BE), run (AE) a ~ (she ran a ~ and was fined) 2. at a ~ (to stop at a ~) 3. on a ~ (he went right through the intersection on a ~)

redolent adj. (formal) (cannot stand alone) ~ of, with (~ of honeysuckle)

redound v. (formal) (d; intr.) to ~ to ("to affect") (her success ~s to the credit of her teachers)

redress n. 1. to seek ~ 2. legal ~

red tape n. 1. to get caught up in, get involved in ~ 2. to cut, eliminate (the) ~ 3. bureaucratic; government ~

reduce v. 1. (D; tr.) to ~ by (the crime rate was ~d by ten percent) 2. (D; tr.) to ~ from; to (they ~d the dosage from four to three) 3. (d; tr.) to ~ in (he was ~d in rank) 4. (d; tr.) to ~ to (she was ~d to poverty; the corporal was ~d to the rank of private)

reduction n. 1. to take a ~ (in salary) 2. to make a (price) ~ 3. risk; stress; weight ~ 4. a ~ in (a ~ in salary) 5. a ~ to 6. at a ~ (to sell merchandise at a substantial ~)

reef n. 1. to strike a ~ (the ship struck a ~) 2. a barrier; coral ~

reek v. 1. (d; intr.) to ~ of (to ~ of alcohol) 2. (d; intr.) to ~ with (to ~ with sweat)

reel v. 1. (D; intr.) ("to stagger") to ~ under (to ~ under blows) 2. (misc.) it made my head ~

reelect v. (D; tr.) to ~ to (they were ~ed to Parliament)

reelection n. 1. to seek; win ~ 2. ~ to (~ to Congress)

reeling adj. to send smb. ~

reentry n. a ~ into (a spaceship's ~ into the atmosphere)

refer v. (d; intr., tr.) to ~ to (in her autobiography she never ~red to her parents; the problem was ~red to a committee; they ~red me to the manager)

refer back v. (d; tr.) to ~ to (the report was ~red

back to the committee)

reference *n.* ["mention, allusion"] 1. to make (a) ~ (she made no ~s to her opponents) 2. to contain a ~ (the statement contains several ~s to me) 3. a direct; indirect, oblique; passing ~ 4. (a) ~ to (without ~ to age) ["regard, relation"] 5. in, with; without ~ to 6. a frame of ~ ["recommendation"] ["statement"] 7. to give, provide a ~ 8. a good, positive, satisfactory; negative ~ 9. a character ~ (her employer gave her a good character ~) ["consultation"] ["source of information"] 10. easy; further; future; quick ~ 11. for ~ (to file for future ~)

referendum *n.* 1. to conduct, hold a ~ on 2. a ~ to + inf. (a ~ to determine the status of a territory) 3. (misc.) to decide (a question) by ~

referral *n.* 1. to make a ~ 2. a ~ from; to

refer to *v.* (D; tr.) to ~ as (he ~red to his opponent as a liar)

refill *n.* 1. to give smb. a ~ 2. a ~ for (a ~ for a ballpoint pen)

refine *v.* (d; intr.) (esp. BE) to ~ on, upon ("to improve") (to ~ on a method)

refinery *n.* an oil; sugar ~

reflect *v.* 1. ("to think about") to ~ closely; seriously 2. (D; intr.) to ~ on, upon ("to think about") (to ~ on one's past mistakes) 3. (d; intr.) to ~ on ("to discredit") (her unfounded accusations ~ed on her credibility) 4. (d; intr.) to ~ on ("to show") (her actions ~ badly/well on her upbringing) 5. (d; tr.) to ~ on ("to bring to") (the team's victory ~ed credit on the coach) 6. (Q) does this answer ~ how you feel?

reflection *n.* ["criticism"] 1. a ~ on (this is no ~ on your qualifications) ["meditation, thought"] 2. quiet; serious; sober ~ 3. ~ on (~s on the war) 4. after, on ~ (on further ~ she saw her mistake)

reflex *n.* 1. to test smb.'s ~es 2. a conditioned ~ 3. abnormal; diminished; hyperactive; normal ~es

reform *n.* 1. to carry out, effect a ~ 2. a far-reaching; radical, sweeping ~ 3. (an) agrarian, land; economic; educational; labor; penal, prison; political; social; tax; welfare ~ 4. (an) orthographic, spelling ~

reformatory *n.* (now AE; obsol.) at, in a ~ (he spent time at/in a ~)

reformer *n.* an economic; political; social ~

refraction *n.* ["eye examination"] (AE) to do a ~ (the oculist did a ~)

refrain I *n.* to repeat; sing a ~

refrain II *v.* (D; intr.) to ~ from (to ~ from smoking)

refresh *v.* (d; refl., tr.) to ~ by; with (they ~ed themselves with a dip in the pool)

refreshing *adj.* ~ to + inf. (it was ~ to find such honesty)

refreshments *n.* 1. to offer, provide, serve ~ 2. light; liquid ~

refrigeration *n.* under ~ (to keep food under ~)

refrigerator *n.* 1. to defrost a ~ 2. a frostfree ~ 3. an electric; gas ~ 4. (misc.) to raid the ~ ("to consume large quantities of food from the refrigerator, esp. at night")

refueling, refuelling *n.* inflight, midair ~

refuge *n.* 1. to give, provide ~ 2. to find, take; seek ~ 3. a wildlife ~ 4. a place of ~ 5. ~ from (to take ~ from the storm)

refugee *n.* 1. a political; stateless ~ 2. a ~ from

refund I *n.* 1. to give, pay a ~ 2. to get, receive a ~ 3. a tax ~

refund II *v.* 1. (A) (BE) they ~ed the money to us; or: they ~ed us the money 2. (B) (AE) the manager ~ed the purchase price to the customer

refusal *n.* 1. an adamant, brusque, categorical, curt, flat, out-and-out, outright, point-blank, unyielding ~ 2. a polite ~ 3. a straightforward ~ 4. a first ~ (BE; CE has *first option*) 5. a ~ to + inf. (I could not comprehend her ~ to help) 6. (misc.) to meet with a ~

refuse I *n.* (BE) to collect the ~ (see also **garbage, trash**)

refuse II *v.* 1. to ~ categorically, completely, flatly, outright, point-blank 2. (E) she ~d to see him 3. (O; can be used with one object) he ~d them nothing

refute *v.* to ~ completely

regain *v.* (D; tr.) to ~ from

regale *v.* (d; tr.) to ~ by; with (to ~ one's guests with funny stories)

regalia *n.* in full ~

regard I *n.* ["consideration"] 1. to show ~ 2. ~ for (she shows no ~ for the feelings of others; you must have ~ for our safety) 3. little, scant ~ ["esteem"] 4. high; low ~ (to hold smb. in high ~) ["aspect, relation"] 5. in a ~ (in this ~) 6. in, with ~ to (in ~ to your request, no decision has been made)

regard II *v.* 1. to ~ highly (highly ~ed in the scientific community) 2. (d; tr.) to ~ as (to ~ smb. as a friend) 3. (d; tr.) to ~ with (to ~ smb. with contempt)

regardless *adj.* ~ of

regards *n.* ["greetings"] 1. to convey smb.'s ~; to send one's ~ 2. to give smb. one's ~ 3. best, cordial, friendly, kind, kindest, sincere, warm, warmest; personal ~ (with best personal ~) 4. ~ from; to (best ~ to your family from all of us)

regatta *n.* an annual ~

regime *n.* 1. to establish a ~ 2. to bring down, overthrow a ~ 3. an authoritarian, dictatorial, totalitarian; puppet; repressive ~ 4. under a ~ (we all suffered under the repressive regime)

regimen *n.* to put smb. on a ~ 2. to follow a ~ 3. a daily; strict ~

regiment *n.* 1. a Guards (GB); infantry ~ 2. a colonel commands a ~

region *n.* 1. a border; mountainous; outlying, remote; polar; tropical; unpopulated ~ 2. an autonomous ~ 3. (misc.) in the ~ of the lungs

register I *n.* ["record, record book"] 1. to keep a ~ 2. a case; hotel ~ ["roster"] 3. (BE) an electoral ~ 4. the Social Register ["machine that registers the amount of each sale"] 5. a cash ~

register II *v.* 1. (D; intr., tr.) to ~ as (she ~ed as a Republican; he was not ~ed as a voter) 2. (D; intr., tr.) to ~ for (she ~ed for two courses; our department(al) secretary has ~ed ten students for the seminar) 3. (D; intr., tr.) to ~ in (how many ~ed/are ~ed in the course?) 4. (D; intr., tr.) to ~ with (he had to ~ with the authorities; to ~ a pistol with the police) 5. (E) have you ~ed to vote? 6. (misc.) the earthquake ~ed six on the Richter scale

registration *n.* 1. to conduct ~ 2. gun; voter ~ 3. ~ for (~ for this course has been completed)

regress *v.* (D; intr.) to ~ to (to ~ to one's childhood)

regret I *n.* 1. to express; have ~(s) 2. to feel; show ~ 3. bitter; deep, great, keen, sincere ~ 4. a token of (one's) ~ 5. ~ at, over; for (to express ~ at not being able to accept an invitation; ~ for one's mistake) 6. to smb.'s ~ (to my ~, she retired last year) 7. with ~ (with sincere ~ we announce that he passed away last night)

regret II *v.* 1. to ~ deeply, very much 2. (formal) (E) we ~ to inform you that your position has been eliminated 3. (G) I ~ having to leave so early 4. (K) everyone ~ted his being dismissed 5. (L) we ~ that we cannot accept your invitation

regrets *n.* ["expression of regret at declining an invitation"] 1. to send (one's) ~ 2. (esp. AE) ~ only (appears on invitations instructing recipients to respond only if they are unable to accept)

regrettable *adj.* ~ that + clause (it was ~ that they could not attend)

regulation *n.* 1. to adopt, enact a ~ 2. to apply, enforce a ~ 3. to obey, observe a ~ 4. to ignore; violate a ~ 5. rigid, strict ~s 6. army; government; health; police; safety, security; traffic ~s 7. a ~ that + clause; subj. (we obeyed the ~ that no cars be/should be parked there)

rehabilitation *n.* physical ~

rehearsal *n.* 1. to conduct, have, hold; schedule a ~ 2. a dress, final ~ 3. a ~ for 4. at a ~ (I'll see you at the dress ~) 5. in ~ (the play is in ~)

rehearse *v.* (D; intr., tr.) to ~ for (to ~ for a concert)

reign I *n.* during smb.'s ~

reign II *v.* 1. (D; intr.) to ~ as (she ~ed as queen for many years) 2. (D; intr.) to ~ over 3. (s) to ~ supreme

reimburse *v.* 1. to ~ amply, fully, generously 2. (rare) (B) all expenses will be ~d to you 3. (D; tr.) to ~ for (you will be ~d for all expenses)

reimbursement *n.* ~ for

rein I *n.* ["control"] 1. to keep a ~ on 2. to give free, full ~ to ("to remove restraints on") 3. a tight ~ (to keep a tight ~ on smb.) 4. (misc.) to seize the ~s of government

rein II *v.* (D; tr.) to ~ to (to ~ a horse to the left)

reinforcements *n.* to bring up; commit; send ~

reins *n.* ["straps used to control an animal"] 1. to draw in, tighten the ~ 2. to pull on the ~ ["control"] 3. to hold; take over the ~ (of government)

reinstate *v.* 1. (D; tr.) to ~ as (she was ~d as treasurer) 2. (D; tr.) to ~ in (to ~ smb. in her/his former position)

reissue *v.* (B) the supply sergeant ~d ammunition to the platoon

reiterate *v.* 1. (B) she ~d her story to the police 2. (L) he ~d that he would resign

reject *v.* to ~ completely, flatly, outright, totally

rejection *n.* complete, flat, outright, total ~

rejoice *v.* 1. (D; intr.) to ~ at, in, over (they ~d at the good news) 2. (E) (rare) she ~d to see her old comrades again 3. (L) we ~d that the war was over

rejoinder *n.* 1. a sharp; telling ~ 2. a ~ to

relapse I *n.* (esp. medical) 1. to have, suffer a ~ 2. a complete, total ~ 3. a ~ into

relapse II *v.* (D; intr.) to ~ into (to ~ into a coma; to ~ into bad habits)

relate *v.* 1. (B) she ~d her version of the incident to the police 2. (d; intr.) to ~ to (this law does not ~ to your case; how do they ~ to each other?) 3. (L; to) she ~d to the police that the attack was unprovoked 4. (Q; to) they ~d to the police how the robbery had been planned

related *adj.* 1. closely; distantly ~ 2. ~ by; to (I am ~ to him by marriage)

relation *n.* 1. to bear; have a ~ to (X bears no ~ to Y) 2. a ~ between 3. in ~ to

relations *n.* 1. to establish; have, maintain; normalize; renew ~ 2. to cement, improve, promote, strengthen ~ 3. to break off, sever; strain ~ (to break off diplomatic ~ with a country) 4. close, intimate; cordial, friendly, harmonious; strained, troubled ~ 5. business, commercial, economic, trade; diplomatic; foreign; industrial, labor; international ~ 6. human; public; race ~ 7. extramarital; marital; premarital; sexual ~ (to have sexual ~ with smb.) 8. ~ among, between; with 9. (misc.) friends and ~ ("friends and relatives")

relationship *n.* 1. to build; cement; enter into, establish, strike up a ~ (to establish a ~ with smb.) 2. to have a ~ with smb. 3. to bear, have a ~ (to bear a ~ to smt.) 4. to break off a ~ (to break off a ~ with smb.) 5. a casual; close, intimate; direct; indirect; meaningful; solid; stormy, tempestuous; symbiotic; tenuous; warm ~ 6. a doctor-patient ~ 7. an extramarital; incestuous ~; interpersonal; spatial ~s 8. an inverse ~ 9. a ~ between; to, towards; with

relative I *adj.* ~ to

relative II *n.* a blood; close; distant ~; smb.'s closest, nearest ~s

relax *v.* (G) they ~ watching TV

relaxant *n.* a muscle ~

relaxation *n.* for ~ (what do you do for ~?)

relaxing *adj.* ~ to + inf. (it is ~ to spend a few days on the beach)

relay I *n.* 1. to run a ~ 2. (misc.) to work in ~s

relay II *v.* (B) she ~ed the information to us

release I *n.* ["liberation"] 1. to bring about, effect, secure smb.'s ~ 2. a ~ from (a ~ from prison) ["surrender of a claim or right"] (legal) 3. to agree to; sign a ~ ["handing over"] 4. ~ to (the ~ of information to the press) 5. a news, press ~ ["recording"] 6. a new ~; the latest ~s

release II *v.* 1. (D; tr.) to ~ from (he has been ~d from prison) 2. (D; tr.) to ~ into; to (the judge ~d the youthful culprit to his parents; the film has been ~d to various movie theaters; the information was ~d to the press; some offenders were ~d into the community)

relegate *v.* 1. (d; tr.) to ~ to (to ~ smb. to second-class status) 2. (misc.) (GB) to ~ a club to the second division

relevance *n.* 1. to have ~ to 2. of ~ to (his testimony is of no ~ to the case)

relevant *adj.* ~ to (the evidence is ~ to the case)

reliance *n.* ~ on

reliant *adj.* (cannot stand alone) ~ on

relics *n.* ancient; holy ~; ~ of the past

relief *n.* ["easing of pain, of a burden"] 1. to bring; give ~ 2. to seek ~ 3. to find; receive ~ (they found ~ in looking at their late son's photographs) 4. to express; feel ~ 5. great, immense; instant; permanent; temporary ~ 6. (esp. BE) (eligible for) tax ~ 7. ~ from (the rain brought instant ~ from the heat) 8. ~ to (the news was a great ~ to us) 9. a ~ to + inf. (it was a ~ to get home) 10. ~ that + clause (they expressed ~ that the crisis was over) 11. in ~ (to sigh in ~) 12. to smb.'s ~ (to my ~ they got there safely) ["welfare, government aid"] (esp. AE; obsol.) 13. on ~ (in the 1930s they were on ~) ["comic scenes"] 14. comic; mock (AE) ~ ["differences in height"] 15. in ~ (to show terrain in ~) ["sharpness of outline"] 16. in bold ~ against (a light background) ["material help"] 17. to provide, send ~ 18. emergency; famine; flood ~

relieve *v.* 1. (D; tr.) to ~ of (the general was ~d of her command) 2. (R) it ~d me to learn that they were safe

relieved *adj.* 1. ~ at (we were ~ at the news) 2. ~ to + inf. (we were ~ to learn that they had arrived safely) 3. ~ that + clause (we were ~ that they had arrived safely)

religion *n.* ["formal belief in a divine power"] 1. to adhere to; embrace; practice a ~ 2. to abjure, recant, renounce a ~ 3. a fundamentalist; monotheistic; polytheistic ~ 4. (an) established, organized ~ 5. a personal; state ~ ["study of systems of worship"] 6. comparative ~(s)

religious *adj.* deeply, profoundly, very ~

relinquish *v.* (B) ("to yield") he ~ed his business interests to his children

relish I *n.* ["enjoyment"] 1. to show ~ for 2. with ~ (we listened to their story with great ~)

relish II *v.* 1. (G) I don't ~ confronting him 2. (K) no one ~es his coming here

relocate *v.* (D; intr., tr.) to ~ in, to (the firm has ~d to a southern state)

reluctance *n.* 1. to display, show ~ 2. extreme, great ~ 3. ~ to + inf. (her ~ to get involved was understandable) 4. with ~ (they agreed with great ~)

reluctant *adj.* (usu. does not stand alone) ~ to + inf. (we were ~ to act)

rely *v.* 1. to ~ heavily 2. (d; intr.) to ~ on, upon (to ~ on smb. for advice) 3. to ~ on, upon to + inf. (we ~ on them to lock up after we leave)

remain *v.* 1. (D; intr.) to ~ of (did anything ~ of the wreckage?) 2. (E) that ~s to be seen 3. (S) she ~ed a widow for the rest of her life; to ~ silent

remains *n.* 1. to exhume ~ 2. animal; human; mortal ~

remand I *n.* on ~ ("in prison awaiting trial")

remand II *v.* 1. (d; tr.) ("to send") to ~ to (the judge ~ed the accused to the county jail) 2. (misc.) ~ed in custody ("sent back to prison")

remark I *n.* 1. to drop, make a ~ 2. to pass a ~ (they passed several sarcastic ~s about the food) 3. a complimentary; flattering; friendly; kind; reassuring; timely ~ 4. a droll; facetious; tongue-in-cheek; witty ~ 5. a pertinent; pithy; pointed ~ 6. a casual; innocent; innocuous; off-the-cuff; passing ~ 7. a controversial; cryptic, puzzling; provocative; suggestive ~ 8. an inane; indiscreet; tasteless; trite; trivial ~ 9. a biting, catty, caustic, cutting, nasty, sarcastic, scathing, snide; cruel, unkind; cynical; derogatory; disparaging, insulting, offensive, rude; impertinent; slanderous ~ 10. smb.'s closing, concluding; introductory, opening ~s 11. a ~ about 12. a ~ that + clause (she made the ~ that being interviewed was boring)

remark II *v.* 1. (d; intr.) to ~ on, upon (the visitors ~ed on the excellent condition of the streets) 2. (L; to) she ~ed (to us) that she found our story very strange

remarkable *adj.* 1. ~ for 2. ~ to + inf. (it's ~ to see such clean streets) 3. ~ that + clause (it's ~ that the streets are so clean after the parade)

remedy *n.* 1. to resort to, use a ~ 2. to prescribe a ~ 3. to provide a ~ (for) 4. (legal) to pursue a (legal) ~ 5. (legal) to exhaust all (legal) ~ies 6. a certain, reliable, sure; effective, efficacious ~ 7. a cold; cough ~ 8. a folk; herbal; home; homeopathic ~ 9. a ~ for

remember *v.* 1. to ~ clearly, distinctly; dimly, vaguely 2. (B; colloq. the direct object is always a personal pronoun) please ~ me to your family ("please give my regards to your family") 3. (D; tr.) to ~ about (do you ~ anything about the incident?) 4. (D; tr.) to ~ as (I ~ her as a young girl) 5. (D; tr.) to ~ of (what do you ~ of them?) 6. (E) she ~ed to buy a newspaper 7. (G) she ~ed buying the newspaper 8. (J) I ~ him being very generous 9. (K) I ~ his being very generous 10. (L) she ~ed that she had an appointment 11. (Q) I could not ~ how to open the safe
USAGE NOTE: The sentence *she didn't remember to buy a newspaper* means "she forgot to buy a newspaper". The sentence *she didn't remember buying a newspaper* means "she had no memory of buying a newspaper", whether she bought one or not.

remembrance *n.* in ~ of

remind *v.* 1. (d; tr.) ("to cause to remember") to ~ about, of (he ~ed me of my promise) 2. (d; tr.) ("to call to mind") to ~ of (she ~s me of my cousin) 3. (H) she ~ed me to buy a newspaper 4. (L; must have an object) we ~ed them that the meeting had been postponed 5. (Q; must have an object) we ~ed them why the meeting had been postponed

reminder *n.* 1. to serve as a ~ 2. a bitter; eloquent; final; gentle; grim ~ 3. a ~ to + inf. (we received a ~ to pay the rent) 4. a ~ that + clause (we received a ~ that the rent was due)

reminisce *v.* (D; intr.) to ~ about

reminiscences *n.* 1. personal ~ 2. ~ about

reminiscent *adj.* (cannot stand alone) ~ of (that melody is ~ of the old days)

remiss *adj.* (formal) 1. ~ about, in (~ in performing one's duties) 2. ~ to + inf. (it was ~ of me not to write)

remission *n.* ["lessening of the effects of a disease"] (med.) in ~

remit I *n.* (BE) ["assignment, area of responsibility"] 1. a limited; wide ~ 2. a ~ to + inf. (they have a ~ to investigate the company's affairs)

remit II *v.* 1. (BE) (A) they ~ted the money to us; or: they ~ted us the money 2. (AE) (B) they ~ted the money to us

remittance *n.* 1. to enclose; send a ~ 2. (obsol.) (BE) a ~ man ("one living abroad on money sent from home") 3. on ~ of (you will receive the book on ~ of the balance)

remonstrate *v.* (formal) (D; intr.) to ~ about, against; with (they ~d with the neighbors about the noise)

remorse *n.* 1. to display, exhibit, show ~ 2. to express; feel ~ 3. bitter, deep, profound ~ 4. a feeling; stab; twinge of ~ 5. ~ for, over (he displayed no ~ for his crimes)

remote *adj.* ~ from

removal *n.* 1. snow ~ 2. (BE) furniture ~ 3. ~ from

remove *v.* (D; tr.) to ~ from; to (to ~ a dressing from a wound)

removed *adj.* 1. easily ~ 2. once; twice ~ (a first cousin once ~) 3. far ~ from

remover *n.* (a) nail-polish, nail-varnish (BE); paint; rust; spot ~

remunerate *v.* (formal) (D; tr.) to ~ for

remuneration *n.* 1. to offer ~ 2. to accept ~ 3. ~ for

rename *v.* (N; used with a noun) the file has been ~d "miscellaneous"

rend *v.* (D; tr.) ("to tear") to ~ into (to ~ one's clothes into shreds)

render *v.* 1. (A) she ~ed a valuable service to me; or: she ~ed me a valuable service 2. (formal) (D; tr.) to ~ into (to ~ a text into English) 3. (N; used with an adjective) her remark ~ed me speechless

rendezvous *n.* 1. to have; make a ~ with 2. a secret ~

rendition *n.* 1. to give a ~ 2. a letter-perfect (AE), word-perfect (BE) ~

renege *v.* (D; intr.) to ~ on (to ~ on a commitment)

renewal *n.* urban ~

renounce *v.* (D; tr.) to ~ for (to ~ wealth for happiness)

renovations *n.* to make ~

renown *n.* 1. to achieve, attain, win ~ 2. great, wide ~ 3. international, worldwide; national ~ 4. of ~ (an artist of great ~)

renowned *adj.* 1. internationally; nationally; widely ~ 2. ~ as; for (~ as a pianist; ~ for one's inventions)

rent I *n.* 1. to pay ~ for 2. to raise the ~ 3. (AE) for ~ (the house is for ~) (BE has *the house is to let*) 4. (misc.) ~ control; to pay five hundred dollars (in) ~

rent II *v.* 1. (A) she ~ed a room to me; or: she ~ed me a room 2. (D; tr.) to ~ from (to ~ a house from smb.) 3. (esp. AE) (d; intr.) to ~ to (she ~s to students) 4. (esp. AE) (d; intr., tr.) to ~ at, for (the room ~ed at five hundred dollars a month)

rental *n.* 1. car; film; office ~ 2. ~ to

rent out *v.* (B) to ~ rooms to students (see also **let out**)

reorganization *n.* to undergo ~

repair I *n.* ["process of restoring to working order"] 1. to do, make a ~ (we have done the necessary ~s) 2. extensive, major; minor; necessary ~s 3. ~s to (the ~s to our roof cost one hundred dollars) 4. under ~ (the road is under ~) ["condition"] 5. in ~ (to keep a car in good ~; in poor ~)

repair II *v.* (formal or humorous) (d; intr.) ("to go") to ~ to (to ~ to the drawing room)

reparations *n.* 1. to pay ~ 2. war ~ 3. ~ for

repartee *n.* witty ~

repast *n.* (formal or humorous) a light, meager ~

repatriate *v.* (D; tr.) to ~ from; to

repatriation *n.* 1. forced ~ 2. ~ from; to

repay *v.* 1. (A) she repaid the money to me; or: she repaid me the money 2. (D; tr.) to ~ by; with (the firm repaid me with a promotion for my hard work) 3. (D; tr.) to ~ for (I repaid him for his expenses) 4. (D; tr.) to ~ to (to ~ a loan to a bank)

repeat *v.* 1. (B) she ~ed her story to us 2. (D; intr.) ("to cause an unpleasant aftertaste") to ~ on (this type of food ~s on me) 3. (L; to) he ~ed (to me) that he would buy some stamps 4. (misc.) ~ after me; to ~ verbatim

repellent I *adj.* 1. ~ to 2. (misc.) a water-repellent fabric

repellent II *n.* an insect; mosquito ~

repent *v.* 1. to ~ sincerely 2. (D; intr.) to ~ for, of (to ~ of one's sins) 3. (rare) (G) he ~ed having stolen the car

repentance *n.* 1. to show ~ for 2. genuine, sincere ~

repercussions *n.* 1. to have ~ on 2. far-reaching; serious; unexpected ~

repertoire *n.* 1. the standard ~ 2. in a ~ (our company has several new plays in its ~)

repertory *n.* in ~ (to play in ~)

replace *v.* 1. (D; tr.) to ~ as (when my sister fell ill, they asked me to ~ her as secretary) 2. (D; tr.) to ~ by, with

replacement *n.* 1. to make a ~ 2. to get, receive a ~ for 3. (misc.) the ~ of smt. by smt. else

replay *n.* action (BE), instant (AE) ~

replenish *v.* (D; tr.) to ~ with

replete *adj.* ~ with

reply I *n.* 1. to give a ~ 2. to send a ~ 3. to get, receive a ~ 4. to draw, elicit a ~ 5. a favorable; witty ~ 6. a straightforward; succinct ~ 7. an immediate, prompt ~ 8. a brusque, curt, gruff; stinging; sullen; terse ~ 9. a ~ to 10. in ~ (to nod in ~) 11. in ~ to (in ~ to your letter)

reply II *v.* 1. to ~ immediately, promptly 2. (D; intr.) to ~ to (she did not ~ to my letter) 3. (D; intr.) to ~ with (she replied to my letter with one of her own) 4. (L; to) she replied that she would be happy to accept our invitation

report I *n.* 1. to file, give, make, present, submit a ~ 2. to do, draw up, make out, write, write out, work up a ~ 3. to confirm a ~ 4. an accurate; balanced; confirmed; detailed, exhaustive, full; favorable, positive; impartial, objective ~ 5. a biased, slanted; negative, unfavorable; sketchy; unconfirmed ~ 6. an annual; daily; monthly; morning; weekly ~ 7. a final; interim; preliminary; status ~ 8. an oral; written ~ 9. an eyewitness; firsthand ~ 10. an accident; incident ~ 11. a live; news; newspaper; press; radio; traffic; TV; weather ~ 12. a classified; committee; confidential; intelligence; official; restricted; secret; special; top secret ~ 13. a majority; minority ~ 14. a school ~ (BE; AE has *report card*) 15. a ~ about, on; to (she filed a ~ about the incident; the annual ~ to stockholders)

16. a ~ that + clause (we have heard ~s that the road is closed)

report II *v.* 1. (B) ("to relate") we ~ed the information to the authorities 2. (D; intr.) to ~ about, on ("to describe") (the correspondent ~ed on the situation at the front) 3. (d; intr.) ("to describe") to ~ as (the fire was ~ed as burning out of control) 4. (D; intr.) ("to present oneself") to ~ for; to (to ~ to headquarters for duty) 5. (D; tr.) ("to inform on") to ~ for; to (to ~ smb. to the police for violating an ordinance) 6. (d; intr.) ("to send information") to ~ from (during the war, she ~ed from London) 7. (pol.) (D; tr.) to ~ out of ("to return smt. for further action") (to ~ a bill out of committee) 8. (d; intr.) to ~ to ("to answer to") (she ~s directly to the dean) 9. (D; intr.) ("to give information") to ~ to (I'll be ~ing to you soon) 10. (G) ("to make known") several people ~ed having seen the stolen car 11. (K) ("to make known") smb. ~ed their leaving early 12. (L; to) ("to relate") she ~ed (to us) that she had accomplished her mission 13. (M) ("to describe") the fire was ~ed to be burning out of control 14. (N; used with an adjective, past participle) ("to describe") the patrol ~ed the entire area clear/cleared; he was ~ed missing in action 15. (Q; to) ("to describe") they ~ed to us how the incident took place 16. (esp. BE) (s) to ~ sick

report back *v.* 1. (D; intr.) to ~ to (you will ~ to the chairperson of the committee) 2. (L; to) they will ~ to the committee that all goals have been reached

reported *adj.* (cannot stand alone) 1. ~ to + inf. (they were ~ to be safe) 2. ~ that + clause (it was ~ed that they were safe)

reporter *n.* a court; cub; financial; free-lance; investigative; news; police; radio; roving; science; society; sports; TV ~

report in *v.* (AE) (s) to ~ sick

reporting *n.* 1. balanced; impartial, objective ~ 2. biased, slanted ~ 3. investigative ~

repose *n.* in (a state of) ~

represent *v.* 1. ("to depict") to ~ graphically 2. (B) ("to be the equivalent of") this room ~ed home to them 3. (esp. BE) (B) ("to convey") to ~ one's grievances to the authorities 4. (d; refl., tr.) ("to depict") to ~ as (she was ~ed as an heroic pioneer) 5. (S; used with nouns) ("to be") this ~s a serious problem

representation *n.* ["statement"] ["protest"] 1. to make ~s to (our ambassador made ~s to their government) ["act of representing"] 2. legal ~ (they insisted on having legal ~) 3. proportional ~

representative I *adj.* ~ of

representative II *n.* 1. a sales ~ (BE also had *commercial traveller*) 2. an elected ~

repression *n.* 1. political; sexual ~ 2. (to live) under ~

repressive *adj.* ~ of

reprieve *n.* 1. to give, grant a ~ 2. to get, receive a ~ 3. a last-minute ~ 4. a ~ from

reprimand I *n.* 1. to administer, give, issue a ~ (the judge issued a ~ from the bench) 2. to receive a ~ 3. a mild; severe, sharp, stern ~ 4. an oral, verbal; written ~ 5. a public ~

reprimand II *v.* (D; tr.) to ~ for (to ~ an employee for being late)

reprint *n.* to issue a ~ (of a book)

reprisal *n.* 1. to carry out ~s 2. a harsh ~ 3. a ~ against, on 4. in ~ (for) 5. (misc.) as a ~; by way of ~

reproach I *n.* 1. a bitter ~ 2. a term of ~ 3. above, beyond ~

reproach II *v.* 1. to ~ bitterly 2. (D; refl., tr.) to ~ for

reproduce *v.* (D; tr.) to ~ from (to ~ a photograph from an old negative)

reproduction *n.* ["copy"] 1. (a) high-fidelity; stereophonic ~ ["biological process of reproducing"] 2. animal; human; plant ~ 3. asexual; sexual ~

reprove *v.* (formal) (D; tr.) to ~ for

reptile *n.* ~s crawl, creep, slither

republic *n.* 1. to establish a ~ 2. an autonomous; banana (obsol.); democratic; people's ~

Republican *n.* (US) a registered ~

repugnance *n.* 1. to feel ~ 2. (a) deep, profound ~

repugnant *adj.* ~ to

repulsive *adj.* ~ to

reputation *n.* 1. to acquire, earn, establish, gain, get a ~ 2. to enjoy, have a ~ (he had the ~ of being a heavy drinker) 3. to guard, protect one's ~ 4. to compromise, blacken, blemish, damage, destroy, ruin, smear, tarnish smb.'s ~ 5. an enviable, excellent, fine, good, impeccable, spotless, unblemished, unsullied, untainted, untarnished ~ 6. a tainted, tarnished, unenviable ~ 7. an international, worldwide; local; national ~ 8. a ~ suffers 9. a ~ as, for (that judge has a ~ for being fair) 10. by ~ (to know smb. by ~) 11. (misc.) to live up to one's ~; to stake one's ~ on smt.

repute *n.* 1. high ~ (to be held in high ~) 2. ill, low ~ (a place of ill ~; to be held in low ~) 3. by ~

reputed *adj.* (cannot stand alone) 1. generally, widely ~ 2. ~ to + inf. (she is ~ to be very generous)

request I *n.* 1. to file, make, submit a ~ (to file a ~ with the appropriate authorities; she has a ~ to make of us; to submit a ~ to the mayor's office) 2. to act on, agree to; grant, honor a ~ 3. to deny, refuse, reject, turn down a ~ 4. a moderate, modest; polite; reasonable ~ 5. a desperate, urgent; unreasonable ~ 6. a formal; official; written ~ 7. an informal; oral; unofficial ~ 8. a ~ for (to make a ~ for more money) 9. a ~ to + inf. (a ~ to be allowed to leave) 10. a ~ that + clause; subj. (we submitted a ~ that more lights be/should be installed on our street) 11. at smb.'s ~ (she did it at my ~) 12. by,

on, upon ~ (brochures are mailed out on ~) 13. (misc.) this radio station takes and plays ~s if you phone them in

request II *v.* 1. (D; tr.) to ~ from; of (to ~ a favor of smb.) 2. (H) to ~ smb. to do smt. 3. (L; subj.) she ~ed that I be/should be there

require *v.* 1. (D; tr.) to ~ from, of (she ~s a term paper of each student) 2. (G) the house ~s painting 3. (H) we ~ all incoming students to take placement examinations 4. (K) this position ~s your getting here on time every day 5. (L; subj.) she ~d that everyone attend/should attend the meeting

requirement *n.* 1. to establish, set ~s 2. to fill, fulfill, meet, satisfy a ~ 3. to waive a ~ 4. admission, entrance; distributional (AE); legal; minimum; physical ~s 5. a ~ that + clause; subj. (this candidate does not meet the ~ that secondary school be/should have been completed)

requisite *n.* a ~ for

requisition I *n.* 1. to make out, write out a ~ 2. to send in, submit a ~ 3. to fill a ~ 4. a ~ for 5. on ~ (that item is on ~)

requisition II *v.* (D; tr.) to ~ for

rerun *n.* to show a ~ (that channel keeps showing ~s of old TV programs)

rescue I *n.* 1. to attempt; effect, make, mount a ~ 2. to come/go to smb.'s ~ 3. a daring, heroic ~ 4. a ~ from

rescue II *v.* (D; tr.) to ~ from

research I *n.* 1. to carry out, conduct, do, pursue ~ 2. to publish one's ~ 3. detailed, diligent, laborious, painstaking, solid, thorough ~ 4. independent; original ~ 5. qualitative; quantitative ~ 6. animal; biological; historical; medical; scientific ~ 7. market; operations; space ~ 8. ~ in, into, on (~ on the development of an electric engine)

research II *v.* (BE) (D; intr.) to ~ into (to ~ into new methods)

researcher *n.* an independent ~

resemblance *n.* 1. to bear, have a ~ to 2. a close, strong; faint, remote, slight; striking; superficial; uncanny ~ 3. a family ~ 4. a ~ between; to

resemble *v.* to ~ closely, strongly; remotely, slightly

resent *v.* 1. to ~ bitterly, deeply, strongly 2. (G) she ~s having to wait 3. (J) we ~ him being the center of attraction 4. (K) we ~ed his being the center of attraction

resentful *adj.* 1. bitterly, very ~ 2. ~ about, at, of

resentment *n.* 1. to arouse, cause, stir up ~ 2. to bear, feel, harbor ~ 3. to express, voice ~ 4. bitter, deep, profound, sullen ~ 5. widespread ~ 6. ~ about, over; against; at, towards 7. ~ that + clause (they felt ~ that nobody paid attention to their request)

reservation *n.* ["booking"] 1. to make a ~ (we made a ~ at a very good hotel) 2. to confirm a ~ 3. to have a ~ (we have a ~ at the restaurant) 4. to cancel a ~ 5. an advance ~ 6. a hotel, motel ~ ["qualification"] 7. a mental ~ 8. without ~ ["tract of land"] 9. an Indian; military ~ 10. on a ~ ["strip of land"] (BE) 11. a central ~ (on a road)

reservations *n.* ["doubts"] 1. to have ~ 2. to express ~ (they expressed strong ~ about the plan) 3. deep, strong ~ 4. ~ about (do you have any ~ about the agreement?)

reserve I *n.* ["restraint, coolness"] 1. to display, show ~ 2. to break down smb.'s ~ ["limitation, restriction"] 3. without ~ (to accept a proposal without ~) ["availability"] 4. in ~ (to hold/keep smt. in ~) ["tract of land"] 5. an Indian (in Canada); nature; wild-life ~ ["military force kept available for future use"] 6. the active; inactive ~ ["store"] 7. to build up a ~

reserve II *v.* 1. (D; tr.) ("to set aside") to ~ for (these seats are ~d for the handicapped) 2. (esp. AE) (D; tr.) ("to order in advance") to ~ for (we have ~d a room for you) (BE also has *to book*)

reserved *adj.* ["restrained, reticent"] 1. ~ about 2. ~ towards, with

reserves *n.* ["forces kept available for future use"] (usu. mil. and sports) 1. to call out, call up the ~ 2. to commit one's ~ 3. limited; unlimited ~ ["stores"] 4. to build up ~ 5. to deplete, exhaust the ~ 6. coal; currency; gas; oil ~ 7. abundant; limited, meager; limitless, unlimited; untapped ~

reservoir *n.* 1. an artificial; natural ~ 2. (misc.) an untapped ~ of talent

reside *v.* (P; intr.) they ~ in London

residence *n.* ["home, abode"] 1. to establish, take up ~ 2. to change one's (place of) ~ 3. one's legal; permanent ~ ["state of being officially present"] 4. in ~ (a poet in ~; the Queen is in ~ at Balmoral)

resign *v.* 1. (D; intr.) to ~ from (she ~ed from her job) 2. (d; refl.) to ~ to (he ~ed himself to his fate)

resignation *n.* ["act of resigning"] 1. to hand in, offer, submit, tender one's ~ 2. to withdraw one's ~ 3. to accept; reject smb.'s ~ 4. a ~ from

resigned *adj.* ["submissive"] ~ to (~ to one's fate)

resist *v.* 1. to ~ strenuously, vigorously 2. (G) they couldn't ~ making fun of him

resistance *n.* 1. to offer, put up ~ 2. to break down, crush, overcome, overpower, put down, smash, wear down ~ 3. to encounter, meet with, run into ~ 4. determined, fierce, stiff, strong, stubborn, valiant ~ 5. armed; non-violent, passive; spotty; token; weak ~ 6. ~ hardens, stiffens 7. ~ crumbles 8. ~ to (~ to a disease) 9. (misc.) a pocket of ~; the line/path (AE) of least ~; her ~ was low and she came down with a severe cold

resistant *adj.* ~ to (~ to change)

resolute *adj.* ~ in (~ in one's decision to do smt.)

resolution *n.* ["decision"] 1. to draft; propose a ~ 2. to adopt, pass a ~ 3. to reject a ~ 4. a joint ~ (of

Congress) 5. a ~ to + inf. (they adopted a ~ to increase membership dues) 6. a ~ that + clause; subj. (a ~ was passed that aid to farmers be/should be increased) ["vow"] 7. to make a (New Year's) ~ ["resolve"] 8. (a) firm ~ ["fine detail"] (optics) 9. sharp ~

resolve I *n.* 1. to display, show ~ 2. to strengthen one's/smb.'s ~ 3. to shake, weaken smb.'s ~ 4. (a) firm ~ 5. a ~ to + inf. (nothing shook his ~ to become an engineer)

resolve II *v.* 1. (BE) (d; intr.) ("to decide") to ~ against (they ~d against going out on strike) 2. (D; tr.) to ~ into (to ~ a problem into simple components) 3. (BE) (d; intr.) ("to decide") to ~ on, upon (they ~d on leaving early) 4. (E) she ~d to work harder 5. (L) we ~d that we would resist to the end

resolved *adj.* (usu. does not stand alone) 1. firmly ~ 2. ~ to + inf. (we are ~ to finish the work on time) 3. (formal) ~ that + clause; subj. (be it ~ that an official delegation be/should be sent)

resort I *n.* ["recourse"] 1. (formal) to have ~ to 2. a last ~ (as a last ~) ["recreational center"] 3. a beach; health; holiday, vacation (esp. AE); popular; ski; summer; winter ~

resort II *v.* (d; intr.) to ~ to (to ~ to trickery)

resound *v.* (P; intr.) applause ~ed in the hall; the shouts of the hunters ~ed through the forest; the auditorium ~ed with cheers

resourceful *adj.* ~ to + inf. (it was ~ of them to find the solution so quickly)

resources *n.* 1. to develop; exploit, tap; mobilize ~ 2. to conserve, husband; marshall; pool, share one's ~ 3. to deplete, exhaust, squander, use up, waste ~ 4. abundant; limited, meager; limitless, unlimited; untapped ~ 5. economic; natural ~ (to exploit natural ~) 6. human; inner ~ 7. the ~ to + inf. (we have the ~ to do the job) 8. (misc.) to leave people to their own ~

respect I *n.* ["esteem"] 1. to have; pay, show ~ to 2. to command, inspire ~ (she commands ~ from everyone = she commands everyone's ~) 3. to earn, gain, get, win ~ 4. to lose smb.'s ~ 5. deep, great, profound, sincere, utmost; due; grudging; mutual ~ 6. a mark, sign, token of ~ 7. ~ for (~ for the law) 8. out of ~ (she did it out of ~ for her parents) 9. in ~ (to hold smb. in ~) 10. with ~ (with all due ~, I disagree) ["regard"] 11. in a ~ (in this ~; in all ~s) 12. in, with ~ to; (esp. BE) in ~ of

respect II *v.* 1. to ~ deeply; widely 2. (D; tr.) to ~ as (to ~ smb. as a scholar) 3. (D; tr.) to ~ for (I ~ them for their integrity)

respected *adj.* highly; universally, widely ~

respectful *adj.* ~ of; to (~ of one's elders)

respects *n.* to pay; send one's ~ (to pay one's last ~ after smb.'s death)

respiration *n.* artificial; labored; normal ~ (to give smb. artificial ~)

respite *n.* 1. to allow, give ~ (we allowed them no ~) 2. to get, have a ~ (we finally got a brief ~) 3. a brief, temporary; welcome ~ 4. a ~ from (there was no ~ from the cold) 5. without ~

resplendent *adj.* ~ in; with (~ in their academic gowns)

respond *v.* 1. to ~ brusquely; immediately; promptly 2. (D; intr.) ("to react") to ~ by (they ~ed by walking out) 3. (D; intr.) to ~ to ("to answer") (to ~ to a letter) 4. (D; intr.) ("to react") to ~ to (to ~ to treatment) 5. (D; intr.) ("to react") to ~ with (they ~ed to our demands with an immediate walkout) 6. (L; to) she ~ed that she would not attend the conference

response *n.* 1. to call forth, draw, elicit, evoke a ~ 2. to give, make a ~ 3. to get, have, receive a ~ 4. an enthusiastic; favorable; witty ~ 5. a glib; lukewarm; sullen ~ 6. a delayed; immediate ~ 7. an affirmative, positive; negative ~ 8. a ~ to 9. in ~ to

responsibility *n.* ["accountability"] ["obligation"] 1. to accept, assume, bear, shoulder, take, take on (a) ~ 2. to exercise, have (a) ~ 3. to discharge a ~ 4. to abandon, abdicate, disclaim, dodge, evade, shirk (a) ~ 5. to delegate; share; shift (a) ~ 6. an awesome, grave, great, heavy, terrible (colloq.); clear ~ 7. (a) collective; joint; moral; personal ~ 8. the ultimate ~ (the ultimate ~ rested with the president) 9. (a) ~ falls on; lies, rests with smb. 10. (a) ~ for (to bear the ~ for the smooth operation of the assembly line) 11. the ~ to + inf. (everyone has a/ the ~ to pay taxes) 12. ~ that + clause; subj. (it was her ~ that all members be/should be notified) 13. on one's ~ (she did it on her own ~) ["blame"] 14. to lay the ~ at smb.'s door 15. to admit, claim ~ (a shadowy group claimed ~ for the hijacking) 16. to disclaim (all) ~ 17. ~ for

responsible *adj.* 1. ~ for; to (politicians are ~ to the voters; people are ~ for their actions) 2. (misc.) to hold smb. ~ for smt.

responsive *adj.* ~ to (~ to flattery)

responsiveness *n.* ~ to

rest I *n.* ["repose"] 1. to have, take a ~ 2. to get some ~ 3. a well-earned ~ 4. bed; complete ~ 5. ~ from 6. at ~ 7. (misc.) to come to ~ ("to stop); to go to one's eternal ~ ("to die"); laid to ~ ("buried"); at parade ~ (mil.); to set one's mind at ~ ["support"] 8. an armrest; chin ~

rest II *v.* 1. (d; tr.) ("to support") to ~ on (~ your head on my shoulder) 2. (d; intr.) ("to stand") to ~ on (the statue ~s on a pedestal) 3. (d; intr.) ("to depend") to ~ with (the decision ~s with the court) 4. (misc.) to ~ in peace ("to lie buried")

restaurant *n.* 1. to manage, operate, run a ~ 2. an elegant, first-class ~ 3. a dairy; fast-food; kosher; seafood; vegetarian ~ 4. (BE) a licensed ~ (that may sell alcoholic drinks)

restful *adj.* ~ to + inf. (it's ~ just to sit and read =

it's ~ just sitting and reading)

restitution *n.* 1. to make; offer ~ 2. full ~ 3. ~ for 4. ~ to

restock *v.* (D; tr.) to ~ with (to ~ a pond with fish)

restore *v.* (d; tr.) to ~ to (to ~ smb. to her/his former position)

restrain *v.* (D; refl., tr.) to ~ from (to ~ smb. from committing violence)

restraint *n.* ["control"] ["act of restraining"] 1. to display, exercise, show ~ 2. to cast off, fling off, shake off (all) ~ 3. (legal) prior ~ 4. ~ in (they showed ~ in responding to the provocation) 5. in ~ of (in ~ of trade) ["device for restraining"] 6. to apply, put on ~s

restrict *v.* (D; refl., tr.) to ~ to (the chair ~ed discussion to items on the official agenda; she ~ed herself to two meals a day)

restriction *n.* 1. to impose, place, put ~s on 2. to lift a ~ 3. ~s on

result I *n.* 1. to achieve, get, produce, show ~s 2. to announce; evaluate, measure; tabulate ~s 3. to negate, nullify, undo a ~ 4. an end, final; direct; lasting; logical; negative; net; positive; striking; surprising ~ 5. overall; surefire ~s

result II *v.* 1. (d; intr.) to ~ from (her death ~ed from an overdose of pills) 2. (d; intr.) to ~ in (the argument ~ed in a fight)

resume *v.* (G) she ~d working

resurrect *v.* (D; tr.) to ~ from (to ~ smb. from the dead)

resurrection *n.* ~ from

resuscitation *n.* 1. to give ~ (the victim was given mouth-to-mouth ~) 2. cardiopulmonary (= CPR); mouth-to-mouth ~

retail I *adv.* to buy; sell ~

retail II *v.* to ~ at, for (it ~s for fifty dollars)

retainer *n.* ["advance fee"] to pay, put down a ~

retaliate *v.* 1. (D; intr.) to ~ against; for (to ~ against the enemy for shelling civilian targets) 2. (D; intr.) to ~ by, with (the enemy ~d by shelling our positions; they ~d with a bombardment)

retaliation *n.* 1. massive ~ 2. military ~ 3. ~ against; for 4. an act of ~ 5. in ~ (for)

retardant *n.* a fire; rust ~

retardation *n.* mental ~

retarded *adj.* mentally ~

retell *v.* (usu. B; occ. A) she has retold the story to us many times

reticence *n.* 1. to display, show ~ 2. ~ about

reticent *adj.* ~ about

retina *n.* a detached ~

retire *v.* 1. (D; intr.) ("to end one's working career") to ~ from (to ~ from one's job) 2. (D; intr.) ("to withdraw") to ~ to (the troops ~d to safer positions; let's ~ to the drawing room)

retirement *n.* 1. to go into ~ 2. to come out of ~ 3. compulsory, forced; early ~; semi-retirement; voluntary ~ 4. in ~ (to live in ~) 5. (misc.) to take early ~

retool *v.* 1. (D; intr., tr.) to ~ for (to ~ for wartime production) 2. (H) to ~ a plant to build prefabricated houses

retort I *n.* 1. to make a ~ 2. a quick; sharp, stinging; witty ~ 3. a ~ to

retort II *v.* (L) she ~ed heatedly that she needed no favors

retraction *n.* to issue, publish a ~ (they issued a quick and unqualified ~)

retreat I *n.* ["withdrawal"] 1. to beat, carry out, make a ~ (they made good their ~; the regiment carried out its ~ in good order) 2. a hasty, precipitate ~ 3. full ~ (in full ~) 4. a strategic; tactical ~ 5. a ~ from ["signal for withdrawal"] 6. to sound ~ ["music for a flag-lowering ceremony"] (mil.) 7. to play, sound ~ ["secluded gathering"] 8. to go on (a) ~ 9. a religious; weekend ~ ["secluded spot"] 10. a country ~

retreat II *v.* (D; intr.) to ~ from; to (our troops ~ed from the border to safer positions; our government has ~ed from its hard-line position)

retribution *n.* 1. to exact ~ from; to visit ~ on 2. divine; swift ~ 3. ~ against (~ against the invaders was swift) 4. in ~ for (he was punished in ~ for sins)

retrieval *n.* data, information ~

retrieve *v.* (D; tr.) to ~ from (to ~ data from a computer)

retroactive *adj.* ~ to

retrorocket *n.* to activate, fire a ~

retrospect *n.* in ~

retrospection *n.* in ~

return I *n.* ["statement about income"] 1. to file a (tax) ~ 2. a joint; tax ~ ["going back, coming back"] 3. a safe ~ (home) 4. a ~ from; to (his ~ to civilian life) 5. on smb.'s ~ (on their ~ from a trip abroad) 6. the point of no ~ ["profit"] 7. to bring in, produce, yield a ~ (this investment will yield a ~ of ten percent) 8. a ~ from, on ["compensation"] 9. in ~ (to give smt. in ~) 10. in ~ for ["next post"] (BE) 11. by ~ (of post) (send us an answer by ~)

return II *v.* 1. (BE) (A) she ~ed my book to me; or: she ~ed me my book 2. (AE) (B) she ~ed my money to me 3. (D; intr., tr.) to ~ from; to (to ~ from a holiday/vacation; she ~ed to her home; to ~ books to the library)

returns *n.* ["election results"] 1. early; election; final; late ~ ["misc."] 2. many happy ~ of the day ("happy birthday"); the law of diminishing ~

reunion *n.* 1. to hold a ~ 2. a touching ~ 3. an annual; class; family ~

reunite *v.* (D; tr.) to ~ with (to ~ smb. with her/his family)

reveal *v.* 1. (B) she ~ed the secret to us 2. (L; to) he ~ed (to us) that he had been ill for years 3. (M) the

document ~ed her to be a conscientious employee 4. (Q; to) she ~ed (to us) how long she had been ill

reveille *n.* (mil.) 1. to play, sound ~ 2. to fall out for ~

revel *v.* (D; intr.) to ~ in

revelation *n.* 1. to make a ~ 2. an amazing, astonishing, astounding, startling, stunning, surprising ~ 3. (a) divine ~ 4. a ~ about 5. a ~ to (the story was a ~ to us) 6. a ~ that + clause (the ~ that she had been in prison surprised everybody)

revenge I *n.* 1. to exact, get, have, take ~ on 2. to plot, seek ~ 3. sweet ~ 4. ~ for; on (to take ~ on smb. for smt.) 5. in ~ for

revenge II *v.* (BE) (d; refl.) to ~ on, upon (to ~ oneself on an enemy)

revenue *n.* ["income"] 1. to generate, produce, raise, yield ~ 2. to collect ~ 3. government; tax ~ 4. smb.'s annual, yearly; monthly; weekly ~ 5. oil ~s 6. falling; rising ~s

USAGE NOTE: The UK *Inland Revenue* corresponds to the US *Internal Revenue Service*.

reverberate *v.* (P; intr.) the cheers ~d through the arena; the stadium ~d with boos; the news ~d around the world

revere *v.* 1. (D; tr.) to ~ as (to ~ smb. as a saint) 2. (D; tr.) to ~ for

reverence *n.* 1. to feel ~ 2. to show ~ 3. deep, profound ~ 4. ~ for 5. in ~ (to hold smb. in ~)

reverie *n.* 1. to indulge in ~s 2. to be lost, sunk in ~ 3. (misc.) to fall into a ~; to wake from a ~

reversal *n.* 1. to suffer a ~ 2. a complete; minor ~

reverse *n.* ["setback"] 1. to suffer, sustain a ~ 2. a serious; slight; tactical ~ 3. financial ~s ["reverse gear"] 4. to put a transmission into ~ 5. to change into, go into, shift (AE) into ~ 6. in ~ ["reversing mechanism"] 7. a/an (automatic) ribbon ~ (on a typewriter)

reversion *n.* ~ to

revert *v.* (d; intr.) to ~ to (her property ~ed to the state; to ~ to enlisted status)

review I *n.* ["renewed study"] 1. to do a ~ 2. a comprehensive ~ ["military ceremony"] 3. to hold a ~ (of troops) 4. to pass in ~ ["critical evaluation"] 5. to do, write a ~ (of a book) 6. to conduct a ~ 7. to get, receive a ~ 8. a complimentary, favorable, glowing, positive, rave; negative, unfavorable ~ (the play got rave ~s) 9. a book ~ 10. (legal) judicial ~ 11. (a) peer ~ 12. under ~ (the entire matter is under ~)

review II *v.* (AE) (D; intr., tr.) ("to study again") to ~ for (to ~ for an exam)

revise (BE) see **review II**

revision *n.* ["renewed study"] (BE) 1. to do ~ (he had to do some ~ for the examination) ["revised version"] 2. to do a ~ (we had to do a complete ~ of the manuscript) ["change"] 3. they made several ~s in/to their plans

revival *n.* a ~ in; of (a ~ in faith healing)

revolt I *n.* 1. to incite, stir up a ~ 2. to crush, quash, quell, put down, stifle a ~ 3. a peasant ~ 4. a ~ breaks out, erupts 5. a ~ against 6. in ~ (to rise in ~)

revolt II *v.* (D; intr.) to ~ against, at

revolting *adj.* 1. ~ to 2. ~ to + inf. (it's ~ to contemplate such a possibility) 3. ~ that + clause (it's ~ that they use such obscene language)

revolution *n.* ["complete change"] 1. to foment, stir up a ~ 2. to organize a ~ 3. to carry out, conduct, fight a ~ 4. to crush, defeat, put down a ~ 5. a cultural; industrial; palace; political; sexual; social ~ 6. a ~ in (a ~ in hair styles) ["complete orbital turn"] 7. to make a ~ 8. a ~ about, around, round

revolve *v.* (D; intr.) to ~ about, around, round (the earth ~s around the sun)

revolver see **pistol** 1-5, 7

revue *n.* to produce, put on, stage a ~

revulsion *n.* 1. to express; feel ~ 2. deep, utmost, utter ~ 3. a feeling of ~ 4. ~ against, at, towards 5. in ~ (they drew back in ~)

reward I *n.* 1. to offer, post; pay a ~ 2. to claim; reap; receive a ~ 3. an ample, handsome; just; tangible; well-deserved ~ 4. a ~ for

reward II *v.* 1. to ~ amply, handsomely 2. (D; tr.) to ~ by; for; with (she was ~ed with a bonus for her outstanding work)

rhapsodize *v.* (d; intr.) to ~ over

rhapsody *n.* to compose; play a ~

rhetoric *n.* 1. to resort to, spout ~ 2. eloquent; impassioned, passionate; soothing ~

rheumatism *n.* 1. to develop ~ 2. to suffer from ~ 3. chronic ~

rhubarb *n.* ["argument"] (slang) (AE) 1. to get into a ~ 2. a ~ about

rhyme I *n.* 1. a nursery ~ 2. (poetry) a feminine; masculine ~ 3. an eye ~ 4. a ~ for (what is a ~ for *singe*?) 5. in ~ (poetry in ~) 6. (misc.) without ~ or reason ("with no apparent reason")

rhyme II *v.* (D; intr., tr.) to ~ with (this word ~s with that word); to ~ one word with another)

rhythm *n.* 1. to beat (out) a ~ 2. (a) frenzied; pulsating; steady; undulating ~ 3. to a ~ (to dance to the ~ of drums) 4. a sense of ~

rib I *n.* 1. to poke smb. in the ~s 2. a false; floating ~ 3. (misc.) to break, fracture a ~

rib II *v.* (colloq.) (D; tr.) to ~ about; for (they ~bed me about my new hair color)

ribbing *n.* ["teasing"] to get, take a ~

ribbon *n.* ["strip of ink-impregnated cloth on a typewriter"] 1. to change a ~ 2. a typewriter ~ 3. the ~ reverses (automatically) ["misc."] 4. a blue ~ ("a first prize"); to cut to ~s ("to destroy completely")

rice *n.* 1. to mill, winnow ~ 2. brown; enriched; polished; quick-cooking; wild ~ 3. a bowl of ~

rich *adj.* 1. ~ in (~ in coal deposits) 2. (misc.) the idle ~; to strike it ~; ~ and poor (alike)

riches *n.* 1. to amass ~ 2. great, untold, vast ~

ricksha, rickshaw *n.* 1. to pedal; pull a ~ 2. to ride in a ~

ricochet *v.* (D; intr.) to ~ off

rid *v.* 1. (d; refl., tr.) to ~ of (to ~ the town of rats) 2. to get ~ of

riddance *n.* (colloq.) ["act of getting rid of smt."] good ~! (good ~ to bad rubbish!)

riddle I *n.* 1. to pose a ~ 2. to solve a ~ 3. a ~ to (the whole business was a ~ to me) 4. (misc.) to speak in ~s

riddle II *v.* (d; tr.) to ~ with (the plane was ~d with anti-aircraft fire)

ride I *n.* ["short trip by vehicle, on horseback"] 1. to catch, get a ~ 2. to go for, go on, have (esp. BE), take (esp. AE) a ~ 3. (colloq.) to bum (AE), hitch, thumb a ~ (as a hitchhiker) 4. to give (smb.) a ~ 5. to take (smb.) for a ~ 6. a bicycle; bus; joy; train ~ (to go on a joy ~ in a stolen car) 7. a bumpy, rough; smooth ~ 8. a ~ on (a ~ on a camel) 9. a ~ into, to (a ~ into/to town) ["attraction"] (in an amusement park) 10. to go on the ~s ["misc."] 11. to take smb. for a ~ ("to victimize smb.")

ride II *v.* 1. (d; intr.) to ~ by, in, on (to ~ in a car/on a bus) 2. (d; intr.) to ~ from; to (we ~ to work by bus) 3. (d; intr.) to ~ on ("to be wagered on") (a lot of money was ~ing on one horse) 4. (P; intr.) to ~ across town; to ~ through a forest; to ~ around the neighborhood 5. (misc.) to ~ bareback; to ~ sidesaddle; to ~ roughshod over smb. ("to treat smb. in an abusive manner"); the ship was ~ing at anchor

ride out *v.* (d; intr.) to ~ to (he rode out to the procession)

rider *n.* ["amendment, addition"] to attach a ~ to (a bill)

ridicule *n.* 1. draw, incur ~ 2. to heap, pour ~ on smb. 3. public ~ 4. (misc.) to hold smb. up to ~

ridiculous *adj.* 1. absolutely, completely, downright, perfectly, totally, truly, utterly ~ 2. ~ to + inf. (it's ~ to apply for that position) 3. ~ that + clause (it's ~ that they could not receive visas)

rife *adj.* ["abounding"] (cannot stand alone) ~ with (the city was ~ with rumors)

riffle *v.* (d; intr.) to ~ through (to ~ through documents)

rifle I *n.* 1. to load a ~ 2. to aim, point; level a ~ 3. to fire a ~ 4. to handle, operate a ~ 5. to assemble; disassemble a ~ 6. an air; assault; automatic; high-powered; hunting; recoilless; semiautomatic ~ 7. a ~ fires, goes off; jams; misfires

rifle II *v.* (d; intr.) to ~ through ("to search") to ~ through the drawers)

rift *n.* 1. to cause a ~ 2. to heal a ~ 3. an ideological ~ 4. a ~ among, between

rig *n.* ["large vehicle"] (AE) 1. to drive a ~ ["equipment"] 2. an oil-drilling ~

right I *adj.* 1. ~ about (to be ~ about smt.) 2. ~ in (you were ~ in assuming that) 3. ~ to + inf. (it was ~ of her to refuse = she was ~ to refuse) 4. ~ that + clause (it's not ~ that they should be treated in that manner) 5. (misc.) all ~; everything went all ~ at the office; that picture is just ~ for this room; she is the ~ person for the job = she is ~ for the job (colloq.); to be in one's ~ mind ("to be sane"); to put things ~ ("to straighten things out")

right II *adv.* 1. to bear, go, turn ~ 2. ~ away; now 3. to do smt. ~ 4. (misc.) go ~ back; go ~ home after dinner; ~ in front of us; to go ~ the way through (BE)

right III *n.* ["that which is due"] 1. to assert, claim a ~ 2. to demand one's ~s 3. to achieve, gain, get a ~ (to achieve full civil ~s) 4. to enjoy, exercise, have a ~ 5. to give up, relinquish, renounce, sign away, waive a ~ 6. to defend, protect, safeguard, uphold smb.'s ~s 7. to give, grant a ~ (to) 8. to deny (smb.) a ~ 9. to violate smb.'s ~s 10. a divine; exclusive, sole; inalienable; inherent; legal; natural ~ 11. animal; civil; constitutional; political; reproductive; states'; voting ~s 12. children's; consumers'; gay; human; individual; patients'; squatters'; veterans'; women's ~s 13. film; grazing; mineral; property; publishing ~s 14. conjugal; visiting, visitation ~s 15. the ~ of assembly; asylum; free speech 16. a ~ to (the ~ to privacy; the ~ to a free press; everyone has the ~ to a fair trial) 17. the ~ to + inf. (the ~ to protest; you have the ~ to remain silent) 18. within one's ~s (she was within her ~s to remain silent) 19. (misc.) a bill of ~s; to read the accused her/his ~s ["right side"] 20. to keep to the ~ 21. on the ~; to the ~ ["conservative group"] 22. the extreme, far, radical ~ 23. the religious ~ ["punch delivered with the right hand"] 24. to deliver, throw a ~ 25. a hard, stiff ~ 26. a ~ to (a ~ to the jaw) ["turn to the right"] 27. (colloq.) to take a ~ 28. to make a sharp ~ ["misc."] 29. in the ~ ("in accordance with the truth, accepted standards"); she has a promising career in her own ~; as of (BE), by ~ ("properly"); by ~ of conquest; ~ and wrong; by ~s ("ideally")

right-of-way *n.* 1. to have the ~ 2. to give (esp. AE), yield the ~ 3. the ~ over (ambulances have the ~ over other vehicles)

right-winger *n.* an extreme ~

rigid *adj.* ~ about, in, on (~ on points of procedure; they are ~ in their views)

rigor mortis *n.* ~ sets in

rig out, rig up *v.* 1. (D; tr.) to ~ as (to ~ smb. out as a clown) 2. to ~ in (to ~ smb. out in a period costume)

rile *v.* (R) it ~d me that they were paying no taxes

riled *adj.* (colloq.) ["annoyed"] 1. ~ at 2. ~ that + clause (she was ~ that nobody believed her story)

rim *n.* along; on; up to a ~ (on the ~ of a crater)

rind *n.* 1. to scrape the ~ 2. lemon; melon ~
USAGE NOTE: One usu. speaks of the *rind* of a melon, the *peel* or the *rind* of a lemon, the *peel* of an orange, the *skin* or the *peel* of a banana.

ring I *n.* ["circular band"] 1. a diamond; gold; platinum; sapphire ~ 2. an earring; engagement; signet; wedding ~ 3. a key; napkin; teething ~ 4. a piston ~ 5. smoke ~s (to blow smoke ~s) 6. (misc.) to have, wear a ~ on one's finger ["group"] 7. a drug; smuggling; spy; vice ~ ["enclosed square area"] 8. the prize ~ 9. to climb into, step into the ~ ["telephone call"] 10. to give smb. a ~ ["misc."] 11. to run ~s (a)round smb. ("to far outperform smb.")

ring II *n.* ["sound"] 1. a false, hollow; familiar ~ (there was a false ~ to his words) 2. (misc.) it has a nice ~ to it; her story had a ~ of truth to it

ring III *v.* 1. (D; tr.) to ~ for ("to call by ringing") (to ~ for the maid) 2. (s) to ~ false; hollow; true (her words ~ false)

ringer *n.* (colloq.) to be a dead ~ for smb. ("to resemble smb. very closely")

ringside *n.* at ~

ring up *v.* (D; tr.) ("to record") to ~ on (to ~ a bill on a cash register)

rink *n.* 1. an ice-hockey; ice-skating; roller-skating ~ 2. at a ~

rinse I *n.* to give smt. a ~

rinse II *v.* (D; tr.) to ~ from, out of (~ the soap out of your hair)

riot *n.* 1. to cause, foment, incite, instigate, spark (AE), spark off (BE), stir up, touch off a ~ 2. to crush, put down, quell a ~ 3. a communal; food; race ~ 4. a ~ breaks out, erupts, flares up 5. ~s swept the country 6. a ~ subsides 7. (misc.) to run ~ ("to act wildly")

riot act *n.* ["stern warning"] to read the ~ to

rioting *n.* 1. to put down, quell ~ 2. communal ~ 3. sporadic; widespread ~ 4. ~ breaks out, erupts, flares up 5. ~ subsides 6. an outbreak of ~

rip *v.* 1. (d; intr.) to ~ into ("to attack") (colloq.) (the politician ~ped into her opponent) 2. (misc.) an explosion ~ped through the laboratory; she ~ped her skirt on a nail; to ~ smt. to pieces

ripcord *n.* to pull the ~

ripe *adj.* ~ for (~ for the picking; the time is ~ for action)

ripen *v.* (d; intr.) to ~ into (their friendship ~ed into love)

ripple *v.* (P; intr.) applause ~d through the auditorium

rise I *n.* ["origin"] 1. to give ~ to ["angry reaction"] 2. to get a ~ out of smb. ["pay increase"] (BE) 3. an across-the-board pay, wage ~ 4. a ~ in (wages) (AE has *raise*) ["increase"] 5. a sharp, steep ~ 6. a ~ in (a ~ in prices) 7. on the ~ (prices are on the ~)

["success"] 8. a meteoric ~ ["move upwards"] 9. a dramatic, sharp; steady ~ 10. a ~ to (a steady ~ to the top)

rise II v. 1. ("to ascend") to ~ sharply, steeply 2. (D; intr.) ("to ascend") to ~ above (to ~ above last year's level) 3. (D; intr.) ("to ascend") to ~ by (prices rose by ten percent) 4. (D; intr.) ("to revolt") to ~ against (to ~ against tyranny) 5. (D; intr.) ("to ascend") to ~ from, out of (smoke rose from the chimney; after many years they rose out of poverty) 6. (d; intr.) ("to be resurrected") to ~ from (to ~ from the dead; to ~ from the ashes) 7. (D; intr.) ("to ascend") to ~ into (the smoke rose into the air) 8. (d; intr.) ("to ascend") to ~ to (to ~ to the surface; to ~ to one's feet) 9. (d; intr.) ("to be equal") to ~ to (to ~ to the challenge; can you ~ to the occasion?)

riser n. an early; late ~

rise up v. (D; intr.) to ~ against (they rose up against the dictator)

risk I n. 1. to assume, incur, run, take a ~ (to run the ~ of being outvoted) 2. to face a ~ 3. to entail, involve a ~ 4. to outweigh a ~ (the advantages outweigh the ~s) 5. to reduce a ~ 6. a grave, great, high ~ 7. a low ~ 8. a calculated ~ (to take a calculated ~) 9. a health; safety; security ~ (she is a security ~) 10. a ~ to (a ~ to safety) 11. a ~ to + inf. (it was a ~ to enter that area) 12. a ~ that + clause (there was a ~ that a fire might break out) 13. at (a) ~ (at one's own ~; the ~ of being ridiculed; lives were at ~; esp. BE: children at ~) 14. (misc.) we diversified our investments in order to spread the ~

risk II v. 1. (G) she ~ed losing everything 2. (K) he ~ed their turning against him

risky adj. ~ to + inf. (it's ~ to play with fire)

rite n. 1. to administer, perform a ~ 2. a pagan; religious; solemn ~ 3. last ~s (to administer the last ~s to a dying person) 4. funeral; initiation; marriage ~s 5. fertility ~s

ritual n. 1. to go through; perform a ~ 2. to make a ~ of smt. 3. a pagan; religious; solemn ~

rival I n. 1. an arch, bitter, keen ~ 2. a political ~ 3. a ~ for; in

rival II v. (D; tr.) to ~ in (to ~ smb. in skill)

rivalry n. 1. to stir up ~ 2. (a) bitter, deep, fierce, intense, keen, strong ~ 3. (a) friendly ~ 4. sibling ~ 5. interservice ~ 6. ~ among, between; for; in; with (keen ~ between them for the award)

river n. 1. to cross; ford a ~ 2. to dam; drag; dredge a ~ 3. a broad, wide; deep ~ 4. a ~ floods; flows (into the sea); narrows; overflows (its banks); recedes; rises; widens 5. the bank; course; mouth; source of a ~ 6. down ~; up ~ 7. (misc.) to sell down the ~ ("to betray")

rivet n. to drive a ~ (into metal)

riveted adj. (cannot stand alone) ~ on, to (all eyes

were ~ on the door; she stood ~ to the spot)

road n. 1. to pave; resurface; surface a ~ 2. to widen a ~ 3. to block, cordon off a ~ 4. to cross a ~ 5. a macadam; metalled (BE); paved, surfaced; smooth (also fig.); straight; wide ~ 6. a connecting; main, trunk (BE); ring (BE); toll ~ 7. a service; slip (BE) ~ 8. a back, country; deserted, lonely; mountain; narrow; secondary; winding ~ 9. a bumpy; dirt (AE), unpaved; icy; impassable; rocky (also fig.); rough (also fig.); unmetalled (BE) ~ 10. intersecting; merging ~s 11. the right; wrong ~ (they took the wrong ~; we were on the right ~) 12. a ~ goes, leads, runs somewhere 13. a ~ curves, winds; forks; zigzags 14. a ~ from; to (the ~ to town) 15. across a ~ 16. down; up a ~ 17. in, on a ~ 18. (also fig.) on the ~ (on the ~ to recovery) 19. (misc.) to take a ~ (they took the wrong ~); one for the ~ ("a final drink"); follow this ~ for two miles; the car holds the ~ well; a stretch of the ~; the ~ is clear (also fig.); some drivers hog the ~; to take the high ~ (usu. fig.)

road block n. 1. to establish, put up, set up a ~ 2. to remove a ~ 3. to break through, crash through, run a ~

roadhouse n. at a ~ (to stop at a ~ for a drink)

roadside n. by, on the ~

road sign n. to put up a ~

roadwork n. ["running"] to do ~ (the boxer did ~ every day)

roam v. (P; intr.) to ~ around town

roar I n. a deep, thunderous ~

roar II v. 1. (D; intr.) to ~ at 2. (D; intr.) to ~ with (to ~ with laughter)

roast n. 1. to cook, do, make a ~ 2. to have a ~ (we had a ~ for dinner) 3. a chuck; eye (AE); lamb; pork; pot; rib; veal ~

rob v. 1. (D; tr.) to ~ of (the bandits ~bed the passengers of their money) 2. (misc.) to ~ smb. blind

robbery n. 1. to commit (a) ~ 2. armed; bank; daylight (BE) ("overcharging"); highway (fig.) ~

robed adj. ~ in (the judges were ~ in red)

robot n. an industrial ~

rock I n. ["stone"] 1. to throw a ~ at (see Usage Note) 2. jagged; rugged ~s 3. falling ~s 4. solid ~ 5. (misc.) as hard/solid as a ~

USAGE NOTE: In BE, a *rock* is typically too big to be thrown. Thus, *to throw a rock at smb.* is esp. AE. However, the figurative expression *to throw rocks at smb.* ("to criticize smb.") is CE.

rock II n. ["type of music"] hard; punk ~; rock-and-roll

rock III v. (D; tr.) ("to lull") to ~ to (to ~ a baby to sleep)

rock bottom n. to hit, reach ~ (prices have reached ~)

rocket I n. ["device propelled by a rocket engine or

explosives"] 1. to fire; launch a ~ 2. a booster; liquid-fuel; long-range; multistage; solid-fuel; space ~ 3. a ~ blasts off; goes into orbit ["reprimand"] (colloq.) (BE) 4. to give smb. a ~ 5. to get a ~ (from)

rocket II v. (d; intr.) to ~ to (she ~ed to stardom)

rocket ship see the Usage Note for **ship I**

rocks n. 1. on the ~ ("with ice") (scotch on the ~) 2. on the ~ ("ruined")

rod n. ["bar, shaft"] 1. a connecting; divining; lightning; piston ~; ramrod ["pistol"] (slang) (AE) 2. to pack ("carry") a ~ ["metal track"] 3. a curtain; traverse ~ ["pole"] 4. a fishing ~ ["misc."] 5. to ride the ~s (AE) ("to ride illegally in the framework below a railroad car")

rodent n. ~s gnaw

rodeo n. to hold, stage a ~

roe n. 1. to spawn ~ 2. hard; soft ~

role n. 1. to assume, take (on) a ~ 2. to assign, hand out ~s 3. to do, perform, play; interpret; understudy a ~ 4. a decisive; important; key; leading; prominent ~ 5. a cameo; starring; supporting; title ~ 6. an active; passive ~ 7. a major; minor ~ 8. a primary; secondary ~ 9. a ~ in (they played a key ~ in the uprising) 10. (misc.) cast in the ~ of

roll I n. ["list of names"] 1. to call, take the ~ 2. an honor ~ (AE; BE has *roll of honour*) ["small cake or bread"] 3. to bake ~s 4. a bread (BE); hamburger; jelly (AE), Swiss (BE); kaiser (esp. US); poppyseed; sweet ~

roll II v. 1. (A) ~ the ball to me; or: ~ me the ball 2. (C) ~ a cigarette for me; or: ~ me a cigarette 3. (d; intr., tr.) to ~ down (the children ~ed down the hill; we ~ed the barrels down the incline) 4. (d; intr.) to ~ in (to ~ in the mud) 5. (d; intr.) to ~ off (the football ~ed off the field; new cars ~ed off the assembly line) 6. (d; intr.) to ~ with ("to lessen the impact by moving in the same direction") (he ~ed with the punch) 7. (P; intr., tr.) they ~ed the barrels down the chute; the ball ~ed across the field

rollaway, rollaway bed n. (AE) to fold up; open up a ~

roll up v. 1. (d; tr.) to ~ in (to ~ smt. up in a blanket) 2. (D; intr., tr.) to ~ into (to ~ smt. into a ball) 3. (D; intr., tr.) to ~ to (the ball ~ed up to me)

romance n. 1. to find ~ 2. a shipboard; wartime; whirlwind ~

romanticize v. (D; intr.) to ~ about

romp v. 1. (d; intr.) ("to deal with easily") to ~ through (she ~ed through the test) 2. (D; intr.) ("to play") to ~ with (to ~ with the children) 3. (misc.) our team ~ed home first ("our team won easily")

romp around v. (D; intr.) ("to play") to ~ with the children

roof n. 1. to install a ~ 2. a gabled; shingled; slate; thatched; tiled ~ 3. a ~ leaks 4. (misc.) to raise the ~ ("to complain vociferously"); to hit the ~ ("to

lose one's temper"); to have a ~ over one's head ("to have shelter")

room I n. ["partitioned part of a building"] 1. to rent a ~ from 2. to let (BE), let out (BE), rent, rent out a ~ to 3. to book (BE), reserve a ~ 4. a back ~; bathroom; bedroom; boxroom (BE); dining; drawing, front (BE), living, reception (BE), sitting; family (AE); game, recreation; guest; spare; utility ~; workroom 5. a banquet; board; common (BE); reading ~; showroom; waiting ~ 6. a baggage (AE); lumber (BE); storage ~ 7. an adjoining ~, the next ~ 8. a changing (BE), dressing; locker ~ 9. a double; single ~ 10. (in a hospital) a delivery; emergency (AE); hospital; operating (esp. AE; BE prefers *operating theatre/theatre*); private; recovery; semiprivate ~ 11. a ladies' (esp. AE), powder; men's (esp. AE); rest (AE) ~; (BE; euphemism) the smallest ~ ("the room with the toilet") 12. a furnished; rented ~; (a) ~ to let (BE) ["space"] 13. to make ~ for 14. to occupy, take up ~ 15. elbow ~; headroom; legroom 16. (in a theater) standing ~ only 17. ~ for (there is ~ for another bed) 18. ~ to + inf. (the children have ~ to play) ["possibility"] 19. ~ for (there is no ~ for doubt)

USAGE NOTE: In the US, a *bathroom* usu. contains a toilet, sink, and bathtub or shower. In GB, it must contain a bath or shower and may have a toilet and washbasin. In CE, a *cloakroom* is a place in a public building where coats, umbrellas, etc. may be left temporarily. In GB, it can also denote a small room on the ground floor of a house near the front door; this room often contains a toilet and a place for hanging coats. *Ladies' room* and *men's room* are especially AE. BE has *ladies'* and *gents'*.

room II v. (d; intr.) ("to reside") to ~ at; with

room service n. to call, call for, get ~

rooster n. (esp. AE) a ~ cock-a-doodle-doos, crows, goes cock-a-doodle-doo (BE has *cock* or *cockerel*)

root I n. 1. to strike, take ~ 2. (mathematics) a cube; square ~ to 3. (misc.) to get at, to the ~ of smt. ("to tackle smt. at the source"); (BE) ~ and branch ("wholly"); the ~ of all evil

root II v. (D; intr.) to ~ for ("to support") (AE) (to ~ for a team)

root about, root around v. (D; intr.) to ~ for ("to search for") (to ~ in a stack of papers for a specific document)

rooted adj. 1. deeply ~ 2. ~ in (~ in poverty) 3. ~ to (~ to the spot)

rooter n. (AE) an ardent ~

roots n. 1. to put down ~ 2. to go back to one's ~ 3. to search for one's ~ 4. deep ~ 5. ethnic ~ 6. by the ~ (to pull smt. up by the ~) 7. (misc.) her ~ are in Canada

rope I n. 1. to pull; tie a ~ 2. to jump (esp. AE), skip ~ 3. to ease up on; tighten a ~ 4. a loose, slack; tight ~ 5. a coil; length; piece of ~ 6. by a ~ (to lower smt. by a ~) 7. (misc.) (boxing and fig.) on the ~s ("in a weak, vulnerable position"); at the end of one's ~ (esp. AE) ("in a desperate situation"); to know the ~s ("to be well informed")

rope II v. 1. (colloq.) (d; tr.) to ~ into ("to induce") (to ~ smb. into doing smt.) 2. (D; tr.) to ~ to (the horse was ~d to a tree)

rosary n. to pray, recite, say the ~

rose n. 1. a long-stemmed; rambling; wild ~ 2. a bouquet of ~s 3. (misc.) a bed of ~s ("an ideal situation")

roster n. 1. to make up a ~ 2. a duty; personnel ~

rostrum n. 1. to get up on, mount the ~ 2. from; on a ~

rot n. 1. black; creeping; dry ~ 2. (misc.) to talk ~ ("to talk nonsense")

rotate v. 1. (D; intr.) to ~ around (to ~ around an axle) 2. (D; intr.) to ~ on (the earth ~s on its axis)

rotation n. 1. to make a ~ 2. crop ~ 3. in ~

rote n. ["repetition"] by ~ (to learn by ~)

rotten adj. 1. (colloq.) to feel ~ about smt. 2. (colloq.) ~ to + inf. (it was ~ of him to do that) 3. (misc.) ~ to the core

rouge n. to apply, put on ~

rough I adj. (colloq.) ["not gentle"] 1. ~ on, with (you've been pretty ~ on the children) ["difficult"] 2. ~ to + inf. (it's ~ to work at night = it's ~ working at night) 3. (misc.) it was ~ on her, losing her job like that

rough II n. ["unpolished condition"] in the ~ (a diamond in the ~) (AE)

roughshod adv. to ride, run ~ over smb. ("to treat smb. in an inconsiderate manner")

roulette n. 1. to play ~ 2. Russian ~

round n. ["unit of ammunition"] 1. to fire a ~; to get a ~ off 2. an incoming ~ (of artillery fire) 3. the ~ jammed ["drinks served to everyone in a group"] 4. to buy; order a ~ (of drinks) ["complete game"] 5. to play, shoot a ~ (of golf) ["song sung in unison in which each part is repeated"] 6. to sing a ~ ["part of a boxing match"] 7. in a ~ (the challenger was knocked out in the seventh ~)

roundabout n. to ride a ~ (BE; CE has *merry-go-round*)

roundhouse n. ["type of blow"] to throw a ~

rounds n. 1. to do, go on, make one's ~ (the doctor was making her ~) 2. on one's ~ (the doctor is on/on his ~)

roundup n. a police ~ (of all suspects)

rouse v. 1. (D; tr.) to ~ from, out of (to ~ smb. out of bed) 2. (D; tr.) to ~ to (to ~ smb. to action)

rouser n. a rabble ~

rout I n. 1. a complete, total, utter ~ 2. (misc.) to put the enemy to ~

rout II v. 1. to ~ completely, utterly 2. to ~ smb. out of bed

route I n. 1. to map out, plan a ~ 2. to follow, take a

~ 3. to introduce a ~ 4. to discontinue a ~ 5. an alternate (AE), alternative; circuitous; direct; devious; indirect; roundabout ~ 6. an escape ~ 7. a scenic ~ (to take the scenic ~) 8. a bus; newspaper; streetcar (AE), tram (BE); truck (esp. AE) ~ 9. an air; overland; sea; trade ~ 10. a ~ between; from; to

route II v. (P; tr.) they ~d the shipment around the war zone; to ~ a memorandum to the appropriate persons

routine n. 1. to change; vary a ~ 2. (a) daily, ordinary; dull ~ 3. a dance ~

rove v. (P; intr.) they ~d around the lobby; we ~d through the mall

row I /rou/ n. ["arrangement in a straight line"] 1. an even, straight ~ 2. a back; front ~ 3. in a ~ 4. (misc.) the third year in a ~ ["misc."] 5. death ~ ("cell block where prisoners await execution") (on death ~); skid ~ (AE) ("area in a city where destitute persons congregate") (on skid ~); her hair was (arranged) in cornrows

row II v. (P; intr, tr.) we ~ed across the lake; they ~ed us down to the bridge

row III /rau/ n. 1. to kick up, make, raise a ~ 2. to have a ~ 3. an awful ~ 4. a ~ about, over; with (to have a ~ with smb. about a trifle)

row IV v. (D; intr.) to ~ about, over; with

rowboat n. (AE) to row a ~

rowing n. 1. to go ~ 2. to go in for ~

rowing-boat (BE) see **rowboat**

row out v. (d; intr.) to ~ to (to ~ to an island)

royalty n. ["percentage of revenue"] 1. to pay a ~/~ties on (the publisher paid them ~ties on their dictionaries) 2. to bring in, earn ~ties (the book brings in handsome ~ties) 3. to earn, get, receive ~ties (the author received ~ties) 4. author's ~ties

rub v. 1. (D; intr, tr.) to ~ against (one part was ~bing against the other; ~ your hand against this surface) 2. (d; tr.) to ~ into, on (to ~ lotion into one's skin) 3. (N; used with an adjective) ~ it dry

rubber n. 1. crude; foam; sponge; synthetic ~ 2. ~ stretches (see the Usage Note for **eraser**)

rubbers n. (AE) ["rubber overshoes"] 1. to put on; wear ~ 2. a pair of ~

rubbish n. 1. (esp. BE) to collect the ~ 2. (esp. BE) household ~ (AE usu. has *trash*) 3. an accumulation, heap, pile of ~ 4. (misc.) to talk ~

rubble n. 1. a heap, pile of ~ 2. (misc.) to reduce smt. to ~

rubdown n. to give smb. a ~

Rubicon n. to cross the ~ ("to commit oneself irrevocably")

rub off v. 1. (D; intr.) to ~ on, onto (the paint ~bed off on my shirt) 2. (colloq.) (D; intr.) to ~ on, onto ("to affect") (we hoped that some of these cultural activities would ~ on our children)

rub up v. 1. (d; intr.) to ~ against ("to touch") (don't let the wire ~ against the pipe) 2. (colloq.) (d; intr.)

to ~ against ("to have contact with") (she used to ~ against many famous movie stars)

ruck *n.* (esp. BE) ["mass of undistinguished people"] 1. the common ~ 2. above; out of the ~

ruckus *n.* (esp. AE) to create, kick up, make, raise, stir up a ~

rude *adj.* 1. ~ about 2. ~ of (that was ~ of him) 3. ~ to 4. ~ to + inf. (it's ~ to talk during a concert)

rudeness *n.* 1. to display, show ~ 2. ~ to

rug *n.* 1. to braid; weave a ~ 2. to clean; shampoo; vacuum a ~ 3. a scatter, throw (AE) ~ 4. a hooked; oriental; Persian; rag ~ 5. a prayer ~

ruin I *n.* 1. to cause, spell ~ 2. to fall into ~ 3. complete, utter ~ 4. financial ~ (to face financial ~) 5. (misc.) on the brink of ~

ruin II *v.* to ~ completely, utterly

ruins *n.* 1. ancient; charred, smoking ~ 2. a heap, pile of ~ 3. (misc.) to sift through the ~; to lie in ~

rule I *n.* ["regulation"] ["principle"] 1. to establish, lay down, make (the) ~s 2. to formulate, set down a ~ 3. to adopt a ~ 4. to apply, enforce a ~ 5. to bend, relax, stretch; waive a ~ 6. to rescind, revoke a ~ 7. to abide by, comply with, obey, observe a ~ 8. to break, violate a ~ 9. a cardinal; firm, hard-and-fast, inflexible, ironclad, strict ~ 10. an un-written ~ 11. a general; ground ~ 12. an exclusionary (AE); gag; parliamentary ~ 13. (ling.) a deletion; grammatical; rewrite; substitu-tion ~ 14. a ~ against 15. a ~ for 16. a ~ to + inf. (it's our ~ not to smoke at staff conferences) 17. a ~ that + clause (they established a ~ that everyone must share the expenses) 18. (to be) against, in violation of the ~s 19. (misc.) the golden ~; a ~ of thumb; as a ~ ("generally"); the ~ of law ["govern-ment, reign"] 20. to establish; extend one's ~ 21. to overthrow smb.'s ~ 22. benevolent; despotic ~ 23. civilian; military; mob; popular ~ 24. major-ity; minority ~ 25. colonial; foreign; home ~ 26. ~ over 27. under smb.'s ~ (under foreign ~) ["straightedge, ruler"] 28. a slide ~

rule II *v.* 1. (d; intr.) to ~ against (the judge ~d against the plaintiff) 2. (D; intr.) to ~ in favor of 3. (D; intr.) to ~ on (to ~ on a question) 4. (D; intr.) to ~ over (to ~ over a country) 5. (L; can be subj.) the court ~d that the witness be/should be disqualif-ied; they ~d that the law was unconstitutional 6. (M) the judge ~d her to be incompetent 7. (N; used with an adjective) the judge ~d him incompetent to stand trial 8. (misc.) the judge ~d her out of order

ruler *n.* ["person who rules"] 1. to put a ~ into power 2. to overthrow, unseat a ~ 3. an absolute, authoritarian, despotic, dictatorial, tyrannical; strong; weak ~ 4. a colonial; military ~

ruling *n.* 1. to give, hand down (AE), make a ~ (the court handed down a ~) 2. a fair, just ~ 3. an unfair, unjust ~ 4. a court; official ~ 5. a ~ about, on 6. a ~

that + clause (the court's ~ that the company had violated the law was appealed)

rumblings *n.* ["rumors"] ~ about; of (~ of discon-tent were heard)

ruminate *v.* (D; intr.) ("to reflect") to ~ about, on, over

rummage *v.* 1. (D; intr.) to ~ for (he was ~ging in his pockets for change) 2. (D; intr.) to ~ through (to ~ through old clothes)

rumor, rumour *n.* 1. to circulate, spread a ~ 2. to confirm; trace, track down a ~ 3. to deny; dispel, quash, spike, squash a ~ 4. a malicious; persistent; vicious; widespread; wild ~ 5. a baseless, uncon-firmed, unfounded; idle, vague ~ 6. ~s circulate, fly, go around, spread 7. a ~ that + clause (we heard a ~ that she was back in town) 8. a ~ about 9. (misc.) ~ has it/~s are rife that she will be getting married soon

rumored *adj.* (cannot stand alone) 1. ~ to + inf. (he is ~ to have escaped to Canada) 2. ~ that + clause (it is ~ that she has returned home)

rumpus *n.* (colloq.) to kick up, raise a ~

run I *n.* ["course"] 1. a ski ~ ["freedom of move-ment"] 2. to have the ~ of the house ["race"] 3. a cross-country ~; the mile ~ ["series of demands"] 4. a ~ on a bank ["running away"] 5. on the ~ 6. (misc.) to make a ~ for it ("to flee") ["trial"] 7. a dry, dummy (BE), trial ~ ["flight"] 8. to make a ~ (over a target) 9. a bombing ~ ["point scored"] (baseball, cricket) 10. to score a ~ 11. (baseball) a home ~ ["unraveled stitches in a stocking"] (BE often has *ladder*) 12. to get, have a ~ (in a stock-ing) ["duration"] 13. in the long; short ~ ["period of performance of a play"] 14. to have a ~ 15. a brief, short; long; record ~ (the play had a record ~ on Broadway)

run II *v.* 1. (C) ("to fill") ~ a bath for me; or ~ me a bath 2. (d; intr.) to ~ across ("to meet by chance") (to ~ across an old friend) 3. (d; intr.) to ~ after ("to chase") (to ~ after a bus) 4. (d; intr.) to ~ against ("to oppose") (I would not like to ~ against her in the senatorial race; popular feeling was ~ning against the president) 5. (d; intr.) to ~ ply") to ~ between (this train ~s between New York and Philadelphia) 6. (d; intr.) to ~ down ("to descend quickly"); ("to pour") (to ~ down the stairs; tears ran down her face) 7. (esp. AE; BE has *stand*) (D; intr.) ("to be a candidate") to ~ for (to ~ for office; to ~ for Congress) 8. (d; intr.) ("to extend") to ~ from; to (the sale will ~ from the first of the month to the tenth; the fence ~s from the house to the road) 9. (d; intr.) to ~ in ("to be present") (ability for languages ~s in their blood; talent ~s in the family) 10. (d; intr.) to ~ into ("to meet") (to ~ into an old friend; to ~ into trouble) 11. (d; intr.) to ~ into ("to hit") (he ran into a pole) 12. (d; intr.) to ~ into ("to enter quickly") (to ~ into the house) 13.

(d; intr.) to ~ into ("to amount to") (the expenses will ~ into thousands of dollars) 14. (d; intr.) ("to move quickly") to ~ off (the car ran off the road) 15. (d; tr.) ("to force") to ~ off (she ran the other car off the road) 16. (d; intr., tr.) to ~ on ("to operate") (the engine ~s on diesel oil; they ran the business on borrowed money) 17. (d; intr.) to ~ out of ("to use up") (she ran out of money) 18. (d; intr.) to ~ out of ("to leave quickly") (to ~ out of the room) 19. (d; intr.) to ~ over ("to crush") (to ~ over an animal) 20. (d; intr.) ("to pass") to ~ through (a blue thread ~s through the cloth; a strange thought ran through her mind) 21. (d; intr.) to ~ through ("to examine") (let's ~ through the material again) 22. (d; tr.) to ~ through ("to process") (~ the data through the computer again) 23. (d; intr.) ("to go quickly") to ~ to (she ran to the doctor) 24. (d; intr.) to ~ to ("to seek help from") (he keeps ~ning to his mother; don't ~ to the police) 25. (d; intr.) to ~ to ("to amount") (the dictionary ~s to a thousand pages) 26. (d; tr.) ("to drive") to ~ to (I'll ~ you to the station) 27. (d; intr.) to ~ up ("to ascend quickly") (to ~ up the stairs) 28. (P; intr., tr.) ("to go") ("to move") ("to move quickly") the road ~s south; to ~ across the street; to ~ for the doctor; the children ran through the park; the smugglers are ~ning guns across the border 29. (s) supplies are ~ning low; the differences ~ deep 30. (misc.) the trains are ~ning behind schedule; she ran her hand through her hair; we are ~ning short of coffee; things are ~ning smoothly; to ~ against the clock (esp. AE) ("to time one's performance"); to ~ fast ("to be ahead of schedule"); to ~ slow ("to be behind schedule"); to ~ smb. out of town ("to expel smb. from a town"); to ~ rampant/riot ("to run wild"); (colloq.) ~ that by me again ("repeat that for me")

run afoul v. (AE) (d; intr.) to ~ of (to ~ of the law)

run aground v. (D; intr.) to ~ on (the boat ran aground on a sandbank)

runaround n. (colloq.) ["delaying action"] to give smb. the ~

run around v. (D; intr.) to ~ with (he ~s around with a fast crowd)

run away v. 1. (D; intr.) to ~ from (to ~ from home) 2. (D; intr.) to ~ to (she ran away to California) 3. (D; intr.) to ~ with (he ~ with his firm's money)

run back v. (D; intr.) to ~ to (she ran back to her room)

run counter v. (d; intr.) to ~ to (their actions ~ to their promises)

rundown n. ["summary"] 1. to give smb. a ~ 2. to get a ~ 3. a ~ on

run down v. 1. (d; intr.) ("to go") to ~ to (to ~ to the grocery store) 2. (D; intr.) ("to descend quickly") to ~ to (to ~ to the bottom of the hill)

run foul v. see **run afoul**

rung n. the bottom, lowest; highest, top ~ (of a ladder)

run-in n. ["clash"] to have a ~ with smb.

run low v. (D; intr.) to ~ on (to ~ on fuel)

runner n. ["one who runs"] 1. a distance, long-distance ~ ["unraveled stitches in a stocking"] (AE) 2. see **run I** 12

runner-up n. a ~ to

running n. ["competition"] 1. in the ~ 2. out of the ~ ["racing"] 3. cross-country ~

run off v. 1. (D; intr.) to ~ to (they ran off to Alaska) 2. (D; intr.) to ~ with (he ran off with his company's funds)

run out v. 1. (D; intr.) to ~ into (to ~ into the street) 2. (D; intr.) to ~ on ("to abandon") (he ran out on his family)

run over v. (d; intr.) to ~ to (she ran over to her friend's place)

run short v. (d; intr.) to ~ of (they never ~ of money)

run-up n. (BE) ["preparatory period"] a ~ to (the ~ to the election)

run up v. 1. (d; intr.) to ~ against ("to encounter") (to ~ against strong competition; to ~ against difficulties) 2. (D; intr.) to ~ to ("to approach quickly") (she ran up to me)

runway n. 1. to clear a ~ (for an emergency landing) 2. to overshoot a ~ 3. on a ~ (the plane was still on the ~)

ruse n. 1. a clever, subtle ~ 2. a ~ to + inf. (it was a ~ to get their money)

rush I n. 1. to make a ~ (to make a ~ for the door) 2. to beat the ~ (let's leave early and beat the ~) 3. a gold ~ 4. a mad; sudden ~ 5. a ~ for (there was a sudden ~ for tickets) 6. a ~ to + inf. (there was a ~ to buy tickets for the concert) 7. in a ~ 8. (misc.) I felt a ~ of dizziness after I drank the punch; a ~ to judgment

rush II v. 1. to ~ headlong, pell-mell 2. (d; intr.) to ~ at ("to attack") 3. (D; intr.) to ~ into (to ~ headlong into a business deal) 4. (d; intr., tr.) to ~ to (to ~ to the office; to ~ to smb.'s assistance; to ~ smb. to the hospital) 5. (P; intr., tr.) they were ~ing across the street; I had to ~ home 6. (misc.) she ~ed to catch the train

rush around v. (P; intr.) they are always ~ing around from one place to another

rush away v. (D; intr.) to ~ from (we had to ~ from the party)

rush off v. 1. (D; intr.) to ~ to (they ~ed off to the theater) 2. (E) she ~ed off to catch the bus

rut n. ["groove, furrow"] 1. a deep ~ (in a road) ["dreary routine"] 2. to get into a ~ 3. in a ~

ruthless adj. ~ in (he is ~ in his methods)

rye n. 1. winter ~ 2. a sheaf of ~ 3. (misc.) a ham sandwich on ~

S

sabbath *n.* 1. to keep, observe the ~ 2. to break, desecrate, violate the ~ 3. on the ~

sabbatical *n.* 1. to give, grant a ~ 2. to get; have; take a ~ 3. (to be, go) on (a) ~ (she was on a ~)

saber, sabre *n.* 1. to draw one's ~ 2. to brandish a ~ 3. (misc.) saber-rattling ("threatening to wage war")

sabotage *n.* 1. to commit ~ 2. an act of ~

sack *n.* ["bag"] 1. a mail ~ ["bed"] (colloq.) (AE) 2. to hit the ~ ("to go to bed") ["dismissal"] (colloq.) 3. to get the ~ 4. to give smb. the ~

sackcloth *n.* in ~ and ashes ("in deep repentance")

sacrament *n.* 1. to administer a ~ 2. to receive a ~

sacred *adj.* ~ to (the shrines were ~ to them)

sacrifice I *n.* 1. to make; offer a ~ 2. to entail a ~ 3. a great; heroic; personal ~ 4. a human ~ 5. the supreme, ultimate ~ 6. a ~ to 7. at (a) ~ (they achieved success at great personal ~)

sacrifice II *v.* 1. (D; refl., tr.) to ~ for (to ~ oneself for a just cause) 2. (D; intr., refl., tr.) to ~ to (to ~ an animal to the gods)

sacrilege *n.* 1. to commit (a) ~ 2. (a) ~ to + inf. (it was ~ to speak like that)

sacrilegious *adj.* ~ to + inf. (it's ~ to speak like that)

sad *adj.* 1. ~ about (we felt ~ about the accident) 2. ~ to + inf. (it is ~ to be alone) 3. ~ that + clause (it's ~ that we could not see each other)

sadden *v.* (R) it ~ed me to watch him turn into an alcoholic; it ~ed her that she would never see them again

saddened *adj.* ~ to + inf. (we were ~ to learn of her death)

saddle I *n.* 1. to put a ~ on (a horse) 2. an English; stock, western ~ 3. in the ~

saddle II *v.* 1. (D; tr.) to ~ for (they ~d a gentle pony for the child) 2. (d; tr.) to ~ with (to ~ smb. with an unpleasant task)

saddle sore *n.* to develop ~s

sadism *n.* to display ~

sadness *n.* 1. to express; feel ~ 2. deep, profound ~ 3. ~ over

sad sack *n.* (slang) (AE) ["inept person"] a hopeless ~

safari *n.* 1. to organize a ~ 2. to go on a ~ 3. a ~ to

safe I *adj.* 1. absolutely, completely, very ~ 2. ~ for (~ for children) 3. ~ from (~ from attack) 4. ~ to + inf. (it is not ~ to lean out of the window; it's ~ to say that their party will win) 5. (misc.) ~ and sound

safe II *n.* 1. to open; unlock a ~ 2. to close; lock a ~ 3. to break open, crack a ~ 4. a wall ~

safe-conduct *n.* to issue a ~

safeguard I *n.* 1. a built-in ~ 2. a ~ against

safeguard II *v.* (D; refl., tr.) to ~ against, from (to ~ one's property from theft)

safekeeping *n.* in ~

safety *n.* ["security"] 1. to assure smb.'s ~ 2. to jeopardize smb.'s ~ 3. air; industrial; public ~ 4. in ~ (to live in ~) 5. (misc.) a margin of ~; there is ~ in numbers; ~ first! ["device that prevents accidental discharge of a firearm"] 6. to set the ~ 7. to release the ~

safety factor *n.* a built-in ~

sag *v.* 1. (D; intr.) to ~ to (to ~ to one side) 2. (D; intr.) to ~ under (the floor ~ged under the weight)

saga *n.* a ~ about, of

sagacity *n.* the ~ to + inf. (she had the ~ to diversify her investments)

said *adj.* 1. ~ to + inf. (she is ~ to be very wise) 2. ~ that + clause (it is ~ that they own five cars)

sail I *n.* 1. to hoist, raise the ~s 2. to let out the ~s 3. to furl, take in a ~; to reduce; slacken ~ 4. to trim ("adjust") the ~s 5. to lower, strike the ~s 6. (misc.) to set ~ for ("to leave for by ship, boat"); to go for a ~

sail II *v.* 1. (d; intr.) to ~ along (to ~ along the coast) 2. (d; intr.) to ~ around, round (to ~ around the world) 3. (d; intr.) to ~ down (to ~ down a river) 4. (d; intr.) to ~ for (to ~ for Europe) 5. (d; intr.) to ~ from; to (to ~ from New York to Liverpool) 6. (d; intr.) to ~ into (the ship ~ed into port) 7. (colloq.) (d; intr.) to ~ into ("to attack") (the opposing candidates ~ed into each other) 8. (d; intr.) to ~ through (to ~ through the straits) 9. (colloq.) (d; intr.) to ~ through ("to cope with easily") (she just ~ed through her finals) 10. (d; intr.) to ~ up (to ~ up the river) 11. (P; intr.) to ~ across the ocean; to ~ towards the coast; to ~ east

sailing *n.* smooth ~ ("unimpeded progress")

saint *n.* a patron ~

sake *n.* 1. for smb.'s ~ (do it for my ~) 2. for old times' ~ 3. for the ~ of (for the ~ of argument) 4. for pity's ~ 5. for argument's ~ 6. (misc.) it's worth doing for its own ~

salad *n.* 1. to make a ~ 2. to garnish; season a ~ 3. a fruit; green; mixed; potato; tomato; tossed ~

salad dressing *n.* to make (a) ~

salary *n.* 1. to pay a ~ 2. to command, draw, get, receive; earn a ~ 3. (colloq.) to pull down (AE), pull in (BE) a ~ 4. to boost, raise ~ries 5. to cut, reduce, slash ~ries 6. to attach smb.'s ~ 7. to withhold smb.'s ~ 8. an annual, yearly; monthly; weekly ~ 9. a fixed; full ~ 10. a big, handsome, high; decent, good; low, meager, poor; small; modest ~ 11. (misc.) to negotiate a ~

sale *n.* ["selling"] 1. to make a ~ 2. a cash ~ 3. for, on

~ ("being sold") (house for ~; the book will be on ~ next month) 4. to put smt. up for ~ ["selling at reduced prices"] 5. to conduct, have, hold, run (colloq.) a ~ 6. an annual; boot, car-boot (BE); clearance; closeout; fire; garage (AE), yard (AE); going-out-of-business; jumble (BE), rummage (AE); storewide; warehouse ~ 7. on ~ (AE) = at, in a ~ (BE) ("being sold at a reduced price")

sales n. 1. to boost ~ 2. brisk ~ 3. gross; net ~ 4. ~ drop off; pick up 5. (misc.) all ~ are final

salesmanship n. high-pressure ~

salient n. (mil.) 1. to form a ~ 2. a ~ juts out (into enemy lines)

saliva n. 1. to dribble ~ 2. ~ dribbles

sally n. ["sortie"] 1. to make a ~ against ["trip"] 2. a ~ into (a ~ into strange territory)

salmon n. pink; red; smoked ~

salon n. a beauty; hair; literary ~

salt n. 1. to pour ~ (pour the ~ into the saltshaker; pour some ~ on the icy driveway) 2. to put, sprinkle ~ in, on (sprinkle some ~ on the meat; put some ~ in the soup) 3. common, table; fine; garlic; mineral; onion; rock ~ 4. a dash, pinch; grain of ~ 5. a spoonful of ~ 6. (misc.) to take smt. with a grain of ~ ("to regard smt. with skepticism"); the ~ of the earth ("the very best"); to be worth one's ~ ("to be worthy of respect")

salts n. bath; smelling ~

salute I n. 1. to fire; give a ~ (the president was given a 21-gun ~) 2. to return; take a ~ 3. a smart, snappy ~ 4. a military; naval; 19-gun; rifle; royal; 21-gun ~ 5. a ~ to 6. in ~ (to) (in ~ to our fighting forces we will play a march)

salute II v. 1. to ~ smartly (the soldier ~d smartly) 2. (D; tr.) to ~ for, on (I ~ you for your magnificent achievement)

salvage v. (D; tr.) to ~ from (to ~ records from a fire)

salvation n. 1. to bring; preach ~ 2. to find; seek ~ 3. ~ from

salve n. 1. to apply, rub in, rub on (a) ~ 2. a ~ for; to (it was a ~ to my wounded feelings)

salvo n. 1. to fire a ~ 2. an opening ~

Samaritan n. a good ~ ("a person who helps those in need")

same n. it's all the ~ to me ("it makes no difference to me")

sample n. ["representative item"] 1. to distribute, hand out (free) ~s 2. a floor; free ~ ["selected segment"] (statistics) 3. a random; representative ~

sampler n. ["needlework"] to work a ~

sampling n. (a) random ~

sanction I n. ["approval"] 1. to give ~ to 2. to receive ~ 3. legal ~

sanction II v. (K) no one ~ed his smoking marijuana

sanctions n. ["coercive measures"] 1. to apply, impose ~ 2. to clamp ~ on 3. to lift ~ 4. economic, trade; military ~ 5. ~ against

sanctuary n. 1. to give, grant, offer, provide (a) ~ 2. to find; seek ~ 3. a bird; wildlife ~ 4. (a) ~ for 5. (a) ~ from

sanctum n. an inner ~

sand n. 1. to scatter, spread, sprinkle, strew ~ 2. coarse; fine ~ 3. a grain of ~ 4. a pile of ~

sandals n. 1. beach ~ 2. a pair of ~

sandwich I n. 1. to make a ~ out of 2. a cheese; club (AE); corned-beef; doorstep (BE); double-decker; grilled-cheese (AE), toasted-cheese (BE); ham; open-face; tomato-and-lettuce; tuna ~

sandwich II v. (d; tr.) to ~ between (to ~ a meeting between a staff conference and lunch)

sanitation n. environmental ~

sanity n. 1. to keep, maintain, preserve, retain one's ~ 2. to lose one's ~

sarcasm n. 1. biting, devastating, keen, piercing, scathing, withering; mild; (thinly) veiled ~ 2. ~ about 3. (misc.) dripping with ~ (her remarks were dripping with ~)

sardines n. 1. a can (AE), tin (BE) of ~ 2. (misc.) to pack in like ~

satellite n. 1. to launch; orbit a ~ 2. an artificial (earth); communications; spy; weather ~

satire n. 1. (a) biting, scathing ~ 2. political ~ 3. a ~ on

satisfaction n. ["act of satisfying"] ["state of being satisfied"] 1. to afford, give ~ to 2. to express; feel ~ 3. to find, take ~ in 4. deep, great, profound ~ 5. quiet ~ 6. ~ that + clause (they felt ~ that a fair compromise had been reached) 7. ~ about, with 8. to smb.'s ~ (the work was done to my ~) ["compensation for a wrong or injury"] 9. to demand; seek ~ 10. to get, receive; have ~ 11. ~ for (to receive ~ for an insult)

satisfactory adj. 1. completely; highly, very ~ 2. ~ for; to

satisfied adj. 1. completely, fully, perfectly, thoroughly ~ 2. ~ with (we are ~ with the results) 3. ~ to + inf. (she is not ~ to spend her days doing nothing) 4. ~ that + clause (we are ~ that all requirements have been met)

satisfy v. 1. to ~ completely, thoroughly 2. (L; refl.) she ~fied herself that all doors were locked)

satisfying n. emotionally ~

SATS n. ["Scholastic Aptitude Tests"] (US) 1. (for admission to US universities) to take the ~ ["Standard Assessment Tasks"] (GB) 2. (given to school children since 1991 as part of the national curriculum) to do the ~

saturate v. (D; tr.) to ~ in; with

sauce n. 1. to savory; sweet ~

saunter v. (P; intr.) to ~ along the street

sausage n. 1. liver ~ (CE; AE has *liverwurst*) 2.

beef; garlic; pork ~

savagery *n.* 1. to display, show ~ 2. an outburst of ~

save I *n.* ["action that prevents an opponent from scoring"] 1. to make a ~ 2. a brilliant, spectacular ~

save II *v.* 1. (C) ~ a place for me; or: ~ me a place 2. (D; intr., tr.) to ~ for (they are ~ing for a new car; to ~ money for a new TV) 3. (D; tr.) to ~ from (to ~ valuable records from destruction) 4. (D; intr.) to ~ on (during the mild winter we ~d on fuel) 5. (J) (esp. BE) it will ~ you having to make a second trip 6. (O) it will ~ you the trouble of making a second trip; the computer will ~ (us) a lot of time 7. (misc.) to ~ money towards retirement

save up *v.* (D; intr.) to ~ for (to ~ for a new tape recorder; to ~ for a rainy day)

saving *n.* to make a ~ (on) (you can make a huge ~ on fuel bills)

savings *n.* 1. to set aside ~ 2. to deposit; invest one's ~ 3. to withdraw one's ~ (from a bank) 4. to dip into; squander one's ~

savings bond *n.* (AE) 1. to issue a ~ 2. to cash (in), redeem a ~ 3. to roll over a ~

savings certificate *n.* 1. to issue a ~ 2. to cash (in), redeem a ~ 3. (AE) to roll over a ~

savor, savour *n.* (d; intr.) to ~ of ("to suggest") (to ~ of arrogance)

savvy *n.* ["knowledge"] (colloq.) 1. to demonstrate ~ 2. political ~ (to demonstrate considerable political ~)

saw I *n.* 1. to set ("put an edge on") a ~ 2. a band; buzz (AE); circular (BE); carpenter's; chain; coping; hand; musical; power; two-handed ~

saw II *v.* 1. (d; intr.) to ~ through (to ~ through a cable) 2. (misc.) to ~ smt. up into little pieces

say I *n.* ["decision"] 1. to have the final ~ ["opportunity to speak"] 2. to have one's ~ ["role"] 3. to have a ~ in

say II *v.* 1. (B) ("to utter") she said a few words to us 2. (d; tr.) ("to state") to ~ about, of (what did they ~ about our offer?) 3. (d; tr.) ("to say in justification of") (what can you ~ for yourself?) 4. (d; tr.) to ~ to ("to respond to") (what do you ~ to the charges?) 5. (colloq.) (E) ("to state") the instructions ~ to take one tablet every morning 6. (L; to) ("to state") they said (to us) that they would be late 7. (Q; to) ("to state") she did not ~ when our next meeting would be 8. (misc.) to ~ smt. in jest; to ~ smt. under one's breath; ~ no more; that ~s it all

saying *n.* 1. a common, old, popular, wise ~ 2. a ~ goes, runs 3. (misc.) it goes without ~ that we will help

say-so *n.* (colloq.) ["statement"] on smb.'s ~ (I believed it was true on her ~)

scab *n.* a ~ falls off; forms

scabies *n.* to catch, get ~

scaffolding *n.* 1. to erect, put up ~ 2. to remove, take

down ~

scald *v.* (D; tr.) to ~ with (he was ~ed with boiling water)

scale I *n.* ["series of notes arranged in a certain sequence"] (mus.) 1. to play; sing a ~ 2. a chromatic; diatonic; major; minor; natural ~ ["system of classifying in a series of steps"] 3. a sliding; social ~ 4. a pay, salary, wage; union ~ ["relative size"] 5. an enormous, grand, large; moderate; monumental; small ~ 6. on a certain ~ (everything was planned on a monumental ~; on a ~ of one to ten) 7. (misc.) drawn to ~

scale II *n.* ["weighing machine"] 1. a bathroom; kitchen; spring; table ~ 2. on a ~ (to weigh smt. on a ~)

scale down *v.* (D; tr.) to ~ to (to ~ production to decreased demand)

scales *n.* ["weighing machine"] 1. see **scale II** 2. a pair of ~ 3. (misc.) to tip the ~ at one hundred fifty pounds ["decisive influence"] 4. to tip the ~ ("to have a decisive influence") (the event tipped the ~ in their favor)

scallions *n.* (esp. AE; BE often prefers *spring onions*) a bunch of ~

scalp *n.* a dry; itchy; oily ~

scamper *v.* (P; intr.) to ~ across the field

scan *n.* ["radiographic image"] 1. to do, perform; interpret a ~ 2. to have, undergo a ~ 3. a bone; brain; CAT; CT; heart; liver; lung ~

scandal *n.* 1. to cause, create a ~ 2. to cover up, hush up; expose, uncover a ~ 3. a juicy, sensational ~ 4. an open; political; public ~ 5. a ~ breaks, erupts; brews (a juicy ~ is brewing) 6. a breath, hint, suggestion of ~ 7. a ~ about, over 8. a ~ that + clause (it's a ~ that the buses are always so late)

scandalize *v.* (R) it ~d public opinion that the mayor had taken bribes; we were ~d to hear the news

scandalized *adj.* ~ at (they were ~ at the news)

scandalous *adj.* 1. ~ to + inf. (it is ~ to behave like that) 2. ~ that + clause (it is ~ that this road has so many potholes)

scanner *n.* a code; ultrasound ~

scapegoat *n.* to make a ~ of smb.

scar *n.* 1. to leave a ~ 2. to bear, carry, have a ~ 3. an emotional, psychological; hideous, ugly; identifying; noticeable, prominent; permanent ~ 4. a ~ on (she has a ~ on her arm) 5. a ~ forms

scarcity *n.* 1. to cause a ~ 2. a severe ~

scare I *n.* (colloq.) 1. to give smb. a ~; to put, throw a ~ into smb. 2. to get, have a ~ 3. a bomb ~

scare II *v.* (colloq.) 1. (D; tr.) to ~ into (to ~ smb. into doing smt.) 2. (D; tr.) to ~ out of (she ~d me out of my wits) 3. (N; used with an adjective) to ~ smb. stiff 4. (R) it ~d us that no one answered the doorbell 5. (misc.) to ~ smb. to death

scared *adj.* (colloq.) 1. ~ stiff, to death 2. ~ at, of (~ at the sound of the air raid siren) 3. ~ to + inf. (they are ~ to say anything) 4. ~ that + clause (we were ~ that the roof would collapse)

scare up *v.* (colloq.) (AE) to ~ for; from (to ~ a meal from leftovers)

scarf *n.* 1. to knit a ~ 2. to wear a ~ (around one's neck) 3. to tie, wrap a ~ (around smb.'s head) 4. a knitted; silk; woolen ~

scarlet fever *n.* to develop; have ~

scar tissue *n.* ~ forms

scatter *v.* (P; intr., tr.) they ~ed through the woods; the pamphlets were ~ed around the neighborhood; the groups are ~ed throughout the various states; the rioters ~ed in all directions

scavenge *v.* 1. (D; intr.) to ~ for 2. (d; tr.) to ~ from (they were ~ging items from wrecked cars)

scenario *n.* ["film outline"] 1. to write a ~ 2. a film ~ ["potential situation"] 3. a doomsday; likely ~ 4. a worst-case ~ (in the worst-case ~)

scene *n.* ["division of a play"] 1. to play; rehearse a ~ 2. to steal ("dominate") a ~ 3. the ~ shifts 4. a love ~ 5. a change of ~ ["display of anger, feelings"] 6. to make a ~ 7. an awkward, painful, ugly ~ ["location"] 8. to come on the ~ ("to appear") 9. at, on a ~ (she was at the ~ of the crime) 10. on the national ~ ["spectacle, picture"] 11. to depict a ~ 12. a beautiful; idyllic; touching ~ 13. a funny; ridiculous ~ 14. a familiar ~ 15. a disgraceful, shameful; distressing; gruesome; revolting; tragic ~ ["misc."] 16. behind the ~s ("in secret"); a change of ~ (usu. fig.); to set the ~ ("to describe a situation") ("to prepare for the occurrence of smt.")

scenery *n.* ["stage props"] 1. to set up ~ 2. to move, shift ~ 3. to dismantle ~ 4. stage ~ ["landscape"] 5. beautiful, majestic, picturesque; wild ~ 6. (misc.) (usu. fig.) a change of ~

scent *n.* ["track, trail"] 1. to have; follow; pick up a (the) ~ (the dogs picked up the ~) 2. to leave a ~ 3. a cold; false; hot ~ 4. (misc.) to throw smb. off the ~ ["intuition"] 5. a ~ for (a ~ for news) ["odor"] 6. a delicate; faint; pungent, strong ~ ["sense of smell"] 7. a keen ~

sceptical see **skeptical**

scepticism see **skepticism**

schedule I *n.* 1. to draw up, make out, make up, plan, prepare, set up, work out a ~ 2. to follow, stick to a ~ 3. to issue a ~ 4. a fixed; flexible; full; heavy; rigid; rotating ~ 5. (esp. AE) an airline; bus; train ~ (BE prefers *timetable*) 6. a production ~ 7. a ~ for 8. according to, on; ahead of; behind ~ (our work is coming along according to/on ~; the trains are running behind ~) 9. to be on smb.'s ~ (what's on your ~ tomorrow/for tomorrow?)

schedule II *v.* 1. (D; tr.) to ~ for (we will ~ her for surgery next week) 2. (H) we're ~d to arrive at one o'clock; can you ~ her to speak in the afternoon?

scheme I *n.* 1. to concoct, cook up, devise, think up a ~ 2. to foil, thwart a ~ 3. a diabolical; fantastic; get-rich-quick; grandiose; harebrained; ill-conceived; nefarious; preposterous, wild-eyed ~ 4. a ~ to + inf. (she concocted a ~ to get publicity) 5. (misc.) in the overall ~ of things

USAGE NOTE: In CE, a *scheme* can be dishonest or crafty; this connotation is probably encountered more frequently in AE than in BE.

scheme II *v.* (derog.) 1. (D; intr.) to ~ against; for 2. (E) they are ~ing to take over the government

schism *n.* 1. to cause, create a ~ 2. a ~ between

scholar *n.* 1. an eminent; productive ~ 2. a ~ in residence

scholarship *n.* ["systematized knowledge, research"] 1. to foster, promote ~ 2. productive; scientific; solid, sound, thorough ~ ["aid to a student, researcher, writer"] 3. to establish, found a ~ 4. to award, grant a ~ 5. to apply for a ~ 6. to get, receive, win a ~ (she won a ~ to a leading university) 7. to have, hold a ~ 8. a ~ for (to receive a ~ for language study) 9. a ~ to 10. a ~ to + inf. (she won a ~ to study abroad)

school I *n.* ["educational institution"] 1. to direct; operate, run a ~ 2. to accredit a ~ 3. to attend, go to (a) ~ (they go to a good ~) 4. to start ~ 5. to enter (a) ~ 6. to finish, graduate from (AE), leave (BE) ~ (she left ~ and went to university) 7. to drop out of, leave, quit (esp. AE) ~ 8. (by level) an elementary, grade (AE), grammar (AE), primary; first (BE); infant (BE); junior (BE); nursery ~ 9. (by level) a junior high (AE); middle; prep (BE) ~ 10. (by level) a comprehensive (BE), high (esp. AE), secondary; grammar (BE); prep (AE), public (BE) ("private secondary"); secondary modern (BE; now rare) ~ 11. (by level) a graduate, postgraduate (esp. BE); undergraduate ~ 12. (by subject) an art; ballet; beauty; business; dancing; divinity; driving; fencing; military; naval; riding; secretarial; technical; trade, vocational ~ 13. (by type) a boarding; church; consolidated; correspondence; progressive; public (AE), state (BE); day; evening; finishing; magnet; night; parochial; preparatory; private; reform (AE; now rare); religious; special; summer; Sunday ~ 14. (at a university; see also **faculty** 1) a business; dental; divinity; engineering; law; medical; nursing (US; CE has *school of nursing*); professional ~ 15. at, in (a) ~ (she works at/in a ~; their son is still at ~; AE also has: their son is still in ~) 16. a ~ for (a ~ for gifted children) 17. (misc.) to be kept after ~; late for ~; (AE) ~ lets out (at three o'clock); (BE) ~ breaks up for the holidays ["group of persons holding similar views"] 18. an avant-garde ~ of artists; a radical ~ of economists 19. a ~ of opinion, thought 20. (misc.) of the old ~ ("adhering to established traditions") ["misc."] 21. the ~ of hard knocks ("life with all its difficulties")

USAGE NOTE: One says *to attend school* and *to go to school*, but with a modifier an article must be included—*to attend a good school, to go to a good school, they go to the school of their choice*. Note that one can say either *they go to a school in California* or *they go to school in California*. (see the Usage Note for **university**)

school II *v*. 1. to ~ thoroughly 2. (D; tr.) to ~ in (to ~ smb. in the martial arts) 3. (H) they were ~ed to obey instantaneously

schooled *adj*. ~ in (well ~ in military tactics)

schooling *n*. 1. to receive one's ~ 2. formal ~ 3. ~ in

schoolwork *n*. to do one's ~

science *n*. 1. to advance, foster, promote ~ 2. an exact; hard; inexact; pure; soft ~ 3. applied; basic; popular ~ 4. computer, information; library; linguistic ~ 5. agricultural; medical; nursing; veterinary ~ 6. military; naval; space ~ 7. behavioral; natural; physical; political; social ~ 8. the life ~s

scientist *n*. a nuclear; political; social ~

scissors *n*. 1. to use ~ 2. to grind, sharpen ~ 3. bandage (AE); manicure; nail ~ 4. a pair of ~

scoff *v*. (D; intr.) to ~ at

scold *v*. 1. to ~ severely 2. (D; intr.) to ~ about, for (they ~ed me for being late)

scolding *n*. 1. to give smb. a (good) ~ 2. to get, receive a ~

scoop I *n*. ["utensil for scooping"] 1. a coal; flour; grain; ice-cream ~ ["hot news item"] (colloq.) 2. to get the latest ~

scoop II *v*. (d; tr.) to ~ out of

scoop up *v*. (D; tr.) to ~ from, off (she ~ed up the ice cream from the plate)

scoot *v*. (P; intr.) the boys ~ed out of the room

scooter *n*. 1. to ride a ~ 2. a motor ~

scope *n*. 1. to broaden, widen the ~ of smt. 2. a broad; narrow ~ 3. beyond, outside the ~ of smt. 4. within the ~ of smt.

score I *n*. ["tally"] (usu. sports) 1. to keep ~ 2. a close; even; lopsided ~ 3. (AE) (usu. baseball) a box ~ 4. a ~ stands (the ~ stood five to three (AE) = the ~ stood five—three (AE) = the ~ stood at five to three; how does the ~ stand?) 5. by a ~ (we won by a lopsided ~) ["points"] (sports) 6. (esp. AE) to run up a ~ 7. a lopsided ~ (our team ran up a lopsided ~) 8. a perfect ~ (the judges gave her a perfect ~) ["grievance"] ["matter"] 9. to pay off, settle a ~ 10. an old ~ (they had some old ~s to settle) 11. a ~ between (there are some old ~s between them) ["musical composition"] 12. to play; write a ~ ["copy of a musical composition"] 13. a film; full; orchestra; piano; vocal ~ ["matter"] 14. on a certain ~ (we are even on that ~) ["facts of a situation"] (colloq.) 15. to know the ~

score II *v*. 1. (D; intr., tr.) ("to make a score") to ~ against (to ~ against a team; they ~d five points against the visiting team) 2. (D; intr., tr.) ("to make a score") to ~ for (she ~d ten points for her team; who ~d for their team?) 3. (d; intr., tr.) ("to write music") to ~ for (to ~ for full orchestra) 4. (colloq.) (BE) (d; intr.) to ~ off ("to beat in an argument") (it's difficult to ~ off him in an argument) 5. (colloq.) (D; intr.) ("to achieve success") to ~ with (I really ~d with the boss) 6. (s) to ~ high; low (they ~d high in/on the proficiency tests)

scoreboard *n*. an electronic ~

scorer *n*. (sports) a high; low ~ (who was the game's high ~?)

scorn I *n*. 1. to express; feel ~ 2. to heap, pour ~ on 3. bitter, withering ~ 4. ~ for (to feel ~ for smb.) 5. with ~

scorn II *v*. (formal) 1. (D; tr.) to ~ as (he was ~ed as a traitor) 2. (BE) (E) she ~s to compromise 3. (G) she ~s compromising

scornful *adj*. ~ of

scorpion *n*. ~s sting

scot-free *adj*. to get off, go (AE) ~

scourge *n*. a ~ to (a ~ to the human race)

scout I *n*. 1. a boy ~ (esp. AE; BE usu. has *scout*) 2. a girl ~ (AE; BE has *girl guide*) 3. a talent ~

scout II *v*. (D; intr., tr.) to ~ for (to ~ the city for building sites; to ~ for new talent)

scout about, scout around *v*. (D; intr.) to ~ for (to ~ for new talent)

scowl I *n*. 1. to wear a ~ 2. to have a ~ on one's face 3. a permanent, perpetual ~

scowl II *v*. (D; intr.) to ~ at

Scrabble *n*. (T) ["game"] to play ~

scramble I *n*. 1. a mad, wild ~ 2. a ~ for (a wild ~ for tickets) 3. a ~ to + inf. (there was a ~ to buy tickets)

scramble II *v*. 1. (C) ~ a couple of eggs for me; or: ~ me a couple of eggs 2. (d; intr.) to ~ for, over (AE) (to ~ for government subsidies) 3. (P; intr.) the hikers were ~ling down the mountain; the children ~d through the forest; the passengers ~d aboard

scrap I *n*. ["waste metal"] to sell (smt.) for ~

scrap II *v*. (colloq.) (D; intr.) ("to fight") to ~ over

scrapbook *n*. to keep a ~

scrape I *n*. ["awkward predicament"] ["fight"] to get into a ~

scrape II *v*. 1. (D; intr., tr.) to ~ against (she ~d against the wall; I ~d the chair against the table 2. (D; tr.) to ~ from, off (to ~ paint off furniture) 3. (D; intr.) to ~ through ("to manage to get through") (to ~ through a crisis) 4. (N; used with an adjective) (she ~d the dishes clean) 5. (misc.) to bow and ~ ("to be obsequious")

scrape along *v*. (D; intr.) to ~ on; with (to ~ on a small salary)

scratch I *n*. ["injury produced by scratching"] 1. (to come through a fight) without a ~ 2. a deep; slight; superficial ~ ["beginning"] 3. from ~ ["prescribed level"] 4. up to ~

scratch II *v.* 1. (d; intr.) to ~ at (the cat was ~ing at the door) 2. (d; tr.) to ~ off (he ~d the paint off the wall 3. (D; tr.) to ~ on (I ~ed my hand on a nail)

scrawl *n.* ["bad handwriting"] 1. to decipher a ~ 2. an illegible; incomprehensible ~ (to write in an illegible ~)

scream I *n.* 1. to give, let out a ~ 2. a bloodcurdling, loud, shrill ~

scream II *v.* 1. to ~ hysterically; to ~ in agony 2. (B) she ~ed a few words to me 3. (D; intr.) to ~ at (he ~ed at the children for making noise) 4. (d; intr.) to ~ for (to ~ for help) 5. (D; intr.) to ~ with (to ~ with pain) 6. (E) she ~ed at/to the children to stop making noise 7. (L; to) she ~ed (to us) that the house was on fire 8. (N; used with a reflexive pronoun and an adjective) (she ~ed herself hoarse)

screech I *n.* to let out a ~

screech II *v.* 1. (D; intr.) to ~ with (to ~ with delight) 2. (misc.) to ~ to a halt

screen I *n.* 1. to put up a ~ 2. a computer; radar; television, TV ~ 3. a smoke ~ 4. the big, silver ~ (in the movies) 5. the small ~ (TV) 6. a blank ~ 7. a ~ between 8. on a ~ (there was no picture on the TV ~) 9. (misc.) to clear a ~ (as on a computer)

screen II *v.* 1. (D; intr., tr.) to ~ for (to ~ for cancer) 2. (d; tr.) to ~ from

screening *n.* 1. to do a ~ 2. (a) mass ~ 3. a ~ for

screen off *v.* (D; tr.) to ~ from (to ~ a bed from the rest of the ward)

screen test *n.* 1. to get, have a ~ 2. to give smb. a ~ 3. to do a ~ (they did a ~ on her)

screw I *n.* 1. to loosen; tighten; turn a ~ 2. a loose ~

screw II *v.* 1. (d; tr.) to ~ into (to ~ a bracket into a wall) 2. (d; tr.) to ~ onto, to (they ~ed the desk to the floor) 3. (slang) (D; tr.) to ~ out of ("to cheat out") (they ~ed him out of his bonus) 4. (N; used with an adjective) ~ the cap tight

screw around *v.* (colloq.) (AE) (D; intr.) ("to fool around") to ~ with

USAGE NOTE: This verb also has an obscene meaning.

screw on *v.* (N; used with an adjective) ~ the cap on tight

scribble *v.* 1.(A) she ~d a note to me; or: she ~d me a note 2. (D; intr.) to ~ with (to ~ with a pencil)

scrimp *v.* 1. (D; intr.) ("to be frugal") to ~ on (to ~ on food) 2. (misc.) to ~ and save

script *n.* ["alphabet"] 1. cuneiform; phonetic ~ (transcribed in phonetic ~) ["text"] 2. a film ~

Scriptures *n.* the Holy ~ (to be found in the Holy ~)

scrounge *v.* (colloq.) 1. (D; intr.) ("to scavenge") to ~ for 2. (D; tr.) ("to wheedle") to ~ from, off (he ~d a cigarette from me)

scrounge around *v.* (colloq.) (D; intr.) ("to scavenge") to ~ for

scrub *v.* (N; used with an adjective) we ~bed the tables clean

scruff *n.* (to take smb.) by the ~ of the neck

scruples *n.* 1. to have ~ 2. moral; religious ~ 3. ~ about

scrupulous *adj.* ~ in (she was ~ in avoiding references to her opponent)

scrutinize *v.* to ~ closely, intently, thoroughly

scrutiny *n.* 1. to bear ~ (his record will not bear close ~) 2. to subject smt. to ~ 3. close, intense, strict, thorough; constant; public ~ 4. open to ~ 5. under ~ (under constant ~; to come under ~)

scud *v.* (P; intr.) the clouds ~ded across the sky

scuffle I *n.* 1. to get into a ~ (with) 2. to have a ~ (with) 3. an angry; loud ~ 4. a ~ breaks out 5. a ~ about, over 6. a ~ between; with

scuffle II *v.* (D; intr.) to ~ about, over; with

sculpture I *n.* 1. to create, do, produce a ~ 2. to cast a ~ 3. an abstract ~ 4. modern ~ 5. a piece of ~

sculpture II *v.* 1. (d; tr.) to ~ into (I ~d the stone into a figure) 2. (d; tr.) to ~ out of (she ~d a head out of the marble)

sculptured *adj.* ~ in (~ in marble)

scurry *v.* 1. (d; intr.) to ~ for (to ~ for cover) 2. (P; intr.) to ~ along the street

sea *n.* 1. to sail the ~s 2. a calm, smooth; choppy, heavy, high, raging, rough, stormy, turbulent ~ 3. the deep; open ~ 4. at ~ (buried at ~) 5. (esp. BE) by the ~ (a holiday by the ~) 6. (misc.) (at) the bottom of the ~; to drift out to ~; to go to ~("to become a sailor"); to put out to ~; (all) at ~ ("bewildered")

seaboard *n.* (esp. AE) 1. the eastern ~ 2. on the (eastern) ~

seal I *n.* ["sea mammal"] 1. ~s bark 2. a colony, pod of ~s 3. a young ~ is a pup 4. a female ~ is a cow 5. a male ~ is a bull

seal II *n.* ["piece of molten wax"] 1. a privy; wax ~ ["closure"] 2. to break a ~ 3. a hermetic ~ ["stamp, symbol"] 4. to affix a ~ 5. an official; royal ~ 6. a ~ of approval (they got/received the official ~ of approval)

seal III *v.* 1. to ~ firmly, tightly; hermetically 2. (N; used with an adjective) they ~ed the area shut

sea level *n.* above; at; below ~

sea lion *n.* a colony of ~s

seal off *v.* (D; tr.) to ~ from

seam *n.* 1. to let out; rip open, tear open a ~ 2. (misc.) to be bursting at the ~s (also fig.); to come apart at the ~s (also fig.)

seaman *n.* an able, able-bodied; junior (BE) ordinary; merchant ~

seance *n.* 1. to conduct, hold a ~ 2. at a ~

seaport *n.* a bustling, busy ~

search I *n.* 1. to conduct, do, make a ~ 2. to abandon, call off a ~ 3. a careful, exhaustive, painstaking, systematic, thorough ~ 4. a fruitless ~ 5. a body, strip; door-to-door, house-to-house ~ 6. a literature ~ 7. a computer; online ~ (to do a computer ~) 8. a ~ for (the ~ for truth) 9. in ~ of 10. (misc.) (legal) unwarranted ~ and seizure

search II v. 1. to ~ carefully, thoroughly 2. to ~ all over, everywhere, high and low 3. (D; intr.) to ~ for (to ~ for a lost child) 4. (d; intr.) to ~ through (she ~ed through her purse for the keys)

searching n. online ~

searchlight n. 1. to direct, focus, shine a ~ 2. ~s play on (a wall)

search party n. to organize; send out a ~

search warrant n. to issue a ~

seared adj. ~ into (that day is ~ into my memory)

seas n. 1. the high ~ (on the high ~) 2. see **sea** 2; calm, smooth; choppy, etc.

seashore n. at the ~

seasick adj. to get; feel ~

seaside n. (BE) at, by the ~ (a holiday at the ~) (AE has *shore*)

season I n. 1. to open, usher in the (a) ~ 2. to close, usher out the (a) ~ 3. the dead, low, off, slack ~ 4. the high ~ 5. (sports) the baseball; basketball; fishing; football; hunting; open ~ 6. the dry; hurricane; monsoon; rainy ~ 7. the harvest; planting ~ 8. the holiday; tourist ~ 9. the breeding, mating, rutting ~ 10. at a ~ (at that ~ of the year) 11. in ~; out of ~ 12. (misc.) the height of the ~; it's open ~ on members of the opposition ("members of the opposition are being subjected to attack")

season II v. 1. (D; tr.) to ~ with (we will ~ the salad with dill) 2. (misc.) mix the ingredients and ~ to taste

seasoned adj. highly; lightly ~

seat n. ["place to sit"] 1. to get; have a ~ 2. to take one's ~ 3. to assign ~s 4. to book (esp. BE), reserve a ~ 5. to give up, relinquish one's ~ 6. to keep one's ~ 7. to save a ~ (for smb.) 8. a back; bucket; car; front; jump ~ 9. a box; front-row; ringside ~ 10. the driver's (AE), driving (BE) ~ 11. this ~ is free, vacant; occupied, taken 12. (misc.) please have, take a ~ ("please sit down") ["right to sit"] ["public office"] 13. to hold; win a ~ 14. to contest a ~ 15. to lose one's ~ ["administrative center"] 16. a county ~ (AE; BE has *county town*) ["dominant position"] 17. the catbird (AE), driver's (AE), driving (BE) ~

seatbelt n. 1. to buckle, fasten a ~ 2. to unbuckle, unfasten a ~ 3. to adjust a ~ 4. to wear a ~

seated adj. 1. to be ~ 2. to remain ~

secateurs n. (esp. BE) a pair of ~ (see also **shears**)

secede v. (D; intr.) to ~ from (a township cannot ~ from a county)

secession n. ~ from

seclude v. (D; refl., tr.) to ~ from

seclusion n. in ~

second I adj. ["inferior"] 1. ~ to (~ to none) ["placing after the first"] 2. to come in ~ (in a race)

second II n. ["one who ranks after the first"] 1. a close ~ ["assistant"] 2. a ~ to smb. 3. (misc.) ~s away! (in wrestling); ~s out! (in boxing) ["second gear"] 4. in ~ (don't start in ~) ["vote of endorsement"] 5. (do I hear) a ~ to (the motion?)

second III n. ["sixtieth part of a minute"] ["short time"] 1. a split ~ 2. for a ~ (I'm stepping out into the corridor for a ~) 3. in a ~ (she'll be here in a ~) 4. (misc.) wait a ~; it will take a ~

second IV /si'kond/ v. (BE) (D; tr.) ("to assign temporarily") to ~ from; to (she was ~ed from the British Council to a university)

secondary adj. ~ to

second best adj. 1. to come off ~ 2. to settle for ~

second-class adv. to travel ~

second fiddle n. ["subordinate role"] to play ~ to

second hand n. at ~ ("indirectly")

secondment n. (BE) on ~ from; to

second nature n. 1. ~ for, to 2. ~ + inf. (it was ~ for her to help)

second opinion n. to get a ~

second place n. to take ~ to (her personal life took ~ to her job)

seconds n. ["second portion of food"] 1. to ask for ~ 2. to offer ~

second thought n. 1. to have ~s about smt. 2. on ~ (AE)/on ~s (BE) ("after reconsideration") 3. (misc.) without giving the matter a ~

second wind n. to get one's ~

secrecy n. 1. to ensure ~ 2. strict ~ 3. ~ about 4. ~ in (~ in conducting negotiations) 5. in ~ (to meet in ~; the meetings were held in the strictest ~; cloaked/shrouded/veiled in ~) 6. (misc.) to swear smb. to ~; a veil of ~

secret I adj., n. 1. strictly ~ 2. most; top ~ 3. to keep smt. ~ (from smb.) 4. (misc.) in ~ in

secret II n. 1. to make a ~ of smt. 2. to guard, keep a ~ 3. to betray, blurt out, divulge, reveal a ~ 4. to ferret out, uncover, unearth a ~ 5. a dark, deep, ugly ~ 6. a closely guarded; military; open; state; trade ~ 7. a ~ that + clause (it was no ~ that they were engaged)

secretary n. ["administrative assistant"] 1. a corresponding; executive; personal; press; recording; social ~ 2. a private ~ (AE; BE has *personal assistant*) 3. a ~ of, to ["company officer"] (BE) 4. a company ~ ["officer supervising a government department"] 5. (GB) the Defence; Foreign; Home Secretary (etc.) 6. (US) the Secretary of Labor; Secretary of State (etc.)

secretion n. 1. an internal ~ 2. a ~ from

secretive adj. ~ about (~ about one's plans)

sect n. a religious ~

section n. ["division of a newspaper"] 1. the business; classified; news; sports; travel ~ ["plane figure"] (geometry) 2. a conical; cross; vertical ~ ["group of instruments"] 3. a brass; percussion;

string; woodwind ~ 4. in a ~ (to play in the woodwind ~) ["group"] (esp. AE) 5. a cheering ~ (in a
grandstand) ["surgical cutting"] 6. an abdominal;
caesarean/cesarean ~ ["area"] 7. a business; residential ~ 8. a non-smoking; smoking ~ ["department"] 9. the political ~ (of an embassy) ["part"]
10. in ~s (the bookcases come in ~s)

sector *n.* 1. the private; public ~ 2. in a ~ (in the
private ~)

secure I *adj.* 1. ~ about (to feel ~ about the future) 2.
~ against, from (~ against attack) 3. ~ in (~ in
one's beliefs)

secure II *v.* 1. (D; refl., tr.) to ~ against (to ~ borders
against attack) 2. (D; tr.) to ~ for; from (I ~d a loan
for the project from the bank)

securities *n.* 1. to issue; register ~ 2. corporate; gilt-
edged; government; negotiable; tax-exempt ~

security *n.* ["safety"] 1. to ensure, provide ~ 2. to
beef up, strengthen, tighten ~ 3. to compromise;
undermine ~ 4. collective; financial; internal; job;
maximum; national; personal; state ~ (to compromise national ~) 5. heightened; lax; strict, tight ~
6. ~ against (~ against attack) 7. (misc.) a feeling,
sense of ~; a breakdown in ~; a lapse in/of ~
["system of social insurance"] 8. (on) social ~
USAGE NOTE: In GB, *social security* refers to the
whole system of public welfare provision. In
the US, *social security* refers to the federal program that provides old-age, survivors', and disability benefits.

sedation *n.* under ~

sedative *n.* 1. to administer, give a ~ 2. to take a ~ 3.
a mild; strong ~

sediment *n.* to deposit ~

sedition *n.* 1. to foment, incite, stir up ~ 2. an act of
~

see *v.* 1. (d; intr.) to ~ about, after ("to take care of")
(to ~ about an important matter) 2. (d; tr.) to ~ as
("to visualize") ("to consider acceptable") (I can't
~ them as members of our organization; can you ~
him as Hamlet?) 3. (d; tr.) ("to find attractive") to
~ in (what does she ~ in him?) 4. (d; tr.) to ~ of ("to
encounter") (we haven't seen much of you recently; you haven't seen the last of them) 5. (d;
intr.) to ~ through ("to comprehend") (she saw
through the scheme immediately) 6. (d; tr.) to ~
through ("to assist, guide") (they saw me through
my period of grief) 7. (d; tr.) ("to accompany") to
~ to (she saw him to the door) 8. (d; intr.) to ~ to
("to attend to") (I had to ~ to the arrangements; he
saw to it that the same mistake was not repeated)
9. (d; tr.) to ~ (through) to ("to be sufficient for")
(this money will have to ~ us through to the end of
the month) 10. (I) we saw her enter the building
11. (J) we saw her entering the building 12. (L)
("to perceive") they saw that further resistance
was hopeless 13. (L) ("to make certain") ~ that

you get there on time 14. (N; used with a past
participle) ("to watch") we saw the play performed
in New York 15. (Q) ("to perceive") I could not ~
how the trick was done 16. (P; tr.) ("to accompany") I'll ~ you home 17. (P; intr.) ("to look") to
~ over the fence; to ~ into the room; to ~ through
the window 18. (misc.) they are ~ing each other
regularly ("they are dating each other"); I ~ by/
from/in the newspapers that...

seed I *n.* 1. to plant, sow, spread ~s 2. ~s germinate,
sprout; grow 3. (misc.) to go to ~ ("to be neglected
and become useless")

seed II *v.* 1. (D; tr.) to ~ with (to ~ a field with rye)
2. (misc.) (tennis) to be ~ed third

seeding *n.* cloud ~

seek *v.* 1. (D; tr.) to ~ from (to ~ help from smb.) 2.
(E) she sought to help

seeker *n.* a status ~

seem *v.* 1. (d; intr.) to ~ like (she ~s like a reasonable person) 2. (E) they ~ to be pleasant; they ~ to
like me 3. (L; to) it ~s (to me) that there will be
more rain 4. (S) they ~ pleasant; it ~ed a waste of
time; she ~s a reasonable person 5. (misc.) it ~s as
if they will win

seen *adj.* ["considered"] ~ as (a new tax cut is ~ as
likely)

seep *v.* (P; intr.) the water ~ed into the basement;
the rain ~ed through the ceiling

seesaw *v.* (d; intr.) ("to alternate") to ~ between (the
lead ~ed between the two teams)

seethe *v.* (D; intr.) to ~ with (to ~ with rage)

segregate *v.* 1. (D; tr.) to ~ by (the pupils were ~d
by age) 2. (D; tr.) to ~ from (to ~ one group from
another) 3. (D; tr.) to ~ into (to ~ people into
different groups)

segregation *n.* 1. to maintain, practice ~ 2. racial;
religious ~ 3. ~ by (~ by age)

seize *v.* 1. (D; tr.) to ~ by (he ~d me by the arm) 2.
(d; intr.) to ~ on, upon (to ~ upon a chance remark)

seized *adj.* ~ with (an acute illness)

seizure *n.* ["convulsion, paroxysm"] 1. to have a ~
2. a cardiac, heart; epileptic; uncontrollable ~
["act of seizing"] 3. search and ~

select *v.* 1. (D; tr.) to ~ as (we ~ed her as our
candidate) 2. (D; tr.) to ~ for (who was ~ed for the
assignment?) 3. (D; tr.) to ~ from among (we ~ed
her from among many candidates) 4. (H) we ~ed
her to represent us

selection *n.* ["choice"] 1. to make a ~ 2. natural ~ 3.
a wide ~ 4. a ~ as (her ~ as party candidate was not
popular) ["selected piece of music"] 5. to play a ~
6. a musical ~

self *n.* 1. smb.'s inmost, inner; real, true ~ 2. one's
old; usual ~ (she performed like her old ~)

self-assurance see **self-confidence**

self-confidence *n.* 1. to acquire, gain; display,
show; have ~ 2. to instill ~ 3. to restore smb.'s ~ 4.

to shake, undermine smb.'s ~ 5. to lose one's ~ 6. the ~ to + inf. (she doesn't have the ~ to run for public office)

self-conscious *adj.* ~ about

self-consciousness *n.* 1. to display ~ in 2. ~ about

self-control *n.* 1. to display, exhibit, show; exercise, maintain ~ 2. to lose one's ~ 3. admirable, complete, great, total ~

self-defense, self-defence *n.* 1. in ~ (to kill smb. in ~) 2. the art of ~

self-denial *n.* to exercise, practice ~

self-determination *n.* 1. to give, grant ~ 2. to achieve, realize; enjoy ~ 3. national ~

self-discipline *n.* 1. to display, exhibit; exercise; have ~ 2. admirable; great, tremendous ~ 3. the ~ to + inf. (who has the ~ to write a dictionary?)

self-evident *adj.* ~ that + clause (it is ~ that she will be chosen)

self-examination *n.* 1. to do a ~ 2. a frank, honest ~

self-flattery *n.* to indulge in ~

self-fulfillment, self-fulfilment *n.* to achieve; seek ~

self-government *n.* 1. to grant ~ 2. to enjoy ~

self-image *n.* 1. to improve one's ~ 2. a good; poor ~

self-interest *n.* 1. enlightened ~ 2. in one's own ~

selfish *adj.* ~ to + inf. (it was ~ of them to do that)

self-pity *n.* 1. to indulge in ~ 2. to wallow in ~

self-portrait *n.* to do, paint a ~

self-respect *n.* to keep one's ~

self-restraint *n.* to display, exercise, practice, show ~

self-rule *n.* 1. to grant ~ 2. to enjoy ~

self-sufficiency *n.* 1. to achieve, attain ~ 2. economic ~ 3. ~ in

self-sufficient *adj.* ~ in

self-treatment *n.* to resort to ~

sell I *n.* (colloq.) ["method of selling"] a hard; soft ~

sell II *v.* 1. to ~ retail; wholesale 2. (A) we sold our old car to him; or: we sold him our old car 3. (d; intr., tr.) to ~ for (it sold for ten pounds; we sold the car to them for three thousand dollars) 4. (D; tr.) to ~ into (to ~ smb. into slavery) 5. (colloq.) (d; tr.) to ~ on ("to convince of") (to ~ smb. on an idea) 6. (misc.) to ~ as is ("to sell with no guarantee as to quality"); to ~ smt. at a loss; to ~ by the dozen; to ~ in bulk; to sell like hot cakes ("to be sold very quickly in large quantities"); to ~ smb. down the river ("to betray and ruin smb.")

seller *n.* a best ~ (this book was a best ~)

selling *n.* panic ~

sell out *v.* (D; intr., tr.) to ~ to (she sold out to her partner)

semantics *n.* general; generative ~

semester *n.* (esp. US) the fall; spring; summer ~

semicircle *n.* 1. to form a ~ 2. in a ~

semicolon *n.* to place, put in a ~

seminar *n.* 1. to conduct, hold a ~ 2. to attend a ~ 3. a ~ on

senate *n.* 1. to convene, convoke a ~ 2. to disband, dissolve a ~ 3. a university ~ 4. a ~ meets, is in session 5. a ~ adjourns

senator *n.* (US) a junior; senior ~ (the junior senator from Idaho)

send *v.* 1. (A) we sent the manuscript to her; or: we sent her the manuscript 2. (D; tr.) to ~ as (he was sent as our representative) 3. (D; tr.) to ~ by (to ~ a letter by airmail) 4. (d; intr.) to ~ for ("to ask to come") (to ~ for the doctor) 5. (d; tr.) to ~ for ("to send smb. to fetch smt.") (she sent me for some beer) 6. (d; tr.) ("to insert") to ~ into (the coach sent some new players into the game) 7. (d; tr.) to ~ on (to ~ students on a field trip) 8. (d; tr.) to ~ out of (the teacher sent the unruly pupils out of the room) 9. (d; tr.) to ~ to (her parents sent her to camp) 10. (H) we sent him to buy beer 11. (J) the explosion sent things flying; we sent him packing ("we dismissed him summarily")

send around *v.* 1. (D; tr.) ("to circulate") to ~ to (the director sent a memo around to the staff) 2. (H) ("to dispatch") I'll ~ a car around to pick you up

send away *v.* (d; intr.) to ~ for; to (we had to ~ to the factory for spare parts)

send back *v.* (A) she sent the money back to me; or: she sent me back the money

send down *v.* 1. (BE) (D; tr.) ("to expel") to ~ from (he was sent down from Oxford) 2. (esp. BE) (D; tr.) ("to sentence") to ~ for (he was sent down for five years) 3. (misc.) we sent down to the restaurant for coffee

send in *v.* (D; intr., tr.) to ~ for (the children sent in box tops for prizes)

send-off *n.* to give smb. a (big) ~ (they gave her quite a ~)

send off *v.* 1. (D; tr.) to ~ to (we sent the children off to Europe) 2. see **send away**

send on *v.* (D; tr.) to ~ to (they sent the package on to my new address)

send out *v.* 1. (B) they sent out invitations to many people 2. (d; tr.) to ~ as (they were sent out as our representatives) 3. (d; intr., tr.) to ~ for (to ~ for pizza; they sent him out for beer) 4. (d; tr.) to ~ on (the young reporter was sent out on her first assignment)

send up *v.* 1. (D; tr.) to ~ to (they sent tea up to my room) 2. (misc.) (AE) he was sent up for five years ("he was sent to prison for five years")

senior I *adj.* ~ to (she is ~ to me by one year)

senior II *n.* (AE) a college; graduating; high-school ~

seniority *n.* according to, by ~ (to promote according to ~)

sensation *n.* ["excitement"] 1. to cause, create a ~ 2. a great ~ (her appearance created a great ~) 3. an

overnight ~ ["feeling"] 4. to feel; have a ~ 5. a
pleasant ~ 6. a burning; choking; numbing; tin-
gling; unpleasant ~ 7. a ~ in (I had a choking ~ in
my throat) 8. a ~ that + clause (I had the sensation
that smb. was in the room)

sense I n. ["judgment"] 1. to display, have, show ~
2. common, good, horse (colloq.); innate ~ 3. a
grain of ~ 4. the ~ to + inf. (they don't have the ~ to
admit defeat) 5. (misc.) to bring smb. to her/his ~s;
to come to one's ~s; to take leave of one's ~s
["logic"] 6. to make ~ (her choice makes ~; it
makes ~ to file an application; can you make any ~
out of this?) 7. to talk ~ 8. to talk ~ into smb. 9. ~ in
(there is no ~ in losing your temper) 10. (misc.)
that makes no ~ (to me) ["reaction to stimuli"] 11.
to sharpen the ~s 12. to dull the ~s 13. an intuitive;
keen ~ 14. the five ~s 15. a sixth ~ ("intuition")
["feeling"] 16. (to have) a false ~ (of security) 17.
(misc.) a ~ of humor ["meaning"] 18. a figurative;
literal, narrow, strict ~ 19. in a ~ (in the literal ~ of
the word; in every ~ of the word; in a certain ~,
you are right) ["appreciation"] 20. a ~ of beauty; a
~ of timing

sense II v. 1. (L) she ~d immediately that smt. was
wrong 2. (Q) I ~d where the problem was

senseless adj. ~ to + inf. (it was ~ to lie)

sense of humor n. 1. to demonstrate, display, have
a ~ 2. a subtle; wry ~

sensibility n. ~ to (~ to pain)

sensible adj. ["reasonable"] 1. ~ about 2. ~ to + inf.
(it was ~ of her to postpone the trip) ["aware"]
(formal) (BE) 3. ~ of (they were ~ of the danger
that they faced)

sensitive adj. 1. highly, very ~ 2. ~ about 3. ~ to (~
to charges of corruption; ~ to criticism)

sensitivity n. 1. great ~ 2. ~ to (~ to criticism)

sensitize v. (D; tr.) to ~ to

sensor n. to activate, set off, trip a ~

sentence I n. ["judgment of a court"] 1. to impose,
pass, pronounce (a) ~ (on) 2. to carry out, execute
a ~ 3. to serve (out) a ~ 4. to commute; reduce,
remit; suspend; vacate a ~ (her ~ was reduced to
five years) 5. a harsh, heavy, severe, stiff ~ 6. a
light ~ 7. a death; jail, prison; life ~ 8. an indefinite, indeterminate; suspended ~ 9. under ~ 10.
(misc.) to get off with a light ~ ["independent
group of words"] 11. to form, formulate, make up;
generate a ~ 12. an affirmative; complex; compound; declarative; elliptical; embedded; exclamatory; impersonal; interrogative; negative;
simple ~

sentence II v. 1. (D; tr.) to ~ for; to (the judge ~d her
to five years for theft; the convicted murderer was
~d to death; to ~ smb. to hard labor) 2. (H) the
judge ~d him to do community service

sentiment n. ["feeling"] 1. to echo; express a ~ 2. to
display, show ~ 3. to share a ~ 4. a growing; lofty;

patriotic; public; shocking; strong ~ 5. (a) ~
against; for, in favor of (there is growing ~ in favor
of a tax reduction) 6. (a) ~ that + clause (there was
strong ~ that the government should step down)

sentimental adj. ~ about, over

sentimentality n. 1. cloying, maudlin, mawkish ~
2. ~ about

sentimentalize v. (D; intr.) to ~ about, over

sentry n. 1. to post a ~ 2. to relieve a ~

separate I adj. ~ from (to keep ~ from)

separate II v. 1. (D; intr., tr.) to ~ from (she was ~d
from her family; to be ~d from the service; the
little girl got ~d from her parents) 2. (D; intr., tr.)
to ~ into (the children were ~d into two groups)

separation n. ~ from

separatism n. political; racial; religious ~

sequel n. a ~ to (as a ~ to)

sequence n. 1. a chronological; natural ~ 2. in ~

serenade n. 1. to play, sing a ~ 2. a ~ to

sergeant n. 1. a buck (AE); color; drill; first, top;
flight (BE); gunnery; master; platoon; recruiting;
staff; technical ~ 2. a ~ major; (BE) a company ~
major

series n. ["sequence"] (math.) 1. an alternating;
convergent; divergent; geometric; harmonic; infinite ~ ["succession"] 2. an unbroken ~ 3. in a ~
["cycle of programs, publications"] 4. a concert;
lecture ~; a miniseries; TV ~

serious adj. 1. deadly ~ 2. ~ about (she is ~ about
her work)

seriousness n. in all ~

sermon n. 1. to deliver, give, preach a ~ 2. a lay ~ 3.
a ~ against; on (a ~ against drinking; a ~ on
business ethics)

servant n. 1. a civil, public; domestic; personal ~ 2.
a faithful, loyal, trusted ~ 3. a ~ to

serve I n. (tennis) 1. to break; return smb.'s ~ 2. to
hold; lose one's ~ 3. the ~ was good, in 4. the ~
was long; out; wide 5. a ~ to (a ~ to the backhand)

serve II v. 1. (A) ("to bring") she ~d dinner to us;
or: she ~d us dinner 2. (d; intr.) to ~ as ("to fulfill
the functions of") (his illness ~d as an excuse; to ~
as mayor) 3. (D; intr.) to ~ on ("to be a member
of") (to ~ on a jury) 4. (D; tr.) to ~ on ("to deliver
to") (to ~ a summons on smb.) 5. (tennis) (D; intr.)
("to put the ball in play") to ~ to (I hate to ~ to her
— she always returns the ball to my backhand) 6.
(D; intr.) ("to be in service") to ~ under (he ~d
directly under a general) 7. (d; tr.) to ~ with ("to
deliver to") (to ~ smb. with a summons) 8. (E) ("to
have an effect") it ~d to calm everyone's nerves 9.
(N; used with an adjective) they ~d the meat cold
10. (misc.) it ~s him right ("he got what he deserved")

server n. an online ~

service n. ["work done for others"] 1. to do, offer,
perform, provide, render a ~ 2. custom (AE); meri-

torious; outstanding; public; yeoman ("loyal") ~
3. professional; social (BE) ~s (a fee for professional ~s) 4. ~ to (she received an award for meritorious ~ to the community) 5. (misc.) to press smb. into ~ ["facility that satisfies a need"] 6. to introduce; maintain; offer, provide; restore (a) ~ 7. to cut, suspend; terminate (a) ~ 8. an ambulance; counseling; emergency; health-care; health-visitor (BE), visiting-nurse (AE); social ~ 9. an answering; clipping (AE), press-cutting (BE); news, wire; online ~ 10. (a) bus; ferry; limousine; rail (BE), train (AE); shuttle ~ 11. a dating; employment (esp. AE); placement ~ 12. (a) diaper (AE); janitorial (AE); laundry; repair ~ 13. (a) delivery; door-to-door; towing ~ 14. customer; maid; room ~ 15. express; postal; telephone ~ ["operation, use"] 16. to go into ~ 17. to see ~ (this equipment has seen plenty of ~) 18. in; out of ~ (the bus was not in ~) 19. (misc.) to put smt. into ~ ["disposal"] 20. to be at smb.'s ~ ["help, benefit"] 21. to be of ~ (to) ["solemn ceremony"] 22. to hold a ~; to hold ~s 23. a burial, funeral; marriage; memorial ~ 24. an ecumenical; prayer, religious ~ 25. an evening; mid-day, noontime (esp. AE); morning; sunrise ~ (they hold sunrise ~s once a week) ["set of utensils"] 26. a coffee; dinner; tea ~ 27. a ~ for ["administrative division of government"] 28. the civil; consular; diplomatic; foreign; intelligence, secret ~ 29. human ~s ("social services") ["game during which one serves"] (tennis) 30. to hold; lose one's ~ 31. to break; return smb.'s ~ ["duty in the armed forces"] 32. to see ~ (she saw ~ during the Second World War) 33. military; national (BE), selective (AE) ~ 34. active; inactive ~ 35. in the ~ ["position as a servant"] (esp. BE) 36. domestic ~ 37. to be in ~ 38. to go into ~ 39. ~ as (to go into ~ as a housekeeper; he recalled his years in ~ as a valet) ["scheduled routes, flights"] 40. to introduce; offer, provide ~ 41. to suspend ~ 42. (a) daily; regular ~ 43. ~ between; from; to (regular ~ between two cities; that airline provides daily ~ from New York to London) ["manner of dealing with customers"] 44. fast; fine; slow ~ ["misc."] 45. lip ~ ("meaningless promises")

serving n. ["portion"] a generous, large, liberal; second; small ~

servitude n. 1. involuntary; penal ~ 2. in ~ to

session n. 1. to hold a ~ 2. a briefing; debriefing ~ 3. a bull (AE; colloq.), rap (colloq.); jam ~ 4. an emergency; joint; legislative; plenary; secret; special ~ 5. a practice; working ~ 6. a summer; winter ~ 7. a ~ on (to hold a special ~ on problems of air pollution) 8. in ~ (in secret ~; the court was in ~)

set I adj. ["opposed"] 1. (cannot stand alone) ~ against (her parents were dead ~ against the marriage) ["ready"] 2. ~ for (we are ~ for the big celebration) 3. ~ to + inf. (we are ~ to begin) ["in

favor of"] 4. ~ on (they were ~ on going) 5. (misc.) to get ~ for; (before a race): get ready, get ~, go! (BE has *ready, steady, go!*; AE also has *on your marks, get ~, go!*)

set II n. ["collection of things used together"] 1. to complete, make up a ~ 2. to break, break up a ~ 3. a carving; chemistry; chess; tea ~ 4. a complete; incomplete ~ ["group of six or more games"] (tennis) 5. to play a ~ 6. to lose; win a ~ ["apparatus"] 7. a radio; television, TV ~ ["clique"] 8. the fast (old-fashioned); international; jet; smart (old-fashioned) ~ (to belong to the jet ~) ["stage, film scenery"] 9. to dismantle, strike a ~ ["misc."] 10. to make a dead ~ at smb. ("to attack smb."); ("to attempt to win smb.'s favor")

set III v. 1. (BE) (C) ("to assign") the teacher set several problems for the pupils; or: the teacher set the pupils several problems 2. (d; tr.) ("to place") to ~ against (to ~ a ladder against a wall) 3. (d; tr.) ("to pit") to ~ against (to ~ brother against brother) 4. (D; tr.) ("to arrange") to ~ for (to ~ the stage for smt.; to ~ a trap for smb.; to ~ a date for a wedding) 5. (d; tr.) ("to incite") to ~ on (to ~ dogs on a trespasser) 6. (D; tr.) ("to put") to ~ on (to ~ a price on an article) 7. (d; tr.) ("to adapt") to ~ to (to ~ a poem to music) 8. (d; intr.) to ~ upon ("to attack") (the wolves set upon the sheep) 9. (BE) (H) ("to assign as a task") she set them to write reports; I set myself to study these problems 10. (J) ("to compel") that set me thinking 11. (N; used with an adjective) to ~ smb. free 12. (P; tr.) ("to place") she set the lamp on the table 13. (misc.) that set me to thinking; to ~ an example for smb.; to ~ smt. apart; to ~ store by smb. ("to rely on smb."); to ~ fire to ("to ignite"); to ~ a match to ("to ignite"); to ~ one's mind to do smt. ("to resolve to do smt."); to ~ smt. in motion; to ~ one's sights on ("to aspire to") to ~ sail for ("to leave by ship for")

set about v. 1. (E) ("to begin") he set about to undo the damage that he had caused 2. (G) ("to begin") we set about undoing the damage

set apart v. (D; tr.) to ~ from (certain traits ~ them apart from the others)

set aside v. (D; tr.) to ~ for (to ~ money for one's old age)

setback n. 1. to have, receive, suffer a ~ 2. a serious; severe; temporary; unexpected ~ 3. a business; diplomatic; financial; military; personal; political; professional ~ 4. a ~ to (it was a ~ to her hopes)

set down v. (BE) (L) ("to establish") it was set down that taxes are due in March

set forth v. see **set out** 2

set off v. (D; intr.) ("to start") to ~ for, on (to ~ for home; to ~ on a trip)

set out v. 1. (D; intr.) ("to leave") to ~ for; from (to ~ for town) 2. (d; intr.) to ~ on ("to begin") (to ~ on a new career) 3. (E) ("to resolve") he has set out to get revenge 4. (misc.) to ~ in search of smt.

setting *n.* ["set of tableware"] 1. a place ~ (for) ["frame in which a gem is set"] 2. to fashion a ~ for ["surroundings"] 3. a natural ~ ["arrangement of stage props"] 4. a stage ~ ["point at which a measuring device is set"] 5. to adjust, change, switch the ~ (of a thermostat) 6. to lower; raise the ~

settle *v.* 1. to ~ peacefully (to ~ a dispute peacefully) 2. (d; intr.) to ~ for ("to be content with") (they had to ~ for a very modest house with no garage) 3. (d; intr.) ("to decide") to ~ on (have you ~d on a place for your vacation?) 4. (D; intr., tr.) ("to adjust accounts; to adjust") to ~ with (to ~ with one's creditors; we have ~d our accounts with our creditors) 5. (misc.) to ~ (a case) out of court; to ~ oneself in an armchair; to ~ on the land; to ~ into a routine; she ~d a large portion of her holdings on her children

settled *adj.* to get ~

settle down *v.* 1. (D; intr.) to ~ into, to (to ~ into a routine; to ~ to family life) 2. (D; intr.) to ~ with (she ~d down for the evening with a good book) 3. (E) to ~ to study 4. (misc.) to ~ for the night

settlement *n.* 1. to come to, hammer out, make, negotiate, reach a ~ (on) 2. to mediate a ~ 3. a fair, reasonable; tentative ~ 4. a divorce; lump-sum; marriage; out-of-court; wage ~ 5. in ~ of

set up *v.* 1. (d; refl.; tr.) ("to establish") to ~ as (she set herself up as a real estate agent) 2. (BE) (d; refl.) ("to claim to be") to ~ as (she ~s herself up as an expert on Chinese art) 3. (D; tr.) ("to establish") to ~ in (to set smb. up in business)

several *determiner, pronoun* ~ of (~ of them)
USAGE NOTE: The use of the preposition *of* is necessary when a pronoun follows. When a noun follows, the use of *of the* limits the meaning—we saw several students; we saw several of the students whom we had discussed earlier.

sew *v.* (C) she ~ed a dress for me; *or:* she ~ed me a dress

sewage *n.* 1. to treat ~ 2. raw, untreated ~

sewer *n.* a sanitary; storm ~

sex *n.* ["sexual relations"] 1. to have ~ (with smb.) 2. good, great ~ 3. casual; consensual ~ 4. extramarital; marital; premarital ~ 5. safe; unsafe ~ (to practice safe ~) 6. illicit; kinky (slang), perverse ~ 7. anal; oral ~ 8. explicit ~ (pictures of explicit ~ were cut from the film) ["division of organisms into male and female"] 9. the female; male ~ 10. a member of the opposite ~ 11. (misc.) the equality of the ~es

sex organs *n.* female; male ~

sexual intercourse *n.* to have ~ (with)

sexuality *n.* female; human; male ~

shack *n.* a dilapidated, run-down; jerry-built ~

shackle *v.* (d; tr.) to ~ to (the prisoner was ~d to the bars)

shackles *n.* to cast off, throw off one's ~

shade I *n.* ["gradation of color"] 1. a delicate, pale, pastel, soft ~ 2. a dark; light ~ ["window cover"] (AE; BE has *blind*) 3. to draw, pull down; raise the ~s 4. a window ~ ["shaded place"] 5. in the ~ ["misc."] 6. a lampshade

shade II *v.* 1. (D; tr.) to ~ from (I must ~ my head from the sun) 2. (d; intr.) to ~ into (the colors ~ into each other)

shades *n.* in ~ (this fabric comes in several ~)

shadow *n.* 1. to cast, produce, throw a ~ (the setting sun cast long ~s) 2. ~s deepen, fall 3. (misc.) a (mere) ~ of one's former self; to walk in smb.'s ~ ("to be subservient to smb."); under a ~ ("under suspicion"); to be afraid of one's (own) ~ ("to fear everything"); beyond a (CE)/the (AE) ~ of a doubt, beyond a ~ of doubt (BE)

shaft *n.* 1. to bore, sink a ~ 2. a cardan (BE), drive (AE) ~ 3. an air; elevator (AE), lift (BE); mine ~

shake I *n.* ["act of shaking"] 1. to give smb. or smt. a ~ (she gave the rug a good ~) ["opportunity"] (colloq.) (AE) 2. a fair ~ (she got a fair ~)

shake II *v.* 1. to ~ hard, vigorously; violently 2. (D; tr.) to ~ at (he shook his fist at me) 3. (d; tr.) to ~ from, out of (to ~ apples from a tree) 4. (D; intr.) to ~ with (to ~ with fear) 5. (N; used with an adjective) the dog shook itself dry 6. (misc.) ~ well before using; let's ~ on it (to show that we agree)

shake down *v.* (D; tr.) to ~ from (to ~ fruit down from a tree)

shaken *adj.* badly, deeply; easily; visibly ~

shaker *n.* 1. a cocktail ~ 2. a pepper ~ (AE; BE has *pepper pot*); saltshaker (esp. AE; CE has *saltcellar*)

shake-up *n.* a personnel ~

shall *v.* (F) we ~ see

shamble *v.* (P; intr.) to ~ across the field; to ~ through the streets

shambles *n.* 1. to make a ~ of; to turn smt. into a ~ 2. in (a) ~ (their economy is in ~)

shame I *n.* 1. to bring ~ on, to, upon 2. to feel ~ at (they felt ~ at accepting bribes) 3. (colloq.) an awful, crying, dirty ~ 4. a ~ to + inf. (it's a ~ to waste so much time = it's a ~ wasting so much time) 5. a ~ that + clause (it was a ~ that they could not come) 6. in ~ (to hang one's head in ~) 7. to smb.'s ~ (to my ~, I never did help them) 8. with ~ (his cheeks burned with ~) 9. (misc.) to have no (sense of) ~; to put smb. to ~; a damn/damned ~; ~ on you!

shame II *v.* 1. (d; tr.) to ~ into (to ~ smb. into doing smt.) 2. (d; tr.) to ~ out of 3. (R) it ~s me to admit it

shameful *adj.* 1. ~ to + inf. (it was ~ of them to surrender 2. ~ that + clause (it was ~ that they surrendered)

shameless *adj.* ~ to + inf. (it was ~ of them to do

that)

shampoo *n.* ["washing of the hair"] 1. to give smb. a ~ 2. to get, have a ~ ["soapy liquid"] 3. to apply ~ 4. an anti-dandruff ~

shape I *n.* ["form"] 1. to give ~ to 2. to assume a ~; to take ~; to take the ~ of (our plans are beginning to take ~; to take the ~ of a human being) ["good physical condition"] 3. to get (oneself) into ~ 4. to keep (oneself) in ~ 5. in ~ 6. out of ~ ["physical condition"] 7. excellent, fine, tip-top; good ~ 8. bad, poor ~ 9. in ~ (to be in bad ~) 10. (misc.) she is in no ~ to give a speech

shape II *v.* 1. (D; tr.) to ~ into (to ~ clay into a jug) 2. (D; tr.) to ~ from, out of (to ~ a jug out of clay)

shape up *v.* 1. (d; intr.) to ~ as (the debate ~d up as a major event) 2. (E) the election is ~ping up to be a surprise

share I *n.* 1. to do one's ~ 2. an equal; fair; full; large, major; minor ~ 3. the lion's ~ 4. a ~ in, of (to have a ~ in the profits)

share II *v.* 1. to ~ equally 2. (D; tr.) to ~ among (the thieves ~d the loot among themselves) 3. (D; intr.) to ~ in (to ~ in the profits) 4. (D; tr.) to ~ with (we ~d our food with them)

shares *n.* ["units of capital stock"] 1. to buy; sell ~ (on the stock market) 2. ordinary ~ (BE; AE has *common stock*) 3. preference ~ (BE; AE has *preferred stock*)

sharing *n.* 1. profit ~ 2. revenue ~ (by the states)

shark *n.* 1. a man-eating ~ 2. (fig.) a loan ~

sharp *adj.* 1. razor ~ ["severe"] 2. ~ with (the boss was rather ~ with the workers)

sharpener *n.* a knife; pencil ~

shatter *v.* (D; intr.) to ~ into (the glass ~ed into many small pieces)

shave I *n.* 1. to give smb. a ~ 2. to get, have a ~ 3. a close ~ 4. (misc.) a close ~ ("a narrow escape")

shave II *v.* 1. (d; tr.) to ~ from, off (the carpenter ~d an inch off the door; the runner ~d ten seconds off the record) 2. (N; used with an adjective) she ~d me close; he ~d his head bald

shavings *n.* wood ~

shears *n.* 1. garden; pinking; pruning (AE) ~ 2. a pair of ~

shed I *n.* a tool ~

shed II *v.* (D; tr.) to ~ on (to ~ light on a mystery) ("to clear up a mystery")

sheen *n.* ["brightness"] a high ~

sheep *n.* 1. to raise, rear (BE) ~ 2. to shear ~ 3. baa, bleat, go baa 4. ~ graze 5. a flock, herd of ~ 6. the meat of the ~ is mutton 7. a young ~ is a lamb; its meat is lamb 8. a female ~ is a ewe 9. a male ~ is a ram 10. (misc.) ~ are tended by a shepherd; to round up stray ~

sheet *n.* ["piece of bed linen"] 1. a cotton; flannel; percale; silk ~ 2. a double; king-sized; queen-sized; single; twin ~ 3. a fitted; flat ~ 4. (misc.) to

change the ~s = to put on clean ~s ["financial statement"] ["record"] 5. a balance ~ 6. (BE) a wages ~ ["diagram"] 7. a flow ~ ["piece of paper"] 8. a blank ~ ["newspaper"] (colloq.) 9. a scandal ~ ["statement"] 10. a charge ~ ("a statement of charges brought against an accused person") ["pan"] (AE) 11. a cookie ~

shelf *n.* 1. to put up a ~ 2. adjustable; built-in shelves 3. a continental ~ 4. (misc.) on the ~ ("no longer in demand"); to stock shelves with supplies

shell I *n.* ["projectile"] 1. to fire a ~ at 2. to fuse a ~ 3. to lob a ~ (our artillery was lobbing ~s into enemy positions) 4. an armor-piercing; high-explosive; hollow-charge; incendiary; mortar; smoke ~ 5. ~s burst, explode ["outer cover"] 6. to come out of, emerge from one's ~ 7. to go into, withdraw into one's ~

shellacking *n.* ["beating"] (colloq.) (AE) 1. to give smb. a ~ 2. to get, take a ~

shelling *n.* constant, round-the-clock; heavy; light ~

shell out *v.* (colloq.) ("to pay") 1. (B) they had to ~ money to their creditors 2. (D; intr., tr.) to ~ for (to ~ a lot for a new car)

shelter I *n.* 1. to afford, give, offer, provide ~ 2. to seek; take ~ from 3. an air-raid, bomb, underground; fallout; homeless; tax ~

shelter II *v.* (D; tr.) to ~ from

shelving *n.* to put up ~

shepherd *v.* (P; tr.) to ~ children around the museum

sheriff *n.* a deputy ~

sherry *n.* dry; sweet ~

shield I *n.* a heat ~ (of a spacecraft)

shield II *v.* (D; tr.) to ~ against, from

shift I *n.* ["change"] 1. to bring about, produce a ~ in 2. (ling.) a consonant; functional; vowel ~ 3. a gradual; dramatic; sudden ~ 4. a ~ away from; to, towards (there was a gradual ~ away from democracy to dictatorship) ["work period"] 5. a day; eight-hour; night; split; swing ~ (she works the night ~; to work an eight-hour ~) ["transmission"] 6. an automatic; standard, stick ~

shift II *v.* 1. (D; intr., tr.) to ~ from; onto, to (to ~ responsibility to smb. else); (AE) (to ~ from first to second gear) 2. (misc.) to ~ for oneself ("to live independently"); to ~ into neutral (AE)

shift key *n.* (as on a typewriter) to press a ~

shin *n.* to bark ("scrape") one's ~s

shine I *n.* ["liking"] (colloq.) 1. to take a ~ to ["shining of shoes"] 2. to give smb. a ~ ("to shine smb.'s shoes")

shine II *v.* 1. to ~ brightly 2. (D; intr.) ("to give light") to ~ on (the hot sun was ~ing directly on our heads) 3. (d; tr.) ("to direct") to ~ on (~ the floodlights on this part of the field)

shiner *n.* ["black eye"] (colloq.) (old-fashioned) 1.

to give smb. a ~ 2. to sport a ~

shingle *n.* ["small sign designating a professional office"] (colloq.) (AE) to hang out one's ~

shingles I *n.* ["building material on a roof"] to lay ~

shingles II *n.* ["herpes zoster"] to develop, get, have ~

ship I *n.* 1. to build; refit a ~ 2. to christen; launch a ~ 3. to navigate; pilot, sail, steer a ~ 4. to scuttle; sink; torpedo a ~ 5. to abandon ~ (when it is sinking) 6. to jump ~ ("to desert from a ship's crew") 7. to raise a sunken ~ 8. to load; unload a ~ 9. a battleship; capital; naval; supply; troop ~; warship 10. a cargo; cruise; hospital; merchant; passenger ~ 11. an oceangoing; sailing ~; steamship 12. a rocket ~; spaceship 13. a ~ heaves; pitches; rolls; sinks 14. a ~ comes into harbor; docks; sails 15. by ~ (to travel by ~) 16. the bow; stern of a ~ 17. (misc.) to board a ~; to disembark from a ~; to run a tight ~ ("to operate efficiently") USAGE NOTE: The term *rocket ship* is now used chiefly in science fiction. The terms *spacecraft* and *space vehicle* are now used for the real thing. The term *spaceship* is sometimes used for "space shuttle".

ship II *v.* 1. (A) they have ~ped the merchandise to us; or: they have ~ped us the merchandise 2. (P; tr.) to ~ cargo through the Panama Canal; to ~ goods to South America from New York

shipboard *n.* on ~

ship off *v.* (D; tr.) to ~ to (they ~ped their children off to camp)

shipping *n.* merchant ~

ship out *v.* (D; intr., tr.) to ~ from; to (they ~ped the goods out from New York to London; we ~ped out from Philadelphia)

shipwreck *n.* 1. to experience, suffer (a) ~ 2. to survive a ~

shipyard *n.* a naval ~

shirk *v.* (G) no one should ~ doing her/his duty

shirt *n.* 1. to put on; take off a ~ 2. to tuck in one's ~ 3. a body; dress; polo (AE); sport (AE), sports ~; sweatshirt; tee ~, T-shirt; undershirt 4. a long-sleeve; short-sleeve ~ 5. a wash-and-wear ~ 6. (misc.) to lose one's ~ ("to lose everything")

shiver I *n.* 1. to feel a ~ 2. (misc.) a ~ went up and down my spine

shiver II *v.* 1. (D; intr.) to ~ at (she ~ed at the thought of getting up) 2. (D; intr.) to ~ from, with (to ~ from the cold)

shivers *n.* (colloq.) 1. to get; have the ~ 2. (misc.) it gives me the ~

shock I *n.* 1. to give smb. a ~ 2. to express; feel a ~ 3. to get; have a ~ 4. to absorb a ~ 5. to get over, recover from a ~ 6. to come as a ~ (to smb.) 7. a mild, slight ~ 8. a deep, great, nasty, profound, severe, terrible; rude, sudden ~ 9. (a) culture ~; future ~ 10. (an) electric ~; insulin ~ (she got an electric ~ when she touched the wire) 11. (an) emotional ~ (it came as a deep emotional ~ to her) 12. a ~ to (her arrest was a ~ to everybody) 13. a ~ to + inf. (it was a ~ to learn of her death = it was a ~ learning of her death) 14. a ~ that + clause (it came as a ~ that he had been released from prison) 15. ~ at (everyone expressed ~ at the hijacking) 16. in ~ (she seemed to be in ~) 17. (misc.) a bit of a ~ (it was a bit of a ~ to everyone); in a state of ~ (it left them in a state of ~)

shock II *v.* 1. to ~ deeply, greatly 2. (D; tr.) to ~ by, with (she ~ed me by her behavior) 3. (D; tr.) to ~ into (to ~ smb. into doing smt.) 4. (R) it ~ed me (to learn) that he had been in prison 5. (misc.) their campaign ~ed us out of our complacency

shocked *adj.* 1. deeply, greatly; easily ~ 2. ~ at (~ at the results) 3. ~ to + inf. (we were ~ to learn that he had been fired) 4. ~ that + clause (everyone was ~ that she had been arrested)

shocking *adj.* 1. ~ to + inf. (it is ~ to read of such crimes) 2. ~ that + clause (it's ~ that the article was censored)

shock therapy, shock treatment *n.* 1. to administer ~ 2. to get, receive ~

shock wave *n.* to send a ~ (the uprising sent ~s through the country)

shoelace *n.* 1. to tie; untie a ~ 2. to knot a ~ 3. a pair of ~s

shoes *n.* 1. to put on; wear ~ 2. to slip off; take off ~ 3. to break in (new) ~ 4. to lace (up) (one's) ~ 5. to brush; polish, shine ~ 6. to fix, mend (esp. BE); repair ~ 7. tight; well-fitting ~ 8. high-heeled; low-heeled ~ 9. ballet; basketball; earth; gym ~; overshoes; running; saddle ~ (esp. AE); snowshoes; sports; tennis; track; walking ~ 10. ~ fit; pinch 11. a pair of ~ 12. (misc.) to fill smb.'s ~ ("to replace smb.")

shoestring *n.* (colloq.) ["limited funds"] on a ~ (to operate a business on a ~)

shoo *v.* (colloq.) (D; tr.) ("to chase") to ~ away from, out of (~ the cat out of the room)

shoot I *n.* ["young plant"] 1. a bamboo ~ ["hunting trip"] (esp. BE) 2. (to go on) a tiger ~

shoot II *v.* 1. (D; tr.) ("to execute by shooting") to ~ as (he was shot as a deserter) 2. (D; intr.) ("to fire") to ~ at (to ~ at smb.) 3. (colloq.) (esp. AE) (d; intr.) ("to aim") to ~ for (to ~ for the top) 4. (D; intr., tr.) ("to fire") to ~ from (to ~ an arrow from a bow) 5. (D; intr., tr.) ("to fire") to ~ into (to ~ into the air) 6. (N; used with an adjective) ("to hit with gunfire") to ~ smb. dead 7. (P; intr.) ("to move quickly") they shot past us in a sports car 8. (misc.) to ~ on sight; to ~ to kill; to ~ it out with smb.

shoot-out *n.* to have a ~ (with)

shoot up *v.* (D; intr.) to ~ into (to ~ into the sky)

shop I *n.* ["store"] 1. to manage, operate a ~ 2. an

antique ~; bookshop; butcher (AE), butcher's (BE); chemist's (BE); duty-free; gift; novelty; pastry ~; pawnshop; pet; stationer's (BE) ~; sweetshop (BE); thrift; toy ~ 3. a draper's ~ (BE; AE has *dry-goods store*) 4. at, in (she works in a ~) ["workshop"] 5. a barbershop (esp. AE), barber's ~ (BE); beauty (esp. AE); body; machine; paint; printing; repair ~ ["place of work"] 6. a closed ~ ("firm that hires only union members") 7. an open ~ ("firm that hires union members and non-union members") 8. a union ~ ("firm that hires only workers who will join the union if they are not already members") ["misc."] 9. to close down (a) ~ ("to stop operations"); to set up ~ ("to begin operations"); to talk ~ ("to discuss one's work while not at work"); a coffee ~ (AE; BE has *coffee bar*); a betting ~ (BE; CE has *bookmaker's*)

USAGE NOTE: *Shop* and *store* are CE. In BE, *store* tends to be used for a very large retail establishment (*department store*) and *shop* for the others (*bookshop, sweetshop*). In AE, *store* is used for all, regardless of size (*department store, book store, candy store*). However, AE can also use *shop* for a small specialized store (*bookshop, millinery shop*). In BE *a chemist* is more likely than *a chemist's shop*.

shop II *v.* 1. (D: intr.) to ~ for (to ~ for food) 2. (misc.) to go ~ping; let's go window ~ping; to ~ smb. to the police (BE; slang) ("to inform on smb. to the police")

shop around *v.* (D; intr.) to ~ for (to ~ for bargains)

shopper *n.* a Christmas; comparison; window ~

shopping *n.* 1. to do the ~ 2. Christmas; comparison; window ~ (to do the Christmas ~; to do comparison ~)

shore *n.* 1. (AE; BE has *seaside*) at the ~ (a vacation at the ~) 2. off ~ (two miles off ~) 3. on a ~ (smb. was standing on the ~) 4. to reach (a) ~

short I *adj.* 1. ~ in (~ in stature) 2. ~ of, on (colloq.) (~ of funds; to go/BE; run/CE ~ of food; to fall ~ of one's goal; he is a nice fellow, but a bit ~ on brains) 3. (misc.) to be caught ~ ("to find oneself in acute need"); to be caught ~ (BE; colloq.) ("to feel the need to go to the toilet"); the boss was ~ ("impatient") with me; a bit, little ~

short II *n.* 1. (we called him Bill) for ~ 2. in ~ (in ~, it was a disaster)

shortage *n.* 1. an acute, desperate, severe ~ 2. a food; fuel; housing; labor; teacher; water ~; war-time ~s

shortcut *n.* 1. to take a ~ 2. a ~ to (a ~ to success)

shorten *v.* 1. (D; tr.) to ~ by (to ~ trousers by two inches) 2. (D; tr.) to ~ to (to ~ a manuscript to acceptable length)

shortening *n.* (esp. AE) vegetable ~

shorthand *n.* 1. to take; transcribe ~ 2. (to take smt. down) in ~

short haul (esp. AE) see **short run**

short run *n.* ["brief period"] in the ~

shorts *n.* 1. Bermuda; boxer ~ 2. a pair of ~

short shrift *n.* ["quick work"] 1. to make ~ of ("to finish with quickly") 2. to give smb. ~ ("to deal with smb. summarily") 3. to get ~ from smb. ("to be treated summarily by smb.")

shortsighted *adj.* ~ to + inf. (it was ~ of her not to make a reservation)

short term see **short run**

short way *n.* 1. to take the ~ (home) 2. (misc.) it's just a ~ to the station

shot *n.* ["act of shooting"] 1. to fire, take a ~ at (she took a ~ at him) 2. a random; warning ~ (to send a warning ~ across the bow of a ship) 3. a pistol; rifle ~ ["marksman"] 4. a bad; crack, good ~ ["throw, kick of the ball to score points"] 5. (esp. basketball) to make, sink; miss; take a ~ (to take a ~ at the basket) 6. (basketball) a dunk, stuff; foul; jump; lay-up ~ 7. (tennis) a drop; passing ~ 8. (ice hockey) a penalty ~ ["metal ball used in the shot put"] 9. to put the ~ ["injection"] 10. to give smb. a ~ 11. to get; have a ~ 12. a booster ~ ["critical remark"] 13. a cheap; parting ~ ["attempt"] (colloq.) 14. to get; have a ~ at (the boxer never got a ~ at the title) ["chance"] (colloq.) (AE) 15. a ~ that + clause (it's a five to one ~ that she'll find out) ["misc."] 16. to call the ~s ("to direct matters"); a ~ in the arm ("a stimulus"); a ~ in the dark ("a wild guess")

shotgun *n.* a sawed-off (AE), sawn-off (BE) ~ (see also **gun** 1, 2, 4, 5, 6)

should *v.* (F) she ~ help

shoulder I *n.* 1. to shrug one's ~s 2. to square, straighten one's ~s 3. broad, square ~s 4. a dislocated ~ 5. (misc.) ~ to ~ (to work ~ to ~) ("to work closely together"); to give smb. the cold ~ ("to be unfriendly to smb."); to put one's ~ to the wheel ("to work very hard"); to rub ~s with ("to associate with"); straight from the ~ ("in a direct manner"); we parked our car on the ~ (AE)/hard ~ (BE) of the road

shoulder II *v.* (d; tr.) to ~ through (she ~ed her way through the crowd)

shout I *n.* 1. to give a ~ 2. a jubilant; loud; piercing; triumphant ~ 3. a ~ rang out, went up

shout II *v.* 1. (B) she ~ed a few words to me 2. (D; intr.) to ~ at (don't ~ at me) 3. (d; intr.) to ~ for, with (she ~ed for/with joy) 4. (E; at; to) she ~ed at/to us to call the police 5. (L; at; to) he ~ed (at/to us) that we should call the police 6. (misc.) he ~ed himself hoarse

shove I *n.* to give smb. a ~

shove II *v.* (P; tr.) ~ the suitcases under the bed; she ~d the files into the drawer

shovel I *n.* a snow; steam ~

shovel II *v.* (P; tr.) they ~ed the snow to the side; I

~ed the coal into the bin

show I *n*. ["performance"] ["program"] 1. to direct; do, produce, put on, stage; promote; sponsor a ~ 2. to attend, catch (colloq.), go to, see, take in a ~ 3. a chat (BE), talk; quiz; TV ~ (to sponsor a TV ~) 4. a one-man, one-woman; talent; variety ~ 5. a floor; peep ~ 6. an air; horse; ice ~ 7. a Punch-and-Judy; puppet; sound-and-light ~ ["display, exhibition"] 8. to produce, put on, stage; promote; sponsor a ~ 9. to attend, go to, see, take in a ~ 10. an antique; art; auto (AE), motor (BE); fashion; flower ~ ["misc."] 11. for ~ ("designed to make an impression"); bad ~ ("very bad"); good ~ ("very good"); to put on a ~ ("to pretend"); to steal the ~ ("to draw the most attention"); to stop the ~ ("to receive a great deal of applause, attention"); a ~ of strength; who is running the ~? ("who is in charge here?"); to get the ~ on the road (slang) ("to get things going")

show II *v*. 1. (A) ("to display") ~ the book to me; or: show me the book 2. (d; tr.) ("to guide") to ~ around, over, round (esp. BE), through (she ~ed me through the museum) 3. (d; tr.) to ~ for ("to have as a result of") (what can we ~ for our efforts?) 4. (d; tr.) ("to guide") to ~ to (I ~ed her to her seat) 5. (J) ("to display") the photograph ~ed them conversing 6. (L; may have an object) ("to demonstrate") the research ~ed (us) that our theory was correct 7. (M) ("to demonstrate") she ~ed herself to be an excellent worker; history ~ed her to be a prophet 8. (Q; usu. has an object) ("to demonstrate") can you ~ me how to operate the copying machine? 9. (misc.) to ~ to advantage ("to show in the best light"); to ~ oneself in public

showdown *n*. 1. to come to, have; force a ~ with 2. a ~ over (we had a ~ over the change in plans)

shower I *n*. ["bath using an overhead spray"] 1. to have (BE), take a ~ ["short period of rain"] ["brief downpour"] 2. a heavy; light ~ 3. April; intermittent; passing; scattered ~s 4. a meteor; rain; snow; thunder ~ 5. a sun ~ (esp. AE) ("rain that falls while the sun is shining") ["party to which the guests are expected to bring gifts"] (AE) 6. to make a ~ for smb. 7. a baby; bridal ~

shower II *v*. 1. (d; tr.) to ~ on, upon (to ~ gifts on smb.) 2. (d; tr.) to ~ with (to ~ smb. with gifts)

showing *n*. ["performance"] 1. to make a ~ 2. a good; poor ~ (he made a good ~)

show off *v*. 1. (B) they ~ed off their new car to all the neighbors 2. (D; intr.) to ~ to (she was ~ing off to everyone)

show up *v*. 1. (D; tr.) to ~ as (the incident ~ed him up as a charlatan) 2. (s) he ~ed up drunk

shrapnel *n*. to catch a piece of ~ (in the leg)

shreds *n*. 1. to cut, rip, tear smt. to ~ 2. (misc.) her clothing was in ~

shrewd *adj*. 1. ~ at, in 2. ~ to + inf. (it was ~ of her

to do that)

shrewdness *n*. 1. to display ~ 2. ~ at, in 3. the ~ to + inf. (she had the ~ to buy real estate when the market was depressed)

shriek I *n*. 1. to let out a ~ 2. a loud ~

shriek II *v*. 1. (D; intr.) to ~ at 2. (D; intr.) to ~ in, with (to ~ with laughter) 3. (H; at) they ~ed at us to stop

shrine *n*. 1. to consecrate; create, establish a ~ 2. to desecrate a ~ 3. a holy, sacred ~ 4. a ~ to 5. at a ~ (to pray at a ~)

shrink *v*. (d; intr.) to ~ from (to ~ from responsibility)

shrouded *adj*. ~ in (~ in mystery)

shrubbery, shrubs *n*. 1. to prune; trim ~ 2. ornamental ~

shrug I *n*. 1. to give a ~ (of the shoulders) 2. with a ~ (of the shoulders)

shrug II *v*. (D; intr.) to ~ at ("to express indifference to") (she ~ged at the suggestion)

shudder I *n*. 1. to send a ~ (through the audience) 2. to give a ~ 3. a ~ ran (through the audience) 4. (misc.) the news sent a ~ through our competitors; the shock sent a ~ down my spine

shudder II *v*. 1. (D; intr.) to ~ at (to ~ at the thought of going back to work) 2. (E) I ~ed to contemplate what lay ahead 3. (misc.) the car ~ed to a stop

shudders *n*. 1. to give smb. the ~ (her weird appearance gave me the ~) 2. to get the ~ (I get the ~ whenever I think about our narrow escape)

shuffle *v*. (P; intr.) they ~d idly along the street; they ~d slowly through the park

shufty *n*. (slang) (BE) ["quick look"] to have a ~ at

shunt *v*. 1. (d; tr.) to ~ from (the trains were ~ed from the station) 2. (d; tr.) to ~ onto, to (to ~ a train onto a siding)

shut *v*. 1. (D; tr.) to ~ on (to ~ the door on smb.) 2. (D; tr.) to ~ to (they shut their eyes to poverty) 3. (N; used with an adjective) she shut the door tight

shut off *v*. (D; refl., tr.) to ~ from (they shut themselves off from their neighbors)

shutter *n*. ["shield in a camera"] 1. to release the ~ ["window cover"] 2. to close; open the ~s

shuttle I *n*. ["vehicle used on an established route"] 1. to take a ~ 2. a space ~ 3. a ~ between

shuttle II *v*. 1. (d; intr.) to ~ between (these ships ~ between the two ports) 2. (P; tr.) to ~ tourists to the terminal

shy I *adj*. ["wary"] ["nervous"] 1. painfully ~ 2. ~ about, of (BE) 3. ~ with (he was very ~ with girls) ["lacking"] (esp. AE) 4. ~ of (we are still a little ~ of our quota)

shy II *v*. (D; intr.) to ~ at (the horse shied at the noise)

shy away *v*. (d; intr.) to ~ from (they shied away from contact with their neighbors)

sic *v*. (D; tr.) ("to urge to attack") to ~ on (to ~ a dog on smb.)

sick *adj.* 1. ~ at (~ at heart; ~ at the prospect of leaving home) 2. ~ of (we are ~ of the red tape) 3. (misc.) ~ to one's stomach (AE); worried ~; to be ~ and tired of smt.; to be taken ~; to make smb. ~ ("to disgust smb.")

sick call *n.* (mil.) to go on ~

sicken *v.* 1. (BE) (d; intr.) to ~ for; of (they ~ed of the endless parties; she's ~ing for the flu) 2. (R) it ~ed me to watch him drink himself to death

sickening *adj.* ~ to + inf. (it was ~ to watch them bicker constantly)

sickness *n.* 1. altitude, mountain; car; decompression; morning; motion, travel; radiation; sea; sleeping ~ 2. in ~ (and in health)

sick parade (BE) see **sick call**

side I *n.* ["right or left part"] 1. the left; right ~ 2. the credit; debit ~ (of a ledger) 3. on a ~ (on the sunny ~ of the street) ["faction, party"] 4. to take smb.'s ~; to take ~s ("to support a faction") 5. the losing; right; winning; wrong ~ 6. on smb.'s ~ (of a dispute) ["direction"] 7. the opposite ~ 8. from a certain ~ (from the other ~; from all ~s) 9. (to turn) to one ~ ["surface"] ["part"] 10. a far; near; reverse ~ 11. the east; north; south; west ~ 12. on a ~ (on the other ~; on the north ~ of the town square) ["aspect"] 13. the bright; dark, gloomy; humorous; practical ~ (of things); the seamy ~ of life 14. a ~ to (there are two ~s to every question) 15. (misc.) to study all ~s of a problem ["area near a person"] 16. at, by smb.'s ~ (she sat at my ~) ["shore, bank"] 17. on a ~ (on the other ~ of the river) ["misc."] 18. to be on the safe ~; I have a pain in my ~; to tutor smb. on the ~ ("to tutor smb. part-time"); we split our ~s laughing ("we laughed long and hard"); time is on our ~ ("time is working for us"); on smb.'s ~ (of the family); he's a bit on the short ~ (see the Usage Note for **team**)

side II *v.* (d; intr.) to ~ against; with

sidelines *n.* on the ~ ("out of action")

sidestroke *n.* to do, swim the ~

siding *n.* ["material attached to the outside of a building"] (AE) 1. to install ~ 2. aluminum ~ ["short stretch of railway track"] 3. a railway ~ 4. on a ~

sidle up *v.* (d; intr.) to ~ to (she ~d up to me)

siege *n.* 1. to conduct a ~ of; to lay ~ to 2. to lift, raise a ~ 3. a state of ~ (in a state of ~) 4. at, during a ~ (he was killed at the ~ of Leningrad) 5. under ~ (a city under ~)

siesta *n.* to have, take a ~

sieve *n.* to pass smt. through a ~

sift *v.* 1. to ~ carefully 2. (d; tr.) to ~ from (to ~ fact from fiction) 3. (d; intr.) to ~ through (to ~ through the debris)

sigh I *n.* 1. to breathe, heave a ~ (of relief) 2. to give, let out a ~ 3. an audible; deep, profound; inaudible

~ 4. a ~ of contentment; a ~ of relief

sigh II *v.* to ~ in, with relief

sight *n.* ["view"] 1. to catch; keep ~ of 2. to lose ~ of 3. at (the) ~ (to faint at the ~ of blood; to fall in love at first ~) 4. by ~ (to know smb. by ~) 5. in, into, within ~ (the ship was no longer in ~; the ship came into ~) 6. on ~ (to shoot looters on ~) 7. out of ~ ["something seen"] 8. a beautiful; interesting; memorable; pleasant; spectacular; thrilling ~ 9. a comical, funny ~ 10. a familiar ~ 11. a miserable; pitiful; sorry ~ 12. a disturbing; horrendous, horrible; ugly; unpleasant ~ ["device used to aim a gun"] 13. to adjust one's ~s 14. to line up one's ~s (on) 15. a front; panoramic; peep; rear; telescopic ~ 16. (misc.) to have smb. in one's ~s ["ability to see"] 17. failing; keen ~ 18. to lose one's ~

sighting *n.* a confirmed; radar; visual ~

sights *n.* ["aspirations"] 1. to set one's ~ on (she set her ~ on a career in politics) 2. to lower; raise one's ~ 3. (misc.) to set one's ~ high ["something worth seeing"] 4. to see, take in the ~ (the tourists took in the ~) 5. to show smb. the ~

sign I *n.* ["indication"] 1. to give, show a ~ (he showed ~s of advanced emphysema; they showed no ~s of life) 2. a clear; sure, telltale, unmistakable ~ 3. an encouraging ~ 4. a danger; warning ~ 5. vital ~s ("basic indications of life") 6. a ~ that + clause (there had been no ~ that the volcano would erupt) ["mark, symbol"] 7. a minus; plus ~ 8. a dollar; pound ~ 9. a call ~ ("identifying letters of a radio station") ["marker"] ["placard"] 10. to post, put up; set up a ~ 11. a for rent (AE), to let (BE); for sale; no smoking; no trespassing; road, traffic ~ (follow the road ~s; they put up a for sale ~) 12. (esp. AE) a ~ that + clause (the police put up a ~ that the road was closed) ["misc."] 13. to make the ~ of the cross

sign II *v.* 1. (D; intr.) to ~ for (she had to ~ for the letter) 2. (D; intr.) to ~ with (the player ~ed with the team yesterday) 3. (misc.) to ~ on the dotted line

signal I *n.* ["sign"] ["message"] 1. to flash, give, send, send out; transmit a ~ 2. to get, pick up; receive a ~ 3. to unscramble a ~ 4. a clear, unmistakable ~ 5. a danger, distress; prearranged; warning ~ 6. a smoke ~ (Indians used to send up smoke ~s) 7. a turn ~ (AE; BE has *indicator*) 8. (AE) a traffic ~ 9. a storm ~ 10. a ~ from; to 11. a ~ to + inf. (the ~ to attack) 12. a ~ that + clause (the troops received the ~ that the attack was to begin) 13. at, on a ~ (the raid began at a given ~) 14. (misc.) she made a ~ for us to leave; (Am. football) to call the ~s (also fig.) ["electrical impulses"] 15. a radar; radio; shortwave ~ 16. a strong; weak ~ 17. ["misc."] to send mixed ~s ("to be vague about one's intentions")

signal II *v.* 1. to ~ wildly 2. (B) they ~ed their

position to us 3. (d; intr.) to ~ for (to ~ for help) 4. (E; to) she ~ed to us to come closer 5. (H) he ~ed us to come closer 6. (L; to; may have an object) the radio operator ~ed (to us)/~ed (us) that the ship was in distress 7. (Q; to) she ~ed (to) us how close we should come 8. (misc.) she ~ed for us to come closer

signatory *n*. a ~ to (the ~ries to the treaty)

signature *n*. 1. to affix; scrawl; write one's ~ 2. to put one's ~ on, to 3. to bear a ~ (the treaty bore the president's ~) 4. to notarize; witness a ~ 5. to forge smb.'s ~

significance *n*. 1. to acquire; have ~ for 2. to attach ~ to 3. deep, great; statistical ~ 4. to be of ~ for, to

significant *adj*. 1. ~ for, to 2. ~ to + inf. (it is ~ to note that the story did not appear in the newspapers) 3. ~ that + clause (it is ~ that our ambassador was not invited)

signify *v*. 1. (L; to) their statements ~ (to us) that no action will be taken 2. (misc.) she ~fied her assent with a nod; all those in favor, ~ by saying "aye"

sign on *v*. 1. (D; intr.) to ~ as (to ~ as a seaman) 2. (D; intr.) (BE) to ~ for (to ~ for the dole)

sign out *v*. (D; tr.) to ~ from (we ~ed out three books from the library)

sign over *v*. (B) she ~ed over the property to her children

sign up *v*. 1. (D; intr.) to ~ as (to ~ as a volunteer) 2. (D; intr., tr.) to ~ for (she ~ed up for an evening course; to sign smb. up for a course) 3. (D; intr., tr.) to ~ with (they ~ed up with the volunteers) 4. (E) they ~ed up to serve as volunteers 5. (H) they ~ed us up to serve as volunteers

silence *n*. 1. to impose ~ 2. to keep, maintain, observe ~ 3. to break (the) ~ 4. (an) absolute, complete, perfect, total, utter ~ 5. a deep, profound; prolonged; respectful, reverent ~ 6. (an) awkward; pained; shocked; stony; stunned ~ 7. a dead; eerie; hushed; ominous ~ 8. ~ reigns 9. in ~ (we were received in ~) 10. (misc.) radio ~; a conspiracy of ~; a vow of ~; a wall of ~

silent *adj*. 1. to become, fall ~ 2. to keep, remain ~ 3. ~ about

silhouette *n*. in ~ (I saw it only in ~)

silhouetted *adj*. ~ against, on (~ against a light background)

silk *n*. ["fine fabric"] 1. to spin ~ 2. fine ~ 3. artificial, synthetic; natural; pure; raw ~ ["misc."] (BE) to take ~ ("to become a King's Counsel or Queen's Counsel")

silkworm *n*. 1. to keep (BE), raise (esp. AE), rear (BE) ~s 2. ~s spin cocoons

silly *adj*. 1. ~ about 2. ~ to + inf. (it was ~ of her to say that) 3. (misc.) to make smb. look ~

silver *n*. pure, sterling ~

similar *adj*. 1. strikingly ~ 2. ~ in (~ in outlook) 3. ~ to (this specimen is ~ to that one)

similarity *n*. 1. to bear, have (a) ~ 2. a striking ~ 3. a ~ among, between; to

simmer *v*. (D; intr.) to ~ with (to ~ with excitement)

simple *adj*. ~ to + inf. (it was ~ to do the job = it was ~ doing the job = it was a ~ job to do)

simultaneous *adj*. ~ with

sin I *n*. 1. to commit a ~ 2. to expiate a ~ 3. to absolve smb. of ~ 4. to forgive smb.'s ~ 5. a cardinal; deadly; inexpiable; mortal, unforgivable, unpardonable; venial ~ 6. original ~ 7. a ~ against 8. a ~ to + inf. (it's a ~ to tell a lie) 9. a ~ that + clause (it's a ~ that her talents are being wasted) 10. (misc.) (obsol.) to live in ~ ("to live together without being married")

sin II *v*. (D; intr.) to ~ against

since *adv*. 1. ever ~ 2. long ~

sincere *adj*. 1. ~ about (she was ~ about her promise to retire) 2. ~ in (~ in one's beliefs)

sincerity *n*. 1. to demonstrate, show ~ 2. (misc.) to doubt smb.'s ~; in all ~

sinful *adj*. ~ to + inf. (it is ~ to waste so much food)

sing *v*. 1. (C; more rarely A) ~ a song for/to us; or: ~ us a song 2. (D; intr.) to ~ about, of 3. (D; intr.) to ~ to (to ~ to a piano accompaniment) 4. (D; intr.) to ~ with 5. (misc.) to ~ in tune; to ~ out of tune; to ~ a baby to sleep

sing along *v*. (D; intr.) to ~ with (~ with me)

singer *n*. a blues; folk; jazz; opera; pop ~

single file *n*. 1. to form a ~ 2. (to walk) in ~

single-minded *adj*. ~ about

single out *v*. 1. (D; tr.) to ~ as (she was ~d out as the leading candidate) 2. (D; tr.) to ~ for (to ~ smb. out for special treatment) 3. (H) to ~ smb. out to get special treatment

singles *n*. (tennis) 1. to play ~ 2. ladies' (BE), women's; men's ~

singular *n*. in the ~

sink I *n*. 1. a kitchen ~ 2. a ~ backs up; leaks

sink II *v*. 1. (d; intr.) to ~ below (to ~ below the surface) 2. (d; intr., tr.) to ~ into (to ~ into oblivion; to ~ one's teeth into a good steak) 3. (D; intr.) to ~ to (to ~ to the bottom)

sink back *v*. 1. (D; intr.) to ~ against (she sank back against the cushions) 2. (D; intr.) to ~ into (to ~ into the bed)

sink down *v*. (D; intr.) to ~ into (his head sank down into the soft pillows)

sip *n*. 1. to have, take a ~ 2. (misc.) to drink water in ~s

siphon *v*. (D; tr.) to ~ from, out of (we had to ~ some gasoline/petrol from another car)

siphon off *v*. (D; tr.) to ~ from; onto, to (the police ~ed off traffic from the main road onto/to a secondary road)

siren *n*. 1. to sound, turn on a ~ 2. an air-raid; ambulance; fire; police ~ 3. a ~ blares, goes off, sounds, wails

sister *n.* ["relative"] 1. a big, elder, older; kid (colloq.), little, younger; twin ~ 2. a foster; half ~; stepsister 3. a sister-in-law 4. a lay; soul ~ 5. a ~ to (she was like a ~ to us) ["senior nurse"] (BE) 6. a nursing; ward ~

sit *v.* 1. to ~ quietly, still; upright 2. (D; intr.) ("to be seated") to ~ around, at (to ~ around a table) 3. (d; intr.) ("to pose") to ~ for (to ~ for a portrait) 4. (d; intr.) to ~ on ("to be a member of") (to ~ on a committee) 5. (d; intr.) to ~ through (we had to ~ through the whole boring speech) 6. (misc.) to ~ tight ("to refrain from taking action"); to ~ for an examination/to ~ an examination (BE) ("to take an examination"); to ~ on the bench ("to be a judge"); to be ~ting pretty ("to be well off")

sit down *v.* 1. to ~ hard 2. (d; intr.) to ~ to (to ~ to a meal)

site *n.* 1. to excavate a ~ 2. an archeological; battlefield; building, construction; burial; camping; caravan (BE) ~ 3. a web ~ 4. on a certain ~ (the new church will be built on the ~ of the old cathedral) 5. (misc.) protective clothing must be worn on ~

sit-in *n.* to conduct, hold; organize, stage a ~

sit in *v.* 1. (D; intr.) ("to attend") to ~ as (she sat in as our representative) 2. (D; intr.) to ~ for ("to replace") (she sat in for me while I was out of town) 3. (D; intr.) to ~ on ("to attend") (we sat in on a few meetings)

sitter *n.* a baby; house ~

sitting duck *n.* ["easy target"] a ~ for

situated *adj.* conveniently ~

situation *n.* 1. to comprehend, grasp, size up, take in, understand a ~ 2. to accept; face, face up to a ~ 3. to deal with, handle a ~ 4. a pleasant; stable ~ 5. an awkward; delicate; embarrassing; tense; ticklish, touchy; tricky ~ 6. a complex, complicated; involved ~ 7. a crisis, emergency; critical; desperate; grave, serious; hopeless, no-win (colloq.); life-and-death ~ 8. a fluid, unstable; explosive; intolerable; unpleasant ~ 9. the current, present ~ 10. the economic; housing; political; social ~ 11. the international; world; local; national ~ 12. a ~ deteriorates; improves 13. in a certain ~ (in the present ~) 14. (misc.) to take stock of the ~
USAGE NOTE: Some purists prefer the simple nouns *crisis* and *emergency* to phrases such as *crisis situation* and *emergency situation*.

sit-up *n.* ["exercise"] to do ~s

sit up *v.* 1. (D; intr.) to ~ with (to ~ with a sick child) 2. (misc.) to ~ late; to ~ straight 3. to ~ and take notice

sit well *v.* (D; intr.) to ~ with ("to be accepted by") (such behavior doesn't ~ with them)

six-shooter see **pistol** 1-5, 7

size *n.* 1. (often clothing) to take; wear (a) certain ~ (what ~ do you wear? I take a large ~) 2. an

enormous, tremendous; large; moderate; small ~ 3. (clothing) an extra-large; large; medium; small ~ 4. a standard ~ 5. the right; wrong ~ (they gave me the wrong a ~) 6. (clothing) boys'; children's; girls'; junior (esp. AE); men's; misses'; women's ~s 7. life ~ 8. of a certain ~ (of enormous ~) 9. (misc.) what ~ shirt do you take? to cut to ~

skate I *n.* 1. an ice; roller ~ 2. a pair of ~s

skate II *v.* (P; intr.) we ~d across the lake; the children ~d onto the thin ice

skate over *n.* (D; intr.) to ~ to (she ~d over to us)

skater *n.* a figure; ice; roller; speed ~

skating *n.* figure; ice; roller; speed ~

skeleton *n.* a human ~

skeptical, sceptical *adj.* ~ about, of

skepticism, scepticism *n.* 1. to demonstrate, display ~ 2. to maintain (a) ~ 3. ~ about (to maintain a healthy ~ about smt.) 4. (misc.) an air of ~; to regard/view smt. with ~

sketch *n.* ["drawing"] 1. to do, draw, make a ~ 2. a charcoal; composite; freehand; pencil ~ 3. a rough ~ ["short essay"] 4. a brief, thumbnail ~ 5. a biographical ~

ski I *n.* a pair of ~s

ski II *v.* (P; intr.) they skied across the valley; I skied down the trail

skid *v.* 1. (D; intr.) to ~ on (cars often ~ on ice) 2. (P; intr.) the bus ~ded into the ditch; the car ~ded off the road

skid row see **row I** 5

skids *n.* on the ~ ("having difficulty")

skiing *n.* cross-country ~

skill *n.* 1. to acquire, develop, learn, master; hone a ~ 2. to demonstrate, display, show ~ 3. a basic ~ 4. consummate, great ~ 5. diplomatic; entrepreneurial; management, managerial; professional; technical; verbal ~ 6. coping; marketable; survival ~s 7. ~ at, in; with (~ at/in using a computer; ~ with one's hands) 8. the ~ to + inf. (she had the ~ to cope with a difficult job) 9. (misc.) to market one's ~s

skilled *adj.* 1. highly ~ 2. ~ at, in; with

skillful, skilful *adj.* ~ at, in; with (~ at tying knots; ~ with one's hands)

skim *v.* 1. (d; tr.) ("to remove") to ~ from (to ~ the fat from the soup) 2. (d; intr.) to ~ through ("to read quickly") (to ~ through an article) 3. (P; intr., tr.) ("to bounce") the boy ~med stones along the surface of the water; the birds ~med across the lake

skimp *v.* (D; intr.) to ~ on (to ~ on food)

skin I *n.* 1. to tan a ~ 2. to cast, shed, slip (esp. AE) one's ~ (the snake shed its ~) 3. clear; delicate; fair; fine; sensitive; tender; smooth; soft ~ 4. chapped; dry; coarse, rough; mottled; oily ~ 5. dark; light ~ 6. human ~ 7. (sunburned) ~ blisters; peels 8. (misc.) to save one's ~ ("to save one's life"); a thick ~ ("insensitivity"); a thin ~ ("excessive sensitivity"); to get under smb.'s ~ ("to irritate smb.")

skin II *v.* to ~ smb. alive ("to punish smb. severely")

skip *v.* (P; intr.) to ~ from one topic to another; the child ~ped across the playground

skirmish I *n.* 1. a border; brief; minor ~ 2. a ~ between; with

skirmish II *v.* (D; intr.) to ~ with

skirt I *n.* 1. to hem; lengthen; shorten a ~ 2. a divided; full; gored ~; miniskirt; pleated; slit; wraparound ~

skirt II *v.* (d; intr.) to ~ (a)round (they ~ed around the problem)

skis *n.* water ~

skit *n.* to do, perform a ~ on

skunk *n.* (misc.) to smell a ~ (esp. AE; colloq.) ("to sense trouble")

sky *n.* 1. a blue, clear, cloudless, fair; starry ~ 2. a cloudy; dull, gray, overcast, sullen ~ 3. a ~ clears up; clouds up, clouds over 4. a patch of (blue) ~ 5. in the ~

skyline *n.* 1. to dominate the ~ (the cathedral spire dominates the ~) 2. an imposing; jagged ~

skyscraper *n.* a tall ~

slab *n.* a concrete; marble; mortuary; stone ~

slack *n.* ["part that hangs loose"] to take up the ~ (of a rope)

slacks *n.* a pair of ~

slam *v.* (P; intr., tr.) she ~med the books down on the table; they ~med right into me; he ~med the door in my face

slander *n.* to spread ~

slang *n.* 1. army; prison; (Cockney) rhyming; student; underworld ~ 2. ~ for ("scram" is ~ for "go away")

slanted *adj.* ["biased"] ~ against; towards (the article was ~ against our viewpoint)

slap I *n.* 1. to give smb. a ~ (in the face) 2. (misc.) a ~ in the face ("a direct insult"); a ~ on the wrist ("a gentle reprimand")

slap II *v.* 1. (d; intr.) ("to strike") to ~ against (the waves were ~ping against the sides of the boat) 2. (D; tr.) ("to strike") to ~ in (to ~ smb. in the face) 3. (d; tr.) ("to impose") to ~ on (to ~ new restrictions on exporters) 4. (misc.) to ~ smb. on the wrist ("to reprimand smb. gently")

slash *v.* (D; intr.) to ~ at (to ~ at smb. with a knife)

slate I *n.* ["record of past performance"] 1. a clean ~ (to start off with a clean ~) 2. (misc.) to wipe the ~ clean

slate II *v.* (colloq.) (BE) (D; tr.) ("to criticize severely") to ~ for (the play was ~d for its dialogue)

slated *adj.* (AE) ["scheduled"] (cannot stand alone) 1. ~ for (~ for promotion) 2. ~ to + inf. (she is ~ to be promoted soon)

slaughter *n.* indiscriminate, mass, wanton, wholesale ~

slave I *n.* 1. to free, liberate a ~; to emancipate ~s 2. a fugitive, runaway ~ 3. (fig.) a ~ to (a ~ to a habit) 4. (misc.) to buy; sell ~s

slave II *v.* (d; intr.) to ~ over (to ~ over a hot stove)

slave away *v.* (D; intr.) to ~ at; over (to ~ over a hot stove)

slavery *n.* 1. to establish, introduce ~ 2. to abolish ~ 3. to free from ~ 4. to sell into ~ 5. white ~

sledding *n.* (colloq.) (AE) ["progress"] rough, tough ~

sleep I *n.* 1. to induce ~ 2. to get (enough) ~ 3. deep, heavy, profound, sound; fitful; light; restful ~ 4. (misc.) to fall into a deep ~; to go to ~; to walk in one's ~; to put to ~ ("to kill"); ("to make unconscious"); to lose ~ over ("to worry a great deal about"); one's beauty ~; to get/have a good night's ~

sleep II *v.* 1. to ~ fitfully; lightly; soundly, well 2. (D; intr.) to ~ on ("to postpone for a day") (to ~ on a decision) 3. (d; intr.) to ~ through (I slept through the lecture) 4. (d; intr.) to ~ with ("to have sexual relations with") 5. (misc.) my foot went to ~; to ~ late; to ~ like a log

sleeper *n.* a heavy, sound; light ~

sleeve *n.* 1. to roll up one's ~s 2. long; short ~s (I always wear short ~s during the summer) 3. (misc.) to have smt. up one's ~ ("to have a secret"); to roll up one's ~s and get down to work ("to get down to serious work"); to laugh up one's ~ ("to laugh secretly")

slice I *n.* 1. to cut off a ~ (of) 2. a thick; thin ~

slice II *v.* 1. (C) ~ a piece of meat for me; or: ~ me a piece of meat 2. (d; intr., tr.) to ~ into (to ~ into the bread; she ~d the cake into several portions) 3. (d; tr.) to ~ off (please ~ a small piece off that end of the roast) 4. (d; intr.) to ~ through (the icebreaker ~d through the ice) 5. (N; used with an adjective) she ~d the bread thin

slice up *v.* (D; tr.) ~ into (she ~d up the roast into several helpings)

slick *n.* an oil ~

slide I *n.* a hair ~ (BE; AE has *barrette*)

slide II *v.* 1. (d; intr.) to ~ down (to ~ down a hill) 2. (d; intr.) to ~ from, out of (the glass slid from her hand) 3. (d; intr.) to ~ into (the car skidded and slid into a ditch) 4. (AE) (baseball) (D; intr.) to ~ into ("to occupy by sliding") (he slid into second base) 5. (P; intr., tr.) to ~ across a frozen pond

slide rule *n.* to operate, use a ~

slides *n.* 1. to project, show ~ 2. to make; mount ~ 3. to look at ~

slight *n.* (lit.) ["slur"] a ~ on, to (a ~ on smb.'s honor)

slime *n.* ~ oozes

sling I *n.* in a ~ (her arm was in a ~)

sling II *v.* 1. (D; tr.) to ~ at (to ~ stones at smb.) 2. (P; tr.) she slung the knapsack over her shoulder 3. (misc.) to ~ mud at smb. ("to slander smb.")

slink *v.* (P; intr.) to ~ through the bushes

slip I *n.* ["error"] 1. to make a ~ (of the tongue) 2. a Freudian ~ ["escape"] (colloq.) 3. to give smb. the ~ ["piece of paper"] 4. a credit (BE), deposit, paying-in (BE) ~ (in a bank); a sales ~ (AE) 5. a call ~ ("request for a library book") 6. a pink ~ ("notice of termination of employment") 7. a rejection ~ ("notification that a manuscript has been rejected by a publisher") 8. ["cover"] a pillow ~ USAGE NOTE: In AE, a *credit slip* indicates a credit for merchandise returned. BE uses *credit note*

slip II *v.* 1. (A) ("to hand") she ~ped a note to me; or: she ~ped me a note 2. (d; intr.) to ~ by, past ("to get by unnoticed") (they easily ~ped by the roadblock; they ~ped past the sentry) 3. (D; intr.) to ~ from, out of ("to fall from") (the glass ~ped out of her hand) 4. (d; intr.) ("to move quickly") to ~ into (to ~ into a room) 5. (d; intr.) to ~ into ("to change into") (to ~ into smt. more comfortable; to ~ into a dressing gown) 6. (d; tr.) to ~ into ("to insert surreptitiously") (to ~ a clause into a contract; she ~ped a note into his hand) 7. (D; intr.) ("to slide and fall") to ~ on (he ~ped on a banana peel) 8. (d; intr.) ("to move quickly") to ~ out of (to ~ out of a house) 9. (d; intr.) to ~ out of ("to take off") (he ~ped out of his sweat suit) 10. (d; intr., tr.) to ~ through ("to pass through; to cause to pass through") (several scouts ~ped through their lines; we were able to ~ an agent through their security net; the opportunity ~ped through his fingers) 11. (misc.) she let it ~ that she was going to retire

slipcovers *n.* (AE) 1. to make ~ 2. to put on ~ 3. custom-made ~

slip out *v.* 1. (D; intr.) to ~ for (she ~ped out for a walk) 2. (D; intr.) to ~ to (they ~ped out to the bar/pub)

slippers *n.* 1. house ~ 2. a pair of ~

slip up *v.* (D; intr.) ("to blunder") to ~ on (she ~ped up on the last question)

slit I *n.* a narrow ~

slit II *v.* (N; used with an adjective) she slit the envelope open

slither *v.* (P; intr.) to ~ along the ground

slobber *v.* (colloq.) to ~ all over smb.

slog I *n.* (esp. BE) a hard ~

slog II *v.* (P; intr.) to ~ through the mud

slogan *n.* 1. to coin a ~ 2. to chant a ~ 3. a catchy ~

slog away *v.* (D; intr.) to ~ at (to keep ~ging away at one's homework)

slope I *n.* 1. a gentle, gradual; steep ~ 2. a slippery ~ (may be fig.) 3. a ski ~

slope II *v.* 1. to ~ gently, gradually 2. (P; intr.) the river bank ~s to the east 3. (colloq.) (BE) (P; intr.)

("to slink") to ~ off to a pub; they ~d off home

slosh *v.* (P; intr.) to ~ through the snow

slot *n.* (colloq.) ["position"] to fill; fit into a ~

slot machine *n.* (AE) ["gambling device"] to play a ~ (BE has *fruit machine*)

slouch I *n.* (colloq.) ["incompetent person"] no ~ at (she is no ~ at getting things done)

slouch II *v.* (D; intr.) to ~ over (she was ~ing over the table)

slouch down *v.* (D; intr.) to ~ behind (she ~ed down behind the steering wheel)

slow I *adj.* 1. ~ at, in (she was ~ in reacting) 2. ~ to + inf. (she was ~ to react) 3. (misc.) ~ of speech

slow II *v.* (D; intr., tr.) to ~ to (the influx of immigrants has ~ed to a trickle; she ~ed the car to a stop)

slow burn *n.* (slang) (AE) to do a ~ ("to become angry gradually")

slowdown *n.* 1. an economic ~ 2. a ~ in, of

slow motion *n.* ["slow-motion photography"] in ~ (they showed the finish in ~)

sludge *n.* activated ~

slug *v.* (colloq.) (esp. AE) 1. (O) (can be used with one animate object) ("to punch") I'll ~ you one 2. (misc.) to ~ it out with smb.

slum *v.* to go ~ming

slumber *n.* deep ~

slump I *n.* 1. a business, economic ~ 2. a ~ in (a ~ in the housing market) 3. in a ~ (housing starts are in a ~)

slump II *v.* 1. (D; intr.) to ~ to (the ground) 2. (P; intr.) she was ~ed over her typewriter; profits ~ed from a record high to a new low

slums *n.* 1. to clean up, clear away, tear down ~ 2. festering, squalid; inner-city, urban ~

slur I *n.* ["insult"] 1. to cast a ~ 2. an ethnic, racial ~ 3. a ~ on (his remark was a ~ on my character)

slur II *v.* (d; intr.) to ~ over ("to minimize") (to ~ over a blunder)

sly *n.* on the ~ (to do smt. on the ~)

smack I *n.* ["heroin"] (slang) to be on ~

smack II *v.* (colloq.) (O) (can be used with one animate object) I'll ~ you one

smack III *v.* (d; intr.) to ~ of ("to suggest") (to ~ of treason)

smallpox *n.* 1. to contract, develop, get; have ~ 2. to eradicate ~

small talk *n.* to make ~

smart I *adj.* ["impudent"] (colloq.) 1. to get ~ with (don't get ~ with me) ["shrewd"] 2. ~ to + inf. (she was ~ to refuse; it was ~ of him to reinvest his money)

smart II *v.* 1. (D; intr.) to ~ at, over (to ~ at an insult) 2. (D; intr.) to ~ from (her eyes were ~ing from the smoke) 3. (D; intr.) to ~ under (to ~ under injustice)

smash *v.* 1. (d; intr., tr.) to ~ into (to ~ into another car) 2. (d; intr.) to ~ through (to ~ through a fence) 3. (misc.) she ~ed her fist down on the table

smattering *n.* to acquire, pick up a ~ of (they have picked up a ~ of the language)

smear I *n.* (med.) 1. to do, take a ~ 2. a Pap ~ (they did a Pap ~ on each patient)

smear II *v.* 1. (D; tr.) to ~ with (to ~ bread with butter) 2. (P; tr.) to ~ lotion all over one's body; to ~ ointment on one's skin

smell I *n.* 1. to give off; have a ~ 2. a clean; delicious, good; sweet ~ (the food has a delicious ~) 3. a faint, slight ~ 4. a lingering; persistent; strong ~ 5. an acrid; bad, dirty, disagreeable, foul, putrid, rank; musty; sour ~ (the room has a dirty ~) 6. a ~ of (the ~ of paint) 7. a sense of ~

smell II *v.* 1. (D; intr.) to ~ like; of (to ~ of fish) 2. (J) we ~ed smt. burning 3. (L) I could ~ that smt. was burning 4. (Q) I could ~ where the coffee was 5. (s) the food ~s good

smile I *n.* 1. to crack a ~; flash a ~ (at) 2. to give smb. a ~ 3. to evoke a ~ 4. to hide, repress a ~ 5. a beautiful, pretty; beguiling, intriguing; cheerful, happy; dazzling; disarming, engaging; friendly; infectious; pleasant; radiant; ready; sunny; sweet ~ 6. a bitter; fixed; forced; sardonic; supercilious ~ 7. with a ~ (to answer with a ~ on one's face) 8. (misc.) they are all ~s at the good news

smile II *v.* 1. to ~ bitterly; cheerfully; coldly; sweetly 2. (D; intr.) to ~ at (she ~d at me) 3. (D; intr.) to ~ on ("to favor") (fortune ~d on us) 4. (misc.) to ~ from ear to ear

smirk *v.* (D; intr.) to ~ at

smite *v.* (formal) (N; used with an adjective) to ~ smb. dead

smithereens *n.* to blow, break, smash smt. into, to ~

smitten *adj.* ["affected"] (formal) 1. ~ by, with (~ by disease) ["infatuated"] (colloq.) 2. ~ by, with (he was totally ~ with her)

smoke *n.* ["gaseous products of burning"] 1. to belch, emit, give off ~ (chimneys belch ~) 2. to exhale; inhale ~ 3. heavy, thick; light ~ 4. acrid; black ~ 5. cigar; cigarette ~ 6. (as of cigarettes) active; passive ~ 7. ~ pours, rises from (a chimney) 8. ~ eddies, spirals (upward) 9. a cloud; column; pall; pillar; puff; whiff; wisp of ~ 10. (misc.) to go up in ~ ("to disappear completely") ["act of smoking"] 11. to have a ~ 12. (to go out) for a ~

smoker *n.* a chain; habitual, heavy, inveterate; light ~

smoke ring *n.* to blow ~s

smoke screen *n.* 1. to lay down a ~ 2. (fig.) to throw up a ~

smoking *n.* 1. to cut down on; give up, stop ~ 2. to ban, prohibit ~ 3. teenage ~ 4. (misc.) no ~!

smolder, smoulder *v.* (d; intr.) to ~ with (to ~ with discontent)

smooth *adj.* 1. ~ to (~ to the touch) 2. (misc.) as ~ as

silk

smother *v.* (D; tr.) to ~ with (we ~ed the flames with a heavy blanket)

smuggle *v.* 1. (D; tr.) to ~ across (to ~ goods across a border) 2. (D; tr.) to ~ by, past, through (to ~ a diamond past customs) 3. (D; tr.) to ~ into (to ~ currency into a country) 4. (D; tr.) to ~ out of (to ~ stolen goods out of a country)

smuggling *n.* 1. to engage in ~ 2. arms; drug ~

smut *n.* a ~ peddler

snack I *n.* 1. to have a ~ 2. to fix ("prepare") a ~ 3. a between-meal(s); light; midnight; quick ~ 4. party ~s

snack II *v.* (D; intr.) to ~ on (to ~ on peanuts)

snag I *n.* ["obstacle"] (colloq.) 1. to hit a ~ ["jagged tear"] 2. to get; have a ~ (in one's stocking)

snag II *v.* (D; tr.) to ~ on (I ~ged my sleeve on a nail)

snake I *n.* 1. a poisonous, venomous ~ 2. ~s bite, strike; coil; crawl; hibernate; hiss; slither 3. ~s molt, shed their skin 4. (misc.) a ~ in the grass ("a treacherous person")

snake II *v.* (colloq.) he ~d his way through the crowd

snap I *n.* ["spell of weather"] 1. a cold ~ ["something easy"] (colloq.) 2. a ~ to + inf. (it was a ~ to find information about that author = it was a ~ finding information about that author)

snap II *v.* 1. (D; intr.) to ~ at (the dog ~ped at him; to ~ at the bait) 2. (L; at) she ~ped (at me) that she had no time to see us 3. (misc.) to ~ to attention; to ~ out of a bad mood; the lid ~ped shut

snap back *v.* (L) when I asked her to help, she ~ped back that she was too busy

snappy *adv.* (colloq.) to make it ~ ("to hurry")

snapshot *n.* to take a ~

snarl *v.* 1. (B) she ~ed a few words to me 2. (D; intr.) to ~ at 3. (L) he ~ed that he would be late

snatch I *n.* ["fragment"] to catch; overhear ~es (of conversation)

snatch II *v.* 1. (d; intr.) to ~ at (she ~ed at the line that the sailors threw to her) 2. (D; tr.) to ~ from, out of (he ~ed the purse from her hand)

sneak *v.* (P; intr.) they ~ed into the theater; to ~ around in the bushes

sneak away *v.* see **sneak off**

sneak off *v.* 1. (D; intr.) to ~ from (she ~ed off from the others) 2. (D; intr.) to ~ to (he ~ed off to the football game)

sneak up *v.* 1. (D; intr.) to ~ behind (smb. ~ed up behind us) 2. (D; intr.) to ~ on, to (he ~ed up to them)

sneaky *adj.* (colloq.) ~ of (that was ~ of him)

sneer *v.* (D; intr.) to ~ at

sneeze *v.* (colloq.) (d; intr.) to ~ at ("to consider lightly") (their offer is not to be ~d at)

sneezing *n.* a fit of ~

snicker *v.* (D; intr.) to ~ at

sniff I *n.* to get, have a ~

sniff II *v.* (D; intr.) to ~ at (the dog ~ed at her)

sniffles *n.* to have the ~

snigger *v.* (esp. BE) (D; intr.) to ~ about, at

snipe *v.* (D; intr.) to ~ at (the press keeps ~ing at her)

snit *n.* (colloq.) (AE) ["state of agitation"] in a ~

snitch on *v.* (slang) (AE) (D; tr.) ("to inform on") to ~ to (she ~ed on him to the police)

snob *n.* 1. an intellectual ~ 2. (BE) an inverted ~

snook *n.* (colloq.) (BE) to cock a ~ at ("to thumb one's nose at")

snore I *n.* a heavy, loud ~

snore II *v.* to ~ heavily, loudly

snow I *n.* 1. to have ~ (we had ~ yesterday) 2. deep; drifting; driving, heavy; falling; powdery; light; wet ~ 3. crisp; new-fallen ~ 4. ~ accumulates; falls; melts; sticks 5. a blanket; coating, dusting of ~ 6. in the ~ (to play in the ~) 7. (misc.) to clear away, remove, shovel ~; as white as ~

snow II *v.* to ~ hard, heavily; lightly

snowball I *n.* to throw a ~ at

snowball II *v.* (D; intr.) ("to expand") to ~ into

snowball fight *n.* to have a ~

snowfall *n.* a heavy; light ~

snow job *n.* (colloq.) (esp. AE) ["deception, flattery"] to give smb. a ~

snowman *n.* to build, make a ~

snowshoes *n.* 1. a pair of ~ 2. (to walk) on ~

snowstorm *n.* see **storm I** 2

snub *n.* a deliberate; obvious ~

snuff *n.* 1. to take ~ 2. a pinch of ~ 3. (misc.) not up to ~ ("not up to an acceptable standard")

snuggle *v.* (d; intr.) to ~ against (the children ~d against each other)

snuggle up *v.* (d; intr.) to ~ to (the little girl ~d up to her doll)

soak *v.* 1. (D; intr., tr.) to ~ in (to ~ the laundry in cold water) 2. (d; intr.) to ~ into (the water ~ed into the soil) 3. (d; intr.) to ~ through (the blood ~ed through the bandages)

soaked *adj.* 1. ~ to the skin 2. ~ through and through 3. thoroughly ~

soaking *n.* 1. to get a (good; thorough) ~ 2. to give smt. a (good) ~

soap *n.* 1. face; laundry; liquid; powdered; saddle; scented; toilet ~ 2. a bar, cake of ~

soar *v.* (d; intr.) to ~ into, to (the temperature ~ed into the eighties; the mercury ~ed to ninety)

sob I *n.* 1. to let out a ~ 2. to stifle a ~ 3. a bitter; choking ~

sob II *v.* 1. to ~ bitterly 2. (B) the child ~bed a few words to the teacher 3. (L) she ~bed that she wanted to go home 4. (misc.) to ~ oneself to sleep

sober *adj.* cold, stone (AE) ~

socialism *n.* 1. to build ~ 2. Fabian; state; utopian ~

3. under ~ (to live under ~)

socialize *v.* (D; intr.) to ~ with (she likes to ~ with her neighbors)

social work *n.* to do ~

society *n.* ["group, association"] 1. to establish, found, set up a ~ 2. to disband, dissolve a ~ 3. a burial; historical; honor; humane; learned; literary; medical; musical; secret ~ 4. a friendly (BE), mutual-aid (AE) ~ 5. a building ~ (BE; AE has *building and loan association*) ["community"] 6. to polarize; unite a ~ 7. an advanced; affluent; civilized; classless; primitive ~ 8. a multicultural; pluralistic ~ 9. a closed; open ~ 10. a matriarchal; patriarchal ~ 11. a capitalist; socialist ~ ["class"] 12. high; polite ~ 13. in ~ (such words are not used in polite ~)

sock I *n.* 1. to knit ~s 2. to darn, mend a ~ 3. ankle, ankle-length; athletic; knee; stretch; tube ~s 4. a pair of ~s

sock II *v.* (colloq.) (D; tr.) ("to punch") to ~ in, on (he ~ed me on the jaw)

socket *n.* a wall ~

soda *n.* ["form of sodium"] 1. baking; caustic; washing ~ ["beverage"] (esp. AE) 2. (a) club; cream; ice-cream ~ ["soda water"] 3. a dash of ~ 4. (misc.) (a) whiskey and ~

sodomy *n.* to commit, practice ~

soft *adj.* ["lenient"] ~ on (this judge is not ~ on drunk drivers)

soft spot *n.* ["weakness"] to have a ~ for

software *n.* 1. to write (the) ~ 2. to download ~ 3. computer; proprietary; public-domain ~

soil I *n.* 1. to cultivate, till, work the ~ 2. to fertilize; irrigate the ~ 3. barren, poor; clayey; fertile; firm; packed; porous; rich; sandy; soggy; swampy ~

soil II *v.* (D; tr.) to ~ on, with (she would not ~ her hands with such trash)

solace *n.* 1. to find ~ in 2. to derive, get ~ from 3. a ~ to (she was a ~ to her parents)

solder *n.* to apply; melt ~

soldier *n.* 1. a career; common; foot; professional; seasoned ~ 2. a ~ enlists; fights; reenlists; serves; trains 3. a ~ defects, deserts; goes AWOL 4. (misc.) the Unknown Soldier; a ~ of fortune; a toy ~

sole I *n.* ["bottom part of a shoe"] 1. to put (new) ~s on shoes 2. a half ~

sole II *n.* ["type of fish"] 1. Dover; lemon ~ 2. (a) fillet of ~

solicit *v.* (D; intr., tr.) to ~ for (she was ~ing funds for the Red Cross)

solicitor *n.* 1. The Solicitor General ("the assistant attorney general") 2. (GB) barristers and ~s

solicitous *adj.* ~ about, of

solicitude *n.* to show ~ for

solid *adj.* to be in ~ with smb. (colloq. AE)

solidarity *n.* 1. to declare, express; feel; show ~ 2. ~

with (to express one's ~ with the protestors)

solitaire *n.* (AE) ["card game"] to play ~ (BE has *patience*)

solitary confinement *n.* 1. to put smb. in(to) ~ 2. in ~

solitude *n.* 1. complete, utter ~ 2. in ~ (to live in complete ~)

solo I *adv.* to dance; fly; perform; play; sing ~

solo II *n.* to perform a ~

solstice *n.* the summer; winter ~

soluble *adj.* ~ in

solution *n.* ["answer"] ["explanation"] 1. to come up with, find a ~ 2. to apply a ~ 3. a definitive; effective; equitable; neat; satisfactory ~ 4. a creative; ideal; ingenious ~ 5. an easy; simple ~ 6. a military; political ~ 7. a permanent; temporary ~ 8. a ~ for, to (a ~ to a problem) ["mixture"] 9. to dilute a ~ 10. a strong; weak ~ 11. an antiseptic; chemical; saline ~ 12. in ~ (salt in ~)

some *pronoun, determiner* 1. ~ to + inf. (we have ~ to sell; we have ~ books to sell) 2. ~ of (~ of them) USAGE NOTE: The use of the preposition *of* is necessary when a pronoun follows. When a noun follows, the use of *of the* limits the meaning—we saw some people; we saw some of the people whom we had discussed earlier. (see also the Usage Note for **something**)

somebody *pronoun* ~ to + inf. (we have ~ to talk to) (see also the Usage Note for **something**)

someone see **somebody**

someplace (AE) see **somewhere**

somersault *n.* to do, execute, turn a ~

something *n., pronoun* 1. a certain, indefinable, indescribable, intangible ~ 2. ~ for (she has ~ for you) 3. ~ to + inf. (we have ~ to say) 4. (misc.) to make ~ of oneself ("to have success in life"); ("slang") I don't know if he wants to make ~ of it ("I don't know if he wants to make an issue of it"); there is ~ unusual about them; she is ~ of a celebrity

USAGE NOTE: The form *some* and its compounds are often used in affirmative statements, whereas *any* and its compounds are often used in neg. and interrogative statements. Compare *we have some books to sell—we don't have any books to sell; we have something to say—do you have anything to say? we have somebody to talk to—we don't have anybody to talk to; we have somewhere to go—do you have anywhere to go?* However, in the meaning "no matter", *any* and its compounds occur in affirmative statements—*we will take any of these; they can say anything they want; we will talk to anyone; we will go anywhere. Some* and its compounds can occur in questions, especially when an affirmative answer is expected—*don't you have something to say to me? would you like some brandy?*

somewhere *adv.* ~ to + inf. (we have ~ to go) (see also the Usage Note for **something**)

son *n.* 1. to adopt a ~ 2. to marry off a ~ 3. an older; only; younger ~ 4. an adopted; foster ~; stepson 5. a son-in-law 6. a ~ to (he was like a ~ to them) 7. (misc.) a favorite ~ (AE; pol.); a prodigal ~ (fig.)

song *n.* 1. to compose, write a ~ 2. to belt out (colloq.), sing; hum; play; whistle a ~ (the orchestra was playing our ~) 3. a drinking; folk; love; marching; popular; theme ~ 4. smb.'s swan ("farewell") ~ 5. (misc.) the same old ~ ("the same story, complaint"); to burst into ~; for a ~ ("inexpensively")

sonic barrier *n.* to break the ~

sonic boom *n.* to cause, generate, produce a ~

sonnet *n.* 1. to compose, write a ~ 2. an Italian; Petrarchan; Shakespearean; Spenserian ~

soot *n.* covered in ~

sop *n.* ["concession"] to throw a ~ to

sophistication *n.* the ~ to + inf. (will she have enough ~ to deal with their questions?)

sophistry *n.* 1. pure ~ 2. ~ to + inf. (it's pure ~ to rationalize such behavior)

soprano *n.* 1. to sing ~ 2. a coloratura ~

sorcery *n.* to practice ~

sore I *adj.* ["angry"] (colloq.) (esp. AE) 1. to get ~ 2. ~ about, over (~ over smb.'s remark) ~ 3. ~ at (why is she ~ at me?) ["hurt"] 4. ~ from (~ from riding horseback)

sore II *n.* a bedsore; canker; cold; open, running; saddle ~

soreness *n.* to reduce ~

sore throat *n.* to come down with; have a ~

sorority *n.* (US) 1. to pledge a ~ ("to agree to join a sorority") 2. a college ~ (see also **fraternity**)

sorrow *n.* 1. to cause ~ 2. to express; feel; show ~ 3. to alleviate smb.'s ~ 4. deep, great, inexpressible, keen, profound ~ 5. personal ~ 6. ~ at, over (to feel deep ~ at the death of a friend) 7. in ~ 8. to smb.'s ~ (to my great ~ I never saw them again) 9. (misc.) an expression; feeling of ~

sorry *adj.* 1. dreadfully, terribly, very ~ 2. ~ about 3. ~ for (she is ~ for him; we are ~ for being late; I feel ~ for you) 4. ~ to + inf. (I am ~ to inform you that your application has been rejected) 5. ~ that + clause (we are ~ that you weren't able to come)

sort I *n.* 1. a bad; curious; good ~ (a curious ~ of a life) 2. (misc.) to be out of ~s ("to be annoyed")

sort II *v.* 1. (D; tr.) to ~ by (to ~ merchandise by size) 2. (D; tr.) to ~ into (to ~ socks into various sizes) 3. (D; intr.) to ~ through (to ~ through old documents)

sortie *n.* 1. to carry out, make a ~ 2. to fly a ~

sort of *adv.* (colloq.) ["more or less"] I ~ expected it (to happen)

sort out *v.* 1. (D; tr.) to ~ from (to ~ the current receipts from the old ones) 2. (misc.) we had to ~

how many votes each one received

SOS *n.* 1. to broadcast, send an ~ 2. to receive an ~

soul *n.* 1. to save smb.'s ~ 2. to bare; search one's ~ 3. an artistic; immortal; kindly; kindred; lost; poor; timid ~ 4. (misc.) body and ~

sound I *adj.* ["healthy"] 1. ~ in, of (~ in mind and body) 2. (misc.) safe and ~

sound II *n.* 1. to emit, make, produce, utter a ~ 2. to transmit (a) ~ 3. to articulate, enunciate, pronounce a ~ 4. to turn down; turn up the ~ (on a radio, TV set) 5. to carry ~ (air carries ~s) 6. a clear; faint; hollow; loud; muffled; rasping; soft ~ 7. (a) ~ travels (~ travels much slower than light) 8. a ~ dies away, dies down; rings out 9. at a ~ (at the ~ of the bell, they all assembled) 10. to a ~ (to the ~ of music)

sound III *v.* 1. (D; intr.) to ~ for (the bell ~ed for dinner) 2. (d; intr.) to ~ like (that ~s like a great idea) 3. (BE) (S) that ~s a great idea 4. (s) their excuse ~ed reasonable 5. (misc.) it ~s as if/as though/like (colloq.) they don't know what to do; how does that ~ to you?

sound barrier *n.* to break the ~

sound off *v.* (colloq.) (D; intr.) to ~ about, against ("to criticize") (to ~ against an idea)

sound out *v.* (D; tr.) ("to inquire") to ~ about (to ~ smb. out about a problem)

soup *n.* 1. to eat; make ~ 2. clear; cold; hot; thick; warm ~ 3. cabbage; celery; chicken; mushroom; noodle; onion; pea; tomato; vegetable ~ 4. a bowl; cup of ~

sour I *adj.* to go, turn ~ (things went ~; the whole affair turned ~)

sour II *v.* (d; intr.) to ~ on (they quickly ~ed on the idea)

source *n.* 1. to locate, track down a ~ 2. to tap a ~ 3. to cite; disclose, indicate, reveal one's ~s 4. an impeccable, unimpeachable; informed; well-informed; reliable, reputable, trustworthy ~ 5. an unreliable ~ 6. an undisclosed, unnamed ~ 7. an original, primary; secondary ~ 8. an energy; renewable ~ 9. ~s dry up 10. at a ~ (it is best to make inquiries at the original ~) 11. (misc.) ~s close to the government revealed that...; (BE) tax deducted at ~

south I *adj., adv.* 1. directly, due, straight ~ 2. ~ of (~ of the city) 3. down ~ 4. (misc.) to face; to go, head ~; southeast by ~; southwest by ~

south II *n.* 1. from the ~; in the ~; to the ~ 2. (misc.) the Deep South ("certain areas of the southern United States")

southeast I *adj., adv.* 1. ~ of (to be ~ of the city) 2. (misc.) to go, head ~; south by ~

southeast II *n.* from; in; to the ~

South Pole *n.* at the ~

southwest I *adj., adv.* 1. ~ of (to be ~ of the city) 2. (misc.) to go, head ~; south by ~

southwest II *n.* from; in; to the ~

sovereignty *n.* 1. to grant ~ 2. to establish ~ 3. to violate a country's ~ 4. ~ over

space *n.* 1. to save ~ 2. to clear a ~ 3. to take up ~ 4. to fill (in) the ~s 5. breathing ~ 6. (a) blank, empty ~ 7. a crawl (AE); parking ~ 8. office; storage ~ 9. airspace; interplanetary; interstellar; outer ~ 10. (a) ~ between 11. (a) ~ for 12. in ~ (to travel in ~) 13. (misc.) the (wide) open ~s; to indent several ~s; to violate a country's airspace

space bar *n.* (on a typewriter) to press a ~

spacecraft *n.* 1. a manned; unmanned ~ (see the Usage Note for **ship**) 2. a ~ docks

spaceflight *n.* 1. to abort a ~ 2. a manned; unmanned ~ 3. a ~ to (a ~ to the moon)

space probe *n.* to launch a ~

space vehicle *n.* to launch a ~ (see the Usage Note for **ship**)

spacing *n.* (on a typewriter or word processor) double; single ~

spadework *n.* ["preparations"] to do the ~

span *n.* 1. a brief, short ~ 2. an attention; life; memory ~ 3. a wing ~ 4. in a certain ~ (in the brief ~ of ten years) 5. (misc.) over a ~ of five years

spanking *n.* 1. to give smb. a (good) ~ 2. to get a ~ 3. (misc.) to deserve a ~

spanner *n.* a box ~ (BE; AE has *lug wrench*)

spar *v.* (D; intr.) ("to fight") to ~ over; with

spare *v.* 1. (C) can you ~ a few minutes for me today? or: can you ~ me a few minutes today? 2. (O; can be used with one animate object) ~ us the details; he wanted to ~ you embarrassment

sparing *adj.* (cannot stand alone) ~ of

spark *n.* 1. to emit, produce a ~ 2. ~s fly 3. (misc.) a shower of ~s

sparkle *v.* (D; intr.) to ~ with (to ~ with humor)

sparrow *n.* 1. ~s chirp 2. a flock of ~s

spasm *n.* (a) muscle ~

spat I *n.* ["quarrel"] to have a ~ with

spat II *v.* (D; intr.) ("to quarrel") to ~ with

spatter *v.* 1. (D; tr.) to ~ with (the car ~ed me with mud) 2. (P; intr.) the paint ~ed all over the floor

speak *v.* ("to talk") 1. to ~ glibly; loudly; quickly, rapidly; quietly, softly; slowly 2. to ~ clearly, distinctly; coherently; correctly; fluently; politely 3. to ~ bluntly, candidly, frankly, freely; openly; responsibly; truthfully 4. to ~ incorrectly; irresponsibly; rudely 5. (D; intr.) to ~ about, of, on (to ~ about politics) 6. (d; intr.) to ~ against (to ~ against a bill) 7. (d; intr.) to ~ as (to ~ as the party candidate) 8. (d; intr.) to ~ for ("to be a spokesperson for") (she spoke for all of us; who will ~ for the accused?) 9. (d; intr.) to ~ from (to ~ from the heart; to ~ from experience) 10. (d; intr.) ("to converse") to ~ in (they were ~ing in English; more usu. is: they were ~ing English) 11. (d; intr.) to ~ to ("to address") (she spoke to the crowd; to ~

to the subject; to ~ to the question on the agenda; don't ~ to him) 12. (D; intr.) ("to converse") to ~ to, (esp. AE) with (she spoke to me about several things); (esp. AE — I spoke with them for an hour) 13. (misc.) to ~ well of smb. ("to praise smb."); to ~ ill of smb. ("to criticize smb."); it ~s for itself ("it is self-evident"); roughly ~ing ("approximately"); strictly ~ing ("in exact terms"); generally ~ing

speaker *n.* ["one who speaks"] 1. a native ~ (of a language) 2. an effective, good; eloquent; fluent ~ 3. a poor ~ 4. a guest; public ~ (she is a good public ~) ["device that amplifies sound"] 5. an extension ~; loudspeaker ["misc."] 6. (US) the Speaker of the House

speaking *n.* public ~

speaking terms *n.* to be on ~ with smb.

speak out *v.* 1. (D; intr.) to ~ about, concerning, on (to ~ on a subject) 2. (d; intr.) to ~ against ("to oppose") (to ~ against a proposal) 3. (d; intr.) to ~ for ("to support") (to ~ for a proposal)

speak up see **speak out**

spear *n.* 1. to hurl, throw a ~ at 2. to thrust a ~ into

spearhead *n.* 1. to send out a ~ 2. an armored ~

special I *adj.* 1. ~ about (there was smt. ~ about her) 2. ~ to 3. extra-special

special II *n.* ["special program"] 1. a TV ~ ["reduced price"] 2. to offer a ~ (on)

specialist *n.* 1. to call in; consult a ~ 2. a ~ in, on (a ~ in plastic surgery; a ~ on Milton)

specialize *v.* (D; intr.) to ~ in

species *n.* 1. an endangered; protected ~ 2. a ~ becomes extinct, dies out; survives

specific *adj.* 1. ~ about 2. ~ to (these symptoms are ~ to liver disease)

specifications *n.* 1. to adhere to, meet ~ 2. rigid ~

specifics *n.* to get down to ~

specify *v.* 1. (D; tr.) to ~ by (to ~ smb. by name) 2. (L) the contract ~fies that a penalty must be paid if the work is not completed on time 3. (Q) the instructions ~ how the medicine is to be taken

specimen *n.* 1. to get; take a ~ 2. a blood; sputum; stool; urine ~

specs (colloq.) see **specifications**, **spectacles**

spectacle *n.* ["show, exhibition"] 1. to stage a ~ 2. a dramatic ~ ["object of curiosity"] 3. to make a ~ of oneself 4. a curious; magnificent; pitiful; ridiculous ~

spectacles *n.* (now esp. BE) a pair of ~

spectators *n.* to seat ~ (the stadium seats sixty thousand ~)

spectrum *n.* a broad, wide ~

speculate *v.* 1. (D; intr.) ("to meditate, think") to ~ about, on (to ~ about what might have been) 2. (D; intr.) ("to conduct business by taking risks") to ~ in; on (to ~ in oil shares; to ~ in gold; to ~ on the stock market) 3. (L) ("to assume, think") they ~d that the election results would be close

speculation *n.* ["meditation, thinking"] 1. to indulge in ~ 2. idle; pure; widespread; wild ~ 3. ~ is rife 4. a flurry of ~ 5. ~ about, over (~ about the upcoming elections) 6. ~ that + clause (there was ~ that a treaty would be signed) ["risky business methods"] 7. to engage in ~ 8. ~ in (~ in stocks and bonds)

speculator *n.* a property (BE), real-estate (AE); stock-market ~

speculum *n.* a nasal; vaginal ~

speech *n.* ["address, talk"] 1. to deliver, give, make a ~ (to) 2. to ad-lib, improvise a ~ 3. an eloquent; passionate; rousing, stirring ~ 4. a brief, short; impromptu, unrehearsed ~ 5. a boring; long; long-winded; rambling ~ 6. an acceptance; after-dinner; campaign; farewell; inaugural; keynote; nominating; political; welcoming ~ 7. a ~ about ["communication in words"] 8. free ~ = freedom of ~ 9. a figure of ~ ["pronunciation"] 10. clipped ~ 11. impaired; slurred ~ ["smb.'s words"] 12. direct; indirect ~

speechless *adj.* 1. to be left ~ 2. ~ with (~ with anger)

speed I *n.* ["swiftness, velocity"] 1. to build up, gain, gather, increase, pick up; maintain (a) ~ 2. to reach a ~ (to reach cruising ~; to reach a ~ of one hundred miles an hour) 3. to decrease, reduce ~ 4. (a) breakneck, breathtaking, high, lightning; cruising; deliberate; full, top; low; moderate; steady; supersonic ~ 5. a burst of ~ 6. at a certain ~ (at top ~; to travel at a ~ of one hundred miles per hour) 7. with a certain ~ (they finished the work with great ~; with all deliberate ~) 8. (misc.) to adjust the idling ~ on an engine; full ~ ahead! ["amphetamine"] (slang) 9. to shoot; snort ~ 10. to be on ~

speed *v.* (P; intr., tr.) to ~ south; to ~ smb. to the airport

speed limit *n.* 1. to enforce; establish, impose, set a ~ 2. to observe a ~ 3. to exceed a ~ 4. at; below, under; over; within the ~

speed trap *n.* to set up a ~

spell I *n.* ["incantation"] 1. to cast a ~ on, over 2. to put smb. under a ~ 3. to break, remove a ~ 4. to fall under smb.'s ~ 5. a magic ~ 6. under a ~

spell II *n.* ["period"] 1. a cold; hot; rainy; sunny; warm ~ 2. a long; short ~ ["period of illness"] 3. a coughing; dizzy; fainting ~ (she has been having dizzy ~s)

spellbinding *adj.* ~ to + inf. (it's ~ to read her memoirs)

spell check *n.* to do, run a ~ (she ran a ~ on her computer)

spelling *n.* 1. phonetic ~ 2. (a) correct; incorrect; variant ~ 3. in (phonetic) ~

spell out *v.* 1. (B) they ~ed out their demands to us 2. (Q; to) do I have to ~ (to you) why I did it?

spend *v.* 1. (D; tr.) to ~ for, on (to ~ a lot of money for a new car; to ~ a lot on repairs) 2. (D; tr.) to ~ in (to ~ a great deal of time in studying) 3. (J) they spent the whole week hiking through the mountains

spender *n.* a big ~

spending *n.* 1. to boost, increase ~ 2. to curtail, cut, cut back (on), decrease ~ 3. deficit; defense; government; military; welfare ~

sperm count *n.* a low; normal; high ~

spew *v.* 1. (d; intr.) to ~ from, out of (lava ~ed from the crater) 2. (d; intr.) to ~ into (fumes ~ed into the atmosphere)

spice I *n.* 1. to add ~(s) 2. ground ~(s)

spice II *v.* (d; tr.) to ~ with (to ~ a cake with cinnamon)

spider *n.* 1. ~s crawl 2. ~s spin webs

spike *v.* (D; tr.) to ~ with (to ~ the punch with rum)

spill I *n.* ["accidental pouring"] 1. an oil ~ ["fall"] 2. to take a ~ (from a horse) 3. a nasty ~

spill II *v.* 1. (D; tr.) to ~ all over, on (I ~ed the milk all over her) 2. (d; intr.) ("to pour") to ~ into (the crowd was ~ing into the streets) 3. (d; intr.) ("to flow") to ~ out of (the liquid was ~ing out of the container)

spill over *v.* (D; intr.) to ~ into (the mob ~ed over into the adjoining streets)

spin I *n.* ["fast drive"] (colloq.) 1. to go for, take a ~ (let's go for a ~ around town) ["fall"] 2. to go into a ~ (the plane went into a ~; the market went into a ~) 3. to come out of a ~ ["rotation"] 4. to put a ~ on smt. (to put a ~ on a tennis ball) ["interpretation"] 5. to put a ~ on smt. 6. a political; positive ~

spin II *v.* 1. (D; tr.) ("to make") to ~ from, out of; into (to ~ wool into thread) 2. (D; intr.) ("to turn") to ~ on (a wheel ~s on its axle)

spinal tap *n.* to do a ~ (on smb.)

spin-off *n.* a ~ from

spiral I *n.* an inflationary; wage-price ~ (a vicious inflationary ~)

spiral II *v.* (d; intr.) to ~ to (the plane ~ed to earth)

spirit *n.* ["vigor"] ["enthusiasm"] 1. to display, show ~ 2. to catch the ~ (of the times) 3. to break smb.'s ~ (her ~ was broken) 4. (a) civic; community; ecumenical; patriotic ~ 5. (a) religious; scientific ~ 6. (a) class; college; school; team ~ 7. (a) competitive; partisan; rebellious ~ 8. a dauntless, hardy ~; (a) fighting; indomitable ~ 9. a guiding; moving ~ 10. with ~ (to work with great ~) 11. (misc.) a ~ of good will pervaded the conversation ["supernatural being, ghost"] 12. to call up, conjure up, invoke a ~ 13. an evil; holy ~ ["soul"] 14. a kindred ~ 15. in ~ (we are with you in ~) ["attitude"] 16. in a ~ (in a ~ of cooperation) 17. (misc.) the letter and the ~ of the law

spirit away *v.* (D; tr.) to ~ from; to (she was ~ed away to the islands for a vacation)

spirit off *v.* (D; tr.) to ~ to (he was ~ed off to prison)

spirits *n.* ["mood"] 1. to boost, lift, raise smb.'s ~ 2. to dampen smb.'s ~ 3. good, high; low ~ 4. ~ droop, flag, sink; rise 5. in ~ (in high ~) ["alcohol"] 6. to drink ~

spit *v.* 1. (D; intr.) to ~ at; on 2. (d; intr.) to ~ in, into (to ~ in smb.'s face) 3. (d; tr.) to ~ out of (to ~ smt. out of one's mouth)

spite *n.* 1. in ~ of 2. out of ~ (they did it out of ~)

spiteful *adj.* ~ to + inf. (it was ~ of him to say that)

splash I *n.* (colloq.) ["vivid impression"] to make a (big) ~

splash II *v.* 1. (D; intr.) to ~ against, on, over (the waves ~ed against the rocks) 2. to ~ with (they ~ed me with water) 3. (misc.) the boys ~ed through the puddle; the children were ~ing around in the water

splashdown *n.* to make a ~ (in)

splatter *v.* 1. (d; intr.) to ~ against (mud ~ed against the windows) 2. (d; tr.) to ~ with (they ~ed the car with eggs)

spleen *n.* ["bad temper"] 1. to vent one's ~ on ["ductless organ near the stomach"] 2. a ruptured ~

splendid *adj.* ~ to + inf. (it was ~ of you to make the offer)

splendor, splendour *n.* 1. regal ~ 2. in ~ (to dine in regal ~)

splice *v.* 1. (D; tr.) to ~ to (to ~ a wire to a cable) 2. (D; tr.) to ~ with (to ~ a wire with tape)

splint *n.* 1. to apply a ~ to; to put a ~ on 2. a ~ for (a fractured leg)

splinter *n.* 1. to get; have a ~ (in one's finger) 2. to extract, get out, remove a ~ (she got the ~ out of my finger)

split I *n.* ["breach"] 1. a formal; irreparable ~ 2. a ~ between 3. a ~ in (the party)

split II *v.* 1. (d; tr.) ("to divide") to ~ among, between; with (we split the profits with them) 2. (d; intr., tr.) ("to divide") to ~ into (they split into several factions; the teacher split the class into two groups) 3. (misc.) the vote was split along party lines

split ticket *n.* (AE) to vote a ~ ("to distribute one's vote among candidates of more than one party")

split up *v.* 1. (D; intr.) to ~ into (they split up into several factions) 2. (colloq.) (D; intr.) to ~ with (she split up with her boyfriend)

splurge *v.* (colloq.) (D; intr.) ("to spend extravagantly") to ~ on (to ~ on a new car)

splutter *v.* (D; intr.) to ~ with (to ~ with rage)

spoil *v.* (d; intr.; usu. in a progressive form) to ~ for ("to seek") (to be ~ing for a fight)

spoils *n.* to divide the ~ (of war)

spoken *adj.* ~ for ("reserved")

spokesman see **spokesperson**

spokesperson *n.* a ~ for (a ~ for the strikers)

spokeswoman see **spokesperson**

sponge I *n.* ["spongy substance"] 1. to squeeze a ~

["symbol of surrender"] 2. to throw in, toss in the ~

sponge II *v.* (colloq.) 1. (D; tr.) ("to wheedle") to ~ from, off, off of (AE) (he ~d a cigarette from me) 2. (d; intr.) to ~ off (of), on ("to impose on") (to ~ on one's friends)

sponsor I *n.* 1. a radio; television, TV ~ 2. a ~ for, of

sponsor II *v.* (D; tr.) to ~ for (she ~ed me for membership)

sponsorship *n.* under smb.'s ~

spoof *n.* ["parody"] a ~ of, on (it was a ~ on the political campaign)

spoon *n.* a dessert; measuring; soup ~; tablespoon; teaspoon

spoon-feed *v.* 1. (D; tr.) to ~ to (she spoon-fed the material to her students) 2. (D; tr.) to ~ with (they spoon-fed their students with theory)

spoonful *n.* a heaping; level ~

sport *n.* ["person judged by her/his ability to take a loss or teasing"] 1. a bad, poor; good ~ 2. a ~ about (she was a good ~ about losing the bet) ["mockery"] (old-fashioned) 3. to make ~ of smb. ("to mock smb.") ["type of physical activity"] 4. a contact; spectator; team ~ 5. an exciting; strenuous, vigorous ~ (skiing is an exciting ~) ["physical activity"] (BE) 6. to go in for ~ 7. fond of ~; in the world of ~ (AE has *sports*)

sporting *adj.* ~ to + inf. (it was ~ of them to give us a chance)

sports *n.* ["physical activity"] (AE) 1. to go in for ~ 2. fond of ~; in the world of ~ (BE has *sport*) ["types of physical activity"] 3. amateur; aquatic, water; competitive; indoor; intercollegiate (AE), inter-university (BE); intramural; outdoor; professional; varsity; winter ~ ["track meet"] (BE) 4. school ~; ~ day

sportsmanship *n.* to display, show ~

spot I *n.* ["mark, stain"] 1. to leave, make a ~ 2. to get out, remove a ~ 3. a grease ~ ["mark on the skin"] 4. a beauty ~ ["area, place"] 5. a high; isolated, secluded; low ~ 6. (soccer) the penalty ~ 7. at a ~ (let's meet at this same ~ tomorrow) ["place of entertainment"] (colloq.) 8. to hit ("visit") all the night ~s ["point, position"] 9. a bright ~; the high; the low ~ (the high ~ of our visit) 10. (misc.) X marks the ~ ["misc."] 11. on the ~ ("immediately"); ("at the center of activity"); ("exposed to the worst danger"); on the ~ ("to expose smb. to danger"); a blind ~ ("an area that cannot be seen") (also fig.); to have a soft/tender/warm ~ (in one's heart) for ("to have a weakness for"); to be in a tight ~ ("to be in a difficult situation"); a trouble ~ (that reporter has been in many trouble ~s throughout the world); (BE; colloq.) a ~ of bother ("a bit of trouble")

spot II *v.* 1. (d; tr.) ("to identify") to ~ as (the police ~ted him as a known criminal) 2. (J) ("to see") we ~ted them going through the gate 3. (esp. AE) (O) ("to give as a handicap") he ~ted me ten points 4. (misc.) (BE) it is ~ting with rain

spot check *n.* to do, make a ~

spotlight *n.* 1. to direct, focus, shine, turn a ~ on 2. (fig.) in the ~

spouse *n.* a beloved; faithful; unfaithful ~

spout *v.* (d; intr.) ("to spurt") to ~ from

sprawl I *n.* urban ~

sprawl II *v.* (P; intr.) to ~ on the sofa

sprawling *adj.* to send smb. ~

spray I *n.* an aerosol; hair; insect ~

spray II *v.* 1. (D; tr.) to ~ on, onto, over (to ~ paint on the walls) 2. (D; tr.) to ~ with (to ~ the walls with paint)

spread I *n.* ["expansion"] 1. to arrest, check; prevent the ~ (of a disease) ["food"] 2. a cheese ~ ["misc."] 3. (the) middle-age(d) ~

spread II *v.* 1. to ~ smt. evenly (to ~ paint evenly) 2. to ~ quickly; unchecked (the epidemic spread unchecked) 3. (D; tr.) to ~ on (to ~ butter on bread) 4. (D; tr.) to ~ over (to ~ a blanket over a bed; to ~ payments over a year) 5. (D; intr.) to ~ to (the epidemic spread to neighboring countries) 6. to ~ with (to ~ the bread with jam) 7. (misc.) to ~ like wildfire; this butter ~s easily

spree *n.* 1. to go on a ~ 2. a crime; shopping; spending; weekend ~

spring I *n.* ["season"] 1. an early ~ 2. during, in (the) ~ 3. (misc.) there is a touch of ~ in the air; a harbinger of ~ ["source of water"] 4. a hot, thermal; mineral; subterranean ~ ["bounce, elasticity"] 5. a ~ in, to (there was a ~ to her step) ["device of coiled metal"] 6. a box; watch ~

spring II *v.* 1. (D; intr.) to ~ at (the lion sprang at the hunter) 2. (d; intr.) ("to arise, result") to ~ from 3. (D; tr.) ("to prepare") to ~ on (to ~ a surprise on smb.) 4. (d; intr.) ("to jump") to ~ over (to ~ over a wall) 5. (d; intr.) ("to jump") to ~ to (to ~ to smb.'s defense; to ~ to one's feet) 6. (s) the trap sprang shut 7. (misc.) they sprang into action

springboard *n.* 1. a ~ for (a ~ for a new campaign) 2. a ~ to (a ~ to success)

spring-clean *n.* (BE) to do, have a ~

spring-cleaning (esp. AE) see **spring-clean**

sprinkle *v.* (D; tr.) to ~ on; with (to ~ water on clothes; to ~ smb. with water)

sprout (D; intr.) to ~ from

spruce up *v.* (D; refl.) to ~ for (they ~d themselves up for the big party)

spunk *n.* (colloq.) ["courage"] 1. to show ~ 2. the ~ to + inf. (she had the ~ to defend her rights)

spur I *n.* ["incentive, stimulus"] 1. a ~ to ["misc."] 2. on the ~ of the moment ("without planning")

spur II *v.* 1. (D; tr.) to ~ to (to ~ smb. to action) 2. (H) what ~red her to do that?

spur on *v.* 1. (D; tr.) to ~ to (to ~ smb. on to greater effort) 2. (H) we ~red them on to make a greater effort

spurs *n.* ["recognition"] 1. to win one's ~ ["devices worn on a rider's heel"] 2. to dig, drive one's ~ (into the side of a horse) 3. ~ jingle

spurt I *n.* 1. a sudden ~ 2. a growth ~ 3. in a ~ (to work in ~s; the blood came out in a ~)

spurt II *v.* (D; intr.) to ~ from (blood ~ed from the wound)

sputum *n.* to cough up, produce ~

spy I *n.* a foreign ~

spy II *v.* 1. (d; intr.) to ~ for (to ~ for a foreign power) 2. (D; intr.) to ~ on, upon 3. (J) we spied them coming through the gate

squabble I *n.* a ~ about, over; between; with

squabble II *v.* (D; intr.) to ~ about, over; with

squad *n.* 1. a bomb; demolition; firing; flying (BE) ~ 2. a vice ~

squalor *n.* in ~ (to live in ~)

squander *v.* (D; tr.) to ~ on (to ~ a fortune on bad investments)

square I *n.* 1. to draw, make a ~ 2. (misc.) back to ~ one ("back to the beginning")

square II *v.* (D; intr., tr.) to ~ with (their story doesn't ~ with the facts; to ~ accounts with smb.)

square root *n.* to find, extract the ~

squash I *n.* (BE) ["fruit drink"] lemon; orange ~

squash II *n.* (AE) ["marrow-like plant"] summer; winter ~ (BE has *marrow*)

squawk I *n.* to let out a ~

squawk II *v.* (colloq.) 1. (D; intr.) ("to complain") to ~ about 2. (L; to) she ~ed (to us) that the decision was unfair

squeak *n.* ["shrill cry"] 1. to emit, let out a ~ ["escape"] (colloq.) 2. a close (AE), narrow (BE) ~

squeal I *n.* to emit, let out a ~

squeal II *v.* 1. (slang) (D; intr.) ("to inform") to ~ on; to (he ~ed on them to the police) 2. (D; intr.) to ~ in, with (to ~ with delight)

squeamish *adj.* ~ about

squeeze I *n.* (colloq.) ["hug"] 1. to give smb. a ~ 2. a gentle; tight ~ ["misc."] 3. in a tight ~ ("in difficulty"); to put the ~ on smb. ("to put pressure on smb.")

squeeze II *v.* 1. (C) ~ some orange juice for me; or: ~ me some orange juice 2. (d; tr.) to ~ from, out of (~ some toothpaste out of the tube) 3. (d; intr., tr.) to ~ into (to ~ into a small room; to ~ juice into a glass) 4. (d; intr.) to ~ through (to ~ through a narrow passage) 5. (N; used with an adjective) ~ the mops dry

squelch *n.* (colloq.) ["crushing rebuke"] a perfect ~

squint *v.* (D; intr.) to ~ at

squirm *v.* (d; intr.) to ~ out of ("to evade") (to ~ out of an obligation)

squirt I *n.* ["instance of squirting"] 1. to give smt. a ~ ["insignificant person"] (colloq.) 2. a little ~

squirt II *v.* 1. (d; intr., tr.) to ~ from, out of (the liquid ~ed out of the bottle; to ~ a liquid out of a bottle) 2. (D; tr.) to ~ on (he ~ed water on us) 3. (D; tr.) to ~ with (she ~ed me with perfume)

stab I *n.* ["attempt"] (colloq.) 1. to have, make a ~ at ["sensation"] 2. a sharp; sudden ~ (of pain) ["thrust of a pointed weapon"] 3. a ~ in the back (also fig.)

stab II 1. (D; tr.) to ~ in (to ~ smb. in the leg) 2. (D; tr.) to ~ with (to ~ smb. with a knife) 3. (misc.) to ~ smb. to death; to ~ smb. in the back (usu. fig.)

stability *n.* 1. to lend ~ to 2. economic; emotional; political ~ 3. ~ in

stabilization *n.* economic; price ~

stable *n.* a livery; riding (esp. AE) ~

stack I *n.* 1. a bookstack; haystack; smokestack (esp. AE) 2. (misc.) to pile books in a ~; (colloq.) (AE) to blow one's ~ ("to lose one's temper")

stack II *v.* 1. (D; tr.) ("to arrange underhandedly") to ~ against (the cards were ~ed against her) 2. (d; tr.) to ~ with (the floor was ~ed with books) 3. (P; tr.) ~ the books on the top shelf; ~ the boxes against the door; ~ the merchandise in piles

stacks *n.* (in a library) 1. closed; open ~ 2. in the ~

stack up *v.* (colloq.) (esp. AE) (D; intr.) to ~ against (to ("to compare to") (how do we ~ to the competition?)

stadium *n.* 1. to crowd, fill, jam, pack a ~ 2. to empty a ~ 3. a baseball; football; Olympic ~ 4. a ~ empties; fills

staff I *n.* ["personnel"] 1. to recruit ~ 2. an administrative; coaching; editorial; hospital; medical; nursing; office; teaching ~ 3. a skeleton ~ 4. junior; senior ~ 5. on the ~ 6. (misc.) to join a ~ (she joined the ~ as an editor) ["group of officers serving a commander"] 7. a general; joint; military; personal; special ~ 8. on a ~ (he was on the general ~) 9. (misc.) to assign smb. to a ~ (she was assigned to the ~ as an intelligence officer); a chief of ~

staff II *v.* (d; tr.) to ~ by, with (the office was ~ed with part-time workers)

stag *adj., adv.* to go ~ ("unaccompanied by smb. of the opposite sex"=AE, "unaccompanied by smb. of the female sex"=CE)

stage *n.* ["platform on which plays are performed"] 1. a revolving; sinking; sliding ~ 2. on (the) ~ (she has appeared many times on ~; to go on ~) ["scene, setting"] 3. to set the ~ for (the ~ was set for a showdown) ["level, degree, step"] 4. to go through; reach a ~ 5. an advanced; beginning; elementary; closing, final, last; critical, crucial; early; intermediate; late; opening ~ 6. flood ~ 7. at a ~ (negotiations were at a crucial ~; the river was at flood ~) 8. in a ~ (in this ~ of one's development) ["portion, part"] 9. easy ~s 10. by, in ~s (to cover a distance by easy ~s; to learn a language in

stagefright *n.* 1. to get; have ~ 2. a (bad) case of ~

stagger *v.* 1. (D; intr.) to ~ from; into (to ~ into a room) 2. (D; intr.) to ~ out of (to ~ out of a building) 3. (D; intr.) to ~ to; toward 4. (R) it ~ed me to learn of his defection 5. (misc.) to ~ to one's feet; to ~ under a heavy burden

staggered *adj.* 1. ~ at, by (~ at the news of the earthquake) 2. ~ to + inf. (she was ~ to learn of the fire)

staggering *adj.* ~ to + inf. (it was ~ to total up the losses)

stain I *n.* ["discolored spot"] 1. to leave a ~ 2. to get out, remove a ~ 3. a stubborn ~ 4. (fig.) a ~ on (a ~ on one's reputation)

stain II *v.* 1. (D; tr.) to ~ with (he ~ed his shirt with ink) 2. (N; used with an adjective) we ~ed the wood dark brown

staircase *n.* a circular, spiral; winding ~

stairs *n.* 1. to climb, go up, walk up the ~ 2. to come down; go down, walk down the ~ 3. moving ~ 4. service ~ 5. (misc.) a flight of ~; at the bottom/top of the ~

stairway see **staircase**

stake I *n.* ["piece of wood"] 1. to drive a ~ (into the ground) 2. to plant a ~ (in the ground) ["post"] 3. (to burn smb.) at the ~ ["share"] 4. to have a ~ in smt. 5. a personal ~ ["risk"] 6. at ~ (our whole future is at ~)

stake II *v.* 1. (d; tr.) to ~ on (to ~ one's hope on an investment) 2. (misc.) to ~ a claim to smt.

stakeholder *n.* a ~ in

stake out *v.* (D; tr.) to ~ on, to (esp. AE) (to ~ a claim to a mine)

stakes *n.* ["wager"] ["prize"] 1. to lower; raise the ~s 2. big, high ~ (to play for high ~) ["misc."] (AE) 3. to pull up ~ ("to move elsewhere")

stalemate *n.* 1. to break; reach a ~ 2. a continuing ~ 3. (misc.) to end a ~

stalk *v.* (P; intr.) to ~ out of the room

stall I *n.* (BE) 1. see **stand I** 9 2. (misc.) a stallholder

stall II *v.* 1. (D; intr.) to ~ on (they were ~ing on handing over the documents) 2. (misc.) to ~ for time

stamina *n.* the ~ to + inf. (she lacked the ~ to finish the race)

stammer I *n.* (to have) a nervous ~

stammer II *v.* 1. (B) she ~ed a few words to us 2. (L; to) she ~ed to us that she was sorry

stamp I *n.* ["postage stamp"] 1. to put, stick a ~ on (an envelope) 2. to lick, moisten a ~ 3. to issue a ~ (the post office has issued a new commemorative ~) 4. to collect ~s 5. to cancel a ~ 6. an airmail; commemorative; postage; revenue; tax ~ 7. a book; roll; sheet of ~s ["coupon"] 8. a food; trading ~ ["device for imprinting"] 9. a rubber ~ ["misc."] 10. to get, receive a/the ~ of approval

stamp II *v.* 1. (d; tr.) to ~ as ("to mark") (these revelations ~ed him as a cheat) 2. (d; tr.) to ~ in, on ("to affix") (to ~ a date in a passport) 3. (d; intr.) to ~ on ("to crush") (to ~ on an insect) 4. (N; used with an adjective) ("to mark") she ~ed the document *secret* 5. (P; intr.) ("to stomp") she ~ed out of the room

stampede I *n.* 1. to cause, create a ~ 2. a ~ to + inf. (there was a ~ to get to the exit)

stampede II *v.* 1. (D; tr.) to ~ into (they were ~d into selling their homes) 2. (E) they ~d to get to the exit

stance *n.* ["attitude"] 1. to adopt, take a ~ (the party leaders have adopted an unpopular ~ on the deficit) 2. a ~ on (the president took a tough ~ on foreign trade)

stand I *n.* ["defense"] 1. to make, put up a ~ 2. a last ~ ["position"] 3. to take a ~ 4. a defiant; firm, resolute, strong; uncompromising ~ 5. a ~ against; for; on (they took a resolute ~ on the issue of tax reform) ["rack, small table"] 6. a music; umbrella ~ ["place taken by a witness"] 7. to take the ~ 8. a witness ~ (AE; BE has *witness box*) ["small structure used for conducting business"] (BE often prefers *stall*) 9. a fruit; hot-dog ~; newsstand; vegetable ~ ["performance, engagement"] 10. a one-night ~ (also fig.: "a single sexual encounter") ["row"] 11. a taxi ~ (BE prefers *taxi rank*)

stand II *v.* 1. ("to hold oneself") to ~ firm; still; straight; tall 2. (BE) (d; intr.) ("to be a candidate") to ~ as (to ~ as a Labour candidate) 3. (d; intr.) ("to hold oneself erect") to ~ at (to ~ at attention; to ~ at ease) 4. (d; intr.) to ~ by ("to support") (her family stood by her throughout the trial) 5. (d; intr.) to ~ for ("to represent") (our party used to ~ for progress) 6. (BE) (d; intr.) to ~ for ("to be a candidate") (to ~ for Parliament) 7. (d; intr.) to ~ for ("to tolerate") (we will not ~ for such conduct) 8. (d; intr.) to ~ on ("to insist on") (to ~ on one's rights; to ~ on ceremony) 9. (d; intr.) to ~ over ("to watch") (he always ~s over me when I work) 10. (d; intr.) ("to be regarded") to ~ with (how do you ~ with your boss?) 11. (E) ("to face") ("to have as a prospect") we stood to gain a great deal 12. (esp. BE) (E; usu. with cannot — can't — couldn't) ("to tolerate") she couldn't ~ to wait any longer 13. (G; usu. with cannot — can't — couldn't) ("to tolerate") she can't ~ waiting 14. (K; usu. with cannot — can't — couldn't) ("to tolerate") I can't ~ his boasting 15. (esp. BE) (O) ("to buy") can I ~ you another round of drinks? 16. (P; tr.) ("to place") she stood the bottle on the table; I stood the books in a row; ~ the paintings against the door 17. (s) she stood first in her class; to ~ accused of murder; I ~ corrected 18. (misc.) to ~ in smb.'s way; your balance ~s at one thousand dollars; the building ~s five hundred feet high; the inflation rate ~s at sixteen percent; (AE) to ~ by one's guns ("to defend one's viewpoint stubbornly"); to ~ on one's own (two) feet ("to support oneself"); to ~ tall (esp. AE; colloq.) ("to be resolute")

stand apart *v.* (D; intr.) to ~ from (she stood apart from the others)

standard *n.* 1. to establish, set a ~ 2. to apply a ~ 3. to have a ~ (to have high ~s) 4. adhere to, maintain a ~ 5. to come up to, meet a ~ 6. to lower; raise ~s/a ~ (to raise the ~ of living; to raise academic ~s) 7. to abandon a ~ (the gold ~ was abandoned) 8. a high; low ~ 9. a double; moral ~ (to apply a double ~) 10. a rigorous, strict ~ 11. the gold ~ (to go off the gold ~) 12. a living ~ (or: a ~ of living) 13. academic, scholastic; educational; professional ~s 14. below; up to ~ 15. by a certain ~ (by our ~s the candidate is not satisfactory) 16. ~s are falling, going down; going up, rising 17. on a ~ (on a gold ~)

standardization *n.* to achieve, bring about ~

standard of living *n.* 1. to raise the ~ 2. a high; low ~ 3. a ~ falls, goes down; goes up, rises

stand back *v.* (D; intr.) to ~ from

standby *n.* ["alert"] to be on ~

stand by *v.* ("to be ready") 1. (D; intr.) to ~ with (they were ~ing by with additional supplies) 2. (E) to ~ to land

stand clear *v.* (d; intr.) to ~ of

stand down *v.* (esp. BE) (D; intr.) ("to withdraw") to ~ in favor of (the other candidate)

stand for *v.* (K) ("to allow") I will not ~ their behaving like that

stand in *v.* (d; intr.) to ~ for ("to substitute for") (can anyone ~ for her?)

standing *n.* ["duration"] 1. of (long) ~ (a custom of long ~) ["status"] 2. academic; advanced ~ (at a university) 3. ~ among, with (~ among the voters) 4. the ~ to + inf. (who has the ~ to take over the leadership of the party?) 5. (misc.) in good ~; an artist of high ~ ["misc."] 6. (US; on a traffic sign) No Standing/No Stopping (GB has *No Waiting*)

stand out *v.* 1. (D; intr.) ("to be clearly visible") to ~ against (to ~ against a dark background) 2. (D; intr.) ("to be noticeable") to ~ among, from, in (to ~ among the others; to ~ in a crowd; to ~ from the rest of the group) 3. (D; intr.) ("to be noticeable") to ~ as (she ~s out as the leading candidate) 4. (colloq.) (BE) (d; intr.) to ~ for ("to insist on") (to ~ out for higher wages)

standpoint *n.* from a ~ (from a practical ~; from our ~)

stands *n.* ["benches for spectators"] in the ~

standstill *n.* 1. to bring smt. to a ~ 2. to come to a ~ 3. a complete, total ~ 4. at a ~ (negotiations were at a complete ~) 5. (misc.) to fight smb. to a ~

stand up *v.* 1. to ~ straight 2. (d; intr.) to ~ for ("to defend") (to ~ for one's rights) 3. (d; intr.) to ~ to ("to resist") (no one dared to ~ to the boss; this jacket will ~ to rough wear) 4. (misc.) the charges will not ~ ("be accepted")

staple *v.* (D; tr.) to ~ to (~ this page to that sheet)

star I *n.* ["heavenly body"] 1. a bright ~ 2. a falling, shooting ~ 3. a fixed ~ 4. the evening; morning; north ~ 5. a distant ~ 6. ~s come out; shine, twinkle 7. (misc.) a galaxy of ~s ["prominent performer"] 8. a baseball; basketball; box-office; film, movie (AE); football; guest; rock; rugby; soccer; sports; track; TV ~ ["fortune"] 9. smb.'s ~ rises; sets, wanes (her ~ was rising) 10. under a ~ (she was born under a lucky ~) ["award"] 11. a battle; gold ~ ["shape"] 12. a five-pointed; six-pointed ~ 13. (misc.) the Star of David

star II *v.* 1. (D; intr., tr.) to ~ as (in his last film he ~red as a cowboy) 2. (D; intr., tr.) to ~ in (to ~ in a new play)

starch I *n.* cornstarch (AE); potato ~

starch II *v.* to ~ stiffly

stardom *n.* to achieve ~

stare I *n.* a blank; cold, icy; fixed; haughty; vacant; wide-eyed ~

stare II *v.* 1. to ~ fixedly; vacantly; wide-eyed 2. (D; intr.) to ~ at 3. (D; intr.) to ~ into (to ~ into space) 4. (misc.) the solution was ~ring us in the face ("the solution was obvious")

starlight *n.* 1. by ~ 2. in the ~

start I *n.* 1. to get off to, make a ~ 2. to have a ~ 3. a flying, running ~ (to get off to a flying ~) 4. a head ~ (to have a head ~) 5. a fresh, new ~ (they got off to/made a fresh ~) 6. a promising ~ (the project got off to/had a promising ~) 7. a false; shaky ~ (they got off to a shaky ~) 8. a ~ at, on (they made a fresh, new ~ at working out their problems; they got off to a shaky ~ on the project) 9. at the ~ 10. for a ~ (for a ~, let's agree where we should meet) 11. from the ~

start II *v.* 1. to ~ afresh, anew 2. (d; intr., tr.) to ~ as (she ~ed her career as a dancer) 3. (d; intr., tr.) ("to begin") to ~ at (prices ~ at five dollars; they ~ed the bidding at fifty dollars) 4. (D; intr.) to ~ by (they ~ed by reviewing the facts of the case) 5. (D; intr.) ("to leave") to ~ for (when did they ~ for the airport?) 6. (d; intr.) ("to leave") to ~ from (we ~ed from Philadelphia) 7. (d; intr.) to ~ on (to ~ on a trip; to ~ on another case) 8. (d; intr., tr.) to ~ with (we'll ~ with you) 9. (E) she ~ed to cough 10. (G) she ~ed coughing 11. (J) what ~ed them drinking? 12. (misc.) to ~ young; she ~ed towards the door; don't ~ anything ("don't cause any trouble")

start back *v.* (P; intr.) let's ~ for home; before it gets dark, we should ~ to the city; while the ferries are still running, we should ~ across the river; we should ~ from this point at dawn

starter *n.* for ~s ("to begin with")

start in v. 1. (D; intr.) to ~ by (they ~ed in by discussing the facts of the case) 2. (AE) (d; intr.) to ~ on ("to put pressure on") (then they ~ed in on her) 3. (misc.) they ~ed in on me to buy a new car (AE); they're ~ing in again with their critical remarks

startle v. (R) it ~d me to see them dressed like that

startled adj. 1. ~ at (~ at the news) 2. ~ to + inf. (she was ~ to hear of their divorce)

startling adj. ~ to + inf. (it was ~ to realize that we were completely cut off from the rest of the world)

start off v. 1. see **start II** 1-8 2. (D; intr.) to ~ to (they ~ed off to the airport without saying goodbye) 3. (misc.) to ~ on a new tack; to ~ on the wrong foot

start out see **start off**

starve v. 1. (D; tr.) to ~ into (to ~ smb. into submission) 2. (misc.) to ~ to death; to ~ oneself to death

starved adj. ~ for, of (BE) (~ for company)

state I n. ["government"] 1. to establish, found, set up a ~ 2. to govern, rule a ~ 3. a free; independent; sovereign ~ 4. a buffer; client; puppet ~ 5. a capitalist; communist; socialist; welfare ~ 6. a garrison; police; totalitarian ~ 7. a secular; theocratic ~ 8. a member ~ (the member ~s of the UN) 9. (misc.) a head of ~; affairs/matters of ~["condition"] 10. a good; satisfactory; unspoiled ~ 11. a permanent; temporary; transitional ~ 12. a comatose; moribund; unconscious ~ 13. a bad, poor; sorry; unsatisfactory; weakened ~ 14. a confused; hysterical; nervous ~ 15. an emotional; mental ~ 16. a financial ~ 17. a gaseous; liquid; solid ~ 18. in a ~ (in a good ~ of repair; in a poor ~ of health; in a highly nervous ~) 19. (misc.) the ~ of the art ("the level of development") ["nervous condition"] 20. in a ~ (she was in quite a ~) ["pomp"] 21. to lie in ~ ["one of the fifty American states"] 22. a dry ~ ("a state in which the sale of alcoholic beverages is prohibited") 23. (historical; US) a border; free; slave ~

state II v. 1. to ~ clearly; emphatically; openly; solemnly; unreservedly 2. (B) we ~d our views to them 3. (L; to) they ~d (to the reporters) that a summit conference would take place soon 4. (Q) she did not ~ how she expected to win the election

statehood n. 1. to achieve ~ 2. to seek, strive for ~

statement n. ["act of stating"] ["something stated"] 1. to issue, make a ~ 2. to confirm; sign a ~ 3. to deny; refute; retract, withdraw a ~ 4. a brief, short; preliminary; succinct; terse ~ 5. a clear; definitive ~ 6. a categorical; controversial; sweeping ~ 7. a prepared; sworn; voluntary ~ 8. a rash; vague ~ 9. an oral; written ~ 10. a false; truthful ~ 11. a ~ that + clause (she has issued a ~ that she intends to be a candidate) 12. (misc.) to take down smb.'s ~; a ~ to the effect that... ["report"] 13. to issue a ~ 14. a bank; financial; official; policy; political; public ~

15. a ~ about (the government issued a ~ about the strike)

state's evidence n. (AE) to turn ~ (see also **King's evidence, Queen's evidence**)

statesman n. an elder; prominent ~

statesmanship n. to practice ~

stateswoman n. an elder; prominent ~

static n. to produce ~

station I n. ["building or place used for a specific purpose"] 1. a broadcasting; radio; television, TV ~ 2. a bus, coach (BE); freight (AE); railroad (AE), railway (esp. BE), train; subway (AE), tube (BE), underground (BE) ~ 3. a fire; police ~ 4. a coast-guard; naval; recruiting ~ 5. a hydroelectric; power ~ 6. a radar; radar-tracking; space; tracking; weather ~ 7. a polling ~ (esp. BE) ["place where motor vehicles are serviced"] 8. a filling, gas (AE), gasoline (AE), petrol (BE), service ~ ["place of duty"] 9. an action; battle ~ ["position"] 10. smb.'s ~ in life 11. above; beneath one's ~ in life ["misc."] 12. to pick up a radio ~

station II v. (P; tr.) they were ~ed in Germany; our unit was ~ed near the coast

statistics n. 1. to collect, gather; tabulate ~ 2. to bandy ~ (about); to cite, quote ~ 3. to manipulate ~ 4. cold, hard ~ 5. vital ~ ("essential data about a population") 6. crime ~ 7. official ~ 8. reliable; valid ~ 9. ~ indicate, show

statue n. 1. to carve; sculpt, sculpture (esp. AE) a ~ 2. to cast a ~ (in bronze) 3. to erect, put up a ~ 4. to unveil a ~ 5. an equestrian ~

stature n. 1. considerable; imposing ~ (a person of imposing ~) 2. the ~ to + inf. (does she have the ~ to run for national office?) 3. in ~ (to grow in ~; small in ~)

status n. 1. to achieve ~ 2. to confer, give, grant ~ 3. celebrity ~ 4. most-favored nation ~ 5. legal ~ (to enjoy/have legal ~) 6. smb.'s financial; marital; social ~ 7. equal ~ 8. smb.'s ~ as (this will not affect your ~ as an asylum-seeker)

status quo n. 1. to maintain, preserve; restore the ~ 2. to disrupt; overturn the ~

statute n. a penal ~

statute of limitations n. 1. the ~ takes effect, goes into effect (or: colloq. and illogically — the ~ expires, runs out) 2. under the ~

stay I n. ["delay"] (legal) 1. to issue; vacate a ~ 2. (misc.) a ~ of execution ["time spent"] 3. a long; short ~ 4. (misc.) we had a very pleasant ~ at the hotel

stay II v. 1. (D; intr.) ("to remain") to ~ for (to ~ for dinner) 2. (d; intr.) to ~ off ("to keep off") (to ~ off the grass) 3. (d; intr.) to ~ out of ("to avoid") (to ~ out of trouble) 4. (d; intr.) to ~ with smb. ("to be smb.'s guest") (they ~ed with us) 5. (s) to ~ calm; seated 6. (misc.) to ~ from Monday to Wednesday

stay abreast v. (D; intr.) to ~ of (to ~ of the news;

the runners ~ed abreast of each other)

stay ahead *v.* (D; intr.) to ~ of

stay away *v.* (D; intr.) to ~ from (to ~ from smb.)

staying power *n.* the ~ to + inf. (does she have the ~ to finish the race?)

stay on *v.* 1. (D; intr.) to ~ as (she ~ed on as deputy) 2. (D; intr.) to ~ for (to ~ for the evening entertainment)

stay out *v.* 1. to ~ late 2. to ~ on strike

stay up *v.* 1. (D; intr.) to ~ for (they allowed the children to ~ for the party) 2. (D; intr.) to ~ until (we ~ed up until midnight) 3. (misc.) to ~ late; the parents ~ed up with the sick child all night

stead *n.* to stand smb. in good ~ ("to be useful to smb.")

steady *adj.* 1. (colloq.) (AE) to go ~ with smb. ("to be smb.'s boyfriend or girlfriend") 2. (misc.) to hold smt. ~; (before a race) ready, ~, go! (BE; AE has *get ready, get set, go!*)

steak *n.* 1. to broil (AE), grill a ~ 2. a juicy; tender; tough ~ 3. to like one's ~ medium; medium-rare; rare; well-done 4. a beefsteak; club (esp. US); cube (esp. US); flank; minute; Porterhouse; rump; Salisbury (US); salmon; sirloin; Swiss (esp. US); T-bone ~

steal *v.* 1. (D; tr.) ("to give surreptitiously") to ~ at (to ~ a glance at smb.) 2. (D; intr., tr.) ("to take illegally") to ~ from (to ~ from the rich; he stole money from his employer) 3. (d; intr.) ("to depart silently") to ~ from, out of (she stole out of the room) 4. (P; intr.) ("to move silently") she stole into the house; we stole quietly across the field; the intruder stole through the rooms

stealth *n.* by ~ (to enter a building by ~)

steal up *v.* (D; intr.) ("to sneak up") to ~ on, to (he stole up on me in the dark)

steam *n.* 1. to emit ~ 2. to get up, produce, work up ~ 3. ~ condenses; forms 4. ~ hisses 5. a cloud; wisp of ~ 6. (misc.) (colloq.) to blow off, let off ~ ("to vent one's feelings"); to run out of ~ ("to use up one's energy")

steam II *v.* 1. (d; intr.) to ~ into; out of (to ~ into a harbor) 2. (N; used with an adjective) she ~ed the envelope open

steamed up *adj.* (colloq.) ["angry"] ~ about, over

steamer *n.* an oceangoing; paddle; tramp ~

steam out *v.* (d; intr.) to ~ to (to ~ to sea)

steamroller *v.* (d; tr.) to ~ through (to ~ a bill through Congress)

steel I *n.* 1. to make, produce ~ 2. to temper ~ 3. stainless ~ 4. a bar; ingot; sheet; slab; strip of ~ 5. (misc.) cold ~ ("bayonet, knife used in close combat")

steel II *v.* 1. (D; refl.) to ~ for (to ~ oneself for the next attack) 2. (H; refl.) to ~ oneself to face an ordeal

steeped *adj.* (cannot stand alone) ~ in (~ in local traditions)

steeple *n.* a church ~

steer I *n.* ["castrated bovine"] to rope a ~

steer II *v.* (P; intr., tr.) we ~ed for port; they ~ed into the hotel

steerage *n.* ["section in a passenger ship"] 1. to travel ~ 2. in ~ (to cross the ocean in ~)

steer clear *v.* (d; intr.) to ~ of (to ~ of danger)

steering *n.* power ~

steering wheel *n.* 1. to turn a ~ 2. at the ~ (who was at the ~?) (see **wheel I**, 7-9)

stem I *n.* (ling.) a consonant; verb ~

stem II *v.* (d; intr.) to ~ from

stench *n.* a dreadful, horrible, unbearable ~

stencil *n.* to cut, make a ~

step I *n.* ["placing the foot"] 1. to make, take a ~ (to take a ~ backward) 2. to retrace one's ~s 3. a giant (usu. fig.); long; mincing; short ~ 4. (usu. fig.) ~ by ~ ["sequence of movements"] (dancing) 5. to execute, perform; learn a ~ ["stride in marching"] (mil.) 6. to keep in ~ 7. to change ~ 8. an even, steady ~ 9. half; route ~ 10. in ~; out of ~ (also fig.: she was out of ~ with everyone else) ["action"] 11. to take a ~ 12. a careful, prudent; positive; precautionary; preventive ~ 13. a bold; critical; decisive; giant; historic ~ (to take a giant ~ forward) 14. a dangerous; drastic; fatal ~ 15. a false; rash, risky ~ 16. (misc.) to keep a ~ ahead of everyone; watch your ~! ("be careful!") ["gait"] 17. a heavy; light ~ ["distance"] 18. a ~ from (their place is just a few ~s from the station)

step II *v.* 1. (d; intr.) to ~ around (to ~ around a puddle) 2. (d; intr.) to ~ between (the referee ~ped between the two boxers) 3. (d; intr.) to ~ into (to ~ into a room) 4. (d; intr.) to ~ off (to ~ off a train) 5. (d; intr.) to ~ on (she ~ped on my foot; to ~ on the brake) 6. (d; intr.) to ~ out of (to ~ out of the room) 7. (d; intr.) to ~ over (she ~ped over the body) 8. (d; intr.) to ~ to, towards (the pupil ~ped to the blackboard) 9. (misc.) to ~ out of line ("to behave inappropriately")

step aside *v.* 1. (D; intr.) to ~ for (he ~ped aside for a younger person) 2. (misc.) she ~ped aside in favor of a younger candidate

step back *v.* (D; intr.) to ~ from (to ~ from the abyss)

step down *v.* 1. (D; intr.) to ~ from (to ~ from the presidency) 2. (D; intr.) to ~ in favor of (he ~ped down in favor of his sister)

step out *v.* 1. (D; intr.) to ~ into (to ~ into the corridor) 2. (D; intr.) to ~ on, onto (she ~ped out on the terrace) 3. (misc.) (esp. AE) he was ~ping out on his wife ("he was betraying his wife")

steppingstone *n.* a ~ to (a ~ to advancement)

steps *n.* ["stairs"] 1. to come up, go up the ~ 2. to come down, go down the ~ 3. steep ~ 4. a flight of ~

step up *v.* (D; intr.) to ~ to (he ~ped up to me and told me who he was)

stereo *n.* (to broadcast) in ~

stereotype *n.* 1. to perpetuate; reinforce a ~ 2. to conform to, fit a ~ 3. a cultural; ethnic; negative; racial ~

stern *adj.* ~ towards; with

stew *n.* 1. (a) beef; Irish; lamb; mulligan (esp. US); veal; vegetable ~ 2. (misc.) in a ~ ("agitated")

steward *n.* a chief; shop ~

stick I *n.* 1. a hiking; hockey; lacrosse; walking ~ 2. a celery ~ 3. a composing ~ ("device for typesetting") 4. a swagger ~ (carried by a military officer) 5. (misc.) to carry a big ~ ("to threaten to use force to settle a dispute")

stick II *v.* 1. ("to remain fixed") to ~ fast (the car is stuck fast in the mud) 2. (d; intr.) to ~ by ("to be loyal to") (to ~ by one's friends) 3. (d; tr.) ("to thrust") to ~ into (to ~ a needle into a cushion; to ~ one's hands into one's pockets) 4. (d; tr.) ("to fasten, paste") to ~ on, to (to ~ a stamp on an envelope) 5. (d; tr.) ("to thrust") to ~ through (she stuck her head through the window) 6. (d; intr.) ("to adhere") to ~ to (the stamp didn't ~ to the envelope) 7. (d; intr.) ("to limit oneself") to ~ to (to ~ to the subject) 8. (d; intr.) to ~ to ("to be loyal to") (to ~ to one's principles) 9. (d; intr.) ("to remain") to ~ with (~ with me, and you will not get lost) 10. (P; tr.) ("to put") she stuck it behind the door; she stuck it under the chair 11. (misc.) it stuck in her mind that she might never see them again; to ~ in smb.'s throat ("to be hard to say"); ("to be a source of irritation")

sticker *n.* a bumper; price ~

stickler *n.* ["one who insists on exactness"] a ~ for (a ~ for protocol)

stick out *v.* 1. (D; intr.) ("to protrude") to ~ from; into (the nail stuck out from the wall; his feet stuck out into the aisle) 2. (D; tr.) ("to extend") to ~ to, towards (she stuck out her hand to us) 3. (misc.) to ~ like a sore thumb ("to be very conspicuous")

sticks *n.* (colloq.) ["rural area"] in the ~ (to live way out in the ~)

stick shift *n.* (colloq.) (AE) to operate a ~

stick up *v.* (d; intr.) to ~ for (colloq.) ("to defend") (to ~ for one's friend)

stiff *adj.* frozen; scared ~

stigma *n.* 1. to attach a ~ to 2. a ~ attaches to (no ~ attaches to being poor) 3. a ~ about, in, to (esp. AE) (there is no ~ to being poor)

stigmatize *v.* (D; tr.) to ~ as (to be ~d as a traitor)

still I *adj., adv.* 1. deathly; perfectly ~ (to stand perfectly ~) 2. to keep; sit; stand ~

still II *n.* in the ~ of the night

stilts *n.* 1. (to walk) on ~ 2. a pair of ~

stimulant *n.* a ~ to (a ~ to the local economy)

stimulate *v.* 1. (d; tr.) to ~ into (they ~d us into

action) 2. (H) to ~ smb. to do smt.

stimulating *adj.* 1. intellectually ~ 2. ~ to + inf. (it is intellectually ~ to live in a large city)

stimulation *n.* 1. to provide ~ 2. erotic, sexual; intellectual ~

stimulus *n.* 1. to give, provide a ~ 2. a powerful, strong ~ 3. a ~ to

sting I *n.* ["skin wound"] 1. a bee; wasp ~ ["con, swindle"] ["trap"] (colloq.) 2. to set up a ~ ["misc."] 3. to take the ~ out of smt. ("minimize disappointment")

sting II *v.* (D; intr.) to ~ from (my eyes ~ from the smoke)

stingy *adj.* ~ with (~ with one's money)

stink I *n.* ("outcry") (colloq.) to cause, kick up, make, raise a ~ (about)

stink II *v.* (D; intr.) to ~ of (the place ~s of rotten fish)

stint I *n.* ["period of service"] to do, serve a ~ (he did his ~ as a soldier)

stint II *v.* (D; intr.) ("to economize") to ~ on (don't ~ on the food)

stipend *n.* 1. to receive a ~ 2. to pay a ~ 3. a modest ~ (to live on a modest ~)

stipulate *v.* 1. (L) the contract ~s that the work must be finished by the end of the year 2. (Q) did they ~ how the job was to be done?

stipulation *n.* 1. to make a ~ 2. a ~ that + clause (there was a ~ that court costs would be shared equally)

stir I *n.* ["disturbance"] 1. to cause, create, make a ~ 2. a big ~ 3. a ~ about, over

stir II *v.* 1. (D; intr., tr.) to ~ from, out of (we could not ~ him from his depression; they would not ~ out of their lethargy; she would not ~ from her desk) 2. (D; tr.) to ~ into (to ~ one ingredient into another) 3. (D; tr.) to ~ to (the news ~red them to greater efforts) 4. (H; usu. refl.) they couldn't ~ themselves to act

stitch *n.* 1. to make a ~ 2. to drop; pick up, take up a ~ 3. to cast on ~es 4. (med.) to put ~es in 5. (med.) to remove, take out ~es 6. a cable; chain; cross; knit, plain (BE); purl; running ~

stitches *n.* in ~ ("convulsed with laughter")

stock I *n.* ["inventory, supply"] 1. to take ~ 2. in ~; out of ~ (this item is not in ~) ["share, shares in a corporation"] 3. to buy; issue; sell ~ 4. common ~ (AE; BE has *ordinary shares*) 5. blue-chip; over-the-counter; preferred (AE; BE has *preference shares*) ~ ["equipment"] 6. rolling ~ ("railway vehicles") ["confidence, trust"] 7. to put ~ in smb. ["evaluation"] 8. to take ~ (we must take ~ of the situation) ["stage productions"] (AE) 9. summer ~ ["livestock"] 10. to graze ~ ["lineage"] 11. of good ~ ["misc."] 12. smb.'s ~ in trade ("smb.'s customary practice")

stock II *v.* (D; tr.) to ~ with (they ~ed their store

with new merchandise)

stock exchange see **stock market**

stocking *n.* 1. mesh; nylon; seamless; silk; surgical ~s 2. a pair of ~s 3. (misc.) she got a ladder (BE)/ run (esp. AE) in her ~

stocking feet *n.* in one's ~

stock market *n.* 1. to gamble, speculate on the ~ 2. the ~ closes; opens (the ~ closed strong) 3. the ~ goes up, rises; rallies 4. the ~ collapses, crashes; falls, goes down, slumps

stocks *n.* ["shares on the stock market"] (esp. AE; CE has *shares*) 1. ~ close; open (did ~ close strong or weak?) 2. ~ go up; rally 3. ~ fall, go down, slump

stock up *v.* (D; intr.) to ~ on, with (to ~ on supplies)

stockyards *n.* at, in the ~ (to work at/in the ~)

stoical *adj.* ~ about

stoicism *n.* 1. to display ~ 2. great ~ 3. with ~ (to meet adversity with great ~)

stole *n.* a fur; silk; woolen ~

stomach *n.* ["digestive organ"] 1. to settle; turn, upset smb.'s ~ 2. an empty; full; queasy; sick; sour; strong; upset; weak ~ 3. smb.'s ~ aches, hurts; growls, rumbles 4. on an empty ~ 5. (misc.) it turns my ~ ("it disgusts me") ["inclination"] 6. to have no ~ for smt.

stomachache *n.* to get; have a ~ (BE also has *to get, have ~*)

stomp *v.* (P; intr.) she ~ed into my office; they ~ed out of the room

stone I *n.* ["piece of rock"] 1. to hurl, throw a ~ 2. a foundation; paving ~ 3. a block, slab of ~ 4. (misc.) to leave no ~ unturned ("to try all methods of achieving an end") ["gem"] 5. to set a (precious) ~ 6. a precious ~ ["stony mass in the body"] 7. a gallstone; kidney ~

stone II *v.* to ~ smb. to death

stone's throw *n.* a ~ away; away from

stool *n.* 1. a bar; ducking ~; footstool; piano; step ~ 2. (misc.) (BE) to fall between two ~s ("to fail to achieve either of two goals")

stoop *v.* 1. (d; intr.) to ~ to ("to lower oneself to") (to ~ to cheating) 2. (E) she ~ed to pick it up

stop I *n.* ["halt"] ["cessation"] 1. to make a ~ 2. to put a ~ to (the teacher put a ~ to the cheating) 3. to bring to a ~ (the driver brought the bus to a ~) 4. to come to a ~ (the train came to a ~) 5. an abrupt, sudden; brief; dead; full; smooth ~ 6. a comfort, rest; flag (AE); request (BE); regular, scheduled; unscheduled; whistle (AE) ("very brief") ~ 7. a bus; pit; refueling; streetcar (AE), tram (BE) ~ 8. at a ~ (at the bus ~) 9. (misc.) to miss one's ~ ["place for resting"] 10. a truck ~ (esp. AE; BE has *transport cafe*) ["punctuation mark"] 11. a full ~ (BE; AE has *period*)

stop II *v.* 1. to ~ dead; short 2. (D; intr.) to ~ at (to ~ at the intersection) 3. (D; intr.) to ~ for (to ~ for lunch; to ~ for a red light) 4. (D; tr.) to ~ from (to ~ smb. from doing smt.) 5. (G) they ~ped talking 6. (BE) (J) to ~ smb. doing smt. 7. (K) I can't ~ his interrupting 8. (misc.) to ~ dead in one's tracks; to ~ at nothing ("to allow no scruples to interfere with one's efforts to achieve an end"); they ~ped (in order) to chat

stop by *v.* 1. (D; intr.) to ~ at (we'll ~ at your place) 2. (D; intr.) to ~ for (to ~ for tea)

stop in *v.* 1. (D; intr.) to ~ at (they ~ped in at my place) 2. (D; intr.) to ~ for

stop off *v.* 1. (D; intr.) to ~ at (we all ~ped off at a bar) 2. (D; intr.) to ~ for (to ~ off for a quick swim)

stopover *n.* 1. to make a ~ (for) 2. at a ~

stop over *v.* 1. (D; intr.) to ~ at 2. (D; intr.) to ~ for (AE) (let's ~ at my place for a cup of coffee)

stoppage *n.* a work ~

stopping see the Usage Note for **standing**

stop short *v.* (d; intr.) to ~ of (they ~ped short of imposing new taxes)

stop sign *n.* to go through, run (AE) a ~

storage *n.* ["storing"] 1. to put smt. into ~ 2. to take smt. out of ~ 3. cold ~ 4. in ~ ["memory of a computer"] 5. external; internal; magnetic ~

store *n.* ["shop, establishment where goods are sold"] (esp. AE; see the Usage Note for **shop**) 1. to manage, operate, run a ~ 2. a bookstore; candy; clothing ~; drugstore; food, grocery; furniture; hardware; jewelry; music; shoe; stationery; toy ~ 3. a chain, multiple (BE); company; convenience; department; discount; general; retail; self-service ~ 4. (AE) a dry-goods ~ (BE has *draper's shop*) 5. (AE) a liquor, package ~ (BE has *off licence*) 6. (AE) a five-and-dime, five-and-ten-cent; (AE) a variety ~ (BE has *haberdashery*) 7. at, in a ~ (she works at/in a ~) ["misc."] 8. to set (great; little) ~ by ("to attribute importance to"); to lie/be in ~ ("to be imminent"); to have smt. in ~ for smb. ("to have smt. prepared for smb.")

stores *n.* ["supplies"] 1. naval ~ 2. a cache of ~

storm I *n.* ["atmospheric disturbance"] 1. to brave, ride out, weather a ~ (the ship finally rode out the ~) 2. a blinding; fierce, heavy, raging, severe, violent ~ 3. a dust; electrical ~; firestorm; hailstorm; ice ~; rainstorm; sandstorm; snowstorm; thunderstorm; tropical ~ 4. a ~ comes up; hits, strikes; rages 5. a ~ blows itself out, blows over, dies down, subsides 6. a ~ was gathering (also fig.) 7. the eye of a ~ (also fig.) ["disturbance, commotion"] 8. to cause, raise, stir up a ~ 9. a ~ was brewing, gathering ["assault, attack"] (mil. and fig.) 10. to take by ~ (the new play took Broadway by ~) ["misc."] 11. to talk up a ~ (colloq.) (esp. AE) ("to talk a great deal")

storm II *v.* (d; intr.) ("to rush angrily") to ~ into; out of (to ~ out of a room)

story I *n.* ["tale"] 1. to narrate, recount, relate, tell a

~ 2. to concoct, fabricate, invent, make up a ~ 3. to spread a ~ 4. to hear; listen to a ~ 5. to change, revise; embellish, embroider a ~ 6. an amusing, funny, humorous; charming; fascinating; nice, pleasant ~ 7. a coherent; likely, plausible; true ~ 8. an unknown; untold ~ 9. a boring; complicated, involved; long ~ 10. a gripping; hard-luck; moving; sad; sob; tragic ~ 11. a horror; ugly; unpleasant ~ 12. a cock-and-bull, farfetched; implausible; improbable; unlikely ~ 13. a dirty, off-color, risqué; juicy ~ 14. an adventure; bedtime, children's, fairy; detective; ghost; hard-luck; love ~ 15. conflicting ~ries (they told conflicting ~ries to the police) 16. a shaggy dog ~ ("a long rambling joke with an illogical punch line") 17. a short ~ ("a short prose narrative") 18. the whole ~ (who knows the whole ~ of the incident?) 19. a ~ about, of (she told charming ~ries about her travels; to narrate gripping ~ries of wartime heroism) 20. a ~ that + clause (have you heard the ~ that she intends to resign?) ["newspaper account"] 21. to carry, circulate, print, run a ~ (all the newspapers carried the ~ about the fire) 22. to feature a ~ 23. to edit; rewrite; write a ~ 24. to file a ~ 25. to cover up, hush up, kill, suppress a ~ 26. a breaking ("very new"); cover; exclusive; feature; follow-up; front-page; human-interest; lead; sensational ~ 27. the inside ~ (you can read the inside ~ in tomorrow's edition) 28. a ~ breaks ("becomes known"); circulates ["background information"] 29. to get the (whole) ~ ["misc."] 30. the ~ goes that she is retiring soon; I have not heard your side of the ~; to stick to one's ~; the police could not make a coherent ~ out of his ravings; a success ~ ("a successful career")

story II storey n. ["floor level"] a lower; top; upper ~

stove n. 1. to light a ~ 2. a coal; gas; kerosene (AE), paraffin (BE); kitchen; oil; pot-belly ~ 3. on a ~ (to cook smt. on a ~)

stow away v. to ~ on a ship

straggle v. (P; intr.) to ~ across the border; they ~d into the lecture hall

straight adj. (misc.) to go ~ ("to become law-abiding"); to set smb. ~ ("to disabuse smb.")

straightforward adj. 1. ~ about 2. ~ with

straight ticket n. (AE) to vote a ~ ("to vote for all the candidates of one party")

strain I n. ["exertion"] ["tension"] 1. to impose, place, put a ~ on 2. to feel; stand the ~ 3. to ease, relieve the ~ 4. (a) considerable, great; terrible, tremendous ~ 5. (an) emotional, mental; financial; physical ~ 6. back ~; eyestrain 7. a ~ on (a ~ on relations between the two countries) 8. under a ~

strain II v. 1. (d; intr.) to ~ at (the dog ~ed at the leash/BE lead) 2. (E) they were ~ing to get the car out of the mud

strain III n. ["variety of microorganism"] a strong, virulent; attenuated, weak ~

straits n. ["difficulties"] 1. desperate, dire; financial ~ 2. in certain ~ (they were left in desperate ~)

stranded adj. to leave smb. ~

strange adj. 1. ~ to 2. ~ to + inf. (it was ~ to work at night = it was ~ working at night) 3. ~ that + clause (it is ~ that she hasn't written for a whole month) 4. (misc.) it was ~ how she kept coming back

stranger n. 1. a complete, perfect, total, utter ~ 2. a mysterious ~ 3. a ~ to (she's no ~ to us) 4. (misc.) I don't know the way — I'm a ~ here myself

strangle v. 1. (D; tr.) to ~ with (he ~d her with a scarf) 2. (misc.) to ~ smb. to death

stranglehold n. 1. to get; have a ~ on smb. (a few multinationals have a ~ on their economy) 2. to loosen; release; tighten a ~

strap I n. a chin; shoulder ~; watchstrap (BE; CE has *watchband*)

strap II v. (D; tr.) to ~ onto, to (they ~ped the suitcase to the top of the car)

strapped adj. (colloq.) 1. financially ~ 2. ~ for cash

stratagem n. 1. to resort to, use a ~ 2. a subtle; wily ~

strategist n. an armchair ("amateur") ~

strategy n. 1. to adopt, design, devise, formulate, map out, plan, work out a ~ 2. to apply, pursue a ~ 3. to outline, unveil a ~ 4. a global; grand, long-range, long-term ~ 5. a campaign, political; defense, military; economic, financial ~ 6. a matter; point of ~ 7. a ~ for (to work out a ~ for balancing the budget) 8. a ~ to + inf. (they unveiled a ~ to win the campaign)

straw n. ["tube"] 1. (to drink) through a ~ 2. (misc.) to decide smt. by drawing ~s (also fig.) ["misc."] 3. a ~ in the wind ("a hint of smt. to come"); to clutch at (any) ~s ("to try in desperation"); the last ~, or: the ~ that broke the camel's back ("a final burden that exceeds smb.'s endurance")

stray v. (D; intr.) 1. to ~ from (to ~ from the subject) 2. (d; intr.) to ~ into, onto (to ~ onto smb.'s property)

streak I n. ["tendency, trait"] (usu. derog.) 1. a cruel; jealous; mean, nasty, vindictive; stubborn ~ 2. a yellow ~ ("cowardice") ["series"] 3. a losing; lucky; winning ~

streak II v. (P; intr.) to ~ across a field

streaked adj. ~ with (~ with gray)

stream I n. 1. to ford a ~ 2. a mountain; running; swollen ~ 3. an endless; steady ~ (a steady ~ of refugees) 4. the jet ~ ("band of high-velocity winds moving from west to east")

stream II v. (P; intr.) people were ~ing towards the town square; the audience came ~ing out of the auditorium

street n. 1. to pave a ~ 2. to name; number ~s 3. to block, cordon off a ~ 4. to cross a ~ 5. a bustling, busy; congested; crowded ~ 6. a deserted, lonely; quiet ~ 7. a back; high (BE), main (AE) ~ 8. a cross; dead-end; one-way; through ~ 9. a broad, wide; narrow; winding ~ 10. a ~ curves; goes; runs (in a certain direction) 11. across the ~ 12. down; up the ~ 13. in (esp. BE), on (esp. AE) the ~ (the children were playing in/on the ~) 14. (BE) in the high ~ 15. (AE) on the main ~; on Main Street 16. (misc.) to take a ~ (they took the wrong ~); follow this ~ for two blocks; the ~ is clear; (the) mean ("squalid") ~s; (AE; military) a battery; company ~

streetcar n. (AE) 1. to drive, operate a ~ 2. to go by ~; to ride a ~; to ride in, on a ~; to take a ~ 3. a ~ runs; stops (BE has *tram*)

strength n. ["power"] 1. to build up, develop (one's) ~ 2. to find; gain, gather (the) ~ 3. to conserve, husband, save (one's) ~ 4. to recoup, regain (one's) ~ 5. to overtax, sap, tax smb.'s ~ 6. brute, great; inner; physical; tensile ~ 7. a position; show of ~ 8. the ~ to + inf. (do you have the ~ to lift this weight?) 9. in ~ ("in large numbers") ["number of personnel, units"] 10. full, maximum ~ (to bring a department up to full ~) 11. at; below ~ (our police force was at full ~; it is now five officers below ~) ["misc."] 12. on the ~ of smt. ("relying on smt.") (on the ~ of your recommendation); on the ~ (BE; colloq.) ("on the full-time permanent staff")

stress I n. ["emphasis"] 1. to lay, place, put (the) ~ on 2. to shift the ~ from; to ["intensity of sound"] (ling.) 3. to place, put the ~ on (a syllable) 4. to shift the ~ from; to 5. (a) dynamic; free; fixed; pitch; primary; qualitative; quantitative; secondary; strong; weak ~ 6. sentence; word ~ ["tension"] 7. to cause, create, generate; increase ~ 8. to alleviate, reduce, relieve; control; decrease ~ 9. emotional, mental, psychological; perceived; physical ~ 10. under ~

stress II v. (L) the police ~ed that all regulations would be strictly enforced

stretch I n. ["final phase"] (esp. AE) 1. the final ~ 2. to fade in the ~ ["period of time"] 3. to do a ~ (in prison) 4. (misc.) for hours at a ~

stretch II v. 1. (N; used with an adjective) we ~ed the rope tight 2. (P; intr.) the prairie ~es for miles

stretched adj. ~ to the limit; ~ tight; tightly ~

stretcher n. (to carry smb.) on a ~

stretch out v. (D; tr.) to ~ to (she ~ed her hand out to us in friendship)

strew v. 1. (d; tr.) to ~ with (the field was strewn with bodies) 2. (P; tr.) their equipment was strewn across the floor; they ~ed flowers around the auditorium

stricken adj. ["afflicted"] 1. ~ by, with 2. (misc.) conscience-stricken; grief-stricken; panic-stricken; poverty-stricken

strict adj. 1. ~ about, concerning, in 2. ~ towards, with

strictly adv. ~ speaking

stricture n. a ~ against, on

stride I n. ["normal speed"] 1. to hit one's ~ 2. to break one's ~ ["progress"] 3. to make great ~s (in) 4. considerable, giant, great, tremendous ~s ["misc."] 5. to take smt. in (one's) ~ ("to confront a problem calmly")

stride II v. 1. to ~ confidently; purposefully 2. (P; intr.) she strode confidently into the room; he strode towards the lectern; they strode angrily out of the room

strident adj. ~ in (they were ~ in their demands)

strife n. 1. to cause, create, stir up ~ 2. bitter ~ 3. civil; communal; domestic; factional; industrial; internal; internecine; political; sectarian ~ 4. ~ among, between; in (to create ~ between two sisters)

strike I n. ["refusal to work"] 1. to call, go (out) on; organize a ~ 2. to conduct, stage a ~ 3. to avert; break (up); mediate; settle a ~ 4. a buyers'; hunger; rent ~ (the prisoners went on a hunger ~) 5. a general; lightning (BE); nationwide; sit-down; sympathy; token ~ 6. an official (BE); unofficial (BE), wildcat ~ 7. on ~ (some of the workers were on ~) ["attack"] 8. to carry out a ~ 9. an air; first, preemptive; retaliatory; second ~ ["disadvantage"] (from baseball) (AE) 10. they have two ~s against them ("they are at a decided disadvantage") ["discovery"] 11. an oil ~

strike II v. 1. (D; intr.) ("to refuse to work") to ~ against; for (the workers struck against the company for higher pay) 2. (D; tr.) ("to hit") to ~ against, on (she struck her head against the door) 3. (d; tr.) ("to impress") to ~ as (the idea struck me as silly) 4. (d; intr.) to ~ at ("to attack") (to ~ at the root causes of poverty; to ~ at the enemy) 5. (d; tr.) to ~ from, off (they struck her name off the list) 6. (N; used with an adjective) ("to make") to ~ smb. dead 7. (BE) (O) ("to give") he struck me a heavy blow 8. (R) it struck me that the inflation rate has been going down

strike back v. (D; intr.) to ~ at (to ~ at the enemy)

strikebreaker n. to bring in ~s

strike out v. 1. (d; intr.) ("to act") to ~ against, at (to ~ against injustice) 2. (d; intr.) to ~ for ("to set out for") (to ~ for shore) 3. (misc.) to ~ on one's own ("to begin an independent existence")

striking distance n. ["effective range"] within ~

string n. ["cord"] 1. to tie a ~ 2. to untie a ~ 3. a ball; piece of ~ ["grouping of players according to ability"] (esp. AE) 4. first; second ~ (see also **strings**)

string along v. (D; intr.) to ~ with

strings n. ["strips used for fastening"] 1. apron ~; shoestrings ["cords on a musical instrument"] 2.

to pick (esp. AE), pluck ~ ["influence"] (colloq.) 3. to pull ~

strip I *n.* ["runway"] 1. an airstrip, landing ~ ["dividing patch"] 2. a centre (BE), median (AE) ~ (on a road)

strip II *v.* 1. (D; intr.) to ~ for (to ~ for a physical examination) 2. (d; tr.) to ~ of (to ~ smb. of all civil rights) 3. (D; intr., tr.) to ~ to (to ~ to the waist) 4. (N; used with an adjective) to ~ smb. naked

strip down *v.* (d; intr.) to ~ to (he ~ped down to his underwear)

stripe *n.* ["strip, band"] 1. a horizontal; vertical ~ 2. a sergeant's ~s 3. a service ~ (worn on a soldier's sleeve to indicate length of service) ["sort"] (esp. AE) 4. of a certain ~ (people of their ~)

stripping *n.* 1. weather ~ 2. (BE) (commercial) asset ~

striptease *n.* to do, perform a ~

strive *v.* 1. (d; intr.) to ~ for (to ~ for peace) 2. (formal) (E) we ~ to please

stroke *n.* ["apoplexy"] 1. to have, suffer a ~ 2. a crippling, massive, severe ~ 3. a slight ~ ["movement, series of movements"] 4. (tennis) a backhand; forehand ~ 5. (swimming) to swim a few ~s 6. a backstroke; breast; butterfly ~; sidestroke ["sound of striking"] 7. at, on a ~ (at the ~ of midnight) ["movement of a piston"] 8. an exhaust; exhaust-suction; intake; suction ~ ["action"] 9. a brilliant ~ 10. (misc.) a ~ of genius; to reduce inflation at one ~; their hard-won freedoms were abolished with the ~ of a pen ["misc."] 11. a ~ of luck

stroll I *n.* 1. to go for, have, take a ~ 2. to take smb. for a ~ (she took the children for a ~) 3. a leisurely ~

stroll II *v.* (P; intr.) to ~ through the park

stroller *n.* (esp. AE) to push a ~ (BE has *pushchair*)

strong *adj.* 1. ~ in (I'm not ~ in mathematics) 2. (misc.) she's still going ~

structure *n.* 1. (ling.) to generate a ~ 2. (ling.) (a) deep; grammatical; intermediate; surface ~ 3. (pol.) a power ~ 4. bone; cellular; molecular ~ 5. a basic; complex; solid ~ 6. a corporate; economic, financial; political; price; tax; wage ~

struggle I *n.* 1. to carry on, put up, wage a ~ 2. a bitter, desperate, fierce, frantic, violent; ceaseless, unending, unrelenting; uphill ~ 3. an armed; internecine; life-and-death ~ 4. a power ~ 5. the class ~ 6. a ~ about, over (a ~ over property rights) 7. a ~ against, with (a ~ against poverty; a ~ with one's conscience) 8. a ~ between (a ~ between the two factions) 9. a ~ for (a ~ for justice) 10. a ~ to + inf. (it was a ~ to make ends meet = it was a ~ making ends meet) 11. in ~ (locked in ~) 12. (misc.) a ~ to the death

struggle II *v.* 1. to ~ bravely; desperately 2. (D;

intr.) to ~ against, with (to ~ against tyranny) 3. (D; intr.) to ~ for (to ~ for freedom) 4. (D; intr.) to ~ over (to ~ over property rights) 5. (E) they ~d to remain alive 6. (misc.) to ~ to one's feet

strung out *adj.* (slang) ~ on (~ on heroin)

strut *v.* 1. (d; intr.) to ~ into (to ~ into a room) 2. (d; intr.) to ~ out of (to ~ out of a meeting) 3. (P; intr.) they were ~ting around the auditorium

stub *n.* 1. a cigarette; pencil; ticket ~ 2. a check (AE), cheque (BE) ~

stubborn *adj.* ~ about

stubbornness *n.* 1. sheer ~ 2. ~ about 3. ~ to + inf. (it was sheer ~ not to agree) 4. out of ~ (she refused to compromise out of ~)

stuck *adj.* ["burdened"] (colloq.) 1. ~ with (he always gets ~ with the worst jobs; I am ~ with the chore of breaking the bad news) ["infatuated"] (colloq.) 2. ~ on (he's ~ on her) ["fully involved"] (colloq.) (BE) 3. ~ into (there is no holding him once he gets ~ into smt.) ["fixed"] 4. to get ~ (they got ~ in the mud) 5. ~ fast

stud *n.* at ~ ("for breeding") (the retired racehorses are at ~)

student *n.* 1. an excellent, outstanding; good, strong ~ 2. a poor, weak ~ 3. a day; evening; external (BE); foreign, overseas (BE); full-time; part-time; special; transfer; work-study ~ 4. a college, university; degree; graduate, postgraduate (esp. BE); high-school (AE); undergraduate ~ 5. (misc.) a student-teacher

USAGE NOTE: In GB, *students* usu. refer to those in post-secondary education. Younger ones are usu. called *pupils*. However, secondary-school pupils in Britain have begun to call themselves *school students*. In the US, the term *students* is used for those at a university and in secondary school—*college students, high-school students*. Children at (BE)/in (esp. AE) primary schools are usu. called *pupils* in the US, and almost always in GB. In CE, one can differentiate between a *student of Freud* ("a student of Freud's ideas") and *Freud's student/a student of Freud's* ("one who was taught personally by Freud").

studies *n.* 1. to begin, take up; complete, finish; pursue one's ~ 2. advanced; graduate, postgraduate (esp. BE); undergraduate ~ 3. Black; classical; liberal (BE); peace; social; women's ~

studio *n.* 1. an art; dance ~ 2. a film; radio; recording; television, TV ~ 3. a soundproof ~

study I *n.* ["investigation"] 1. to conduct, do, make a ~ 2. a careful, detailed, exhaustive, in-depth, intensive, rigorous, thorough ~ 3. a feasibility; follow-up; pilot; statistical ~ 4. a classic, classical; definitive ~ 5. a case; empirical; epidemiological; experimental; scientific; time-and-motion ~ 6. under ~ (the matter is under ~) ["branch of learning, subject"] 7. nature ~ ["learning"] 8. advanced ~ 9.

supervised ~

study II *v.* 1. to ~ closely; diligently, hard, seriously 2. (D; intr.) to ~ for (to ~ for a degree) 3. (d; intr.) to ~ under (to ~ under a well-known professor) 4. (Q) to ~ how to ~ing to be a nurse 5. (misc.) he is ~ing to survive in the wilderness

study up *v.* (colloq.) (AE) (D; intr.) to ~ on (to ~ on a topic)

stuff I *n.* (colloq.) ["subject matter"] 1. to know one's ~ 2. heady ("exciting"); kid ("elementary") ~; the same old ~ ["knowledge, ability"] 3. to show, strut one's ~ 4. (AE) the ~ to + inf. (she has the ~ to succeed) 5. (misc.) (esp. AE) the right ~ ["duties"] 6. to do one's ~

stuff II *v.* 1. (d; tr.) to ~ into (she ~ed her things into a suitcase) 2. (D; tr.) to ~ with (they ~ed their suitcases with all sorts of things)

stumble *v.* 1. (d; intr.) to ~ across, into, on, onto, upon ("to meet by chance") (to ~ across an old manuscript) 2. (D; intr.) to ~ over ("to trip over") (she ~d over every sentence)

stumbling block *n.* 1. an insurmountable ~ 2. a ~ to (a ~ to progress)

stump I *n.* to remove a ~ (of a tree)

stump II *v.* (d; intr.) to ~ for (esp. AE) ("to support by making speeches") (to ~ for a candidate)

stun *v.* (R) it ~ned me to see him drunk

stunned *adj.* ~ to + inf. (we were ~ to learn of his defection)

stunt *n.* 1. to do, perform a ~ 2. (colloq.) to pull a ~ ("to do smt. unexpected") 3. a publicity ~ 4. a daredevil ~

stupid *adj.* 1. ~ about 2. ~ to + inf. (it was ~ of him to lie; I was ~ to agree)

stupidity *n.* 1. to display ~ 2. sheer ~ 3. the height of ~ 4. ~ to + inf. (it was sheer ~ to believe him) 5. ~ that + clause (it was sheer ~ that she decided to drop out of school)

stupor *n.* 1. to fall into a ~ 2. a drunken ~

stutter *n.* a nervous ~ (he speaks with a nervous ~)

style I *n.* ["manner of expression"] 1. to develop; polish, refine one's ~ 2. an affected; classic, classical; elegant; flowery, ornate; formal; informal; pedestrian; plain; vigorous ~ ["manner of acting"] 3. to cramp smb.'s ~ 4. an abrasive; grand ~ 5. in (a) ~ (to live in a/in grand ~) ["fashionable elegance"] 6. high ~ 7. in ~ (to live in ~) ["excellence of expression or behavior"] 8. to lack ~ ["fashion"] 9. to keep up with the latest ~s 10. in ~ (running shoes are in ~) 11. out of ~ (dresses like that never go out of ~)

style II *v.* (D; tr.) to ~ for (to ~ shoes for comfort)

suasion *n.* ["persuasion"] moral ~

subconscious *n.* in one's ~

subdivide *v.* (D; tr.) to ~ into

subject I *adj.* (cannot stand alone) ~ to (~ to change)

subject II *n.* ["topic, theme"] 1. to bring up, broach; mention; pursue; tackle a ~ 2. to address, cover, deal with, discuss, take up, treat a ~ 3. to dwell on; exhaust; go into a ~ 4. to avoid; drop a ~ 5. to change the ~ 6. an appropriate, suitable; everyday, mundane; favorite; pleasant ~ 7. a controversial, thorny, delicate, ticklish; inappropriate; taboo; unpleasant ~ 8. a ~ comes up (for discussion) 9. a ~ for (a ~ for debate) 10. on a ~ (we have nothing to say on that ~) ["area, course of study"] 11. to study, tackle, take up a ~ 12. to master a ~ 13. an elective (AE), optional (BE); required ~ 14. a major (AE), main (BE); minor (AE), secondary (BE) ~ ["noun, noun phrase in a clause"] 15. a compound; grammatical; impersonal; logical; simple ~ ["citizen of a monarchy"] (esp. BE) 16. a British; loyal; naturalized ~

subject III *v.* (d; tr.) to ~ to (to ~ smb. to torture)

subjection *n.* ~ to

subject matter *n.* related; unrelated ~

subjugate *v.* (D; tr.) to ~ to

subjugation *n.* in ~

sublease see **sublet**

sublet *v.* 1. (B) to ~ a house to smb. 2. (D; tr.) to ~ from (to ~ a house from smb.)

sublimate *v.* (D; tr.) to ~ into

sublime *n.* from the ~ to the ridiculous

submarine *n.* 1. a conventional; midget; nuclear, nuclear-powered ~ 2. ~s dive; hunt in packs; submerge; surface

submerge *v.* (D; refl., tr.) to ~ in (she ~d herself in her work)

submission *n.* ["giving in"] 1. in ~ to (they lived in ~ to the conqueror) ["argument"] (legal) 2. to make a ~ 3. a ~ that + clause (her lawyer made a ~ that she had not been informed of her rights)

submissive *adj.* ~ to

submit *v.* 1. (B) ("to present") they ~ted their report to us 2. (D; intr.) ("to yield") to ~ to (to ~ to superior force) 3. (d; intr.) ("to agree to undergo") to ~ to (to ~ to arbitration) 4. (usu. legal) (L) ("to claim") their lawyer ~s that there are no grounds for denying bail

subordinate I *adj.* ~ to

subordinate II *v.* (D; refl., tr.) to ~ to (they had to ~ their own needs to the needs of the group)

subordination *n.* ~ to

subpoena I *n.* 1. to issue a ~ 2. to serve a ~ on 3. a ~ to + inf. (she received a ~ to appear in court in two weeks)

subpoena II *v.* 1. (D; tr.) to ~ as (to ~ smb. as a witness) 2. (H) to ~ smb. to testify

subscribe *v.* 1. (D; intr.) to ~ for ("to agree to purchase") (they ~d for a large number of shares) 2. (D; intr.) to ~ to ("to receive regularly") (to ~ to a magazine) 3. (d; intr.) to ~ to ("to agree with") (to ~ to an opinion)

subscriber *n.* a ~ to (a ~ to a magazine)

subscription *n.* ["arrangement for receiving a periodical"] 1. to get, take out; have a ~ to 2. to renew a ~ 3. to cancel a ~ 4. an annual ~ 5. a ~ lapses 6. a ~ to (a ~ to a magazine) ["amount of money pledged"] 7. a public ~

subsequent *adj.* (cannot stand alone) ~ to

subservience *n.* ~ to

subservient *adj.* ~ to

subsidiary *adj.* ~ to

subsidized *adj.* heavily ~

subsidy *n.* 1. to provide a ~ for 2. to grant a ~ to 3. a farm; government, public, state ~ 4. a generous ~ 5. a ~ for; to

subsist *v.* (d; intr.) to ~ on

subsistence *n.* 1. (a) bare, hand-to-mouth ~ 2. a means of ~

substance *n.* ["drug"] 1. (AE) a controlled ~ ("a drug regulated by law") 2. an illegal ~ 3. (misc.) ~ abuse ["meaningful quality"] 4. ~ to (is there any ~ to their claim?) 5. (misc.) a matter of ~; a person of ~; a rumor without (any) ~ ["matter"] 6. a chemical; hard; oily; pure; radioactive; toxic ~

substitute I *n.* 1. a poor ~ 2. a ~ for (a ~ for sugar)

substitute II *v.* (D; intr., tr.) to ~ for (the coach ~d Smith for Jones)

substitution *n.* 1. to make a ~ 2. a ~ for

subsume *v.* (formal) (d; tr.) ("to classify") to ~ under (to ~ an item under a more inclusive category)

subterfuge *n.* to resort to, use a ~

subtract *v.* (D; tr.) to ~ from (to ~ five from ten)

subtraction *n.* to do ~

suburb *n.* 1. a fashionable; leafy (BE); residential ~ 2. in the ~s (to live in the ~s)

subvention see **subsidy**

subversion *n.* to engage in ~

subway *n.* ["underground railway"] (esp. US) (GB has *tube, underground*) 1. to take a ~ 2. (to go/travel) by ~ 3. (misc.) crime in the ~

succeed *v.* 1. (D; tr.) ("to come after") to ~ as (she ~ed me as treasurer) 2. (D; intr.) to ~ in (to ~ in doing smt.; to ~ in business) 3. (D; intr.) to ~ to ("to inherit") (to ~ to the throne)

success *n.* 1. to achieve, attain (a) ~ 2. to enjoy ~ 3. to score a ~ 4. to make a ~ of smt. 5. a brilliant, dazzling, great, howling (AE), huge, resounding, roaring, rousing, signal, spectacular, thorough, total, tremendous, unequivocal, unqualified ~ 6. (an) immediate; instant, overnight ~ 7. a modest ~ 8. a box-office; commercial; critical ~ 9. (a) ~ in; with

successful *adj.* 1. highly, very; moderately ~ 2. ~ at, in; with (~ in business)

succession *n.* ["right to succeed to an office, position"] 1. the ~ to (the ~ to the throne) ["misc."] 2. in ~ ("successively, one after the other"); in quick ~; in rapid ~

successor *n.* 1. a worthy ~ 2. a ~ to (the ~ to the throne)

succumb *v.* (D; intr.) to ~ to (to ~ to smb.'s urging; to ~ to a disease)

suck *v.* 1. (d; tr.) to ~ from (to ~ the juice from an orange) 2. (d; tr.) to ~ into (they were ~ed into the family quarrel) 3. (D; intr.) to ~ on (she was ~ing on an orange) 4. (D; tr.) to ~ through (she ~ed the juice through a straw) 5. (N; used with an adjective) she ~ed the lemon dry 6. (misc.) the baby ~ed at its mother's breast

suck away *v.* (D; intr.) to ~ at (to ~ at a lollipop)

sucker *n.* ["easily deceived person"] (colloq.) 1. to make a ~ out of smb. 2. a ~ for (she's a ~ for any hard-luck story) 3. a ~ to + inf. (he's a ~ to believe her)

sue *v.* 1. (d; intr.) to ~ for ("to request") (to ~ for peace) 2. (D; intr., tr.) ("to seek in court") to ~ for (to ~ for damages; she ~d him for a large sum of money) 3. (E) ("to seek in court") they ~d to get their property back

suffer *v.* 1. (D; intr.) to ~ for (to ~ for one's sins) 2. (D; intr.) to ~ from (to ~ from insomnia)

suffering *n.* 1. to inflict ~ on 2. to bear, endure ~ 3. to alleviate, ease, relieve ~ 4. chronic; great, incalculable, intense, untold ~

suffice *v.* 1. (D; intr.) to ~ for (my salary ~s for our basic needs) 2. (E) it should ~ to cite her previous accomplishments; my salary ~s to meet our basic needs 3. (misc.) ~ it to say that we will do our duty

sufficient *adj.* 1. ~ for 2. ~ unto oneself ("independent") 3. ~ to + inf. (it would have been ~ to send a brief note)

suffix *n.* a derivational; diminutive; inflectional ~

suffrage *n.* 1. to extend, grant ~ 2. universal; women's ~

sugar *n.* 1. to produce; refine ~ 2. beet; brown; cane; confectioner's (AE), icing (BE); crude; demerara (BE); granulated; lump; maple ~ 3. (med.) blood ~ 4. a lump; spoonful of ~ 5. (misc.) as sweet as ~

suggest *v.* 1. (B) she ~ed a compromise to us 2. (G) I ~ed waiting 3. (K) who ~ed his taking part? 4. (L; can be subj.; to) she ~ed (to us) that an exception be/should be made; it was ~ed that a mistake had been made 5. (Q; to) did she ~ where we should meet?

suggestion *n.* ["proposal"] 1. to advance, make, offer, put forward a ~ 2. to ask for, call for, invite ~s 3. to act on; adopt; consider; take; welcome a ~ 4. to decline, reject, turn down a ~ 5. an appropriate; constructive; good; helpful; pertinent ~ 6. an inappropriate; outrageous; preposterous, ridiculous ~ 7. a ~ about, concerning 8. a ~ that + clause; subj. (she made a ~ that each worker contribute/ should contribute one day's pay) 9. at smb.'s ~ (at my ~ we went on a picnic) ["hint, overtone"] 10. the merest, slightest ~ (there was just the slightest ~ of menace in his voice; there was just the merest ~ of garlic in the sauce)

suggestive *adj.* ~ of

suicide *n.* 1. to commit ~ 2. to attempt; contemplate ~ 3. political ~ 4. attempted ~ 5. ~ to + inf. (it would be ~ to try to climb that mountain in this weather)

suit I *n.* ["legal claim"] 1. to bring (a), file (a), institute a ~ against 2. to contest; press a ~ 3. to lose; win a ~ 4. to dismiss a ~ 5. a civil; class-action; libel; malpractice; pending ~ ~ ["set of clothes"] 6. to have a ~ made 7. to put on; take off; try on a ~ 8. a bathing, tank; diving; gym; ski; space; sweat ~ 9. a bespoke (BE), custom-made, made-to-measure (BE), made-to-order; off-the-peg (BE), ready-made ~ 10. a business (AE), lounge (BE); dress; leisure; sailor ~ 11. a double-breasted; single-breasted; three-piece; two-piece ~ 12. (for women) a pants (AE), trouser (BE) ~ 13. (BE) a boiler ~ ("overalls") 14. a ~ fits (well) 15. (misc.) a ~ of armor; (humorous) in one's birthday ~ ("naked") ["set of similar playing cards"] 16. to follow ~ (also fig.) 17. a major; minor; trump ~ ["trait"] 18. smb.'s strong ~

suit II *v.* 1. to ~ perfectly 2. (R) it ~ed her to keep him guessing 3. (misc.) to ~ smb. down to the ground (BE), to ~ to a T ("to be perfectly appropriate for")

suitability *n.* ~ for

suitable *adj.* 1. eminently ~ 2. ~ for, to 3. ~ to + inf. (would it be ~ to discuss this matter at lunch?)

suitcase *n.* 1. to pack; unpack a ~ 2. (esp. AE) to check a ~ (through) 3. to label a ~

suite *n.* ["group of connected rooms"] 1. a bridal; executive; hospitality; hotel; luxury; office; penthouse ~ ["set of matched furniture"] 2. a bedroom; living-room; three-piece (BE) ~

suited *adj.* 1. ideally ~ 2. ~ for, to (~ for the job; ~ to each other) 3. ~ to + inf. (is he psychologically ~ to be a police officer?)

sulk *v.* (D; intr.) to ~ about, over

sum *n.* 1. to raise a ~ (of money) 2. a considerable, large, substantial, tidy; equivalent; flat; lump; nominal; round; trivial ~ 3. (formal) in ~ (in ~, it could not have been worse)

summarize *v.* (D; tr.) to ~ for (she ~d the plot for the class)

summary *n.* 1. to give, make a ~ 2. a brief ~ 3. a news ~ 4. in ~

summer *n.* 1. Indian; St. Luke's (BE; rare); St. Martin's (BE; rare) ~ 2. during, over (esp. AE) the ~ 3. in (the) ~

summit *n.* ["peak"] (also fig.) 1. to reach a ~ 2. at a ~ (to stand at the ~) ["summit conference"] 3. to convene, have, hold a ~ 4. at a ~ (we met at the ~ in Geneva)

summit conference *n.* 1. to hold a ~ 2. at a ~ (to meet at a ~)

summon *v.* 1. (D; tr.) to ~ as (to ~ smb. as a witness) 2. (D; tr.) to ~ before (to be ~ed before a judge) 3. (D; tr.) to ~ to (we were ~ed to the director's office) 4. (H) to ~ smb. to do smt.

summons I *n.* 1. to issue a ~ 2. to serve a ~ on smb.; to serve smb. with a ~ 3. a ~ to + inf. (I received a ~ to appear in court)

summons II *v.* (BE) (H) she was ~ed to appear in court

sums *n.* to do ~

sun *n.* 1. to blot out the ~ 2. the blazing; bright; hot; midday; tropical ~ 3. the ~ is down; up 4. the ~ is in; out 5. the ~ beats down; comes out; comes up, rises; goes down, sets; goes in (behind a cloud); shines 6. in, under the ~ (to sit in the ~) 7. (misc.) there's nothing new under the ~

sunburn *n.* 1. to get; have a ~ 2. a painful ~

sundae *n.* a butterscotch; chocolate; hot-fudge; strawberry ~

sundown *n.* at ~

sunlight *n.* 1. bright, brilliant, glaring, strong ~ 2. in the ~ 3. a patch; shaft of ~

sunrise *n.* at ~

sunscreen *n.* to apply, put on ~

sunset *n.* at ~

sunshine *n.* 1. to soak up ~ 2. bright, dazzling; warm ~ 3. a ray of ~

sunstroke *n.* to get; have ~

suntan *n.* to get; have a ~

supercilious *n.* ~ about

superfluous *adj.* ~ to + inf. (it would be ~ to add anything to their remarks)

superhighway *n.* the Information Superhighway

superimpose *v.* (D; tr.) to ~ on (to ~ one image on another; to ~ a new way of life on old customs)

superintendent *n.* a building (AE); school ~

superior I *adj.* 1. clearly, decidedly, definitely, far, much, vastly ~ 2. ~ in (~ in numbers) 3. ~ to (~ to all other competitors)

superior II *n.* 1. smb.'s immediate ~ 2. (misc.) a mother ~

superiority *n.* 1. to achieve, establish ~ 2. to enjoy, hold ~ 3. clear ~ 4. numerical ~ 5. (so-called) racial ~ 6. ~ in; over, to 7. see **air superiority**

superlative *n.* (to express oneself) in ~s

supermarket *n.* at, in a ~ (to shop at/in a ~)

supersensitive *adj.* ~ to

superstition *n.* 1. a common ~ 2. a ~ about 3. a ~ that + clause (it is a common ~ that thirteen is an unlucky number)

superstitious *adj.* ~ about

supervision *n.* 1. to exercise ~ of, over 2. to tighten ~ 3. to ease up on, relax ~ 4. close, strict; lax, slack ~ 5. joint ~ 6. under smb.'s ~

supper *n.* 1. to eat, have ~ 2. to make, prepare; serve ~ 3. a light ~ 4. at ~ (what did they discuss at ~?) 5. for ~ (what was served for ~?)

supplement I *n.* 1. a literary; Sunday ~ (to a newspaper) 2. a dietary; iron; mineral; vitamin ~ (to take a vitamin ~ every day) 3. a ~ to

supplement II *v.* (D; tr.) to ~ by; with (she ~ed her regular income with a part-time job)

supplementary *adj.* ~ to

supplicate *v.* (formal) (H) to ~ smb. to do smt.

supply I *n.* 1. to bring up, provide ~lies 2. to lay in, receive; replenish; store ~lies 3. an abundant, liberal, plentiful; inexhaustible ~ 4. a fresh ~ 5. emergency; relief ~lies 6. military; office ~lies 7. the coal; money; water ~ 8. ~lies hold out 9. ~lies run out; run short 10. in short ~

supply II *v.* 1. (D; tr.) to ~ to (to ~ power to industry) 2. (D: tr.) to ~ with (to ~ industry with power)

supply lines *n.* 1. to overextend ~ 2. to cut ~

support I *n.* 1. to give, lend, offer, provide ~ 2. to pledge one's ~ 3. to drum up, enlist, line up, mobilize, muster, rally, round up ~ 4. to seek (smb.'s) ~ 5. to gain, get, receive, win (smb.'s) ~ 6. to have the ~ of 7. to derive, draw ~ from 8. to cut off, terminate, withdraw (one's) ~ 9. ardent, complete, enthusiastic, firm, full, solid, strong, unflagging, unqualified, unstinting, unwavering, wholehearted ~ 10. lukewarm, qualified ~ (to give lukewarm ~ to a candidate) 11. active; bipartisan; liberal; loyal; vocal; wide ~ 12. emotional, psychological; financial; moral ~ 13. government, state; popular, public ~ 14. child ~ 15. farm; price ~s 16. ~ for; in 17. ~ from 18. in ~ (of) (she came out in ~ of the party)

support II *v.* 1. to ~ completely, enthusiastically, strongly, wholeheartedly 2. (D; tr.) to ~ in (we ~ you in your efforts) 3. (K) we ~ed their seeking office 4. (misc.) we ~ed her financially all through college

supporter *n.* ["fan"] 1. to attract ~s 2. an ardent, enthusiastic, fervent, firm, loyal, stalwart, staunch, steady, strong ~ 3. a lukewarm ~ 4. an active; vocal ~ (see also the Usage Note for **fan II**)

supportive *adj.* 1. very ~ 2. ~ of

suppose *v.* 1. (L) we ~ that the situation will improve 2. (formal) (M) we ~d him to be guilty

supposed *adj.* ~ to + inf. (it was ~ to rain; she was ~ to work today)

supposition *n.* 1. to make a ~ 2. (a) mere, pure ~ 3. a ~ that (I reject the ~ that she stole the money) 4. on (a) ~ (to condemn smb. on mere ~)

suppository *n.* 1. to insert a ~ 2. a rectal; vaginal ~

supremacy *n.* 1. to achieve, establish, gain ~ (over) 2. to acknowledge smb.'s ~ 3. air; military; naval ~ 4. ~ in; over

supreme *adj.* to reign ~

surcharge *n.* 1. to add a ~ to 2. to impose a ~ (on); to put a ~ on (the candidates vowed not to impose any ~s after the election; the new government put a ~ on all imported cars) 3. a ~ on (there is a ~ on these goods)

sure *adj.* 1. ~ about (are you ~ about this?) 2. ~ of (~ of success) 3. ~ to + inf. (she is ~ to pass the exam) 4. ~ that + clause (I am ~ that they will come; please make ~ that there will be enough light and heat)

surety *n.* to act as, stand ~ for

surf *n.* to ride the ~

surface *n.* 1. a bumpy, rough, uneven; even, smooth; flat; plane ~ 2. the calm; frozen ~ (of a body of water) 3. below, beneath, under, underneath the ~ (also fig.) 4. on the ~ (also fig.) 5. (misc.) to scratch, skim (esp. AE) the ~ ("to treat superficially")

surge I *n.* (technical) a voltage ~

surge II *v.* (P; intr.) the crowd ~d around the entrance

surgeon *n.* 1. a brain; dental; flight; orthopedic (AE), orthopaedic (BE); plastic; veterinary (BE) ~ 2. a tree ~ 3. a ~ performs operations, operates (on patients)

surgery *n.* ["branch of medicine"] 1. to perform ~ 2. to undergo ~ 3. corrective, remedial; cosmetic; elective; plastic ~ 4. major; minor ~ 5. brain; bypass; open-heart; transplant ~ 6. keyhole (BE); laser ~ 7. emergency; heroic; radical ~ ["office"] (BE) 8. a doctor's ~ (CE has *doctor's office*) ["consultation period"] (BE) 9. to hold a ~ (our MP holds a ~ every week) 10. an MP's ~ ["misc."] 11. tree ~ (see the Usage Note for **office**)

surmise *v.* (L) I ~d that the situation would improve

surplus I *adj.* (BE) ~ to (this merchandise is ~ to requirements)

surplus II *n.* 1. to accumulate a ~ 2. to run ("have") a ~ 3. a budget; trade ~ 4. a ~ in 5. (BE) in ~ (our foreign trade is in ~)

surprise I *n.* 1. to spring a ~ on smb. 2. (mil.) to achieve ~ 3. to express; register ~ 4. to show ~ 5. (a) complete, outright, total ~ (we achieved complete ~) 6. a pleasant; unpleasant ~ (they sprang an unpleasant ~ on us) 7. ~ at (to express ~ at recent events) 8. a ~ to (the results were a complete ~ to everyone) 9. a ~ to + inf. (it was a pleasant ~ to learn of her promotion) 10. a ~ that + clause (it was a ~ that he got here on time) 11. by ~ (our troops took the fortress by ~) 12. to smb.'s ~ (to our ~ he was not drunk) 13. (misc.) it came as no ~; it will come as no ~ (to anyone) that she has been promoted; the element of ~

surprise II *v.* 1. to ~ greatly, very much 2. (J) I ~d him lurking in the undergrowth 3. (R) it ~d me to see them drunk; it ~d us that their party won the election

surprised *adj.* 1. ~ at (~ at the news) 2. ~ to + inf. (I was ~ to see her) 3. ~ that + clause (everyone was ~ that we attended the meeting)

surprising *n.* 1. ~ to + inf. (it was ~ to see her there) 2. ~ that + clause (it was ~ that she was nominated) 3. (misc.) it is ~ how much they have grown

surrender I *n.* 1. unconditional ~ 2. a ~ to (there will be no ~ to pressure)

surrender II *v.* (D; intr., tr.) to ~ to (to ~ to the enemy; to ~ a fortress to the invader)

surrounded *adj.* ~ by, with

surroundings *n.* 1. comfortable; elegant; luxurious; pleasant; sumptuous ~ 2. austere; unpleasant ~

surtax *n.* to impose, put a ~ (on)

surveillance *n.* 1. to conduct, maintain ~ 2. to keep; place smb. under ~ 3. (a)round-the-clock, constant; close, strict; police ~ (she was placed under strict ~) 4. electronic ~ 5. under ~

survey *n.* 1. to carry out, conduct, do, make a ~ 2. a brief; comprehensive ~ 3. an aerial; geodetic; topographical ~

survival *n.* 1. to assure smb.'s ~ 2. (misc.) the ~ of the fittest

survive *v.* 1. (D; intr.) to ~ on (to ~ on bread and cheese; we can barely ~ on our income) 2. (E) she ~d to tell the tale

survivor *n.* 1. to pick up ~s (at sea) 2. the sole ~

susceptibility *n.* ~ to (~ to disease)

susceptible *adj.* ~ to

suspect I *n.* 1. to arrest a ~ 2. to interrogate, question a ~ 3. to place a ~ under surveillance 4. to identify a ~ 5. the prime ~ 6. (misc.) to round up the usual ~s

suspect II *v.* 1. to ~ strongly 2. (D; tr.) to ~ as (to be ~ed as an accomplice) 3. (D; tr.) to ~ of (the police ~ed him of participation in the robbery) 4. (L) we ~ strongly that she is guilty

suspend *v.* 1. (D; tr.) ("to hang") to ~ from (to ~ a hook from the ceiling) 2. (D; tr.) ("to bar temporarily") to ~ from (to ~ smb. from duty)

suspenders *n.* (AE) a pair of ~ (that hold up trousers) (BE has *braces*)

suspense *n.* 1. to break the ~ 2. great; mounting; unbearable ~ 3. in ~ (to keep smb. in ~; to wait in ~ 4. in ~ over (everyone was in ~ over the outcome) 5. (misc.) we cannot bear the ~

suspension *n.* independent ~ (on a car)

suspicion *n.* ["suspecting"] ["mistrust"] 1. to arouse, cause, create, evoke, give rise to, sow, stir (a) ~ 2. to entertain, harbor, have a ~ 3. to confirm a ~ 4. to cast ~ on 5. to allay, dispel ~ 6. a groundless, unfounded ~ 7. a lingering, lurking; slight, sneaking; strong; vague; well-founded ~ 8. a ~ about, of (there was some ~ about her motives) 9. (the) ~ falls on smb. 10. a ~ that + clause (these events confirmed my strong ~ that she was guilty)

11. above ~ ("not suspected") 12. on ~ of (arrested on ~ of murder) 13. under ~ ("suspected") 14. (misc.) a cloud of ~; the finger of ~ points at you; to regard smt. with ~ ["slight trace"] 15. a ~ of (not even the slightest ~ of scandal)

suspicious *adj.* ["suspecting"] 1. ~ about, of (the police were ~ of the butler) ["causing suspicion"] 2. ~ that + clause (it was ~ that no story appeared in the press)

suture *n.* 1. to put in a ~ 2. to remove, take out a ~

swagger *v.* (P; intr.) he ~ed into the room; they ~ed down the street

swallow I *n.* ["act of swallowing"] to take a ~

swallow II *v.* 1. to ~ hard 2. (misc.) to ~ smt. whole

swamp I *n.* to drain a ~

swamp II *v.* (d; tr.) to ~ by, with (they were ~ed with work)

swan *n.* as graceful as a ~

swap I *n.* ["exchange"] to make a ~ for; with

swap II *v.* 1. (D; tr.) to ~ for (she ~ped her bicycle for a hi-fi) 2. (D; tr.) to ~ with (I ~ped places with my friend) 3. (O) I'll ~ you my bicycle for your hi-fi

swarm *v.* 1. (d; intr.) ("to crowd") to ~ around (the autograph seekers ~ed around the actor) 2. (d; intr.) ("to congregate") to ~ in (the tourists were ~ing in the streets) 3. (d; intr.) ("to throng") to ~ into (to ~ into an auditorium) 4. (d; intr.) ("to throng") to ~ over, through (to ~ through the streets) 5. (d; intr.) ("to teem") to ~ with (the streets were ~ing with tourists) 6. (P; intr.) the spectators were ~ing across the field

swarming *adj.* ~ with

swath, swathe *n.* ["path"] to cut a ~ (to cut a wide ~ of destruction through the ranks of the enemy)

swathe *v.* (d; tr.) ("to wrap") to ~ in (she was ~d in mink)

sway I *n.* ["dominance"] 1. to hold ~ over 2. under smb.'s ~

sway II *v.* 1. to ~ gently 2. (D; intr.) to ~ to (to ~ to the music) 3. (misc.) to ~ from side to side; to ~ back and forth; to ~ in the breeze

swayed *adj.* easily ~

swear *v.* 1. to ~ solemnly 2. (B) ("to promise solemnly") they swore allegiance to the government 3. (D; intr.) ("to curse") to ~ at (he swore at them) 4. (d; intr.) ("to rely completely") to ~ by (everyone ~s by her remedy for a cold) 5. (d; intr.) to ~ ("to confirm solemnly") (to ~ to the truth of a statement) 6. (d; tr.) ("to bind solemnly") to ~ to (to ~ smb. to secrecy) 7. (E) ("to promise solemnly") she swore to tell the truth 8. (L; to) ("to promise solemnly") she swore (to us) that she would tell the truth 9. (misc.) to ~ on the Bible; to ~ like a trooper ("to use obscene language freely")

swear in *v.* (D; tr.) to ~ as (she was sworn in as president)

sweat *n.* 1. to break out in a cold ~ 2. beads of ~ 3. (misc.) to work up a good ~; to be dripping with ~; by the ~ of one's brow ("by working very hard")

sweater *n.* 1. to crochet; knit a ~ 2. to put on; take off a ~ 3. to wear a ~ 4. a light; warm ~ 5. an angora; mohair; turtleneck; woolen ~

sweep I *n.* ["reconnaissance"] 1. to make a ~ (behind enemy lines) ["winning of a series of contests"] 2. to make a clean ~ (of a series) ["sweeper"] 3. a chimney ~

sweep II *v.* 1. (d; tr.) ("to remove") to ~ off (we swept the snow off the car) 2. (d; tr.) ("to remove") to ~ out of (to ~ the debris out of the room) 3. (N; used with an adjective) ("to clean with a broom") to ~ a floor clean 4. (P; intr., tr.) ("to move swiftly and overwhelmingly") the other party swept into office; they were swept into the sea; our troops swept through the village; the enemy column swept across the border 5. (misc.) to ~ smt. under the carpet (BE)/rug (AE) ("to conceal smt.")

sweep away *v.* (D; tr.) to ~ from (the children swept the snow away from the house)

sweep down *v.* (d; intr.) to ~ on (the storm swept down on the village)

sweep in *v.* (D; intr.) to ~ from (the hurricane swept in from the sea)

sweepstakes, sweepstake *n.* to win the ~

sweet *adj.* (colloq.) 1. ~ on ("in love with") (he is ~ on her) 2. ~ to + inf. (it was ~ of you to think of me)

swell *v.* (d; intr.) to ~ with (to ~ with pride)

swelling *n.* 1. (to have) a painful ~ 2. (the) ~ goes down, subsides (the ~ went down)

swerve *v.* (D; intr.) to ~ from; to (to ~ from a course; to ~ to the right)

swift *adj.* 1. (lit.) ~ of (~ of foot) 2. ~ to + inf. (she was ~ to react)

swig *n.* (colloq.) ["swallow"] to take a ~

swim I *n.* 1. to have, take a ~ 2. to go for a ~

swim II *v.* (P; intr.) to ~ for shore; to ~ around the island; to ~ into the wrong lane

swimming pool *n.* an indoor; outdoor ~

swindle I *n.* to perpetrate a ~

swindle II *v.* (D; tr.) to ~ out of (to ~ smb. out of money)

swing I *n.* ["punch"] 1. to take a ~ at smb. 2. a wild ~ ["shift"] 3. a ~ in (there was a ~ in public opinion) 4. a ~ to (in the last elections there was a ~ to the right) 5. (misc.) with that new medication, patients may be subject to frequent mood ~s ["operation"] 6. in full ~ (the work was in full ~)

swing II *v.* 1. (D; intr., tr.) to ~ at (he swung at me; I swung the bat at the ball) 2. (D; intr.) to ~ from; to (to ~ from right to left) 3. (P; intr., tr.) public opinion swung towards the right; the cranes swung the cargo onto the ship 4. (misc.) ~ your partner round and round

swings *n.* (children play) on the ~

swipe *n.* (colloq.) ["critical remark"] to take a ~ at

swirl *v.* (P; intr.) she ~ed (a)round the room

switch I *n.* ["change"] 1. to make a ~ 2. a ~ from; to 3. a ~ in (there was a sudden ~ in official policy) ["device used to open or close an electrical circuit"] 4. to flick on, turn on a ~ 5. to flick off, turn off a ~ 6. to throw a ~ ("to turn off or turn on a switch") 7. a master; power; time; toggle ~ ["movable section of railroad track"] (AE) 8. a railroad ~ (BE has *point*)

switch II *v.* (D; intr., tr.) to ~ from; into; to (to ~ to the metric system; she ~ed her support to the other candidate; to ~ from English into Russian)

switchboard *n.* 1. at, on a ~ (to work at a ~) 2. calls jammed the ~

switch over *v.* (D; intr.) to ~ to (we ~ed over to French)

swoon I *n.* 1. to fall into a ~ 2. in a ~

swoon II *v.* 1. (d; intr.) to ~ over (to ~ over a new film idol) 2. (d; intr.) to ~ with (to ~ with joy)

swoop *n.* ["stroke"] at one fell ~ ("at one time")

swoop down *v.* (D; intr.) to ~ on (the hawk ~ed down on the sheep)

swop (colloq.) (BE) see **swap I, II**

sword *n.* 1. to draw, unsheathe a ~ 2. to brandish, wield a ~ 3. to cross ~s with smb. (now usu. fig.) 4. to thrust a ~ into 5. to sheathe a ~ 6. (misc.) a double-edged, two-edged ~ ("smt. that can have opposite results to those intended")

syllable *n.* 1. to stress a ~ 2. a closed; open; stressed; unstressed ~

syllabus *n.* to draw up, make up a ~

symbiosis *n.* 1. (a) ~ between 2. in ~ with

symbol *n.* 1. a chemical; phallic; phonetic; religious; status ~ 2. (misc.) a ~ of authority

symbolic *adj.* ~ of

symmetrical *adj.* ~ to, with

sympathetic *adj.* ~ to, with

sympathize *v.* 1. to ~ deeply 2. (D; intr.) to ~ with

sympathy *n.* 1. to arouse, stir up ~ for 2. to capture; command; gain, get, win ~ 3. to express, extend; feel, have ~ for 4. to display, show ~ for 5. to lavish ~ on 6. to accept smb.'s ~ 7. deep, deepest, great, heartfelt, profound, strong ~ (please accept our deepest ~) 8. little ~ for (to have little ~ for smb.) 9. one's ~ goes out to smb. 10. a token of one's ~ 11. ~ for (to have ~ for the underdog) 12. in ~ with (to be in complete ~ with smb.'s cause) 13. out of ~ (we did it out of ~ for your family) 14. (misc.) an expression of smb.'s ~; a message of ~

symphony *n.* 1. to compose, write a ~ 2. to perform, play a ~

symposium *n.* 1. to conduct, hold a ~ (on) 2. to attend a ~ (on)

symptom *n.* 1. to develop; have, manifest, show ~s (of) 2. an acute; chronic ~ 3. a classic; specific ~ 4.

a ~ appears, develops; disappears, goes away; per-
sists 5. withdrawal ~s
symptomatic *adj.* ~ of
synch *n.* (colloq.) ("synchronization") 1. in ~ (with)
2. out of ~ (with) (their ideas are out of ~ with the
times)
synchronize *v.* (D; tr.) to ~ with
syndicate *n.* 1. to form a ~ 2. a crime; drug ~
syndrome *n.* 1. the China; Stockholm ~ 2. acquired
immune deficiency ~ (AIDS); Down (AE),
Down's ~; premenstrual ~; sudden infant death ~
(SIDS); toxic shock ~; (post-)traumatic stress ~
synonymous *adj.* ~ with
synopsis *n.* to give; make, prepare a ~
synthesis *n.* to make a ~
syphilis *n.* 1. to spread, transmit ~ 2. to catch,
develop, get; have ~ 3. acquired; congenital; early;
late; latent; primary; secondary; tertiary ~
syringe *n.* a disposable; hypodermic ~
syrup *n.* 1. chocolate; corn; maple ~ 2. cough ~
system *n.* ["group of items serving a common purpose"] 1. an air-conditioning; drainage; heating;
sprinkler ~ 2. an amplifying; communications;
intercommunication; public-address; stereo ~ 3. a
brake; steering ~ 4. a data-processing; filing ~ 5.
an early-warning; guidance ~ 6. a highway (AE),
motorway (BE); road; postal; rail, railroad (AE),
railway (BE); sewage; transit (esp. AE), transport

(esp. BE), transportation (esp. AE) ~ 7. (misc.) a
life-support ~ ["form of organization, principles
pertaining to a form of organization"] 8. a philosophical ~ 9. an honor; merit; quota; seniority ~
10. an economic; educational, school; governmental; justice; political; social ~ 11. a capitalist;
communist; democratic; socialist ~ 12. an electoral; multiparty; one-party; two-party ~ 13. a
banking; monetary ~ 14. a caste; hierarchical ~ 15.
a patronage; spoils ~ 16. (colloq.) (AE) a buddy ~
17. under a ~ (under our political ~) 18. (misc.) to
beat; buck (AE) the ~ ("to challenge established
procedures") ["group of items forming a unified
whole in nature"] 19. an ecosystem; mountain;
river; solar ~ ["functionally related group of bodily
elements or structures"] 20. the cardiovascular;
central nervous; circulatory; digestive; excretory;
genito-urinary; immune; muscular; reproductive;
respiratory; skeletal ~ ["classification"] ["type of
measurement"] 21. a decimal; metric; monetary;
number; taxonomic ~ ["group of substances in or
approaching equilibrium"] (chemistry) 22. a binary; ternary ~ ["set of meteorological conditions"] 23. a high-pressure; low-pressure ~
["procedure"] 24. the touch ~ (of typing) ["elements that allow the operation of a computer"]
25. to boot up; reboot a ~ 26. a disk-operating,
operating; retrieval ~ ["misc."] 27. ~s analysis; ~s
theory

T

T *n.* to a ~ ("precisely") (you fit the role to a ~)

tab I *n.* ["tabulator, device for setting a margin"] 1. to set a ~ ["bill"] (colloq.) (AE) 2. to pick up the ~ for (she picked up the ~ for everyone) 3. the ~ for

tab II *v.* (colloq.) (AE) 1. (d; tr.) ("to identify") to ~ as (she was ~bed as a leading contender) 2. (d; tr.) ("to designate") to ~ for (large sums were ~bed for school construction)

tabernacle *n.* to build a ~

table *n.* ["piece of furniture"] 1. to lay (esp. BE), set (esp. AE) a ~ 2. to clear a ~ 3. a bedside; coffee; dressing; end; night; tray; writing ~ 4. a dining-room; dinner; kitchen ~ 5. a card; drop-leaf; folding ~ 6. a billiard; ping-pong; pool ~ 7. the operating ~ (in a hospital) 8. (AE) a training ~ (for members of a team) 9. around, round a ~ (to sit around a ~) 10. at the ~/at ~ (BE) ("while eating") (we never discuss politics at the dinner ~) 11. on a ~ 12. the foot; head of a ~ 13. (misc.) to book(BE)/reserve (AE) a ~ in a restaurant ["table for conducting discussions, negotiations"] ["negotiating session"] 14. a bargaining, conference, negotiating; round ~ 15. at the ~ (at the negotiating ~) 16. on the ~ (a new offer was put on the ~) ["enumeration, list"] 17. to compile, draw up a ~ 18. a conversion; genealogy; life, mortality; multiplication; periodic ~s 20. in a ~ (to give data in ~s) ["level"] 21. a water ~ ["misc."] 22. to turn the ~s on smb. ("to reverse the roles in a struggle with smb."); under the ~ ("illegally")

tablespoon *n.* a heaping; level ~

tablet *n.* ["pad"] (AE) 1. a writing ~ ["pill"] 2. to take a ~ 3. an aspirin ~ 4. a scored ~ ["slab"] 5. a bronze; clay; marble; stone ~

taboo *n.* 1. to break, violate a ~ 2. a rigid ~ 3. a ~ against, on 4. (to place smt.) under (a) ~

tabs *n.* (colloq.) ["watch, surveillance"] to keep ~ on

tack I *n.* ["short nail"] 1. a carpet; thumb (AE; BE has *drawing pin*) ~ ["direction of a sailing ship"] 2. the port; starboard ~ ["course of action"] ["direction"] 3. to take a new ~ 4. (misc.) to go off, start off on the wrong ~

tack II *v.* (d; tr.) ("to attach") to ~ onto, to

tackle *n.* fishing ~

tack on *v.* 1. (D; tr.) to ~ as (the bill was ~ed on as an amendment) 2. (D; tr.) to ~ to (an amendment was ~ed on to the bill

tact *n.* 1. to display, exercise, show, use ~ 2. to have ~ 3. considerable, exemplary, great; subtle ~ 4. the ~ to + inf. (does she have the ~ to conduct the negotiations?)

tactful *adj.* 1. ~ of 2. ~ to + inf. (it was of you not ~ to mention that)

tactic *n.* 1. a scare ~ (see **tactics**) 2. a ~ fails; pays off, succeeds

tactics *n.* 1. to adopt; devise; employ; use ~ 2. aggressive; bullying; delaying; diversionary; pressure; questionable; roughhouse (AE); scare; smear; strong-arm; wily ~ (to employ questionable ~) 3. defensive; military; offensive ~ 4. (esp. AE) Madison Avenue ~ ("reliance on sophisticated promotion, advertising")

tactless *adj.* ~ to + inf. (it was ~ of him to speak like that)

taffy *n.* (esp. AE) 1. to make; pull ~ 2. saltwater ~

tag I *n.* ["children's game"] 1. to play ~ 2. a game of ~

tag II *n.* ["label, marker"] 1. to put a ~ on smt. 2. a baggage; name; price ~ 3. (AE) license ~s (on a car) 4. (AE) (mil.) dog (colloq.), identification ~s (BE has *identification disc*) ["short phrase"] (ling.) 5. a question ~

tag III *v.* (colloq.) 1. (d; intr.) to ~ after ("to follow") (the child ~ged after the others) 2. (d; tr.) ("to label") to ~ as (he was ~ged as a quitter) 3. (AE) (d; tr.) ("to fine") to ~ for (she was ~ged for going through a red light) 4. (N; used with a noun) they ~ged her a failure

tag along *v.* 1. (D; intr.) to ~ behind (she would always ~ behind them) 2. (D; intr.) to ~ with

tag end *n.* (esp. AE) ["very end"] at the ~ (of smt.)

tail *n.* ["rear appendage to an animal's body"] 1. to swish; wag a ~ (a dog wags its ~; a horse swishes its ~) 2. to dock ("shorten") a ~ 3. a bushy ~ 4. (misc.) to turn ~ ("to flee") ["person who conducts surveillance"] (colloq.) 5. to put a ~ on smb. ["misc."] 6. a car was right on my ~ ("a car was following me very closely")

tail end *n.* ["very end"] at the ~ (of smt.)

tailor I *n.* a bespoke (BE), custom; ladies'; men's ~

tailor II *v.* (d; tr.) to ~ to (to ~ an insurance policy to the needs of the insured)

tailored *adj.* 1. ~ for (~ed for a young audience) 2. ~ to + inf. (~ to meet the needs of our clients)

tailor-made *adj.* ~ for; to (~ for the assignment)

tailspin *n.* to go into a ~

tainted *adj.* ~ by, with

take I *n.* (colloq.) ["reaction"] 1. a double ~ ("delayed reaction") (to do a double ~) ["illegal payments"] 2. on the ~ (they were all on the ~) ("they were all accepting bribes") ["view"] (colloq.) 3. to have a ~ on (she has an interesting ~ on the subject)

take II *v.* 1. to ~ hard; lightly; personally; philo-sophically; seriously 2. (A) ("to carry") she took a cup of tea to him; or: she took him a cup of tea 3. (d; intr.) to ~ after ("to resemble") (he ~s after his father) 4. (d; tr.) ("to construe") to ~ as (we took her gesture as a sign of friendship; I took his remark as a compliment) 5. (d; tr.) ("to grasp") to ~ by (she took him by the hand) 6. (D; tr.) ("to lead, accompany") to ~ for (she took her daughter for a walk; he took us for a ride) 7. (D; tr.) ("to obtain, secure") to ~ for (I took the book for him) 8. (d; tr.) to ~ for ("to assume to be") (do you ~ me for a fool?) 9. (D; tr.) ("to obtain"); ("to remove") to ~ from (he took the book from her; I took the money from the safe) 10. (d; tr.) ("to subtract") to ~ from (~ five from ten) 11. (d; tr.) ("to carry") to ~ into (~ the chairs into the house) 12. (d; tr.) to ~ into ("to bring into") (to ~ smb. into one's confi-dence; they took the prisoner into custody) 13. (d; tr.) to ~ into ("to include") (to ~ smt. into consider-ation; we took all the facts into account) 14. (d; tr.) ("to remove"); ("to deduct") to ~ off (I took the books off the shelf; they took ten pounds off the bill) 15. (d; tr.) ("to carry") to ~ out of (~ the chairs out of the house) 16. (d; intr.) to ~ to ("to like") (to ~ kindly to an offer; she took to them at once) 17. (d; intr.) to ~ to ("to begin"); ("to engage in") (to ~ to drink; she took to gambling at the casinos; he took to fishing with great gusto) 18. (d; intr.) ("to go"); ("to have recourse") to ~ to (to ~ to one's bed; to ~ to the streets; to ~ to the lifeboats; to ~ to the airwaves) 19. (d; tr.) ("to lead, accompany, transport") to ~ to (to ~ smb. to dinner; she took us to the art museum; we took them to the station) 20. (d; tr.) ("to carry") to ~ to (I took the books to the library; she took the money to the bank) 21. (d; tr.) ("to move, transfer") to ~ to (they took the case to the supreme court) 22. (D; tr.) ("to accept, bear") to ~ with (he took his punishment with a smile; to ~ a remark with a grain of salt) 23. (d; tr.) ("to lead; accompany") to ~ with (they took their daughter with them) 24. (G) ("to tolerate") I just can't ~ being ignored 25. (H) ("to interpret") I took your silence to mean disapproval 26. (H) ("to require") it took us two hours to do the job 27. (M) ("to consider"); ("to accept") I took him to be a friend; do you ~ this man to be your lawful wedded husband? 28. (O) ("to require") the job took us two hours 29. (O) ("to seize") we took him pris-oner; to ~ smb. hostage 30. (P; tr.) her work often ~s her abroad; he threatened to ~ his business elsewhere; the guide took us through the museum; she took them across the street 31. (R) ("to de-mand, require") it sometimes ~s courage to tell the truth; it took (us) two hours to do the job 32. (s) ("to become") to ~ sick 33. (misc.) she took it on herself to break the news; to ~ five (esp. AE;

colloq.) ("to have a five minute break"); they took the law into their own hands ("they dispensed justice without a trial"); to ~ smb. to court ("to sue smb."); to ~ smb. under one's wing ("to protect and help smb."); to ~ to one's heels ("to flee"); to ~ by storm ("to overwhelm completely"); to ~ by surprise ("to surprise"); to ~ smt. lying down ("to accept a defeat without protest"); to ~ smt. for granted (see **granted**)

take away *v.* (D; tr.) ("to remove") to ~ from (she took the scissors away from the child)

take back *v.* 1. (D; tr.) ("to accept") to ~ from (they took the furniture back from the customer) 2. (D; tr.) ("to return") to ~ into (they took the furniture back into the house) 3. (D; tr.) ("to return") to ~ to (she took the book back to the library; the song took me back to my childhood) 4. (P; tr.) they took the chairs back up to the attic; they took the boxes back down to the basement; they took the visitors back across the river

take down *v.* 1. (D; tr.) ("to remove") to ~ from, off (she took the suitcase down from the attic; I took the books down off the shelf) 2. (D; tr.) ("to write down") to ~ in (to ~ testimony down in shorthand) 3. (D; tr.) to ~ to ("to move") (they took the suitcase down to the basement)

take in *v.* 1. (D; tr.) ("to accept") to ~ as (we took her in as a partner) 2. (D; tr.) ("to fool") to ~ by (he was taken in by flattery) 3. (misc.) to ~ a car in for service; we took them in out of the cold

taken *adj.* ["impressed"] ["infatuated"] ~ with (he was very much ~ with her)

takeoff *n.* ["parody"] (colloq.) 1. to do a ~ of (esp. BE), on (esp. AE) ["departure of an airplane"] 2. to abort a ~ 3. a smooth ~ 4. on ~

take off *v.* 1. (colloq.) (D; intr.) ("to leave") to ~ for (they took off for town) 2. (D; intr.) ("to begin flight") to ~ from (we took off from a small land-ing strip) 3. (D; intr.) ("to leave") to ~ with (he took off with their money)

take on *v.* (D; tr.) ("to accept") to ~ as (we took her on as a partner)

take out *v.* 1. (D; tr.) ("to remove") to ~ from (I took out ten dollars from my purse) 2. (D; tr.) ("to carry") to ~ into (they took the chairs out into the garden) 3. (d; tr.) ("to vent") to ~ on (don't ~ your anger out on me) 4. (D; tr.) ("to accompany") to ~ to (she took them out to a nice restaurant) 5. (misc.) he took her out on a date; to ~ it out on smb. ("to make smb. else suffer for one's own problem")

takeover *n.* 1. a friendly; hostile ~ (of a firm) 2. a corporate; military ~ 3. (misc.) a ~ bid

take over *v.* 1. (D; intr., tr.) to ~ from (the new government has taken over from the outgoing government; we will ~ power from them) 2. (D; tr.) to ~ to (I took some soup over to my neighbor)

take up *v.* 1. (D; tr.) ("to carry") to ~ from (they took up the chairs from the basement) 2. (D; tr.) ("to remove") to ~ from (they took up the carpeting from the floor) 3. (d; tr.) to ~ on ("to accept, adopt") (he took me up on my offer) 4. (D; tr.) ("to carry") to ~ to (she will ~ the books up to the bedroom) 5. (d; intr.) to ~ with ("to join") (he took up with a rough crowd) 6. (misc.) I'll ~ ("discuss") the matter with my lawyer

taking *n.* (colloq.) for the ~ (it's there for the ~) ("it can be taken by anyone who wants it")

tale *n.* 1. to concoct, make up a ~ 2. to narrate, tell a ~ 3. to hear a ~ 4. to listen to a ~ 5. an absorbing, exciting, fascinating, gripping, incredible; fanciful; grizzly; hair-raising, harrowing, shocking ~ 6. a fairy; folk ~ 7. a tall ("unbelievable") ~ 8. a cautionary ~ 9. a ~ about 10. (misc.) to tell ~s out of school ("to reveal secrets")

talent *n.* 1. to demonstrate, display, show (a) ~ 2. to cultivate, develop a ~ 3. to have (a) ~ 4. to squander one's ~(s) 5. (a) great; mediocre; outstanding; rare; real ~ 6. (a) natural ~ 7. fresh; local; young ~ 8. the ~ to + inf. (she has the ~ to go far) 9. (a) ~ for (a ~ for painting) 10. of ~ (a person of considerable ~)

talented *adj.* 1. highly, very ~ 2. ~ at, in 3. ~ with (~ with one's hands)

talk I *n.* ["address, lecture"] 1. to deliver, give a ~ 2. a pep; sales ~ 3. a ~ about, on (she gave an interesting ~ on bringing up children) ["conversation"] ["chatter"] 4. to have a ~ (with) 5. blunt, plain; idle, small; loose; table ~ 6. a long; short ~ (she had a long ~ with him about his work) 7. sweet ~ ("flattery") 8. double, fast ~ ("deception") 9. a heart-to-heart ("frank") ~ 10. straight ("frank") ~ 11. (colloq.) big ~ ("boasting") 12. ~ about, of; with (there is ~ of her resigning) 13. ~ that + clause (there is ~ that there will be a strike) ["type of speech"] 14. baby ~ ["misc."] 15. it's all ~ but no action; the ~ of the town ("the topic being discussed by everyone") (see also **talks**)

talk II *v.* 1. to ~ bluntly, candidly, frankly, freely, openly 2. to ~ loud, loudly 3. to ~ quietly, softly 4. (D; intr.) to ~ about, of, on (they were ~ing about the elections; she was ~ing of her trip; to ~ on a topic) 5. (d; tr.) to ~ into ("to persuade") (to ~ smb. into doing smt.) 6. (d; tr.) to ~ out of ("to dissuade") (to ~ smb. out of doing smt.) 7. (d; intr.) ("to speak") to ~ to, with (esp. AE) (I will ~ to them about this problem) 8. (misc.) to ~ big ("to boast"); to ~ turkey ("to speak frankly"); to ~ oneself hoarse

talk back *v.* (D; intr.) to ~ to (to ~ to one's boss)

talk down *v.* (d; intr.) to ~ to (to ~ to an audience)

talker *n.* (colloq.) a fast, glib, smooth ~ ("one who speaks glibly, in a deceptive manner")

talking *n.* to do the ~ (she did all the ~)

talking-to *n.* (colloq.) ["scolding"] 1. to give smb. a (good) ~ 2. to get a ~

talk over *v.* (D; tr.) ("to discuss") to ~ with (we ~ed it over with them)

talks *n.* ["negotiations"] 1. to conduct, hold; to resume ~ (about) 2. to break off ~ 3. candid, frank ~ 4. arms-control, arms-limitation; contract; peace ~ 5. exploratory; private ~ 6. formal; informal ~ 7. high-level; top-level ~ 8. ~ break down, collapse; are deadlocked 9. ~ about; between, with (~ about smt.; ~ with smb.) 10. (misc.) the next round of ~ will be held in the summer

tall *adj.* 1. to stand ~ ("to be resolute") 2. to walk ~ ("to be self-confident") 3. (misc.) she is five feet ~

tally I *n.* to keep; make a ~

tally II *v.* (D; intr.) ("to correspond") to ~ with

tambourine *n.* to play (on) the ~

tamper *v.* (d; intr.) to ~ with (to ~ with a lock; one should not ~ with a jury)

tampon *n.* to insert a ~

tan I *n.* 1. to get; have a ~ 2. a deep ~

tan II *v.* (intr.) to ~ easily, readily

tandem *n.* in ~ (with)

tangent I *adj.* ~ to (~ to a circle)

tangent II *n.* ["digression"] to go off at, on (esp. AE) a ~

tangential *adj.* (formal) ["incidental"] ~ to

tangle I *n.* 1. to unravel a ~ 2. to get into; get out of a ~

tangle II *v.* (colloq.) (d; intr.) ("to quarrel") to ~ about, over; with (don't ~ with him over money)

tangled *adj.* ~ in

tango *n.* to dance, do the ~

tank *n.* ["armored combat vehicle"] 1. to drive a ~ 2. a heavy; light; medium ~ 3. a column of ~s ["receptacle, container"] 4. a fish; fuel; gas (AE), gasoline (AE), petrol (BE); oil; oxygen; septic; water ~ 5. a ~ holds twenty gallons ["prison"] (slang) (esp. AE) 6. in the ~ ["misc."] 7. a think ~ ("a group of thinkers, planners")

tanker *n.* an oil ~; a supertanker

tantamount *adj.* (cannot stand alone) ~ to

tantrum *n.* 1. to have, throw a ~ 2. to fly into a ~ 3. a temper ~ (he threw a temper ~)

tap I *n.* 1. on ~ ("ready to be drawn") (beer on ~) 2. on ~ ("available"); ("imminent") (what's on ~ for tonight?) 3. see **faucet**

tap II *v.* 1. (d; tr.) ("to ask") to ~ for (to ~ smb. for information) 2. (d; intr.) to ~ into ("to use") (to ~ into reserves) 3. (D; tr.) to ~ on ("to strike lightly") (to ~ smb. on the shoulder)

tape I *n.* ["narrow strip of material"] 1. adhesive, sticky (BE); friction; insulating; magnetic; masking; measuring; name; ticker ~ ["string stretched across the track at the end of a race"] 2. to reach the ~ (both runners reached the ~ together) ["tape recording"] 3. to make a ~ 4. to fast-forward; play, put on, run; play back a ~ 5. to rewind; wind a ~ 6. to erase a ~ 7. a blank ~ 8. on ~ (I have their testimony on ~) 9. audiotape; videotape (see also **red tape**)

tape II v. (d; tr.) ("to attach") to ~ onto, to (she ~d the announcement to the bulletin board)

taper v. (d; intr., tr.) to ~ to (~ed to a point)

tape recorder n. 1. to start; turn on a ~ 2. to operate, play a ~ 3. to stop; turn off a ~ 4. a cassette; reel-to-reel ~

tape recording n. 1. to make a ~ 2. to play, play back a ~

tapestry n. 1. to weave a ~ 2. (misc.) (BE) (it's all part of) life's rich ~

taps n. ["signal played on a bugle"] (AE; BE has *last post*) 1. to play, sound ~ 2. at ~ (lights go out at ~)

tar n. coal ~

tardiness n. ~ in

target I n. 1. to aim at; destroy; hit; shoot at a ~ 2. to track a ~ 3. to miss; overshoot a ~ 4. a civilian; military; moving; stationary ~ 5. an easy; inviting; sitting ~ 6. off ~ ("not accurate") 7. on ~ ("accurate") 8. (misc.) to use smt. as a ~

target II v. (d; tr.) to ~ as (she was ~ed as the next victim)

tariff n. 1. to impose, levy a ~ 2. to pay a ~ 3. a protective ~ 4. a high; low ~ 5. a ~ on (a stiff ~ was imposed on tobacco products)

tarpaulin n. 1. to spread a ~ 2. a piece, sheet of ~

tarry v. (formal) to ~ long (do not ~ long over dinner)

task n. 1. to carry out, do, fulfill, perform; cope with; take on, undertake a ~ 2. to assign smb. a ~ 3. an enviable; pleasant; welcome ~ 4. a delicate, ticklish; fruitless, hopeless ~ 5. an arduous; difficult; enormous; formidable; Herculean, monumental; strenuous ~ 6. a dreary; irksome; menial; onerous; thankless; unenviable; unpleasant; unwelcome ~ 7. (misc.) to take smb. to ~ for smt. ("to criticize smb. for smt.")

task force n. 1. to form, set up a ~ 2. an army; navy ~

taskmaster n. a hard, rigid, severe, stern ~

taste I n. ["appreciation"] ["sense of what is proper"] 1. to acquire, cultivate, develop a ~ 2. to demonstrate, display, show (a) ~ 3. to have ~ 4. (an) acquired; artistic; discriminating; elegant, excellent, exquisite, impeccable; good; simple ~ (she has excellent ~ in clothes) 5. bad, poor ~ (it is bad ~ to ignore an invitation to a wedding) 6. a ~ for (to develop a ~ for music) 7. ~ in (they showed good ~ in planning the decor; excellent ~ in music) 8. in (a certain) ~ (everything was done in good/the best possible ~) 9. to smb.'s ~ (these paintings are not to my ~) 10. (misc.) ~s differ; a sense of ~ ["sensation obtained from tasting, eating"] (also fig.) 11. to leave a ~ (the fruit left a

pleasant ~; the whole affair left a bitter ~ in my mouth) 12. to spoil the ~ 13. a bad, foul; bitter; mild; nice, pleasant, sweet; sour; strong ~ 14. (misc.) the sense of ~; add salt to ~ ["small amount tasted"] 15. to have, take (esp. AE) a ~ (of) 16. to give smb. a ~ of smt. (often fig.) (they gave him a ~ of his own medicine)

taste II v. 1. (d; intr.) to ~ like; of (a nectarine ~s like a peach; the food ~s of garlic) 2. (s) the food ~s good

tasteless adj. ~ to + inf. (it was ~ of them to bring up that subject)

taster n. a wine ~

tatters n. in ~ (the beggars were in ~)

tattle v. (colloq.) (D; intr.) ("to inform") to ~ on

taunt I n. 1. to hurl a ~ at smb. 2. a cruel ~

taunt II v. 1. (D; tr.) to ~ about 2. (d; tr.) to ~ into (to ~ smb. into doing smt.)

tax I n. 1. to impose, levy, put a ~ on 2. to collect a ~ from 3. to pay a ~ (to pay a ~ on a new car; to pay a large sum in ~es; to pay a ~ to the government) 4. to avoid (esp. BE), evade a ~ 5. to increase, raise ~es 6. to cut, lower, reduce ~es 7. to rescind, revoke a ~ 8. an amusement; cigarette; gasoline (AE), petrol (BE); liquor (esp. AE); road (BE) ~ 9. a direct; indirect ~ 10. an excise; nuisance; purchase (BE), sales ~; a value-added tax (= VAT) (GB) 11. a federal (AE); local; state (US) ~ 12. a capital gains; corporate; excess-profits; windfall-profits ~ 13. an income; negative income; social-security ~; withholding ~ (esp. AE; BE has *PAYE*) 14. a personal-property; property; real-estate; transfer ~ 15. a capital transfer ~ (BE; has replaced *death duty*); death (AE), estate, inheritance; gift ~ 16. a flat; graduated, progressive ~ 17. a ~ on (a ~ on cigarettes) 18. (AE) delinquent ~es 19. (misc.) heavy ~es; ~ evasion; a ~ haven; ~ relief; a ~ shelter; (BE) these purchases attract value-added ~ at twelve percent

tax II v. 1. to ~ heavily 2. (formal) (d; tr.) ("to accuse") to ~ with (to ~ smb. with negligence)

taxation n. direct; indirect ~

taxi I see **cab**

taxi II v. (P; intr.) the plane ~ed along the runway; the jet ~ed to a complete stop

tax return n. 1. to complete, fill in, fill out (esp. AE), make out a ~ 2. to file, send in, submit a ~

tax shelter n. a foreign ~

tea n. ["plant"] 1. to grow ~ ["beverage"] 2. to brew, make; steep ~ 3. to drink, have, take ~ (to take ~ with sugar) 4. to have, take (old-fashioned) ~ with smb. 5. strong; weak ~ 6. hot; iced ~ 7. black; green ~ 8. decaffeinated; herbal; scented ~ 9. camomile; jasmine; lemon; mint ~ 10. beef ~ (BE; CE has *beef broth*) 11. the ~ is brewing 12. a cup; glass; pot of ~ (bring us two cups of ~; or: bring us two ~s) ["meal"] (GB) 13. to have ~ 14. afternoon;

cream; high ~

USAGE NOTE: In Britain, *high tea* and *tea* can mean "early dinner", "dinner", or "supper".

teach *v.* 1. (A) she taught history to us; or: she taught us history 2. (D; tr.) to ~ about (to ~ children about their heritage) 3. (H) she taught them to swim 4. (L; may have an object) he taught (us) that the best policy is to tell the truth 5. (Q; must have an object) she taught me how to drive

teacher *n.* 1. to certify; license; train a ~ 2. an exchange; practice, student ~ 3. (BE) a supply ~ (AE has *substitute*) 4. a ~ of (a ~ of English)

teaching *n.* 1. practice, student ~ 2. team ~ 3. health ~ 4. (misc.) to go into ~

teachings *n.* to follow smb.'s ~

teacup *n.* a storm in a ~ (BE) ("much ado about nothing") (for AE, see **teapot**)

teakettle see **kettle**

team *n.* 1. to field; organize a ~ 2. to coach; manage a ~ 3. to disband, split up a ~ 4. an all-star (AE); losing; winning ~ 5. a home; opposing, rival; visiting ~ 6. a baseball; basketball; cricket; drill; football; hockey; lacrosse; relay; soccer; track, track-and-field; volleyball ~ 7. (Am. professional football) a wild-card ~ 8. (mil.) a combat ~ 9. a negotiating ~ 10. (misc.) (AE) to make a ~ ("to succeed in becoming a member of a team")

USAGE NOTE: AE uses *team* more often than BE — Chicago has fielded a strong team for today's game; Chicago is the strongest team in the league. BE prefers *side* when referring to a competitive match — Liverpool have fielded a strong side for today's match. BE often uses *club* when referring to a team in general — United is/are the strongest club in the Premier League. In BE, a player can be *in a side; in a team.* In AE, a player cen be *on a side; on a team.* In CE, a player can be *in a club.* In references to international competition, *team* is standard in BE — the England team in the World Cup.

team up *v.* (D; intr.) to ~ against; with (we ~ed up with them against our common enemy)

teapot *n.* a tempest in a ~ (AE) ("much ado about nothing") (for BE, see **teacup**)

tear I /tiy(r)/ *n.* ["drop of fluid secreted by the lacrimal gland"] 1. to burst into ~s 2. to shed a ~ 3. to weep (bitter) ~s 4. to choke back, hold back one's ~s 5. bitter ~s 6. ~s flowed, ran, rolled, streamed down their cheeks 7. ~s welled up in my eyes 8. (misc.) crocodile ("false") ~s; to be in ~s over smt.; eyes fill with ~s; bored to ~s; a flood of ~s; ~s of joy; ~s of gratitude

tear II /tey(r)/ *n.* ["rip"] 1. to make a ~ 2. to mend a ~

tear III *v.* 1. (d; intr.) to ~ at (to ~ at the bandages) 2. (d; tr.) to ~ from, out of (she tore several pages out of the book) 3. (d; intr.) to ~ into ("to attack

verbally") (he tore into his opponent) 4. (D; tr.) to ~ into, to (she tore the paper into/to pieces; to ~ an argument to shreds) 5. (d; tr.) to ~ off (he tore a button off the coat) 6. (D; tr.) to ~ on (she tore her blouse on a nail)

tear away *v.* (D; refl., tr.) to ~ from (she couldn't ~ herself away from the book)

tear gas *n.* to use ~ (on)

tease I *n.* ["person who teases"] a terrible ~

tease II *v.* 1. (D; tr.) to ~ about (they ~d her about her new hairdo) 2. (D; tr.) to ~ into (to ~ smb. into doing smt.)

teaspoon *n.* a heaping; level ~

teatime *n.* 1. at ~ 2. past ~

technicality *n.* 1. a legal ~ 2. on a ~ (we lost the case on a ~)

technician *n.* a dental; lab, laboratory; medical; radar; television, TV ~

Technicolor (T) *n.* in ~

technique *n.* 1. to acquire; develop, devise, work out; perfect a ~ 2. to apply a ~ 3. an acting; dance ~ 4. a diagnostic ~ 5. relaxation ~s 6. a ~ for 7. a ~ to + inf. (they worked out a ~ to analyze the data)

technology *n.* 1. to create, develop (a) ~ 2. to apply, employ, use ~ 3. to export, transfer ~ (to developing countries) 4. computer; information ~ 5. high ~ (also *high tech*) 6. advanced, latest, modern, state-of-the-art ~ 7. a ~ to + inf. (they developed a ~ to analyze the data)

teed off *adj.* (colloq.) (AE) ["angry"] ~ about, at

teem *v.* (d; intr.) to ~ in; with (fish were ~ing in that brook; the river was ~ing with fish)

teens *n.* 1. early; late ~ 2. in one's ~ (they are still in their ~)

teeter *v.* (d; intr.) to ~ on (to ~ on the edge of a cliff)

teeth see **tooth**

telegram *n.* 1. to send a ~ 2. to get, receive a ~ 3. a ~ from; to (a ~ from London to Paris)

telegraph I *n.* by ~ (the news was sent by ~)

telegraph II *v.* 1. (A) they ~ed the information to us; or: they ~ed us the information 2. (H; no passive) they ~ed us to leave immediately 3. (L; may have an object) she ~ed (us) that the manuscript had been received 4. (Q; may have an object) they ~ed (us) where we should meet

telepathy *n.* mental ~

telephone I *n.* 1. to hook up, install a ~ 2. to answer a ~ 3. to tap a ~ 4. to disconnect a ~ 5. a car; cellular; cordless; dial; mobile; pay, public ~ 6. a ~ rings 7. by ~; on, over (esp. AE) the ~ (she spoke to him by ~; I enjoyed our chat on/over the ~; to speak on/over the ~; he is always on the ~) 8. (BE) on the ~ ("connected to the telephone system") 9. (misc.) to be wanted on the ~; to call smb. to the ~ (see also **phone I**)

telephone II *v.* 1. (B) they ~d the message to us 2. (D; tr.) to ~ about (they ~d me about the meeting)

3. (H; no passive) she ~d us to return home 4. (L; may have an object) he ~d (us) that he would be late 5. (Q; may have an object) I ~d (them) when to come

telephone call see **call I** 13-22

telephone directory *n.* to be in the ~

telephone receiver see **receiver** 1-2

telescope I *n.* 1. to focus, train a ~ on 2. a reflecting; refracting ~

telescope II *v.* (D; tr.) to ~ into (to ~ a syllabus into a brief outline)

televised *adj.* nationally ~

television *n.* 1. to put on, switch on; turn on the ~ 2. to watch ~ 3. to switch off, turn off the ~ 4. to turn down; turn up the ~ 5. black-and-white; color ~ 6. cable; closed-circuit; educational; local; national; pay; peak-time (BE), peak-viewing-time (BE), prime-time (esp. AE); public; satellite ~ 7. on ~ (I saw her on ~) 8. (misc.) she works in ~

television set *n.* 1. to plug in a ~ 2. to put on, switch on, turn on a ~ 3. to switch off, turn off a ~ 4. to unplug a ~

tell *v.* 1. (A; usu. without *to*) ("to relate") she told the news to everyone; or: she told everyone the news; he told me his name; she told them a story; ~ me the truth 2. (D; intr.) ("to be certain") to ~ about (you can never ~ about people like that) 3. (d; intr., tr.) ("to inform") to ~ about, of (he didn't want to ~ about the incident; ~ me about the game; she told everyone of her success) 4. (BE; formal) (d; intr.) to ~ against ("to count against") (their past misdemeanors will ~ against them) 5. (d; intr.) ("to ascertain") to ~ from (can you ~ anything from a quick examination?) 6. (d; tr.) to ~ from ("to differentiate") (can you ~ one twin from another?) 7. (colloq.) (d; intr., tr.) to ~ of (BE), on ("to inform on") (he told on her when the teacher returned; I'm going to ~ my father on you) 8. (D; intr.) to ~ on ("to affect") (the strain was beginning to ~ on her) 9. (H) ("to order") she told me to leave 10. (L; must have an object) ("to inform") we told them that we would be late 11. (Q; must have an object) ("to inform") ~ me how to get there 12. (Q) ("to ascertain") can you ~ from a quick examination where his injuries are? 13. (misc.) I told you so!

tell apart *v.* (D; tr.) to ~ from (I cannot ~ them apart from each other)

teller *n.* (AE) a bank ~ (BE has *cashier*)

telling *n.* ["certainty"] 1. there is no ~ what will happen ["act of narrating"] 2. in the ~ (the story changed in the ~)

temerity *n.* the ~ to + inf. (he had the ~ to file a grievance)

temper I *n.* 1. to control, curb, keep one's ~ 2. to lose one's ~ 3. a bad, explosive, foul, hot, nasty, quick, uncontrollable, ungovernable, violent ~ 4. a calm, even, mild ~ 5. ~s cool down; flare (up) 6. a display, fit of ~ (she said that in a fit of ~) 7. (misc.) she was in a bad ~ this morning; he flew into a ~

temper II *v.* (D; tr.) to ~ with (to ~ discipline with compassion)

temperament *n.* 1. to have a certain ~ (she has a nervous ~) 2. an artistic; poetic ~ 3. a calm, even, mild, quiet ~ 4. an excitable; fiery; nervous ~

temperance *n.* ~ in

temperate *adj.* ~ in

temperature *n.* ["degree of heat or cold"] 1. to adjust, control the ~ 2. to take smb.'s ~ 3. a high; low; normal ~ 4. (smb.'s) body ~ 5. room ~ (at room ~) 6. the average ~ 7. a ~ drops, falls; goes down 8. a ~ goes up, rises 9. a ~ remains steady 10. at a (certain) ~ (water boils at a certain ~) 11. an increase, rise in ~ 12. a decrease, drop in ~ ["excess over normal body heat"] 13. to have, run a ~ 14. a high; slight ~

tempo *n.* 1. to increase, step up the ~ 2. to slow down the ~ 3. a fast; slow ~

tempt *v.* 1. (D; tr.) to ~ into (to ~ smb. into doing smt.) 2. (H) to ~ smb. to do smt.

temptation *n.* 1. to overcome, resist ~ 2. to be exposed to, face, feel ~ 3. to succumb to ~ 4. to place, put ~ in smb.'s way 5. irresistible, strong ~ 6. a ~ to + inf. (she resisted the ~ to answer back)

tempted *adj.* ~ to + inf. (I am ~ to go)

tempting *adj.* ~ to + inf. (it's ~ to stay home when the weather is bad)

tenacity *n.* 1. to demonstrate, display, show ~ 2. to have ~ 3. bulldog; great; sheer ~ (to demonstrate great ~) 4. the ~ to + inf. (she had the ~ to finish the job) 5. by ~ (she finished the job by sheer ~)

tend *v.* 1. (AE) (d; intr.) to ~ to (to ~ to one's own business) (CE has *attend to*) 2. (d; intr.) to ~ towards 3. (E) he ~s to exaggerate

tendency *n.* 1. to demonstrate, display, show a ~ 2. a growing; mounting; natural; pronounced; strong; universal ~ 3. artistic; homicidal; suicidal; vicious ~cies (for years he has displayed suicidal ~cies) 4. a ~ towards 5. a ~ to + inf. (she has a ~ to exaggerate)

tender I *adj.* ~ to, towards, with

tender II *n.* ["offer, bid"] (esp. BE) 1. to make, put in, send in, submit a ~ 2. to invite ~s 3. to lose; win a ~ 4. the highest; lowest ~ 5. a ~ for ["currency"] 6. legal ~

tender III *v.* 1. (B) ("to offer") she ~ed her resignation to the government 2. (BE) (d; intr.) to ~ for ("to bid on") (to ~ for the construction of a new motorway)

tenderness *n.* ["kindness, care"] 1. to show ~ 2. ~ towards

tendon *n.* 1. to pull a ~ 2. the Achilles' ~

tenet *n.* 1. a basic, fundamental ~ 2. a ~ that + clause (our basic ~ is that all people are equal) 3. (misc.) to embrace the ~s of a new philosophy

tennis *n.* 1. to play ~ 2. court (AE), real (BE); lawn; paddle; table ~ 3. (misc.) a ~ match; a game of ~ (let's play a game of ~; she won the first game and went on to win the set and match)

tennis racket *n.* to restring; string a ~

tenor *n.* to sing ~

tenpins *n.* (AE) to play ~

tense I *adj.* ~ with (~ with anxiety)

tense II *n.* (grammar) the future; future perfect; past; past perfect; present; progressive ~

tension *n.* ["strained relations"] ["strain"] 1. to cause, create ~ 2. to exacerbate, heighten, increase ~ 3. to alleviate, ease, lessen, reduce, relieve ~ (to alleviate/ease ~ between the adversaries) 4. acute; mounting ~ 5. arterial; nervous; premenstrual ~ 6. international; racial ~ 7. ~ builds up, increases, mounts, rises 8. ~ decreases, eases, subsides 9. ~ between 10. under ~ ["tautness"] 11. fan-belt ~ ["voltage"] 12. high; low ~

tent *n.* 1. to erect, pitch, put up a ~ 2. to dismantle, take down a ~ 3. a circus; pup; pyramidal; wall ~ 4. a croup; oxygen ~

tenterhooks *n.* on ~ ("in suspense")

tenure *n.* ["permanence of employment as a teacher"] 1. to give, grant ~ 2. to acquire, get, receive ~ 3. academic ~

term I *n.* ["expression, word"] 1. an abstract; concrete, specific; general ~ 2. a clear; comprehensible ~ 3. an incomprehensible; vague ~ (the lecturer used an incomprehensible ~ in making her point) 4. a general; generic; legal; medical; technical ~ ["period of time served"] 5. to serve a ~ (in office) 6. an unexpired ~ 7. a ~ expires, runs out 8. a jail, prison ~ ["division of a school year"] 9. the autumn (BE), fall (AE); school; spring; summer ~ 10. at the end of a/of (BE) ~ ["time at which a normal pregnancy terminates"] 11. to have a baby at ~ (see also **terms**)

term II *v.* (formal) (rare) (N; used with a noun or adjective) ("to call") they ~ed the compromise acceptable; by what right does he ~ himself an artist?

terminal *n.* ["point on an electric circuit"] 1. a negative; positive ~ ["device by which information enters or leaves a computer"] 2. a computer ~; Visual Display Terminal = VDT (AE; CE has *Visual Display Unit* = VDU) ["passenger, freight station"] 3. an airline; bus, coach (BE); freight; rail; shipping; trucking ~ 4. at a ~ (let's meet at the bus ~)

terminate *v.* 1. (D; intr.) to ~ in (their efforts ~ed in success) 2. (BE) (P; intr., tr.) this train ~s here

termination *n.* ["cessation of employment"] voluntary ~

terminology *n.* 1. to codify, create, establish, stan-

dardize (a) ~ 2. basic; legal; scientific; technical ~

terminus *n.* (esp. BE) 1. a bus, coach; main-line; rail ~ 2. at; in a ~

termites *n.* a colony of ~

terms *n.* ["expressions, words"] 1. absolute; general; relative ~ 2. bold; flattering; glowing ~ (she described him in glowing ~) 3. in ~ (to speak in general ~; in the strongest possible ~; in no uncertain ~; a contradiction in ~) ["conditions, provisions"] 4. to dictate; set; specify, stipulate (the) ~ 5. to state the ~ 6. easy; favorable ~ 7. surrender ~ (to stipulate surrender ~ to an enemy) 8. by the ~ (of an agreement) 9. on certain ~ (on one's own ~; on our ~) 10. under (the) ~ of the agreement ["acceptance"] ["agreement"] 11. to come to ~ with smb. ["relationship"] ["footing"] 12. equal, even; unequal ~ 13. familiar, intimate; speaking ~ 14. friendly, good; unfriendly ~ 15. on certain ~ (with) (to be on speaking ~ with smb.; to negotiate with smb. on equal ~; they are not on good ~ with each other) ["aspects"] 16. in certain ~ (in economic ~, that country is a superpower; in ~ of its foreign trade, that country is a serious competitor) 17. (misc.) ~ of reference

terrace *n.* from; on a ~

terraces *n.* (BE) (as in football stadiums) from; on the ~ (cheers from the ~)

terrain *n.* harsh, rough, rugged; hilly; mountainous; rocky; swampy ~

terrible *adj.* 1. ~ at (she is ~ at bridge) 2. ~ to + inf. (it was ~ to work there = it was ~ working there; it was ~ of them to do that) 3. ~ that + clause (it is ~ that she lost her wallet; I feel ~ that you cannot accept our invitation)

terrified *adj.* 1. ~ at, by, of ~ 2. ~ to + inf. (we are ~ to think that there might be a hurricane) 3. ~ that + clause (we are ~ that there may be another earthquake)

terrify *v.* 1. (D; tr.) to ~ into (she was ~fied into handing over the keys) 2. (R) it ~fied me to contemplate the consequences of your actions; it ~fies us that there may be another earthquake

terrifying *adj.* 1. ~ to + inf. (it was ~ to watch that movie = it was ~ watching that movie) 2. ~ that + clause (it's ~ that there are so many drunk drivers on the road)

territory *n.* 1. to annex; occupy ~ 2. to cede ~ 3. a neutral; trust ~ 4. (an) occupied; unoccupied ~ 5. unexplored ~ 6. (misc.) to reconnoiter enemy ~

terror *n.* 1. to employ, engage in, resort to, sow, unleash ~ 2. to inspire ~; to strike ~ into (to strike ~ into the hearts of people) 3. to feel ~ 4. blind, mortal, sheer, stark ~ 5. (colloq.) a holy ~ 6. in ~ (to live in ~ of smt.) 7. (misc.) a campaign, reign of ~; a shriek of ~

terrorism *n.* 1. to combat, fight ~ 2. indiscriminate; international; state; urban ~ 3. an act of ~ 4. see

terror 1
terrorist *n.* an armed; international; urban ~
terrorize *v.* (D; tr.) to ~ into
test I *n.* ["examination, set of questions"] 1. to administer, conduct, give a ~ 2. to draw up, make up, prepare, set (BE) a ~ 3. to sit (for) (BE), take a ~ 4. to fail, flunk (colloq.; esp. AE) a ~ 5. to pass a ~ 6. a demanding, difficult ~ 7. an easy ~ 8. an achievement; aptitude; intelligence ~ 9. a placement; proficiency ~ 10. a cloze; completion; multiple-choice; objective; true-false ~ 11. a driving; road ~ 12. a breath ~ 13. a lie-detector, polygraph ~ 14. a competency; means ~ 15. a ~ in, of, on (a ~ in mathematics; a ~ on new material) ["ordeal, trial"] 16. an acid, demanding, exacting, litmus, rigorous, severe ~ 17. an endurance ~ ["experiment, trial"] ["examination"] 18. to carry out, conduct, do, perform, run a ~ 19. to have, undergo a ~ 20. exhaustive, extensive, thorough ~s 21. a blood; breathing; diagnostic; DNA; drug; PAP; patch; saliva; skin; scratch; tuberculin ~ 22. a personality; psychological ~ 23. a laboratory; nuclear ~ 24. a road ~ 25. a ~ for (to do a skin ~ for tuberculosis) 26. a ~ on (they conducted a series of ~s on me at the health center) 27. (misc.) to stand the ~ of time; the ~ turned out (to be) negative/positive; the ~ was negative/positive; to put smb. to the ~
USAGE NOTE: In AE, a *road test* is ambiguous; it can test a vehicle or a driver. In BE, a *road test* tests the vehicle only. In CE, a *test drive* tests the vehicle, and a *driving test* tests the driver.
test II *v.* 1. (D; intr., tr.) to ~ for (to ~ for excessive air pollution; to ~ the urine for sugar) 2. (D; tr.) to ~ in, on (we ~ed them in English/on their knowledge of English) 3. (P; intr.) (esp. AE) some of our students ~ed in the top percentile 4. (esp. AE) (s) some students ~ high, others low; to ~ negative/positive for a disease
testament *n.* 1. the New; Old Testament 2. a ~ to 3. (misc.) smb.'s last will and ~
tested *adj.* sorely ~
test flight *n.* to conduct a ~
testicle *n.* an undescended ~
testify *v.* 1. (D; intr.) to ~ about (to ~ about a case) 2. (D; intr.) to ~ against; for, on behalf of (to ~ for the plaintiff) 3. (d; intr.) to ~ to (the results ~ to the quality of their work) 4. (L) she ~fied that she had not seen the accident 5. (misc.) to ~ under oath
testimonial *n.* 1. to give, offer a ~ 2. an eloquent ~ 3. a ~ to (a ~ to smb.'s accomplishments)
testimony *n.* 1. to give, offer ~ 2. to cite ~ 3. to recant, repudiate, retract (one's) ~ 4. to contradict, discount, refute (smb.'s) ~ 5. reliable ~ 6. false, perjured; unreliable ~ 7. expert ~ 8. ~ about 9. ~ against (she gave ~ against the plaintiff) 10. ~ for, on behalf of 11. (a) ~ to (her Nobel Prize is a real ~

to her achievement) 12. ~ that + clause (nobody could refute her ~ that the driver was drunk)
test paper *n.* 1. to hand in a ~ 2. to mark a ~
testing *n.* 1. proficiency ~ 2. drug; mandatory; voluntary ~
tetanus *n.* to develop ~
tether *v.* (D; tr.) to ~ to (the horse was ~ed to the hitching-post)
text *n.* 1. to set a ~ (in type) 2. to edit a ~ 3. to annotate a ~ 4. an annotated ~ 5. a machine-readable ~ 6. to stray from the ~
textbook *n.* 1. an introductory ~ 2. a ~ of, on (a ~ on advanced grammar)
texture *n.* delicate, fine; rough; smooth ~
thank *v.* 1. to ~ profusely; sincerely 2. (D; tr.) to ~ for (she ~ed me profusely for my help) 3. (H; no passive) I'll ~ you to make less noise in the future! 4. (L; must have an object) we can ~ you that we got there on time 5. (misc.) ~ you very much!
thankful *adj.* 1. ~ for; to 2. ~ to + inf. (~ to be alive) 3. ~ that + clause (we were ~ that you offered to help)
thanks *n.* 1. to express; give one's ~; to say ~ 2. to accept smb.'s ~ 3. one's heartfelt, sincere, warm ~ 4. ~ for; to 5. (misc.) many ~; ~ a lot; I finished the whole job on time, no ~ to you; we completed the work on time, ~ to your help; we owe her a vote of ~
that *pronoun* 1. at ~ ("in addition") (she was a thief and a clever one at ~) 2. (misc.) take ~! ("I'm going to punch you!")
thaw *n.* 1. the spring ~ 2. a ~ sets in (also fig.)
theater, theatre *n.* ["building in which plays are performed or (esp. AE) films shown"] 1. to crowd, jam, pack a ~ 2. an art; dinner (esp. AE); movie (AE; BE has *cinema*); open-air; repertory ~ 3. at the ~ (we were at the ~ last night) ["theatrical profession"] 4. the legitimate ~ 5. in the ~ (she was well thought of in the ~) ["operating room in a hospital"] (BE) 6. an operating ~ 7. to ~ (we rushed her to ~ for an emergency operation)
theft *n.* 1. to commit (a) ~ 2. petty ~ 3. a ~ from (a daring ~ from a museum)
theme *n.* 1. a basic; central, dominant, main; underlying ~ 2. a contemporary ~ 3. a recurrent, recurring ~ 4. a ~ for (a ~ for discussion) 5. (misc.) variations on a ~
then *adv., n.* 1. before; by ~ 2. from ~ on
theorem *n.* 1. to deduce; formulate a ~ 2. to prove; test a ~ 3. to disprove a ~ 4. the binomial ~
theorize *v.* 1. (D; intr.) to ~ about 2. (L) the police ~d that the burglar had entered through a window
theory *n.* 1. to formulate a ~ 2. to advance, advocate, present, propose, put forth, set forth, suggest a ~ 3. to develop; test a ~ 4. to confirm a ~ 5. to debunk, discredit, disprove, explode, refute a ~ 6. to challenge a ~ 7. a pet ~ 8. an economic; political

~ 9. game; information; number; quantum; set; scientific; systems ~ 10. the big bang; steady state ~ 11. the germ ~ (of disease) 12. a ~ evolves 13. a ~ holds (up) 14. a ~ that + clause (she has a ~ that drinking milk prevents colds) 15. in ~ (in ~ their plan makes sense) 16. on a ~ (they proceeded on the ~ that the supplies would arrive on time) 17. (misc.) the ~ of evolution; the ~ of relativity; to combine ~ and practice

therapist *n.* a family; group; occupational; physical ~; psychotherapist; speech ~

therapy *n.* 1. to employ, use ~ (on, with) 2. to get, have; undergo ~ 3. art; dance; music ~ (to employ/use music ~) 4. massage; occupational; physical; recreational; speech ~ (to get speech ~; to employ/use recreational ~) 5. electro-convulsive (BE), electro-shock (AE); shock ~ (to get/undergo shock ~; to employ/use electro-shock ~) 6. behavior(al); cognitive; family; group ~; psychotherapy 7. chemotherapy; hormone replacement therapy (HRT); inhalation; radiation, X-ray ~ (to get/have/undergo radiation ~) 8. ~ for 9. in ~ (she was in ~)

there *adv.* over ~

thermometer *n.* 1. a clinical; meat; oral; oven; rectal ~ 2. a ~ shows a temperature

thermostat *n.* 1. to adjust, set; turn down; turn up a ~ 2. to calibrate a ~

thesis *n.* ["research paper"] 1. to write a ~ (about, on) 2. a doctoral, Ph.D.; graduate; master's ~ ["proposition, hypothesis"] 3. to advance, propose; test a ~ 4. to challenge; refute a ~ 5. smb.'s main, major ~ 6. a ~ about, on 7. a ~ that + clause (these developments disprove their ~ that high taxes stifle investment) (see the Usage Note for **dissertation**)

thick I *adj.* 1. (colloq.) (esp. BE) ~ with (they are ~ with each other) 2. (misc.) as ~ as thieves ("very closely allied"); to lay it on ~ ("to exaggerate")

thick II *n.* ["most intense part"] in the ~ (of the battle)

thick and thin *n.* ["all difficulties"] through ~ (to remain friends through ~)

thief *n.* 1. a car; jewel ~ 2. a common, petty; sneak ~ 3. a band, gang of thieves

thing *n.* ["deed"] ["event"] 1. to do a ~ (she did a nice ~ when she offered to help; to do great ~s; to do the right ~) 2. a good; great; nice ~ 3. a funny; strange ~ 4. a bad; mean; nasty; terrible ~ 5. a big; small ~ 6. a difficult; easy ~ 7. a sensible; stupid ~ 8. the decent, right; wrong ~ 9. a ~ happens; ~s happen (a strange ~ happened this morning; when bad ~s happen to good people) 10. a ~ to + inf. (it was an easy ~ to do; it was the wrong ~ to do) ["object"] 11. to use a ~ for (don't use this ~ for removing paint) ["facts, details"] 12. to discuss; say ~s (about) 13. to get a ~ out of smb. (I couldn't get a ~ out of her) 14. to know a ~ about (he

doesn't know a ~ about music); to know a ~ or two ("to know quite a bit") 15. (misc.) the way ~s stand ["fact, point"] (colloq.) 16. the ~ is that + clause (the ~ is that I still have a great deal of work to do; the other ~ is that I really don't want to go) ["article of clothing"] 17. not to have a ~ to wear (I don't have a ~ to wear) 18. to put on; take off one's ~s ["possessions, effects"] 19. to pack one's ~s ["step"] 20. the first; last; next ~ (the next ~ is to submit your application) ["person of a certain type"] 21. a pretty; poor ~ (a pretty little ~; you poor ~) 22. to say the right ~ ["matters"] (used in the plural) 23. to even ~s up 24. to see ~s (as they are) 25. (misc.) all ~s considered ("with everything taken into account"); ~s don't look good; ~s are looking up for us; how do ~s stand? how are ~s? ["utensils"] 26. to clear the (breakfast) ~s away ["individual"] 27. a living ~ (there wasn't a living ~ in sight) ["fear"] ["obsession"] (colloq.) 28. a ~ about (she has a ~ about flying) ["misc."] 29. let's forget the whole ~; to be seeing ~s ("to be imagining things"); to do one's (own) ~ ("to do what one feels competent or motivated to do"); any old ~ ("anything at all"); a sure ~ ("smt. that is certain to succeed"); of all ~s ("most surprisingly"); to tell smb. a ~ or two ("to tell smb. frankly what one thinks")

think I *n.* (colloq.) (BE) 1. to have a ~ about 2. a long hard ~

think II *v.* 1. to ~ aloud; clearly; fast; hard (I thought hard and finally remembered the name) 2. (D; intr.) ("to reflect") to ~ about, of (I was ~ing about you; to ~ of the past) 3. (d; intr.) ("to be concerned") to ~ about, of (I was only ~ing of your welfare when I declined the offer) 4. (d; intr.) to ~ of ("to have an opinion of") (to ~ highly; ill; well of smt.) 5. (d; intr.) to ~ of ("to consider; to intend") (she never thought of telephoning; to ~ of resigning) 6. (E) ("to remember") she never thought to call 7. (L) ("to anticipate") we thought that it would rain 8. (L) ("to believe") I ~ that he is a fool 9. (M; used in the passive) ("to consider") she is thought to be irreplaceable 10. (N; used with an adjective) ("to consider") many people ~ her charming 11. (Q) I cannot ~ where it could be 12. (misc.) to ~ nothing of walking five miles every morning; I thought to myself that it would be nice to have some hot soup; he doesn't ~ of himself as a politician; to ~ better of doing smt. ("to change one's mind about doing smt."); to ~ on one's feet ("to decide or respond quickly")

think about *v.* (J and K) ("to direct one's thoughts to") I thought about you/your working out there in the hot sun

think ahead *v.* (D; intr.) ("to direct one's thoughts ahead") to ~ to (to ~ to the future)

think back *v.* (D; intr.) ("to direct one's thoughts

back") to ~ on, to (to ~ to the old days)

thinker *n.* a clear; deep, profound; great; independent; logical; muddled; original ~

thinking *n.* 1. to do some (serious) ~ 2. clear; good; logical; positive; quick ~ 3. creative; independent; original ~ 4. critical; deep ~ 5. muddled; wishful ~ 6. (misc.) to my way of ~

thinking cap *n.* (old-fashioned) to put on one's ~ ("to ponder a problem")

third degree *n.* (colloq.) ["brutal, harsh interrogation"] to give smb. the ~

thirst I *n.* 1. to experience ~; more usu. is: to be thirsty 2. to quench, slake, satisfy smb.'s ~ 3. unquenchable; unquenched ~ 4. (to have) a ~ for (a ~ for knowledge)

thirst II *v.* 1. (d; intr.) to ~ after (formal), for (to ~ for knowledge) 2. (E) (formal) they were ~ing to know the truth

thirsty *adj.* ~ for (~ for power)

thorn *n.* 1. to remove, take out a ~ (from one's finger) 2. (misc.) a ~ in smb.'s side ("a source of irritation")

thorough *adj.* ~ in

thoroughfare *n.* ["road"] (formal) 1. a busy, crowded; main ~ ["through road"] 2. No Thoroughfare (BE)

thought *n.* ["reflection"] ["idea"] 1. to entertain, harbor, have a ~ (to harbor ~s of revenge) 2. to relish a ~ 3. to express, present a ~ 4. to collect, compose, gather; sum up one's ~s 5. a happy; intriguing; refreshing ~ 6. a fleeting, passing ~ 7. a disconcerting, upsetting; evil; sobering; ugly ~ 8. the ~ occurred to me/struck me that... 9. a ~ about, on (what are your ~s on this matter?) 10. a ~ that + clause (the ~ that we would soon reach home gave us courage) 11. at a ~ (my mind boggles at the very ~) 12. in smb.'s ~s (she was always in my ~s) 13. (misc.) the ~ has crossed my mind that...; to read smb.'s ~s; a train of ~; in ~ and deed; one's innermost ~s ["consideration"] 14. to give ~ to 15. to abandon, give up all ~(s) (of doing smt.) 16. (misc.) with no ~ for one's own safety; don't give it a ~; perish the ~! ("one should not even consider the possibility!") ["ideas, principles"] 17. liberal; logical; modern ~ 18. a school of ~ ["opinion"] 19. to express a ~ 20. a ~ about, on 21. a ~ that + clause (she expressed her ~ that the case should be settled without litigation) ["concentration"] 22. (deep) in ~ ["intention"] 23. to have no ~ (of doing smt.) (see also **second thought**)

thoughtful *adj.* 1. ~ about 2. ~ to + inf. (it was ~ of her to do that)

thoughtless *adj.* 1. ~ of 2. ~ to + inf. (it was ~ of them to make noise)

thousand *n.* by the ~s, in the ~, in their (BE) ~s (the crowd streamed into the stadium by the ~s)

thrall *n.* (formal) ["slavery"] in ~ to

thrash *v.* 1. to ~ soundly 2. (misc.) to ~ from side to side; to ~ about/around in one's sleep; to ~ smb. within an inch of her/his life

thrashing *n.* 1. to get a ~ 2. to give smb. a ~ 3. a good, sound ~

thread I *n.* ["fiber, cord"] 1. to make, spin; wind ~ 2. coarse; fine; heavy; thin ~ 3. cotton; lisle; nylon; polyester; rayon; silk ~ 4. a piece; reel (BE), spool (AE) of ~ 5. (misc.) the ~ gets tangled; a loose ~; to hang by a ~ ("to be very uncertain") ["theme"] ["train of thought"] 6. to lose the ~ (of an argument) 7. the common ~ (of the stories) 8. a tenuous ~ 9. (misc.) a common ~ runs through all of her stories; to pull all the loose ~s of the story together

thread II *v.* (C) ~ a needle for me; or: ~ me a needle

threat *n.* 1. to issue, make, utter; mutter a ~ 2. to carry out, fulfill a ~ 3. to be, constitute, pose, represent a ~ 4. to defy; ignore a ~ 5. to give in to a ~ 6. a constant; dire, grave, serious; direct; explicit; imminent ~ 7. a covert; empty, idle; implicit; veiled ~ 8. a death; security; terroristic ~ (their group poses a security ~; they issued a death ~ against the leader of the rival group; they made terroristic ~s before the rally) 9. a ~ against, to (to constitute a ~ to the party leadership) 10. a ~ to + inf. (she carried out her ~ to resign) 11. a ~ that + clause (she carried out her ~ that she would resign) 12. under ~ of (under ~ of reprisals) 13. (misc.) to take a ~ seriously; a constant ~ hung over them

threaten *v.* 1. (D; tr.) to ~ with (to ~ smb. with reprisals) 2. (E) she ~ed to resign

threshold *n.* ["entrance"] 1. (also fig.) to cross a ~ 2. (also fig.) on the ~ (to be on the ~ of a promising career) 3. (med.) a renal ~ ["tolerance"] 4. a pain ~ 5. a high; low ~ (to have a low pain ~)

thrift *n.* to practice ~

thrifty *adj.* ~ in

thrill I *n.* 1. to give, provide a ~ 2. to experience, feel, get, have a ~ 3. a ~ for smb. 4. a ~ to + inf. (it was a ~ to ride in your new car = it was a ~ riding in your new car) 5. (misc.) a cheap ~; to gamble for the ~ of it ("to gamble for the sheer excitement of gambling")

thrill II *v.* 1. (d; intr.) to ~ to (she ~ed to the sound of their voices) 2. (R) it ~ed me to learn of your success

thrilled *adj.* 1. ~ at; with (we were ~ at the thought of meeting the princess; they were ~ with the gift) 2. ~ to + inf. (she was ~ to receive an invitation) 3. ~ that + clause (we were ~ that he would give a concert in our town)

thrilling *adj.* 1. ~ to + inf. (it was ~ to see them) 2. ~ that + clause (it was ~ that we finally met her)

thrive *v.* (D; intr.) to ~ on (to ~ on hard work)

throat *n.* 1. to clear one's ~ 2. to gargle one's ~ 3. to cut, slash, slit smb.'s ~ 4. a clear ~ 5. an inflamed, red, sore; scratchy; strep ~ 6. (misc.) to cut one's own ~ ("to ruin oneself"); to jump down smb.'s ~ ("to criticize smb."); to ram smt. down smb.'s ~ ("to impose smt. on smb."); the words stuck in her ~ ("she found it difficult to say them"); to have a lump in one's ~ ("to be overcome by emotion"); to be at each other's ~s ("to be constantly quarreling")

throb v. (D; intr.) to ~ with (to ~ with excitement)

throes n. 1. death ~ 2. in the ~ (in the ~ of a severe economic crisis)

thrombosis n. a cerebral; coronary ~

throne n. 1. to ascend, mount, succeed to a ~ 2. to seize, usurp; topple a ~ 3. to occupy, sit on a ~ 4. to abdicate, give up a ~ 5. to lose one's ~ 6. (misc.) the power behind the ~

throng v. (P; intr.) they all ~ed (a)round the speaker

thronged adj. ~ with (the beaches are ~ with people)

throttle n. 1. to open a ~ 2. at full ~ ("at full speed")

through adj. 1. right, straight ~ (to) (when I dialed, I got right/straight ~; the call went right/straight ~; from spring right/straight ~ to winter) 2. ~ with (after thirty years, he is ~ with teaching) (see also **come through; get through; go through**)

throw I n. 1. (basketball) a free ~ 2. (baseball) a wild ~

throw II v. 1. to ~ hard; high; straight (she threw the ball hard) 2. (A) ~ the ball to her; or: ~ her the ball 3. (D; tr.) to ~ across, over (to ~ a ball over a fence) 4. (D; tr.) to ~ at (she threw a stone at me) 5. (d; refl., tr.) to ~ into (he threw himself into his work; they threw the ball into the air; the news threw everyone into confusion) 6. (d; refl., tr.) to ~ on (she threw herself on the mercy of the court; to ~ light on a subject) 7. (d; tr.) to ~ out of (they were thrown out of work) 8. (d; refl., tr.) to ~ to (I threw myself to the ground) 9. (P; tr.) she threw the plate against the wall; he threw the tools under the car 10. (misc.) to ~ smb. off balance; he threw himself at her ("he made a maximum effort to win her affections")

throw away v. (D; tr.) ("to squander") to ~ on (to ~ one's money on gambling)

throwback n. ["reversion"] a ~ to

throw back v. 1. (B) she threw the ball back to me 2. see also **throw II** 3-8

throw down v. 1. (D; tr.) to ~ on, onto, to (she threw the books down onto the table) 2. see also **throw II** 5, 8

throw up v. 1. (B) ("to reproach") (esp. AE) I was late, but she didn't ~ it up to me 2. (D; tr.) ("to toss") to ~ in, into; to (she threw the ball up in the air)

thrust I n. ["push"] 1. to make a ~ 2. a deep ~ (they made a deep ~ into enemy lines) 3. a ~ at; into ["main point"] 4. the main, principal ~ (the main ~

of their argument)

thrust II v. 1. to ~ deeply 2. (d; tr.) to ~ at (she thrust the money at me) 3. (d; tr.) to ~ into (she thrust the money into my hand) 4. (misc.) to ~ one's way through a crowd

thud n. 1. a dull; loud; sickening ~ 2. (misc.) it fell to the ground with a loud ~

thumb I n. ["finger"] 1. babies often suck their ~s ["misc."] 2. under smb.'s ~ ("dominated by smb."); to twiddle one's ~s ("to be idle")

thumb II v. (d; intr.) to ~ through (to ~ through a book)

thumbs-down n. ["rejection"] (colloq.) to get; give the ~

thumbs-up n. ["approval"] (colloq.) to get; give the ~

thunder I n. 1. ~ booms, reverberates, roars, rolls, rumbles 2. a clap, crash, peal, roll of ~ (a deafening clap of ~) 3. (misc.) to steal smb.'s ~ ("to do first what smb. else was going to do")

thunder II v. (L; at) he ~ed at us that he would never agree

thunderbolt n. a ~ struck (a tree)

thunderstruck adj. 1. ~ at (~ at the news) 2. ~ to + inf. (they were ~ to learn that the train had already left)

thwart v. (D; tr.) to ~ in (we were ~ed in our efforts to help)

tic n. a nervous ~

tick I n. (colloq.) (esp. BE) ["credit"] on ~ (to let smb. have smt. on ~)

tick II n. (colloq.) (BE) ["moment"] in a ~ (she'll be down in a ~)

tick III n. (BE) ["check mark"] to make, put a ~ (beside, by)

ticket I n. ["document showing that a fare or admission fee has been paid"] 1. to issue a ~ 2. to book, reserve; buy; get a ~ 3. to honor ("accept") a ~ 4. an airplane; bus, coach (BE); platform (BE); rail, train ~ 5. a day-return (BE); one-way (AE), single (BE); return (BE), round-trip (AE) ~ 6. a commutation (AE); season ~ 7. a library (BE; CE has *library card*); meal (AE; BE has *luncheon voucher*) ~ 8. a pawn ~ 9. a theater ~ 10. a complimentary, free; valid ~ 11. a ~ for, to (a ~ for a concert; a ~ to a game; a ticket to Birmingham) ["list of candidates"] (pol.) (AE) 12. to split a ~ 13. a split; straight ~ (to vote a split ~) 14. (misc.) who is running on the party ~? ["printed card indicating participation in a game of chance"] 15. a winning ~ (she held the winning ~) 16. a lottery; sweepstake (BE), sweepstakes (AE) ~ ["citation for a traffic violation"] 17. to give (smb.); issue, write out a ~ (the police officer wrote out a ~ for speeding) 18. to get; pay a ~ 19. a parking; speeding; traffic (AE) ~ 20. a ~ for (she got a ~ for illegal parking) 21. (misc.) to fix a ~ (colloq.) (AE) ("to get a traffic ticket nullified") ["misc."] 22. to write one's own ~ (esp. AE; colloq.) ("to have complete freedom of action")

ticket II v. (D; tr.) to ~ for (AE) (I was ~ed for illegal parking)

tickled adj. (colloq.) (esp. AE) ["happy"] 1. ~ at (~ at the prospect) 2. ~ to + inf. (they would be ~ to come to the party) 3. ~ that + clause (we're ~ that you'll be at our party) 4. (misc.) ~ pink/silly (AE), ~ to death ("very much pleased")

tide n. ["rising and falling of the surface of bodies of water"] 1. a daily; ebb; falling; high, spring; flood; low, neap; strong ~ 2. a ~ comes in; ebbs, goes out 3. (misc.) to sail with the ~ ["trend, tendency"] 4. to buck (AE), go/swim against the ~ 5. to go/swim with the ~ 6. to stem; turn the ~

tide over v. (D; tr.) to ~ until (this money will ~ us over until next month)

tidings n. 1. to bear, bring ~ 2. to receive ~ 3. glad; sad ~

tidy up v. (D; intr., tr.) to ~ after smb. (we always have to ~ after them)

tie I n. ["necktie"] 1. to knot; tie; loosen a ~ 2. (GB) a regimental; school ~ ["draw"] (sports) 3. to break a ~ 4. a goalless (esp. BE), scoreless ~ 5. (to end) in a ~ ["match"] (BE) (sports) 6. a cup ~ ["link, bond"] 7. to establish ~s with 8. to cement, strengthen ~s 9. to cut, sever; loosen ~s with 10. close, intimate, strong ~s 11. family ~s 12. ~s between; to, with (~s between nations) ["support for rails"] (AE) 13. a railroad ~ (BE has *sleeper*) ["misc."] 14. the old school ~ (BE) ("mutual aid of former fellow-students; the old-boy network")

tie II v. 1. (d; tr.) ("to fasten") to ~ (a)round (she ~d the cord around the package) 2. (D; tr.) ("to equal the score of") to ~ for (to ~ smb. for the lead) 3. (D; tr.) ("to fasten") to ~ onto, to (they ~d him to a post) 4. (D; intr.) ("to equal the score") to ~ with (our team ~d with them for the lead) 5. (D; tr.) ("to fasten") to ~ with (I ~d the books with a string) 6. (N; used with an adjective) she ~d the rope tight

tied adj. ["connected"] ~ to (the raise was ~ to the cost of living)

tie down v. (D; tr.) to ~ to (she was ~d down to her job)

tied up adj. ["busy"] 1. ~ with (I'm ~ with appointments all week) ["connected"] 2. ~ with (they are ~ with several multinational corporations)

tie-in n. (colloq.) ["relation"] a ~ between; with

tiers n. ["rows"] in ~

tie-up n. ["stoppage"] 1. to cause a ~ 2. a traffic ~ ["link"] 3. a ~ to; with

tie up v. 1. (D; tr.) to ~ in (they ~d up their money in bonds) 2. (D; tr.) to ~ into (she ~d up everything into a bundle) 3. (D; tr.) to ~ to (she tied the horse up to the fence) 4. (D; tr.) to ~ with (I ~d up the package with string)

tiff n. ["quarrel"] 1. to have a ~ with 2. a minor ~

tiger n. 1. a Bengal; man-eating; saber-toothed; Siberian ~ 2. ~s growl; roar 3. a young ~ is a cub 4. a female ~ is a tigress 5. (misc.) to fight like a ~ ("to fight very fiercely"); a paper ~ ("one who only seems to pose a threat")

tight adj. ["stingy"] (colloq.) 1. ~ with (~ with money) ["misc."] 2. to sit ~ ("to maintain one's position")

tighten up v. (D; intr.) to ~ on (the police are ~ing up on illegal parking)

tightrope n. to walk a ~ (also fig.)

tile n. ceramic; vinyl ~

till n. ["money drawer"] to have one's finger(s) in the ~ ("to steal from a money drawer")

tilt I n. ["attack"] (colloq.) (BE) 1. to have, make a ~ at ["inclination"] 2. a ~ to, towards ["misc."] 3. at full ~ ("at full speed")

tilt II v. 1. (D; intr.) to ~ to (to ~ to the right) 2. (misc.) to ~ at windmills ("to fight imaginary enemies")

timber n. 1. to float, raft ~ (down a river) 2. seasoned; unseasoned ~

time I n. ["unlimited duration"] ["entire period of existence"] 1. ~ flies; goes by, passes 2. in ~ (we exist in ~ and space) ["unlimited future period"] 3. (only) ~ will tell (~ will tell if we are right) 4. in ~ (in ~ everything will be forgotten) ["moment"] ["fixed moment"] ["appropriate moment"] 5. to fix, set, specify a ~ for (to fix a ~ for a meeting) 6. to bide (one's) ~ ("wait patiently for") one's ~ 7. bedtime; check-in; check-out; curtain ~; lunchtime; mealtime; starting ~ 8. the appointed; present; right; wrong ~; an appropriate, suitable ~ 9. a closing; opening ~ 10. (a) ~ for (it's ~ for lunch) 11. ~ to + inf. (it's ~ for us to leave) 12. ~ that + clause (it's high ~ that she returned/was returning home) 13. at a certain ~ (at a bad ~; at the present ~; at that ~; at any old ~) 14. by a certain ~ (by that ~ she had left) 15. (misc.) in good ~; in plenty of ~; there's a ~ and place for everything; smb.'s ~ has come ["duration"] ["period"] ["interval"] 16. to pass, spend ~ (she spends her ~ reading) 17. to gain, save ~ 18. to find ~ (she somehow finds ~ to jog every day) 19. to take ~ (it takes quite a bit of time to get there; how much ~ will this job take?) 20. to lose; waste ~; to fritter away, idle away, while away one's ~ 21. a long; short ~ 22. ancient; Biblical; former; modern; olden; prehistoric; recent ~s (in ancient ~s) 23. (AE) compensatory ~ ("free time given to an employee for previously worked overtime") (BE has *time off in lieu*) 24. equal ~ (for political candidates on TV and radio) 25. peak-time (BE), peak-viewing ~ (BE), prime ~ (what's on TV tonight during prime ~?) 26. (a) record ~ (she ran the distance in record ~) 27. released ~ ("time given for extracurricular activities") 28. travel ~ ("time spent in going to and returning from work") 29. (the) running ~ (of a film) 30. (the) ~ drags; is up; runs out 31. (the) ~ flies 32. ~ for (will you have ~ for an interview?) 33. (misc.) to kill ~ ("to make time pass"); to play for ~ ("to seek delay"); to take one's ~ (about); ("to act slowly"); for a ~; for the ~ being ("for now"); ~ hangs heavy on our hands ["conditions during a period"] 34. to keep up with the ~s 35. bad, difficult, hard, rough ~s (during/in hard ~s) ["available period"] 36. to find; get; have; take (the) ~ (she doesn't find/get/have/take the ~ to relax; he never finds ~ for his family) 37. to budget; plan one's ~ 38. to run out of ~ 39. to devote ~ to; to put ~ into 40. free, leisure, spare ~ (what do you do in your leisure ~?) 41. ~ to + inf. (there is no ~ to lose; will you have ~ to see me tomorrow?) 42. ~ for (~ for relaxation; I have no ~ for my family) ["period worked"] 43. double; full ~; overtime; part ~; time-and-a-half (I work part ~) 44. lost ~ (to make up lost ~; to make up for lost ~) ["period of serving, service"] 45. to do, serve ~ (to do/serve ~ in prison) ["tempo, rhythm"] 46. to beat; keep ~ (to music, to a song) 47. (mus.) common ~ 48. (usu mil.) double; quick ~ (quick ~, march!) 49. in ~ to (the music) ["system of measuring duration"] 50. to gain; keep; lose ~ (my watch gains ~; your watch keeps good ~; her watch loses ~) 51. to show the ~ (that clock shows the ~) 52. to tell ~ (esp. AE)/the ~ (esp. BE) (a clock tells ~/the ~; the child is learning how to tell ~/the ~) 53. central (US); daylight-saving (AE), summer (BE); eastern (US); Greenwich (mean); local; mountain (US); Pacific (US); solar; standard (AE) ~ 54. (misc.) what ~ is it? = what is the ~? ["schedule"] 55. ahead of ~ 56. behind ~ 57. in (good, plenty of) ~ for (we arrived in ~ for the concert) 58. on ~ (they got there on ~) ["experience"] 59. to have a (good) ~ 60. a delightful, good, great, lovely, pleasant, wonderful ~ (we had a great ~ on our trip) 61. a bad, hard, miserable, rough, tough, unpleasant ~ (they gave us a hard ~) ["timeout"] (sports) 62. to call ~ ["occasion"] 63. the first; last; next ~; that; this ~ ["end of pregnancy"] 64. her ~ is near ["misc."] 65. at the same ~ ("however"); at ~s ("occasionally"); for the ~ being ("at present"); behind the ~s ("not abreast of recent events"); from ~ immemorial ("from the earliest period"); (all) in good ~ ("when appropriate"); in no ~ (at all) ("very soon"); to have the ~ of one's life ("to enjoy oneself thoroughly"); it's about ~ ("we must act now"); to keep up with the ~s ("to keep abreast of the latest developments"); to make good ~ ("to travel quickly"); to make ~ with smb. (esp. AE; colloq.) ("to be successful in attracting smb."); to mark ~ ("to be inactive"); ~ and ~ again; or ~ after ~ ("frequently"); to live on

borrowed ~ ("to live beyond the expected time of death"); pressed for ~ ("in a hurry"); to work against ~ ("to work to meet a deadline"); the ~ is ripe for action ("it is time to act"); he died before his ~ ("he died prematurely"); (sports) extra ~ (BE), overtime (AE)
USAGE NOTES: 1. The phrase *in time* can mean "eventually"—in time everything will be forgotten. 2. The phrase *in time* can also mean "with some time to spare"—we arrived in time for the concert. 3. The phrase *on time* means "neither early nor late"—they got there on time. (see also **big time**)
time II *v.* 1. to ~ smt. badly; well 2. (misc.) to ~ smt. (down) to the last second
time bomb *n.* 1. to set off a ~ 2. a ~ ticks away 3. (misc.) they are sitting on a ~ ("disaster is imminent")
time clock *n.* to punch a ~
time limit *n.* to set a ~ for
time-out *n.* 1. to take (a) ~ for 2. a ~ to + inf. (they took a ~ to rest)
timer *n.* ["timing device"] to set a ~
timetable *n.* 1. to draw up, make out, make up, prepare, work out a ~ 2. to issue a ~ 3. to follow, stick to a ~ 4. to upset a ~ 5. (esp. BE) an airline; bus; railway, train ~ (AE prefers *schedule*) 6. a ~ for (we have worked out a ~ for our trip)
timid *adj.* ~ about; with
timing *n.* bad; flawless, perfect; good ~
tin *n.* (BE) a baking; cake ~ (AE has *baking pan; cake pan*)
tinged *adj.* (cannot stand alone) ~ with (~ with regret)
tingle *v.* (D; intr.) to ~ with (my ears ~d with the cold)
tinker *v.* (colloq.) (D; intr.) to ~ with
tint *v.* (N; used with an adjective) the windshield is ~ed blue
tip I *n.* ["gratuity"] 1. to give, leave a ~ 2. a big, generous, handsome ~ (I left a generous ~ for the waitress)
tip II *v.* 1. to ~ generously, handsomely, liberally 2. (O) we ~ped the waiter (five dollars)
tip III *n.* ["information"] 1. give smb. a ~ 2. to get, receive a ~ 3. to take a ~ 4. an anonymous; hot ~ 5. a ~ about, on
tip IV *n.* ["pointed end"] 1. a filter ~ ["end"] 2. at the ~ (at the northern ~ of the island) 3. on the ~ of smb.'s tongue (the word was on the ~ of my tongue; it was on the ~ of my tongue to say something)
tip V *v.* (d; tr.) ("to cover") to ~ with (they ~ped their arrows with poison)
tip VI *v.* (BE) see **tipped**
tip off *v.* 1. (D; tr.) ("to inform") to ~ about 2. (L; must have an object) ("to inform") a friend ~ped

them off that the police were coming

tipped *adj.* ["considered likely"] (BE) 1. widely ~ 2. ~ as (~ as the next prime minister) 3. ~ for (widely ~ for the job) 4. ~ to + inf. (she is ~ to win the contest)

tiptoe I *n.* (to stand, walk) on ~

tiptoe II *v.* (P; intr.) she ~d into the room; they ~d up the stairs

tirade *n.* 1. to deliver; launch into a ~ 2. a blistering, lengthy ~ 3. a ~ against

tire I tyre *n.* 1. to deflate; inflate a ~ 2. to mount a ~ 3. to change; patch, repair; recap; retread a ~ 4. to crisscross, rotate ~s (to reduce wear) 5. to slash a ~ 6. a flat ~ (we had a flat ~ during our trip) 7. a worn ~ 8. a balloon; radial; rubber; snow; spare; steel-belted; studded; tubeless ~ 9. whitewall ~s 10. a ~ blows (out); goes flat

tire II *v.* (d; intr.) to ~ of (to ~ of watching television)

tired *adj.* 1. to get ~ 2. dead ~ 3. ~ of (I'm ~ of waiting)

tiresome *adj.* ~ to + inf. (it's ~ to do the same thing every day = it's ~ doing the same thing every day)

tissue *n.* ["structural material"] 1. cellular; conjunctival; connective; fatty; granulation; muscular; scar ~ ["soft paper"] 2. absorbent; cleansing; toilet ~ ["misc."] 3. a ~ of lies

title I *n.* ["appellation"] 1. to bestow, confer a ~ on 2. to renounce a ~ 3. an official ~ ["exclusive possession"] 4. to give, grant smb. ~ to smt. 5. to hold ~ to smt. 6. clear ~ 7. ~ to (they hold ~ to the property) 8. (misc.) there is a cloud on the ~ ["championship"] 9. to fight for; win a ~ 10. to hold a ~ 11. to clinch a ~ 12. to defend a ~ 13. to give up; lose a ~

title II *v.* ("to call, name") (esp. AE) (N) they ~d their dictionary *The BBI*

titter *v.* (D; intr.) 1. to ~ nervously 2. to ~ at

toady (CE), **toady up** (esp. AE) *v.* (d; intr.) to ~ to (he ~died to the boss = he ~died up to the boss)

toast I *n.* ["browned bread"] 1. to make ~ 2. buttered; cinnamon; dry; French; melba ~ 3. a piece, slice of ~ 4. on ~ (butter on ~)

toast II *v.* (C) ~ two slices for me; or: ~ me two slices

toast III *n.* ["act of drinking to honor smb."] 1. to drink; propose a ~ 2. a ~ to (we drank a ~ to her) 3. (misc.) to join smb. in a ~ ["highly admired person"] 4. the ~ of (the ~ of the town; the ~ of high society)

tobacco *n.* 1. to grow, raise ~ 2. to cure ~ 3. to chew ~ 4. mild; strong ~ 5. chewing; pipe ~ 6. a plug of (chewing) ~

toddy *n.* a hot ~ (for a cold)

to-do *n.* ["fuss"] to make a (big) ~ over

toe *n.* 1. to stub one's ~ (on) 2. to curl one's ~s 3. the big; little ~ 4. (misc.) to keep on one's ~s ("to be

alert"); to tread on smb.'s ~s ("to offend smb.")

toehold *n.* ["footing"] to gain, get a ~

toenail *n.* an ingrowing (BE), ingrown (AE) ~

together *adv.* 1. to go ~ ("to match") 2. ~ with

toil I *n.* ["hard work"] 1. arduous, backbreaking, unremitting ~ 2. physical ~

toil II *v.* (D; intr.) ("to work hard") to ~ over

toilet *n.* 1. to go to, use the ~ 2. to flush a ~ 3. a pay; public ~ 4. down the ~ (to flush smt. down the ~)

token *n.* ["symbol, sign"] 1. to be, constitute a ~ 2. to give, provide a ~ of 3. a tangible ~ 4. (misc.) by the same ~ ("for a similar reason"); in ~ of ("as evidence of") ["metal or plastic disc used as a substitute for money"] 5. to drop in, insert, put in a ~ (to insert a ~ into a slot) 6. to accept, take a ~ (will this machine take ~s?) 7. a bus; subway (AE) ~ ["coupon, voucher"] (BE) 8. a book; gift; record ~

told *adj.* all ~ ("altogether")

tolerance *n.* 1. to display, show ~ 2. to have (a) ~ 3. ~ for, of, towards 4. (misc.) zero ~ (of crime)

tolerant *adj.* 1. ~ of (~ of criticism) 2. ~ towards

tolerate *v.* (K) I will not ~ his smoking

toleration *n.* 1. to display, show ~ 2. ~ for

toll I *n.* ["amount levied"] 1. to charge, impose a ~ 2. to collect ~s (on a bridge, road) 3. to pay a ~ 4. a bridge; tunnel; turnpike (AE) ~ 5. (misc.) ~ free ["damage"] 6. to take a ~ (on) (the storm took a heavy ~; the earthquake took a heavy ~ on several villages) 7. a heavy ~ ["casualties"] 8. the death ~

toll II *v.* (D; intr.) to ~ for (the bell ~ed for those who had made the supreme sacrifice)

tomato *n.* 1. to grow ~es 2. to can ~es 3. a rotten ~ (also fig. in AE)

tome *n.* ["volume"] a scholarly; weighty ~

tom-tom *n.* 1. to beat a ~ 2. the beat of the ~

ton *n.* 1. a gross; long; metric; short ~ 2. (misc.) (BE; slang) to do the ~ ("to go one hundred miles per hour")

USAGE NOTE: The ton in GB is the *long ton* (two thousand two hundred forty pounds). In the US, the ton is the *short ton* (two thousand pounds). The *metric ton* is one thousand kilograms and is officially spelled *tonne* in GB.

tone *n.* ["style, trend"] 1. to set the ~ ["sound"] 2. dulcet, sweet; harsh; strident ~(s) ["manner of speaking that reveals the speaker's feelings"] 3. to adopt, take a certain ~ 4. a conversational; friendly; normal ~ 5. a businesslike; decisive; emphatic; firm ~ 6. an apologetic; subdued ~ 7. a flippant; ironic ~ 8. a serious; solemn ~ 9. a condescending, patronizing; unctuous ~ 10. an arrogant; imperious ~ 11. an abusive; angry, querulous; strident; threatening ~ 12. in a ~ (in angry ~s; she spoke in a normal ~ of voice) 13. (misc.) don't take that ~ with me! smb.'s ~ of voice ["signal"] 14. a dial (AE), dialling (BE); engaged (BE; AE has *busy signal*) ~ ["pitch"] (ling.) 15. a falling; high; low; rising ~

tongs *n.* 1. coal; curling; ice; sugar ~ 2. a pair of ~

tongue *n.* ["language"] 1. smb.'s mother, native ~ 2. a foreign ~ ["organ of speech"] ["speech"] 3. to hold one's ~ ("to be silent") 4. to find one's ~ ("to begin to speak") 5. to stick out one's ~ (the child stuck out its ~ at me) 6. to click one's ~ 7. a coated ~ 8. (misc.) a ~ depressor; on everyone's ~ ("discussed by everyone"); on the tip of one's ~ ("not quite recalled"); ~s were wagging ("people were gossiping"); to speak with a forked ~ ("to be deceitful"); with ~ in cheek ("wryly"); the brandy loosened her ~ ("after drinking she became very talkative") ["manner of speaking"] 9. a caustic, foul, nasty, sharp, vile; civil; glib; loose ~ (he has a nasty ~)

tongue-lashing *n.* 1. to give smb. a (good) ~ 2. to get, receive a ~

tonic *n.* 1. to take a ~ 2. a ~ for 3. (misc.) a gin and ~ ("type of mixed drink")

tonnage *n.* dead-weight; displacement; gross; net, registered ~

tonsillectomy *n.* 1. to do, perform a ~ 2. to have a ~

tonsils *n.* 1. enlarged; inflamed ~ 2. (misc.) to have one's ~ out/removed/taken out

tool *n.* 1. to use a ~ 2. a garden; machine; power ~ 3. burglar's; farm ~s 4. (misc.) the ~s of smb.'s trade; (BE) to down ~s ("to go out on strike")

toot *n.* (colloq.) to give a ~ (on a horn)

tooth *n.* 1. to cut, get teeth (babies are often fretful when they are cutting teeth) 2. to lose a ~ 3. to brush (esp. AE), clean one's teeth 4. to cap; crown; drill; extract, pull, take out; fill a ~ 5. to pick one's teeth 6. to bare; clench, gnash, grind, grit one's teeth 7. a false; baby (AE), milk; back; front; lower; permanent; upper; wisdom ~ 8. an abscessed; decayed; loose ~ 9. teeth ache; chatter; decay, rot; erupt ("appear"); fall out; get discolored 10. a (full) set of teeth 11. (misc.) to have a sweet ~ ("to love sweets"); to sink one's teeth into smt. ("to become completely engrossed in smt."); to show one's teeth ("to show hostile intentions"); ~ and nail ("with all one's strength"); to cut one's teeth on smt. ("to gain one's first experience with smt.")

toothache *n.* to get, have a ~ (AE)/get, have (a) ~ (BE)

toothbrush *n.* to use a ~

toothpaste *n.* a tube of ~

top I *n.* ["device that spins"] 1. to spin a ~ ["misc."] 2. to sleep like a ~ ("to sleep soundly")

top II *n.* ["highest point"] 1. to reach the ~ 2. a mountain ~; rooftop 3. from; to (the) ~ (from ~ to bottom; we climbed to the ~; to fill smt. to the ~) 4. at, on the ~ ["cover, cap"] 5. to put on, screw on a ~ 6. to screw off, take off, unscrew a ~ 7. a bottle; box; screw ~ ["misc."] 8. to blow one's ~ ("to explode in anger"); to go over the ~ ("to begin a charge by going over a parapet"); ("to exceed a limit"); to be on ~ of a situation ("to be in control of a situation")

top III *v.* (d; tr.) to ~ with (the cake was ~ped with whipped cream)

topic *n.* 1. to bring up, broach, consider; discuss, explore a ~ 2. a controversial; current; everyday; special ~ 3. a ~ comes up (for discussion) 4. (misc.) a ~ of conversation; a ~ for discussion

top off *v.* (d; tr.) to ~ with (to ~ a lunch with a nice dessert)

topple *v.* (D; intr., tr.) to ~ from (he was ~d from the throne)

topsy-turvy *adv.* to turn (smt.) ~

torch *n.* ["portable electric light"] (BE; AE has *flashlight*) 1. to turn on a ~ 2. to flash, shine a ~ on 3. to turn off a ~ 4. an electric ~ ["burning stick"] 5. to light a ~ 6. to bear, carry, hold a ~ 7. a flaming ~ ["device used to produce a very hot flame"] 8. a blowtorch; welding ~ ["misc."] 9. to put smt. to the ~ ("to set fire to smt."); to carry a ~ for smb. (colloq.) ("to remain in love with smb. who does not return that love")

torment I *n.* in ~

torment II *v.* (D; tr.) to ~ into (to ~ smb. into doing smt.)

torn *adj.* ["divided"] (cannot stand alone) ~ between (she was ~ between her family and her job)

tornado *n.* a ~ hits, strikes (the ~ struck several cities)

torpedo *n.* 1. to fire, launch a ~ 2. an acoustic; aerial; bangalore; magnetic ~ 3. a ~ explodes 4. a ~ hits; misses its target

torrent *n.* 1. an angry, raging ~ 2. a mountain ~ 3. (misc.) the rain came down in ~s

tort *n.* (legal) to commit a ~

torture I *n.* 1. to employ, practice, resort to, use ~ 2. 2. to subject smb. to ~ 3. to undergo ~ 4. cruel; plain, sheer; sadistic; severe ~ 5. the water ~ 6. an act of ~ 7. ~ to + inf. (it was sheer ~ to listen to her sing = it was sheer ~ listening to her sing) 8. under ~ (he confessed under ~)

torture II *v.* 1. (D; tr.) to ~ into (he was ~d into confessing) 2. (misc.) to ~ smb. to death

toss I *n.* ["flipping of a coin to decide an issue"] to lose; win the ~ (who won the ~ to go first?)

toss II *v.* 1. ("to turn and twist") to ~ (and turn) restlessly (in one's sleep) 2. (A) ("to throw") ~ the ball to me; or: ~ me the ball 3. (D; intr., tr.) to ~ for ("to decide by flipping a coin") (let's ~ for it) 4. (P; tr.) to ~ a ball into the air; the children ~ed stones over the fence

toss-up *n.* 1. a ~ between (it was a ~ between the two leading candidates) 2. (misc.) it was a ~ who would win; it was a ~ whether to go or stay

total *n.* 1. to add up, calculate, tally up a ~ 2. a combined; grand; sum ~

touch I *n.* ["social contact"] 1. to be; get in ~ 2. to keep, stay in ~ 3. to lose ~ (with) 4. close ~ 5. in ~ with smb. (keep in close ~ with me) 6. out of ~ with (I am out of ~ with the present situation) ["feel"] 7. to the ~ (smooth to the ~) ["physical contact"] 8. a deft; delicate; gentle, light, soft, soothing; heavy ~ ["sensitivity"] 9. to have the common ~ ("to have the ability to appeal to the common people") 10. the human ~ ("the ability to relate with compassion to others") ["ability"] 11. to lose one's ~ ["manner"] 12. a bold; distinctive; magic; man's; personal; woman's ~ ["detail, stroke"] 13. the finishing ~es (to put the finishing ~es on/to smt.) ["misc."] 14. a soft ~ ("an overly generous person")

touch II *v.* 1. (d; intr.) ("to stop briefly") to ~ at (the ship will ~ at three ports) 2. (colloq.) (d; tr.) to ~ for ("to ask for") (to ~ smb. for a loan) 3. (d; intr.) to ~ on ("to treat briefly") (to ~ on a topic)

touchdown *n.* (esp. Am. football) to score a ~

touched *adj.* 1. deeply ~ 2. ~ to + inf. (she was ~ to be invited) 3. ~ that + clause (I was ~ that I was singled out for such an honor)

touching *adj.* ~ to + inf. (it was ~ to watch)

touchy *adj.* (colloq.) ~ about (he's ~ about his appearance)

tough *adj.* (colloq.) ["strict"] 1. to be, get ~ (on) 2. ~ on, with (they are ~ on drunk drivers) ["difficult"] 3. (cannot stand alone) ~ to + inf. (he is ~ to work with = it is ~ to work with him = it is ~ working with him = he is a ~ person to work with) ["unfortunate"] 4. ~ that + clause (it's ~ that you can't be with your family) ["misc."] 5. to hang ~ (esp. AE; slang) ("to be very firm"); to talk ~ ("to take a very firm bargaining position")

tour *n.* 1. to conduct, operate a ~ 2. to organize a ~ 3. to go on, make a ~ of 4. a barnstorming (AE); campaign; goodwill; lightning ~ 5. a bus; city; walking ~ 6. a concert; lecture, speaking; study ~ 7. a conducted, guided; organized; package ~ 8. a city; sightseeing ~ 9. on (a) ~ (to be on ~)

tourist *n.* a flock; party of ~s

tournament *n.* 1. to conduct, hold a ~ 2. to enter a ~ 3. a bridge; chess; invitational (AE); rapid-transit (for chess) (AE); tennis ~

tourniquet *n.* 1. to apply, put on a ~ 2. to loosen; tighten a ~

tour of duty *n.* 1. to do a ~ 2. on a ~ (they were on a ~ in the Far East)

tout I *n.* (BE) a ticket ~ (AE has *scalper*)

tout II *v.* (colloq.) ("to praise") 1. (d; tr.) to ~ as (he was ~ed as the next middleweight champion) 2. (misc.) highly ~ed; (BE) to ~ for ("to solicit")

tow I *n.* 1. to give a ~ (to) 2. a ski ~ 3. to have, take in ~ (she had her little sister in ~; they took the ship in ~)

tow II *v.* 1. (D; tr.) to ~ into (to ~ a barge into a port) 2. (D; tr.) to ~ out of (to ~ a boat out of a harbor) 3. (D; tr.) to ~ to (to ~ a car to a garage) 4. (P; tr.) they ~ed the bus across town

towel *n.* ["cloth, paper for drying"] 1. a bath; dish (AE), tea (esp. BE); face; guest; hand; linen; paper; roller; Turkish ~ 2. a sanitary ~ (BE; AE has *sanitary napkin*) 3. a disposable ~ ["symbol of surrender"] 4. to throw, toss in the ~

tower I *n.* 1. a bell; clock; conning; control; fire; TV; water ~ 2. a signal ~ (AE; BE has *signal box*) 3. a ~ stands (one hundred feet high) 4. (misc.) an ivory ~ ("a sheltered place where life's realities may be avoided")

tower II *v.* (d; intr.) to ~ above, over (as a thinker, she ~s over her colleagues)

town *n.* 1. a boom; border; college; ghost ("deserted"); jerkwater (AE; colloq.), one-horse, provincial, sleepy, small; market (BE) ~ (they live in a sleepy little ~) 2. a company ~ 3. (BE) a dormitory ~ (AE has *bedroom community*) 4. smb.'s hometown 5. a county ~ (BE; AE has *county seat*) 6. in ~; out of ~ (they were out of ~ for six weeks; they are back in ~) 7. (misc.) to come to ~; to go to ~ (colloq.; fig.) ("to go all out"); to leave ~; to blow/skip ~ (esp. AE; colloq.) ("to leave town suddenly"); (out) on the ~ ("enjoying city nightlife")

USAGE NOTE: In GB, many places are called *towns* that would be called *cities* in the US. In the US, many places are called *towns* or *small towns* that are *villages* in GB. AE rarely uses *village* for places in the US.

tow out *v.* (d; tr.) to ~ into, to (the boat was ~ed out into the channel; they ~ed the barge out to the freighter)

toy I *n.* 1. to make a ~ 2. to wind, wind up a ~ 3. an educational; executive (BE); mechanical; musical ~ (to wind a mechanical ~) 4. (misc.) to play with ~s; a ~ car; plane; train

toy II *v.* (d; intr.) to ~ with (to ~ with smb.'s affections; cats ~ with mice)

trace I *n.* 1. to leave a ~ 2. to show a ~ of (to show no ~ of remorse) 3. to lose (all) ~ of 4. a slight ~ (he didn't show the slightest ~ of intoxication) 5. without (a) ~ (they disappeared without a ~)

trace II *v.* (D; tr.) to ~ to (the letter was ~d to its sender)

traceable *adj.* ~ to

trace back *v.* (d; tr.) to ~ to (she ~d her origins back to the twelfth century)

tracer *n.* ["inquiry"] (esp. AE) 1. to put out, send out a ~ on ["tracer bullet"] 2. to fire a ~ ["substance used to follow a reaction in the body"] (med.) 3. to inject, introduce a ~ (into the body) 4. to scan (for) a ~ 5. a radioactive ~

traces *n.* to kick over the ~ ("to free oneself")

tracing *n.* to do, make a ~

track I *n.* ["awareness"] 1. to keep ~ of (to keep ~ of expenses) 2. to lose ~ of 3. close ~ (to keep close ~ of smt.) ["course for racing"] 4. a fast; muddy; slow ~ 5. a cinder; indoor ~; racetrack; running ~ ["path, road"] 6. a cart ~ (BE; AE has *dirt road*) 7. off ~ ("straying from one's goals") 8. on ~ ("proceeding towards one's goals") 9. (misc.) on the right ~ ("proceeding correctly"); on the wrong ~ ("proceeding incorrectly"); off the beaten ~ ("isolated") ["rail"] 10. to lay ~s 11. a double; main; railroad (AE), railway (BE); single ~ 12. (misc.) on the wrong side of the ~s (esp. AE; colloq.) ("in the poor section of a city") ["recording"] 13. a sound ~ ["misc."] 14. the fast ~ ("the quickest route to success"); the inside ~ ("an advantageous position")
USAGE NOTE: For footraces, *track* is CE. For horseracing, AE uses *track* and *racetrack*; BE prefers *course* and *racecourse*.

track II *v.* (D; tr.) to ~ to (the hunters ~ed the animal to its lair)

track-and-field *n.* (AE) to go in for ~ (BE has *athletics*)

tracks *n.* ["trail"] 1. to leave ~ 2. to make ~ for ("to go directly to") 3. to cover one's ~ ["misc."] 4. they are hard on the ~ of a scientific discovery; to stop (dead) in one's ~ ("to stop instantaneously"); tire ~

tract *n.* ["system of organs"] the digestive; gastrointestinal; genitourinary; intestinal; respiratory ~

traction *n.* 1. to apply ~ 2. in ~ (her leg is in ~)

tractor *n.* to drive, operate a ~

trade I *n.* ["commerce, business"] 1. to carry on, conduct, engage in ~ 2. to build up, develop, drum up, promote; lose ~ 3. to stimulate ~ 4. to restrain, restrict ~ 5. (a) brisk, lively, thriving ~ (they built up a lively ~) 6. fair ~ 7. the arms; tourist ~ 8. domestic; export; foreign, international, overseas; free; illicit; maritime; retail; wholesale ~ (to promote international ~) 9. (the) slave ~ 10. the carriage ~ ("business with wealthy people") 11. ~ is dropping off, falling off; picking up 12. ~ among, between; with (to conduct ~ with many countries) 13. ~ in 14. (misc.) (in) restraint of ~; balance of ~ ["exchange"] 15. to make a ~ with smb. 16. a fair ~ ["occupation"] 17. to ply, practice a ~ 18. to learn a ~ 19. by ~ (she is a bookbinder by ~) 20. (misc.) a jack of all ~s

trade II *v.* 1. (D; tr.) to ~ for (she ~d a knife for a hat) 2. (D; intr.) to ~ in (to ~ in furs) 3. (D; intr.) to ~ with (to ~ with various countries) 4. (O) she ~d me a knife for a spoon

trade in *v.* (D; tr.) to ~ for (she ~d in her old car for a newer one)

trademark *n.* 1. to issue a ~ 2. to receive, register a ~ 3. to bear; display a ~ 4. to infringe a ~

trade-off *n.* a ~ between

trade off *v.* (D; tr.) to ~ against

trader *n.* 1. a fur ~ 2. a ~ in

trade up *v.* (colloq.) (D; intr.) to ~ from; to (to ~ to a larger car)

trading *n.* 1. brisk; heavy; slow, sluggish ~ (slow ~ on the stock market) 2. insider ~ 3. ~ in

tradition *n.* 1. to hand down, pass down a ~ 2. to establish, start a ~ (we started a new ~) 3. to cherish; have; keep up, maintain, preserve, uphold a ~ 4. to break with; defy (a) ~ 5. an ancient, old; deep-rooted, deep-seated, established; long ~ (they have a long ~ of spending summers in the country) 6. a cherished; great; hallowed; popular ~ 7. a family; oral; religious ~ 8. according to, by ~ (according to ancient ~; by popular ~) 9. in a ~ (in our ~; a new release in the great ~ of Hollywood musicals)

traditional *adj.* ~ to + inf. (it's ~ around here to fly the flag on holidays)

traffic I *n.* ["movement of vehicles, aircraft"] 1. to direct ~ (the police officer was directing ~) 2. to control, regulate ~ (traffic lights control/regulate ~) 3. to block, hold up, obstruct, tie up ~ 4. to divert ~ 5. bumper-to-bumper, heavy; light; rush-hour; slow-moving ~ 6. air; highway (AE), motorway (BE); vehicular ~ 7. inbound; outbound ~ 8. local; long-distance ~ 9. merging; through, thru (AE) ~ 10. one-way; two-way ~ 11. ~ backs up; builds up; thins out 12. (misc.) the flow of ~; the volume of ~; a lane of ~; an update on ~ conditions; a ~ report ["commerce, trade"] 13. brisk, lively ~ 14. illegal, illicit ~ 15. ~ in (illicit ~ in drugs) ["misc."] 16. (colloq.) to charge what the ~ will bear ("to charge as much as people are willing to pay")

traffic II *v.* (d; intr.) to ~ in (to ~ in drugs)

traffic light see **light II** 16-19

traffic ticket (AE) see **ticket I** 17-21

tragedy *n.* 1. to avert a ~ 2. a great; personal; terrible ~ 3. (a) ~ strikes (~ struck their family) 4. a ~ that + clause (it was a ~ that there were no survivors) 5. (misc.) a Greek ~

tragic *adj.* ~ that + clause (it was ~ that they all perished)

trail I *n.* 1. to blaze, make; lay out a ~ 2. to leave a ~ (the wounded animal left a ~ of blood) 3. to follow a ~ 4. to cover up a ~ 5. a steep; winding ~ 6. a hiking; ski; vapor ~ (to lay out a ski ~) 7. a campaign ~ (she was on the campaign ~ for months) 8. on smb.'s ~ (the police were on his ~) 9. (misc.) the ~ winds through the forest; to leave a paper ~ ("to leave a record of one's activities behind")

trail II *v.* 1. (D; intr.) to ~ after, behind (to ~ behind the leaders) 2. (D; tr.) to ~ to (the police ~ed them to the hideout)

trailer *n.* 1. a house ~ (AE; BE has *caravan*) 2. a flatbed ~ 3. the ~ jackknifed

trail off *v.* to ~ to a whisper

train I *n.* ["row of connected railroad cars"] 1. to drive a ~ 2. to shunt ~s (onto different tracks) 3. to board, get on; catch; get off; miss; take a ~ (we took a ~ to the city) 4. to change ~s (we'll have to change ~s in Chicago) 5. to flag down; hold; stop a ~ (to stop a ~ by pulling the communication/ emergency cord) 6. a boat; commuter; express; intercity (BE); local (AE), stopping (BE); long-distance; shuttle; suburban; through ~ 7. a down (BE) ("from a city"); up (BE) ("to a city") ~ 8. an inbound; outbound ~ 9. a freight (AE), goods (BE); hospital; passenger; troop ~ 10. an electric; elevated ~ 11. a ~ arrives, pulls in; leaves, pulls out; runs late; runs on time; stops 12. a ~ for, to; from (the ~ from Exeter to London) 13. by ~ (to travel by ~) 14. aboard, on a ~ (we met on the ~) ["column"] 15. a mule; supply; wagon ~ ["mechanism for transmitting power"] 16. a power ~

USAGE NOTE: In BE, a *train, tram,* or *underground/tube (train)* is driven by an "engine/train driver". In AE, a *train* or *subway* is driven or operated by an "engineer", and a *streetcar* is run by an "operator".

train II *v.* 1. (D; intr., tr.) to ~ as (she ~ed as a runner) 2. (D; intr., tr.) to ~ for (to ~ for the Olympics) 3. (D; tr.) to ~ in (to ~ smb. in defensive driving) 4. (d; tr.) ("to aim") to ~ on (he ~ed his gun on the intruder) 5. (d; intr.) to ~ with (she ~ed with a champion) 6. (E) to ~ to be a dancer 7. (H) they were ~ed to react instantaneously to an attack; they ~ed the workers to be precise

trained *adj.* 1. poorly; well ~ 2. ~ to + inf. (the dogs are ~ to attack) 3. (misc.) house-trained (esp. BE; AE prefers *house-broken*); potty-trained (BE), toilet-trained

trainer *n.* an animal ~

training *n.* 1. to give, provide ~ 2. to get, receive ~ 3. intense; thorough ~ 4. basic; specialized ~ 5. hands-on; in-service, on-the-job (AE); professional; vocational ~ 6. assertiveness; manual; military; physical; sensitivity; toilet; voice ~ 7. ~ in (hands-on ~ in the use of computers) 8. the ~ to + inf. (the soldiers did not have the necessary ~ to carry out the mission) 9. by ~ (she's an engineer by ~) 10. in ~ (he was in ~ for the big fight)

traipse *v.* (colloq.) (P; intr.) they were ~sing along the road

USAGE NOTE: In AE, the verb *traipse* has the connotation of "saunter"; in BE, it typically has the connotation of "trudge" or "tramp heavily".

trait *n.* an acquired; character; genetic, hereditary; negative; personality; positive ~

traitor *n.* 1. a ~ to (a ~ to one's country) 2. (misc.) to turn ~

tram (BE) see **streetcar**

tramp *v.* (P; intr.) to ~ through the woods

trample *v.* 1. (d; intr.) to ~ on, upon (to ~ on smb.'s rights) 2. (misc.) to ~ underfoot; to ~ smb. to death

trance *n.* 1. to fall, go into a ~ 2. to come out of a ~ 3. a deep; hypnotic; light ~ 4. (to be) in a ~

tranquillity, tranquility *n.* 1. to disturb; shatter smb.'s ~ 2. domestic; inner ~ 3. (misc.) an air of ~

tranquillizer *n.* 1. to take a ~ 2. to prescribe a ~ (for) 3. (to be) on ~s

transaction *n.* 1. to conduct ~s 2. a delicate ~ 3. business, financial ~s 4. ~s between

transcribe *v.* 1. (D; tr.) to ~ from; into (to ~ testimony from a tape; to ~ a text into Cyrillic) 2. (D; intr., tr.) to ~ in (to ~ speech in phonetic script)

transcript *n.* 1. an official ~ 2. (AE) a grade ~ ("a student's record")

transcription *n.* 1. to make a ~ 2. (ling.) a broad; narrow; phonemic; phonetic ~

transfer I *n.* ["act of transferring"] 1. to make a ~ 2. an electronic; technology ~ 3. a ~ from; to 4. (misc.) a peaceful ~ of power ["ticket allowing a passenger to change from one vehicle to another on public transportation"] (esp. AE) 5. a bus; streetcar; subway ~

transfer II *v.* (D; intr., tr.) to ~ from; to (she was ~red from New York to Toronto)

transfixed *adj.* ~ with (~ with horror)

transform *v.* (D; tr.) to ~ from; into; to (to ~ current from one voltage to another)

transformation *n.* ["radical change"] 1. to undergo a ~ 2. a complete, radical, total ~ ["transformational rule"] (ling.) 3. to formulate a ~ 4. to apply a ~ 5. to order ~s 6. a dative-movement; indirect-object; imperative; insertion; negative; particle-movement; passive; question ~ 7. a ~ applies

transformer *n.* a step-down; step-up ~

transfuse *v.* (D; tr.) to ~ into, to

transfusion *n.* 1. to administer, do, give a ~ 2. to get, have, receive a ~ 3. a blood; plasma ~

transgress *v.* (formal) (D; intr.) to ~ against

transgression *n.* to commit a ~ against

transistor *n.* a solid-state ~

transit *n.* 1. (esp. AE) mass, rapid ~ 2. in ~ (damaged in ~)

transition *n.* 1. to make; undergo a ~ 2. a gradual; peaceful; rapid ~ 3. a ~ from; to 4. a ~ between (the country is in a state of ~ between socialism and capitalism) 5. in ~ (at present, our economy is in ~) 6. (misc.) in a state of ~

transitional *adj.* ~ between

translate *v.* 1. to ~ freely; literally; simultaneously; word-for-word 2. (D; tr.) to ~ as (to ~ *chien* as *dog*) 3. (D; tr.) to ~ from; into (to ~ a book from Russian into Spanish) 4. (misc.) to ~ at sight

translation *n.* 1. to do, make a ~ 2. (a) close, literal, word-for-word; free, loose, rough; on-sight ~ 3. an authorized ~ 4. (a) loan ~ 5. (a) machine; running; simultaneous ~ 6. a ~ from; into (a ~ from German into English) 7. in ~ (to read a novel in ~; the poem is very effective in free/in a free ~; some poetry loses a lot in ~)

transliterate *v.* 1. (D; tr.) to ~ as (to ~ a Russian letter as *ch*) 2. (D; tr.) to ~ from; into (to ~ a text from Cyrillic into Roman letters)

transliteration *n.* to do a ~

transmission *n.* ["gearbox"] 1. an automatic; standard; synchromesh ~ ["act of transmitting"] 2. a ~ from; to

transmit *v.* 1. (D; tr.) to ~ from; to (the results were ~ted to all local stations from the network) 2. (D; tr.) to ~ through (the infection was ~ted through contaminated food) 3. (misc.) to ~ by satellite; to ~ live

transmitted *adj.* sexually ~

transmitter *n.* 1. a longwave; radar; radio; shortwave ~ 2. a television, TV ~

transmute *v.* (formal) (D; tr.) to ~ from; into (to ~ base metal into gold)

transpire *v.* 1. (L) ("to become apparent, evident, known") it ~d that he had gone out of town before the crime occurred 2. (misc.) as it ~d, she had gone out of town before the crime occurred

transplant I *n.* 1. to do a ~ 2. to reject a ~ (her body rejected the ~) 3. a bone-marrow; corneal; gene; heart; kidney; organ; skin ~ 4. a ~ takes; is rejected

transplant II *v.* (D; tr.) to ~ from; to

transport I *n.* 1. (esp. BE) see **transportation** 2. a supersonic ~ (also *SST*) 3. a troop ~

transport II *v.* 1. to ~ bodily 2. (d; tr.) to ~ from; to

transportation *n.* (esp. AE; BE usu. has *transport*) 1. to provide ~ 2. air; bus; ground, surface; mass, public ~ 3. ~ from; to (to provide ~ from the city to the airport)

transpose *v.* (D; tr.) to ~ from; into, to (to ~ a song into a different key)

transposition *n.* a ~ from; into, to

transship *v.* (D; tr.) to ~ from; to

trap *n.* ["device for catching animals or people"] ["stratagem for tricking unsuspecting people"] 1. to bait; lay, set a ~ (for) 2. to spring a ~ on 3. to fall into a ~ 4. to lure smb. into a ~ 5. a booby; death ~; mousetrap; radar; speed ~; a sand ~ (in golf) ["mouth"] (slang) 6. to shut one's ~

trapeze *n.* 1. on a ~ 2. (misc.) to hang from a ~

trapper *n.* an animal; fur ~

trash *n.* (esp. AE; CE has *refuse, rubbish*) 1. to accumulate ~ 2. to collect, pick up ~ 3. to dispose of, dump ~ (BE prefers *to tip refuse*) 4. to put out the ~ 5. (misc.) (derog.) white ~ ("poor white people in the southern US")

trauma *n.* 1. to cause (a) ~ 2. to suffer (a) ~ 3. (an)

emotional; physical; psychological ~

travel I *n.* 1. air; rail; sea; space ~ 2. foreign, international ~ 3. ~ from; to (~ from the United States to Japan)

travel II *v.* 1. to ~ extensively, widely; far; far and wide 2. to ~ deluxe; first-class; second-class; tourist-class 3. to ~ incognito; light 4. (D; intr.) to ~ across; in; through (to ~ in Canada; to ~ through the Rockies) 5. (D; intr.) to ~ by (to ~ by air) 6. (D; intr., tr.) to ~ from; to (to ~ from London to Tokyo) 7. (d; intr.) to ~ with (to be ~ing with a group of students) 8. (misc.) to ~ on business; to ~ downstream; to ~ upstream; to ~ the world

traveler, traveller *n.* 1. an experienced, seasoned ~ 2. an air ~ 3. a commercial ~ (old-fashioned; BE; CE has *traveling salesman*) 4. (misc.) a fellow ~ ("a Communist sympathizer")

travels *n.* on one's ~ (on our ~ we saw many interesting places)

travesty *n.* 1. to make a ~ of 2. a shocking ~ 3. a ~ of, on (a ~ of justice)

tray *n.* 1. a serving ~ 2. on a ~

treachery *n.* 1. an act of ~ 2. ~ to + inf. (it was ~ to reveal such secrets to the enemy)

tread I *n.* ["step"] 1. a firm; heavy; light ~ ["mark"] 2. tire ~s (as left on mud) ["pattern of ridges"] 3. a worn ~ 4. a tire ~

tread II *v.* 1. (can be fig.) (d; intr.) to ~ on, upon (to ~ on smb.'s toes) 2. (P; intr.) to ~ softly

treadle *n.* to work a ~

treadmill *n.* on a ~ (often fig.)

treason *n.* 1. to commit; plot ~ 2. high ~ 3. an act of ~ 4. ~ to + inf. (it is ~ to sell military information to a foreign power)

treasonable see **treasonous**

treasonous *adj.* ~ to + inf. (it is ~ to deal with the enemy during wartime)

treasure *n.* 1. an art ~ 2. a national; priceless; real ~ 3. (a) buried; sunken ~ (to find buried/a buried ~; to raise sunken ~ from the bottom of the sea)

treat I *n.* ["source of joy"] 1. to provide a ~ 2. a ~ for (their visit was a real ~ for us) 3. a ~ to + inf. (it was a ~ to watch them dance) ["paying for the food or entertainment of others"] 4. to stand ~ (esp. AE) 5. (misc.) it's my ~

treat II *v.* 1. ("to describe") to ~ (a subject) exhaustively, painstakingly, thoroughly 2. ("to deal with") to ~ badly; cruelly; fairly; harshly; kindly; leniently; unfairly; well 3. (d; tr.) to ~ as ("to deal with") (they ~ed us as honored guests) 4. (D; tr.) ("to cure") to ~ for; with (to ~ smb. for a cold with a new drug) 5. (d; tr.) ("to deal with") to ~ like (he ~ed him like his own brother; she ~s me like dirt) 6. (formal) (d; intr.) to ~ of ("to deal with") (her books ~ of economic problems) 7. (D; refl., tr.) to ~ to ("to provide with at one's own expense") (to ~ smb. to a decent meal) 8. (d; tr.) ("to deal with") to

~ with (to ~ smb. with kindness)

treatise *n.* (formal) 1. to write a ~ 2. a learned; scientific; theoretical ~ 3. a ~ on, upon

treatment *n.* ["care"] ["cure"] 1. to administer, give, provide ~ 2. to get, have, receive, undergo ~ 3. to respond to ~ 4. inpatient; medical; outpatient; radiation; shock ~ 5. the ~ was effective; ineffective 6. ~ for (to undergo ~ for alcoholism) 7. under ~ 8. (misc.) a beauty ~ ["method of dealing with"] 9. gentle; humane; kid-glove; kind ~ 10. equal, equitable; fair ~ 11. preferential; red-carpet; special ~ (to receive preferential ~) 12. shabby; uneven; unfair ~ 13. atrocious, barbarous, brutal, cruel, harsh, inhumane ~ (brutal ~ of prisoners) 14. (colloq.) the full; VIP ("special") ~ (they got the full/VIP ~) 15. the silent ~ (to give smb. the silent ~) ["description, study"] 16. a definitive; exhaustive, lengthy ~ 17. a cursory; superficial ~

treaty *n.* 1. to conclude, sign; negotiate, work out a ~ 2. to confirm, ratify a ~ (the senate must confirm all ~ties) 3. to honor a ~ 4. to break, violate a ~ 5. to abrogate, denounce a ~ 6. a draft ~ 7. a bilateral, bipartite ~ 8. a commercial, trade; extradition ~ 9. a nonaggression; peace ~ 10. a nonproliferation; test-ban ~ 11. a ~ between; with (a ~ between former foes) 12. a ~ to + inf. (they signed a ~ to settle all border disputes by arbitration) 13. (misc.) the terms of a ~

tree *n.* ["woody plant with a trunk"] 1. to grow; plant a ~ 2. to prune, trim a ~ 3. to chop down, cut down, fell a ~ 4. to uproot a ~ (the gale uprooted several ~s) 5. a Christmas; shade ~ 6. a deciduous; evergreen ~ 7. a tall ~ 8. a ~ grows 9. a cluster; grove; stand of ~s 10. in; on a ~ (monkeys live in ~s; fruit grows on ~s) 11. (misc.) to climb a ~; (colloq.) up a ~ (AE), up a gum ~ (BE) ("stymied"); to bark up the wrong ~ ("to be mistaken") ["something resembling a tree"] 12. a family, genealogical ~ 13. a clothes; shoe ~ ["misc."] 14. they cannot see the forest (AE)/wood (BE) for the ~s ("they see all of the details, but they do not recognize the essence of the problem")

trek I *n.* ["long trip"] to go on, make a ~ from; to

trek II *v.* (P; intr.) to ~ across the fields

tremble *v.* 1. (d; intr.) to ~ at (to ~ at the thought of going back to the front) 2. (D; intr.) to ~ from, with (to ~ from the cold; to ~ with fear)

tremor *n.* 1. a nervous ~ 2. a perceptible; slight ~ 3. uncontrollable; violent ~s 4. an earth ~

trench *n.* 1. to dig a ~ 2. a slit ~ 3. (misc.) in the ~es (during World War I)

trend *n.* 1. to create, set, start a ~ 2. to buck (colloq.) (AE); reverse a ~ 3. a discernible, noticeable; general; marked ~ 4. a growing; recent ~ 5. a downward; upward ~ 6. an unwelcome; welcome ~ 7. an economic; political ~ 8. a ~ towards

trespass I *n.* criminal ~

trespass II *v.* 1. (obsol.) (D; intr.) to ~ against 2. (D; intr.) to ~ on, upon (to ~ on a neighbor's property)

trespassing *n.* no ~!

trial *n.* ["legal proceedings"] 1. to conduct, hold a ~ 2. to bring smb. to ~; to put smb. on ~ 3. to await ~ 4. to face; stand ~ for (he stood ~ for embezzlement) 5. to come, go to ~ (the case went to ~) 6. to waive a (jury) ~ (the accused waived a jury ~) 7. a fair; speedy ~ (to get a fair ~) 8. a closed; open, public; show ~ 9. a court; jury (or: a ~ by jury); summary ~ 10. a murder; war-crimes ~ 11. at a ~ (she testified at his ~) 12. on ~ (for) (he was on ~ for murder) ["test, experiment"] 13. to carry out, conduct a ~ 14. to undergo ~s 15. a clinical; field ~ 16. (misc.) by ~ and error ["source of worry"] 17. a ~ to (they are a ~ to their parents)

trial balloon *n.* to float, send up a ~

trial run see **dry run**

triangle *n.* 1. to draw, make a ~ 2. an acute; congruent; equilateral; isosceles; obtuse; right (AE), right-angled (BE); scalene ~ 3. the apex of a ~ 4. (fig.) the eternal ~; a love ~

tribe *n.* 1. to lead a ~ 2. a native; nomadic, wandering; primitive ~ 3. (misc.) to belong to a ~; a member of a ~

tribulation *n.* 1. to bear, endure a ~ 2. (misc.) trials and ~s

tribunal *n.* 1. to set up a ~ 2. a military; war-crimes ~ 3. (GB) an industrial ~ 4. at, before a ~ (to appear before a military ~)

tribute *n.* ["money paid under duress"] 1. to exact ~ from 2. to pay ~ to ["testimonial"] 3. to pay (a) ~ to 4. a fitting; glowing; moving, touching ~ 5. a floral ~ ("a bunch of flowers") 6. a ~ to 7. in ~ to

trick I *n.* ["dexterous feat, sleight of hand"] 1. to do, perform a ~ 2. a card ~ ["prank"] ["deceitful act"] 3. to play a ~ on smb. 4. a clever ~ 5. a cheap, contemptible, dirty, low, mean, nasty, shabby, sneaky ~ 6. a confidence ~ (BE; AE has *confidence game*) ["scoring unit in a card game"] 7. to lose; take, win a ~ ["misc."] 8. to do the ~ ("to be exactly what is needed"); smb.'s bag of ~s ("smb.'s expertise"); ~ or treat! (at Halloween); she doesn't miss a ~ ("she notices everything") (see also **tricks**)

trick II *v.* 1. (D; tr.) to ~ into (to ~ smb. into doing smt.) 2. (D; tr.) to ~ out of (she was ~ed out of her money)

trickle I *n.* 1. a mere ~ 2. (misc.) to slow to a ~

trickle II *v.* (P; intr.) stragglers kept ~ling into camp; blood ~d from the cut

trickle down *v.* (D; intr.) to ~ to (to ~ to the general population)

tricks *n.* 1. (often pol.) dirty ~ 2. (misc.) they are up to their old ~ again

trifle I *n.* a mere ~

trifle II *v.* (d; intr.) to ~ with (they are not to be ~d with)

trigger *n.* ["device for releasing the hammer of a firearm"] 1. to press, pull, release, squeeze a/the ~ 2. a hair ("delicate") ~ 3. (misc.) quick on the ~ ["device that fires an explosive"] 4. a ~ for

trim I *n.* ["good condition"] ["condition"] 1. fighting ~ (in fighting ~) 2. in ~ (to be in ~) ["ornamental metalwork on a car"] 3. chrome ~ (he scratched my chrome ~)

trim II *v.* (d; tr.) to ~ from, off (to ~ the fat from the budget)

trimmings *n.* ["garnishings"] ["extras"] with all the ~ (turkey with all the ~; they got the full treatment with all the ~)

trip I *n.* 1. to go on, make, set off on, take a ~ (she went on a ~; I've made three ~ many times; we would like to take a ~) 2. to arrange, organize, plan a ~ 3. to cancel; postpone a ~ 4. an extended, long; short ~ 5. a business; camping; day; field; pleasure; return; round; round-the-world; wedding ~ (we are planning a round-the-world ~) 6. a ~ along; around 7. a ~ from; to (they went on a ~ to Canada; to take a ~ from England to Australia) 8. a ~ through (a ~ through the west) 9. on a ~ (she was away on a ~) 10. (misc.) a bad ~ (on drugs); an ego ~ ("behavior that satisfies one's ego")

trip II *v.* (D; intr.) ("to stumble") to ~ on, over (to ~ on a rock; she was ~ping over every word)

triplets *n.* a set of ~

triplicate *n.* in ~ (to prepare all documents in ~)

tripod *n.* 1. to set up a ~ 2. on a ~ (the camera rested on a ~)

triumph I *n.* 1. to achieve, score a ~ 2. a glorious, splendid; short-lived ~ 3. a ~ over (a ~ over evil) 4. in ~ (to return home in ~)

triumph II *v.* (D; intr.) to ~ over

triumphant *adj.* ~ in; over

trolley *n.* ["small wheeled conveyance"] (BE) 1. a (shopping) ~ (in a supermarket) (AE has *shopping cart*) 2. a tea ~ (AE has *tea wagon*) 3. a sweet ~ (in a restaurant) ["streetcar, tram"] (AE) 4. see **streetcar**

USAGE NOTE: Wheeled conveyances that are called *trolleys* in BE are often called *carts* in AE. In a library, books are moved on a *trolley* (BE) or on a *cart* (AE).

trombone *n.* to play the ~

troop I *n.* 1. a cavalry ~ 2. a (Boy) Scout; Girl Scout (AE) ~

troop II *v.* (P; intr.) the children ~ed into school

trooper *n.* 1. (US) a state ~ 2. (misc.) to swear like a ~ ("to use vile language")

troops *n.* 1. to commit; deploy; dispatch; lead; rally ~ 2. to review ~ 3. to station ~ (in a country) 4. green; seasoned ~ 5. victorious ~ 6. defeated; demoralized ~ 7. airborne; armored; ground; motorized; mounted; ski ~ 8. elite; irregular; regular;

shock ~

trophy *n.* 1. to award, give, present a ~ 2. to get, receive, win a ~ 3. to display a ~ 4. a sports; war ~

tropic *n.* the Tropic of Cancer; Capricorn

tropics *n.* in the ~ (to live in the ~)

trot I *n.* 1. at a ~ 2. (misc.) (BE; colloq.) on the ~ all day ("busy all day"); that horse won four races on the ~ ("that horse won four races in succession")

trot II *v.* (P; intr.) the horses ~ted (a)round the track

troth *n.* (old-fashioned) to pledge, plight one's ~ ("to make a promise of marriage")

trouble I *n.* 1. to cause, foment, make, start, stir up ~ 2. to give smb. ~ (they gave their parents a lot of ~) 3. to ask for, invite, look for ~ 4. to go through, have, run into ~ (she had a lot of ~ with her back) 5. to go to ~ (they went to a great deal of ~ to arrange the interview) 6. to get (smb.) into ~ (we got into ~ during our trip; she got herself into serious ~ with the police; they got me into ~ at school) 7. to take the ~ to do smt. (I took the ~ to check on her story) 8. to get (smb.) out of ~ (I got out of ~; she got herself out of ~; they got him out of ~) 9. to avoid, steer clear of ~ 10. to prevent ~ 11. deep, real, serious ~ 12. back; engine; heart ~ (to develop engine ~) 13. ~ is brewing 14. ~ blows over 15. ~ about, over; with (we had ~ with our neighbors over the noise that they were making) 16. a bit of ~ 17. no ~ to + inf. (it's no ~ to call them) 18. in ~ (with) (they were in ~; he was in ~ with the police) 19. out of ~ (to keep out of ~) 20. (misc.) to put smb. to a lot of ~; it is not worth the ~; sending a telegram will save you the ~ of making a second trip; she has ~ going up steps; he had no ~ memorizing the material for the test

trouble II *v.* 1. (d; refl., tr.) to ~ about (don't ~ yourself about the arrangements) 2. (d; tr.) to ~ for (could I ~ you for the salt?) 3. (colloq.) (E; in neg. sentences) she didn't even ~ to lock the door 4. (colloq.) (H; in interrogative sentences; no passive) could I ~ you to open the window? 5. (R) it ~d me to read that no negotiations were scheduled; it ~d us that they did not write of their plans

troubled *adj.* 1. deeply ~ 2. ~ by, with (she is ~ with arthritis) 3. ~ to + inf. (we were ~ to learn of her problems)

troublesome *adj.* ~ to + inf. (it is ~ to be without electricity)

trousers *n.* 1. to have ~ on, to wear ~ 2. to put on ~ 3. to take off ~ 4. to button up; unbutton; unzip; zip up one's ~ 5. baggy; long; short ~ 6. a pair of ~ 7. (misc.) a trouser leg

trowel *n.* a bricklayer's; gardener's; plasterer's ~

truant *n.* 1. to play ~ 2. (misc.) (AE) a ~ officer

truce *n.* 1. to agree (BE), agree on, agree to, arrange, call, work out a ~ 2. to announce, declare a ~ 3. to violate a ~ 4. to denounce a ~ 5. an armed; uneasy ~ 6. a ~ between

truck I *n.* ["vehicle"] 1. (esp. AE; BE often has *lorry, van*) to drive, operate; steer a ~ 2. to load; unload a ~ 3. (AE) a delivery, panel ~ (BE has *delivery van*) 4. a dump (esp. AE), dumper (BE), tipper (BE) ~ 5. (AE) a garbage, trash ~ (BE has *dustbin lorry, dustcart*) 6. (AE) a pickup; trailer ~ (BE has *articulated lorry*) 7. a breakdown (BE), tow (AE) ~ (BE also has *breakdown lorry, breakdown van*) 8. a railway ~ (BE; AE has *flatcar*) 9. a sound ~ 10. a ~ jackknifes

truck II *n.* ["dealings"] to have no ~ with

trudge *v.* (P; intr.) to ~ through the mud

true *adj.* 1. historically ~ 2. ~ to (~ to one's principles; ~ to form; ~ to life) 3. ~ that + clause (it is not ~ that she has resigned) 4. (misc.) to come ~; to ring ~; it is not ~ to say that she will resign; to hold ~ ("to be valid")

true colors *n.* to reveal, show one's ~

truly *adv.* (usu. at the close of a letter) (esp. AE) yours ~; yours very ~; very ~ yours (see **yours**)

trump *n.* ["winning card"] to play a ~

trump card *n.* ["final resource"] to play one's ~

trumpet *n.* 1. to play the ~ 2. ~s blare

trumps *n.* to lead ~ (when playing cards)

trunk *n.* ["main stem"] 1. a tree ~ ["large piece of luggage"] 2. to pack; unpack one's ~ 3. to ship a ~ 4. a steamer; wardrobe ~

USAGE NOTE: On cars, *trunk* is AE; *boot* is BE.

trunks *n.* 1. swimming ~ 2. a pair of ~

trust I *n.* ["reliance"] 1. to place, put one's ~ in 2. to earn, gain, win; have smb.'s ~ 3. to abuse, betray, violate smb.'s ~ 4. absolute; blind, unquestioning; universal ~ 5. public ~ 6. on ~ (to sell on ~) 7. a breach of ~ ["cartel"] 8. to break up a ~ ["fund"] 9. to set up a ~ (for a child) 10. a unit ~ (BE; AE has *mutual fund*) 11. a blind; perpetual ~ (to place one's holdings in a blind ~ during one's term of office) 12. in ~ for

trust II *v.* 1. to ~ blindly, implicitly 2. (d; intr.) ("to believe") to ~ in (to ~ in God) 3. (d; intr.) to ~ to ("to rely on") (to ~ to one's memory) 4. (d; tr.) ("to entrust") to ~ with (to ~ smb. with one's savings) 5. (H) ("to entrust") I ~ed her to deposit the funds 6. (L) ("to believe") we ~ that you will keep your word 7. (misc.) (ironic) ~ them to do smt. silly!

trust fund *n.* to set up a ~ for smb.

truth *n.* 1. to ascertain, elicit, establish, find; face, face up to; get at; search for, seek the ~ 2. to admit; expose, reveal; speak, tell the ~ 3. to distort, pervert, stretch the ~ 4. the absolute, basic, fundamental, gospel, naked, plain, unvarnished, whole ~ 5. the awful; bitter; ultimate ~ 6. (the) historical ~ 7. an element, grain, kernel of ~ 8. (there is) not an iota, shred of ~ (in that) 9. the ~ about (I finally discovered the ~ about their origins) 10. ~ in (in there is some ~ in their allegations; is there any ~ in that?) 11. in ~ 12. (misc.) where does the ~ lie? it

had a ring of ~ about it; the ~ is that she served in the army

truthful *adj.* ~ about; in

try I *n.* 1. to have, make a ~ at 2. (colloq.) to give smt. a ~ 3. (rugby) to score a ~ 4. a valiant ~ 5. a ~ at, for 6. a ~ to + inf. (they made another ~ to have the decision reversed) 7. (misc.) (AE; colloq.) to give it the old college ~ ("to make a determined effort"); it's worth a ~

try II *v.* 1. to ~ hard; to ~ one's best 2. (D; intr.) ("to attempt") to ~ for (to ~ for a prize) 3. (D; tr.) ("to subject to trial") to ~ for (they tried her for murder) 4. (E) ("to attempt") she tried to telephone us 5. (G) ("to attempt") he tried jogging, but his ankles would hurt

USAGE NOTES: 1. The phrase *try and do smt.* is a colloq. variant of *try to do smt.*, but has no past tense. 2. The sentence *she tried to jog* usu. means that she never was able to jog; *she tried jogging* means that she was able to jog, but gave it up after a while.

try on *v.* to ~ smt. on for size

tryout *n.* a ~ for

try out *v.* 1. (D; intr., tr.) to ~ for (esp. AE) (to ~ for a major part in a play) 2. (D; tr.) to ~ on (to ~ a new drug on animals)

tryouts *n.* to hold ~ for

tryst *n.* (formal) 1. to keep a ~ 2. a ~ with

tsar (BE) see **czar**

tub *n.* ["bathtub"] (esp. AE; BE prefers *bath*) 1. to fill the ~ (for a bath) 2. to empty the ~ (after a bath) 3. to clean out; scrub (out) a ~

tube *n.* ["channel within the body"] 1. bronchial; Eustachian; Fallopian ~s ["rubber casing"] 2. an inner ~ ["hollow cylinder"] 3. an electron; picture, television; test ~ 4. a vacuum ~ (AE; BE has *valve*) 5. (slang) the boob ~ ("television") ["container"] 6. to squeeze a ~ (of toothpaste) ["underground"] (BE) 7. to take the ~ 8. by ~ (to go to work by ~) 9. on the ~ (to travel to work on the ~) (AE has *subway*)

tuberculosis *n.* to contract, develop, get; have ~

tubing *n.* copper; glass; flexible; plastic; rubber ~

tuck *v.* 1. (d; tr.) to ~ into (to ~ a child into bed; he ~ed his shirt into his trousers) 2. (d; tr.) to ~ under (she ~ed the napkin under her chin)

tug I *n.* ["pull"] 1. to give a ~ on ["tugboat"] 2. a seagoing ~

tug II *v.* 1. (D; intr.) to ~ at (to ~ at a rope) 2. (P; tr.) they ~ged the ship out of the harbor

tuition *n.* ["instruction"] (BE) 1. to give ~ 2. to get, have, receive ~ 3. private ~ (in) ["payment for instruction"] 4. to pay ~ for 5. free; full; half ~ (to pay full ~; to get/have/receive free ~)

tumble I *n.* (colloq.) ["fall"] 1. to take a ~ 2. a bad, nasty ~ (she took a nasty ~) 3. a ~ from ["sign of recognition"] (AE) 4. to give smb. a ~ (they wouldn't give us a ~)

tumble II v. 1. (d; intr.) to ~ into (to ~ into bed) 2. (d; intr.) to ~ out of (to ~ out of a chair) 3. (colloq.) (d; intr.) to ~ to ("to catch on to, comprehend") (they didn't ~ to the meaning of the clues) 4. (P; intr.) ("to fall") to ~ down the stairs

tumor, tumour n. 1. to excise, remove, take out a ~ 2. a benign; inoperable; malignant ~

tumult n. ["violent, noisy agitation"] 1. to cause ~ 2. in ~ over

tune n. ["melody"] 1. to compose, write a ~ 2. to hum; play; sing; whistle a ~ (to play a ~ on the piano) 3. to carry ("sing the notes of") a ~ 4. a ~ of, to (the ~ to a song) 5. a catchy; lilting ~ 6. in ~; out of ~ (to sing in ~; she was playing out of ~) 7. to a ~ (to dance to a ~) 8. (misc.) (BE) a signature ~ ("theme song of a program") ["agreement"] 9. in ~ with (in ~ with the times) 10. out of ~ with ["attitude"] (colloq.) 11. to change one's ~ ["misc."] (colloq.) 12. to call the ~ ("to be in command"); to sing a different ~ ("to begin to act differently"); to the ~ of ("approximately")

tune II v. (d; tr.) to ~ to (we ~d our sets to the local station)

tune in v. (D; intr.) to ~ on (esp. AE), to (to ~ to a station)

tuner n. a piano ~

tune-up n. 1. to do a ~ (of an engine); to give (an engine) a ~ 2. an engine ~

tuning n. fine ~

tunnel I n. 1. to bore, build, construct, dig a ~ 2. a pedestrian; railroad (AE); railway (BE); wind ~ 3. a ~ caves in 4. through a ~ (to drive through a ~) 5. (misc.) (fig.) the light at the end of the ~

tunnel II v. (P; intr.) to ~ under the Channel; termites ~ through wood

turbulence n. clear-air ~

turkey n. 1. to raise ~s 2. to carve; roast; stuff a ~ 3. a wild ~ 4. ~s gobble 5. a female ~ is a hen 6. a male ~ is a gobbler

turmoil n. 1. complete ~ 2. in (a) ~ (the country was in ~) 3. (misc.) the city was thrown into ~

turn I n. ["change of direction"] ["direction"] 1. to make, negotiate a ~ (to negotiate a difficult ~) 2. to take a ~ (the conversation took an interesting ~) 3. a left; right; sharp ~; U-turn (to make a U-turn) 4. a ~ to (a ~ to the right) ["proper order, opportunity"] 5. to have, take one's ~ 6. to take ~s at; with (we took ~s with them standing/at standing guard) 7. to wait one's ~ 8. to miss one's ~ 9. smb.'s ~ comes (my ~ came) 10. smb.'s ~ to + inf. (it's my ~ to drive) 11. by ~s 12. in ~; out of ~ ["change"] 13. to take a ~ (the situation took a ~ for the better) 14. a dramatic; favorable; unexpected; unfavorable ~ (events took a dramatic ~ for the worse) 15. (usu. of business conditions) a downward; upward ~ (the market took an upward ~) 16. at the ~ (of the

century) ["short walk"] 17. to take a ~ (let's take a ~ around/round the park) ["shock"] 18. to give smb. a ~ (the revelation gave me quite a ~) ["misc."] 19. at every ~ ("on every occasion"); to do smb. a good ~ ("to do smb. a favor")

turn II v. 1. ("to change direction") to ~ abruptly, sharply 2. (d; intr., tr.) to ~ against ("to become antagonistic towards"); ("to make antagonistic towards") (to ~ against one's friends; what ~ed him against us?) 3. (d; intr.) to ~ for; to ("to resort to") (she ~ed to her family in her time of need; they had to ~ somewhere for help) 4. (d; intr.) ("to shift") to ~ from; to (let's ~ from this topic to a more pleasant one; to ~ to a new field) 5. (D; intr.) ("to change direction") to ~ into; onto (to ~ into a side street) 6. (d; intr., tr.) to ~ into ("to be converted, transformed into"); ("to convert, transform into") (caterpillars ~ into butterflies; freezing water ~s (in)to ice; his love ~ed to hate; they ~ed the meeting into a brawl; the incident ~ed her into a better person) 7. (D; intr.) to ~ off ("to leave") (to ~ off the main road) 8. (d; intr.) to ~ on ("to attack") (to ~ on smb. in anger; the speaker finally ~ed on the hecklers) 9. (d; intr.) to ~ on, upon ("to depend, hinge on") (everything ~s on the judge's interpretation of the law) 10. (D; intr.) ("to change direction") to ~ to (to ~ to the right) 11. (d; intr.) ("to direct one's attention, efforts") to ~ to (to ~ to a new subject; she ~ed to the study of art) 12. (d; tr.) ("to direct") to ~ to, towards (to ~ one's attention to a new problem; ~ your face towards the mirror; you should not ~ your back to the audience) 13. (D; intr.) to ~ towards ("to face") (~ towards me) 14. (N; used with an adjective) ("to cause to become") we ~ed the dog loose; anger ~ed her hair gray 15. (S) to ~ traitor; she ~ ed pale 16. (misc.) to ~ anticlockwise (BE)/counterclockwise (AE); to ~ left/right; to ~ smt. inside out; to ~ smt. upside down; to ~ one's back on smb. ("to reject smb."); to ~ sixteen ("to reach one's sixteenth birthday") (see the Usage Note for **grow**)

turnabout n. ["reversal"] to do a ~

turn away v. (D; intr.) to ~ from

turn back v. (D; intr.) to ~ from; to

turn down v. 1. (D; tr.) to ~ to (please ~ the heater down to a lower setting) 2. (misc.) to ~ the radio down low; to ~ down cold (AE)/flat ("to reject outright")

turn in v. 1. (B) ("to hand over") they ~ed him in to the police; she ~ed the assignment in to the teacher; he refused to ~ himself in to the authorities 2. (D; tr.) ("to trade in") (esp. AE) to ~ for (she ~ed her old car in for a new one) 3. (misc.) to ~ early ("to go to sleep early")

turning n. (esp. BE) to take a ~ (take the first ~ on the right)

turning point n. 1. to be, mark a ~ (in history) 2. to

reach a ~ 3. a ~ for 4. a ~ in 5. at a ~ (we are at a ~ in history)

turn off v. 1. (D; intr.) to ~ from; into (we ~ed off from the main road into a side road) 2. they ~ed off at the last corner

turn on v. (slang) 1. (D; intr.) to ~ to ("to become excited about") (to ~ to Beethoven) 2. (D; tr.) to ~ to ("to excite about") (to ~ smb. on to Beethoven) 3. (R) it really ~s me on to hear Beethoven

turnout n. ["attendance"] ["participation"] 1. to attract a (large) ~ 2. a big, enormous, heavy, large; good; record ~ 3. a light, poor, small ~ 4. (a) voter ~

turn out v. 1. (D; intr.) ("to appear") to ~ for (a large crowd ~ed out for her first concert) 2. (E) ("to prove") the test ~ed out to be positive 3. (L) it ~ed out that they were away on a trip 4. (s) the test ~ed out negative

turnover n. ["movement of goods or personnel"] 1. a brisk, quick, rapid ~ 2. a high; low ~ 3. (a) staff ~ ["filled pastry"] 4. an apple ~

turn over v. (B) ("to hand over") to ~ a thief over to the police

turnpike n. (AE) ["toll expressway"] 1. (to travel) by ~ 2. (to drive) on a ~

turn signal n. (AE) to put on, use a ~ (BE has *indicator*)

turnstile n. 1. to pass through a ~ 2. a subway (AE), underground (BE) ~

turn up v. ("to appear") 1. (D; intr.) to ~ as (she ~ed up as the new principal of the school) 2. (D; intr.) to ~ for (they did not ~ for the ceremony) 3. (D; intr.) to ~ in (she finally ~ed up in London) 4. (D; tr.) to ~ to (please ~ the heater up to a higher setting) 5. (D; intr.) to ~ with (she ~ed up with the missing money) 6. (s) he ~ed up drunk at/for work 7. (misc.) they ~ed up unexpectedly; they ~ed the radio up high ("they turned the radio on very loud")

turpitude n. moral ~

turtle n. 1. a fresh-water; land (AE); mud; sea; snapping ~ 2. (misc.) to turn ~ ("to capsize")

tusk n. an elephant; walrus; wild-boar ~

tussle I n. (colloq.) 1. to get into, have a ~ 2. a ~ about, over; between; with

tussle II v. (colloq.) (D; intr.) to ~ about, over; with

tutelage n. under smb.'s ~

tutor I n. 1. a course (BE); private ~ 2. a ~ to

tutor II v. (D; intr., tr.) to ~ in (to ~ smb. in physics)

tutorial n. ["course"] 1. to give smb. a ~ 2. to have a ~ with 3. a ~ about, on

TV see **television; television set**

TV set see **television set**

twang n. 1. a nasal ~ 2. (misc.) to speak with a ~

tweed n. 1. Harris; herringbone ~ 2. in ~s (dressed in ~s)

tweezers n. a pair of ~

twilight n. 1. at ~ 2. in the ~ (in the ~ of smb.'s career)

twin v. (D; tr.) to ~ with

twine I n. a ball of ~

twine II v. (d; intr., refl.) to ~ around, round (the vines ~d around the tree)

twinkle I n. 1. a ~ in smb.'s eyes 2. with a ~ in one's eyes

twinkle II v. (D; intr.) to ~ with (her eyes ~d with amusement)

twins n. 1. fraternal; identical; Siamese ~ 2. a pair, set of ~

twirl v. (D; intr., tr.) to ~ around (she ~ed the baton around her finger)

twist I n. ["type of dance"] 1. to dance, do the ~ ["twisting or being twisted"] 2. to give smt. a ~ 3. to have a ~ (the rope has a ~ in it) ["unexpected turn"] 4. to take a ~ 5. a bizarre, strange, unusual; ironic ~ (the matter took a bizarre ~) ["interpretation"] 6. to give a (new) ~ (to the news) ["approach, method"] 7. a new ~ (to)

twist II v. 1. (D; tr.) to ~ (a)round (she ~ed the thread around her finger) 2. (D; tr.) to ~ into (to ~ smt. into a certain shape) 3. (D; tr.) to ~ off (he ~ed the cap off the bottle) 4. (D; tr.) to ~ out of (to ~ smt. out of shape) 5. (D; tr.) to ~ to (~ the knob to the right) 6. (misc.) to ~ smb.'s arm ("to coerce smb."); to ~ smb. around one's little finger ("to manipulate smb."); the road ~s and turns

twitch I n. a nervous; uncontrollable ~

twitch II v. 1. to ~ nervously; uncontrollably 2. (D; intr.) to ~ with (~ with pain)

two n. to put ~ and ~ together ("to comprehend the significance of smt.")

two cents' worth n. (slang) (AE) ["opinion"] to get in, put in one's ~

tycoon n. a business ~

type I n. ["metal blocks used in printing"] 1. to set ~ (to set ~ by hand) 2. bold, boldface, boldfaced; elite; italic; pica; regular; roman ~ 3. a font (esp. AE)/fount (BE) of ~ 4. in ~ (to set a book in ~) ["sort, category"] 5. a blood ~ 6. of a certain ~ (a person of that ~ = that ~ of person) 7. (misc.) true to ~

type II v. (D; tr.) ("to typewrite") to ~ for (~ this letter for me)

typecast v. (D; tr.) to ~ as; in (to be typecast in a certain role; that actor has been typecast as a villain)

typewriter n. 1. to operate, use; pound (colloq.) a ~ 2. an electric; electronic; manual; portable ~ 3. a ~ skips 4. on a ~ (I did the letter on my electric ~)

typhoid n. to contract, develop, get; have ~

typhoon n. the ~ hit/struck (several islands)

typhus n. to contract, develop, get; have ~

typical adj. 1. ~ of 2. ~ to + inf. (it was ~ of her to say such things)

typing *n.* to do (the) ~

typist *n.* 1. a shorthand ~ (BE; AE has *stenographer*) 2. a clerk-typist

tyranny *n.* 1. to impose ~ on 2. to overthrow (a) ~ 3. cruel, merciless; ruthless ~ 4. an act of ~ 5. ~ over

tyrant *n.* 1. to overthrow a ~ 2. a cruel, merciless; ruthless ~

tyre (BE) see **tire I**

U

UFO *n.* ["unidentified flying object"] 1. to sight a ~ 2. (misc.) a ~ sighting
ukase *n.* ["edict"] to issue a ~
ulcer *n.* 1. to have an ~ 2. a bleeding; duodenal; gastric, stomach; mouth; peptic; perforated ~
ultimate *n.* ["acme"] 1. the ~ in (the ~ in comfort) 2. (carried) to the ~
ultimatum *n.* 1. to deliver, give, issue, present an ~ 2. to get, receive an ~ 3. to accept an ~ 4. to defy; ignore; reject an ~ 5. to withdraw an ~
umbilical cord *n.* 1. to tie (off) an ~ 2. to cut the ~ (also fig.)
umbrage *n.* ["offense"] 1. to give ~ 2. to take ~ at
umbrella *n.* 1. to open an ~ 2. to fold (up) an ~ 3. a beach ~ 4. under an ~ (also fig.)
unable *adj.* (cannot stand alone) ~ to + inf. (she is ~ to work today; she wants to work, but she is ~ to)
unacceptable *adj.* 1. completely, totally ~ 2. ~ to 3. ~ to + inf. (it's ~ to behave like that)
unaccountable *adj.* ~ to
unaccounted *adj.* ~ for (several items are still ~ for)
unaccustomed *adj.* (cannot stand alone) ~ to (~ to public speaking)
unaffected *adj.* 1. ~ by 2. to remain ~
unafraid *adj.* 1. ~ of 2. ~ to + inf. (she was ~ to dive off the high board)
unaided *adj.* ~ by; in
unamenable *adj.* (formal) ~ to
unanimity *n.* ~ in
unanimous *adj.* ~ in
unanswered *adj.* to go, remain ~ (that question remained ~)
unappreciative *adj.* ~ of
unasked *adj.* ~ for
unattended *adj.* to leave smt. ~
unaware *adj.* (cannot stand alone) 1. blissfully ~ 2. ~ of 3. ~ that + clause (they were ~ that the road had been closed)
unawares *adv.* ["unexpectedly"] to catch, take smb. ~
unbalanced *adj.* mentally ~
unbeatable *adj.* ~ at, in (~ at chess)
unbecoming *adj.* ~ of; to (conduct ~ to an officer = conduct ~ an officer)
unbeknown *adj.* (cannot stand alone) ~ to (~ to us, they had already left)
unbeknownst *adj.* (formal) (cannot stand alone) ~ to
unbelievable *adj.* 1. ~ to 2. ~ that + clause (it's ~ to me that she would commit such a blunder)
unbending *adj.* ~ in (~ in one's manner)
unbiased *adj.* ~ towards

unburden *v.* 1. (B; refl.) he finally ~ed himself to his family 2. (D; refl.) to ~ of (to ~ oneself of a secret)
uncalled *adj.* ~ for (that remark was completely ~ for)
uncanny *adj.* 1. positively ~ 2. ~ to + inf. (it was ~ to see how closely they resemble each other) 3. ~ that + clause (it's ~ that we both arrived on the same day after traveling for three months) 4. (misc.) it's ~ how much the twins resemble each other
uncared *adj.* (cannot stand alone) ~ for (the children were ~ for)
uncensured *adj.* to go ~
uncertain *adj.* 1. ~ about, as to, of (~ about the outcome) 2. (misc.) I am still ~ (as to) whether (or not) they are coming
uncertainty *n.* 1. to express ~ 2. grave, great ~ 3. ~ about, as to (there was no ~ about the matter; there is still some ~ as to whether they are coming)
unchallenged *adj.* to go, pass ~
unchanged *adj.* to remain ~
uncharacteristic *adj.* 1. ~ of 2. ~ to + inf. (it was ~ of her to leave early)
uncharitable *adj.* 1. ~ of 2. ~ to + inf. (it was ~ of her to say that)
unchecked *adj.* to go, remain ~
unclaimed *adj.* to go, remain ~
uncle *n.* (misc.) (colloq.) (AE) to say ~ ("to admit defeat")
unclear *adj.* 1. ~ how; whether; why (it was ~ why she quit her job; it was ~ whether they would attend) 2. ~ to (it was ~ to us how they were able to do it)
uncomfortable *adj.* 1. to feel ~ 2. to make smb. ~ 3. ~ about; with (I felt ~ about discussing this matter in public) 4. ~ to + inf. (it is ~ to wear shoes like that = it is ~ wearing shoes like that)
uncommitted *adj.* ~ to
uncommon *adj.* ~ to + inf. (it is not ~ to find people here who know several languages)
uncommunicative *adj.* ~ about, regarding
uncompromising *adj.* ~ in; on; towards (~ in one's attitude; ~ towards their proposal)
unconcerned *adj.* ~ about, over; with (see Usage Note for **concerned**)
unconscious *adj.* 1. to become; remain ~ 2. ~ of 3. to beat smb. ~
unconsciousness *n.* to lapse into ~
unconstitutional *adj.* ~ to + inf. (it is ~ to censor the press)
unconventional *adj.* 1. ~ in (~ in one's tastes) 2. ~

to + inf. (it is ~ to go to work in shorts)

unconvinced *adj.* 1. to remain ~ 2. ~ of 3. ~ that + clause (they remained ~ that it would work)

uncooperative *adj.* ~ about; in; towards (~ in working out a compromise)

uncorrected *adj.* to go, remain ~

uncritical *adj.* ~ of

unction *n.* (rel.) 1. to give ~ 2. to receive ~ 3. Extreme Unction
USAGE NOTE: The term *the Anointing of the Sick* is now preferred to *Extreme Unction.*

undaunted *adj.* ~ by; in (~ in one's resolve)

undecided *adj.* 1. ~ about, as to (we are ~ as to when we will leave) 2. ~ whether (I am ~ whether I will attend) 3. ~ whether + inf. (he is ~ whether to go) 4. to remain ~

undemonstrative *adj.* ~ towards

undeniable *adj. adj.* ~ that + clause (it's ~ that she is the best candidate)

underbrush *n.* (AE) in the ~ (see **undergrowth**)

undercoating *n.* (AE) (on a car) to apply ~ (BE has *underseal*)

undercover *adv.* ["acting in secret"] 1. to work ~ 2. to go ~

undergraduate *n.* a college, university ~

underground I *adv.* 1. to go ~ (during the war they went ~) 2. buried ~

underground II *n.* ["transportation"] (BE) 1. by ~ (I always travel by ~) 2. on the ~ (we went there on the ~) (AE has *subway*)

undergrowth *n.* 1. to chop away, clear, remove the ~ 2. dense, heavy; thick ~ 3. in the ~

underseal (BE) see **undercoating**

understand *v.* 1. to ~ clearly, fully, perfectly 2. (D; intr., tr.) to ~ about (they do not ~ anything about computers) 3. (d; tr.) to ~ by (what do you ~ by this term?) 4. (H) I understood her to say that she would attend the meeting 5. (K) I cannot ~ his behaving like that 6. (L) I ~ that you will be moving here soon 7. (Q) we do not ~ why she left 8. (misc.) she gave me to ~ that the bill would be paid

understandable *adj.* 1. barely; perfectly ~ 2. ~ that + clause (it was perfectly ~ that they would refuse)

understanding I *adj.* ~ about, of

understanding II *n.* ["agreement"] 1. to arrive at, come to, reach an ~ 2. to have an ~ 3. a clear; complete, full; secret; tacit; verbal; written ~ 4. an ~ about; with (we have a tacit ~ with them about the matter) 5. an ~ to + inf. (we reached an ~ to keep the dispute out of the newspapers) 6. an ~ that + clause (it was my ~ that we would share the expenses) 7. on an ~ (we bought the supplies on the ~ that we would be reimbursed) ["harmony"] ["comprehension"] 8. to bring about, create, develop, promote ~ 9. to display, show ~ (for, of) 10. deeper; mutual ~ 11. ~ between (to promote

deeper ~ between nations; to develop mutual ~)

understatement *n.* 1. to make an ~ 2. to go in for ~ 3. (misc.) a masterpiece of ~; the ~ of the year

understood *adj.* ~ that + clause (it was ~ that everyone would help)

undertake *v.* (E) she undertook to complete the project in six months

undertaking *n.* ["promise"] (esp. BE) 1. to give smb. an ~ 2. an ~ to + inf. (an ~ to complete a project in six months) ["task, enterprise"] 3. a joint; large-scale ~

underwear *n.* long; thermal ~

underworld *n.* in the ~

underwriter *n.* an insurance ~

undeserving *adj.* ~ of

undesirable *adj.* ~ to + inf. (it is ~ to raise taxes at this time)

undeterred *adj.* ~ by (~ by our advice)

undignified *adj.* ~ to + inf. (it was ~ to behave like that)

undiminished *adj.* ~ by; in (~ in stature)

undisturbed *adj.* ~ by (~ by the commotion)

undoing *n.* ["ruin"] to prove to be smb.'s ~ (alcohol proved to be his ~)

undone *adj.* to come ~ (her necklace came ~)

undreamed, undreamt *adj.* ~ of

undressed *adj.* to get ~

uneasiness *n.* 1. to cause ~ 2. to allay smb.'s ~ 3. ~ about

uneasy *adj.* ~ about

unemployed *n.* ["unemployed people"] the hardcore; long-term ~

unemployment *n.* 1. to cause, create ~ 2. to eliminate; reduce ~ 3. falling; high; low; mass; mounting, rising; seasonal; widespread ~

unemployment compensation *n.* (esp. AE) 1. to pay ~ 2. to draw, get, receive ~ 3. to be on ~ 4. to go on ~ 5. to apply for ~

unemployment insurance (esp. AE) see **unemployment compensation** 1, 2, 5

unequal *adj.* 1. ~ in (they are ~ in every way) 2. ~ to (she felt ~ to the task)

unequaled, unequalled *adj.* ~ at, in; by

unerring *adj.* (usu. does not stand alone) ~ in (~ in her judgment)

unessential *adj.* ~ for; to

unethical *adj.* ~ to + inf. (it was ~ of them to do that)

unexcelled *adj.* ~ in

unfair *adj.* 1. grossly, very ~ 2. ~ to (~ to certain groups) 3. ~ to + inf. (it was ~ to take advantage of the situation) 4. ~ that + clause (it's ~ that she has to work so hard)

unfaithful *adj.* ~ in; to

unfaithfulness *n.* ~ in; to

unfaltering *adj.* ~ in (they were ~ in their efforts to reduce crime)

unfamiliar *adj.* ~ to; with (the area was ~ to me; I was ~ with the situation)

unfamiliarity *n.* ~ with (my ~ with the area)

unfashionable *adj.* ~ to + inf. (it is ~ to wear boots to a formal reception)

unfasten *v.* 1. (D; tr.) to ~ from 2. (misc.) to come ~ed

unfavorable, unfavourable *adj.* ~ for, to

unfed *adj.* to go ~

unfeeling *adj.* 1. ~ towards 2. ~ to + inf. (it was ~ of them to turn down her request)

unfit *adj.* 1. mentally, psychologically; physically ~ 2. ~ for (~ for military service) 3. ~ to + inf. (~ to serve)

unfortunate *adj.* 1. ~ for 2. ~ in 3. ~ that + clause (it's ~ that they cannot attend)

unfriendly *adj.* 1. ~ of (that was ~ of them) 2. ~ to, towards 3. ~ to + inf. (it was ~ of him to refuse)

ungrateful *adj.* ~ for; to (he was ~ to us for our help)

unhappy *adj.* 1. bitterly, very ~ 2. ~ about, at, over; in; with (she was ~ about/at/over the news; he was ~ in his work; they were ~ with the results) 3. ~ to + inf. (she was ~ to learn the news) 4. ~ that + clause (we are ~ that you cannot visit us) 5. (misc.) she will be ~ working here

unharmed *adj.* 1. to go, remain ~ 2. ~ by 3. (misc.) to escape ~

unhealthy *adj.* 1. ~ for (smoking is ~ for you) 2. ~ to + inf. (it's ~ to smoke)

unheard-of *adj.* ~ to + inf. (it's ~ to come to a reception without an invitation)

unheeded *adj.* 1. to go ~ (her advice went ~) 2. ~ by

unheedful *adj.* (cannot stand alone) ~ of (~ of threats)

unification *n.* to achieve, bring about (the) ~ (to achieve the ~ of a country)

uniform I *adj.* ~ in; with

uniform II *n.* 1. to don, put on a ~ 2. to wear a ~ 3. to take off a ~ 4. a dress, full-dress; fatigue; military; naval; nurse's; parade; police; regulation; school ~ 5. in ~; out of ~ (he was out of ~ when he was picked up by the military police)

uniformity *n.* ~ in

unify *v.* 1. (D; tr.) to ~ into (they were ~fied into one nation) 2. (D; tr.) to ~ with

unimportant *adj.* ~ for; to

uninformed *adj.* ~ about, of

uninterested *adj.* ~ in (~ in politics)

uninvited *adj.* to appear, show up, turn up ~

union *n.* 1. to form a ~ 2. to break up, dissolve a ~ 3. a company; craft; credit; currency, monetary; customs; industrial; labor (AE), trade (BE); postal; student ~ 4. a ~ between 5. (misc.) to recognize a labor/trade ~

union shop *n.* to introduce a ~

unique *adj.* 1. ~ in 2. ~ to (~ to a certain area)

unison *n.* in ~ (with)

unit *n.* ["single constituent of a whole"] 1. a basic, primary ~ ["military formation"] 2. to activate; form a ~ 3. to commit a ~ (to combat) 4. to deactivate; disband a ~ 5. an advance, advanced; airborne; armored; combat; crack, elite; mechanized, motorized; naval; tactical ~ (advance armored ~s have reached the river) ["standard"] 6. a message ~ (used for telephone calls) 7. a currency; monetary ~ (the pound is the monetary ~ of Great Britain) ["single residence"] 8. a rental ~ ["computer terminal"] 9. a Visual Display Unit = VDU (CE; AE also has *Video Display Terminal* = VDT)

unite *v.* 1. (D; intr., tr.) to ~ against (to ~ against aggression; to ~ one's allies against the common foe) 2. (D; intr.) to ~ for (we must ~ for the common good; the nation was ~d for the struggle against terrorism) 3. (D; intr., tr.) to ~ in (we must ~ in our struggle against terrorism; to ~ a nation in the fight against inflation) 4. (D; intr., tr.) to ~ into (we had to ~ the competing factions into a cohesive whole) 5. (D; intr.) to ~ with (our countries must ~ with each other against the common enemy)

united *adj.* ~ in

United States *n.* the contiguous ~ (without Alaska and Hawaii)

unity *n.* 1. to achieve, bring about ~ 2. to destroy, shatter ~ 3. national; party ~ (to achieve national ~) 4. in ~ (in ~ there is strength)

universe *n.* the known ~

university *n.* 1. to establish, found a ~ 2. to go to a ~/to go to ~ (BE) (she goes to a good ~) 3. a free, open; people's ~ 4. an Ivy-League (US); redbrick (GB); state (US) ~ 5. at; in a ~ (to teach at a ~; there is a spirit of cooperation at/in our ~; BE: what did you read at ~? = AE: what did you major in at college?)

USAGE NOTE: In BE, one goes *to university*; in AE, *to a university* or *to college*. CE has *to go to a good university*. See the Usage Notes for **college, school.**

unjust *adj.* 1. ~ of 2. ~ to 3. ~ to + inf. (it was ~ of him to accuse you without proof) 4. ~ that + clause (it's ~ that our side of the story was never heard)

unjustified *adj.* 1. completely, totally ~ 2. ~ in (she was ~ in complaining)

unkind *adj.* 1. ~ of 2. ~ to 3. ~ to + inf. (it was ~ of him to say that)

unknown *adj.* ~ to (the facts were ~ to us)

unlawful *adj.* ~ to + inf. (it's ~ to drive without a license)

unleash *v.* (D; tr.) to ~ against, on (to ~ a new arms race on the world)

unlike *prep.* ~ to + inf. (it's ~ her to be late)

unlikely *adj.* 1. highly, very ~ 2. ~ to + inf. (they are ~ to accept our invitation) 3. ~ that + clause (it's ~

that she will attend)

unload v. 1. (D; tr.) to ~ from (to ~ cargo from a ship) 2. (D; tr.) (fig.) to ~ on (they were ~ing defective merchandise on unsuspecting customers)

unlucky adj. 1. ~ at, in; for; with (~ at cards; ~ in love; ~ for some people; they were ~ with their new car) 2. ~ to + inf. (some people feel that it is ~ to walk under a ladder) 3. ~ that + clause (it was ~ that we got there late)

unmarked adj. ~ by

unmarred adj. ~ by (the ceremony was ~ by any untoward incidents)

unmatched adj. 1. ~ as (she was ~ as a dancer) 2. ~ by; for, in

unmerciful adj. ~ to, towards

unmindful adj. (cannot stand alone) ~ of (~ of danger)

unmoved adj. ~ by (they were left ~ by her tears)

unnamed adj. to remain ~

unnatural adj. 1. ~ to + inf. (it's ~ of parents to reject their own children) 2. ~ that + clause (it's ~ that members of the same family should fight so much)

unnecessary adj. 1. ~ for 2. ~ to + inf. (it's ~ for us to wait) 3. ~ that + clause (it's ~ that you should get involved)

unnoticed adj. to go, pass ~ (the incident went/ passed ~)

unobserved adj. to go, pass ~

unopposed adj. ~ to

unorthodox adj. ~ to + inf. (it is ~ to bypass the channels of command in the army)

unparalleled adj. ~ in (~ in ferocity)

unperturbed adj. ~ by (she was ~ by the loud noise)

unpleasant adj. 1. ~ to (he is ~ to everyone) 2. ~ to + inf. (it's ~ to talk to him = it's ~ talking to him = he's ~ to talk to = he's an ~ person to talk to)

unprepared adj. 1. ~ for 2. ~ to + inf. (I am unprepared to take on such a responsibility)

unprofessional adj. ~ to + inf. (it was ~ of her not to investigate the matter)

unpunished adj. 1. to go, remain ~ (the criminals went ~) 2. ~ for

unqualified adj. 1. clearly; grossly ~ 2. ~ for 3. ~ to + inf. (she is ~ to work as a teacher)

unrealistic adj. 1. ~ about 2. ~ to + inf. (it is ~ to hope for an improvement so soon)

unreasonable adj. 1. ~ about (they were very ~ about the price) 2. ~ of (that was ~ of you) 3. ~ to + inf. (it is ~ to demand that employees work without a break)

unrecognized adj. 1. to go, pass, remain ~ 2. ~ by

unreported adj. to go, remain ~ (the story went ~)

unresponsive adj. ~ to

unrest n. 1. to foment, stir up ~ 2. to crush, quell ~

3. civil; industrial; labor; political; social ~ 4. violent ~ 5. (misc.) a wave of ~

unrivaled, unrivalled adj. 1. ~ as 2. ~ in

unsafe adj. 1. ~ for (it is ~ for children) 2. ~ to + inf. (it's ~ to drive without putting on seat belts)

unsaid adj. to leave smt. ~

unsanctioned adj. ~ by (~ by custom)

unsatisfactory adj. 1. highly, very ~ 2. ~ for (her qualifications are ~ for our needs) 3. ~ in (they were ~ in their job performance) 4. ~ to (~ to all concerned)

unscathed adj. 1. ~ by 2. to emerge ~ 3. to go ~

unschooled adj. ~ in

unscrupulous adj. 1. ~ in (~ in his business dealings) 2. ~ to + inf. (it was ~ of their lawyer to withhold evidence)

unseemly adj. (formal) ~ to + inf. (it was ~ of them to show up at the reception without an invitation)

unseen adj. 1. to remain ~ 2. (misc.) to buy smt. sight ~

unselfish adj. ~ to + inf. (it was ~ of her to make the offer)

unsettle v. (R) it ~d me to see them quarrel

unsettling adj. 1. profoundly, very ~ 2. ~ to + inf. (it was ~ to hear them quarrel)

unshakable adj. ~ in (~ in one's faith)

unshaken adj. ~ in (~ in one's beliefs)

unshaven adj. to go ~ (he went ~ for a week)

unsightly adj. ["not pleasing to the sight"] it was ~ to behold

unskilled adj. ~ at, in

unsound adj. structurally ~

unsparing adj. ~ in, of (~ in one's criticism; ~ of praise)

unspoiled, unspoilt adj. ~ by (~ by success)

unstinting adj. (cannot stand alone) ~ in (~ in one's praise)

unstuck adj. ["ruined"] (colloq.) to come ~ (the whole scheme came ~)

unsuccessful adj. ~ at, in; with

unsuitable adj. 1. highly, very ~ 2. ~ for; to

unsuited adj. ~ for; to

unsure adj. 1. ~ about 2. ~ of

unsurpassed adj. 1. ~ at, in (~ at learning languages) 2. ~ by (~ by any competitor)

unsuspicious adj. ~ of

unswerving adj. ~ in (~ in one's determination to stamp out corruption)

unsympathetic adj. ~ to

untainted adj. ~ by, with (~ by scandal)

untarnished adj. ~ by

unthanked adj. to go ~

unthinkable adj. 1. ~ to + inf. (it would be ~ to build a house so close to the river) 2. ~ that + clause (it is ~ that they would even make such an offer)

untiring adj. (usu. does not stand alone) ~ in (~ in

one's efforts)

untold *adj.* to remain ~ (the story remained ~ for years)

untouched *adj.* ~ by

untreated *adj.* to go, remain; leave ~ (the disease went ~; the disease was left ~)

untroubled *adj.* ~ by

untrue *adj.* ~ to

untruth *n.* 1. to tell an ~ 2. a blatant, deliberate, transparent ~

untruthful *adj.* 1. ~ about, in 2. ~ to + inf. (it would be ~ to deny it)

untutored *adj.* ~ in

untypical *adj.* 1. ~ of 2. ~ to + inf. (it was altogether ~ of them to come without calling first)

unusable *adj.* ~ for

unused *adj.* ["unaccustomed"] (cannot stand alone) ~ to (they are ~ to hard work)

unusual *adj.* 1. ~ for 2. ~ to + inf. (it is ~ to see snow in this region; it's ~ for two world records to be set in/on one day) 3. ~ that + clause (it's ~ that two world records should be set in/on one day)

unversed *adj.* (cannot stand alone) ~ in (~ in the ways of big business)

unwarranted *adj.* ~ by

unwavering *adj.* ~ in (~ in one's support)

unwilling *adj.* ~ to + inf. (she is ~ to participate)

unwillingness *n.* an ~ to + inf. (everyone deplored their ~ to compromise)

unwise *adj.* 1. ~ of 2. ~ to + inf. (it would be ~ to walk through the park at midnight)

unworthy *adj.* ~ of (~ of your help; such behavior is ~ of you)

unyielding *adj.* ~ in (~ in one's demands)

up I *adj.* (cannot stand alone) ["abreast"] 1. ~ on (are you ~ on the news?) ["dependent"] 2. ~ to (the decision is ~ to you; it's ~ to you to decide; it's ~ to you whether we go) ["misc."] 3. inflation is ~ by ten percent; the dollar was ~ against the yen; she is ~ for reelection; that topic was ~ for discussion; my car is ~ for sale

up II *v.* 1. (D; tr.) ("to increase") to ~ by (they ~ped the price by ten percent) 2. (misc.) (colloq.) they just ~ped and left

upbraid *v.* (D; tr.) to ~ for (they ~ed him for his sloppy work)

upbringing *n.* 1. a bad; good; strict ~ 2. smb.'s family; religious ~ 3. (misc.) she had a good ~

update I *n.* (colloq.) ["bringing up-to-date"] 1. to give an ~ on (I'll give you an ~ on the situation) 2. an ~ on (here is an ~ on the situation)

update II *v.* (colloq.) (D; tr.) to ~ on (could you ~ me on the situation?)

up front *adv.* (colloq.) ~ with ("candid with")

upgrade *v.* (D; tr.) to ~ to (our legation was ~d to an embassy)

upheaval *n.* 1. a big, great; dramatic; violent ~ 2. a political; social ~

upholstery *n.* leather; plastic; vinyl ~

upkeep *n.* ["cost of maintenance"] the ~ of, on (esp. AE) (the ~ on this machinery is very costly)

upper hand *n.* ["control"] 1. to gain, get; have the ~ 2. to lose the ~ 3. the ~ in; over (we gained the ~ over them in that contest)

upright *adv.* to sit bolt ~

uprising *n.* 1. to foment, incite, spark (esp. AE), spark off (BE) an ~ 2. to crush, put down, quell an ~ 3. an armed; peasant; popular ~ 4. an ~ against

uproar *n.* 1. to cause, create an ~ 2. an ~ over 3. in an ~

uproot *v.* (D; tr.) to ~ from (they were ~ed from their homes)

upset I *adj.* 1. to be, feel; get ~ about, over 2. ~ with (she was ~ with me about my expenses) 3. ~ to + inf. (she was ~ to learn of their attitude) 4. ~ that + clause (we were ~ that they could not attend)

upset II *n.* ["unexpected victory"] 1. (sports) to score an ~ over ["malaise"] 2. a stomach ~

upset III *v.* 1. (R) it upset me to learn of their attitude 2. (misc.) it ~s me when they behave like that

upsetting *adj.* 1. ~ to (recent events have been very ~ to us) 2. ~ to + inf. (it was ~ to learn of their attitude)

upside down *adv.* to turn smt. ~

upstanding *adj.* be ~ ("stand up") (esp. BE) (be ~ for the judge; be ~ for a toast)

upstairs *adv.* to come; go; run; walk ~

upsurge *n.* an ~ in (there was an ~ in violence)

uptake *n.* ["comprehension"] (colloq.) (quick) on the ~

uptight *adj.* (colloq.) 1. ~ about 2. (misc.) just don't get all ~ about it

up-to-date *adj., adv.* ~ on (to bring smb. ~ on smt.; to be ~ on the issue)

upturn *n.* 1. a modest, slight ~ 2. a sharp ~ 3. an ~ in (there was a sharp ~ in the economy) 4. (misc.) the economy took a slight ~

upwards *adv.* ~ of (~ of an hour) ("somewhat more than an hour")

uranium *n.* enriched ~

urchin *n.* a street ~

urge I *n.* 1. to feel; get; have an ~ 2. to satisfy an ~ 3. to control; resist; stifle an ~ 4. an irrepressible, irresistible, uncontrollable; natural; sudden ~ 5. an ~ to + inf. (she felt an ~ to respond)

urge II *v.* 1. to ~ forcefully, strongly 2. (H) she ~d me to accept the compromise 3. (L; subj.) we ~d that the bill be/should be passed

urgency *n.* 1. great, utmost ~ 2. ~ about, in (there is no ~ about this matter) 3. with ~ (she spoke with great ~) 4. (misc.) a matter of great ~; a sense of ~

urgent *adj.* 1. ~ in (she was ~ in her demands) 2. ~ that + clause; subj. (it is ~ that they all be/should be present)

urge on *v.* 1. (D; tr.) to ~ to (they ~d me on to greater efforts) 2. (H) she ~d me on to try harder

urging *n.* at smb.'s ~ (at our ~ they accepted the invitation)

urn *n.* a burial; coffee ~

usable, useable *adj.* ~ for

usage *n.* 1. common; constant; correct; incorrect ~ 2. in ~ (this word is not in common ~)

use I /ju:s/ *n.* 1. to make ~ of 2. to put smt. to (good) ~ 3. to find, have a ~ for 4. to have; lose; regain the ~ of (she lost the ~ of one arm) 5. to deny; grant (the) ~ of (the visitors were denied ~ of the library) 6. constant; daily; emergency; official; practical ~ 7. exclusive; extensive; full; universal; wide ~ (they made extensive ~ of computers) 8. external; internal ~ 9. (legal) fair ~ 10. ~ for (do you have any ~ for this old paper?) 11. ~ in (is there any ~ in trying again?) 12. ~ of (what's the ~ of worrying?) 13. for ~ (for official ~ only) 14. in ~ (the copying machine is in ~) 15. of ~ to (it was of no earthly ~ to us; can I be of any ~ to you?) 16. (misc.) she has no ~ for them ("she dislikes them"); to come into ~; to go out of ~ USAGE NOTE: The following constructions are variants; the constructions with no prepositions are colloquial—*is there any use in trying again?—is there any use trying again? what's the use of worrying?—(AE) what's the use worrying?*

use II /ju:z/ *v.* 1. to ~ widely 2. (D; tr.) to ~ as (she ~d the candlestick as a paperweight) 3. (D; tr.) to ~ for (let's ~ paper plates for the picnic) 4. (E; in positive sentences and negative sentences with *never* this verb is used only in the past tense to denote a former practice or state; in interrogative sentences the infinitive of this verb occurs with *didn't, did not*) she ~d to work there; there ~d to be an open field here; she never ~d to work there; didn't he ~ to work here? USAGE NOTE: In negative sentences with *didn't*,

did not, this verb occurs with the infinitive and, colloquially, with the past tense—she didn't use/ used to work there. In old-fashioned BE, constructions such as the following may occur—used she (not) to work there? she used not to work there.

used I /ju:st/ *adj.* (cannot stand alone) ["accustomed"] to be; get ~ to (she is ~ to working hard; to get ~ to hard work)

used II /ju:zd/ *adj.* ["employed"] 1. ~ for (this machine is ~ for making copies) 2. ~ to + inf. (this machine is ~ to make copies)

useful *adj.* 1. highly, very ~ 2. ~ for, to (a combinatory dictionary is ~ for/to students) 3. ~ for, in (computers are ~ in compiling statistics) 4. ~ to + inf. (it's ~ to know several foreign languages when you are traveling abroad = it's ~ knowing several foreign languages when you are traveling abroad)

usefulness *n.* ~ for; to

useless *adj.* 1. absolutely ~ 2. ~ at 3. ~ to + inf. (it's ~ to try to convince her = it's ~ trying to convince her)

user *n.* a casual ~ (of drugs)

usher *v.* 1. (d; tr.) to ~ into (they ~ed the guests into a large waiting room) 2. (d; tr.) to ~ out of 3. (d; tr.) to ~ to (we were ~ed to our seats)

usual *adj.* 1. ~ for 2. ~ to + inf. (it's ~ to ask/ask for permission before visiting a class)

usury *n.* 1. to engage in, practice ~ 2. to condemn; outlaw ~

utensils *n.* cooking, kitchen; household ~

utility *n.* ["company providing a public service"] a public ~

utilize *v.* 1. to ~ fully 2. (D; tr.) to ~ for

utmost *n.* ["maximum effort"] to do one's ~ (we did our ~ to help)

utter *v.* (B) she ~ed a few words to them

utterance *n.* 1. (formal) to give ~ to 2. a prophetic; public ~

U-turn *n.* to do, make a ~

363

varied

V

vacancy *n.* 1. to create a ~ 2. to have a ~ 3. to fill a ~ 4. a ~ for (we have a ~ for a clerk) 5. (misc.) no ~ (the sign reads *no vacancy/vacancies*)

vacation *n.* ["period of rest"] (AE; CE has *holiday*) 1. to spend; take a ~ 2. to be on; go on ~ 3. an extended, long; paid; short ~ 4. a spring; summer; winter ~ 5. a ~ from 6. during a ~; on ~ (she was away on ~) ["period during which a college or university is closed"] 7. (BE) the long ~ USAGE NOTE: Soldiers and sailors go on *leave*; civilians go on *holiday* (BE) or on *vacation* (AE). British students go on *holiday* during the long *vacation/vac*.

vaccinate *v.* (D; tr.) to ~ against (to ~ smb. against a disease)

vaccination *n.* 1. to carry out, do a (mass) ~ (of the population) 2. (a) compulsory; mass ~ 3. a ~ against (to carry out a mass ~ against tuberculosis)

vaccine *n.* 1. to administer, give a ~ 2. BCG; influenza; polio; Sabin; Salk; smallpox; tetanus; yellow-fever ~

vacillate *v.* (D; intr.) to ~ between; in

vacuum *n.* 1. to create, leave, produce a ~ 2. to break; fill a ~ 3. a partial ~ 4. a power ~ 5. in a ~ (nothing can live in a ~)

vague *adj.* ~ about (she was ~ about her plans)

vain *adj.* 1. ~ about (~ about one's appearance) 2. ~ to + inf. (it is ~ to protest) 3. (misc.) in ~ ("without success") (to work in ~); to take the Lord's name in ~ ("to treat the Lord's name in a disrespectful manner")

valedictory *n.* ["farewell speech"] to deliver, give a ~

valid *adj.* 1. ~ for (~ for one year) 2. ~ to + inf. (is it ~ to say that Olympic athletes are amateurs?)

valise *n.* to pack; unpack a ~

valley *n.* 1. a ~ between (high mountains) 2. in a ~ (they live down in the ~)

valor, valour *n.* 1. to demonstrate, display, show ~ 2. uncommon ~ 3. for ~ (to get a medal for ~) 4. (misc.) (discretion is the better part of ~

valuable *adj.* 1. ~ for; to 2. ~ to + inf. (it's ~ to know languages if you work in an export firm)

valuables *n.* to check (esp. AE); deposit one's ~

value I *n.* ["worth"] ["monetary, numerical worth"] 1. to attach ~ to 2. to place, put, set a ~ on 3. to acquire, have ~ 4. to have (a) ~ (of) (their holdings have little ~) 5. (a) great, high; inestimable ~ 6. (a) little; low ~ 7. a book; cash; face; market; nominal; trade-in ~ (your car has a cash ~ of five thousand dollars) 8. (an) intrinsic; material; nuisance; sentimental; strategic; symbolic, token ~ 9. (math.) an absolute; numerical; relative ~ 10.

a fair ~ (the commission set a fair ~ of five million dollars on the property) 11. (economics) surplus ~ 12. (economics) present ~ 13. a (market) ~ falls, goes down; goes up, rises 14. at a certain ~ (at face ~) 15. of ~ (to) (a discovery of great ~) 16. (misc.) they took her story at face ~; to get ~ for your money; the street ~ (as of illegal drugs) ["principles, qualities"] 17. to cherish; foster ~s 18. basic; core; enduring; lasting; traditional ~s (a return to traditional ~s) 19. esthetic; family; human; moral; religious, spiritual; social ~s 20. middle-class; Victorian ~s

value II *v.* 1. to ~ greatly, highly, very much 2. (d; tr.) to ~ as (to ~ smb. as a friend) 3. (d; tr.) to ~ at (to ~ a painting at five thousand pounds) 4. (D; tr.) to ~ for (to ~ smt. for sentimental reasons)

valve *n.* ["device that regulates flow"] 1. to grind ~s 2. a ball; butterfly; check; exhaust; gate; globe; needle; safety; shunt; suction ~ ["membranous fold that permits body fluids to flow in one direction"] (anat.) 3. a heart ~ (the patient has a defective heart ~)

van I *n.* ["road vehicle"] 1. to drive a ~ 2. (BE) a breakdown ~ (BE also has *breakdown lorry, breakdown truck*; AE has *tow truck*) 3. (BE) a delivery ~ (AE has *delivery truck, panel truck*) 4. a moving (AE), removal (BE) ~ ["rail vehicle"] 5. a guard's ~ (BE; AE has *caboose*) 6. a luggage ~ (BE; AE has *baggage car*) 7. a minivan (AE)

van II *n.* ["vanguard"] in the ~

vandalism *n.* 1. to commit ~ 2. an act of ~

vane *n.* a weather ~

vanguard *n.* in the ~ (of)

vanish *v.* 1. to ~ completely 2. (D; intr.) to ~ from (to ~ from sight) 3. (D; intr.) to ~ into (to ~ into thin air)

vanity *n.* 1. to flatter, tickle smb.'s ~ 2. sheer ~

vantage point *n.* from a certain ~

vapor, vapour *n.* 1. to emit (a) ~ 2. water ~ 3. (a) ~ rises

vapor trail, vapour trail *n.* to leave a ~ (high flying aircraft leave ~s)

variable *n.* (math.) a dependent; independent; random ~

variance *n.* ["permission to bypass a regulation"] (legal) (US) 1. to grant a ~ 2. to apply for a ~ 3. a zoning ~ ["disagreement"] 4. at ~ with (a theory at ~ with the facts)

variation *n.* ["deviation, change"] 1. (a) slight; wide ~ 2. ~ in ["modified repetition of a theme"] 3. a ~ on a theme (the government's new position is merely a ~ on the same old theme)

varied *adj.* highly ~

variety *n.* 1. to add, lend ~ to 2. (a) great; wide ~ 3. a limited ~ 4. in a ~ of (in a ~ of roles)

varnish *n.* 1. to apply ~ 2. nail ~ (BE; CE has *nail polish*)

varsity *n.* ["college or secondary-school team"] (AE) 1. to make ("be selected to join") the ~ 2. the junior ~ 3. on the ~ (we play on the ~)

vary *v.* 1. to ~ considerably, greatly; slightly 2. (D; intr.) to ~ between 3. (D; intr.) to ~ from; to (prices ~ from ten to fifteen dollars) 4. (d; intr.) to ~ in (to ~ in size; they ~ in their opinions)

VAT *n.* (BE) to attract ~ at seventeen percent

vault I *n.* 1. a bank ~ 2. a family ~ (for burial) 3. (misc.) to keep one's valuables in a ~

vault II *v.* 1. (d; intr.) to ~ into (to ~ into prominence) 2. (d; intr.) to ~ over (he ~ed over the bar)

VCR *n.* to program a ~

veal *n.* 1. to roast ~ 2. roast ~

veer *v.* 1. (D; intr.) to ~ from; to (to ~ from one's course; to ~ to the right) 2. (P; intr.) to ~ across the field

veer away *v.* (D; intr.) to ~ from

vegetables *n.* 1. to grow ~ 2. canned/tinned (BE); fresh; frozen ~ 3. green; leafy; root ~ 4. garden ~ 5. cooked; raw; steamed; stir-fried ~

vegetation *n.* dense, lush, rank; sparse; subtropical; tropical ~

vehicle *n.* ["conveyance"] 1. to drive, operate a ~ 2. an all-purpose; amphibious; armored; half-tracked; motor; passenger; recreational (esp. AE); re-entry; space ~ 3. a hired (BE), rented, self-drive (BE) ~ ["means"] 4. a ~ for (a ~ for spreading propaganda)

veil *n.* 1. to draw a ~ (over) 2. to lift, raise a ~ 3. a bridal ~ 4. (misc.) under a ~ of mystery; to take the ~ ("to become a nun")

veiled *adj.* 1. thinly ~ (a thinly ~ reference) 2. (misc.) ~ in secrecy

vein *n.* ["blood vessel"] 1. to open a ~ 2. the jugular ~ 3. varicose ~s ["mood"] ["manner"] 4. a happy; humorous; light; lighter; merry ~ 5. a gloomy; melancholy; serious ~ 6. a different; similar ~ 7. in a certain ~ (let's continue our discussion in a lighter ~) 8. (misc.) a rich ~ of humor runs through her works

velocity *n.* 1. to develop; gain; lose ~ 2. high; low ~ 3. muzzle ~ 4. at a certain ~ (at the ~ of sound)

velvet *n.* (misc.) as smooth as ~

vendetta *n.* 1. to conduct, lead, wage a ~ 2. a personal ~ 3. a ~ against

vending machine *n.* to use a ~

vendor *n.* a fruit; street ~

veneer *n.* ["superficial gloss"] 1. a polished; superficial, thin ~ 2. beneath a ~ of

venerate *v.* 1. (D; tr.) to ~ as (she is now ~d as an elder stateswoman) 2. (D; tr.) to ~ for

veneration *n.* 1. deep, profound ~ 2. ~ for 3. to hold

smb. in ~

venetian blinds *n.* 1. to close, shut; lower; open; raise ~ 2. to install ~

vengeance *n.* 1. to exact, take, wreak ~ on, upon 2. to vow ~ 3. to seek ~ for 4. ~ for (to take ~ on smb. for smt.) 5. (misc.) with a ~ ("to an extreme degree") (it started snowing with a ~)

venom *n.* ["poison"] 1. to neutralize ~ 2. snake ~ ["malice"] 3. to spew, spout ~ 4. with ~

vent I *n.* ["opening"] 1. an air ~ ["outlet"] 2. to give ~ to (he gave ~ to his pent-up feelings)

vent II *v.* (d; tr.) to ~ on (to ~ one's fury on smt.)

ventriloquism *n.* to practice ~

venture I *n.* 1. to undertake a ~ 2. a business, commercial; collaborative, cooperative, joint ~ 3. (misc.) to join smb. in a ~

venture II *v.* (formal) 1. (E) I ~ to suggest that your whole idea is unworkable 2. (L; to) (rare) ("to express") she ~d (to us) that our idea might be flawed 3. (P; intr.) to ~ into the unknown; to ~ out of doors

venue *n.* ["site of a trial"] (AE) 1. a change of ~ (her lawyer requested a change of ~) ["site"] (BE) 2. a ~ for (the best ~ for a pop concert)

veracity *n.* (formal) to doubt, question smb.'s ~

veranda see **porch** 1, 3

verb *n.* 1. to conjugate, inflect; passivize a ~ 2. an auxiliary, helping; compound; copular (esp. BE), copulative, linking; defective; irregular; main; modal; phrasal; prepositional; regular; strong; weak ~ 3. an active; passive ~ 4. an intransitive; reflexive; transitive ~ 5. an imperfective; perfective ~ 6. ~s agree (with); ~s govern, take a case (a ~ agrees with its/the subject in number) 7. a ~ has aspect; mood; tense; voice 8. ~s have complements; objects

verdict *n.* 1. to arrive at, reach a ~ 2. to announce; bring in, deliver, hand down (AE), render, return a ~ 3. to sustain ("uphold") a ~ (the higher court sustained the ~) 4. to overturn, quash, set aside a ~ 5. to appeal (AE), appeal against a ~ 6. a fair, just; unfair, unjust ~ 7. an adverse, unfavorable; directed; favorable; sealed; unanimous ~ 8. a ~ comes down 9. a ~ of guilty; or: a guilty ~; a ~ of not guilty; a ~ for the defendant; a ~ for the plaintiff (the jury brought in a ~ of not guilty) 10. a ~ that + clause (they appealed the court's ~ that fraud had been committed) 11. (misc.) to defy/ignore a ~

verge I *n.* ["brink"] 1. on the ~ of (he was on the ~ of a nervous breakdown) 2. (misc.) driven to the ~ of bankruptcy

verge II *v.* (d; intr.) to ~ on, upon (her actions ~d on the ridiculous)

verification *n.* official; written ~

verify *v.* 1. (L) the police ~fied that she had an airtight alibi 2. (Q) they could not ~ where the money had been deposited

vermin *n.* 1. to exterminate ~ 2. (misc.) infested with ~

vernacular *n.* in the ~ (to express oneself in the ~)

versatile *adj.* ~ at, in

versatility *n.* 1. to demonstrate, display, show ~ 2. ~ at, in; with

verse *n.* 1. to compose, write; memorize; recite ~(s) 2. to scan ~ 3. blank; free; heroic; macaronic; rhymed, rhyming; unrhymed ~ 4. in ~ 5. (misc.) to cite/give/quote chapter and ~ ("to indicate one's sources very precisely")

versed *adj.* (cannot stand alone) (well) ~ in

version *n.* 1. to give one's ~ (of a story) 2. to corroborate smb.'s ~ (of an event) 3. an abridged, condensed; expurgated; watered down ~ 4. an unabridged, uncut; unexpurgated ~ (an uncut ~ of a film) 5. an accepted, authorized, official ~ 6. a conflicting; different, differing ~ (the police heard conflicting ~s of the incident) 7. an unauthorized, unofficial ~ 8. a censored; uncensored (an uncensored ~ of the book was smuggled into the country) 9. an oral; written ~ 10. a film, movie (AE); stage ~ (of a novel)

vertebra *n.* a cervical; lumbar; sacral; thoracic ~

vessel *n.* ["tube in the body"] 1. a blood ~ ["ship, boat"] 2. to charter a ~ 3. to launch a ~ 4. a cargo; escort; fishing; naval; oceangoing, seagoing ~

vest I *n.* a bulletproof; life (AE) (CE has *life jacket*); string (BE) ~

USAGE NOTE: In BE, the basic meaning of *vest* is "undershirt"; in AE, it is "waistcoat".

vest II *v.* (formal) 1. (d; tr.) to ~ in (to ~ power in smb.) 2. (d; tr.) to ~ with (to ~ smb. with power)

vested *adj.* (cannot stand alone) 1. ~ in (the power to impose taxes is ~ in Congress; by the power ~ in me) 2. ~ with (Congress is ~ with the power to impose taxes)

vestiges *n.* ["traces"] 1. to lose all (remaining) ~ of 2. the last ~ of

veteran *n.* a disabled (AE); war ~ (to retrain disabled ~s)

USAGE NOTE: The basic BE meaning of *veteran* is "smb. with long experience". The basic AE meaning of *veteran* is "person who has served in the armed forces". However, AE also has the meaning of "smb. with long experience". The basic AE meaning is now coming into BE, and such phrases as *war veteran*, *Falklands veteran*, and *veteran of WWII* are CE.

veto *n.* 1. to exercise, impose, use a ~ 2. to sustain a ~ 3. to override a ~ (Congress overrode the President's ~) 4. (US) a line-item; pocket; presidential ~ 5. (AE) (legal) a heckler's ~ 6. a ~ of, over 7. (misc.) European Union members have the power of ~ in certain cases

vex *v.* (R) it ~es me to read such things in the

newspapers; it ~es me that they are always late

vexation *n.* in ~ (she shouted in ~)

vexed *adj.* (formal) 1. deeply ~ 2. ~ about, at, with (we were ~ at the mix-up) 3. ~ to + inf. (they were ~ to learn of the delay) 4. ~ that + clause (they were ~ that things had been delayed)

vexing *adj.* 1. ~ to + inf. (it is ~ to read such things in the newspapers) 2. ~ that + clause (it is ~ that such things are published) 3. (misc.) it is ~ how such lies can be printed

viability *n.* commercial, financial ~

vibes *n.* (slang) 1. to get (certain) ~ (from) 2. bad; good ~ (to get good ~ from smb.)

vibration *n.* 1. to feel a ~ 2. a slight; strong; weak ~

vice I *n.* 1. to stamp out ~ 2. legalized ~

vice II (BE) see **vise**

vicinity *n.* 1. the close, immediate ~ 2. in the ~ (in the immediate ~ of the school)

vicious *adj.* ~ to + inf. (it was ~ of him to make such an accusation)

vicissitude *n.* the ~s of life

victim *n.* 1. to fall ~ to 2. an innocent; unsuspecting ~ (of) 3. an accident; amnesia; earthquake; flood; hurricane; murder; storm ~

victorious *adj.* ~ in; over

victory *n.* 1. to achieve, chalk up, gain, pull off (colloq.), score, win a ~ 2. a clear, clear-cut, decisive, outright, signal ~ 3. a landslide, overwhelming, resounding, stunning, sweeping ~ 4. a glorious; hard-won ~ 5. a bloodless; easy ~ 6. a narrow; upset ~ 7. a cheap; hollow; Pyrrhic ~ 8. a military; moral ~ 9. a ~ in; over (a ~ in a long and bloody struggle; a ~ over an enemy) 10. (misc.) to snatch, wrest ~ from the jaws of defeat

video *n.* 1. to make, produce, record a ~ (of) 2. to play, run, show a ~ 3. to watch a ~ 4. a blank ~ 5. on ~ (to record on ~; the film came out on ~)

videotape *n.* see **video**

vie *v.* 1. (formal) (d; intr.) to ~ for; with (she had to ~ for the prize with formidable competitors) 2. (E) they ~d to keep out all foreign competition

view I *n.* ["opinion"] ["outlook"] 1. to air, express, make known, present, put forth, put forward, voice a ~ 2. to harbor, hold a ~ 3. to advance, advocate, support a ~ 4. to exchange ~s 5. to have; take a ~ 6. a cheerful, favorable, optimistic, rosy; positive; sound ~ (she expressed very optimistic ~s about the project) 7. a cynical; dim; grave, grim, pessimistic; slanted; unpopular ~ (she took a dim ~ of the matter) 8. a contrary, unfavorable; divergent; diverse; opposing ~ (they hold opposing ~s on various matters) 9. an extreme; strong ~ (they aired strong ~s about the candidates) 10. a conservative; liberal, progressive; moderate; radical; reactionary ~ (she presented moderate ~s at the rally) 11. an ideological; philosophical; political ~ (we do not support that political ~) 12. an view | 366

advanced; modern ~ 13. a popular; prevailing ~ 14. an old-fashioned; outdated, outmoded ~ 15. a ~ about, on 16. a ~ that + clause (they disputed my ~ that taxes should be raised) 17. in smb.'s ~ (in my ~ the offer is unacceptable) ["sight"] 18. to get a ~ of 19. to block smb.'s ~ 20. a beautiful, breathtaking, magnificent, majestic, marvelous, superb, wonderful ~ 21. a clear, unhampered, unimpaired ~ 22. a bird's-eye; close-up; full; full-length; panoramic; sectional ~ 23. in, within ~ (in full ~ of the public) 24. (misc.) to come into ~ ["perspective"] 25. an exploded ~ ["what can be seen"] 26. a rear ~ 27. a ~ from (the ~ from the window) 28. (misc.) a room with a (nice) ~ (of the ocean) ["aim"] 29. with a ~ (with a ~ to reestablishing diplomatic relations) ["misc."] 30. in ~ of ("in consideration of"); a point of ~

view II *v.* ("to consider") 1. to ~ favorably; unfavorably 2. (d; tr.) to ~ as (she was ~ed as a serious threat to the party leadership) 3. (d; tr.) to ~ with (to ~ recent developments with alarm)

viewer *n.* 1. a regular ~ 2. younger ~s

viewpoint *n.* 1. a ~ that + clause (he explained his ~ that taxes should be increased) 2. from smb.'s ~ (see also **view I** 1-17)

vigil *n.* 1. to hold a ~; to keep (a) ~ 2. an all-night; lonely; prayer ~ 3. a ~ over

vigilance *n.* 1. to display, show; exercise ~ 2. constant; eternal ~

vigor, vigour *n.* 1. to regain one's ~ 2. to lose one's ~ 3. to sap smb.'s ~ 4. great ~ (he rejected the accusation with great ~) 5. the ~ to + inf. (does he have enough ~ to get everything done?)

vile *adj.* (formal) ~ to + inf. (it was ~ of them to issue such a statement)

village *n.* an agricultural, farming; fishing ~ (see the Usage Note for **town**)

village green *n.* on the ~

villain *n.* an arch, consummate ~
USAGE NOTE: In AE, *villain* is mostly literary or humorous; in colloq. BE, it can still mean "criminal".

vim *n.* ["energy"] with ~ and vigor; full of ~ and vigor

vindictive *adj.* ~ of (that was ~ of him)

vinegar *n.* 1. balsamic; cider; malt; wine ~ 2. oil and ~ (as a salad dressing)

vintage *n.* ["period"] 1. of a certain ~ (a mansion of prewar ~; a car of ancient ~) 2. (misc.) a ~ wine

viola *n.* to play the ~

violation *n.* 1. to commit a ~ 2. a brazen, flagrant, gross; major ~ 3. a minor ~ 4. a human-rights ~ 5. a moving; parking; traffic ~ (by a motorist) 6. in ~ of (he acted in ~ of the law)

violence *n.* ["devastating force"] 1. to resort to, use ~ 2. excessive ~ 3. domestic; sexual ~ 4. an act of ~ 5. ~ against ["distortion"] ["harm"] 6. to do ~ to

(the decision does ~ to our whole judicial tradition) ["rioting"] 7. to incite, stir up ~ 8. to crack down on ~ 9. communal; continuing; ethnic; mob; racial; sporadic; urban ~ 10. ~ breaks out, erupts, flares up 11. ~ ceases, dies down 12. an eruption, flare-up, outbreak, outburst of ~

violin *n.* 1. to play the ~ 2. to string; tune a ~

virgin *n.* a vestal ~ (historical)

virginity *n.* to keep one's ~; to lose one's ~

virtue *n.* ["admirable feature"] ["moral excellence"] 1. to have a ~ (our budget has the ~ of providing for a small surplus) 2. a cardinal ~ 3. (misc.) a paragon of ~; to extol the ~s of smt. ["misc."] 4. by ~ of ("because of"); of easy ~ (old-fashioned) ("sexually promiscuous"); to make a ~ of necessity ("to make the best of smt. bad")

virus *n.* 1. to culture a ~ 2. to isolate a ~ 3. to come down with a ~ 4. a (common) cold; influenza; intestinal ~ 5. a computer ~ (a computer ~ is spreading) 6. a ~ is going around, spreading

visa *n.* 1. to apply for a ~ 2. to get, receive a ~ 3. to overstay; violate a ~ 4. to grant, issue a ~ 5. to extend; renew a ~ 6. to deny smb. a ~ 7. to cancel a ~ 8. an entry; exit; student; tourist; transit ~ 9. a ~ expires, runs out

vise, vice *n.* ["tool for holding an object being worked on"] 1. to loosen; tighten a ~ 2. in a ~
USAGE NOTE: The AE form is *vise*; the BE form is *vice*.

visibility *n.* ["degree of being visible"] 1. clear; good; unlimited ~ 2. limited; poor; marginal; zero ~ (all planes were grounded because of poor ~) 3. (misc.) ~ is down to fifty yards ["exposure to publicity"] 4. high; low; maximum ~

visible *adj.* 1. barely; clearly, plainly ~ 2. ~ from; to (~ to the naked eye) 3. (misc.) (fig.) a highly ~ public figure

vision *n.* ["sight"] 1. acute; clear; keen; normal; twenty-twenty ~ 2. blurred; dim; double; failing; impaired; tunnel ~ 3. peripheral ~ 4. to lose one's ~ 5. (misc.) a field of ~; a ~ of the future; a ~ of loveliness ["foresight"] 6. the ~ to + inf. (she had the ~ to make wise investments several years ago) 7. of ~ (a person of great ~) 8. (misc.) tunnel ~ ("narrow horizons") ["imaginary picture"] 9. a ~ that + clause (she had a ~ that her country would be liberated) 10. in a ~ (to see smt. as if in a ~)

visit I *n.* 1. to make, pay a ~ (to) 2. to schedule a ~ (to) 3. to have a ~ from 4. to cancel; postpone a ~ 5. to cut short a ~ 6. a brief, flying, short; extended, lengthy, long ~ 7. a formal; friendly; informal; official; return; state; unscheduled; weekend ~ 8. a ~ to (this is my first ~ to your country) 9. on a ~ (on a ~ to South America)

visit II *v.* 1. (obsol. and formal) (d; tr.) to ~ on (the Lord's anger was ~ed on the people) 2. (AE) (d; intr.) to ~ with (we ~ed with several friends)

visitor *n.* 1. to have, receive a ~ (we had some ~s this weekend) 2. a frequent ~ 3. a weekend ~ 4. (BE) a prison ~ 5. (BE) a health ~ (AE has *public-health nurse*) 6. a ~ from (~s from abroad) 7. a ~ to (~s to our city)

vista *n.* ["view"] 1. to open up new ~s (of the future) 2. a broad, wide ~

visual aids *n.* to employ, use ~

visualize *v.* 1. (d; tr.) to ~ as (I cannot ~ her as a famous star) 2. (J) I cannot ~ him becoming a famous star 3. (K) I cannot ~ his becoming a famous star 4. (Q) I could not ~ how she could become a famous star

vital *adj.* 1. ~ for, to (their aid is ~ to our success) 2. ~ to + inf. (it is ~ to be prepared for any eventuality) 3. ~ that + clause; subj. (it is ~ that we be/should be kept informed of all developments)

vital signs *n.* to check, take smb.'s ~

vital statistics *n.* to gather; record; report ~

vitamins *n.* 1. to take ~ 2. multivitamins

vocabulary *n.* 1. to command a ~ 2. to build, develop, enlarge one's ~ 3. an extensive, huge, large, rich ~ 4. a limited, meager, restricted, small ~ 5. a basic; technical ~ 6. an active; passive ~

vocation *n.* 1. to have a ~ 2. a genuine, real ~ 3. (misc.) to have missed one's ~ ("not to have chosen an occupation or vocation at which one is particularly adept"); to have a (genuine) ~ for the priesthood

vogue *n.* ["popularity"] ["current fashion"] 1. to be the ~ (home computers are the latest ~) 2. to be in ~; to come into ~; to have a ~ (BE) 3. to go out of ~ 4. the current; latest ~ 5. (misc.) to be all the ~

voice I *n.* ["sound produced by vocal cords"] 1. to raise one's ~ 2. to drop, lower one's ~ 3. to keep one's ~ down 4. to disguise one's ~ 5. to lose one's ~ 6. a friendly, gentle, good, kind, pleasant, soft; mellifluous, melodious, sweet ~ 7. a clear; firm, steady ~ 8. a deep; mellow; resonant; rich ~ 9. a high; high-pitched; low, low-pitched ~ 10. a booming; loud; stentorian; strident; thundering ~ 11. a quaking, quivering, shaking, shaky, trembling ~ 12. a guttural; hoarse; husky; muffled; subdued ~ 13. a gruff, harsh, raucous; shrill ~ 14. a ~ breaks, cracks; carries; changes; drops, falls; quivers, shakes, trembles 15. in a certain ~ (in a loud ~) 16. (misc.) (to shout) at the top of one's ~; a ventriloquist throws her/his ~; an actor must learn to project her/his ~ ["expression"] 17. to give ~ to ["verbal form indicating the relation of the verb to its subject"] 18. the active; middle; passive ~ ["influence"] 19. to have a ~ in smt. ["misc."] 20. an inner ~ ("conscience"); the ~ of reason

voice II *v.* (B) she ~d her concerns to us

void I *adj.* ["devoid"] (cannot stand alone) ~ of

void II *n.* 1. to fill a ~ 2. to leave a ~ 3. a painful ~ 4.

a ~ in

volatile *adj.* highly ~

volcano *n.* 1. an active, live; dead, extinct; dormant, inactive; intermittent ~ 2. a ~ erupts 3. a ~ spews lava 4. (misc.) the mouth of a ~

volition *n.* ["act of choosing"] of, on one's own ~ (they agreed of their own ~; to act on one's own ~)

volley I *n.* ["simultaneous discharge of weapons"] to fire a ~

volley II *v.* (P; tr.) she ~ed the ball across the court

volleyball *n.* to play ~

voltage *n.* 1. to step up (the) ~ 2. high; low ~ 3. (misc.) a ~ surge

volume *n.* ["loudness"] 1. to amplify; increase, turn up the ~ 2. to decrease, turn down the ~ 3. at a certain ~ (at full ~) ["space occupied in three dimensions"] 4. molecular ~ ["book"] 5. a rare ~ 6. a companion ~ (this work is a companion ~ to our first dictionary) 7. bound ~s (of a journal) 8. (misc.) to speak ~s ("to imply a lot") (a single glance can speak ~s)

volunteer I *n.* 1. to recruit ~s 2. a ~ for (I recruited several ~s for the job)

volunteer II *v.* 1. (D; intr.) to ~ as (to ~ as a tutor) 2. (D; intr.) to ~ for (who will ~ for this job?) 3. (E) she ~ed to water our plants

vomiting *n.* 1. to cause, induce ~ 2. projectile ~

voodoo, voodooism *n.* to practice ~

vortex *n.* to draw, suck into a ~

vote I *n.* ["collective opinion as determined by voting"] 1. to take a ~ on (a motion) 2. to put a motion to a ~; to bring a motion to a ~ 3. to influence, swing a ~ (recent events swung the ~ in our favor; the press can influence the ~) 4. to count, tabulate, tally; recount the ~ 5. a close; lopsided; majority; solid; unanimous ~ 6. a straw; voice; write-in ~ 7. a ~ on (a ~ on an issue) 8. (esp. BE) a ~ to + inf. (we took a ~ to adjourn) 9. by a ~ (by a unanimous ~) 10. a ~ of censure; confidence; no-confidence; thanks 11. (misc.) to fix, rig a ~; the ~ went in our favor ["individual expression of opinion, ballot"] 12. to cast a ~ 13. to change, switch one's ~ 14. to get, receive smb.'s ~ (you'll never get my ~) 15. the deciding ~ (to cast the deciding ~) 16. a write-in ~ 17. a ~ against; for; on (to cast a ~ for a proposal) 18. the ~s to + inf. (we have enough ~s to carry the state) ["group of voters"] 19. the conservative; floating (BE) ("unattached); independent; labor; liberal; undecided ~ ["voters as a group"] 20. to deliver the ~(s); to get out the ~ (the party machine delivered the ~s; a series of interesting debates helped to get out the ~) 21. a heavy; light ~ ["right to vote, franchise, suffrage"] 22. to get, receive the ~ (in some countries women got the ~ after World War I)

vote II *v.* 1. (C; usu. used without *for*) Congress ~d him a pension 2. (D; intr.) to ~ against; for (to ~

against a bill) 3. (d; tr.) to ~ into (to ~ smb. into office) 4. (D; intr.) to ~ on, upon (to ~ on a resolution) 5. (d; tr.) to ~ out of (to ~ smb. out of office) 6. (E) the committee ~d to approve the report 7. (L; subj.) Parliament ~d that the allocation be/should be reduced 8. (N; used with an adjective, noun) she was ~d most likely to succeed 9. (misc.) to ~ by a show of hands

voter *n.* 1. an absentee; floating (BE) ("unattached"); independent; registered ~ 2. a ~ registers (to vote)

voting *n.* 1. absentee; bloc ~ 2. (misc.) ~ irregularities

voting lists *n.* to tamper with ~

vouch *v.* (d; intr.) to ~ for (I can ~ for the truth of her statement)

voucher *n.* a gift (BE); hotel; luncheon (BE; AE has *meal ticket*); travel; tuition (AE) ~

vouchsafe *v.* (formal; rare) 1. (B) ("to grant") she ~d me a word 2. (E) ("to condescend") she ~d to help

vow I *n.* 1. to make, take a ~ 2. to keep one's ~ 3. to break, violate a ~ 4. a formal, solemn ~ 5. clerical; marriage; monastic; religious ~s (priests take religious ~s) 6. a ~ to + inf. (she made a solemn ~ not to smoke again) 7. a ~ that + clause (we took a ~ that we would always help each other) 8. (misc.) to exchange; renew marriage ~s; a ~ of silence

vow II *v.* 1. (E) she ~ed to return 2. (L; to) I ~ed (to them) that he would be avenged

vowel *n.* a back; closed; front; high; lax; long; middle; nasal; open; reduced; rounded; short; stressed; tense; unstressed ~

voyage *n.* ["journey"] 1. to go on, set off on a ~ 2. a long; maiden; ocean, sea; round-the-world; short; space ~ 3. a ~ around (a ~ around the world) 4. a ~ from; to (a ~ to the islands) 5. a ~ through (a ~ through the Panama Canal)

V sign *n.* 1. to give, make the ~ (showing triumph or encouragement) 2. (BE) to give, make a ~ (showing vulgar contempt or rage)

vulgar *adj.* ~ to + inf. (it's ~ to spit in public)

vulnerable *adj.* ~ to

vulture *n.* ~s feed on carrion

vying see **vie**

W

wad *n.* (slang) (AE) ["a large amount, as of money"] to shoot one's ~ ("to spend all of one's money" or "to make a last-ditch effort")
waddle *v.* (P; intr.) to ~ across the road
wade *v.* 1. (d; intr.) to ~ across (to ~ across a stream) 2. (d; intr.) to ~ into (to ~ into a river) 3. (d; intr.) to ~ into ("to attack") (the speaker ~d into the opposing candidate) 4. (d; intr.) to ~ through (to ~ through deep water) 5. (d; intr.) to ~ through ("to read through with difficulty") (to ~ through a long report)
wade in *v.* (colloq.) (D; intr.) to ~ with (she ~d in with a few choice comments)
waft *v.* (P; intr.) an aroma ~ed in from the kitchen
wage I *n.* 1. to draw, earn, get, receive a ~ 2. to pay a ~ 3. to boost, increase, raise ~s 4. to cut, reduce, slash ~s 5. to freeze ~s 6. to attach, garnishee ~s 7. a decent, living; minimum; subsistence ~ (to pay workers a decent ~) 8. an annual, yearly; daily; hourly; monthly; weekly ~ 9. a union ~ 10. (misc.) the union successfully negotiated (for) a higher ~
wage II *v.* (D; tr.) to ~ against (to ~ a campaign against smoking)
wage bracket *n.* in a (certain) ~
wager I *n.* 1. to lay, make, place a ~ on 2. a ~ that + clause (she made a ~ that her team would win)
wager II *v.* 1. (D; intr., tr.) to ~ on (did you ~ a lot of money on that horse?) 2. (L; may have an object) she ~ed (me) that I could not guess the riddle 3. (O; can be used with one object or two objects followed by a clause) we ~ed ten dollars; we ~ed him ten dollars that it would rain
wages *n.* 1. see **wage I** 2. starvation ~
waggon (BE) see **wagon**
wagon *n.* 1. a station ~ (AE; BE has *estate car*) 2. a tea ~ (AE; BE has *tea trolley*) 3. a patrol ~ 4. (AE) a welcome ~ ("a car sent with gifts from local merchants to a family that has just moved into a neighborhood") 5. a Conestoga; covered ~ 6. a goods ~ (BE; AE has *freight car*) 7. (colloq.) (AE) a chuck ("food") ~ (on a ranch) 8. (misc.) on the ~ ("pledged not to drink alcoholic beverages")
waist *n.* 1. a slender, slim ~ 2. around, round the ~ (she wore a belt around her ~)
wait I *n.* 1. to lie in ~ for 2. to have a (long) ~ for (we had a long ~ for the bus) 3. a long; short ~
wait II *v.* 1. (BE) (d; intr.) to ~ at (to ~ at table) (cf. 3) 2. (D; intr.) to ~ for (they ~ed for me; they ~ed for me to leave) 3. (AE) (d; intr.) to ~ on (to ~ on tables) (cf. 1) 4. (d; intr.) to ~ on, upon ("to attend to") (to ~ on smb. hand and foot) 5. (E) we are ~ing to go 6. (misc.) to keep smb. ~ing; they ~ed until she returned; ~ and see; ~ a minute

waiting *n.* (GB; on a traffic sign) no ~ (US has *no standing* or *no stopping*)
waiting game *n.* to play a ~
waiting list *n.* (to put smb.) on a ~
wait up *v.* (D; intr.) to ~ for (they ~ed up for her until she returned)
waiver *n.* to agree to, sign a ~
wake I *n.* ["vigil over a corpse"] to hold a ~
wake II *n.* ["aftermath"] in the ~ (of) (war brings misery in its ~; security was beefed up in the ~ of the explosion)
wake III *v.* 1. (D; intr.) to ~ from, out of (she woke from a deep sleep) 2. (d; intr., tr.) to ~ to (they woke to the sound of music; it woke the community to the danger of pollution) 3. (E) they woke to find themselves surrounded by the enemy 4. (s) I woke refreshed
wake up *v.* 1. (D; intr., tr.) to ~ from, out of (to ~ out of a sound sleep) 2. (d; intr., tr.) to ~ to (to ~ to the danger of inflation) 3. (E) I woke up to find the house on fire 4. (s) I woke up refreshed 5. (misc.) to ~ with a start
walk I *n.* ["journey by foot"] 1. to have (BE), take a ~ 2. to take smb. for a ~ (BE also has: to take smb. a long ~ round the grounds) 3. to go for, go on a ~ 4. a brisk; easy; leisurely; long; nature; short ~ (to take a brisk ~) 5. a ~ from; to (we took a ~ from our house to the center of town; it's an easy ~ from here to school) ["profession"] ["class"] 6. from every ~/all ~s of life
walk II *v.* 1. to ~ fast; slow 2. (d; intr.) to ~ across (to ~ across the street) 3. (d; intr.) to ~ along (to ~ along a river bank) 4. (d; intr.) to ~ around, round (to ~ around a house) 5. (d; intr.) to ~ by, past (to ~ past the library) 6. (d; intr.) to ~ down (to ~ down the street) 7. (D; intr., tr.) to ~ from; to, towards (we ~ed from the park to the station; I ~ed her to the library) 8. (d; intr.) to ~ into (to ~ into a room; to ~ into an ambush) 9. (d; intr.) to ~ on, over (don't ~ on the wet floor!) 10. (d; intr.) to ~ out of (to ~ out of a meeting) 11. (d; intr.) to ~ (all) over ("to treat badly") (they ~ed all over us) 12. (d; intr.) to ~ through (to ~ through the park; to ~ through a puddle) 13. (d; tr.) to ~ smb. through ("to help with smt. complicated") (she ~ed me through the procedure) 14. (misc.) she ~ed her dog in the park; they ~ed off the job in protest against the long hours; they ~ed me home; to ~ up and down/back and forth
walkabout *n.* (colloq.) ["a walk through a crowd by an important person"] (BE) 1. to do, go on a ~ (the Queen went on a ~ after the ceremony) ["misc."] 2. my camera seems to have gone ~ ("my

camera seems to be missing")
walk away *v.* 1. (D; intr.) to ~ from (he ~ed away from me without saying a word; to ~ from an accident) ("to survive an accident unhurt") 2. (d; intr.) to ~ with ("to win") (she ~ed away with all the top prizes)
walk down *v.* (d; intr.) to ~ from; to (they ~ed down to the river bank)
walker *n.* a tightrope ~
walk in *v.* 1. (d; intr.) to ~ from (they ~ed in from the street) 2. (d; intr.) to ~ on ("to come across unexpectedly") (I ~ed in on an interesting scene)
walking *n.* 1. heel-and-toe ~ 2. power ~
walking papers *n.* (colloq.) (AE) ["notice of dismissal"] to give smb. her/his ~ (BE has *marching orders*)
walk off *v.* (d; intr.) to ~ with ("to win") (she ~ed off with the first prize)
walkout *n.* 1. to stage a ~ 2. to end a ~ 3. a sympathy ~
walk out *v.* 1. (D; intr.) to ~ on ("to leave") (she ~ed out on her husband) 2. (D; intr.) to ~ onto (they ~ed out onto the veranda)
walk over *v.* (d; intr.) to ~ from; to (he ~ed over to her table; she ~ed over from her house to our house)
walk up *v.* (d; intr.) to ~ to (I ~ed up to them and said a few words)
wall *n.* 1. to build, erect, put up a ~ 2. to demolish, tear down a ~ 3. to climb, scale a ~ 4. to paint; panel; paper; plaster a ~ 5. to line a ~ (to line a ~ with bookshelves) 6. a high; low; solid, thick ~ 7. a brick; fire; inside; outside; retaining ~; seawall; stone; supporting ~ 8. (also fig.) a ~ between (the ~ between church and state) 9. against the ~ (they were lined up/stood up against the ~ and shot) 10. on a ~ (there were several pictures on the ~) 11. (misc.) we had our backs to the ~ ("we were in a desperate situation"); (slang) to drive smb. up the ~ ("to frustrate smb. completely")
wallet *n.* 1. a leather ~ 2. (misc.) his ~ was bulging with banknotes
wall off *v.* (D; tr.) to ~ from
wallop *n.* (colloq.) ["force"] 1. to pack a ~ (the winds packed a real ~) ["blow"] 2. to give smb. a ~ (on)
wallow *v.* (d; intr.) to ~ in (to ~ in the mud; to ~ in self-pity)
wallpaper *n.* 1. to hang, put up ~ 2. to scrape (off), take off ~ 3. a roll of ~
waltz I *n.* 1. to play a ~ 2. to dance, do a ~
waltz II *v.* 1. (colloq.) (d; intr.) to ~ through ("to complete with ease") (she just ~ed through the test) 2. (P; intr.) they ~ed around the room together
waltz off *v.* (d; intr.) to ~ with (she ~ed off with first prize)
wand *n.* 1. to wave a ~ 2. a magic ~

wander *v.* 1. (d; intr.) ("to stray") to ~ from (to ~ from the subject) 2. (P; intr.) we ~ed across the park; they ~ed along the river bank; she ~ed into the village; he ~ed through the town
wander away *v.* (D; intr.) to ~ from (the children ~ed away from their parents)
wanderer *n.* a homeless ~
wane I *n.* ["decrease"] ["period of decrease"] on the ~ (the moon is on the ~)
wane II *v.* 1. (D; intr.) to ~ into (to ~ into insignificance) 2. (misc.) to wax and ~
wangle *v.* (colloq.) 1. (C) could you ~ an invitation for me? or: could you ~ me an invitation? 2. (D; tr.) to ~ from, out of (she ~d an invitation out of them) 3. (misc.) to ~ one's way into a party
want I *n.* ["need"] 1. to fill, meet, satisfy a ~ 2. to minister to smb.'s ~s 3. for ~ of (to die for ~ of medical care) 4. in ~ of (in ~ of a job) ["poverty"] 5. in ~ (to live in ~)
want II *v.* 1. to ~ badly, desperately, very much (they ~ed very badly to see us) 2. (d; intr.) to ~ for ("to be in need of") (they will never ~ for anything) 3. (D; tr.) ("to seek") to ~ for (he is ~ed for murder in three states) 4. (D; tr.) ("to desire") to ~ for (we ~ you for our team) 5. (E) ("to desire") I ~ to help 6. (E) ("ought") you ~ to think carefully about what you say to them 7. (BE) (G) ("to be in need of") your shirts ~ mending; the house ~s painting; her hair ~s cutting 8. (H; no passive) ("to desire") they ~ us to finish the job in two weeks 9. (J) I ~ them singing in tune! 10. (M) ("to desire") I ~ them to be kept busy at all times 11. (N; used with an adjective, past participle) ("to desire") we ~ the troublemakers removed; I ~ them ready in one hour; she ~s the house painted tomorrow 12. (misc.) I ~ them out of the house by tomorrow; (esp. AE) they ~ out of the deal
USAGE NOTE: It should be noted that the construction *want + for + to +* inf. can be acceptable in CE as in—*what they want is for us to finish the job today; they want very much for us to finish the job today*. In addition, a construction such as *they want very much that we should finish the job is* acceptable in CE only when a modifier such as *very much* appears between *want* and the dependent clause introduced by *that*.
want ad *n.* (colloq.) (esp. AE) 1. to place a ~ 2. to answer a ~ 3. to follow, read the ~s
wanted *adj.* ["sought"] 1. ~ by (~ by the police) 2. ~ for (~ for murder)
wanting *adj.* ["deficient"] 1. ~ in 2. (misc.) to be found ~
war I *n.* 1. to conduct, fight, wage ~ against, with 2. to make ~ 3. to declare ~ on; to go to ~ over 4. to drift into; plunge into (a) ~ 5. to provoke (a) ~ 6. to escalate, step up a ~ 7. to avert (a) ~ 8. to survive (a) ~ 9. to lose; win a ~ 10. to ban, outlaw ~ 11. to

end a ~ 12. an all-out, full-scale, total; global, world ~ 13. a limited, local ~ 14. a civil; guerrilla; revolutionary ~ 15. a cold; hot, shooting ~ 16. a defensive; offensive ~ 17. a holy; religious ~ 18. a trade ~ 19. an atomic, nuclear, thermonuclear ~ 20. star ~s 21. a gang; price ~ 22. a ~ of aggression; attrition; extermination; nerves 23. a ~ breaks out; rages; spreads (the ~ spread to the north) 24. an act of ~ 25. a ~ against; between (a ~ against an aggressor; a ~ between former allies) 26. a ~ on (a ~ on drugs) 27. at ~ (with) (to be at ~ with one's neighbors) 28. (misc.) a theater of ~; a state of ~ (to be in a state of ~ with a country)

war II *v.* 1. (d; intr.) to ~ against, with (to ~ with one's neighbors) 2. (d; intr.) to ~ over (to ~ over disputed territory)

war clouds *n.* ~ gather

war crime *n.* 1. to commit a ~ 2. to prosecute ~s

ward *n.* ["hospital room"] 1. an emergency; maternity, obstetrics; pediatrics; private (BE) ("not under the National Health Service") ~ 2. in, on a ~ (to work in the emergency ~; who works in/on this ~?)

warden *n.* 1. a prison ~ (AE; BE has *governor*) 2. (BE) a traffic ~ 3. an air-raid ~
USAGE NOTE: An AE *prison warden* should not be confused with a BE *prison warder*, who in AE is a *prison guard*.

wardrobe *n.* ["clothes"] 1. an autumn (esp. BE), fall (AE); spring; summer; winter ~ 2. (misc.) I bought a whole new ~ for the cruise

warehouse *n.* a bonded ~

wares *n.* to display; hawk, peddle one's ~

warfare *n.* 1. to engage in ~ 2. armored; guerrilla; naval; trench ~ 3. conventional; push-button ~ 4. atomic, nuclear, thermonuclear ~ 5. bacteriological, germ; biological; chemical ~ 6. desert; jungle; tribal ~ 7. all-out; global; total ~ 8. economic; psychological; modern ~

war games *n.* to hold, stage ~

warhead *n.* 1. to fire, launch a ~ 2. a conventional; multiple; nuclear ~

warm *v.* (d; intr.) to ~ to ("to begin to like") (I was just ~ing to the task)

warm front *n.* a ~ approaches; forms

warming *n.* global ~

warmth *n.* body ~

warm up *v.* 1. (D; intr.) to ~ for (the players were ~ing up for the game) 2. (d; intr.) to ~ to (after a few drinks he ~ed up to the other guests)

warn *v.* 1. (D; intr., tr.) to ~ about, against, of (they ~ed me about his bad temper; I ~ed him against driving on ice; the police ~ed us of the pickpockets; the economists are ~ing of an impending slump) 2. (H) they ~ed him to be careful; I ~ed her not to go 3. (L; may have an object) she ~ed (us) that the winter would be severe 4. (misc.) (esp.

BE) my doctor has ~ed me off smoking

warn away *v.* (D; tr.) to ~ from (the police ~ed us away from the burning building)

warning *n.* 1. to give, issue, send, sound a ~ 2. to shout a ~ 3. to heed; receive a ~ 4. to disregard, ignore a ~ 5. a cryptic; dire; tacit; timely ~ 6. (an) advance ~ 7. ample ~ 8. a storm ~ 9. a ~ against 10. a ~ to (a ~ to all; let this be a ~ to you) 11. a ~ to + inf. (a ~ to watch out for pickpockets) 12. a ~ that + clause (they issued a ~ that the escaped criminals were dangerous) 13. without ~

warpath *n.* (usu. colloq. and humorous) 1. to go on the ~ 2. to be on the ~ (they are on the ~ again)

warrant I *n.* 1. to issue a ~ (the court issued a search ~) 2. (AE) to swear out a ~ against smb. 3. to serve a ~ on (a ~ was served on her) 4. an arrest; bench; death; search ~ (to sign smb.'s death ~) (also fig.) 5. a ~ for (the court issued a ~ for her arrest) 6. a ~ to + inf. (the police have a ~ to search the house) 7. (misc.) a ~ is out for her arrest

warrant II *v.* 1. (K) ("to justify") nothing ~ed his behaving like that 2. (L) ("to guarantee") I cannot ~ that the coins are genuine 3. (formal and rare) (M) I cannot ~ the coins to be genuine

warranty *n.* 1. to give a ~ 2. an implied; limited; special ~ 3. a ~ expires, runs out 4. a ~ on (a two-year ~ on a new car) 5. under ~ (the new car is still under ~)

warren *n.* a rabbit ~

warship *n.* 1. to commission; launch a ~ 2. to command a ~

wart *n.* to remove a ~

wartime *n.* during, in ~

wary *adj.* ~ of (be ~ of strangers)

wash I *n.* ["laundry"] 1. to do the ~ 2. to hang out the ~ (to dry) 3. the weekly ~ ["installation for washing"] 4. a car ~

wash II *v.* 1. (d; intr.) to ~ against (the waves ~ed against the pier) 2. (D; tr.) to ~ for (would you please ~ the dishes for me?) 3. (d; tr.) to ~ off, out of (she ~ed the marks off the wall; I ~ed the mud out of my shirt) 4. (D; tr.) to ~ over (the waves ~ed over the deck) 5. (D; tr.) to ~ with (I ~ed my hands with soap) 6. (misc.) to be ~ed overboard
USAGE NOTE: In AE, *to wash up* means "to wash one's hands and face"; in BE, it means "to do the dishes".

wash down *v.* (D; tr.) to ~ with (to ~ a meal with a glass of beer)

washing (esp. BE) see **wash I** 1-3

washing machine *n.* 1. to run, use a ~ 2. to load; unload a ~

washing-up *n.* (BE) to do the ~ ("to wash the dishes") (see the Usage Note for **wash II**)

wash up *v.* (D; intr.) to ~ on (the wreckage ~ed up on shore)

wasp *n.* ~s buzz; sting

wastage *n.* (esp. BE) natural ~ (the staff will be reduced by natural ~) (CE has *attrition*)

waste I *n.* 1. to cause ~ 2. to cut down on ~ 3. hazardous; nuclear; radioactive; solid; toxic ~s 4. complete, sheer, total, utter ~ 5. (misc.) to go to ~ ("to be wasted"); to lay ~ to ("to destroy"); a terrible ~ of time and money

waste II *v.* 1. (D; tr.) to ~ on (we ~d a lot of time on that project) 2. (misc.) we ~d a lot of time going through the files

wasteful *adj.* 1. ~ of (~ of natural resources) 2. ~ to + inf. (it's ~ to use so much fuel)

wasteland *n.* 1. to reclaim ~ 2. (a) barren, desolate; cultural; industrial ~

watch I *n.* ["timepiece"] 1. to adjust; set; wind (up) a ~ 2. to synchronize ~es 3. to clean; repair a ~ 4. a pocket; self-winding ~; stopwatch; waterproof; wrist ~ 5. an analog; digital ~ 6. a ~ is fast; right; slow 7. a ~ goes; keeps time; runs; tells time 8. a ~ gains time; loses time; runs down; stops 9. the dial, face; hands of a ~ 10. (misc.) to set, turn a ~ ahead/back (by) one hour ["surveillance"] 11. to keep, maintain a ~ on 12. a close ~ 13. on the ~ (for) (to be on the ~ for bargains) ["sailor's duty"] 14. to stand ~ 15. on ~ (several sailors were on ~) ["volunteers organized to prevent crime"] 16. a crime (esp. AE); neighborhood; town (esp. AE) ~ ["preliminary warning"] (esp. AE) 17. a storm ~

watch II *v.* 1. to ~ closely 2. (d; intr.) to ~ for (to ~ for the train) 3. (d; intr.) to ~ over (to ~ over one's property) 4. (I) we ~ed them enter the auditorium 5. (J) we ~ed them entering the auditorium 6. (L; used in the imper.) ~ that they don't take everything 7. (Q) ~ how it's done

watchdog *n.* (esp. BE) a consumer ~ (profiteers exposed by consumer ~s)

watcher *n.* ["observer"] a poll ~

watching *n.* ["observation"] 1. to bear ~ (her activities bear ~) ("her activities should be watched") ["act of watching"] 2. bird ~

watch out *v.* 1. (D; intr.) to ~ for 2. (esp. AE) (L; used in the imper.) ~ that she doesn't fool you

water I *n.* 1. to turn on the ~ 2. to turn off the ~ 3. to cut off, disconnect the ~ 4. to draw, run ~ (for a bath) 5. to add ~ 6. to drink; sip ~ 7. to pour; spill ~ 8. to drain (off) ~ (from) 9. to splash; sprinkle; squirt ~ on 10. to boil, sterilize; chlorinate; distill; filter; fluoridate; purify; soften ~ 11. to pollute ~ 12. drinking; safe ~ 13. carbonated, fizzy (BE); mineral; soda ~ 14. clear; fresh; running ~ 15. distilled; rain; soft ~ 16. hard ~ 17. salt, sea ~ 18. holy ~ 19. heavy ~ 20. boiling; hot ~ 21. cold; cool; ice ~ 22. lukewarm; tepid; warm ~ 23. contaminated, polluted; murky; stagnant ~ 24. ~ boils; evaporates; freezes; vaporizes 25. ~ flows, pours, runs; leaks; oozes; rises 26. a body of ~ 27. by ~ (to travel by ~) 28. under ~ (after the flood our basement was under ~) 29. (misc.) a bottle of ~; a glass of ~; to make/pass ~ ("to urinate"); to hold ~ ("to be valid") (your theory doesn't hold ~); to tread ~ (when swimming); ~ under the bridge ("past events that are done with"); to pour cold ~ on ("to discourage"); to keep one's head above ~ ("to keep out of difficulty"); toilet ~ ("liquid used as a skin freshener"); to be in hot ~ ("to be in trouble"); the boat was shipping ~ ("the boat was taking in water")

water II *v.* (misc.) to make smb.'s mouth ~ ("to create a desire or appetite in smb."); her mouth ~s at the sight of popcorn

watercolors *n.* to paint in ~

waterfront *n.* along, on the ~

watermark *n.* 1. to reach a ~ 2. a high; low; record ~

waters *n.* 1. flood ~ (the flood ~ receded/subsided) 2. coastal; international; navigable; territorial; uncharted ~ 3. in ~ (the ship was in international ~) 4. (misc.) to fish in muddy (AE)/troubled ~ ("to attempt to stir up trouble"); to take the ~ ("to take a water cure")

water table *n.* the ~ is high; low

waterway *n.* an inland ~

waterworks *n.* a municipal ~

wave I *n.* ["moving ridge on the surface of water"] 1. a high, tall; mountainous ~ 2. a tidal ~ 3. ~s break (on the rocks); crest 4. beneath the ~s ["upsurge"] 5. a crime ~ 6. in ~s ["physical disturbance that is transmitted in the propagation of sound or light"] 7. light; radio; sound; transverse ~s 8. long; medium; short ~s ["brain rhythm"] 9. an alpha; brain ~ ["period of weather"] 10. a cold; heat ~ ["reaction"] 11. a shock ~ ["waviness of the hair"] 12. a natural; permanent ~ ["misc."] 13. to attack in ~s; to make ~s ("to have an impact"); (BE) a Mexican ~ ("a wave-like motion made by a crowd at a sporting event")

USAGE NOTE: In colloq. BE, a *brain wave* can also mean a "sudden bright idea", which in AE is a *brainstorm*. In colloq. BE, a *brainstorm* is a "sudden mental aberration". However, the verb *to brainstorm* (as in *a brainstorming session*) is now CE.

wave II *v.* 1. (A) ~ goodbye to them; or: ~ them goodbye 2. (D; intr., tr.) to ~ at, to (~ to them; she ~d her arm at me; she ~d to them to come closer; she ~d at us from the airplane)

wave back *v.* (D; intr.) to ~ at, to (she ~d back at/to us)

wavelength *n.* ["manner of thinking"] (colloq.) to be on the same ~; to operate on different ~s

waver *v.* (D; intr.) to ~ between (to ~ between two possibilities)

wax I *n.* beeswax; sealing ~

wax II *v.* 1. (s) ("to become") to ~ indignant; to ~

eloquent over ("to express one's enthusiasm concerning") 2. (misc.) to ~ and wane

way *n.* ["path, route"] 1. to blaze, clear, cut, open, pave, prepare the ~ for (to pave the ~ for reform) 2. to smoothe the ~ for 3. to take the easy ~ out (of a difficult situation) 4. to lead; point, show the ~ 5. to edge; elbow; fight; force; hack; inch; jostle; make; muscle; push; shoulder; shove; slash; squeeze; thread; tunnel; wedge; work one's ~ through; to (to elbow one's ~ through a crowd; the battalion fought its ~ through enemy lines to the coast; he pushed his ~ through the mob; to shove one's ~ through the revelers; we made our ~ to the door; to tunnel one's ~ to freedom) 6. to twist; weave, wend, wind one's ~ (the river winds its ~ to the sea) 7. to feel; find one's ~ 8. to wangle, worm one's ~ (into smb.'s confidence) 9. to know the ~ to (do you know the ~ to the station?) 10. to lose one's ~ 11. to bar, block the ~ 12. (BE) a permanent ~ ("a railroad track") 13. the ~ from; to (he kept chattering all the ~ from our house to the airport) 14. the ~ into, to (the ~ into the park; can you show me the ~ to the station?) 15. the ~ out of (the ~ out of the city; show me the ~ out of this building; there is no easy ~ out of this mess) 16. on the ~ (a letter is on the ~; she is on her ~ to the airport) 17. (misc.) to work one's ~ through college; out of harm's ~; to make one's ~ in life; to see one's ~ clear to do smt.; they went their separate ~s; my gift is winging its ~ to you by airmail; to come to a parting of the ~s; by ~ of ("via"); to go the ~ of all flesh ("to be mortal"); to know one's ~ around ("to be familiar with procedures"); to bluff one's ~ out of a predicament ["room for movement"] 18. to make ~ for 19. in the ~ (to be/ stand in the ~; to get in smb.'s ~) 20. out of the ~ (to get out of the ~) ["progress"] 21. under ~ (an investigation is under ~) ["distance"] 22. to come; go a long ~ ["direction"] 23. this ~; that ~; the other ~ (she went that ~; please step this ~; they went the other ~) ["aspect, respect"] 24. in a certain ~ (in every ~; in no ~; in more ~s than one) ["manner, method"] 25. to find a ~ (they found a ~ to spend less money on electricity) 26. the proper, right; wrong ~ 27. the easy; hard ~ (to do smt. the hard ~; let's do it the easy ~) 28. charming, winsome ~s 29. that; this ~ (do it this ~) 30. the ~ to + inf. (show me the ~ to work this washing machine; that's the ~ to do it; there is no easy ~ to learn a new language) 31. in a certain ~ (in her own ~; in such a ~ that...; in a small ~) 32. (misc.) to my ~ of thinking; to mend one's ~s; to fall into evil ~s ["purpose"] 33. by ~ of (by ~ of apology; by ~ of example; by ~ of illustration) ["effective manner"] 34. to have a ~ with (she has a ~ with children) ["goal"] 35. to get, have one's (own) ~ (she always gets her ~) ["misc."] 36. to know the ~s of the world; to know one's ~ around; to make one's ~ in the world; to get under ~ ("to start out"); in a ~ ("to some degree"); to go out of one's ~ ("to make a special effort"); to give ~ ("to collapse") ("to yield"); under ~ ("in progress"); to pay one's own ~ ("to pay for oneself"); (old-fashioned) to be in the family ~ ("to be pregnant"); by the ~ ("incidentally"); on the ~ out ("becoming obsolescent"); there are no two ~s about it ("it is definitely true"); out our ~ ("where we live"); we are in a fair ~ to get our new library ("it appears as if we will get our new library"); this compromise goes a long ~ towards resolving our differences; the ~ to smb.'s heart; to my ~ of thinking; a ~ of life
USAGE NOTE: Constructions such as *to hack one's way through the jungle* cannot be passivized. Compare *they hacked a path through the jungle—a path was hacked (by them) through the jungle.*

wayside *n.* to fall by the ~

weak *adj.* 1. ~ at, in (he's ~ in mathematics) 2. ~ from, with (~ with hunger)

weakened *adj.* ~ by

weakness *n.* ["quality of being weak"] 1. to reveal, show (a) ~ 2. a basic; glaring; inherent; structural ~ 3. ~ in (his ~ in mathematics) ["fondness"] 4. to have a ~ 5. a ~ for (a ~ for chocolate)

wealth *n.* ["abundance of material possessions"] 1. to accumulate, acquire, amass, attain ~ 2. to dissipate, squander ~ 3. to flaunt one's ~ 4. enormous, fabulous, great, untold ~ 5. hereditary ~ ["abundance of resources"] 6. mineral; natural ~ (the natural ~ of a country) ["abundance, profusion"] 7. a ~ of information

wean *v.* 1. (D; tr.) to ~ from (to ~ a calf from its mother) 2. (d; tr.) to ~ on (the children were ~ed on television) 3. (misc.) to ~ smb. away from bad company

weapon *n.* 1. to load a ~ 2. to fire a ~ 3. to brandish; carry; draw; handle a ~ 4. to calibrate; zero in a ~ 5. to lay down, throw down one's ~s 6. a concealed; deadly, lethal ~ 7. automatic; defensive; heavy; light; offensive; semiautomatic ~s 8. atomic, nuclear, thermonuclear; chemical; conventional ~s 9. (misc.) (they entered the building) with drawn ~s/with ~s drawn; the ultimate ~ ("nuclear bombs or missiles"); to stockpile ~s

wear I *n.* ["clothing"] 1. beach; bridal; casual; children's; evening ~; footwear; infants'; ladies', women's; men's; sports; everyday ~ ["wearing out"] 2. to save ~ and tear (on)

wear II *v.* 1. (N; used with an adjective) she ~s her hair short 2. (s) my patience is ~ing thin 3. (misc.) she wore a hole through her sock

weary I *adj.* ~ of (they grew ~ of his preaching)

weary II *v.* (d; intr.) to ~ of (to ~ of one's job)

weasel *v.* (colloq.) (AE) (d; intr.) to ~ out of ("to

evade") (to ~ out of one's obligations)
weather *n.* 1. to forecast, predict the ~ 2. (good)
beautiful; clear, fair; dry; fine, good, nice, pleasant; mild; seasonable ~ (we had nice ~ all week) 3.
(bad) atrocious, bad, beastly, bleak, dismal,
dreary, foul, gloomy, inclement, nasty, stormy;
threatening; ugly ~ 4. (rainy) cloudy, overcast;
damp; foggy; overcast; rainy; unsettled; wet ~ 5.
(warm) hot; humid, muggy; sultry; sunny; sweltering; tropical; warm ~ 6. (cold) arctic; cold; cool;
freezing; windy; wintry ~ 7. the ~ clears up; the ~
turns cold/warm 8. ~ sets in (bad ~ set in) 9. in ~
(restaurants lose customers in bad ~) 10. (misc.)
under the ~ ("slightly ill")
weather forecast see **weather report**
weather report *n.* to give the ~
weather stripping *n.* to install, put on ~
weave I *n.* a coarse; fine; loose; plain; satin; tight;
twill ~
weave II *v.* 1. (C) she wove a basket for us; or: she
wove us a basket 2. (d; tr.) to ~ around, round (she
wove the story around a specific theme) 3. (d; tr.)
to ~ from, out of; into (she wants to ~ a scarf from
this wool; they want to ~ this wool into a scarf) 4.
(d; tr.) ("to insert") to ~ into (to ~ some humor into
a plot) 5. (misc.) to ~ in and out of traffic
web *n.* 1. to spin; weave a ~ 2. an intricate, tangled ~
(a tangled ~ of intrigue) 3. a spider ~ 4. (computers) to browse; surf the ~ 5. the World Wide Web
USAGE NOTE: Spiders *spin* webs. People *weave*
webs (the author wove a web of mystery).
web site *n.* (computers) to access; build, create;
design; visit a ~
wedded *adj.* (cannot stand alone) ~ to (~ to tradition)
wedding *n.* ["ceremony"] 1. to have, hold a ~ 2. to
officiate at, perform a ~ 3. to attend a ~ 4. a big;
(humorous) shotgun ~ 5. at a ~ ["anniversary"]
(esp. BE) 6. see **wedding anniversary**
wedding anniversary *n.* a diamond; golden; silver
~
wedding cake *n.* to cut the ~
wedding date *n.* to set a ~
wedding day *n.* on smb.'s ~
wedge I *n.* to drive a ~ between; into
wedge II *v.* 1. (d; intr., tr.) to ~ between; into 2. (N;
used with an adjective) she ~d the door open
wedged *adj.* (cannot stand alone) ~ between; in
wedlock *n.* 1. to join in ~ 2. out of ~ (born out of ~)
weed out *v.* (D; tr.) to ~ from
weeds *n.* 1. to pull ~ 2. to kill ~
week *n.* 1. to spend a ~ (somewhere) 2. last; next;
this ~ 3. a ~ from (Tuesday) 4. by the ~ (she is paid
by the ~) 5. during the ~ 6. for a ~ (they came here
for a ~) 7. for ~s (she hasn't been here for ~s; esp.
AE is: she hasn't been here in ~s) 8. in a ~, in a ~'s
time (esp. BE) (they'll be here in a ~) 9. (misc.) the

working ~; (AE) freshman ~
USAGE NOTE: In the meaning "a week from
Tuesday", BE also has—a week on Tuesday, (on)
Tuesday week. Note also the BE expressions—she
arrived a week last Tuesday; she will arrive a week
next Tuesday.
weekday *n.* on ~s; AE also has: ~s (she works ~s/on
~s)
weekend *n.* 1. to spend a ~ somewhere 2. at (BE),
during, over (esp. AE) the ~ 3. (AE) on ~s (I work
on ~s) 4. (AE) ~s (she works ~s) 5. (BE) at ~s, at
the ~ (he works at ~s) 6. (misc.) a long ~; a holiday
~; have a nice ~!
weeknight *n.* on ~s; AE also has: ~s (she works ~s/
on ~s)
weep *v.* 1. to ~ bitterly 2. (d; intr.) to ~ about, over
(to ~ over one's misfortune) 3. (d; intr.) to ~ for,
with (to ~ for joy) 4. (E) she wept to see them so
poor 5. (misc.) I wept at seeing them so poor
weevil *n.* an alfalfa; boll ~
weigh *v.* 1. to ~ heavily 2. (d; intr.) ("to count") to ~
against (his testimony will ~ heavily against you)
3. (d; tr.) ("to balance") to ~ against (to ~ one
argument against another) 4. (d; intr.) ("to press")
to ~ on (legal problems ~ed heavily on her mind)
5. (P; intr.) ("to have a weight") the suitcase ~s
quite a lot 6. (misc.) to ~ in smb.'s favor
weigh down *v.* 1. (D; tr.) to ~ by, with (we were ~ed
down with packages) 2. (esp. AE) (D; intr.) to ~ on
(snow ~ed down on the roof)
weigh in *v.* (D; intr.) to ~ at (the boxer ~ed in at one
hundred fifty pounds)
weight I *n.* ["amount weighed, heaviness"] 1. to
gain, put on ~ 2. to lose, take off ~ 3. to check;
control; watch one's ~ 4. to bear a ~ (the central
beam must bear a very heavy ~) 5. (a) dead; gross;
minimum; net ~ 6. atomic; avoirdupois; birth;
molecular ~ 7. under a ~ (the table collapsed under
the ~ of the food) 8. (misc.) excess ~ (as in air
travel) ["device used in athletic exercises for its
heaviness"] 9. to lift ~s 10. heavy; light ~s 11. a set
of ~s ["importance"] 12. to carry ~ (with) 13. to
add; attach, give, lend ~ to 14. considerable ~ 15.
(misc.) to throw one's ~ about (BE)/around ("to
flaunt one's influence"); to pull one's ~ ("to do
one's fair share"); it was a (great) ~ off my mind
("I felt relieved")
weight II *v.* 1. to ~ heavily 2. (D; tr.) ("to slant") to
~ against (the evidence was ~ed heavily against
me)
weighting *n.* (BE) ["salary supplement"] to get
(the) London ~
weigh up *v.* (BE) (Q) to ~ whether to do smt.
weird *adj.* (colloq.) 1. ~ about (there is smt. ~ about
them) 2. ~ to + inf. (it was ~ to see her again = it
was ~ seeing her again) 3. ~ that + clause (it's ~
that you never noticed her)

welcome I *adj.* 1. perfectly ~ 2. ~ to (you are ~ to my share; ~ to New York!) 3. ~ to + inf. (you are ~ to borrow my car at any time) 4. (misc.) to make smb. feel ~; ~ home!
welcome II *n.* 1. to bid, extend, give a ~ to 2. to receive a ~ 3. to outstay, overstay one's ~ 4. a cordial, effusive, enthusiastic, hearty, rousing, royal, warm ~ (we gave them a rousing ~) 5. a chilly, cool ~ 6. a ~ from; to (we received a warm ~ from the mayor; the immigrants received a cool ~ to their new country)
welcome III *v.* 1. to ~ cordially, enthusiastically, warmly 2. to ~ coolly 3. (D; tr.) to ~ from (they ~ inquiries from readers) 4. (D; tr.) to ~ to (we ~d them to our city)
welcome mat *n.* (colloq.) (esp. AE) to put out the ~ for smb.
weld *v.* (D; tr.) to ~ onto, to
welfare *n.* ["government financial aid"] 1. public ~ 2. (esp. US) on ~ (to be on ~; to go on ~) ["well-being"] 3. to promote the public ~ 4. the general; public ~ 5. child; social ~ 6. for smb.'s ~
well I *adv.* 1. to leave ~ enough alone (AE)/to leave ~ alone (BE) ("not to interfere with smt. that is satisfactory") 2. to do ~ (at, in, on) 3. (misc.) are things going ~ for/with you? you did ~ to tell me; to mean ~; to think ~ of
well II *n.* ["hole dug to tap a supply of oil or water"] 1. to bore, dig, drill, sink a ~ 2. an abandoned; deep ~ 3. an artesian; oil ~ 4. a ~ dries up
well-advised *adj.* ~ to + inf. (you would be ~ to come early)
well-being *n.* 1. to threaten smb.'s ~ 2. material; physical; psychological ~ 3. (misc.) a sense of ~
well-disposed *adj.* ~ towards
well-grounded *adj.* ~ in
well-informed *adj.* ~ about, on
well-intentioned *adj.* ~ towards
well-known *adj.* 1. ~ for 2. ~ to 3. ~ that + clause (it's ~ that she intends to retire next year)
well up I *adv.* 1. (AE) ~ in years 2. ~ on (the latest styles)
well up II *v.* (D; intr.) to ~ in (tears ~ed up in his eyes)
welt *n.* to raise a ~ (on the skin)
west I *adj., adv.* 1. directly, due, straight ~ 2. ~ of (~ of the city) 3. (misc.) to face; go, head ~; northwest by ~; southwest by ~
west II *n.* 1. from the ~; in the ~; to the ~ 2. (AE) out ~ ("in the western part of the US") 3. (misc.) the Wild West (old-fashioned colloq.) ("the western part of the US"); (BE) up ~ (London slang) ("to the West End of London from the East End"); to go ~ (esp. BE; old-fashioned) ("to die")
wet *adj.* 1. dripping, soaking, sopping, wringing ~ 2. ~ from; with (~ with dew) 3. (misc.) she got her shoes ~; he got ~ through and through

whack I *n.* (colloq.) ["blow"] 1. to give smb. a ~ ["attempt"] 2. to take a ~ at 3. to have the first ~ at ["share"] (colloq.) (BE) 4. a fair; full ~ (of) ["misc."] 5. out of ~ (esp. AE) (she threw her shoulder out of ~); to have a ~ at smt. (esp. BE) ("to give smt. a try")
whack II *v.* (colloq.) (O) ("to strike") I'll ~ you one
whale *n.* ["sea mammal"] 1. to harpoon a ~ 2. a blue; bowhead; right; sperm; white ~ 3. a pod, school of ~s 4. a young ~ is a calf 5. a female ~ is a cow 6. a male ~ is a bull ["misc."] 7. a ~ of a good time ("a very good time")
whammy *n.* (slang) (esp. AE) ["jinx"] 1. to put a (the) ~ on smb. 2. a double ~
wharf *n.* at; on a ~ (the ship was tied up at a ~)
what *determiner, pronoun* 1. ~ about, of (~ about them?) 2. (used in exclamatory sentences) ~ a (~ a day!) 3. (misc.) (colloq.) she has ~ it takes ("she is very capable"); to know ~'s ~ ("to understand clearly what the situation is"); ~ else is new? (esp. AE); so ~? ~ on earth can she mean? ~'s new?
wheat *n.* 1. to grow; harvest; plant ~ 2. to grind; thresh ~ (to grind ~ into flour) 3. summer; winter ~ 4. club; common; drum; hybrid ~ 5. cracked; whole ~
USAGE NOTE: AE has *whole wheat bread, whole wheat flour;* BE has *wholemeal bread, wholemeal flour.*
wheedle *v.* 1. (d; tr.) to ~ from, out of (to ~ information from smb.) 2. (d; tr.) to ~ into (to ~ smb. into doing smt.)
wheel I *n.* ["circular rim or solid disc joined to a hub that turns"] 1. to spin; turn a ~ 2. to align; balance; rotate ~s (on a car) 3. a balance; driving; front; idler; mill; paddle; potter's; ratchet; rear; retractable; roulette; spinning; sprocket; undershot; water ~ 4. a big (BE), Ferris ~ (in an amusement park) 5. a ~ spins; turns 6. (misc.) to break on the ~; (humorous) to reinvent the ~ ["device that turns a car"] 7. to take the ~ 8. a steering ~ (to turn the steering ~) 9. (to be) at the ~ (who was at the ~ when the accident occurred?) ["misc."] 10. a big ~ ("an influential person")
wheel II *v.* (P; tr.) she ~ed the chair into the room
wheelbarrow *n.* to push, roll a ~
wheelchair *n.* 1. to push a ~ 2. a motorized ~
wherewithal *n.* ["resources"] 1. the ~ for (to have the ~ for a trip abroad) 2. the ~ to + inf. (they didn't have the ~ to conduct a successful political campaign)
which *determiner, pronoun* ~ of (~ of them do you know?)
USAGE NOTE: The use of the preposition *of* is necessary when a pronoun follows. When a noun follows, the use of *which of the* limits the meaning—which student(s) did you see? which of the students whom we had discussed did you see?

whiff *n.* (colloq.) ["smell, odor"] 1. to catch; get; have; take a ~ of (to get a good ~ of tear gas) 2. to give smb. a ~ of smt. 3. at a ~ (she lost consciousness at the first ~ of ether)

while *n.* 1. a good, long, little ~ (I had to wait a long ~) 2. (misc.) it was worth our ~

whim *n.* 1. to have, pursue; satisfy a ~ 2. to indulge a ~ 3. an idle; passing; sudden ~ 4. a ~ to + inf. (I had a sudden ~ to go for a walk) 5. at; on a ~ (they went there on a ~)

whine *v.* 1. (B) she ~d a few words to them 2. (D; intr.) to ~ about (he kept ~ing about his bad luck) 3. (L; to) she ~d (to us) that she had been cheated

whinge *v.* (colloq.) (BE) see **whine** 2, 3

whip I *n.* ["lash used for whipping"] 1. to crack, snap a ~ ["dessert made by whipping"] 2. a prune ~ ["member of a political party who enforces party discipline"] 3. a government (GB); majority; minority; opposition (GB); party ~ ["official party edict"] (GB) 4. to defy a ~ (against) 5. a three-line ~ ("most insistent") (to defy a government three-line ~)

whip II *v.* 1. (d; tr.) ("to beat") to ~ into (to ~ eggs into a froth) 2. (colloq.) (d; tr.) ("to bring") to ~ into (the sergeant ~ped the recruits into shape) 3. (d; tr.) ("to incite") to ~ into (the speaker ~ped the crowd into a frenzy) 4. (P; intr.) ("to move very quickly") they ~ped into position

whip hand *n.* ["control"] to get; have the ~ over

whipping *n.* ["beating"] 1. to get, receive, take a ~ (from) 2. to give smb. a ~

whip-round *n.* (BE) ["collection"] to have a ~

whirl I *n.* (colloq.) ["try"] 1. to give smt. a ~ ["hectic activity"] 2. the social ~ 3. (misc.) my mind is in a ~

whirl II *v.* (P; intr.) the leaves ~ed through the air

whirlpool *n.* to be drawn into a ~

whisk I *n.* an egg ~ (BE; AE has *eggbeater*)

whisk II *v.* (P; tr.) ("to move quickly") they were ~ed into the hotel; the important visitors were ~ed through customs

whisk away see **whisk off**

whiskers *n.* ["beard"] 1. to grow ~ 2. to shave off one's ~ 3. rough ~

whiskey, whisky *n.* 1. to age; distill, produce ~ 2. straight ("undiluted") ~ 3. blended; bonded (US); corn; Irish; malt; rye; Scotch ~ 4. ~ ages 5. a shot of ~

USAGE NOTE: The spelling *whiskey* is usu. used in Ireland and the US.

whisk off *v.* (colloq.) (d; tr.) to ~ to (they were ~ed off to prison)

whisper I *n.* 1. a stage ~ 2. in a ~ (to speak in a ~)

whisper II *v.* 1. (B) he ~ed a few words to her 2. (d; intr.) to ~ about (what were they ~ing about?) 3. (d; intr., tr.) to ~ into (I ~ed a few words into her ear) 4. (E) she ~ed to us to be careful 5. (L; to) she

~ed (to us) that she was preparing a surprise party

whistle I *n.* ["instrument that produces a whistling sound"] 1. to blow (on) a ~ 2. a bird; factory; police; referee's ~ 3. a ~ blows, sounds ["act of whistling"] 4. to give a ~ 5. a loud; shrill ~ ["misc."] 6. as clean as a ~ ("very clean"); to blow the ~ on smb. ("to reveal smb.'s evil intentions")

whistle II *v.* 1. (B) she ~d a song to me 2. (D; intr.) to ~ at; to (who ~d at you?) 3. (D; intr.) to ~ with (to ~ with surprise)

USAGE NOTE: One whistles *to* smb. to attract her/his attention. One whistles *at* smb. to express one's feelings about that person.

white I *adj.* 1. lily; snow ~ 2. (misc.) as ~ as a sheet; ~ with anger

white II *n.* ["a color"] 1. dressed in ~ ["the albumen of an egg"] 2. an egg ~ (for this recipe, beat two egg ~s until stiff)

white feather *n.* ["symbol of cowardice"] to show the ~

white flag *n.* ["symbol of surrender"] to hoist, show the ~

white lie *n.* to tell a ~

white paper *n.* ["official government report"] 1. to issue a ~ 2. a ~ on

white slavery *n.* to sell smb. into ~

whittle *v.* 1. (D; intr.) to ~ at (to ~ at a piece of wood) 2. (D; tr.) to ~ into (to ~ a reed into a whistle) 3. (D; tr.) to ~ out of (to ~ a whistle out of a reed)

whittle away *v.* (D; intr.) to ~ at (to ~ at smb.'s alibi)

whiz, whizz I *n.* (colloq.) a ~ at (she is a ~ at languages)

whiz, whizz II *v.* (P; intr.) to ~ through the air

whole *n.* 1. to constitute, form a ~ 2. a complete; integrated ~ 3. as a ~ 4. on the ~ (the situation is, on the ~, satisfactory)

whole hog *n.* (colloq.) ["the whole way"] to go ~ (AE)/the ~

wholesale *adv.* to buy; sell ~

whoop *n.* ["loud cry"] to emit, let out a ~

whoopee *n.* (colloq.) ["boisterous fun"] to make ~

whooping cough *n.* to catch (the) ~

whopper *n.* (colloq.) ["a big lie"] to tell a ~

wicked *adj.* 1. ~ of (that was ~ of her) 2. ~ to + inf. (it's ~ to lie)

wide *adj.* ["deviating"] (cannot stand alone) ~ of (you are ~ of the mark)

widow *n.* 1. a war ~ 2. (humorous) a golf; grass ~

widower *n.* (humorous) a grass ~

width *n.* in ~ (ten feet in ~)

wife *n.* 1. (old-fashioned) to take a ~ 2. to beat; desert, leave a ~ 3. an abused, battered; common-law; estranged ~; ex-wife, former; jealous; unfaithful ~ 4. (misc.) he had two children by his first ~

wig n. 1. to wear a ~ 2. to put on; take off a ~
wild I adj. ["enthusiastic"] (colloq.) 1. to go ~ (the spectators went ~) 2. ~ about, over (the audience went ~ over the new play) ["furious"] 3. ~ with (~ with anger) 4. (misc.) to drive smb. ~ ["out of control"] 5. to run ~
wild II n. ["wilderness"] in the ~ (to live in the ~)
wilderness n. 1. a desolate; trackless; unexplored ~ 2. in the ~
wildfire n. to spread like ~ ("to spread very quickly")
wild oats n. ["youthful excesses"] to sow one's ~
wilds n. see **wild II**; lost in the ~ of the Yukon
will I n. ["desire"] 1. to impose one's ~ (on) 2. to implement the ~ (of the majority) 3. the ~ to + inf. (lacking the ~ to survive) 4. at ~ 5. (misc.) to lose the ~ to live; a clash of (strong) ~s; against smb.s ~; with a ~ (to work with the ~ to succeed) ["attitude"] 6. to show good ~ 7. to bear no ill ~ ["choice"] 8. free ~ (of their own free ~) 9. at ~ (to fire at ~) ["legal document disposing of an estate"] 10. to draw up, make, make out a ~ 11. to change a ~ 12. to administer; execute a ~ 13. to probate, validate a ~ 14. to challenge, contest a ~ 15. to break, overturn a ~ 16. to repudiate a ~ 17. a deathbed ~ 18. a living ~ 19. (misc.) to be cut out of a ~; to be named in a ~; to be remembered in smb.'s ~ ["spirit"] ["power to make decisions"] 20. to break smb.'s ~ 21. an indomitable, iron, strong; inflexible, unbending ~
will II v. (A) he ~ed his entire estate to her; or: he ~ed her his entire estate
will III v. (auxiliary) (F) she ~ return
willies n. (colloq.) ["jitters"] 1. to get the ~ 2. to give smb. the ~ (her behavior gives me the ~)
willing adj. 1. ~ to + inf. (she is ~ to help) 2. (misc.) we are ~ for them to share in the benefits
willingness n. 1. to demonstrate, show ~ 2. to express ~ 3. the ~ to + inf. (she expressed her ~ to work for us)
willpower n. 1. to demonstrate, show ~ 2. great, sheer ~ 3. the ~ to + inf. (do you have the ~ to stick to the diet?)
wily adj. ~ of (that was ~ of him)
win I n. to chalk up a ~
win II v. 1. to ~ easily, handily, hands down 2. (D; intr.) to ~ against (to ~ against considerable odds) 3. (D; intr.) to ~ at (to ~ at cards) 4. (O) her perseverance won her the award 5. (misc.) to ~ by a mile
wince v. 1. (D; intr.) to ~ at (to ~ at the thought of going back to work) 2. (misc.) to ~ in pain
win back v. (D; tr.) to ~ from (she won the trophy back from her chief rival)
winch I n. to operate, use a ~
winch II v. (P; tr.) they ~ed the victims to safety
wind I n. /wind/ ["movement, current of air"] 1. a

balmy, gentle, light; fair, favorable ~ 2. a brisk, heavy, high, stiff, strong; gale-force; gusty ~ 3. a biting, cold, cutting, icy; raw ~ 4. an adverse; head; tail ~ 5. a trade ~ 6. the prevailing ~s 7. the ~ blows; picks up; shifts 8. the wind dies down, drops, falls, subsides 9. the ~ howls; whistles 10. a blast, gust; puff of ~ 11. a down; up ~ 12. (misc.) as free as the ~ ["knowledge"] 13. to get ~ of smt. ["breath"] 14. to catch, get one's second ~ 15. out of ~ ["misc."] 16. to break ~ ("to expel rectal gas"); in the ~ ("imminent"); to take the ~ out of smb.'s sails ("to deflate smb."); to see how the ~ blows ("to see what is likely to happen")
wind II v. /waynd/ 1. (d; tr.) to ~ around, round (she wound the string around her finger) 2. (P; intr.) the procession wound through the town 3. (misc.) to ~ smb. around one's little finger ("to manipulate smb.")
winded adj. ["out of breath"] easily ~
windfall n. ["good fortune"] 1. to get, have a ~ 2. a sudden, unexpected ~
windmill n. 1. a ~ turns 2. (misc.) to tilt at ~s ("to struggle with imaginary opponents")
window n. 1. to open a ~; to roll down a ~ (in a car) 2. to close, shut a ~; to roll up a ~ (in a car) 3. to clean, wash a ~ 4. a bay; bow; French; lattice; picture; storm ~ 5. a shop, store (esp. AE) ~ 6. a back, rear; front; side ~ (as of a car) 7. a ~ fogs up, sweats; frosts over
window shade n. (AE) 1. to lift, raise a ~ 2. to draw, drop, lower a ~ (BE has *blind*)
wind up v. ("to end up") 1. (d; intr, tr.) to ~ by (she wound up her affairs by selling all her stock) 2. (d; intr.) to ~ with 3. (G) I wound up paying for everyone 4. (misc.) to ~ out in the cold; she wound up worse off than when she started
wine n. 1. to make, produce ~ (a) 2. to decant, pour ~ 3. (a) dry; sweet ~ 4. (a) cooking; dessert; table; vintage ~ 5. (a) red; rosé; sparkling; white ~ 6. (a) communion; sacramental ~ 7. mulled ~ 8. (a) domestic; imported ~ 9. a house ~ (of a restaurant) 10. ~ ferments 11. a bottle; carafe; decanter; glass of ~
USAGE NOTE: The phrase *domestic wine* seems to be reserved for wine produced in English-speaking countries. English-speakers in France or Italy, for example, usu. do not refer to French or Italian wine as *domestic*.
wing n. ["faction of a political party"] 1. a conservative; left; liberal; radical; right ~ ["a bird's appendage used for flying"] 2. a bird beats, flaps, flutters; spreads its ~s (the bird spread its ~s and flew off) 3. (misc.) to clip smb.'s ~s ("to restrict smb.'s freedom"); to spread one's ~s ("to develop one's full potential") ["protection"] 4. to take smb. under one's ~ ["act of flying"] 5. to take ~ (also fig.) 6. on the ~ ["extension, annex of a building"] 7. to

add a ~ (to a building) 8. (BE) see **fender** ["misc."]
9. to wait in the ~s ("to await the opportunity to
take over a job"); the political ~ ("the political
section of an organization")
wink I *n.* 1. to give smb. a ~ 2. a suggestive ~ 3.
(misc.) I didn't get a ~ of sleep last night; I didn't
sleep a ~ last night; to get, have forty ~s ("to take a
brief nap"); (BE) to tip smb. the ~ ("to give smb.
secret information")
wink II *v.* (D; intr.) to ~ at (also fig.: the police ~ed
at illegal gambling)
winkle I *v.* (colloq.) (BE) (d; tr.) ("to obtain") to ~ out
of (to ~ the truth out of smb.)
winner *n.* 1. a clear; likely; real; sure ~ 2. (misc.) to
be on to a (sure) ~ (at a racetrack)
winning number *n.* to draw a ~
win out *v.* (d; intr.) to ~ over (we won out over the
opposition)
win over *v.* (d; tr.) to ~ to (we won them over to our
side)
winter *n.* 1. a cold, cruel, hard, harsh, severe, terrible ~ 2. a mild ~ 3. in, over (the) ~ 4. (misc.) in
the dead of ~
wipe *v.* 1. (d; tr.) to ~ off ("to erase from") (to ~ a
city off the map) 2. (D; tr.) to ~ on (she ~d her
hands on the towel) 3. (N; used with an adjective)
he ~d the dishes dry
wipers *n.* 1. to turn on the ~ 2. windscreen (BE),
windshield (AE) ~
wire I *n.* ["long metal thread"] 1. to string ~ 2.
barbed; chicken; copper ~ 3. a trip ~ ["cable conducting electric current"] 4. to cross, jump ~s (in
order to start a car) 5. (esp. AE) to tap ~s 6.
telephone ~s 7. (an) electric; high-tension ~ 8.
heavy-duty ~ ["cablegram, telegram"] (esp. AE) 9.
to send a ~ ["finish line"] (esp. AE) (also fig.) 10.
(right) down to the ~ ("to the very end") 11.
(misc.) to get in under the ~ ("to enter barely in
time")
wire II *v.* (esp. AE) (CE has *telegraph*) 1. (A) ("to
send by wire") we ~d the money to her; or: we ~d
her the money 2. (d; intr.) ("to request by sending
a wire") to ~ for (she ~d home for some money) 3.
(H; no passive) ("to inform by wire") we ~d them
to return home immediately 4. (L; may have an
object) ("to inform by wire") she ~d (us) that the
manuscript had arrived 5. (Q; may have an object)
we will ~ (you) where to meet
wire III *v.* 1. (D; tr.) ("to provide with wire") to ~
for (the auditorium was ~d for sound) 2. (d; tr.)
("to connect") to ~ to (the explosives were ~d to
the door)
wire back *v.* (esp. AE) (see **wire II**) 1. (L; to) they
~d back (to us) that they would attend the conference 2. (Q; to) they ~d back where we should meet
wireless *n.* (BE) (now less common than *radio*) see
radio 1-4, 6

wiring *n.* 1. defective, faulty ~ 2. electric ~
wisdom *n.* 1. to impart ~ 2. to doubt, question
smb.'s ~ (to question the ~ of an action) 3. (the)
conventional, (the) received ~ 4. folk, homespun ~
5. the ~ to + inf. (will they have the ~ to make the
correct choice?) 6. of ~ (a person of great ~) 7.
(misc.) in their infinite ~, the council members
voted to cut the police budget in the midst of a
crime wave
wise *adj.* ["sagacious"] 1. ~ to + inf. (it was ~ of you
to remain silent = you were ~ to remain silent)
["aware of"] (colloq.) 2. ~ to (she was ~ to their
scheme; I finally got ~ to their tricks; they put me
~ to his tricks)
wisecrack I *n.* ["flippant remark"] 1. to make a ~ 2.
a ~ about
wisecrack II *v.* (colloq.) (L) ("to remark flip-
pantly") she ~ed that she could earn more money
at home
wise up *v.* (colloq.) (AE) (D; intr.) to ~ to (I finally
~d up to his tricks)
wish I *n.* ["desire"] 1. to make a ~ 2. to fulfill,
realize a ~ 3. to get one's ~ 4. to express a ~ 5. to
respect smb.'s ~(es) 6. to grant smb.'s ~ 7. a
fervent, strong; unfulfilled ~ 8. smb.'s dying ~
(her dying ~ to see her children was granted) 9. the
death ~ 10. a ~ comes true 11. a ~ for (a ~ for
peace) 12. a ~ to + inf. (they expressed a ~ to visit
the museum) 13. a ~ that + clause; subj. (the editor
respected her ~ that the contribution not be/should
not be announced publicly) 14. against smb.'s ~es
(the project was carried out against our ~es) 15. in
accordance with smb.'s ~es ["greetings"] 16. to
extend, offer, send one's (best) ~es 17. one's best,
good, warm, warmest ~es 18. one's ~es for (one's
best ~es for the New Year)
wish II *v.* 1. (A; usu. without *to*) they ~ed us good
luck 2. (D; intr.) to ~ for (we were ~ing for cool
weather) 3. (formal) (E) I ~ to lodge a complaint 4.
(formal) (H; no passive) do you ~ me to stay? 5.
(L) we ~ that she would settle down 6. (misc.) to ~
smb. well ("to hope that things will go well for
smb.")
wit I *n.* 1. to display, show ~ 2. (a) keen, penetrating, sharp; sophisticated; sparkling ~ 3. (a) dry;
quick, ready; sly ~ 4. (an) acerbic, acid, biting,
caustic, cutting, mordant, trenchant ~ 5. (misc.) at
one's ~'s end (see also **wits**)
wit II to ~ ("namely")
witchcraft *n.* to practice ~
witch-hunt *n.* to conduct a ~ against
withdraw *v.* (D; intr., tr.) to ~ from; into, to (our
troops have withdrawn from the border area; to ~
money from a bank; to ~ to a safer area; to ~ into
one's shell)
withdrawal *n.* ["removal of funds"] 1. to make a ~
2. mass ~s 3. a ~ from (a ~ from an account)

["retreat"] (often mil.) 4. to carry out, make a ~ 5. to complete a ~ 6. an orderly; phased; precipitate; strategic; tactical; unilateral ~ 7. a ~ from; into, to (a ~ to higher ground)

withhold *v.* (D; tr.) to ~ from (to ~ information from the police)

within *n.*, *prep.* 1. ~ a mile of 2. (misc.) an attempt to reform the system from ~

witness I *n.* ["testimony"] 1. to bear ~ to 2. false ~ (to bear false ~) ["one who testifies"] 3. to produce a ~ (the district attorney finally produced a credible ~) 4. to call, subpoena; swear in a ~; to hear ~es 5. to cross-examine; examine, interrogate, question; interview a ~ 6. to badger; bribe; confuse; discredit; lead; suborn; trap a ~ 7. a defense; expert ~; eyewitness; prosecution ~ 8. a competent; credible; reliable ~ 9. a character; hostile ~ 10. a key; material ~ 11. a ~ is sworn in = a ~ takes the oath 12. a ~ testifies (under oath) 13. a ~ stands down, steps down 14. a ~ against (a ~ against one's former accomplices) 15. a ~ for (a ~ for the prosecution) 16. a ~ to (a ~ to an accident)

witness II *v.* (K) who ~ed his signing the documents?

witness box *n.* (BE) to go into the ~

witness stand *n.* (AE) to take the ~

wits *n.* 1. to collect one's ~ 2. to match ~ with smb. 3. the ~ to + inf. (he didn't have enough ~ to realize what was happening) 4. (misc.) keep your ~ about you! ("stay alert!"); to live by one's ~; at one's wits' end; a battle of ~; to drive smb. out of her/his ~; to be frightened out of one's ~

witty *adj.* ~ of (that was ~ of her)

wizard *n.* 1. a financial; mathematical ~ 2. a ~ at (a ~ at solving crossword puzzles)

wizardry *n.* sheer ~

woe *n.* a tale of ~

wolf *n.* 1. ~ves howl 2. ~ves hunt in packs 3. a pack of ~ves 4. a young ~ is a pup 5. (misc.) to cry ~ ("to give a false alarm"); to keep the ~ from the door ("to provide the necessities"); a ~ in sheep's clothing ("one who disguises hostile intentions")

woman *n.* 1. to deliver a ~ (of a baby) 2. an attractive, beautiful, pretty; average; fat; grown; handsome; middle-aged; old; short; tall; thin; ugly; wise; young ~ 3. a divorced; married; single ~ 4. a career; liberated; professional; self-made; stunt; working ~ 5. an anchor ~; businesswoman; newspaperwoman 6. (AE) a cleaning ~ (BE has *charwoman, char*) 7. (BE) a lollipop ~ (AE has *crossing guard*) 8. (AE) enlisted women (BE has *other ranks*) 9. a battered ~ 10. the other ~ ("a married man's paramour") 11. (misc.) a ~ of letters; a ~ of action; a ~ of the world; the ~ of the year

USAGE NOTE: The terms *career woman* and *working woman* are becoming old-fashioned. (see

also the Usage Note for **girl**)

womanhood *n.* to reach ~

wonder I *n.* 1. to perform, work a ~ 2. to achieve ~s 3. to do ~s for 4. a natural ~ 5. a ~ that + clause (it's a ~ that we didn't get lost; it's no small ~ that they had so much trouble) 6. in ~ (to look around in ~) 7. (misc.) the seven ~s of the world; the eighth ~ of the world

wonder II *v.* 1. to ~ really, very much (I really ~ if/ whether they'll come) 2. (D; intr.) to ~ about, at (to ~ about a problem) 3. (L) I shouldn't ~ that you are tired after all that work 4. (Q) I ~ why they left 5. (misc.) one's ~ that + clause (it was ~ that we could see each other)

wonderful *adj.* 1. ~ to + inf. (it was ~ to visit our national parks; it was ~ of them to come) 2. ~ that + clause (it was ~ that we could see each other)

wonderland *n.* a scenic ~

wonderment *n.* in ~

wont I *adj.* (formal) (rare) ["accustomed"] (cannot stand alone) ~ to + inf. (she is ~ to call at any time; she got here late, as she is ~ to do)

wont II *n.* (formal) (rare) ["custom"] 1. it is her ~ to arrive late 2. she arrived late, as was/is her ~

wood *n.* 1. to chop, cut ~ 2. to gather ~ 3. firewood; kindling ~ 4. a block; cord; piece; sliver of ~ 5. (misc.) out of the ~ (BE)/~s (AE) ("safe from danger"); in our neck of the ~s ("where we live")

wool *n.* 1. to produce ~ 2. to comb; process; sort ~ 3. lamb's; steel, wire (BE) ~ 4. (one hundred percent) pure ~ 5. (CE) cotton ~ (AE has *absorbent cotton*) 6. a ball; skein of ~ 7. (misc.) to pull the ~ over smb.'s eyes ("to deceive smb.")

woozy *adj.* (colloq.) ["dazed, dizzy"] ~ from (~ from lack of sleep)

word I *n.* ["independent, meaningful linguistic form"] 1. to coin, make up a ~ 2. to define a ~ 3. to spell; write a ~ 4. to pronounce, say, utter a ~ 5. to mispronounce a ~ 6. an archaic, obsolete ~ 7. a compound; simple ~ 8. a monosyllabic; polysyllabic ~ 9. a borrowed; dialectal, regional; foreign; native ~ 10. a ghost; nonce ~ 11. a four-letter, obscene; taboo ~ 12. a portmanteau ~ 13. a guide ~ (at the top of a page in a dictionary, reference work) 14. (misc.) (upon) my ~! ("really!"); ~ for ~ ("verbatim"); a household ["common"] ~; to get a ~ in edgewise (AE)/edgeways (BE) ("to manage to say smt. in a dispute"); to have the last ~ ("to conclude an argument"); to put in a good ~ for smb. ("to plead smb.'s case"); in a ~ ("briefly"); begin at the ~ *go*; a buzz ~; a code ~ ["promise"] 15. to give one ~s 16. to take smb.'s ~ 17. to take smb. at her/his ~ 18. to break one's ~ 19. one's solemn ~; one's ~ of honor 20. one's ~ that + clause (she gave me her ~ that she would deliver the message) 21. of one's ~ (she's a woman of her ~) ("she keeps her promises") ["command"] 22. to give the ~ ["information, news"] 23. to bring; send ~ 24. to breathe, say a ~ (don't breathe a ~ about it

to anyone) 25. to get ~ (we got ~ that the contract would be signed) 26. the latest ~ 27. (esp. AE) advance ~ 28. ~ about, of (there was no ~ of the incident in the newspapers) 29. ~ that + clause (they sent ~ that they would be late) 30. (misc.) there has been no ~ from them ["conversation"] 31. to have a ~ with smb. about smt. (see also **words**) USAGE NOTE: The construction *I'd like to have a word with you* usu. indicates that the conversation will be of a serious nature. Compare *I had words with him* "I had an argument with him".
word II *v.* to ~ smt. carefully; strongly; tactfully
wording *n.* the exact ~
word order *n.* (a) fixed; flexible; normal; reverse ~
word processor *n.* a dedicated ~
words *n.* ["text"] 1. (the) ~ of, to (a song) ["discussion"] 2. to bandy, exchange ~ with smb. ["argument"] 3. to have ~ with smb. 4. (misc.) ~ passed between them ["words that constitute a statement"] 5. to say a few ~ about smt. 6. to weigh ("consider with care") one's ~ (carefully) 7. to distort smb.'s ~ 8. to not mince any ~ ("to speak frankly") 9. (misc.) smb.'s dying ~ ["words that express strong feeling"] 10. kind; sincere; warm ~ 11. choice; eloquent; high-sounding ~ 12. angry, cross, sharp; fighting; harsh; hasty; heated, hot; threatening ~ 13. hollow, hypocritical; weasel ~ ["misc."] 14. to choose one's ~ carefully; in so many ~ ("precisely"); of few ~ ("not talkative"); to hang on (to) smb.'s ~ ("to listen to smb. very attentively"); she took the ~ right out of my mouth ("she said exactly what I wanted to say"); a play on ~ ("a pun")
work I *n.* ["labor"] 1. to do ~ (they never do any ~) 2. to begin, start; quit (AE), stop ~ (they quit ~ at one o'clock) 3. to take on ~ 4. delicate; easy, light ~ 5. meticulous, precise ~ 6. backbreaking, hard, heavy; demanding; exhausting, tiring ~ 7. dirty, scut (AE); physical ~ 8. shoddy, slipshod, sloppy ~ 9. clerical, office; paper ~ 10. fieldwork 11. full-time; part-time ~ 12. (misc.) he never does a lick/ stitch (AE)/stroke of ~; to make short ~ of ("to dispose of quickly"); to undo smb.'s ~ ("to destroy the results of smb.'s labor") ["employment"] 13. to get to, go to ~ 14. to begin, start ~ 15. to finish, stop ~ 16. to return to ~ 17. to take (time) off from ~ 18. to leave ~ (early) 19. at ~ (they are still at ~) 20. (BE) in ~ ("employed") 21. out of ~ (they have been out of ~ for a week) ["result of research, labor, artistic effort"] 22. to exhibit; hang one's ~s (in a gallery) 23. a literary; scholarly ~ 24. collected; published; selected ~s 25. (misc.) ~ in progress; a ~ of art; their life's ~ was writing novels ["service"] 26. social ~ (to do social ~) 27. undercover ~ (to do undercover ~ for the police) 28. volunteer ~ ["treatment"] 29. root-

canal ~ (to do root-canal ~ on smb.) ["misc."] 30. to go to ~ on smb. ("to put pressure on smb.") (see also **works**)
work II *v.* 1. ("to labor") to ~ effectively; full-time; hard, strenuously; part-time 2. (d; intr.) to ~ against ("to oppose") (to ~ against a proposed law) 3. (D; intr.) ("to labor") to ~ as (to ~ as a teacher) 4. (d; intr.) ("to labor") to ~ at, on (they were ~ing on a new book; you have to ~ at being friendlier with people) 5. (d; intr.) ("to be employed; to labor") to ~ for (she ~s for a large firm; to ~ for a living) 6. (d; intr.) to ~ for ("to support") (to ~ for a good cause) 7. (d; refl.) ("to excite") to ~ into (she ~ed herself into a rage) 8. (d; tr.) to ~ into ("to insert") (she ~ed a few jokes into her speech) 9. (d; intr.) to ~ through ("to go through") (to ~ through difficult material) 10. (d; intr.) ("to progress") to ~ towards (to ~ towards a common goal) 11. (d; intr.) ("to labor") to ~ under ("to ~ under a noted scientist") 12. (d; intr.) ("to collaborate") to ~ with (to ~ closely with one's colleagues) 13. (misc.) to ~ far/ late into the night; to ~ one's way through college; to ~ one's way through a crowd; I slowly ~ed my way through the long report; the committee ~ed to reduce tension; to ~ against the clock; they are ~ing us to death; the screw ~ed (itself) loose; the drug needs time to ~ through the system; to ~ one's fingers to the bone; (BE) to ~ to rule ("to conform to all rules governing work so as to do only the minimum")
worked up *adj.* (colloq.) ~ about, over (he got himself all ~ over a trifle)
worker *n.* 1. to hire, take on a ~ 2. to retrain; train ~s 3. to organize, unionize ~s 4. to dismiss, fire, lay off, sack (colloq.) a ~; to make a ~ redundant (as by eliminating her/his job) (BE) 5. a diligent, efficient, good, hard, indefatigable; meticulous ~ 6. an idle; poor ~ 7. an assembly-line; blue-collar (esp. AE); construction; dock; factory ~ 8. an office; research; white-collar ~ 9. an immigrant; migrant; undocumented (AE) ~ 10. a full-time; part-time ~ 11. a skilled; unskilled ~ 12. (misc.) a social ~
workforce *n.* to cut, downsize, reduce the ~
working hours *n.* regular; staggered; unsocial (BE) ~ (during regular ~)
workings *n.* the inner ~
workload *n.* a heavy; light ~ (to carry a heavy ~)
workmanship *n.* 1. conscientious; meticulous, sound; delicate, exquisite, fine ~ 2. poor, shoddy ~
workout *n.* ["exercise"] 1. to get, have a ~ 2. a daily ~
work out *v.* 1. (D; intr.) to ~ with (to ~ with weights) 2. (Q) we ~ed out how to proceed
workplace *n.* at, in the ~ (to maintain harmony in the ~)
works *n.* ["construction projects"] 1. public ~

["preparation"] (colloq.) 2. in the ~ ["opera-tions"] 3. to gum up, mess up the ~ ["everything available"] (colloq.) 4. to give smb. the ~ ["misc."] 5. ~ of art (see **work I** 22-24)

workshop *n.* ["working seminar"] 1. to conduct a ~ 2. a ~ on

workup *n.* ["series of tests"] (esp. AE) 1. to do a ~ (on) 2. a diagnostic ~

work up *v.* 1. (d; refl., tr.) ("to excite") to ~ into (he ~ed himself up into a rage) 2. (d; refl., tr.) ("to incite") to ~ to (the orator ~ed the crowd up to a fever pitch) 3. (misc.) she ~ed her way up to the top; she ~ed her way up through the ranks; to get all ~ed up over smt.; he finally ~ed up the courage to ask for a promotion

world *n.* ["earth"] 1. around, round the ~ (to travel around the ~) 2. (misc.) to see the ~ ("to travel to many parts of the earth") ["area, **part of the** **earth**"] 3. the free; known; New; Old; Third ~ (in the Third ~) ["domain, realm, sphere"] 4. the ani-mal ~ 5. the academic; business; financial; liter-ary; scientific ~ 6. the civilized; outside; real ~ (out in the real ~) ["period"] 7. the ancient; medi-eval; modern ~ (there are many problems in the modern ~) ["life, being"] 8. to bring a child into the ~ 9. to come into the ~ 10. the next ~ ("life after death") ["misc."] 11. the whole ~; dead to the ~; in an ideal ~; it makes a ~ of difference; out of this ~ ("remarkable"); ~s apart ("very far apart")

world's fair *n.* to hold, stage a ~

World Wide Web *n.* 1. to browse; cruise the ~ 2. on the ~

worm *v.* 1. (d; tr.) to ~ into (how did they ~ their way into the meeting?) 2. (d; intr., tr.) to ~ out of (to ~ out of an obligation; to ~ information out of smb.) 3. (misc.) to ~ one's way into smb.'s confi-dence

worried *adj.* 1. unduly; very ~ 2. ~ about 3. ~ that + clause (we were ~ that she might not arrive on time) 4. (misc.) ~ sick; ~ to death

worry I *n.* 1. to cause ~ 2. deep, serious ~ 3. financial ~ries 4. ~ about, over 5. a ~ that + clause (their constant ~ that smt. bad would happen was understandable)

worry II *v.* 1. (D; intr.) to ~ about, over (they ~ about you; I ~ried about them working so hard; to ~ over trifles) 2. (L) I ~ that smt. might go wrong 3. (R) it ~ried me that they did not answer the telephone

worse *adj.* any ~ (will it be any ~ living in the city?)

worship I *n.* 1. ancestor; hero; idol; nature; public ~ (to practice ancestor ~) 2. (misc.) a house of ~

worship II *v.* 1. to ~ reverently 2. (D; tr.) to ~ as (to ~ smb. as a god) 3. (misc.) I ~ the ground she walks on

worst *n.* 1. to prepare for the ~ 2. to bring out the ~ in smb. 3. to expect; fear the ~ 4. to get the ~ of

smt. 5. at one's ~ (I'm at my ~ in the morning) 6. (misc.) if ~ comes to ~ (AE)/if the ~ comes to the ~; at (the) ~, our team may lose five matches

worth I *adj., prep.* 1. well ~ (the cost) 2. ~ to (how much is it ~ to you?) 3. ~ + -*ing* (it's not ~ keeping) 4. (misc.) ~ one's salt ("worthy of respect for one's work"); it's ~ a try; what is it ~? it would be (well) ~ your while to visit the exhibition

worth II *n.* 1. intrinsic; true ~ 2. net ~ 3. (legal) comparable ~ (the theory of comparable ~) 4. of ~ (books of great ~) 5. (misc.) she bought ten dollars ~ of vegetables; the fire did thousands of dollars ~ of damage

worthwhile *adj.* 1. ~ for (that experience was very ~ for them) 2. ~ to + inf. (it's ~ to visit the exhibit = it's ~ visiting the exhibit)

worthy *adj.* (usu. does not stand alone) ~ of (~ of praise)

would *v.* (F) ~ you do it?

wound *n.* 1. to inflict a ~ on/upon smb. 2. to re-ceive, sustain a ~ 3. to bandage, dress; cauterize; clean, cleanse; suture; swab a ~ 4. a deep; fatal, mortal; festering; flesh; gaping; light, slight; self-inflicted; serious, severe; superficial ~ (to receive a slight ~) 5. a bullet, gunshot; knife ~ 6. a ~ festers; weeps 7. a ~ heals 8. (misc.) to lick one's ~s ("to recover from a beating"); to open old ~s ("to stir up bad memories")

wounded *adj.* 1. badly; fatally, mortally; lightly, slightly; seriously ~ 2. (fig.) deeply ~ (I was deeply ~ by your remarks) 3. ~ in (she was ~ in the arm)

wracked *adj.* ~ with (~ with pain)

wrangle *v.* 1. to ~ constantly, incessantly 2. (D; intr.) to ~ about, over; with

wrangling *n.* 1. constant, incessant ~ 2. ~ about, over; with

wrap I *n.* (esp. AE) (a) freezer; plastic ~

wrap II *v.* 1. (d; refl., tr.) to ~ (a)round (to ~ a blanket around oneself) 2. (d; tr.) to ~ in (to ~ a child in a blanket)

wrapped up *adj.* ["engaged, busy"] ~ in (they are all ~ in campaigning)

wrapper *n.* a cellophane ~

wraps *n.* to keep a plan under ~ (colloq.) ("to keep a plan secret")

wrath *n.* (formal) 1. to arouse; incur smb.'s ~ 2. to bring down smb.'s ~ (on smb.) 3. to visit one's ~ upon smb.

wreak *v.* 1. (d; tr.) to ~ on (to ~ vengeance on smb.) 2. (misc.) to ~ havoc with smt.

wreath *n.* 1. to make, weave a ~ 2. to lay, place a ~ (they laid a ~ at the Tomb of the Unknown Sol-dier) 3. a bridal; Christmas; floral; funeral; laurel ~

wreathed *adj.* ~ in (~ in flowers; ~ in smiles)

wreck *n.* ["wrecked car"] 1. to tow a ~ 2. (misc.) the car was a total ~ ["person who has suffered a breakdown"] 3. a nervous ~ 4. (misc.) he was a total ~ after his wife died ["wrecked ship"] 5. to raise a ~ (to the surface)

wreckage *n.* 1. to strew ~ (over a wide area) 2. to clear, remove ~ 3. to raise ~ 4. twisted ~

wrench I *n.* 1. a monkey ~ 2. a lug ~ (BE also has *box spanner*)

wrench II *v.* 1. (d; tr.) to ~ from, off (he ~ed the handbag from the old woman) 2. (misc.) she ~ed her handbag free

wrest *v.* (d; tr.) to ~ from (to ~ power from a dictator)

wrestle *v.* 1. (D; intr.) to ~ with (to ~ with various problems) 2. (misc.) they ~d me to the ground

wrestler *n.* to pin; throw a ~

wrestling *n.* arm; catch-as-catch-can; Greco-Roman; Indian ~

wretch *n.* a homeless; miserable, poor ~

wretched *adj.* 1. to feel ~ 2. ~ about ~ (they felt perfectly ~ about the failure of the experiment) 3. ~ of (that was ~ of him)

wriggle *v.* 1. (d; intr.) to ~ out of (he ~d out of my grip) 2. (s) to ~ free, loose

wring *v.* 1. (d; tr.) ("to extract") to ~ from, out of (the police finally succeeded in ~ing a confession from the prisoner) 2. (N; used with an adjective) ("to squeeze") to ~ a towel dry

wrinkle *n.* ["crease"] 1. to make a ~ 2. to iron out, press out ~s ["innovation"] (colloq.) 3. the latest ~ in (the latest ~ in marketing home computers)

wrist *n.* 1. to sprain one's ~ 2. (misc.) to slash one's ~s; a slap on the ~ ("a minor rebuke")

writ *n.* ["legal order"] 1. to issue; serve a ~ (to serve a ~ on smb.) 2. to quash a ~

write *v.* 1. ("to form letters") to ~ illegibly; legibly 2. (A) ("to compose and send") she wrote a letter to me; or: she wrote me a letter 3. (C) ("to compose") he wrote a recommendation for me; or: he wrote me a recommendation 4. (d; intr.) to ~ about, of ("to describe") (to write about/of the war) 5. (D; tr.) to ~ about ("to compose about") (she wrote a book about her experiences) 6. (D; intr.) ("to be a writer") to ~ for (she ~s for popular magazines) 7. (d; intr.) to ~ for ("to request") (she wrote for a recommendation; she wrote to me for a recommendation; AE also has: she wrote me for a recommendation) 8. (d; intr.) to ~ to ("to compose and send a letter to") (he ~s to her every day; AE also has: he ~s her every day) 9. (D; tr.) to ~ to ("to compose for") (to ~ the words to a song) 10. (d; intr.) ("to order, command") to ~ to + to + inf. (she wrote to me to come home) 11. (AE) (H; no passive) ("to order, command") she wrote me to come home 12. (L; to; may have an object in AE) ("to

inform") they wrote to us/wrote us (AE) that they would come home 13. (Q; to; may have an object in AE) ("to inform") she wrote to us/wrote us (AE) where we were to meet 14. (misc.) she ~s home every week; she ~s extensively and publishes many books; his part was written out of the script; I ~ with a pen; she ~s poetry in French

write away *v.* 1. (d; intr.) to ~ for (the children wrote away for a puzzle book) 2. (D; intr.) to ~ to (the children wrote away to the company)

write back *v.* 1. (A) ("to answer") she wrote a long letter back to me; or: she wrote me back a long letter 2. (D; intr.) to ~ for (she wrote back for more information) 3. (D; intr.) to ~ to ("to answer") she wrote back to me 4. (L; to) she wrote back (to me) that they would attend the conference

write off *v.* (D; tr.) to ~ as (he was written off as a has-been)

write out *v.* (A) she wrote out a receipt to me; or: she wrote me out a receipt

writer *n.* 1. a free-lance; screen; sports ~ 2. a hack; professional ~ 3. a prolific ~

write-up *n.* (colloq.) ["account"] to get a (good) ~ (in the newspapers)

write up *v.* 1. (D; tr.) to ~ for (to ~ a story for a newspaper; to ~ smb. up for a decoration)

writhe *v.* (D; intr.) to ~ in (to ~ in pain)

writing *n.* 1. to decipher smb.'s ~ 2. cuneiform; cursive; hieroglyphic; picture ~ 3. illegible; legible ~ 4. creative; travel ~ 5. (misc.) to have smt. in ~; to put smt. in ~; to see the ~ on the wall (for AE, see **handwriting**, 3) ("to see impending failure")

writing paper *n.* personalized ~

writings *n.* ["written works"] 1. collected; selected ~ 2. scientific ~ (her latest scientific ~ appeared in a recent journal)

wrong I *adj.* 1. completely, dead (colloq.), totally ~ 2. morally ~ 3. ~ about 4. ~ in (I was ~ in going there) 5. ~ with (what's ~ with her?) 6. ~ to + inf. (it was ~ of them to gossip = they were ~ to gossip; I was ~ to disregard your advice; it is ~ to lie) 7. ~ that + clause (it's ~ that they should be treated so badly) 8. (misc.) everything went ~; she is the ~ person for the job = she is ~ for the job USAGE NOTE: The expression *what's wrong?* can express sympathy; *what's wrong with you?* is often critical.

wrong II *adv.* 1. to do smt. ~ 2. to go ~

wrong III *n.* 1. to do (smb.) ~ 2. to redress, right, undo a ~ 3. a grievous; irreparable ~ 4. in the ~ (you were in the ~) 5. (misc.) two ~s do not make a right; to know right from ~

wrought up *adj.* ["upset"] ~ over (he gets ~ over trifles)

X ray *n.* 1. to do (colloq.), make, take an ~ (the physician decided to take an ~ of my back) 2. to interpret, read an ~ (the radiologist will read your ~ before you leave) 3. to get an ~ 4. to go for an ~

xylophone *n.* to play the ~

Y

Y *n.* (= YMCA, YWCA, YMHA, YWHA, which are abbreviations of Young Men's or Women's Christian or Hebrew Association) at the ~ (they are staying at the ~)

yacht *n.* 1. to sail a ~ 2. on a ~ (they spent the summer on their ~)

yammer *v.* (colloq.) (D; intr.) to ~ about; for

yank I *n.* ["tug"] to give a ~

yank II *v.* (colloq.) 1. (d; intr.) ("to tug") to ~ at, on (the little girl kept ~ing at her mother's apron) 2. (d; tr.) to ~ out of ("to withdraw") (they ~ed their children out of school)

yap I *n.* ["mouth"] (colloq.) to shut one's ~

yap II *v.* (colloq.) 1. (D; intr.) to ~ about 2. (d; intr.) to ~ at

yard I *n.* ["enclosed area"] a barnyard (esp. AE), farmyard; brickyard; coalyard; dockyard (BE), navy ~ (AE); graveyard; junkyard (esp. AE), scrapyard (BE); lumberyard (AE), timberyard (BE); prison; railroad (AE), railway (BE) ~
USAGE NOTE: In BE, a plot of land adjoining a house is called a *garden* if grassy (a *back garden*, a *front garden*) or a *yard* if paved (a *backyard*, a *front yard*). In AE, such a plot is called a *yard*, whether grassy or paved; a large, grassy plot can also be called a *garden*.

yard II *n.* ["unit of measure"] 1. a cubic; square ~ 2. by the ~ (to sell carpeting by the square ~)

yardstick *n.* ["standard"] to apply a ~ to

yarn *n.* ["fiber"] 1. to spin ~ 2. to unsnarl ~ 3. wool(en); worsted ~ 4. (misc.) a ball; hank; skein of ~ ["tale, story"] (colloq.) 5. to spin, tell a ~ about

yawn I *n.* 1. to give a ~ 2. to stifle, suppress a ~ 3. a loud ~

yawn II *v.* to ~ loudly

year *n.* 1. to spend a ~ (somewhere) 2. a banner (AE), good; happy; healthy; memorable; peak, record; profitable ~ (our firm had a very profitable ~; their team had a good ~) 3. a bad, lean ~ 4. smb.'s formative; golden ~s 5. every; last; next; this ~ 6. the coming; current; past ~ 7. an academic; school; calendar ~ 8. an election; presidential (US) ~ 9. a jubilee; sabbatical ~ 10. a financial (esp. AE), fiscal; tax ~ 11. a common; leap ~ 12. a light; sidereal ~ 13. a lunar; solar ~ 14. early; future; past; recent ~s 15. by the ~ (to be paid by the ~) 16. by ("before or in") a ~ (by the ~ 2020, the population in many countries will have doubled) 17. for a ~ (they went abroad for a ~) 18. for, in (esp. AE) ~s (they have not been here for/in ~s) 19. in a ~, in a ~'s time (BE) (they'll be back in

a ~) 20. in a (certain) ~ (he died in the ~ of the great flood; in future ~s; in ~s to come; in past ~s) 21. (misc.) once a ~; ~ in, ~ out; the first time in (esp. AE), for (BE) a ~; she is five ~s old; light ~s away; for ~s to come; up to last ~; children of tender ~s; she had three ~s of college

yearn *v.* 1. (d; intr.) to ~ for (to ~ for freedom) 2. (E) she ~s to return home

yearning *n.* 1. to express; feel a ~ for 2. a strong ~ 3. a ~ for 4. a ~ to + inf. (she has a ~ to visit the village where she was born)

yeast *n.* brewer's ~

yell I *n.* 1. to give, let out a ~ 2. a bloodcurdling; rebel ~

yell II *v.* 1. (B) she ~ed smt. to them 2. (D; intr., tr.) to ~ at (she ~ed at them; he ~ed smt. at me) 3. (D; intr.) to ~ with (to ~ with fear) 4. (H; at, to) she ~ed at me to go away 5. (L; to) he ~ed (to us) that the house was on fire 6. (N; refl.; used with an adjective) he ~ed himself hoarse 7. (misc.) she was ~ing at the top of her voice

yellow *n.* bright; pale ~

yellow fever *n.* to catch, contract, get; have ~

yelp I *n.* to give, let out a ~

yelp II *v.* (D; intr.) to ~ at

yen *n.* ["desire"] (colloq.) 1. to have a ~ for 2. a ~ to + inf. (she had a ~ to go bowling)

yes *n.* ["positive response"] 1. to say "yes" 2. an emphatic ~

yield I *n.* ["earnings"] 1. the current ~ (of an investment) 2. an annual ~ 3. a high; low ~

yield II *v.* 1. (B) I ~ed the right-of-way to the other driver 2. (D; intr.) to ~ to (they finally ~ed to our demands; to ~ to temptation)

yoga *n.* to do, practice ~

yoke I *n.* ["wooden frame"] 1. to put a ~ on (oxen) ["servitude, bondage"] 2. to cast off, throw off the ~ (of bondage) 3. a foreign ~ 4. under a (foreign) ~

yoke II *v.* (D; tr.) to ~ to (to ~ oxen to a cart)

young I *adj.* 1. ~ at heart 2. ~ in spirit

young II *n.* ["offspring of an animal"] 1. to bring forth ~ (wild animals bring forth their ~ in the wilderness) 2. with ~ ("pregnant")

yours *pronoun* 1. (at the close of a letter) Yours faithfully (esp. BE), Yours sincerely, Yours truly (AE) 2. Sincerely ~ (AE)
USAGE NOTE: At the end of letters, the following combinations can occur—Yours (esp. BE; informal); Yours ever (BE; friendly); Yours faithfully (esp. BE); Yours sincerely; Sincerely yours (AE); Yours truly (AE); Very truly yours (AE); AE also commonly uses Sincerely. In BE,

Yours faithfully usually ends a letter beginning with *Dear Sir/Madam/Colleague*; *Yours sincerely* usually ends a letter beginning with *Dear Mr/Mrs/Ms/Dr/Prof Smith.*

youth *n.* 1. gilded ~ 2. in smb.'s ~ 3. (misc.) a gang of ~s

Z

zap v. (colloq.) (P; intr., tr.) she ~ped the incident out of her memory (esp. AE); I ~ped through the exam

zeal n. 1. to demonstrate, display, show ~ 2. great; excessive ~ 3. evangelical; missionary; religious; righteous ~ 4. ~ for (to show ~ for one's work) 5. the ~ to + inf. (does she have enough ~ to finish the project?) 6. in one's ~ (in her ~ to impress others, she made many blunders) 7. with ~ (they worked with great ~)

zealot n. a religious ~

zealous adj. ~ about, in

zebra n. a herd of ~(s)

zenith n. 1. to attain, reach a ~ 2. at a ~ (at the ~ of their power)

zero n. 1. absolute ~ 2. above; below ~ (it was five degrees below ~ Fahrenheit)

zero in v. (d; intr.) ("to concentrate") to ~ on (they all ~ed in on me)

zest n. 1. to add ~ to 2. boundless; great; youthful ~ 3. a ~ for (a ~ for life) 4. with (great) ~

zigzag I n. to make a ~

zigzag II v. (P; intr.) the road ~s across the county

zip I (BE), **zipper** (AE) n. 1. to do up, zip up a ~ 2. to undo, unzip a ~ 3. a ~ gets stuck

zip II v. (P; intr.) they ~ped past us

zodiac n. the signs of the ~

zone I n. 1. to establish, set up a ~ 2. a climatic; frigid; temperate; torrid ~ 3. a buffer; combat; communications; demilitarized; drop; military; neutral; no-fly; occupation; war ~ 4. a danger; nuclear-free; safety; security ~ 5. a no-parking; no-passing; school; towaway ~ 6. a postal; time ~ 7. an erogenous ~ (of the body) 8. (misc.) a twilight ("transitional") ~

zone II v. 1. (d; tr.) to ~ as (they ~d the area as residential) 2. (d; tr.) to ~ for (this area has been ~d for residential use)

zoning n. exclusionary ~ (esp. AE)

zoo n. at, in a ~ (she works at the ~; wild animals are well cared for in our zoo)

zoom in v. (d; intr.) to ~ on (the camera ~ed in on the podium)